FIFTH EDITION

Economics

S0-AAB-041

Stephen L. Slavin

Union County College   Cranford, New Jersey
The New School for Social Research   New York City

Irwin
McGraw-Hill

Boston   Burr Ridge, IL   Dubuque, IA   Madison, WI   New York   San Francisco   St. Louis
Bangkok   Bogotá   Caracas   Lisbon   London   Madrid
Mexico City   Milan   New Delhi   Seoul   Singapore   Sydney   Taipei   Toronto

Irwin/McGraw-Hill

A Division of The **McGraw·Hill** *Companies*

ECONOMICS

Copyright © 1999, 1996, 1994, 1991, and 1989 by The McGraw-Hill Companies, Inc. All rights reserved. Printed in the United States of America. Except as permitted under the United States Copyright Act of 1976, no part of this publication may be reproduced or distributed in any form or by any means, or stored in a data base or retrieval system, without the prior written permission of the publisher.

 This book is printed on recycled acid-free paper containing a minimum of 50% total recycled fiber with 10% post-consumer de-inked fiber.

3 4 5 6 7 8 9 0 QPD QPD 9 0 0 9

ISBN 0–256–26326–4

Editorial director: *Michael W. Junior*
Publisher: *Gary Burke*
Executive editor: *Paul Shensa*
Developmental editor: *Kezia Pearlman*
Marketing manager: *Nelson W. Black*
Project manager: *Robert A. Preskill*
Production supervisor: *Pam Augspurger*
Senior designer: *Francis Owens*
Cover illustrator: *Alan E. Cober*
Compositor: *Shepherd, Inc.*
Typeface: *10/12 Times Roman*
Printer: *Quebecor Printing Book Group, Dubuque*

Library of Congress Cataloging-in-Publication Data

Slavin, Stephen L.
    Economics / Stephen L. Slavin.—5th ed.
        p.   cm.
    Includes bibliographical references and index.
    ISBN 0-256-26326-4
    1. Economics.   I. Title.
HB171.5.S6276   1998
330—dc21   98-16402
                                        CIP

http://www.mhhe.com

ABOUT THE AUTHOR

Stephen L. Slavin received his B.A. in economics from Brooklyn College and his M.A. and Ph.D. in economics from New York University. He has taught at New York Institute of Technology, Brooklyn College, St. Francis College (Brooklyn), and in the M.B.A. program at Fairleigh Dickinson University, and he now teaches at the New School for Social Research in New York City and at Union County College in Cranford, New Jersey.

He has written eight other books: *The Einstein Syndrome: Corporate Anti-Semitism in America Today* (University Press of America); *Jelly Bean Economics: Reaganomics in the Early 1980s* (Philosophical Library); *Economics: A Self-Teaching Guide, All the Math You'll Ever Need, Math for Your First- and Second-Grader, Quick Business Math: A Self-Teaching Guide* (all four published by John Wiley & Sons); *Chances Are: The Only Statistics Book You'll Ever Need* (University Press of America); and *Everyday Math in 20 Minutes a Day* (LearningExpress). He is the co-author of two other Wiley books, *Practical Algebra* and *Quick Algebra Review*.

Dr. Slavin's articles have appeared in *Studies in Family Planning, Economic Planning, Journal of BioSocial Science, Business and Society Review, Bankers Magazine, Education for Business, Public Management, Better Investing, Northwest Investment Review, U.S.A. Today Magazine, Patterns in Prejudice, Culturefront,* and *Conservative Review.* In addition, he has written more than 500 newspaper commentaries on public policy, demographic economics, politics, urban economics, international trade, investments, and economic fluctuations.

PREFACE TO THE INSTRUCTOR

More than 25 years ago, while still a graduate student, I got a part-time job helping to ghostwrite an introductory text for a major publisher. I asked my editor why so many economics texts were ghostwritten. She smiled and said, "Economists can't write."

Economics can be a rather intimidating subject, with its extensive vocabulary, complicated graphs, and quantitative tendencies. Is it possible to write a principles text that lowers the student's anxiety level without watering down the subject matter? To do this, one would need to be an extremely good writer, have extensive teaching experience, and have solid academic training in economics. In this case, two out of three is just not good enough.

Why did I write this book? Probably my moment of decision arrived about nine years ago when I mentioned to my macro class that Kemp-Roth cut the top personal income tax bracket from 70 percent to 50 percent. Then I asked, "If you were rich, by what percentage were your taxes cut?"

The class sat there in complete silence. Most of the students stared at the blackboard, waiting for me to work out the answer. I told them to work it out themselves. I waited. And I waited. Finally, someone said, "Twenty percent?"

"Close," I replied, "but no cigar."

"Fourteen percent?" someone else ventured.

"No, you're getting colder."

After waiting another two or three minutes, I saw one student with her hand up. One student knew that the answer was almost 29 percent—*one* student in a class of 30.

When do they teach students how to do percentage changes? In high school? In junior high or middle school? Surely not in a college economics course.

How much of *your* time do you spend going over simple arithmetic and algebra? How much time do you spend going over simple graphs? Wouldn't you rather be spending that time discussing economics?

Now you'll be able to do just that, because all the arithmetic and simple algebra that you normally spend time explaining are covered methodically in this book. All you'll need to do is tell your students which pages to look at.

The micro chapters offer scores of tables and graphs for the students to plot on their own; the solutions are shown in the book. This will cut down on the amount of time you'll need to spend putting these problems on the board.

As an economics instructor these last 31 years at such fabled institutions as Brooklyn College, New York Institute of Technology, St. Francis College (Brooklyn), and Union County College, I have used a variety of texts. But each of their authors assumed a mathematical background that the majority of my students did not have. Each also assumed that his graphs and tables were comprehensible to the average student.

The biggest problem we have with just about any book we assign is that many of our students don't bother to read it before coming to class. Until now, no one has written a principles text in plain English. I can't promise that every one of your students will do the readings you assign, but at least they won't be able to complain anymore about not understanding the book.

Distinctive Qualities

My book has six qualities that no other principles text has.

1. **It reviews math that students haven't covered since middle school and high school.** (See, e.g., the box, "A Word About Numbers," Chapter 5, page 82, or "Calculating Percentage Changes," Chapter 8, page 166.)

2. **It's an interactive text, encouraging active rather than passive reading.** (See, e.g., the calculation of average fixed, variable, and total cost, Chapter 21, pp. 483–84.)

3. **It's a combined textbook and workbook.** Each chapter is followed by workbook pages that include multiple-choice and fill-in questions, as well as numerical problems.

4. **It costs less than virtually every other text on the market.** The fifth edition has the lowest list price on the market for this combined textbook-workbook.

5. **It's written in plain English without jargon.** See for yourself. Open any page and compare my writing style with that of any other principles author. This book is written to communicate clearly and concisely with the students' needs in mind.

6. **It is written with empathy for students.** My goal is to get students past their math phobias and fear of graphs by having them do hundreds of problems, step-by-step, literally working their way through the book. Students learn economics best by actively "doing."

Current Economic News

The study of economic needs to be conducted within an empirical context. We start, in Chapter 1, with a brief economic history of the United States. In virtually every chapter that follows, we weave current economic news into the discussion. We look at the aftermath of the collapse of the Soviet empire in Chapter 4. In Chapter 11, we talk about the disappearing federal budget deficit, and its implications on fiscal policy. The ongoing Microsoft antitrust case, whose outcome will shape how we use PCs, is examined in Chapter 28.

The 1997 Teamsters strike against United Parcel Service provided labor with its greatest victory in at least a couple of decades. And the merger of the National Education Association and the American Federation of Teachers announced in early 1998 created what will be the nation's largest labor union. These two events are discussed within the context of labor's long-term decline in Chapter 30.

The Welfare Reform Act of 1996 was the most far-reaching piece of welfare legislation since the New Deal. Its requirements and their possible effects are discussed in Chapter 33. And finally, in Chapter 35, we look at the Asian financial crisis that has centered in South Korea, Thailand, and Indonesia. After the 1995 Mexican peso crisis and current one in East Asia, one wonders where and when the next crisis will occur.

Special Features

Three special features of my book are its integrated coverage of the global economy, its extra help boxes, and its advanced work boxes.

The Global Economy

Until the early 1970s our economy was largely insulated from the rest of the world economy. All of this changed with the oil price shock of 1973, our subsequent growing appetite for fuel-efficient Japanese compact cars, as well as for TVs, VCRs, camcorders, and other consumer electronics made in Asia. As our trade deficits grew, and as foreigners bought up more and more American assets, every American became quite aware of how integrated we had become within the global economy.

Traditionally, principles texts included a couple of chapters at the back of the book on international trade and finance. However, in recent years it has become very apparent to authors that we needed to integrate international material throughout our texts. The fifth edition of my own text follows this practice, and more than ten percent of the book deals specifically with the global economy.

Here are some of the things we look at:

- The "Isms": Capitalism, Communism, Fascism, and Socialism (Ch. 4, p. 72)
- China: The Premier Communist Power (Ch. 4, p. 75)
- Why the Japanese Savings Rate Has Been So High (Ch. 5, p. 83)
- Foreign Investment in the United States (Ch. 6, p. 117)
- The Cost of Living in the U.S. and Russia: An Alternate Comparison (Ch. 8, p. 172)
- The Effectiveness of Monetary Policy in an Open Economy (Ch. 13, p. 324)
- The global economy: Let them eat bread (Ch. 17, p. 417)

- How the Japanese Drove American T.V. Manufacturers Out of Business (Ch. 34, p. 768)
- The Asian Financial Crisis (Ch. 35, p. 787)
- Will Foreigners Soon Own America? (Ch. 35, p. 792)

Extra Help Boxes

Students taking the principles course have widely varying backgrounds. Some have no problem doing the math or understanding basic economic concepts. But many others are lost from day one.

I have provided dozens of extra help boxes for the students who need them. They are especially useful to instructors who don't want to spend hours of class time going over material that they assume should be understood after one reading.

Of course these boxes can be skipped by the better prepared students.

Here are some of the topics covered in the extra help boxes:

- Read only if you still don't understand why C is 1,000 (Ch. 5, p. 89)
- More on finding autonomous and induced consumption (Ch. 5, p. 94)
- Calculating percentage changes (Ch. 8, p. 166)
- Read only if you're not sure how to calculate the unemployment rate (Ch. 9, p. 192)
- Finding percentage changes in the price level (Ch. 9, p. 199)
- Differentiating between the deficit and the debt (Ch. 11, p. 263)
- Differentiating between changes in demand and changes in the quantity demanded (Ch. 18, p. 430)
- Calculating marginal utility and total utility (Ch. 19, p. 453)
- What's the difference between shutting down and going out of business? (Ch. 21, p. 480)
- How to read a graph (Ch. 24, p. 540)
- Finding the imperfect competitor's MRP (Ch. 29, p. 630)
- Finding the percentage of income share of the quintiles in Figure 1 (Ch. 33, p. 711)

Advanced Work Boxes

There are some concepts in the principles course that many instructors will want to skip. (Of course, if they're not included in principles texts, this will make some instructors quite unhappy.) These boxes are intended for the better prepared students who are willing to tackle these relatively difficult concepts.

Here is a sampling of my advanced work boxes:

- Post-World War II recessions (Ch. 1, p. 13)
- APCs greater than one (Ch. 5, p. 86)

- Progressive in name vs. progressive in effect (Ch. 7, p. 134)
- Why NNP is better than GDP (Ch. 8, p. 161)
- The accelerator principle (Ch. 9, 187)
- The paradox of thrift (Ch. 11, p. 256)
- Three modifications of the deposit expansion multiplier (Ch. 13, p. 316)
- Rational expectations vs. adaptive expectations (Ch. 14, p. 347)
- Maximizing total profit and maximizing profit per unit (Ch. 23, p. 523)
- Technological advance and decreasing costs (Ch. 23, p. 528)
- Perfect price discrimination (Ch. 25, p. 565)
- Who created the land? (Ch. 32, p. 693)
- The negative income tax (Ch. 33, p. 731)

Changes in the Fifth Edition

Two basic ways my book is different from all other principles texts is that it is a smoother read and it is interactive. The fifth edition improves on these features.

Most of the really hard stuff is in advanced work boxes and appendices. This relatively difficult material can be skipped, or perhaps assigned for extra credit. The really easy stuff—e.g., math that should have been learned in high school—is covered in extra help boxes. These boxes save professors hours of valuable class time. For example, students who can't figure out percentage changes can get help from the boxes on pages 166 and 199. In the fifth edition I've added a dozen new boxes. I've also moved the equation of exchange and the quantity theory of money from Chapter 12 (Money and Banking) to Chapter 14 (Twentieth-Century Economic Theory). I wanted to lessen the load of more difficult theory for the student to learn at one time.

Unlike all other principles texts, which encourage passive reading, my book encourages active reading. Students work their way through each chapter, tackling numerical problems, filling in tables, and drawing graphs. Then, at the end of each chapter is a workbook section with multiple-choice and fill-in questions, and problems. In the fifth edition we now have about 100 problem sheets in the Instructor's Manual, which can be torn out, photocopied, and handed out to the students. Let's say a professor assigned the first 10 pages of Chapter 11 (Fiscal Policy and the National Debt). A problem sheet would have a graph and three questions: (1) Is this an inflationary gap or a deflationary gap? (2) How big is it? (3) What two fiscal policy measures would you use to remove it? There's a problem like this in the workbook section of Chapter 11, but this problem comes up at the beginning of a very long chapter. Having these problem sheets saves the professor from having to put this graph on the board and having students spend class time figuring out the answers.

The Supplement Package

In addition to the workbook, which is built in, *Economics* has a supplemental package to help students and instructors as they use the text.

Instructor's Manual

I prepared the instructor's manual to give instructors ideas on how to use the text. The manual includes a description of the textbook's special features, a chapter-by-chapter discussion of material new to the fifth edition, and a rundown of chapter coverage to help instructors decide what they can skip. The answers to the workbook sections of the text are in this manual. New to this edition in the IM are over 30 problem sets designed to supplement almost every chapter.

Test Bank (Micro and Macro Versions)

I have thoroughly revised the test bank so that it offers more than 7,000 questions. Multiple-choice questions, fill-in questions, and problems are classified by degree of difficulty.

Teaching Transparencies

The most important graphs and tables from the text are reproduced as two-color transparencies. Use of these acetates will aid the instructor's classroom presentations and the students' understanding.

Computerized Testing

The Micro and Macro test banks are available in computerized versions, both for IBM-PC and compatibles and for Macintosh computers. Developed by the Brownstone Research Group, this state of the art software has the capability to create multiple tests, "scramble," and produce high-quality graphs.

Videos

A selection of videos is available to adopters, including both tutorial lessons and programs that combine historical footage, documentary sequences, interviews, and analysis to illustrate economic theory. There is also a 15-minute video that explains how to get the most out of the book. This may be played during the first day of class.

One-Semester Courses

Here are some syllabi for one-semester courses with varying orientations:

Macro oriented:

Chapters 1–8; 11–13; 17; 31–35.
Chapters 1–2; 9; 11–13; 16–17; 28; 31–35.
Chapters 1–9; 16–17; 28; 33–35.

Micro oriented:

Chapters 2–4; 9; 16–28.

Chapters 1–4; 16–26; 34–35.

Chapters 2–3; 17–22; 29–35.

Balanced approach:

Chapters 1–8; 17–22; 34–35.

Chapters 1–4; 16–22; 28–33.

Here's another possibility—a one-semester course that focuses on contemporary problems:

Chapters 2–4; 9; 11–13; 16; 28; 31–35.

Acknowledgments

It is one thing to write an unconventional, even controversial, principles text, and it is quite another to get it published. Gary Nelson, the sponsoring editor at the time my book was signed, saw the project through from its inception to its completion, and I want to thank him for making this book possible. Gary oversaw the development from a bare bones text to a full-fledged principles package.

Paul Shensa, who succeeded Gary Nelson as sponsoring editor, has been a great advocate of my book, both inside and outside the company. I also wish to thank Gary Burke, my publisher, who put together the group that edited and produced the book.

Kezia Pearlman, the developmental editor, saw this project through from the first reviews, the chapter-by-chapter revisions, the test bank revisions, and the dozens of deadlines that we met, to the time the book finally went to press.

Project manager Rob Preskill, with whom I worked day to day, managed the copyediting, artwork, and page proofs, and saw to it that we stayed not just on schedule, but ahead of schedule.

Peter de Lissovoy, the copyeditor with the light touch, suggested hundreds of improvements, large and small, while smoothing out the rough edges of the manuscript.

Francis Owens oversaw the design of the book from cover to cover. Supplements coordinators Louis Swaim and Florence Fong made sure the supplement production process went smoothly.

Finally, I want to thank Nelson Black, the marketing manager, and all of the Irwin/McGraw-Hill sales reps for the great job they did selling my book.

I'd also like to thank the many reviewers who helped improve this text over the last four editions.

Carlos Aguilar, *El Paso Community College*
James Q. Aylsworth, *Lakeland Community College*
Robert G. Bise, *Orange Coast College*
Steve Cole, *Bethel College*
Ana-María Conley, *DeVry Institute of Technology–Decatur*
Daniel Fischer, *University of Arizona*
Russell L. Flora, *Pikes Peak Community College*
Joseph W. Ford, *Iona College*
Arthur Friedberg, *Mohawk Valley Community College*
Harold Friesen, *Friends University*
Cindy Goodyear, *Webster University*
Sanford B. Helman, *Middlesex County College*
Mark G. Johnson, *Lakeland Community College*
James Kelly, *Rio Hondo College*
Kenneth E. Kimble, *Sinclair Community College*
Jack Klauser, *Chaminade University of Honolulu*
Wayne Klutarits, *Jefferson College*
Harry Kolendrianos, *Danville Community College*
Stephen E. Lile, *Western Kentucky University*
Steven B. McCormick, *Southeastern Illinois College*
John E. Michaels, *University of Phoenix*
Green Miller, *Morehead State University*
Louis A. Patille, *University of Phoenix*
Eric Rahimian, *Alabama A&M University*
W. H. Segur, *University of Redlands*
Don M. Soule, *University of Kentucky*
Bruno Stein, *New York University*
Stephen Steller, *University of Phoenix*
Edward Stevens, *Nebraska College of Business*
James Watson, *Jefferson College*
Elaine Gale Wrong, *Montclair State College*

Many reviewers helped me to improve the text as it developed into the fifth edition. I thank the following reviewers for their suggestions:

Kevin Baird, *Montgomery Community College*
Michael Cohik, *Collin Community College*
Eugene Gendel, *Woodbury University*
Paul Lockard, *Black Hawk College*
Joan O'Brien, *Quincy College*
Alannah Orrison, *Saddleback College*
James Watson, *Jefferson College*
Marc Weglarski, *Macomb Community College*

Finally, to all adopters of the past four editions, thank you. Your comments and concerns have helped me to write the 1999 edition of *Economics*.

Stephen L. Slavin

PREFACE TO THE STUDENT

What have you heard about economics? That it's dull, it's hard, it's full of undecipherable equations and incomprehensible graphs? If you were to read virtually any of the introductory economics textbooks, that's exactly what you would find.

How is this book different from all other books? For starters, this is the first economics book that is reader friendly. While you're reading, I'll be right there with you, illustrating various points with anecdotes and asking you to work out numerical problems as we go along.

Are you a little shaky about the math? Your worries are over. If you can add, subtract, multiply, and divide (I'll even let you use a calculator), you can do the math in this book.

How do you feel about graphs? Do you think they look like those ultramodernistic paintings that even the artists can't explain? You can relax. No graph in this book has more than four lines, and by the time you're through, you'll be drawing your *own* graphs.

In nearly every chapter you'll find one or two boxes labeled "Extra Help." Sometimes you can master a concept when additional examples are given. Don't be too proud to seek extra help when you need it. And when you don't need it, you may skip the boxes.

Unlike virtually every other economics text, this one includes a built-in workbook. Even if your professor does not assign the questions at the end of each chapter, I urge you to answer them because they provide an excellent review.

I can't guarantee an *A* in this course, but whether you are taking it to fulfill a college requirement or planning to be an economics major, you will find that economics is neither dull nor all that hard.

Stephen L. Slavin

CONTENTS IN BRIEF

CONTENTS

12 Money and Banking   279

13 The Federal Reserve and Monetary Policy   309

14 Twentieth-Century Economic Theory   333

15 A Guide to Macropolicy   371

INTRODUCTION

What Is Economics All About, How Do We Use This Book, and Why Is This Book Different from All Other Introductory Economics Textbooks?

An economist is a man who states the obvious in terms of the incomprehensible.

—Alfred A. Knopf

You've just started reading what may be the shortest introduction with the longest title ever to appear in an introductory economics textbook. Why is this introduction so short? Mainly because I believe in economizing. What is economizing? Funny you should ask.

Economics deals with efficiency—getting rid of waste. That's why this introduction is so short. In fact, that's why this entire book—a textbook and a workbook combined—is so short. We've eliminated most of the extraneous material, the stuff that almost no one reads and virtually no one can understand. What you'll be getting here is 99.44 percent pure introductory economics. If this book were sold in supermarkets, you'd find it with the rest of the no-frills products.

What is economics? Basically, economics is a set of tools that enables us to use our resources efficiently. The end result is the highest possible standard of living.

Economics operates on two levels, the macro level and the micro level. *Macroeconomics* deals with huge aggregates like national output, employment, the money supply, bank deposits, and government spending; and how we can deal with inflation and recession. The first half of the book *Economics* (through Chapter 16) is devoted to macroeconomics.

Microeconomics operates on the level of the individual business firm, as well as that of the individual consumer. How does a firm maximize its profits, and how do consumers maximize their satisfaction? These are the types of questions answered by microeconomic analysis, which begins with Chapter 17 of *Economics* (or Chapter 5 of *Microeconomics*).

This book differs from every other introductory text in several ways. Not only is it shorter, but it is much more readable. To modify an old computer term, it is reader-friendly. There are plenty of jokes and anecdotes to illustrate points. And you will be able to do the math even if you are mathphobic.

The format of the book encourages you to read actively rather than passively. You will be asked to answer questions and do calculations. Then you'll check your work against my answers.

Before you are asked to do any calculations (and we rarely go beyond eighth-grade arithmetic), there will be a section that reviews the math. For example, just before we explore the subject of consumption (Chapter 5 of *Economics* and *Macroeconomics*), which is expressed in trillions of dollars, there is a section showing you how to deal with large numbers. If you happen to be one of those people who doesn't know billions from trillions, then this section is for you. But if you do know your billions and trillions, you can pass this section, go directly into the chapter, collect $200, and roll the dice again.

Actually, I won't claim that reading this book will be quite as much fun as playing Monopoly, or that you will get to collect $200 whenever you skip a section. But you do get to save some money.

This text gives you two books in one: the conventional textbook and the workbook. Go into any college bookstore and check out the prices. Almost every standard textbook/ workbook package will cost you over $60, so you're already economizing. And yet, in the words of the Carpenters' golden oldie, "We've only just begun."

1

A Brief Economic History of the United States

It was the best of times, it was the worst of times, it was the age of wisdom, it was the age of foolishness, it was the epoch of belief, it was the epoch of incredulity, it was the season of Light, it was the season of Darkness, it was the spring of hope, it was the winter of despair.[1]

Introduction

These are the opening words of *A Tale of Two Cities,* which Charles Dickens wrote about 140 years ago. He was writing about Paris and London at the time of the French Revolution, but his words could also describe America today.

Our economy is a study in contrasts. We have poverty in the midst of plenty; we have rapidly expanding industries like computer software and medical technology, and we have dying industries like shipbuilding and consumer electronics; we have won the cold war against communism, but we may be losing the trade war against Japan and China.

Which country has the largest economy in the world, the United States or Japan? Believe it or not, our national output is nearly double that of Japan. Then again, there are twice as many Americans as there are Japanese. But Japan has been gaining on us so quickly that the Japanese may overtake us within a couple of generations.

America is the sole superpower and has one of the highest standards of living in the world. Communism, to borrow a phrase from Karl Marx, has been "swept into the dustbin of history"—at least, the version that dominated the former Soviet Union after the 1920s and Eastern Europe after World War II is no more.

But there are many discordant notes sounding in the United States, ranging from rampant crime and drug use to a permanent underclass to large foreign trade deficits to a standard of living that has not improved much since the early 1970s. Perhaps most alarming, for the first time in our history, the generation that came of age in the 1980s and early 1990s has not done as well as their parents did when *they* came of age.

The generation that just came of age did not do as well as their parents did.

The baby-boom generation has earned higher incomes than any other generation in history. Indeed, Americans once considered it their birthright to do better than their parents. But that ended some 25 years ago, and a lot of young people are worrying about their futures.

Since the end of the 1990–91 recession, our economy has generated nearly 15 million new jobs. That's the good news. The bad news is that half of them pay less than $12,000 per year. These so-called McJobs are often low-level, minimum wage, dead-end positions with no health benefits.

The children of the first baby boomers are now entering the job market. And their parents, after paying $25,000 or more a year to educate them, are wondering about their children's job prospects. In the early 1990s job placement counselors were saying that the job market for college graduates was the worst in recent memory. After four years of decline, hiring of college graduates finally rose in 1994 by about 2 percent over the

The job market for college graduates is the worst it's been in recent memory.

---

[1]Charles Dickens, *A Tale of Two Cities* (New York: MacMillan, 1955), p. 3. Original work published 1859.

previous year. The job market in 1997 and 1998 was the strongest in memory, partly because large corporations, in their aggressive downsizing drives, may have laid off too many workers of their parents' generation. Jim Morin, a cartoonist, put it this way: "Hi dad. The good news is I found a job. The bad news is it's the same job you were downsized out of last year."

In these first few chapters, we'll be looking at how our economy uses its basic resources, at the workings of the law of supply and demand, and at how capitalism and other economic systems actually work. But first we need to ask how we got here. After all, the American economic system evolved over a period of more than 300 years.

Those who cannot remember the past are condemned to repeat it.

—George Santayana

What did the great philosopher mean by this? Perhaps he meant that those who do not learn enough history the first time around will be required to repeat History 101. But whatever he meant, it is clear that to understand our economy today, we need to know how it developed over the years.

Did you see *Back to the Future?* You may have seen parts 1, 2, and 3, but let's stick with just part 1. Imagine being sent back to the 1950s. The way people lived then was very different from the way we live today—and the 1950s represented life on the fast track compared to daily existence during the first decade of this century. So before we worry about today's economy, we'll take a few steps back and look at life in this country about 200 years ago.

Part 1: The American Economy in the 19th Century

Agricultural Development

America has always had a large and productive agricultural sector. At the time of the American Revolution, 9 out of every 10 Americans lived on a farm; 100 years later, however, fewer than 1 out of every 2 people worked in agriculture. Today, it's fewer than 2 in 100, but those 2 not only feed America but also produce a huge surplus that is sold abroad.

America had an almost limitless supply of land.

Unlike Europe, 200 years ago America had an almost limitless supply of unoccupied fertile land. The federal government gave away farmland—usually 160-acre plots (one-quarter of a square mile)—to anyone willing to clear the land and farm on it. Although sometimes the government charged a token amount, it often gave away the land for free.

The great abundance of land was the most influential factor in our economic development during the 19th century. Not only did the availability of very cheap or free land attract millions of immigrants to our shores, but it also encouraged early marriage and large families, since every child was an additional worker to till the fields and handle the animals. Even more important, this plenitude of land, compared to amount of labor, encouraged rapid technological development.

At the time of George Washington's inauguration in 1789, there were about 4 million people living in the United States. By the time of the War of 1812, our population had doubled. It doubled again to 16 million in 1835, and had doubled still again by 1858. Our numbers continued to grow, but at a somewhat slower pace, reaching the 100 million mark in 1915 and the 200 million mark in 1968. Our population reached 248.7 million in 1990, according to the U.S. census, and is now about 270 million.

America's large and growing population has been extremely important as a market for our farmers and manufacturers. After World War II, Japanese manufacturers targeted the American market, while the much smaller Japanese market remained largely closed to American manufactured goods. Japan—with just half our population and, until very recently, much less purchasing power than the United States—has largely financed its industrial development with American dollars. (See box titled "Mass Production and Mass Consumption.")

Mass Production and Mass Consumption

Mass production is possible only if there is also mass consumption. In the late 19th century, once the national railway network enabled manufacturers to sell their products all over the country, and even beyond our shores, it became feasible to invest in heavy machinery and to turn out volume production, which, in turn, meant lower prices. Lower prices, of course, pushed up sales, which encouraged further investment and created more jobs. At the same time, productivity, or output per hour, was rising, which justified companies in paying higher wages. And a high-wage workforce could easily afford all the new low-priced products.

So we had a mutually reinforcing relationship. Mass consumption enabled mass production, while mass production enabled mass consumption. As this process unfolded, our industrial output literally multiplied and our standard of living soared. And nearly all of this process took place from within our own borders with only minimal help from foreign investors, suppliers, and consumers.

After World War II, the Japanese were in no position to use this method of reindustrialization. Not only had most of their plants and equipment been destroyed by American bombing, but also Japanese consumers did not have the purchasing power to buy enough manufactured goods to justify mass production of a wide range of consumer goods. And so the Japanese industrialists took the one course open to them: As they rebuilt their industrial base, they sold low-priced goods to the low end of the American market. In many cases they sold these items—textiles, black-and-white TVs, cameras, and other consumer goods—at half the prices charged in Japan.

Japanese consumers were willing to pay much higher prices for what was often relatively shoddy merchandise, simply because that was considered the socially correct thing to do. Imagine American consumers acting this way! Within a couple of decades, Japanese manufacturers, with a virtual monopoly in their home market and an expanding overseas market, were able to turn out high-volume, low-priced, high-quality products. We will look much more closely at Japanese manufacturing and trade practices in the chapter on international trade.

Southern economic development remained agricultural.

Although all regions of the United States remained primarily agricultural in the years following the Civil War, New England, the Middle Atlantic states, and the Midwest—with their already well-established iron, steel, textile, and apparel industries—were poised for a major industrial expansion, which would last until the Great Depression. In contrast, the South, whose economy was based on the cash crops of cotton, tobacco, rice, and sugar, as well as on subsistence farming, remained primarily an agricultural region well into the 20th century. Its railroads had been largely destroyed by invading Northern armies during the war. Indeed, to this day there are places in Georgia where you can see evidence of the destruction caused by General William Tecumseh Sherman's army. Do you know what the twisted rails were called? Sherman's bow ties.

The South continued to be the poorest section of the country, a relative disadvantage that was not erased until the growth of the Sun Belt took off in the 1960s. The post–Civil War rallying cry "The South will rise again" did not even *begin* to ring true until 100 or so years later. (See box titled "Two Economic Conflicts Leading to the Civil War.")

Southern agriculture developed very differently from agriculture in the other regions of the nation. We know, of course, that most of the labor was provided by slaves whose ancestors had been brought here in chains from Africa. On the average, Southern farms were large. By 1860, four-fifths of the farms with over 500 acres were in the South. The plantation owners raised commercial crops such as cotton, rice, sugar, and tobacco, while the smaller farms, which were much less dependent on slave labor, produced a wider variety of crops.

In the North and the West, self-sufficient, 160-acre family farms were most common. Eventually, corn, wheat, and soybeans became important commercial crops. But in the years following the Civil War, increasing numbers of people left the farms of the North to take jobs in manufacturing.

Bad times for agriculture

Times were bad for agriculture from the end of the Civil War until the close of the century. The government's liberal land policy, combined with increased mechanization, vastly expanded farm output. The production of the nation's three basic cash crops—corn, wheat, and cotton—rose faster than did its population through most of that period. Why did production rise so rapidly? Mainly because of the rapid technological progress made during that period (see box titled "American Agricultural Technology"). This

Two Economic Conflicts Leading to the Civil War

In the decades before the Civil War, the economic interests of the North and South came into sharp conflict. Northern manufacturers benefited from high protective tariffs, which kept out competing British manufacturers. The Southern states, which had only a small manufacturing sector, were forced to buy most of their manufactured goods from the North and to pay higher prices than they would have paid for British goods had there been no tariff.*

As the nation expanded westward, another conflict reached the boiling point: the expansion of slavery into the new territories. In 1860, when Abraham Lincoln had been elected president, most of the land between the Mississippi River and the Pacific Ocean had not yet been organized into states. As newly formed states applied for membership in the Union, the big question was whether they would come in as "free states" or "slave states." Lincoln—and virtually all the other leaders of the new Republican Party—strenuously opposed the extension of slavery into the new territories of the West.

The Southern economy, especially cotton agriculture, depended heavily upon slave labor. The political leaders of the South realized that if slavery were prohibited in the new territories, it would be only a matter of time before these territories entered the Union as free states and the South was badly outvoted in Congress. And so, as Abraham Lincoln was preparing to take office in 1861, 11 Southern states seceded from the Union, touching off the Civil War, which lasted four years, cost hundreds of thousands of lives, and largely destroyed the Southern economy.

The two major consequences of the war were the freeing of 4 million black people who had been slaves and the preservation of the Union with those 11 rebel states. It would take the nation a full century to overcome the legacies of this conflict.

*Tariffs are fully discussed in the chapter on international trade.

Supply and demand

brings us to supply and demand, which is covered in Chapter 3, and which explains why times were bad for agriculture despite expanded output. If the supply of corn increases faster than the demand for corn, what happens to the price of corn? It goes down. And this happened to wheat and cotton as well. Although other countries bought up much of the surpluses, the prices of corn, wheat, and cotton declined substantially from the end of the Civil War until the turn of the century.

The National Railroad Network

The completion of the transcontinental railroads

The completion of a national railroad network in the second half of the 19th century made possible mass production, mass marketing, and mass consumption. In 1850, the United States had just 10,000 miles of track, but within 40 years the total reached 164,000 miles. The transcontinental railroads had been completed, and it was possible to get virtually anywhere in the country by train. Interestingly, however, the transcontinental lines all bypassed the South, which severely retarded its economic development well into the 20th century.

In 1836, it took a traveler an entire month to get from New York to Chicago. Just 15 years later, he could make the trip by rail in less than two days. What the railroads did, in effect, was to weave the country together into a huge social and economic unit, and eventually into the world's first mass market (see again box titled "Mass Production and Mass Consumption").

The Age of the Industrial Capitalist

Andrew Carnegie, American industrial capitalist (National Portrait Gallery/Art Resource)

The last quarter of the 19th century was the age of the industrial capitalist. The great empire builders—Carnegie (steel), Du Pont (chemicals), McCormick (farm equipment), Rockefeller (oil), and Swift (meat packing), among others—dominated this era. John D. Rockefeller, whose exploits will be discussed in the chapter on corporate mergers and antitrust, built the Standard Oil Trust, which controlled 90 percent of the oil business. In 1872, just before Andrew Carnegie opened the Edgar Thomson works, the United States produced less than 100,000 tons of steel. Only 25 years later, Carnegie alone was turning out 4 million tons, almost half of the total American production. Again, as supply outran demand, the price of steel dropped from $65 to $20 a ton.

American Agricultural Technology

In the 19th century, a series of inventions vastly improved farm productivity. In the late 1840s, John Deere began to manufacture steel plows in Moline, Illinois. These were a tremendous improvement over the crude wooden plows that had previously been used.

Cyrus McCormick patented a mechanical reaper in 1834. By the time of the Civil War, McCormick's reaper had at least quadrupled the output of each farm laborer. The development of the Appleby twine binder, the Marsh brothers' harvesting machine, and the Pitts thresher, as well as Eli Whitney's cotton gin, all worked to make American agriculture the most productive in the world.

Part 2: The American Economy from 1900 through World War I

Until the last quarter of the 19th century, American economic history was largely agricultural history. Thereafter, the emphasis shifted to manufacturing. By the end of World War I, agriculture played a relatively minor role in our economic development.

Industrial Development

On the world's technological cutting edge

Henry Ford, American automobile manufacturer (The Granger Collection, New York)

By the turn of the century, America had become an industrial economy. Fewer than 4 in 10 people still lived on farms. We were among the world's leaders in the production of steel, coal, steamships, textiles, apparel, chemicals, and agricultural machinery. Our trade balance with the rest of the world was positive every year. And although we continued to export most of our huge agricultural surpluses to Europe, increasingly we began to send the countries of that continent our manufactured goods as well.

We were also well on our way to becoming the world's first mass-consumption society. The stage had been set by the late-19th-century industrialists. At the turn of the century, we were on the threshold of the automobile age (see box titled "The Development of the Automobile Industry"). The Wright brothers would soon be flying their plane at Kitty Hawk, but commercial aviation was still a few decades away.

American technological progress—or, if the South can forgive me, Yankee ingenuity— runs the gamut from the agricultural implements previously mentioned to the telegraph, the telephone, the radio, the TV, and the computer. It includes the mass-production system perfected by Henry Ford, which made possible the era of mass consumption and the high living standards that the people of all industrialized nations enjoy today. America has long been on the world's technological cutting edge, as well as being the world's leader in manufacturing.

The Development of the Automobile Industry

Nothing is particularly hard if you divide it into small jobs.

—Henry Ford

Who was the first automobile manufacturer to use a division of labor, to use a moving assembly line, and to bring the materials to the worker instead of the worker to the materials? Was it Henry Ford? Close, but no cigar. The man was Henry Olds, who turned the trick in 1901 when he started turning out Oldsmobiles on a mass basis. Still another Henry, Henry Leland, believed it was possible and practical to manufacture a standardized engine with interchangeable parts. By 1908, he did just that with his Cadillac.

Henry Ford was able to carry mass production to its logical conclusion. His great contribution was the emphasis he placed on an expert combination of accuracy, continuity, the moving assembly line, and speed, through the careful timing of manufacturing, materials handling, and assembly. In a sense, then, Henry Ford was the precursor to today's Japanese automaker.

Back in 1908, just 200,000 cars were registered in the United States. In 1915, Ford produced over one-third of the 880,000 motor vehicles built that year. In 1923, Ford built 57 percent of the 4 million cars and trucks produced. But soon General Motors supplanted Ford as the country's number one automobile firm, a position it continues to hold. In 1929, motor vehicle production peaked at 5.3 million units, a number that was not reached again until 1949.

This technological talent, a large agricultural surplus, the world's first universal public education system, and the entrepreneurial abilities of our great industrialists combined to enable the United States to emerge as the world's leading industrial power by the time of World War I. Then, too, fortune smiled upon this continent by keeping it out of harm's way during the war. This same good fortune recurred during World War II; so once again, unlike the rest of the industrial world, we emerged from the war with our industrial plant intact.

Agricultural Development

Agricultural conditions really turned around in the first two decades of the 20th century. Production stabilized, and agriculture enjoyed mild prosperity from 1900 to 1913. Then came World War I, which brought the farmer unprecedented prosperity despite a huge increase in output. Wheat production, for example, which exceeded 1 billion bushels in 1915, passed the 3-billion-bushel mark in 1920.

But in the years immediately after the war, agriculture went into a terrible slump. The price of corn, which had been $1.50 a bushel in 1919, fell to just 30 cents. Wheat fell from $2.15 to 40 cents. And cotton went from 36 cents a pound all the way down to a nickel. It was not until the New Deal, World War II, and the massive federal farm-subsidy program that followed the war that farmers finally were able to get on their feet again.

Part 3: The American Economy between the Wars

When did the United States emerge as a mature industrial economy? We'll take as our starting point the decade of the 1920s, when America truly became a mass-consumption economy. But that economy did not have any distinct time of departure. It evolved from a set of powerful forces that were described in the first part of this chapter.

Let's proceed with a brief decade-by-decade account of the country's economic performance these last 70-odd years. Actually, not all these decades are *exactly* 10 years long, but nobody's perfect. Like the rest of life, economic history does not unfold into uniform periods of ups and downs.

The Roaring Twenties

The postwar boom

World War I ended on November 11, 1918. After a mild and very brief recession, during which our economy reverted to peacetime production, we enjoyed a short economic boom from the spring of 1919 through January 1920. This boom was set off mainly by pent-up consumer demand for housing, clothing, and automobiles; the existence of a large amount of cash, bank deposits, and savings bonds just waiting to be spent; a high foreign demand for American products; and continuing high spending by the federal government. (These same forces, albeit on a much larger scale, were to fuel the prosperity enjoyed in the years immediately following World War II.)

The postwar depression

The Roaring Twenties actually began and ended with depressions. In early 1920, consumers, upset with high prices, began cutting back on their purchases. The Federal Reserve,[2] which controls our money supply, had already begun to tighten credit. Meanwhile, the federal government quickly managed to cut its large wartime budget deficit to zero, which also depressed the economy.[3]

Retailers, stuck with heavy inventories, curtailed their purchases from manufacturers. Wholesale prices dropped 45 percent. Within months, a worldwide depression was in the works. But recovery began very quickly in the United States as excess inventory was

---

[2]I'll discuss how the Federal Reserve controls the growth of our money supply in the chapter on the monetary policy of the Federal Reserve in *Economics* and *Macroeconomics*.

[3]Federal budget deficits and their effect on our economy are discussed in a later chapter of *Economics* and *Macroeconomics*.

worked off. The most important factor in the recovery was that the long-term investment opportunities that existed in 1919–20 were still present in 1921.

Like the pent-up demand for residential housing, there was a tremendous demand for commercial buildings. The automobile industry was growing rapidly and required a further expansion of auxiliary industries such as steel, glass, and rubber, as well as service stations and new roads.

The spreading use of electricity

Another important development in the 1920s was the spreading use of electricity. During this decade, electric power production doubled. Not only was industrial use growing, but by 1929 about two out of every three homes in America had been wired and were now using electrical appliances. The telephone, the radio, the toaster, the refrigerator, and other conveniences became commonplace during the 1920s.

Between 1921 and 1929, national output rose by 50 percent. Despite two minor recessions in 1924 and 1927, most Americans thought the prosperity would last forever. The stock market was soaring, and instant millionaires were created every day, at least on paper.

How to become a millionaire in the stock market

It was possible, in the late 1920s, to put down just 10 percent of a stock purchase and borrow the rest on margin from a stockbroker, who, in turn, borrowed that money from a bank. If you put down $1,000, you could buy $10,000 worth of stock. If that stock doubled (i.e., if it was now worth $20,000), you just made $10,000 on a $1,000 investment. Better yet, your $10,000 stake entitled you to borrow $90,000 from your broker, so you could now own $100,000 worth of stock.

This was not a bad deal—as long as the market kept going up. But as you've heard so many times, what goes up must come down. And as you well know, the stock market came crashing down in October 1929 (see box titled "Our Financial House of Cards"). Although no one knew it at the time, the economy had already begun its descent into a recession a couple of months before the crash. And as the economy continued to sink, that recession became the Great Depression.

Curiously, within days after the crash, several leading government and business officials—including President Hoover and John D. Rockefeller—each described economic conditions as "fundamentally sound." The next time you hear our economy described in those terms, you'll know we're in big trouble.

The Great Depression

The August 1929 recession

By the summer of 1929, the country had clearly built itself up for an economic letdown. The boom in sales of cars and electrical appliances was over. The automobile market was saturated. Nearly three out of four cars on the road were less than six years old, and model changes were not nearly as important then as they are today. The tire industry had been overbuilt, and textiles were suffering from overcapacity. Residential construction was already in decline, and the general business investment outlook was not that rosy.

Had the stock market not crashed and had the rest of the world not gone into a depression, we might have gotten away with a moderate business downturn. Also, had the federal government acted more expeditiously, it is quite possible that the prosperity of the 1920s, after a fairly short recession, could have continued well into the 1930s. But that's not what happened. What did happen completely changed the lives of the people who lived through it, as well as the course of human history itself.

Even through 1930 there was no clear indication that we were in anything worse than a bad recession.[4] There was a slight, abortive recovery in the early months of 1930, with rises in both automobile production and residential construction. Wage rates were well maintained throughout the year. But prices began to decline, investment in plant and equipment collapsed, and a drought wiped out millions of farmers. In fact, conditions grew so bad in what became known as the Dust Bowl that millions of people from the Midwest just packed their cars and drove in caravans to seek a better life in California.

The Dust Bowl and the "Okies"

---

[4] I'm putting off defining a recession until we talk about business cycles in the chapter on economic fluctuations in *Economics* and *Macroeconomics*.

Our Financial House of Cards

Buying stocks on margin was one of the more visible financial excesses of the Roaring Twenties. The Florida real estate boom, which included thousands of spectacular underwater properties, was another. But the major abuse was the erection of a financial superstructure of holding companies and investment trusts that came crashing down in the early 1930s.

When the crash came, the banks that had financed these ventures began to fail, since the speculators were in no position to repay their loans. And as these banks failed, other banks around the country began to fail as well, either because they had large deposits at the failing banks or because depositors, nervous about the safety of their deposits, began withdrawing their savings. So even the banks that had little or nothing to do with the financial excesses of the 1920s were forced to close. And when they did, millions of depositors found that they had lost their entire life savings.

Their flight was immortalized in John Steinbeck's great novel *The Grapes of Wrath,* which was later made into a movie. Although most of these migrants came from other states, they were collectively called Okies, because it seemed at the time as if the entire state of Oklahoma had picked up and moved west.

The bank failures

By the end of 1930, thousands of banks had failed and the generally optimistic economic outlook had given way to one of extreme pessimism. Yet in the early months of 1931, the economy seemed to be attempting to stage another recovery. But whatever chance it had was crushed that spring by the collapse of the entire international financial structure. From here on, it was all downhill. By the beginning of 1933, banks were closing all over the country; by the first week in March, every single bank in the United States had shut its doors.

Hitting bottom

By the time the economy hit bottom, in March 1933, national output was about one-third lower than it had been in August 1929. The official unemployment rate was 25 percent, which meant that some 16 million Americans were out of work at a time when our country's population was less than half its present size. To lend some perspective, at the low point of the 1990–91 recession, nearly 10 million Americans were officially unemployed.

But official figures tell only part of the story. Millions of additional workers had simply given up looking for work during the depths of the Great Depression, as there was no work to be had. Yet according to the way the government compiles the unemployment rate, these people were not even counted since they were not actually looking for work.[5]

Herbert Hoover, thirty-first president of the United States (National Portrait Gallery/Art Resource)

Herbert Hoover and the Depression

Why did the downturn reverse itself?

The Depression was a time of soup kitchens, people selling apples on the street, large-scale homelessness, so-called hobo jungles where poor men huddled around garbage-pail fires to keep warm, and even fairly widespread starvation. "Are you working?" and "Brother can you spare a dime?"[6] were common greetings. People who lived in collections of shacks made of cardboard, wood, and corrugated sheet metal scornfully referred to them as Hoovervilles. Although Herbert Hoover did eventually make a few halfhearted attempts to get the economy moving again, his greatest contribution to the economy was apparently his slogans. When he ran for the presidency in 1928, he promised "two cars in every garage" and "a chicken in every pot." As the Depression grew worse, he kept telling Americans that "prosperity is just around the corner." It's too bad he didn't have Frank Perdue in those days to stick a chicken in every pot.

Why did the downturn of August 1929 to March 1933 finally reverse itself? Well, for one thing, we were just about due. Business inventories had been reduced to rock-bottom levels, prices had finally stopped falling, and there was a need to replace some plant and equipment. The federal budget deficits of 1931 and 1932, even if unwillingly incurred, did provide a mild stimulus to the economy.

---

[5]How the Department of Labor computes the unemployment rate is discussed in the chapter on economic fluctuations in *Economics* and *Macroeconomics.* In Chapter 2, we'll be looking at the concept of full employment, but you can grasp intuitively that when our economy enters even a minor downturn, we are operating at less than full employment.

[6]"Brother, Can You Spare a Dime?" was a depression era song written by Yip Harburg and Jay Gorney.

The New Deal

When Franklin D. Roosevelt ran for president in 1932, he promised "a new deal for the American people." Action was needed, and it was needed fast. In the first 100 days Roosevelt was in office, his administration sent a flurry of bills to Congress that were promptly passed.

The New Deal is best summarized by the three Rs: relief, recovery, and reform. Relief was aimed at alleviating the suffering of a nation that was, in President Roosevelt's words, one-third "ill-fed, ill-clothed, and ill-housed." These people needed work relief, a system similar to today's workfare (work for your welfare check) programs. About 6 million people on average were put to work at various jobs ranging from raking leaves and repairing public buildings to maintaining national parks and building power dams. Robert R. Russell made this observation:

> The principal objects of work-relief were to help people preserve their self-respect by enabling them to stay off the dole and to maintain their work habits against the day when they could again find employment in private enterprises. It was also hoped that the programs, by putting some purchasing power into the hands of workers and suppliers of materials, would help prime the economic pump.*

The government hoped that all of this spending would bring about economic recovery, but the most lasting effect of the New Deal was reform. The Securities and Exchange Commission (SEC) was set up to regulate the stock market and avoid a repetition of the speculative excesses of the late 1920s, which had led to the great crash of 1929. After the reform, bank deposits were insured by the Federal Deposit Insurance Corporation (FDIC) to prevent future runs on the banks by depositors, like those experienced in the early 1930s. Also, an unemployment insurance benefit program was set up to provide temporarily unemployed people with some money to tide them over. The most important reform of all was the creation of Social Security. Although even today retired people need more than their Social Security benefits to get by, there is no question that this program has provided tens of millions of retired people with a substantial income and has largely removed workers' fears of being destitute and dependent in their old age.

*Robert R. Russell, *A History of the American Economic System* (New York: Appleton-Century-Crofts, 1964), p. 547.

Franklin D. Roosevelt, thirty-second president of the United States (Franklin D. Roosevelt Library)

The recession of 1937–38

Clearly a lot of the credit must go to the new administration of Franklin D. Roosevelt, which reopened the banks, ran large budget deficits, and eventually created government job programs that put millions of Americans back to work (see box titled "The New Deal"). A 50-month expansion began in March 1933 and lasted until May 1937. Although output did finally reach the levels of August 1929, more than 7 million people were still unemployed.

By far, the most important reason for the success of the New Deal's first four years was the massive federal government spending that returned millions of Americans to work. This huge infusion of dollars into our economy was just what the doctor ordered. In this case, the doctor was John Maynard Keynes, the great English economist, who maintained that it didn't matter *what* the money was spent on—even paying people to dig holes in the ground and then to fill them up again—as long as enough money was spent. But in May 1937, just when it had begun to look as though the Depression was finally over, we plunged right back into it again.

What went wrong? Two things: First, the Federal Reserve Board of Governors, inexplicably more concerned about inflation than about the lingering economic depression, greatly tightened credit, making it much harder to borrow money. Second, the Roosevelt administration suddenly got that old balance-the-budget-at-all-costs religion. The cost of that economic orthodoxy—which would have made sense during an economic boom— was the very sharp and deep recession of 1937–38. Tight money and a balanced budget are now considered the right policies to follow when the economy is heating up and prices are rising too quickly, but they are prescriptions for disaster when the unemployment rate is 12 percent.[7]

The ensuing downturn pushed up the official unemployment count by another 5 million, industrial production fell by 30 percent, and people began to wonder when this depression would ever end. But there really *was* some light at the end of the tunnel.

---

[7]These policies will be discussed in later chapters of *Economics* and *Macroeconomics*.

In April 1938, both the Roosevelt administration and the Federal Reserve Board reversed course and began to stimulate the economy. By June, the economy had turned around again, and this time the expansion would continue for seven years. The outbreak of war in Europe, the American mobilization in 1940 and 1941, and our eventual entry into the war on December 7, 1941, all propelled us toward full recovery.

When we ask what finally brought the United States out of the Great Depression, there is one clear answer: the massive federal government spending that was needed to prepare for and to fight World War II.

Part 4: From World War II to the Vietnam War

For most Americans the end of the Depression did not bring much relief because the nation was now fighting an all-out war. For those who didn't get the message in those days, there was the popular reminder, "Hey, bub, don't yuh know there's a *war* goin' on?"

The country that emerged from the war was very different from the one that had entered it less than four years earlier. Prosperity had replaced depression. Now inflation had become the number one economic worry.

The United States and the Soviet Union were the only superpowers left standing in 1945. When the cold war quickly developed, we spent tens of billions of dollars to prop up the sagging economies of the nations of Western Europe and Japan, and we spent hundreds of billions more to provide for their defense. In the four decades since the close of World War II we expended 6 percent of our national output on defense, while the Soviet Union probably expended more than double that percentage. This great burden certainly contributed to the collapse of the Soviet Union a few years ago, and our own heavy defense spending continues to divert substantial resources that might otherwise be used to spur our economic growth.

The 1940s: World War II and Peacetime Prosperity

Just as the Great Depression dominated the 1930s, World War II was the main event of the 1940s, especially from the day the Japanese bombed Pearl Harbor until they surrendered in August 1945. For the first time in our history, we fought a war that required a total national effort. Although the Civil War had caused tremendous casualties and had set the South back economically for generations, we had never before fought a war that consumed half of our nation's total output.

At the peak of the war, more than 12 million men and women were mobilized and, not coincidentally, the unemployment rate was below 2 percent. Women, whose place was supposedly in the home, flocked to the workplace to replace the men who had gone off to war. Blacks, too, who had experienced great difficulty finding factory jobs, were hired to work in the steel mills and the defense plants in the East, the Midwest, and the West.

Between 1939 and 1944, national output of goods and services nearly doubled, while federal government spending—mainly for defense—rose by more than 400 percent. By the middle of 1942, our economy reached full employment for the first time since 1929. To hold inflation in check, the government not only instituted price and wage controls but also issued ration coupons for meat, butter, gasoline, and other staples.

During the war, 17 million new jobs were created, while the economy grew 10 or 11 percent a year. Doris Kearns Goodwin attributed "a remarkable entrepreneurial spirit" not only to the opportunity to make huge wartime profits but to a competitiveness "developed within each business enterprise to produce better than its competitors to serve the country." A sign hanging in many defense plants read: "PLEDGE TO VICTORY: The war may be won or lost in this plant."[8]

---

[8]Doris Kearns Goodwin, "The Way We Won: America's Economic Breakthrough during World War II," *The American Prospect*, Fall 1992, p. 68.

The United States entered a very slight recession for a few months in 1945, as the economy underwent reconversion to put it on a peacetime footing. A somewhat longer, but still mild, downturn occurred from late 1948 through late 1949 (see box titled "Post–World War II Recessions"), but the decade was basically one of rapid economic expansion.

Within a year after the war ended, some 12 million men and several hundred thousand women returned home to their civilian lives. Very little housing had been built during the war and the preceding depressed period, so most veterans lived in overcrowded houses and apartments, often with three generations under one roof. The first thing they wanted was new housing.

ADVANCED WORK ········· Post–World War II Recessions
···

Since World War II, the United States has had 10 recessions of varying length and severity. Although I won't define *recession* until a later chapter, I'll briefly note some of the highlights of each downturn. How much of this do you *have* to know? Probably not a whole lot, but as a minimum, you should have some idea of when the recessions took place and how bad they were.

February 1945–October 1945 Even though the war had not yet ended, we began to reconvert into peacetime production. This process was relatively painless, and the recession was perhaps the mildest in the last six decades.

December 1948–October 1949 This was another very mild downturn, really a pause after consumers had satisfied their pent-up demand for cars, major appliances, and new homes.

August 1953–May 1954 A decline in defense spending after the end of the Korean War and a reduction in business inventories built during the last months of the war were the main culprits. This was the third mild recession in a row.

August 1957–April 1958 Business, which had been flat from early 1956 through the summer of 1957, finally sank into a recession. Although brief, the decline was rapid. Investment in plant and equipment fell sharply, but spending by consumers fell only slightly. This was the worst recession since the Great Depression, but it ended in just nine months.

April 1960–February 1961 A long steel strike in 1959 and a swing to a balanced federal budget set off this very mild recession. National output fell almost imperceptibly.

December 1969–November 1970 This was another very mild downturn with another almost imperceptible decline in national output. The downturn coincided with an automobile strike and a strike at General Electric.

November 1973–March 1975 This was the worst downturn since the end of the Great Depression. It was set off by a fourfold increase in the price of oil engineered by the OPEC nations (which we'll talk a lot more about in the chapter on economic fluctuations in *Economics* and *Macroeconomics*). Simultaneously, there was a worldwide shortage of foodstuffs, which drove up food prices. To make matters worse in *this* country, we struck a deal to export about one-quarter of our wheat and other grains to the Soviet Union. Output fell about 5 percent, and to make matters still worse, the rate of inflation remained unacceptably high.

January 1980–July 1980 A doubling of oil prices by OPEC and a credit crunch set off by the Federal Reserve Board of Governors, which had been alarmed by an inflation rate that had reached double-digit levels, pushed us into a very brief, but fairly sharp, recession. When interest rates rose above 20 percent, the Federal Reserve allowed credit to expand and the recession ended.

August 1981–November 1982 This downturn was also set off by the Federal Reserve, which was now determined to wring inflation out of our economy. By the end of the recession—which now held the dubious distinction of being the worst downturn since the Great Depression—the unemployment rate had reached almost 11 percent. But the inflation rate had been brought down, and in late summer 1982, the Federal Reserve once again eased credit, setting the stage for the subsequent recovery. At the same time, the federal government had been cutting income tax rates, further helping along the business upturn.

July 1990–March 1991 After the longest uninterrupted peacetime expansion in our history, a fairly mild downturn was caused by a combination of sharply rising oil prices (due to Iraq's invasion of Kuwait on August 2 and the ensuing Persian Gulf War), tight money, and a deficit-cutting budget agreement between President George Bush and Congress in October. The agreement, which called for a package of tax increases and federal government spending reductions totaling nearly $500 billion over five years, was supposed to bring down the deficit. What it *did* was make the recession somewhat worse than it might otherwise have been and also retard the ensuing recovery. President Bush himself termed the recovery "anemic," and its slow pace was largely responsible for his loss of the 1992 election to Bill Clinton. Unemployment continued to rise—to a peak of 7.8 percent—well into the recovery, which took an unusually long 18 months. Indeed, it was not until the very last week of 1992 that economists were certain that the recession was over and that we had fully recovered.

The federal government obligingly facilitated this by providing Veterans Administration (VA) mortgages at about 1 percent interest and often nothing down to returning veterans. The Federal Housing Administration (FHA) supplemented this program with FHA mortgages to millions of other Americans. Where were these houses built? In the suburbs. By 1945, little land was available in the cities, so suburbanization was inevitable.

And how would these new suburbanites get to work? By car. Thus more highways were needed. Once again, the federal government stepped in. Before long a federally subsidized interstate highway network was being built, along with thousands of state and local highways, parkways, and freeways, as well as local streets and roads.

Hence the late 1940s and the 1950s were one big construction boom. Highway building and home construction provided millions of jobs. The automobile industry, too, was prospering after a total shutdown during the war. In the postwar era, we not only supplied all the new suburbanites with cars, but we also became the world's leading auto exporter. The industrial plants of West Germany and Japan had been destroyed or damaged during the war; it wasn't until the mid-1960s that those nations reentered the world market, and it took them another decade to capture more than 10 percent of the American car market.

The returning veterans, like the nation, had a lot of catching up to do. Couples had been forced to put off having children, but after the war the birthrate shot up and stayed high until the mid-1960s. This baby boom and low gasoline prices added impetus to the nation's suburbanization. Why continue to live in cramped urban quarters when a house in the suburbs was easily affordable?—as it was to most middle-class and working-class Americans (see box titled "Levittown, U.S.A.").

The only jarring economic notes were very minor recessions in 1945 and 1948–49 (see again the box titled "Post–World War II Recessions") and a serious bout of inflation immediately after the war when consumer prices rose 35 percent in three years. Then, just when inflation had been brought under control, the Korean War, which the country entered in June 1950, brought on another wave of price increases.

The 1950s: The Eisenhower Years

The economy was further stimulated by the advent of television in the early 1950s, as well as by the Korean War. It didn't really matter what individual consumers or the government spent their money on, as long as they spent it on something.

General Dwight D. Eisenhower, one of the great heroes of World War II, made two key promises in his 1952 campaign for the presidency: He would end the war in

Levittown, U.S.A.

Levittown, Long Island, a tract development of 17,000 nearly identical homes, was built right after World War II, largely for returning veterans and their families. These 800-square-foot, prefabricated homes sold for $8,000 each, with no down payment for veterans. William Levitt described the production process as the reverse of the Detroit assembly line:

There, the car moved while the workers stayed at their stations. In the case of our houses, it was the workers who moved, doing the same jobs at different locations. To the best of my knowledge, no one had ever done that before.[*]

Levittown became the prototype of suburban tract development, and the Levitts themselves built similar developments in New Jersey, Pennsylvania, and Maryland. And so, while tens of millions of Americans were able to move into new suburban homes in the decades after World War II, a popular cartoon of the 1950s depicted this scene: Ten men with briefcases are getting out of their cars. Ten identical dogs rush out of 10 identical homes to greet them while 10 wives, each with two children, wait at the front doors.

In 1963, civil rights demonstrations targeted William Levitt's housing development in Bowie, Maryland. Levitt admitted he had refused to sell houses to black families, because, he said, integrating his developments would put him at a competitive disadvantage. Levitt's discriminatory sales policy was no different from most other developers, who did not relent until well into the 1960s, when government pressure forced them to do so. To this day, most of the communities built by the Levitts remain overwhelmingly white.

*Eric Pace, "William J. Levitt, 86, Pioneer of Suburbs, Dies," *New York Times,* January 29, 1994, p. A1.

The Consequences of Suburbanization

Suburbanization was the migration of tens of millions of middle-class Americans—nearly all of them white—from our nation's large central cities to newly developed suburban towns and villages. Instead of getting to work by public transportation, these commuters now went by car. Truck transport replaced railroads as the primary way to haul freight. Millions of poor people—the large majority of whom were black or Hispanic—moved into the apartments vacated by the whites who had fled to the suburbs.

Suburbanization left our cities high and dry. As middle-class taxpayers and millions of factory jobs left the cities, their tax bases shrank. There were fewer and fewer entry-level jobs for the millions of new arrivals, largely from the rural South. Throughout the 1950s, 1960s, and 1970s, a huge concentration of poor people was left in the cities as the middle-class workers—both black and white—continued to flee to the suburbs. By the mid-1970s, the inner cities were rife with poverty, drugs, and crime, and had become socially isolated from the rest of the country.

Still other consequences of suburbanization were our dependence on oil as our main source of energy and, eventually, our dependence on foreign sources for half our oil. Indeed, America's love affair with the automobile has not only depleted our resources, polluted our air, destroyed our landscape, and clogged our highways, but also has been a major factor in our imbalance of trade.*

*The damage we are doing to our nation's environment and to that of our planet is alarming, but discussing it goes beyond the scope of this book. However, in the chapter on international trade, we do have a lengthy discussion of our trade imbalance and how our growing oil imports have contributed to it.

Korea, and he would end the inflation. Eisenhower made good on both promises. Although three recessions occurred during his eight years in office, the country continued to suburbanize, and economic growth, although not as fast as it had been in the 1940s, was deemed satisfactory by most Americans (see the box "The Consequences of Suburbanization").

What may be most significant about the Eisenhower years is what *didn't* happen rather than what did. Eisenhower made no attempt to undo the legacies of the New Deal such as Social Security, unemployment insurance, or the regulatory reforms that had been instituted. The role of the federal government as a major economic player had become a permanent one. Twenty-eight years later, when President Ronald Reagan left office after having paid great lip service to "getting the government off the backs of the American people," that role had grown even greater.

The Soaring Sixties: The Years of Kennedy and Johnson

When John F. Kennedy ran for president in 1960, the country was mired in the third Eisenhower recession. Kennedy pledged to "get the country moving again." The economy *did* quickly rebound from the recession, and embarked on an uninterrupted eight-year expansion. An assassin shot Kennedy before he could complete his first term; he was succeeded by Lyndon Johnson, who in his first speech as president stated simply, "Let us continue." A major tax cut, which Kennedy had been planning, was enacted in 1964 to stimulate the economy. That and our growing involvement in the Vietnam War helped bring the unemployment rate down below 4 percent by 1966. But three major spending programs, all initiated by Johnson in 1965, have had the most profound long-term effect on the economy: Medicare, Medicaid, and food stamps.

However, as the federal deficit mounted and as the money supply grew too quickly, another round of inflation began; it was not brought under control until the mid-1980s.

Part 5: From the Vietnam War to the Breakup of the Soviet Empire

Our country has been at relative peace—with the exception of the very brief war against Iraq in 1990–91—since our withdrawal from Vietnam in the early 1970s. Nevertheless, we have continued to spend about 4 percent of our national output on defense. With the breakup of the Soviet Union and its Eastern European military alliance came great hopes of a "peace dividend," but the government has made only minimal cuts in defense spending since 1990, and these hopes have been receding.

Since the early 1970s, our economic growth, no longer stimulated by suburbanization or war, has slowed markedly. By the presidential election of 1992, virtually everyone, including President George Bush, seemed to agree that our economy had somehow strayed far off course and would need to undergo major adjustments before things could be expected to pick up again.

The Sagging Seventies: The Stagflation Decade

In 1968, Richard Nixon said he had a plan to end the Vietnam War and to bring inflation under control. Soon after taking office, he was greeted by a relatively minor recession (see again the box titled "Post–World War II Recessions"), but his main problem was with inflation. On August 15, 1971, Nixon suddenly announced wage and price controls, but these were applied halfheartedly and did not seem to make much of an impact. Nevertheless, Nixon was reelected by a landslide in 1972, though by then he seemed unwilling or unable to get our economy back on course—perhaps because he had other things to worry about, such as getting impeached.

Stagnation + inflation = stagflation.

The 1970s brought Americans crashing back to economic reality. In 1973, we were hit by the worst recession in more than 30 years. This came on the heels of an oil price shock: The Organization of Petroleum Exporting Countries (OPEC) had quadrupled oil prices in the fall of 1973, and by then, too, we were mired in double-digit inflation, an annual rate of increase in prices of at least 10 percent. About the only good thing during this period was that we were able to add a new word to our vocabularies—*stagflation*. The first part of this word is derived from stagnation. Our rate of economic growth, which had been fairly rapid for 25 years after World War II, had slowed to a crawl. Usually when this happened, prices would stop rising or would at least slow their rate of increase. But now the opposite had happened: We had a bad case of inflation, which gave us the second part of the word *stagflation*.

Nixon's successor, Gerald Ford, did have a little success with respect to inflation, although his main weapon seemed to be a button he liked to wear that said WIN, which stood for "Whip Inflation Now."

Jimmy Carter's economic problems

The president who seemed to have the worst economic luck of all was Jimmy Carter. He presided over mounting budget deficits that, coupled with a rapid growth of the money supply, pushed up the inflation rate to nearly double-digit levels. And then suddenly, in 1979, the Iranian revolution set off our second oil shock. Gasoline prices went through the ceiling, rising from about 70 cents a gallon to $1.25 in June and July of that year.

Alarmed at the inflation rate, which had nearly doubled in just three years, the Federal Reserve literally stopped the growth of the money supply in October 1979. By the following January we were in another recession, while the annual rate of inflation reached 18 percent. Talk about stagflation!

Still another disturbing development was a slowing of our nation's productivity growth, or output per hour worked. By the late 1970s, it had dropped to only 1 percent, just about one-third its postwar rate.[9] Until we found a way to boost our productivity, our economy would continue to stagnate.

The 1980s: The Age of Reagan

Ronald Reagan, who overwhelmingly defeated incumbent Jimmy Carter in the 1980 presidential election, offered the answers to our most pressing economic problems. For too long, he declared, we had allowed the federal government to "tax, tax, tax, spend, spend,

---

[9]Productivity is output per hour worked, a concept we'll examine further in a chapter on economic growth and productivity in *Economics* and *Macroeconomics* and a chapter on unions, labor markets, and wage rates in *Economics* and *Microeconomics*.

spend." Big government was not the answer to our problems. Only private enterprise could provide meaningful jobs and spur economic growth. If we cut tax rates, said Reagan, people would have more incentive to work, output would rise, and inflation would subside. After all, if inflation meant that too many dollars were chasing too few goods, why not produce more goods?

Supply-side economics

This brand of economics, supply-side economics, was really the flip side of Keynesian economics. Both had the same objective: to stimulate output, or supply. The Keynesians thought the way to do this was to have the government spend more money, which, in turn, would give business firms the incentive to produce more. The supply-siders said that if tax rates were cut, people would have more of an incentive to work and would increase output.

Personal income taxes were cut by a whopping 23 percent in 1981 (stretched over a three-year period), and business taxes were also slashed. This was the heart of the supply-side program.

In January 1981, it was Ronald Reagan's ball game to win or lose. At first he seemed to be losing. He presided over still another recession, which, by the time it ended, was the new postwar record holder, at least in terms of length and depth. The second-worst recession since World War II had been that of 1973–75. But the 1981–82 recession was a little longer and somewhat worse.

The recession of 1981–82

By the end of 1982, the unemployment rate reached nearly 11 percent, a rate the country had not seen since the end of the Depression. But on the upside, inflation was finally brought under control. In fact, both the inflation and unemployment rates fell during the next four years, and stagflation became just a bad memory.

Still, some very troubling economic problems surfaced during the period. The unemployment rate, which had come down substantially since the end of the 1981–82 recession, seemed stuck at around 6 percent, a rate that most economists consider to be unacceptably high. A second cause for concern was the megadeficits being run by the federal government year after year. Finally, there were the foreign trade deficits, which were getting progressively larger throughout most of the 1980s.

"Read my lips."

In 1988, George Bush, who had served as Reagan's vice president for eight years and claimed to be a convert to supply-side economics, made this famous campaign promise: "Read my lips: no tax increase." Of course, the rest is history. Bush won the election, and a couple of years later, in an effort to reduce the federal budget deficit, he agreed to a major tax increase. Not only did his words come back to haunt him when he ran for reelection in 1992, but the deficit continued to rise. And to completely ruin his party, we suffered a lingering recession that began in the summer of 1990 and from which we did not completely recover until the end of 1992, with the unemployment rate still hovering above 7 percent.

The budget deficit has become a concern to all Americans. When Ronald Reagan took office in 1981, the deficit was $79 billion, but just 11 years later it had climbed to $290 billion. By 1998, however, it had virtually disappeared, and there was speculation that we would soon be running surpluses. We'll return to the deficit and the humongous national debt in the chapter on fiscal policy in *Economics* and *Macroeconomics*.

The State of American Agriculture

It is fitting that we close out our brief summary of American economic history with the present state of American agriculture because that's where we started some 200 years ago. While agriculture is perhaps the most productive sector of our economy, only about 4.5 million people live on farms today, and less than half of them farm full-time.

Despite the hundreds of billions of dollars in price-support payments to farmers for crops in the years since World War II, the family farm is rapidly vanishing (see box titled "The Farm Program: Hunger in the Midst of Plenty"). Within a generation, nearly all our food will come from huge corporate farms.

Expanding agricultural productivity

The story of American agriculture is the story of vastly expanding productivity. The output of farm labor doubled between 1850 and 1900, doubled again between 1900 and

The Farm Program: Hunger in the Midst of Plenty

We pay our farmers billions of dollars a year *not* to produce food. The reasoning is that these payments are needed to save the family farm. During the six decades this program has been in operation, 7 out of every 10 family farms have disappeared, while three-quarters of the payments go to large corporate farms.

There are nearly 1 million family farms still being operated, but farm subsidy payments are being drastically reduced in accordance with the farm bill of 1990. In fact, from 1986 to 1997, these payments were reduced from $25.8 billion to $6.2 billion. Who will be producing our food? Large corporate farms will grow the bulk of our food on huge plantations, employing millions of laborers at or below the minimum wage. One by one, the dairy farmers, the poultry farmers, the grain growers, and the feedlot operators are being squeezed out by the huge agricultural combines. The vast corporate farms of California's San Joaquin Valley are our future.*

On the supply side of the agricultural equation, we have a mismanaged farm program, which was supposed to help preserve the family farm and hold down agricultural surpluses but somehow managed to attain the opposite results. Yet amid all this plenty, there is widespread hunger in America. According to a recent study by Second Harvest, the largest charitable hunger-relief organization in the United States, 30 million Americans go hungry. And more than 30 million Americans make use of food pantries, soup kitchens, and other food distribution programs.

So we've got the U.S. Department of Agriculture paying farmers not to grow food, while millions of Americans—many of them children—go to bed hungry every night. In a land as bountiful as America, widespread hunger is not just a sign of inefficiency; it is a crime.

*The author is grateful to Dennis Olson, an organizer for the Great Plains Resource Council, for providing much of this information.

1947, and doubled a third time between 1947 and 1960. In 1800 it took 370 hours to produce 100 bushels of wheat. By 1960 it took just 15 hours. In 1820 one farmer could feed 4.5 people. Today that farmer could feed about 100 people.

In the chapter on economic growth and productivity in *Economics* and *Macroeconomics,* we'll talk about the Malthusian theory of population. At the beginning of the 19th century, Thomas Robert Malthus predicted that the world's population growth would eventually outrun its food supply. Although there is widespread starvation in some parts of the world and even in the United States (see again the box titled "The Farm Program: Hunger in the Midst of Plenty"), American farmers have been feeding a rapidly growing number of people. The amazing thing is that they have done this with fewer and fewer workers as the exodus from the land has continued to deplete their ranks.

Part 6: The American Economy near the End of the Century

All of our major wars have had very strong influences on our economy, generally setting off bouts of inflation and often speeding up our economic growth and reducing our unemployment as well. But our country has been more or less at peace since the early 1970s, when we withdrew from Vietnam. The 1990–91 Persian Gulf war against Iraq was too brief an encounter to have had a major economic impact, especially since it occurred in the middle of a recession and neither drove up prices nor reduced unemployment.

As the century draws to a close, Americans are focusing almost entirely on the country's economic problems. Although defense spending continues at over the $250 billion level, for the first time in at least six decades, our nation has virtually no military rivals. Even our rivalry with Japan is purely economic. It is somewhat ironic that at the height of our military power, most Americans see a rather bleak economic future.

For one thing, the average American worker is not doing nearly as well as she or he did some 25 years ago. In dollar wages, of course, we're *all* making more money, but in *real* wages—that is, wages paid in dollars of constant purchasing power—most of us are not doing all that well.

Our standard of living has not risen since the early 1970s.

Any way you measure it, our standard of living has not risen since the early 1970s. Average family incomes rose 111 percent (i.e., they more than doubled) between 1947

The New Vocabulary of Corporate Downsizing

It may be no consolation to the millions of Americans who have been "downsized" during the 1990s, but this phenomenon has certainly enriched our vocabulary. Here is some of the euphemistic new corporate lingo that tries to put a positive spin on these massive layoffs.

AT&T—"Force management program"
Bank of America—"Release of resources"
Bell Labs—"Involuntary separation from payroll"
Clifford of Vermont—"Career-change opportunity"
Digital Equipment Corp.—"Involuntary severance"
GM—"Career-transition program"
Harris Bank of Chicago—"Rightsizing the bank"

National Semiconductor—"Reshaping"
Newsweek—"Reduction in force (RIF)"
Pacific Bell—"Elimination of employment security policy"
Procter & Gamble—"Strengthening global effectiveness"
Stanford University—"Repositioning"
Stouffer Foods Corp.—"Schedule adjustments"
Tandem Computers—"Reducing duplication or focused reduction"
Wal-Mart—"Normal payroll adjustment"

Source: Compiled by William Lutz, appearing in *Newsweek,* August 12, 1996, p. 57.

and 1973. But over the next 24 years, they rose only 10 percent.[10] And the only reason they rose at all is because so many women joined the workforce.

If you *really* want to know how we're doing, you need to look at real median hourly pay for nearly 100 million workers. (The number of workers above the median, or middle, is the same as the number below it.) According to *Newsweek,* back in 1973 "the average nonsupervisory worker in the private sector earned $8.55 an hour (in 1982 dollars)." But in October 1997, "in those same 1982 dollars, the average hourly wage is $7.59—a stunning 11 percent drop over 24 years."[11] This is a striking statistic, especially when compared to the 50 percent increase in real wages enjoyed by American workers between 1950 and 1970.

Why have real wages fallen since 1973? There are numerous explanations. Plant closings and corporate downsizing have done away with millions of well-paid jobs. (See box, "The New Vocabulary of Corporate Downsizing.") The weakening of labor unions and the alternative of cheaper workers abroad have exerted downward pressure on wages. Still another factor has been the increasing tendency of business to replace full-time workers with temporary and part-time employees. Apparently about half the new jobs our economy has generated in the 1990s have been part-time or temporary.

The problem of poverty

In the second half of the chapter on income distribution and poverty in *Economics* and *Microeconomics,* we will discuss poverty in America. There are 36 million Americans below the poverty line[12] and perhaps 2 million homeless. In Santa Fe, the beautiful capital of New Mexico, where several hundred homeless people have staked out places to sleep, there's a sign under a bridge: "This is a home." In downtown Seattle, you can see

Signs of the times

people with signs around their necks: "No Job, No Food, No Hope." They don't even bother to add "No Home." Former vice presidential candidate Geraldine Ferraro remembers a little girl she saw near a shut-down steel mill near Pittsburgh holding up a sign that said, "My daddy needs a job." And all over America there are people with signs that say, "I will work for food."

Our mayors and governors go, hat in hand, to Japanese industrialists and beg them to set up factories in America. When the factories are built, these industrialists *do* provide jobs for Americans. But almost always they're semiskilled, relatively low-paying assembly-line jobs—and, incidentally, nonunion jobs as well.

---

[10]Peter Passell, "Harder Times, Softer Politics," *New York Times,* September 5, 1990, p. D2; Bureau of the Census, *Current Population Reports,* 1997, P-60.

[11]Marc Levinson, "Living on the Edge," *Newsweek,* November 4, 1991, p. 23; *Economic Indicators,* November 1997.

[12]The poverty line is the amount of money needed by a family to maintain a minimal standard of living. It is computed each year by the federal government.

Our problems threaten to overwhelm us.

Ours is a society beset with monumental problems that are threatening to overwhelm us. Crime, drugs, the disposal of nuclear waste, the spread of AIDS, and our dying central cities are becoming crises screaming out for solutions. After years of neglect, our interstate highway network remains, at best, a work-in-progress, highlighted by those orange signs, plastic barrels, flashing arrows, and one-lane stretches that seem to have become a permanent part of our landscape. And we have become a nation of consumption junkies who have run up a public and private debt exceeding $17 trillion—more than twice the value of our annual national output.

On a personal level, you might be asking: Will I be able to find a decent job when I graduate? Will I be able to live as well as my parents did? Or will I have to live with them because I won't be able to afford a place of my own? Will I be able to collect Social Security benefits when I retire, or will the whole system go bankrupt before then?

Which company is the largest employer in the U.S.A.? General Motors? Exxon? Wal-Mart? Do you give up? Our largest employer is Manpower, Inc., a temporary employment agency. And temp agencies like Manpower are our future. Bank of America, which has been cutting its full-time employees for years, hopes to soon reach its goal of having 80 percent of its staff made up of part-time employees working less than 20 hours a week—and ineligible for benefits like medical insurance.

We have certainly gotten ourselves into a fix. Why did the most prosperous nation in the history of the world fall so quickly from economic grace? Less than 15 years ago we were the world's largest creditor, but now we're the largest debtor. The American standard of living, which was long the highest in the world, has barely increased in 25 years. We are steadily losing our manufacturing base while hemorrhaging millions of well-paid blue-collar jobs. Our educational system turns out 1 million functional illiterates every year. One out of every 10 Americans is on public assistance, and there is a growing permanent underclass of hundreds of thousands of fourth- and fifth-generation welfare families. And even though we hold more than 1.6 million people in prison, our streets remain unsafe and drug dealers operate with impunity.

Not all the economic news is bad. Since the end of the last recession in March 1991, our economy has been expanding. From mid-1992 it grew at an annual pace of nearly 3 percent, and since September 1994, the unemployment rate has been below 6 percent. Moreover, the rate of inflation has averaged less than 3 percent since the beginning of 1992.

In April 1998 our economy reached the seven-year mark of uninterrupted expansion. At the time of this writing it is not known for sure what will happen, but if this expansion continues for another seven months, it will set a peace-time record. And if it were to continue through April 1999, then it would be the longest economic expansion in our entire history. That record was set between March 1961 and November 1969 and was stimulated by very large military expenditures during the Vietnam War.

President Reagan used to say that rather than fight over how the economic pie gets divided, let's just bake a bigger pie. Economics deals with how large a pie we bake (we call this production) and how that pie gets sliced up (which is distribution).

In order to bake a pie, you start with ingredients. The ingredients of our economic pie are our resources—land, labor, capital, and entrepreneurial ability—which we'll be taking up in the next chapter.

Questions for Further Thought and Discussion

1. Describe, in as much detail as possible, the impact of the Great Depression on the lives of those who lived through it.
2. What were the main agricultural developments over the last two centuries?
3. How have wars affected our economy? Use specific examples.
4. Inflation has been a persistent problem for most of the 20th century. What were some of its consequences?

WORKBOOK FOR CHAPTER 1

Name _____ Date _____

Multiple-Choice Questions

Circle the letter that corresponds to the best answer.

1. Which statement is true?

   a. Twenty-five million Americans were officially unemployed in 1933. b. Our economy expanded steadily from 1933 to 1945. c. Once the Great Depression began in 1929, our economy moved almost steadily downhill until the beginning of 1940.

   d. None of the above.

2. In the early 19th century, the United States suffered from a scarcity of

   a. land and labor b. land—relative to labor

   c. labor—relative to land d. neither land nor labor

3. Which statement is false?

   a. President Eisenhower presided over three recessions.

   b. Our economy has not had full employment since the early 1940s. c. There were six straight years of economic expansion under President Reagan.

   d. None of the above. (All of the above are true.)

4. Which statement is true?

   a. There was a great deal of stagflation in the 1970s.

   b. We had full employment for most of the 1980s.

   c. We have had seven recessions since World War II.

   d. None of the above.

5. Each of the following were elements of the New Deal except

   a. relief, recovery, reform b. a massive employment program c. unemployment insurance and bank deposit insurance d. a balanced budget

6. In which of the following years was there a recession?

   a. 1928 b. 1942 c. 1950 d. 1957

   e. 1965

7. At the time of the American Revolution, about _____ of every 10 Americans lived on a farm.

   a. one b. three c. five d. seven

   e. nine

8. Between 1939 and 1944, federal government spending rose by

   a. 100% b. 200% c. 300% d. 400%

   e. 500%

9. Each of the following was a year of high unemployment except

   a. 1933 b. 1938 c. 1944 d. 1975

   e. 1982

10. Which one of the following recessions was the mildest?

    a. 1948 b. 1957 c. 1973 d. 1980

    e. 1981

11. Between 1929 and 1933, output fell _____.

    a. by about one-tenth b. by about one-third

    c. by about one-half d. by about two-thirds

12. The inflation rate declined during the presidency of

    a. both Eisenhower and Reagan b. neither Eisenhower nor Reagan c. Reagan d. Eisenhower

13. Our national output is _____ that of Japan.

    a. one-half b. a little smaller than c. a little larger than d. almost twice

14. The transcontinental railroads completed in the 1860s, 1870s, and 1880s all bypassed the

    a. Northeast b. Midwest c. South

    d. mountain states e. Far West

15. Which statement is true?

    a. About 10 percent of all Americans live on farms today. b. The job prospects of college graduates today are better than ever. c. There were two recessions in the 1970s and two in the 1980s.

    d.   None of the above.

16. In general, the children of the baby-boom generation are _____ their parents did when they got out of school.

    a.   doing much better than   b.   doing a little better than   c.   doing about as well as   d.   not doing as well as

17. The age of the great industrial capitalists like Carnegie, Rockefeller, and Swift was in the

    a.   second quarter of the 19th century   b.   third quarter of the 19th century   c.   fourth quarter of the 19th century   d.   first quarter of the 20th century   e.   second quarter of the 20th century

18. We had a business downturn at the end of, or soon

    a.   after World War I and World War II   b.   after neither World War I nor World War II   c.   after World War II, but not World War I   d.   after World War I, but not World War II

19. Medicare and Medicaid were inaugurated under the administration of

    a.   Franklin Roosevelt   b.   Harry Truman   c.   Dwight D. Eisenhower   d.   John F. Kennedy   e.   Lyndon B. Johnson

20. Most of the recessions since World War II lasted

    a.   less than 6 months   b.   6 to 12 months   c.   12 to 18 months   d.   18 to 24 months   e.   24 to 36 months

21. Which statement is true?

    a.   President Eisenhower attempted to undo most of the New Deal.   b.   There was a major tax cut in 1964.   c.   The federal budget deficit was reduced during President Lyndon Johnson's administration.   d.   None of the above.

22. There was a major tax cut in

    a.   both 1964 and 1981   b.   neither 1964 nor 1981   c.   in 1964, but not in 1981   d.   in 1981, but not 1964

23. Our economic growth began to slow markedly

    a.   in the early 1940s   b.   in the early 1960s   c.   in the early 1970s   d.   between 1982 and 1985

24. Wage and price controls were introduced by President

    a.   Eisenhower   b.   Kennedy   c.   Johnson   d.   Nixon   e.   Ford

25. In the 1970s, our economy suffered from

    a.   inflation, but not stagnation   b.   stagnation, but not inflation   c.   inflation and stagnation   d.   neither inflation nor stagnation

26. The recession of 1990–91 was _____ and the ensuing recovery was _____.

    a.   deep, slow   b.   deep, fast   c.   shallow, slow   d.   shallow, fast

27. Our longest uninterrupted peacetime economic expansion took place mainly in the decade of the

    a.   1940s   b.   1950s   c.   1960s   d.   1970s   e.   1980s   f.   1990s

Fill-In Questions

1. The low point of the Great Depression was reached in the year _____.

2. In 1790, about _____ of every 10 Americans lived on farms.

3. The worst recession we had since World War II occurred in _____.

4. The country with the world's largest output is _____.

5. In 1933, our official unemployment rate was _____%.

6. Bills providing for Medicare and Medicaid were passed during the administration of President _____.

7. Today one American farmer feeds about_____ _____ people.

8. During President Dwight D. Eisenhower's two terms, there were _____ recessions.

9. Rapid technological change in agriculture during the first half of the 19th century was brought on mainly by _____ _____.

10. The main factor in finally bringing us out of the Great Depression was _____.

11. Since World War II there have been _____ recessions.

12. The quarter century that was completely dominated by the great industrialists like Andrew Carnegie and John D. Rockefeller began in the year _____.

Resource Utilization

Economics is defined in various ways, but scarcity is always part of the definition. We bake an economic pie each year, which is composed of all the goods and services we have produced. No matter how we slice it, there never seems to be enough. Some people feel the main problem is how we slice the pie, while others say we should concentrate on baking a larger pie.

Chapter Objectives

In this chapter you'll learn:

- The definition of economics.
- The central fact of economics.
- The four economic resources.
- The concepts of opportunity cost, full employment, and full production.
- Productive and allocative efficiency.
- What enables an economy to grow.
- The law of increasing costs.

Economics Defined

Economics is the efficient allocation of the scarce means of production toward the satisfaction of human wants.

Economics is the efficient allocation of the scarce means of production toward the satisfaction of human wants. You're probably thinking, *What* did he say? Let's break it down into two parts. The scarce means of production are our resources, which we use to produce all the goods and services we buy. And why do we buy these goods and services? Because they provide us with satisfaction.

The only problem is that we don't have enough resources to produce all the goods and services we desire. Our resources are limited while our wants are relatively unlimited. In the next few pages, we'll take a closer look at the concepts of resources, scarcity, and the satisfaction of human wants. Keep in mind that we can't produce everything we'd like to purchase—there's scarcity. This is where economics comes in. We're attempting to make the best of a less-than-ideal situation. We're trying to use our resources so efficiently that we can maximize our satisfaction. Or, as François Quesnay put it back in the 18th century, "To secure the greatest amount of pleasure with the least possible outlay should be the aim of all economic effort."[1]

Economics is the science of greed.

—F. V. Meyer

The Central Fact of Economics: Scarcity

Scarcity and the Need to Economize

Most of us are used to economizing; we save up our scarce dollars and deny ourselves various tempting treasures so we will have enough money for that one big-ticket item—a

---

[1]François Quesnay, *Dialogues sur les Artisans,* quoted in Gide and Rist, *A History of Economic Doctrines,* 1913, pp. 10–11.

new car, a stereo system, a trip to Europe. Since our dollars are scarce and we can't buy everything we want, we economize by making do with some lower-priced items—a Cadillac instead of a Rolls Royce, chicken instead of steak, a videotape rental instead of a neighborhood movie.

If there were no scarcity, we would not need to economize.

If there were no scarcity, we would not need to economize, and economists would need to find other work. Let's go back to our economic pie to see how scarcity works. Most people tend to see scarcity as not enough dollars, but as John Maynard Keynes[2] pointed out over 60 years ago, this is an illusion. We could print all the money we want and still have scarcity. As Adam Smith noted in 1776, the wealth of nations consists of the goods and services they produce, or, on another level, the resources—the *land, labor, capital,* and *entrepreneurial ability*—that actually produce these goods and services.

The Economic Problem

In the 1950s, John Kenneth Galbraith coined the term *the affluent society,* which implied that we had the scarcity problem licked. Americans were the richest people in the world (we've since slipped to fourth or fifth). Presumably, we had conquered poverty. But within a few years, Michael Harrington's *The Other America*[3] challenged that contention.

The economic problem, however, goes far beyond ending poverty. Even then, nearly all Americans would be relatively poor when they compared what they have with what they would like to have—or with what the Rockefellers, Du Ponts, Mellons, and Gettys have.

Human wants are relatively limitless (see box titled "E.T. and the Satisfaction of Human Wants"). Make a list of all the things you'd like to have. Now add up their entire cost. Chances are you couldn't earn enough in a lifetime to even begin to pay for all the things on your list.

John Kenneth Galbraith, American economist and social critic (UPI/Bettmann)

The Four Economic Resources

We need four resources, often referred to as "the means of production," to produce an output of goods and services. Every society, from a tiny island nation in the Pacific to the most complex industrial giant, needs these resources: *land, labor, capital,* and *entrepreneurial ability.* Let's consider each in turn.

---

[2]Keynes, whose work we'll discuss in later chapters of *Economics* and *Macroeconomics,* was perhaps the greatest economist of the 20th century.

[3]Michael Harrington, *The Other America* (New York: Macmillan, 1962).

E.T. and the Satisfaction of Human Wants

Remember the movie *E.T.?* Well, suppose E.T. were to return to Earth and hand each person $50 million. What would happen when everyone rushed out to spend this money? There simply would not be enough goods and services available. Still, assuming E.T.'s money was good, storekeepers would accept it. But since there would not be enough goods and services to go around, they would have to raise their prices. After all, what would you do if a line eight miles long formed outside *your* store?

Now an extraterrestrial like E.T. would never want to cause inflation, so you can be sure he would have made some provision for more goods and services to be made available. Imagine that he and his friends set up an E.T. shopping mall in every city and town in the world and continued to charge the old prices rather than the new in-flated prices. Everyone would be able to buy as much as he or she desired without having to worry about inflation.

Now we come to the greatest benefit of all. No one would ever have to take a course in economics. Why not? Because E.T. has eliminated the two conflicting forces that made economics necessary in the first place. Since we now have all the goods and services we desire, human wants are finally satisfied. Or, alternatively, the means of production are sufficient to produce everything people desire. We can no longer call them the "scarce means of production."

Of course, there may well be some people who would want even more than $50 million worth of goods and services. These people would still need to economize. And they'd still need to take courses in economics.

Land

As a resource, land has a much more general meaning than our normal understanding of the word. It includes natural resources (such as timber, oil, coal, iron ore, soil, and water) as well as the ground in which these resources are found. Land is used not only for the extraction of minerals but for farming as well. And, of course, we build factories, office buildings, shopping centers, and homes on land. The basic payment made to the owners of land is rent.

Labor

Labor is the work and time for which employees are paid. The police officer, the computer programmer, the store manager, and the assembly-line worker all supply labor. About two-thirds of the total resource costs are paid to labor in the form of wages and salaries.

Capital

Capital is "man"-made goods used to produce other goods or services. It consists mainly of plant and equipment. The United States has more capital than any other country in the world. This capital consists of factories, office buildings, and stores. Our shopping malls, the Empire State Building, and automobile plants and steel mills (and all the equipment in them) are examples of capital. The return paid to the owners of capital is interest.

Entrepreneurial ability

Entrepreneurial ability is the least familiar of our four basic resources. The entrepreneur sets up a business, assembles the needed resources, risks his or her own money, and reaps the profits or absorbs the losses of this enterprise (see the box titled "The Young Entrepreneur"). Often the entrepreneur is an innovator, such as Andrew Carnegie (U.S. Steel), John D. Rockefeller (Standard Oil), Henry Ford (Ford Motor Company), Steven Jobs (Apple Computer), or William Gates (Microsoft).

We may consider land, labor, and capital passive resources, which are combined by the entrepreneur to produce goods and services. A successful undertaking is rewarded by profit; an unsuccessful one is penalized by loss.

In the American economy, the entrepreneur is the central figure, and our long record of economic success is an eloquent testimonial to the abundance of our entrepreneurial talents. The owners of the nearly 20 million businesses in this country are virtually all entrepreneurs. The vast majority either work for themselves or have just one or two employees. But they have two things in common: each runs a business, and each risks his or her own money.

These resources are scarce because they are limited in quantity. There's a finite amount of land on this planet, and at any given time a limited amount of labor, capital, and entrepreneurial ability is available. Over time, of course, the last three resources can be increased.

Our economic problem, then, is that we have limited resources available to satisfy relatively unlimited wants. The reason why you, and everyone else, can't have three cars, a town house and a country estate with servants, designer clothing, jewels, big screen TVs in each room, and a $50,000 sound system is that we just don't have enough resources to produce everything that everyone wants. Therefore, we have to make choices, an option we call opportunity cost.

The Young Entrepreneur

An entrepreneur is a person who sees an opportunity to make a profit and is willing and able to risk his or her funds. I went to school with such a person.

When he was 14, he was standing in line with several hundred other boys waiting for an application for a summer job. He got hungry, so he asked the guy in back of him to hold his place in line while he got a hot dog. On his way back, several boys along the line asked him where he had gotten that hot dog. Dollar signs immediately danced before his eyes.

"I went back to the store and bought as many as I could carry. They gave me a carton of them. I went up and down the line, and I charged 10 cents more than I paid." He quickly ran out. Then, using the money he had collected, he went back to that store again and again.

He made more money working that line than he made for the first two weeks on that summer job. Before he was 30, he became a vice president of Helmsley-Spear, the giant real estate company. I don't know if he's still peddling hot dogs.

Opportunity Cost

Because we can't have everything we want, we must make choices. The thing we give up (i.e., our second choice) is called the opportunity cost of our choice. Therefore, *the opportunity cost of any choice is the forgone value of the next best alternative.*

Suppose a little boy goes into a toy store with $15. Many different toys tempt him, but he finally narrows his choice to a Monopoly game and a magic set, each costing $15. If he decides to buy the Monopoly game, the opportunity cost is the magic set. And if he buys the magic set, the opportunity cost is the Monopoly game.

If a town hires an extra police officer instead of repaving several streets, the opportunity cost of hiring the officer is not repaving the streets. Opportunity cost is the cost of giving up the next best alternative.

In some cases the next best alternative—the Monopoly game or the magic set—is virtually equal no matter what choice is made. In other cases, there's no contest. If someone were to offer you, at the same price, your favorite eight-course meal or a Big Mac, you'd have no trouble deciding (unless, of course, your favorite meal *is* a Big Mac).

The state of California has a limited number of tax dollars to spend. Two of its biggest expenditures are college education and prisons. The opportunity cost of building more prisons is building fewer colleges. Between 1967 and 1997 California built 21 prisons and only one new state university. Between 1990 and 1997, California's universities laid off 10,000 employees, while in the same period the number of state prison guards rose by 10,000. What then, is the opportunity cost of 10,000 more prison guards? It's 10,000 fewer university employees. Even more alarming, some of those laid off were economics professors.

Perhaps the most vivid example of opportunity cost occurred in the movie *Sophie's Choice*. When Sophie arrived at a concentration camp during World War II, a sadistic official ordered her to make a choice: she could save either her little boy or her little girl. In either case, the opportunity cost was inhumanly high. Fortunately, most choices confronting us are much more mundane.

In the next section we will be dealing with the production possibilities frontier, and once again, we will have to make choices. As we shall see, the more we produce of one product, the less we can produce of another product.

Full Employment and Full Production

Everyone agrees that full employment is a good thing, even if we don't all agree on exactly what full employment means. Does it mean that every single person in the United States who is ready, willing, and able to work has a job? Is *that* full employment?

The answer is no. There will always be some people between jobs. On any given day thousands of Americans quit, get fired, or decide that they will enter the labor force by finding a job. Since it may take several weeks, or even several months, until they find the "right" job, there will always be some people unemployed.[4]

If an unemployment rate of zero does not represent full employment, then what rate does? Economists cannot agree on what constitutes full employment. Some liberals insist that an unemployment rate of 4 percent constitutes full employment, while there are conservatives who feel that an unemployment rate of 6 percent would be more realistic.

Similarly, we cannot expect to fully use all our plant and equipment. A capacity utilization rate of 85 or 90 percent would surely employ virtually all of our usable plant and equipment.[5] At any given moment there is always some factory being renovated or some machinery under repair. During wartime we might be able to use our capacity more fully, but in normal times 85 to 90 percent is the peak.

In a global economy, not only has it become increasingly difficult to define which goods and services are made in America and which originate abroad, but one may even

---

[4]See the second part of Chapter 9 in *Economics* and *Macroeconomics*.

[5]Technically, this is the rate at which the nation's factories, mines, and utilities are operating.

question the relevance of a plant's location. If our steel industry were operating at full capacity, we could get still more steel from Germany, Japan, Korea, Brazil, and other steel-producing nations. In the context of the global economy, our capacity utilization ratio is clearly much less important than it was just a few decades ago.

As long as all available resources are fully used—given the constraints we have just cited—we are at our production possibilities frontier. A few additional constraints should also be considered because they too restrict the quantity of resources available. These are institutional constraints, the laws and customs under which we live.

The so-called blue laws restrict the economic activities that may be carried out in various cities and states, mainly on Sundays. Bars and liquor stores must be closed certain hours. In some places, even retail stores must be closed on Sundays.

State and federal law carefully restrict child labor. Very young children may not be employed at all, and those below a certain age may work only a limited number of hours.

Traditionally, Americans dislike working at night or on weekends, particularly on Sundays. Consequently, we must leave most of our expensive plant and equipment idle except during daylight weekday hours. We don't consider that plant and equipment unemployed, nor do we consider those whose labor is restricted by law or custom unemployed. All of this is already allowed for in our placement of the location of the production possibilities frontier (shown in Figure 1 in the next section).

By full production, we mean that our nation's resources are being allocated in the most efficient manner possible. Not only are we using our most up-to-date technology, but we are using our land, labor, capital, and entrepreneurial ability in the most productive way.

We would not want to use the intersection of Fifth Avenue and 57th Street in Manhattan for dairy farming, nor would we want our M.D.s doing clerical work. But sometimes we do just that.

Until recently in our nation's history, very few blacks were allowed to go to medical school (or law school or business school). Why? Because they were not white (see box titled "The Jackie Robinson Story").

And until recently only a tiny minority of women employed in the offices of American business were not typists or secretaries. In the 1950s and even into the 1960s, virtually every article in *Fortune* was written by a man and researched by a woman. What a waste of labor potential!

These are just a few of the most blatant examples of employment discrimination, a phenomenon that has diminished but has not yet been wiped out. Employment discrimination automatically means that we will have less than full production because we are not efficiently allocating our labor. In other words, there are millions of Americans who really should be doctors, engineers, corporate executives, or whatever but have been condemned to less exalted occupations solely because they happen not to be white Protestant males (see the box titled "The Glass Ceiling: Employment Discrimination at the Top").

The Jackie Robinson Story

Blacks had been banned from almost all professional sports since the turn of the century, but most notoriously by major league baseball. For decades there was a parallel association for blacks called the Negro leagues. Finally, the color barrier was broken in 1947 when Jackie Robinson began playing for the Brooklyn Dodgers.

Looking back, then, to all those years when black ball players were not permitted to play major league baseball, basketball, and football, hundreds of athletes were underemployed. Not only did they suffer economically and psychologically, but the American public was deprived of watching innumerable talented athletes perform.

In 1991 I met a few of the men who played in the Negro leagues when I was visiting Kansas City, where the Negro League Baseball Museum is located. They all knew Satchel Paige, a legendary pitcher whose fastball was so fast, the batters often couldn't even see it, let alone hit it. Sometimes Paige would wind up and pretend to throw a pitch. The catcher pounded his glove and the umpire called a strike. Then the catcher, who had the ball all along, threw it back to Paige. As great as he was, Satchel Paige didn't play in the major leagues until the twilight of his career, when he was in his late forties.

The Glass Ceiling: Employment Discrimination at the Top

You probably never heard of Linda Wachner or Jill Elikann Barad. They happen to be the only female chief executive officers (CEOs) of Fortune 500 industrial companies. Indeed, *Fortune* magazine found a female CEO so unusual that it did a feature article on Ms. Wachner.* For the record, Ms. Barad heads Mattel and Ms. Wachner runs Warnaco, which, among other things, manufactures Calvin Klein underwear.

They are the exceptions that prove the rule: In today's wonderful world of equal opportunity, you need to be a white male to get ahead in large corporations. There is a glass ceiling beyond which female executives do not rise. Although the barriers are coming down—at once exclusively male dining clubs; at country clubs; in executive recruitment programs; and in law school, business school, and medical school admission—there's an invisible "Men Only" sign posted on the entrances to most corporate executive suites.

Surveys by Catalyst, a nonprofit women's research and advocacy group, found that women held only 2.4 percent of the top jobs (chairman, president, CEO, and executive vice president) at the nation's largest 500 companies. And it can evidently get quite lonely at the top. Only three companies—Sallie Mae, Avon Products, and H. F. Abmanson—had more than one woman in their roster of the five top officers.†

Elite business schools began admitting large numbers of women in the mid-1970s. Because senior executives of major corporations usually have an MBA and at least 25 years of experience, we should see further increases in the number of women in senior corporate posts by the beginning of the new millennium. But according to the Federal Glass Ceiling Commission report released in 1995, "At the highest levels of business there is indeed a barrier only rarely penetrated by women or persons of color."

*Susan Caminiti, "America's Most Successful Businesswoman," *Fortune*, June 29, 1992.
†See *Business Week*, February 17, 1997, p. 6.

Using the best available technology

Finally, there is the question of using the best available technology. Historically, the American economy has been on the cutting edge of technological development for almost 200 years; the sewing machine, mechanical reaper, telephone, airplane, automobile, assembly line, and computer are all American inventions.

Perhaps the best case in point is the industrial robot, which illustrates both our historical innovative role and how that role has been altered. *Robotics,* a term coined by science fiction writer Isaac Asimov, was essentially an American development. But where are most industrial robots currently used? You win if your first guess was Japan.

Is this such a bad thing?

The reasons for this state of affairs are complex, but one thing should be perfectly clear. Americans have been losing their ability to use the best available technology, even if they invented that technology. Consequently, the country is operating below its full-production level.

Full employment and underemployment

We need to tie up one more loose end before moving on to the main focus of this chapter, the production possibilities frontier. We need to be clear about distinguishing between less than full employment and underemployment of resources.

If we are using only 70 percent of our capacity of plant and equipment, as we do during some recessions, this would be a case of our economy operating at less than full employment of its resources. Anything less than, say, an 85 percent utilization rate would be considered below full employment.

More familiarly, when the unemployment rate is, say, 10 percent, there is clearly a substantial amount of labor unemployed. But how much *is* full employment? We never really answered that one.

As a working definition, we'll say that an unemployment rate of 5 percent represents full employment. Why not use 4 percent, as the liberal economists suggest, or the 6 percent figure favored by the conservatives? Because 5 percent represents a reasonable compromise. So we'll be working with that figure from here on, but keep in mind that not everyone agrees that a 5 percent unemployment rate represents full employment.

Unemployment means that not all our resources are being used. Less than 95 percent of our labor force is working, and less than 85 percent of our plant and equipment is being used. It also means that our land and entrepreneurial ability are not all being used.

What is underemployment of resources? To be at full production, not only would we be fully employing our resources, we would also be using them in the most efficient way

Underemployment of College Graduates

According to the Bureau of Labor Statistics, one in five college graduates has a job that does not require a college degree. And many of the jobs they hold that *do* require a bachelor's degree are dead-end, low-wage positions.

There are about 1 million college graduates working as salesclerks; 1.5 million as typists, file clerks, and receptionists; and another 1.3 million as construction or assembly-line workers.

That's the *good* news. The bad news is that by 2005, according to Labor Department economists, 3 out of every 10 college graduates will have jobs like these.

Thomas Geoghegan, a labor lawyer, tried to learn exactly what was the difference between a college job and a noncollege job:

> What does the Bureau of Labor Statistics define as a college job?
> Manager of a Blockbuster video store? Yes.
> Assistant manager of Blockbuster? Maybe.
> Legal secretary? Can be.
> Police officer? Perhaps.
> Claims adjuster? Maybe.*

Members of the 1994 graduating class of the University of Illinois at Urbana-Champaign were asked a year after they graduated whether their college training was being put to good use. Almost 40 percent considered themselves underemployed, nearly double the percentage of recent years, according to David S. Bechtel, director of the university's career services center.

When I graduated from college, I met a recruiter from the Continental Baking Company who wanted to hire economics majors to be truck drivers. "How will I use my economics?" I asked. He had a great answer: "You can economize on the gasoline." I told him that I didn't go to college for four years so that I could drive a truck. He might have answered by asking if I would rather be *under*employed or *un*employed.

You are spending a great deal of time and money on your education. Unless our economic prospects improve substantially, you and your friends may spend a large part of your working lives underemployed. Who knows, that truck driving job may still be open.

*Thomas Geoghegan, "Overeducated and Underpaid," *New York Times,* June 3, 1997, p. A23.

[handwritten margin note: MORE COLLEGE GRADUATES THAN COLLEGE LEVEL JOBS]

The production possibilities frontier represents our economy at full employment and full production.

possible. To make all women become schoolteachers, social workers, or secretaries would grossly underuse their talents. Equally absurd—and inefficient—would be to make all white males become doctors or lawyers and all black and Hispanic males become accountants or computer programmers (see the box "Underemployment of College Graduates").

Similarly, we would not want to use that good Iowa farmland for office parks, nor would we want to locate dairy farms in the middle of our cities' central business districts. And finally, we would certainly not want to use our multimillion-dollar computer mainframes to do simple word processing.

These are all examples of underemployment of resources. Unfortunately, a certain amount is built into our economy, but we need to reduce it if we are going to succeed in baking a larger economic pie.

This brings us, at long last, to the production possibilities frontier. As we've already casually mentioned, the production possibilities frontier represents our economy at full employment and full production. However, a certain amount of underemployment of resources is also built into our model. How much? Although the exact amount is not quantifiable, it is fairly large. But to the degree that employment discrimination has declined since the early 1960s, it may be holding our output to 10 or 15 percent below what it would be if there were a truly efficient allocation of resources.

The Production Possibilities Frontier

Since scarcity is a fact of economic life, we need to use our resources as efficiently as possible. If we succeed, we are operating at full economic capacity. Usually there's some economic slack, but every so often we *do* manage to operate at peak efficiency. When this happens, we are on our production possibilities frontier (or production possibilities curve).

Often economics texts cast the production possibilities frontier in terms of guns and butter. A country is confronted with two choices: it can produce only military goods or only civilian goods. The more guns it produces, the less butter, and, of course, vice versa.

If we were to use all of our resources—our land, labor, capital, and entrepreneurial ability—to make guns, we would obviously not be able to make butter at all. Similarly, if we made only butter, there would be no resources to make any guns. Virtually every country makes *some* guns and *some* butter. Japan makes relatively few military goods, while the United States devotes a much higher proportion of its resources to making guns.

You are about to encounter the first graph in this book. This graph, and each one that follows, will have a vertical axis and a horizontal axis. Both axes start at the origin of the graph, which is located in the lower left-hand corner and usually marked with the number 0.

In Figure 1 we measure units of butter on the vertical axis. Each line or box stands for one unit. On the horizontal axis we measure units of guns. As we move to the right, the number of guns increases—1, 2, 3, 4, 5.

The curve shown in the graph is drawn by connecting points A, B, C, D, E, and F. Where do these points come from? They come from Table 1. Where did we get the numbers in Table 1? They're hypothetical. In other words, I made them up.

Guns and butter

Table 1 shows six production possibilities ranging from point A, where we produce 15 units of butter and no guns, to point F, where we produce 5 units of guns but no butter. This same information is presented in Figure 1, a graph of the production possibilities curve or frontier. We'll begin at point A, where a country's entire resources are devoted to producing butter. If the country were to produce at full capacity (using all its resources) but wanted to make some guns, they could do it by shifting some resources away

Figure 1   Production Possibilities Curve

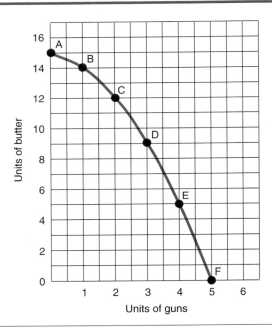

**Table 1   Hypothetical Production Schedule
for Two-Product Economy**

Point	Units of Butter	Units of Guns
A	15	0
B	14	1
C	12	2
D	9	3
E	5	4
F	0	5

from butter. This would move them from point A to point B. Instead of producing 15 units of butter, they're making only 14.

Before we go any further on the curve, let's go over the numbers at points A and B. We're figuring out how many guns and how much butter is produced at each of these points. Starting at the origin, or zero, let's check out point A. It's directly above the origin, so no guns are produced. Point A is at 15 on the vertical scale, so 15 units of butter are produced.

Now we'll move on to point B, which is directly above 1 unit on the guns axis. At B we produce 1 unit of guns and 14 units of butter (shown vertically). Incidentally, to locate any point on a graph, first go across, or horizontally, then up, or vertically. Point B is 1 unit to the right, then 14 units up.

Now locate point C: 2 units across and 12 up. At C we have 2 guns and 12 butters. Next is D: 3 across and 9 up (3 guns and 9 butters). At E: 4 across and 5 up (4 guns and 5 butters). And finally F: 5 across and 0 up (5 guns and no butter).

The production possibilities curve represents a two-product economy at full employment.

The production possibilities curve is a hypothetical model of an economy that produces only two products—in this case, guns and butter (or military goods and civilian goods). The curve represents the various possible combinations of guns and butter that could be produced if the economy were operating at capacity, or full employment.

Since we usually do not operate at full employment, we are seldom on the production possibilities frontier. So let's move on to Figure 2, which shows, at point X, where we generally are. Sometimes we are in a recession, with unemployment rising beyond 8 or 9 percent, represented on the graph by point Y. A depression would be closer to the origin, perhaps shown by point Z. (Remember that the origin is located in the lower left-hand corner of the graph.)

What if we were at the origin? What would that represent? Think about it. What would be the production of guns? How about the production of butter? They would both be zero. Is that possible? During the Great Depression in the 1930s, the U.S. economy sank to point Z, but no economy has ever sunk to the origin.

Move back to the production possibilities curve, say, at point C, where we are producing 2 units of guns and 12 units of butter. Is it possible to produce more guns? Certainly. Just move down the curve to point D. Notice, however, that we now produce fewer units of butter.

Figure 2   Points Inside and Outside the Production Possibilities Curve

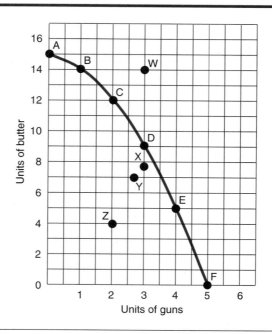

At D we have 3 units of guns and 9 units of butter. When we go from C, where we have 2 guns, to D, where we have 3, gun production goes up by 1. But at the same time, butter production declines from 12 at C to only 9 at D (a decline of 3).

If we're at point C, then, we can produce more guns, but only by sacrificing some butter production. The opportunity cost of moving from C to D (i.e., of producing 1 more gun) is giving up 3 units of butter.

Let's try another one, this time moving from C to B. Butter goes up from 12 to 14—a gain of 2. Meanwhile, guns go down from 2 to 1, a loss of 1. Going from C to B, a gain of 2 butters is obtained by sacrificing 1 gun. The opportunity cost of producing 2 more butters is 1 gun.

Except at point A, we can go somewhere else on the production possibilities curve and increase our output of butter. Similarly, anywhere but at point F, we can go somewhere else on the curve and raise our output of guns. It is possible to increase our output of *either* guns *or* butter by moving somewhere else on the curve, but there is an opportunity cost involved. The more we produce of one (by moving along the curve), the less we produce of the other. It is not possible, then, if we are anywhere on the curve, to raise our production of both guns *and* butter. Of course, over time it is possible to produce beyond our current production possibilities curve as our economy grows. We'll get to economic growth in a few minutes.

What if we're somewhere inside the production possibilities frontier? Would it be possible to produce more guns *and* more butter? The answer is yes. At point Z we have an output of 2 guns and 4 butters. By moving to point D we would have 3 guns and 9 butters. Or, by going to point E, output would rise to 4 guns and 5 butters.

We are able to increase our output of both guns and butter when we move from Z to D or E because we are now making use of previously unused resources. We are moving from depression conditions to those of full employment. But when we go from C to D, we stay at full employment. The only way we can produce more guns is to produce less butter, because resources will have to be diverted from butter to gun production.

Productive Efficiency and Allocative Efficiency

So far we've seen that our economy generally falls short of full production. Now we'll tie that failure in to our definition of economics.

At the beginning of this chapter, we defined economics as *the efficient allocation of the scarce means of production toward the satisfaction of human wants.* The scarce means of production are our resources, land, labor, capital, and entrepreneurial ability. So how efficiently do we use our resources?

Productive efficiency is attained when the maximum possible output of one good is produced, given the output of other goods.

An economy is efficient whenever it is producing the maximum output allowed by a given level of technology and resources. *Productive efficiency is attained when the maximum possible output of any one good is produced, given the output of other goods.* This state of grace occurs only when we are operating on our production possibilities curve. Attainment of productive efficiency means that we can't increase the output of one good without reducing the output of some other good.

As we've seen, our economy rarely attains productive efficiency, or full production. We did manage this state of grace from the summer of 1997 into early 1998 when the unemployment rate dipped below 5 percent. The last time our economy actually operated on its production possibilities frontier was during the Vietnam War, in 1968 and 1969.

Now we come to allocative efficiency, which occurs when no resources are wasted. *When an efficient allocation of resources is attained, it is not possible to make any person better off without making someone else worse off.* No society has ever come anywhere close to allocative efficiency.

When an efficient allocation of resources is attained, it is not possible to make any person better off without making someone else worse off.

In our hypothetical examples of production possibilities curves, we assumed that our economy produced just two goods or services. If our economy limited its production to two goods or services—or even 10—would this be an *efficient* allocation of our resources? Remember that the goal of economics is to satisfy human wants. Could *your*

AGAIN, IS THIS NECESSARY?

wants be satisfied with just 10 goods and services? Most people could easily make up lists totaling dozens of different goods and services which they consider basic necessities, and perhaps hundreds of additional goods and services which they would *like* to have.

Economists have long puzzled over the question of allocative efficiency, but we have more pressing things to consider—such as economic growth, which happens to be the subject of the next section.

Economic Growth

If the production possibilities curve represents the economy operating at full employment, then it would be impossible to produce at point W (of Figure 2). To go from C to W would mean producing more guns *and* more butter, something that would be beyond our economic capabilities, given the current state of technology and the amount of resources available.

The best available technology

Every economy will use the best available technology. At times, because a country cannot afford the most up-to-date equipment, it will use older machinery and tools. That country really has a capital problem rather than a technological one.

As the level of available technology improves, the production possibilities curve moves outward, as it does in Figure 3. A faster paper copier, a more smoothly operating assembly line, or a new-generation computer system are examples of technological advances. And increasingly, industrial robots and bank money machines are replacing human beings at relatively routine jobs.

Our economic capacity is also expanded when there is an expansion of labor or capital. More (or better trained) labor and more (or improved) plant and equipment would also push the production possibilities curve outward. This is illustrated in Figure 3, as we go from PPC_1 to PPC_2, and from PPC_2 to PPC_3.

In the 1950s, when Nikita Khrushchev, then the head honcho of the Politburo, said, "We will bury you," he wasn't trying to drum up business for his funeral parlor. He meant that the Soviet Union would overtake the United States in output of goods and services. At that time the U.S.S.R. was growing much faster than we were. But in the 1960s, our rate of economic growth sped up, while the Soviet rate slowed down.

Figure 3   Production Possibilities Curves

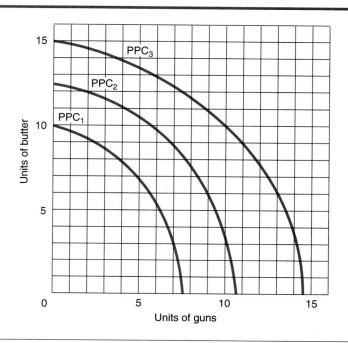

Handwritten margin notes: WHAT ABOUT TRADE DEFICIT? PER CAPITA?   WHAT ABOUT CHEAPER LABOR OVERSEAS?   SO WHAT IF WE UNDER UTILIZE RESOURCES?

However, since the early 1970s, our rate of growth, which had averaged over 3 percent a year during the last two centuries, slowed to only a little more than 2 percent.

There is no question that the American economy is in trouble. Another indication is the huge trade deficits that we have been running for more than a decade. What it all comes down to is that Americans are consuming too much and producing too little. Another way of putting this is that Americans are not saving enough and business firms are not investing enough. This is shown by the two alternate graphs of Figure 4.

Margin note: Americans are not saving enough.

Why can't we operate at point B of Figure 4 rather than at point A? That's a very good question. Probably the best answer is that Americans, for whatever reason, have come to believe in the adage "Buy today, pay tomorrow."

Buying "on time" became popular after World War II, along with relatively easy-to-obtain home mortgages, federal income tax preferential treatment for home ownership and personal borrowing,[6] and, over the last two decades, the tremendous expansion in the use of credit cards. In addition, Americans are bombarded by more than $125 billion worth of advertising a year. The products may vary, but the message remains the same: Buy! Buy! Buy!

The more we buy, the less we save. In fact, by 1986, Americans were saving only about 2 percent of their incomes after taxes, which was just one-third the rate of the 1960s. Also contributing to our shortfall of savings has been the federal government, which ran budget deficits approaching $300 billion by the early 1990s.

It all came down to this: The funds needed by business firms for investment in plant and equipment were no longer being provided in sufficient quantity by private savers, and the federal government was sopping up much of the savings that were available. Foreign investors, who had been accumulating surplus dollars from our trade deficits, were lend-

---

[6]Until 1987, interest paid on all consumer loans—for example, car loans, credit card loans, bank personal loans, and installment loans—was deductible from federal personal income taxes.

People who own their homes can deduct mortgage interest and property taxes from their federal personal income tax.

Figure 4   Production Possibilities Curves Over Time

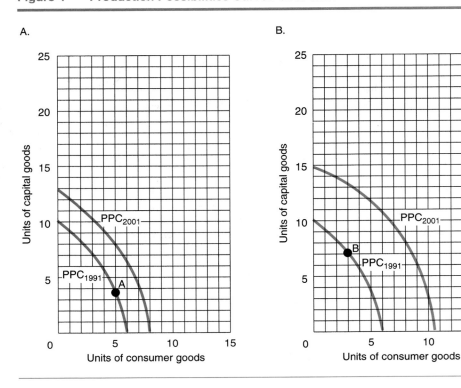

The Production Possibilities Frontier during World War II

World War II was a classic case of guns and butter, or, more accurately, guns *or* butter. Almost two years before we became actively involved in the war, we began increasing our arms production and drafting millions of young men into the armed services. Did this increase in military goods production mean a decrease in the production of consumer goods?

Gee, that's a very good question. And the answer is found when you go from point A to point B on the first figure shown here.

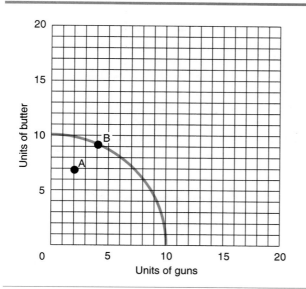

possible? Can we raise our production of both guns *and* butter to a point beyond our production possibilities frontier without jumping to a still higher production possibilities curve?

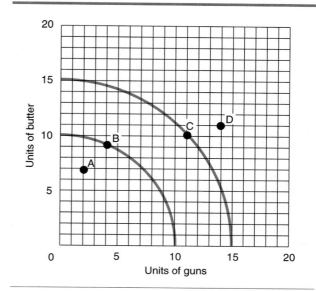

How were we able to increase the production of both guns and butter in 1940 and 1941? Because there was still a great deal of economic slack in those years. It was the tail end of the Great Depression described so eloquently in Chapter 1, and there were still millions of people out of work and a great deal of idle plant and equipment that could be pressed into use.

Now we're in the war, and we're at point B in the first figure. Is it possible to further expand our output of both guns and butter? Think about it.

Is there any way we could do it? How about if there's economic growth? In the second figure shown here, we went from point B to point C by moving to a higher production possibilities curve. Is this *possible?* Over a considerable period of time, yes. But in just a couple of years? Well, remember what they used to say: There's a *war* going on. So a move from point B to point C in just a couple of years is possible during a war.

Now we're really going to push it. How about a move from point C to point D in the second figure? Is *this* move

Well, what do you think? Remember, there's a war going on. The answer is yes. In 1942, 1943, and 1944 we did push our official unemployment rate under 3 percent, well below the 5 percent rate we would consider full employment today. Employers were so desperate for workers that they would hire practically anybody, and people who wouldn't ordinarily be in the labor market—housewives, retired people, and teenagers—were flocking to the workplace.

Meanwhile, business firms were pressing older machinery and equipment into use, because it was almost impossible to get new machinery and equipment built during the war. And so we were not only operating at full capacity, but well beyond that point.

How long were we able to stay at point D? Only as long as there was a war going on. Point D represents an output of guns and butter that our economy can produce temporarily if it operates beyond its production possibilities frontier. It's almost like bowling 300. You can't expect to go out and do it every night.*

*One can argue that we were temporarily operating on a higher production possibilities frontier and, at the end of the war, we returned to the lower production possibilities frontier.

ing us back some of our own money. But this was insufficient to provide all of the investment funds needed to spur our rate of economic growth.

We noted earlier in the chapter (in the full-employment and full-production section) that our investment in new technology was lagging. The United States, which had always been on the cutting edge of technological advance, was giving up this leadership role as well. Although American inventors were no less inventive, the application of their technological discoveries required investments that we were sometimes unable to make. I'll come back to this problem from time to time in subsequent chapters.

Let's go back again to the days of World War II when our economy began to expand at an extremely rapid rate. The question I raise in the box titled "The Production Possibilities Frontier during World War II" is this: Can we have more guns *and* more butter?

Finally, let's consider how we can get our economy to grow faster. We've talked about increasing our savings rate so that we'd have more money to invest in new capital goods. As our technology improves (most recently through computerization), our capital will be more productive.

Another important stimulant to growth is a growing labor force. Even more important, the better educated and trained our labor force is, the more productive it will be, and the faster will be our rate of growth. Examples of countries which experienced rapid economic growth due largely to their well-trained and well-educated labor forces are Germany, Japan, South Korea, Taiwan, Singapore, and Hong Kong.

The main factors spurring growth are an improving technology, more and better capital, and more and better labor. Using our resources more efficiently and reducing the unemployment of labor and capital can also raise our rate of growth. This topic is discussed more extensively in Chapter 16 of *Economics* and *Macroeconomics*.

Questions for Further Thought and Discussion

1. If you were in a position to run our economy, what steps would you take to raise our rate of economic growth?
2. Under what circumstances can we operate outside our production possibilities curve?
3. Give an example of an opportunity cost for an individual and a nation.
4. Would it be harder for a nation to attain full employment or full production? Explain.

[Handwritten margin notes:]

THE FED IS INCREASING RATES TO SLOW ECONOMY DOWN

AGAIN, GROWTH IS MEANINGLESS W/OUT CONSUMER GROWTH.

CONSUMER GROWTH IS ALREADY NEARLY PEAKED, IDENTIFIED BY LOW SAVINGS RATE

THIS AUTHOR CONTRADICTS HIMSELF OFTEN:

1) WANTS "BETTER EDUCATED LABOR" (P. 38) VS. "UNDEREMPLOYMENT OF COLLEGE GRADUATES" (P. 31)

2) COMPLAINS ABOUT LOWER NONUNION JOBS, (P. 19) VS. TRADE DEFICIT

3) PUSHES FOR MORE PRODUCTION GROWTH, (P. 38) & (P. 30) VS. AMERICANS CONSUMING TOO MUCH (P. 36)

WORKBOOK FOR CHAPTER 2

Name _____ Date _____

Multiple-Choice Questions

Circle the letter that corresponds to the best answer.

1. The word that is central to the definition of economics is
   a. resource   b. wants   c. scarcity   d. capital

2. We would not need to economize if
   a. the government printed more money   b. there
   was no scarcity   c. there was less output of goods and
   services   d. everyone received a big pay increase

3. Human wants are
   a. relatively limited   b. relatively unlimited
   c. easily satisfied   d. about equal to our productive
   capacity

4. Which of the following is an economic resource?
   a. gold   b. scarcity   c. labor   d. rent

5. Each of the following is an example of capital except
   a. land   b. an office building   c. a computer
   system   d. a factory

6. The opportunity cost of spending four hours studying a
   review book the night before a final exam would be
   a. the cost of the review book   b. missing four
   hours of TV   c. a higher grade on the exam
   d. the knowledge gained from studying

7. An economy operating its plant and equipment at full
   capacity implies a capacity utilization rate of
   a. 40 percent   b. 70 percent   c. 85 percent
   d. 100 percent

8. The full-production level of our economy implies
   a. an efficient allocation of our resources   b. zero
   unemployment   c. our plant and equipment being
   operated at 100 percent capacity   d. a high
   unemployment rate

9. Underemployment means
   a. the same thing as unemployment
   b. underutilization of resources   c. a recession
   d. slow economic growth

10. The production possibilities frontier represents
    a. our economy at full employment but not full
    production   b. our economy at full production but not
    full employment   c. our economy at full production
    and full employment

11. If we are operating inside our production possibilities
    frontier
    a. there is definitely a recession going on   b. there
    is definitely not a recession going on   c. there is
    definitely less than full employment   d. there is
    definitely inflation

12. The closer we are to the origin and the farther away we
    are from the production possibilities frontier
    a. the more unemployment there is   b. the less
    unemployment there is   c. the more guns we are
    producing   d. the more butter we are producing

13. Economic growth will occur if any of the following occur
    except
    a. a better technology becomes available   b. the
    level of consumption rises and the savings rate falls
    c. more capital becomes available   d. more labor
    becomes available

14. To attain a higher rate of economic growth, we need to
    devote
    a. a higher proportion of our production to capital goods
    and a lower proportion to consumer goods   b. a
    higher proportion of our production to consumer goods
    and a lower proportion to capital goods   c. a higher
    proportion of our production to both consumer goods and
    capital goods   d. a lower proportion of our
    production to both consumer goods and capital goods

15. Each of the following has contributed to our low rate of
    economic growth except
    a. our high rate of savings   b. our high rate of
    consumption   c. our federal budget deficits
    d. our low rate of investment

16. Statement 1: As we move toward a more global economy, our capacity utilization rate becomes more relevant.

    Statement 2: A capacity utilization rate of 100 percent means that our economy is operating at full capacity.

    a. Statement 1 is true and statement 2 is false.

    b. Statement 2 is true and statement 1 is false.

    c. Both statements are true.   d. Both statements are false.

17. Statement 1: The old Negro leagues provide an example of underemployment.

    Statement 2: Underemployment means basically the same thing as unemployment.

    a. Statement 1 is true and statement 2 is false.

    b. Statement 2 is true and statement 1 is false.

    c. Both statements are true.   d. Both statements are false.

18. Employment discrimination is most closely related to

    a. specialization   b. technology

    c. unemployment   d. underemployment

19. A woman who has a Harvard MBA who is working as a secretary would almost definitely be

    a. unemployed   b. underemployed   c. both unemployed and underemployed   d. neither unemployed nor underemployed

20. Which of the following is the most accurate statement?

    a. Women now hold about one-third of the senior management positions in Fortune 500 companies.

    b. The Glass Ceiling no longer exists.

    c. Underemployment of women, blacks, and other Americans has declined substantially since the 1950s.

    d. Although there was substantial employment discrimination in the past, there is virtually none today.

21. Which statement is true?

    a. America has always had a shortage of entrepreneurs.   b. Our economic problem is that we have limited resources available to satisfy relatively unlimited wants.   c. America has less economic resources today than we had 40 years ago.

    d. Aside from a few million poor people, we have very little scarcity in the United States.

22. Suppose you had $1,000 to spend. If you spent it on a vacation trip rather than on new clothes, your second choice, or 1,000 lottery tickets, your third choice, what was your opportunity cost of going on a vacation trip?

    a. $1,000   b. the vacation trip itself   c. not buying the new clothes   d. not buying the lottery tickets   e. missing out on the $10 million lottery prize

Fill-In Questions

1. The main reason for our lagging rate of economic growth has been not enough _____.

2. The central fact of economics is (in one word) _____.

3. Human wants are relatively _____, while economic resources are relatively _____.

4. List the four economic resources (1) _____;

   (2) _____; (3) _____;

   and (4) _____.

5. Opportunity cost is defined as _____

   _____.

6. If you went into a store with $25 and couldn't decide whether to buy a pair of jeans or a jacket, and you finally decided to buy the jeans, what would be the opportunity cost of this purchase? _____

7. Full employment implies an unemployment rate of about _____ percent.

8. List some constraints on our labor force that prevent our fully using our plant and equipment 24 hours a day, seven days a week.

   (1) _____;

   (2) _____;

   and (3) _____.

9. Employment discrimination results in the _____

_____ of our labor force.

10. When we are efficiently allocating our resources and

using the best available technology, we are operating on

our _____.

11. Most of the time our economy is operating _____

_____ its production possibilities frontier.

12. Economic growth can be attained by:

(1) _____ and

(2) _____.

13. Economics is defined as the allocation of the _____

toward the _____.

Problems

1. If we were at point C of Figure 1, could we quickly produce substantially more houses *and* more cars?

Figure 1

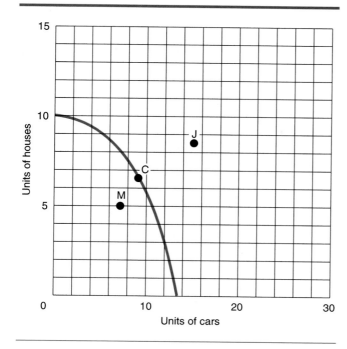

2. If we were at point M of Figure 1, could we quickly produce substantially more houses *and* more cars?

3. If we were at point C on Figure 1, could we quickly go to
point J?

4. Fill in the following points on Figure 2.
Point X: where our economy generally operates
Point Y: a serious recession
Point Z: a catastrophic depression
Point W: economic growth

Figure 2

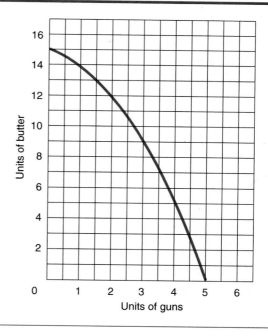

5. In Figure 3, fill in a new production possibilities frontier representing substantial economic growth.

6. In Figure 3, place point M where there is 100 percent unemployment.

7. Fill in the following points on Figure 4.
   Point A: an unemployment rate of 100 percent.
   Point B: an unemployment rate of 20 percent.
   Point C: an unemployment rate of 2 percent.

Figure 3

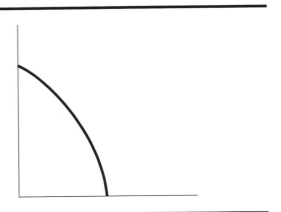

Figure 4

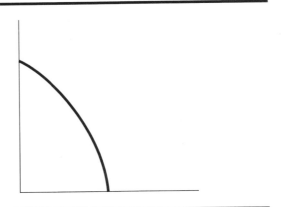

The Law of Increasing Costs[1]

You may notice that Figure A-1 is an exact duplication of Figure 1. You may also notice that as we shift production from guns to butter, we have to give up increasing units of guns for each additional unit of butter. Or, shifting the other way, we would have to give up increasing units of butter for each additional unit of guns we produce.

Figure A-1   Production Possibilities Curve

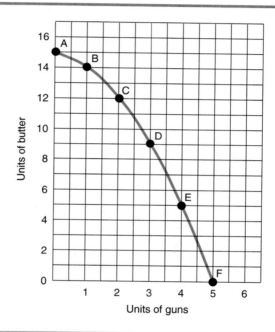

The law of increasing costs

We will be calling this "the law of increasing costs." Stated formally, this law says that *as the output of one good expands, the opportunity cost of producing additional units of this good increases.* In other words, as more and more of a good is produced, the production of additional units of this good will entail larger and larger opportunity costs.

The law of increasing costs is based on three concepts: (1) the law of diminishing returns, (2) diseconomies of scale, and (3) factor suitability. We've already alluded to factor suitability when we talked about using our resources in the most efficient way possible. One example was to use our computer mainframe for sophisticated data analysis rather than for simple word processing.

The law of diminishing returns, which we'll take up more formally in a later chapter, is defined this way: *If units of a resource are added to a fixed proportion of other resources, eventually marginal output will decline.* Suppose one farmer working with one tractor can produce 100 bushels of wheat on one acre of land. Two farmers, working together, can produce 220 bushels. And three, working together, can produce 350.

[1]Never content to give one name when we can come up with three, economists sometimes call this the law of increasing relative costs. The latter name may make some sense to you as you continue reading.

Diminishing Returns in the New York Region

The New York region, which includes the 15 counties in and around New York City, is extremely overcrowded, particularly with respect to getting around. In a sense, then, diminishing returns have set in when it takes 90 minutes to make a 20-mile trip to work, when daytime traffic moves at less than five miles per hour in midtown Manhattan, and when rush-hour gridlock threatens to prevent any movement whatsoever. The Houston area provides another example of overdevelopment resulting in near immobility.

The marginal output of the first farmer is 100. (In other words, the first farmer added 100 bushels to output.) The marginal output of the second farmer is 120. And the marginal output of the third farmer is 130. So far, so good. We call this increasing returns.

If we keep adding farmers, do you think we'll continue to enjoy increasing returns? Won't that single acre of land start getting a little crowded? Will that one tractor be sufficient for four, five, and six farmers? Suppose we did add a fourth farmer and suppose output rose from 350 to 450. By how much did marginal output rise?

It rose by only 100. So marginal output, which had been rising by 120 and 130, has now fallen to 100. We call this diminishing returns. (See box for another example of diminishing returns.) And it is one of the bases for the law of increasing costs.

Diseconomies of scale is a new term. As a business firm grows larger, it can usually cut its costs by taking advantage of quantity discounts, the use of expensive but highly productive equipment, and the development of a highly specialized and highly skilled workforce. We call these *economies of scale*. But as the firm continues to grow, these economies of scale are eventually outweighed by the inefficiencies of managing a bloated bureaucracy, which might sometimes work at cross-purposes. Most of the day could be spent writing memos, answering memos, and attending meetings.[2] Labor and other resources become increasingly expensive, and not only are quantity discounts no longer available, but now suppliers charge premium prices for such huge orders. As costs begin to rise, diseconomies of scale have now overcome economies of scale.[3]

Let's look at some increasing costs. We have already seen how we have had to give up the production of some guns to produce more butter and vice versa. We'll now take this a step further. To produce additional units of guns—one gun, two guns, three guns—we will have to give up increasing amounts of butter. Similarly, to produce additional units of butter, we will have to give up increasing numbers of guns.

How many units of butter would we have to give up to produce each additional gun? This is shown in Table A-1, which is derived from Figure A-1, or, if you prefer, from Table 1 of Chapter 2.

Table A-1   Production Shifts from Butter to Guns

Shift from Point to Point	Change in Gun Production	Change in Butter Production
A to B	+1	−1
B to C	+1	−2
C to D	+1	−3
D to E	+1	−4
E to F	+1	−5

In Table A-1, as we begin to switch from butter to guns, we move from point A to point B. We give up just one unit of butter in exchange for one unit of guns. But the move from B to C isn't as good. Here we give up two butters for one gun. C to D is still worse: We give up

---

[2]The time wasted performing these "managerial functions" is aptly described by Maryann Keller in *Rude Awakening* (New York: William Morrow, 1989), a book about General Motors Corporation.

[3]Economies and diseconomies of scale are more fully discussed in a later chapter.

three butters for one gun. D to E is even worse: We give up four units of butter for one gun. And the worst trade-off of all is from E to F: We lose five butters for just one gun.

This is why we call it the law of increasing relative costs. To produce more and more of one good, we have to give up increasing amounts of another good. To produce each additional gun, we have to give up increasing amounts of butter.

Three explanations for the law of increasing relative costs

There are three explanations for the law of increasing relative costs. First, there's diminishing returns. If we're increasing gun production, we will need more and more resources—more land, more labor, more capital, and more entrepreneurial ability. But one or more of these resources may be relatively limited. Perhaps we will begin to run out of capital—plant and equipment—or perhaps entrepreneurial ability will run out first.

Go back to our definition of the law of diminishing returns. *If units of a resource are added to a fixed proportion of other resources, eventually marginal output will decline.* Had we been talking about farming rather than producing guns, the law of diminishing returns might have set in as increasing amounts of capital were applied to the limited supply of rich farmland.

A second explanation for the law of increasing costs is diseconomies of scale. By shifting from butter to guns, the firm or firms making guns will grow so large that diseconomies of scale will eventually set in.

The third explanation, factor suitability, requires more extensive treatment here. We'll start at point A of Table 1, where we produce 15 units of butter and no guns. As we move to point B, gun production goes up by one, while butter production goes down by only one. In other words, the opportunity cost of producing one unit of guns is the loss of only one unit of butter.

Why is the opportunity cost so low? The answer lies mainly with factor suitability. We'll digress for a moment with the analogy of a pickup game of basketball (see Figure A-2). The best players are picked first, then the not-so-good ones, and finally the worst. If a couple of players from one side have to go home, the game goes on. The other side gives them their worst player.

Figure A-2   Choosing Players for a Basketball Team

Picking from right to left, the tallest player is picked first, then the next tallest, and so forth. So the most suitable players are picked first. And presumably, if you were choosing a football team, you'd pick from left to right.

If we're shifting from butter to guns, the butter makers will give the gun makers their worst workers. But people who are bad at producing butter are not necessarily bad at making—or shooting—guns.

When all we did was make butter, people worked at that no matter what their other skills. Even if a person were a skilled gun maker, or a gun user, what choice did he have?

Presumably, then, when given the choice to make guns, those best suited for that occupation (and also poorly suited for butter making) would switch to guns.

As resources are shifted from butter to guns, the labor, land, capital, and entrepreneurial ability best suited to guns and least suited to butter will be the first to switch. But as more resources are shifted, we will be taking resources that were more and more suited to butter making and less and less suited to gun making.

Take land, for example. The first land given over to gun making might be terrible for raising cows (and hence milk and butter) but great for making guns. Eventually, however, as nearly all land was devoted to gun making, we'd be giving over fertile farmland that might not be well suited to gun production.

Each of these three reasons—diminishing returns, diseconomies of scale, and factor suitability—helps explain the law of increasing costs. But now that the law is explained, we won't have to worry too much about it, because we would never devote all of our production to just one, or even a few, goods and services. Nevertheless, the law does have an applicability in certain localities and regions, or in particular economic sectors that may grow too large relative to the rest of the economy.

The law of increasing costs explains why we don't expand certain industries or sectors too far and what would happen if we did. That there are few examples of such overexpansion is eloquent testimony to the potency of the law.

Questions for Further Thought and Discussion

1. Explain the law of increasing costs, using a numerical example.
2. Discuss the three concepts upon which the law of increasing costs is based.

WORKBOOK FOR APPENDIX TO CHAPTER 2

Name _____ Date _____

Multiple-Choice Questions

Circle the letter that corresponds to the best answer.

1. As we produce increasing amounts of a particular good, the resources used in its production
   a. become more suitable   b. become less suitable
   c. continue to have the same suitability

2. The law of increasing costs is explained by each of the following except
   a. the law of diminishing returns   b. diseconomies of scale   c. factor suitability
   d. overspecialization

3. As a firm grows larger,
   a. economies of scale set in, then diseconomies of scale   b. diseconomies of scale set in, then economies of scale   c. economies of scale and diseconomies of scale set in at the same time
   d. neither economies of scale nor diseconomies of scale set in

4. The law of increasing costs states that as
   a. output rises, cost per unit rises as well   b. the output of one good expands, the opportunity cost of producing additional units of this good increases   c. economies of scale set in, costs increase   d. output rises, diminishing returns set in

Fill-In Questions

1. Large firms are able to lower their costs by taking advantage of _____.

2. When firms get too big _____ set in.

3. The law of increasing costs states that as the output of one good expands, _____.

4. The law of diminishing returns, diseconomies of scale, and factor suitability each provide explanations for the law of _____.

Problem

1. Given the information in Table A-2, what is the opportunity cost of going from point B to point C? And of going from point D to point C?

Table A-2   **Hypothetical Production Schedule for Two-Product Economy**

Point	Units of Butter	Units of Guns
A	15	0
B	14	1
C	12	2
D	9	3
E	5	4
F	0	5

2. Use Figure A-3 to answer these questions:
   a. What is the opportunity cost of going from point B to point C?
   b. What is the opportunity cost of going from point D to point C?
   c. What is the opportunity cost of going from point B to point A?
   d. What is the opportunity cost of going from point C to point D?

3. Use the data in Figure A-3 to illustrate the law of increasing costs numerically. (Hint: Start at point E and move toward point A.)

Figure A-3

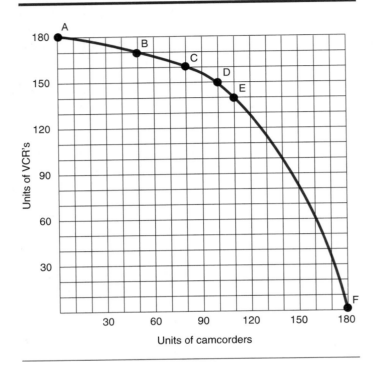

Units of camcorders

Supply and Demand

Our economy has a built-in guidance system that allocates resources efficiently. The interaction of the forces of supply and demand in the marketplace is known as the price system. How does it work? You're about to find out.

How are you at reading graphs? Economists love to draw them, so if you're going to get through this course, you'll need to be able to read them. The main graph we like to draw has just two curves: the demand curve and the supply curve. By observing where they cross, we can easily find not only the price of a good or service, but the quantity sold. In this chapter, you need to read only a few graphs. Later, if the book you're reading is titled *Economics,* you'll be drawing and analyzing graphs in Chapter 17. If your book is *Microeconomics,* drawing and analyzing graphs is covered in Chapter 5. But if your book is *Macroeconomics,* you won't have to worry about any of this until you take a course in microeconomics, probably next semester.

Chapter Objectives

In this chapter we'll answer four questions:

- What is demand?
- What is supply?
- What is equilibrium?
- What are shifts in demand and supply?

Demand

Definition of demand: the schedule of quantities of a good or service that people will buy at different prices.

We define demand as *the schedule of quantities of a good or service that people will buy at different prices.* And as you would suspect, the lower the price, the more people will buy.

How much would people living in Denver or in Chicago be willing to pay for a round-trip plane ticket for weekday travel between the two cities? Suppose we conducted a survey and were able to draw up a demand schedule like the one shown in Table 1.

Notice that as the price declines, increasing quantities of tickets are demanded. Now look at Figure 1 to see how a graph of this demand schedule looks.

The demand curve moves downward and to the right. That's because of the way we've set up our graph. Prices are on the vertical axis, with the highest price, $500, at the top. From here on, the vertical axis of every graph in this book will be measured in terms of money. The horizontal axis of Figure 1 measures the quantity sold, beginning with zero, at the origin of the graph, and getting to progressively higher quantities as we move to the right. In all the demand and supply graphs that follow, price will be on the vertical axis, and quantity on the horizontal.

Supply

Definition of supply: the schedule of quantities of a good or service that people will sell at different prices.

Supply is defined as *the schedule of quantities of a good or service that people are willing to sell at different prices.* If you compare the definition of supply with that of demand, you'll find that only one word is changed. Can you find that word?

Table 1   Hypothetical Daily Demand for Coach Seats on Round-Trip Weekday Flights between Denver and Chicago

Price	Quantity Demanded
$500	1,000
450	3,000
400	7,000
350	12,000
300	19,000
250	30,000
200	45,000
150	57,000
100	67,000

Figure 1   Hypothetical Daily Demand for Coach Seats on Round-Trip Weekday Flights between Denver and Chicago

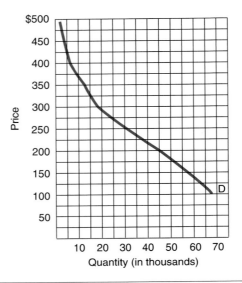

If you are a supplier, then you are willing to *sell* a schedule of quantities at different prices, while if you are a buyer, then you are willing to *buy* a schedule of quantities at different prices. What's the difference, then, between supply and demand? At higher prices the suppliers are willing to sell larger and larger quantities, while the buyers are willing to buy smaller and smaller quantities. Similarly, as price declines, buyers are willing to buy more and sellers are willing to sell less. But we're getting a little ahead of ourselves, as you haven't yet been formally introduced to a supply schedule. So first check out Table 2, and then Figure 2, which is a graph drawn from the numbers in the table.

What happens, then, to quantity supplied as the price is lowered? It declines. As Ross Perot has said, it's as simple as that.

But on the other hand, as economists like to say, we have skipped over a couple of very important considerations. In our definitions of demand and supply, we talked about a schedule of quantities of a good or service that people will buy or sell at different prices. One assumes that they are *able* to. But what if they just don't have the money? Then those buyers are simply not counted. We say that they are not in the market. Similarly, we would exclude from the market any sellers who just don't have the goods or services to sell. I'd *love* to sell my services as a $500-an-hour corporate lawyer, but quite frankly, I just don't have those services to sell.

That brings us to a second consideration not included in our definitions of supply and demand. The supply and demand for any good or service operates within a specific mar-

Table 2   Hypothetical Daily Supply for Coach Seats on Round-Trip Weekday Flights between Denver and Chicago

Price	Quantity Supplied
$500	62,000
450	59,000
400	54,000
350	48,000
300	40,000
250	30,000
200	16,000
150	7,000
100	2,000

Figure 2   Hypothetical Daily Supply for Coach Seats on Round-Trip Weekday Flights between Denver and Chicago

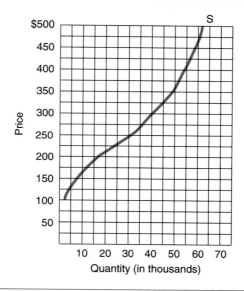

ket. That market may be very local, as it is for food shopping; regional, as it is for used cars; national; or even international. We'll have a lot more to say about markets near the beginning of Chapter 18 in *Economics* and Chapter 6 in *Microeconomics*.

Equilibrium

You've heard a lot about supply and demand—or is it demand and supply? It doesn't matter whether you put demand or supply first. What *does* matter is placing them together on the same graph. Look at Figure 3.

Can you find the equilibrium price? Did you say $250? Good! And how much is equilibrium quantity? Right again! It is 30,000.

Let's step back for a minute and analyze what we've just done. We've figured out the equilibrium price and quantity by looking at the demand and supply curves in Figure 3. So we can find equilibrium price and quantity by seeing where the supply and demand curves cross.

What is equilibrium price? It's the price at which quantity demanded equals quantity supplied. What is equilibrium quantity? It's the quantity sold when the quantity demanded is equal to the quantity supplied.

Equilibrium price is the price at which quantity demanded equals quantity supplied.

Figure 3   Demand and Supply Curves

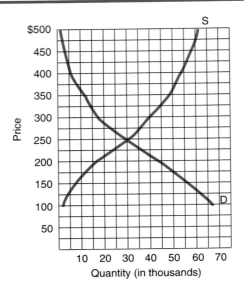

Surpluses and Shortages

Is the actual price, or market price, always equal to the equilibrium price? The answer is no. It could be higher and it could be lower. Suppose the airlines were selling tickets for $400. How many tickets would be demanded? Look back at Table 1 or, if you prefer, Figure 1 or Figure 3.

A total of 7,000 tickets would be demanded. And at a price of $400, how many tickets would be supplied?

A surplus occurs when the market price is above the equilibrium price.

The quantity supplied would be 54,000. What we've got here is a surplus. This occurs when the actual price, or the market price, is greater than the equilibrium price. How much is that surplus? You can measure it by finding the horizontal distance between quantity demanded and quantity supplied in Figure 3. Or, you can subtract the quantity demanded that you found in Table 1 (at a price of $400) from the quantity supplied in Table 2 (also at a price of $400). Either way, the surplus comes to 47,000.

What happens when there's a surplus? The forces of demand and supply automatically work to eliminate it. In this case, some of the airlines, which would be very unhappy about all those empty seats, would cut their prices. If the market price fell to $300, would there still be a surplus?

A glance at Figure 3 tells us that there would be. And how much would that surplus be? It would be 21,000 seats. So *then* what would happen?

Some of the airlines would cut their prices to $250, and the buyers would flock to them. The other airlines would have no choice but to cut their price—or stop flying the Denver–Chicago route altogether. At $250, these flights would be at the equilibrium point. There would be no tendency for the price to change, unless, of course, there's a shift in either the demand curve or the supply curve. But we won't deal with those shifts until the next section.

A shortage occurs when the market price is below the equilibrium price.

What if the market price were below equilibrium price? Then we'd have a shortage. How much would that shortage be if the equilibrium price were $200?

At a price of $200, quantity demanded would be 45,000, while quantity supplied would be just 16,000. So the shortage would be 29,000.

This time the buyers would be unhappy, because they would be quite willing to pay $200 for a round-trip ticket, but most would be unable to get one without waiting for months. Many of the buyers would be willing to pay more. So what do you think would happen?

You guessed it! The market price would rise to $250. At that price—the equilibrium price—quantity demanded would equal quantity supplied, and the shortage would be eliminated.

Thus we can see that the forces of demand and supply work together to establish an equilibrium price at which there are no shortages or surpluses. At the equilibrium price, all the sellers can sell as much as they want and all the buyers can buy as much as they want. So if we were to shout, "Is everybody happy?" the buyers and sellers would all shout back yes!

Shifts in Demand and Supply

So far we've seen how the forces of demand and supply, or the price mechanism, send signals to buyers and sellers. For example, the surplus that resulted from a price of $400 sent a clear signal to sellers to cut their prices. Similarly, a price of $200 was accompanied by a shortage, which made many buyers unhappy. And sellers quickly realized that they could raise their price to $250 and *still* sell all the tickets they wanted to sell.

Now we'll see how shifts in supply curves and shifts in demand curves change equilibrium price and quantity, thereby sending new sets of signals to buyers and sellers. Figure 4 has a new demand curve, D_2. This represents an increase in demand because it lies entirely to the right of D_1, the original demand curve. There has been an increase in demand if the quantity demanded is larger at every price that can be compared.

I'd like you to find the new equilibrium price and the new equilibrium quantity. When you do, please write down your answers.

The new equilibrium price is $300, and the new equilibrium quantity is 40,000. So an increase in demand leads to an increase in both equilibrium price and quantity.

Next question: What would happen to equilibrium price and quantity if there were a decrease in demand?

There would be a decrease in both equilibrium price and quantity. Need a little extra help? Then see the box "How Changes in Demand Affect Equilibrium."

OK, one more set of shifts and we're out of here.

Figure 5 shows an increase in supply. You'll notice that the new supply curve, S_2, is entirely to the right of S_1. There has been an increase in supply if the quantity supplied is larger at every price that can be compared.

Please find the new equilibrium price and quantity, and write down your answers.

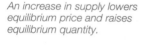
An increase in supply lowers equilibrium price and raises equilibrium quantity.

The new equilibrium price is $200, and the new equilibrium quantity is 45,000. So an increase in supply lowers equilibrium price and raises equilibrium quantity. One last question: If supply declines, what happens to equilibrium price and equilibrium quantity?

Figure 4   Increase in Demand

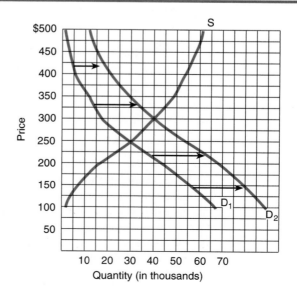

How Changes in Demand Affect Equilibrium

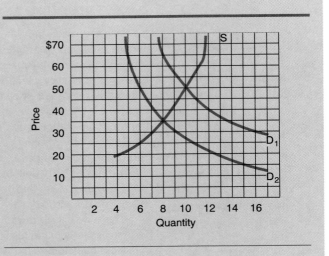

If demand falls and supply stays the same, what happens to equilibrium price and equilibrium quantity? To answer those questions, sketch a graph of a supply curve, S, and a demand curve, D_1. Then draw a second demand curve, D_2, representing a decrease in demand. I've done that in this figure.

The original equilibrium price was $50, and the original equilibrium quantity was 10. Equilibrium price fell to $35, and equilibrium quantity fell to 8. So a decrease in demand leads to a decrease in equilibrium price and quantity.

What would happen to equilibrium price and equilibrium quantity if demand rose and supply stayed the same? Equilibrium price and quantity would rise.

Figure 5   Increase in Supply

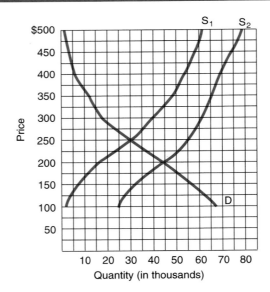

When supply declines, equilibrium price rises and equilibrium quantity declines. As you make your way through this text, supply and demand graphs will pop up from time to time. In every case you'll be able to find equilibrium price and quantity by locating the point of intersection of the demand and supply curves. If you need extra help, see the box "How Changes in Supply Affect Equilibrium."

Now let's work out a couple of problems. First, look at Figure 6 and write down your answers to this set of questions: (*a*) If the supply curve is S_1, how much are the equilib-

How Changes in Supply Affect Equilibrium

If supply rises and demand stays the same, what happens to equilibrium price and equilibrium quantity? Again, to answer those questions, sketch a graph of a demand curve, D, and a supply curve, S_1. Then draw a second supply curve, S_2, representing an increase in supply. I've done that in this figure.

The original equilibrium price was $12, and the original equilibrium quantity was 20. Equilibrium price fell to $9, and equilibrium quantity rose to 26. So an increase in supply leads to a decrease in equilibrium price and an increase in equilibrium quantity.

What happens to equilibrium price and equilibrium quantity if supply falls and demand stays the same? Equilibrium price rises and equilibrium quantity falls.

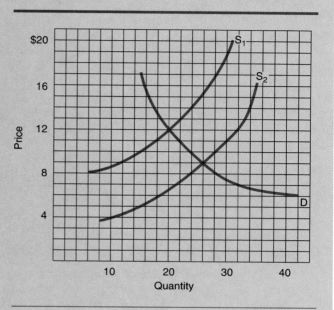

Figure 6

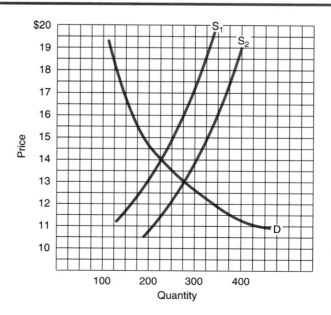

Figure 7

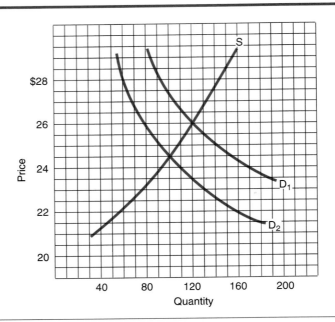

rium price and quantity? (*b*) If supply changes from S_1 to S_2, does that represent an increase or decrease in supply? (*c*) How much are the new equilibrium price and quantity?

Here are the answers: (*a*) $14; 225; (*b*) increase; and (*c*) $13; 275.

Next problem: Use Figure 7 to answer these questions: (*a*) If the demand curve is D_1, how much are the equilibrium price and quantity? (*b*) If demand changes from D_1 to D_2, does that represent an increase or decrease in demand? (*c*) How much are the new equilibrium price and quantity?

Here are the answers: (*a*) $26; 120; (*b*) decrease; and (*c*) $24.50; 100.

At the beginning of the next chapter, we'll see how the price mechanism plays the central role in allocating resources under capitalism. The forces of demand and supply operate as an automatic guidance system that enables our economy, and others like it, to provide consumers with an endless stream of goods and services.

Questions for Further Thought and Discussion

1. a. If market price is above equilibrium price, explain what happens and why. **b.** If market price is below equilibrium price, explain what happens and why.

2. Explain the concept of equilibrium.

3. What is demand? What are the two ways to depict a demand schedule?

4. a. As the price of theater tickets rises, what happens to the quantity of tickets that people are willing to buy? Explain your answer. **b.** As the price of theater tickets rises, explain what happens to the quantity of tickets that people are willing to sell. Explain your answer.

WORKBOOK FOR CHAPTER 3

Name _____   Date _____

Multiple-Choice Questions

Circle the letter that corresponds to the best answer.

1. When demand rises and supply stays the same,

    a. equilibrium quantity rises   b. equilibrium quantity declines   c. equilibrium quantity stays the same

2. When supply rises and demand stays the same,

    a. equilibrium quantity rises   b. equilibrium quantity falls   c. equilibrium quantity stays the same

3. At equilibrium price, quantity demanded is

    a. greater than quantity supplied   b. equal to quantity supplied   c. smaller than quantity supplied

4. When quantity demanded is greater than quantity supplied,

    a. market price will rise   b. market price will fall   c. market price will stay the same

5. What happens to quantity supplied when price is lowered?

    a. It rises   b. It falls   c. It stays the same   d. It cannot be determined if it rises, falls, or stays the same

6. What happens to quantity demanded when price is raised?

    a. It rises   b. It falls   c. It stays the same   d. It cannot be determined if it rises, falls, or stays the same

7. When market price is above equilibrium price,

    a. market price will rise   b. equilibrium price will rise   c. market price will fall   d. equilibrium price will fall

8. At equilibrium, quantity demanded is _____ equal to quantity supplied.

    a. sometimes   b. always   c. never

9. Market price _____ equilibrium price.

    a. must always be equal to   b. must always be above   c. must always be below   d. may be equal to

10. A demand schedule is determined by the wishes of

    a. sellers   b. buyers   c. buyers and sellers   d. neither sellers nor buyers

11. In Figure 1, if market price were $110, there would be

    a. a shortage   b. a surplus   c. neither a shortage nor a surplus

12. In Figure 1, if market price were $140, there would be

    a. a shortage   b. a surplus   c. neither a shortage nor a surplus

Figure 1

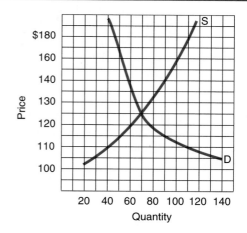

Fill-In Questions

1. If demand fell and supply stayed the same, equilibrium price would _____ and equilibrium quantity would _____.

2. If supply rose and demand stayed the same, equilibrium price would _____ and equilibrium quantity would _____.

3. If quantity supplied were greater than quantity demanded, market price would _____.

4. Equilibrium price is always determined by _____ and _____.

5. As price is lowered, quantity supplied _____.

Problems

1. In Figure 2, find equilibrium price and quantity.
2. Draw in a new demand curve, D_1, on Figure 2, showing an increase in demand. What happens to equilibrium price and quantity?

Figure 2

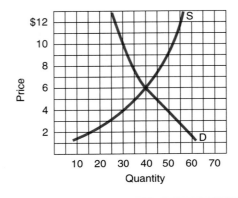

3. In Figure 3, find equilibrium price and quantity.
4. Draw in a new supply curve, S_1, on Figure 3, showing a decrease in supply. What happens to equilibrium price and quantity?

Figure 3

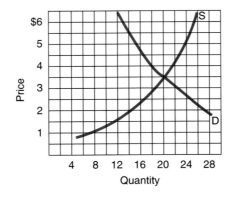

5. **a.** In Figure 4, if the demand curve is D_1, how much are equilibrium price and quantity? **b.** If demand changes from D_1 to D_2, does that represent an increase or decrease in demand? **c.** How much are the new equilibrium price and quantity?

Figure 4

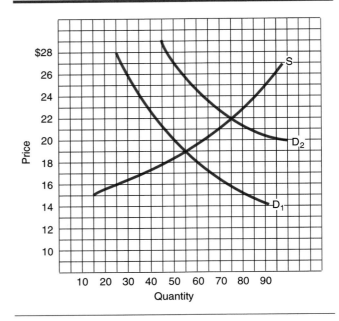

6. **a.** In Figure 5, if the supply curve is S_1, how much are equilibrium price and quantity? **b.** If the supply changes from S_1 to S_2, does that represent an increase or decrease in supply? **c.** How much are the new equilibrium price and quantity?

Figure 5

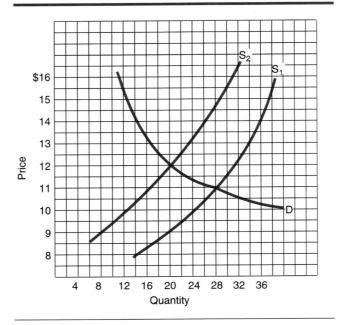

4 The Mixed Economy

Ours is a mixed economy because there is a private sector and a public sector. Close to 90 percent of our goods and services originate in the private sector, although the government co-opts some of this production for its own use. China also has a mixed economy, although the public sector produces the large majority of goods and services. As we shall see, the Chinese are, to some degree, lackeys of the capitalists while Americans are, to some degree, running dogs of the communists.

Chapter Objectives

In this chapter we'll cover:

- The three questions of economics.
- The concepts of the profit motive, the price mechanism, competition, and capital.
- The circular flow model.
- Market failure and externalities.
- The economic role of capital.
- Specialization and its consequences.
- The "isms": capitalism, fascism, communism, and socialism.
- The decline and fall of the communist system.

The Three Questions of Economics

Because every country in the world is faced with scarce (limited) resources, every country must answer three questions: (1) What shall we produce? (2) How shall these goods be produced? (3) For whom shall the goods be produced? We'll take up each in turn.

What shall we produce?

What Shall We Produce?   In the United States, most of our production is geared toward consumer goods. Almost 4 percent goes toward military goods. In the former Soviet Union, a much higher proportion was devoted to armaments, with a proportionately smaller percentage devoted to consumer goods. Japan has concentrated on building up its plant and equipment but devotes just 1 percent of its production to military goods.

Who makes these decisions? In the United States and Japan, there is no central planning authority but rather a hodgepodge of corporate and government officials, as well as individual consumers and taxpayers. The Soviets, as you probably guessed, *did* have a central planning authority. In fact, every five years the Soviet government used to come up with a new plan that set goals for its economy in numbers of cars, TVs, factories, and bushels of wheat and corn to be produced.

The resulting shortage of consumer goods was a perennial source of jokes in the former Soviet Union. One that was making the rounds a few years ago went like this:

A man walks into a store and asks the manager, "Is this the store that has no meat?"

"No," the manager replies, "This is *not* the store that has no meat."

"What store *is* this, then?"

"This is the store that has no fish. The store that has no meat is around the corner."

Shortages of consumer goods generally mean long lines, even when there is only a rumor that a shipment has arrived. In a *New York Times* article about his experiences while living in the Soviet Union, Marc Greenfield told this anecdote:

On a bus one summer day, I overheard this conversation between two women, one of them with a pair of Austrian boots:

"Did you have to stand long?"

"Not very. Only overnight."

"Overnight! You call that not long?"

"It's worse in winter, when you have to sleep in the doorways. This time it was fine. It was warm."

"Do they fit?"

"No; two sizes too big. But I wasn't going to stand in line for nothing."[1]

Here's another one:

A man goes into a Leningrad car dealership and orders a new car. The salesman tells him that the car will be delivered to him on June 15, 2006.

"Morning or afternoon?"

"What difference could it possibly make?" asks the salesman.

"Well, on the morning of June 15, 2006, the plumber is coming to fix the toilet."

How Shall These Goods Be Produced?   In our country—and in most others as well—nearly everything is produced by private businesses. Not only are all the goods and services that consumers purchase produced by businesses, but so are most of what the government purchases. For example, when our astronauts landed on the moon, a long list of contractors and subcontractors was released. It read like a who's who in American corporations.

In socialist countries, of course, the government is the main producer of goods and services. But even in the most strictly communist country, China, there is still a substantial role for private enterprise.

For Whom Shall the Goods Be Produced?   Economics may be divided into two parts: production, which we dealt with in the first two questions, and distribution. In the first question, we asked what the economic pie should be made of; in the second, we talked about how the pie would be made. Now we are ready to divide up the pie.

Our distribution system is a modified version of one dollar, one vote. In general, the more money you have, the more you can buy. But the government also has a claim to part of the pie. Theoretically, the government takes from those who can afford to give up part of their share (taxes), spends some of those tax dollars to produce various government goods and services, and gives the rest to the old, the sick, and the poor. (Nevertheless, the rich reap a major share of the subsidies to airlines, shipping companies, defense contractors, and agriculture.)

In theory, the Soviets' distributive system was diametrically opposed to ours. The communist credo "From each according to his ability, to each according to his needs" was something the Soviet leaders claimed to follow, and it does have a nice ring to it. But in actuality, their income distribution system, with its jerry-built structure of wage incentives, bonus payments, and special privileges, was probably no more equitable than our own.

This point is illustrated by a story about Leonid Brezhnev. His mother visited him at the Kremlin just after he took power in the mid-1960s. He wanted to show off, so he told her how well he was living, but she didn't say anything. He showed her his magnificent quarters, but she didn't seem very impressed. He took her for a ride out to his country estate. Still, nothing. No reaction. He couldn't understand how his aged mother, a woman of humble peasant origin, could fail to be impressed with how well her son was doing. So finally he blurted out, "Babushka![2] Tell me! What do you think?" "Leonid," the old lady replied, "what if the communists come back?"

---

[1]Marc Greenfield, "Life among the Russians," *New York Times,* sect. 6, October 24, 1982, p. 96.

[2]*Babushka* is an affectionate term that is roughly translated as "little grandmother." It really sounds much better in Russian, and it's OK to address an old peasant woman, not necessarily your grandmother, in this manner.

How shall these goods be produced?

For whom shall the goods be produced?

Henry Fairlie has come up with a capitalist credo: From each according to his gullibility. To each according to his greed.

The Invisible Hand, the Price Mechanism, and Perfect Competition

We have just set the stage for a comparison between our economic system and those of several other countries. We'll start with the competitive economic model, which is based on the law of supply and demand, then talk about the economic roles of government and of capital, and then discuss specialization. These concepts, common to all economies, need to be understood before we can make comparisons among the economies of different nations.

Back in the 1950s, there was a popular song that went:

Love and marriage
Love and marriage
Go together like a horse and carriage
Dad was told by mother
You can't have one without the other.

Just as love and marriage go together, so do the invisible hand, the price mechanism, and perfect competition.[3] Maybe a little less catchy than the words to a popular song, it admittedly has a beat; most economists kind of like to dance to it.

And like love and marriage, the invisible hand, the price mechanism, and perfect competition really do go together like a horse and carriage. In fact, you never can have one without the others.

The Invisible Hand

Adam Smith, Scottish professor of philosophy (Historical Pictures/Stock Montage)

Some students go through their entire principles of economics course believing that the invisible hand is something that once grabbed them in a dark movie theater. But when Adam Smith coined the term, he was actually thinking about some kind of economic guidance system that always made everything come out all right.

In fact, he believed that if people set out to promote the public interest, they will not do nearly as much good as they would if they pursued their own selfish interests. That's right! If all people are out for themselves, everyone will work harder, produce more, and we'll all be the richer for it. And that premise underlies the free-enterprise system.

Smith said that the entrepreneur is motivated by self-interest:

He generally, indeed, neither intends to promote the public interest, nor knows how much he is promoting it. By preferring the support of domestic to that of foreign industry, he intends only his own gain, and he is in this, as in many other cases, led by an invisible hand to promote an end which was no part of his intention. . . . By pursuing his own interest he frequently promotes that of the society more effectually than when he really intends to promote it.[4]

Whenever a businessperson runs for public office, he or she invariably brings up the fact that his or her opponent never met a payroll. This businessperson, motivated solely by a quest for profits, provided jobs for perhaps hundreds, or even thousands, of people. His or her firm produced some good or service so desirable that buyers were willing to pay for it. And so, this aspiring politician, who went into business solely to make money, now claims credit for creating jobs and promoting the public interest. And not a word of thanks to the invisible hand.

President Reagan was long a believer in supply-side economics, which placed great faith in the workings of the free-enterprise system. Supply-side economics is aimed at providing people with tax-cut incentives to work, save, and invest. Instead of appealing to their sense of patriotism, supply-side economics appeals to their self-interest by letting

---

[3]Perfect competition is the topic of Chapter 23 in *Economics* and Chapter 11 in *Microeconomics*. It exists only in industries in which there are many firms selling an identical product, where there are no legal, technical, or economic barriers keeping new firms from entering the industry.

[4]Adam Smith, *The Wealth of Nations,* Book IV (London: Methuen, 1950), chap. II, pp. 477–78.

them keep more of their earnings. One might add, parenthetically, that if all people wanted to do good, we might not have needed such strong incentives.

Perhaps the central axiom of supply-side economics is that the government's economic role has been too big. Ideally, if we reduce that role, individuals will take up the slack by performing charitable or public-spirited acts on a voluntary basis. Unfortunately, however, the response of our economy during the Reagan years was somewhat underwhelming.[5]

Less than a decade ago, about one-third of the food in the Soviet Union was produced on just 2 percent of the land under cultivation. That 2 percent was made up of small, privately owned plots; the other 98 percent was in the form of large collective farms. Obviously, the same farmers worked much harder on their own land than on the land whose produce was owned by the entire society. As Adam Smith said, a person pursuing his own interest "frequently promotes that of society more effectively than when he really intends to promote it."

After more than seven decades of communism, the Soviet Union still had not attained agricultural self-sufficiency. Indeed, since the early 1970s the Soviets had been purchasing up to a quarter of our wheat crop as well as smaller portions of our other agricultural staples. But now the acreage under private cultivation is expanding rapidly. It will be interesting to see if the Commonwealth of Independent States, as the former Soviet Union is known these days, will become agriculturally self-sufficient, as Adam Smith might have expected.

The invisible hand, then, is really the profit motive or, more broadly, economic self-interest, which guides us. It motivates us to do good by helping us do well.

The invisible hand is really the profit motive.

The Price Mechanism[6]

It is often said that everyone has a price, which means that nearly all of us, for a certain sum of money, would do some pretty nasty things. The key variable here is *price*. Some of us would do these nasty things for $100, others for $1,000, others perhaps only for $1 million.

Not only does everyone have a price, but everything has a price as well. The price of a slice of pizza or a gallon of gasoline is known to all consumers. Although they vary somewhat, gas prices rarely fall below a dollar, nor would anyone pay $5 for a slice of pizza.

Prices send signals to producers and consumers.

Just as prices send signals to consumers, they also signal producers or sellers. If pizza goes up to $5 a slice, I'll put an oven in my living room and open for business the next day.

The price system, which we examined in Chapter 3, is based on the law of supply and demand. When the sugar supply was curtailed about a dozen years ago, prices soared. And when people began driving less and the economy was in a recession, gasoline prices dropped in early 1982.[7]

When consumers want more of a certain good or service, they drive the price up, which, in turn, signals producers to produce more. If the price rise is substantial and appears permanent, new firms will be attracted to the industry, thereby raising output still further.

During the 1970s, when we experienced some of the worst inflation in our history, many people called for price controls. These were very briefly and halfheartedly instituted by President Nixon, and their results in controlling inflation were decidedly mixed. Critics

---

[5]Supply-side economics and four other economic policy schools are covered in Chapter 14 of *Economics* and *Macroeconomics*. Three major accomplishments of the Reagan years were sharply reduced rates of inflation and interest and the longest peacetime economic expansion on record.

[6]By the way, economists sometimes refer to the price system as the price mechanism. What's the difference between these two terms? There is none. To avoid confusion, I'll try to use just the price system from now on.

[7]Not only did demand for gasoline fall in the early 1980s, but a glut of oil developed in the world market. Price declines may result, then, from declines in demand, increases in supply, or some combination of the two.

of controls believe they interfere with our price mechanism and the signals that mechanism sends to producers and consumers. Others, most notably John Kenneth Galbraith, have argued that the prices of our major products are administered or set by the nation's largest corporations rather than in the marketplace. What this disagreement boils down to is whether our economic system is basically competitive, with millions of buyers and sellers interacting in the marketplace, or whether our economy is dominated by a handful of corporate giants who have subverted the price system by setting prices themselves.

Competition[8]

What is competition? Is it the rivalry between Chase and Citibank? GM and Ford? Most economists will tell you that to have real competition, you need many firms in an industry. How many? So many that no firm is large enough to have any influence over price. Thus, by definition, an industry with many firms is competitive.

Competition makes the price system work.

When GM or Ford announces its new prices, *those* are the prices for American cars. When Bank of America, Chase, Citibank, or any of the other six or eight leading banks announces the new prime lending rate, *that* is the benchmark interest rate on which nearly every loan will be based.[9] No ifs, ands, or buts. No give-and-take in the marketplace. And the price mechanism? It just doesn't apply here.

To allow the price mechanism to work, we need many competing firms in each industry. Would seven or eight U.S. auto firms be considered many? Or the 16 oil firms that refine over half the oil sold in the American market? Surely some among a handful of companies can influence price. Although there's no clear dividing line, probably most economists would consider the automobile industry at least somewhat competitive if there were 15 or 20 firms. And if there were about double the number of oil companies, that industry would also have a considerable degree of competition.

If large sectors of American industry are not very competitive, then the price system doesn't work all that well and the invisible hand becomes even more invisible. On the other hand, even without a perfectly competitive economic system, we can't just toss the price mechanism out the window. The forces of supply and demand, however distorted, are still operating. With all their price manipulation, even the largest corporations must guide themselves by the wishes of their consumers. In conclusion, then, let's just say that we have an imperfectly functioning price system in a less than competitive economy that is guided by a not too vigorous invisible hand.

Equity and Efficiency

Under our economic system, most of the important decisions are made in the marketplace. The forces of supply and demand (i.e., the price system) determine the answers to the three basic questions we raised at the beginning of the chapter: What? How? And for whom? Most economists would agree that this system leads to a very efficient allocation of resources, which, incidentally, happens to conform to our definition of economics: *Economics is the efficient allocation of the scarce means of production toward the satisfaction of human wants.*

Is our income distributed fairly?

So far, so good. But does our system lead to a fair, or equitable, distribution of income? Just look around you. You don't have to look far to see homeless people, street beggars, shopping-bag ladies, and derelicts. Indeed, there are about 36 million Americans whom the federal government has officially classified as "poor." Later in this chapter, we'll see that one of the basic functions of our government is to transfer some income from the rich and the middle class to the poor. Under the capitalist system, there are huge

---

[8]I use the terms competition and perfect competition interchangeably. We won't define perfect competition until later, but, for now, let's go with the definition given in the first paragraph of this section.

[9]This is not to say that the nation's leading banks are free to set the prime at 50 percent, or, for that matter, at 5 percent. However, within parameters set by credit market conditions—monetary policy, credit demand, availability of funds, and inflation—the banks are free to set the prime rate.

differences in income, with some people living in mansions and others in the streets. One of the most controversial political issues of our time is how far the government should go in redistributing some of society's income to the poor.

Very briefly, the case for efficiency is to have the government stand back and allow everyone to work hard, earn a lot of money, and keep nearly all of it. But what about the people who don't or can't work hard, and what about their children? Do we let them starve to death? The case for equity is to tax away some of the money earned by the rich and the middle class and redistribute it to the poor. But doing so raises two questions: (1) How much money should we redistribute? and (2) Won't this "handout" just discourage the poor from working? We'll discuss this further in the chapter on Income Distribution and Poverty toward the end of the book.

The Circular Flow Model

In Chapter 2 we talked about the four basic resources—land, labor, capital, and entrepreneurial ability. Who owns these resources? We all do. Nearly all of us sell our labor, for which we earn wages or salaries. In addition, many people own land or buildings for which they receive rent. A landlord may have just one tenant paying a few hundred dollars a month, or he or she may own an office building whose rent is reckoned by the square foot.

We also may receive interest payments for the use of our funds. Since most of the money we put into the bank is borrowed by businesses to invest in plant and equipment, we say that interest is a return on capital.

Finally, there are profits. Those who perform an entrepreneurial function (that is, own a business) receive profits for income.

The question we are asking here is, What do people do with their incomes? What happens to the tremendous accumulation of rent, wages and salaries, interest, and profit? Mostly, it is spent on consumer goods and services, which are produced by private businesses.

This is the essence of what economists call the *circular flow model.* A model is usually a smaller, simplified version of the real thing. (Think of a model plane or a model ship.) An economic model shows us how our economy functions, tracing the flow of money, resources, and goods and services. Let's take the circular flow model step by step.

First we have some 100 million households receiving their incomes mainly from the business sector. A household may be a conventional family—a father, mother, and a couple of children—it may be a person living alone, or it may be two cohabiting adults. Any combination of people under one roof—you name it—is defined as a household.

We diagram the household's income stream in Figure 1. Businesses send money income (rent, wages and salaries, interest, and profits) to households. We've ignored the government sector (i.e., Social Security checks, welfare benefits, food stamps).

In Figure 2 we show where this money goes. It goes right back to the businesses as payment for all the goods and services that households buy. In sum, the households provide business with resources—land, labor, capital, and entrepreneurial ability—and use the income these resources earn to buy the goods and services produced by these same resources.

In effect, then, we have a circular flow of resources, income, goods and services, and payments for these goods and services. By combining Figures 1 and 2, we show this circular flow in Figure 3.

We can distinguish two circular flows in Figure 3. In the inner circle, we have resources (land, labor, capital, and entrepreneurial ability) flowing from households to business firms. The business firms transform these resources into goods and services, which then flow to the households.

The outer circular flow is composed of money. Households receive wages and salaries, rent, interest, and profits from business firms. This money is spent on goods and services, so it is sent back to business firms in the form of consumer expenditures.

Who owns our resources? It is not the employer who pays wages—he only handles the money. It is the product that pays wages.

—Henry Ford

There are two circular flows.

Figure 1   The Flow of Resources and Payments for Them

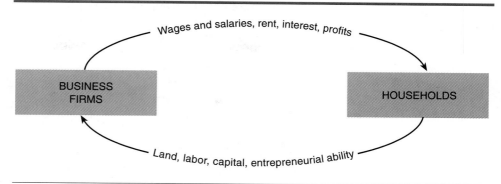

Figure 2   The Flow of Goods and Services, and Payments for Them

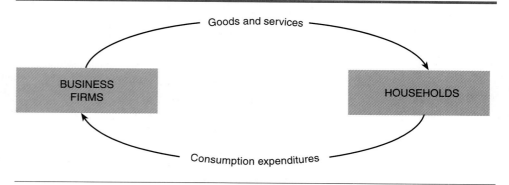

Figure 3   The Circular Flow

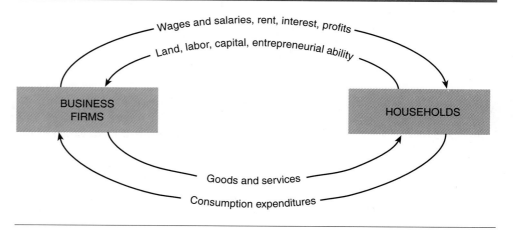

Thus we have two circular flows: (1) money and (2) resources, and goods and services. These two flows represent the economic activities of the private sector. Whenever any transaction takes place, someone pays for it, which is exactly what *does* happen whenever we do business.[10]

Although the circular flow model may appear fairly complex, it actually oversimplifies the exchanges in our economy by excluding imports, exports, and the government

---

[10]Resource markets and the determination of rent, interest, wages, and profits are fully discussed in later chapters of *Economics* and *Microeconomics*.

sector. I leave it to your imagination to picture the additional flow of taxes, government purchases, and transfer payments such as unemployment and Social Security benefits. We shall now look at the government's economic role, but our analysis will be separate from our analysis of the private sector.

The Economic Role of Government

The government under our federal system has three distinct tiers. At the top is the federal, or national, government, which we generally refer to as "the government." There are also 50 state governments and tens of thousands of local governments.

Each of these units of government collects taxes, provides services, and issues regulations that have a profound effect on our economy. By taxing, spending, and regulating, the government is able somewhat to alter the outcome of the three questions: What? How? and For whom?

The government provides the legal system under which our free enterprise economy can operate. It provides for the enforcement of business contracts, and defines the rights of private ownership. Our legal system works so well that bribery is the very rare exception, rather than the rule, as it is in so many other countries, especially many in Asia and Africa.

The government also maintains our competitive system and ensures the relatively unfettered operation of the law of supply and demand. Barriers to competition are sometimes broken down by the government, particularly when a few large firms attempt to squeeze their smaller competitors out of a market. We'll discuss those efforts more fully in the chapter on corporate mergers and antitrust in *Economics* and in *Microeconomics*.

Some of what we produce is done in response to government demand for roads, schools, courthouses, stamp pads, and missile systems. Government regulations have prevented business firms from producing heroin, cyclamates (from the mid-1960s to the late 1970s), and alcoholic beverages (from 1920 to 1933), as well as prostitutes' services (except in part of the state of Nevada, where they are legal).

How things are produced is also influenced by child labor laws, health and safety regulations, and pollution control. And finally, the government, by taking over $1.3 trillion away from wage earners in taxes, redistributes some of these funds to the old and the poor, thus strongly altering the outcome of the question "For whom?"

The size of our government depends largely on how well private enterprise does the job of efficiently allocating our resources. In the next section, we'll see that our price system does not always work perfectly, so the government is called upon to fix problems.

Market Failure

If our price system worked perfectly, there would be no such thing as market failure, and you wouldn't need to read these next couple of pages. *When our resources are not allocated efficiently, we have market failure.*

We'll examine two basic classes of market failure: externalities and public goods. Both provide the government with the opportunity to improve upon the work of Adam Smith's invisible hand. Another cause of market failure, monopoly, is the subject of a later chapter in *Economics* and *Microeconomics*.

Externalities

When you drive to school, how much does your ride cost you? Once you figure in the cost of gas, oil, and the depreciation on your car, you might come up with a figure of, say, 25 cents a mile. We call that 25 cents the *private cost* of driving to school.

External cost

But there's also an *external cost.* You cause a certain amount of pollution and congestion, and we could even factor in the cost of highway construction and maintenance. It would be hard to actually come up with a monetary figure, but there is no question that your drive to school imposes a definite social, or external, cost on society.

You probably never thought that driving to school was such a terrible thing, especially if there is no convenient public transportation. But you will be happy to know that you are capable of doing many socially beneficial things as well. If you paint your house and plant a beautiful garden in your front yard, you will not only add to the beauty of your neighborhood, but you will also enhance its property values. So now you will provide an *external benefit*.

External benefit

Definition of external cost and benefit

Let's define external cost and external benefit. An external cost occurs when the production or consumption of some good or service inflicts costs on a third party without compensation. An external benefit occurs when some of the benefits derived from the production or consumption of some good or service are enjoyed by a third party.

The private market, governed solely by the forces of supply and demand, does not take into account external costs and external benefits. This is market failure. When the market failure imposes a high cost on society, we demand that the government do something about it.

Basically, the government can take three types of action. If you are doing something that provides an external benefit, such as running a family farm, the government may provide you with a subsidy to encourage you to continue farming. As we saw back in Chapter 1, although the federal government has paid out hundreds of billions of dollars in farm subsidies since World War II, not only have most family farms disappeared, but huge corporate farms have gotten most of the subsidies.

If you are incurring external costs, the government can discourage these activities in two ways. It can tax you, or it can impose stringent regulations.

Let's consider what the government can do about air and water pollution. It could tax these activities highly enough to discourage them. A hefty tax on air pollution will force the biggest offenders to install pollution-abatement equipment. What about the disposal of nuclear waste? Do we let nuclear power plants dump it into nearby rivers, but make them pay high taxes for the privilege? Hardly. The federal government heavily regulates nuclear plants.

Basically, we want to encourage activities that provide external benefits and discourage those that incur external costs. One method now used in many states is the five-cent deposit on cans and bottles. Millions of people have a monetary incentive to do the right thing by returning these bottles and cans for recycling.

Lack of Public Goods and Services

A wide range of goods and services is supplied by our federal, state, and local governments. These include national defense; a court system; police protection; the construction and maintenance of streets, highways, bridges, plus water and sewer mains; environmental protection; public parks; and public schools. Few of these would be supplied by private enterprise because entrepreneurs would not be able to make a profit.

Interestingly, many of these goods and services *were* once supplied by private enterprise. The nation's first toll road, Pennsylvania's Lancaster Turnpike, was built two centuries ago. Private toll bridges were constructed all over the country. Even today, there are more than twice as many people who work in private security ("rent-a-cops," store and hotel detectives, building security, campus security, and private investigators, for example) than there are city and state police. Our national rail lines were once privately owned, with such fabled names as the Pennsylvania (or Pennsy) Railroad; the Baltimore and Ohio (you'll still find the B&O on the Monopoly board); the Seaboard; the Southern; the Great Northern; the New York Central; the New York, New Haven, and Hartford; the Boston and Maine; the Southern Pacific; and the storied Atchison, Topeka, and the Santa Fe.

Difference between public and private goods

Let's talk about the difference between *public* goods and *private* goods. Private goods are easy. You buy a car. It's your car. But a public good is something whose consumption by one person does not prevent its consumption by other people. Take our national defense. If you want to pay to have your home defended from nuclear attack, then everyone on your block is defended as well, even though they don't chip in a cent. Or, if

Karl Marx, German economist, historian, and philosopher (Historical Pictures/Stock Montage)

Capital consists of plant and equipment.

The central economic role of capital

Where did capital come from?

your block association hires a private security firm to patrol your neighborhood, even your neighbors who were too cheap to pay their dues are protected.

Public goods tend to be indivisible; they usually come in large units that cannot be broken into pieces for purchase or sale in private markets. Often there is no way they can be produced by private enterprise because there is no way to exclude anyone from consuming the goods even if she or he did not pay for them. National defense is a classic example. Could you imagine putting *that* service on a pay-as-you-go basis? "I think this year I'll just skip being defended." We can't exactly move the nuclear umbrella away from my house while continuing to shield those of all my neighbors.

Capital

Capital is the crucial element in every economic system. Karl Marx's classic *Das Kapital*[11] examined the role of capital in the mid-19th-century industralizing economy of England. According to Marx, the central figure of capitalism is the capitalist, or business owner, who makes huge profits by exploiting his workers. Capitalism is denigrated by communist societies whose own economic system has been labeled *state capitalism.*

Capital consists of plant and equipment. Marx said that whoever controlled a society's capital controlled that society. In today's economy, it takes a great deal of wealth to control much capital, so whether or not you agree with Marx's conclusions, you'd have to agree that the people who own large chunks of America's leading corporations are not exactly without influence.

Furthermore, Marx observed that one's social consciousness was determined by one's relationship to the means of production. Inevitably, he believed, there would be a clash between the capitalists and the workers, leading to an overthrow of capitalism and the establishment of a communist society. Then the workers would own the means of production. In the Soviet Union, incidentally, the means of production *were* owned by the workers, but the ruling elite, the top Communist Party officials, had real economic and political control.

The role of capital in the production process is central to why our country is rich and most of the rest of the world is poor. The reason an American farmer can produce 10 or 20 times as much as a Chinese farmer is that the American has much more capital with which to work—combines, tractors, harvesters, and reapers. And the reason the American factory worker is more productive than the Brazilian factory worker is that our factories are much better equipped. We have a tremendous stock of computers, assembly lines, warehouses, machine tools, and so on.

Take the example of the word processor. In the past, a lot of business letters had to be personally or individually typed, although they were really only form letters. Today we have a word processor that can be programmed to type out identical texts with different addressees at better than a letter a minute.

Our stock of capital enables us to turn out many more goods per hour of labor than we could produce without it. Much backbreaking as well as tedious labor has been eliminated by machines. Without our capital, we would have the same living standard as that of people throughout Asia, Africa, and Latin America.

Where did capital come from? Essentially from savings. Some people would set aside part of their savings, go into business, and purchase plant and equipment (see box "Where Capital Comes From"). But we're really skipping a step.

Initially there was no capital, except for some crude plows and other farm tools. People worked from sunrise to sunset just to produce enough food to put on the table. But a few farmers, a little more prosperous than their neighbors, were able to spare some time to build better farm tools. Or they might have had enough food stored away to employ someone to build these tools. Either way, some productive resources were diverted from producing consumer goods to producing capital goods.

---

[11]Karl Marx, *Das Kapital* (New York: International Publishers, 1967).

Where Capital Comes From

The following hypothetical situation will illustrate the value of capital. Suppose it takes a man 10 hours to make an optical lens, while someone working with a machine can make one in just 5 hours. Let's assume that it would take 1,000 hours to build such a machine.

Assume, however, that a person working 10 hours a day is barely able to support himself and his family. (Karl Marx observed that in most working-class families, not only did wives work, but they didn't have to worry about day care centers or baby-sitters for the children because factories employed six- and seven-year-olds.) If he could not afford to spend 100 days (1,000 hours) building the machine, he still had two choices. He could cut back on his consumption—that is, lower his family's standard of living—by working nine hours a day on the lenses and one hour a day on building the machine. Or he could work, say, an extra hour a day on the machine.

In either case, it would take 1,000 days to build the machine. If he cut back on his consumption *and* worked an extra hour a day, it would take him 500 days to build the machine.

Once he had the machine, he'd really be in business. He could double his daily output from one lens a day to two a day (remember that a person working with a machine can turn out a lens in just five hours).

Each day, if he held his consumption to the same level, he would produce two lenses and sell one for food, rent, and other necessities. The other lens he'd save. At the end of just 100 days, he'd have saved 100 lenses. Those 100 lenses represent 1,000 hours of labor, which is exactly the same amount of labor that went into building a machine. He would probably be able to buy another machine with those 100 lenses.

Now he's really a capitalist! He'll hire someone to run the second machine and pay him a lens a day. And in another 100 days, he'll have a surplus of 200 lenses and he'll be able to buy two more machines, hire a foreman to run his shop, retire to a condominium in Miami Beach at the age of 36, and be the richest kid on the block.

The factory conditions of the 19th-century England that Marx described in *Das Kapital* were barbaric, but the end result was that a surplus of consumer goods was produced. The factory owner, by paying his workers meager wages, was able to use this surplus to buy more capital goods. These enabled his factory to be more productive, creating still greater surpluses that were used to purchase still more plant and equipment.

Under Joseph Stalin, the Russians devoted a large part of their production to capital goods, literally starving the Russian population of consumer goods. To this day there is a great shortage of consumer goods in the former Soviet Union. But this shortage is no longer due to diversion of resources from production of consumer goods to the production of capital goods. It is due to the inefficiencies of the economic system itself—something we'll be looking at more closely in the closing pages of this chapter.

Capital is past savings accumulated for future production.
—Jackson Martindell

In the years following World War II, Japan and the countries of Western Europe, struggling to rebuild their shattered economies, held down their consumption as they concentrated on building new plant and equipment. The South Koreans and Taiwanese have followed this model of building capital by holding down consumption.

Capital is the key to our standard of living.

Capital, then, is the key to every society's standard of living. In the late 1980s, as our productivity and economic growth continued to lag, economists pointed to our slow rate of capital growth as the basic problem. Americans, they told us, were consuming too much and saving too little. There is no question that U.S. society cannot continue on this spending binge indefinitely, but Americans should also keep in mind that we have the largest stock of capital of any country in the world. Whether we are sufficiently modernizing that stock of plant and equipment and adding to it is an entirely different question.[12]

The world's developing nations face nearly insurmountable obstacles—rapidly growing populations and very little plant and equipment. The experience of the industrializing nations in the 19th century was that as people moved into cities from the countryside and as living standards rose, the birthrate invariably declined. But for industrialization to take place, capital must be built up. There are two ways to do this: cut consumption or raise production. Unfortunately, most developing nations are already at subsistence levels, so no further cuts in consumption are possible without causing even greater misery. And production cannot easily be raised without at least some plant and equipment.

---

[12]We'll have a lot more to say about our lagging rates of saving in Chapter 16 of *Economics* and *Macroeconomics*.

With the exception of the OPEC nations, which have been able to sell their oil in exchange for plant and equipment, the poorer nations of Africa, Asia, and Latin America have little hope of rising from extreme poverty.[13] An exchange of letters that legend has it took place between Mao Tse-tung and Nikita Khrushchev when China and the Soviet Union were allies in the early 1960s illustrates the futility of a third way out—foreign aid.

Mao: Send us machinery and equipment.

Khrushchev: Tighten your belts.

Mao: Send us some belts.

Specialization and Its Consequences

We could not have a modern, highly productive economy without specialization and exchange. Imagine if we all had to be self-sufficient. Each of us would live on a farm where we would grow our own food, weave our own cloth, build our own homes, make our own tools and clothes—even our pins and needles and nails.

In modern economies, virtually everyone specializes. We can sell whatever good or service we produce. By specializing, we get good at producing something, and we are able to sell it for a relatively low price. So instead of spending hours trying to make your own nails, you can buy all the nails you need at the hardware store for less than a dollar.

But specialization may lead to boredom and alienation, especially if our job requires us to do repetitive tasks. A certain degree of work alienation is inevitable in a modern economy, but some employers have been more successful at minimizing it than others.

Specialization and Exchange

When people specialize, they are usually far more productive than if they attempt to be jacks-of-all-trades. Doctors, lawyers, accountants, engineers, and, of course, college professors, all specialize (see box "Specialization in Economics").

If all of us become really good at something and concentrate on that one specialty, we will produce much more than if we try to do everything. A family that tries to be self-sufficient will have a relatively low standard of living because it takes a lot of time to do the hundreds of things that need to be done—all on an individual basis. Imagine not just making your own nails and pins, but weaving your own cloth, growing all your food, and building your own means of transportation. Think how many hours it would take you to weave a yard of cloth when you could buy it in the store for a couple of dollars.

Specialization is fine only if there is a demand for your specialty. One way there would be a demand for what you make or do is if someone wants what you have. If this person has what you want, you can trade. This is called barter. Today we use money to facilitate exchange. Thus, instead of having to find someone who has what you want and wants what you have, all you need to do is buy what you want and find someone to buy what you have.

Barter, unlike buying something for money, can get pretty complicated. When we use money, we can pay for something and be out of the store in a minute. But when we need to barter, we may be there all day trying to think of something that we have that the storekeeper will accept as payment.

Without money, very little exchange; without exchange, no specialization.

The lack of money obviously inhibits trade, or exchange, and without exchange, people can't specialize. Imagine calling someone to fix your air conditioner and trying to pay this person with piano lessons, a psychotherapy session, or by correcting their overbite or fixing their transmission. It's much easier to specialize when you don't have to buy from the same person who buys from you.

---

[13]Many of these less developed countries have only one or two primary exports, usually agricultural products, with which to obtain foreign exchange. Furthermore, most are deeply in debt to banks in developed countries as well as to foreign governments and international lending organizations.

Specialization in Economics

People specialize in every field of learning. Your economics professor, for example, may have specialized in banking, and not only can tell you all the dirt on the 1980s savings and loan scandal, but can explain exactly how banks operate, how they determine the creditworthiness of borrowers, and even how you can wire money to other countries.

Of course, you can overspecialize. A colleague of mine was the nation's leading expert on the Bland-Allison Act of 1878, which authorized the secretary of the treasury to purchase 2 to 4 million ounces of silver every month. Now that's a great thing to know, but the man tried to teach economics by relating most things to the Bland-Allison Act.

Specialization and Alienation

Working the line at G.M. was like being paid to flunk high school for the rest of your life.

—Ben Hamper, Rivethead: Tales from the Assembly Line

Many factory workers have become little better than cogs in some huge industrial wheel. People whose sole function is to tighten a couple of bolts or place front right fenders on auto bodies eight hours a day for most of their lives understandably get a little bored. Some express their unhappiness by frequent absences, while some, like the workers in a Chevy Vega plant in Lordstown, Ohio, many years ago, actually sabotage some of the cars they are assembling.

One of the most boring jobs in the world has got to be that of a telemarketer. "Hello, may I speak with Mr. Smith?" (which he manages to mispronounce) . . . "How are *you* this evening?" (Fine, until you interrupted my dinner.) And then he goes into his canned talk, which, I can tell you from painful memories of selling cemetery plots on the phone, is tacked to the wall in front of him. Imagine calling dozens of people a night and delivering, *verbatim,* the same talk again and again and again.

In a book simply titled *Working,* Studs Terkel recounted tape-recorded interviews with hundreds of American workers. Here's what a spot welder in a Chicago Ford auto assembly plant said about his work:

> I stand in one spot, about a two- or three-foot area, all night. The only time a person stops is when the line stops. We do about thirty-two jobs per car, per unit. Forty-eight units an hour, eight hours a day. Thirty-two times forty-eight times eight. Figure it out. That's how many times I push that button.[14]

One of the problems here is that the workers never see the product of their labor. Attempts have been made in Western Europe, particularly in Sweden, as well as in Japan, to involve the workers in making a larger segment of the product. Some degree of specialization is sacrificed in an effort to bolster employee morale. Although these new production modes have been successful, American factories have made only a few tentative efforts in this area.

No one seems to be asking what we can do to make jobs more interesting. Why must clerical workers do repetitive tasks instead of switching off with one another? Perhaps the classic boring job is that of elevator operator. Let's face it: being enclosed in a box riding up and down all day long is enough to drive anyone up a wall. Maybe my observations are not completely accurate, but most of these people seem ready to jump out of their skins. Couldn't they be given desk jobs for half the day and let the deskbound people ride the elevators—or be given the shaft, as they say in the trade when they're not saying the job has its ups and downs—thereby keeping everybody at least half happy and half sane?

Seymour Melman, a longtime observer of the corporate scene, had this to say about how the factory floor bred worker alienation:

> Managements that have long viewed the industrial worker as a replaceable, animated, special-purpose machine have given little, if any, thought to the impact of the physical conditions of the workplace on the men and women employed there. As a result, the environment is often dangerous, or noisy, or dirty, or poorly ventilated, too hot or too cold, or some combination of these.[15]

---

[14]Studs Terkel, *Working* (New York: Avon Books, 1972), pp. 221–22.

[15]Seymour Melman, *Profits without Production* (Philadelphia: University of Pennsylvania Press, 1987), p. 123.

In some respects, office workers glued to a video display terminal or a word processor are no better off than assembly-line operators. They are often isolated, completely out of contact with other workers, and very likely to become bored, apathetic, and alienated. Each worker must discipline herself or himself to the system imposed by the machine, most often working with computer terminals that have been strictly programmed to perform only one task.

A developed or industrial economy must necessarily have most of the features we have discussed in this chapter. Obviously, a huge capital stock is required, and a fairly large government sector is inevitable. Specialization is also inevitable, but worker alienation could probably be avoided, at least to a greater degree than it has been in this country.

The "Isms": Capitalism, Communism, Fascism, and Socialism

> Q: *What is the difference between capitalism and socialism?*
> A: *Under capitalism, man exploits man. Under socialism, it's just the opposite.*
> —Overheard in Warsaw[16]

> *Property is the exploitation of the weak by the strong.*
> *Communism is the exploitation of the strong by the weak.*
> —Pierre-Joseph Proudhon[17]

During the 20th century, perhaps no three opprobriums have been hurled more often at political opponents than those of Communist! Capitalist! and Fascist! Depending on where and when you lived, you might have been called any of these three. In the United States in the 1920s, it was bad to be a communist. In the 1930s and the first half of the 1940s, being a communist was acceptable in many quarters, but being a fascist was not. Although being a fascist had gone completely out of style in Germany and the rest of Europe by 1945, communism was "in" only in Eastern Europe. In Western Europe in the late 1940s and the 1950s, it was tolerated; but in the United States, many politicians made careers by claiming to hunt down "card-carrying" communists in all walks of life. "Excuse me, ma'am, may I see your card?" And heaven help you if your card was red.

All of this time, in the Soviet Union, if you were a bad guy in the 1930s and early 1940s, you were probably a fascist (except between 1939 and 1941, when the Soviet Union and Germany were nominal allies). That alliance vanished when Hitler's armies invaded the Soviet Union in mid-1941, and suddenly a new alliance was born as we American capitalists shipped the Soviets billions of dollars in war material. But after 1945, the capitalists in that country became the oppressed minority, card or no card. Then in the 1990s, of course, communism is out and capitalism is in throughout the length and breadth of Russia and the rest of what was once the Soviet empire.

Capitalism

Enough about political freedom. Let's compare the four great economic systems. Capitalism, as we've already seen, is characterized by private ownership of most of the means of production—that is, land, labor, capital, and entrepreneurial ability. Individuals are moved to produce by the profit motive. Production is also guided by the price system. Thus, we have millions of people competing for the consumer's dollar. The government's role in all of this is kept to a minimum; basically, it ensures that everyone sticks to the rules.

Communism

"The theory of the Communists may be summed up in the single sentence: Abolition of private property," declared Karl Marx and Friedrich Engels in *The Communist Manifesto.* Who would own everything? The state. And eventually the state would wither away and we would be left with a workers' paradise.

In the Soviet version of communism, under which the state had evidently not yet withered away, most of the capitalist roles were reversed. Instead of a guidance system of prices

---

[16]Lloyd G. Reynolds, *Microeconomic Analysis and Policy,* 6th ed. (Burr Ridge, IL: Richard D. Irwin, 1988), p. 435.

[17]Pierre-Joseph Proudhon, *What Is Property?* chap. V, Part II.

to direct production, a government planning committee dictated exactly *what* was produced, *how* it was produced, and *for whom* the goods and services were produced. After all, the state owned and operated nearly all of the means of production and distribution.

All of the resources used had to conform to the current five-year plan. If the goal was 2 million tractors, 100 million tons of steel, 15 million bushels of wheat, and so on, Soviet workers might have expected to be putting in a lot of overtime.

The big difference between the old Soviet economy and our own is what consumer goods and services are produced. In our economy, the market forces of supply and demand dictate what gets produced and how much of it gets produced. But a government planning agency in the Soviet Union dictated what and how much was made. In effect, central planning attempted to direct a production and distribution process that works automatically in a market economy.

How well did the Soviet communist system work? Remember the chronic shortages of consumer goods we mentioned earlier in the chapter? Although Soviet president Mikhail Gorbachev went to great lengths to shake up the bureaucracy and get the economy moving again, his efforts were futile. In order to raise output, he found he needed to somehow remove the heavy hand of bureaucracy from the economic controls. But as he stripped away more and more of the Communist Party's power, he found that his own power had been stripped away as well.

One of the fundamental economic problems with *any* economy that attempts to substitute government planning for the price system (or to replace the law of demand and supply with government decrees) is that changes in price no longer help producers decide what and how much to produce. In a capitalist country, higher microwave oven prices would signal producers to produce more microwave ovens. But in the Soviet Union, there was very little inflation even though there were widespread shortages of consumer goods. In fact, the Soviets came up with a great cure for inflation. Just let everyone wait in line.

The entire Soviet economy was a Rube Goldberg contraption[18] of subsidies, fixed prices, bureaucratic rules and regulations, special privileges, and outright corruption. Had Gorbachev not acted, the entire Soviet system may well have come apart by itself over another couple of generations.

A joke that circulated in the late 1980s went like this: Under communism your pockets are full of money, but there isn't anything in the stores you can buy with it. Under capitalism, the stores are full, but you have no money in your pockets.

Fascism

Fascism hasn't been in vogue since Hitler's defeat in 1945, but it does provide another model of an extreme. In Nazi Germany the ownership of resources was in private hands, while the government dictated what was to be produced.

The problem with describing the fascist economic model is that there really *is* no model. The means of production are left in private hands, with varying degrees of governmental interference. Generally those in power are highly nationalistic, so a high proportion of output is directed toward military goods and services.

Fascists have been virulently anticommunist but have also been completely intolerant of any political opposition. The one-party state, suppression of economic freedom, and a militaristic orientation have been hallmarks of fascism.

The early 1940s were evidently the high-water mark of fascism. Although from time to time a fascist state does pop up, it appears to be a temporary phenomenon. With the possible exception of Hitler's Germany, which did put most Germans back to work after the Great Depression, albeit largely at military production, most fascist states have been economic failures that apparently collapsed of their own weight.

No countries today are admittedly fascist, although Salazar's Portugal and Franco's Spain, both holdouts from the 1930s, functioned as fascist regimes until fairly recently. The military dictatorships of Africa, South America, and Saddam Hussein's Iraq have also been likened to the fascist model, but there is nothing today to compare with Hitler's Germany or Mussolini's Italy.

---

[18]Such a device is designed to accomplish by complex means what seemingly could be done simply.

Socialism

The vice of capitalism is that it stands for the unequal sharing of blessings; whereas the virtue of socialism is that it stands for the equal sharing of misery.
—Winston Churchill

Socialism has not gotten the bad press that capitalism, fascism, and communism have received, perhaps because those who dislike the socialists prefer to call them communists. In fact, even Soviet government officials used to refer to themselves as socialists and their country, the U.S.S.R., was formally called the Union of Soviet Socialist Republics, although President Ronald Reagan referred to the Soviet Union as the evil empire. And the countries with socialist economies were our military allies.

The economies of such countries as Sweden, Canada, Great Britain, and, recently, France and Greece have been described as socialist, not only by government officials in those countries but by outside observers as well. In general, these economies have three characteristics: (1) government ownership of some of the means of production; (2) a substantial degree of government planning; and (3) a large-scale redistribution of income from the wealthy and the well-to-do to the middle class, working class, and the poor.

One of the most familiar characteristics of socialist countries is cradle-to-grave security. Medical care, education, retirement benefits, and other essential needs are guaranteed to every citizen. All you need to do is be born.

Where does the money to pay for all of this come from? It comes from taxes. Very high income taxes and inheritance taxes fall disproportionately on the upper middle class and the rich. In Israel several years ago, a joke went around about a man who received an unusually large paycheck one week. He couldn't figure out what had happened until his wife looked at his check stub and discovered that he had been sent his deductions by mistake. Although only the very wealthy must give the government over half their pay in socialist countries, the story *did* have a ring of truth to it.

Rather than allow the market forces to function freely, socialist governments sometimes resort to very elaborate planning schemes. And since the government usually owns the basic industries and provides the basic services, this planning merely has one hand directing the other.

Sweden is often considered the archetypal socialist country, although perhaps 90 percent of the country's industry is privately owned. It is the government's massive intervention in the private economy that gives Swedish society its socialist tone. Not only has the Swedish government kept the unemployment rate generally below 3 percent for several decades by offering industry and workers a series of subsidies and incentives, but it provides one of the most elaborate cradle-to-grave programs in the world. The government doles out $100 monthly allowances for each child and provides day care centers, free education from nursery school through college, free medical care, and very generous unemployment and retirement benefits. Women may take a year off work after the birth of a child while receiving 80 percent of their pay.

Of course, taxes are very high in Sweden. In 1996 about 60 percent of the nation's output was paid out in taxes, compared to just 32 percent in the United States. Critics of the Swedish system have questioned whether the high tax rates haven't hurt work incentives. Even if they have, Sweden not only has one of the most equal income distributions in the world, but also has one of the highest living standards. So the Swedes must be doing something right.

But Sweden's brand of socialism pales in comparison to that of Norway, its Scandinavian neighbor. In addition to free day care, subsidized housing and vacations, and free medical care, Norwegians receive annual stipends of over $1,600 for every child under 17, retirement pay for homemakers, and 42 weeks of fully paid maternity leave. How do they pay for all of this? Not only does Norway have the world's highest income tax rates, but a 23 percent sales tax and a gasoline tax of about $5 a gallon. Hallmarks of Norwegian society are a great disdain for the trappings of wealth and power and a profound sense of equality, which militate against a wide disparity in pay.

In much of Western Europe the unemployment rate was over 10 percent in 1996 and 1997. Critics of the socialist welfare states have noted that extremely high jobless benefits provide a disincentive to work. Why bother working when you can collect benefits equal to, say, 90 percent of what you could have earned? In addition, employers must pay very high taxes for each worker they hire. In France there are taxes for family allowances, for a fund offering low-cost housing loans, for unemployment insurance, for pensions, for the improvement of security on building sites, for professional training, and even for reducing the social security deficit.

Perhaps this joke, which has made its rounds on the Internet, may best sum up the four isms:

Socialism: You have two cows. State takes one and gives it to someone else.
Communism: You have two cows. State takes both of them and gives you milk.
Fascism: You have two cows. State takes both of them and sells you milk.
Capitalism: You have two cows. You sell one and buy a bull.

The Decline and Fall of the Communist System

In the closing months of 1989, the communist governments of Eastern Europe came tumbling down like falling dominoes. As democratically elected governments replaced Soviet-backed dictatorships, there was a strong movement away from government-owned and operated economies to market economies. These transitions are still evolving, and the final mix of private enterprise and government ownership is far from certain in any of these countries.

Two basic problems—inflation and rising unemployment

Two basic problems they have encountered are inflation and rising unemployment. The lifting of government price controls, as well as the removal of government subsidies for such basic necessities as meat, bread, eggs, milk, and butter, made price increases inevitable. And as some of the less efficient government enterprises have been shut down, hundreds of thousands of workers have been thrown out of work.

In the Soviet Union, the economic power of the government had been based largely in Article 10 of the Soviet constitution:

> The foundation of the economic system of the USSR is socialist ownership of the means of production in the form of state property (belonging to all the people), and collective farm and cooperative property.

In March 1990, the Soviet parliament passed a property law giving private citizens the right to own small factories, stores, and other businesses. It also permitted the creation of worker-owned cooperatives. But it remains to be seen whether these plans will create a truly mixed economy. A lot depends on whether the bureaucrats who control the huge state-run enterprises will cooperate with or sabotage these new competitors by refusing to sell them needed machinery, equipment, and supplies.

The communists ran the Soviet Union for more than 70 years, so even if their entire bureaucratic structure of state-owned farms, factories, offices, and stores were to be privatized, the process would take years, even decades. The whole system of economic planning and the millions of bureaucrats whose jobs depend on the state will not just disappear in a puff of smoke. The process of privatization so far has been relatively limited in comparison to what has already taken place in Poland, the former East Germany, Hungary, and a few of the other Eastern European countries.

Russia has made tremendous strides toward ridding itself of the old, inefficient Soviet bureaucracy, but it is also greatly burdened by the problems of transforming into a market economy. Rampant inflation, high unemployment, and a huge budget deficit have threatened to derail economic reform, while President Boris Yeltsin's poor health may have weakened his ability to govern. The income of the average Russian is barely half what it was before the collapse of the communist system in 1990–91. Even more ominous, a Russian mafia, estimated by the police to consist of some 5,700 gangs totaling 100,000 members, is not only responsible for about 80 murders a day but has stifled competition, encouraged official corruption, and deterred foreign investment. In mid-1994, *Newsweek* reported, "According to a U.S. Embassy official in Moscow, at least 80 percent of all Russian businesses are believed to have links with organized crime.[19]

---

[19]*Newseek,* July 25, 1994, p. 28.

And yet a great deal of progress has been made. In early 1993 the government employed about 97 or 98 percent of the Russian industrial workforce, but by early 1998 more than 75 percent worked for private enterprises. More than 100,000 state companies—from small shops to huge, enormously inefficient factories—have been transferred to private ownership. The question remains whether these largely inefficient enterprises can be transformed into lean and mean competing business firms.

Will the Soviet Union go capitalist?

Will the Soviet economy evolve into a clone of American capitalism? Probably not. For one thing, seven decades of egalitarian ideology have left their mark on every facet of Russian life. A new class of rich and superrich would cut against the grain of that deepseated belief.

Collapse of communism is not a vote of confidence in American capitalism.

And one other thing: The economic performance of the American economy has been nothing to write home about—or to the former Soviet Union, for that matter. Our lagging economic growth, massive federal budget and trade deficits, not to mention our problems with drugs, crime, and education, do not exactly recommend us as a role model.[20] So while the cold war may finally be over and communism may be dead, or at least dying, we would do well to heed the words of newspaper columnist William Raspberry: "The collapse of communism isn't necessarily the same thing as the vindication of American-style capitalism."[21] (See box titled "Was the Decline of Communism the Triumph of American Capitalism?")

Perhaps a word of caution is in order about the political and economic changes that have swept across Eastern Europe and the Soviet Union over the last few years. The situation in each country will be fluid, if not volatile, for years to come. It is very possible that most or all of these nations will peacefully evolve into socialist or capitalist democracies. But then again, the pendulum may swing back toward communist autocracy. Either way, the next few years will be very interesting.

China: The Premier Communist Power

With the demise of the Soviet Union, China became the world's premier communist power. The communists came to power in 1949, taking over one of the world's poorest nations. For the first three decades, largely under Mao Tse-tung (his friends called him Chairman Mao, and he liked the rest of the Chinese to refer to him as "the Great Helmsman"), the Chinese economy was dominated by Soviet-style central planning. Even though the economy absorbed two extremely disruptive setbacks—the Great Leap Forward (1958–60), during which perhaps 30 million people starved to death, and the Cultural Revolution (1966–75), both of which Mao used to consolidate power—economic growth may have averaged 10 percent a year. China was pulled up from a backward country plagued by periodic famine to one in which everyone had enough to eat and many could afford to buy TVs, refrigerators, cameras, and some of the other amenities we in the United States take for granted.[22] In 1978 there were 1 million TV sets in China; by 1998 there were nearly 300 million.

Major economic reforms in 1978 and again in 1984 introduced freer markets in agriculture, allowed individuals to set up small businesses, and diluted the ideological purity that had marked the first 30 years of communist rule. Indeed, by 1984 the Communist Party's Central Committee went so far as to depart from the traditional communist credo "From each according to his ability, to each according to his needs." The new slogan was "More pay for more work; less pay for less work." What this did, implicitly, was to say to budding entrepreneurs, "It's OK if you get rich—you worked hard for your money." Apparently the reformers, led by Deng Xiaoping, the nonagenarian revolutionary who had survived Mao's purges, believed that a large degree of economic freedom should be toler-

To get rich is glorious.
  —Deng Xiaoping

---

[20]Each of these economic and social problems will be taken up in Chapter 16 of *Economics* and *Macroeconomics*.

[21]Syndicated column of the same title, *Washington Post,* March 14, 1990.

[22]Chinese economic development is also outlined in Chapter 16 of *Economics* and of *Macroeconomics*.

Was the Decline of Communism the Triumph of American Capitalism?

Several years ago, I knew a history professor at St. Francis College in Brooklyn who loved to shock his students by telling them that he had been a communist. As a young man, he had joined a Catholic religious order, lived in a commune, and shared all his possessions with his fellow seminarians. "What could be more communist than living in a commune with no private property?" he asked his students.

And so we may ask whether what they had in the Soviet Union and in Eastern Europe was really communism. How would Karl Marx have reacted to those huge bureaucratic dictatorships? Marx had foreseen "the withering away of the state," until all that was left was a society of workers who followed his credo "From each according to his ability; to each according to his needs." This sounds a lot more like that history professor's seminary than what was passing for communism in the old Soviet empire.

The Soviet regime collapsed not just because of its bureaucratic inefficiencies but also because it supported a huge military establishment that claimed between one-fifth and one-quarter of its resources and national output. One might note that our country, too, has supported a huge military establishment, which had claimed about 6 percent of our national output since the close of World War II. The fall of the Soviet empire may well have been a great triumph for capitalism, but not necessarily for the American model.

We might also keep in mind that one out of every four people living on this planet still lives under communism. Some 1.2 billion people live in China, whose government remains militantly communist. Of course, even in China there is a strong capitalist sector, most notably in the southern provinces closest to Hong Kong.

In the new Commonwealth of Independent States, most of the giant state enterprises—the manufacturing operations, the collective farms, and the distribution system—have continued to function. Although privatization is proceeding, it will take perhaps at least another generation until we will be seeing economies that even approximate what might be termed private enterprise, or capitalism.

Back in the early 1970s, two great heavyweight champions, Muhammed Ali and Joe Frazier, fought each other in epic 15-round battles. Both fighers absorbed such terrible punishment that neither was ever the same. Indeed, it seems apparent that having taken so many punches to the head had a lot to do with Ali's contracting Parkinson's disease.

Think of the United States and the Soviet Union as two heavyweight superpowers, pounding each other almost nonstop for 45 years. The Soviets probably expended over 20 percent of their national output on armaments, while we averaged 6 percent of a much larger national output. What was the opportunity cost of all this spending? *Think* about it. Both nations could have been building capital goods, providing better education and health care, advancing their technology—or simply providing their citizens with more consumer goods and services. In retrospect, we certainly *did* win the cold war, but our economy would have been a lot larger and more productive today if that war had never been fought.

ated but that free political expression was an entirely different matter, as the student demonstrators in Beijing's Tienanmen Square were to learn in 1989.[23]

Over 70 percent of all investment in China goes into state-owned factories run by managers appointed by the Communist Party, up from about 60 percent in 1990. Although they soak up a growing percentage of investment funds, these factories produce a shrinking share of China's economic output. Indeed, privately owned factories now produce about 60 percent of all output.

In September 1997, the Chinese government announced that it would sell off more than 10,000 of the nation's 13,000 large and medium-sized state enterprises, but it is unclear to whom they will be sold. At a time when the economy is rapidly expanding, the private sector may be able to absorb most of the workers who will be laid off.

Although average family income has at least quintupled since 1978, China remains a relatively poor agricultural nation with three-quarters of its population living in rural areas. But it has 1.2 billion people (one out of every five people on this planet lives in China), and it has become a middle-rank industrial power. Should its economy continue to grow at its present pace, within less than a generation China may well replace Japan as our most formidable economic rival.

---

[23]Deng died in 1997, at the age of 92.

Will China eventually overtake the United States as the world's leading economic power? China is already the world's largest producer of coal, cement, grain, fish, and cotton; it ranks third in steel production and fifth in crude oil output. If today's trends continue, sometime around the year 2025, China may supplant the United States as the world's leader in total economic output.

Last Word: The Mixed Economy

The first words of this chapter were these: Ours is a mixed economy because there is a private sector and a public sector. The next time you're in the supermarket, pick up a jar of mixed nuts and see if the label proclaims, "No more than 70 percent peanuts." Think of our economy as a jar of mixed nuts. If the privately held sector were peanuts, what would the label say? Probably, "No more than 90 percent peanuts."

No economy is wholly government owned and operated. In the old Soviet Union, there were privately held plots of farmland and hundreds of thousands of tiny business firms. And in China today, there is a huge and rapidly growing private sector that includes millions of manufacturing firms, retailers, and service providers. Indeed, the largest chunk of private property is held by officers of the Peoples' Liberation Army. The Chinese government has had great difficulty preventing these enterprises from producing and selling pirated American computer software, CDs, jeans, and videos. Although most Chinese still work for government-owned and -operated factories, stores, and farms, perhaps one-third of the Chinese economy is in private hands.

So where does all of this leave us? It leaves us with one conclusion: Every nation in the world has a mixed economy.

Questions for Further Thought and Discussion

1. The circular flow model is a simplified version of our economy. Describe how this model works.
2. What are the three basic economic questions that all economies must answer? Describe the differences in the ways capitalism and socialism answer these questions.
3. What was Adam Smith's invisible hand, and what economic function did it serve?
4. What are the two basic classes of market failure? What would be an example of each?
5. What are the consequences of overspecialization? Give an example of a job that is overspecialized.

WORKBOOK FOR CHAPTER 4

Name _____   Date _____

Multiple-Choice Questions

Circle the letter that corresponds to the best answer.

1. We have a mixed economy because

    a. we produce guns and butter   **b.** we consume domestically produced goods as well as imports
    c. we consume both goods and services   **d.** there is a private sector and a public sector

2. Which does not fit with the others?

    a. competition   **b.** government planning and regulation   **c.** the invisible hand   **d.** the price mechanism

3. Adam Smith believed the best way to promote the public interest was to

    a. have the government produce most goods and services   **b.** let people pursue their own selfish interests   **c.** wait for individuals to set out to promote the public interest   **d.** get rid of the price mechanism

4. Supply-side economists believe cutting taxes will

    a. hurt the economy   **b.** give people an incentive to work, save, and invest   **c.** have little or no economic effect   **d.** help during recessions, but be less effective than government spending increases

5. In the Soviet Union

    a. the most productive plots of land were privately owned   **b.** there was no private ownership of agricultural land   **c.** private plots produced more food than collective farms   **d.** there was more privately owned land than government-owned land

6. Adam Smith believed people are guided by all of the following except

    a. the profit motive   **b.** self-interest
    c. the public good   **d.** the invisible hand

7. The price system is based on

    a. government regulation (i.e., the government sets most prices)   **b.** the individual whim of the businessperson   who sets it   **c.** the feelings of the individual buyer   **d.** supply and demand

8. Which statement is true?

    a. American industry is very competitive.   **b.** There is no competition in American industry.   **c.** To have competition, you need to have many firms in an industry.   **d.** The American automobile industry is very competitive.

9. In the United States, nearly all resources are owned by

    a. the government   **b.** business firms
    c. individuals   **d.** foreigners

10. Most of the money that people receive as income

    a. goes to the government in taxes   **b.** is saved
    c. is spent on consumer goods and services
    d. is unaccounted for

11. Wages, rent, interest, and profits flow from

    a. business firms to households   **b.** households to business firms   **c.** business firms to the government
    d. the government to business firms

12. The government performs each of the following economic functions except

    a. collecting taxes   **b.** spending   **c.** issuing regulations   **d.** operating the price mechanism

13. Private ownership of most of the means of production is common to

    a. capitalism and communism   **b.** capitalism and fascism   **c.** capitalism and socialism   **d.** fascism and communism

14. The price mechanism is least important under

    a. capitalism   **b.** socialism   **c.** fascism
    d. communism

15. The five-year plan had been the main economic plan of

    a. the United States   **b.** Sweden
    c. Nazi Germany   **d.** the U.S.S.R.

16. Fascism peaked in the
    a. 1920s   b. 1930s   c. 1940s   d. 1950s

17. The strongest criticism of Sweden's economic system has
    been that
    a. it provides too many benefits   b. its taxes are too
    high   c. its taxes are too low   d. it doesn't
    provide enough benefits

18. The strongest indictment of the capitalist system was
    written by
    a. Adam Smith   b. John Maynard Keynes
    c. Rose D. Cohen   d. Karl Marx

19. Karl Marx said that
    a. whoever controlled a society's capital controlled that
    society   b. in the long run, capitalism would survive
    c. the U.S.S.R.'s communist system was "state
    capitalism"   d. capitalists and workers generally had
    the same economic interests

20. The main reason the American farmer can produce more
    than the farmer in China is that he
    a. has more land   b. has more capital   c. has
    more labor   d. is better trained

21. Capital comes from
    a. gold   b. savings   c. high consumption
    d. the government

22. All modern economies depend on
    a. alienation   b. government ownership of the
    means of production   c. free enterprise
    d. specialization

23. Alienation is one result of
    a. exchange   b. overspecialization
    c. underspecialization   d. self-sufficiency

24. An individual can build up his/her capital by
    a. working longer hours only   b. cutting back on
    consumption only   c. both cutting back on
    consumption and working longer hours
    d. only by borrowing

Fill-In Questions

1. The invisible hand is generally associated with (1) the

   _____ and (2) _____.

2. Adam Smith believed that if people set out to promote the

   public interest, they will not do nearly as much good as

   they will if they _____.

3. Supply-side economists believe the way to provide people

   with incentives to work, save, and invest is to _____.

4. Supply-side economists feel that the government's

   economic role is _____.

5. In the ex-Soviet Union most of the farmland was in the

   form of _____.

6. Under private enterprise, production is guided by

   _____.

7. The price system is based on the law of _____

   _____.

8. Critics feel that price controls interfere with the

   _____.

9. Under competition, there are so many firms that no firm is

   large enough to _____.

10. According to the circular flow, businesses send money

    income to _____.

11. _____ provide business firms with

    resources.

5

The Household-Consumption Sector

In this chapter we begin our examination of the three main sectors of gross domestic product (GDP): C (consumption), I (investment), and G (government spending). We look at consumption: why people spend money, what they buy, and why they save so little of their incomes. We will also introduce graphing techniques as a tool for macroeconomic analysis, which will be covered in Chapters 10 and 11.

Chapter Objectives

In this chapter we will introduce eight economic concepts:

- The average propensity to consume.
- The average propensity to save.
- The marginal propensity to consume.
- The marginal propensity to save.
- The consumption function.
- The saving function.
- The determinants of consumption.
- The permanent income hypothesis.

GDP and Big Numbers

Consumption, investment, and government spending are the three main sectors of GDP. But what, exactly, is GDP? Gross domestic product is a term that you'll find quite frequently in the financial section of your newspaper, as well as in the *Wall Street Journal, BusinessWeek, Fortune,* and other financial publications. Gross domestic product, which is the subject of Chapter 8, is the *nation's expenditure on all the final goods and services produced during the year at market prices.*

*What's the difference between mathematics and economics?
Mathematics is incomprehensible, economics just doesn't make sense.*

I'm going to be throwing very large numbers at you—millions, billions, and trillions. The box titled "A Word about Numbers" provides a lucid explanation of how to deal with these numbers; so if you don't know your billions from your trillions, you definitely need to read it.

Speaking of numbers, so they don't have to write out 12 zeros, economists write one trillion dollars like this: 1,000, or sometimes, 1000. It's a lot faster than writing, $1,000,000,000,000.

How would they write $100 billion? See if you can do it. The answer is 100. Now maybe you *do* need to read "A Word about Numbers."

Consumption

The average American spends about 95 percent of her income after taxes. The total of everyone's expenditures is consumption, designated by the letter C. The largest sector of GDP, C, is now just over two-thirds of GDP.[1]

---

[1]In 1997, C was 67.9 percent of GDP. Since 1980, C averaged about two-thirds of GDP. There's a graph of C as a percentage of GDP in Figure 5 of Chapter 8.

A Word about Numbers

The time has come to talk about numbers—big numbers. We need to keep our thousands, millions, billions, and trillions straight, so I've devised a little test. This will help you gauge what you know and don't know. And by the time you finish this section, believe me, you will know.

I'd like you to express some numbers in words. I'll do the first one.

(a) 1,591 <u>One thousand, five-hundred, and ninety-one</u>

(b) 4,338,500,000 _____

(c) 468,374 _____

(d) 2,847,600,000,000 _____

(e) 216,129,000 _____

You'll find the answers at the end of the box. But don't look yet—I have a few more problems for you. OK, I'll do the first one—then you do the rest. This time we translate words into numbers.

(f) Seventy-six billion, three-hundred million
   76,300,000,000 _____

(g) Two-hundred nineteen thousand, four hundred
   _____

(h) Six trillion _____

(i) Forty-five million, three-hundred eighty-eight thousand _____

Summary

1. Thousands come after the first comma: for example, 17,000 (seventeen thousand); 391,000 (three-hundred ninety-one thousand).

2. Millions come after the second comma: for example, 6,000,000 (six million); 410,000,000 (four-hundred ten million).

3. Billions come after the third comma: for example, 924,500,000,000 (nine-hundred twenty-four billion, five-hundred million); 86,000,000,000 (eighty-six billion).

4. Trillions come after the fourth comma: for example, 31,000,000,000,000 (thirty-one trillion); 570,000,000,000,000 (five-hundred seventy trillion).

Answers

(b) four billion, three-hundred thirty-eight million, five-hundred thousand

(c) four-hundred sixty-eight thousand, three-hundred and seventy-four

(d) two trillion, eight-hundred forty-seven billion, six-hundred million

(e) two-hundred sixteen million, one-hundred twenty-nine thousand

(g) 219,400

(h) 6,000,000,000,000

(i) 45,388,000

Consumers spend more than half their money on services such as medical care, eating out, video rentals, life insurance, and legal fees. The rest is spent on durable goods, such as television sets and furniture, or on nondurable goods, such as food and gasoline. All consumption falls into one of the two categories of goods or services.

The consumption function states that as income rises, consumption rises, but not as quickly.

Although consumption is not a steady percentage of disposable income, it is almost always between 90 and 95 percent. John Maynard Keynes (pronounced "canes") noted that consumption is a stable component of income. His theory, called the consumption function, states that *as income rises, consumption rises, but not as quickly.* For example, if a country's disposable income rises by 300 (from 2,000 to 2,300), its C will rise, but by less than 300. If C were 1,800, it might rise by 250 to 2,050.[2]

The consumption function is illustrated by the hypothetical figures in Table 1. Let's start with a disposable income of 1,000 (read as $1,000 billion, or $1 trillion) and consumption of 1,400 ($1,400 billion, or $1.4 trillion). Now let's move up to a disposable income of 2,000. You'll notice that C rose to 2,200. So an increase of 1,000 (from 1,000 to 2,000) in disposable income pushes up C by 800 (from 1,400 to 2,200). This relationship remains the same as we raise disposable income to 3,000, 4,000, and 5,000. Each 1,000 increase in disposable income gives us an 800 increase in C.

---

[2]No more Mr. Nice Guy. From here on I'll refer to billions of dollars in this shorthand way. The number 2,050 represents $2,050 billion (or $2.05 trillion). Remember that 2,000 represents $2,000 billion, or $2 trillion. This is a convention all economists use when writing about billions and trillions of dollars.

Table 1   Consumption and Disposable Income

Disposable Income	Consumption
1,000	1,400
2,000	2,200
3,000	3,000
4,000	3,800
5,000	4,600

So, as disposable income rises in increments of 1,000, C rises in increments of 800, which conforms to the consumption function: *As income rises, consumption rises, but not as quickly.*

When we say, then, that consumption is a function of disposable income, we mean that it *varies* with disposable income. When disposable income goes up, so does consumption, though by a smaller amount. And when disposable income declines, so does consumption, but again, by a smaller amount.

Saving

When one has had to work so hard to get money, why should he impose on himself the further hardship of trying to save it?
—Don Herold

Saving is simply not spending. Since the average family spends more than 95 percent of its disposable income, it saves something less than 5 percent, one of the lowest savings rates among industrialized nations. In recent years Japan has had a savings rate of about 20 percent (see box "Why the Japanese Savings Rate Has Been So High"), Italy and Korea have averaged over 20 percent, and Taiwan has averaged over 30 percent. But the prize for savings may go to China which has a rate of 35 to 40 percent.

Figure 1 shows our savings record over the last three decades. During that entire period the savings rate was under 10 percent of disposable personal income, and there has been a marked downward trend since the mid-1980s. A low savings rate and a high consumption rate are just flip sides of the same coin. The more we spend, the less we save. And a low savings rate leads to a low rate of productivity growth. Why? Because without savings to invest in new and better capital, we can't raise our productivity very quickly.

Why has the savings rate sunk so low, or, alternatively, why are Americans spending about 95 percent of their take-home pay? These are good questions. But never mind the why and wherefore—at least for now. We'll get into the mechanics of saving and consuming, run a few graphs by you, and then, near the end of the chapter, get around to answering why we save so little and spend so much. Let's let the suspense build for a while. (See the box titled "Total Savings.")

Why the Japanese Savings Rate Has Been So High

Until 1988, when there were extensive revisions of the tax law, about 70 percent of Japanese personal savings was tax free. Not only was interest on bank deposits of up to $20,000 tax free, but so was interest on government and corporate bonds. And up to $5,000 of savings deducted from paychecks was also tax free.*

The Japanese system is described this way by Bill Emmott:

Japanese are workaholics who save lots of money and refuse to consume; their government spends very little; their industry is fearsomely efficient and has such a strong cash flow that it no longer borrows much.†

*See Jim Powell, *The Gnomes of Tokyo* (New York: American Management Association, 1989), p. 14.
†Bill Emmott, *The Sun Also Sets* (New York: Times Books, 1989), p. 21.

Figure 1   Savings as a Percentage of Disposable Personal Income, 1960–97

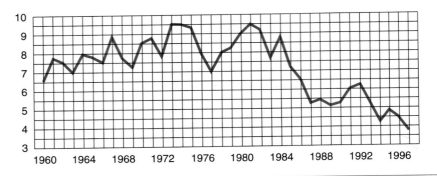

Source: *Economic Report of the President,* 1998.

Average Propensity to Consume (APC)

The average propensity to consume is the percentage of disposable income spent. Using the data in Table 2, let's calculate the APC.

To find the percentage of disposable income spent, we need to divide consumption by disposable income.

$$APC = \frac{Consumption}{Disposable\ income}$$

$$APC = \frac{Consumption}{Disposable\ income} = \frac{\$30,000}{\$40,000} = \frac{3}{4} = .75$$

Let's review how this is done. We use the three-step method of solving this problem. First, write the formula. Then, substitute the numbers into the formula. Finally, solve the formula.

You know that $30,000/$40,000 can easily be reduced to 3/4. To change the fraction (3/4) into decimal form, divide 3 by 4. (Remember always to divide the bottom number into the top number.)

$$4\overline{)3.00}^{\ .75}$$

Average Propensity to Save (APS)

The APS is the mirror image of the APC. It is the percentage of disposable income saved. Using the data in Table 2, calculate the APS.

Table 2

Disposable Income	Consumption
$40,000	$30,000

Use the same three-step method we used to calculate the APC: (1) write the formula, (2) plug in your numbers, and (3) solve. Do it right here.

Now we'll check your work. The formula is:

$$APS = \frac{\text{Saving}}{\text{Disposable income}}$$

Next we'll substitute into the formula. You already know from Table 2 that disposable income is $40,000. How much is saving? It's not in Table 2, but since consumption is $30,000, we can find saving by subtracting consumption from disposable income: $40,000 − $30,000 = $10,000. Now we can complete the problem.

$$APS = \frac{\text{Saving}}{\text{Disposable income}} = \frac{\$10,000}{\$40,000} = \frac{1}{4} = .25\,^3$$

Notice that the APC and the APS add up to 1. Let's work out another one, using the data in Table 3.

Table 3

Disposable Income	Saving
$20,000	$1,500

Use the space below to calculate the APC and the APS.

Solutions:

$$APC = \frac{\text{Consumption}}{\text{Disposable income}} = \frac{\$18,500}{\$20,000} = \frac{185}{200} = \frac{37}{40}$$

$$40\overline{)37.000} = 4\overline{)3.7^10^20}\quad .925$$

$$APS = \frac{\text{Saving}}{\text{Disposable income}} = \frac{\$1,500}{\$20,000} = \frac{15}{200} = \frac{3}{40}$$

$$40\overline{)3.00} = 4\overline{).30^20}\quad .075$$

---

[3]To convert ¼ into a decimal, we must divide the bottom number, 4, into the top number, 1.

ADVANCED WORK................................

APCs Greater than One

Is it possible to have an APC greater than one? You bet it is! How much would your APC be if you had a disposable income of $10,000 and your consumption was $12,000? Figure it out:

$$APC = \frac{Consumption}{Disposable\ income} = \frac{\$12,000}{\$10,000} = \frac{12}{10} = 1.2$$

Where would this extra $2,000 come from? Let's round up the usual suspects. You might take money out of the bank, borrow on your credit cards, take out a car loan, or buy on the installment plan. The bottom line is that many people find it quite easy to spend more than

they earn year after year, whether by drawing down their savings, borrowing money, or some combination thereof.

Incidentally, if your APC *were* 1.2, how much would your APS be? Work it out right here:

$$APS = \frac{Saving}{Disposable\ income} = \frac{-\$2,000}{\$10,000} = \frac{-2}{10} = -0.2$$

Is it possible to have a negative APS? If your savings happens to be negative (i.e., you spend more than your income), then your APS will definitely be negative. And you'll notice that your APC (1.2) plus your APS (−0.2) add up to 1.0.

APC + APS = 1

Notice that once again APC (.925) and APS (.075) add up to 1. This is your check to ensure that you haven't made a mistake in your calculations. (But can the APC ever be greater than 1? See the box "APCs Greater than One.")

Now that we've done all this work, what does it mean to say that a person has an APC of .925 and an APS of .075? Think about it for a moment. Go back to the formulas for the APC and the APS. Think of the APC and the APS as percentages. Obviously, then, the APC is the percentage of a person's income that he or she spends. And the APS? It is the percentage of the person's income that is saved. In other words, 92.5 percent is spent and 7.5 percent is saved.

Just two more questions: How much is the APC for the United States? How much is the country's APS? In recent years the APC has been about .95 and the APS .05. In other words, Americans spend about 95 percent of their disposable incomes and save the remaining 5 percent.

Marginal Propensity to Consume (MPC)

When income changes, so does consumption. When income rises, consumption also rises, but by less than does income. This is the consumption function, introduced at the beginning of the chapter.

The formula for calculating the MPC is:

$$MPC = \frac{Change\ in\ C}{Change\ in\ income}$$

$$\frac{Change\ in\ C}{Change\ in\ income}$$

Using the data in Table 4, calculate the MPC in the space below.

Solution:

$$MPC = \frac{Change\ in\ C}{Change\ in\ income} = \frac{\$8,000}{\$10,000} = \frac{8}{10} = .8$$

Marginal Propensity to Save (MPS)

When income changes, not only does consumption change, but so does saving. When income rises, both consumption and saving will rise. Similarly, when income falls, both consumption and saving fall.

The formula for calculating the MPS is:

$$MPS = \frac{Change\ in\ saving}{Change\ in\ income}$$

$MPS = \frac{Change\ in\ saving}{Change\ in\ income}$

Table 4

Year	Disposable Income	C
1998	$30,000	$23,000
1999	40,000	31,000

Using Table 4 again, calculate the MPS. (Note: Remember how to find saving when you have disposable income and consumption.)[4]

Solution:

$$MPS = \frac{Change\ in\ saving}{Change\ in\ income} = \frac{\$\,2,000}{\$10,000} = \frac{2}{10} = .2$$

Graphing the Consumption Function

Through the ages, generations of economics students have been traumatized by graphs. The consumption function, savings, and, later, investment, aggregate demand, and equilibrium GDP have been undecipherable quantities. Estimating these variables on a graph is like being called on to read an exotic foreign language—without being permitted to use a dictionary.

Our first step will be to learn how to read a graph. The key to reading economic variables from a graph is knowing where to look for them; so before we even look at graphs, let's just talk about them for a moment. There is a vertical line on the left side of every graph called the vertical scale, and there is a horizontal line on the bottom of every graph called the horizontal scale. Take a peek at Figure 2 to see what I'm talking about.

Every graph you will ever see in an economics text will have these two dimensions: the horizontal and the vertical. The vertical scale is almost always measured in dollars. In Figure 2 we have an expenditures scale with the numbers 1,000, 2,000, and 3,000, which represent expenditures of $1 trillion, $2 trillion, and $3 trillion, respectively. Notice that the distances between each of the successive numbers are equal. If you used a ruler to measure the distances between 0 and 1,000; 1,000 and 2,000; and 2,000 and 3,000, they would be exactly the same. This is a very important point because in a few pages you'll need to estimate distances between these numbers.

---

[4]From Table 4: Disposable income – Consumption = Savings

(1998) $30,000 – $23,000 = $7,000

(1999) $40,000 –   31,000 = 9,000

Figure 2   Disposable Income and Expenditures

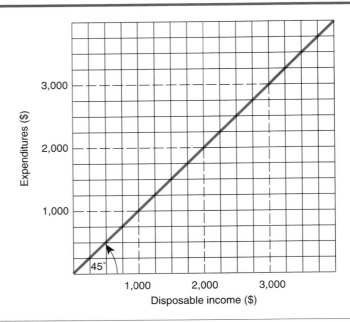

Expenditures are measured on the vertical scale and disposable income along the horizontal scale.

The horizontal axis in Figure 2 measures disposable income, also in units of 1,000, 2,000, and 3,000. In the graphs you'll encounter in future chapters, the horizontal scale will sometimes be based on units of time or units of output, but here we are measuring disposable income, which is measured in terms of dollars.

Nearly every variable is read from the vertical scale. The only exception we will encounter is disposable income, which is read from the horizontal scale.

The graph in Figure 2 shows expenditures along the vertical scale and disposable income along the horizontal scale. Figure 2 has only one line: a 45-degree line. This line has one purpose: to equate the horizontal scale with the vertical scale, that is, expenditures with disposable income.

Notice the dotted line rising from a disposable income of 1,000. It meets the 45-degree line and then moves horizontally to the vertical scale. For a disposable income of 2,000, there is another dotted line rising to the 45-degree line and then moving straight across to the vertical scale. The same pattern occurs at a disposable income of 3,000.

Let's take that first point on the 45-degree line, just above 1,000 on the disposable income scale and directly across from 1,000 on the expenditures (vertical) scale. That point is exactly 1,000 units from both the vertical and horizontal scales. Point 2 is 2,000 units from each scale. Thus, we see that points on the vertical scale are equal to their corresponding points on the horizontal scale.

Now we're ready to graph the consumption function. First we'll review it: *as income rises, consumption rises, but not as quickly.* How should it look on a graph? Suppose disposable income rises by 1,000. By how much should C rise? According to our definition of the consumption function, it should rise by less than 1,000.

If the consumption function stated that C rises as quickly as income, can you guess what a graph of the consumption function would look like? That's a hard one. It would look like the 45-degree line. Each point would be the same number of units from the two scales.

Figure 3 illustrates that consumption does not rise as quickly as the 45-degree line. Since C does not rise quickly as disposable income, the consumption line is flatter than the 45-degree line in Figure 2.

OK, now we're ready to read the graph in Figure 3. How much is consumption when disposable income is 1,000? Don't wait for me to tell you. Find a disposable income of 1,000 on the horizontal axis and work your way vertically (that means straight up) to the

Figure 3   Consumption and Disposable Income

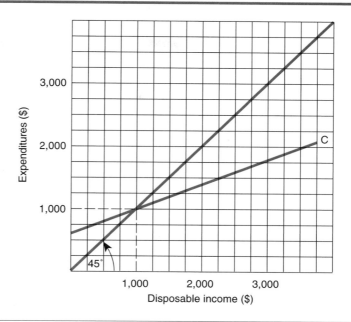

consumption line (C line). Then move across to the vertical axis. Now how much is C? You're not sure? OK, get a ruler or some other straightedge. Don't worry. I'll wait for you right here. Now let's go back to that disposable income of 1,000. Using the ruler, draw a line straight up to the C line. Now draw another line, this one perfectly horizontal (that means straight across), to the vertical axis. Now read the number. It is 1,000. Voilà! (If you need extra help, see the Extra Help box.)

We both know that I really did that one. Those lines were already on the graph. There are no guidelines for the next one. Find the level of C when disposable income is 2,000. Are you ready? Go ahead then. Just remember: up from a disposable income of 2,000 to the C line and then straight across. Oops! I'm giving it away. Go ahead: you do it and I'll let you know if you're right or not.

Read Only If You Still Don't Understand Why C Is 1,000

If you're still trying to figure out why C is 1,000, we'll use the analogy of football. Suppose your team is about to receive a kickoff. One of your players catches the ball on the goal line and runs it out to your own 10-yard line. How far was his return yardage? Obviously 10 yards. How do you know it was exactly 10 yards? Because you saw him start at the goal line and get tackled at the 10. In fact, there are even markers on the sideline.

If we were to ask how much C is when disposable income is 1,000, we go vertically (or downfield) from the horizontal axis to the 1,000 mark, which we find on the

vertical axis. How far did we go? We went 1,000. We have a scale on the vertical axis that enables us to measure how far we've gone—just like in football.

Now suppose a team has a first down, say, on the 25-yard line. On the next play it moves the ball to about the 35. Is this another first down? What will the referees do? They'll measure. How? That's right, they'll bring out the chains.

You may do the same thing to measure C or any other variable measured against the vertical axis. Not only is there a scale on the vertical axis (or yard markers), but you may use a ruler (chains) to make your measurements.

What did you get? To me it looks like about 1,400. Anything close to 1,400 is fine. But if you got 1,300, then you probably thought that each box is worth 200. Check Figure 3 again. Each box is worth 250, because there are four boxes between 1,000 and 2,000. Incidentally, how much is the marginal propensity to consume? Figure it out in the space below using the three-step method: formula, substitute, and solve.

Solution:

$$MPC = \frac{\text{Change in C}}{\text{Change in disposable income}} = \frac{400}{1,000} = \frac{4}{10} = .4$$

Let's try another problem. How much is C when disposable income is 3,000?

What did you come up with? Your answer should be around 1,800. While we're at it, how much is the average propensity to consume? Again, use the three-step method.

Solution:

$$APC = \frac{\text{Consumption}}{\text{Disposable income}} = \frac{1,800}{3,000} = \frac{18}{30} = \frac{3}{5} = .6$$

Remember that C is measured vertically. Notice that as disposable income (which is measured horizontally) increases, C moves higher and higher. But it doesn't rise as quickly as disposable income.

At low income levels, C is greater than disposable income.

At very low levels of disposable income, notice that the C line is higher than the 45-degree line. When that happens, consumption is greater than disposable income. How is that possible? Believe me, it happens—especially during depressions. Besides, didn't your consumption ever exceed your income? What's that? Your consumption always exceeds your income? Well, then, you might not have any money in the bank, but you should intuitively grasp the notion that a nation can spend more than its disposable income.

Some nations have gone into debt for tens of billions of dollars. A few years ago, Mexico, Brazil, and Argentina headed the list of big debtors. However, the new champion is the United States, whose external net debt is approaching $1 trillion.[5]

The Saving Function

The saving function: as income rises, saving rises, but not as quickly.

The saving function is virtually the same as the consumption function: *as income rises, saving rises, but not as quickly.*

Now we're ready to find saving on the graph in Figure 4. First, how much is saving when disposable income is 1,000? Go ahead and figure it out. Even with no listing of saving on the graph, you can figure out how much saving is from the information you already have—you already figured the level of C when disposable income is 1,000.

Your answer should be zero. If disposable income is 1,000 and C is 1,000, saving must be zero. Note that saving is the vertical distance between the C line and the 45-degree line.

Next problem. How much is saving when disposable income is 2,000? After you do that, find saving when disposable income is 3,000.

The answers to both questions are worked out in the graph in Figure 4. All you need to do is take the vertical distance between the C line and the 45-degree line. (To figure

---

[5]In the last chapter of this book, we'll examine this problem in detail.

Figure 4   Consumption, Saving, and Disposable Income

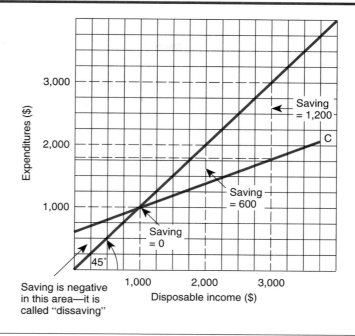

Autonomous Consumption versus Induced Consumption

You may have noticed in Figure 4 that when disposable income is zero, C is about 600. We call this *autonomous consumption* because people will spend a certain minimum amount on the necessities of life—food, clothing, and shelter. Whether one has to dig into one's savings, go on welfare, or else beg, borrow, or steal, one will spend that minimum amount. And on a national level, we will all spend a minimum amount—what we are calling autonomous consumption—even if national disposable income is zero.*

If the autonomous level of consumption were 600, then it would continue to be 600 no matter what the level of disposable income was. We know from the consumption function that consumption rises as disposable income rises; therefore an increase in consumption is induced. At any given level of disposable income there is a corresponding level of consumption. Part of that consumption is autonomous and part is induced. Because autonomous consumption stays the same—no matter how much disposable income varies—we can easily figure out how much consumption is induced. Just subtract autonomous consumption from total consumption.

Let's start with a disposable income of zero in Figure 4. Autonomous consumption *is* total consumption because a disposable income of zero cannot induce any consumption.

Let's go to a disposable income of 1,000. How much are autonomous consumption and induced consumption? Autonomous consumption would continue to be 600. Because total consumption is 1,000, induced consumption is 400.

We'll try one more. How much is autonomous consumption and how much is induced consumption when disposable income is 3,000? Autonomous consumption continues to be 600. If total consumption is estimated at 1,800, then induced consumption is 1,200 (1,800 − 600).

*Of course, national disposable income would never actually fall to zero because people are always spending that minimum amount, so other people are receiving most of that amount in income. For example, if people spent $20 each on food, clothing, and shelter each week, this money would end up in the pockets of those who supplied these goods and services. They, in turn, would spend most of this money on their own necessities. This analysis anticipates our discussion of the multiplier, which we will get to in Chapter 11.

out what C is when disposable income is zero, see box "Autonomous Consumption versus Induced Consumption.")

Let's stop for a minute to define two terms—autonomous consumption and induced consumption. *Autonomous consumption is our level of consumption when disposable income is 0.* It's called autonomous consumption because it's autonomous, or independent, of changes in the level of disposable income. *Induced consumption is that part of consumption which varies with the level of disposable income.* As disposable income rises,

autonomous consumption

induced consumption

induced consumption also rises, and when disposable income falls, induced consumption also falls. We say that changes in the level of disposable income **induce** changes in the level of consumption.

If you are having any trouble measuring these vertical distances, remember that all vertical distances are measured on the vertical axis. Horizontal dotted lines have been drawn in Figure 4 to locate points on the vertical axis.

Let's try another graph to make sure we're clear on how to measure consumption and saving at various levels of disposable income. In Figure 5, find the levels of consumption and saving when disposable income is (a) 1,500, (b) 3,000, and (c) 4,500. To check your work, see Figure 6. (For extra help on reading graphs, see the boxes "On Reading Graphs" and "More on Finding Autonomous and Induced Consumption.")

Each box is 250. From 1,500 to 3,000 is a distance of 1,500. Divide 1,500 by 6 and you get 250. The C line begins two lines or boxes above 1,500, which means that autonomous C is 2,000—that is, $1,500 + (2 \times 250)$.

Once you know autonomous consumption, you can figure out induced consumption for any level of disposable income. Start with a disposable income of zero. How much is induced consumption? Figure it out.

The answer is zero. At a disposable income of zero, total consumption is 2,000. Because autonomous consumption is also 2,000, induced consumption must be zero. Remember: Total consumption, or C, is the sum of autonomous consumption and induced consumption.

Next question: How much is induced consumption when disposable income is 1,500?

The answer is 200. Total consumption is 2,200. Total consumption (2,200) – autonomous consumption (2,000) = induced consumption (200). Remember: Autonomous consumption stays the same for all levels of disposable income. So once you find autonomous consumption, you can find induced consumption for any amount of disposable income by subtracting autonomous consumption from total consumption.

How much is induced consumption when disposable income is 3,000?

It's 325. Total consumption (2,325) – autonomous consumption (2,000) = induced consumption (325).

One more. How much is induced consumption when disposable income is 4,500?

Figure 5   Consumption, Saving, and Disposable Income

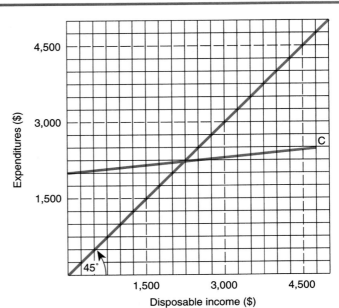

Figure 6   Consumption , Saving, and Disposable Income

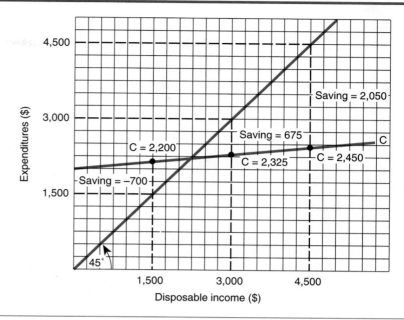

Please note that C is the vertical distance between the horizontal axis and the C line. Saving is the vertical distance between the C line and the 45-degree line. C and saving always add up to disposable income.

When disposable income is 1,500, C is 2,200, so saving must be –700.

When disposable income is 3,000, C is 2,325 and saving is 675.

When disposable income is 4,500, C is 2,450 and saving is 2,050.

These are only approximations. Your answers may vary slightly as long as your saving and consumption add up to disposable income.

On Reading Graphs

So far, we've had graphs with just two lines—the C line and the 45-degree line. In Chapter 6 we'll be adding the C + I line and in Chapter 7 the C + I + G line.

Not everyone can read a graph the first time out, but usually, with a little practice reading graphs becomes easier. So if you're not yet comfortable with graphs, I'd like you to go back a few pages to the section headed Graphing the Consumption Function. After you've reread it and reworked each of the problems, you should be considerably more comfortable with graphs.

The answer is 450. Total consumption (2,450) – autonomous consumption (2,000) = induced consumption (450).

What the Consumer Buys

The consumer buys durables, nondurables, and services.

Consumption is traditionally divided into three categories: durables, nondurables, and services. Durables are things that last a while—say, at least a year or two. Nondurables, such as food, gasoline, and children's clothing, don't last long. (In fact, a case could be made that the clothing worn by fashion-conscious adults doesn't last either, although the reason it doesn't last is that fashions change rather than that it wears out.)

More on Finding Autonomous and Induced Consumption

We are going to find autonomous and induced consumption in Figure 6. That is, you're going to find them, and then I'll tell you whether you're right. Ready? Good. How much is autonomous consumption? Did you get 2,000? That's correct.

How much is induced consumption when disposable income is (1) 0; (2) 1,500; (3) 3,000; and (4) 4,500? Write your answers here: (1)_____; (2)_____; (3)_____; and (4)_____.

Your answers should be: (1) 0; (2) 200; (3) 325; and (4) 450. (If you got everything right, then you know how to find autonomous and induced consumption, so you may skip the rest of this box.)

First we'll go over the autonomous consumption, which is the level of consumption when disposable income is zero. In Figure 6, when disposable income is zero, which is at the lower left-hand corner of the graph, you can see that consumption is between 1,500 and 3,000, but somewhat closer to 1,500. The distance between 1,500 and 3,000 is six boxes or lines. How much is each box (the distance between two consecutive lines)? Figure it out.

Each box is 250. From 1,500 to 3,000 is a distance of 1,500. Divide 1,500 by 6 and you get 250. The C line begins two lines or boxes above 1,500, which means that autonomous C is 2,000—that is, 1,500 + (2 × 250).

Once you know autonomous consumption, you can figure out induced consumption for any level of disposable income. Start with a disposable income of zero. How much is induced consumption? Figure it out.

The answer is zero. At a disposable income of zero, total consumption is 2,000. Because autonomous consumption is also 2,000, induced consumption must be zero. Remember: Total consumption, or C, is the sum of autonomous consumption and induced consumption.

Next question: How much is induced consumption when disposable income is 1,500?

The answer is 200. Total consumption is 2,200. Total consumption (2,200) – autonomous consumption (2,000) = induced consumption (200). Remember: Autonomous consumption stays the same for all levels of disposable income. So once you find autonomous consumption, you can find induced consumption for any amount of disposable income by subtracting autonomous consumption from total consumption.

How much is induced consumption when disposable income is 3,000?

It's 325. Total consumption (2,325) – autonomous consumption (2,000) = induced consumption (325).

One more. How much is induced consumption when disposable income is 4,500?

The answer is 450. Total consumption (2,450) – autonomous consumption (2,000) = induced consumption (450).

Durable goods include appliances, cars, and furniture. They last—or, at least, they're supposed to last. The big change in our economy since World War II has been in the service sector, which now produces over half of what consumers buy. Medical care, education, legal and financial services, and entertainment are some of the fields that have grown rapidly in the last four decades.

Figure 7 summarizes where the consumer's dollar went in 1955 and where it went in 1997. There has been a huge shift from expenditures on durables and nondurables to expenditures on services.

In 1955 Americans spent only 36 cents out of every consumer dollar on services; but today, 59 cents goes toward services. Why this massive shift? For one thing, Americans are spending a much larger part of their incomes on medical care than they did in the 1950s. This trend has been reinforced as our population grows older. More Americans are going to college, eating out, and suing each other than ever before. Computer services, financial services, and personal services have expanded rapidly. Basically, we're paying people to do things for us that we either did for ourselves 40 years ago or didn't do at all.

Do you bring your lunch to school every day? Do you know anyone who does? Had you gone to college 40 years ago, the chances are you would have brown-bagged it. How does a homemade lunch go into GDP? It goes into the category of nondurable goods. But the lunch you buy in the cafeteria or at Burger King is classified as a service. Similarly, if

Figure 7   Consumer Spending, 1995 and 1997 ($ billions)

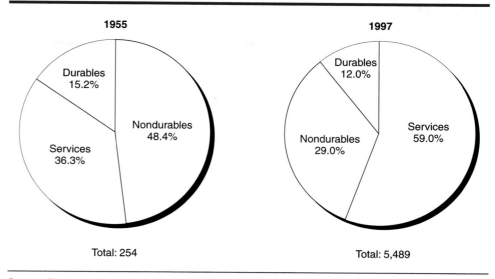

Source: *Economic Report of the President,* 1998.

Table 5   The Components of Consumption, 1997*

Durable goods	659
Nondurable goods	1,593
Services	3,237
Consumption	5,489*

*The figures, as well as all the 1997 data that follows, are preliminary.
Source: *Survey of Current Business,* March 1995.

you buy lettuce, tomatoes, carrots, and other raw vegetables, cut them up at home, and eat a salad, the components of that salad classify as nondurables. But if you stop at a salad bar and buy the identical components, which have been cut up for you—and pay about 10 times as much per pound—then this expenditure would count as a service.

Americans spent nearly $5.5 trillion on consumer goods and services in 1997 (see Table 5). This came to over two-thirds of GDP. In Chapter 6 we'll look at the investment sector, and in Chapter 7, the government sector. At the end of Chapter 8, after we tack on net exports, we'll add up $C + I + G + X_n$ and get GDP.

Determinants of the Level of Consumption

A budget tells us what we can't afford, but it doesn't keep us from buying it.

—William Feather

Why do people spend money? Some hate to spend a penny, and others spend every penny they can lay their hands on. The aphorism "If you don't have it, you can't spend it" is especially relevant to any discussion of the determinants of consumption. The six basic determinants are listed below. (As we shall see, however, a person's level of spending is determined largely by how much money he or she has.)

1. Disposable income.
2. Credit availability.
3. Stock of liquid assets in the hands of consumers.
4. Stock of durable goods in the hands of consumers.
5. Keeping up with the Joneses.
6. Consumer expectations.

The Level of Disposable Income

Many factors influence how much money people spend; by far the most important is disposable income. As illustrated with the consumption function, as income rises, consumption rises, but not as quickly.

At very low income levels, people not only don't save, they actually dissave. Suppose, for example, you lose your job. Do you simply stop spending money? If you did, you'd sure lose a lot of weight. How do you get by? If you collect unemployment benefits, then that's your disposable income. But the chances are, you would spend more each week than your unemployment checks, especially if you support a family. You still have to pay rent, car payments, other installment payments, utilities, and food bills, as well as the cost of looking for another job.

To manage all this you might borrow—if you can get credit—and you will go into your savings. So, at very low levels of income, you tend to spend more than your disposable income.

At the other end of the economic spectrum are the rich, who usually manage to save some of their disposable income. Every so often we'll read about a wealthy professional athlete or entertainer who has gone bankrupt, but these are the rare exceptions. The Rockefellers, the Du Ponts, the Mellons, the Waltons, the Perots, the Fords, the Gateses, the Buffets, and the Kluges all spend a lot of money. Still, they somehow manage to save several million dollars a year.

The more you've got, the more you spend. Or, alternatively, if you ain't got it, you can't spend it. So you can be sure that the working-class family spends more than the poor family. And that the upper-middle-class family spends more than the working-class family. Almost every family spends most of its income, so clearly the level of disposable income largely determines the level of consumption.

The main point here is that rich people spend a lot more money than do poor people. Why? Because they *have* more money. What is the most important determinant of consumption? Disposable income.

Credit Availability

You can't borrow money if you don't have credit. The most popular ways of borrowing are credit cards, especially VISA and MasterCard. Bank loans, home mortgages, home equity loans, and auto loans are other ways of borrowing. When credit is eased, people tend to borrow more.

For example, suppose a furniture store, which had been asking its customers to put down 50 percent of their purchases in cash and pay out the balance in six months, now offered new terms: nothing down and two years to pay. Many people would buy furniture on these terms.

This is not to say that everyone stretches his or her credit to the limit, although some people do. However, credit availability has some influence on the level of consumption.

Credit availability varies inversely with the level of consumer debt. That is, the more you owe, the less likely you are to have more credit available. If your credit card limit is $5,000 and you already owe $4,900, you have only $100 of credit available. Furthermore, people who owe a great deal are somewhat reluctant to take on still more debt.

Stock of Liquid Assets in the Hands of Consumers

People own things that can be quickly turned into cash. These are called liquid assets. Prime examples include government and corporate bonds, corporate stocks, savings accounts, bank certificates of deposit (CDs), and money market funds.

In the United States today, people hold a stock of liquid assets of a few trillion dollars. This makes some people feel rich. Suppose, for example, you hold 1,000 shares of IBM and the price of that stock rises $2. You are $2,000 richer (at least on paper). This may induce you to go out and spend some of that money you just made.

In addition to *feeling* rich, if your liquid assets rise, you do indeed have more money to spend. That is, you can quickly convert some of these assets into money, then go out and spend it. Economists have found that there is some correlation between consumption and the amount of liquid assets held. The reasoning here is that if you don't have it, you can't spend it, and if you do have it, you will spend some of it.

Thorstein Veblen, American sociologist and economist (Historical Pictures/Stock Montage)

Stock of Durable Goods in the Hands of Consumers

In 1929, radios, toasters, vacuum cleaners, waffle irons, and other appliances were relatively new because most of the country had been electrified only over the last decade and a half. More than 95 percent of the cars on the road were under 10 years old. By 1930, the market for consumer durables was temporarily saturated.

When few people own items such as personal computers, VCRs, or video games, sales will rise. But when the market is saturated (and people own relatively late models), it will be some time before sales pick up again.

Consumer durables are now a relatively small part of total consumption—only 12 percent of all goods and services sold to consumers in 1997. However, their sales are somewhat erratic, largely because they vary inversely with the stock of consumer durables in the hands of consumers. When people hold a large stock of consumer durables, consumer durable sales tend to be low; when that stock is low, sales tend to be high.

Wealth has never been a sufficient source of honor in itself. It must be advertised, and the normal medium is obtrusively expensive goods.

—John Kenneth Galbraith, *The Affluent Society*

Conspicuous consumption

Keeping Up with the Joneses

Most of us, at least a few times in our lives, have been guilty of showing off our expensive clothes, our jewelry, our cars, or even our Florida tans. And most of us have been tempted to keep up with our neighbors, relatives, and friends. When the Joneses buy something, we have to go out and buy one, too—even if we can't afford it—because if we don't buy it, we won't be keeping up.

Why do some people spend $2,000 on a wristwatch, $150 for a pair of sneakers, or $5,000 for an evening gown? To a large degree, they're showing off. I have so much money, they seem to be saying, that I can afford these indulgences.

More than 80 years ago Thorstein Veblen coined the term *conspicuous consumption.* In a marvelous book titled *The Theory of the Leisure Class,* Veblen stated, "Conspicuous consumption of valuable goods is a means of reputability to the gentleman of leisure." He went on to say, "With the exception of the instinct of self-preservation, the propensity for emulation is probably the strongest and most alert and persistent of the economic motives proper."[6]

Consumer Expectations

When people expect inflation, they often buy consumer durables before prices go up. On the other hand, when they expect recession, they tend to reduce their purchases of such big-ticket items as cars, furniture, and major appliances. Many people fear being laid off or having their income reduced because of recessions, so they tend to postpone major purchases until times get better.

The Permanent Income Hypothesis

According to Milton Friedman, a prominent conservative economist, the strongest influence on consumption is one's estimated average lifetime income. No one knows what his or her average lifetime income will actually be, but people can generally figure out if they are earning more or less than that average.

If a factory worker earning $22,000 a year expects to remain a factory worker, she can estimate her future earnings until she retires. According to Friedman, people gear their consumption to their expected earnings more than to their current income.

Suppose someone's income temporarily contracts, say, because of a factory layoff. Would the person cut back very sharply on her consumption? No, she would not, says

Milton Friedman, winner of Nobel prize, 1976, for work on monetary theory (© The Nobel Foundation)

---

[6]Thorstein Veblen, *The Theory of the Leisure Class,* Chapters 4 and 5.

this theory, since she knows she will be back on the job within a few months. She has to continue paying her rent, meeting her car payments, and eating three times a day.

Earnings tend to rise until late middle age (about 55 or so) and then decline. Therefore the permanent income hypothesis would predict that most people's consumption is greater than their income until their mid or late 20s. From the late 20s to the early 60s, current disposable income is usually greater than consumption. In old age, the relationship between consumption and current disposable income is again reversed, so consumption is greater than income.

Thus, our consumption is determined by our average expected income, or permanent income. That income is a constant; consumption is a constant percentage of that income. For most Americans, consumption would be about 90 to 95 percent of permanent income.

According to Friedman's hypothesis, if you suddenly win the lottery, make a huge sum of money on a quiz show, or experience some other windfall, you will not spend much of it. You will spend *some* of it because it will raise your permanent income, but you will spend only a small part of it.

For example, suppose you receive a windfall of $100,000. If the permanent income hypothesis applies, you might spend $6,000 or $8,000 a year over the next 15 years or so. Is this how most lottery winners have handled their windfalls? Apparently there are quite a few deviations from the behavior predicted by the permanent income hypothesis.

Determinants of the Level of Saving

Savings may be viewed as a residual of disposable income, what is left after most or nearly all of it has been used on consumption. Some people spend virtually all of their income, while others manage to spend more than they earn year after year.

There are many reasons why people save.

Still, most Americans manage to save at least a small part of their income. Some people are saving for a big-ticket item like a couch, a new bedroom set, a car, or a VCR. Others are saving for a vacation or perhaps the down payment on a house. Many Americans try to put away some money each year for their children's education. Some people save money every year for a rainy day or their old age, while still others are simply penny-pinchers.

On the average, Americans save about 5 percent of their disposable income. Can you figure out from this one fact how much our APS and APC are?

APS =   APC =

If you remembered what we covered near the beginning of the chapter, you said that the APS is .05 and APC is .95. In other words, we spend, on the average, 95 percent of our disposable income and save 5 percent.

For most of the 20th century, Americans saved between 7 and 10 percent of their disposable incomes. A decline to 5 percent (and even less in recent years) may not seem like much, but it amounts to an enormous amount of money when we consider that our disposable personal income is almost $6 trillion. Now figure out by how many dollars our savings would decline if the savings rate fell by 2 percent. Work it out here and then check the solution in the space below.

Solution: $6,000,000,000,000 × .02 = $120,000,000,000 (or $120 billion).

Incidentally, this problem can be reduced to a very simple problem in arithmetic. How much is $6 trillion × 2? It's $12 trillion. Write it out: $12,000,000,000,000. OK. Now when you multiply a number by .02, how many zeros do you take from it? I hope you said two. Thus we have $12,000,000,000,000. When we move the commas over, we get $12,000,000,000.

A much easier way to do this calculation is to write $5 trillion as 5000 (which stands for 5 thousand billion). Then 5000 × .02 = 100.

A $120 billion shortfall is particularly important at a time when we need all the savings we can lay our hands on to finance the hundreds of billions of investment funds that large corporations need to build new plant and equipment.

Why Do We Spend So Much and Save So Little?

Murray Weidenbaum, President Reagan's first chief economic advisor (© 1993 Susan Muniak)

It seems a lot of trouble if, instead of having to earn money and save it, you can just go and borrow it.
—Winston Churchill

Nobody goes to the mall anymore because they're too crowded.
—Standard retail industry joke

Americans have been on a spending binge these last dozen years. In fact, the national motto might well be "Buy now, pay later," "Shop till you drop," or "We want it all, and we want it now!" The "me generation" has had a fascination for every conceivable type of electronic gadget, has had to buy new wardrobes every six months as the fashions change, and has had to drive the latest-model fully loaded luxury foreign car. In fact, much of what we buy is made by foreigners. Murray Weidenbaum, who served as President Ronald Reagan's first chief economic advisor, summed up our profligacy this way:

> As citizens of the United States, we are consuming more than we are producing, borrowing more than we are saving, and spending more than we are earning. We are rapidly approaching the time when we will have to pay the piper.[7]

The federal government has actually underwritten our spending binge. Until 1987, interest paid on consumer loans was fully deductible from our federal income taxes. Mortgage interest and property taxes remain fully deductible. So buy a home and charge part of your costs to Uncle Sam.[8] And if you need to borrow still more money, just take out a second mortgage and use this money to finance your ever-growing consumption expenditures.

The tremendous expansion of bank credit cards, installment credit, and consumer loans has further fueled the consumer binge of the last dozen years. Every day Americans are offered millions of credit cards, whether they asked for them or not. In fact, from 1991 to 1997, consumer debt rose by 57 percent. Some people call credit cards "mall money."

Young Americans getting married, buying their first homes, and starting families will not be able to begin saving until they are well into their 30s. Traditionally, it is the middle-aged who do the bulk of the nation's saving. But today's middle-aged, the baby boomers born in the late 1940s and in the 1950s, are spending as if there were no tomorrow. Much of this spree is financed by tax-deductible home equity loans (see box "Home Equity Loans: A Tax Subsidy for Consumption").

In America, we like to say that the consumer is king. See the box "Is the Consumer Really King?" for a view almost diametrically opposed to the one I've been expressing all this time. Does the consumer really have all that many choices, or does our suburban lifestyle make it almost impossible for most families to save?

Our saving rate might not have been so low were it not for two factors that have become increasingly important over the last five decades—Social Security and widespread home ownership. Most Americans do not feel the pressing need to save for their old age because they will receive Social Security benefits, not to mention private pensions. Similarly, home ownership is seen as a form of saving, especially during a period of rising real estate prices.

How *have* we been able to put off paying the piper for so long? By borrowing. As individual consumers, we borrow; as giant corporations, we borrow; and as the federal government, we borrow. And who lends us this money? Increasingly, the answer is foreigners.

Foreigners have been financing about half the federal budget deficit and our purchase of hundreds of billions of dollars of imported manufactured goods, and foreigners have been pouring hundreds of billions of dollars into commercial real estate as well as corporate stocks and bonds. In other words, foreigners have been making up for most of the shortfall in American savings.[9]

---

[7]Murray Weidenbaum, *Rendezvous with Reality* (New York: Basic Books, 1988). p. 4.

[8]Tax deductions are a marvelous way to reduce your tax bill. In Chapter 7 we'll talk about how the tax system works and how you can beat it.

[9]Foreign investments in the United States will be fully discussed in the last chapter of this book.

Home Equity Loans: A Tax Subsidy for Consumption

Until the Tax Reform Act of 1986, consumer spending was subsidized by the federal government in two ways. Money spent on sales tax could be deducted from federal taxes. Also deductible was interest on consumer loans. These two subsidies were taken away, but a loophole the size of a house was left in place.

Homeowners are able to continue taking the interest paid on home equity loans off their taxes. So if you need money for a new car, a trip around the world, or a plain old-fashioned shopping spree, just take out a home equity loan. Since it's treated by the IRS as mortgage borrowing, it's tax deductible.

One of the consequences of this spending binge by the middle-aged is that they will leave much less to their children than *their* parents left to them. Alfred Malabre observes that "the coming generation of Americans won't be able to afford the standard of housing enjoyed by their parents, since their parents will have spent their inflated equity and left behind a mountain of debt."*

*Alfred L. Malabre, Jr., *Beyond Our Means* (New York: Random House, 1987), p. 46.

Is the Consumer Really King?

Before we even receive our paychecks today, nearly all those dollars already have someone else's name on them. *Think* about it. How much of *your* family's paychecks goes toward paying off your mortgage, credit card debt, your cars, school tuition, insurance, medical bills, and home repair? Of course you would have had a lot more to spend if the government hadn't already taken *its* share of your pay before you even saw your paycheck.

Let's start with what is, by far, our most important purchase—a home. Once that purchase is made, there aren't a whole lot of choices with respect to mortgage payments, real estate taxes, heating bills, homeowner's insurance, upkeep, and repairs. Back in 1949, the average 30-year-old head of household needed to spend just 14 percent of his paycheck to make the payments on his home. By 1970 it took more than 21 percent of his paycheck to pay for that home. And today the average 30-year-old has to shell out over 40 percent of his take-home pay.

The American dream has gradually become a financial nightmare. I recently asked my students how many cars their families owned. The majority owned three or four.

Suburban sprawl has almost completely obviated the use of mass transit. Indeed, it is economically unfeasible to have any kind of mass transit—even express bus service during peak travel times—unless there's a minimum population density of five families per acre. This means that the typical suburban family must be completely dependent on its cars. The trip to work, to school, to the store, to little league practice, and to virtually anywhere else must be made by car.

The cost of car payments, insurance, gas, maintenance, and repairs takes another large chunk—often more than 25 percent—out of the typical suburban family's income. So it's no wonder that most households depend on two full-time incomes, and often one or two additional part-time incomes as well.

What's so terrible about a low rate of saving? It means that we are spending nearly all of our earnings on consumer goods and services. It means that we are devoting little of our resources toward the production of plant and equipment, toward research and development, and toward the fostering of economic growth in general. Rather than investing in the future, we are bound and determined simply to live for today. We will examine the consequences of our low saving rate in the next chapter when we consider investment.

Questions for Further Thought and Discussion

1. Explain the relationship between consumption and saving.
2. Explain the difference between autonomous consumption and induced consumption.
3. Explain how the stock of consumer durables in the hands of consumers and credit availability each affect the level of consumption.
4. Since the 1950s a massive shift in consumption patterns with respect to nondurable goods and services has taken place. What is this shift and how can it be explained?

WORKBOOK FOR CHAPTER 5

Name _____ Date _____

Multiple-Choice Questions

Circle the letter that corresponds to the best answer.

1. Since 1955 Americans have been spending
   a. a larger percentage of their incomes on services
   b. a smaller percentage of their incomes on services
   c. about the same percentage of their incomes on services

2. When the C line crosses the 45-degree line, saving is
   a. positive   b. negative   c. zero
   d. impossible to calculate because there is not enough information to know.

3. When disposable income is zero
   a. autonomous consumption is equal to induced consumption   b. autonomous consumption is equal to total consumption   c. induced consumption is equal to total consumption

4. The minimum amount that people will spend even if disposable income is zero is called _____ consumption.
   a. autonomous   b. induced   c. total

5. According to the permanent income hypothesis, if a person received a windfall, of $100,000, he would spend _____ that year.
   a. some of it   b. most of it   c. nearly all of it
   d. all of it

6. As disposable income rises
   a. autonomous C rises   b. autonomous C falls
   c. induced C rises   d. induced C falls

7. The largest component of GDP is
   a. net exports   b. investment   c. consumption
   d. government purchases

8. The largest component of C is
   a. durable goods   b. services   c. nondurable goods

9. The consumption function tells us that as income rises, consumption
   a. declines   b. remains the same   c. rises more slowly than income   d. rises more quickly than income

10. When income levels are very low, C is
    a. zero   b. lower than income   c. higher than income

11. When income is equal to consumption, saving is
    a. negative   b. zero   c. positive
    d. impossible to calculate because there is insufficient information

12. Which of the following relations is *not* correct?
    a. MPC + MPS = 1   b. APC + APS = 1
    c. MPS = MPC + 1   d. 1 – APS = APC
    e. 1 – MPC = MPS

13. Induced consumption expenditures
    a. fall as income rises   b. are always equal to autonomous consumption expenditures   c. plus saving equals total consumption expenditures
    d. represent consumption that is independent of income   e. are influenced mainly by income

14. Autonomous consumption expenditures are
    a. equal to induced consumption expenditures
    b. proportional to disposable income   c. not influenced by income   d. influenced primarily by the saving function

15. The average propensity to save
    a. is disposable income divided by savings   b. is a measure of the additional saving generated by additional income   c. is negative at very high income levels
    d. varies directly with income; as income rises, the APS rises

Fill-In Questions

1. About _____ percent of what Americans spend on consumption is spent on services.

2. The average propensity to consume is found by dividing _____ by _____.

3. The APS + the APC = _____.

4. The consumption function states that _____ _____.

5. Dissaving takes place when _____.

6. Induced consumption is induced by _____.

7. According to the saving function, as disposable income rises, _____.

8. The most important determinant of the level of consumption is _____.

9. The average propensity to consume in the United States today is about _____.

10. $1 - MPS =$ _____.

11. When the C line crosses the 45-degree line, saving is equal to _____.

Problems

1. Given the information shown in Table 1, calculate the APC and the APS.

Table 1

Disposable Income	Consumption
$10,000	$8,400

2. Given the information shown in Table 2, calculate the MPC and MPS. (Assume disposable income rises from $35,000 to $37,000.)

Table 2

Year	Disposable Income	Saving
2002	$35,000	$4,600
2003	37,000	5,300

3. Using the information in Figure 1, how much are consumption and saving when disposable income is:

		C	Saving
a.	1,000	____	____
b.	2,000	____	____
c.	3,000	____	____

4. Using your answers from question 3a, calculate the APC and the APS.

5. Using your answers from questions 3a and 3b, calculate the MPC and the MPS when disposable income rises from 1,000 to 2,000.

6. Using the data in Figure 1, how much is autonomous consumption?

7. Using the data in Figure 1, determine induced consumption when disposable income is:
   a. 1,000   b. 2,000   c. 3,000

8. If C is $4 trillion, disposable income is $5 trillion, and autonomous consumption is $3 trillion:
   a. How much is saving? b. How much is induced consumption? c. How much is the APS? d. If the APS falls by .01, how much does saving fall?

Figure 1

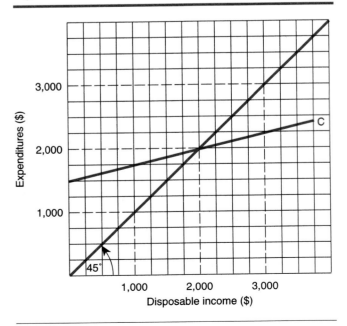

6 The Business-Investment Sector

Unlike China, Vietnam, Cuba, and dozens of other communist and socialist nations, most investment in the United States is carried out by private business firms rather than by the government. That investment consists of the production of new plant and equipment, residential housing, and additions to our inventories.

Chapter Objectives

In this chapter you'll learn about:

- The three types of business firms.
- How investment is carried out.
- The difference between gross investment and net investment.
- How capital is accumulated.
- The determinants of the level of investment.
- The graphing of the C + I line.

Proprietorships, Partnerships, and Corporations

There are over 20 million business firms in the United States. About 7 out of 10 are proprietorships, 1 out of 10 is a partnership, and 2 out of 10 are corporations. Proprietorships are owned by individuals and are almost always small businesses. Partnerships, which are also usually small, are owned by two or more people. There are relatively few large businesses in our country, and virtually all of them are corporations. Most corporations, like most businesses, are small.

Most businesses are small.

The Proprietorship

A typical proprietorship would be a grocery, a barbershop, a candy store, a restaurant, a family farm, or a filling station. Chances are, nearly all of the places in the neighborhood where you shop are proprietorships.

The Partnership

Two or more people can own a partnership. Although the typical partnership has two people, some law and accounting firms have hundreds of partners. Two key advantages of forming a partnership are being able to raise more capital and to divide the work and responsibility of running the business.

Advantages of a partnership

A typical division of labor between partners would be production and sales, or, in the parlance of business, inside and outside. The advantages of forming a partnership must be weighed against two basic disadvantages. The first is that the partnership must be dissolved when one of its members dies or wants to leave the business. A second disadvantage is that of unlimited liability.

Disadvantages of a partnership

Both proprietors and partners are liable for all debts incurred by their businesses. For example, if the firm is sued for negligence, the owners are personally liable to pay the amount awarded if the firm cannot do so. If one partner absconds with funds, the other partners may lose their homes and cars even though they were innocent victims. The way to avoid ever having to face this dilemma is to incorporate.

The Corporation

The key advantage of the corporation is limited liability. That is, each owner's liability is limited to the amount of money he has invested in the business. If there's a negligence suit or someone absconds with funds, the most you can lose is your investment. No one can touch your house, car, or any other personal property.

A corporation is a legal person. As such, it can sue and be sued. What is significant about this attribute is that the people who own the corporation—the stockholders—cannot be sued no matter how grievous the transgressions of the corporation. However, the courts have, on occasion, found stockholders liable (e.g., when stockholders form a corporation for fraudulent purposes).

A second advantage of a corporation is its potentially perpetual life. While a partnership must be dissolved when one of the partners leaves the business, a corporation can continue indefinitely: the stock owned by the principal who wants to pull out is purchased by someone else. In the case of large, publicly held corporations, such transactions take place routinely at the major stock exchanges.

Still another advantage of incorporating is that the company can sell stock to the public to raise more money. Because the owners have limited liability and the firm itself has ongoing life, the corporation is in a better position than the proprietorship or partnership to go to the public to raise funds.

Of course, only a tiny fraction of all corporations ever go public. Nearly all are relatively small businesses that are completely owned by a few individuals. (See box "Big Corporations and Small Corporations.") However, virtually all large companies in the United States are corporations.

Perhaps all of this can be cleared up by a syllogism:[1] (1) Nearly all large companies are corporations. (2) Nearly all corporations are small companies. (3) Therefore, a small minority of corporations constitutes nearly all the large companies. In other words, of nearly 4 million corporations, about 2,000 are large companies, and these 2,000 large corporations constitute the vast majority of the nation's large companies.

Although accounting for only 20 percent of the nation's business firms, corporations collect more than 90 percent of all business receipts. While most corporations are tiny enterprises that incorporated to limit the liability of the owners, there are perhaps 2,000 really large corporations. These companies do most of the nation's business.

Only a very small percentage of corporations actually sell stock, but it should be obvious that the limited liability of the stockholders would be a great advantage in raising capital. I have already emphasized that there are only a few really large businesses out of the nearly 20 million in the United States. Each large firm is a corporation, and virtually each one is publicly held (that is, it sells stock to the public).

The largest 10 corporations are shown in Table 1. Who's number one? It's General Motors, with sales of nearly $178 billion.

You'll notice that *Fortune* ranks corporations in terms of sales. They may also be ranked in size of assets, profits, number of employees, or some other attribute. If you're curious, in 1996, Exxon led the nation in profits with $7.5 billion, followed closely by General Electric with $7.3 billion, and Philip Morris ($6.3 billion).

There are two disadvantages to incorporating. First, you have to have papers drawn up and pay a fee for a charter. The expense of doing this varies, but two of the most popular states in which to incorporate, Delaware and New Jersey, appear to make things the easiest. A second disadvantage is that you will have to pay federal, and possibly state, corporate income tax. Although the rates are very low for small corporations, those with profits of more than $10 million must pay 35 percent of anything above that amount to the

---

[1]What is a syllogism? It is a form of reasoning consisting of two statements and a conclusion drawn from them.

Big Corporations and Small Corporations

The typical corporation is very small, like the old North American Uniform Cap Corporation. Although the company had a rather impressive name, its officers were Jonas Lewy, president; Nadja Lewy, vice president; and their son, Henry Lewy, secretary-treasurer. They ran their business out of a tiny loft in Manhattan's garment district, sewing up work caps, military caps, and what are now called "gimme caps." They had about a half-dozen sewing machines, and Henry's parents—the president and the vice president—operated two of them. During the "busy season," they hired another three or four operators.

The North American Uniform Cap Corporation never grew into a large enterprise, although the Lewys were always waiting for that one big order—like maybe a few million caps for the Chinese communist army. But the big order never came, and like 85 percent of all corporations, North American Uniform Caps never managed to do a million dollars worth of business in a single year.

But some corporations *are* really big. According to *Business Week,* 83 corporations do more than $10 billion in sales.* And the 15 percent of all corporations that do more than $1 million in sales take in 85 percent of the receipts of all corporations.†

Business Week, March 6, 1995, pp. 101–116.

†See Janet Lowe, *The Secret Empire: How 25 Multinationals Rule the World* (Burr Ridge, IL: Business One Irwin, 1992), p. 6.

Table 1   The Top Ten in U.S. Sales, 1997

	1997 Sales in Billions
1 General Motors	$178
2 Ford Motor	154
3 Exxon	122
4 Wal-Mart Stores	119
5 General Electric	91
6 IBM	79
7 Chrysler	61
8 Mobil	60
9 Philip Morris	56
10 AT&T	53

Source: *Fortune,* April 27, 1998.

Internal Revenue Service.[2] Still another disadvantage of incorporating is being subject to double taxation. After a corporation's profits are subject to the corporate income tax, much of what remains is paid out in dividends, on which one must pay personal income taxes.

The box titled "The New Hybrid Varieties" describes companies that are a cross between partnerships and corporations.

Stocks and Bonds

Stockholders are owners of a corporation. Bondholders lend money to a company and are therefore creditors rather than owners. This distinction becomes important when we consider the order in which people are paid off when the corporation is doing well and when it goes bankrupt.

Two types of stock

There are two types of corporate stock: common and preferred. The advantage of owning preferred is that you will receive a stipulated dividend, say 6 percent of the face value of your stock, provided there are any profits out of which to pay dividends. After you are paid, if some profits remain, the common stockholders will be paid.

Why bother to own common stock? Mainly because only common stockholders may vote on issues of concern to the corporation as well as on who gets to run the corporation. Both preferred and common stockholders own the corporation, or hold equity in the company, but only common stockholders vote.

Bondholders are creditors—not owners.

Bondholders are creditors rather than owners of a corporation. Like the preferred stockholders, they must be paid a stipulated percentage of the face value of their bonds,

[2]Corporations earning smaller profits pay lower rates.

ADVANCED WORK..........   The New Hybrid Varieties

Some companies seem to fall into the cracks between partnerships and corporations. There are limited partnerships, which not only avoid paying corporate income taxes but, as their name implies, also minimize legal risk to their investors. There are S corporations—named after the subchapter of the Internal Revenue Code that authorizes them—which offer their shareholders limited liability and pay no corporate income tax. Since 1988, the Internal Revenue Service has also authorized limited liability companies, which have the legal insulation of a corporation and the preferred tax treatment of a limited partnership.

You can also form a limited liability company, or limited liability partnership, to protect your personal assets if your business is sued. A suit can place only the assets of your business at risk. Between 1992 and 1994 more than 40 states—with California a prominent exception—passed limited liability legislation. A limited liability company carries the same benefits as the S corporation, with taxes assessed solely at the individual level; the owners pay personal income tax on their profits but do not have to pay corporate income tax.

But all of this said, these are still the exceptions that prove the rule. The vast majority of businessowners incorporate to secure limited liability, and are then subject to paying corporate income taxes. The hybrid entities do provide loopholes, but so far only a small minority of businessowners have crawled through.

say 8 percent, in the form of interest, but they must be paid whether or not the company makes a profit. In fact, the interest they receive is considered one of the costs of doing business. And should a company go bankrupt, the bondholders, as creditors, have to be paid off before the owners of preferred and common stock see any money.

Capitalization and Control

A corporation's total capital, or capitalization, consists of the total value of its stocks and bonds. For example, a $4 billion corporation may have $1 billion in bonds, $500 million in preferred stock, and $2.5 billion in common stock. Similarly, a corporation with $200 million in bonds, $100 million in preferred stock, and $300 million in common stock would be capitalized at $600 million.

One might ask how much money would be needed to gain control of a large corporation. Let's consider a corporation that's capitalized for $500 million—$300 million in bonds, $120 million in preferred stock, and $80 million in common stock. Theoretically, you would need slightly over $40 million, or 50 percent plus one share of the common stock.

But most large corporations are rather widely held; that is, there are many stockholders with only a few holding even 1 percent. Furthermore, many stockholders either don't bother to vote their shares or they give proxies to others who will. Usually, then, holding about 5 percent of the common stock of a company will be sufficient for control. So, in this case, by holding $4 million worth of common stock (5 percent of $80 million), you should be able to control this $500 million corporation.

Now let's work out a problem testing your knowledge of capitalization and control: If the XYZ corporation has $4 billion in preferred stock, $6 billion in common stock, and $3 billion in bonds: (*a*) How much is its capitalization? (*b*) Theoretically, how much would it take to control it? (*c*) Practically speaking, it may take only about how much to control it?

Work out your answers here:

Solutions: (*a*) $4 billion + $6 billion + $3 billion = $13 billion
(*b*) $6 billion × .50 = $3 billion, or, technically speaking, $3 billion + $1
(*c*) $6 billion × .05 = $300 million

Many economists believe that you really need to hold about 10 percent of the common stock to be assured of control. In *that* case, we have: $6 billion × .10 = $600 million. So to be fair, we would have to accept an answer of either 5 percent of the common stock or 10 percent of the common stock. Or, for that matter, any percentage between 5 and 10.

Investment

Investment is really the thing that makes our economy go. When we have prosperity, investment is high and rising. And when we're in a recession, it is low and falling. Let's define investment and then see how it varies.

Investment is any new plant, equipment, additional inventory, or residential housing.[3] Plant includes factories, office buildings, department and other retail stores, and shopping malls. Examples of equipment are assembly lines, machine tools, display cases, cash registers, computer systems, typewriters, and office furniture—as long as businesses purchase them. For example, if you buy a car for your personal use, it's a consumption expenditure. But if Shell Oil buys a car for its executives to ride around in (on company business), then it's an investment. The key question we must ask is whether the purchase adds to a company's plant, equipment, or inventory. If not, then it's not investment. What if your town buys a new police car or a new word processor, or puts up a new school? Is this investment? Close, but no cigar. When the government makes these purchases, it's government spending rather than investment. This may sound arbitrary, but it's part of the rules of national income accounting, which we discuss fully in Chapter 8.

You are investing if you are adding to your firm's plant, equipment, or inventory.

What if you were to purchase 100 shares of Mobil Oil stock? Would that be investment? Does that add (directly) to Mobil Oil's plant, equipment, or inventory? It doesn't? Then it isn't investment. It's merely a financial transaction. When Mobil Oil uses those funds to buy plant, equipment, or inventory, *then* it's investment. (See box "Are We Counting All Our Investment?")

Calculating inventory investment is a little tricky. We include only the net change from January 1 to December 31 of a given year. For example, how much was inventory investment for General Motors in 1996 (using the figures in Table 2)?

How to calculate inventory investment

How much was GM's inventory investment in 1996? $25 million? Nope. $395 million? Nope. The answer is $10 million. All you have to do is look at the levels of inventory on January 1 and December 31 and calculate the difference.

---

[3]Economists are not in complete agreement (what else is new?) about whether new residential housing is a category of investment or consumption. Since the quasi-official position of the profession is that it belongs in the investment category, we'll go along with that and classify residential housing as investment.

Residential construction does not properly belong in a chapter on business investment, but I am prepared, just this once, to dispense with propriety, because I don't know where else to put it.

Are We Counting All Our Investment?

When Kmart opens 15 new stores or U.S. West installs a new switching system, the U.S. Department of Commerce counts these as investment. But as *Business Week* points out, "...the 10 largest software companies have a total market capitalization of $80 billion—yet, according to the government, none of them produces any investment goods."* This is simply because software isn't classified as equipment.

While a new personal computer is classified as investment, what about the software that makes it run? And what about the huge investment U.S. companies have been making since the early 1980s to train the workforce to use computers? None of this is counted as investment, and yet it all clearly adds to our economic capacity. In 1995 the Commerce Department began a major overhaul of its statistics, so we may soon see some changes.

Business Week, November 7, 1994, p. 113.

Table 2   Hypothetical Inventory Levels
           of General Motors

Date	Level of Inventory
January 1, 1996	$120 million
July 1, 1996	145 million
December 31, 1996	130 million

Let's try another one. Using Table 3's data, calculate the inventory investment for Shell Oil in 1999.

Your answer should be –$10 million. Between the first day of the year and the last day of the year, the level of Shell's inventory went down by $10 million. In other words, inventory investment was negative.

Table 3   Hypothetical Inventory Levels
           of Shell Oil

Date	Level of Inventory
January 1, 1999	$230 million
May 15, 1999	215 million
September 1, 1999	240 million
December 31, 1999	220 million

The fact that we can have negative inventory investment is significant. Because investment is one sector of GDP, declining inventories will be a drag on GDP. That's what happens during recessions.

A glance at Figure 1 shows just how unstable inventory investment has been over the last 35 years. In fact, you've probably never been on a roller coaster that had as many steep ups and downs as inventory investment. Nearly all the steep drops are associated with recessions, and the years of negative investment (when inventories were being depleted) all occurred during recession years—1975, 1980, 1982, and 1990–91.

Investment in plant and equipment is more stable than investment in inventory, but it should be clear from Figure 2 that plant and equipment spending also has its ups and downs. Unlike inventory investment, even in a bad year companies will still invest a substantial

Figure 1   Inventory Investment, 1960–97 (in billions of 1987 dollars)

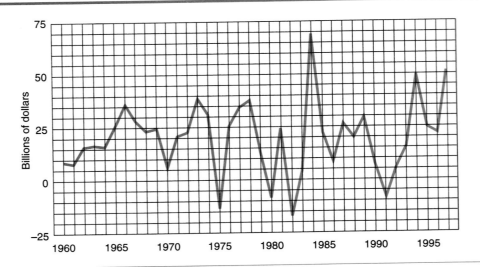

Source: *Economic Report of the President,* 1998.

amount in new plant and equipment, mainly because old and obsolete factories, office buildings, and machinery must be replaced. This is the depreciation part of investment.

A second reason for the stability of plant and equipment investment is that most of it is planned years ahead and will be carried out on schedule regardless of what phase the business cycle is in. Since this plant and equipment is being built to meet the needs of the years ahead, little would be gained by postponing construction for the duration of a recession.

A final reason for carrying out capital investment during a recession is that interest rates tend to come down at that time. As the cost of borrowing money is a major part of construction costs, it can be advantageous to carry out construction projects during times of recession. Other resources, too, would tend to be available at lower costs.

Figure 2   Investment in Plant and Equipment, 1960–97 (in 1987 dollars)

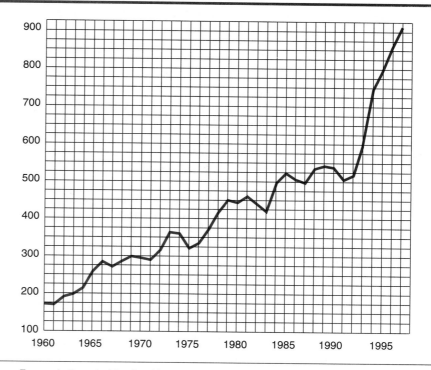

Sources: *Economic Report of the President, 1998.*

Each of these factors places a floor under investment spending during recessionary years. Nevertheless, as we can see by the dips in Figure 2 for 1975, 1982, and 1991, there have been major declines in spending on new plant and equipment during years of recession.

The three reasons for the stability of investment during business downturns were overwhelmed by the general economic collapse of the Great Depression. Why replace worn-out or obsolete plant and equipment when your plant is half idle? Why carry out long-term investment plans when your firm may not survive the next few weeks? Why bother to borrow at low interest rates when your expected rate of profit is negative?

Investment in plant and equipment plummeted from $59.2 billion in 1929 to $16.5 billion in 1933 (in 1997 dollars).[4] While some people believe another depression could happen at any time, we shall see in subsequent chapters the country has several safeguards built into its economy to prevent a collapse of such proportions. Nevertheless, investment remains the loose cannon on our economic deck, a destabilizing element that

---

[4]In 1929, plant and equipment spending was $10.6 billion (in current, 1929 dollars). It sank to $2.4 billion in 1933 (in current, 1933 dollars). During that period the prices of newly constructed plant and equipment fell by more than 20 percent, so the decline in investment wasn't quite as bad as it appeared. To show this we need to correct for price changes (in this case, price declines, or deflation). We do that by using 1997 dollars.

ADVANCED **W**ORK ......   **Shifting Resources to Investment Goods** ....

Our country's lagging investment is usually expressed in terms of dollars spent, but it can also be thought of in terms of resources used. Back in Chapter 2, when discussing the production possibilities frontier, I mentioned that a nation will grow faster if it devotes more of its resources to producing capital goods rather than consumer goods. And in the last chapter, I talked about how Americans spend about 95 percent of their incomes on consumer goods and services, and save only 5 percent. Think of all the land, labor, capital, and entrepreneurial ability that is devoted solely to turning out those consumer goods and services.

Japan, Germany, Italy, France, Taiwan, South Korea, and our other industrial competitors devote much higher proportions of their resources to capital goods production than we do. It will become increasingly difficult to compete in the international economic arena unless we substantially raise our investment in new factories, machinery, and equipment, as well as in research and development and in worker training. This would require a massive shift of resources away from the production of consumer goods and services, and into the production of capital goods.

tends to push our economy to its highs and lows. (See the box titled "Shifting Resources to Investment Goods.")

Residential construction involves replacing our aging housing stock as well as adding to it. During the 25 years following World War II, the United States had a tremendous spurt in residential building, as nearly half of the American population moved to the suburbs. Today there is continued building, particularly in the outlying areas of the suburbs (the exurbs) 50 to 100 miles from the nearest city, but the postwar housing boom has been over for about two decades.

Residential home building fluctuates considerably from year to year. Mortgage interest rates play a dominant role. For example, from 1979 to 1982, when mortgage rates reached 15 and 16 percent in most parts of the country, new housing starts plunged by nearly 40 percent. Another factor that causes steep declines in home construction is periodic overbuilding. Once the surplus of new homes on the market is worked off, residential construction goes into another boom period.

Investment is very unstable.

What this all comes down to is that investment is the most volatile sector in the economy. Fluctuations in GDP are largely fluctuations in investment. More often than not, the country's recessions are touched off by declines in investment, and recoveries are brought about by rising investment.

How Does Savings Get Invested?

How *does* savings get invested? A good question. Well, for starters, what do *you* do with the money you save? Put it in the bank? Buy stocks? Buy corporate bonds?

If you buy corporate stocks or bonds, then your money is going directly to a large corporation, which uses it to invest in plant and equipment.[5] It may also use some of it for advertising; to build up inventory; or to pay wages and salaries, rent, insurance, or taxes. But most of the money that large corporations raise from issuing stocks and bonds is invested in new plant and equipment.

If you deposit your money in a bank, much of it will end up being invested by large business borrowers. What the banks do is package a large number of deposits into a much smaller number of substantial business loans. When IBM, Exxon, General Motors, and AT&T come calling on their bankers, they're going to borrow hundreds of millions of dollars—so much, in fact, that loan syndicates of dozens of banks are often formed to raise the total amount needed.

Corporations also raise a substantial portion of their investment funds internally, through retained earnings and depreciation allowances. Retained earnings are the portion

---

[5]When a corporation issues stocks or bonds, the proceeds go directly to that company. But when you buy a company's stock in the stock market or when you buy a company's bonds in the bond market, your money goes to the person who sold that stock or those bonds.

of profits not paid to the owners of the business. Depreciation allowances are the tax-deductible funds that have been set aside to replace worn-out or obsolete plant and equipment.

Let's make a clear distinction between "financial" investment and "real" investment. When you buy corporate stocks and bonds, a bank certificate of deposit (CD), or any other financial security, you may consider that an investment. But economists will tell you that although you made a personal financial investment, it was not a "real" investment. The only investment that is real to economists is the purchase of a new home or the purchase by a business firm of new plant, equipment, or inventory. Only "real" investment is counted in GDP. (See the box "When Is an Investment Not an Investment?")

Gross Investment versus Net Investment

In Chapter 8 we will be distinguishing between gross domestic product (GDP) and net national product (NNP): GDP – Depreciation = NNP.

We can even do a little generalizing now. *Gross domestic product is the sum of consumption, gross investment, government purchases, and net exports.* And how about net national product? *Net national product is the sum of consumption, net investment, government purchases, and net exports.* This leaves us with two simple relationships:

1. GDP – Depreciation = NNP
2. Gross investment – Depreciation = Net investment

Gross investment – Depreciation = Net investment

Most of us are painfully familiar with the distinction between gross income (what your boss says you are earning) and net income (what you actually take home after taxes and other deductions). Gross and net investment are parallel concepts. In fact, when you subtract depreciation from gross investment, you get net investment.

We've said that investment is our nation's expenditure on any new plant, equipment, additional inventory, or residential housing. That's *gross* investment. To get net investment we need to subtract depreciation on plant and equipment and residential housing. (There is no depreciation on inventory accumulation.)

Each year our stock of residential housing depreciates by a certain percentage, say 2 or 3 percent. This depreciation takes place every year even though the market value of that housing stock may be rising. What we're really doing is accounting for the physical deterioration of those buildings. Now we'll take a closer look at depreciation on plant and equipment.

Let's say you started the year with 10 machines and bought another 6 during the year. Your gross investment would be 6. If 4 machines (of your original 10) wore out or became obsolete during the year, your depreciation would be 4. Therefore, your gross investment (6) – depreciation (4) = net investment (2). In other words, you added 2 machines during the year, raising your total from 10 to 12.

Now we're ready to work out a hypothetical problem. Given all the information in Table 4, calculate the nation's gross investment and net investment.

In Chapter 8 we'll be using an equation for GDP: $GDP = C + I + G + X_n$, where C is consumption, I is investment, G is government spending, and X_n is net exports (exports

When Is an Investment Not an Investment?

Suppose you bought 100 shares of Southwestern Bell, or you invested $10,000 in a U.S. Treasury bond, or you bought part of Rockefeller Center from the Mitsubishi Corporation. These were all investments, right? Wrong!

Remember that in economics there are only two types of investment: the purchase of (1) new plant, new equipment, and new residential housing, and (2) additional inventory. What about all that money you "invested" in stocks, bonds, and real estate? If those aren't investments, what *are* they? They are financial transactions—mere exchanges of assets. Now, there's nothing wrong with these transactions, but they don't go into GDP. And if they don't, then they're not investments.

Table 4   Hypothetical Inventory Levels and Investment and Depreciation Schedules of Nation, 1996

Date	Level of Inventory
January 1, 1996	$60 billion
July 1, 1996	55 billion
December 31, 1996	70 billion
Expenditures on new plant and equipment: $120 billion	
Expenditures on new residential housing: $90 billion	
Depreciation on plant and equipment and residential housing: $30 billion	

Solution:

Inventory investment	$10 billion
Plus: Expenditures on new plant and equipment	120 billion
Expenditures on new residential housing	90 billion
Gross investment	$220 billion
Minus: Depreciation	−30 billion
Net investment	$190 billion

minus imports). I represents gross investment. From now on, I'll often refer to gross investment with the letter I.

Building Capital

At the end of Chapter 4 I stressed that capital (plant, equipment, and inventory) is built up by producing more, consuming less, or some combination thereof. Suppose you want to open a factory with one machine. You have various alternatives.

You might be able to borrow the money to buy the machine. But the person from whom you borrow has saved this money by not consuming all of his or her income. And someone else, who built the machine, spent many hours working on it.

Investment involves sacrifice.

Investment, or the building up of capital, takes sacrifice. If you decide to save the money yourself, you may have to work overtime, take on a second job, or cut back on your lifestyle.

Finally, if you decide to build the machine yourself, think of all the hours this might take you. These are hours you could be working at a paid job, or maybe just lying around watching TV. So no matter how you go about building up capital, there's a great deal of sacrifice involved.

To invest, we must work more and consume less.

Essentially, then, to build up our plant, equipment, and inventory, we need to work more and consume less. On this all economists agree. But Karl Marx parted company with the classical economists of the 19th century when he wrote his landmark *Das Kapital*. Capital, according to Marx, is created by labor but expropriated by the capitalist, the factory owner. He wrote:

> The owner of the money has paid the value of a day's labour-power; his, therefore, is the use of it for a day; a day's labour belongs to him. . . . On the one hand the daily sustenance of labour-power costs only half a day's labour, while on the other hand the very same labour-power can work during a whole day, that consequently the value which its use during one day creates, is double what he pays for that use.[6]

---

[6]Karl Marx, *Das Kapital,* Vol. 1 (New York: International Publishers, 1967), pp. 193–94.

In other words, if it costs three shillings to keep a person alive for 24 hours and this person produces three shillings' worth of cloth in six hours, pay him three shillings for 12 hours of work. And if he objects, just tell him to look out the window at the factory gate where hundreds of people stand waiting for a chance to have his job.

These people are, incidentally, the *reserve army* of the unemployed, a term I used to think referred to the Army Reserve unit to which I once belonged. Every other Wednesday night or Sunday, we'd put on our uniforms and sit around playing cards, reading, or listening to the football game. But Karl Marx's reserve army was evidently much more anxious to do some work.

The Determinants of the Level of Investment

Many factors determine the level of investment. We'll confine ourselves to four.[7]

(1) The Sales Outlook

You won't invest if your sales outlook is bad.

If you can't sell your goods or services, there's no point in investing, so the ultimate determinant of the level of investment is the business firm's sales outlook. If business is good and sales are expected to be strong for the next few months, then business firms will be willing to take on more inventory. And if sales look good for the next few years, additional plant and equipment will probably be purchased.

(2) Capacity Utilization Rate

The capacity utilization rate is the percentage of plant and equipment that is actually being used at any given time. Since it would be virtually impossible to use every single factory, office, and piece of machinery day in and day out, we will always have *some* idle plant and equipment.

Generally, manufacturing firms use about 80 to 85 percent of their capacity. When business really gets good, the capacity utilization rate approaches 90 percent; during severe recessions, like those of 1974–75 and 1981–82, this rate dips close to 70 percent (see Figure 3).

You won't invest if you have a lot of unused capacity.

For our purposes, we can count on the capacity utilization rate as an important influence on the level of investment in plant and equipment. At high rates, companies have considerable incentive to build more plant and equipment because sales are pressing against factory capacity. During really bad recessions, when demand is slack, one-third of our factories and equipment may be idle. Why build more?

We must temper this analysis by taking note of three additional factors. First, it is likely that we are understating the capacity utilization rate by counting much obsolete or

---

[7]Additional factors are corporate income tax rates, depreciation allowances, the level of technology, and the cost of constructing new plant and equipment.

Figure 3   Capacity Utilization Rate in Manufacturing, 1965–97

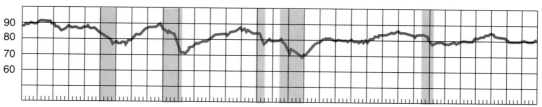

Source: *Survey of Current Business,* March 1994; January 1998.

unusable capacity.[8] For example, steel mill and auto plant closings in the early 1980s indicated that some of the plant and equipment in those industries had been counted for several years when their use was economically unfeasible. Second, manufacturing has been a shrinking part of our economy for at least four decades. It now accounts for less than one out of every five jobs in our economy.

Third, the growing importance of imports—along with increasing investment in overseas manufacturing facilities by U.S. multinational corporations—has reduced the significance of our capacity utilization rate. To illustrate, let's suppose that our economy is approaching full capacity. Although we may invest in new capacity, we may also increase our imports and our multinational corporations may build new manufacturing capacity abroad.

(3) The Interest Rate

The interest rate is the cost of borrowing money. There are actually many different interest rates, depending on a firm's creditworthiness and the size of the loan.

Suppose you want to borrow $1,000 for one year and the bank will charge you 12 percent interest. How much interest will you have to pay if you borrow the $1,000 for one year?

Go ahead. Work it out.

I hope your answer is $120. If it isn't, here's how to calculate the interest:

$$\text{Interest rate} = \frac{\text{Interest paid}}{\text{Amount borrowed}}$$

$$.12 = \frac{x}{\$1,000}$$

Now, multiply both sides by $1,000:

$$\$120 = x$$

You won't invest if interest rates are too high.

In general, the lower the interest rate, the more business firms will borrow. But to know how much they will borrow—or whether they will borrow at all in any particular instance—we need to compare the interest rate with the expected rate of profit on the investment.

(4) The Expected Rate of Profit

Economists are not happy unless they give virtually the same concept at least three different names. Therefore, the expected rate of profit is sometimes called the marginal efficiency of capital or the marginal efficiency of investment. We'll define it this way:

$$\text{Expected rate of profit} = \frac{\text{Expected profits}}{\text{Money invested}}$$

---

[8]Suppose our capacity utilization rate is 80 percent, but 10 percent of our plant and equipment is obsolete or unusable. Then our true capacity utilization would be 89 percent (80/90).

Now, of course, we have to work out a problem. Here's an easy one: How much is the expected profit rate on a $10,000 investment if you expect to make a profit of $1,650? You know how things work around here. Do it yourself, then check your result against mine. I'm always right. But you can't be unless you try.

$$\text{Expected rate of profit} = \frac{\text{Expected profits}}{\text{Money invested}}$$

$$= \frac{\$1,650}{\$10,000}$$

$$= 16.5 \text{ percent}$$

You won't invest unless the expected profit rate is high enough.

The relationship between the interest rate and the expected profit rate was underscored by John Maynard Keynes in his landmark *The General Theory of Employment, Interest, and Money*. Keynes said that every profit opportunity would be exploited as long as the expected profit rate (which he called the "marginal efficiency of capital") exceeded the interest rate: "The rate of investment will be pushed to . . . where the marginal efficiency of capital in general is equal to the market rate of interest."[9]

Suppose your business firm is interested in borrowing $100,000 at the going interest rate of 15 percent to buy inventory. If your expected profit rate is 18 percent, would it pay to borrow? In other words, after you paid off the interest, how much money would you have left? ($18,000 − $15,000 in interest = $3,000.) You would stand to make $3,000 profit. Of course you would borrow the money.

Now we're ready for an easy three-part problem. Suppose you could borrow money at 20 percent interest and someone offered to buy 100 pounds of a certain substance from you at $1,300 a pound. It costs you only $1,000 a pound to grow this substance. The only problem is that the money you borrow will be tied up for a year until you are able to pay it back.

Answer yes or no to each of these three questions:

(*a*) Would you accept the deal as it stands?

(*b*) Would the deal be acceptable if the interest rate were 10 percent?

(*c*) Would the deal be acceptable if the interest rate were 30 percent?

You stand to make a profit of 30 percent using borrowed money. From those profits, you need to pay interest on your loan. If you borrowed the money at (*a*) 20 percent interest, you would still have money left over (net profit) after you paid the interest, so it would pay to accept the deal. If you borrowed money at (*b*) 10 percent interest, it would be even more profitable than at 20 percent interest. But if you accepted the deal at (*c*) 30 percent interest, after you paid the interest from your 30 percent profit, there would be no money left over from your sales. (See the box titled "Investing Your Own Money.")

---

[9]John Maynard Keynes, *The General Theory of Employment, Interest, and Money* (New York: Harcourt Brace Jovanovich, 1958), pp. 136–37.

Investing Your Own Money

Business firms do not always borrow the money that they use for investment projects. Actually, American businesses invest hundreds of billions of dollars a year that they have accumulated in depreciation allowances and retained earnings. If this money is not borrowed and no interest needs to be paid on it—it would be kind of silly to pay interest to yourself—then why even *think* about the interest rate?

If a firm didn't invest this money internally, what would it *do* with this money? Suppose that it lent the money to another firm at the going rate of interest. Back in Chapter 2 we talked about the concept of opportunity cost. Do you remember its definition? *The opportunity cost of any choice is the forgone value of the next best alternative.* The firm has two choices: it can use the money itself, or it can lend it to another firm and collect interest. If it uses the money itself, it forgoes the interest it would have otherwise been able to collect. That's why a firm must take the interest rate into account even if it is using its own funds.

Let's use a concrete example. The political consulting firm of Nixon, Ford, Reagan, and Bush is thinking of opening a branch office. It already has the $1 million it would need. It has an expected profit rate of 14 percent on its investment. Its other choice is to lend the money to its competitor, McGovern, Carter, Mondale, and Dukakis.

Question: What does it do? You need to ask *me* a question before you can answer. And what question is that? You need to ask me how much the going interest rate happens to be. Suppose that the going interest rate is 5 percent. What should Nixon, Ford, Reagan, and Bush do? Lend the money to their competitor or use it themselves? Your answer? They should use it themselves. Why? Because their expected profit rate is substantially higher than the interest rate. In terms of opportunity cost, they can get a much higher rate of return by investing the money in their own firm than by lending it to someone else.

What should Nixon, Ford, Reagan, and Bush do if the going rate of interest is 18 percent? Lend the money to their competitor or use it themselves? What do you think? I think they should lend the money to their competitor, because they would collect a sure 18 percent interest, which is 4 percentage points higher than their *expected* (but not guaranteed) profit rate. Again in terms of opportunity cost, by lending the money out, they would be getting a return 4 points higher than if they invested it in their own firm.

Why Do Firms Invest?

We've talked about *when* firms tend to invest—(1) when their sales outlook is good; (2) when their capacity utilization rate is high; (3) when interest rates are low; and (4) when their expected profit rate is high. But *why* do they invest?

Some firms invest merely to replace worn-out equipment. A related purpose is to replace this equipment with equipment that is more technologically advanced. For example, an old photocopy machine that did 10 copies a minute may be replaced with a high-speed machine that can do more tricks than Houdini. In effect, then, we are replacing machinery and equipment that may not only be dilapidated but obsolete as well. A firm may have to do this just to keep up with the competition. So, in a large sense, just keeping up with current technology requires a substantial amount of investment.

A business may also invest to become larger. Of course, the incentive to invest is based on the sales outlook. No one will want to grow if it means operating at only 50 percent of capacity. In that case, you might be the biggest kid on the block, but you would certainly not be the richest—*or* the smartest.

What Accounts for Our Low Rate of Investment?

Chapter 4 talked about the importance of capital in the production of goods and services. The rate of growth in our country's capital stock has fallen sharply over the last decade. Compared to that of other leading industrial nations, it is downright anemic.

In the 1950s, 1960s, and 1970s, our nation's net business investment rate (net investment in plant and equipment as a percentage of GDP) was more than 3 percent every year, but since 1981 it has been below 3 percent every year. In several other industrial nations (including Japan, the former West Germany, South Korea, and Taiwan), the net investment rate through the mid-1990s was more than 5 percent.

We've seen how our high interest rates have discouraged investment and how investment has also been depressed by our low savings rate. So a business firm thinking about adding new plant and equipment is hit with a double whammy. First, does it really want to pay such a high rate of interest? Second, even if it does, is there money out there that it can borrow?

Japan, a country with less than half our population, invests more in plant and equipment than we do. Even more embarrassing, a major part of the funds we do invest is provided by Japanese and other foreign savers. (See the box "Foreign Investment in the United States.")

What went wrong? Let's round up the usual suspects—our low savings rate, the short time horizon of many corporate officials (who seem more concerned about the next quarterly profit figure than about their firm's long-term profitability), and, more generally, the quality of management and labor. There is plenty of blame to go around, but for now we need to reiterate two related points: (1) The less we save, the less we can invest. (2) The less we invest, the slower our rate of economic growth.[10]

Graphing the C + I Line

Do you remember the consumption function from Chapter 5? As income rises, consumption rises, but not as quickly. Do you remember induced consumption? As income rises, more consumption is induced.

Figure 4 reproduces the consumption function graphed in Figure 3 of Chapter 5. You'll notice that as income rises, the C line slopes upward. Higher income levels induce higher levels of consumption.

Would it be reasonable to assume that there is a parallel concept of induced investment? That as income rises, the level of investment rises as well? What do *you* think?

At very low levels of income, the country is in a depression. Nobody invests. At somewhat higher levels of income, more and more investment takes place, because people are able to save *some* money and those funds are invested. So it would be reasonable to say that as income rises, higher levels of investment are induced.

That would be a reasonable assumption, but we need to keep things simple here, because we want to be able to read our graphs. So we're going to assume the level of investment stays the same for all levels of income. We know that in the real world, as income rises, I rises, but we're going to trade off some reality for some simplicity.

So far we've had a graph with just two lines—the 45-degree line and the C line, or consumption function. From this two-line graph, C and savings could be calculated. To

---

[10]I'll have a lot more to say about our lagging investment and our sluggish economic growth in Chapter 16.

Foreign Investment in the United States

Why have foreigners been so happy to invest in America? Mainly because of our relatively high interest rates. As our trade deficits topped $100 billion for most of the 1980s and 1990s, foreigners found themselves awash in U.S. dollars. Many of those dollars were recycled through the purchase of U.S. government securities, corporate stocks and bonds, real estate, and an increasing amount of direct investment, which entailed setting up shop in the United States. A prime example of foreign direct investment is the Japanese automobile transplants, most significantly Honda, Toyota, and Nissan.

Given our shortage of savings, this inflow of foreign investment has been a tremendous help. Not only has it provided needed funds to corporate borrowers and helped finance the federal deficit, but it has kept interest rates from going sky-high. However, a significant side effect, which we'll examine closely in the chapter on international finance, is the implication of foreign ownership on our national economic sovereignty.

Figure 4   The Consumption Function

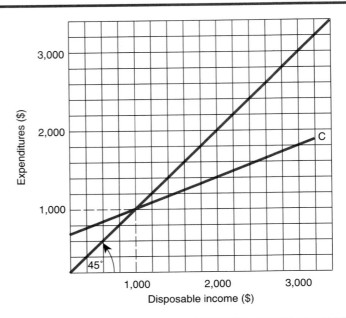

calculate I (actually the C + I line), a third line is necessary. Figure 5 graphs a C + I line, which is drawn parallel to the C line. This is the same graph as in Figure 4, with the C + I line added.

The question for you to solve has three parts: How much is I when disposable income is (a) 1,000, (b) 2,000, and (c) 3,000? Look at the graph and figure out the answers. Keep in mind that the C line and the C + I line are parallel.

The answer to the question "How much is I when disposable income is (a) 1,000, (b) 2,000, and (c) 3,000?" is "around 425" (400, 410, 420, 430, 440, or 450 are acceptable). More important, since the C line and the C + I line are parallel, the vertical distance

Figure 5   Measuring the Level of Investment

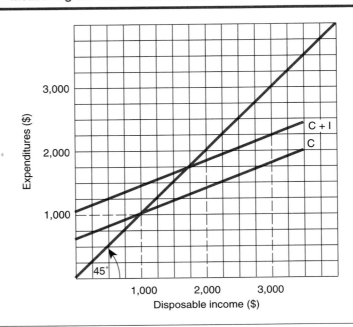

Reading the C + I Graph

Do you remember how, in the last chapter, we found C, or consumption, at various levels of disposable income? All we did was take the vertical distance between the horizontal axis and the C line. For

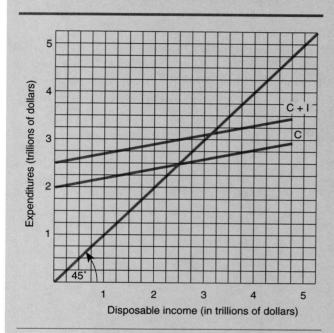

example, in the figure shown here, how much is C at a disposable income of $4 trillion? It's just a tad over $2.75 trillion—say $2.8 trillion.

How do we find I? Well, you tell *me*. How much is I, or investment, at a disposable income of $4 trillion? If you're not sure, just guess. Did you come up with about $500 billion, or $.5 trillion? The way we measure I is to take the vertical distance between the C line and the C + I line. At a disposable income of $4 trillion, that vertical distance is about two boxes. Since each box counts for one-quarter of a trillion dollars (because there are four boxes between each trillion dollars), then two boxes equal half a trillion dollars, or $500 billion. Incidentally, if you're still having trouble distinguishing between millions and billions, and between billions and trillions, then you definitely need to reread the box "A Word about Numbers," which appears near the beginning of Chapter 5.

Now we'll do one more. How much is I when disposable income is $2.5 trillion? Did you get $500 billion, or $.5 trillion? I certainly hope so. Just remember that we measure I by taking the vertical distance between the C line and the C + I line. It's as easy as counting the boxes.

between them remains the same. If you estimated I at 410 with a disposable income of 1,000, it remains 410 when disposable income is 2,000 or 3,000.

We're about halfway through our graphs. Before you go any further, you need to ask yourself this question: Self, do I really know how to measure I, or investment, in Figure 5? If the answer is a definite yes, then go directly to the last section of this chapter, The Summing Up of Investment. But if you'd like a little extra help, you'll find it in the box "Reading the C + I Graph."

The Summing Up of Investment

We're finally ready to include the last part of investment: residential construction spending. The data shown in Table 5 indicate the relative size of the components of investment.

Table 5   Gross Investment, 1997

Plant and equipment	845
Residential construction	328
Inventory change	65
Total	1238

Source: *Economic Report of the President,* 1998.

The figures here are in current dollars rather than in 1987 dollars to make them comparable with the data from the other two chapters dealing with GDP components. We've now covered two of the three main components of GDP—C (in the last chapter) and I (in this chapter). Which component comes next?

Questions for Further Thought and Discussion

1. What are the advantages and disadvantages of the corporation as a form of business organization?
2. Explain how the capacity utilization rate and the interest rate affect the level of investment.
3. Explain why building up capital takes a great deal of sacrifice.
4. The Carolina Textile Corporation is capitalized at $200 million. If you wanted to buy control of this company, how much money would you have to invest? Since you don't have nearly enough information to make this decision, just make some reasonable assumption about its bonds, preferred stock, and common stock.

WORKBOOK FOR CHAPTER 6

Name _____   Date _____

Multiple-Choice Questions

Circle the letter that corresponds to the best answer.

1. In the United States, investment is done

    a. entirely by the government   b. mostly by the government   c. about half by the government and half by private enterprise   d. mainly by private enterprise

2. Which of these is not investment?

    a. additional inventory   b. the building of a county courthouse   c. the building of a shopping mall   d. the building of an automobile assembly line

3. There are nearly _____ business firms in the United States.

    a. 2 million   b. 12 million   c. 20 million
    d. 32 million

4. A business firm with one owner is

    a. a proprietorship   b. a partnership
    c. a corporation   d. none of these

5. A partnership

    a. must have exactly two owners   b. must have more than two owners   c. must have more than one owner   d. may have more than one owner

6. A key advantage of a partnership over a proprietorship is

    a. limited liability   b. division of responsibility
    c. perpetual life of the business firm   d. none of these

7. A _____ is a legal person.

    a. proprietorship   b. partnership   c. corporation
    d. business firm

8. Most corporations are

    a. publicly held   b. very large   c. very small
    d. none of these

9. Corporations collect about _____ percent of all business receipts.

    a. 10   b. 30   c. 60   d. 90

10. A key disadvantage of incorporating is that

    a. you will have to pay corporate income tax
    b. you will have to charge sales tax   c. you will have to sell stock   d. you will have to reorganize the corporation whenever an officer resigns or dies

11. Corporations are controlled by the

    a. employees   b. bondholders   c. common stockholders   d. preferred stockholders

12. The last to be paid off, whether the corporation does well or goes bankrupt, are the

    a. employees   b. bondholders   c. common stockholders   d. preferred stockholders

13. Ownership of a corporation is based on

    a. whether you work for the company   b. whether you buy from the company   c. whether you hold the bonds of the company   d. whether you hold stock in the company

14. A corporation's capitalization is based on all of the following except

    a. preferred stock   b. common stock   c. bonds
    d. sales

15. Which is not investment?

    a. the purchase of 100 shares of IBM   b. the construction of a new factory   c. the purchase of a new delivery truck   d. the purchase of inventory

16. Inventory investment is

    a. always positive   b. always negative   c. can be either positive or negative   d. can be neither positive nor negative

121

17. Inventory investment is

    a. very stable   b. fairly stable   c. fairly unstable

    d. very unstable

18. During severe recessions, inventory investment is

    a. negative   b. stable   c. fairly high

    d. very high

19. Gross investment

    a. plus depreciation equals net investment

    b. minus depreciation equals net investment

    c. plus net investment equals depreciation

    d. equals net investment minus depreciation

20. Each of the following might be used to acquire capital except

    a. working more   b. consuming less

    c. borrowing   d. consuming more

21. Karl Marx said that capital is produced by

    a. the worker   b. the capitalist   c. the government

    d. money

22. Which is the least stable?

    a. investment in plant and equipment

    b. investment in residential housing   c. investment in inventory   d. overall investment

23. Business firms invest in plant and equipment during recession years for each of these reasons except

    a. interest rates are lower   b. it has been planned years ahead   c. it replaces worn-out plant and equipment   d. it is needed because capacity may be fully utilized

24. During bad recessions, investment in plant and equipment will

    a. be negative   b. fall by around 15–20 percent

    c. fall somewhat   d. rise

25. Each of the following is business investment except

    a. inventory investment   b. investment in new plant   c. investment in new equipment

    d. investment in new residential housing

26. Investment will be high when the capacity utilization rate is _____ and the interest rate is _____.

    a. high, high   b. low, low   c. high, low

    d. low, high

27. Our capacity utilization rate is usually between

    a. 10 and 30   b. 30 and 50   c. 50 and 70

    d. 70 and 90

28. Firms will most likely borrow money for investment when

    a. interest rates are low   b. interest rates are high   c. the interest rate is higher than the expected profit rate   d. the expected profit rate is higher than the interest rate

Fill-In Questions

1. Of the big three spending sectors of GDP, the least stable is _____.

2. There are nearly _____ million business firms in the United States.

3. A business firm owned by one person is called a _____.

4. A partnership is owned by _____ people.

5. The key advantage of incorporating is _____.

6. Nearly all large companies are corporations, and nearly all corporations are small companies. Therefore, _____.

7. Most of the business in this country is done by about _____ corporations.

8. The two main disadvantages of incorporating are

    (1) _____ and (2) _____ .

9. A corporation is owned by its _____ and its _____.

10. A corporation is controlled by its _____

    _____ .

11. The creditors of a corporation are mainly its

    _____ .

12. Theoretically, you would need an investment of about

    $ _____ to control a

    corporation that had $100 million in preferred stock,

    $50 million in common stock, and $350 million in bonds.

13. The least stable form of investment is _____

    _____ investment.

14. Gross investment – _____ =

    Net investment.

15. According to Karl Marx, capital was created by the

    _____ and expropriated by the

    _____ .

16. In Marx's terms, the people who wait outside the factory

    gates for work are the _____ .

17. The four main determinants of the level of investment are

    (1) _____ ; (2) _____ ;

    (3) _____ ; and (4) _____ .

18. During severe recessions, our capacity utilization rate

    falls to around _____ percent.

19. The expected profit rate is found by dividing

    _____ by _____ .

20. An investment will be undertaken if the expected profit

    rate is higher than the _____

    _____ .

21. Total investment is found by adding

    (1) _____ ; (2) _____ ;

    and (3) _____ .

Problems

1. If a corporation has $100 million in preferred stock, $150 million in common stock, and $250 million in bonds: **a.** How much is its capitalization? **b.** Theoretically, how much would it take to control it? **c.** Practically speaking, it may take only about how much to control it?

2. If a corporation has gross investment of $150 million and depreciation of $40 million, how much is its net investment?

3. Given the information in Table 1, find inventory investment in 1996.

Table 1

Date	Level of Inventory
January 1, 1996	$500 million
July 1, 1996	530 million
December 31, 1996	485 million

4. Given the information in Table 2, how much was total gross investment? How much was net investment?

Table 2

Item	Amount ($ millions)
Expenditures on new plant and equipment	$100
Depreciation	15
Inventory investment	10
Residential housing investment	30

5. Use the information in Figure 1 to fill in Table 3:

Figure 1

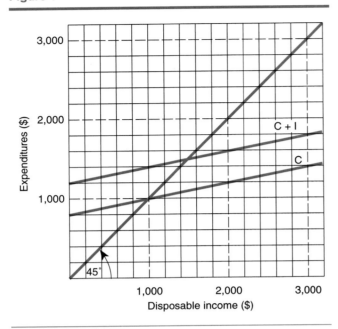

Table 3

Disposable Income	Consumption*	Savings*	Investment
(a) 1,000	————	————	————
(b) 2,000	————	————	————
(c) 3,000	————	————	————

*If you don't remember how to find consumption and savings, you'll need to review parts of Chapter 5.

6. If a corporation has $2 billion in common stock, $1 billion in preferred stock, and $4 billion in bonds: **a.** How much is its capitalization? **b.** Theoretically, how much would it take to control it? **c.** Practically speaking, it may take only about how much to control it?

7. If net investment is 400 and depreciation is 175, how much is gross investment?

8. Given the information in Table 4, find inventory investment in 1997.

Table 4

Date	Level of Inventory
January 1, 1997	$2.0 billion
May 1, 1997	2.1 billion
Sept. 1, 1997	1.8 billion
Dec. 31, 1997	2.3 billion

9. Suppose you could borrow $200,000 for one year at an interest rate of 10 percent. You are virtually certain that you can invest this money in inventory that you could sell over a year for $300,000. If your selling costs were $50,000 and you were to pay your interest out of your profits, how much would your expected profit rate be on your investment?

10. Hideki Irabu, George Steinbrenner, and Tino Martinez would like to gain control of the Sports Trading Card Corporation of America. If that corporation has $200 million in common stock, $300 million in preferred stock, and $500 million in bonds: **a.** Theoretically, how much would they need to invest to control it? **b.** Practically speaking, how much would they need to invest to control it?

11. In Angola, the level of inventory was $11 billion on January 1, 1998. $50 billion was spent on new plant and equipment during the year, $20 billion was spent on new residential housing, depreciation was $10 billion, and on December 31, 1998, the level of inventory was $13 billion. Capital stock was $90 billion on January 1, 1998.
    a. How much was gross investment in 1998?
    b. How much was net investment in 1998?
    c. What was the level of capital stock on December 31, 1998?
    d. How much was inventory investment in 1998?

The Government Sector

The last two chapters covered consumption and investment. In this chapter we'll look at the last of the three main sectors of GDP: government spending. While we're at it, we'll see how the government affects our economy through spending, taxation, regulation, and income redistribution.

Chapter Objectives

We'll be looking at these topics:

- Government spending.
- The graphing of the C + I + G line.
- Types of taxes.
- The average and marginal tax rates.
- Sources of government revenue.
- Principles of taxation.
- The economic role of the government.

Introduction: The Growing Economic Role of Government

Most of the growth was due to the Depression and World War II.

The role of government has grown tremendously over the past six decades. Actually, most of that growth took place between 1933 and 1945, during the administration of Franklin Delano Roosevelt. The two major crises of that period—the Great Depression and World War II—dwarfed anything our nation has faced since. In fact, we would have to go back to the Civil War to find an event as cataclysmic as either the Depression or what people over 55 still refer to as "the war."

Government is not the solution to our problem. Government is the problem.

—Ronald Reagan

Since 1945, the roles of government at the federal, state, and local levels have expanded, but the seeds of that expansion were sown during the Roosevelt administration. Americans seem determined never to experience again the traumatic events that overtook us during the 30s and 40s. *Never again* will we leave ourselves vulnerable to a depression or a military attack by another nation.

The government exerts four basic economic influences: it spends over $2.5 trillion, levies almost that amount in taxes, redistributes hundreds of billions of dollars, and regulates our economy. For the last three and a half decades, the state and local governments have managed to raise enough money in taxes to pay for their expenditures and still run a surplus each year. In other words, total tax revenue of all state and local government has exceeded total spending. But over this same period, the federal government has spent much more than it has raised in taxes. It has made up the difference each year by borrowing.

What does the government *do* with all our money? Some of it is spent on goods and services (i.e., highways, police protection, defense), and some of it is redistributed to the poor, to retirees, and to the holders of government bonds.

What does the government do with all our money?

The government also has an important regulatory role in our economy. We are subject to myriad local, state, and federal laws governing how business may be conducted. These will be examined toward the end of this chapter.

Government Spending

Federal Government Spending

In fiscal year 1998 the federal government spent nearly $1.7 trillion. Who got the biggest bite of the pie? As you can see from the right side of Figure 1, it went to individuals who received direct benefit payments. These include Social Security benefits as well as Medicare, Medicaid, food stamps, public assistance, and veterans' benefits. (For an explanation of budget preparation and the fiscal year, see the boxes "The Chronology of Federal Budget Preparation" and "Why the Fiscal Year Starts on October 1.")

During the last 30 years, federal transfer payments have gone through the roof. How come? There are several explanations for this huge increase in social spending. Much of it reflects continued expenditures on the Great Society programs of the 1960s,

Figure 1   The Federal Government Dollar—Fiscal Year 1999 Estimate

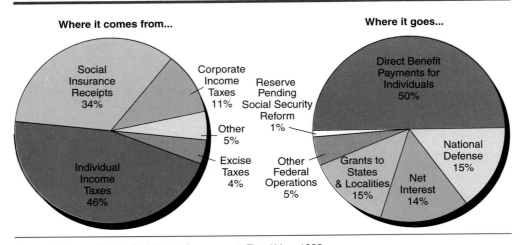

Source: *Budget of the United States Government,* Fiscal Year 1999.

The Chronology of Federal Budget Preparation

Preparation of the budget begins about two years before the beginning of the fiscal year. We'll be looking at the timetable for the preparation of the budget for fiscal year 1999, which began on October 1, 1998.

During early 1997, after months of internal studies, each department presented its budget for fiscal year 1999 to the Office of Management and Budget (OMB). That agency has the job of coordinating all budget requests to ensure that they are consistent with the president's economic program. The OMB then put together a tentative budget for the president.

President Bill Clinton was concerned not just with individual spending programs—foreign aid, defense, food stamps, Social Security—but with the bottom line, or total spending. The president and the director of the OMB then established spending ceilings for each department and the federal agencies, which were then asked to prepare a second round of expenditure plans over the summer.

During the fall of 1997 the OMB reviewed these revised programs, and in the late fall the budget was presented to President Clinton for final approval. The final budget message was then drafted for submission to Congress in January 1998.

Over the next eight months the ball was in Congress's court. Both houses of Congress have budget committees that prepare "concurrent resolutions" to be reported to their respective houses by April 15. These resolutions contain two key figures: overall expenditures and overall revenue. By May 15 Congress must pass a single concurrent resolution.

Between May 15 and October 1, Congress passed various appropriations bills—agricultural subsidies, veterans' benefits, aid to mass transit, public assistance—while trying to stay within the limits set by the concurrent resolution. Finally, a second budget resolution had to be passed by October 1, the first day of the fiscal year.

As a footnote to these proceedings, at the start of fiscal year 1988 (October 1, 1987), Congress had not yet passed even 1 of 13 regular appropriation bills. To keep the government afloat, a stopgap bill was passed. In October 1990, the federal government was almost forced to shut down until President George Bush agreed to a huge tax increase in exchange for major spending cuts.

Why the Fiscal Year Starts on October 1

The federal government, as you might expect, often has to do things a little differently. While nearly all business firms issue annual reports based on the normal calendar year—January 1 to December 31—the federal government's financial, or fiscal, year begins on October 1 and runs through September 30 of the following year.

Do they start on October 1 just to be different, or is there a reason for this unorthodox starting time? There actually *is* a reason. A new Congress is elected every second November and takes office the following January. This gives congresspeople eight months to work on the next year's federal budget. Of course, if the new budget did not go into effect until January 1, they'd have 11 months. Since Congress tends to leave its most important business for last, it would be trying to wrap up busi-

ness while worrying about getting home for Christmas. So members *do* have a reason for starting on October 1— maybe not a great reason, but a reason nevertheless.

By the way, what has probably been lost in my cogent explanation of why the fiscal year starts on October 1 is what a fiscal year actually is. It is a 12-month period over which the government projects a certain amount of spending and a certain level of tax receipts. The government might budget expenditures of $1.8 trillion and tax receipts of $1.7 trillion, leaving a deficit of how much?

The deficit would come to $100 billion (or $.1 trillion). If this math still bothers you, you would do well to reread the box "A Word about Numbers" on the second page of Chapter 5.

---

particularly Medicare, Medicaid, and food stamps. A second reason for the increase is that the prosperity our nation has enjoyed in recent years has not spread to tens of millions of poor Americans. Consequently, spending on public assistance, unemployment insurance benefits, and food stamps has shot up since the early 1970s. Finally, in 1955 relatively few people were collecting full Social Security benefits, as that program was then only 20 years old. Today, however, the number of retired people on the rolls is more than twice that of 1955, and benefits have gone up substantially because they are indexed for inflation. For example, if the consumer price index were to go up by 1.2 percent in the third quarter of 1999, then Social Security benefits would rise by 1.2 percent in the fourth quarter of that year.

The next big-ticket item is defense expenditures, budgeted in fiscal 1999 at $271 billion. This comes to $1,000 for each person in the United States. President Ronald Reagan had long been an advocate of a strong national defense; he managed to get Congress to nearly double military spending between 1981 and 1986. Ironically, Mr. Reagan was critical of Democratic social programs "for throwing money at problems."

One of the fastest-growing federal expenditures is interest on the national debt. The national debt is six times its 1980 size. When you owe six times as much, you have to pay a lot more interest.

So far we've covered the big three of federal spending. If you'd like to see more, I've summarized President Bill Clinton's spending proposals for fiscal year 1999 in Figure 2. But none of these figures is written in stone. After all, the president proposes and Congress disposes. In fact, much of the data presented in these last few chapters will be out of date before the book even gets to the printer. I'd even be willing to place a little side bet that defense spending, which is budgeted at $271 billion, will come in at more than $280 billion, once the Republican majorities in the House and the Senate have a chance to vote on the defense appropriations bill. So it would be extremely helpful for you to consult newspapers, news magazines, and government periodicals (the Commerce Department's *Survey of Current Business* is *my* favorite) for more up-to-date figures.

If you're like most taxpayers, you'd like to see the government trim some of the fat from its budget. So I'd like you to pick up your heaviest ax and start hacking away at Figure 2. But be careful—as soon as you lift your ax, a lot of people will start howling.

Begin with defense. You'll not only make the president unhappy, but you'll incur the wrath of the secretary of defense, the armed forces' top brass, and thousands of defense contractors—not to mention the millions of your fellow citizens who think any cut in the defense budget is the same as just handing the country over to our enemies, whoever they are. And besides, even if everyone agreed to major cuts, we are legally obligated to pay defense contractors hundreds of billions of dollars for the next few years for weapons

Government is the great fiction, through which everybody endeavors to live at the expense of everybody else.

—Frédéric Bastiat, *Essays on Political Economy,* 1872

Figure 2   1999 Proposed Spending by Category*

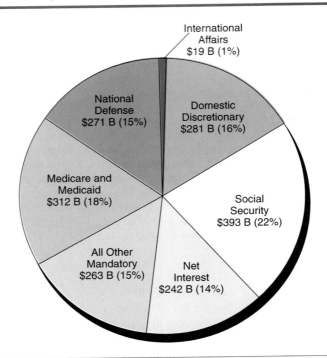

International
Affairs
$19 B (1%)

National
Defense
$271 B (15%)

Domestic
Discretionary
$281 B (16%)

Medicare and
Medicaid
$312 B (18%)

Social
Security
$393 B (22%)

All Other
Mandatory
$263 B (15%)

Net
Interest
$242 B (14%)

*Percentages add to more than 100 due to rounding.
Source: *Budget of the United States Government,* Fiscal Year 1999.

systems already in the pipeline. And just one other thing—can you actually "fire" the Army? That elusive "peace dividend" we heard so much about when the Soviet Union disappeared along with the communist menace has yet to materialize. Although defense spending is down substantially from its $350 billion levels of 1989 and 1990 (in 1997 dollars), it has probably bottomed out, and may be rising substantially as long as the Republicans continue to control Congress.

OK, let's cut Social Security and Medicare. Just try it! There are more than 44 million recipients of these benefits, and nearly all of them vote. What about federal pensions? It's too late—we're legally obligated for the next 40 years or so.

Want to cut the other mandatory spending? First, we're legally obligated to pay pensions and other benefits to retired federal employees and veterans. Second, there's a political problem. Veterans' benefits have a powerful constituency. Just drop by your local American Legion hall and ask the people there how *they* would feel about the government cutting these benefits.

Can we cut the interest we pay on the national debt? Now, this is something *everyone* would like to cut. The only problem is that the debt keeps getting bigger, and so does the interest that we have to pay. But as the deficit falls to zero, and budget surpluses are a real possibility, perhaps we'll see a declining national debt. Near the end of Chapter 11 we'll see just why the debt is such a problem.

State and Local Government Spending

Big state and local expenditures are: education, health, and welfare.

State and local government spending has been rising rapidly since World War II, but it is still just a little more than half the level of federal spending. Well over half of all state and local government expenditures goes toward education, health, and welfare. One of the problems faced by these governments is that they are expected to provide more and more services with limited tax bases. For example, more than 20 million teenagers are currently attending high school or college. Fifty or 60 years ago most people were

Are We Giving Away the Store?

Many taxpayers are asking whether it makes sense to be spending so much money to help foreigners when we have so many poor people in the United States. During fiscal year 1996, we provided our friends, our allies, and many of the poorer nations of the world with about $13 billion in economic and military aid. About half went to Israel, Egypt, Russia, and the other states of the former Soviet Union.

How does foreign aid spending stack up against what the federal, state, and local governments spend on public assistance, food stamps, Medicaid, and public housing? It turns out that we spend more than 10 times as much on our own poor as we do on foreigners. Recent polls found that two out of five Americans believe foreign aid is the largest single item in the federal budget.

In the chapter on income distribution and poverty I'll argue that the government could do a lot more about poverty in the United States, but just now I'm trying to put the federal government's spending programs in perspective. Our foreign aid bill comes to less than 1 percent of the federal budget, or less than 0.2 percent of our GDP. Thirteen billion dollars is a lot of money, and much of it, especially the military aid, is being questioned in light of the receding Russian military threat. But in relative terms, it's just a drop in the federal budgetary bucket.

working by the time they were 14, but now they are still in school. Supporting public education has traditionally been the role of the state and local governments, although in recent years Washington has provided supplementary funds covering about 6 percent of the costs of educating children through high school.

Another expenditure that has increased enormously is police protection. Although this is another traditional function of local government, rising crime and perhaps the deterioration of neighborhoods have made it necessary to hire many more police officers. Until the 1950s, neighborhoods largely policed themselves informally, mainly because people spent a great deal of time on the street, most urban areas were more densely populated, and people tended to know one another. All this has changed, and now the police are being called on to perform functions that neighborhoods used to handle.

The twin epidemics of crime and crack cocaine have strained local resources to the breaking point. Add the problem of homelessness, which is ubiquitous in cities and towns across the nation, and it becomes clear that we may be asking our local and state governments to do a lot more than we are willing to pay for in the form of higher taxes.

Government Purchases versus Transfer Payments

$GDP = C + I + G + X_n$

The federal, state, and local governments spend over $2.5 trillion a year. Nearly half goes to individuals as transfer payments, and the rest is government purchases. We represent these purchases by the letter G, and they go into our GDP equation: $GDP = C + I + G + X_n$.

What do you think the biggest government purchase is? It's defense, which accounts for 20 cents out of every dollar that goes into G. Other biggies are education, police, health, and highway construction. A government purchase is the spending of government funds to purchase or provide the public with some good or service.

Transfer payments cannot be counted because they do not represent that kind of spending. What is the largest government transfer payment? I'm sure you know that it's Social Security. Of the trillion dollars that the federal, state, and local governments pay out in transfer payments, near $400 billion goes to Social Security recipients.

You may want to ask why we bother to distinguish between government purchases and transfer payments. OK, go ahead and ask. The reason is that we need to come up with a figure for GDP—the nation's expenditures on all final goods and services produced during the year at market prices. So we want to add in only what we produced and purchased that year. Don't people receiving transfer payments spend that money on consumer goods and services, or C in our GDP equation? Yes, they do. And so as soon as they spend those Social Security, public assistance, or government employees' retirement and veterans' benefits, that money will go into GDP.

The point to remember is that what the government gives it must first take away.

—John Strider Coleman

What Do We Want the Government to Do?

We want a lot from the government. We want police protection, good schools, unclogged highways, a clean environment, a strong defense, and money and medical care in our old age. We want the government to do something about the homeless, crack, and AIDS. In general, then, we look to the government to provide us with services that we either used to perform for ourselves or considered unnecessary a few generations ago. The question is, where does the money come from?

Graphing the C + I + G Line

In Chapter 5 we graphed the C line. In the last chapter we graphed the C + I line. Now we add another line to our graph: the C + I + G line. By now this should be old hat to you, so I'm going to ask you to figure out how much G is in Figure 3 (assuming the C + I + G line is parallel to the C + I line).

What did you get? You should have gotten 400 or thereabouts (each box is 200). You'll notice that the level of G remains at 400 no matter what the level of disposable income. Is this realistic? It can be argued that at low levels of income, the government might spend more money than at higher income levels. Why? Because low income levels represent periods of recession and depression, when the government might well be spending a lot of money to get the economy moving again. We'll see just how the government would do this in the chapter on fiscal policy.

It could also be argued that at higher levels of disposable income, the government would be taking in more tax dollars and thus have more money to spend. So, rather than take sides here, I'll just say that the government spends a constant amount of money, no matter what the level of disposable income. The main reason for doing this is to keep our graph as simple as possible.

We're not quite finished with our graphs. We still need to draw the C + I + G + X_n line, but that won't happen until the beginning of the next chapter.

Figure 3   Measuring Government Spending

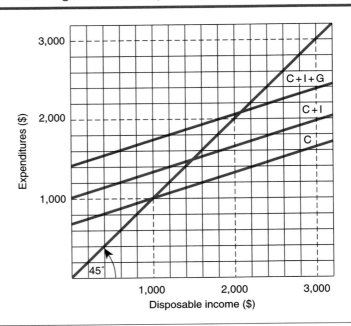

Taxes

Taxes are so pervasive that over half the chapter will be devoted to them. Before we even begin to consider how much taxes are, we'll need to understand something about tax rates and the types of taxes that exist. Once that's done, we'll see just how onerous the American tax system really is.

The Average Tax Rate and the Marginal Tax Rate

If someone asked you what your tax rate was, would you have a ready answer? Generations of attorneys have taught us that the best answer to any question (and especially those to which you don't know the answer) is another question. So the answer to the question "What's your tax rate?" is "Which tax rate are you referring to? My average tax rate or my marginal tax rate?"

But what if your questioner replies, "Tell me your average tax rate"? What do you do then? You tell her. And if she then happens to ask you your marginal tax rate, you tell her that as well.

The art of taxation consists in so plucking the goose as to obtain the largest possible amount of feathers with the smallest amount of hissing.

—Jean-Baptiste Colbert

We all pay tax at two different rates: the average rate and the marginal rate. The average rate is the overall rate you pay on your entire income, while the marginal rate is the rate you pay on your last few hundreds (or thousands) of dollars earned. Your marginal rate is often referred to as your tax bracket. In nearly all cases, I'm talking about the average and marginal rates that you're paying in personal income tax, but I'll apply the average tax rate to the Social Security tax as well.

The Average Tax Rate   I kind of left you hanging there, didn't I? How do you answer the question "Tell me your average tax rate"?

Let's try a simple problem. The average tax rate is calculated by dividing taxes paid by taxable income:

$$\text{Average tax rate (ATR)} = \frac{\text{Taxes paid}}{\text{Taxable income}}$$

Suppose a person paid $3,000 on a taxable income of $20,000. How much is the average tax rate? Do your calculations right here:

$ATR = \dfrac{Taxes\ paid}{Taxable\ income}$

$$\text{Average tax rate} = \frac{\text{Taxes paid}}{\text{Taxable income}} = \frac{\$3,000}{\$20,000} = .15, \text{ or } 15\%$$

If you correctly calculated 15 percent, go on to the marginal tax rate in the next section. If not, let's go over all the steps in finding the average tax rate. How do we get from $^{\$3,000}/_{\$20,000}$ to .15? First, reduce the fraction to $^{3}/_{20}$. Whatever you do to the top of the fraction, you do to the bottom. Get rid of the three zeros on top and get rid of three zeros on the bottom. (While you're at it, you can get rid of the dollar signs as well.)

The next step is to divide 3 by 20. Remember, whenever you have a fraction, you may divide the bottom number into the top number. If you divide the top into the bottom, you will <u>not</u> only violate a basic <u>law</u> of arithmetic, but you will also get the wrong answer. $20\overline{)3}$ is the same as $20\overline{)3.00}$. We are allowed to put a decimal point after any whole number. And we are allowed to put zeros after the decimal point, because they don't change the number's value. These are more laws of arithmetic.

$$20\overline{)3.00} = 20\overline{)3.00}$$
$$\underline{-20x}$$
$$100$$
$$\underline{-100}$$

The average tax rate is .15, or 15 percent. Our final law of arithmetic is that whenever you want to convert a decimal into a percentage, you move the decimal point two places to the right and write a percent sign after the number. Examples would be .235 = 23.5%; or, .71 = 71%; or, .406 = 40.6%. If a baseball player is hitting .406, he is getting a hit 40.6 percent of the times he bats. And if your average tax rate comes to .406, it means you are paying 40.6 percent of your taxable income to the Internal Revenue Service.

Let's try one more problem. Suppose you pay $12,000 on a taxable income of $50,000. How much is your average tax rate? To solve this problem: (1) write the formula, (2) substitute numbers into the formula, and (3) solve.

$$\text{Average tax rate} = \frac{\text{Taxes paid}}{\text{Taxable income}} = \frac{\$12,000}{\$50,000} = \frac{12}{50} = \frac{6}{25}$$

$$25\overline{)6.00} \quad .24 = 24\%$$
$$\underline{-50x}$$
$$100$$
$$\underline{-100}$$

The Marginal Tax Rate   The average tax rate is the overall rate you pay on your entire income, while the marginal tax rate is the rate you pay on the last few hundred dollars you earned. Suppose you made $100 in overtime and the government took $70. Would you work overtime? Chances are you wouldn't, and that supposition forms a cornerstone of supply-side economics. The supply-siders' basic belief is that our high marginal tax rates rob people of the incentive to work as hard and as long as they would with a lower tax burden.

The marginal tax rate is calculated by dividing additional taxes paid by additional taxable income:

$$\text{Marginal tax rate (MTR)} = \frac{\text{Additional taxes paid}}{\text{Additional taxable income}}$$

Suppose you had to pay an additional $420 on an additional taxable income of $1,000. How much is the marginal tax rate?

$$\text{Marginal tax rate} = \text{Additional taxes paid/Additional taxable income}$$

$$= \frac{\$420}{\$1,000} = \frac{42}{100} = .42 = 42\%$$

Did you get the right answer? If so, you might as well skip the rest of this section. If not, we'll go over the problem step-by-step.

How did we get from 42/100 to .42? The fraction 42/100 means we have to divide 42 by 100. When you divide a number by 100, you move its decimal two places to the left. If you do that, you get .42:

$$
\begin{array}{r}
.42 = 42\% \\
100\overline{)42.00} \\
-400x \\
\hline
200 \\
-200 \\
\hline
\end{array}
$$

Now we'll get a little fancier. Suppose your taxable income rose from $20,000 to $22,000 and the taxes you paid rose from $4,500 to $5,200. How much is your marginal tax rate?

$MTR = \dfrac{\textit{Additional taxes paid}}{\textit{Additional taxable income}}$

$$\text{Marginal tax rate} = \frac{\text{Additional taxes paid}}{\text{Additional taxable income}}$$

$$= \frac{\$700}{\$2,000} = \frac{7}{20} = .35 = 35\%$$

$$
\begin{array}{r}
.35 = 35\% \\
20\overline{)7.00} \\
-60x \\
\hline
100 \\
-100 \\
\hline
\end{array}
$$

Types of Taxes

There are two basic divisions of taxes. First we'll be looking at the difference between direct and indirect taxes. Then we'll take up progressive, proportional, and regressive taxes.

Direct Taxes   A direct tax is a tax with your name written on it. The personal income and Social Security taxes are examples. They are taxes on particular persons. If you earn a certain amount of money, you must pay these taxes.

The corporate income tax is also a direct tax. You might not think so, but a corporation is considered a legal person. For example, in court, you would sue a corporation rather than its owners or officers. Thus, if a corporation makes a profit, it must pay a corporate income tax, and this is a direct tax.

In this world nothing can be said to be certain, except death and taxes.

—Benjamin Franklin

Indirect Taxes   These are not taxes on people, but on things. Some of us may have trouble making this distinction, especially given our problematic relationships with some of our family, friends, and co-workers, but in economics we *do* make a sharp distinction between people and things. Taxes on things include sales and excise taxes. Examples are a state sales tax on most retail purchases and the excise taxes on tires, gasoline, movie tickets, cigarettes, and liquor.

The distinction between direct and indirect taxes was made by John Stuart Mill more than a century ago:

John Stuart Mill, English
philosopher and economist
(Brown Brothers)

A direct tax is one which is demanded from the very persons who, it is intended or desired, should pay it. Indirect taxes are those which are demanded from one person in the expectation and intention that he shall indemnify himself at the expense of another.[1]

Now we shall take up, in turn, progressive, proportional, and regressive taxes. The key variable we use to differentiate them is where the tax burden falls.

Progressive Taxes   A progressive tax places a greater burden on those best able to pay and little or no burden on the poor. The best example is, of course, the federal personal income tax. For the vast majority of American taxpayers today, the more they earn, the higher percentage they pay. In terms of the average tax rate, then, people in higher income brackets pay a substantially higher average tax rate than those in lower brackets.

But the federal income tax was much more progressive before the passage of the Economic Recovery Tax Act of 1981 and the Tax Reform Act of 1986. At the upper end of the income scale, the maximum marginal tax rate of 70 percent before 1981 went to just 50 percent that year, and to just 28 percent in 1988.[2] Also, the number of tax brackets was reduced from 14 in 1986 to just 2 in 1988 and then nudged up to 3 in 1990. By lumping all taxpayers into only three brackets, the government further cut down on the progressiveness of the personal income tax.[3]

In 1991 the New Jersey tax rates were raised. All income under $20,000 was taxed at 2.2 percent. There were now three intermediate brackets, taxed at 2.8 percent, 5.5 percent, and 7.2 percent, and all income above $75,000 was taxed at 7.7 percent. Question: Did this tax increase make the New Jersey state income tax more progressive? Yes, it did. But it also made Governor Jim Florio the most unpopular person in the state. In fact, he was so unpopular that in 1993 he was beaten by Christine Todd Whitman, who then made good on her promise to cut the state income tax by 10 percent a year for three years.

Proportional Taxes   Proportional taxes place an equal burden on the rich, the middle class, and the poor. Sometimes a flat tax rate is advanced as a "fair" or proportional tax, but it is neither. For example, a flat income tax rate of, say, 15 percent, with no deductions, would place a much greater burden on the poor and the working class than on the rich. (See box "Nominally Progressive, Proportional, and Regressive Taxes.") It would be much harder for a family with an income of $10,000 to pay $1,500 in income tax (15 percent of $10,000) than it would be for a family with an income of $100,000 to pay $15,000 (15 percent of $100,000).

---

[1]John Stuart Mill, *Principles of Political Economy*, Book IV, ed. William J. Ashley (Philadelphia: Porcupine Press, 1979), p. 823.

[2]In 1990 the maximum marginal tax rate was raised to 31 percent, and in 1993 to 39.6 percent.

[3]This loss of progressivity can best be illustrated by looking at the marginal tax brackets of upper-middle-class families and of millionaires. A family earning, say, $75,000 of taxable income is in the 28 percent tax bracket, while the family with a taxable income of $75 million is in the 39.6 percent bracket. Back in 1980 the $75,000 family had a marginal tax rate of about 40 percent and the millionaire family had a marginal tax rate of 70 percent.

ADVANCED WORK .... Progressive in Name vs. Progessive in Effect

Let's distinguish between progressiveness in name and progressiveness in effect by looking at a real-life example. Until 1991 New Jersey's state personal income tax called for a 2 percent rate on all income below $20,000, a 2.5 percent rate on income between $20,000 and $50,000, and a 3.5 percent rate on all income above $50,000. Nominally then, it was a progressive tax.

But, in effect, it was hardly progressive because it was a much greater burden on the family with an income of $10,000 to pay $200 tax (2 percent of $10,000) than it was on the $100,000 family to pay $2,900 (2 percent on the first $20,000 = $400, plus 2.5 percent on the next $30,000 = $750, plus 3.5 percent on the next $50,000 = $1,750; $400 + $750 + $1,750 = $2,900).

A regressive tax falls mainly on the poor.

Regressive Taxes   A regressive tax falls more heavily on the poor than on the rich. The examples I have already given illustrate this (a tax may be set forth as progressive or proportional when it may be regressive in actuality). Another example is the Social Security tax. In 1998 the rate was 6.2 percent on all wages and salaries up to $68,400. The maximum you had to pay was $4,240.80. Where did this figure come from? I'll give you some space to come up with the answer:

ADVANCED WORK

Nominally Progressive, Proportional, and Regressive Taxes

We have already defined these taxes in accordance with their effect, or burden, on taxpayers in different income groups. The burden of a progressive tax falls most heavily on the rich; the burden of a proportional tax falls equally on all income groups; and the burden of a regressive tax falls most heavily on the poor.

This three-part graph presents an alternative view of these types of taxes. I'll tell you up front that I strongly disagree with the implications of this view. Let's look at each part of this graph and see how *you* feel.

The graph in part (*a*) is nominally progressive because higher-income people pay a higher tax rate than lower-income people. For example, those earning $10,000 pay only 4 percent of their incomes, while those earning $100,000 pay 8 percent. But is this, in effect, a progressive tax? Is it as easy for a poor family to pay $400 as it is for a rich family to pay $8,000? We could argue it either way. And, unfortunately, economic analysis cannot supply an answer. Now, I personally feel that a $400 tax bill imposes a greater burden on a family earning $10,000 than an $8,000 tax bill imposes on a family earning $100,000. What do *you* think?

Let's move on to the next part of the graph, (*b*), which shows a nominally proportional tax rate of 10 percent. Here's the question: Is it as easy for a poor family to hand over 10 percent of its income to the IRS as it is for a middle-class family, or a rich family? What do *you* think? My own view is that it isn't and that this nominally proportional tax is, in effect, a regressive tax.

The last part, (*c*), is easy. This is a nominally regressive tax because the tax rate declines as income rises. Obviously, by any measure, the burden falls most heavily on the poor.

Economists should avoid making value judgments, so perhaps I have gone a bit too far in claiming that nominally progressive taxes *could* be regressive in effect. And that nominally proportional taxes *are* regressive in effect (although this is somewhat less controversial). So if you disagree with my conclusions it doesn't make one of us wrong and the other right. It means only that our values are different.

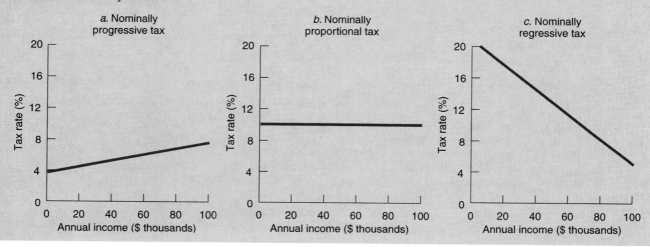

That's right: multiply $68,400 by 6.2 percent, or .062.

$$
\begin{array}{r}
\$68{,}400 \\
\times\,.062 \\
\hline
136\,800 \\
4104\,00 \\
\hline
\$4{,}240.800 \\
\end{array}
$$

Now that I've had you do all these calculations, I have some bad news for you. The 6.2 percent of your wages deducted from your paycheck is not *all* the government takes. The Medicare tax of 1.45 percent is also taken out, but unlike the Social Security tax, there's no wage-base limitation. If you earned $1 million, you'd pay a Medicare tax of $14,500.

So let's go back to the drawing board. The deduction from your pay is 7.65 percent (6.2 percent for Social Security and 1.45 percent for Medicare). How much, then, is deducted per year for these programs from the pay of a person earning $10,000? Work it out right here:

The answer is $765 ($10,000 × .0765). Of course, your employer also withholds money from your check for personal income taxes. But guess what! More than 70 percent of all taxpayers pay more in payroll taxes (i.e., Social Security and Medicare) than they do in personal income tax.

Table 1 shows the Social Security taxes paid by people with various incomes. Only earned income (wages and salaries) is subject to this tax; rental income, interest, dividends, and profits are not. It might appear at first glance that the Social Security tax is proportional; but as you examine Table 1, you should observe that it is not only regressive in effect, but nominally as well.

Take a yearly income of $100,000, for example. This person pays the maximum of $4,240.80 (i.e., 6.2 percent of the first $68,400). Now, what percentage of a $100,000 income is taxed? It comes to just 4.24 percent. Not bad. Everyone with an income below $68,400 paid 6.2 percent. What happens, then, is that as income rises above $68,400, people pay the same tax—$4,240.80—while the proportion of their income that goes to the Social Security tax falls steadily. In fact, the person making $1 million a year also pays $4,240.80, which comes to just 0.424 percent of his or her income.

What would be an ideal tax—one that would not fall disproportionately on the poor, the middle class, *or* the rich? In principle, an ideal tax would be a tax that is proportional *in effect*. It would therefore be a tax that is nominally progressive, looking something like the one in graph (*a*) in the box "Nominally Progressive, Proportional, and Regressive Taxes."

So far, so good. The only problem is that when we try to come up with actual tax rates for different income groups, there is a great deal of screaming and carrying on by

Table 1   The Incidence of the Social Security Tax at Various Income Levels in 1998*

Level of Earned Income	Taxes Paid	Average Tax Rate
$ 10,000	$ 620.00	6.2%
68,400	4,240.80	6.2%
100,000	4,240.80	4.24%
1,000,000	4,240.80	0.424%

*The Social Security tax rate is set by law at 6.2 percent. Each year, however, the inflation rate of the previous year raises the wage base.

those who feel they are being forced to pay too much. Remember that in 1980 Ronald Reagan was elected president largely because he promised—and delivered—a massive personal income tax cut. In 1984, when he ran for reelection, he declared that taxes would be increased only "over my dead body." In 1988 George Bush made his fateful "Read my lips: no new taxes" pledge, which he broke less than two years later. Finally, in the 1992 election, Bush tried to make up for his indiscretion by pledging new tax cuts, while Bill Clinton, not to be outdone, also said he would cut the taxes of the middle class. But only a few weeks after taking office, Clinton announced that no one would be getting a tax cut after all. And in 1993 we had a substantial tax increase that fell almost entirely on the rich.

Sources of Federal Revenue

The largest source of federal revenue is the personal income tax.

The Personal Income Tax   As we saw in Figure 1, the federal government has three main sources of tax revenue, the largest of which is the personal income tax. This tax was only a minor source of federal revenue until World War II. It now accounts for 46 cents out of every tax dollar collected by the Internal Revenue Service. (To find out how to save on your income tax, see box with this title.)

The Economic Recovery Tax Act of 1981

The personal income tax would be an even greater source of revenue were it not for two landmark tax laws passed in the 1980s. First, the Economic Recovery Tax Act of 1981, better known as the Kemp-Roth tax cut,[4] lowered the average citizen's tax bill by 23 percent over a three-year period. The maximum rate was cut from 70 percent to 50 percent, and, most analysts agreed, the wealthiest third of the population got most of the benefits.

The Tax Reform Act of 1986

Where there is an income tax, the just man will pay more and the unjust less on the same income.
—Plato

People want just taxes more than they want lower taxes. They want to know that every man is paying his proportionate share according to his wealth.
—Will Rogers

Then came the Tax Reform Act of 1986, which cut personal income taxes still further. The maximum rate was lowered to 28 percent, and most taxpayers ended up in the lower bracket—15 percent. This meant the nation's wealthiest people had marginal tax rates of 28 percent, the upper middle class was taxed at 28 percent, and the working class and lower middle class were taxed at 15 percent. At the same time, millions of poorer families were taken off the income tax rolls entirely. In 1990, however, the top marginal rate was raised to 31 percent, and in 1993 the top bracket was raised to 36 percent, with a 10 percent surtax on incomes over $271,000. That makes the top bracket 39.6 percent (36 + 10 percent of 36 or 3.6). Figure 4 shows changes in the maximum marginal tax rate since 1979. In 1981 the top marginal tax rate was lowered in stages to 50 percent, a rate that was maintained from 1983 to 1987. Under the Tax Reform Act of 1986, it was lowered in stages to 28 percent in 1988. In 1990 the top marginal tax rate was raised to 31 percent, a rate that was in effect from 1991 through 1993. In 1993 the top tax bracket was raised to 36 percent, with a 10 percent surtax for those making more than $250,000. In effect, then, since 1994, the top marginal tax rate has been 39.6 percent (36 percent + 3.6 percent).

You don't have to pay tax on your entire income. In 1997, married couples were entitled to a standard deduction of $6,900, which meant that the first $6,900 was not subject to personal income tax. In addition, they were entitled to exemptions of $2,650 for each dependent. Suppose we're looking at the tax return of a couple with two children. They are entitled to four exemptions, totaling $10,600 ($2,650 × 4). They would not have to pay any federal personal income tax on their first $17,500 of income. Suppose they earned $18,500. How much tax would they have to pay? Work it out here:

---

[4]Kemp was Representative Jack Kemp from upstate New York. He had been a star quarterback for the Buffalo Bills and was a 1988 Republican presidential contender. In 1989, he joined President Bush's cabinet as secretary of housing and urban development, and in 1996 he was Bob Dole's vice presidential running mate. William Roth was, and still is, a Republican senator from Delaware.

How to Save on Your Income Tax

The personal income tax would be even more progressive in effect were it not for two methods of beating the Internal Revenue Service out of some of its tax proceeds. One method is tax evasions, which are illegal. The other, tax avoidance, is not only legal but has been purposely put into the Internal Revenue Code by Congress. These provisions are commonly known as "loopholes."

The most popular way of evading taxes is to not report income. We may think first of cabdrivers, waiters and waitresses, barbers and beauticians, and domestics, who often don't report all their income from tips. People who work "off the books" and those engaged in illegal activities are also frequently cited. But we usually miss the big boys—the businesspeople, doctors, dentists, and others who work for themselves.

According to the IRS, the worst tax cheats are auto dealers, restaurateurs, and clothing store operators, who underreport 40 percent of their taxable income. The IRS estimates that small businesses that deal mostly in cash are reporting only 20 cents of each dollar they receive.

Often you can tell when a businessperson isn't reporting income. He will tell you that there's no sales tax if you pay cash. Now isn't that nice of him?

Another way of evading income tax is to take phony deductions. Even President Richard Nixon was not above cheating on his taxes. He had made a gift of his vice presidential papers to the National Archives and valued them at $482,018. So far, so good. The only trouble was that a year before he made this gift, Congress had passed a law that made such gifts nondeductible. No

problem. Nixon simply predated his gift to reflect the time before the law's passage. The president could have pleaded ignorance of the law. The only problem was that Nixon himself had signed the bill into law.

Tax avoidance, unlike evasion, is quite legal. In fact, the Internal Revenue Code is set up to help rich people avoid a large chunk of their tax liability. Perhaps the most blatant example is the treatment of interest on state and municipal bonds. Unlike interest you might earn on savings accounts or corporate bonds, you pay no federal income tax on the interest earned from state and municipal bonds.* The reason for this is to make it easier for state and local governments to borrow by making their securities more attractive to investors.

Now, guess who the *big* investors are in state and municipal bonds? The rich. They hold most of these bonds. Why? Because they're tax exempt.

Imagine you have $100 million lying around the house. If you were to buy some of these bonds, you might earn 7 percent interest, or $7 million a year. With other bonds you would have to pay 39.6 percent of this income to the federal government, but because the interest on these bonds isn't taxed, you don't have to pay one penny. When the rich invest in these securities, we call that tax avoidance. And what's so nice about it is that it's perfectly legal.

*Nearly 1 million people with incomes of more than $100,000 earned more than $20 billion in interest on their tax-exempt bond holdings in 1992 and saved about $6 billion on their income tax.

The solution: $18,500 − $17,500 = $1,000 taxable income. At a marginal tax rate of 15 percent, they have to pay $150.

Most poor people pay little or no personal income tax. For example, a family of four would need to earn more than $17,500 before it would have to pay any taxes, and that income would place the family well above the poverty line ($16,036 in 1996). But what really kills the working poor is the payroll tax, which begins with the first dollar earned.

Giving money and power to the government is like giving whiskey and car keys to teenage boys.
—P. J. O'Rourke

The Payroll Tax   What's the payroll tax? Remember the Social Security and Medicare taxes that you pay? What you pay is matched by your employer. When you pay 7.65 percent of your wages, your employer also pays 7.65 percent of your wages.

The payroll tax is the federal government's fastest-growing source of revenue and now stands second in importance to the personal income tax. But the Social Security trust fund may be running out of money, because in the coming years medical and retirement payments may rise even faster than tax collections. (See the box titled "The Arithmetic of Social Security.")

We have seen that the Social Security tax is extremely regressive. This regressiveness lessened somewhat over the years as the earnings ceiling was raised. Recently, however, the ceiling has been raised each year at the same rate at which the consumer price index rose the previous year. In effect, then, the regressive structure of the Social Security tax is written in stone, at least until such time as the president and Congress change the law.

As we hear from time to time (see again the box about the arithmetic of Social Security), when the baby boomers begin to retire starting in the year 2011, the Social Security

Figure 4   Federal Personal Income Tax: Top Marginal Tax Rate, 1954–98*

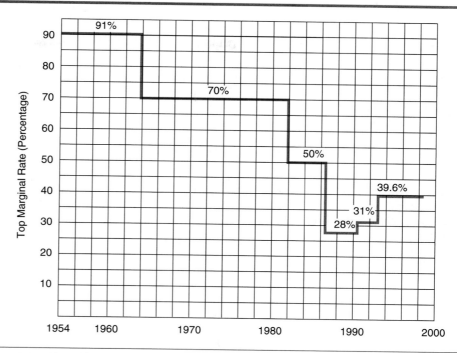

*During World War II the top MTR was 94%.

The Arithmetic of Social Security

Will Social Security be there for you when you retire? If you were born after 1950, the answer is no. The way things stand right now, in the year 2013, the Social Security system, which is currently accumulating huge surpluses, will begin paying out more in benefits than it will receive in tax revenue. Of course, the chances are very good that sometime in the next few years, Congress will get around to dealing with this impending disaster.

Today more than 40 million Americans—retired, survivors, and disabled—collect Social Security benefits. As the baby boomers—those born between 1946 and 1964—begin reaching retirement age, the number of Social Security beneficiaries will swell to more than 50 million in the year 2010, to 65 million in 2020, and to 75 million in 2030. Look at it this way: In 1945, there were 42 workers for every beneficiary. In 1965, this ratio fell to 4 to 1. It's 3 to 1 today. And in 2030, it will be less than 2 to 1.

What it all comes down to is that our population is aging, so more and more people will be receiving Social Security payments while fewer and fewer people will be paying into the system. So if you think we have problems now, just wait until 2030. You should only *live* so long!

trust fund will be in big trouble. Around 2013 the Social Security trust fund will begin taking in less in payroll taxes than it is paying out in benefits.

So what should we do? Raise the age at which you can collect full benefits? We already did that. Right now people who are retiring can collect full benefits at the age of 65, but this will be raised gradually to 67 by 2022. Should we raise the wage base? This, too, is being done. Each year the wage base is raised to keep pace with inflation. Of course we could raise the wage base *faster* than the inflation rate and we could also raise the tax rate from 6.2 percent to, say, 7 or 8 percent.[5] But further increases in Social Security taxes would surely meet with tremendous political opposition, especially from workers in their 20s and 30s, who are wondering whether there will be any money left in the trust fund for *their* retirement benefits.

As we can't immediately resolve this dilemma, let's make sure we're clear on what the Social Security, Medicare, and payroll taxes are. Our employers deduct 6.2 percent of

---

[5]Because the Social Security tax is very regressive, the burden of an increase in its rate would fall disproportionately on the working poor and the working class. Furthermore, an increase in its rate would discourage employers from hiring more workers because employers also pay this tax.

our pay (up to $68,400) in Social Security taxes and 1.45 percent of our pay in Medicare taxes. In other words, we pay 7.65 percent in payroll tax on wages of up to $68,400, and 1.45 percent on all wages. The employer matches the employee's payments dollar for dollar. So how much payroll tax would the government collect on wages of $20,000?

Solution: It would collect $3,060 ($20,000 × .153). The employee would pay $1,530 ($20,000 × .0765), and this would be matched by the employer.

The power to tax involves the power to destroy.
—Chief Justice John Marshall

The Corporate Income Tax   Until the late 1970s the corporate income tax was the second-largest source of federal revenue, but it is now a distant third. Under the Tax Reform Act of 1986, the maximum rate was lowered from 46 percent to just 34 percent, but most large corporations have ended up paying more tax because several deductions were reduced. At the present time the maximum rate is 35 percent.[6]

The corporate income tax is a tax on a corporation's profits. Those who believe profits provide our economy with its main incentive to produce goods and services are uneasy that they are so heavily taxed.

Excise Taxes   An excise tax is a sales tax, but it is aimed at specific goods and services. The federal government taxes such things as tires, cigarettes, liquor, gasoline, and phone calls. Most excise taxes are levied by the federal government, although state and local governments often levy taxes on the same items. Cigarettes and gasoline, for example, are subject to a federal excise tax as well as to excise taxes in many states. In fact, the differential in state excise taxes encourages many people to "smuggle" cigarettes from North Carolina into New York.

Excise taxes, which account for about 3 percent of federal revenue, have another purpose beside serving as a source of revenue. They tend to reduce consumption of certain products of which the federal government takes a dim view. The surgeon general not only warns us about cigarettes but looks on approvingly as the government taxes them.

Excise taxes are usually regressive.

Excise taxes are generally regressive because they tend to fall more heavily on the poor and working class. The tax on a pack of cigarettes is the same whether you're rich or poor, but it's easier for the rich person to handle 60 or 80 cents a day it than it is for a poor person. The same is true of liquor and gasoline. In fact, a tax on most consumer goods is regressive because the poor tend to spend a higher proportion of their incomes on consumption than the rich (who save 20 to 25 percent of their incomes). (See the boxes regarding cigarette and gasoline excise taxes.)

Sources of State and Local Revenue

The sales tax is regressive.

The Sales Tax   More than half the taxes collected by the states come from the sales tax. This is a highly regressive tax. Although most food items are exempt, the poor consume a higher proportion of their incomes than the rich, who are able to save. In other words, a higher proportion of poor people's income is subject to this tax.

Furthermore, the rich can avoid or evade a large proportion of the sales tax by buying their big-ticket items—stereos, TVs, cars, and so on—in states that have low or no sales tax. They can also evade the sales tax by buying expensive items for cash (an option not feasible for the poor) from merchants who don't declare their cash incomes.

---

[6]All corporations earning profits of at least $335,000 pay an average tax rate of 35 percent. Of course, using loopholes in the tax law, virtually all major corporations are legally able to report much lower profits, and consequently, pay much lower taxes.

ADVANCED WORK . . . . Should Cigarettes Be Taxed?

Economists don't like to get into issues involving value judgments, but this one is too good to pass up. Should cigarettes be taxed to discourage their consumption? Do cigarettes cause lung cancer, heart disease, and other terrible things? No less an authority than the surgeon general of the United States says that they do. Indeed, he provides us with a gentle reminder on every pack of cigarettes.

Should cigarettes be taxed? Why not? If the tax is high enough, it will discourage smoking. Of course, we don't want to make it too high, or nobody will smoke and the federal government will be out about $6 billion a year.*

But there are two good reasons why a tax on cigarettes is unfair (a word economists never use). OK, there are two reasons why it's inequitable. Whatever. First, it's regressive. We can see that it's harder for a poor person to pay 50 cents a pack (or $547.50 a year, if that person has a three-pack-a-day habit) than it is for a rich person to pay 50 cents a pack. But if you're poor, you're much more likely to smoke than if you're rich.

According to the U.S. Centers for Disease Control in Atlanta (where I actually once worked as a management trainee), 16 percent of all college graduates smoke, while 36 percent of all high school dropouts continue to puff away. Your average college student is much more affluent than your average high school dropout, which means a cigarette tax is almost targeted at the poor.

Here's a second good reason why a tax on cigarettes is inequitable. John Shover, a Stanford University economics professor, has calculated that "premature death saves society about $20,000 in Social Security benefits for each smoker."† So you can see that these guys are really paying their dues, so to speak. We single out relatively poor people, we tax them on something they really like to do, we overcharge them on Social Security taxes, and then, to add insult to injury, we make them stand outside the building. So put *that* in your pipe and smoke it.

---

* Smokers pay over a dollar a pack in state and federal taxes in 40 states in January 1988.

†See Peter Passell, "So Long, Marlboro Man," *New York Times,* February 28, 1990, p. D2.

Should the Gasoline Tax Be Raised?

Are our gas taxes too high? They certainly are not too high relative to the taxes paid in other industrial countries. The table below shows gasoline prices per gallon before and after taxes in selected industrial countries for mid-June 1994.

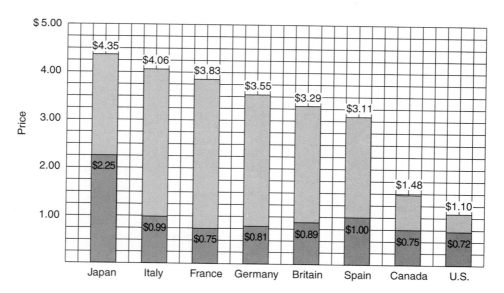

Source: International Energy Agency.

The Property Tax   More than 80 percent of all local tax revenue is derived from the property tax. There is some disagreement about whether this is a regressive tax, but it *is* a deduction that you may take on your federal income tax. For example, if you paid $3,000 in property tax, you are entitled to a $3,000 deduction on your federal income tax return.

The State and Local Fiscal Dilemma

Since World War II, state and local governments have been expected to provide an increasing number of services, most notably health, welfare, education, and police protection. In 1945 state and local taxes were about 5 percent of GDP; now they are just over 14 percent (see Figure 5). During the 1960s and 1970s the federal government accommodated the fiscal needs of states and cities through increasing grants-in-aid and general revenue sharing. The Reagan administration not only stemmed this increase, but strongly reversed it.

At a time when they can no longer look to Washington for increased aid, some of the states and cities are finding that they have gone to the well once too often with respect to raising taxes. In 1978 Proposition 13 was passed in California, limiting the growth of property taxes. Other states, most notably Massachusetts, soon followed suit.

Furthermore, under our federal system, neighboring states and local governments are in direct competition with one another for tax dollars. If one government's tax rates—particularly the sales and property taxes—rise too far above the levels of its neighbors, its citizens will vote with their feet. They will shop or even move to the areas that have lower tax rates. Were there a uniform national sales or property tax, it could be more easily raised when necessary. As long as neighboring government units are in direct competition, raising the necessary tax revenues will be difficult.

Figure 5   **Government Tax Receipts as Percentage of GDP, 1929 and 1996**

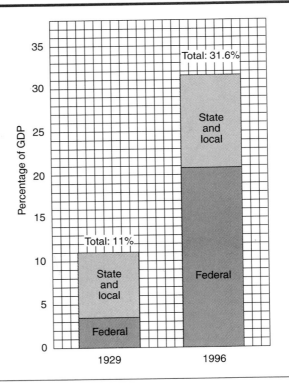

Source: *Economic Report of the President,* 1998.

Comparison of Taxes in the United States and Other Countries

Contrary to popular opinion, Americans are not heavily taxed in comparison with the citizens of other industrial countries. As we see in Figure 6, our taxes, which were 32.6 percent of our GDP in 1994, are at the low end of the world's leading industrial countries. Keep in mind that these taxes include federal, state, and local taxes, and that about half of that total is redistributed in the form of transfer payments, such as Social Security, public assistance, food stamps, and unemployment insurance payments.

So what's our problem? Why all this whining and carrying on about our high taxes when people in other countries pay so much more? Much of the dissatisfaction has to do with the tangible benefits we get in return for our taxes. In many European countries medical care is free, college is free, and day care is heavily subsidized. Indeed, parents of young children actually receive $1,000 or more every year in child care allowances from their governments. So the United States would definitely have many more happy campers if its citizens got to see more of what they've been paying for.

A tax is a compulsory payment for which no specific benefit is received in return.
—U.S. Treasury

Two Principles of Taxation: Ability to Pay versus Benefits Received

Economists, politicians, moralists, and other people concerned with the fairness of taxation ponder and debate this issue endlessly: (1) Should the amount of taxes that people pay be based on their ability to pay? or (2) Should taxes be based on the benefits that

That which angers men most is to be taxed above their neighbors.
—Sir William Petty, *A Treatise of Taxes and Contributions*, 1662

Figure 6   Tax Receipts as a Percentage of GDP in United States and Selected Western European Countries, 1994

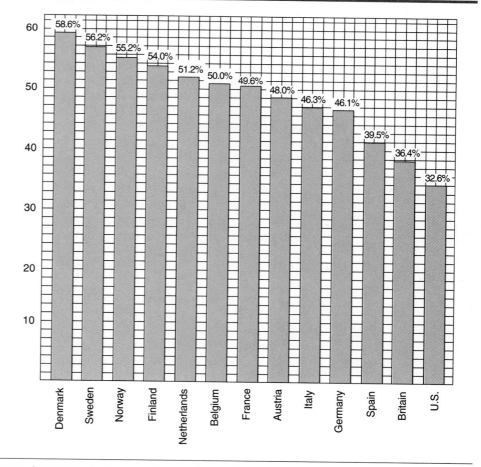

Source: Organization for Economic Cooperation and Development.

Paying for Education with the Property Tax

Every so often a tax comes along that balances ability to pay with benefits received. Such a confluence occurred in the 1950s and 1960s when millions of 20- and 30-something couples with children moved into thousands of new suburban developments.

Few of these couples minded paying property taxes, which were used to pay for their children's schools. To paraphrase Marx and Engels's communist credo, "from each according to his ability, to each according to his needs," from each according to his property tax assess-ment, to each according to the number of his school-age children.

By the 1980s these children had all grown up and moved away, but their parents, now in retirement, were still paying high property taxes. And they began asking what they were getting in return for these taxes: "We're paying taxes to educate other people's children. Let them pay for it. We've already paid for ours. Now let somebody else pay for theirs."

It is generally allowed by all, that men should contribute to the publick charge but according to the share and interest they have in the public peace; that is, according to their estates or riches.

—Sir William Petty, *A Treatise of Taxes and Contributions*, 1662

people receive? Not surprisingly, the ability-to-pay and the benefits-received principles were quickly discovered.

If taxes were based solely on ability to pay, rich people would pay much higher pro-portions of their incomes to the Internal Revenue Service than middle-class people, who, in turn, would be paying a much higher proportion of their incomes than poor people. Is this fair? Yes—if we are concerned only with people's incomes.

But what if some people receive more benefits from the proceeds of these tax dollars than other people? If my house caught fire, I would receive the benefits of the fire depart-ment's services, whereas all my neighbors would not (unless, of course, the fire depart-ment, by putting out the fire in my house, prevented it from spreading to my neighbors' houses). Even more to the point, the family receiving food stamps or welfare payments is receiving greater benefits from the government than those who receive nothing.

Quite clearly, then, some people receive more benefits from the government than others. If we were to apply the benefits-received principle strictly, we would obtain some rather absurd results. We would take away in tax payments the food stamps or welfare payments that a poor family received. Would *this* make sense? And if you had the misfor-tune of a fire starting in your house, it might pay not to call the fire department; your in-surance would probably cover most of your losses, while the fire department might charge you thousands of dollars for its services. And if your neighbors also opted to col-lect on *their* insurance policies as the fire spread, we'd end up with very few houses in your town—all because of the benefits-received principle.

Still another problem with the benefits-received principle is that we are not always clear about the value of the benefits we are receiving. Take, for instance, the so-called nu-clear umbrella that the Department of Defense was kind enough to install several miles above our country. Even though our military leaders tell us that the Russians can easily get several thousand missiles through this umbrella, we are still paying more than $1,000 per capita every year for this protection. Talk about protection money!

Police protection is another case in point. How do we *know* when we are being pro-tected? Does a masked man on a white horse perform some heroic act and then, just to make sure we get the message, leave behind a silver bullet? When a police patrol car drives by, this action may well avert a mugging, but does the potential muggee realize that he has just been saved?

So what we're left with are two undeniably noble principles that are not easily ap-plied. The federal personal income tax is an attempt to apply the ability-to-pay principle, as it is fairly progressive. Local sewer taxes are based on water usage; they are, therefore, an application of the benefits-received principle. Another such application is the federal and state tax on gasoline, which is geared to the number of miles we drive on public roads. And, of course, all the highway and bridge tolls we pay are also based on the benefits-received principle. (See the box "Paying for Education with the Property Tax" for a discussion of education and taxes.)

We cannot, however, devise a tax based on both principles because they appear to be mutually exclusive. Unless we have a society in which everyone earns the same income and receives the same government benefits, we will have to compromise by basing some taxes on individuals' ability to pay and others on the benefits they receive.

The Economic Role of Government

This chapter has talked a lot about taxes and government spending. In short, the government giveth and the government taketh away.

One fact that should be readily apparent is that the federal government and, to a lesser degree, state and local governments have a tremendous impact on the economy. This analysis, however, will be confined to the federal government. Although there is a great deal of overlap, we are going to consider, sequentially, four specific economic functions of government: provision of public goods and services, redistribution of income, stabilization, and economic regulation. We covered some of these functions back in Chapter 4, but now we'll talk about them in greater detail

(1) Provision of Public Goods and Services

Near the beginning of the chapter, I enumerated the range of goods and services provided by our federal, state, and local governments. Private enterprise would supply few of these because they are not profitable. Back in the 1950s, most of the country was served by private intercity bus lines. In New Jersey, when these companies began losing money, the state had to subsidize them just to keep the buses running. Finally, more than 20 years ago the state was forced to take over all the remaining private bus lines. Other states and regions were also forced to form public transportation authorities, while the federal government formed Amtrak to take over the national rail lines. Add to these all the other government operations and you're talking about some $1.5 trillion of public goods and services.

(2) Redistribution of Income

Does the government take from the rich and give to the poor—or is it the other way around?

The government is sometimes seen as a modern-day Robin Hood, redistributing money from rich taxpayers to poor welfare recipients, or from huge corporations to unemployment benefit recipients. Food stamps, Medicaid, and disability payments are all programs aimed mainly at the needy, while the relatively well-to-do taxpayer foots the bill.

Some would dissent from this view by arguing that there is also welfare for the rich, whether in the form of subsidies to corporate farmers and shipbuilders; tax breaks for defense contractors, oil companies, and other large corporations; or huge government contracts for missile systems.

While one may well question whether the government takes from the rich and gives to the poor or vice versa, as former President Richard Nixon was fond of saying, "Let me make one thing perfectly clear": the government does redistribute hundreds of billions of dollars every year. We now have a federal budget of some $1,700 billion. In effect, then, the government taxes about $1,700 billion a year, spends less than half of it, and gives the rest of it away in the form of transfer payments.

What is the economic impact of all this churning? The largest expenditure, Social Security, redistributes money from those currently working to those who have retired. The next largest expenditure, defense, provides contractors and subcontractors with hundreds of billions of dollars for building all those tanks, planes, guns, and missiles. But perhaps the most important economic impact of all this spending is the stabilization function, which we shall consider next.

(3) Stabilization

It is the aim of good government to stimulate production, of bad government to encourage consumption.

—Jean-Baptiste Say

Two basic goals of the federal government are stable prices and low unemployment. Stated somewhat differently, the goals may be seen as a fairly high rate of economic growth (which would hold the rate of unemployment to a minimum) with no inflation.

How the government might go about attaining these goals is the subject of Chapters 10 through 16. But at this time we can already gauge some of the economic impact of the federal budget and how that budget might affect the stability of our economy.

The $1,800 billion that the federal government now dispenses annually puts a floor under our economy's purchasing power. During the early stages of the Great Depression, the federal government was only a minor economic player. The total federal budget was less than 5 percent of GDP. Now it's over 20 percent. Thus, no matter how bad things get, at least the government will provide a floor under total spending.

(4) Economic Regulation

Another important function of government is to provide the economic rules of the game and, somewhat more broadly, the social and political context in which the economy operates. Some of these rules are easily understood: the fostering of competition among business firms, environmental protection laws, child labor laws, the setting of a minimum hourly wage rate, consumer protection laws, and a court system to adjudicate disputes and punish offenders. Beyond these, the government helps provide the social and political framework within which individuals and business firms are able to function smoothly.

In Chapter 4 we talked about the role of competition and the price mechanism in our economic system. A competitive system will function only as long as there is competition. If there are only a handful of firms in several industries, there is no competition. The government's job is to make sure this doesn't happen.

Within our political and social framework, the government must also allow individuals and business firms to operate with the maximum degree of freedom. There are those who consider the current level of government regulation blatant interference with their economic freedom.

Does that freedom imply the right to pollute the environment or to monopolize an industry by driving competitors out of business? Perhaps Justice Oliver Wendell Holmes put it best when he noted that a person's freedom to swing his fist extended only as far as his neighbor's nose. Unfortunately, in the economic environment, there is little agreement as to how far economic freedom may be extended without interfering with society as a whole or the economic rights of specific individuals or business firms.

Conclusion

Until the early 1930s, just before the advent of President Roosevelt's New Deal, the federal government more or less followed the role prescribed by Adam Smith. Although Smith never would have approved of high protective tariffs, land subsidies to railroads, and possibly not even the antitrust legislation and trust-busting of the 1890–1915 period, until the 1930s the basic economic policy of the government could well have been described as laissez-faire.[7]

Big government, like rock 'n' roll, is here to stay.

In 1980 Ronald Reagan campaigned for the presidency by promising to "get the government off the backs of the American people." While he did attain a certain measure of success by cutting back some government spending programs, lowering income tax rates, and fostering a less rigorous approach to government regulation, it is obvious that big government is here to stay. An open question, though, is just how big big government will be.

Adam Smith's dos and don'ts

Adam Smith, in his monumental *The Wealth of Nations,* published in 1776, summed up the dos and don'ts of economic endeavor: "Every man, as long as he does not violate the laws of justice, is left perfectly free to pursue his own interest his own way, and to bring both his industry and capital into competition with those of any other man, or order of men."[8]

---

[7]This is a French expression that means "to leave alone" or "hands off." In this context, a laissez-faire policy means that the government keeps its hands off business, allowing it to operate without interference.

[8]Adam Smith, *The Wealth of Nations* (London: Methuen, 1950), p. 208.

Smith went on to define the economic role of government:

> According to the system of natural liberty, the sovereign has only three duties to attend to; three duties of great importance, indeed, but plain and intelligible to common understandings: first, the duty of protecting the society from the violence and invasion of other independent societies; secondly, the duty of protecting, as far as possible, every member of the society from the injustice or oppression of every other member of it, or the duty of establishing an exact administration of justice; and, thirdly, the duty of erecting and maintaining certain public works and certain public institutions, which it can never be for the interest of any individual, or small number of individuals, to erect and maintain; because the profit could never repay the expense to any individual or small number of individuals, though it may frequently do much more than repay it to a great society.[9]

If we were to take Adam Smith's description of the government's economic role as our starting point, let's see how far it might be expanded. Should the government try to curb air and water pollution? What about prohibiting the dumping of toxic waste or regulating the disposal of nuclear waste?

In the 1992 presidential election, President George Bush tried to frame the issue of environmental protection as the balancing of two opposing forces—protecting jobs or protecting the spotted owl. Vice presidential candidate Albert Gore (whom Bush nicknamed "ozone man") countered that environmental protection actually generated a net gain of jobs. But the underlying issue was how far we want the federal government to go in protecting our environment.

How much should the government be involved in helping the homeless and the 36 million Americans officially classified as poor?[10] And what more should be done about crime and drugs? Other problems—many of which were also raised in the 1992 presidential election—include our failing educational system, our inefficient and extremely expensive health care system, our crumbling infrastructure of highways and bridges, our shrinking manufacturing base, the AIDS epidemic, our low rate of economic growth, and our shaky financial system.[11] As this century winds down, our government will become increasingly involved in dealing with these problems. The government's economic role has grown tremendously these last six decades, and it will continue to grow in coming years. Indeed, when your children take macroeconomics, the author of their textbook may look back at the late 1990s as a period when the economic role of government was still relatively small.

Questions for Further Thought and Discussion

1. If a political candidate said that if she were elected to Congress, she would work toward cutting federal government spending by one-third over the next four years, would she stand much chance of fulfilling her promise? Why not?
2. When you retire, will you be able to collect Social Security benefits? Give the reasons why you might not be able to collect.
3. Discuss the pros and cons of having a high cigarette excise tax.
4. Make up a numerical example to show why the Social Security tax is regressive.
5. If Adam Smith were alive today, to what degree would he approve of the present economic role of the American government?

---

[9]Ibid., pp. 208–9.

[10]Poverty is the subject of a later chapter.

[11]These problems will come up in subsequent chapters. Our financial system is the subject of Chapters 12 and 13.

WORKBOOK FOR CHAPTER 7

Name _____ Date _____

Multiple-Choice Questions

Circle the letter that corresponds to the best answer.

1. The role of government grew most rapidly during the period
   a. 1920–1933   b. 1933–1945   c. 1945–1960
   d. 1960–1975

2. The seeds of the expansion of the federal government's economic role were sown during the administration of
   a. Franklin Roosevelt   b. Dwight Eisenhower
   c. Richard Nixon   d. Ronald Reagan

3. The federal government spends about $_____ a year.
   a. $1,800 million   b. $1,800 billion
   c. $1,800 trillion   d. $1,800 quadrillion

4. The key agency in the preparation of the president's budget is
   a. the Treasury   b. the OMB   c. the Comptroller of the Currency   d. the Department of Defense

5. The federal government's fiscal year begins on
   a. January 1   b. July 1   c. October 1
   d. November 1

6. Transfer payments to individuals are _____ percent of the federal budget.
   a. 25   b. 50   c. 65   d. 85

7. Which federal spending program grew the fastest in the 1980s?
   a. defense   b. interest on the national debt
   c. aid to mass transit   d. aid to education

8. Compared to federal spending, state and local spending is
   a. twice as large   b. about the same   c. half as large   d. one-quarter as large

9. The largest federal government purchase of final goods and services is
   a. Social Security   b. defense   c. interest on the national debt   d. foreign aid

10. If one person earns $10,000 and another person earns $100,000 a year, they both will pay Social Security tax
    a. at the same average tax rate   b. but the poorer person will pay at a higher average tax rate   c. but the richer person will pay at a higher average tax rate
    d. but it is impossible to tell what their average tax rates are

11. The least regressive tax listed here is the
    a. Social Security tax   b. federal personal income tax   c. federal excise tax   d. state sales tax

12. Each of the following is a direct tax except the _____ tax.
    a. Social Security   b. federal personal income
    c. corporate income   d. federal excise

13. Which is true?
    a. The rich are hurt more than the poor by regressive taxes.   b. The poor are hurt more than the rich by progressive taxes.   c. The federal personal income tax is a regressive tax.   d. None of these statements is true.

14. A tax with an average tax rate of 20 percent for the rich and 2 percent for the middle class is
    a. progressive   b. regressive   c. proportional
    d. none of these

15. In 1998 a person earning $200,000 paid Social Security tax on
    a. none of her income   b. all of her income
    c. nearly all of her income   d. less than half of her income

16. You can legally cut down on how much income tax you pay by means of
    a. tax avoidance   b. tax evasion   c. both tax evasion and tax avoidance   d. neither tax evasion nor tax avoidance

17. In 1998 a person making $5 million in interest on municipal bonds was taxed on this income at an average tax rate of
    a. 39.6 percent   b. 31 percent   c. 28 percent   d. 0 percent

18. The most important source of federal tax revenue is the
    a. personal income tax   b. corporate income tax   c. federal excise tax   d. payroll tax

19. Until 1981 the maximum marginal tax rate on the federal income tax was
    a. 70 percent   b. 50 percent   c. 40 percent   d. 33 percent

20. Today for every retired person there is (are) _____ person(s) in the labor force.
    a. one   b. two   c. three   d. four

21. In 1998 the maximum corporate income tax rate was _____ percent.
    a. 50   b. 46   c. 40   d. 35

22. Each of the following is subject to a federal excise tax except
    a. phone calls   b. gasoline   c. cigarettes   d. paper products

23. Taxes (including federal, state, and local) are about _____ of our GDP.
    a. 10 percent   b. 25 percent   c. 30 percent   d. 45 percent

24. The most important source of state tax revenue is the _____ tax.
    a. property   b. income   c. excise   d. sales

25. The most important source of local tax revenue is the _____ tax.
    a. property   b. income   c. excise   d. sales

26. Compared with the citizens of other industrial countries, Americans are
    a. much more heavily taxed   b. somewhat more heavily taxed   c. taxed at about the same rate   d. not as heavily taxed

27. As a redistributor of income, the federal government plays
    a. no role   b. a very minor role   c. a major role   d. a completely dominating role

28. Adam Smith endorsed each of the following roles of government except
    a. providing for defense   b. establishing a system of justice   c. erecting a limited number of public works   d. guaranteeing a job to every person ready, willing, and able to work

29. An example of a public good is
    a. a Honda Accord   b. a movie theater   c. a Boeing 747   d. a lighthouse

30. Public goods are usually
    a. very low-priced   b. efficiently produced   c. indivisible   d. sold by private firms

31. Which statement is true?
    a. Americans pay the highest taxes in the world.
    b. Public goods are provided by private enterprise.
    c. The economic role of the federal government has shrunk over the last 30 years.   d. In 1990 and in 1993 taxes for the rich were increased substantially.

32. A person in which one of these occupations is least likely to cheat on his taxes?
    a. auto dealer   b. restaurateur   c. clothing store operator   d. postal clerk

33. Statement 1: Americans pay a higher percentage of their income in taxes than most Western Europeans but also receive much greater benefits from the government. Statement 2: Public education is traditionally funded largely by local property taxes.
    a. Statement 1 is true and statement 2 is false.
    b. Statement 2 is true and statement 1 is false.
    c. Both statements are true.   d. Both statements are false.

34. Gasoline taxes in the United States are _____ than they are in other leading industrial nations.
    a. much higher   b. a little higher   c. a little lower   d. much lower

35. Statement 1: Payroll taxes and Social Security taxes are identical. Statement 2: The Social Security tax was 6.2 percent of your earnings on a wage base of $68,400 in 1998.

   a.   Statement 1 is true and statement 2 is false.

   b.   Statement 2 is true and statement 1 is false.

   c.   Both statements are true.   **d.**   Both statements are false.

36. Statement 1: The Medicare tax is 1.45 percent on a wage base of $68,400. Statement 2: The Medicare tax is slightly less regressive than the Social Security tax.

   a.   Statement 1 is true and statement 2 is false.

   b.   Statement 2 is true and statement 1 is false.

   c.   Both statements are true.   **d.**   Both statements are false.

37. Statement 1: The wage base for the Social Security tax is raised each year to keep pace with inflation. Statement 2: About one out of every three taxpayers pays more in payroll taxes than in personal income taxes.

   a.   Statement 1 is true and statement 2 is false.

   b.   Statement 2 is true and statement 1 is false.

   c.   Both statements are true.   **d.**   Both statements are false.

Fill-In Questions

1. The economic role of the federal government began to get very large in the year _____.

2. Name basic economic influences of the federal government: (1) _____; (2)_____; and (3) _____.

3. Fiscal year 1993 began on _____ _____(fill in month, day, and year).

4. The federal government agency that plays the central role in the preparation of the president's budget is _____ _____.

5. In 1998 we spent about $ _____ on defense.

6. Interest on the federal debt in 1998 was about _____ _____.

7. In 1998 the federal government spent about $ _____ _____.

8. Total government spending in 1998 (including federal, state, and local) came to $ _____.

9. The largest federal government transfer payment is _____.

10. The average tax rate is found by dividing _____ by _____.

11. Progressive taxes place the greatest burden on the _____.

12. Examples of regressive taxes include _____ _____ and _____.

13. In 1998 the Social Security tax rate was _____ percent.

14. The most important source of federal tax revenue is the _____ tax.

15. The Economic Recovery Act of 1981 was better known as the _____.

16. The maximum marginal tax rate today is _____ percent.

17. Most Americans are taxed at marginal rates of _____ percent and _____ percent.

18. If you earned $10,000 in 1998, how much would the federal government collect in payroll tax? $_____ _____.

19. There is currently a federal excise tax on

    (1) _____ ; (2) _____ ;

    (3) _____ ; (4) _____ ;

    and (5) _____ .

20. The state and local governments have been faced with a

    dilemma since World War II. They have been expected to

    _____ but they have had difficulty

    _____ .

21. The ability-to-pay principle of taxation states that

    _____ .

22. The benefits-received principle of taxation states that

    _____ .

23. The federal government has several economic roles.

    Name three: (1) _____ ;

    (2) _____ ; and (3) _____ .

24. If Adam Smith were alive today, he would say that our

    government is too _____ .

Problems

1. If a person earned $80,000 in 1998, how much Social Se-curity tax did he pay?

2. If a person earned $10,000 in 1998, how much Social Se-curity tax did she pay?

3. If you earned $20,000 and paid $1,000 in federal income tax, how much was your average tax rate?

4. If you had a marginal tax rate of 28 percent and earned an extra $10,000, how much tax would you pay?

5. If you earned an extra $1,000 and paid $150 in taxes on that income, how much would your marginal tax rate be?

6. If you were in the lowest personal income tax bracket, how much personal income tax would you have to pay on $5,000 of taxable income?

7. Suppose that Ross Perot's income were to increase by $100 million. How much more personal income tax would he have to pay?

8. If your taxable income rose from $30,000 to $40,000 and your tax bill rose from $4,500 to $7,000, how much is your marginal tax rate?

9. If you pay $5,000 on a taxable income of $40,000, how much is your average tax rate?

10. The Speedy Delivery Service paid its 10 drivers $30,000 each. How much did the company owe in payroll tax?

11. If you earned $100,000, how much would you pay in So-cial Security tax and in Medicare tax?

12. Prove that a married person with three dependents (in-cluding himself) and an income of $12,000 pays more in Social Security tax than in federal income tax.

8

Gross Domestic Product

When was the last time someone said to you, "Mine is bigger than yours?" My *what* is bigger than your *what?* My GDP is bigger than your GDP? Well, it just so happens that our country's GDP is bigger than everyone else's. Even Japan's. Gross domestic product, or GDP, measures a country's output over a year—which means the United States produces more goods and services every year than any other nation in the world.

Chapter Objectives

When you have finished this chapter, you will know the answers to these questions:

■ How do we graph the $C + I + G + X_n$ line?

■ What is GDP?

■ How is GDP measured?

■ What are the national income accounts?

■ What is the difference between GDP and real GDP?

■ How does our GDP compare to those of other nations?

■ How is per capita GDP calculated?

■ What are the shortcomings of GDP as a measure of national economic well-being?

What Is Gross Domestic Product?

What is GDP? *It is the nation's expenditure on all the final goods and services produced during the year at market prices.* For example, if we spent $10,000 per car on 7 million American cars, that $70 billion would go into GDP. We'd add in the 10 billion Big Macs at $1.80 for another $18 billion and the 1.6 million new homes at $80,000 each for $128 billion. Then, for good measure, we'd add the 5 billion visits to doctors' offices at $50 apiece for $250 billion and the 16 billion nightclub admissions at $10 each for $160 billion. Add everything up and we'd get something a bit more than $8 trillion in 1997.

Definition of GDP

Did you notice the word *final* in the definition of GDP? We include only those goods and services that consumers, businesses, and governments buy for their own use. So when you buy a telephone answering machine or you get your hair cut, or if the government repaves a highway, we count those goods and services in GDP. But if Liz Claiborne buys 10,000 yards of fabric to make dresses, that purchase is not recorded in GDP. When the dresses are sold, they are then counted in GDP.

A Summing Up: $C + I + G + X_n$

Subtract imports from exports to get net exports.

The last three chapters examined the three main components of GDP: C, or consumption; I, or investment; and G, or government spending. One more variable goes into GDP: net exports. *Net exports = Exports – Imports.* If we subtract all the money the United States spends on foreign goods and services from what foreigners spend on U.S. goods and services, we get net exports. This number represents the difference between what we sell to foreigners and what they sell to us.

Until recently most economists more or less ignored this last item in the GDP equation. The figure for net exports, while positive, was usually less than 1 percent of GDP. More significantly, since the turn of the century net exports was a positive figure every year until 1971.

For the first seven decades of the 20th century, we sold more to foreigners every single year than they sold to us. But in the early 1970s our balance of trade turned negative, with net exports reaching a low of −$142 billion in 1987. Why did net exports turn negative in the early 1970s, and what accounts for the fluctuations in the negative trade balance since then? You'll find out when you reach the next-to-last chapter, "International Trade."

Let's get back to our GDP equation:

$$GDP = C + I + G + X_n$$

Substituting 1994 data into this equation, we get:

$$GDP = 5,489 + 1,238 + 1,454 - 97$$

$$GDP = 8,083$$

In 1997 we produced over $8 trillion worth of final goods and services (see Table 1). Over two-thirds were consumer goods and services, followed in size by government purchases, investment spending, and, finally, net exports, which were negative. Now we'll draw a few graphs and then move on to how GDP is measured.

Table 1 offers a detailed compilation of the components of GDP in 1997. As you can see, C was the largest, followed by G, I, and then X_n, which was negative.

$GDP = C + I + G + X_n$

Table 1   The Components of GDP, 1997 (in $ billions)*

Consumption:		
Durable goods	659	
Nondurable goods	1,593	
Services	3,237	
C	5,489	5,489
Investment:		
Plant and equipment	845	
Residential housing	328	
Inventory change	65	
I	1,238	1,238
Government purchases:		
Federal	525	
State and local	929	
G	1,454	1,454
Net exports:		
Exports	959	
− Imports	− 1,056	
X_n	− 97	− 97
GDP		8,083

*Figures may not add up due to rounding.

Source: *Economic Report of the President,* 1998.

For our final trick, we're going to graph the $C + I + G + X_n$ line. We'll take as our starting point the graph of the $C + I + G$ line, shown in Figure 1. Now keep in mind that X_n has been negative since the early 1970s and will probably continue to be negative for at least the rest of this century.[1]

Draw a $C + I + G + X_n$ line in Figure 1. You might as well make it parallel to the $C + I + G$ line. Are you done? OK, let's see what your line looks like. I hope it looks a lot like *my* line in Figure 2. It doesn't have to be as close to the $C + I + G$ line, and it doesn't have to be exactly parallel, but your $C + I + G + X_n$ line should lie *below* the $C + I + G$ line.

---

[1]The next-to-last chapter in this book is devoted to the topic of foreign trade. I deal there with the whys and wherefores of the country's negative balance of trade at much greater length.

Why do we draw the C + I + G + X$_n$ line *below* the C + I + G line? Because X$_n$ is a negative number, so the sum of C + I + G + X$_n$ is *less* than the sum of C + I + G.

This graph completes an odyssey we began back in Chapter 5 when we graphed the C line, and continued with the C + I line in Chapter 6, and the C + I + G line in Chapter 7. I'll give you a chance to catch your breath in this chapter and the next, but in Chapter 10 the graph of the C + I + G + X$_n$ line returns.

Figure 1   Measuring GDP

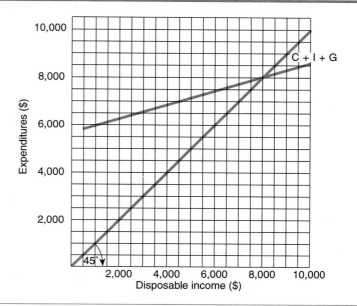

Figure 2   Measuring GDP (solution)

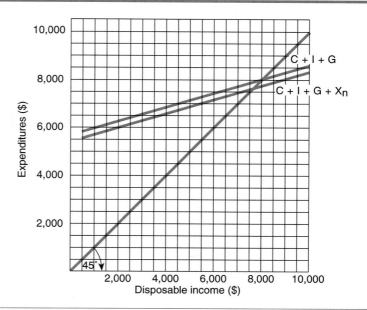

How GDP Is Measured

Two ways to measure GDP are the flow-of-income approach and the expenditures approach.

There are two basic ways of measuring GDP: the flow-of-income approach and the expenditures approach (which happens to be my favorite). Both are illustrated in Figure 3.

Both approaches are parts of the national income accounts, a series of numbers that only an economist could love. Figure 3 has the flow of income (resources and resource payments) on the top and the expenditures flow (consumer goods and services and consumer expenditures) on the bottom.

Unfortunately, Figure 3 is a gross simplification (no pun intended) of the way our economy works. We've left out business investment, savings, government purchases and transfer payments, and taxes, as well as imports and exports. These will be added to our model of the economy in the next three chapters.

By the way, haven't you seen Figure 3 someplace before, or do you use that line on all the graphs you meet? Well, it turns out you did see virtually the same flowchart a few chapters ago. Check out Figure 3 in Chapter 4 and you'll see for yourself.

Before we go any further, we need to clarify one point. Until December 1991, when the U.S. Department of Commerce started publishing gross domestic product data instead of gross national product data, virtually all of our national output was expressed in terms of gross national product, or GNP. What's the difference between GNP and GDP? If you're curious, this question is answered in the box "The Switch from GNP to GDP."

The Expenditures Approach

This approach will be used in the next few chapters. People buy consumer goods from business firms and pay for them. Notice that we have a circular flow of expenditures and income by connecting the top and bottom loops of Figure 3. People receive incomes from business firms for their land, labor, and capital. This money flows right back to the firms in exchange for consumer goods and services. Hence the money keeps flowing around and around as more goods are produced and paid for.

We've excluded business investment expenditures and government expenditures until now. If we included them with consumer expenditures, they would add up to GDP: *Consumer expenditures + Investment expenditures + Government expenditures = GDP.* We'll be adding a smaller sector, net exports, in a minute.

The big three spenders of GDP

GDP, then, represents spending by three major groups, the largest of which is consumers, who spend more than two out of every three dollars of GDP. *Consumption* spending is designated by the letter C.

Business firms spend hundreds of billions of dollars on plant, equipment, and inventory. We call this sector *investment* and use the letter I to represent it.

Next, if we add up all the spending on goods and services by the federal, state, and local governments, we have government expenditures, which is represented by the letter G.

Figure 3   The Circular Flow

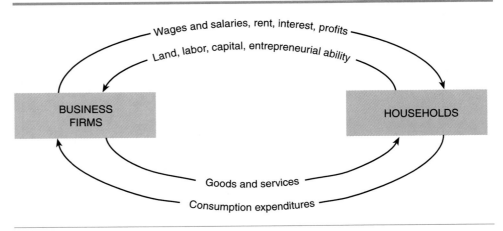

ADVANCED WORK

The Switch from GNP to GDP

Generations of economics students were steeped in tales of gross national product, how it was measured, and why it was or wasn't a wonderful way of evaluating our nation's economic performance. Well, it was fun while it lasted, but in 1991, the great minds that head up the Bureau of Economic Analysis of the U.S. Department of Commerce decided that gross domestic product, or GDP, a term that had been kicking around for decades, more accurately measured the nation's output than did GNP.

Exactly what is the difference between GDP and GNP? GDP measures the value of all the final goods and services produced *within* the borders of the United States, while GNP measures the output of all Americans, whether the goods and services are produced here or abroad.

A few million foreigners live and work in the United States. What they earn in wages, rent, interest, and profits is counted in our GDP. What was counted in the old GNP—but is not in GDP—was the wages, rent, interest, and profits earned by Americans working abroad.

For instance, the value of cars produced by the Japanese Nissan factory in Smyrna, Tennessee, including its profits, is included in the U.S. GDP. What about the wages earned by Americans employed by Toys R Us in Japan or the profits earned by the Motorola TV factory in Mexico? Sorry, but neither goes into our GDP. If it isn't made in the United States, then it doesn't belong in our GDP.

Using GDP gives us a few advantages over using GNP. GDP corresponds more closely than GNP to many important series of economic data, such as employment and industrial production. It is also more useful for making international comparisons, because most other nations now express their output in terms of GDP.

We'll stick with the definitions of GDP that we started with at the beginning of the chapter. But some prefer this alternate definition: GDP is the value of all goods and services produced within a nation's boundaries.

Finally, we have X_n, or net exports. Although our imports exceed our exports by a relatively small amount (What's a hundred billion or so, compared to a GDP of over $8 trillion?), the sum of our imports and exports is growing much faster than our GDP. Figure 4 shows the relationship of the foreign sector of our economy to our entire economy.

The growing foreign economic sector

Figure 4   Sum of U.S. Imports and Exports as Percentage of GDP, 1970–97

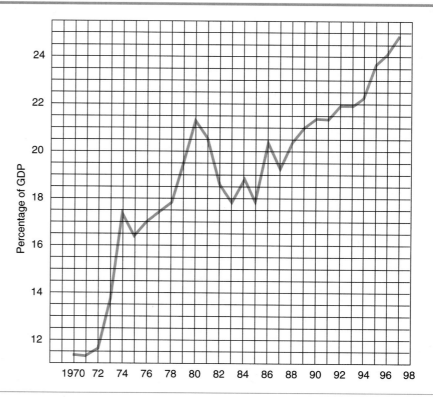

Source: *Economic Report of the President,* 1998.

As you'll observe, the sum of U.S. imports and exports jumped from 11.5 percent of GDP in 1972 to 17.3 percent just two years later. You won't see this in Figure 4, but prior to 1966, imports and exports did not reach 10 percent of GDP. The big jump in 1973–74 was due mainly to skyrocketing oil prices, something we'll talk more about in the next chapter. Another long-term factor was Americans' increasing appetite for Japanese cars and consumer electronics from Japan and other countries in Southeast Asia. Now our foreign trade sector has reached 25 percent of our GDP.

GDP is the nation's expenditure on all the final goods and services produced during the year at market prices.

From time to time we will go back to the definition of GDP: *the nation's expenditure on all the final goods and services produced during the year at market prices.* Only "final" goods and services are counted. These include those goods and services purchased by their ultimate consumers. They are represented by the variables in our equation:

$$GDP = C + I + G + X_n$$

Substituting 1997 data for these variables, we get:

$$8,083 = 5,489 + 1,238 + 1,454 - 97$$

A careful perusal of Figure 5 will disclose three trends. Between the late 1970s and the late 1990s, the consumption percentage share of GDP rose from the low 60s to the high 60s. The government share stayed between 18 and 20 percent. And the investment share fluctuated within a range of 12 to 18 percent.

The upward trend in consumption and the downward trend in investment reinforce what I warned you about in previous chapters. If these trends continue, our economy is headed for big trouble. The only way we can raise our sluggish rate of economic growth is to curb our consumption, save more, and invest more. Unless we can reverse the consumption and investment trends shown in Figure 5, our economy will continue along its path of very slow growth.[2]

[2]Our lagging economic growth is the subject of Chapter 16.

Figure 5   C, I, and G as Percentages of GDP, 1979–97

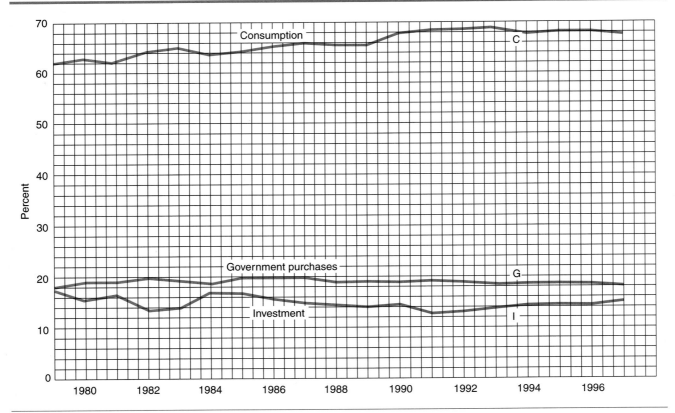

Source: *The Economic Report of the President,* 1998.

The Flow-of-Income Approach

Business firms produce nearly all our goods and services. The firms pay people wages to get them to turn out these goods and services. Those who own the land and buildings used are paid rent, and those who supply the capital are paid interest. Add up all the goods and services produced and you have GDP. Or, alternatively, add up the incomes received by the factors of production (plus a couple of other things we'll be talking about) and you have GDP.

The flow-of-income approach to GDP is shown in the top part of Figure 3. Households provide business firms with resources (land, labor, capital, and entrepreneurial ability) and are paid by business firms in the form of rent, wages and salaries, interest, and profits.

We need to look at the flow of income in more detail than we looked at the expenditures flow because it has more components. Indeed, this approach is so complex, we'll divide it into three parts: national product (Table 2), national income (Figure 6), and personal income (Figure 6).

GDP – Depreciation = NNP

1. National Product   Now we come to the fun part. Many economists are unhappy with the concept of gross domestic product. It's simply too gross. They much prefer net national product (see box "Why NNP Is Better than GDP"). What's the difference? The main difference is depreciation.

Gross domestic product – Depreciation = Net national product

GDP includes, among other things, $845 billion worth of plant and equipment spending (see Table 1). This is money spent on new office buildings, shopping malls, factories, stores, assembly lines, office machines, computers, and a host of other machinery and equipment.

Why are we so anxious to get rid of depreciation? Depreciation represents the buildings and machinery (plant and equipment) that have worn out or become obsolete over the course of the year. Usually these are replaced with new plant and equipment, but this doesn't represent a net gain because the company ends up right where it started. For example, if a firm begins the year with eight machines and replaces three that wore out during the year, it still has eight machines at the end of the year.

Table 2   National Product, 1997 (billions of dollars)

Consumption	$5,489
Investment	1,238
Government spending	1,454
Net exports	– 97
GDP	$8,083
(Plus) Receipts of factor income from rest of world	234
(Less) Payments of factor income to rest of world	– 232
GNP	8,085
(Less) Depreciation	– 868
Net national product	7,217
(Less) Indirect business taxes and subsidies†	– 560*
National income	$6,657†

*Indirect business taxes constitute nearly 90 percent of this figure. Subsidies are very small and positive. Also included are business transfer payments ($30 billion) and a statistical discrepancy (which, in 1997, was $69 billion which we somehow could not account for).

†The figures do not add up exactly because of rounding.

Source: *Economic Report of the President,* 1998.

Figure 6   National Product and Income, 1997

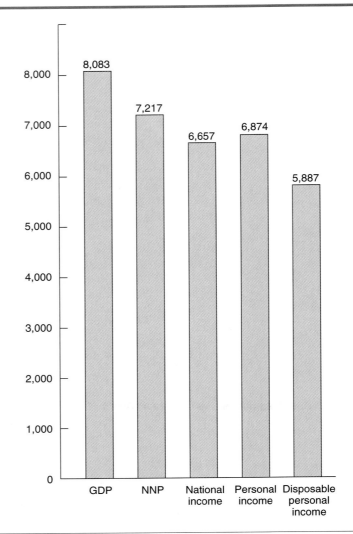

Source: *Economic Report of the President*, 1998.

Similarly, when we measure a nation's GDP, one of the things we are counting is the replacement of plant and equipment, which can lead to some dubious conclusions about a nation's economic well-being. For example, suppose Sweden and Canada each have a GDP of 200, but depreciation in Sweden is 50, while in Canada it is only 30. The NNP of Sweden would be 150 (GDP of 200 – Depreciation of 50); Canada's NNP would be 170 (GDP of 200 – Depreciation of 30). A more elaborate example appears in the box "Why NNP Is Better than GDP."

Are you ready for a big question? All right then, here it comes. What's the difference between gross investment and net investment? *Gross* investment is the total amount we invest in new plant and equipment (as well as new residential housing and additional inventory). *Net* investment is the additional plant and equipment with which we end up by the end of the year. So we have this equation:

Gross investment – Depreciation = Net investment

The *I* in the equation GDP = C + I + G + X_n is *gross* investment. We distinguished between *gross* investment and *net* investment back in Chapter 6.

Let's go over the arithmetic. In Table 2, we have a GDP of $8,083 billion (the sum of C + I + G + X_n). We add net receipts of factor income from the rest of the world (+$2

ADVANCED WORK .... Why NNP Is Better than GDP

Although people commonly use GDP when they talk about national output, most economists prefer NNP. Why? Because it allows for depreciation of plant and equipment. Let's illustrate this with two hypothetical countries in the table below:

North Atlantis		South Atlantis	
GDP	500	GDP	500
– Depreciation	50	– Depreciation	100
NNP*	450	NNP*	400

We see that North Atlantis and South Atlantis had identical GDPs, but that North Atlantis had depreciation of $50 billion while South Atlantis's depreciation was $100 billion.† Consequently, North Atlantis ended up with an NNP of $450 billion, while South Atlantis had an NNP of just $400 billion.

This distinction is important. North and South Atlantis had the same GDP, but North Atlantis's NNP was $50 billion greater than that of South Atlantis. Why? Because South Atlantis had to replace $100 billion of worn-out or obsolete plant and equipment that year, while North Atlantis had to replace just $50 billion of plant and equipment.

In 1930 Babe Ruth held out for a salary of $80,000. A reporter asked him if it would be fair for a baseball player to earn more than Herbert Hoover, the president of the United States. "Why not? I had a better year than he did," the Babe replied. And so, we too may ask, who had a better year, North or South Atlantis? Based on GDP, they did equally well; based on NNP, North Atlantis did better.

South Atlantis had a lower NNP because it had to devote twice as much production to replacing worn-out and obsolete plant and equipment as did North Atlantis. When you are devoting such a large portion of your resources to replacing plant and equipment, these resources can't go toward adding to your stock of plant and equipment or, for that matter, to producing consumer goods and services.

Suppose North Atlantis devoted that extra $50 billion to production of more plant and equipment. It would now have $50 billion worth of additional plant and equipment. Or if it had produced $50 billion worth of consumer goods and services, its citizens would have enjoyed a much higher standard of living.

So who enjoyed a better year? Virtually every economist would tell you that North Atlantis did because it had a higher NNP. Stated differently, it's not as significant to know how much a country grossed as to know how much it netted.

* We are ignoring receipts from and payments of factor income to the rest of the world because they almost cancel each other out.

†Economists use this shorthand way of writing billions (e.g., 50 = $50 billion; 100 = $100 billion).

billion) and subtract depreciation ($868 billion) from GDP to get net national product ($7,217 billion). Are you ready to take up national income? All right then, here it comes.

2. National Income   Now we need to subtract indirect business taxes (mainly general sales taxes and taxes on specific items such as gasoline, liquor, and cigarettes) and subsidies (such as government payments to farmers).

We've talked about indirect taxes (sales taxes and taxes on cigarettes, gasoline, and liquor) and we've also talked about income taxes and Social Security taxes, which are direct taxes. Direct taxes are on *people* and indirect taxes are on *things*. (Direct and indirect taxes were discussed in Chapter 7.)

NNP – Indirect business taxes and subsidies = National income

NNP – Indirect business taxes and subsidies = National income

The big three of national product—GDP, NNP, and national income—are lined up by size in Figure 6 for 1997. For other years, could they be in some other order? Could NNP, for example, be larger than GDP? The answer is no. Since GDP – Depreciation = NNP, the only way for NNP to be larger would be if depreciation were negative.[3]

Our national income was $6,657 billion in 1997. The largest part, by far, was compensation of employees (see Figure 7). This compensation includes wages, salaries, and fringe benefits (such as medical insurance and sick, holiday, and vacation pay). Corporate profits are either paid out as dividends or plowed back into the corporation. Net interest is the total interest income of individuals minus interest paid by consumers to businesses and net interest paid by the government. (No one ever asks you to define net interest on

---

[3] Negative depreciation is a logical absurdity. It would mean that plant and equipment had somehow become *less* obsolete and *less* worn out during the year. Negative depreciation is actually appreciation.

Figure 7   Distribution of National Income, 1997

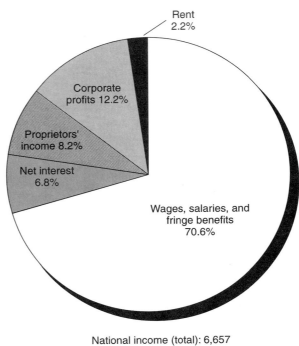

National income (total): 6,657

Source: *Economic Report of the President,* 1998.

an economics exam.) Rental income is the rent received by individuals (rent received by businesses is counted elsewhere). And finally, we have the fifth part of national income: proprietors' income. This includes the total incomes of all unincorporated businesses (i.e., rent, interest, profits, and compensation for labor).[4]

National income, then, is the sum of compensation to employees, corporate profits, net interest, rental income, and proprietors' income. These are all resource payments for the use of land, labor, capital, and entrepreneurial ability.

So far we've dealt with the national product and national income. OK, two down, one to go.

3. Personal Income   Now we'll work our way down to personal income and disposable personal income. Starting with national income, we subtract earnings not received (almost all Social Security taxes and corporate profits that were not paid out as dividends), add receipts not earned (mainly Social Security benefits and other government transfer payments, and interest income), and we get personal income, which was $6,874 billion in 1997.

You probably noticed in Figure 6 that personal income is larger than national income. Why? Because receipts not earned were larger than earnings not received. But personal income is really just what we earn on paper, so to speak. The bottom line is disposable personal income, because it's the money that's ours to keep.

Starting with personal income, we need to subtract personal taxes (chiefly personal income taxes) and a few relatively minor items, such as traffic tickets and charges for government services. Disposable personal income gets its name because it is ours to dispose of, to spend and save as we see fit. In 1997 it came to $5,887 billion.

Do you need to know all of this stuff? Will you ever get to use it? The answer to both questions is a qualified no. GDP you definitely need to know (see the box "Reviewing the Two Approaches to GDP"). The other terms will crop up from time to time over the next eight chapters.

---

[4] These are proprietorships and partnerships, which were discussed early in Chapter 6.

Reviewing the Two Approaches to GDP

First we'll go over the flow-of-income approach. If wages and salaries are $4.7 trillion, rent is $.1 trillion, interest is $.7 trillion, profits are $.5 trillion, indirect business taxes are $.8 trillion, and depreciation is $.6 trillion, find national income, NNP, and GDP:

Solution:

Wages and salaries	$4.7 trillion
Rent	.1
Interest	.7
Profits	.5
National income	6.0
+ Indirect business tax	.8
NNP	6.8
+ Depreciation	.6
GDP	7.4

Now we'll do a problem that starts off with GDP and works its way down to national income. Given: GDP = 6,700, Indirect business taxes = 500, Depreciation = 700, and Direct taxes = 500. Find NNP and national income.

Solution:

GDP	6,700
– Depreciation	– 700
NNP	6,000
– Indirect taxes	– 500
National income	5,500

I hope you didn't try to use direct taxes. Clearly, they don't belong in our calculations. Just because they're listed doesn't mean we should use them. Suppose you were baking a cake and you had placed your flour, sugar, butter, and other ingredients on a counter. If someone left out a can of turpentine there, would you pour it into your mixing bowl? I hope not, especially if you were planning to offer me a slice of that cake.

Well, then, why did I put direct taxes into the last problem? Because I wanted to see what you would do with it. Remember, just because something is there doesn't mean we have to use it.

Moving right along, let's work out a problem using the expenditures approach to GDP. Given: C = 4,100, I = 900, G = 1,200, Imports = 750, Exports = 650. Find GDP:

Solution: First we'll find net exports:

$$X_n = \text{Exports} - \text{Imports}$$

$$X_n = 650 - 750$$

$$X_n = -100$$

Next we'll write down our equation:

$$\text{GDP} = C + I + G + X_n$$

Then we substitute numbers for the letters:

$$\text{GDP} = 4,100 + 900 + 1,200 - 100$$

And finally, we solve:

$$\text{GDP} = 6,200 - 100$$

$$\text{GDP} = 6,100$$

We'll follow this general procedure for problem-solving throughout the book: (1) Write down the equation, (2) substitute, and (3) solve.

Two Things to Avoid When Compiling GDP

Two mistakes are commonly made when GDP is compiled. First we'll talk about multiple counting, that is, counting a particular good at each stage of production. Then we'll look at the inclusion of transfer payments. To compile GDP correctly, we count each good or service only once, and we don't count transfer payments as part of GDP.

Multiple Counting

We need to avoid multiple counting when we compile GDP. Only expenditures on final products—what consumers, businesses, and government units buy for their own use—belong in GDP. This is clearly illustrated by the journey wheat makes from the farm to the supermarket.

The farmer gets about 2 cents for the wheat that goes into a loaf of bread. This wheat is ground into flour at a mill and is now worth, say, 4 cents. When it is placed in 100-pound packages, it is worth 5 cents, and when it is shipped to a bakery, it is worth 10 cents. Baked bread is worth 20 cents, packaged baked bread is worth 23 cents, and bread delivered to the supermarket is worth 35 cents. The supermarket sells it for 89 cents.

How much of this goes into GDP? Do we add up the 2 cents, 4 cents, 5 cents, 10 cents, 20 cents, 23 cents, 35 cents, and 89 cents? No! That would be multiple counting. We count only what is spent on a final good, 89 cents, which is paid by the consumer. Of this entire process, only 89 cents goes into GDP.

GDP counts only what we spend on final goods and services.

GDP, then, counts only what we spend on final goods and services—not those of an intermediate nature. We are not interested in the money spent on wheat or flour, but only that which the buyer of the final product, bread, spends at the supermarket. If we count intermediate goods, we will greatly inflate GDP by counting the same goods and services over and over again.

Value-added approach to measuring GDP

An alternate way of measuring GDP is the value-added approach.[5] The farmer grows 2 cents' worth of wheat, to which the flour mill adds 2 cents by grinding the wheat into flour and 1 cent by packaging it. The shipper adds 5 cents by getting that flour to the bakery. The baker adds 10 cents by baking the flour into bread and 3 cents more by packaging it. The person who delivers the bread to the supermarket adds another 12 cents to the value of the bread, and finally, the supermarket, by providing a convenient location for the sale of the bread, adds 54 cents. If you sum the value added by each stage—2 cents + 2 cents + 1 cent + 5 cents + 10 cents + 3 cents + 12 cents + 54 cents—you should get 89 cents. If you didn't, you better get a new battery for your calculator. Or if you got a different answer in your head, perhaps your own battery is beginning to run down.

Just as we don't include intermediate goods in GDP, we don't count used goods either. If you buy a used car, a 10-year-old house, or virtually anything from a flea market, your purchase does not go into GDP. Remember, we count only final goods and services that were purchased in the current year.

However, anything done this year to make a used product salable is counted (e.g., a paint job for a used car). What if you add a room to your house? If you do it yourself, then the cost of materials will be included in GDP. If you pay someone to build the addition, then we'll include the full cost of the job.

Treatment of Transfer Payments

At first glance, transfer payments appear to belong in GDP. When the government issues a Social Security or unemployment insurance check, isn't this a form of government spending? Shouldn't it be part of G, like defense spending or the salaries paid to government employees?

GDP includes only payments for goods and services produced this year. A person receiving a Social Security check is not being reimbursed for producing a good or service this year. But a government clerk or a defense contractor *is* providing a good or service this year and their pay would therefore be included under government purchases, designated by the letter G.

Transfer payments don't go directly into GDP.

Because Social Security, public assistance, Medicare, Medicaid, and other government transfer payments—which now make up more than half of the federal budget—are not payments for currently produced goods and services, they are not included in GDP. However, those who receive these payments will spend nearly all of that money, so, ultimately, the payments will go toward GDP in the form of consumer spending. Note that

---

[5] The value-added approach to measuring GDP is rarely used. It amounts to summing the values added by all firms in the economy, plus any value added by the government.

consumer spending does involve the purchase of final goods and services produced in the current year.

Financial transactions don't go into GDP.

Something else not counted in GDP is financial transactions. The purchase of corporate stocks and bonds does not add anything to GDP. Isn't it an investment? It certainly is from an individual's point of view; but in strictly economic terms, the purchase of corporate stocks and bonds, government securities, real estate, and other financial assets does not constitute investment because it does not represent the purchase of new plant and equipment. But aren't these funds used to buy new plant and equipment? Perhaps. If and when they are, those purchases qualify as investment and therefore as part of GDP.

GDP versus Real GDP

Suppose you have a birthday party every year and invite the same three guests, and every year you send out to the same pizzeria for a large pie with everything. Pretty wild, eh? In 1995 the pie cost you $8; in 1996, $9; in 1997, $10; and in 1998, $11. The pie was exactly the same size each year; the only thing that got bigger was its price. It's the same way with real GDP (the pie) and GDP (the price of the pie).

To make year-to-year GDP comparisons, we have to get rid of inflation.

If we want to compare our national economic pie, or total production (real GDP), from one year to the next, we have to get rid of inflation. For example, the pizza pie that cost us $8 in 1995 and $11 in 1998. But we were getting exactly the same amount of pizza.

If our economy produced the same amount of output in 1998 as it did in 1995, then real GDP did not change. Prices may have gone up 37.5 percent (from $8 to $11), but we're still producing exactly the same amount of pizza.

To understand the concept of real GDP, you're going to need to calculate percentage changes. Here's one virtually all my students (and quite a few of my fellow economists) get wrong. If a number is tripled, by what percentage has it increased? Go ahead and try to figure it out.

Solution: Pick any number. An easy one is 100. Triple it. You have 300. Now find the percentage change.

Have you figured it out? Did you get 200 percent? If you did, then you might be able to skip the box that shows how to calculate percentage changes. If you're at all shaky on how to do this, this extremely helpful box will probably change your life.

GDP is the basic measure of how much the country produced in a given year. However, comparisons of GDP from one year to the next can be misleading. For example, say GDP went from $3 trillion in 1982 to $3.3 trillion in 1983. At first, it appears the United States has done extremely well, because GDP leapt by 10 percent. But before we get too excited, we should remember that GDP is a measure of all the final goods and services produced during a given year *at market prices*. For all we know, the entire 10 percent increase in GDP may be due to inflation. This would obviously be the case if prices *did* rise by 10 percent in 1983.

The GDP deflator

We need to be able to correct GDP for price increases so we can measure how much actual production rose. To do this we use the GDP deflator, which is calculated quarterly by the Department of Commerce. The GDP deflator is really a price index, like the consumer price index,[6] and it is used to measure price changes in the items that go into GDP (i.e., consumer goods and services, investment goods, and government goods and services).

Let's go back to the problem we posed earlier: GDP rose from $3 trillion in 1982 to $3.3 trillion in 1983. We need to deflate 1983's GDP to find out how much production rose. In other words, if GDP was $3 trillion in 1982, how much was GDP one year later in 1982 dollars? To find this we use the formula:

Deflating GDP to get real GDP

$$\text{Real GDP (current year)} = \text{GDP (current year)} \times \frac{\text{GDP deflator (base year)}}{\text{GDP deflator (current year)}}$$

---

[6] The consumer price index is examined near the end of Chapter 9. The GDP deflator is a much broader concept, covering not just consumer goods and services but also investment goods and government goods and services.

Calculating Percentage Changes

When we go from 100 to 120, that's an increase of 20 percent. From 150 to 200 is an increase of 33⅓ percent. When we go from 50 to 25, that's a percentage decline of 50 percent. How do we know? We use this formula:

$$\% \text{ change} = \frac{\text{Change}}{\text{Original number}}$$

Using the first example, from 100 to 120 is a change of 20, and as our original number is 100, we have $^{20}\!/_{100}$. Any number divided by 100 may be read as a percentage—in this case, 20 percent.

Another way of figuring this out—and we'll need this method most of the time because 100 will rarely be the original number—is to divide the bottom number into the top number. Remember, whenever you have a fraction, you may divide the bottom number into the top:

$$\frac{\text{Change}}{\text{Original number}} = \frac{20}{100} \quad 100\overline{)20.00}^{\;.20\,=\,20\%}$$

.20 is 20 percent. Any decimal may be read as a percent if you move the decimal point two places to the right and add the percent sign (%).

Now let's do the other two. First, the percentage change when we go from 150 to 200. Work it out yourself in the space provided here, and then go on to the last one—when we go from 50 to 25.

$$\frac{\text{Change}}{\text{Original number}} = \frac{50}{150} = \frac{5}{15} = \frac{1}{3} = 33\tfrac{1}{3}\%$$

And finally:

$$\frac{\text{Change}}{\text{Ordinal number}} = -\frac{25}{50} = -\frac{1}{2} = -.50\% = -50\%$$

$$50\overline{)-25.00}^{\;-.50}$$

We'll adapt this general formula to our specific years. We're comparing 1983 (our current year) to 1982 (the base year). Therefore, our formula will now read:

$$\text{Real GDP}_{83} = \text{GDP}_{83} \times \frac{\text{GDP deflator}_{82}}{\text{GDP deflator}_{83}}$$

To solve this equation, we need to substitute actual numbers for the three variables on the right side of the equation. We already know that GDP was $3.3 trillion in 1983. By convention, this number is written as 3,300. The GDP deflator for 1982, the base year, is 100, again by convention. The base year of virtually every index is 100.

We still need to know the GDP deflator for 1983. The Commerce Department publishes this figure, but let's assume it is 110. In other words, prices rose by 10 percent in 1983. Now we'll see if our formula works because our answer should be obvious. We're looking for the real GDP in 1983, and we see that GDP rose by 10 percent and prices also rose by 10 percent. Real GDP in 1983 should be equal to that of 1982. The formula is as follows:

$$\text{Real GDP}_{83} = \text{GDP}_{83} \times \frac{\text{GDP deflator}_{82}}{\text{GDP deflator}_{83}}$$

$$= \frac{3,300}{1} \times \frac{100}{110}$$

$$= \frac{\cancel{3,300}\,30}{1} \times \frac{100}{\cancel{110}\,1}$$

$$= 3,000$$

Let's go over a few of the mechanics of our solution. We put the 3,300 over 1 because this makes it easier to do cross division followed by multiplication. Incidentally, you are allowed to put any number over 1 because this means you are dividing that number by 1 (which doesn't change the number). For example, 5 is equal to 5/1. It means that 1 goes into 5 five times.

Another thing we did was reduce the fractions by division: 110 goes into 3,300 30 times. You don't have to reduce fractions, but usually you'll find that smaller numbers are easier to work with.

Here's one more problem: GDP rises from $3 trillion in 1982 to $5 trillion in 1988. The GDP deflator in 1988 is 150. Find the real GDP in 1988. Find the percentage increase in real GDP between 1982 and 1988.

Solution:

$$\text{Real GDP}_{88} = \text{GDP}_{88} \times \frac{\text{GDP deflator}_{82}}{\text{GDP deflator}_{88}}$$

$$= \frac{5,000}{1} \times \frac{100}{150}$$

$$= \frac{33.33}{1} \times \frac{100}{1}$$

$$= 3,333$$

Percentage change in real GDP from 1982 to 1988:

$$\frac{\text{Change}}{\text{Original number}} = \frac{333}{3,000} = 11.1 \text{ percent}$$

Real GDP in the current year enables us to compare the economy's output, or production, with that of the base year. This problem shows that output was 11.1 percent higher in 1988 than in 1982.

Now let's take a look at the record, which is shown in Figure 8. GDP rose steadily between 1960 and 1997. Not even during recession years (1970, 1973–75, 1980, 1981–82, and 1990–91) were there any declines. But real GDP *did* fall during those bad periods. How come? You tell *me*.

Real GDP reflects just our output, or production. Output falls during recessionary years; therefore real GDP, by definition, must also fall. But GDP, by definition, is *the nation's expenditure on all final goods and services produced during the year at market prices.* If prices rise by a larger percentage than output falls, then GDP will increase. For example, if output goes down by 4 percent and prices go up by 7 percent, by what percentage does GDP go up?

It goes up by 3 percent. Take another look at Figure 8. Real GDP starts out much higher than GDP in 1960. By 1992—the base year—they're equal. And after 1992, GDP soars far above real GDP. Why? Because prices are rising.

The GDP curve begins at a level of just over $500 billion in 1960 (much lower than the real GDP curve). But the GDP curve crosses the real GDP curve in 1992, and ends much higher than real GDP. What's going on here? What's going on is that GDP measures changes in output *and* prices. Real GDP measures just changes in output. GDP rose every year from 1960 to 1997. Even in recession years like 1974 and 1975 GDP rose. That's because price increases during those years were greater than output declines. How do we know that output went down in 1974 and 1975? Just look at the real GDP curve. It dipped

Figure 8   GDP and Real GDP (in 1992 dollars), 1960–97

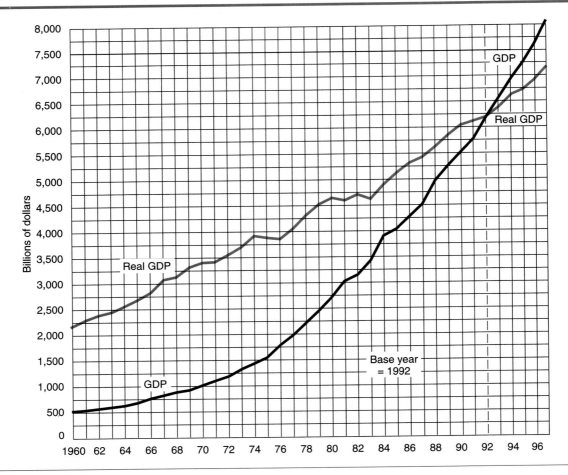

Source: *Economic Report of the President*, 1998.

in 1974 and 1975. In 1982 the same thing happened: GDP went up, but real GDP went down. What happened? It was another recession year. But it was also a year of inflation. In fact, so *much* inflation that the increase in prices was greater than the drop in output.

Now let's see if you can work out some verbal GDP problems. If GDP rises and real GDP falls, explain what happened.

Answer: The GDP deflator (or, rate of inflation) rose more than real GDP fell. For instance, if GDP rose by 3 percent, while real GDP fell by 2 percent, then the GDP deflator must have risen by 5 percent.

Next problem: Real GDP remains unchanged, while GDP falls. What happened?

Answer: What happened was deflation, or a decline in the price level (i.e., the GDP deflator dropped below 100). Although those of us under 68 never experienced much deflation in our lifetimes, deflation *does* happen. We'll talk more about deflation toward the end of the next chapter.

One more problem: GDP doubles and the price level doubles. What happened to real GDP?

Answer: Real GDP stayed the same. Let's make up a problem with real numbers: GDP rises from 1000 to 2000, and the GDP deflator is 200 in the current year. What happened to real GDP?

$$\begin{array}{c} \text{Real GDP} \\ \text{(current year)} \end{array} = \begin{array}{c} \text{GDP} \\ \text{(current year)} \end{array} \times \frac{\text{GDP deflator (base year)}}{\text{GDP deflator (current year)}}$$

$$= \frac{\overset{10}{\cancel{2000}}}{1} \times \frac{100}{\underset{1}{\cancel{200}}} = 1,000$$

International GDP Comparisons

Which country has the world's largest GDP? I hope you didn't forget that the United States does. Which country has the second largest? That's right; it's Japan. In Figure 9 we have the 1996 GDPs of the world's six largest economies.

Different countries use different national income accounting systems, and international exchange rates fluctuate (we'll take up international exchange rates in the last chapter of this book). Hence GDP comparisons among countries cannot be made with great precision. Yet it's reasonable to say that such comparisons do give us fairly close approximations.

America has had the world's largest economy since the 1920s, but over the last 40 years we have spent a lot of time looking over our shoulders. In the 1950s and 1960s, we thought that the Soviet Union might overtake us. Then, in the 1970s and 1980s, it was the Japanese who were catching up. And now, as we approach the millennium, it appears that our biggest economic rival may soon be China.

Per Capita Real GDP

In spite of all this information, you may still be wondering, how *are* we doing? How are we doing in comparison to what? Or to whom? OK, how are we doing in comparison to other countries? We're doing just great—kind of.

Figure 9   Trillion Dollar Economies, 1996*

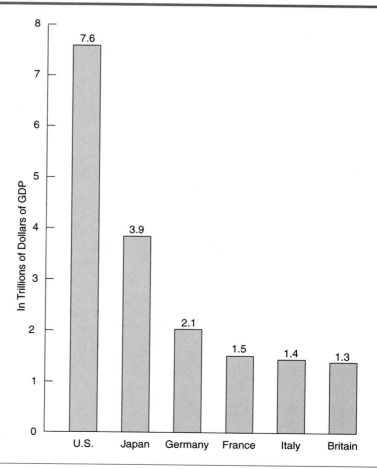

*China and Russia each have GDPs of nearly $1 trillion.
Source: *Wall Street Journal Almanac,* 1998.

How can we tell? We can measure our GDP against that of any other nation. And ours is bigger. How much bigger? Well, our GDP is nearly $3 trillion larger than Japan's. Of course, Japan happens to have half as many people.

You'll notice a decline between 1929 and 1939 in Table 3. What happened? What happened was the Great Depression. In fact, per capita real GDP probably declined by 50 percent between 1929 and 1933. By 1939, per capita real GDP had made it most of the way back to its 1929 level. There were substantial increases in the 1940s, 1950s, and 1960s, but since then our economic growth has slowed. We'll keep coming back to this slowdown in subsequent chapters, and then, in Chapter 16, we'll finally get around to asking why our growth has slowed and what we can do to speed it up again.

GDP may be used to compare living standards among various countries or living standards during different time periods within one country. Such comparisons would usually be on a per capita basis. Per capita GDP = GDP/Population. In the United States, per capita GDP in 1994 was:

$$\frac{GDP}{Population} = \frac{\$8,083,400,000,000}{267,901,000} = \$30,173$$

This means that in 1997 we produced $30,173 worth of final goods and services for every man, woman, and child in this country.

To compare 1997 per capita GDP with that of another year, we would have to correct for inflation. In other words, we really need to revise our formula:

$$Per\ capita\ real\ GDP = \frac{Real\ GDP}{Population}$$

Per capita real GDP = Real GDP/Population

Per capita real GDP comparisons over time

How does our per capita real GDP compare with earlier years? Just take a look at Table 3. Since 1939 per capita real GDP has nearly quadrupled. But in recent years, especially during the early 1970s to early 1980s, the gains have been less impressive. In fact, between 1978 and 1982 (not shown in Table 3) there was virtually no change. The calculation of per capita real GDP is shown in the accompanying Advanced Work box.

How valid are per capita real GDP comparisons over time? Over the short run, say, up to 10 years, they are quite valid. But comparisons over 20, 30, or 40 years become more and more like comparing apples and oranges, or, more to the point, like comparing video games and pocket calculators with nine-inch RCA TVs and those big old office adding machines whose lever you pulled every time you entered a number. Still more to the point, compare Ford T-birds with Model-T Fords. Over long periods of time, not only do different goods and services go into GDP, but the quality of those goods and services changes as well.

International per capita real GDP comparisons

International comparisons of per capita real GDP must be made with even more caution. The per capita real GDP of America is perhaps 80 times the size of India's. Do we produce 80 times as much per capita? Probably not. The typical Indian, a farmer living in a rural village, is not subject to the psychological stresses, commuting problems, pollution, or crime that the average American is. Furthermore, the average Indian family pro-

Table 3   Per Capita Real GDP, Selected Years, 1929–97 (in 1997 dollars)

Year	Per Capita Real GDP
1929	$ 8,663
1939	8,166
1949	11,026
1959	13,565
1969	17,934
1979	21,646
1989	24,052
1997	30,173

Source: *Economic Report of the President,* 1998.

ADVANCED WORK

Calculating Per Capita Real GDP

Earlier in the chapter we worked out several problems in which we converted GDP into real GDP. And we've just done some per capita GDP problems. So what's left to do? Calculating per capita real GDP.

Suppose our GDP were to rise from $12 trillion in 2006 to $18 trillion in 2016, when the GDP deflator is 120. And suppose that our population rose from 280 million in 2006 to 300 million in 2016. What we want to find is (1) How much is per capita real GDP in 2016, and (2) By what percentage did per capita real GDP rise between 2006 and 2016?

See if you can work this out. I would suggest doing this problem in four steps: (1) Find real GDP in 2016; (2) find per capita real GDP in 2016; (3) find per capita real GDP for 2006; and (4) find the percentage rise in per capita real GDP between 2006 and 2016.

Solution:

(1) $\text{Real GDP}_{2016} = \text{GDP}_{2016} \times \dfrac{\text{GDP deflator}_{2006}}{\text{GDP deflator}_{2016}}$

$$= \dfrac{\overset{150}{\cancel{18,000}}}{1} \times \dfrac{100}{\underset{1}{\cancel{120}}}$$

$$= 15,000$$

(2) $\text{Per capita real GDP}_{2016} = \dfrac{\text{Real GDP}_{2016}}{\text{Population}_{2016}} = \dfrac{15,000}{.3} = \$45,000$

(3) $\text{Per capita real GDP}_{2006} = \dfrac{\text{Real GDP}_{2006}}{\text{Population}_{2006}} = \dfrac{12,00\cancel{0}}{.28\cancel{0}}$

$$= \dfrac{6000}{.14} = \dfrac{3000}{.07}$$

$$.07\overline{)3000} = 7\overline{)30^2 0^6 0^4 0^5 0} \overset{42857}{} = \$42,857$$

(4) $\text{Percentage change} = \dfrac{\text{Change}}{\text{Original number}} = \dfrac{\$2,143}{\$45,000}$

$$45\overline{)2.143} \overset{.047}{} = 4.8\%$$
$$\underline{-1\,8\,0}x$$
$$3\,4\,3$$
$$\underline{-3\,1\,5}$$
$$2\,8$$

duces most of its own food, clothing, and shelter—items that are not counted in GDP. Therefore, we are seriously underestimating India's real GDP.

Perhaps the American real GDP is not 80 times that of India, but just 25 times as high. Per capita real GDP is not an accurate measure of international differences in production levels, but it does provide a rough measure. Comparisons of countries at similar stages of economic development are much more accurate, however, than comparisons of countries at different stages.

How does our per capita GDP compare with those of other leading industrial nations? Twenty-five years ago, we were clearly number one. By 1996, however, we had definitely lost our lead. As you can see in Figure 10, Luxembourg, Switzerland, Japan, Bermuda, Denmark, and Norway have passed us. But using an alternate measure, the World Bank placed the United States second in terms of actual living standard.

There are problems with translating the value of yen, marks, pounds, krona, and other currencies into dollars, and vice versa. Currency swings and different price levels make comparisons less than precise. So the best we can say is that our living standard is somewhere in the top eight.

From the close of World War II until 1990, the Soviet Union was our bitter rival. Since that nation's breakup, the standard of living of its main component, Russia, has progressively worsened. In the box "Cost of Living in the United States and Russia: An

The Cost of Living in the United States and Russia: An Alternate Comparison

One way around the problems of dealing with currency exchange rates and different national income accounting systems is to measure living standards in terms of the number of minutes of work needed to buy certain goods. The table below shows the minutes of work that were required in 1994 to pay for selected goods in the United States and Russia. Clearly, our standard of living is perhaps six to eight times the Russian standard.

Good	U.S.	Russia
Sugar, per pound	3 minutes	29 minutes
Bread, per pound	5 minutes	14 minutes
Milk, half-gallon	9 minutes	1 hour, 10 minutes
Sausage, per pound	12 minutes	2 hours, 27 minutes
Gasoline, per gallon	8 minutes	1 hour, 16 minutes
Television, average	6 days	71 days

Source: Russian State Statistics Committee, U.S. Bureau of Labor Statistics, U.S. Department of Agriculture, Electronic Industries Association.

Does our eighth-place per capita GDP ranking mean our standard of living is falling? No. Our standard of living has been rising, although at a much slower rate these last 25 years than it was in the 1950s and 1960s. It means several nations have caught up with us, and if present trends continue, by the turn of the century our standard of living will be slightly higher than today's, but it will be only the 10th or 12th highest in the world. But in the immortal words of baseball great Satchel Paige, "Don't look back, because somebody may be gaining on you."

We've used the terms *per capita GDP* and *standard of living* interchangeably, but what if half of our GDP were spent on defense—as it was during the Second World War? During those years our per capita GDP was about double our standard of living. Similarly, a nation like Japan, which devotes significantly more of its resources to capital production, has a much higher per capita GDP than living standard. Still another qualification is a nation's housing stock. Although the Japanese have a comparable per capita GDP, Americans live better. The average American family has three times the living space of its Japanese counterpart. So when we use per capita GDP and standard of living interchangeably, we need to take each of these additional factors into account.

We've also used *per capita GDP* and *per capita real GDP* interchangeably. Technically, we use per capita real GDP comparisons over time. But if we're talking about just one year's per capita GDP, we drop the "real" because we're not making a year-to-year comparison.

Alternate Comparison," we've used another method to compare the living standards of the United States and Russia.

Shortcomings of GDP as a Measure of National Economic Well-Being

Production That Is Excluded

Household Production   Household production consists mainly of the work done by homemakers—care of children, cleaning, shopping, and cooking. Were a housekeeper hired to do these tasks, this would be counted in GDP. Were two homemakers to work for each other as housekeepers (why, I don't know), their work would be counted in GDP. So why not count homemakers' work in their own homes? Because no money changes hands. No payments are recorded.

Food grown in backyard plots, home repairs, clothes made at home, and any other do-it-yourself goods and services that people make or do for themselves, their families, or their friends are not counted in GDP. (The National Gardening Association reports that about 35 million households have garden plots that produce over $1 billion worth of food. The most popular crop is tomatoes, which are grown on 85 percent of the plots.) When you buy these goods and services from other people, the goods and services are counted (assuming they are reported by the sellers as income).

Illegal Production   Illegal goods and services are not counted in GDP. The big three—dope, prostitution, and gambling—are ignored even though people spend hundreds of billions on these goods and services. Of course, if you place a bet at a racetrack or an offtrack betting parlor, it is legal and counts in GDP. But a bet placed with a bookie

Figure 10   Per Capita GDP of the 10 Leading Nations, 1996

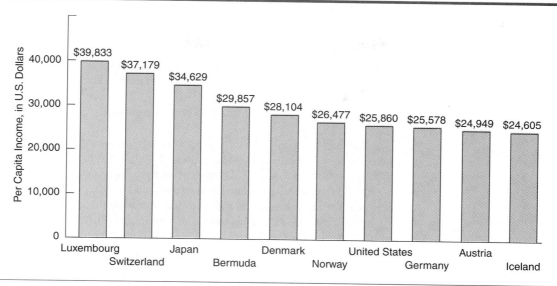

Source: *Top 10 of Everything 1998* (New York: D. K. Publishing, 1997).

is illegal. If you play the state lottery, your bet is counted toward GDP, but not if you play the numbers.

Prostitution was legal in France before World War II. Although the same services continued to be provided after the war on an illegal basis, anyone scanning France's GDP figures right after the war might think that the country had been hit by a depression.

California is our leading agricultural state. Do you know its number one crop? Lettuce? Grapes? Citrus fruit? Sorry, it's none of the above. California's number one crop is grass—that's right, grass, as in marijuana.

How much do Americans spend on illegal drugs? Estimates vary widely, but it is likely that more than $100 billion a year is spent on heroin and cocaine alone. Crack, which is the drug of choice among the poor, has become a cottage industry in the ghettos of our nation's cities.

The Underground Economy   In every large city, on country roads, in flea markets, and even in suburban malls, there are people selling everything from watches to watermelons, and from corn to collectibles. Chances are, the proceeds of these sales are not reported to the government. Not only are no taxes paid, but the sales are not reflected in GDP.

Some of the items sold were stolen, but most are simply goods produced without the government's knowledge. Together with illegal goods and services, these markets form a vast underground economy. How vast? Maybe 10 or 15 percent of GDP.[7] Who knows? How much of *your* income is spent in the underground economy? Or perhaps I should be asking, how much of your income *comes* from the underground economy?

Our underground economy is not composed of only the street peddlers, cabdrivers, and low-life entrepreneurs who underreport their incomes. Oh no. The underground economy gets a very nice class of people—doctors, dentists, lawyers, and even, heaven forbid, accountants. In fact, there is a whole branch of accounting dedicated to the underground economy. It's called creative accounting. Often it involves keeping three separate sets of books—one for your creditors, showing an inflated profit, one for the government, and one for yourself, so you know how you're doing. The next time you're having your teeth realigned, just ask your dentist, "Would you prefer a check or cash?" Then, to make absolutely certain, ask if there's a discount for paying cash.

---

[7]*Fortune* magazine (September 5, 1994, p. 104) reports that in India "the underground economy adds anywhere from 20% to 50% to the official GDP."

Let's step back for a minute and look once again at our definition of GDP: *the nation's expenditure on all the final goods and services produced during the year at market prices.*

What exactly *is* production? What we produce? For once economists are in agreement and quite clear as well about what something means. *Production is any good or service that people are willing to pay for.* And that means anything!

You go to a concert and fall asleep. How much was your ticket? $10? That was $10 worth of production.

You went to a brilliant lecture on the future of the universe. It was free. The speaker wasn't paid. No production.

You grow tomatoes in your backyard for your family's consumption. No production.

You take a course in philosophy. The professor walks into the room and lies down on the floor in the front of the class. This happens all term. How much tuition did you pay to take this course? That's how much production took place.

The problem we have, then, is an inconsistency between the definition of GDP and the way it is compiled by the U.S. Department of Commerce. There's a lot of stuff going on out there that the department misses. Why? Is it understaffed (one of the all-time favorite words of bureaucrats)? Perhaps. The government not only refuses to count the underground economy—legal *or* illegal—but it will not even admit its existence. The bottom line is that it does not go into GDP, even as an estimate. As a result, we are grossly (no pun intended) undercounting GDP.

Treatment of Leisure Time

GDP does not take leisure time into account. We have no way of telling if the people of a country enjoy a 30-hour week or have to work 60 hours a week. In the United States recent immigrant groups, whether the Vietnamese and Koreans in the 1970s and 1980s, the Cubans in the 1960s, the eastern and southern Europeans from the 1880s to the 1920s, or the Irish in the 1840s, have been resented for putting in longer hours than native-born Americans. For these immigrants, long hours were necessary for survival, not only in America, but in their native lands. The rice farmer in Egypt, the factory worker in Mexico, and the manual laborer in India do not have seven-hour workdays, paid sick leave, long vacations, 10 paid holidays, and a couple of days off for Christmas shopping.

The average workweek in the United States, as in the rest of the industrial world, has gradually declined. Until the close of World War II, most workers still put in five and a half or six days a week. In 1900 the 10-hour day was common, and when you wanted to take a vacation, if your boss liked you he reached into his pocket and gave you $5 spending money.

All of this is to show that we have made marvelous gains in leisure time, but these gains are not reflected in GDP. Nor, for that matter, are differences in the respective workweeks of various countries whose GDPs might be compared. For example, the Japanese have nearly caught up with Americans in per capita real GDP, but they work longer hours.

Human Costs and Benefits

Another problem with comparing our GDP with those of other countries, or with our own GDP in previous years, is that the physical and psychological costs of producing that GDP and any human benefits associated with producing it are ignored (see the box "Measure of Economic Welfare").

First the costs. The strain of commuting long distances along congested routes, the tedium, the dangers, the low status, and other unpleasant factors associated with certain jobs are some of the costs. Other jobs cause anxiety because the worker is always worrying about getting ahead or just getting along. Advertising account executives, air traffic controllers, and bomb squad members are all under the gun, so to speak, during most of their working hours. Economists call the psychological strain associated with work

Measure of Economic Welfare

Two economists, James Tobin (who won a Nobel Prize in economics and served on President John F. Kennedy's Council of Economic Advisors) and William Nordhaus (who served on President Jimmy Carter's Council of Economic Advisors) have developed an alternative way of measuring national output. In some respects, they say, GDP is too big because it includes certain things that either add nothing to our standard of living or actually detract from it. However, GDP does *not* include certain things that should be counted.

Some of the "economic bads" are congestion, pollution, and littering. These unfortunate by-products of our industrial society should be subtracted from our GDP, according to Tobin and Nordhaus, because they detract from our standard of living. An example they did not use, but that illustrates the point, is a cartoon of a slave galley. You might recall that in the movie *Ben Hur,* which you probably never saw or heard of, the galley's rowing speed is controlled by a drummer (like the coxswain's count controls the rowing speed in crew races). Anyway, in the cartoon, this slave is passing the hat among his fellow rowers. One of them asks what the collection is for. "It's going toward a new drum."

Think about it. A lot of what we produce—perhaps hundreds of billions of dollars' worth—goes toward dealing with bad things like pollution. Think of how much we need to spend not only on cleaning up our rivers and streams, but on air pollution–control devices, garbage disposal, as well as time lost and aggravation due to congestion. What Tobin and Nordhaus do is arrive at a figure of a few hundred billion dollars and subtract it from GDP.

They also subtract the "regrettable necessities" of defense spending, police protection, and private security measures. Defense and police you already know, but did you know that more than 2 million people work in private security—private detectives, store detectives, hotel detectives, security guards (also known as "rent-a-cops" and "phony cops"), night watchmen, and private housing police. In fact, call up any medium- or large-size company and ask for "security." Most places have their own security departments.

So we subtract these "regrettable necessities" from GDP along with the "economic bads." But we have to add to GDP all the goods and services it should have counted and didn't. We have to add household production as well as the production of illegal goods and services, not to mention unreported production. Sometimes illegal production and unreported (but otherwise legal) production are lumped together as the "underground economy," but that's actually a rather misleading label because nearly all of it takes place above ground, right on the street. And if you know where to find it, you have what is called "street smarts." Sounds a lot better than underground smarts, unless you happen to be a groundhog or a gopher.

To put this all together, the measure of economic welfare is:

GDP – The economic bads

– The regrettable necessities

+ Household, unreported, and illegal production

Do you think the measure of economic welfare is larger or smaller then GDP? It's larger. In other words, the additions are greater than the subtractions.

Psychic cost

psychic cost. Psychic costs detract from one's enjoyment of a job, while *psychic income* adds to that enjoyment.

There are also physical strains and benefits associated with work. As we've already noted, the average workweek is much shorter than it was 80 years ago. Further, the amount of physical labor performed on the average job has declined. Not only have we shifted nearly completely from human power to mechanical power, but the nature of work has also changed from farming and manufacturing to service jobs, most of which require no physical labor.

This is not to say that there are no longer any jobs requiring physical labor or being performed under unpleasant circumstances. Just ask the people who work in toy, purse, textile, or automobile factories (see the section on specialization and alienation in Chapter 4). Or talk to coal miners, migrant farm workers, and police officers. Or watch the mail sorters who work the graveyard shift in a large post office.

Some people, on the other hand, really enjoy their jobs. Take actors. They are willing to hold all kinds of stopgap jobs—waitress, hotel clerk, theater doorman, short-order cook, office temporary—while waiting for that big chance. For most, of course, it never comes. In New York, where there are no more than 2,000 people who earn their entire livelihood from acting, there are tens of thousands of aspiring actors. Why are they willing to buck such outrageous odds? Because they love acting. The *psychic income* from

Psychic income

working in the theater—the roar of the grease paint, the smell of the crowd, the adulation, the applause—is the compensation they seek.

Another case of someone who really enjoyed his job was reported by Dr. David Reuben in his best-selling *Everything You Always Wanted to Know about Sex but Were Afraid to Ask*. It seems there was a foot fetishist who worked in a women's shoe store. Only my strong sense of propriety prevents me from disclosing the details of this man's work. Suffice it to say, he reported that he was so happy at his job he would have worked for nothing.

Finally, let's consider the physical benefits from work. Literally. My friend Marty, the gym teacher, is always in great shape. What do you expect? But I really want to talk about Mr. Spalter, a little bald-headed man who taught gym (how can you *teach* gym?) at Brooklyn's James Madison High School in the 1950s. The guy had to be at least 80. Anyway, Mr. Spalter could go up a 30-foot rope in less than 15 seconds—and do it in perfect form, with his legs exactly perpendicular to his body. The physical benefits of being a gym teacher, farmer, or a health club employee are obvious.[8]

Today's GDP is produced by an entirely different type of labor force doing different work from that of 50 or 100 years ago. And our labor force works very differently from those of developing countries. This makes GDP comparisons that much less valid.

What Goes into GDP?

James Tobin, winner of Nobel Prize, 1981, for work on the interrelationship between money and the real economy (© The Nobel Foundation)

Other problems with GDP as a measure of national economic well-being have to do with what goes into GDP (see again the box titled "Measure of Economic Welfare"). When a large part of our production goes toward national defense, police protection, pollution control devices, repair and replacement of poorly made cars and appliances, and cleanups of oil spills, a large GDP is not a good indicator of how we're doing. And if a large part of our labor force staffs the myriad bureaucracies of state, local, and federal governments, as well as those of the corporate world, we're not all that well off. GDP tells us how much we produce. We need to ask: how much of what?

In general, the problem with using GDP as a measure of national economic well-being is that GDP is just one number, and no single number can possibly provide us with all the information we need. Try these examples.

My daughter is doing very well on her diet. She's down to 120 pounds. Of course she's only 3 feet 6 inches.

How's the weather? It's great; the temperature is 50. Oh yes, there's a hurricane.

My son got all A's in his college courses this semester. Unfortunately, he's taking them in jail where he is serving 10 consecutive life sentences for mass murder. Oh well, like I always say, nobody's perfect.

The Last Word on GDP

I've said some nasty things about GDP that I hope you won't be repeating to your friends. I said it includes some things that really shouldn't be counted. And GDP has excluded some things that should be included. We've even attempted to refine GDP by correcting it for inflation (real GDP) and by subtracting depreciation (NNP). As pointed out in the box "Measure of Economic Welfare," James Tobin and William Nordhaus have actually come up with an alternative measure of national output. Nevertheless, if we can accept GDP while acknowledging all of its limitations, it serves us well, not only for the analysis of the next eight chapters, but in any discussion of macroeconomics beyond the pages of this book.

William Nordhaus, economist who served on President Jimmy Carter's Council of Economic Advisors (J. D. Levine/Yale University)

---

[8] Mr. Spalter must have been doing *something* right. Two Madison graduates have won the Nobel Prize in economics. Robert Solow, who graduated in 1940, won it in 1987, and Gary Becker, class of 1948, won it in 1992. Thus the high school I attended has had more economics Nobel Prize winners than any other high school in the country. And who knows, maybe lightning will strike a third time. If you're curious, I graduated in 1957.

I'd like to close this chapter with some words that Robert Kennedy wrote more than a quarter of a century ago:

> We will find neither national purpose nor personal satisfaction in a mere continuation of economic progress, in an endless amassing of worldly goods. We cannot measure national spirit by the Dow Jones average, nor national achievement by the gross national product. For the gross national product includes air pollution and advertising for cigarettes, and ambulances to clear our highways of carnage. It counts special locks for our doors, and jails for the people who break them. The gross national product includes the destruction of the redwoods, and the death of Lake Superior.[9]

Questions for Further Thought and Discussion

1. Suppose we want to compare this year's GDP with those of previous years. As we go back in time—to 1980, to 1970, to 1960, and to still earlier years—what happens to the validity of these comparisons. Why does this happen?

2. If our GDP rose from 7,500 to 7,700, there could be a few different explanations. List each of these possibilities.

3. Which has been increasing faster, GDP or real GDP? Explain your answer.

4. GDP is not an ideal measure of national economic well-being. Make a list of all the things you would do to improve this concept. Include in your list the goods and services that GDP does not count.

5. "Americans enjoy the highest standard of living in the world." Discuss why this statement is not perfectly accurate.

---

[9] Robert Kennedy, *To Seek a Newer World* (Garden City, NY: Doubleday, 1967), p. 264.

Name _____ Date _____

Multiple-Choice Questions

Circle the letter that corresponds to the best answer.

1. Nearly all of our output is produced by

    a. the government   b. private business firms

    c. individual consumers

2. GDP may be found by

    a. adding together money spent on goods and services and incomes received by the factors of production

    b. subtracting incomes received by the factors of production from the money spent on goods and services

    c. subtracting the money spent on goods and services from the incomes received by the factors of production

    d. adding the money spent on final goods and services

3. Which equation is correct?

    a. GDP – Depreciation = NNP   b. NNP – Depreciation = GDP   c. GDP + NNP = Depreciation

4. Each of the following is an indirect business tax except

    a. sales tax   b. excise tax   c. business property tax   d. corporate income tax

5. If Mexico had a GDP of 700 and depreciation of 100, while Italy had a GDP of 710 and a depreciation of 180, most economists would say that

    a. Italy had a better year   b. Mexico had a better year   c. There is no way of determining which country had a better year

6. Which statement is true?

    a. Both direct and indirect taxes are on things rather than on people.   b. Both direct and indirect taxes are on people rather than on things.   c. A direct tax is on people.   d. An indirect tax is on people.

7. In declining order of size, which of these is the proper ranking?

    a. GDP, NNP, national income   b. NNP, GDP, national income   c. National income, GDP,

NNP   d. National income, NNP, GDP   e. GDP, national income, NNP   f. NNP, national income, GDP

8. Wages, salaries, and fringe benefits constitute about _____ of national income.

    a. 25 percent   b. 50 percent   c. 75 percent

    d. 95 percent

9. The largest sector of GDP is

    a. investment   b. government spending   c. net exports   d. consumer spending

10. Which is not counted in GDP?

    a. a Social Security check sent to a retiree

    b. government spending on highway building

    c. money spent on an airline ticket   d. money spent by a company to build a new office park

11. Which one of these goes into the investment sector of GDP?

    a. the purchase of a new factory   b. the purchase of 100 shares of Mobil Oil stock   c. the purchase of a 10-year-old office building   d. the purchase of a U.S. savings bond

12. When there is inflation

    a. real GDP increases faster than GDP   b. GDP increases faster than real GDP   c. GDP and real GDP increase at the same rate   d. there is no way of telling whether GDP or real GDP increases faster

13. If GDP rose from $6 trillion to $9 trillion and prices rose by 50 percent over this period

    a. real GDP fell by 100 percent   b. real GDP fell by 50 percent   c. real GDP stayed the same   d. real GDP rose by 50 percent   e. real GDP rose by 100 percent

14. Which of the following is counted in GDP?

   a. household production   b. illegal production
   c. leisure time   d. government spending

15. Which statement is true?

   a. There is an inconsistency between the definition of GDP and the way it is compiled by the U.S. Department of Commerce.   b. GDP is an accurate measure of production in the United States.   c. U.S. GDP figures include estimates for production in the underground economy.   d. Our GDP would grow faster if we had less inflation.

16. Suppose the GDP of Argentina were 10 times that of Uruguay. Which statement would be most accurate?

   a. There is no way of comparing the output of Argentina and Uruguay.   b. Argentina's output is greater than that of Uruguay.   c. Argentina's output is probably around 10 times that of Uruguay.
   d. Argentina's output is 10 times that of Uruguay.

17. Which statement is true?

   a. GDP tells us how much we produce as well as what we produce.   b. GDP tells us neither how much we produce nor what we produce.   c. GDP tells us what we produce.   d. GDP tells us how much we produce.

18. The measure of economic welfare formulated by Tobin and Nordhaus starts with GDP and then
   a. subtracts the economic bads and the regrettable necessities and adds household, unreported, and illegal production   b. subtracts the economic bads, the regrettable necessities, and household, unreported, and illegal production   c. adds the economic bads and the regrettable necessities and subtracts the household, unreported, and illegal production   d. adds the economic bads and subtracts the regrettable necessities and household, unreported, and illegal production

19. Per capita real GDP is found by
   a. dividing population by real GDP   b. dividing real GDP by population   c. adding population to real GDP   d. multiplying real GDP by population

20. Which statement is true?

   a. Over longer and longer periods of time, comparisons of real per capita GDP become increasingly valid.
   b. Over the short run, say, up to 10 years, comparisons of per capita real GDP are quite valid.
   c. International comparisons of per capita real GDP may be made with less caution than comparisons over time within a given country.   d. None of these statements is true.

21. Since 1929 our per capita real GDP has
   a. declined   b. stayed about the same   c. doubled   d. more than tripled

22. Which statement is true?

   a. The Japanese have a higher standard of living than we do.   b. The Japanese have a larger GDP than we do.   c. The typical Japanese family has more living space than the typical American family.   d. None of the above.

23. $C + I + G + X_n$ is _____ approach(es) to GDP.

   a. the flow-of-income   b. the expenditures
   c. both the expenditures and the flow-of-income
   d. neither the expenditures nor the flow-of-income

24. Which statement is true about the period since 1984?

   a. Both the consumption and investment percentage shares of GDP rose.   b. Both the consumption and investment percentage shares of GDP fell.   c. The consumption percentage share of GDP rose, while the investment percentage share of GDP fell.   d. The investment percentage share of GDP rose, while the consumption percentage share of GDP fell.

Fill-In Questions

1. The nation's expenditure on all the final goods and services produced during the year at market prices is

   _____.

2. Nearly all our goods and services are produced by

   _____.

3. GDP – _____ = NNP.

4. NNP – _____ = national income.

5. A tax with your name on it is a(n) _____ tax.

6. A sales tax is a(n) _____ tax.

7. The four basic economic resources are

    (1) _____;

    (2) _____;

    (3) _____;

    and (4) _____.

8. Using the expenditures approach, GDP consists of four

    things:

    (1) _____;

    (2) _____;

    (3) _____;

    and (4) _____.

9. Net exports = _____ minus _____.

10. GDP includes only payments for _____

    _____.

11. _____ measures total production in one year.

12. Goods and services produced without the government's

    knowledge are part of the _____ economy.

13. Economists call any good or service that people are

    willing to pay for _____.

14. Economists call the psychological strain associated with

    work _____.

15. The measure of economic welfare developed by Tobin

    and Nordhaus begins with GDP and subtracts

    _____ and _____

and adds _____ and _____

and _____ .

16. Per capita real GDP is found by dividing _____

    _____ by _____ .

17. Over time, per capita real GDP comparisons become

    _____ valid.

Problems

1. Given the following information, calculate NNP and national income: GDP = $5 trillion, Indirect business taxes = $300 billion, and Depreciation = $500 billion.

2. If national income is $3 trillion, depreciation is $400 billion, and indirect business taxes are $300 billion, how much are NNP and GDP?

3. If wages, salaries, and fringe benefits are $4 trillion, profit is $500 billion, interest is $300 billion, rent is $100 billion, and depreciation is $600 billion, how much is national income?

4. If wages, salaries, and fringe benefits are $3 trillion, profit is $400 billion, interest is $200 billion, rent is $100 billion, depreciation is $400 billion, and indirect business taxes are $300 billion, how much is national income, NNP, and GDP?

5. If consumption spending is $3 trillion, investment is $800 billion, government spending is $1 trillion, imports are $1.2 trillion, and exports are $900 billion, how much is GDP?

6. If consumption is $3.8 trillion, investment is $1.1 trillion, government spending is $1.1 trillion, imports are $1.6 trillion, and exports are $1.4 trillion, how much is GDP?

7. GDP rises from $4 trillion in 1986, the base year, to $5 trillion in 1989. The GDP deflator in 1989 is 120. Find real GDP in 1989. Find the percentage increase in real GDP between 1986 and 1989.

8. GDP rises from $5 trillion in 1990, the base year, to $7 trillion in 1994. The GDP deflator in 1994 is 140. Find real GDP in 1994. Find the percentage increase in real GDP between 1990 and 1994.

9. Find the Tobin and Nordhaus measure of economic welfare if GDP is $5 trillion, the economic bads are $500 billion, the regrettable necessities are $400 billion, and the sum of household, unreported, and illegal production is $1 trillion.

10. Find per capita GDP when population is 100 million and GDP is $2 trillion.

11. Find per capita GDP when GDP is $1.5 trillion and population is 300 million.

12. Suppose our GDP were to rise from $10 trillion in 2007 to $20 trillion in 2027, when the GDP deflator is 125. And suppose that our population rose from 300 million in 2007 to 330 million in 2027. **a.** How much is per capita real GDP in 2027? **b.** By what percentage did per capita real GDP rise between 2007 and 2027? [Hint: Do the problem in four steps: (1) Find real GDP in 2027; (2) find per capita real GDP in 2027; (3) find per capita real GDP for 2007; and (4) find the percentage rise in per capita real GDP between 2007 and 2027.]

13. Suppose the GDP of South Korea were to rise from $600 billion in 2005 to $1.5 trillion in 2015, when the GDP deflator is 150. And suppose that Korea's population rose from 40 million in 2005 to 50 million in 2015. **a.** How much is per capita real GDP in 2015? **b.** By what percentage did per capita real GDP rise between 2005 and 2015?

Economic Fluctuations, Unemployment, and Inflation

As the chapter title indicates, we'll be covering the major problems the U.S. economy has encountered, especially in the years since World War II. In later chapters we'll consider how the government can deal with these problems.

Chapter Objectives

In this chapter we will:

- Examine the business cycle.
- Consider various business cycle theories.
- Show how economic forecasting is done.
- Measure the GDP gap.
- Learn how the unemployment rate is computed.
- Look at the types of unemployment.
- Construct a consumer price index.
- Consider the theories of inflation.

Economic Fluctuations

> *Let's look at the record.*
> —Alfred E. Smith[1]

Figure 1 shows the country's economic record since 1964, but before we are in a position to analyze that record, we need a little background information on the business cycle.

Is There a Business Cycle?

Economists and noneconomists have long debated whether there is a business cycle. It all depends on what is meant by the term. If *business cycle* is defined as increases and decreases in business activity of fixed amplitude that occur regularly at fixed intervals, then there is no business cycle. In other words, business activity does have its ups and downs, but some ups are higher than other ups and some downs are lower than others. Furthermore, there is no fixed length to the cycle. For example, as Figure 1 shows, the United States went for nearly the entire decade of the 1960s without a recession but had back-to-back recessions in 1980 and 1981.

If we define the business cycle as alternating increases and decreases in the level of business activity, of varying amplitude and length, then there is definitely a business cycle. What goes up will eventually come down, and what goes down will rise again.

Cycle Turning Points: Peaks and Troughs

Peaks

At the end of economic expansion, business activity reaches a peak (see Figure 1). Usually there is a certain degree of prosperity, but the last time there was full

---

[1]Smith, the governor of New York in the 1920s, was indiscreet enough to run for president in 1928, even though he was a Catholic. An unspoken but widely held sentiment among the American populace prior to the election of John F. Kennedy in 1960 was that no Catholic would ever be elected president.

Figure 1   GDP in 1987 dollars, 1964–97

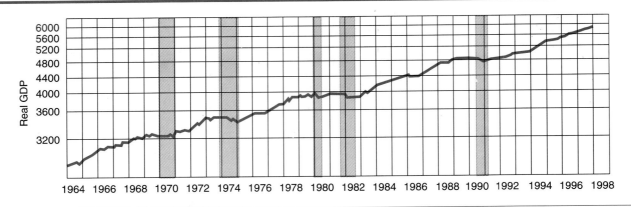

Note: Each shaded vertical column indicates a recession.
Source: U.S. Dept. of Commerce, *Business Conditions Digest,* April 1982; and *Economic Report of the President,* 1998.

employment was at the 1969 peak. In the month following the peak, the economy went into a decline.

Not all economic declines turn out to be recessions. As a rule of thumb, most economists agree that a recession has occurred if real GDP declines for at least two consecutive quarters. However, in the decline that occurred in the second half of 1981, real GDP actually rose slightly in the third quarter, but it is generally accepted that the recession started in August, the second month of the third quarter.

Troughs   When the economy bottoms out, a trough occurs. From this low point, economic recovery sets in, and eventually most sectors share in the expansion.

Business cycles may be measured from peak to peak, or trough to trough. As we have noted, these cycles vary greatly in amplitude and length. Note the severity of the 1973–75 and 1981–82 recessions in Figure 1, and the varying lengths of the cycles shown in the same graph.

Since the end of World War II, the economy's expansions have been as brief as 12 months and as long as 106 months. The contractions fall into a much narrower range—from 6 to 16 months. And so we may conclude that, like snowflakes, no two business cycles are exactly alike. For a blow-by-blow account of the 10 recessions since World War II, see the box "Post–World War II Recessions" in Chapter 1.

The Conventional Three-Phase Business Cycle

We'll begin our analysis with the first peak in Figure 2. The decline that sets in after the peak is called a recession, which ends at the trough. Occasionally there is a false recovery when business activity turns upward for a few months but then turns down again. If the next low point is the lowest since the previous peak, then *that* is the trough.

Recovery begins at the trough, but the expansion must eventually reach the level of the previous peak. Occasionally business activity rises without reaching the previous peak; unless it does, it does not qualify as a recovery.

Once recovery has definitely set it, GDP moves upward until it passes the level of the previous peak, when it enters the third phase of the cycle: prosperity. This phase does not necessarily mean there is full employment, or even that we are approaching full employment. As long as production (real GDP) is higher than it was during the previous peak, we are in the prosperity phase.

Some people say prosperity is when the prices of the things that you are selling are rising, and inflation is when the prices of things that you are buying are rising.

—Anonymous

Prosperity is the second part of the economic expansion and is accompanied by rising production, falling unemployment, and often accelerating inflation. Sooner or later we reach a peak and the process starts all over—recession, recovery, and prosperity.

This is the conventional three-phase cycle. A two-phase cycle would consist of contraction (recession) and expansion (recovery and prosperity) lumped together.

Figure 2   Hypothetical Business Cycles

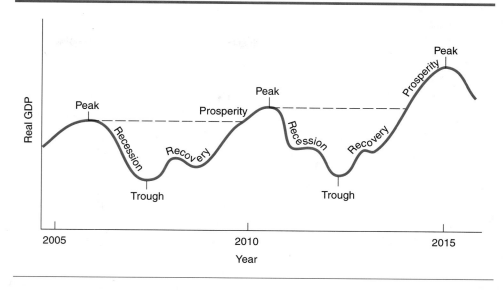

Some people talk of a fourth phase: depression. Although depressions are relatively rare—we have not had one since the 1930s—there is always talk about the possibility that a recession could turn into a depression.

What is the dividing line between a recession and a depression? There is no agreed-on or official definition. Obviously, an unemployment rate of 20 percent would be a depression. But would 10 percent qualify?

Perhaps the best definition was proposed by, among others, the late George Meany, longtime president of the AFL–CIO. He said that if his neighbor were unemployed, it would be a recession. If *he* were unemployed, it would be a depression!

Business Cycle Theories

I have stated that business cycles are inevitable; what goes up must come down, and what goes down must come back up. Although economists generally agree that business cycles exist, they have many competing theories on their causes. We'll briefly consider two types of theories: endogenous (internal) and exogenous (external).

Endogenous Theories

These theories place the cause of business cycles within rather than outside the economy. We'll consider first the theory of innovations, which was advanced primarily by Joseph Schumpeter.

When a businessman attempts to market a new product such as a car or a television set, at first he will encounter resistance ("Get that contraption off the road—it's frightening my horses!"). But when others perceive the profits being made by the innovator, they will imitate his new product with their own versions, and production will soar. Eventually the market will be saturated—as it was by cars in 1929 and televisions in 1953—and an economic downturn will occur. The downturn continues until a new innovation takes hold and the process begins anew.

A second endogenous theory is the psychological theory of alternating optimism and pessimism, which is really an example of a more general theory of the self-fulfilling prophecy. If businessowners are optimistic, they will invest in plant, equipment, and inventory. This will provide more jobs and result in more consumer spending, justifying still more investment, more jobs, and more spending. But eventually businessowners will turn pessimistic, perhaps because they figure this prosperity can't continue. As pessimism sets in, investment, jobs, and consumer spending all decline, and a recession begins. The

What is the dividing line between recession and depression?

Innovation theory

Psychological theory

contraction continues until businessowners figure that things have gone down so far, there's no place to go but back up again.

Inventory cycle theory

Still another endogenous theory is that of the inventory cycle. During economic recovery, as sales begin to rise, businessowners are caught short of inventory, so they raise their orders to factories, thus raising factory employment. As factory workers are called back to work, they begin to spend more money, causing businessowners to order still more from factories. Eventually the owners are able to restock their inventories, so they cut back on factory orders. This causes layoffs, declining retail sales, further cutbacks in factory orders, and a general economic decline. The decline persists until inventory levels are depleted low enough for factory orders to increase once again. (See box "The Accelerator Principle.")

Monetary theory

Yet another endogenous theory of the business cycle is the monetary theory. When inflation threatens, the monetary authorities slow or stop the growth of the money supply. This causes a recession. When they are satisfied that inflation is no longer a problem—or if the recession they have caused has become even more of a concern than inflation—the monetary authorities allow the money supply to grow at a faster rate, which brings about economic recovery. The monetary theory may well explain the 1980 and 1981–82 recessions, when the Federal Reserve stepped heavily on the monetary brakes, as well as our subsequent recoveries, when monetary growth was increased. We'll have a lot more to say about monetary policy in Chapter 13.

Underconsumption theory

One last theory and we're out of here. The underconsumption or overproduction theory stipulates that our economy periodically produces more goods and services than people want or can afford. A variant is the overinvestment theory, which says that business firms periodically overinvest in plant and equipment (again see box "The Accelerator Principle").

Exogenous Theories

Just as endogenous theories place the causes of the business cycle within the economy, exogenous theories place the causes of the business cycle outside the economy.

The sunspot theory

I am perfectly convinced that these decennial crises do depend upon meterorological variations of like period, which again depend, in all probability, upon cosmic variations of which we have evidence in the frequency of sunspots, auroras, and magnetic perturbations.

—W. Stanley Jevons,
Investigations in Currency
and Finance

The very first business cycle theory, the sunspot theory, was formulated by William Stanley Jevons more than a century ago. Jevons believed that storms on the sun, which were observed through telescopes as sunspots, caused periodic crop failures. Because 19th-century economies were primarily agricultural, crop failures, by definition, caused declines in production, or recessions. Subsequent better harvests led to recovery, then prosperity, until the next sunspots occurred.

Is the sunspot theory valid today? Was it ever valid? Not really. Then why even mention it? Because it got people to thinking about what causes business cycles. If it isn't sunspots, it must be something else. Benjamin Franklin once said, "A question is halfway to wisdom." William Stanley Jevons asked the right question, so he deserves at least partial credit for his theory.

The war theory

Another external theory is the war theory. The production surge caused by preparation for war and war itself causes prosperity, and the letdown after war causes a recession. Our experiences before, during, and after World War II, the Korean War, and the Vietnam War seem to validate this theory.

Perhaps no single explanation, whether exogenous or endogenous, can explain each of the cycles we have experienced. The best we can do, then, is to treat each cycle separately, seeking causes that apply.

Business Cycle Forecasting

We have two kinds of forecasters: Those who don't know . . . and those who don't know they don't know.

—John Kenneth Galbraith

There are two main types of business cycle forecasts: analytic and barometric. Analytic forecasts attempt to explain the entire process from start to finish: Such-and-such will happen to real GDP because such-and-such is happening in each sector. These forecasts usually involve economic models, some of which have more than 2,000 equations that are solved simultaneously.

Barometric forecasts are much simpler affairs, usually consisting of tracking only a few economic variables. The reasoning usually runs as follows: If these variables decline, then the economy goes into a recession; similarly, if they rise, then recovery will soon set in.

▲DVANCED ⬛ORK · · · · · · · · · · · · The Accelerator Principle

The accelerator principle is a variant of the overinvestment theory of the business cycle. It is somewhat analogous to the predicament of the Red Queen in *Through the Looking-Glass* (the sequel to *Alice's Adventures in Wonderland*), who had to keep running just to stay where she was. The accelerator principle requires sales to keep increasing at the same rate to prevent investment from falling. The table below presents a hypothetical example of the accelerator principle.

Year	Sales	Machines	Net I (+)	Replacement I (=)	Gross I
1991	100	200	0	10	10
1992	110	220	20	10	30
1993	120	240	20	10	30
1994	130	260	20	10	30
1995	135	270	10	10	20
1996	130	260	−10	10	0

This particular example is based on three assumptions:

1. Two dollars' worth of machinery will produce $1 of output. This ratio of 2:1 is the capital-output ratio.
2. Each machine has a life of 20 years.
3. We'll assume sales have been 100 and we've had 200 machines for the past 20 years. Therefore, we need to replace 10 machines each year just to stay at 200 machines. In other words, each year we start out with 200 machines, 10 wear out, and we have to replace those 10 to still have 200.

Now we're ready to use the table. When sales are 100, we need 200 machines. In 1991 we start with 200 machines, which is the number we'll need that year since sales are 100 and the capital-output ratio is 2:1. We just need to replace the 10 machines that wore out. There's no Net I, but we replace 10 machines and have a Gross I total of 10 [Net I (0) + Replacement I (10) = Gross I (10)]. This, by the way, is the same as saying that Net I plus Depreciation equals Gross I.

In 1992 sales rise from 100 to 110. Because the capital-output ratio is 2:1, we need 220 machines. Net I is 20 machines and we replace 10 machines, so our Gross I is 30.

Machine makers, who had been making 10 machines a year for years, are suddenly deluged with orders. "Thirty machines! What should we do? Should we enlarge our plant and build more equipment to handle these orders? Will business continue to be so good?"

In 1993 sales go up to 120, which means we now need 240 machines. Again Net I is 20 and Replacement I is 10, which adds up to a Gross I of 30.

We've now arrived at what economists call "the Red Queen effect." We're running just to stay where we are. Sales went up by 10 and Gross I stayed at 30.

In 1994 sales again go up 10 to 130, 260 machines are needed, and Gross I stays at 30. Let's see what happens if sales go up by just 5, from 130 to 135. Now we need 270 machines, which leads to a Gross I of only 20.

An increase in sales has led to a decline in Gross I! Sales, which had been increasing by 10 in 1992, 1993, and 1994, rose by only 5 in 1995. So sales, which had been increasing at a constant rate during the previous three years, increased at a decreasing rate in 1995. This led to a decline in Gross I.

When orders for machines fall from 30 to 20, the machine maker must lay off one-third of his employees. And his plant is now being used at only two-thirds of capacity.

In Chapter 11 we will work out problems with the multiplier. Any change in C, I, or G has a multiplied effect on GDP. Now we have a decline of 10 in I. If the multiplier were 5, GDP would decline by 50. This means we are in a recession.

When machine makers lay off their workers, even though they'll collect unemployment insurance, they'll still cut back on their consumption. This, in turn, will depress sales in the following year, 1996. This decline of 5, from 135 to 130, means we need 10 fewer machines. Net I is actually negative, −10, canceling replacement demand of 10 so that Gross I is 0.

This is really a bad year. Gross I has fallen from 20 to 0. Sales are down by 5. The economy sinks still deeper into the recession.

What brings us out? Perhaps more machines wear out and have to be replaced. Maybe sales pick up. If, for some reason, sales eventually start to rise, then Gross I will rise and we'll be back on the ascending part of our roller coaster ride.

Let's recap. The accelerator principle states that if sales or consumption is rising at a constant rate, Gross I will stay the same; if sales increase at a decreasing rate, both Gross I and GDP will fall.

Analytic Forecasts

Econometric models

Econometric models of the economy are the main tool for analytic forecasting. Various universities, such as MIT, the Wharton School of Business, and the University of Michigan, as well as many private economic consulting firms, have developed scores of econometric models. By constantly plugging new data into the hundreds or even thousands of equations used, the model can continually update its forecasts.

Q: Why did God create economists?
A: To make weather forecasters look good.

How good are these forecasts? They are usually better than simple seat-of-the-pants guessing, but the models are only as accurate as the assumptions on which they're based.

Barometric Forecasts

The most widely used barometric forecasting device is the index of leading economic indicators, which is compiled monthly by the Department of Commerce. This series, which is a weighted average of 10 variables, is a valuable forecasting tool, particularly when used with caution.

The 10 leading indicators consist of variables that "lead" general economic activity by several months. Let's note three of these indicators: (1) Contracts and orders for plant and equipment will rise before an increase in the production of plant and equipment. (2) New building permits issued is a good indication of how much construction activity there will be three or four months from now. (3) A change in manufacturers' unfilled orders for durable goods signals how good business will be. If orders are backed up, there will be plenty of work filling these orders in the months ahead.

When the index turns downward, particularly for two or three months in a row, there is a good chance the economy may be heading into a recession. However, as some pundits have put it, the index has predicted 13 of the last 5 recessions. In other words, the index may have turned downward for two or three months a total of 13 times, but in only 5 instances did a recession follow. (See the box "On Economic Forecasting.")

If the index moves steadily upward, there is virtually no chance of a recession in the next few months. But when it begins to move downward, watch out! A downturn *may* be at hand.

Similarly, when the index of leading economic indicators moves down steadily for 11 months in a row, as it did from April 1981 through March 1982, we not only had a recession, but there was virtually no chance of an upturn until later in the year, which is exactly what happened.

Figure 3 presents a record of the performance of the index of leading economic indicators. You may judge for yourself how well the index predicted recessions. (See the box "By How Many Months Do the Leading Indicators Lead?")

Where does all of this leave us? It leaves us with the observation that economics is an inexact science that attempts to forecast certain conditions in an uncertain world. For example, the index of leading indicators turned down eight months before the November 1973 peak, and it turned up one month before the March 1975 trough. Similarly, the index turned down two months before the July 1981 peak and turned up 10 months before the November 1972 trough.

An economist is an expert who will know tomorrow why the things he predicted yesterday didn't happen today.

—Laurence J. Peter,
Peter's Quotations

To err is human; to get paid for it is divine.

—William Freund,
economic consultant

On Economic Forecasting

Economics' claim of being a science is based mainly on its ability to predict the future. Although economists have not often been successful at the art of prediction, they are great at explaining why their forecasts were wrong. Even the boy who cried wolf was right that last time.

In early 1970 Pierre Rinfret, then one of the richest economists (he owned a large consulting firm),* predicted, "There ain't gonna be no recession." Although his grammar was not impeccable, his forecast was technically correct. There wasn't going to be a recession because one had already begun—in December 1969. On the other end of the pay scale, I wrote two articles for the *Journal of Commerce* in 1979 titled respectively "A Recession in April?" (January 24, 1979) and "Recession Likely to Get Worse" (September 18, 1979). There was only one problem. The recession I had been talking about did not actually begin until January 1980. Oh well, nobody's perfect.

The index of leading economic indicators rose five out of six months (April through October) of 1982, prompting me to proclaim the 1981–82 recession finally over in an article titled "Pessimist Sees Economic Breakthrough" in the *Ocean County* (New Jersey) *Reporter,* November 24, 1982, and "Economic Recovery Has Finally Arrived" in the *Boston Post-Gazette,* November 12, 1982. Just so you don't get the impression every economic forecast is wrong, this one was right on the money. The recession of 1981–82 *did* end in November 1982.

*In 1990 Rinfret accepted the Republican nomination for governor of New York (a nomination almost no one else wanted) and ran against Governor Mario Cuomo. Rinfret lost.

By How Many Months Do the Leading Indicators Lead?

Notice those numbers with arrows in Figure 3. The note below the graph states numbers entered on the chart indicate lengths of leads (–) and lags (+) in months from reference turning dates. For example, a recession began in April 1959, but the Index of Leading Indicators turned down 10 months earlier. Similarly, a recovery that began in the second half of 1980 was "predicted" by an upturn in the index two months earlier.

There are two main problems in using the index to forecast business cycle turning points. First, it takes the Department of Commerce a full month to tabulate all the necessary data. That means, for example, that the index for September is not announced until the end of October. A second problem is that we can't be sure for several months whether the index has had a turning point. Suppose the index actually turned downward in January. At the end of February, the Department of Commerce would report that the index had declined. And then again at the end of March. It would still be too early to predict a recession, and yet a recession might have already begun.

Figure 3   The Index of Leading Indicators, 1958–1998

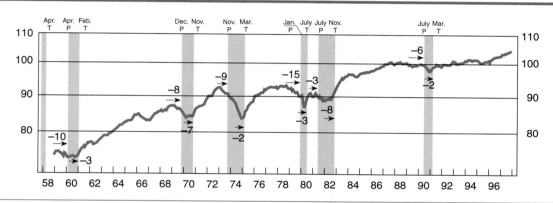

Note: The numbers and arrows indicate length of leads (–) and lags (+) in months from business cycle turning dates.

Source: *Survey of Current Business,* March 1995, *Business Cycle Indicators,* February 1998.

The GDP Gap

The economic effects of unemployment are more quantifiable than the social effects. To measure them we will use the GDP gap, which is the difference between what we could potentially produce and what we actually produce.

We'll try an analogy first. Do you bowl? What's your high game? Suppose your high game were 180. If you went out tonight and bowled 178, how would you feel? Good? What if you bowled 185? Great?

Living up to our potential GDP

Our potential GDP is like our high game at bowling. We know we can do it—not often, but sometimes. And there's always the chance that we can do still better. Our potential GDP, then, is our output when our resources are fully employed and we are using the best available technology. Remember the production possibilities frontier in Chapter 2? If we are attaining our potential GDP, we are on our production possibilities frontier.

How often do we produce our potential GDP? About as often as we bowl our high game; it happens, but it's unusual. Usually our economy operates below our potential GDP.

Potential GDP and the production possibilities curve

What's the difference, then, between the production possibilities curve and potential GDP? They both represent output when the economy is at full employment (that is, with an unemployment rate of 5 percent), but the production possibilities curve (or frontier) represents the economy at a particular moment in time, while the graph of potential GDP shows how much the economy would produce over time if it were to operate at full employment. Thus, the production possibilities frontier is a snapshot of the economy at full employment at a particular time, while a graph of the potential GDP might show how much the economy would produce at full employment over a period of decades.

Figure 4 shows our country's economic record since World War II. In fact, you'll find that it's essentially a reproduction of Figure 1, except it has a smooth curve added to the record of our actual GDP. That's our potential GDP. Notice that potential GDP is greater than actual GDP for almost every year. There is a gap, which we call the GDP gap. It is the amount of production by which potential GDP exceeds actual GDP.

You'll also notice that in some years, most recently 1969, actual GDP exceeds potential GDP; there's no GDP gap at all. This is like having a high bowling game of 180 and going out and bowling a 185. These things *do* happen, but they happen so infrequently that we can safely say we don't expect our actual GDP to exceed our potential GDP. On those rare instances when it happens, we can be pleasantly surprised, and then wait maybe another 20 years for it to happen again.

One of those infrequent instances when our actual GDP exceeded our potential GDP was from mid-1997 into early 1998, when our unemployment rate dipped below 5 percent. Since we consider a rate of 5 percent to represent full employment, then we can say that during that period our economy actually exceeded its potential. The big question in early 1998 was how much longer would our economy remain in this state of grace.

What is the significance of the GDP gap?

What, then, is the significance of the GDP gap? Obviously, it shows by how much we are leaving our potential unfulfilled. In 1992 the Congressional Budget Office made an estimate of the GDP gap. Had the unemployment rate been 5.5 percent that year, instead of 7.3 percent, then the United States would have produced an additional $271 billion in GDP.

Unemployment

The Problem

One of the most devastating experiences a person can have is to be out of work for a prolonged period. Most of us have been unemployed once or twice, but only those who have been unable to find work after looking for six to eight months, or even longer, really know that feeling of hopelessness and self-doubt, not to mention a depressed standard of living.

How can you expect somebody who's warm to understand somebody who's cold?
—Aleksandr Solzhenitsyn, *One Day in the Life of Ivan Denisovich*

The Bureau of Labor Statistics (BLS) defines "discouraged workers" as those who have given up looking for work and have simply dropped out of the labor force.[2] Where have all the discouraged workers gone?

Walk around the slums of our great cities. Walk through East St. Louis, Watts, Bedford-Stuyvesant, and the Hough district of Cleveland. Walk through Roxbury in Boston or central Newark, or through most of our nation's capital. Walk through any of

---

[2]Poverty and welfare are two of the main topics in the chapter on income distribution.

Figure 4   The GDP Gap, 1945–97

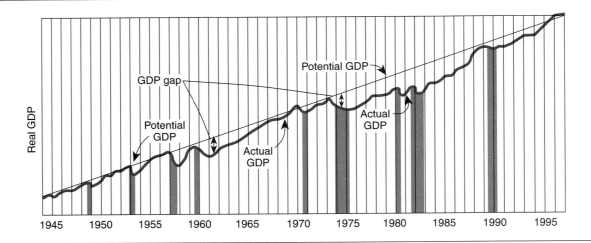

these places in midafternoon and you'll see block after block of teenagers and adults hanging around with nothing to do.

Wanted: a real job

Ask them what they want more than anything else. A bigger welfare check? More food stamps? A bigger TV? Most of them would tell you that all they want is a decent job. Not a dead-end, minimum-wage, low-status, menial job, but a *real* job.

Are these people unemployed? No, these people have given up, dropped out, and are, for all intents and purposes, no longer living in the United States. They may reside here physically, but they are not part of our society.

How the Unemployment Rate Is Computed

Where unemployment data comes from.

The Bureau of Labor Statistics (BLS) is in charge of compiling statistics on the number of Americans who are employed and unemployed. Where does it get its data? Most people believe it gets statistics from unemployment insurance offices, but if you stop and think about it, only about one-third of all unemployed Americans are currently collecting unemployment insurance benefits. The BLS gets its unemployment statistics by conducting a random survey of more than 60,000 households.

Essentially, the bureau asks a series of questions: (1) Are you working? If the answer is no, (2) Did you work at all this week—even one day? Anyone who has answered yes to questions 1 or 2 is counted as employed. For those who have not been working, the BLS has one more question: (3) Did you look for work during the last month (i.e., did you go to an employment agency or union hall, send out a résumé, or go on an interview)? If your answer is yes, you're counted as unemployed. If your answer is no, you're just not counted; you're not part of the labor force. If you want to work but have given up looking for a job, you're a "discouraged worker," but you are not in the labor force and you are not considered "unemployed."

The labor force consists of the employed and the unemployed. For example, in October 1997, 129,894,000 Americans were employed and 6,467,000 were unemployed. We can compute the unemployment rate by using this formula:

Unemployment rate = $\dfrac{\text{Number of unemployed}}{\text{Labor force}}$

$$\text{Unemployment rate} = \frac{\text{Number of unemployed}}{\text{Labor force}}$$

How much was the unemployment rate in March 1987? Work it out right here.

Who are the discouraged workers?

Did you get 4.7 percent? The key here is to figure out how many people are in the labor force. Add the employed (129,894,000) and the unemployed (6,467,000), and you'll get a labor force of 136,361,000. Then divide the labor force (136,361,000) into the unemployed (6,467,000). Thus, in October 1997 the official unemployment rate was 4.7 percent. (If you need more help with this, see the Extra Help box.)

The liberals say the true unemployment rate is higher than the official rate.

The liberal economists (does anyone still call herself a "liberal"?) would say that the true rate of unemployment is somewhat higher, perhaps 8 or 9 percent, because we should count all the jobless people who are ready, willing, and able to work. Do you remember any scenes from the movie *Butch Cassidy and the Sundance Kid?* Paul Newman kept asking Robert Redford about the posse that had been pursuing them through the badlands: "Who *are* those guys?"

Let's ask that same question about all those guys—the 2 or 3 million of them—who are not working but are not officially unemployed. If we asked the BLS, it would tell us that those guys are discouraged workers. Discouraged? Why discouraged? Because they're *so* discouraged they've given up looking for work. Therefore, they don't meet the BLS criteria for being officially unemployed. If a person has not actively looked for a job

Read Only If You're Not Sure How to Calculate the Unemployment Rate

In January 1995, 7,500,000 Americans were unemployed and 124,600,000 held jobs. Go ahead and calculate the unemployment rate:

$$\text{Unemployment rate} = \frac{\text{Number of unemployed}}{\text{Labor force}}$$

$$= \frac{7,500,000}{132,100,000}$$

OK, where did we get the 132,100,000? That's the labor force—the number of unemployed (7,500,000) plus the number of employed (124,600,000).

The next step is simple division: 132,100,000 into 7,500,000, which gives us an unemployment rate of 5.7 percent.

Incidentally, a common mistake in this type of problem is to divide 7,500,000 into 132,100,000. Some people insist on dividing the smaller number into the larger number. But the rule we must always follow is to divide the bottom number into the top number. By the way, if you're interested, you may want to buy another book I wrote, *All the Math You'll Ever Need.**

*It was published by John Wiley & Sons and is available in many bookstores.

---

during the last month—sent out a résumé, gone on a job interview, or visited an employment agency—that person is not counted as unemployed. He is not in the labor force. And as far as our unemployment rate statistics go, he is not there at all.

The liberals have a couple of additional bones to pick with the BLS definition. A person who worked one day in the last month is counted as employed. Also, someone who works part-time but wants to work full-time is counted as employed. The liberals ask, "Doesn't this sort of measurement overstate the number of employed?" When you put it all together, they maintain, the BLS is overstating employment and understating unemployment. The result is an unemployment rate that is perhaps a couple of points too low.

The conservatives say the true unemployment rate is lower than the official rate.

That's the liberal view. As you would expect, the conservatives say the official unemployment rate *over*estimates the true rate of unemployment. Using the BLS definition of an unemployed person—someone who has not worked this month and who has actively sought work—the conservative focuses on those who are required to report to state employment or other government employment offices to remain eligible for unemployment insurance, welfare, or food stamps. Is this, asks the conservative, really an effort to look for work, or are these guys just going through the motions?

The effect of married women on the unemployment rate

Another factor that conservatives cite as boosting the unemployment rate is the change in the composition of the labor force. The percentage of married women who work has risen from 25 percent in the late 1940s (when the birthrate was very high) to about 65 percent today. The advent of married women seeking work raises the unemployment rate in three different ways. First, married women who are reentering the labor force after having had children will have to find jobs (unless their employers held their old positions open for 5, 10, or 20 years). Second, because their husbands are employed, they can shop around some for a job. And third, their husbands, if unemployed, can also shop around for a while if their wives are working.

The rate of unemployment is 100 percent if it's you who is unemployed.

—David L. Kurtz

And so, in each case, the rise in labor force participation by married women has tended to raise the unemployment rate over the last four decades. But it is interesting to note that in recent years there has been virtually no difference between the unemployment rates of women and men. It has also been pushed up as the baby-boom generation (those born from the late 1940s to the mid-1960s) came of age. Young adults tend to have a relatively high unemployment rate because, like the homemakers returning to the labor

When It's a Recession for Whites, It's a Depression for Blacks

In the first part of this chapter, I jokingly referred to the difference between recessions and depressions. For blacks, however, unemployment is no joking matter. Historically, the unemployment rate for blacks has been double that of whites. And black teenagers' "official" unemployment rate during the 1981–82 recession topped 50 percent. We can only guess at their true unemployment rate if all the "discouraged" black teenagers who dropped out of the labor force were counted.

A survey in the early 1980s by the Center for the Study of Social Policy turned up this interesting fact: Black college graduates earn about the same income as white high school graduates. So much for the notion of equal opportunity.

Of course, there have been major strides toward equality of economic opportunity since the mid-1960s, but they have left in their wake a huge black (and Hispanic) underclass. If you are black or Hispanic, your chances of being poor are three times as great, and your chances of being unemployed are twice as great.

It appears that two things can be done to ease the economic burden of minority groups. One is to make greater efforts to end employment discrimination. The other is to avoid recessions and keep the unemployment rate as low as possible.

Figure 5   The Unemployment Rate, 1948–97

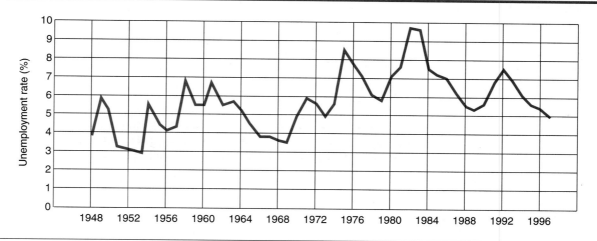

Source: *Economic Report of the President,* 1998.

force, they need time to find that first job. Next, they tend to go from job to job until, like Goldilocks, they find a position that is "just right." Finally, because many young adults still live at home or receive help from their parents, they experience less pressure to take the first job that comes along. On the other hand, as the baby boomers have aged, the proportion of young people in the labor force has been lower than it was 25 years ago. (See "When It's a Recession for Whites, It's a Depression for Blacks" box for a discussion of unemployment among blacks.)

The bottom line, according to the conservatives, is that perhaps a couple of million of the "officially" unemployed are not really looking for work. The liberal bottom line is that at least a couple of million people out there want to work but aren't being counted.

Are the conservatives or the liberals right? Guess what? I'm going to let *you* decide.

Figure 5 is a record of the official unemployment rate from 1948 through 1997. You'll notice a marked upward trend from the late 1960s through the mid-1980s, which apparently lends credence to the conservative interpretation—but all the results are not yet in. In fact, the trend seems to have reversed since the mid-1980s, by which time the baby boomers had all come of age.

The unemployment rate plays an important role in presidential elections. A high unemployment rate in 1992 was a very important factor in President George Bush's loss to Bill Clinton. And four years later, when Clinton defeated challenger Bob Dole, he made our low rate of unemployment a major campaign issue. Moreover, in every election since

A Computerized Job Bank

Imagine a computerized network that lists every job opening in the country and every person seeking employment. Every job opening and every job seeker will be matched instantly. What effect will this have on frictional unemployment? It will practically wipe it out in one fell swoop.

Why don't we set up such a system? Believe it or not, we have. Virtually every state employment office* has a computer data bank of job openings. There are just two problems.

First, only a small minority of employers list their jobs with their state employment services. One reason most employers don't is that they're reluctant to hire people who are collecting unemployment insurance because they are sometimes perceived as being lazy or having low motivation. Also, employers in general will look askance at anyone who is out of work. "*Why* are you unemployed?" You'll always stand a better chance of finding a job if you already have a job, or at least if people think you do.

A second reason why the state employment services can't perfectly match job openings to job seekers is that not everybody out of work registers at their state employment office. If they're collecting unemployment insurance benefits, they *have* to register. If they're not, they may. But in certain lines of work—executive positions, many professional jobs, and, in general, higher-paying positions—job applicants rarely register at their state employment service.

There's another computerized job bank on the Worldwide Web. The Internet can put you in touch with thousands of potential employers. Sounds too good to be true? Here are six job sites you can find on the Web:

America's Job Bank—http://www.ajb.dni.us
CareerMosaic—http://www.careermosaic.com
The Main Quad—http://develop.mainquad.com
The Monster Board—http://www.monster.com
Online Career Center—http://www.occ.com
Yahoo! Classifieds—http://classifieds.yahoo.com

* These are the employment agency counterparts to the state unemployment insurance offices where unemployed people sign up for their unemployment checks.

1948, the party that occupied the White House held on to the presidency if the unemployment rate was falling in the second quarter of that year but lost the election if the unemployment rate was flat or rising. This leading indicator has been right on the money in the last 13 elections; maybe we can dispense with the voting and just tote up the April, May, and June unemployment rates in every presidential year.

Types of Unemployment

The final solution for unemployment is work.
—Calvin Coolidge

Frictional Unemployment   Our economy is far from a well-tuned, efficient, smoothly functioning machine. When a job opening occurs somewhere, it is rarely filled instantaneously, even when there is someone ready, willing, and able to fill it. In a word, our economy has a certain degree of friction (see box "A Computerized Job Bank").

The frictionally unemployed are people who are between jobs or just entering or reentering the labor market. Because our system of filling jobs—newspaper classified ads, employment agencies, corporate recruiters, executive headhunters, help-wanted signs, and word of mouth—is imperfect, usually weeks or months pass before positions are filled.

About 2 to 3 percent of our labor force is always frictionally unemployed.

At any given time, about 2 or 3 percent of the labor force is frictionally unemployed. Students who are looking for their first full-time jobs, homemakers reentering the labor market after 5, 10, or 20 years, and servicemen and -women who have recently been discharged by the armed forces are frictionally unemployed until they find jobs. In addition, there are those who leave their jobs voluntarily, perhaps so they can spend all their time looking for better jobs. Maybe they're looking in another part of the country. Add to these the people who get fired or quit. These people, too, are between jobs, or frictionally unemployed.

About 2 to 3 percent of our labor force is always structurally unemployed.

Structural Unemployment   A person who is out of work for a relatively long period of time, say, a couple of years, is structurally unemployed. The economy does not have any use for this person. The steelworker in Youngstown, Ohio, and the coal miner from Kentucky are no longer needed because the local steel mills and coal mines have closed. (See the box "The Effects of Structural Unemployment.") And the skills of clerical workers, typists, and inventory control clerks who once staffed a corporate office have been made obsolete by a computer system. Add to these the people whose compa-

---

The Effects of Structural Unemployment

In a book titled *Prosperity Lost,* Philip Mattera provides scores of stories of how structural unemployment has affected the lives of ordinary Americans. He talks about Ray Woolaghan, who was laid off his $12-an-hour job at U.S. Steel's Homestead, Pennsylvania, mill back in the mid-1980s, just 17 days short of qualifying for his pension. It took him two years to find steady work. What he found was a $5.23-an-hour custodial position at the University of Pittsburgh.

Then Mattera tells about another person who found himself structurally unemployed:

After Bill Baudendistel of Goshen, Ohio, was laid off from his $13-an-hour factory job with General Electric in 1988, the best work he could find was a position as a night mainte-

nance man at a shopping mall. The pay: $5 an hour. His wife had to take a part-time job as a secretary in a hospital, though she preferred to stay at home with their three children. Nonetheless, the Baudendistels, finding it hard to keep up, began buying their clothes at garage sales and stopped purchasing "luxuries" like fresh fruit.*

As both of these structurally unemployed workers eventually found much lower paying jobs, neither is counted among the unemployed. But both will spend the rest of their working lives at relatively low-paying jobs and adjust their living standards accordingly.

* Philip Mattera, *Prosperity Lost* (Reading, MA: Addison-Wesley, 1991), pp. 66–67.

The "unemployables"

nies have gone out of business or whose jobs have been exported to low-wage countries and you've got another 2 to 3 percent of the labor force structurally unemployed.

One out of five adult Americans is functionally illiterate. These people cannot read, write, or do simple numerical computations. In a workplace that increasingly demands these minimal skills, more and more of these people are finding themselves virtually shut out of the labor force. Each year our educational system turns out 1 million more functional illiterates, most of whom will face long periods of structural unemployment. Many of these young adults come from very poor families where no one has held a job. They have no idea of how to dress for a job interview, what to say, or even the need to show up on time. Unless these people are given some kind of vocational training and provided with entry-level jobs, they will be out of work for most of their lives.

Ours is a dynamic economy, and the opportunities for retraining and subsequent employment *do* exist. But the prospects for a 50- or 60-year-old worker embarking on a second career are not auspicious. To compound the problem, most of the structurally unemployed reside in the Rust Belt of the East and Midwest, while most of the new career opportunities are in the Sun Belt, and in several states on the East and West coasts.[3]

What if someone were "between jobs" for six months, or a year, or even two years? When someone is out of work for a long period of time, he or she is classified as "structurally unemployed." But where do we draw the line between frictional and structural unemployment? The answer is that we don't. There *is* no clear dividing line.

Fluctuations in our unemployment rate are due to cyclical unemployment.

Cyclical Unemployment   As you know, our economy certainly has its ups and downs, a set of fluctuations known as business cycles. During a recession, the unemployment rate rises to 8, 9, or even 10 percent. During the Great Depression, the "official" unemployment rate hit 25 percent, which definitely understated the true unemployment picture.

If we allow for a certain amount of frictional and structural unemployment, anything above the sum of these two would be cyclical unemployment. Let's say that the sum of frictional and structural unemployment is 5 percent. If the actual rate of unemployment is 7.7 percent, then the cyclical rate is 2.7 percent.

If we take a 5 percent unemployment rate as our working definition of full employment, anything above 5 percent would be cyclical unemployment. You may wonder whether 5 percent is a reasonable level for full employment. Surely we can never expect our unemployment rate to reach zero, since we'll always have some frictionally and structurally unemployed people. Our unemployment rate did get down to 1.2 percent in 1944, but as they said then, "There's a war going on." With 12 million men in the armed

---

[3]Many large corporations, including IBM, AT&T, General Motors, Sears, Boeing, and GTE, have been downsizing by offering hundreds of thousands of employees early retirement, while other companies have been closing plants and putting millions of employees out of work.

Are You Eligible to Collect Unemployment Benefits?

A large number of people who are eligible to collect don't know they're eligible. The eligibility requirements are a yes answer to these three questions:

1. Did you work for at least parts of 20 of the last 52 weeks (or 15 of the last 52 weeks and 40 of the last 104)?
2. Did you lose your last job through no fault of your own?
3. Are you ready, willing, and able to work?

The second question is open to interpretation. What if you were fired from your last job? Why were you fired? Did you provoke your own dismissal? Then you can't collect. What if you and your boss had an argument? Then you may be eligible.

What if you were fired because your boss didn't like you, or because you couldn't get the hang of the job, or because there was simply no work for you to do? Then you could collect. But what if you got fired because you were always late, often absent, or refused to do any work? You then provoked your own dismissal and are not eligible for unemployment benefits.

The answer to the second question is not always a clear-cut yes or no. As a onetime employee of the New York State Employment Service, I offer you this advice: If you lose your job and you think you *may* be eligible for unemployment benefits, it pays to apply. Numerous people collecting right now probably had even more dubious claims than you have. Just go down to your state unemployment insurance office and find out whether you're eligible.

forces and the economy going full-steam ahead, employers were desperate for help, and anyone who could walk and spell his or her name had no trouble finding a job.

There are liberal economists who insist that we could realistically get the unemployment rate down to 4 percent, while there are conservative economists who consider 6 percent the lowest attainable rate. We'll split the difference and call 5 percent full employment.

Read the box titled "Are You Eligible to Collect Unemployment Benefits?" You might be eligible, even if you're a full-time student. Hundreds of thousands of people are eligible right now but aren't collecting. Yet millions more are unemployed and ineligible to collect. Why? Many are new entrants or reentrants to the labor market; others are people who left their jobs voluntarily, those who provoked their dismissals, and finally, those whose unemployment insurance benefits ran out. Only one out of every three unemployed people is actually collecting benefits.

Seasonal Unemployment   At any given time a couple of hundred thousand people may be out of work because this is their "slow season." The slack seasons in the ladies' garment industry are in the spring and fall after those seasons' new fashions have been shipped to the stores. The tourist season is slow all summer in Florida, and some employees at Carvels and Dairy Queen are laid off in the winter. My aunt Betty, who worked in the garment industry for nearly 60 years, turned her seasonal unemployment to her advantage by arranging to get laid off each year in early November, registering for unemployment insurance benefits, and then taking off for Florida.

Seasonal unemployment is not nearly as large as frictional, structural, or cyclical unemployment, so it hasn't figured in our discussion of total unemployment. But if it weren't mentioned here, someone would be sure to ask why it wasn't included.

Natural Unemployment Rate

As the unemployment rate falls, and it becomes increasingly difficult to find employees, employers will bid up wage rates, pushing up the rate of inflation. Once the unemployment rate falls below its natural rate, which most economists estimate to be 5 or 6 percent, then inflationary wage pressure emerges.

Whatever the natural rate of unemployment, it is falling, as American businesses can draw more on foreign workers than they could in the past. Multinational corporations can take full advantage of what has become an international labor supply.

In the next part of this chapter, we'll see how rising wages, among other things, contribute to inflation. But first we'll need to answer the question "What is inflation?"

Inflation

Defining Inflation

What exactly *is* inflation? It is a rise in the price level. Generally, we consider inflation a sustained rise in the price level over a period of years. In our own lifetimes, we have known little *but* inflation.

If the rate of inflation had been 4 percent, would that mean the price of every good and service went up by 4 percent? Of course not! The prices of some things went up by much more than 4 percent, and the prices of others rose by less than 4 percent. The prices of some things may not have changed. And when the overall price level is rising, the prices of some goods and services are actually going down. Can you think of any examples? In the 1970s and 1980s TV prices came way down. And then the price of VCRs declined. And more recently, prices of cellular phones, fax machines, CDs and CD players, camcorders, personal computers, laser printers, and pocket calculators have fallen.

U.S. inflation has been persistent since World War II, particularly in the 1970s when, for much of the decade, it was at double-digit proportions. And yet, when compared to an inflation rate of more than 100 percent in several South American countries during the 1980s,[4] ours has been relatively mild.

Ask the man on the street what inflation is and he'll tell you that everything costs more. To be more precise, the U.S. Department of Labor's Bureau of Labor Statistics compiles an average of all items that consumers buy—the prices of cars, appliances, haircuts, TVs, VCRs, steaks, medical services, Big Macs—and figures out how much it costs the average family to live. Every month several hundred BLS employees around the country check the cost of 90,000 items—ranging from airline tickets to cat food. Let's say that in January 1995 it cost the Jones family $20,000 to maintain a certain standard of living. If it cost the Joneses $22,000 to buy the same items in January 1999, we would say that the cost of living went up 10 percent.

The consumer price index (CPI), which measures changes in our cost of living, is reported near the middle of every month by the Bureau of Labor Statistics. For example, you'll hear on the radio, "There was some good news today on the inflation front. Consumer prices rose just two-tenths of 1 percent last month, and the consumer price index now stands at 134.6." Before you have a chance to digest this information, the announcer is doing sports and weather.

First let's consider that prices rose just two-tenths of 1 percent last month. Is that a lot of inflation? If we convert it to an annual rate, it comes to just under 2.7 percent.[5] An inflation rate of 2.7 percent a year certainly does not seem to be all that bad, especially when you compare it to the inflation we experienced from the early 1970s to the early 1980s (see Figure 6).

The radio announcer also said that our consumer price index now stands at 134.6. What does that tell us? Unless you're pretty familiar with the consumer price index, how it's constructed, and what it measures, you won't be able to fully appreciate the significance of that number. Well, your worries are over. In another few pages you'll know exactly what this index is all about.

The number 100 is a magic number. It lends itself well to calculating percentage changes. Suppose, for example, that we want to find out by what percentage prices rose since the base year for the consumer price index. The base year is set at 100. If the CPI were 136.4 today, by what percentage did prices rise since the base year? They rose by 36.4 percent.

---

[4] In 1989 Brazil had an annual inflation rate of 1,700 percent. But Bolivia managed to attain an even more impressive rate of 50,000 percent in 1985.

[5] How did we get from 0.2 percent a month to just under 2.7 percent a year? There are three ways of doing this: (1) use pencil and paper, if you happen to have about half an hour; (2) work it out with your pocket calculator; or (3) look it up in a book that has compound interest tables.

Figure 6   Annual Percentage Change in Consumer Price Index, 1946–97

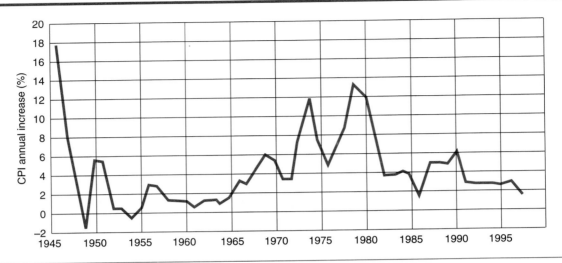

Source: *Economic Report of the President,* 1998.

What I did was subtract 100 from 136.4. Try this one: If the CPI is now 201.6, by what percentage did prices rise since the base year? Work it out right here:

They rose by 101.6 percent (201.6 – 100). Now you're getting it—I hope. You'll notice that we take the CPI in the current year and subtract the CPI in the base year, which is always 100.

No one would complain if the cost of living rose 2 or 3 percent a year, but during the 10-year period from 1972 to 1982 the consumer price index rose from 125.3 to 289.1. By what percentage did the cost of living rise? Figure it out here:

It went up by 130.7 percent. In other words, it cost the typical American family more than twice as much to live in 1982 as it did 10 years earlier.

If you didn't get an increase of 130.7 percent, then it's a pretty good bet that you could use some extra help calculating percentage changes. You'll find that help in the box "Finding Percentage Changes in the Price Level."

Deflation and Disinflation

Deflation.   *Deflation* is a decline in the price level, but once again, not for just a month or two but for a period of years. The last deflation the United States had was from 1929 to 1933, when prices fell 50 percent. Significantly, that deflation was accompanied by the Great Depression.

Until the inflationary recessions of the 1970s, business downturns were called deflations, for they were invariably accompanied by price declines. As much as business-

Finding Percentage Changes in the Price Level*

First we'll work out the arithmetic of finding the percentage change in going from 125.3 to 289.1:

$$\text{Percentage change} = \frac{\text{Change}}{\text{Original number}} \times 100$$

$$= \frac{163.8}{125.3} \times 100$$

$$= 1.307 \times 100$$

$$= 130.7$$

Calculating percentage changes is an essential skill, not just in economics, but in everyday life. If you're *still* not comfortable with the arithmetic, please study the box "Calculating Percentage Changes," which is about halfway through Chapter 8.

If all this is beginning to sound like déjà vu all over again, as baseball great Yogi Berra used to say, it should be. The reason we needed to compute percentage changes in Chapter 8 was to use them to gauge changes in real GDP. And to find real GDP itself, we employed the GDP deflator, which is a price index for GDP compiled by the Bureau of Labor Statistics. This organization also compiles the consumer price index (CPI), which mea-sures changes in consumer prices. So both the CPI and the GDP deflator are price indices, but the GDP deflator measures price changes in a much broader range of goods and services.

Here's a chance to work out a few more problems: Find the percentage change in prices since the base year if the CPI is now 94.7.

The answer is –5.3 percent. The price level declined (94.7 – 100 = – 5.3). OK, one last problem and we're out of here. By what percentage did prices rise since the base year if the CPI is now 485.2?

They rose by 385.2 percent (485.2 – 100 = 385.2). So when you're figuring out the percentage change in prices since the base year, all you have to do is subtract 100 from the current CPI.

*This method varies slightly from that shown in the box "Calculating Percentage Changes" in Chapter 8.

owners dislike inflation, particularly that of double-digit proportions, they hate deflation even more.

Suppose your store sells air conditioners, refrigerators, and other appliances. You place orders with manufacturers a couple of months before delivery and generally hold two months' worth of inventory in your warehouse. If there is a 2 or 3 percent rate of deflation, instead of the 2 or 3 percent rate of inflation you had been counting on, you'll probably have to charge about 5 percent less than you had been planning to charge. You paid your suppliers more than you should have, and you'll collect less from your customers than you had expected to. So just a little deflation can be very bad news to business firms, especially retailers.

But deflation is great news to consumers, because it means that they'll be paying lower prices. If you happen to have a lot of money—in the form of currency or bank deposits—you will be sitting pretty, because each dollar that you hold will be going up in value. And if you're living on a fixed income, you'll be able to buy more for your money.

Disinflation   You now know all about inflation and deflation. Get ready for a new one: *disinflation.* You may ask yourself, Do we really need another term, especially since *dis*inflation sounds a lot like *de*flation?

Until about 35 years ago, we would have had little use for the term *disinflation.* After all, if the price level was rising, that was inflation. If the price level was falling, that was deflation. And if prices were rising and output was going nowhere, we had stagflation. Immediately after World War II we had a great deal of inflation. But when recessions occurred, inflation would disappear and prices actually declined slightly.

By the late 1950s, even though the rate of inflation was quite moderate, recessions no longer eliminated rising prices. They continued to rise, albeit at a slower rate. This gave us our definition of disinflation: *Disinflation occurs when the rate of inflation declines.*

For example, during the recession of 1981–82, the rate of inflation fell from about 12 percent to about 4 percent. And again, since the recession of 1990–91, the rate of inflation fell from a little more than 4 percent to less than 2 percent (see Figure 6).

In late 1997 Federal Reserve Chairman Alan Greenspan stated that deflation was a very real possibility, perhaps in 1998. By January of 1998 several business economists were making similar forecasts. The last year the consumer price index fell was in 1955.

The Post–World War II History of Inflation

During each war in U.S. history, prices rose sharply. Each war was accompanied by a combination of money supply increases and large budget deficits.

In 1945, as World War II ended, a tremendous pent-up demand for consumer goods was unleashed. Consumer prices rose sharply. Too many dollars were chasing too few goods. Just as the inflation was being brought under control, the Korean War broke out. This brought on another wave of consumer spending and price increases.

President Dwight David Eisenhower took office in 1953, pledging to end the war in Korea and the inflation at home. It took him only a couple of months to end the war, but it wasn't until 1960, three recessions later, that inflation was controlled.

Until 1965, consumer prices rose at an annual rate of only 1 percent (see Figure 6). Then the Vietnam War, accompanied by huge federal budget deficits, rekindled another inflationary fire.

By this time most Americans had become conditioned to rising prices; they seemed inevitable. When prices have been rising for some time, it is reasonable to assume they will keep rising. So what did we do? We ran out to buy still more goods and services before prices rose still further. And when businessowners saw that demand for their products was high, they were encouraged to raise *their* prices.

What was taking place was a self-fulfilling prophecy. We thought something would happen, and it did. In other words, so long as people *believe* inflation is inevitable, it is indeed inevitable!

Early in President Richard Nixon's first term, he recognized this self-fulfilling prophecy; he therefore reasoned that all he needed to do was convince people that prices would not be rising in the near future. Then they wouldn't stock up on goods, and prices wouldn't rise.

Nixon's premise was correct, as was his conclusion: If people believe prices will be stable, they won't buy too much and drive up those prices. However, no one believed Nixon when he told the country that prices would be leveling off.

Since then a lot has happened to affect the rate of inflation. Nixon's wage and price freeze didn't really take, perhaps because it was tried only halfheartedly. When OPEC quadrupled oil prices in the fall of 1973, inflation accelerated (see Figure 6). The deep recession that followed did damp down the inflation, but in the late 1970s it returned with renewed vigor. Not until the back-to-back recessions of 1980 and 1981–82 was the rate of inflation finally brought down to acceptable levels.

In the 1970s we did get to add a new word to our vocabulary—*stagflation*—which is a contraction of the words *stagnation* and *inflation.* The new word got a great deal of use during the recessions of 1973–75, 1980, and 1981–82, when we experienced the worst of both worlds: declining output *and* inflation.

Since 1992, the inflation rate has stayed below 3 percent in five of six years. What accounts for this? Three factors come to mind. First is the rising tide of imported goods. When these imports compete with goods made in America, the competition drives down prices. Imported goods reduce our inflation rate by 1 or 2 percent.

A second factor is the rise of huge discounters, like WalMart, Toys R Us, Staples, and Price-Costco. In 1997 discount stores sold almost 50 percent of all general merchandise, up from 37 percent just eight years earlier. Discounters work closely with suppliers

At its present cost, life is worth about 30 cents on the dollar.
—Don Herold

Inflation seems inevitable.

Inflation is like sin; every government denounces it and every government practices it.
—Sir Frederick Keith-Ross,
June 1957

So far I haven't heard of anybody who wants to stop buying on account of the cost.
—Frank McKinney Hubbard

to minimize distribution costs, and these savings are largely passed on to consumers as lower prices.

Finally, the efforts of business firms to become leaner and meaner have been paying off in rising efficiency and productivity. Wage increases have been held down, millions of workers have been discharged, and, again, savings have been passed on to consumers. Are the bad old inflationary days of the 1970s and early 1980s behind us, or will inflation come roaring back again?

Why didn't the low unemployment rate in 1997 lead to a rising rate of inflation, as it had in previous years? An assortment of factors (most of which we've already mentioned) appears to have held down prices. In addition, people no longer expected price increases, as they had back in the 1980s, and those expectations can be self-fulfilling. We'll talk about such self-fulfilling expectations toward the end of the chapter when we consider inflation as a psychological process.

One might have expected that such low unemployment would create labor shortages, forcing employers to bid up wages to keep their current employees, and to entice new ones to come to work for them. But job insecurity, after years of corporate downsizing, and the migration of manufacturing jobs to low-wage countries, has made workers reluctant to press for large wage increases.

Hobson's choice: You lose either way—more inflation or a possible recession.

The Construction of the Consumer Price Index

The most important measure of inflation is the consumer price index. Now we'll see how the Bureau of Labor Statistics goes about constructing this index.

To find the CPI in the current year, divide the cost of living in the current year by the cost of living in the base year and multiply by 100.

First a base year is picked. In early 1998 we used the period 1982–84 as our base, setting the average price level of those years equal to 100. By December 1997 the CPI stood at 161.3, which meant, of course, that the price level had risen 63.1 percent since 1982–84. So the CPI measured the rise in the cost of living from the base years to December 1997.[6]

If you're *really* curious about the mechanics of how the CPI is constructed, it's worked out in the box "Construction of the Consumer Price Index." Of course, this is a very simplified version containing just six items. The Bureau of Labor Statistics compiles a market basket of hundreds of goods and services that the typical urban family buys in 1987. Assuming they buy that same market basket of goods and services in 1995, the BLS figures out how much that family would have had to spend. It then comes up with an index number for 1995. In fact, it does this every month.

In January 1995 Federal Reserve Chairman Alan Greenspan told Congress that the consumer price index overstated inflation by as much as 1.5 percentage points. Officials of the Labor Department disagreed with Greenspan, though they acknowledged a possible overstatement of perhaps as much as five-tenths of a percentage point. In December 1996 a commission headed by Michael Boskin (who had been the chief economic advisor to President George Bush) told Congress that the CPI overstated inflation by 1.1 percent. In any case, federal statisticians have begun a major overhaul of government statistics to remedy mounting deficiencies in measuring the nation's economic performance.

The consumer price index tends to overstate the actual rate of inflation by failing to account completely for gains in the quality of the goods and services that people buy as well as improvements in technology. Back in 1987, when there were personal computers in just 18 percent of all American households, you would have paid a lot more for one than you would have paid 10 years later. By 1997, when there were personal computers in 40 percent of all households, you could have bought one with much greater capabilities for the same money. But the CPI utterly fails to take into account such improvements in product quality.

Suppose that in 1999 the CPI is recalculated so that the rate of inflation is adjusted downward by 1 percent. Because Social Security benefits are raised by the same percent that the CPI rises, the average Social Security recipient would get about $100 less that

---

[6]The Bureau of Labor Statistics usually overhauls the CPI every 10 years, doing a survey of some 10,000 families to find out what they're buying and how much they're paying.

ADVANCED WORK .... Construction of the Consumer Price Index

We're going to calculate how much it cost a family to live in March 1987 and in March 1995. In the table showing hypothetical costs of living for these months, part A has a month's expenditures for 1987, the base year. To find these expenditures, we multiply quantity purchased by price. Then, adding up the money spent on each item, we find the total amount of money spent in March 1987.

Now we'll compare that amount with the amount spent in March 1995, which is shown in part B. What happened, then, was that the family spent $848 for these six items in 1987 and $994 for these same items in 1995. Obviously, their cost of living went up. But by how much?

To find out, we'll construct a consumer price index. To do this, divide the cost of living in the base year, 1987, into the cost of living in the current year, 1995. After you've done that, multiply your answer by 100 to convert it into an index number. Do your work in the space provided and then check it with the calculations shown.

$$994/848 = 1.172$$
$$1.172 \times 100 = 117.2.$$

That's our consumer price index for 1995. You'll notice that we've carried it to one decimal place, which is exactly how the Bureau of Labor Statistics does it, and how you'll find it listed in the newspaper.

One last question: By what percentage did prices rise between 1987 and 1995? The envelope please. Prices rose by 17.2 percent (117.2 − 100).

If you're still having trouble figuring out percentage changes, reread the box titled "Finding Percentage Changes in the Price Level," earlier in this chapter.

A. March 1987

Item	Quantity	Price	Quantity × Price
Loaf of bread	10	.70	7.00
Quart of milk	15	.60	9.00
Pair of jeans	2	23.00	46.00
New car	0.02	7800.00	156.00
Mortgage payment	1	590.00	590.00
Movie admission	8	5.00	40.00
Total			848.00

B. March 1995

Item	Quantity	Price	Quantity × Price
Loaf of bread	10	.90	9.00
Quart of milk	15	.80	12.00
Pair of jeans	2	31.00	62.00
New car	0.02	9000.00	180.00
Mortgage payment	1	675.00	675.00
Movie admission	8	7.00	56.00
Total			994.00

year. In Chapter 11 we'll look at the effects of an adjustment in the CPI on government spending and tax receipts.

Anticipated and Unanticipated Inflation

Why farmers like inflation

Traditionally, inflation has hurt creditors and helped debtors. Throughout our history, the farmers have been debtors. During times of deflation or stable prices, the farmers' cries of anguish are heard loud and clear all the way to Washington; but during times of inflation, there is scarcely a peep out of them.

Creditors have better memories than debtors.
—James Howell, 1659

It is easy to see why. Suppose a farmer borrows $100, which he agrees to repay in one year along with 4 percent interest ($4). In one year he pays back $104. But what if, during the year, prices double? The money he pays back is worth much less than the money he borrowed.

Let's say that when the farmer borrowed the money, wheat was selling at $2 a bushel. He would have been able to buy 50 bushels of wheat ($100/$2). But farmers don't buy wheat; they sell it. So one year later, this farmer harvests his wheat and pays back the loan. If the price level doubles, assume the price of wheat doubles. How much wheat would the farmer need to sell at $4 a bushel to pay off the $104 he owes? He would need to sell only 26 bushels ($104/$4).

This farmer, who is a debtor, benefits magnificently from unanticipated inflation because he has borrowed money worth some 50 bushels of wheat and pays back his loan—with interest—in money worth only 26 bushels of wheat. Debtors, in general, gain from unanticipated inflation because they repay their loans in inflated dollars.

Just as obviously, those hurt by unanticipated inflation are people who lend out the money—the creditors. We generally think of creditors as banks, but banks are really financial middlemen. The ultimate creditors, or lenders, are the people who put their money in banks, life insurance, or any other financial instrument paying a fixed rate of interest. And the biggest debtor and gainer from unanticipated inflation has been the U.S. government. The national debt, which now totals $5.5 trillion, would be a lot easier to pay off if there were a great deal of inflation.

The issuers may have, and in the case of government paper, always have, a direct interest in lowering the value of the currency, because it is the medium in which their own debts are computed.

—John Stuart Mill

Another group helped by unanticipated inflation is businessowners. Just as businesses suffer losses on their inventory during periods of deflation, during inflations they obtain inventory price windfalls. Between the time inventory is ordered and the time it is sold, prices have crept upward, swelling profits.

Who is hurt by inflation?

Those who are hurt by unanticipated inflation are people who live on fixed incomes, particularly retired people who depend on pensions (except Social Security) and those who hold long-term bonds, whether corporate or U.S. government bonds. Finally, people whose wages are fixed under long-term contracts and landlords who have granted long-term leases at fixed rent are hurt by unanticipated inflation. In other words, under unanticipated inflation, some people gain and others lose. In fact, the gains and losses are exactly equal.

When inflation is fully anticipated, there are no winners or losers. The interest rate takes into account the expected rate of inflation. Normally, without anticipated inflation, the interest rate would be around 3 or 4 percent. In 1980, and again in 1981, when the rate of inflation ran at close to 15 percent, the prime rate of interest (paid by top credit-rated corporations) soared over 20 percent.

If all prices and incomes rose equally, no harm would be done to anyone. But the rise is not equal. Many lose and some gain.

—Irving Fisher, 1920

For inflation to be fully anticipated and built into interest rates, people need to live with it for several years. Although the country had relatively high inflation for most of the 1970s, it was only in 1979 that the prime interest rate (which top credit-rated corporate borrowers pay) finally broke the 12 percent barrier. Today, however, unanticipated inflation is largely a thing of the past.

Creditors have learned to charge enough interest to take into account, or anticipate, the rate of inflation over the course of the loan. This is tacked onto the regular interest rate that the lender would charge had no inflation been expected.

Real rate of interest

We'll work out a few examples. If the real rate of interest (the rate that would be charged without inflation) were 5 percent, and there was an expected rate of inflation of 3 percent, then obviously the creditors would charge 8 percent.

If the real rate of interest were 4 percent and the expected inflation rate were 6 percent, how much would the nominal rate (the rate actually charged) be? Good! I know you said 10 percent. Thus, the real rate of interest plus the expected rate of inflation equals the nominal rate of interest.

Are you ready for a tricky one? If the nominal interest rate is 6 percent and the expected rate of inflation is 8 percent, how much is the real rate of interest? Have you found it yet? The real rate of interest is –2 percent. How can a real rate of interest be negative? It can be negative if the rate of inflation is greater than the rate of interest that you pay or receive (i.e., the nominal rate of interest).

If the nominal interest rate accurately reflects the inflation rate, then the inflation has been fully anticipated and no one wins or loses. This is a good thing for the economy because it means no one is hurt and no one is forced out of business because of inflation.

Is a Dollar Worth Only 50 Cents Today?

What this country needs is a good five-cent nickel.
—Franklin Pierce Adams

A dollar is worth only 50 cents today. Is that true? If it is, then would you be willing to give me a dollar for every 50 cents I give you? Think about it.

What you really mean when you say that a dollar is worth only 50 cents today is that a dollar today buys only half as much (or 50 percent of) what it bought, say, 10 years ago.

When you lament that a dollar is worth only 50 cents today—or 25 cents, or even 10 cents for that matter—you need to specify which year's dollar you are comparing with today's dollar. For example, in 1948 you could buy a hot dog for a dime or see a movie for 50 cents. So, in terms of what a dollar bought in 1948, a dollar today is worth only about 10 cents.

But if the rate of inflation keeps growing—even if it is correctly anticipated—our economy will be in big trouble. In a hyperinflation there are ultimately only losers.

In recent years Social Security benefits have been indexed for inflation; that is, they have gone up by the same percentage as the consumer price index, protecting those who collect Social Security from inflation. Many wage-earners, too, are protected against inflation by cost-of-living adjustment clauses (called COLA agreements) in their contracts.[7] One way or another, then, many sectors of our society have learned to protect themselves from at least the short-term ravages of inflation. (But how much is a dollar worth? See box "Is a Dollar Worth Only 50 Cents Today?")

Theories of the Causes of Inflation

Excessive demand causes demand-pull inflation

Demand-Pull Inflation   When there is excessive demand for goods and services, we have demand-pull inflation. What is excessive? When people are willing and able to buy more output than our economy can produce. Something's gotta give. And what gives are prices.

Demand-pull inflation is often summed up as "too many dollars chasing too few goods." The problem is that we can't produce any more goods because our economy is already operating at full capacity.

What happens next if demand keeps rising? What if people have money in their pockets and the desire to spend it? Again, something's gotta give. Output can't rise any more. There's only one thing that can go up: prices.

This usually happens during wars. The government spends a lot of money on uniforms, tanks, planes, rifles, bullets, bombs, and missile systems. Private citizens want more consumer goods and services. Business firms are also bidding for resources to build more plant and equipment, expand their inventories, buy more raw materials, and hire more employees. So everyone's out there spending a lot of money to buy what they want.

Inflation is a form of taxation that can be imposed without legislation.
—Milton Friedman

It would not be unreasonable to ask, Just *where* did all this money come from? Milton Friedman, a Nobel laureate in economics and the world's leading exponent of monetary economics, has long been rounding up the usual suspects: the seven governors of the Federal Reserve System, which controls the money supply's rate of growth. Chapter 13 provides a detailed account of how the Board of Governors exercises that control. Demand-pull inflation is shown graphically in the box "Demand-Pull Inflation and the Aggregate Supply Curve."

The wage-price spiral

Cost-Push Inflation   There are three variants of cost-push inflation. Most prominent is the wage-price spiral. Because wages constitute nearly two-thirds of the cost of doing business, whenever workers receive a significant wage increase, this increase is passed along to consumers in the form of higher prices. Higher prices raise everyone's cost of living, engendering further wage increases.

---

[7]About one worker in four is covered by a COLA. See Chapter 30 of *Economics* or Chapter 18 of *Microeconomics.*

ADVANCED WORK

Demand-Pull Inflation and the Aggregate Supply Curve

To help explain what happens when there's excess demand, we'll select another term from the economist's tool kit: the *aggregate supply curve*. The figure here shows a hypothetical aggregate supply curve. It has a horizontal curve that begins to slope upward to the right and eventually becomes completely vertical. Notice that it becomes vertical at full employment.

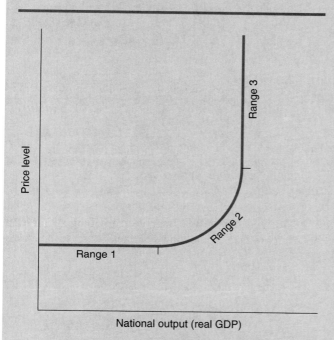

National output (real GDP)

At very low levels of output—depression levels—it is easy to increase output without raising prices. After all, with high unemployment and idle plant and equipment, those resources can be put back to work without raising costs much. For example, if a person who has been out of

work for several months is offered a job at the going wage rate, she will jump at the chance to get back to work.

Look at the aggregate supply curve. In which range are we operating? Clearly we're in range 1.

As output expands, most of the idle resources will be back in production. Firms that need more plant and equipment will have to buy them. Employers will have to raise wages to induce new employees to work for them. In effect, then, businesses will have to bid for resources, and in doing so, they will bid up the prices of land, labor, and capital. We are now in range 2 of the aggregate supply curve.

As their costs go up, business firms will be forced to raise their prices. We're moving closer and closer to full employment. It becomes increasingly difficult to get good help. New workers have to be lured away from other employers. There's only one way to do this: pay them more.

This pushes costs up still further until finally we've reached the full-employment level of output. Any further spending on goods and services will simply bid up prices without any corresponding increase in output. Welcome to range 3.

Our economy rarely operates in either range 1 or range 3. Both depressions and runaway inflations are relatively rare occurrences, though they *do* happen. The twin goals of macroeconomic policy are to avoid these extremes, or anything approaching them. But runaway inflations in particular are sometimes unavoidable. This happens when macroeconomic policy must subordinate itself to military necessity. During World War II, for example, the federal government bought up half the national output for military use. The only problem was that private citizens had plenty of money to spend and not enough output to spend it on. So civilians and the government had a bidding war for the country's limited resources. It was a classic case of too much money chasing too few goods.

We've actually gotten a bit ahead of ourselves. To fully understand the shape of the aggregate supply curve, we need to do some further analysis, which we'll put off until the next chapter.

One man's wage rise is another man's price increase.
—Sir Harold Wilson, 1970

Imagine a 3 percent rise in the cost of living. Labor unions will negotiate for a 3 percent catch-up increase and a 3 percent increase on top of that for an anticipated cost-of-living increase *next* year. That's 6 percent. If every labor union gets a 6 percent increase, prices will undoubtedly rise not 3 percent but you guessed it—6 percent! In the next round of labor negotiations, the unions might want not just a 6 percent catch-up but 12 percent, to take care of next year as well.[8]

All of this can be described as the wage-price spiral. Regardless of who is to blame for its origin, once it gets started it spawns larger and larger wage and price increases. Round and round it goes, and where it stops nobody knows.

This variant of cost-push inflation may well explain a great deal of the inflation the country experienced through the early 1970s. However, in recent years the membership

---

[8]Labor unions are covered in Chapter 30 of *Economics* and Chapter 18 of *Microeconomics*.

Profit-push inflation

and power of U.S. labor unions have been sharply declining, so the wage-price spiral would serve today, at best, as a partial explanation for inflation.

The second variant of cost-push inflation is profit-push inflation. Because just a handful of huge firms dominate many industries (for example, cigarettes, detergents, breakfast cereals, cars, and oil), these firms have the power to administer prices in those industries rather than accept the dictates of the market forces of supply and demand. To the degree that they are able to protect their profit margins by raising prices, these firms will respond to any rise in costs by passing them on to their customers.

Supply-side cost shocks

Finally, we have supply-side cost shocks, most prominently the oil price shocks of 1973–74 and 1979. When the OPEC nations quadrupled the price of oil in the fall of 1973, they touched off not just a major recession but also a severe inflation. When the price of oil rises, the cost of making many other things rises as well, for example, electricity, fertilizer, gasoline, heating oil, and long-distance freight carriage. And as we've seen again and again, cost increases are quickly translated into price increases. Cost-push inflation is shown graphically in the box "Graphing Demand-Pull and Cost-Push Inflation."

Inflation as a Psychological Process

Inflation takes on a life of its own.

Have you noticed that once inflation gets under way, the initial cause is of little consequence because the process takes on a life of its own? To come to grips with inflation, we must get at its roots. We have already discussed the psychology of inflation. If people believe prices will rise, they will act in a way that keeps them rising. The only way to curb inflation is to counter inflationary psychology.

Various things can set off an inflationary spiral—wars, huge federal budget deficits, large increases in the money supply, sudden increases in the price of oil—but once the spiral begins, inflationary psychology takes over.

When prices have been jolted upward, the original cause no longer matters; other forces are activated. Labor unions seek catch-up wage increases. Businesspeople raise their prices to keep up with costs—primarily wage increases. Consumers with money in their pockets spend it before prices rise further.

ADVANCED WORK .... Graphing Demand-Pull and Cost-Push Inflation

Demand-pull inflation is set off by an increase in demand for goods and services without any increase in supply. The left graph shows how prices rise.

Cost-push inflation happens when production costs rise. Sellers can no longer supply the same output at current prices. This results in a decrease in supply. We see how prices go up in the right graph.

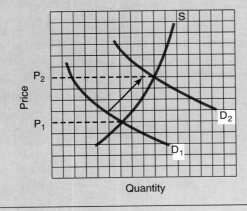

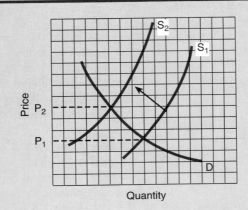

Breaking the back of the inflationary psychology

To stop inflation, then, we need to convince workers, businesspeople, and consumers that prices will stop rising. If we can do that, prices *will* stop rising.

Once we attain a period of price stability, the psychology of inflation will be destroyed. We will enjoy that stability as long as we can avoid triggering another round of inflation. In the early 1960s we attained such a period of stability, but then came the Vietnam War and its attendant federal budget deficits. Again in the mid-1980s we had a very low rate of inflation, but continuing deficits and rapid monetary growth may have rekindled the inflationary fires.

To break the back of the inflationary psychology is to bring down the rate of inflation for a sufficiently long period of time for people actually to expect price stability to continue. This has happened in the recent past only after successive recessions have wrung inflation out of the economy. To date, this has been the only cure we've come up with, and obviously it's a cure with some unpleasant side effects, particularly for those who lose their jobs during these recessions. After we examine creeping inflation and hyperinflation, we'll return to the problem of unemployment.

Creeping Inflation and Hyperinflation

Creeping inflation in one country would be hyperinflation in another.

Because *inflation* is a relative term, what may be considered creeping inflation in one country would be hyperinflation in another. Moreover, what might have been called creeping inflation in one particular country 10 years ago might now be considered hyperinflation in that same country.

For example, when the United States suffered from double-digit inflation in the mid-1970s and again in the late 70s and early 80s, a rate of 6 or 7 percent would have been welcomed as creeping inflation. But by the mid-1980s, some people would have considered anything above 4 percent to be hyperinflation.

Let's take an annual rate of increase in the consumer price index of 1 or 2 percent as something that virtually everyone would agree is creeping inflation. Very few people would be alarmed by this price-level increase. Businesspeople would generally like it because it would swell profits and basically be good for business. And as we have seen, many wage-earners and all Social Security recipients are protected from inflation by cost-of-living increases tied to the consumer price index.

Having a little inflation is like being a little pregnant.
—Leon Henderson

But once we cross the line between creeping inflation and hyperinflation—which keeps shifting—we run into trouble. It becomes increasingly difficult to conduct normal economic affairs. Prices are raised constantly. It becomes impossible to enter into long-term contracts. No one is sure what the government might do.

Prices serve as a signal system for business firms. If prices are rising, business firms will produce more goods and services. But what if costs are rising faster?

Suppose Bethlehem Steel agrees to supply General Motors with 50,000 tons of steel at $300 a ton. Suddenly Bethlehem's costs rise by 50 percent. Would GM go along with a $150 increase, raising the price from $300 to $450 a ton? Would you? Not if you had signed a contract calling for only $300 a ton.

Meanwhile, the government—meaning Congress, the president, and the Federal Reserve Board[9]—may decide to act precipitously. On August 15, 1971, President Nixon suddenly announced the imposition of wage and price controls—based on a law he had been saying he would never use. In October 1979 the Federal Reserve Board suddenly stopped monetary growth, sending interest rates through the roof and touching off a sharp recession.

The German inflation

The classic hyperinflation took place in Germany after World War I. You may think that double-digit inflation (10 percent or more per year) is hyperinflation, but in Germany prices rose 10 percent an hour! The German government had to print larger and larger denominations—100-mark notes, then 1,000-mark notes, and, eventually, 1-million-mark

---

[9]Technically, the Federal Reserve Board is not part of the government. We'll consider its role in regulating the rate of growth of our money supply in Chapter 13.

Hungary's pengö provides an example of inflation

notes. The smaller denominations became worthless; parents gave them to children as play money.

The German inflation eventually led to a complete economic breakdown, helped touch off a worldwide depression, and paved the way for a new chancellor named Adolf Hitler. No wonder the Germans get nervous whenever their inflation rate begins to inch up.

Another classic example is what happened in Hungary during and after World War II. Before the war, if you went into a store with a pengö, you had some money in your pocket. In those days a pengö was a pengö. But by August 1946, you needed 828 octillion pengös—that's 828 followed by 27 zeros—to buy what one pengö bought before the war.

When inflation really gets out of hand, people begin to refuse to accept money as a means of payment. Society is reduced to a state of barter, making it extremely difficult for the economy to function. If you don't have what I want or I don't have what you want, we can't do business.

When there is *any* inflation, even a creeping inflation of just 1 or 2 percent a year, people often worry that the rate will keep increasing until we have a runaway inflation. Does this always happen? The answer is a definite no. However, there's always the chance that things may get out of control. Like fire, a little inflation is not bad at all, but if it gets out of control, we'll be in big trouble.

Conclusion

The misery index

One thing the economy has rarely been able to attain simultaneously is a low unemployment rate and stable prices. A British economist, A. W. Phillips, even had a curve named after him illustrating that there is a trade-off between price stability and low unemployment.

As Phillips showed, in the 1950s and 1960s we attained price stability at the cost of higher unemployment and vice versa. In the 1970s, though, we had high unemployment *and* rapidly rising prices. During the presidential campaign of 1976, Jimmy Carter castigated President Gerald Ford with his "misery index," which was the inflation rate and the unemployment rate combined.[10] Anything over 10 was unacceptable, according to Carter.

In 1980 Ronald Reagan resurrected the misery index for the voters, reminding them that it had gone from 10, when President Carter took office, all the way to 20.

---

[10]During the 1960s Arthur Okun, while he was President Lyndon Johnson's Chairman of the Council of Economic Advisors, coined the term *economic discomfort index,* which Jimmy Carter renamed the *misery index.*

Figure 7   The Misery Index, 1948–97

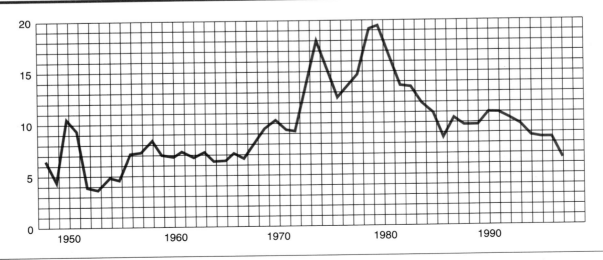

Source: *Economic Report of the President,* 1998.

Although the misery index has obvious political uses, it also provides us with a snapshot view of our economic performance over the last four decades. From Figure 7 we can gauge just how stable our economy has been during this period. When taken together with Figure 1, we can safely say that our economic record, particularly that of the last two decades, is not one we would want to write home about. On the other hand, since 1993 our misery index has stayed below 10 and is still falling.

It would certainly be hard to have a lower misery index then we have had in recent years. We'll begin to examine macroeconomic policy in Chapter 11 to learn how things are supposed to work and why they sometimes don't. But first I'll try to tie things together a bit in the next chapter when we look at equilibrium GDP.

Questions for Further Thought and Discussion

1. Why is a high rate of inflation bad for the economy?
2. Right now, our economy is going through what phase of the business cycle? How do you know this?
3. Explain the difference between deflation and disinflation.
4. Being unemployed means different things to different people. Illustrate this by making up examples of three different unemployed people.
5. How would you improve upon the way the Bureau of Labor Statistics computes the unemployment rate?

WORKBOOK FOR CHAPTER 9

Name _____   Date _____

Multiple-Choice Questions

Circle the letter that corresponds to the best answer.

1. If the CPI rose from 160.5 in 1998 to 168.7 in 1999 to 173.4 in 2000, this would be an example of
   a. deflation   b. disinflation   c. inflation

2. Disinflation generally occurs during
   a. recessions   b. economic booms   c. periods of hyperinflation   d. times of deflation

3. In the three-phase business cycle, the prosperity phase is always followed immediately by
   a. recovery   b. the trough   c. depression
   d. recession

4. If our economy is at full employment, the cyclical rate of unemployment would be
   a. 0   b. 2 percent   c. 5 percent
   d. impossible to find

5. A business cycle forecasting method that tries to explain the entire economic process is
   a. endogenous   b. exogenous   c. barometric
   d. analytic

6. If the CPI rose from 100 to 500, the price level rose by
   a. 100 percent   b. 200 percent   c. 300 percent
   d. 400 percent   e. 500 percent

7. *Prosperity Lost,* a book by _____, recounted scores of instances of structural employment.
   a. Joseph Schumpeter   b. William Stanley Jevons
   c. Philip Mattera   d. Milton Friedman
   e. Alfred Smith

8. If there are 90 million people employed, 10 million unemployed, 5 million collecting unemployment insurance, and 5 million discouraged workers, there are _____ in the labor force.
   a. 90 million   b. 95 million   c. 100 million
   d. 105 million   e. 110 million

9. During the 1970s, we experienced
   a. high inflation and high unemployment   b. low inflation and low unemployment   c. high inflation and low unemployment   d. low inflation and high unemployment

10. The misery index was highest in which of these years?
    a. 1989   b. 1986   c. 1980   d. 1977   e. 1967

11. The last time we had full employment was in
    a. 1929   b. 1945   c. 1957   d. 1969

12. We have business cycles of
    a. the same length and amplitude   b. the same length but different amplitudes   c. the same amplitude but different lengths   d. different lengths and amplitudes

13. During business cycles
    a. troughs are followed by recessions   b. troughs are followed by peaks   c. peaks are followed by troughs   d. peaks are followed by recessions

14. The second part of the expansion phase of the cycle is
    a. recovery   b. prosperity   c. recession
    d. depression

15. An example of an exogenous business cycle theory would be
    a. overinvestment   b. inventory   c. money   d. war

16. The accelerator principle is a variant of the _____ theory.
    a. monetary   b. innovations   c. psychological
    d. overinvestment

17. The GDP gap is found by
    a. subtracting actual GDP from potential GDP
    b. subtracting potential GDP from actual GDP   c. adding potential GDP and actual GDP   d. none of the above

18. When the unemployment rate rises, the GDP gap
    a. will get wider   b. will get narrower   c. will remain the same   d. none of the above is correct

19. The unemployment rate is computed by the
    a. nation's unemployment insurance offices
    b. Bureau of Labor Statistics   c. Department of Commerce   d. Office of Management and Budget

20. If the number of unemployed stays the same and the number of people in the labor force rises
    a. the unemployment rate will rise   b. the unemployment rate will fall   c. the unemployment rate will stay the same   d. there is not enough information to determine what will happen to the unemployment rate

21. Which statement is true?
    a. Both liberals and conservatives feel that the official unemployment rate is too high.   b. Both liberals and conservatives feel that the official unemployment rate is too low.   c. The liberals believe that the official unemployment rate is too high, and the conservatives feel that it is too low.   d. The conservatives feel that the official unemployment rate is too high, and the liberals feel that it is too low.

22. Greater participation by young people in the labor force
    a. tends to push the unemployment rate up   b. tends to push the unemployment rate down   c. has no effect on the unemployment rate   d. has an unknown effect on the unemployment rate

23. Which statement is false?
    a. Over the last two decades there has been an upward drift in the unemployment rate.   b. The unemployment rate for blacks is about twice that for whites.   c. The official unemployment rate includes "discouraged" workers.   d. None of the above is false.

Answer questions 24 through 29 by using one of these three choices:
    a. frictional unemployment   b. structural unemployment   c. cyclical unemployment

24. An autoworker who is still out of work two years after her plant closed is an example of _____.

25. A homemaker returning to the labor market after an absence of 10 years and looking for work is an example of _____.

26. A blue-collar worker who is laid off until business picks up again is an example of _____.

27. People who are "between jobs" are examples of _____.

28. A person in his mid-50s whose skills have become obsolete would be an example of _____.

29. When the unemployment rate goes above 5 percent, anything above that 5 percent level is _____.

30. An example of deflation since the base year would be a CPI in the current year of
    a. 90   b. 100   c. 110   d. 200

31. Inflation generally occurs
    a. during wartime   b. before wars   c. during recessions   d. during peacetime

32. The period of greatest price stability was
    a. 1950–56   b. 1958–64   c. 1968–76   d. 1976–82

33. Traditionally, those hurt by inflation have been _____ _____.
    a. creditors and people on fixed incomes   b. debtors and people on fixed incomes   c. debtors and creditors

34. Farmers have generally been _____ by inflation.
    a. hurt   b. helped   c. neither helped nor hurt

35. Creditors generally do better when inflation is
    a. anticipated   b. unanticipated   c. neither anticipated nor unanticipated

36. Businesspeople generally like a little _____ but dislike a little _____.
    a. inflation, deflation   b. deflation, inflation

37. Inflationary recessions first occurred in the
    a. 1950s   b. 1960s   c. 1970s   d. 1980s

Fill-In Questions

1. The worst recession since World War II began in _____.

2. Stagflation is a contraction of the words _____ and _____.

3. To find the number of people in the labor force we need to add the _____ and the _____.

4. To find the unemployment rate we need to divide the _____ by the _____.

5. A person who is functionally illiterate faces long periods of _____ unemployment.

6. When the overall unemployment rate is 6.5 percent, the cyclical unemployment rate is _____.

7. The upper turning point of a business cycle is called the _____.

8. In the year _____ the OPEC nations quadrupled the price of oil.

9. The low point of a business cycle is the _____; _____the high point is the _____.

10. Theories that place the cause of business cycles within the economy rather than outside are known as _____ _____ theories.

11. According to the inventory theory of the business cycle, a recession is set off when retailers _____.

12. The monetary theory of the business cycle hypothesizes that recessions are set off when _____ and recoveries begin when the monetary authorities _____.

13. The acceleration principle requires sales to keep increasing at the _____ to prevent investment from _____.

14. Two exogenous theories of the business cycle are the

(1) _____ theory and the

(2) _____ theory.

15. Economic forecasts that attempt to explain the entire economic process are _____ forecasts, while those that track only a few economic variables are _____ forecasts.

16. To be eligible for unemployment insurance benefits, you need to be able to answer yes to these three questions:

(1) _____?

(2) _____?

(3)_____?

17. Liberals say the unemployment rate is actually _____ _____ than the BLS says it is; conservatives say it is really _____.

18. Between the mid-1970s and the mid-1980s, our unemployment rate never dipped below _____ percent.

19. The unemployment rate for blacks is about _____ times the white unemployment rate.

20. The misery index is found by adding the _____ _____ and the _____.

21. When the unemployment rate declines, the GDP gap _____.

22. To be eligible for unemployment insurance, you need to have worked at least _____ or _____.

23. During a very severe recession when more than 11 percent of the labor force is out of work, most of the unemployment is _____ unemployment.

24. In 1973 the OPEC nations _____ the price of oil.

25. According to A. W. Phillips, there is a trade-off between _____ and _____.

26. If the consumer price index rises from 150 to 180, the cost of living rose by _____ percent.

27. Deflation is _____.

28. The three variants of cost-push inflation are (1) _____;

_____; (2) _____;

and (3) _____.

29. Once inflation is under way, an _____

takes over.

30. To stop inflation, we need to convince people that _____

_____.

Problems

1. If the unemployment rate is 7 percent, how much is cyclical unemployment?

2. Compute the unemployment rate given the following information: 8 million unemployed, 117 million employed.

3. Given the following information, how many people are in the labor force? 3 million people are collecting unemployment insurance; 7 million people are officially unemployed; 2 million people are discouraged workers; and 110 million people are employed.

4. How much would the nominal interest rate be if the real rate of interest were 6 percent and the expected rate of inflation were 7 percent?

5. How much would the real rate of interest be if the nominal interest rate were 12 percent and the expected rate of inflation were 4 percent?

6. If the CPI is currently 178.9, by what percentage did prices rise since the base year?

7. If the CPI rose from 200 in 1991 to 240 in 1997, by what percentage did prices increase?

8. If the rate of inflation is 5 percent, the prime rate of interest is 6 percent, and the unemployment rate is 7 percent, how much is the misery index?

9. If actual GDP is 4,400 and potential GDP is 4,600, state the GDP gap in dollars.

10. Label the graph in Figure 1 with respect to the three phases of the business cycle and the cycle turning points.

Figure 1

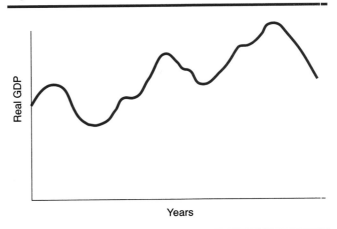

11. Answer these questions, given the following information: **a.** How many people are in the labor force? **b.** What is the unemployment rate? Employed: 90 million; discouraged workers: 4 million; unemployed: 10 million; people collecting unemployment insurance: 8 million.

12. a. If the CPI fell from 180 to 150, by what percentage did the price level fall? **b.** If the CPI rose from 150 to 180, by what percentage did the price level rise?

10 Classical and Keynesian Economics

This chapter is divided into three parts: (1) the classical economic system, (2) the Keynesian critique of the classical system, and (3) the Keynesian system. The basic difference between Keynes and the classicals is whether our economy tends toward full employment.

Chapter Objectives

In this chapter we shall take up:

- Say's law.
- Classical equilibrium
- Real balance, interest rate, and foreign purchases effects.
- Aggregate demand.
- Aggregate supply in the long run and short run.
- The Keynesian critique of the classical system.
- Equilibrium at varying price levels.
- Disequilibrium and equilibrium.
- Keynesian policy prescriptions.

Part I: The Classical Economic System

Say's law

Jean Baptiste Say, French economist and entrepreneur (Historical Pictures/Stock Montage)

The centerpiece of classical economics is Say's law. Named for Jean Baptiste Say, a late-18th-century (that means the late 1700s) French economist, the law stated, "*Supply creates its own demand.*" Think about it. Somehow what we produce—supply—all gets sold.

A few years later the great English economist David Ricardo elaborated on Say's law:

> No man produces but with a view to consume or sell, and he never sells but with an intention to purchase some other commodity which may be immediately useful to him or which may contribute to future production. By producing, then, he necessarily becomes either the consumer of his own goods, or the purchaser and consumer of the goods of some other person.[1]

People who produce things are paid. What do they do with this money? They spend it. On what? On what *other* people produce.

We can illustrate Say's law using the production figures in Table 1. Let's look at Table 1. Everyone eats tomatoes, bread, and butter, and wears Mao jackets and wooden shoes. Joe sells eight bushels of tomatoes, keeping two for his own use. Sally wears one of her Mao jackets and sells the other four. And so forth.

---

[1] David Ricardo, *The Principles of Political Economy and Taxation* (Burr Ridge, IL: Richard D. Irwin, 1963), p. 166.

Table 1	Production in a Five-Person Economy
Joe	10 bushels of tomatoes
Sally	5 Mao jackets
Mike	20 loaves of bread
Bill	10 pounds of butter
Alice	5 pairs of wooden shoes

What do they do with the proceeds from their sales? They use them to buy what they need from each of the others. Joe, for example, buys a Mao jacket from Sally, four loaves of bread from Mike, two pounds of butter from Bill (they all like to put a lot of butter on their bread), and a pair of wooden shoes from Alice.

"Why does anybody work?" asked Say. Because a person wants money with which to buy things. Why do *you* work?

As long as everyone spends everything that he or she earns, we're OK. But we begin having problems when people start saving part of their incomes.

Basically, producers need to sell everything they produce. If some people save, then not everything produced will be sold. In a world with large companies instead of self-employed producers, some workers must be laid off when demand for production falls. In fact, as unemployment mounts, demand falls still further, necessitating further cutbacks in production and employment.

The villain of the piece is clearly saving. If only people would spend their entire incomes, we'd never have unemployment. But people do save, and saving is crucial to economic growth. Without saving we could not have investment—the production of plant, equipment, and inventory.[2]

Think of production as consisting of two products: consumer goods and investment goods (for now, we're ignoring government goods). People will buy consumer goods; the money spent on such goods is designated by the letter C. Money spent by businesses on investment goods is designated by the letter I.

If we think of GDP as total spending, then GDP would be C + I. Once this money is spent, other people receive it as income. And what do they do with their income? They spend some of it and save the rest.

If we think of GDP as income received, that money will either be spent on consumer goods, C, or saved, which we'll designate by the letter S. If we put all this together, we have two equations:

$$GDP = C + I$$

$$GDP = C + S$$

These two equations can be simplified to one short equation. First, because things equal to the same thing are equal to each other:

$$C + I = C + S$$

This step is justified because C + I and C + S are both equal to GDP. Therefore, they are equal to each other.

Next, we can subtract the same thing from both sides of an equation. In this case we are subtracting C:

$$C + I = C + S$$
$$I = S$$

Going back to Say's law, we can see that it holds up, at least in accordance with classical analysis. Supply does create its own demand. The economy produces a supply of consumer goods and investment goods. The people who produce these goods spend part

---

[2] In this chapter we're ignoring investment in residential housing and considering only business investment.

of their incomes on consumer goods and save the rest. Their savings are borrowed by investors who spend this money on investment goods. The bottom line is that everything the economy produces is purchased.

This is a perfect economic system. Everything produced is sold. Everyone who wants to work can find a job. There will never be any serious economic downturns, so there is no need for the government to intervene to set things right.

Supply and Demand Revisited

We're going to be doing a considerable amount of supply and demand analysis, which you may remember dimly from Chapter 3. Rather than ask you to turn back to that chapter, I've drawn another supply and demand graph for you in Figure 1.

I'd like you to observe two things: equilibrium price and equilibrium quantity. How much is the equilibrium price? Good. And the equilibrium quantity? Good—you got that right, too. You followed the horizontal dotted line to a price of about $7.20 and the vertical dotted line to a quantity of 6.

Equilibrium price and quantity

Incidentally, we call the price that clears the market *equilibrium price* and the quantity purchased and sold *equilibrium quantity*. At the equilibrium price the quantity that buyers wish to purchase is equal to the quantity that sellers wish to sell.

Now let's see how the classical economists applied the law of supply and demand to help prove Say's law and, more specifically, to prove that I = S (Investment = Saving). This is done in Figure 2, which graphs the demand for investment funds and the supply of savings.

What if savings and investment were not equal? For instance, if savings were greater than investment, there would be unemployment. Not everything being produced would be purchased.

Savings and investment will be equal.

There's nothing to worry about, according to the classical economists. And they proved this by means of the two curves in Figure 2. If savings were greater than investment, the interest rate would fall. Why? Because some savers would be willing to lend at lower interest rates and some investors would be induced to borrow at lower interest rates.

Prices and wages will fall to bring about equilibrium between saving and investing.

The classical economists had a fallback position. Even if lower interest rates did not eliminate the surplus of savings relative to investment, price flexibility would bring about equilibrium between saving and investing. Business firms, unable to sell their entire output, would simply lower prices. And then people would buy everything produced.

One might ask whether business firms could make a profit if prices were reduced. Yes, answered the classical economists, if resource prices—particularly wages—were also reduced. Although output and employment might decline initially, they would move

Figure 1   Demand and Supply Curves

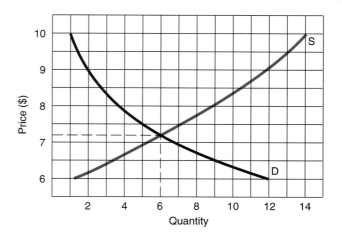

back up again once prices and wages fell. At lower prices people would buy more, and at lower wages employers would hire more.

Falling prices and falling wage rates can also be illustrated by a supply and demand graph. Look at Figure 3. If sellers of a particular good are not selling all they wish to sell *at the price,* some of them will lower their price. In Figure 3 the price falls from $8 to $6, which happens to be the equilibrium price.

Exactly the same thing happens in the labor market (see Figure 4). At a wage rate of $9 an hour, there are many unemployed workers. Some are willing to accept a lower wage rate. When the wage rate falls to $7 an hour, everyone who wants to work at that rate can find a job, and every employer willing to hire workers at that rate can find as many workers as she wants to hire.

Figure 2   The Loanable Funds Market

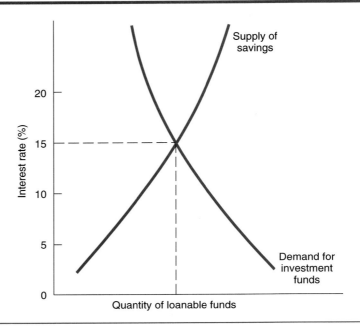

Figure 3   Market for Hypothetical Product

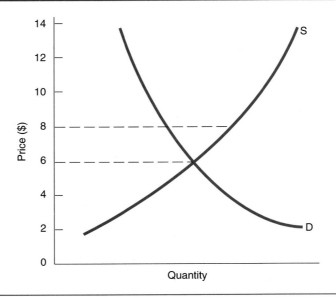

Figure 4   Hypothetical Labor Market

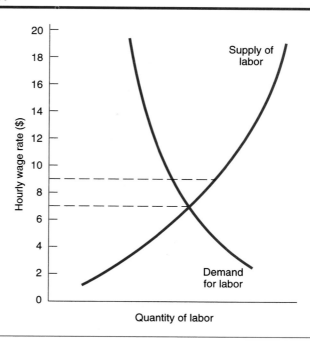

The Classical Equilibrium: Aggregate Demand Equals Aggregate Supply

What exactly *is* equilibrium GDP? We've seen, on a micro level, that when quantity demanded equals quantity supplied, we're at equilibrium. Similarly, on a macro level, when aggregate demand equals aggregate supply, we're at equilibrium. At equilibrium there is a state of balance between opposing forces such that there is no tendency for change.

Our economy is either at or tending toward full employment.

The classical economists believed our economy was either at, or tending toward, full employment. So at the classical equilibrium—the GDP at which aggregate demand was equal to aggregate supply—we were at full employment. And as long as aggregate demand and aggregate supply did not change, our economy would continue operating at full employment.

We've been weaving back and forth between macro and micro analysis. From here on it's going to be macro. We'll begin with the economy's aggregate demand curve, go on to the economy's aggregate long-run and short-run supply curves, and finally put these curves together to derive the economy's equilibrium GDP.

The Aggregate Demand Curve

The aggregate demand curve shows that as the price level declines, the quantity of goods and services demanded rises.

The aggregate demand curve of Figure 5 depicts an inverse relationship between the price level and the quantity of goods and services demanded: as the price level declines, the quantity of goods and services demanded rises. Similarly, as the price level rises, the quantity of goods and services demanded declines. This relationship is illustrated by an aggregate demand curve that slopes downward to the right.

This is different from the aggregate demand curve in Figure 2 of Chapter 8. Why? Because in *that* graph, the price level was held constant. The C + I + G + Xn curve showed that as disposable income rose, there was a corresponding increase in the quantity demanded of goods and services, assuming no change in the price level.

Is it reasonable to assume constant prices? Instinctively, we would reject this assumption because in our lifetimes we have known almost nothing but inflation. Furthermore, as the economy approaches full employment, a certain amount of inflation is inevitable.

Figure 5   Aggregate Demand Curve (in trillions of dollars)

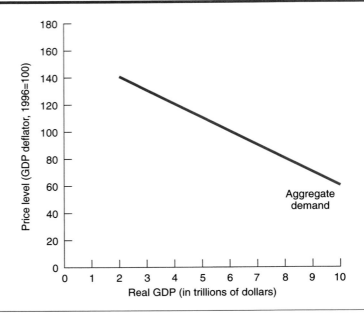

What does this curve tell us? I'll begin by defining aggregate demand as *the total value
of real GDP that all sectors of the economy are willing to purchase at various price levels.*
You'll notice that as the price level declines, people are willing to purchase more and more
output. Alternatively, as the price level rises, the quantity of output purchased goes down.

There are three reasons why the quantity of goods and services purchased declines as
the price level increases: (1) an increase in the price level reduces the wealth of people
holding money, making them feel poorer and reducing their purchases; (2) the higher
price level pushes up the interest rate, which leads to a reduction in the purchase of
interest-sensitive goods, such as cars and houses; and (3) net exports decline as foreigners
buy less from us and we buy more from them at the higher price level. The first of these
reasons is called the real balance effect, the second is the interest rate effect, and the third
is the foreign purchases effect. Let's consider each in turn.

(1) The Real Balance Effect   When the price level goes up, your purchasing
power goes down. The money you have in the bank, your stocks and bonds, and all your
other liquid assets shrink in terms of what they can buy. You *feel* poorer, so you'll tend to
spend less.

The *real balance effect* is the influence of a change in your purchasing power on the
quantity of real GDP that you are willing to buy. Here's how it works. Suppose you are
holding $800 in money and your only other asset is $200 worth of shoes (you are a fan of
Philippine former first lady Imelda Marcos, who managed to accumulate 3,000 pairs of
shoes). Now, what if the prices of most goods and services fell, among them those of
shoes. The $800 that you're holding now buys more goods than before. You've got a
larger real balance.

Before prices fell, you were very happy holding 80 percent of your assets in the form
of money ($800 of $1,000) and 20 percent in the form of shoes ($200 of $1,000). But
now those shoes you're holding are worth less than $200 because their price has fallen,
while your money is worth more. Let's say there was so much deflation that the purchasing power of your money doubled, to $1,600, while the value of your shoes fell to $100.
Question: Wouldn't you like to take advantage of the price decrease to buy more shoes?
Of course you would. And how many more dollars' worth of shoes would you buy if you
wanted to keep 20 percent of your assets in the form of shoes (and 80 percent in the form
of money)? Answer: Your total assets are now $1,700 ($1,600 in money and $100 in

shoes), so you'd want to hold 20 percent of the $1,700, or $340, in shoes. In other words, you'd buy $240 worth of shoes.

Let's sum up. A decrease in the price level increases the quantity of real money. The larger the quantity of real money, the larger the quantity of goods and services demanded. Similarly, an increase in the price level decreases the quantity of real money. The smaller the quantity of real money, the smaller the quantity of goods and services demanded.

(2) The Interest Rate Effect   A rising price level pushes up interest rates, which in turn lower the consumption of certain goods and services and also lower investment in new plant and equipment. Let's look more closely at this two-step sequence.

First, during times of inflation, interest rates rise, because lenders need to protect themselves against the declining purchasing power of the dollar. If you lent someone $100 for one year and there was a 10 percent rate of inflation, you would need to be paid back $110 just to be able to buy what your original $100 would have purchased.

Second, certain goods and services are more sensitive to interest rate changes than others. Can you name some especially sensitive ones? Try auto purchases and home mortgages. Clearly, then, when interest rates rise, the consumption of certain goods and services falls, and when interest rates fall, their consumption rises.

Now let's see how a rising price level (which pushes up interest rates) affects investment spending. We saw in Chapter 6 that rising interest rates choke off investment projects that would have been carried out at lower rates. Some projects, especially in building construction, where interest is a major cost, are particularly sensitive to interest rate changes. So we know, then, that a rising price level pushes up interest rates and lowers both consumption and investment. Similarly, a declining price level, which pushed down interest rates, encourages consumption and investment. Clearly the interest rate effect can be very powerful.

(3) The Foreign Purchases Effect   When the price level in the United States rises relative to the price levels in other countries, what effect does this have on U.S. imports and exports? Because American goods become more expensive relative to foreign goods, our imports rise (foreign goods are cheaper) and our exports decline (American goods are more expensive).

In sum, when our price level increases, this tends to increase our imports and lower our exports. Thus, our net exports (exports minus imports) component of GDP declines. When the price level declines, the net exports component (and GDP) rises.

The Long-Run Aggregate Supply Curve

First I'll define aggregate supply as *the amount of real output, or real GDP, that will be made available by sellers at various price levels.* Next I'll show you what the long-run aggregate supply curve looks like. You'll notice in Figure 6 that it's a vertical line.

This curve is based on two assumptions of the classical economists. First, in the long run, the economy operates at full employment. (In Chapter 9 we decided that because there would always be frictional and structural unemployment totaling about 5 percent of the labor force, a 5 percent unemployment rate meant the economy was operating at full employment.) Second, in the long run, output is independent of prices.

Ready for a little action? We're going to put the aggregate demand curve and the long-run aggregate supply curve together on one graph and see what happens. Figure 7 shows this.

The equilibrium full-employment level of real GDP

What happens is that we find two things: (1) the equilibrium full-employment level of real GDP and (2) the corresponding price level, which happens to be 100.

What does this *mean?* It means that in the long run our economy will produce the level of output that will provide jobs for everyone who wants to work (i.e., the unemployment rate will be 5 percent). In other words, in the long run our economy will produce at full-employment GDP. And how much *is* full-employment GDP, according to Figure 7? It comes to exactly $6 trillion. One of the nice things about working with hypothetical numbers is that they come out so well rounded.

Figure 6   Long-Run Aggregate Supply Curve (in trillions of dollars)

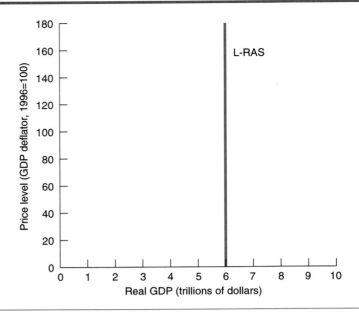

Figure 7   Aggregate Demand and Long-Run Aggregate Supply (in trillions of dollars)

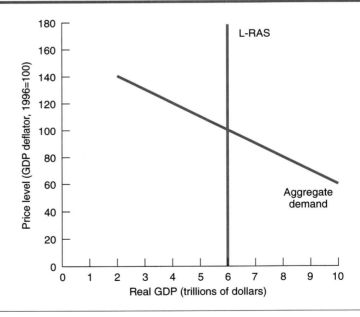

This is what the classical economists predicted and is completely consistent with Say's law: Supply creates its own demand. Our economy, then, will always be at full employment in the long run. But what about in the short run?

The Short-Run Aggregate Supply Curve

The economy may operate below full-employment GDP in the short run.

In the short run, according to the classical economists, some unemployment *is* possible. Some output *may* go unsold. And the economy *may* operate below full-employment GDP. Figure 8 shows all of this.

Why does the short-run aggregate supply curve sweep upward to the right? Because business firms will supply increasing amounts of output as prices rise. Why? Because

Figure 8   Short-Run Aggregate Supply Curve (in trillions of dollars)

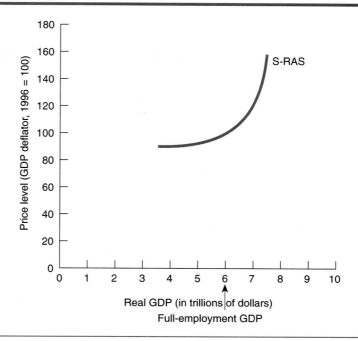

wages, rent, and other production costs are set by contracts in the short run and don't increase immediately in response to rising prices. Your landlord can't come to you while
your lease still has two years to go and tell you that he must raise your rent because *his*
costs are going up. Your employees who are working under two- and three-year contracts
can't ask you to renegotiate. (They can *ask* you to, but you probably won't.) And your
suppliers may also have agreed contractually to send you their goods at set prices. So, in
the short run, higher prices mean higher profit margins, which give business firms like
yours an incentive to increase output.

As output rises, costs rise.

As output continues to rise, land, labor, and capital become more expensive and less-
efficient resources are pressed into service. To get homemakers to work, employers need
to make wage rates attractive enough (and some even go to the expense of setting up
child care facilities) to entice them back into the labor force. As output approaches full
employment, antiquated machinery and less-productive facilities must be used. And so,
as the full-employment level of GDP is approached, the short-run aggregate supply curve
is becoming steeper and steeper. You'll notice that full-employment GDP is still $6 tril-
lion, as in Figure 7.

Beyond full employment

You'll also notice in Figure 8 that output continues to rise even after we've exceeded
full-employment GDP. Is this *possible?* Can our real GDP ever exceed our full-
employment GDP? Yes, it can. But only in the short run.

Do you remember the production possibilities curve back in Chapter 2? When the
economy was operating on that curve, we were at full employment. Occasionally, however, we could exceed that output level and produce beyond the full-employment level.
We also saw this near the beginning of the last chapter in Figure 4, when actual GDP exceeded potential GDP. How can we *do* this?

Let's extend the example of luring homemakers into the labor force with better pay.
How about enticing full-time college students who are working part-time to give up their
education (or perhaps switch to night school) and work full-time? Or how about persuading retired people, or those about to retire, to take full-time jobs? How would we do this?
By paying attractive wage rates and providing whatever other incentives are necessary.
We can also keep putting back into service aging or obsolete plant and equipment, and
make use of marginal land as well.

*Why does the short-run aggregate
supply curve eventually become
vertical?*

Why, then, does the short-run aggregate supply curve eventually become vertical?
Because there is a physical limit to the output capacity of the economy. There is just so

much land, labor, and capital that can be put to work, and when that limit is reached, there is no way to increase production appreciably. During World War II, U.S. factories ran 24 hours a day and millions of people worked 50 or 60 hours a week. But everyone simply could not have kept up this effort year after year. As Americans said at the time, "There's a war going on." Just in case someone hadn't noticed.

So, in the short run, we can push our output beyond the level of full-employment GDP and get our economy to operate beyond full employment. But this is only possible in the short run. In the long run, we're back at the long-run aggregate supply curve.

Figure 9 puts this all together for you. You see the point at which the short- and long-run aggregate supply curves intersect the aggregate demand curve? That's the long-run equilibrium level of GDP. At that point, the price level happens to be 100 and GDP is $6 trillion.

In the classical system, all the parts fit together neatly. The long-run aggregate supply curve, the short-run aggregate supply cost curve, and the aggregate demand curve come together at full employment. If there *is* some unemployment in the short run, it will automatically be eliminated as the economy returns to its long-run, full-employment equilibrium. And if there is more than full employment, this is again only a temporary phenomenon that will end as the level of economic activity returns to its full-employment level. In short, the economy can temporarily slide up and down its short-run aggregate supply curve, but it inevitably returns to its long-run equilibrium at full employment.

Do aggregate demand and aggregate supply remain constant? Of course not. Over time, as an economy grows, they grow, too. And during recessions, of course, they decline. If you're curious about why we won't be covering changes in aggregate demand and aggregate supply, see the box "Changes in Aggregate Demand and Aggregate Supply."

Part II: The Keynesian Critique of the Classical System

Until the Great Depression, classical economics was the dominant school of economic thought. Adam Smith, credited by many as the founder of classical economics, believed the government should intervene in economic affairs as little as possible. Indeed,

Figure 9   Aggregate Demand, Long-Run and Short-Run Aggregate Supply (in trillions of dollars)

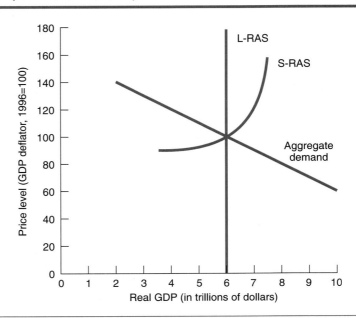

Changes in Aggregate Demand and Aggregate Supply

Life is said to be a series of compromises, and compromises are central to the study of economics. Near the beginning of Chapter 2 we talked about making choices and opportunity cost. Remember that *the opportunity cost of any choice is the forgone value of the next best alternative.* This is just another way of saying you can't have it *all.* What I'm getting at is that we're about to make a choice—actually, I've already made that choice *for* us—and hence we will give something up.

We're giving up on carrying out our analysis still further by looking at changes in aggregate demand and aggregate supply. Consequently, you will be missing out on the dazzling array of graphical analyses that is part of virtually every introductory text. This impressive presentation provides the reader with the opportunity to view material that he can just begin to comprehend after taking another couple of courses in economic analysis. So I want to be completely up front about how you are being short-changed at this particular spot. That's right, you're missing out on the opportunity to be mystified and baffled by changes in aggregate demand and aggregate supply. Now, if you happen to prefer confusion to comprehension and value complexity over clarity, then just get hold of any standard principles-of-economics text and find out what you've been missing.

Our free enterprise system has rightly been compared to a gigantic computing machine capable of solving its own problems automatically. But anyone who has had some practical experience with large computers knows that they do break down and can't operate unattended.

—Wassily Leontief, March 1971

Keynes asked, "What if saving and investment were not equal?"

Keynes: Saving and investing are done by different people for different reasons.

John Maynard Keynes, British economist (The Bettmann Archives)

laissez-faire economics was practiced down through the years until the time of Herbert Hoover, who kept predicting that prosperity was just around the corner. John Maynard Keynes finally proclaimed the end of the classical era when he advocated massive government intervention to bring an end to the Great Depression.

John Maynard Keynes, a prominent classically trained economist, spent the first half of the 1930s writing a monumental critique of the classical system.[3] If supply creates its own demand, he asked, why are we having a worldwide depression? Keynes set out to learn what went wrong and how to fix it.

Keynes posed this problem for the classical economists: What if saving and investment were not equal? For instance, if saving were greater than investment, there would be unemployment. Not everything being produced would be purchased.

You'll recall—at least I *hope* you will—that the classicals figured this was no problem. They just trotted out the graph in Figure 2, which showed that the interest rate would equilibrate savings and investment. If the quantity of savings exceeded the quantity of loanable funds demanded for investment purposes, the interest rate would simply fall. And it would keep falling until the quantity of savings and the demand for investment funds were equal.

Keynes disputed this view. Saving and investing are done by different people for different reasons. Most saving is done by individuals for big-ticket items, such as cars, stereo systems, and major appliances, as well as for houses or retirement. Investing is done by those who run business firms basically because they are trying to make a profit. They will borrow to invest only when there is a reasonably good profit outlook. Why sink a lot of money into plant and equipment when your factory and machines are half idle? Even when interest rates are low, business firms won't invest unless it is profitable for them to do so. This point was discussed at length toward the end of Chapter 6.

Even *this* posed no major problem to the classical economists, because they assumed wages and prices were downwardly flexible. If there were unemployment, the unemployed would find jobs as wage rates fell. And, similarly, if sellers were stuck with unwanted inventory, they would simply lower their prices.

Keynes questioned whether wages and prices were downwardly flexible, even during a severe recession. In the worst recession since the Great Depression, the downturn of 1981–82, there were very few instances of price or wage declines even in the face of declining output and widespread unemployment. Studies of the behavior of highly concentrated industries indicate that prices are seldom lowered, while similar studies of large labor unions indicate that wage cuts (even as the only alternative to massive layoffs) are

---

[3] *The General Theory of Employment, Interest, and Money* is considered one of the most influential books of the 20th century.

We are not always at, or tending toward, full employment.

seldom accepted. Even if wages *were* lowered, added Keynes, this would lower workers' incomes, consequently lowering their spending on consumer goods.

All of this led Keynes to conclude that the economy was not always at, or tending toward, a full-employment equilibrium. Keynes believed three possible equilibriums existed—*below* full employment, *at* full employment, and *above* full employment. Using the same demand and supply analysis as the classicals, Keynes showed that full employment was hardly inevitable.

The Keynesian long-run aggregate supply curve was really a hybrid of the classical short-run and long-run aggregate supply curves. It is drawn in Figure 10.[4] At extremely low levels of real GDP, when output is at, say, $3 trillion, our economy is in a catastrophic depression. As the economy begins to recover, output can be raised to about $4.7 trillion without any increase in prices. Why? Because millions of unemployed workers would be happy to work for the prevailing wage, so wage rates would certainly not have to be raised to entice people back to work. Furthermore, businessowners would also be happy to sell additional output at existing prices. But as real GDP continues to rise above $4.7 trillion, costs begin to rise, and bottlenecks eventually develop in certain industries, making greater and greater price increases necessary. Eventually, of course, at a real GDP of $6 trillion, we are at full employment and cannot, in the long run, raise output above that level. (See the box "The Ranges of the Aggregate Supply Curve.")

The Keynesian and classical aggregate supply analyses are virtually identical.

So, for all intents and purposes, the Keynesian and classical aggregate supply analyses are virtually identical. But they are completely at odds with respect to aggregate demand. Figure 11 shows three aggregate demand curves. AD_1 represents a very low level of aggregate demand, which, Keynes believed, was the basic problem during recessions and depressions. The AD_2 curve shows the same full-employment equilibrium shown in Figure 9. And finally, AD_3 represents excessive demand, which would cause inflation.

In the last chapter we talked about demand-pull inflation, which was described as "too much money chasing too few goods." Demand-pull inflation occurs in the intermediate range of the aggregate supply curve in the figure in the box "The Ranges of the

---

[4] The curve shown in Figure 10 is actually a slightly modified Keynesian aggregate supply curve. Keynes originally assumed prices would not rise at all until full employment was attained (when real GDP was $6 trillion), but we've allowed here for an accelerating rise in prices from a real GDP of about $4.7 trillion to one of $6 trillion.

Figure 10   Modified Keynesian Aggregate Supply Curve

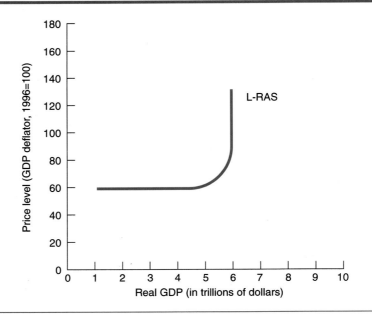

The Ranges of the Aggregate Supply Curve

The curve shown in the figure to the right is just slightly more elaborate than that in Figure 10. Here we have the three ranges: Keynesian, intermediate, and classical. The Keynesian range is thus named because John Maynard Keynes was writing during the Great Depression. People were so anxious to find work that they were happy to take a job—virtually any job—at the going wage rate. Thus, business firms could easily expand output without encountering rising wages.

Would they raise prices? Not for quite a while. After suffering through a few years of extremely low sales, they would be grateful for more business, albeit at the same price.

As the economy expanded, bottlenecks would begin to develop, shortages of resources (especially labor) would occur here and there, and costs would begin to rise in some sectors and eventually spread throughout the economy. And then business firms would begin raising their prices as well.

Eventually the economy would reach the maximum output level, at which point the only give would be in the form of higher prices. This would be the classical range of the aggregate supply curve. Remember that the classical economists believed that full employment was our normal state of affairs.

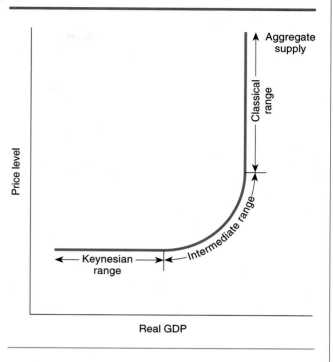

Figure 11   **Three Aggregate Demand Curves**

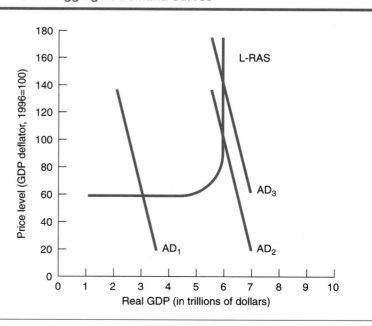

Aggregate Supply Curve." Or, looking at Figure 11, start with an aggregate demand of AD_1 and imagine a series of higher and higher aggregate demand curves. At first we would have increases in real GDP without any price increases, but as aggregate demand moved closer to AD_2, we would eventually be able to keep pushing up real GDP only at the cost of some inflation. And as aggregate demand approached AD_2, we would be obtaining smaller and smaller increments of added output at the cost of larger and larger rises in the price level.

So we see that increases in aggregate demand will eventually lead to inflation. Applying this same analysis but moving in the opposite direction, we'll observe that decreasing aggregate demand leads to declining output and a decline in the rate of inflation. Starting at AD_2 and moving toward AD_1 in Figure 11, we see that real GDP is declining. As we noted toward the beginning of the last chapter, a decline in real GDP for two consecutive quarters is, by definition, a recession. And if continued decreases in aggregate demand pushed real GDP down still further, the recession would deepen and we might even sink into a depression.

Under this Keynesian analysis, we have three distinct possible equilibriums—below full employment, at full employment, and above full employment (with respect to prices, not output). Our economy, according to Keynes, does not necessarily tend toward full employment, as the classicals maintained.

Our economy, said Keynes, can get stuck at an equilibrium that is well below full employment:

> Indeed it seems capable of remaining in a chronic condition of subnormal activity for a considerable period without any marked tendency either toward recovery or toward complete collapse. Moreover, the evidence indicates that full, or even approximately full, employment is of rare and short-lived occurrence.[5]

What we need to do now is examine the Keynesian system in more detail, and then we'll be ready to consider what the government should (or should not) do to prevent or to moderate recessions and inflations.

Part III: The Keynesian System

The classical equilibrium could not explain the Great Depression.

The classical theory of equilibrium was great at explaining why we would be either at full employment or tending toward it. But it wasn't much good at explaining why, in the 1930s, the entire world was in a depression. We needed a new theory to explain what was happening, and we needed a policy prescription to bring us out of this depression. John Maynard Keynes provided both.

Keynes used the same aggregate demand and supply apparatus as the classicals had, but he came up with very different conclusions. The key to his analysis was the role of aggregate demand. According to Keynes, the equilibrium level of GDP was determined primarily by the volume of expenditures planned by consumers, business firms, governments, and foreigners. Keynes concentrated on aggregate demand because he viewed rapid declines in this variable as the villain in recessions and depressions. Changes in aggregate supply—changes brought about by new technology, more capital and labor, and greater productivity—came about slowly and could therefore be neglected in the short run.

What about Say's law that "Supply creates its own demand"? Keynes stood Say's law on its head. In fact, we can summarize Keynesian theory with the statement "Demand creates its own supply."

Keynes: Aggregate demand is our economy's prime mover.

Aggregate demand, said Keynes, is our economy's prime mover. Aggregate demand determines the level of output and employment. In other words, business firms produce only the quantity of goods and services they believe consumers, investors, governments, and foreigners will plan to buy.

---

[5] John Maynard Keynes, *The General Theory of Employment, Interest, and Money* (New York: Harcourt Brace Jovanovich, 1958), pp. 249–50.

The centerpiece of his model was the behavior of the consumer. If consumers decide to spend more of their incomes on goods and services—or less, for that matter—then the effect on output and employment can be substantial.

The Keynesian Aggregate Expenditure Model

Since the Keynesian model assumes a constant price level, we'll return to our original graphic presentation, which we began in Chapter 5. We'll be on familiar ground because we'll be using some of the concepts covered in Chapters 5 through 8. You already have quite a bit of Keynesian analysis under your belt without having known it.

In a nutshell, here's what we're going to be working with: (1) the consumption function; (2) the saving function; and (3) investment, which will be held constant. To keep things as simple as possible, we are including only the private sector, so government purchases (and net exports, as well) are excluded from our model. This means changes in aggregate demand are brought about only by changes in C. And that's why I said the centerpiece of the Keynesian model was the behavior of the consumer.

The Consumption and Saving Functions
Here's the consumption function: *As income rises, consumption rises, but not as quickly.* It is a "fundamental psychological law," said Keynes "that men are disposed, as a rule and on the average, to increase their consumption as their income increases, but not by as much as the increase in their income."[6]

So what people do, then, as incomes rise, is spend some of this additional income and save the rest—which brings us to the saving function: *As income rises, saving rises, but not as quickly.* No surprises here.

Hypothetical consumption and savings functions appear in Figure 12. This should be old hat to you, since we covered the consumption and savings functions back in Chapter 5.

As disposable income rises, consumption and saving rise as well. Because disposable income rises as output, or real GDP, rises, we can say that as real GDP rises, consumption and saving rise. What about investment?

---

[6]Ibid., p. 96.

Figure 12   Disposable Income (in trillions of dollars)

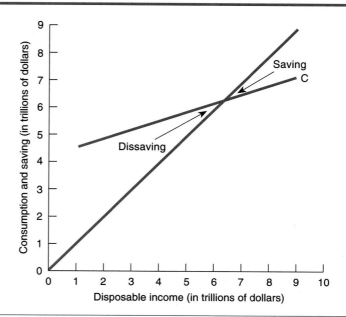

Investment is unstable.

The Investment Sector   We learned in Chapter 6 that investment is the loose cannon on our economic deck. Keynes was well aware of this. What causes recessions in the Keynesian model? A decline in profit expectations, or, as Keynes puts it, in the marginal efficiency of capital, causes recessions. Although rising interest rates may play an important role in setting off recessions, Keynes stressed profit expectations:

> But I suggest that a more typical, and often the predominant, explanation of the crisis is, not primarily a rise in the rate of interest, but a sudden collapse in the marginal efficiency of capital.[7]

How do we allow for planned investment in the Keynesian model? We've seen that planned consumption rises with disposable income and real GDP. What about planned investment? It, too, probably varies directly with disposable income and real GDP. But we need to keep things simple. So we're going to come up with an arbitrary figure for planned investment—$500 billion—and keep it constant for all levels of real GDP.

We'll add just one line to our graph, the C + I line, and then we'll be able to wind up our analysis. We've done that in Figure 13. Assuming C + I constitutes aggregate demand, how much is equilibrium GDP? It comes out to $7 trillion.

And how much is investment? Also $500 billion.

So, at equilibrium GDP, all our ducks are in a line, so to speak. Aggregate demand, C + I (measured vertically), is equal to aggregate supply, or real GDP (measured on the horizontal scale). The level of output produced is exactly equal to the amount that buyers wish to purchase.

Also, saving and investment are equal. Saving is the vertical distance between the C line and the 45-degree line. The vertical distance between the C line and the C + I line is I. Therefore, the vertical distance between the C line and the 45-degree line must be equal to (actually, identical to) the vertical distance between the C line and the C + I line. (For extra help with finding equilibrium GDP, see box "Finding Equilibrium GDP.")

---

[7]Ibid, p. 315.

Figure 13   Real GDP (in trillions of dollars)

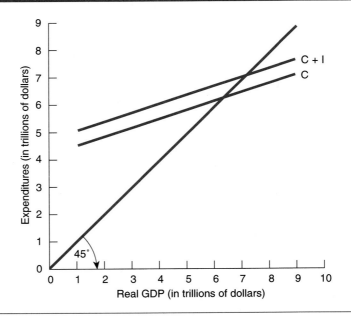

Finding Equilibrium GDP

inding equilibrium GDP is as easy as finding the level of spending at which saving and investment are equal. Try to find that level of spending in the first figure here.

After all the graphs we've gone through in this chapter, in the second figure here we come back to the C + I + G + X_n graph from Chapter 8. $C + I + G + X_n$ is aggregate demand, or GDP. We've simply added the government and foreign sectors to the consumption and investment sectors.

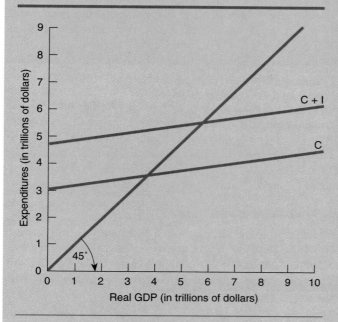

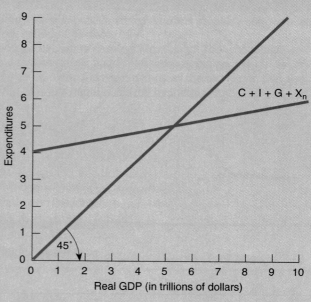

What did you get? Equilibrium real GDP is $5.5 trillion. Now, how much is saving? At equilibrium GDP, saving—the vertical distance between the C line and the 45-degree line—is about $1.7 trillion. And how much is I? It's the vertical distance between the C line and the C + I line—also about $1.7 trillion. And so, at an equilibrium GDP of $5.5 trillion, savings and investment are equal at $1.7 trillion.

How much is equilibrium GDP in the second figure? It's $5 trillion. We'll be making good use of this type of graph at the beginning of the next chapter.

Disequilibrium and Equilibrium

In both Keynesian and classical economic systems, the economy is always tending toward equilibrium, where aggregate demand and aggregate supply are equal. Let's look at this process from two perspectives: first, when aggregate demand is larger than aggregate supply, and second, when aggregate supply is larger than aggregate demand.

(1) Aggregate Demand Exceeds Aggregate Supply

When aggregate demand exceeds aggregate supply, inventories decline.

When aggregate demand exceeds aggregate supply, a chain reaction is set off and continues until the economy is back in equilibrium. The first thing that happens is that inventories start declining. What do business firms do? They order more inventory.

As I said, the first thing that happens when aggregate demand is greater than aggregate supply is that inventories are depleted. Consequently, orders to manufacturers rise, and, of course, production rises. Manufacturers will hire more labor, and eventually, as plant utilization approaches capacity, more plant and equipment is ordered.

Suppose you own an appliance store. You have been ordering 50 blenders a month because that's about how many you sell. But during the last month your blender sales doubled, so you decide to order 100 blenders instead of your usual 50. Think of what this does to the production of blenders, assuming the other appliance stores double their orders as well.

As more people find employment, they will consume more, raising aggregate demand. Business firms may also begin raising their prices. Retailers may perceive that their customers are willing to pay more. Eventually, the manufacturers may have trouble increasing output much farther because of shortages in labor, raw materials, plant and equipment, or the funds to finance expansion. These shortages will occur at some point—and consequently, prices will have to rise—because what is happening in the appliance industry is probably happening in the rest of the economy. As the economy approaches full capacity (and full employment), prices will have begun to rise.

We started with aggregate demand exceeding aggregate supply, but this disparity told manufacturers to increase aggregate supply. First, output was increased; eventually, so were prices. As final GDP (which is identical to aggregate supply) is defined as the nation's output of goods and services at market prices, it appears that there are two ways to raise aggregate supply—by increasing output and by increasing prices. By doing this, we raise aggregate supply relative to aggregate demand and quickly restore equilibrium.

(2) Aggregate Supply Exceeds Aggregate Demand

When aggregate supply exceeds aggregate demand, inventories rise.

When aggregate supply is greater than aggregate demand, the economy is in disequilibrium. Aggregate supply must fall. Because aggregate supply is greater than aggregate demand, production exceeds sales, and inventories are rising. When retailers realize this, what do they do? They cut back on orders to manufacturers. After all, if you found you were accumulating more and more stock on your shelves, wouldn't you cut back on your orders? Remember, not only does it cost money to carry large inventories—shelf space as well as money is tied up—but also there is always the risk that you may not be able to sell your stock.

When manufacturers receive fewer orders, they reduce output and consequently lay off some workers, further depressing aggregate demand as these workers cut back on their consumption. Retail firms, facing declining sales as well as smaller inventories, may reduce prices, although during recent recessions price reductions have been relatively uncommon. Eventually, inventories are sufficiently depleted. In the meantime, aggregate supply has fallen back into equilibrium with aggregate demand.

(3) Summary: How Equilibrium Is Attained

When the economy is in disequilibrium, it automatically moves back into equilibrium.

We can make an interesting observation about the entire process. When the economy is in disequilibrium, it automatically moves back into equilibrium. It is always aggregate supply that adjusts. When aggregate demand is greater than aggregate supply, the latter rises, and when aggregate supply exceeds aggregate demand, aggregate supply declines.

Please keep in mind that aggregate demand (C + I) must equal the level of production (aggregate supply) for the economy to be in equilibrium. When the two are not equal, aggregate supply must adjust to bring the economy back into equilibrium.

Keynesian Policy Prescriptions

The classicals believed recessions were temporary because the economy is self-correcting.

Let's summarize the classical position. Recessions are temporary because the economy is self-correcting. Declining investment will be pushed up again by falling interest rates, while, if consumption falls, it will be raised by falling prices and wages. And because recessions are self-correcting, the role of government is to stand back and do nothing.

Keynes's position was that recessions were not necessarily temporary, because the self-correcting mechanisms of falling interest rates and falling prices and wages might be insufficient to push investment and consumption back up again. The private economy did not automatically move toward full employment. Therefore, it would be necessary for the government to intervene.

What should the government do? Spend money! How *much* money? If the economy is in a bad recession, it will be necessary to spend a lot of money. And if it's in a depression, then it must spend even more. I'll be more specific in the next chapter.

Aggregate demand is insufficient to provide jobs for everyone who wants to work; thus it is necessary for the government to provide the spending that will push the economy toward full employment. Just spend money; it doesn't matter on what. Keynes made this point quite vividly:

> If the Treasury were to fill old bottles with banknotes, bury them at suitable depths in disused coal mines which are then filled up to the surface with town rubbish, and leave it to private enterprise on well-tried principles of laissez-faire to dig the notes up again . . . , there need be no more unemployment. . . . It would, indeed, be more sensible to build houses and the like; but if there are political and practical difficulties in the way of this, the above would be better than nothing.[8]

Why didn't New Deal spending get us out of the economic crisis of the 1930s?

If all it takes is government spending to get us out of a depression, then why didn't President Franklin Roosevelt's massive New Deal spending get us out of the Great Depression? First of all, it did succeed in bringing about rapid economic growth between 1933 and 1937. But then, just when the economy seemed to be coming out of its depression, Roosevelt suddenly decided to try to balance the federal budget; he raised taxes and cut government spending. On top of this, the Federal Reserve sharply cut the rate of growth of the money supply. So back down we went, with output plunging sharply and the unemployment rate soaring once again.

Not until the huge federal government expenditures on World War II in the early 1940s did the United States finally emerge from the Depression. So what, then, did we learn from all of this? One possibility is that the only way to end a depression is to go to war (see the box titled "A Dissertation upon Roast Pig"). But what I hope you learned is that massive government spending of *any* kind—whether on highways, school construction, AIDS

---

[8]Ibid., p. 129.

A Dissertation upon Roast Pig*

This wonderful fable by Charles and Mary Lamb provides an analogy to going to war to end a depression. The story takes place in China many centuries ago.

> The swineherd, Ho-ti, having gone out into the woods . . . to collect mast for his hogs, left his cottage in the care of his eldest son, Bo-bo, a great lubberly boy, who being fond of playing with fire, as younkers of his age commonly are, let some sparks escape.

To make a long story short, the cottage burned down, and nine pigs, who were kept in the hut, were burned to death. Bo-bo touched one of the pigs, burned his fingers, and put them in his mouth to cool them off. And he discovered the joys of tasting roast pig. He proceeded to devour pig after pig. When his father, Ho-ti, returned home, he too burned his fingers on a pig, placed them in his mouth, and tasted roast pig.

Well, there was no question that they were onto something. Neighbors observed that Ho-ti's cottage was burnt down with great frequency. Pretty soon the secret was out, and all the neighbors were burning down *their* cottages to make roast pig.

> Thus this custom of firing houses continued until . . . a sage arose, who made a discovery, that the flesh of swine, or indeed of any other animal, might be cooked . . . without the necessity of consuming a whole house to dress it.

If the analogy isn't clear, let me clarify. To end a depression, or even a bad recession, we certainly don't need to go to war. All we need to do is spend as much money as we would have spent going to war. As Keynes said, it doesn't matter *what* the money is spent on, as long as enough of it is spent.

*Charles and Mary Lamb, "Dissertation upon Roast Pig," *The Works of Charles Lamb,* Vol. III (Boston: Crosby, Nichols, Lee, 1980), pp. 203–12.

research, crime prevention, space exploration, *or* military expansion—will pull us out of a depression.

Over the last six decades, our economy has been racked by repeated bouts of inflation, recession, and, of course, the decade-long Great Depression. According to John Maynard Keynes, our problem during periods of recession and depression has been insufficient aggregate demand. And though he died in 1946, before we encountered periods of sustained inflation, he would have prescribed lowering aggregate demand to bring down the inflation rate.

In the next chapter we shall deal specifically with this Keynesian manipulation of the level of aggregate demand to deal with inflation and recession. Fiscal policy, which is the name that has been assigned to Keynesian taxation and government spending prescriptions, became the basic government policy tool to ensure price stability and high employment from the 1930s through the 1960s.

Questions for Further Thought and Discussion

1. The classical economists believed that our economy was always at full employment or tending toward full employment. If our economy were operating below full employment, what would happen, according to the classicals, to move the economy back toward full employment?

2. When the price level increases, the quantity of goods and services declines. Why does this happen?

3. Explain the difference between the long-run aggregate supply curve and the short-run aggregate supply curve.

4. What were the major areas of disagreement between John Maynard Keynes and the classical economists?

WORKBOOK FOR CHAPTER 10

Name _____ Date _____

Multiple-Choice Questions

Circle the letter that corresponds to the best answer.

1. Until the Great Depression, the dominant school of economic thought was

    a. classical economics   **b.** Keynesian economics

    c. supply-side economics   **d.** monetarism

2. The classical economists believed in

    a. strong government intervention   **b.** laissez-faire

    c. a rapid growth in the money supply   **d.** none of these

3. Say's law states that

    a. we can have an inflation or a recession, but never both at the same time   **b.** the normal state of economic affairs is recession   **c.** demand creates its own supply   **d.** supply creates its own demand

4. People work, according to Jean Baptiste Say, so that they can

    a. spend   **b.** save   **c.** stay busy   **d.** none of these

5. According to the classical economists

    a. people will always spend all their money   **b.** any money that is saved will be invested   **c.** saving will always be greater than investment   **d.** saving will always be smaller than investment

6. Keynes believed

    a. recessions were temporary   **b.** once a recession began, it would always turn into a depression   **c.** the real problem that modern economies faced was inflation

    d. none of these

7. "Our economy is always at full employment" was a claim made by

    a. both Keynes and the classicals   **b.** neither Keynes nor the classicals   **c.** Keynes but not the classicals   **d.** the classicals but not Keynes

8. According to the classical economists, if the amount of money people are planning to invest is greater than the amount that people want to save,

    a. interest rates will rise and saving will rise

    b. interest rates will fall and saving will fall

    c. interest rates will fall and saving will rise

    d. interest rates will rise and saving will fall

9. Each of the following supports the classical theory of employment except

    a. Say's law   **b.** wage-price flexibility   **c.** the interest mechanism   **d.** government spending programs

10. Our economy is definitely at equilibrium in each case except when

    a. saving equals investment   **b.** aggregate demand equals aggregate supply   **c.** the amount people are willing to spend equals the amount that producers are producing   **d.** equilibrium GDP equals full-employment GDP

11. That we are always tending toward full employment is a belief of

    a. Keynes   **b.** the classicals   **c.** the supply-siders

    d. the monetarists

12. Keynes said

    a. the expected profit rate was more important than the interest rate   **b.** the interest rate was more important than the expected profit rate   **c.** the expected profit rate and the interest rate were equally important

    d. neither the expected profit rate nor the interest rate was important

13. John Maynard Keynes is most closely associated with the

    a. American Revolution   **b.** French Revolution

    c. the Great Depression   **d.** inflation

14. The classical economists' aggregate supply curve is vertical

   a. both in the short run and in the long run   b. in neither the short run nor the long run   c. in the short run, but not in the long run   d. in the long run, but not in the short run

15. To end a bad recession, we need to

   a. go to war   b. spend a lot of money

   c. balance the federal budget

16. Which statement best describes the classical theory of employment?

   a. We will always have a great deal of unemployment.

   b. We will usually have a great deal of unemployment.

   c. We will occasionally have some unemployment, but our economy will automatically move back toward full employment.   d. We never have any unemployment.

17. According to Keynes, our economy always tends toward

   a. equilibrium GDP   b. full-employment GDP   c. recessions   d. inflations

18. When saving is greater than investment, we are

   a. at equilibrium GDP   b. at full-employment GDP   c. below equilibrium GDP   d. above equilibrium GDP

19. Keynes considered full-employment GDP to be

   a. the normal state of economic affairs   b. a rare occurrence   c. an impossibility   d. none of these

20. Keynes was concerned mainly with

   a. aggregate supply   b. aggregate demand   c. the interest rate   d. inflation

21. When aggregate demand is greater than aggregate supply

   a. inventories get depleted and output rises

   b. inventories get depleted and output falls

   c. inventories rise and output rises   d. inventories rise and output falls

22. When the economy is in disequilibrium

   a. production automatically rises   b. production automatically falls   c. it automatically moves back into equilibrium   d. it stays in disequilibrium permanently

23. As the price level rises

   a. the quantity of goods and services demanded falls   b. the quantity of goods and services demanded rises   c. the quantity of goods and services demanded stays the same   d. none of the above is correct

24. The slope of the aggregate demand curve is explained by each of the following except

   a. the real balance effect   b. the interest rate effect   c. the foreign purchases effect   d. the profit effect

Fill-In Questions

1. Laissez-faire was advocated by the _____ school of economics.

2. Say's law states that _____ _____.

3. According to Say's law, people work so that they can _____.

4. According to Say's law, people spend _____.

5. The classical economists believed savings would equal _____.

6. If supply creates its own demand, asked Keynes, why are we having a _____?

7. If saving were greater than investment, said the classical economists, they would be set equal by the _____ _____.

8. The classical economists believed that wages and prices were _____ flexible.

9. The classical economists believed recessions were _____ _____.

10. During recessions, said the classical economists, the government should _____.

11. Aggregate supply is _____ _____.

12. Aggregate demand is _____ _____.

13. At equilibrium GDP, _____ will be equal to _____ and _____ will be equal to _____.

14. Our economy always tends toward _____ _____ GDP.

15. When investment is greater than savings, we are _____ _____ equilibrium GDP.

16. Full-employment GDP and equilibrium GDP are _____ _____equal.

17. Keynes was most concerned with one main variable, _____.

18. According to John Maynard Keynes, the level of aggregate supply is determined by the _____ _____.

19. When we are below the full-employment level of GDP, Keynes suggested that the _____ _____.

20. When aggregate supply is greater than aggregate demand, the economy is in _____.

21. When aggregate demand is greater than aggregate supply, inventories will _____ and output will _____.

22. When individuals, business firms, and the government are spending just enough money to provide jobs for everyone willing and able to work, we are at _____ _____ GDP.

23. The real balance effect states that _____ _____ _____.

24. The two reasons why the aggregate supply curve moves upward to the right are: (1) _____; and (2) _____.

25. The interest rate effect states that _____ _____ _____.

26. The three reasons why the aggregate demand curve slopes downward are (1) _____; (2) _____; and (3) _____.

27. The foreign purchases effect states that _____ _____ _____.

Problems

1. If GDP = C + I and if GDP = C + S, then _____ = _____.

2. Given the information in Figure 1, and assuming an interest rate of 15 percent: **a.** Will the economy be at equilibrium? **b.** Will savings equal investment? **c.** What will happen, according to the classical economists?

3. Given the information in Figure 2: **a.** If aggregate demand shifts from AD_1 to AD_2, what happens to the level of prices and to output? **b.** If aggregate demand shifts from AD_2 to AD_3, what happens to the level of prices and to output? **c.** If aggregate demand shifts from AD_3 to AD_4, what happens to the level of prices and to output?

Figure 1

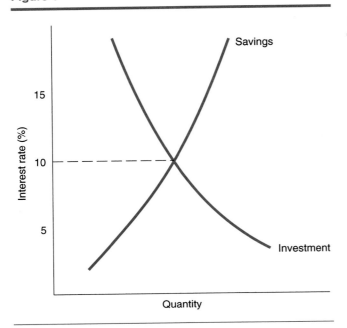

Figure 2

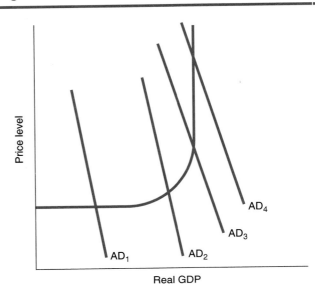

11 Fiscal Policy and the National Debt

Fiscal policy is *the manipulation of the federal budget to attain price stability, relatively full employment, and a satisfactory rate of economic growth.* To attain these goals, the government must manipulate its spending and taxes. Later, in Chapter 13, we'll look at monetary policy, which uses very different means to promote the same ends.

Chapter Objectives

In this chapter you will learn about:

- The deflationary gap.
- The inflationary gap.
- The multiplier and its applications.
- Automatic stabilizers.
- Discretionary fiscal policy.
- Budget deficits and surpluses.
- The public debt.

Putting Fiscal Policy into Perspective

Until the time of the Great Depression, the only advice economists gave the government was to try to balance its budget every year and not to interfere with the workings of the private economy. Just balance the books and then stay out of the way. There was no such thing as fiscal policy until John Maynard Keynes invented it in the 1930s.

He pointed out that there was a depression going on and that the problem was anemic aggregate demand. Consumption was lagging because so many people were out of work. Investment was extremely low because businessowners had no reason to add to their inventories or build more plant and equipment. After all, sales were very low and much of their plant and equipment was sitting idle. So the only thing left to boost aggregate demand was government spending.

What about taxes? Well, certainly, we would not want to *raise* them. That would push aggregate demand even lower. We might even want to *cut* taxes to give consumers and businesses more money to spend. OK, now if we were to follow this advice, would the government be able to balance its budget? No way! But if we ran a big enough budget deficit, we could jump-start the economy and, in effect, spend our way out of this depression.

You don't have to be a great economist to see that we haven't been too successful at attaining our fiscal policy goals, particularly since the mid-1960s. It's important that the aggregate supply of goods and services equals the aggregate demand for goods and services at just the level of spending that will bring about full employment at stable prices.[1]

Equilibrium GDP tells us the level of spending in the economy. Full-employment GDP tells us the level of spending necessary to get the unemployment rate down to 5 percent (which we have been calling full employment). We'll see how fiscal policy is used to push equilibrium GDP toward full-employment GDP.

---

[1]That's a very long sentence whose meaning will become increasingly apparent as you read this chapter.

In terms of equilibrium GDP, sometimes we are spending too much, and at other times we are spending too little. When equilibrium GDP is too big, we have an inflationary gap, and when it's too small, a deflationary gap.[2] Remember Goldilocks and the Three Bears? Remember the porridge that was too hot and the porridge that was too cold? Like Goldilocks seeking the perfect porridge, our policy objective is to find a level of GDP that is just right. We will deal with deflationary and inflationary gaps and GDPs that are just right in the next few pages.

Economics is filled with dicta, some of which make perfect sense—you can't repeal the law of supply and demand—and some of which don't seem to make much sense at all. This chapter is based on two of the second type. First, we'll consider the following dictum: The federal budget must be balanced every year. In fact, during the last decade, the required three-quarters of the state legislatures nearly approved a constitutional convention to consider an amendment that would have made an annually balanced budget the law of the land. Since then, in 1994, 1995, 1996, and in 1997 new efforts to pass a balanced budget amendment have been defeated in Congress. You can read all about this in Part VI of this chapter.

The last part of this chapter will be devoted to a discussion of the public or national debt. The dictum in question is: The public debt is a burden on future generations. In fact, another dictum virtually contradicts this one: We owe it to ourselves. As we shall see, neither holds true, but as we shall also see, neither is completely wrong.

Part I: The Deflationary Gap and the Inflationary Gap

Before we go to the gaps, we need to go over some terms from Chapter 10. First: *equilibrium GDP*. Our economy is always at equilibrium GDP or tending toward it. Equilibrium GDP is the level of output at which aggregate demand equals aggregate supply. What is *aggregate demand?* It's *the sum of all expenditures for goods and services* (i.e., $C + I + G + X_n$). And what is *aggregate supply?* Aggregate supply is *the nation's total output of final goods and services.* So at equilibrium GDP, everything produced is sold.

We need to review one more term: *full-employment GDP*. Full employment means nearly all our resources are being used. For example, if our plant and equipment is operating at between 85 and 90 percent of capacity, *that's* full employment. Or if only 5 percent of our labor force is unemployed, then *that's* full employment. So, what's full-employment GDP? Full-employment GDP is *the level of spending necessary to provide full employment of our resources.* Alternatively, it is the level of spending necessary to purchase the output, or aggregate supply, of a fully employed economy.

The Deflationary Gap

A *deflationary gap occurs when equilibrium GDP is less than full-employment GDP.* Equilibrium GDP is the level of spending that the economy is at or is tending toward. Full-employment GDP is the level of spending needed to provide enough jobs to reduce the unemployment rate to 5 percent. When too little is being spent to provide enough jobs, we have a deflationary gap, which is shown in Figure 1. Another way of expressing this state of economic affairs is to say that we are inside our production possibilities frontier (or curve), as we discussed in Chapter 2.

How much is equilibrium GDP in Figure 1? Write down the number. What did you get? Did you get $5 trillion? That's the GDP at which the $C + I + G + X_n$ line crosses the 45-degree line.

How can we close the deflationary gap?

How do we close this gap? We need to raise spending—consumption (C) or investment (I) or government expenditures (G)—or perhaps some combination of these.[3] John

---

[2]Some economists call this a *recessionary* gap. If this term makes you happier, use it.

[3]We are leaving out net exports (X_n) for purposes of simplification. Increasing our exports and/or reducing our imports would reduce a deflationary gap, but these two variables are not very responsive to fiscal policy.

Figure 1   The Deflationary Gap

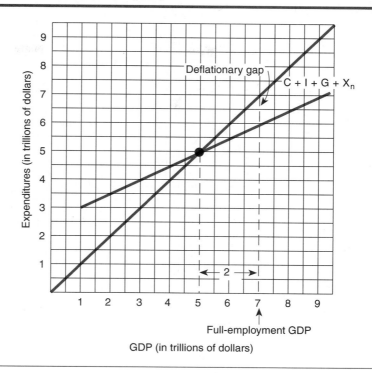

Maynard Keynes tells us to raise G. Or we may want to lower taxes. Lowering business taxes might raise I; lowering personal income taxes would increase C.

How much would we have to raise spending to close the deflationary gap shown in Figure 1? Would you believe $1 trillion? That's right! This is *some* deflationary gap. There would have to be a depression going on, so we would need to raise spending by $1 trillion. Anything less would reduce, but not eliminate, the gap.

Notice that equilibrium GDP is $2 trillion less than the full-employment GDP of $7 trillion. In a few pages we'll do some multiplier analysis. This analysis will show us that raising G by $1 trillion will raise equilibrium GDP by $2 trillion and eliminate the deflationary gap. But let's not get ahead of ourselves.

Notice how the points in Figure 1 line up. Equilibrium GDP is to the left of full-employment GDP. The deflationary gap is directly above the full-employment GDP. It is the vertical distance between the 45-degree line and the $C + I + G + X_n$ line.

The Inflationary Gap

Figure 2 shows the inflationary gap. The key difference between this graph and that of the deflationary gap is the position of equilibrium GDP. When there is an inflationary gap, equilibrium GDP is to the right of full-employment GDP. It is to the left when there's a deflationary gap. In other words, *equilibrium GDP is greater than full-employment GDP when there's an inflationary gap.* When there's a deflationary gap, full-employment GDP is greater than equilibrium GDP.

In both graphs the gap is the vertical distance between the $C + I + G + X_n$ line and the 45-degree line, and in both graphs the gap is directly above full-employment GDP.

In short, when there's a deflationary gap, equilibrium GDP is too small; when there's an inflationary gap, it's too big. To eliminate an inflationary gap, Keynes would suggest cutting G and raising taxes. Both actions are aimed at reducing spending and, therefore, equilibrium GDP.

In Figure 2 the inflationary gap is $200 billion ($1,200 billion – $1,000 billion). If we cut spending by $200 billion, it would have a multiplied effect on GDP. Equilibrium GDP would decline by $500 billion ($1,500 billion – $1,000 billion) to the full-employment level.

Deflationary gap: Equilibrium GDP is too small.

Inflationary gap: Equilibrium GDP is too large.

Figure 2   The Inflationary Gap

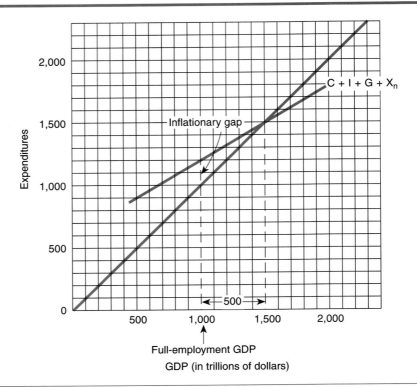

I'm tossing around billions and trillions as if they were pocket change. Remember that 1,000 billion equals 1 trillion. If you need a fast review, reread the box "A Word about Numbers," near the beginning of Chapter 5.

To summarize, if spending is too high, equilibrium GDP is above the full-employment level. To eliminate the inflationary gap, we cut G and/or raise taxes. If equilibrium GDP is less than full-employment GDP, we eliminate the deflationary gap by raising G and/or cutting taxes.

Over the last two decades Republicans have labeled every Democratic presidential candidate a "tax and spend liberal." And by inference these Republicans wanted to be called "low-tax and low-spend conservatives." To generalize, liberals seem to favor a high-spending, high-taxing, big government, and conservatives a low-spending, low-taxing, relatively small government. How would these philosophies lend themselves to fiscal policy?

If there were a recession, conventional fiscal policy calls for tax cuts and more government spending. If the liberal could choose just one of these measures, which would she favor? And which one would the conservative favor? The liberal would choose higher government spending (which would increase the role of government), while the conservative would cut taxes, thereby reducing the government's role.

Now figure out the liberal's and conservative's respective policy prescriptions for dealing with inflation. Write them down right here:

The liberal would raise taxes, and the conservative would cut government spending. To generalize—or perhaps overgeneralize—the liberal tends to favor bigger government, and the conservative, smaller government.

Part II: The Multiplier and Its Applications

We're going to put together some concepts introduced in earlier chapters: aggregate demand (Chapters 8 and 10), the marginal propensity to consume (Chapter 5), and equilibrium GDP (Chapter 10). We know that an increase in G will raise aggregate demand, but by how much? We also know that a tax increase will lower aggregate demand, but, again, by how much? The multiplier will tell us by just how much.

The Multiplier

The multiplier is based on two concepts covered in Chapter 8: (1) GDP is the nation's expenditure on all the final goods and services produced during the year at market prices. (2) GDP = C + I + G + X_n.

It is obvious that if C goes up, GDP will go up. Or if I goes down, so will GDP. Now we'll add a new wrinkle. When there is any change in spending, that is, in C, I, G, or X_n, it will have a multiplied effect on GDP.

When money is spent by one person, it becomes someone else's income. And what do we do with most of our income? We spend it. Once again, when this money is spent, someone else receives it as income and, in turn, spends most of it. And so, if a dollar were initially spent, perhaps someone who received that dollar would spend 80 cents, and of that 80 cents received by the next person, perhaps 64 cents would be spent. If we add up all the spending generated by that one dollar, it will add up to four or five or six times that dollar. Hence, we get the name *the multiplier*.

Any change in spending (C, I, or G) will set off a chain reaction, leading to a multiplied change in GDP. *How much* of a multiplied effect? A $10 billion increase in G might increase GDP by $50 billion. In that case, the multiplier is 5. If a decline of $5 billion in I causes GDP to fall by $40 billion, then the multiplier would be 8.

First we'll concentrate on calculating the multiplier, for which we'll use the formula:

$$\frac{1}{1 - MPC}$$

Then we'll see how it is used to predict changes in GDP. (A reminder: MPC is marginal propensity to consume.)

The formula above is the same as 1/MPS. Remember, MPC + MPS = 1 (or 1 − MPC = MPS). Because the multiplier (like C) deals with spending, 1/(1 − MPC) is a more appropriate formula.

The MPC can thus be used to find the multiplier. If the MPC were .5, find the multiplier. Work this problem out in the space below. Write down the formula first, then substitute and solve.

Multiplier $= \dfrac{1}{1 - MPC}$

Solution:

$$\text{Multiplier} = \frac{1}{1 - MPC} = \frac{1}{1 - .5} = \frac{1}{.5} = 2$$

Many students get lost at the third step. How do we get .5? How come 1 − .5 = .5? Look at it this way:

$$
\begin{array}{r}
1.0 \\
-.5 \\
\hline
.5
\end{array}
$$

If it's still not clear, then think of 1 as a dollar and .5 (or .50) as 50 cents. How much is a dollar minus 50 cents?

Step four is just as easy. How many times does 50 cents go into a dollar? Or, you can just divide .5 into 1.0. Either way, it comes out to 2.

Let's try another problem. When the MPC is .75, how much is the multiplier?

Solution:

$$
\text{Multiplier} = \frac{1}{1 - \text{MPC}} = \frac{1}{1 - .75} = \frac{1}{.25} = 4
$$

After you've substituted into the formula, think of 1 as a dollar and .75 as 75 cents. From there (1/.25) we divide .25 into 1, or a quarter into a dollar.

The multiplier is really a shortcut for addition. In the case illustrated in Table 1, a consumer spends $1,000 of additional money. If the MPC is .5, that means the person who receives this $1,000 in additional income will spend $500. The $500 spent will add to others' incomes, and—still assuming an MPC of .5—they will spend $250. Ad infinitum (that's Latin for "without limit, or forever").

Applications of the Multiplier

The multiplier is used to calculate the effects of changes in C, I, and G on GDP.

Knowing the multiplier, we can calculate the effect of changes in C, I, and G on the level of GDP. If GDP is 2,500, the multiplier is 3, and C rises by 10, what is the new level of GDP?

A second formula is needed to determine the new level of GDP:

New GDP = Initial GDP + (Change in spending × Multiplier)

Notice the parentheses. Their purpose is to ensure that we multiply before we add. In arithmetic you must always multiply (or divide) before you add (or subtract). Always. The parentheses are there to make sure we do this.

Copy down the formula, substitute, and solve.

Table 1   Step-by-Step Working of the Multiplier When MPC Is .5

$1,000.00
500.00
250.00
125.00
62.50
31.25
15.625
7.8125
3.90625
1.953125
.9765625
.48828125
.244140625
.1220703125
.06103515625
.030517578125
.0152587890625
$1,999.9847402109375*

*In arithmetic, addition and multiplication are one and the same. Multiplication is just a shortcut. If we were to carry out even more steps in our addition, we would approach a sum of $2,000. It is surely much easier to use the multiplier of 2 (2 × $1,000 = $2,000) than to add up all these figures.

Solution:

(1) New GDP = Initial GDP + (Change in spending × Multiplier)

(2)   = 2,500   +   (10 × 3)

(3)   = 2,500   + (30)

             = 2,530

Here are a few variations of this type of problem. Suppose that consumer spending rises by $10 billion and the multiplier is 3. What happens to GDP?

Solution: It rises by $30 billion: $10 billion × 3.

Try this one: Government spending falls by $5 billion with a multiplier of 7.

Solution: – $5 billion × 7 = –$35 billion. In other words, if government spending falls by $5 billion with a multiplier of 7, GDP falls by $35 billion.

Two more multiplier applications and we're through. First, how big is the multiplier in Figure 1? If you're not sure, guess. What's your answer? Is it 2? We can find the multiplier by using deductive logic. We know the deflationary gap is $1 trillion. We also know that equilibrium GDP is $2 trillion less than full-employment GDP. (Equilibrium GDP is $5 trillion and full-employment GDP is $7 trillion.) Suppose we were to raise G by $1 trillion. What would happen to the gap? It would vanish! And what would happen to equilibrium GDP? It would rise by $2 trillion and become equal to full-employment GDP.

Still not convinced? Let's redraw Figure 1 as Figure 3 and add $C_1 + I_1 + G_1 + X_{n1}$. You'll notice that $C_1 + I_1 + G_1 + X_{n1}$ is $1 trillion higher than $C + I + G + X_n$. You'll also notice that the deflationary gap is gone. And that equilibrium GDP equals full-employment GDP.

One more question: How big is the multiplier in Figure 2? Again, if you're not sure, guess. Is your answer 2.5? How do we get 2.5? OK, we know that the inflationary gap is 200, and we know equilibrium GDP is 500 greater than full-employment GDP. So if we lower G by 200, the inflationary gap disappears. And now equilibrium GDP falls by 500 and is equal to full-employment GDP.

Here's a formula you can use to find the multiplier whether you have an inflationary gap or a deflationary gap:

$$\text{Multiplier} = \frac{\text{Distance between equilibrium GDP and full-employment GDP}}{\text{Gap}}$$

In Figure 4 the distance is 500 and the inflationary gap is 200. So: 500/200 = 2.5. You can also use this formula to find the multiplier if there is a deflationary gap. For example, in Figure 3 the distance between equilibrium GDP and full-employment GDP is $2 trillion, which we can express as 2,000. And the deflationary gap is $1 trillion, or 1,000. Using the formula:

$$\text{Multiplier} = \frac{\text{Distance between equilibrium GDP and full-employment GDP}}{\text{Gap}} = \frac{2,000}{1,000} = 2$$

If you are still a bit uncertain and want a little more practice, then do the work in the box "Finding the Multiplier."

Because tax cuts and tax increases present a more complex problem, we'll put them in their own box. If you like more complex problems, read the box "Tax Cuts and Tax Increases." And while you're at it, you may also find the box on the paradox of thrift (later in the chapter) of some interest. Otherwise, you may collect $200 and advance to Part III.

Figure 3   Removing the Deflationary Gap

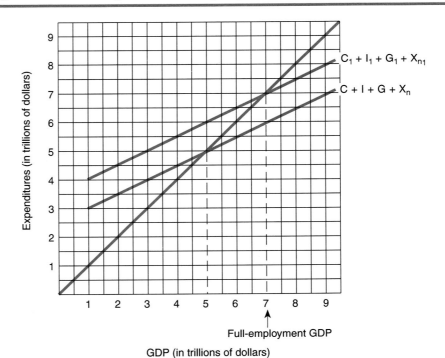

Figure 4   Removing the Inflationary Gap

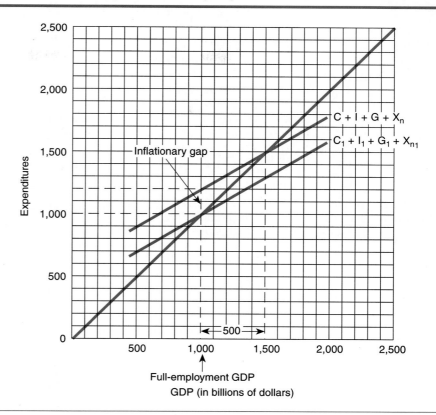

Finding the Multiplier

et's assume that the full-employment GDP is $4 trillion in Figure 3 (use the $C + I + G + X_n$ line; ignore the $C_1 + I_1 + G_1 + X_{n1}$ line). See if you can answer these three questions:

1. Is there an inflationary gap or a deflationary gap?
2. How much is the gap?
3. How much is the multiplier?

Solution:

1. There is an inflationary gap because full-employment GDP is less than equilibrium GDP. If aggregate demand, or total spending, is greater than the spending necessary to attain full employment, that excess spending will cause inflation.
2. The inflationary gap is measured by the vertical distance between the 45-degree line and the $C + I + G + X_n$ line at full-employment GDP. It appears to be

half a trillion, or $500 billion, which we can write as 500.

3. Multiplier = $\dfrac{\text{Distance between equilibrium GDP and full-employment GDP}}{\text{Gap}}$

Now let's assume that full-employment GDP is $6 trillion. Please answer the same three questions.

Solution:

1. There is a deflationary gap.
2. It is $500 billion, or 500.
3. Multiplier = $\dfrac{1,000}{500} = 2$

ADVANCED WORK ..... Tax Cuts and Tax Increases
....

A tax cut will have the same impact on the deflationary gap as an increase in G *only if people spend the entire tax cut.* If personal income taxes were cut by $100 billion, would people spend this entire amount? Maybe. They certainly would if their MPC were 1.0. But what if it were only .9? How much of it would they spend? Just $90 billion. And what would the multiplier be if the MPC were .9? It would be 10 (Multiplier = 1/(1 − MPC) = 1/(1 − .9) = 1/.1 = 10). So, if taxes were cut by $100 billion, by how much would equilibrium GDP rise? It would rise by $900 billion ($90 × 10 = $900 billion).

The same logic applies to a tax increase. If personal income taxes were raised by $100 billion and the MPC were .8, by how much would equilibrium GDP decline?

Solution:

$$\text{Change in GDP} = \text{Change in spending} \times \text{Multiplier}$$
$$= -80^* \qquad\qquad \times 5^\dagger$$
$$= -400$$

*We get −80 by multiplying the tax cut of $100 billion by the MPC of .8. We're assuming that if taxes had not been raised by $100 billion, people would have spent $80 billion of the income.

†Multiplier = 1/(1 − MPC) = 1/(1 − .8) = 1/.2 = 5.

Part III: The Automatic Stabilizers

Have you ever been on an airborne plane when the pilot took a stroll through the cabin and you asked yourself, Who's flying the plane? Let's hope it's the copilot. Or maybe the plane is on automatic pilot, which is fine unless it hits some turbulence. If it does, then the pilot will rush back to the cockpit and take over the manual controls.

An analogy can be made with our economy. Our automatic stabilizers enable us to cruise along fairly smoothly, but when we hit severe economic turbulence, then we hope the president and Congress take the controls. Right now, we'll examine our automatic stabilizers, and in Part IV, we'll talk about discretionary fiscal policy, which is our manual control system.

The automatic stabilizers protect us from the extremes of the business cycle.

In the 1930s the government built a few automatic stabilizers into the economy, mainly to prevent recessions from becoming depressions. Today, when the country hits routine economic turbulence, Congress does not need to pass any laws, and no new bureaucracies have to be created. All the machinery is in place and ready to go.

Each of these stabilizers protects the economy from the extremes of the business cycle—from recession and inflation. They are not, by themselves, expected to prevent booms and busts, but only to moderate them. To do still more, we need discretionary economic policy, which we'll discuss in the next section.

Personal Income and Payroll Taxes

During recessions, tax receipts decline.

During recessions the government collects less personal income tax and Social Security tax than it otherwise would. Some workers who had been getting overtime before the recession are lucky to be hanging on to their jobs even without overtime. Some workers are less lucky and have been laid off. That's the bad news. The good news is that they don't have to pay any personal income tax or payroll tax because they have no income.

During inflations, tax receipts rise.

During prosperous times our incomes rise, and during times of inflation our incomes tend to rise still faster. As our incomes rise, we have to pay more taxes. These taxes tend to hold down our spending, relieving inflationary pressures.

During recessions, as incomes fall, federal personal income and Social Security tax receipts fall even faster. This moderates economic declines by leaving more money in taxpayers' pockets.

Personal Savings

During recessions, saving declines.

As the economy moves into a recession, saving declines. Many Americans lose their jobs and others earn less overtime. As incomes fall, savings must fall as well. Looked at from another perspective, consumption rises as a percentage of income.

During prosperity, saving rises.

Just as the loss of income is cushioned by a fall in saving, the reverse happens when the economy picks up again. Like higher taxes, during times of rapid economic expansion, increased saving tends to damp down inflationary pressures.

Credit Availability

Credit availability helps get us through recessions.

Because most Americans now hold bank credit cards, mainly MasterCard and VISA, we may think of these as automatic stabilizers that work in the same way that personal savings does. During good times, we should be paying off the credit card debts that we run up during bad times.

Although many of us are quite good at running up credit card debt during good times as well as bad, our credit cards, as well as other lines of credit, may be thought of as automatic stabilizers during recessions because they give us one more source of funds with which to keep buying things. You may have lost your job and have no money in the bank, but your credit cards are just as good as money.

Unemployment Compensation

Here's a great example of closing the barn door after the horses ran off. We came up with a great unemployment insurance program back in 1935, which happened to be the sixth year of the Great Depression.

Reason to study economics: When you are in the unemployment line, at least you will know why you are there.

When you lose your job, you can sign up for unemployment benefits if you qualify. To qualify you need to have worked at an insured job for 20 weeks during the last year or 40 weeks during the last two years. Also, you must have lost your job through no fault of your own. If you were laid off or your company moved out of town, you will be able to collect almost automatically.

During recessions, more people collect unemployment benefits.

During recessions, as the unemployment rate climbs, hundreds of thousands and then millions of people register for unemployment benefits. Benefit schedules and maximum payments vary from state to state. Most people who collect get almost 60 percent of their salaries, although those earning more than $40,000 a year get considerably less than half.

A man whose gross income is $200 a week and take-home pay is $160 receives between $110 and $120 in unemployment benefits. For this person, the loss of his job means an income decline of just $40. Without unemployment insurance it would have been a lot worse. Chances are, by dipping into his savings and borrowing a little here and there, he can more or less maintain his standard of living until he finds another job.

But *will* he find another job? There's a recession going on. Actually, the tens of billions of dollars of unemployment benefits being paid out establish a floor under purchasing power. People who are, they hope, only temporarily out of work will continue spending money. This helps keep retail sales from falling much, and even without further government help, the economy has bought some time to work its way out of the recession. As the economy recovers and moves into the prosperity phase of the cycle, people find jobs more easily and unemployment benefit claims drop substantially.

The maximum paid varies from state to state. In 1962, when the author collected for the full 26 weeks from New York, the maximum was just $50.

Sometimes during recessions, Congress will extend the benefit period beyond 26 weeks to 39 or even 52 weeks in certain cases. This action is part of discretionary policy, because it does not happen automatically. You cannot collect beyond 26 weeks unless Congress acts. During the recession of 1969–70, for example, a friend who had been "cut off" after 26 weeks unexpectedly heard from her local unemployment insurance office. "It was a miracle!" she told me. "They called me in and said I could collect for another 13 weeks!"

Clearly most people can protect themselves from relatively short-term losses of income. Because this is so, their continued spending helps provide a floor under consumer spending during recessions, which, in turn, helps keep recessions from turning into depressions. For a more personal example, see box "How the Automatic Stabilizers Help You Survive a Recession."

How the Automatic Stabilizers Help You Survive a Recession

Elizabeth Zimiles, who was earning $500 a week, lost her job during a recession. How was she able to make ends meet?

First of all, she no longer had to pay any federal or state income tax, nor did she have to pay any payroll (Social Security and Medicare) tax. Let's see how this affected her aftertax income.

Before she lost her job, Ms. Zimiles earned $500, paid $100 in taxes, and took home $400. Now she earns nothing and takes home nothing. So her aftertax income fell from $400 to 0.

Suppose that when she was working, she saved $50 a week. Now that she has lost her job, she takes $100 a week out of her savings. Let's see how this affected her spending money.

Before Ms. Zimiles lost her job, she took home $400 a week, saved $50, and had $350 available for spending. But now she takes home no money, and draws $100 a week out of her savings to have available for spending. So her spending money has fallen from $350 to $100.

But you ain't seen nuthin' yet. She applies for unemployment insurance benefits, and receives $260 a week. Add that to her $100 of spending money and now she has $360.

	Earned Income	Aftertax Income	– Savings	+	Unemployment Insurance Benefits	Spending Money
Before job loss	$500	$400	$ 50		0	$350
After job loss	0	0	–$100		$260	$360

Can you see where we're going with this? Before she lost her job, she had $350 to spend each week. But now she has $360. While I'm not suggesting that everyone can live better without a job than with one, I *am* suggesting that the automatic stabilizers can definitely help you survive a recession.

The Corporate Profits Tax

During recessions, corporations pay much less corporate income taxes.

Perhaps the most countercyclical of all the automatic stabilizers is the corporate profit (or income) tax. Corporations must pay 35 percent of their net income above $10 million to the federal government. During economic downturns, corporate profits fall much more quickly than wages, consumption, or real GDP; and, of course, during expansions, corporate profits rise much more rapidly. During the 1981–82 recession, corporate aftertax profits fell from an annual rate of $169 billion in the first quarter of 1981 to $119 billion just one year later. And during the much milder downturn almost a decade later, profits slid from an annual rate of $271 billion in the first quarter of 1989 to just $194 billion two years later.

Part of this decline is cushioned by the huge falloff of federal tax collections from the corporate sector. This leaves more money to be used for investment or distribution to shareholders in the form of dividends. And when corporate profits shoot up during economic booms, the federal government damps down economic expansion by taxing away 35 percent of the profits of the larger corporations.

Other Transfer Payments

Some people think that when a recession hits, the government automatically raises Social Security benefits. This might make sense, but it doesn't happen. Congress would have to pass special legislation to do so.

A safety net for the poor.

Three important payments do rise automatically because of laws on the books. Each is aimed at helping the poor. These are welfare (or public assistance) payments, Medicaid payments, and food stamps.

Whenever a recession hits, millions of people become eligible for welfare, or if they are already getting welfare payments, they become entitled to larger payments. Someone earning the minimum wage of $5.15 an hour brings home just $166.46 (based on a 35-hour week with payroll taxes—but not personal income taxes—deducted). This comes to just $8,656 a year, which most states deem inadequate support for a family of four, making this family eligible for public assistance and food stamps to supplement their income. During a recession, if this person loses her job and she collects unemployment benefits, these benefits will come to only a little more than half her pay, so her family will get larger welfare payments.

At the same time, this family will get more food stamps, as both public assistance and food stamps are based solely on family income. Furthermore, people who join the ranks of those on public assistance become eligible for Medicaid benefits.

These programs are important for two reasons. Not only do they alleviate human suffering during bad economic times, but they also help provide a floor under spending, which helps keep economic downturns from worsening.

The automatic stabilizers smooth out the business cycle, keeping the ups and downs within a moderate range. Since the Great Depression, we have had neither another depression nor a runaway inflation. But the stabilizers, by themselves, cannot altogether eliminate economic fluctuations.

Figure 5 shows the workings of the stabilizers. The solid line shows real GDP in an economy with no automatic stabilizers. The dotted line shows real GDP in an economy such as ours, which does have automatic stabilizers. The latter part of the expansions are held down in the hypothetical business cycle with stabilizers in place, and the contractions are less severe. Basically, then, the automatic stabilizers smooth out the business cycle but don't eliminate it.

The automatic stabilizers may be likened to running our economy on automatic pilot—not well suited for takeoffs and landings, but fine for the smooth part of the flight. However, when the going gets rough, the economy must resort to manual controls. Discretionary policy is our manual control system.

Part IV: Discretionary Fiscal Policy

The first words of this chapter were *Fiscal policy is the manipulation of the federal budget to attain price stability, relatively full employment, and a satisfactory rate of economic growth.* The automatic stabilizers, which swing the federal budget into substantial deficits during recessions and tend to push down those deficits during periods of inflation, would appear to be part of fiscal policy. Because they are built into our economy, one might call them a passive fiscal policy. But our automatic stabilizers are now taken for granted; therefore we consider fiscal policy to be purely discretionary. Let's now consider the discretionary fiscal policy tools that are available to the federal government.

Making the Automatic Stabilizers More Effective

One problem with unemployment benefits is that they run out in six months while a recession can drag on for more than a year and its effects can last still longer. After the

Figure 5   Hypothetical Business Cycles

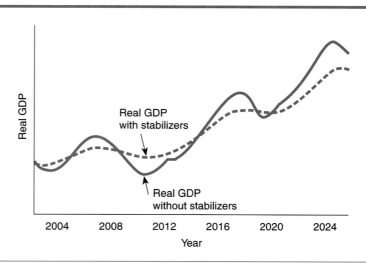

1990–91 recession ended, the unemployment rate continued rising and did not begin to decline until a full year after the start of the recovery. Extending the benefit period is an example of discretionary fiscal policy because benefits are not extended automatically. An increase in the benefit ceiling or a widening of eligibility standards are other ways of making this stabilizer more effective.

One of the most devastating charges against President Bush during the 1992 election campaign was that he was insensitive to the suffering of the unemployed. The fact that he vetoed legislation extending unemployment benefits did not help his case, although he finally *did* relent and sign a bill that extended benefits in states with high unemployment for up to 20 more weeks.

Altering federal personal and corporate income tax schedules to make them more progressive is another example of discretionary fiscal policy. As the economy heats up and personal incomes and corporate profits rise, they would be taxed at progressively higher rates. Of course, the most recent adjustments in personal income taxes, the 1981 Kemp-Roth Act and the Tax Reform Act of 1986, have had the opposite effect, making the tax structure less progressive and therefore less countercyclical. Progressive taxes were more fully discussed in Chapter 7 if you'd like to review this material.

Public Works

The main fiscal policy to end the Depression was public works.

During the Great Depression, the Roosevelt administration set up several so-called alphabet agencies to provide jobs for the long-term unemployed. Among them, the Works Progress Administration (WPA), the Civilian Conservation Corps (CCC), and the Public Works Administration (PWA) put millions of people to work doing everything from raking leaves to constructing government buildings.

One of the problems in getting these public works projects off the ground was a lack of plans. Not only did the government lack ready-to-go blueprints, but it did not even have a list of the needed projects. If the country is ever again to institute a public works program, it needs to be much better prepared than it was in the early 1930s. If not, by the time the program gets started, the recession will be over.

Although criticized as "make-work projects," the public works projects gave jobs to millions of the unemployed. These workers spent virtually their entire salaries, thereby creating demand for goods and services in the private sector, thus creating still more jobs. Unfortunately, in 1937, there was a complete turnaround in both fiscal and monetary policy, plunging the economy into a deep recession from which it did not fully recover until the massive arms buildup just before the country's involvement in World War II.

Public works is probably not the answer to recessions unless the downturns last so long that the projects can be carried out. Yet one might ask, if public works are so necessary, why wait for a recession to carry them out?

It seems ideally conceivable that the state . . . should undertake public works, that must be executed some time, in the slack periods when they can be executed at least expense, and will, at the same time, have a tendency to counteract a serious evil.

—Philip H. Wicksteed, The Common Sense of Political Economy

Transfer Payments

Just as the government could increase the amount of money given for unemployment compensation, it could add to the welfare, Social Security, and veterans' pensions during recessions. Like public works, this would channel money into the hands of consumers, who, by spending this money, would create jobs in the private sector.

Increased transfer payments have the added advantage of working quickly. No plans or blueprints are needed. Just program the computer and put the checks in the mail.

Changes in Tax Rates

So far, the discretionary policy measures have dealt exclusively with recessions. What can we do to fight inflation? We can raise taxes.

This was done in 1968 when Congress, under President Lyndon Johnson, passed a 10 percent income tax surcharge. If your income was $15,000 and your federal income tax was listed in the tax table as $2,300, you had to pay a $230 surcharge, which raised your taxes to $2,530.

In the case of a recession, a tax cut would be the ticket. The recession of 1981–82 was somewhat mitigated by the Kemp-Roth tax cut, which called for a 5 percent cut in personal income taxes in 1981 and a 10 percent cut in July 1982. However salutary its effects, Kemp-Roth was seen by its framers as a long-run economic stimulant rather than an antirecessionary measure.

Corporate income taxes, too, may be raised during inflations and lowered when recessions occur. The investment tax credit, first adopted by the Kennedy administration, is another way of using taxes to manipulate spending.

A key advantage to using tax rate changes as a countercyclical policy tool is that they provide a quick fix. We have to make sure, however, that temporary tax cuts carried out during recessions do not become permanent cuts.

Changes in Government Spending

When we talked about increasing government transfer payments and embarking on public works projects to counter business downturns, we were calling for increased government spending. Looking back at the Depression, what finally pulled the United States out was the massive armament spending at the beginning of World War II. To generalize, then, we can beat any recession by having the government spend enough money.

But too much spending—whether C, or I, or G—will lead to inflation. To help solve that problem, we must cut government spending. Some critics of President Ronald Reagan had asked how he expected to end inflation by cutting social programs if, at the same time, he got Congress to raise defense spending even more. (See the box "The Politics of Fiscal Policy.")

In sum, discretionary fiscal policy dictates that we increase government spending and cut taxes to mitigate business downturns, and that we lower government spending and raise taxes to damp down inflation. In brief, we fight recessions with budget deficits and inflation with budget surpluses.

The Politics of Fiscal Policy

In a sense there really *is* no fiscal policy, but rather a series of political compromises within Congress and between the president and Congress. The reason for this lies within our political system, especially the way we pass laws.

To become a law, a bill introduced in either house of Congress must get through the appropriate committee (most bills never get that far) and then receive a majority vote from the members of that house. It must get through the other house of Congress in the same manner. Then a House–Senate conference committee, after compromising on the differences between the two versions of the bill, sends the compromise bill to both houses to be voted on once again. After receiving a majority vote in both houses, the bill goes to the president for his signature.

If the president does not like certain aspects of the bill, he can threaten to veto it, hoping Congress will bend to his wishes. If he gets what he wants, he now signs the bill and it becomes law. If not, he vetoes it. Overriding a veto takes a two-thirds vote in both houses—not an easy task.

Adding to the political difficulties, there were only six years between 1968 and 1998 when the president and the majority in both houses of Congress were in the same political party.* This necessitated still more compromise. For example, many Democrats in Congress wanted to scrap the third year of the Kemp-Roth tax cut scheduled to take effect July 1, 1983, while the president had considered asking Congress to make it effective January 1, 1983. Neither side got its way: the tax cut went into effect as scheduled, July 1, 1983. President Ronald Reagan wanted to cut social programs and raise military spending—priorities that many congressional Democrats wanted to reverse. Again, compromises had to be reached.

Although the president and the budget committees of the House and Senate come up with budgets for the coming fiscal year, the resulting fiscal policy is necessarily the product of political compromise. It's interesting that Republican and Democratic party leaders point the finger at each other when the economy doesn't improve. The suspicion here is that both sides are right.

*With substantial Democratic majorities in both houses of Congress, Bill Clinton enjoyed this political state of grace in 1993 and 1994, but since January 1995 the Republicans have held majorities in both houses of Congress.

Who Makes Fiscal Policy?

Making fiscal policy is like driving a car. You steer, you keep your foot on the accelerator, and occasionally you use the brake. Basically, you should not go too fast or too slow, and you need to stay in your lane.

Would you mind letting someone else help you drive? Suppose you had a car with dual controls, like the ones driving schools have. Unless you and the other driver were in complete agreement, not only would driving not be much fun, but you'd be lucky to avoid having an accident.

So, if making fiscal policy is like driving a car, let's ask just who is doing the driving. Is it the president? Or is it Congress? The answer is yes to both questions. In other words, the conduct of our fiscal policy is a lot like driving a dually controlled car. Further complicating maneuvers, sometimes one political party controls Congress while the president belongs to the other party. In October 1990 the federal government all but shut down while President George Bush struggled with Congress in an effort to pass a budget. And in 1993, even though President Bill Clinton and a substantial majority of members of both houses were Democrats, each house passed a budget by just one vote. (See again box "The Politics of Fiscal Policy.")

Fiscal policy is indeed a powerful tool that may be used to promote full employment, stable prices, and a satisfactory rate of economic growth. But no one seems to be in charge of *making* fiscal policy. Nor is there widespread agreement among economists as to what effect any given fiscal policy measure has on our economy. Perhaps the words of Robert J. Gordon lend just the right perspective:

> Unfortunately, policymakers cannot act as if the economy is an automobile that can quickly be steered back and forth. Rather, the procedure of changing aggregate demand is much closer to that of a captain navigating a giant super-tanker. Even if he gives a signal for a hard turn, it takes a mile before he can see a change, and 10 miles before the ship makes the turn.[4]

The huge budget deficits we've been running since the early 1980s have sharply limited the government's ability to use discretionary fiscal policy to create jobs and to stimulate the economy. Between legally mandated spending programs and legally mandated entitlement programs such as Social Security, Medicare, and Medicaid, there is little discretionary income to play with. Of course, the Treasury could borrow even more money, but only if Congress and the president were willing to allow the budget deficit to grow.

Part V: The Deficit Dilemma

From time to time you'll read in the papers about *the perils of our twin deficits*—the federal budget deficit and the trade deficit. Right now we'll deal with the budget deficit; we'll worry about the trade deficit in the chapter on international trade.

Deficits, Surpluses, and the Balanced Budget

A deficit is created when the government is paying out more than it's taking in.

To understand how fiscal policy works, we need to understand three basic concepts. First, the deficit. *When government spending is greater than tax revenue, we have a federal budget deficit.* The government is paying out more than it's taking in. How does it make up the difference? It borrows. Deficits have been much more common than surpluses. In fact, the federal government has run budget deficits every year from 1970 through 1997.

This is not to say that deficits are always bad. Indeed, during recessions, they are just what the economic doctor ordered. But as you are certainly aware, we have not had recessions every year since 1970!

We haven't had a budget surplus since 1969.

Second, budget surpluses are the exact opposite of deficits. They are prescribed to fight inflation. *When the budget is in a surplus position, tax revenue is greater than government spending.* The last surplus we did have, in 1969, was rather suspect. President

---

[4]Robert J. Gordon, *Macroeconomics* (Boston: Little, Brown, 1978), p. 334.

Lyndon Johnson had pushed a 10 percent personal income tax surcharge through Congress (this raised everyone's income taxes by 10 percent). He also pushed certain 1969 government expenditures into the 1970 budget. President Jimmy Carter promised a surplus for fiscal year 1981 (we actually had a deficit of $79 billion), and President Ronald Reagan promised a surplus in 1984 (when the deficit came to $185 billion).

Finally, *we have a balanced budget when government expenditures are equal to tax revenue.* We've never had an exactly balanced budget; in many years of the 19th and early 20th centuries, we had small surpluses or deficits. Perhaps if the deficit or surplus were less than $10 billion, we'd call that a balanced budget. Remember, we're dealing with a budget that calls for nearly $3.5 trillion in taxes and spending, so if tax revenue and expenditures were within $10 billion of each other, that would be close enough to call the budget balanced.

Deficits and Surpluses: The Record

Back in Chapter 7, we talked about federal government spending and federal government tax receipts. Let's put all that data together and focus on how well the government has covered its spending with tax revenue. Let's look at the record since the 1950s (see Figures 6 and 7).

Figure 6   The Federal Budget Deficit, Fiscal Years 1975–98

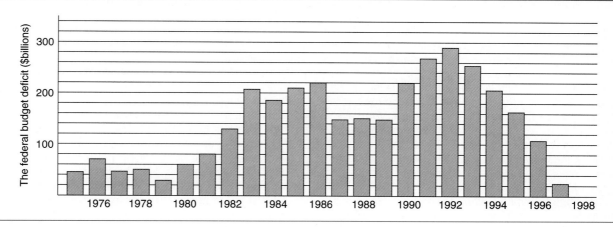

Source: *Economic Report of the President,* 1998; Congressional Budget Office.

Figure 7   Federal Budget Deficit or Surplus as a Percentage of GDP, 1975–98

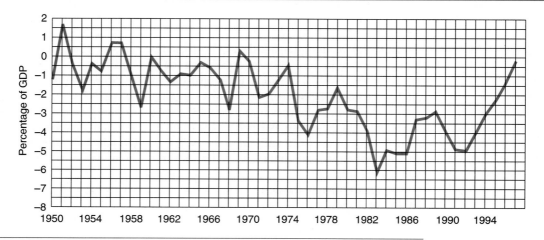

Source: *Economic Report of the President,* 1998.

ADVANCED WORK ....   The Paradox of Thrift*

Since childhood we have been taught that saving is good. Benjamin Franklin once said, "A penny saved is a penny earned." Franklin, it turns out, never followed his own advice. It also turns out that if we all try to save more, we'll probably end up with a really bad recession. This outcome is explained by the paradox of thrift.

You have probably heard that the sum of the parts does not necessarily add up to the whole. Consider, for example, what you would do if you were in a room full of people and that room suddenly burst into flames. Would you politely suggest to your companions that everyone file out of the room in an orderly fashion? Or would you bolt for the door?

What if the door opened inward (i.e., into the room)? Whoever got there first would attempt to pull open the door. But if everyone made a dash for the door, they would all arrive at just about the same time. The person trying to pull open the door wouldn't have space to do this because everyone else would be pushing him against the door. Several people would get injured in the crush. Unless they backed off, no one would get out of the room.

We call this an example of the fallacy of composition. What makes perfect sense for one person to do—rush to the door and pull it open—makes no sense when everyone tries to do it at the same time.

The paradox of thrift is a variant of the fallacy of composition. If everyone tries to save more, they will all end up saving less. Let's say that every week you save an extra $10 from your paycheck. At the end of a year, you will have saved an extra $520. Right? Right! Now, what if everyone tries saving an extra $10 a week? At the end of a year, we should have tens of billions in extra savings. Right? Wrong!

How come? Because what makes sense for one person to do does not make sense for everyone to do. If everyone tries to save more, everyone is cutting back on consumption. Business sales fall by hundreds of millions of dollars a week. If 130 million people each cut back by $10 a week, that comes to a weekly reduction of $1.3 billion. Over the course of a year, this will add up to $67.6 billion!

This $67.6 billion decline in consumption will have a multiplied effect on GDP. If the multiplier is 4, GDP will decline by $270.4 billion; if it is 6, GDP will decline by $405.6 billion. Surely such declines are typical of depressions.

But that's just for starters. When retailers get the idea that business will be off over the next few months, they do two things: lay off employees and cut back on their inventory. The workers who lose their jobs cut back on their consumption. Meanwhile, the retailers have begun canceling their orders for new inventory, prompting factories to lay off people and cut back on their orders for raw materials.

As the recession spreads, more and more people get laid off, and each will cut back on his or her consumption, further aggravating the decline in retail sales.

Now we come back to saving. Millions of people have been laid off and millions more are on reduced hours. Still others no longer get overtime. Each of these people, then, has suffered substantially reduced income. Each is not able to save as much as before the recession. Savings decline.

And so we're back where we started. We have the paradox of thrift: *If everyone tries to save more, they all will end up saving less.*

One of the biggest problems we have had since the early 1980s has been our low savings rate. So one may ask: If our savings rate is too low, don't we really need to save more, and will more saving really lead to a recession? One way that this dilemma can be resolved is to have a growing economy. Everyone's income goes up, everyone saves more and consumes more, and there's no recession.

*The paradox of thrift is not relevant today because we save less than 5 percent of our personal income. Then why talk about it? Because it does a great job of illustrating how the multiplier works.

How do we interpret the data? On the surface, it's obvious that the deficit went through the roof in the 1980s. Indeed, during the late 1940s the government ran three surpluses, in the 1950s it ran four, it ran just one in the 1960s, and it has run none since 1969. Of course, the size of the deficits can largely be explained by inflation. So let's take another look at the deficit as a percentage of GDP, which we've plotted in Figure 7. The increase in the deficit as a percentage of GDP is not as dramatic as the graph in Figure 6 shows, but the trend until the early 1980s was still quite alarming. Since then, however, the deficit as a percentage of GDP has shrunk from over 6 percent in 1983 to less than 1 percent in 1997.

What has brought the deficit down since 1992? Congress passed two huge deficit reduction packages in 1990 and in 1993. To secure the spending cuts he wanted in 1990, George ("Read my lips: no tax increase") Bush agreed with the Democratic leaders of Congress to a tax increase, raising the top personal income tax bracket from 28 percent to 31 percent, which probably cost him reelection in 1992. The $492 billion five-year deficit reduction package had a major impact.

Then, three years later, President Clinton pushed a five-year $433 billion deficit re-
duction package through Congress. About half this package was tax increases and half
was government spending reductions. Its main feature was raising the top personal income tax bracket from 31 percent to 39.6 percent. So, over a three year period, the top income tax bracket went from 28 percent to 39.6 percent.

Is there a "real" deficit that is much larger than the "official" deficit? Should the
taxes earmarked for the Social Security Trust Fund be used to reduce the deficit? In fiscal
year 1997 the Social Security Trust Fund (which exists only as a computer entry in the
federal government's accounts) took in about $80 billion more (in tax receipts and inter-
est on the federal debt it holds) than it paid out. Without these revenues, the federal
deficit for fiscal year 1997 would have been $102 billion, rather than the official figure of
$22 billion. Perhaps our real deficit worries will not begin until the second decade of the
21st century, when the baby boomers begin to retire and the Social Security Trust Fund
surplus turns into a deficit.

How does our deficit compare with those of other nations? Until the late 1990s, we
were among those running the highest deficits. But as you can see by glancing at Figure 8, by 1997 we were in relatively good shape.

Why Are Large Deficits So Bad?

Let us count the ways. Number one: They raise interest rates, which, in turn, discourages
investment. Our real interest rate (the nominal interest rate less the rate of inflation) during the latter half of the 1980s was three times as high as the real interest rate in Japan,
and it was much higher than those in most Western European countries as well. The
Japanese, who have been investing in plant and equipment at more than twice our rate (as
a percentage of GDP)—and more than we have in absolute numbers as well—have been
able to tap a huge domestic pool of savings and *still* have more than $100 billion a year
left over to invest in the United States and other countries. In fact, had it not been for this
vast inflow of savings from Japan and Western Europe, our interest rates would have
been much higher.

Number two: The federal government has become increasingly dependent on foreign
savers to finance the deficit—foreigners currently finance more than half the deficit (until
a few years ago, the Japanese alone were financing 40 percent). It has gotten to the point

Figure 8   The Deficit as a Percentage of GDP, Selected Countries, 1997

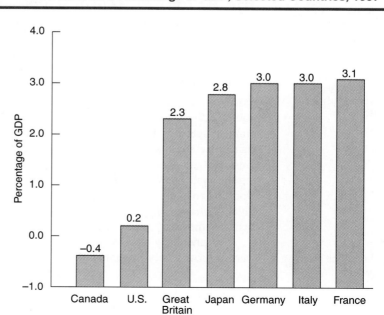

Source: OECD, Economic Outlook, December 1997.

that whenever the Treasury is about to run a big securities auction, everyone always asks, "Where are the Japanese?" When the Japanese did not buy their usual allotment of securities in the late summer and fall of 1987, the ensuing panic may well have set off the stock market crash of that October.

Number three: Until the mid-1990s the deficit sopped up more than half the personal savings in this country, making that much less savings available to large corporate borrowers seeking funds for new plant and equipment. We'll talk about this when we discuss the crowding-out effect in the appendix to this chapter.

Number four: Continuing deficits keep adding to the national debt, a topic we'll be considering in the last section of this chapter. The bigger the debt, the more interest we'll have to pay on it, and the bigger our deficits will be.

Christmas is a time when kids tell Santa what they want and adults pay for it. Deficits are when adults tell the government what they want—and their kids pay for it.
—Richard Lamm

Robert Eisner (a former president of the American Economic Association), Robert Heilbroner (another prominent economist), and Peter Bernstein (a writer billed on the jacket of his book as "one of the nation's keenest financial analysts") have dissented from the prevalent view that our government's deficits have been too large. They raise the question of why the federal government, unlike large corporations, does not have two separate budgets—an operating budget and a capital budget.[5] The operating budget would include the day-to-day costs of providing goods, services, and transfer payments, while the capital budget would include expenditures on improving our highways, airports, and other infrastructure, as well as expenditures on improving our human resources, such as money spent on health and education.

OK, let's have two budgets. And because it could be argued that we are spending well over $200 billion a year on "capital improvements," the operating budget would show a balanced budget. And the capital budget? That would show a deficit of more than $200 billion. So, any way you divide government spending and then add it up again, we're still running the same large deficits.

Eisner, Heilbroner, Bernstein, and others have also pointed out that budget deficits stimulate the economy. The only problem is that we should not have needed this stimulus during the "prosperous" mid- to late 1980s, when we were running huge deficits. And, as Senator Lloyd Bentsen put it during his televised vice presidential debate with Senator Dan Quayle in 1988, anyone could induce prosperity by writing hundreds of billions of dollars of "hot checks." We would do well to remember that John Maynard Keynes advocated writing those checks during recessions and paying them off during prosperity.

Will We Ever Be Able to Balance the Budget?

There are only three ways known to man to reduce the deficit and balance the budget: (1) cut government spending; (2) raise taxes; or (3) maintain a high rate of economic growth. Some combination of these could also work. So what are our chances that this will happen?

Raising taxes and cutting government spending would reduce the deficit.

We can reduce the deficit by raising taxes and cutting government spending. But most Americans oppose tax increases. Remember what happened to President Bush for going back on his pledge not to raise taxes? And when it comes to cutting specific government spending programs, most of them are off-limits—legally *and* politically. For instance, we are contractually obligated to pay defense contractors for *years* even if Congress and the president decide we don't really need all those new tanks and planes and missile systems. We would just love to cut spending on Medicare and Medicaid, but we won't be able to until we manage to put a cap on our escalating national health care costs. Finally, imagine the outcry if *any* elected official proposed cutting Social Security benefits. (See the box "The Special Interest Groups.")

Reducing the deficit through economic growth

Isn't there any other way to bring down the deficit? Actually there is. If our economy were to grow at a fairly rapid clip—say, at an annual rate of more than 3 percent a year—

---

[5]See Robert Eisner, *How Real Is the Federal Deficit?* (New York: Free Press, 1986); and Robert Heilbroner and Peter Bernstein, *The Debt and the Deficit* (New York: W. W. Norton, 1989).

The Special Interest Groups

Government is not a candy store in which every group can pick from any jar it wants.

—Ross Perot*

During every election campaign people make allusions to special interest groups—wealthy contributors, lobbyists, labor unions, defense contractors, and the like—who exert undue political influence and receive special favors. For example, the government has been paying farmers billions of dollars a year in subsidies, ostensibly to save the family farm. But in the six decades that this program has been in operation, 7 out of every 10 family farms have disappeared; three-quarters of the payments go to large corporate farms.

But the group that has fed the most at the government trough is the elderly. Since 1960 the dollars of federal benefit outlays per elderly person has more than quadrupled, from about $3,000 to more than $12,000 (both in constant 1998 dollars). Military pensions, civil service pensions, veterans' benefits, Medicare payments, and, of course, Social Security retirement benefits have all skyrocketed over the last three decades. And the lion's share of this money has gone to the middle-class and wealthy elderly rather than to the elderly poor. Peter G. Peterson and Neil Howe have explained just how the system works:

> In the end, what we wound up with was a kind of "government by grievance." Each nonpoverty entitlement program acquired and nurtured a public constituency, which, with the aid of its corresponding bureaucratic and congressional constituency (not to mention the battalions of special interest lawyers), protected and assured its continual expansion. As time went on, the entire fiscal system acquired a strong bias favoring budget deficits and the current consumption of national resources.†

*Ross Perot, *United We Stand* (New York: Hyperion, 1992), p. 36.
†Peter G. Peterson and Neil Howe, *On Borrowed Time* (New York: Simon & Schuster, 1988), p. 16.

and if we held government spending increases to less than the growth rate, then the deficit would actually begin to shrink. This would happen because tax receipts would be rising faster than government spending. For example, if the economy grew by 3 percent, government spending grew by 1 percent, and tax receipts grew by 3 percent (i.e., as our incomes rose, we would be paying 3 percent more in personal income tax and Social Security tax, while corporations would be paying at least 3 percent more in corporate income tax), then the deficit would fall by about 2 percent a year. So if we could get all our economic ducks lined up—restrained government spending increases, higher economic growth, and rising tax receipts—we could reduce the deficit without either raising taxes or cutting government spending.

We seemed to be following that script in recent years, as the deficit plummeted from $290 billion in fiscal year 1992 to just $22 billion in fiscal year 1997. But in July 1997 President Clinton and Congress made a deal that provided a package of tax cuts and spending increases, but promised to trim future Medicare and Medicaid increases by over $100 billion during the next five years. Apparently both the president and Congress, after years of fiscal discipline and restraint, may reverse the deficit's downward trend.

Next, consider what Nobel prize–winning economist Wassily Leontief had to say about our decaying infrastructure:

> Drastic cuts in public spending (except for military purposes) left the physical infrastructure of this country in ruin. City streets and transportation facilities, water supply and sewage systems, particularly in large metropolitan areas, are collapsing; the once glorious interstate highways are crumbling, and cramped airports are incapable of handling the rapidly increasing traffic. Despite the valiant effort of the underfinanced, underpowered Environmental Protection Agency, our lakes, rivers, and forests are succumbing to deadly acid rain.[6]

While we're hanging out all our dirty laundry, let's continue this laundry list. What will AIDs, drugs, crime, the homeless, and the underclass cost us in the coming years? And what about education, job retraining for workers displaced by foreign competition, and research to find renewable forms of energy? Have we factored in enough money to

Wassily Leontief, winner of Nobel prize, 1973, for work on interrelationship among sectors of the economy (The Nobel Foundation)

[6]Wassily Leontief, letter to *New York Times,* February 4, 1990.

clean up nuclear waste? Not to mention our underfunded pension liabilities and federally guaranteed loans that will go bad?[7] How much over budget will we go?

That's enough *bad* news. The *good* news is that the deficit, which has been declining rapidly since 1992 (see Figure 6), should be very small or even disappear in fiscal year 1998. Few economists—and certainly not yours truly—would have predicted this. We seem to have gotten all our economic ducks in a line—low inflation and interest rates (which hold down interest on the national debt), low unemployment (which lowers government spending and raises tax receipts), high economic growth (which also raises tax receipts), and even a booming stock market (which, at least until early 1998, raised tax receipts). The big question was what to do with expected surpluses in the coming years.

But all good things *do* come to an end. A recession, a decline in stock prices, a tax cut, or an increase in government spending programs can easily push the deficit back up again. And keep in mind that after the year 2010, as the baby boom generation attains senior citizenship, the Social Security Trust Fund will quickly be depleted, and, unless the government has already raised Social Security taxes or cut benefits, the federal budget deficit will skyrocket.

Part VI: The Proposed Balanced Budget Amendment and the Line Item Veto

To come back to the dictum that we must balance our budget each year—something the government really tried to do even into the early 1930s—the economic wisdom today tells us that we should have deficits in lean years and surpluses in fat years. But perhaps over the course of the business cycle, we should balance the budget (see the box "Balancing the Budget over the Business Cycle").

Of course, it hasn't worked out that way. During the last 30-odd years, we managed only one surplus. Our national debt has risen year after year as we ran budget deficits in fat years as well as in lean years. (See the box Micawber's Equation.")

The first step in passing a Constitutional amendment is a two-thirds vote in both houses of Congress. Then it would still need to be ratified by three-quarters of the states before it became part of our Constitution.

Despite some very close votes in 1994, 1995, 1996, and 1997, the balanced budget amendment failed in one or the other house of Congress. However, its prospects for

---

[7]Richard Lamm, former governor of Colorado, has estimated these liabilities to be at least $6 trillion for unfunded military pensions, federal civil service pensions, and the unfunded liability of the Social Security system. See Richard Lamm, "Crisis: The Uncompetitive Society," in *Global Competitiveness: Getting the U.S. Back on Track,* ed. Martin K. Starr (New York: W. W. Norton, 1988), p. 23. Christopher Byron has estimated that the federal government has $4 trillion of liabilities not provided for in its budget. See Christopher Byron, "The Bombs in the Budget," *New York Magazine,* March 5, 1990, p. 19.

Balancing the Budget over the Business Cycle

For most of 1997 the unemployment rate was at or below 5 percent. And yet, in July of that year Congress passed, and President Clinton signed, a substantial tax cut and spending increase, which will tend to push the deficit back up again.

Do you remember the Old Testament story of Joseph, the man who had a real talent for interpreting dreams? One day he was asked by the king to interpret this dream: Seven fat cows walked by, followed by seven emaciated cows. That was an easy one for Joseph. Seven fat years, or good harvests, would be followed by seven lean years, or bad harvests. Joseph's policy pre-

scription: Store up all of the surplus grain grown during the seven years of plentiful harvests and use this bounty to feed everyone during the lean years.

What should we have learned from that story? We should have learned that during years of economic prosperity, we need to run budget surpluses. And that we could use those surpluses to finance the deficits we incur during recessionary years. So, over the entire business cycle, we have balanced the budget.

Have we been following the economic policies prescribed by Joseph? You tell *me.*

Micawber's Equation

Do you remember Mr. Micawber from *David Copperfield?* This poor man was almost always just one step ahead of his creditors. Here is the advice he offered David, who was visiting him in debtors' prison:

> He solemnly conjured me, I remember, to take warning by his fate; and to observe that if a man had twenty pounds a-year for his income, and spent nineteen pounds nineteen shillings and sixpence, he would be happy, but that if he spent twenty pounds one he would be miserable.*

Should we apply Micawber's equation to the federal budget? Will our continuing budget deficits and mounting public debt lead to national misery? There are plenty of people out there who would agree with Mr. Micawber that our government must not spend one penny more than it receives in taxes.

*Charles Dickens, *David Copperfield* (Harmondsworth, Middlesex, England: Penguin Books), p. 221.

---

passage are quite good, especially if the Republicans pick up additional seats in the House and in the Senate in the 1998 elections. On the other hand, now that there's a good likelihood of surpluses in 1998, 1999, and the first few years of the new century, perhaps there will be less support for this measure.

Those advocating a balanced budget amendment to the Constitution use our history of deficits and our mounting national debt to make their case. If our political leaders are unwilling or unable to exercise restraint, they will be required by law to do so.

Do we want to put ourselves in an economic straitjacket?

Most economists oppose such an amendment because it would put us in an economic straitjacket. No longer would we be able to fight recessions with deficits. Even our automatic stabilizers would be taken from us (as they are sure to cause deficits in recession years), leaving us vulnerable not just to recessions but to depressions as well.

The irony and even hypocrisy of this proposed amendment lay with its greatest advocate, President Ronald Reagan. It was remarkable that the man who presided over the eight largest deficits in our entire history was supporting a balanced budget amendment. "Stop me," he seemed to be pleading, "before I spend again!" His successor, George Bush, who went on to run even larger deficits than Reagan, pleaded again and again for the balanced budget amendment, as if that measure would magically wipe out all the red ink. Of course there's plenty of blame to go around considering that the president can't spend one penny without having Congress pass the necessary legislation.

In still another effort to lower the deficit, Congress passed a law in 1996 to permit the president to veto parts of tax and spending bills he opposes, without vetoing the entire legislation. This line item veto can be eventually overridden by a two-thirds vote in each house of Congress. In August 1997 President Clinton used the line item veto to strike down three relatively minor tax and spending items, while declaring, "From now on, presidents will be able to say no to wasteful spending or tax loopholes, even as they say yes to vital legislation." By December 1997 he had vetoed less than $2 billion of spending items, a minuscule fraction of the federal budget. Opponents of the line item veto claim that it can be enacted only by constitutional amendment, and hope to have the issue decided by the Supreme Court.

In February 1998 a federal judge ruled the line item veto unconstitutional because it gave the president powers that Article I of the Constitution reserved for Congress. The Clinton Administration immediately filed an appeal, which the Supreme Court will probably rule upon some time in 1998. Until it does, the legality of the line item veto remains in doubt.

Part VII: The Public Debt

The debt is like a crazy aunt we keep down in the basement. All the neighbors know she's there, but nobody wants to talk about her.

—Ross Perot

The attractiveness of financing spending by debt issue to the elected politicians should be obvious. Borrowing allows spending to be made that will yield immediate political payoffs without the incurring of any immediate political cost.

—James Buchanan, *The Deficit and American Democracy*

The public, or national, debt is the amount of currently outstanding federal securities that the Treasury has issued. Although about 10 percent is held by various federal agencies, most notably the Federal Reserve, it is reasonable to say that the public debt is what the federal government owes to the holders of Treasury bills, notes, bonds, and certificates.

In 1981 the public debt went over the $1 trillion mark. Do you remember how much money $1 trillion is? Write it out with all the zeros right here:

Written out, it looks like this: $1,000,000,000,000.[8] In 1986 the national debt broke the $2 trillion mark. That means it took the federal government just five years to accumulate as much debt as it had accumulated between 1776 and 1981. The $3 trillion barrier was breached in 1989. We passed the $4 trillion mark in 1992 and the $5 trillion mark in 1996 (see Figure 9).

Exactly what is the national debt?

Exactly what *is* the national debt? It is *the cumulative total of all the federal budget deficits less any surpluses.* Much of it was run up during recessions and wars. It is owed to the holders of Treasury bills, notes, certificates, and bonds. For example, if you own any of these, you are holding part of the national debt. (For extra help in differentiating between the deficit and the debt, see the Extra Help box.)

Who holds the national debt? Private American citizens hold about half. Foreigners hold about 20 percent. The rest is held by banks, other business firms, and U.S. government agencies. Those who say we owe it to ourselves are substantially correct. As a taxpayer, you owe part of that debt. And if you happen to own any U.S. government securities, you are also owed part of the debt, so you literally owe it to yourself.

Is the national debt a burden that will have to be borne by future generations? As long as we owe it to ourselves, the answer is no. If we did owe it mainly to foreigners, and if they wanted to be paid off, it could be a great burden. But that is certainly not the case at this point.

In 1960 foreigners held about 3 percent of the national debt. They have increased their holdings so substantially in recent years almost entirely because Americans love to

A nation is not in danger of financial disaster merely because it owes itself money.
—Andrew W. Mellon,
Secretary of the Treasury in the 1920s

---

[8]If big numbers still make you nervous, you would do well to review the box "A Word about Numbers," near the beginning of Chapter 5.

Figure 9   National Debt, 1975–97*

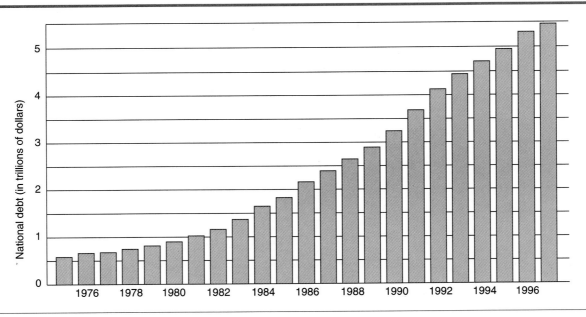

*Debt on January 1 of each year.
Source: *Economic Report of the President,* 1998.

Differentiating between the Deficit and the Debt

It's easy to confuse the federal budget deficit and the national debt. The *deficit* occurs when federal government spending is greater than tax revenue. The *debt* is the cumulative total of all the federal budget deficits less any surpluses.

The last time we had a budget surplus was in 1969. This means that our public debt has been rising steadily since that year. In fact, the deficit has also risen substantially, especially since the early 1980s.

Now suppose that our deficit declined one year, say, from $200 billion to $150 billion. What would happen to the national debt? Can you guess? It would still go up. By how much? By $150 billion. So every year that we have a deficit—even a declining one—the national debt will go up.

spend and hate to save, and because the U.S. federal government has been running megadeficits during the last decade. Today foreigners hold nearly one-quarter percent.

By the mid-1980s the United States was running annual trade deficits of more than $100 billion and budget deficits of more than $200 billion. Because our saving rate was so low, there wasn't enough domestic saving available to finance the federal budget deficits; but foreigners, particularly the Japanese, were awash with dollars, so they simply recycled them by lending them to the U.S. government.

Consequently, foreigners have been holding an increasing percentage of the public debt. While still nothing to be alarmed about, if the present trend continues—huge budget deficits, huge trade deficits, and a low domestic saving rate—soon after the turn of the century the foreign share of the national debt could be approaching 30 percent. At that point, could we keep saying that we owe it to ourselves?

The national debt rose substantially during wars. We paid for these wars partly by taxation and partly by borrowing. It was considered one's patriotic duty during World War II to buy war bonds. Unfortunately, however, it was also a terrible investment because the buyers were locked into low interest rates—between 1 and 1 1/2 percent for 7 to 10 years—while immediately after the war, prices jumped 35 percent in 3 years.

In wartime a nation will invest very little in plant and equipment; all available resources must go toward the war effort. As a result, during the first half of the 1940s, we built no new plant and equipment. Had there been no war, billions of dollars' worth of plant and equipment would have been built. The generation that came of age after the war inherited less capital than it would have had no war been fought. To that degree, a burden was placed on their shoulders.

Those who would point at the huge increase in the national debt during the war as the cause of our having less plant and equipment have misplaced the blame. It was the war, not the increase in the debt, that prevented wartime construction of capital goods.

When do we have to pay off the national debt?

When do we have to pay off the debt? We don't. All we have to do is roll it over, or refinance it, as it falls due. Each year several hundred billion dollars' worth of federal securities fall due. By selling new ones, the Treasury keeps us going. But there is no reason why the national debt ever has to be paid off. (For one economist's view of the debt, see box "Dr. Eisner: How He Learned to Stop Worrying and Love the Debt Bomb.")

A real problem would arise if investors thought the government might go bankrupt. That's what happened to the New York City government in 1975. Suddenly the city was unable to sell its securities, which it needed to do to roll over its debt. Had the pension plans of the municipal labor unions and the federal government not helped out, the city would indeed have gone bankrupt. However, the financial positions of the governments of New York City and the United States are hardly comparable. The federal government has first claim to our tax dollar, which make its securities the safest possible investment.

Dr. Eisner: How He Learned to Stop Worrying and Love the Debt Bomb

Not everyone is depressed about the debt. Like Dr. Strangelove,* someone has managed to see the bright side of a situation that is beginning to alarm the rest of us. I'll let him talk for himself:

> With all the deficits, the general trend of real federal debt—the debt adjusted for inflation—has been downward. On a per capita basis it has indeed gone down very sharply over most of the last 40 years.[†]

He's right. In 1946 (40 years before his book was published) our national debt was actually larger than our GDP. One of the tricks everyone likes to use in statistics is to pick a base year that will enable you to show a trend. Suppose we picked 1966 or 1976 as our base year? Then we'd get very different results. Eisner's downward trend would become an upward trend.

The problem is that Eisner overstated his case. Inflation does depreciate the value of the debt, so even if we never begin to pay it off, it would be somewhat easier to manage interest payments. Of course, there is no guarantee that inflation will continue. And what would happen if we ever saw a period of deflation? Then the debt would become an even greater burden.

Eisner makes another basic point:

> Of fundamental importance . . . is the notion that the federal debt, however frequently viewed as a burden to the government or to future taxpayers, is wealth to those who own it.

Whatever their concerns for the government's fiscal responsibility, the holders of all those deficit-financing Treasury notes, bills, and bonds feel richer for having them. And the richer they feel, the more they try to spend now and plan to spend in the future.[‡]

Again, Eisner makes a good point. The national debt is the government's liability, but it is also an asset of those who hold it. Three problems, however, detract from the view that the debt should be seen in such a positive light.

First, if the debt is indeed depreciating in value because of inflation, as Eisner correctly maintains, then its value as an asset depreciates accordingly. Second, an increasing amount of the debt is being held by foreigners. And third, in times when we need to hold down consumption and raise saving and investment, any inducement to spend rather than save will have a detrimental effect on our economy.

Nevertheless, the points that Eisner raises are valid and should temper our alarm over the rising national debt. It will be interesting to see whether Eisner continues to hold to these views as the debt keeps mounting.

*Your video store may have *Dr. Strangelove.* This movie will bring the joys of nuclear warfare right into your living room.
[†]Robert Eisner, *How Real Is the Federal Deficit?* (New York: Free Press, 1986), p. 4.
[‡]Ibid., p. 5.

Isn't the national debt getting too big? Too big relative to what? Table 2 compares the debt to GDP. Notice how the debt in 1945 was even larger than GDP! Today the national debt is slightly more than two-thirds of GDP. We make that comparison because the federal government does have first claim on our tax dollar. In fact, if the government really wanted to, it could probably pay off the national debt in about 20 years by raising our taxes by about one-quarter.

The public debt, which was just 33 percent of GDP in 1980 (see Table 2), rose to 68 percent in 1997. This gave rise to the question, Can the U.S. Treasury go bankrupt? (see box). This concern has diminished as the federal budget deficit has virtually disappeared in 1998.

Table 2   GDP and the Public Debt, Selected Years (in billions of dollars)

Public Year	Debt	GDP	Public Debt as a Percentage of GDP
1945	260	214	122%
1970	381	1,036	37
1980	909	2,784	33
1985	1,818	4,181	43
1990	3,207	5,744	56
1994	4,644	6,936	67
1997	5,500	8,083	68

Source: *Economic Report of the President,* 1998.

Can the U.S. Treasury Go Bankrupt?

The national debt has been growing rapidly since 1980. In fact, the fastest-growing big-ticket item in the federal budget is interest on the debt. But we are not going bankrupt. Not now. Not in the next 10 years. And, perhaps, not ever.

Perhaps? That's right. We *could* go bankrupt. If the purchasers of U.S. Treasury securities stop buying them, then that's *it.* On the other hand, no matter how fast the debt increases, as long as the Treasury is able to find buyers for its securities, we will not go bankrupt. We don't have to worry about paying off the debt or even about reducing it. All we have to do is be able to keep rolling it over.

As the debt grows and interest payments keep rising, sometime down the road, perhaps 15 or 20 years from now, bondholders may start getting a little nervous. At that time, even the U.S. government may be perceived as unable to continue meeting interest payments and refinancing the debt. To induce bondholders to keep rolling over the debt as it falls due, the Treasury will have to offer higher interest rates. These, in turn, will make the debt still more unmanageable and will lead to even higher interest rates.

Budget deficits and interest payments on the debt have the Treasury in a double bind. Because the debt grows each year (because we run deficits each year), we have to pay more and more interest on the debt. And because interest payments keep rising, our deficits keep growing, further pushing up the national debt.

Let's see how this works by plugging in some actual numbers. In fiscal 1989 the U.S. deficit was about $150 billion, so the national debt rose by that amount. In the following fiscal year, the Treasury had to pay more interest on this larger debt. How *much* more? Since the average rate of interest that the Treasury had to pay that year was 8 percent, the Treasury had to pay an extra $12 billion ($150 billion times .08). So, that $12 billion was tacked onto the deficit for fiscal 1990, which pushed the debt up still further.

The nation is thus locked into the inexorable force of compound interest. The debt is so huge that annual interest payments alone are more than $250 billion. And the interest on *that* interest will keep mounting. Which will add still further to the deficit, making the debt rise still more.

Can the U.S. Treasury go bankrupt? It can and it will if our creditors start thinking that they will never be paid back. At that point, there will be no more buyers for our government securities. We have always thought that it can't happen here. Someday our creditors might make us think again.

Why not go ahead and pay off the debt—or at least reduce it? Economists predict that following this course would have catastrophic consequences. It would bring year after year of budget surpluses and would probably send us into a deep depression. According to our earlier analysis, when the economy is experiencing high unemployment, we need to run budget deficits, not surpluses. But during prosperity, particularly when inflation becomes a problem, we need to run budget surpluses, paying off part of the debt. This is the part of a countercyclical policy we have ignored during most of the last two decades.

How serious a problem is the interest on the debt? The interest payments more than tripled during the 1980s and will continue to climb higher as the debt itself rises. Interest payments are now about one-seventh of the federal budget, one of the "uncontrollable" expenditures not subject to budget cuts. For a long time the Treasury got a free ride. It had contracted most of the debt at relatively low interest rates—less than 2 percent in the 1940s and early 1950s, and until the late 1970s, single-digit rates. Interest rates reached 10- and 15-year lows in late 1993. Although interest rates rose sharply in 1994, they have since fallen to relatively low levels in late 1997 and early 1998.

Some evidence indicates government borrowing has drained funds away from private investment in recent years. To the degree that this is true, the growth rate of our capital stock—our plant and equipment—has been slower than it would have otherwise been. Again, the national debt as such is not causing this problem. Rather, the national debt is merely the symptom of the government's continuing habit of living beyond its means.

Most Americans do not seem particularly concerned that the government is living beyond its means; after all, they are doing the same thing themselves. But there is just so much we as individuals can borrow. Does the federal government have such a credit limit as well? Yes, it does. Every borrower has a limit—even the U.S. Treasury. But because it already owes about $5.5 trillion, it obviously has an extremely high credit limit.

Who sets that limit? Increasingly, foreigners do. When William Proxmire was chairman of the Senate Banking Committee, he had this to say about foreign investors' increasing power: "As time goes on, as foreign investors get a larger and larger share of the national debt, they get into a position where they can impose tough terms or cut off the credit. You lose some part of your sovereignty under those circumstances. You lose your independence."[9]

Let's return to two of the dicta stated at the beginning of this chapter: (1) The public debt is a burden on future generations. (2) We owe it to ourselves. To the degree that the debt is being held increasingly by foreigners, we can no longer say we owe it (only) to ourselves. In the future, even if we never pay back one penny of that debt, our children and our grandchildren will have to pay foreigners hundreds of billions of dollars a year in interest. At least to that degree, then, the public debt *will* be a burden to future generations.

Questions for Further Thought and Discussion

1. Describe the differences between an inflationary gap and a deflationary gap.
2. Explain why large deficits are so bad.
3. It can be argued that there really is no fiscal policy. How would you make this argument?
4. To what degree is the public debt a burden to future generations?
5. Explain how, in general, the automatic stabilizers work. Then use one automatic stabilizer to illustrate this.

---

[9]Quoted in Martin Tolchin and Susan Tolchin, *Buying into America* (New York: Times Books, 1988), p. 198.

WORKBOOK FOR CHAPTER 11

Name _____   Date _____

Multiple-Choice Questions

Circle the letter that corresponds to the best answer.

1. In the late 1970s and early 1980s, the goals of fiscal policy were

    a. completely attained   b. largely attained

    c. largely unattained   d. completely unattained

2. When equilibrium GDP is too small, we have

    a. a deflationary gap   b. a depression   c. an inflationary gap   d. none of these

3. There is an inflationary gap when

    a. equilibrium GDP is equal to full-employment GDP

    b. equilibrium GDP is smaller than full-employment GDP   c. equilibrium GDP is larger than full-employment GDP   d. none of these occur

4. Fiscal policy and monetary policy are

    a. different means used to attain different goals

    b. different means used to attain the same goals

    c. the same means to attain the same goals

    d. the same means to attain different goals

5. Budget surpluses are most appropriate during

    a. depressions   b. recessions   c. inflations

6. Each of the following is an automatic stabilizer except

    a. unemployment compensation   b. direct taxes   c. welfare payments   d. Social Security benefits

7. If you lost a $300-a-week job and were eligible for unemployment insurance, you would probably collect about

    a. $240   b. $200   c. $160   d. $120

    e. $80

8. When there is a recession, the biggest decline is in

    a. Social Security tax receipts   b. personal income tax receipts   c. consumer spending   d. corporate aftertax profits

9. The automatic stabilizers

    a. help smooth out the business cycle

    b. make the business cycle worse

    c. eliminate the business cycle

10. Each of the following is an example of discretionary fiscal policy except

    a. public works spending   b. making the automatic stabilizers more effective   c. changes in tax rates

    d. the unemployment insurance program

11. The proposed balanced budget amendment to the Constitution would have required the federal budget to be balanced

    a. over the business cycle   b. every three years

    c. every year   d. every nonrecession year

12. Fiscal policy is made by

    a. the president only   b. Congress only   c. both the president and Congress   d. neither the president nor Congress

13. The requirement to override a presidential veto is

    a. a majority vote in each house of Congress   b. a two-thirds vote in each house of Congress   c. a three-quarters vote in each house of Congress   d. a majority vote of both houses of Congress combined

14. If we passed a constitutional amendment requiring a balanced budget every year, this would probably

    a. make our recessions into depressions   b. prevent recessions   c. create inflations   d. raise interest rates

15. If equilibrium GDP is $5.5 trillion and full-employment GDP is $5 trillion, there is

    a. definitely an inflationary gap

    b. probably an inflationary gap

    c. definitely a deflationary gap

    d. probably a deflationary gap

16. Statement 1: A tax cut will have the same impact on the deflationary gap as an increase in G only if people spend the entire tax cut.

Statement 2: The paradox of thrift is more relevant today, when savings are so low, than it was back in the 1950s and 1960s.

   a. Statement 1 is true and statement 2 is false.
   b. Statement 2 is true and statement 1 is false.
   c. Both statements are true.
   d. Both statements are false.

17. Statement 1: Although the federal budget deficit was higher in the 1980s than in the 1970s, it was a somewhat smaller percentage of GDP.

Statement 2: The federal budget deficit reached $5.5 trillion in 1998.

   a. Statement 1 is true and statement 2 is false.
   b. Statement 2 is true and statement 1 is false.
   c. Both statements are true.
   d. Both statements are false.

18. Which statement is true?

   a. About one-third of the national debt is rolled over (or refinanced) every year.   b. The national debt is doubling every 10 years.   c. Unless we balance the budget within the next five years, the United States stands a good chance of going bankrupt.   d. None of these statements is true.

19. Since 1945 the national debt has _____ as a percent of GDP.

   a. risen   b. fallen   c. remained about the same

20. Which statement is true?

   a. The national debt is larger than GDP.
   b. The national debt will have to be paid off eventually.
   c. Most of the national debt is held by foreigners.
   d. None of these statements is true.

21. If the federal government attempts to eliminate a budget deficit during a depression, this will

   a. alleviate the depression   b. contribute to inflation   c. make the depression worse   d. have no economic effect

22. During times of inflation, we want to

   a. raise taxes and run budget deficits
   b. raise taxes and run budget surpluses
   c. lower taxes and run budget surpluses
   d. lower taxes and run budget deficits

23. Which statement is true?

   a. The public debt is larger than our GDP.   b. The public debt is the sum of our deficits minus our surpluses over the years since the beginning of the country.   c. We have had budget deficits only during recession years and wartime.   d. None of these statements is true.

24. The public debt has been increasing at the rate of $1 trillion every _____ years.

   a. 2   b. 4–5   c. 8–10   d. 25

25. A major advantage of the automatic stabilizers is that they

   a. simultaneously stabilize the economy and tend to reduce the size of the public debt
   b. guarantee that the federal budget will be balanced over the course of the business cycle
   c. automatically produce surpluses during recessions and deficits during inflations
   d. require no legislative action by Congress to be made effective

26. The most valid argument against the size of the national debt is that it

   a. will ruin the nation when we have to pay it back
   b. is owed mainly to foreigners
   c. leaves future generations less plant and equipment than would be left had there been a smaller debt
   d. will bankrupt the nation because there is a limit as to how much we can borrow

27. The Budget Act of 1990 was designed to lower the deficit over the next five years by a total of nearly $_____ billion.

   a. 100   b. 200   c. 300   d. 400   e. 500

Fill-In Questions

1. The goals of fiscal policy are (1) _____

   _____; (2) _____

   _____; and (3) _____

   _____.

2. The means that fiscal policy uses to attain those goals are

   the manipulation of _____ and

   _____.

3. We could eliminate inflationary gaps and deflationary

   gaps by making _____

   GDP equal to _____ GDP.

4. The two ways of eliminating an inflationary gap are

   (1) _____

   and (2) _____.

5. The two ways of eliminating a deflationary gap are

   (1) _____

   and (2) _____.

6. When there is an inflationary gap, _____

   _____ GDP is greater than _____

   _____ GDP.

7. When there is a deflationary gap, _____

   _____ GDP is greater than _____

   _____ GDP.

8. Inflationary gaps call for budget _____

   _____ while deflationary gaps call for

   budget _____.

9. When there is a budget surplus, _____

   is greater than _____;

   when there is a budget deficit, _____

   is greater than _____.

10. The last year we had a budget surplus was _____

    _____.

11. When there is a budget deficit of $10 billion, essentially

    we have a _____budget.

12. Welfare spending, unemployment compensation, and

    direct taxes are all examples of _____

    _____.

13. If you are earning $200 a week before taxes and then

    collect unemployment insurance benefits, you can expect

    to collect about $_____ a week.

14. Perhaps the most countercyclical of all the automatic

    stabilizers is the _____.

15. In addition to the automatic stabilizer, we have _____

    _____ fiscal policy.

16. Fiscal policy was invented by _____.

17. When equilibrium GDP is equal to full-employment GDP,

    we have an inflationary gap equal to _____.

Problems

1. a. In Figure 1, is there an inflationary gap or a deflationary gap? **b.** How much is it? **c.** How much is the multiplier?

Figure 1

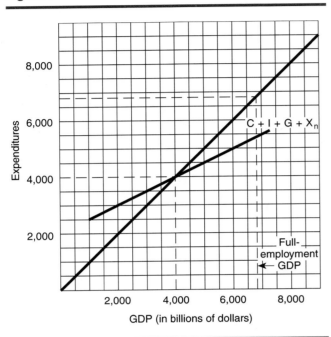

Expenditures — GDP (in billions of dollars)

2. To remove the gap in Figure 1, what two fiscal policy measures would you recommend?

3. When the MPC is .8, how much is the multiplier?

4. If the MPC is .6, how much is the multiplier?

5. If C rises by $10 billion and the multiplier is 4, what happens to the level of GDP?

6. If I falls by $20 billion and the multiplier is 5, what happens to the level of GDP?

7. If GDP is 3,400, the multiplier is 5, and I rises by 15, what is the new level of GDP?

8. If GDP is 3,900, the multiplier is 8, and G falls by 10, what is the new level of GDP?

9. Suppose that Saddam and George each have MPCs of .5. If Saddam receives one dollar of income, how much of that dollar would he be expected to spend? If George receives all of the money that Saddam spent, how much would George be expected to spend?

10. If equilibrium GDP is $400 billion greater than full-employment GDP and there is an inflationary gap of $50 billion, how much is the multiplier?

11. If the full-employment GDP is $1 trillion greater than equilibrium GDP and the multiplier is 5, how much is the deflationary gap?

12. If Bill receives $1,000 from his newly created government job and gives $900 to George for writing him a speech, and then George gives $810 to Ross for installing a computer system, assuming everyone else in the nation has the same spending pattern: **a.** how much is the multiplier? **b.** If $10 billion of new investment had been made, by how much would our GDP rise?

13. Suppose that in the year 2020 our national debt were $10 trillion and our budget deficit were $300 billion. If a plan to gradually reduce the deficit and to balance the budget in the year 2030 were successful, make an estimate of the national debt in 2030.

14. In Figure 2: **a.** Is there an inflationary gap or a deflationary gap? **b.** How much is it? **c.** How much is the multiplier?

15. Krista Chavez was earning $600 a week after taxes and saved $50. If she lost her job, how much did she now spend each week on consumption? Show how you got your answer.

Figure 2

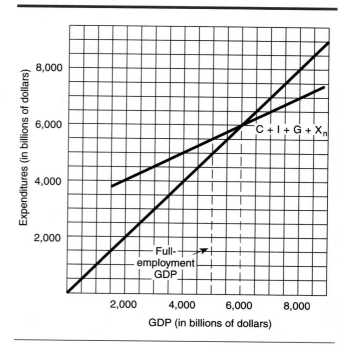

The Full-Employment Budget and the Crowding-Out and Crowding-In Effects

There is fairly widespread agreement among economists that the government needs to run budget deficits during recessions and surpluses during periods of prosperity, full employment, and inflation. But how big should those deficits and surpluses be? That question is answered by setting up the full-employment budget. A second issue, raised by many conservative economists, is whether large budget deficits don't crowd private borrowers out of the financial markets. Or whether, as the Keynesians maintain, these large deficits actually lead to *more* private borrowing. In this appendix we will examine the issue of crowding out versus crowding in.

Appendix Objectives

In this appendix you will learn about:

- The full-employment budget.
- The crowding-out effect.
- The crowding-in effect.

The Full-Employment Budget

How big should our deficits be during recessions?

One question I have sidestepped is the size of deficits or surpluses. Besides saying that if the deficit or surplus is less than $10 billion the budget is virtually in balance and that our country's $200 billion-plus deficits are huge indeed, I have not distinguished among the various sizes of deficits during the past few decades. To do that, I will use the concept of the full-employment budget.

To better understand this concept, let's start with an economy that is at full employment with a balanced budget. The unemployment rate is 5 percent, and federal expenditures are equal to tax revenues. What would happen if the unemployment rate rose just 1 percentage point to 6 percent? Economists have calculated that federal tax revenues would fall and government spending would rise by approximately $30 billion. The government would be taking in less in taxes because 1.3 million workers lost their jobs and corporate profits probably declined somewhat.[1] Also, government expenditures for transfer payments, particularly unemployment benefits, food stamps, welfare, and Medicaid, would rise. Together, then, the decline in tax revenue and the rise in government expenditures would total some $30 billion. In other words, we'd have a budget deficit of $30 billion.

Now we'll take it a step further by raising the unemployment rate to 7 percent, forcing up the deficit another $30 billion to a grand total of $60 billion.

Assuming no changes in the tax structure and no new government spending programs, let's figure out how much of a deficit the government would have been running had the economy been at full employment. Think about it. Tax revenue would have been higher because 2.6 million more people would have been working. Government expendi-

---

[1]We are assuming a labor force of 130 million people.

tures would have been much lower because more than one million fewer people would have been collecting unemployment benefits; food stamp and welfare payments also would have been much lower.[2] In fact, the deficit would have been zero.

When the deficit is zero, the budget is balanced. Had our economy been at full employment then, we would have had a balanced budget. In other words, with a 7 percent unemployment rate and a $60 billion deficit, we would still say that we had a full-employment balanced budget.

A deficit of $60 billion when the unemployment rate is 7 percent would provide the same economic stimulus that a balanced budget would provide when there is full employment. But earlier we said that when there is a recession, it is necessary to have a budget deficit to stimulate the economy. Would a full-employment balanced budget be adequate to reduce the unemployment rate (i.e., is our actual $60 billion deficit high enough)?

Economists do not agree here. (What else is new?) Some feel the actual deficit should run higher, and others say the $60 billion is more than adequate to push the economy back toward full employment. Furthermore, many economists consider a 5 percent unemployment rate a far too optimistic goal and say that 5½ or even 6 percent would be our lowest attainable rate. Were that so, we would base the full-employment budget on a higher unemployment rate. (If this is not entirely clear to you, see the Extra Help box.)

All of this seems to fly in the face of our recent experience. After all, our unemployment rate has been below 5 percent since mid-1997. How can we still define full employment at a 5 percent unemployment level—let alone a level of 5½ or 6 percent? You've just asked a very good question. The answer is that extraordinary circumstances have pushed the unemployment rate below 5 percent, but those circumstances are very temporary. If that's true, then we shall soon see the unemployment rate go back up again. If not, then maybe we'll need to reset the unemployment rate that defines full employment.

The Crowding-Out and Crowding-In Effects

The great debate: Monetarists: Deficits cause crowding-out. Keynesians: Deficits cause crowding-in.

Welcome to the first debate we are going to be sponsoring between the monetarists and the Keynesians over the next few chapters. In this debate the monetarists will argue in favor of the crowding-out effect, while the Keynesians will take the side of the crowding-in effect.

The monetarists maintain that Keynesian deficits designed to raise aggregate demand will have little, if any, positive effect. First, budget deficits drive up interest rates, thus discouraging investment. Second, the more money the government borrows to finance the deficit, the less that will be available to private borrowers.

If the proper fiscal policy during recessions is a large budget deficit, one would wonder where the Treasury will get all this money. Presumably it will go out and borrow it. But from whom?

If it borrows funds from individuals who would have otherwise made this money available for business investment, won't business borrowers be "crowded out" of the financial markets by the government? And won't interest rates be driven up in the process, further discouraging investment? Won't increased government spending financed by borrowing be replacing private investment spending?

The answer is yes to all three questions. Yes—but to what degree?

During recessions business firms cut back on their investing, so the government would be tapping a relatively idle source of funds, and during recessions interest rates tend to fall.

Even during relatively prosperous times, such as the mid-1980s, there is enough money to go around if the Federal Reserve allows the money supply to grow at a fairly rapid clip and if foreign investors are willing to make a few hundred billion dollars available each year to major corporations as well as to the U.S. Treasury.

---

[2]We are assuming that only 40 percent of the unemployed receive unemployment insurance benefits.

Read Only if the Full-Employment Balanced Budget Is Not Clear to You

The full-employment balanced budget means the federal government's spending equals its tax receipts when there is full employment. So if the unemployment rate is 5 percent, the deficit is zero. That's our starting point. For every 1 percent that the unemployment rate rises, the federal budget deficit rises by $30 billion (because such expenditures as unemployment benefits and welfare payments would automatically go up, while tax revenues would decline). OK, so if the unemployment rate were 6 percent, and if the deficit were 30, then we'd have a full-employment balanced budget.

A deficit of 30 would be exactly right for our economy if the unemployment rate were 6 percent. It would stimulate the economy (through more spending and lower tax receipts) and move the country back toward full employment.

What if the deficit were 50? It would be 20 too big. Instead of a full-employment balanced budget, we'd have a full-employment budget deficit of 20.

Now we'll see how much you've learned. If we have an unemployment rate of 8 percent, how large a deficit *should* we run? Work it out here:

The answer is 90. Because the unemployment rate is 3 percent over the full-employment rate of 5 percent, we need to run a deficit of 90 to have a full-employment balanced budget.

Next question: What if the deficit were only 60 and we had an unemployment rate of 8 percent? What would we have? Would it be a full-employment budget surplus or a full-employment budget deficit? It would be a full-employment budget surplus because it would be as if we were running a surplus when we were at full employment.

One more question: If we *did* run an actual deficit of 60 when the unemployment rate was 8 percent, how much of a full-employment budget surplus would we be running? The answer is 30. We *needed* a deficit of 90, but it was only 60; we were 30 short. By running a deficit of just 60, we were, in fact, running a full-employment budget surplus of 30.

Nevertheless, the crowding-out effect cannot be dismissed out of hand, particularly during times of tight money, such as the late 1970s and early 1980s. That any borrower as big as the U.S. government crowds other borrowers out of financial markets is a fact (see box "Is the Federal Government Crowding Out Private Borrowers?"). And as the late Israeli defense minister Moshe Dayan once put it, "You can't argue with a fact."

Let's take a closer look at the Keynesian position. When there is substantial economic slack, one would not expect increased government borrowing to have much impact in financial markets. Not only would there be little effect on interest rates, but the Treasury would be sopping up funds that would otherwise go unclaimed. When orthodox Keynesian fiscal policy is followed, it is precisely during times of economic slack that large budget deficits are incurred.

One might also mention a possible "crowding-in" effect caused by deficit financing. This results from the stimulative effect that the deficit has on aggregate demand. If a massive personal income tax cut causes the deficit, consumption will rise, pulling up aggregate demand and inducing more investment. Similarly, increased government spending

Is the Federal Government Crowding Out Private Borrowers?

In the late 1980s and early 1990s the government was running massive budget deficits, although the unemployment rate was hovering around 5 percent. The Treasury was sopping up over half of all personal saving just to finance these deficits. But foreigners were also financing just over half of the deficit. Because virtually all of our personal savings was indeed available to private borrowers, it could be argued that there was no crowding-out effect.

On the other hand, had the Treasury not been borrowing so heavily from foreigners, *that* money would have been available to American corporations seeking funds to replace and expand their plant and equipment. Furthermore, because of the huge deficits the Treasury was financing, real interest rates were much higher than they would have otherwise been. These high rates further discouraged private borrowing.

In sum, there definitely *was* a large crowding-out effect in the late 1980s. But it would have been a lot larger had it not been for the great inflow of foreign funds.

In the aftermath of the recession of 1990–91, not only did the government run the two largest budget deficits in U.S. history, but the Federal Reserve tried to accommodate private borrowers by pushing interest rates down to 15-year lows. And still President Bush was forced to term the recovery "anemic." One of the problems was that many banks were happy to pay only 2 or 3 percent interest for deposits and then buy U.S. government securities of varying maturities paying more than 5 percent interest. What we had here was a classic crowding-out effect at a time when it clearly hurt our economy.

So in the late 1980s and early 1990s, the conservative critics of an expansionary fiscal policy could point to a tangible crowding-out effect. What is ironic is that during the time under scrutiny, the White House was occupied by two self-proclaimed fiscal conservatives, Ronald Reagan and George Bush.

---

will raise aggregate demand, also inducing more investment. In other words, any rise in aggregate demand will induce a rise in investment.

This leaves us with one last question: which is larger, the crowding-in or the crowding-out effect? It doesn't really matter. The point is that as long as there is a sizable crowding-in effect, every dollar the government borrows will not crowd out a dollar of private borrowing. Thus, all we need to demonstrate is that there is a substantial crowding-in effect.

It appears that if we accept one fact—that the total amount of loanable funds is not fixed—there probably will be a substantial crowding-in effect. If there is indeed a fixed pool of saving, then it follows that every dollar the government borrows is one less dollar available to private savers. But *is* this total pool of saving fixed? If aggregate demand, stimulated by massive budget deficits, *does* rise, won't people save more money (as well as spend more)?

Therefore, as more saving becomes available, not every dollar borrowed by the government will actually be taken from private borrowers. Furthermore, as aggregate demand rises, more investment will be stimulated. If the crowding-in effect dominates the crowding-out effect, not only will government borrowing rise but so will private borrowing and investing. All we need to show is that total borrowing—government and private—rises.

What do *you* think? Are the monetarists right in saying that government borrowing crowds out private borrowing? Or are the orthodox Keynesians correct in saying that the crowding-in effect may dominate the crowding-out effect? The betting here is that the truth lies somewhere between these two extremes.

Questions for Further Thought and Discussion

1. Explain the crowding-in and crowding-out effects. How valid are these two concepts?

2. Why is the concept of the full-employment budget more meaningful than the budget that the federal government uses? Specifically, why are the full-employment budget's deficits and surpluses more meaningful than those reported by the government?

Name _____   Date _____

Multiple-Choice Questions

Circle the letter that corresponds to the best answer.

1. When there is a federal budget deficit, there could be a full-employment budget surplus if there happened to be

    a. inflation   **b.** full employment   **c.** an unemployment rate of more than 5 percent   **d.** a declining national debt

2. When the unemployment rate goes up one percentage point, this increases the federal budget deficit by about

    a. $30 million   **b.** $60 million   **c.** $30 billion
    d. $60 billion

3. The crowding-out effect cancels out at least part of the impact of

    a. expansionary fiscal policy   **b.** expansionary monetary policy   **c.** restrictive fiscal policy
    d. restrictive monetary policy

4. The crowding-out effect is

    a. much stronger during a recession than during prosperity   **b.** much stronger during prosperity than during a recession   **c.** equally strong during a recession and prosperity

5. In 1991 and 1992 we were running

    a. full-employment budget deficits   **b.** full-employment budget surpluses   **c.** full-employment balanced budgets

6. Which of the following is an example of crowding out?

    a. Federal government spending causes changes in state and local government spending.   **b.** Government spending reduces private spending.   **c.** Tax changes perceived as temporary are largely ignored.
    d. Government spending causes the price level to rise.

7. Between 1992 and 1997 the actual deficit

    a. declined, and the full employment deficit rose

    b. declined, and the full employment deficit stayed

about the same   **c.** declined, and the full employment deficit declined   **d.** rose, and the full employment deficit rose   **e.** rose, and the full employment deficit stayed about the same   **f.** rose, and the full employment deficit declined

Fill-In Questions

1. During a recession we need to run a budget deficit; the full-employment balanced budget tells us _____ _____ that deficit should be.

2. The crowding-out effect is associated with _____ _____ economists, while the crowding-in effect is associated with _____ economists.

3. A full-employment balanced budget means the budget

    _____

    _____.

4. The crowding-out effect states that when the Treasury borrows a lot of money to finance a budget deficit,

    _____.

Problems

1. If we had a budget deficit of $135 billion and an unemployment rate of 9 percent, would we have a full-employment surplus or deficit? Of how much?

2. If the unemployment rate were 7.5 percent, how large should our budget deficit be?

3. If we had a budget deficit of $60 billion and an unemployment rate of 8 percent, would we have a full-employment surplus or deficit? Of how much?

4. If the unemployment rate were 10 percent, how large should our budget deficit be?

5. We should run a balanced budget when our unemployment rate is about _____ percent.

6. Given: tax receipts, 1,500; government spending, 1,800; unemployment rate, 8.5 percent. **a.** How much is the actual deficit? **b.** How much is the full-employment budget deficit or surplus?

7. Given: tax receipts, 1,350; government spending, 1,500; unemployment rate, 9 percent. **a.** How much is the actual deficit? **b.** How much is the full-employment budget deficit or surplus?

12

Money and Banking

Banks create money. The rate of monetary growth itself is controlled by the Federal Reserve, which serves as our nation's central bank. In this chapter we'll look at our country's money supply and banking system, and in the next, at the Federal Reserve System.

First we'll talk about the money supply in the United States and the jobs it does. Next we'll work in a little monetary theory; we'll look at the demand for money and how interest rates are set. Then we'll turn to banking, beginning with its origins in medieval times; moving right along, we'll look at modern banking. So fasten your seat belt; and in the words of the late Jackie Gleason, "And away we go!"

Chapter Objectives

We will discuss the following interesting topics:

- The four jobs of money.
- What money is.
- M1, M2, and M3.
- The demand for money.
- The origins of banking.
- The creation and destruction of money.
- Branch banking and bank chartering.
- The FDIC.
- The savings and loan debacle.

Money

The Four Jobs of Money

The four jobs of money are:
(1) medium of exchange
(2) standard of value
(3) store of value
(4) standard of deferred payment

I don't have to tell you how important money is. About 25 years ago, Abbie Hoffman and a bunch of yippies (not hippies or yuppies) created pandemonium at the New York Stock Exchange by throwing dollar bills from the visitors' gallery down to the trading floor. If money were unimportant, surely that multitude of stockbrokers would not have stopped trading to help clean up.

Money's most important job

Medium of Exchange   By far the most important job of money is to serve as a medium of exchange: when any good or service is purchased, people use money.

Money makes it much easier to buy and to sell because money is universally acceptable. With money I can go out and buy whatever I want—provided, of course, I have enough of it. Similarly, a seller will sell to anyone who comes along with enough money; he won't have to wait for a buyer who's willing to trade something the seller needs.

Money, then, provides us with a shortcut in doing business. By acting as a medium of exchange, money performs its most important function.

Is money a good standard of value?

Is money a good store of value?

Standard of Value   Wanna buy a brand name VCR? A new sports car? A Swiss watch?

"Sure," you say. "How much?"

Thus money performs well at its second job—as a standard of value. If I told you that I got gasoline at 50 cents a gallon, you'd want to know the exact location of that gas station. But if I said that I bought a cheeseburger at a fast-food place for $8.50, you might wonder whether I have both oars in the water. A job that pays $2 an hour would be nearly impossible to fill, while one paying $50 an hour would be swamped with applicants.

Does money work well as a standard of value? You tell *me*.

Store of Value   In economics we have a hard time doing scientific experiments because they won't allow us to use those Bunsen burners. We also have a hard time explaining why we need test tubes and litmus paper. So, I'll ask you to excuse my lack of equipment as I try to conduct a scientific experiment. I'll count on your help by asking you to use your imagination.

Imagine that in 1982 you put $100 under your mattress and took out that same hundred dollars in February 1995. (I *do* hope you were changing the sheets regularly.) How much was that $100 worth?

In other words, if you could buy 100 units of goods and services with your $100 in 1982, how many units could you buy with $100 in 1995? Eighty? No, fewer. Seventy? No, but very close. OK, I'll put you out of your misery. You could have bought just 69.9 units.

Did someone sneak into your bedroom in the middle of the night and steal most of your money? No; but over the years, inflation took its toll. During this 13-year period, inflation robbed the dollar of more than 30 percent of its purchasing power.

This brings us back to the third job of money. Is money a good store of value or wealth? Over the long run, and particularly since World War II, it has been a very poor store of value. However, over relatively short periods of time, say, a few weeks or months, money does not lose much of its value. More significantly, during periods of price stability, money is an excellent store of value. Of course, the best time to hold money is during deflation because the longer you hold it, the more it's worth. For example, if you held money under your mattress from late 1929 to early 1933, it would have doubled in value during those years.

Standard of Deferred Payment   Many contracts promise to pay fixed sums of money well into the future. A corporate bond may pay a specified amount of interest every quarter for 30 years and then, upon maturity, pay out the principal as well. A 20-year mortgage obligates the homeowner to send the bank a monthly payment covering interest and principal for the next 240 months. These contracts call for the payment of money years into the future, illustrating how money functions as a standard of deferred payment.

When Dave Winfield signed a 10-year, $23 million contract to play the outfield for the New York Yankees in 1980, he really got stuck, because over the next 10 years the consumer price index went up by almost 59 percent. Today when a professional ballplayer, entertainer, or virtually anyone else signs a long-term contract, she or he is generally protected by an escalator clause, which calls for increased payments to compensate for any future inflation.

How well does money do its job as a standard of deferred payment? About as well as it does its job as a store of value—usually quite well in the short run, but not well at all over the long run of, say, three years or more.

Try to imagine how hard it would be to do business without money. Whenever you shopped, you'd have to have something to trade that the shopkeeper wanted. Your employer would have to pay you with something that you could trade for at least some of the things you needed. You'd have to find a way to make your car payments and your rent or mortgage payments, and pay for electricity, gasoline, food, clothing, appliances, and anything else you needed. In short, to carry out every transaction, you would need to find someone with whom you had a double coincidence of wants.

Everything, then, must be assessed in money; for this enables men always to exchange their services, and so makes society possible.

—Aristotle
Nicomachean Ethics

What does our money supply consist of?

Money versus Barter   Without money, the only way to do business is by bartering. "How many quarter sections of beef do you want for that car?" or "Will you accept four pounds of sugar for that 18-ounce steak?"

For barter to work, I must want what you have and you must want what I have. This makes it pretty difficult to do business. (See the box "Money versus Barter.")

Our Money Supply

What does our money supply consist of? Gold? No! U.S. government bonds? No! Diamonds? No! Money consists of just a few things: coins, paper money, demand (or checking) deposits, and checklike deposits (commonly called NOW—or negotiable order of withdrawal—accounts). Coins (pennies, nickels, dimes, quarters, half-dollars, and silver dollars) and paper money (dollar bills, fives, tens, twenties, fifties, and hundreds) together are considered currency. (By the way, where did the *dollar* come from? See box.)

Six out of every 10 dollars in our money supply are demand deposits and other checkable deposits. Virtually all the rest is currency (see Figure 1). We have to be careful, however, to distinguish between checks and demand (or checking) deposits. Jackie

ADVANCED WORK .... Money versus Barter

Imagine living in a country with no money. Every time you needed something, you would have to find someone who had what you wanted and was willing to trade for something that you had.

But if there were money, a widely accepted medium of exchange, you wouldn't need to barter. You could just go out and buy what you wanted without having to find someone willing to trade.

Money also provides a standard of value. Every good and service has a price that's expressed in terms of dollars and cents. If there were no money, then everything we traded would be valued in terms of what we traded for. For example, a haircut might trade for three movie tickets. Suppose there were just three goods and services in our economy, *a, b,* and *c.* The price of *a* would be expressed in terms of *b* and *c,* and the price of *b* would be expressed in terms of *c.* If there were four goods and services—*a, b, c,* and *d*—then the price of *a*

would be expressed in terms of *b, c,* and *d,* the price of *b* would be expressed in terms of *c* and *d,* and the price of *c* would be expressed in terms of *d.* So four goods would have six prices in a barter economy.

As the number of goods and services in a barter economy increases, the number of prices increases exponentially (see the table below). It sure is hard to do business when you have to keep track of so many prices.

Number of Goods and Services	Number of Prices in a Money Economy	Number of Prices in a Barter Economy
2	2	1
3	3	3
4	4	6
10	10	45
100	100	4,950
1,000	1,000	499,500

Where Did the Dollar Come From?

Our monetary policy is based, believe it or not, on the old Spanish-milled silver dollar. You didn't think it was based on the British system, did you? You'd really have to be crazy to try to copy a system that uses pence, shillings, guineas, and pounds.

Are you any good at trivia questions? In Robert Louis Stevenson's *Treasure Island,* there was a parrot who, as parrots will do, kept repeating the same phrase over and over. OK, what was the phrase? You have eight seconds to answer the question. What was the phrase that the parrot, who, by the way, was acquainted with Long John Silver, kept repeating? Did you guess? Sorry—time's up.

The answer is "Pieces of eight. Pieces of eight." See that? You learn something every day.

By the way, how much money is two bits? It's a quarter. And four bits? That's right—50 cents. Eight bits? A dollar.

What was that parrot getting at with his "Pieces of eight. Pieces of eight"? He was talking dollars, Spanish-milled silver dollars. Those dollars were milled in such a way, that eight pieces—or bits—could be torn from each dollar, like perforated slices in a metal pie. That way, if you had a dollar and wanted to spend just 25 cents, you tore off two pieces or bits. To this day, some South American countries have coins worth 12½ centavos.

Figure 1   The Components of M1, January 1998

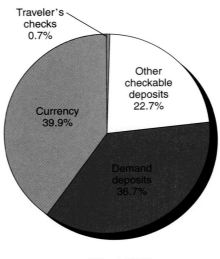

M1 = 1,097.5

Source: *Federal Reserve Statistical Release,* February 5, 1998.

Gleason used to tell a story about two guys who get into an argument in a bar about who is cheaper. Suddenly one of them pulls out a dollar bill and a book of matches, lights the bill on fire, and lets it burn to a crisp. Not to be outdone, the other guy pulls out a five, lights it, and watches it burn to a crisp. So then the first guy does the same thing with a $10 bill. Well, the other guy doesn't want to look bad, so he reaches into his pocket, pulls out his checkbook, writes out a check for $1,000, lights it, and watches it burn to a crisp.

Checks are *not* money. Checking deposits *are.*

Incidentally, demand deposits are so named because they are payable "on demand." When you write a check, your bank must honor it, provided, of course, that you have enough money in your account to cover the check. Banks also insist that a certain number of business days go by before they will cash a specific check. It is usually 5 days for a local check and 7 to 10 days for an out-of-town check. Banks call this waiting period the time it takes for a check to clear. But any money in your checking account that has been cleared is available to depositors on demand.

Our currency is legal tender for all debts, public and private. But don't take *my* word for it. You'll find those words written just to the left of George Washington's portrait on the one dollar bill, or to the left of Abraham Lincoln's on the five. So the government says that your money must be accepted for payment of all debts. Does the government say that about checks and credit cards? No! Now what does it say on the back of each dollar just below "THE UNITED STATES OF AMERICA"? It says, "IN GOD WE TRUST." And as many people say: "In God we trust—all others pay cash."

M1, M2, and M3

Until a few years ago the money supply in the United States was defined as including just two things—currency and demand deposits. But the Federal Reserve was well aware of NOW accounts (accounts that allow negotiable orders of withdrawals) held at savings institutions other than commercial banks. After all, aren't these really checking accounts that just happen to pay interest? Then why not include them in the money supply?

M1 = currency, demand deposits, traveler's checks, and other checkable deposits.

Our money supply now includes not just currency and demand deposits but also traveler's checks and what the Federal Reserve terms "other checkable deposits," which include the NOW accounts and something called "share draft accounts," or checking accounts issued by credit unions. (Are credit cards money? See box with that title.) The components of M1 are shown in Figure 1.

Are Credit Cards Money?

The answer is no. Credit cards are ID cards that enable you to buy a whole range of goods and services without having to pay until the end of the month. Who pays? The bank that issued your credit card pays the merchant; then, a few weeks later, you repay the bank.

What the bank would really like you to do is run up a large balance and pay 18 or 20 percent interest on that balance for years and years. That's the main reason they will give you a credit line of $5,000 or $10,000.

Bank of America issued the first bank credit cards in 1958, but most people didn't begin using them regularly until the 1970s. Through the 1960s people used cash and checks to pay for all purchases. Today Americans hold 1.2 billion credit cards, about 10 for every cardholder. These include not just bank credit cards, but gasoline, department store, restaurant, and telephone credit cards.

Bank credit cards like VISA, MasterCard, and American Express have become extremely important in our economy. Not only can you travel and make major purchases without having to carry hundreds or thousands of dollars in cash, but you won't be able to rent a car, stay in some hotels, or transact certain types of business without such a card. But remember, they're only pieces of plastic—not money.

Figure 2   M1, M2, M3, January 1998

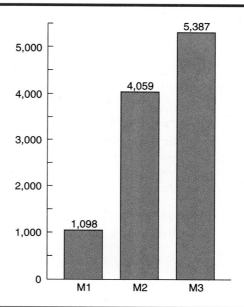

Source: *Federal Reserve Statistical Release,* February 5, 1998.

M1 is shown, along with M2 and M3, in Figure 2. As of January 1998, our money supply totaled $1,098 billion. Virtually everyone considers M1 our money supply, but we're going to consider two broader measures of money, M2 and M3.

By adding savings deposits, small-denomination time deposits, and money market mutual funds to M1, we get M2. You know what savings deposits are. Time deposits hold funds that must be left in the bank for a specified period of time—a week, a month, three months, a year, five years, or even longer.

Remember the bank ads that warn, "There is a substantial penalty for early withdrawal"? These warnings are another way of saying that under the conditions of a time deposit, you are legally required to leave your money in the bank for a specified period of time. And so, unlike a demand deposit, time deposits are not payable until a certain date.

Technically, the money held in time and savings deposits does not have to be paid to the depositors "on demand." When you fill out a withdrawal slip to take money out of your savings account, you are completely confident that you will walk out of the bank with your money. Legally, however, your bank can require up to 30 days' written notice before giving you these funds. In practice, of course, no bank ever does this. Although nearly every bank in the country is insured by the Federal Deposit Insurance Corporation,

M1 + savings, small-denomination time deposits, and money market funds = M2.

it is quite possible that if a 30-day waiting period were enforced, many nervous depositors would rush into their banks to get their money while they could.

Money market mutual funds are issued by stockbrokers and other institutions, usually pay slightly higher interest rates than banks, and offer check-writing privileges. From 1977 to 1982 there was a literal explosion in these funds, whose assets jumped from less than $4 billion to about $240 billion. Since then, however, due to legal restrictions caused by the Depository Institutions Act of 1982, these funds have grown more slowly and now total a little more than $620 billion.

We get from M2 to M3 by adding large-denomination time deposits. How large is large? The dividing line between small-denomination and large-denomination time deposits is $100,000. Any deposit of less than $100,000 is small.

Here's a recap of how we get from M1 to M2 and then from M2 to M3. M1 consists of three main items: currency, demand deposits, and checklike deposits. M1 plus savings deposits, small-denomination time deposits, and money market mutual funds equals M2. M2 plus large-denomination time deposits equals M3. Note two more things: M1 is part of M2, and M2 is the biggest part of M3.

A strong case can be made to designate M2 as our basic money supply rather than M1. First point, it is the monetary measure most closely watched by the Federal Reserve, the agency that controls the growth of our money supply. Second, with the enormous growth of money market deposit accounts, time deposits, and money market mutual funds, which people can quickly convert into cash, attention has shifted to M2. But I'm enough of a traditionalist to keep calling M1 our basic money supply—at least until the next edition of this text.

M2 + large-denomination time deposits = M3

Our Growing Money Supply

Our money supply grows from year to year as the amount of currency in circulation goes up and as our checking deposits and checklike deposits go up as well. How fast does the money supply grow? Figure 3 shows monetary growth from the 1960s through the late 1990s.

Monetary growth has not been smooth. You'll notice a huge jump, for example, in 1985 and 1986. The Federal Reserve controls the rate of monetary growth. How? Read all about it in the next chapter. (To learn how much money is out there, see box.)

Figure 3   Annual Percentage Change in the Money Supply, M1

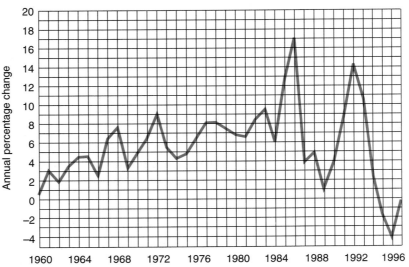

Sources: *Economic Report of the President,* 1993; *Federal Reserve Bulletin,* February 1998.

How Much Money Is out There Anyway?

How much currency do we have circulating in the country? Is the answer $426 billion? The U.S. Treasury said it was in January 1998. There's something comforting about such a precise figure. It assures us that someone has gone to great trouble to calculate something to the nearest 10th. The only problem is that the Treasury and the Federal Reserve have absolutely no idea how much currency is actually circulating in the United States.

The reason they don't know is that about $300 billion American dollars are circulating abroad. In 1994 Federal Reserve officials estimated that this amount was increasing by $15 billion to $20 billion a year. Most of this money is used as a second currency. For example, in Trinidad, Barbados, Jamaica, and other Caribbean nations, the British West Indian dollar—or BWI (pronounced beewee)—is the official currency. But U.S. dollars are gladly accepted.

Try this experiment. Pick a country—any country in the world. Buy a plane ticket and fly there. Get off the plane, go through customs, hop in a cab, and ask the driver to take you to the best restaurant he knows. When you pay the driver, ask whether he accepts U.S. dollars. Then go in the restaurant and order the most expensive thing on the menu, and, again, pay in U.S. dollars. After you've done this, let me know what happened and I'll write about your experiences in the next edition of this book.

Now, back to our story. How do U.S. dollars end up circulating in other countries? Tourists spend them there, Americans send money to their relatives in other countries, and retired Americans often live abroad because of the relatively low cost of living in many countries. But, increasingly, U.S. dollars are being shipped abroad to pay for drugs.

By the way, have you ever heard of "Eurodollars"? These are deposits denominated in U.S. dollars at banks and other financial institutions outside the United States. Why are they called Eurodollars? Because until about 20 years ago, nearly all this money was held in Western Europe. Now Eurodollar deposits are held all over the world. How much? Would you believe well over $1 trillion?

Is any of this money counted in our money supply? It does not show up in M1, but some Eurodollars held by U.S. residents are included in M2 and M3.

How much of our currency is circulating in foreign countries? In 1989 Federal Reserve chairman Alan Greenspan told Congress that "perhaps more than half of U.S. currency is outside the United States." Nice. Here's the guy who's supposed to be in charge of our money supply, and *he* doesn't even have a clue.

Where does all of this leave us? Personally, I find the whole experience humbling. I mean, here I've taught economics for 31 years, and I still don't know how much currency is circulating in the United States. Oh well, maybe the next 31 years will be better.

The Demand for Money

How much of *your* assets do you hold in the form of money? A typical middle-class family might own a home, two cars, several thousand dollars' worth of corporate stock, and perhaps one or two U.S. Treasury bonds. Of course, none of that is money. But the same family may also have a couple of bank accounts and $800 in cash. Let's consider the reasons why people hold some of their assets in the form of money.

Why do people hold money?

The classical economists of the 19th century believed money was merely a medium of exchange, something that burned a hole in your pocket. By that they did not mean that money was hot (in any sense of the word), but that people didn't hold it for very long. But economists today recognize that people hold money for a variety of purposes. John Maynard Keynes noted that people had three reasons for holding money: to make transactions, for precautionary reasons, and to speculate. Economists have since identified four factors that influence the three Keynesian motives for holding money: (1) the price level, (2) income, (3) the interest rate, and (4) credit availability.

The amount of money that people hold is called money balances. It consists of currency, checking deposits, checklike deposits held at financial institutions, and traveler's checks. After we discuss the Keynesian motives for holding money, we shall look at the influences that shape the demand for holding money.

The Keynesian Motives for Holding Money   John Maynard Keynes said people have three motives for holding money. Instead of holding their assets in other forms—stocks, bonds, real estate, commodities—everyone opts to hold at least some of their assets in the form of currency or demand deposits. First we'll look at the transactions motive.

Transactions motive

Precautionary motive

Speculative motive

Individuals have day-to-day purchases for which they pay in cash or by check. You take care of your rent or mortgage payment, car payment, monthly bills, and major purchases by check. Cash is needed for groceries, gasoline, most restaurant meals, the movies, and nearly every other small purchase. Businesses, too, need to keep substantial checking accounts to pay their bills and to meet their payrolls. Individuals and businesses, then, both need to hold a certain amount of money for regular expenses. Keynes called this the transactions motive for holding money.

Next we have the precautionary motive. People will keep money on hand just in case some unforeseen emergency arises. They do not actually expect to spend this money, but they want to be ready if the need arises.

One good example dates to the 1950s and earlier, when women did not have to share the expenses when they went out on dates. In the 1950s many women carried a $10 bill on all their dates—just in case. They called it "mad money," which they would use for cab fare if their date went beyond the limits prescribed by the social mores of those times.

Finally, there is the speculative motive for holding money. When interest rates are very low—as they were during the Great Depression when Keynes was writing—you don't stand to lose much by holding your assets in the form of money. Alternatively, by tying up your assets in the form of bonds, you actually stand to lose money should interest rates rise, because you'd be locked into very low rates. In effect, the speculative demand for money is based on the belief that better opportunities for investment will come along and that, in particular, interest rates will rise.

Four Influences on the Demand for Money   The amount of money we hold is influenced by four factors: (1) the price level, (2) income, (3) interest rates, and (4) credit availability. Changes in these factors change how much money we hold.

(1) The Price Level   As prices rise you need more money to take care of your day-to-day transactions. As a young man during those prosperous years before World War I, I didn't need to carry much money around. After all, those were the days, my friend. The days of nickel beer and nickel hot dogs. And, believe it or not, two kids could see a movie for a nickel.

In the mid-1950s a popular musical starring Sammy Davis, Jr., was *The Most Happy Fella.* One of its songs, "Standin' on the Corner," had this couplet:

> Saturday and I'm so broke
> Couldn't buy a girl a nickel Coke.

Today it costs a family of four about $40 to take in a neighborhood movie and a meal at McDonald's. In Manhattan, where movie tickets are $8 and parking costs more than $10 for the first hour, this outing would cost about $80. Thus, as the price level goes up, so does the demand for money balances. Nobody leaves home with just a nickel anymore.

Today we must pay a substantial penalty for holding our assets in the form of money. In fact, there are two closely related penalties. First, there's inflation. If the inflation rate is 10 percent, then $100 held for a year will be worth only about $90. That is, $100 will buy as much as $90 bought one year ago.

During times of inflation, then, we don't want to hold more than is necessary in currency or checking deposits. In other words, we want to get some kind of return on our money, or in some other way protect its purchasing power.

By holding our assets in the form of money, not only would we be forgoing interest, but our money would be losing its purchasing power from month to month. Therefore, in times of high interest rates and inflation (the two generally go together), people prefer to hold as little as possible of their assets in the form of money.

We should distinguish between two contradictory influences on money balances with respect to the price level. As the price level rises, people need to hold higher money balances to carry out their day-to-day transactions. But as the price level rises (i.e., with inflation), the purchasing power of the dollar declines; so the longer you hold money, the less that money is worth.

A distinction between short run and long run would be helpful. Assume a constant inflation rate of 10 percent so that the price level rises by exactly 10 percent every year. The cost of living would double every seven years.[1] So you would need to carry double the money balance in 2003 that you did in 1996 to handle exactly the same transactions.

On the other hand, with a 10 percent rate of inflation, the longer you hold assets in the form of money, the less that money will buy. Even though there is an inflation penalty for holding money for relatively long periods of time, you will surely keep enough on hand to take care of your day-to-day transactions. And if you compared your money balance in 1996 with that of 2003, you'd find that in 2003 you would be holding about double what you held in 1996, all other things remaining the same.

We are left with this conclusion: Even though people tend to cut down on their money balances during periods of inflation, as the price level rises people will hold larger money balances.

Money is the poor people's credit card.
—Marshall McLuhan

(2) Income   Poor people seldom carry around much money. Check it out. The more you make, the more you spend, and the more you spend, the more money you need to hold as cash or in your checking account. Even if you use a credit card, you still have to pay your bill at the end of the month. Therefore, as income rises, so does the demand for money balances.

(3) The Interest Rate   So far we've had two positive relationships: the quantity of money demanded rises with the level of prices and income. Are you ready for a negative relationship? All right, then. The quantity of money demanded goes down as interest rates rise.

Until recently people did not receive interest for holding money. Cash that you keep in your wallet or under your mattress still pays no interest, and until the late 1970s neither did checking deposits. Even today nearly all checking deposits pay less than 2 percent interest, and some don't pay any interest whatsoever. The alternative to holding your assets in the form of money is to hold them in the form of bonds, money market funds, time deposits, and other interest-bearing securities. As interest rates rise, these assets become more attractive than money balances. Thus, there is a negative relationship between interest rates and money balances.

Do you remember the concept of opportunity cost, which was introduced in Chapter 2? What is the opportunity cost of holding money? It's the interest that you forgo.

(4) Credit Availability   If you can get credit, you don't need to hold so much money. Thirty years ago most Americans paid cash for their smaller purchases and used checks for big-ticket items. The only form of consumer credit readily available was from retail merchants and manufacturers. The last three decades have seen a veritable explosion in consumer credit in the form of credit cards and bank loans. Over this period, then, increasing credit availability has been exerting a downward pressure on the demand for money.

We can now make four generalizations:

1. As interest rates rise, people tend to hold less money.
2. As the rate of inflation rises, people tend to hold more money.
3. As the level of income rises, people tend to hold more money.
4. People tend to hold less money as credit availability increases.

The Demand Schedule for Money

For purposes of analysis, we shall use the Keynesian motives for holding money to derive the demand schedule for money. This schedule, when brought together with the money supply schedule in the next section, will enable us to derive the interest rate. Right now we'll be combining the transactions, precautionary, and speculative demands for money.

---

[1] Any number that increases by 10 percent a year will double in seven years. This is an application of the rule of 70: Any number that increases by 1 percent a year doubles in 70 years. You can check this out on your calculator or by consulting a book of compound interest tables.

The transactions demand

How much money individuals and business firms need to hold for their transactions really depends on the size of GDP, or total spending. The more we spend, the more we need to hold at any given time. The transactions demand for money is somewhat responsive to interest rate changes (see Figure 4A). Corporate comptrollers used to leave relatively large balances in their checking accounts in the 1950s when interest rates were very low and checking accounts paid zero interest. Today those funds might be held in the form of seven-day certificates of deposit or other very short-term, very liquid assets to take advantage of the relatively high interest rates. Individuals, too, because of today's higher interest rates as well as the widespread use of credit cards, carry much smaller money balances than they would have back in the 1950s.

The precautionary demand

The precautionary demand for money is least responsive to interest rate changes (see Figure 4B) because people have a specific purpose for holding these funds. However, even these funds would be at least partially converted into other assets at extremely high interest rates.

The speculative demand

The speculative demand for money is, as we would expect, the most responsive to interest rate changes (see Figure 4C). The people who are holding these funds would obviously hold a lot more at low interest rates than they would at higher rates.

The Liquidity Trap

At very low interest rates, people don't lend out their money.

When John Maynard Keynes carried his speculative motive for holding money to its logical conclusion, he determined that at very low interest rates people would not lend out their money, would not put it in the bank, would not buy bonds with it, but would simply hold it. That's right—they'd sit on it, they'd hoard it, but they wouldn't spend it or make it available to anyone else.

Why should they? When the interest rate declines to, say, 2 percent, why would people risk their money for such a low rate of return? And why would they tie it up at such a low interest rate when within a few months the interest rate might rise? *Then* they would sink it into interest-bearing assets, not now. This reasoning is reflected by the horizontal

Figure 4   The Three Demands for Money

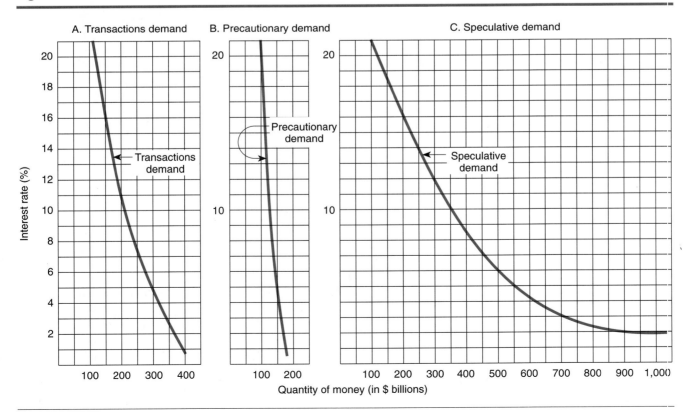

section of the Keynesian money demand curve (which he called a liquidity preference curve) shown in Figure 5.

Using the data from Figure 4, we can derive the total demand schedule for money, shown in Figure 5. This demand curve is the sum of the three demand curves shown in Figure 4—the transactions, precautionary, and speculative demands for money. In the next section we combine this curve with the money supply curve to determine the interest rate.

Determination of the Interest Rate

In Figure 5 we assumed various interest rates and determined that as the interest rate declined, the amount of money that the public wished to hold went up. But what determines the interest rate? If we think of the interest rate as the price of money, then the interest rate, like the price of anything else, is set by the forces of supply and demand.[2]

The supply of money is controlled by the Federal Reserve.[3] At any given time supply is fixed, so we'll represent it as a vertical line at 800 in Figure 6. Taking the demand

The demand for and the supply of money determine the interest rate.

If you would know the value of money, go and borrow some.
—Benjamin Franklin

---

[2]The last section of Chapter 3 provides a cogent explanation of the workings of supply and demand.
[3]We'll go over how the Federal Reserve sets the money supply in the next chapter.

Figure 5   Total Demand for Money

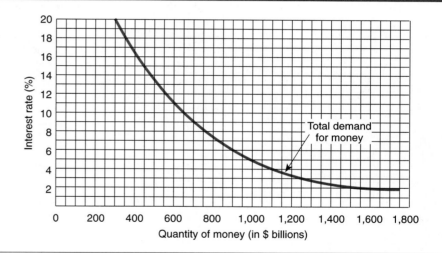

Figure 6   Total Demand for Money and Supply of Money

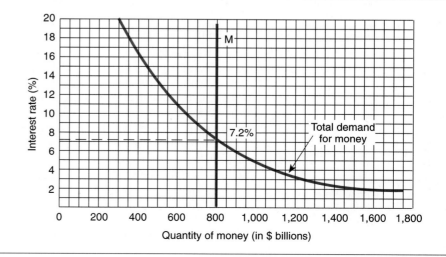

▲DVANCED ▼ORK ·········· Keeping Track of Interest Rates

The Wall Street Journal and other major newspapers track interest rates, often on a weekly basis, so readers can follow the ups and downs of these important series. The graphs below plot the short-term and long-term interest rates for the second half of 1989. The dividing line between the short-term and long-term is one year.

Treasury bills are very short-term borrowing, usually for just 91 days, at $10,000 denominations. "*Federal funds* are loans of reserves [which we'll be discussing in the next chapter] by one bank to another, and *commercial paper* is short-term debt sold on the open market by large corporations (kind of a private T bill)."*

Notice how the rates all move up and down virtually in lockstep while maintaining the same distances from each other. These six are just a few of the interest rates we could have plotted. But no matter which ones you follow, all interest rates move up and down together.

Why are there so many different interest rates? The main reason is the possibility of default. When you buy a three-month U.S. Treasury bill, you know that you will be paid back in three months. But you're taking something of a risk when you purchase a corporate "junk bond." So the riskier the loan, the more interest the borrower must pay. Long-term interest rates are generally higher than short-term rates to protect lenders against the possibility of inflation. For example, in mid–1995 there was a spread of about four points between short-term and long-term rates.

*Michael B. Lehmann, *The Wall Street Journal Workbook*, Instructor's Manual (Burr Ridge, IL.: Richard D. Irwin, 1990), p. 190.

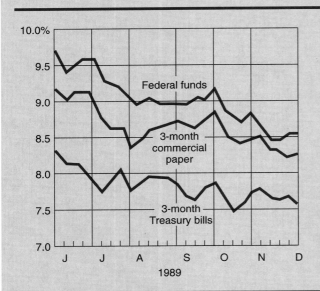

Source: *Federal Reserve Bank of New York,* as reported in *The Wall Street Journal,* December 7, 1989.

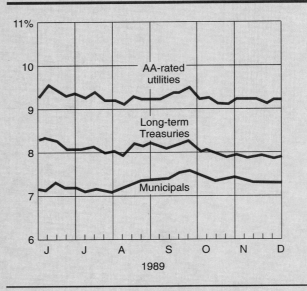

Source: *Merrill Lynch Securities Research,* as reported in *The Wall Street Journal,* December 11, 1989.

---

curve from Figure 5, we find that it crosses the money supply curve in Figure 6 at an interest rate of about 7.2 percent. It's as simple as that. Find the point at which the demand curve and supply curve cross, and you've got the interest rate.

Of course, both our demand and supply curves are hypothetical, so the interest rate we've found is hypothetical as well. OK, then, let's get real. How much is the interest rate right now? 5 percent? 8 percent? 10 percent? How much *is* it? How much is it on *what?* On passbook savings? On home mortgages? On Treasury bills? Are we talking about the interest rate that you *get* for your money or the interest rate that you *pay?* Guess which is always higher?

There are literally scores of interest rates (see box "Keeping Track of Interest Rates"). People may receive between 2 and 5 percent on their savings, and a lot more during times of inflation, and may have to pay somewhere between 6 and 15 percent on a house mortgage. Large corporations with good credit ratings pay the prime rate, while smaller and less creditworthy firms might pay 1 or 2 percent above prime.

In banking it is axiomatic that the richest customers paid the least for borrowed money; highest interest rates were for the poor.
— Arthur Hailey,
The Moneychangers

Figure 7   The Prime Rate of Interest Charged by Banks on Short-Term Business Loans, 1978–98

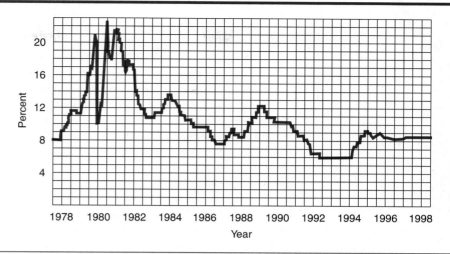

Source: *Federal Reserve Bulletin,* 1978–98.

Interest rates may vary from day to day, and there may be considerable variation over the course of a year or two. Figure 7 shows the average rate of interest that banks charged on short-term business loans from 1978 through early 1998. Because all interest rates move up and down together, you can easily observe their cyclical nature. This particular rate (along with the prime rate, which is generally slightly lower) rose from 11 percent in 1980 to 21 percent in 1981 and then fell to 10 percent in early 1983.

Who controls interest rates?

Who controls interest rates? Is it the people who borrow money? Is it the banks? Is it the Federal Reserve? The answer is yes to all three questions. But most experts point to the Federal Reserve Board of Governors as playing the dominant role. However, board members would probably respond the way Casey Stengel did when he was congratulated (and then fired, incidentally) after managing the Yankees to 10 pennants and 7 World Series wins in 12 years. His exact words were "I couldn't have done it without my players." Neither can the Federal Reserve.

Banking

A Short History of Banking

There are 9,500 commercial banks in the United States. These are defined as banks that hold demand deposits, but other banks—mutual savings banks, savings and loan associations, credit unions, and mutual money market funds—also issue checking accounts. The distinction between commercial banks and other savings institutions is blurring.

We'll talk about the origins of banking before we discuss how banking is conducted today in the United States. The first banks were run by goldsmiths back in the Middle Ages. We'll see that these fellows invented not only banking, but paper money as well.

The origins of banking

In medieval times, about the only secure place for your money was in the safes of the goldsmiths, so anybody who was anybody kept his money with the local goldsmith. These gentlemen would give receipts that possibly looked a little like the hatcheck slips you get at some of the fancier restaurants. If you left 10 gold coins with the smith, he wrote 10 on your receipt. If you happened to be rich, it was very important to be able to count past 10.

Although no one is quite sure who was the first to accept paper money—that is, goldsmiths' receipts—it might well have happened this way:

A knight was having his castle completely redone—new wallpaper, new bearskin rugs, new dungeon, new drawbridge—the works! When the job was finally completed, the contractor handed him a bill for 32 gold pieces.

The knight told the contractor, "Wait right here. I'll hitch up the team and take the oxcart into town. I'll get 32 gold coins from the goldsmith. I shouldn't be gone more than three days."

"Why bother to go all the way into town for the 32 gold coins?" asked the contractor. "When you give them to me, I'll have to ride all the way back into town and deposit the coins right back in the goldsmith's safe."

"You mean you're not going to charge me for the job?" The knight, while able to count past 10, came up short in certain other areas.

"Of course I want to get paid," replied the contractor. "Just give me your receipt for 32 gold coins."

It took the knight a little while to figure this out, but after the contractor went over it with him another six or eight times, he was finally able to summarize their transaction: "If I give you my receipt, we each save a trip to the goldsmith." And with that, paper money began to circulate.

The goldsmiths were not only able to count higher than anyone else in town, but they generally had a little more upstairs as well. Some of them began to figure out that they could really start to mint money, so to speak. First, they recognized that when people did come in to retrieve their gold coins, they did not insist on receiving the identical coins they had left. Second, they noticed that more and more people were not bothering to come in at all to get their money because they were paying their debts with the receipts. And so, the goldsmiths were struck with this evil thought: Why not lend out some of these gold coins just sitting here in the safe?

This was the moment modern banking was born. As long as the total number of receipts circulating was equal to the number of gold coins in the safe, there was no banking system, but when the number of receipts exceeded the number of coins in the safe, a banking system was created. For example, if a goldsmith had 1,000 coins in his safe and receipts for 1,000 coins circulating, he wasn't a banker. What if he knew that his depositors would never all come to him at the same time for their money and he decided to lend out just 10 gold coins? He would then still have receipts for 1,000 coins circulating, but he'd have only 990 coins in his safe.

The "paper money" issued by the goldsmith is no longer fully backed by gold, but there's really nothing to worry about because not everyone will show up at the same time for their gold. Meanwhile, the goldsmith is collecting interest on the 10 gold pieces he lent out.

"But why stop there?" asks the goldsmith. "Why not lend out 100 gold coins, or even 500?" And so he does. With 500 coins lent out, he still has 500 in his safe to cover the 1,000 receipts in circulation. And what are the chances that half his depositors will suddenly turn up demanding their coins?

Now we have 500 coins backing up 1,000 receipts, or a reserve ratio of 50 percent. As long as no panics occur, 50 percent is certainly a prudent ratio. As the ratio declines (from 100 to 50 percent), let's see what happened to the money supply, the gold coins, and the goldsmith's receipts in the hands of the public (Figure 8).

Initially the goldsmith has 1,000 coins in the safe (or bank) and 1,000 receipts circulating. The reserve ratio is 100 percent (1,000 coins backing 1,000 receipts). Next he has 500 coins in the safe and 500 circulating, along with the 1,000 receipts in the hands of the public. His reserve ratio is 50 percent (500 coins backing 1,000 receipts). And the money supply? It's grown to 1,500—1,000 receipts and 500 coins in circulation. Thus, as the reserve ratio declines, the money supply rises.

Let's go a step further and have the goldsmith lend out an additional 250 gold coins. See if you can figure out the reserve ratio and the size of the money supply.

Because there are now 250 coins backing 1,000 receipts, the reserve ratio is 25 percent. Meanwhile the money supply has grown from 1,500 to 1,750, because in addition to the 1,000 receipts, 750 coins are in the hands of the public.

If the goldsmith were to continue lending out gold coins, he would end up with none in his safe. His reserve ratio would sink to zero, and the money supply would be 2,000 (1,000 receipts and 1,000 coins).

Moment at which modern banking was born

Figure 8   Goldsmith's Receipts and Reserves

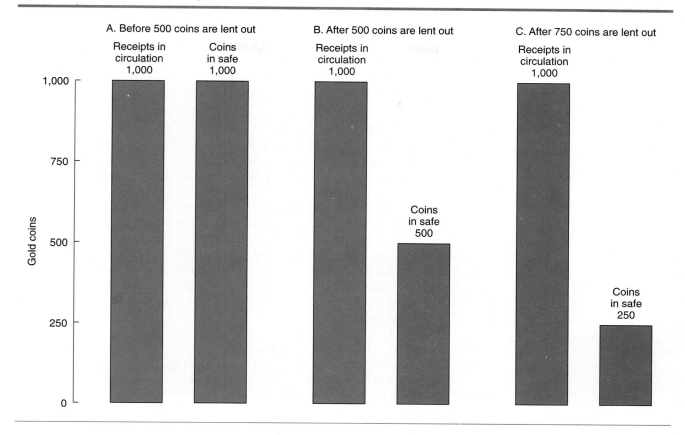

Being a clever fellow, the goldsmith has noticed that his receipts circulate as easily as gold coins. And so, long before he has lent out all his coins, which he really needs as reserves (or backing for his receipts), he begins to make loans in the form of his receipts. For example, suppose you need to borrow 10 gold coins. The goldsmith merely writes up a receipt for 10 gold coins and off you go with your money.

What is to prevent the goldsmith from writing up receipts every time someone wants to borrow? We call this printing money. For example, with his original 1,000 gold coins tucked away in his safe, the goldsmith prints up 1,000 receipts (in addition to the 1,000 receipts he already gave to the owners of the 1,000 gold coins). How much would the reserve ratio be and what would be the size of the money supply?

With 1,000 coins backing up 2,000 receipts, the reserve ratio is 50 percent. The money supply consists of the 2,000 receipts in the hands of the public. Suppose the goldsmith lent out another 2,000 (units) in the form of receipts. The reserve ratio would be 25 percent (1,000 coins backing 4,000 receipts), and the money supply would be the 4,000 receipts.

If the goldsmith so chose, he could even print up 10,000 receipts, which would bring about a reserve ratio of 10 percent (1,000 coins backing 10,000 receipts) and a money supply of 10,000 receipts. Or he could lend out 100,000, bringing the reserve ratio down to 1 percent (1,000 coins backing up 100,000 receipts) and creating a money supply of 100,000 receipts.

The system worked as long as the goldsmiths did not get too greedy.

The system worked as long as the goldsmiths did not get too greedy and as long as the depositors maintained their confidence in their goldsmith's ability to redeem his receipts in gold coins. From time to time, however, individual goldsmiths went too far in lending out money, whether in the form of gold coins or receipts. When depositors began to notice so many receipts in circulation, they asked themselves whether the goldsmith could possibly have enough coins in his safe to redeem them all. And when they thought he might not, they rushed into town to withdraw their gold coins before everyone else tried to.

If too many people reached the same conclusion, a panic ensued and the goldsmith could not possibly meet the demands of his depositors. In effect, then, he went bankrupt, and those left holding his receipts found them worthless. Of course, that was all before the days of the Federal Deposit Insurance Corporation (FDIC), so there was no one to whom depositors could turn.

Modern Banking

Like the early goldsmiths, today's bankers don't keep 100 percent reserve backing for their deposits. If a bank kept all its deposits in its vault, it would lose money from the day it opened. The whole idea of banking is to borrow cheap and lend dear. The more you lend, the more profits you make.

Banks would like to keep about 2 percent of their deposits in the form of vault cash. As long as depositors maintain confidence in the banks—or at least in the FDIC—there is really no need to keep more than 2 percent on reserve.

Unhappily for the banks, however, they are generally required to keep a lot more than 2 percent of their deposits on reserve. All the nation's 9,500 commercial banks, as well as the 11,900 credit unions, 2,900 savings and loan associations, and 800 savings banks, now have to keep up to 10 percent of their checking deposits on reserve. (See Table 1 in the next chapter.)

The Big Banks   Figure 9 lists our country's top 10 banks by size of assets in 1997. Nearly all are familiar names. You may notice that 5 of the top 10 are located in New York City, which was the financial capital of the world for a long time. Although it remains the financial capital of America, New York has been superseded by Tokyo as the preeminent financial center of the world.

Figure 9   The Top Ten American Banks, Ranked by Assets, 1997

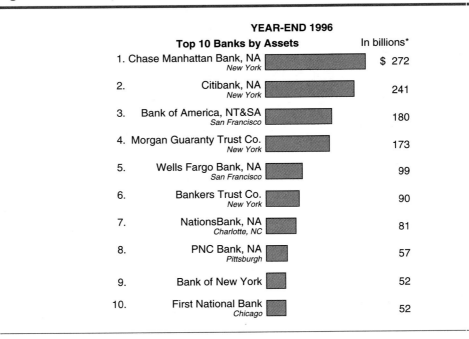

*Rounded to nearest billion.
Source: Keefe, Bruyette & Woods.

How do the banks listed in Figure 9 rank internationally? Seven of the top 10 banks in the world are Japanese. Chase (16) and Citicorp (25) are the only American banks among the world's top 25 banks. Just 25 years ago, BankAmerica, Citicorp, and Chase were the top three banks in the world.

What happened? To a large degree, this change reflects the decline in the status of the United States as the world's preeminent economic power. It also reflects our country's lagging savings rate. But another important factor has been the growing competition in the American banking industry, as well as the growing concentration of banking assets among the 25 leading Japanese banks.

Banking today is not all that different from the banking conducted by goldsmiths back in the Middle Ages. Of course, today's bankers have the Federal Reserve looking over their shoulders, not to mention the state banking authorities and the FDIC. Why all this regulation? Basically because people want to know that their money is safe.

Bank Lending   Banking is based on one simple principle: Borrow money at low interest rates and lend that money out at much higher interest rates. Even when interest rates are very low, as they were in the spring of 1997, banks charge their borrowers a lot more than they pay their depositors. Just look at the rates that banks post in their windows or in their lobbies. They come right out and admit that they pay either zero or up to maybe 3 percent interest on most deposits—and perhaps three or four points more if you leave your money on deposit for a few years—but they charge about 7 percent for fixed-rate mortgages, a bit more for most business loans, and about 18 percent on credit card loans. (See box for a discussion of "welfare banks.")

Financial Intermediaries   Financial intermediaries channel funds from savers to borrowers. Basically they repackage the flow of deposits, insurance premiums, pension contributions, and other forms of savings into larger chunks—$10,000, $1 million, $50 million, or even more—for large business borrowers. And, of course, they pay relatively low rates of interest to their lenders and charge relatively high rates to their borrowers. We're all familiar with banks, but this function is performed by a variety of other financial intermediaries (see box "Nonbank Financial Intermediaries").

"Welfare Banks"

Most of us take for granted the services provided by our neighborhood banks. They cash our paychecks; they operate 24-hour cash machines; and, if we need the money to buy a new car or even a house, they lend it to us.

But where do poor people do their banking? Chances are, they go to the "welfare bank," which is what the check-cashing stores are called. You'll find at least one in virtually every poor neighborhood. Where did the name come from? Well, on "check day," which almost always falls on the 1st and the 16th of every month, nearly 10 million Americans receiving public assistance get their checks in the mail. Why don't they cash them at their neighborhood banks? First of all, many poor neighborhoods don't have banks. Second, you usually need to have a minimum balance of at least $1,500 or the bank will charge you some pretty stiff fees for its services. Third, people receiving public assistance are not allowed to have bank accounts; they have no choice but to find someplace else to cash their checks.

The check-cashing outlets not only cash checks but also sell money orders. Who pays their bills by money order? Poor people do. And, of course, a money order may cost $1, or $2, or even more. To cash a check, you usually pay a fee of 1 to 3 percent of the value of the check, but some check-cashing stores will charge you as much as 20 percent.

You may ask why banks almost always require a minimum balance on checking accounts in the first place. The reason is that every banking transaction—depositing money, withdrawing money, processing checks, even posting interest—costs the banks money. On the other hand, the poor, especially those on welfare, can least afford to pay the fees charged by check-cashing services. Congress, as well as state legislatures, has considered passing laws requiring banks to cash welfare and Social Security checks, and to provide other banking services to people who cannot afford to keep the stipulated minimum balances, but the American Bankers Association, one of the nation's most powerful special interest groups, has easily beaten back this legislation.

Nonbank Financial Intermediaries

Banks offer their customers checking deposits that are included in M1. Some nonbank financial intermediaries may come close, but no cigar. Money market mutual funds, for instance, often allow their investors to write checks on their balances, but usually only a few a month, and for at least $500 or $1,000.

Pension funds, generally set up by large corporations, are another major form of financial intermediary. TIAA-CREF, which nearly all college professors have joined, is the largest, with a stock and bond portfolio worth several hundred billion dollars. Where did it get all this money? From our paychecks, with matching contributions from our employers.

Insurance companies collect billions of dollars in premiums every year, which they invest in real estate, stocks and bonds, and mortgages. Consumer finance companies—such as Beneficial Finance and Household Finance—borrow at very low rates, because they have excellent credit ratings, and charge their customers 25, 30, or even 40 percent interest rates. Why are these people willing to pay so much? Because they don't have much choice—if their credit ratings had been better, they could have borrowed from a bank.

The main financial intermediaries are banks (a category that includes commercial banks, savings banks, savings and loan associations, and credit unions).[4] Traditionally, banks lent money for very short-term commercial loans, but in the last few decades they have branched out into consumer loans, as well as commercial and residential mortgages. Indeed, it has been mainly defaulting commercial mortgage loans that have gotten many banks into serious financial difficulties.

Sometimes business borrowers dispense with financial middlemen altogether by borrowing directly from savers. The U.S. Treasury does this every month by issuing new bonds, certificates, notes, and bills. And increasingly, large business borrowers are doing the same thing by issuing relatively short-term commercial paper and long-term bonds.

The Creation and Destruction of Money

The Creation of Money

Money consists of checking deposits, checklike deposits, and currency in the hands of the public. To create money, banks must increase either currency held by the public or checkable deposits. The way banks do this is by making loans.

Banks create money by making loans.

A businessman walks into Bank of America and requests a loan of $10,000. Later that day he calls the bank and finds out that his loan is granted. Because he already has a checking account at Bank of America, the bank merely adds $10,000 to his balance. In return he signs a form promising to pay back the loan with interest on a specified date. That's it. Money has been created. Checking deposits have just increased by $10,000.

If, for some reason, the businessman had asked to be paid in cash, the public would have held $10,000 more in currency. And the bank? The $10,000 it gave away was merely inventory; it was not counted as part of our money supply.

The point is that the bank just created $10,000. Whether checkable deposits or currency held by the public rose by that amount, our money supply rose by $10,000.

This may sound like a license to print money. It is, but it's a very restricted license. A bank may make loans only if it has some available reserves. And who determines whether banks have these reserves? You *guessed* it—the Federal Reserve. So we really have three parties involved in the creation of money: the person who wants to borrow the

---

[4]Until the passage of the Depository Institutions Deregulation and Monetary Control Act of 1980, which is outlined near the end of the next chapter, only commercial banks were legally allowed to issue checking deposits, and they were the only institutions clearly recognized as "banks."

money, the bank that creates the money, and the Federal Reserve, which allows this creative act to take place.

The Destruction of Money

He who creates can usually destroy as well. That's what happens when the businessman pays back his loan. He'll probably write a check on his account for $10,000 plus the interest he owes, and when the bank deducts that amount from his account, down goes the money supply. Or if he pays back the loan in cash, again—down goes the money supply. In this case the currency leaves the hands of the public (literally) and goes into the bank's inventory. The bank will stamp the loan agreement form "paid," and the transaction is completed.

Money is destroyed when a loan is repaid to the bank.

The creation and destruction of money is a major function of banking. The basic way this is done is through loans. The most important commercial bank loans are commercial and industrial loans, although consumer loans have grown considerably in importance since World War II.

Limits to Deposit Creation

Most bank loans involve giving the borrower an additional deposit in his or her checking account; therefore, it would appear that banks can create all the money they wanted by doing this. All you need is a simple bookkeeping operation. A $20,000 loan means you increase that customer's account by $20,000—on paper or by an entry into a computer.

Remember the goldsmith who kept writing receipts until there were 1,000 gold coins in his safe backing 100,000 receipts? Why can't bankers keep issuing loans by increasing the checking accounts of their customers?

The first limit would be prudence. Most banks would try to keep about 2 percent of their demand deposits on reserve in the form of vault cash; in case some of their depositors came in to cash checks, there would be enough money on hand to pay them. Thus, if left to their own devices, bankers would expand their loans only up to the point at which they had just 2 percent cash reserves, or a reserve ratio of 2 percent. Of course, most bankers would more prudently opt for reserve ratios of 3 or 4 percent.

But no banker has that choice. The Federal Reserve sets legal requirements to which the banks must adhere, and, as I've already mentioned, these limits are substantially higher than those that might be set by the most prudent of bankers.

Bank Regulation

Branch Banking and Bank Chartering

Branch Banking versus Unit Banking   Banking is legally defined as accepting deposits. Branch banking, therefore, would be the acceptance of deposits at more than one location. Branch banking rules are set by the state in which a bank is located. Bank of America, for example, is subject to California banking law, while Citibank and Chase Manhattan are regulated by New York banking law.

Three types of branch banking have evolved under various state laws. First is unrestricted branch banking, under which a bank may open branches throughout the state. Bank of America and Wells Fargo have branches all over California.

The three types of branch banking are:
(1) Unrestricted branching
(2) Limited branching
(3) Unit banking

A second variation is restricted, or limited, branch banking. For example, a bank may be allowed to open branches only in contiguous communities. What is permissible varies from state to state.

Finally, there is unit banking, in which state law forbids any branching whatsoever. A bank that opens an office that receives deposits at a particular location cannot open any other branches. This obviously restricts the size of banks in those states. In fact, banks in unit banking states are, on the average, about one-fifth the size of banks in states that permit unrestricted branching.

Right now two out of five states, nearly all in the East and Far West, have unlimited branching. Another two out of five states, mainly in the Midwest and the South, allow limited branching. And finally, the remaining states, mostly in the Midwest, permit only unit banking.

There are about 58,000 bank branches throughout the nation, but some banks are closing branches and replacing them with automated teller machines. Since 1992 Bank-America has closed more than 400 branches, while Huntington Bancshares, of Columbus, Ohio, recently replaced one-third of its branches with smaller all-electronic sites.

Why the shift to ATMs? Processing a teller transaction costs more than double what an ATM transaction costs. In fact, some banks charge depositors a $3 fee for teller transactions. By the end of 1997 there were about 150,000 ATMs in the United States doing more than 13 billion transactions a year. As this trend continues, we can expect to see a decline in branch offices.

But now, you can withdraw money from your checking account at hundreds of thousands of retail outlets with a debit card. The vast majority of the 70 million debit cards in circulation were issued by MasterCard and VISA. But instead of getting a month to pay off your balance, as you would on your credit card, your money is automatically withdrawn almost instantly from your checking account to pay for your purchases. Like the advent of the ATM, the debit card promises to make personal banking almost obsolete.

Most banks have state charters. **State and Nationally Chartered Banks**   To operate a bank, you must get a charter. More than two-thirds of the nation's banks have state charters; the rest have national charters. National charters are issued by the comptroller of the currency and are generally harder to obtain than state charters. Each of the 50 states issues state charters.

To get a bank charter you need to demonstrate three things: (1) that your community needs a bank or an additional bank; (2) that you have enough capital to start a bank; and (3) that you are of good character.

Most large banks are nationally chartered. Often the word *national* will appear in their names, for example, First National City Bank or Mellon National Bank. Incidentally, all nationally chartered banks must join the Federal Reserve. State banks may join, but few have done so and many left because of the high reserve requirements.[5]

To summarize, all nationally chartered banks must join the Federal Reserve System. All Federal Reserve member banks must join the FDIC. Only a small percentage of the state-chartered banks are members of the Federal Reserve. Nearly all banks are members of the FDIC.

Interstate Banking   Until 1994 interstate banking was technically illegal, although banks managed to engage in the practice by buying banks in other states and operating them as separate entities. But the passage of the Riegle-Neal Interstate Banking and Branching Efficiency Act of 1994 swept away the last barriers to opening branches in different states. Until this law was passed, for example, a customer of a bank branch in North Carolina was not permitted to make a deposit at one of the same bank's South Carolina branches.

The Federal Deposit Insurance Corporation

After the massive bank failures of the 1930s, Congress set up the FDIC—another case of closing the barn door after the horses had run off. This organization taxes its members from 0 to 27 cents for every $100 of deposits in exchange for insuring all member bank deposits of up to $100,000.[6] The amount insured has progressively been raised, the last time in 1980, when the ceiling was raised from $40,000.

---

[5]Until the early 1980s, when reserve requirements for all depository institutions were made uniform, Federal Reserve member banks were subject to higher reserve requirements than nonmember banks.

[6]Until 1995 the FDIC charged a premium of 23 cents. The premium now depends on how safe the FDIC deems each bank's deposits.

The whole idea of the FDIC

The whole idea of the FDIC is to avert bank panics by assuring the public that the federal government stands behind the bank, ready to pay off depositors if it should fail. The very fact that the government is ready to do this has apparently provided enough confidence in the banking system to avoid any situation that could lead to widespread panic.

Until 1977, when Franklin National, then the nation's 20th largest commercial bank, went under, the FDIC had never had to pay out more than $100 million a year to depositors. Since then, however, things have grown a lot worse, particularly with large savings banks, many of which are in the New York area.

Are some banks just too big to fail—because their demise would wreak havoc through the financial world? The too-big-to-fail doctrine was first articulated in 1984 by Todd Conover, comptroller of the currency, regarding the government's $8 billion bailout of Continental Illinois. Since then, the application of this doctrine has apparently been extended to any bank with more than $1 billion in total assets—making about 400 banks too big to be allowed to fail. Table 1 lists the FDIC's biggest bailouts.

The FDIC prefers takeovers to payoffs.

The FDIC would rather have another bank take over an ailing institution than be forced to pay off its depositors. Often, to encourage such takeovers, the FDIC will actually give the cooperating bank up to several hundred million dollars to take certain white elephants off its hands.

When the FDIC has had trouble disposing of failed banks, it has reluctantly acquired certain of their assets. It has held 960 acres of almond groves (in the form of the U.S. National Bank of San Diego), a $40,000 Koran (Islamic bible, courtesy of the Northern Bank of Cleveland), and even part ownership in *The Happy Hooker* (a film acquired in the Franklin National debacle).[7]

But why should our government go for substitutes when it can own the real thing? The U.S. government owns Nevada's Mustang Ranch—a legal brothel—which went bankrupt in September 1990. *Newsweek* quoted assistant bankruptcy trustee Bill Knudson: "That's what our goal is—to keep it in operation until they sell it."[8] The U.S. government even owned a piece of the Dallas Cowboys, the 1993, 1994, and 1996 Super Bowl winners, which means that they really were "America's team."

All told, federal government institutions insure more than $8 trillion in risks. Everything from crops and crime to overseas investments, stockbroker bankruptcies, bank deposits, and private pension plans is covered. All these programs underlie the business adage "Without risk there can be no gain." Some critics feel, however, that the federal government is taking all the risks and private individuals are making all the gains.

Will the FDIC run out of money?

Is the FDIC in any danger of running out of money? Yes and no. In mid-1998 it had $37 billion in assets backing nearly $2.8 trillion in deposits. But can the FDIC actually go bankrupt? Not really. The Congress, the Federal Reserve, the Treasury, and all the financial resources of the U.S. government are committed to the preservation of this institution.

---

[7]See Shirley Hobbs Scheibla, "Call in the Reserves?" *Barron's,* March 8, 1982.

[8]*Newsweek,* October 1, 1990, p. 17.

Table 1   The Biggest Bank Bailouts by the FDIC

Bank	Cost of Bailout
Continental Illinois (Chicago)	$8.0 billion
First Republic (Texas)	3.0
Bank of New England (Boston)	2.1
MCorp (Texas)	1.8
Franklin National (New York)	1.7
First City (Texas)	0.6

Source: FDIC.

More than 99 percent of all banks are members of the FDIC. If you want to make sure that yours is, first check to see whether there's a sign in the window attesting to this fact. If there isn't, ask inside, and if the answer is no, then very calmly walk up to the teller and withdraw all your money. Membership in the FDIC means that your money is safe and that we will probably never have a repetition of what happened back in the 1930s when there were runs on the banks, culminating in the Great Depression.

Is something missing from this rosy picture? You *bet* there is. What about the savings and loan debacle? Thank you for reminding me. All right, then, let's talk about *that.*

The Savings and Loan Debacle

In early 1990 the financial press was calling this the greatest financial scandal in the history of the United States. How could it have happened? How bad *was* it?

The origins

The following may be the greatest understatement I will ever make: The recent decade was not a very good one for the savings and loan industry. But the roots of the problem date to the 1950s and 1960s, when the nation's 3,000 savings and loan associations were handing out millions of 30-year mortgages at 4, 5, and 6 percent fixed interest rates. This was good business—at that time—because the S&Ls were paying just 2 or 3 percent interest to their shareholders.[9]

When interest rates went through the roof from the late 1970s through the early 1980s, the shareholders rushed in to withdraw their money. But their money wasn't just sitting there in the vaults. It was already lent out to homeowners. It was being paid back, a little each month, over a 30-year period.

Why did the shareholders want to take their money out? Because they could get much higher interest rates by purchasing Treasury bills, certificates of deposit, money market mutual funds, corporate bonds, or other financial instruments. Why didn't the savings and loan associations simply pay them more interest? Because they were legally barred from doing so.

In 1980 the law was changed to allow the savings and loan associations to pay much higher rates of interest.[10] In addition, they were freed from making primarily home mortgage loans. What the S&Ls did, then, with their newfound freedom was go out and borrow funds at very high interest rates and lend them out at still higher interest rates. The only trouble was that the loans they tended to make were very risky ones.

Dangerous speculation

Money was lent to farmland speculators in the Midwest and to people buying up oil properties in the Southwest. These seemed like reasonably safe loans because the prices of this land had been rising very rapidly. But what goes up must come down. At least it did during the severe recession of 1981–82. And what was a bad situation nationwide got to be a worse situation in the Southwest and the Midwest as declining oil prices and drought depressed land prices still further. Borrowers defaulted on their loans, and the S&Ls were stuck with large holdings of real estate, which they had to sell in a depressed market. In short, scores of S&Ls—most notably in Texas and Oklahoma—lost their shirts.

And that was just *part* of the problem. Real estate developers, many of them based in California, Florida, and Texas, bought control of many S&Ls and poured billions of dollars into shopping malls, office parks, condos, and other ventures of dubious merit (dubious during a time of sinking real estate prices, anyway). And so another wave of S&Ls was taken to the cleaners.

Junk bonds

Still another aspect of the S&L debacle revolved around junk bonds, which were used extensively to finance corporate takeovers or, alternatively, to stave off hostile

---

[9]Technically, the people who deposit their money in savings and loan associations are *shareholders,* but if you'd rather call them *depositors,* that's fine with me.

[10]Insurance coverage was raised at that time from $40,000 to $100,000 on savings and loan shares and on bank deposits.

takeovers. To raise billions of dollars quickly, corporate raiders—or the boards of the corporations facing hostile bids—would issue bonds given very low credit ratings. Why did anyone want to buy them? Because they paid relatively high interest rates.

Among the biggest buyers of these junk bonds were failing S&Ls. And so, using their shareholders' money, they helped feed the speculative corporate takeover frenzy that dominated Wall Street during the 1980s. When the prices of many of these bonds plunged steeply in the late 1980s, in the wake of the stock market crash of October 1987, several hundred more S&Ls were ruined.

Organized crime

So far we've been talking about the nice guys. Now let's talk about organized crime. Stephen P. Pizzo, who extensively studied the downfall of the S&L industry,[11] had *this* to say about the role that organized crime played:

> Coast to coast, mob families and their associates bellied up to thrifts and sucked out hundreds of millions of dollars. One New York mob associate turned up in the records of 130 thrifts; 125 of those failed. Another organized crime figure, now in jail, was in the federal witness protection program while he defrauded thrifts of tens of millions of dollars. The longer list of those who showed up at now-dead thrifts reads like a Mafia Who's Who.[12]

By the late 1980s it was clear that the insurance fund for the S&L industry, the Federal Savings and Loan Insurance Corporation (FSLIC), had not only run out of money to pay off the shareholders of the failed institutions, but its regulatory arm, the Federal Home Loan Bank Board, had done a less-than-wonderful supervisory job as well. Indeed, the FSLIC ran out of money in 1987 but was provided by Congress with an additional $10.8 billion, which it ran through within a year. Clearly something more was needed.

That something turned out to be a lot more money. In February 1989 the Financial Institutions Reform, Recovery, and Enforcement Act of 1989 was passed by Congress and signed by President George Bush, whose administration had masterminded the whole idea. It provided a more powerful regulatory authority (the Office of Thrift Supervision), and it established the Resolution Trust Corporation, which was empowered to do three things: (1) sell off the assets of the failed S&Ls; (2) close down the failing S&Ls; and (3) borrow enough money to pay off all the shareholders of the failed and failing S&Ls.

The government has already spent a total of more than $150 billion on paying off S&L depositors and reorganizing the failed S&Ls so they could be reopened under new management. It now seems likely that when interest costs are added (the Treasury had to borrow the money to finance the bailout), the total cost may reach $200 billion.

Let's stop right here. Take a deep breath. Now ask yourself one question: Why is the government paying hundreds of billions of dollars to bail out the S&L industry? Why is the government ready to spend perhaps 100 times as much as it spent to bail out such corporate stalwarts as Lockheed and Chrysler when *they* almost went bankrupt? *Why?* Because the government had placed its full faith and credit behind nearly all the money that savers had placed in the savings and loan associations. Remember that every shareholder was insured up to $100,000. So when the S&Ls failed, the government had to pay off every shareholder up to $100,000.

Incompetence, inordinate risk-taking, poor supervision, and outright fraud all played prominent roles in the decline and fall of the savings and loan industry. We leave it to historians and future textbook writers to sort out and apportion the blame. But right now, one thing is perfectly clear. The S&L mess will cost hundreds of billions of dollars to clean up. And guess who will get stuck with the bill?

Will the Commercial Banks Go the Way of the S&Ls?

From 1987 through 1989 the nation's commercial banks were in trouble. Big trouble. Nearly 200 banks were going under each year. Back in the mid- and late 1970s, only

---

[11]Stephen P. Pizzo is coauthor of *Insider Job: The Looting of America's Savings and Loans* (New York: McGraw-Hill, 1990).

[12]Stephen P. Pizzo, "The Real Culprits in the Thrift Scam," *New York Times,* April 2, 1990.

Derivatives: Another Financial Crisis in the Making?

In the mid-1980s was the savings and loan crisis. The late 1980s and early 1990s saw a wave of commercial bank failures. Will the mid- to late 1990s become known as the age of massive derivative losses?

In 1994 the Treasurer of Orange County in California managed to lose $1.7 billion speculating in derivatives. In 1995 Barings, a venerable British bank, went under after a young options trader bet wrong on the Japanese stock market and lost over 1 billion dollars. A year earlier Proctor & Gamble lost $157 million in leveraged currency swaps and Air Products & Chemicals lost $122 million in leveraged interest rate and currency swaps.

What is a derivative? A good description was provided by Terrence P. Paré, writing in *Fortune:*

> Basically, derivatives are financial instruments whose value is tied to something else—called an "underlying" by the trade—such as equity or an indicator like interest rates. When consumers pay extra to get an interest rate cap on an adjustable-rate mortgage . . . they are dealing in derivatives.*

The basic purpose of derivatives is to transfer risk to another party. That party, of course, is willing to bear that risk at a price.

Derivatives are contracts that have a value that varies with an underlying financial asset or index, most commonly interest rates or currencies. For example, Bankers Trust sold a number of corporations derivatives that would have benefited the bank if interest rates had remained steady, but made the bank assume the risk of large losses if the rates increased sharply.

Default swaps are becoming an increasingly common type of derivative. Here is how one is described in

BusinessWeek: (1) A bank makes a five-year loan for a power plant in China, but doesn't want the risk of default. (2) To avoid the risk that the loan might go sour, the bank gets investors to assume the default risk for a fee. (3) If the borrower defaults, investors would reimburse the bank for loss in loan value.†

So what's the problem with derivatives? In most cases there *is* no problem. Many major corporations have successfully employed them to manage the risks of fluctuating interest and exchange rates. The derivative market is huge—about $20 trillion in 1995. Carol J. Loomis summarized the goods and the bads:

> When they are employed wisely, derivatives make the world simpler, because they give their buyers an ability to manage and transfer risk. But in the hands of speculators, bumblers, or unscrupulous peddlers, they are a powerful leveraged mechanism for *creating* risk. Last year the worst sort of crowd grabbed hold of the tool and took over the plant.‡

Five of the six leading players in the derivatives market are banks, led by Chemical, with a portfolio of over $3 trillion in contracts. Undoubtedly there will be more spectacular losses, but derivatives have become an integral part of the financial world.

*Terrence P. Paré, "Learning to Live with Derivatives," *Fortune,* July 25, 1995, p. 107.
†*BusinessWeek,* July 21, 1997, p. 102.
‡Carol J. Loomis, "Untangling the Derivatives Mess," *Fortune,* March 20, 1995, p. 50.

---

about 10 a year failed. So the big question was: Would the banks go the way of the savings and loan associations? And will the taxpayers get stuck with another $500 billion bill? (See the box "Derivatives: Another Financial Crisis in the Making?")

The answer to both questions is no. More banks *will* fail, but while only half of the 2,900 S&Ls that were in operation in 1980 are still open, of the nation's 9,500 commercial banks, there were just six bank failures in 1995 and only five in 1996. How have the commercial banks been able to avoid the same fate as the S&Ls?

To begin with, the banks were never traditional mortgage lenders, so they were not seriously hurt by skyrocketing interest rates in the late 1970s and early 1980s. However, around this time they did make hundreds of billions in loans to less developed countries, most notably in Latin America and Eastern Europe. Today this loan portfolio has been written down to less than half its face value. The banks, like the S&Ls, also lost a substantial amount of money in the junk bond market. But the big losses, which have accounted for most of the bank failures in recent years, have come from the commercial real estate market. The banks poured in some $350 billion. Of all the office space in the United States, 30 percent was built in the 1980s. And if you haven't already guessed, this created a huge glut of office space. This oversupply may last until the turn of the century.

Today hundreds of commercial banks are in serious trouble, and failures may well rise again if defaults from loans in South Korea, Indonesia, and Thailand continue to mount. But the banks have always been fairly closely regulated by the Federal Deposit Insurance Corporation and, in many instances, by the Federal Reserve and the comptroller of the currency. The excesses of the S&Ls—when real estate speculators actually took control—were largely absent. But probably the main reason the banks did not end up like the S&Ls is that they did not enter the 1980s saddled with huge mortgage commitments. The S&Ls were permitted to roll the dice for higher, riskier stakes for a few more years, and basically they lost the game. The bankers, of course, also made mistakes, and, at the end of the 20th century, they are in much better financial shape than they were in the late 1980s and early 1990s.

What happened? They have been helped by a stronger economy, increased loan demand, and a generous interest rate spread. As interest rates rose in 1994 and early 1995, the banks raised the rates they charged their customers, while allowing the rates they paid to depositors to rise more slowly. Consequently bank profits rose sharply, while bank failures plummeted. And so, as we approach the new millennium, our commercial banks are riding high.

Last Word

On October 1, 1993, responsibility for handling the liquidation of the failed savings and loan portfolio shifted from the Resolution Trust Corporation to the FDIC, which may be analogous to hiring a new captain after the Titanic struck an iceberg. This is not to say that the Resolution Trust Corporation did such a poor job, but rather that more decisive regulatory action in the early 1980s might have at least mitigated the worst effects of the S&L disaster.

The ultimate cost to the American taxpayer of the savings and loan debacle—and of the subsequent wave of commercial bank failures as well—will not be known until well past the turn of the century, as it will be determined by future real estate prices and interest rates. If real estate prices rise, the cost will decline, because the FDIC will get more money as it sells off its holdings. On the other hand, if interest rates rise, then the cost of carrying these holdings will go up.

We are continuing to pay for the financial excesses brought on by the deregulation of the financial industry that began in the late 1970s and accelerated in the early 1980s. However, the regulatory pendulum has already begun to swing the other way, and depositors can count on the FDIC and the Federal Reserve to keep a close watch on their money. In the next chapter, we'll consider how the Federal Reserve manages that job and how it controls the rate of growth of our money supply.

Questions for Further Thought and Discussion

1. How does the crude quantity theory of money differ from the modern, sophisticated version?
2. What happens to the demand for money as (*a*) the price level rises; and (*b*) the availability of credit rises? Explain your answers.
3. Describe the conditions that were necessary for modern banking to be born.
4. What were the conditions that led to the savings and loan debacle?
5. Explain the role of financial intermediaries.

WORKBOOK FOR CHAPTER 12

Name _____   Date _____

Multiple-Choice Questions

Circle the letter that corresponds to the best answer.

1. Each of the following except _____ is a job of the money supply.

    a. medium of exchange   b. store of value

    c. standard of value   d. receipt for gold

    e. standard of deferred payment

2. Which is the most important job of money?

    a. medium of exchange   b. store of value

    c. standard of value   d. receipt for gold

    e. standard of deferred payment

3. The basic alternative to money in the United States would be

    a. gold   b. barter   c. stealing   d. the underground economy

4. Barter involves

    a. money   b. specialization   c. a double coincidence of wants   d. demand deposits

5. Which one of the following is not part of our money supply?

    a. dollar bills   b. demand deposits   c. traveler's checks   d. gold

6. Which statement is true?

    a. M1 is larger than M2.   b. M1 + M2 = M3.

    c. M2 + large-denomination time deposits = M3.

    d. M1 × M2 = M3.

7. Which statement is true?

    a. Checks are not money.   b. A small part of our money supply is silver certificates.   c. Most of our money supply is in the form of currency.   d. None of these statements is true.

8. The U.S. dollar is based on _____ currency.

    a. British   b. French   c. Dutch   d. Spanish

9. Which is not in M2?

    a. currency   b. demand deposits   c. small-denomination time deposits   d. large-denomination time deposits

10. Which statement is true?

    a. Credit cards are a form of money.   b. M1 is closer to the size of M2 than M2 is to the size of M3.

    c. M2 is about three and a half times the size of M1.

    d. M3 is about $2 trillion.

11. The Financial Institutions Reform, Recovery, and Enforcement Act of 1989 provided for each of the following, except

    a. selling off the assets of failed S&Ls

    b. the closing down of failing S&Ls

    c. allowing the S&Ls to make commercial loans

    d. the borrowing of enough money to pay off all the shareholders of failed S&Ls

12. In early 1998 M1 was over $_____ billion.

    a. 600   b. 800   c. 1,000   d. 1,400

13. Over the last three decades our money supply

    a. grew steadily at about the same rate   b. fell steadily at about the same rate   c. rose steadily through the 1970s and fell steadily through the 1980s

    d. fell steadily through the 1970s and rose steadily through the 1980s   e. grew every year, but at widely varying rates

14. The interest rate on business loans _____ the interest rate that banks pay their depositors.

    a. is higher than   b. is lower than   c. has no relationship to

15. The too-big-to-fail doctrine

    a. is the basis for the savings and loan bailout

    b. has had little relevance since the Great Depression

    c. was the basis for the bailouts of Franklin National,

Continental Illinois, and other large banks

d. was proclaimed by President Franklin Roosevelt and extended by nearly all of his successors

16. Which statement is true?

a. The too-big-to-fail doctrine covers banks with assets of more than $1 billion.

b. The largest bank bailout in our history was that of the Bank of New England.

c. The FDIC has financed 15 bailouts costing more than $1 billion each.

d. None of these statements is true.

17. John Maynard Keynes identified three motives for holding money. Which motive listed below did Keynes not identify?

a. transactions   **b.** precautionary

c. psychological   **d.** speculative

18. As the price level rises, the transactions demand for money

a. rises   **b.** falls   **c.** remains about the same

19. As the interest rate rises, the quantity of money demanded

a. rises   **b.** falls   **c.** remains about the same

20. People tend to hold more money as

a. incomes rise and credit availability rises

b. incomes fall and credit availability falls

c. incomes rise and credit availability falls

d. incomes fall and credit availability rises

21. The distinction between commercial banks and other banks is

a. very clear   **b.** becoming blurred

c. nonexistent   **d.** none of these

22. Banking began in

a. biblical times   **b.** medieval times   **c.** the 19th century   **d.** the 20th century

23. What led to the bankruptcy of many goldsmiths was that they

a. had a reserve ratio that was too high

b. had a reserve ratio that was too low

c. lent out gold coins instead of receipts

d. lent out receipts instead of gold coins

24. Bankers would like to hold a reserve ratio of about

a. 2 percent   **b.** 10 percent   **c.** 50 percent

d. 100 percent

25. Which statement is true?

a. Most financial institutions are commercial banks.

b. There are currently fewer than 1,000 commercial banks in the United States.   **c.** Nearly all banks today are regulated by both the Federal Reserve and the FDIC.

d. About half the banks in the United States are members of the FDIC.

26. Which statement is false?

a. About 99 percent of all banks are members of the FDIC.   **b.** If the FDIC runs out of money, the federal government will supply it with more funds.   **c.** The FDIC would rather have another bank take over an ailing institution than be forced to pay off its depositors.

d. None of these statements is false.

27. Which statement is true?

a. Most states allow only unit banking.

b. Most states allow unlimited branching.

c. Most banks have national charters.

d. None of these statements is true.

28. To get a bank charter, you need to demonstrate each of the following, except

a. that your community needs a bank or an additional bank   **b.** that you have sufficient banking experience

c. that you have enough capital to start a bank

d. that you are of good character

29. Money is created when someone

a. takes out a bank loan   **b.** pays back a bank loan

c. spends money   **d.** saves money

30. Bank deposit creation is limited by

a. reserve requirements   **b.** the interest rate

c. whether a bank is nationally or state chartered

d. whether a bank is in a large city or a rural area

31. Which statement is true?

    a. About half the savings and loan associations went bankrupt in the early 1980s.   b. The savings and loan associations were helped by high interest rates in the late 1970s and early 1980s.   c. Most savings and loan associations were locked into low-interest-rate mortgages in the 1950s and 1960s.   d. None is true.

Fill-In Questions

1. The most important job of money is as _____ _____. The other three jobs of money are _____,

_____,

and _____.

The job money performs the most poorly is as _____ _____.

2. The alternative to money would be _____ _____. To do this, you would need a _____.

3. The three main components of our money supply are

    (1) _____;

    (2) _____;

    and (3) _____.

4. The U.S. dollar is based on the _____ _____.

5. The basic function of credit cards is _____ _____.

6. To get from M2 to M3, we add _____ _____.

7. M2 is about _____ times the size of M1.

8. Another name for checking deposits is _____ _____.

How did they get this name? _____ _____.

9. About _____ percent of the states allow only unit banking.

10. About _____ percent of all banks have state charters.

11. The main way that banks create money is by _____ _____; the main way that money is destroyed is when _____.

12. The interest rate is set by the _____ _____ and the _____.

13. The total demand for money is the sum of (1) the _____ demand; (2) the _____ _____ demand; and (3) the _____ _____ demand.

14. The four main influences on the amount of money that people tend to hold are (1) _____;

    (2) _____; (3) _____;

    and (4) _____.

15. John Maynard Keynes identified the following three motives to explain why people hold money: (1) _____ _____; (2) _____;

    and (3) _____.

16. People tend to hold more money as _____ and _____ rise; they tend to hold less

money as _____ and

_____ rise.

17. People hold more money for their _____

   motive than for the other two motives.

18. According to Keynes's liquidity trap, at very low interest

   rates, people would _____

   _____.

19. The world's first bankers were the _____

   _____.

20. Modern banking was born when the first bankers noticed

   two things: (1) _____

   _____

   and (2) _____

   _____.

21. The world's first paper money was in the form of _____

   _____.

22. If a goldsmith had 100 gold coins sitting in his safe and

   lent out 50 of them, this would imply a reserve ratio of

   _____ percent.

23. The bankruptcy of the goldsmiths who lent out part of the

   gold they were safekeeping was caused by _____

   _____.

24. Most bankers today would like to hold a reserve of about

   _____ percent.

25. Banks are very heavily regulated. The main reason for

   this is that _____

   _____.

26. The FDIC insures all bank deposits of up to $_____.

27. Rather than pay off depositors of a failed bank, the FDIC

   would prefer that _____.

   _____.

Problems

1. If M2 were 2,500, small-denomination time deposits were
   250, and large-denomination time deposits were 300, how
   much would M3 be?

2. a. A goldsmith has 1,000 gold coins in his safe and 1,000
   receipts circulating. How much are his outstanding loans
   and what is his reserve ratio?

   b. The goldsmith then lends out 100 of the coins. What is
   his reserve ratio?

3. A goldsmith has 100 gold coins in his safe. If there are
   500 receipts in circulation, how much is his reserve ratio?

4. a. A banker lends a businessowner $100,000. How does
   this affect the money supply?

   b. The businessowner pays back the loan. How does this
   affect the money supply?

5. How much would M2 be if M1 were 500; small-
   denomination time deposits, savings deposits, and money
   market mutual funds totaled 1,200; and large-denomination time deposits were 300? How much would M3 be?

13 The Federal Reserve and Monetary Policy

In the first part of the chapter, we'll examine the organization and management of the Federal Reserve System (the Fed), especially how it uses open-market operations, changes in the discount rate, and changes in reserve requirements to control the rate of growth of the money supply.

The goals of monetary policy are price stability, relatively full employment, and a satisfactory rate of economic growth. If you go back to the first page of Chapter 11, you'll see that the goals of fiscal and monetary policy are identical. The melodies are the same, but the lyrics are quite different. Fiscal policy is the use of government spending and taxation to affect the overall economy, while monetary policy uses controls on the money supply's rate of growth to affect the overall economy.

Chapter Objectives

The main topics of this chapter are:

- The organization of the Federal Reserve System.
- Reserve requirements.
- The deposit expansion multiplier.
- The tools of monetary policy.
- The Fed's effectiveness in fighting inflation and recession.
- The Banking Act of 1980.

The Federal Reserve System

Unlike most other industrial nations, the United States was without a central bank until 1913.[1] While the Bank of England and the Bank of France acted as each country's central banking authority, Americans were left defenseless when financial panics set in. Every few years in the 1880s, 1890s, and early 1900s, financial crises developed and eventually receded until, finally, we had the Panic of 1907.

During this panic, people rushed to their banks to take out their money, and business was severely disrupted. The public demanded that the government take steps to prevent this from ever happening again. After six years of intermittent debate, Congress finally passed the Federal Reserve Act of 1913. One of the hopes of its framers was that the 12 Federal Reserve district banks would, at times of crisis, act as a "lender of last resort." In other words, if U.S. bankers were caught with their pants down, someone stood ready to give them a little time to get their affairs back in order.

The Federal Reserve District Banks

The 12 Federal Reserve District Banks

There are 12 Federal Reserve District Banks, one in each of the nation's Federal Reserve districts. These are shown in the map in Figure 1. Each of these banks issues currency to accommodate the business needs of its district.[2] (To learn who actually issues our

---

[1]There had been a First United States Bank (1791–1811) and a Second United States Bank (1816–36), but the charters of both had been allowed to lapse, mainly for political reasons.

[2]The Bureau of Engraving in Washington does the actual printing, but why be picky?

currency, see box.) For example, all the paper currency issued by the Boston Federal Reserve District Bank in the First District has an *A* on the face of the bill about an inch and a half from the left edge. Currency issued by the Second Federal Reserve District Bank in New York has a *B,* while the Philadelphia Bank in the Third District has a *C.*

You'll notice in Figure 1 that the Federal Reserve District Banks are concentrated in the East and Midwest. This reflects the concentration of banks and business activity in 1913. Why haven't we moved some of the banks to the West, perhaps paralleling the movement of the old Brooklyn Dodgers, New York Giants, and Philadelphia Athletics? Evidently, it's a lot easier to move a baseball team than a Federal Reserve District Bank. To accommodate the needs of western banks, branch offices of the San Francisco, Kansas City, Dallas, and Minneapolis Federal Reserve District Banks have been set up in several cities (see Figure 1). For example, in the 12th district, in which the San Francisco bank is situated, there are branches in Los Angeles, Portland, and Salt Lake City.

Each Federal Reserve District Bank is owned by the several hundred member banks in that district. A commercial bank becomes a member by buying stock in the Federal Reserve District Bank. However, effective control is really exercised by the Federal Reserve Board of Governors in Washington, D.C.

The Board of Governors

The seven members of the Federal Reserve Board

The seven members of the Board of Governors are nominated by the president, subject to confirmation by the Senate. Each is appointed for one 14-year term and is ineligible to serve a second term. The terms are staggered so that vacancies occur every two years. That way, in every four-year term, a president appoints two members of the Board of Governors.

Usually, however, a president gets to appoint three or even four members during a single executive term because many Governors do not serve their full 14-year terms. Why not? Mainly because they could make much more money "on the outside." Serving on the Board looks great on your résumé, and it's done in the spirit of serving one's country, but 14 years is a bit long to live on a government paycheck.

The chairman of the Board, who generally exercises considerable influence, serves a 4-year term, which is part of his or her 14-year tenure as a member of the Board. He or she is also appointed by the president and may serve more than one term as chairman.

Who Issues Our Currency?

The U.S. Treasury issues it, right? Wrong! Our currency is issued by the 12 Federal Reserve District Banks.* Check it out. Pull a dollar out of your wallet and look at it. What does it say right near the top, about a half inch above George Washington's picture? That's right—"Federal Reserve Note." Then, to the left of Washington's picture is a letter. If you live anywhere near New York, chances are this letter will be a B. You'll note that the circle around the letter will say "Federal Reserve Bank of New York, New York." There is a 2 printed above and below the B, which stands for Second Federal Reserve District.

Try another dollar—or a 5, 10, 20, or whatever else you happen to have. Got any Ls? That would be the 12th Federal Reserve District Bank in San Francisco. How about As? That's the First Federal Reserve District Bank in Boston. How about Es—Richmond, in the Fifth District.

If you thought the Treasury issues our currency, it used to (and the secretary of the Treasury still signs every bill). The last thing it issued, until the mid-1960s, was $1 and $5 silver certificates. These certificates are now out of circulation, snapped up by collectors. The Treasury still issues our pennies, nickels, dimes, quarters, half dollars, and metal (no longer silver) dollars, but, as you might have suspected, that's just the small change of our money supply.

And what about the backing for the dollar? Look on the back of the bill just above the big "ONE." What's the backing for our currency? That's right—"In God We Trust." Actually, there is backing for our currency—the government's word, as well as its general acceptability.

*As noted in footnote 2, the actual printing is done by the Federal Bureau of Engraving.

Figure 1   The Federal Reserve System

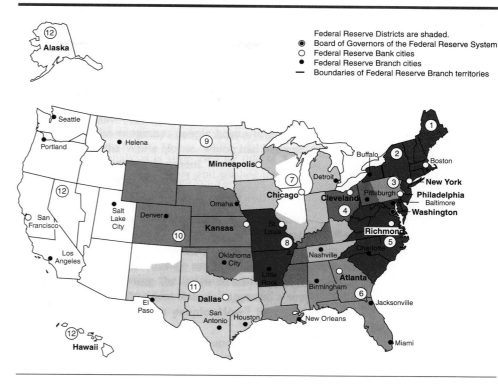

Independence of the Board of Governors

Should the Board of Governors be controlled by or answerable to anyone else?

Does the president "control" the Board of Governors and its chairman? The answer is, generally, no. First, unless there is a vacancy caused by death or resignation, the president would have to serve two terms to appoint four members to the Board.[3] Second, once someone is appointed to the Board, there is no reason to expect that person to do the president's bidding.

The president does get to appoint a chairman sometime during his or her term. However, Jimmy Carter had to deal with Arthur Burns (Richard Nixon's appointee) for the first part of his term; Ronald Reagan did not always see eye-to-eye with Jimmy Carter's appointee, Paul Volcker. And Bill Clinton, who inherited Alan Greenspan from George Bush,[4] could not have been that pleased to see the Federal Reserve push up short-term interest rates seven times between early 1994 and early 1995. There have been proposals that the president be allowed to appoint his own chairman at the beginning of the executive term so that monetary and fiscal policy can be coordinated, but no action has been taken thus far.

Once a Board member or chairman is confirmed by the Senate, she or he is not answerable to the president or Congress. Although the chairman is legally required to make an annual report to Congress, he or she is free to stand before that body and tell them, "We have completely defied your wishes. You wanted us to increase the money supply and we lowered it. You wanted interest rates to drop and they've gone up. That is our report."

Of course, things are much more cordial than that between the Fed and Congress and between the Fed and the president, but the bottom line remains that the Federal Reserve is

---

[3]Because of a slew of resignations, President Ronald Reagan was able to appoint all seven members in his first seven years in office. Interestingly, two of those who resigned did so because the president would not promise them the chairmanship.

[4]George Bush, in turn, inherited Greenspan from Ronald Reagan, who appointed him chairman in 1987. Bill Clinton reappointed Greenspan to a third term.

an independent agency. Some feel that for a group of unelected officials, the members of the Board have too much power. When interest rates soar or inflation rages out of control, these rascals cannot be turned out of office by an angry electorate. About all we can do is hope that better people will eventually be appointed to the Board.

Others feel that the difficult, unpopular decisions of monetary policy must be made by those who are insulated from the wrath of the voters. Tight money is hardly a popular policy, but when the Federal Reserve Board members think it will help control inflation, why should they be inhibited by fears of political reprisal?

Of course, the members of the Board of Governors are not immune to the reactions of their fellow citizens, but their independence permits them to follow unpopular policies if they feel that doing so is in the best economic interest of the nation. Attempts have been made in recent years to make the Federal Reserve Board more responsive to the wishes of Congress and the administration, but none has been successful.

Legal Reserve Requirements

The Federal Reserve's most important job

The Federal Reserve has various jobs, the most important of which is to control the money supply. When it was set up in 1913, the framers of the Federal Reserve Act envisaged the Fed as a "lender of last resort." Obviously, the record of widespread bank failures in the early 1930s is a sad commentary on how well the Fed was able to do that job.

Before we consider how the Fed works today, we will look at the focal point of the Federal Reserve's control of our money supply: legal reserve requirements. Every financial institution in the country is legally required to hold a certain percentage of its deposits on reserve, either in the form of deposits at its Federal Reserve District Bank or in its own vaults. As neither Federal Reserve deposits nor vault cash pays interest, no one is very happy about holding 10 percent of most demand deposits on reserve (see Table 1).

We'll be using some technical terms, so let's be very clear on their meanings. *Required reserves* is the minimum amount of vault cash and deposits at the Federal Reserve District Bank that must be held by the financial institution. *Actual reserves* is what the bank is holding. If a bank is holding more than required, it has excess reserves. Therefore, *actual reserves − required reserves = excess reserves.*

If a bank had $100 million in checking deposits, how much reserves would it be required to hold? Work it out right here, using the information in Table 1:

Table 1   Legal Reserve Requirements, March 1997

Checking accounts:	
$0–$47.8 million*	3%
Over $47.8 million	10
Time deposits	0%

*Up to $4.7 million of deposits has a zero percent reserve requirement. This amount varies from bank to bank, so we shall ignore it.

Source: *Federal Reserve Bulletin,* March 1998.

Solution:

$$3 \text{ percent of } \$47.8 \text{ million} = \$1,434,000$$

$$10 \text{ percent of remaining } \$52.2 \text{ million} = \$5,220,000$$

$$\text{Required reserves} = \$1,434,000 + \$5,220,000$$

$$= \$6,654,000$$

If this bank happened to be holding reserves of, say, $9 million, then it would be holding excess reserves of $2,346,000. Because banks earn no interest on their reserves, they try to keep them down to a bare minimum. In fact, a bank ideally holds no excess reserves whatsoever; its goal is zero excess reserves.

Let's try another question. If a bank had demand deposits of $1 billion and held $120 million in actual reserves (in the form of deposits at the Federal Reserve District Bank and vault cash), calculate (1) its required reserves and (2) its excess reserves.

Solution:

$$(1) \; 3\% \text{ of } \$47.8 \text{ million} = \$1,434,000$$

$$10 \text{ percent of remaining } \$952.2 \text{ million} = \$95,220,000$$

$$\$1,434,000 + \$95,220,000 = \$96,654,000$$

$$\text{Required reserves} = \$96,654,000$$

$$(2) \; \text{Actual reserves} - \text{Required reserves} = \text{Excess reserves}$$

$$\$120,000,000 - \$96,654,000 = \$23,346,000$$

Can a bank ever end up with negative excess reserves? Think about it. Time's up: what do you think? If actual reserves are less than required reserves, then excess reserves are negative. Or, in simple English, the bank is short of required reserves. If a bank does find itself short, it will usually borrow reserves from another bank that has some excess reserves. The reserves it borrows are called *federal funds,* and the interest rate charged for them is called the *federal funds rate.* A bank short of reserves may also borrow at the discount window of its Federal Reserve District Bank, a process we'll discuss later in the chapter.

The Monetary Control Act of 1980 (which will be discussed in detail toward the end of this chapter) called for uniform reserve requirements for all financial institutions—commercial banks, savings banks, savings and loan associations, money market mutual funds, and credit unions. Until 1987, when the uniform reserve requirements were fully phased in, only Federal Reserve member banks, about 5,000 in number, were subject to relatively high reserve requirements. The other 28,000 or so of the nation's financial institutions were subject to much lower requirements.

You'll notice in Table 1 that the reserve requirement for time deposits is zero. Because time deposits, by definition, are held for relatively long periods of time, the Federal Reserve Board eliminated reserve requirements for all time deposits in 1992.

Primary and Secondary Reserves

A bank's *primary reserves are its vault cash and its deposits at the Federal Reserve District Bank.* These reserves pay no interest; therefore the banks try to hold no more than the Federal Reserve requires. Ideally, then, they hold zero excess reserves.

What are the three main aims of bankers?

Bankers are, if nothing else, prudent. Their main aims, other than making high profits, are to protect their depositors and to maintain liquidity. Liquidity is the ability to convert assets quickly into cash without loss.

Even without legal reserve requirements, bankers would keep some cash on reserve to meet the day-to-day needs of their depositors as well as to meet any unforeseen large withdrawals. The cash that banks do keep on hand, together with their deposits at the Federal Reserve District Banks, is sometimes called primary reserves. In addition, every bank holds secondary reserves, mainly in the form of very short-term U.S. government securities.

Treasury bills, notes, certificates, and bonds (that will mature in less than a year) are generally considered a bank's secondary reserves. These can quickly be converted to cash without loss if a bank suddenly needs money, whether because of increased withdrawals or perhaps a shortage of primary reserves. Generally, in the case of a shortage of primary reserves, a bank will borrow on a daily basis from other banks in the federal funds market. Another source of short-term funds is the Federal Reserve District Bank's discount window.

In the spring of 1993, when short-term interest rates had fallen to 15-year lows, banks were paying their depositors less than 3 percent interest on everything except long-term CDs. What did they *do* with these deposits? The banks held hundreds of billions of dollars' worth of short-term U.S. government securities that paid about 4 percent interest. These investments were not only profitable and risk free, but they incurred no administrative costs, as individual and commercial loans would have. And so, well into 1998, banks held a very high level of secondary reserves.

Deposit Expansion

How Deposit Expansion Works

To see how deposit expansion works, we'll assume a 10 percent reserve ratio because that's an easy number with which to work. Suppose someone comes into a bank and deposits $100,000.

We know that banks don't like to have idle reserves because they don't earn any interest on them. So what does the bank do with the $100,000? It lends out as much as it can.

With a 10 percent reserve requirement, the bank can lend $90,000. To keep matters simple, we'll assume the $90,000 was lent to a single company. The bank added $90,000 to the company's checking account by making an entry in its computer.

Normally, the bank would need an additional $9,000 in reserves to cover the new $90,000 demand deposit. But why did the company borrow $90,000? Obviously it was needed for certain business expenses; no one pays interest on borrowed money just to sit on it.

Again, keeping things simple, suppose this company wrote a check for $90,000 to pay for additional inventory. The company receiving the check deposits it in its bank, and the process is repeated. The bank keeps the required 10 percent ($9,000) on reserve and lends out the remaining $81,000. This money is spent and eventually deposited in a third bank, which keeps 10 percent ($8,100) on reserve and lends out $72,900.

We could go on and on. Indeed, we have in Table 2. Were we to continue the process with an infinite number of banks, we would eventually end up with $1 million in deposits and $100,000 in reserves.

The Deposit Expansion Multiplier

Remember the multiplier in Chapter 11? Now we'll look at the deposit expansion multiplier, which is based on the same principle and nearly the same formula.

Any new money injected into the banking system will have a multiplied effect on the money supply. How large this multiplied effect will be depends on the size of the multiplier. In general, when the reserve ratio is low, the multiplier will be high and vice versa.

Table 2 **Hypothetical Deposit Expansion with 10 Percent Reserve Requirement**

Deposits	Reserves
$100,000.00	$10,000.00
90,000.00	9,000.00
81,000.00	8,100.00
72,900.00	7,290.00
65,610.00	6,561.00
59,049.00	5,904.90
53,541.00	5,354.10
48,186.90	4,818.69
43,368.21	4,336.82
39,031.39	3,903.14
35,128.25	3,512.83
31,615.43	3,161.54
28,453.89	2,845.39
25,608.50	2,560.85
23,047.65	2,304.76
20,742.89	2,074.29
18,668.60	1,866.86
16,812.00	1,681.20
15,130.80	1,513.08
13,617.72	1,361.77
—*	—*
—	—
—	—
$1,000,000.00	$100,000.00

*To save space, the rest of the calculations are omitted.

The formula for the deposit expansion multiplier is:

Deposit expansion multiplier $= \dfrac{1}{Reserve\ ratio}$

$$\frac{1}{\text{Reserve ratio}}$$

If the reserve ratio is .10, we substitute and solve to find the multiplier:

$$\frac{1}{\text{Reserve ratio}} = \frac{1}{.10} = 10$$

Remember, how many dimes are in a dollar?

If the reserve ratio is .25, find the deposit expansion multiplier. Do it right here.

Using the formula, we get:

$$\frac{1}{\text{Reserve ratio}} = \frac{1}{.25} = 4$$

How many times does .25 go into 1? How many times does a quarter go into a dollar?

Now that I've made you do these calculations, a confession is in order. The deposit expansion multiplier is a bit less wonderful than I led you to believe. It's just too big. You can probably get on with your life just accepting this fact, but if you happen to be from Missouri (the Show Me State), then you can check out the box "Three Modifications of the Deposit Expansion Multiplier."

Three Modifications of the Deposit Expansion Multiplier

Not every dollar of deposit expansion will actually be redeposited and lent out repeatedly. Some people may choose to hold or spend some of their money as currency. For example, an individual receiving a $300 check may deposit $200 and receive $100 back as cash.

This cash leakage tends to cut down on the deposit expansion multiplier because not all the money lent out is redeposited. For example, if $90,000 is lent out but only $81,000 is redeposited, this would have the same effect on the multiplier as a 10 percent increase in the reserve ratio.

It is also possible, although unlikely in times of inflation, for banks to carry excess reserves. To the degree that they do, however, this cuts down on the deposit expansion multiplier. Why? Because it, in effect, raises the reserve ratio. For example, if the reserve ratio rose from .20 to .25 because banks were carrying a 5 percent excess reserve, the multiplier would fall from 5 ($\frac{1}{2}$ = 5) to 4 ($\frac{1}{25}$ = 4).

Currency leakages do take place, especially during times of recession and low interest rates. During such times, it is quite possible for banks to carry excess reserves. One might also keep in mind that during recessions, banks might carry excess reserves because of a scarcity of creditworthy borrowers.

Finally, there are leakages of dollars to foreign countries caused mainly by our foreign trade imbalance. Our imports far exceed our exports, so there is a large drain of dollars to foreigners. And then, too, there is all the currency that American tourists spend abroad plus the tens of billions sent covertly to international drug traffickers. Some of these dollars return to the United States in the form of various investments (particularly in U.S. government securities, corporate securities, and real estate), but there is a definite net outflow of dollars, which, in turn, depresses still further the deposit expansion multiplier.

Where does all this leave us? It leaves us with the conclusion that the deposit expansion multiplier is, in reality, quite a bit lower than it would be if we based it solely on the reserve ratio. In other words, if the reserve ratio tells us it's 10, perhaps it's only 6.

Cash, Checks, and Electronic Money

One of the jobs of the Federal Reserve is called check clearing. Through this process, once the checks you write are deposited by the people you gave them to, they make their way through our financial system, facilitated by the Fed, and eventually wind up in your mailbox at the end of the month. How did they get there? Read the box "Check Clearing."

Increasingly, money is changing hands electronically rather than in the form of checks. Today, more than $1.7 trillion a day is transferred electronically—80 percent of the total payments made worldwide in dollars. About $600 billion of these transfers are carried out by the Federal Reserve's electronic network, while the other $1.1 trillion are done by the Clearing House Interbank Payments System (CHIPS), which is owned by 11 big New York banks.

Does all this mean that we are well on our way to a checkless, cashless society? Yes and no. We still carry out nearly 85 percent of our monetary transactions in cash—everything from paying for our groceries to tipping the hairdresser. But when we consider the total dollars actually spent, cash covers less than 1 percent of the total value of transactions, while electronic transfers account for five out of every six dollars that move in the economy.

The Tools of Monetary Policy

The goals of monetary policy were outlined at the beginning of the chapter. To attain these goals, the Fed regulates the rate of growth of the nation's money supply. This effort focuses on the reserves held by financial institutions. The most important policy tool used by the Fed to control reserves and, indirectly, the money supply, is open-market operations. To reiterate, the most important job of the Fed is to control the money supply; its most important policy tool to do that job is open-market operations.

How Open-Market Operations Work

What are open-market operations?

Open-market operations are the buying and selling of U.S. government securities in the open market. What are U.S. government securities? They are Treasury bills, notes,

Check Clearing

If you have a checking account at your local bank, at the end of each month you receive a statement listing all your deposits and withdrawals. The withdrawals are more numerous than the deposits because every time you write a check, that money is withdrawn from your account. Together with your statement, your bank encloses a pile of checks you wrote that month.

Did you ever wonder how, if you wrote a check, it ended up with your statement at the end of the month? No? Well, I'm going to tell you anyway. The whole process is called check clearing, and it is a service provided by the Federal Reserve System.

In 1976 we had a series of birthday parties for the nation. The United States of America was 200 years old that year. I was visiting some friends out in San Francisco at the time, and one of them, Bob, sold me a beat-up old bugle, which actually *looked* like it might have dated from the American Revolution.

This bugle has come in quite handy at my 8:00 A.M. classes. At the time I bought it, though, the big question was how I would pay for it. I didn't have $50 in cash I could spare. But what was really good about Bob was that he took out-of-state checks.

I gave Bob my check for $50. It was written on Chemical Bank back in Brooklyn. Bob deposited it in his account at Bank of America. From there it went to Bank of America's main office in San Francisco, which, in turn, sent it on to the San Francisco Federal Reserve District Bank. Bank of America's reserves were raised by $50 (the amount of the check). Doing this was a simple book-keeping operation.

The check was sent to the New York Federal Reserve District Bank, which deducted $50 from the reserves of Chemical Bank. The check then went to Chemical Bank's main office on Park Avenue in Manhattan and then to my branch out on Flatbush Avenue in Brooklyn. The $50 was then deducted from my account, and at the end of the month, the canceled check was mailed to me with my statement.

All of these transactions are shown pictorially in the diagram below. The check I gave Bob in San Francisco was sent back to me by my Brooklyn bank with my statement at the end of the month.

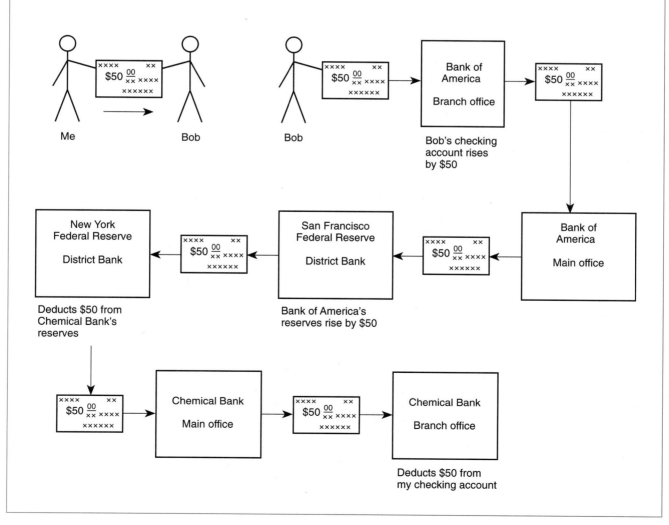

certificates, and bonds. The Fed does not market new securities.[5] That's the Treasury's job. Rather, the Fed buys and sells securities that have already been marketed by the Treasury, some of which might be several years old.

The total value of all outstanding U.S. government securities is more than $4 trillion. If this number is familiar, it should be; it's our national debt. Many students are under the misconception that the Federal Reserve sells newly issued securities for the Treasury, but all it does is buy and sell chunks of the national debt.

What open-market operations consist of, then, is the buying and selling of chunks of the national debt. The Fed does this by dealing with government bond houses, which are private bond dealers. If the Fed wants to buy, say, $100 million of Treasury notes that will mature within the next three months, it places an order with a few of these bond houses, which then buy up the securities for the Fed. When the Fed wants to sell securities, it again goes to the government bond houses and has them do the actual selling.

How the Fed increases the money supply

When the Fed wants to increase the money supply, it goes into the open market and buys U.S. government securities. You might ask, "What if people don't want to sell?" Remember the line from *The Godfather*, "I'll make you an offer you can't refuse"? Well, that's exactly what the Fed does. It tells the government bond houses, "Buy us 30,000 Treasury bills no matter what the price."

Question: What do you get when you cross the Godfather with an economist? Answer: An offer you can't understand.

If the Fed goes on a buying spree in the open market, it will quickly drive up the prices of U.S. government securities. All this buying will push down interest rates. Let's see why.

Suppose a bond is issued by the Treasury with a face value of $1,000 and an interest rate of 8 percent. This means the bond costs the initial buyer $1,000 and pays $80 interest a year. The price of the bond will fluctuate considerably over its life; but when it matures, the Treasury must pay the owner $1,000, its face value. And every year the Treasury must pay the owner $80 interest.

Using the formula

$$\text{Interest rate} = \frac{\text{Interest paid}}{\text{Price of bond}}$$

Interest rate = Interest paid / Price of bond

we can observe that a $1,000 bond paying $80 interest pays an interest rate of 8 percent:

$$\frac{\$80}{\$1,000} = 8 \text{ percent}$$

We have been talking about the Fed going into the open market and buying government securities. Suppose the Fed bought enough securities to bid up their price to $1,200. Remember, these securities still pay $80 interest a year. Let's calculate their new interest rate:

$$\text{Interest rate} = \frac{\text{Interest paid}}{\text{Price of bond}} = \frac{\$80}{\$1,200} = 6\frac{2}{3} \text{ percent}$$

You see that, as previously noted, when the Fed goes into the open market to buy securities, it bids up their price and lowers their interest rates. In the process, as we shall soon see, this also expands the money supply.

How the Fed contracts the money supply

When the Fed wants to contract the money supply, or at least slow down its rate of expansion, it goes into the open market and sells securities. In the process, it lowers bond prices and raises interest rates.

When selling securities, the Fed also uses the "Godfather principle." Again, it makes an offer that can't be refused (in this case, an offer to sell securities at low enough prices to get rid of a certain amount).

---

[5]The Fed is legally limited to buying no more than $5 billion in newly issued government securities a year, which is less than 1 percent of what the Treasury issues.

If the Fed bids bond prices down to $800, we use the same formula to find that the interest rate has risen to 10 percent.

$$\text{Interest rate} = \frac{\text{Interest paid}}{\text{Price of bond}} = \frac{\$80}{\$800} = \frac{1}{10} = 10 \text{ percent}$$

When the Fed sells securities on the open market to contract the money supply, bond prices fall and interest rates rise. Falling bond prices and rising interest rates generally accompany a tightening of the money supply.

You should note that although the Fed deals only with U.S. government securities, interest rates and bond prices move together in a broad range. When the Fed depresses the prices of U.S. government securities, all government and corporate bond prices tend to fall. And when the Fed pushes up the interest on U.S. government securities, all interest rates tend to rise.

Let's try another interest rate problem. Find the interest rate on a bond that pays $100 a year in interest and is currently selling for $800. Work it out right here:

Solution:

$$\text{Interest rate} = \frac{\text{Interest paid}}{\text{Price of bond}} = \frac{\$100}{\$800} = 12.5 \text{ percent}$$

The Federal Open-Market Committee

How the open-market operations are conducted

Open-market operations are conducted by the Federal Open-Market Committee (FOMC), which consists of 12 people. Eight are permanent members—the seven members of the Board of Governors and the president of the New York Federal Reserve District Bank (he or she is a permanent member because nearly all open-market purchases are made in the New York federal securities market). The other four members of the FOMC are presidents of the other 11 Federal Reserve District Banks; they serve on a rotating basis. Incidentally, when Paul Volcker, who had been serving as president of the New York Federal Reserve Bank, was appointed chairman of the Board of Governors by President Carter in 1979, he continued to serve on the FOMC, along with Anthony Solomon, the new president of the New York Federal Reserve Bank.

To fight recessions, the FOMC buys securities.

The FOMC meets about once every six weeks to decide what policy to follow. This is not to say that every three weeks the committee changes directions from buy to sell to buy again.

Assume the FOMC decides to ease credit a bit, perhaps because of the threat of a recession. It might decide to buy $100 million of securities on the open market. The New York Bank, as agent of the Federal Reserve, places an order with several government bond houses. The bonds are paid for by checks written on various Federal Reserve District Banks. Each government bond house deposits the checks in its own commercial bank. From there the checks are sent to the New York Federal Reserve District Bank, which adds the amount of the checks to the banks' reserves.

Say, for example, the Fed gives a $10 million check to bond house number one, which deposits it in its account at Bankers Trust. From there the check is sent a few blocks away to the New York Federal Reserve District Bank, which adds $10 million to the reserves of Bankers Trust.

What does Bankers Trust do with $10 million of reserves? Assuming it now has excess reserves of $10 million, it will lend most of it out. Up goes the money supply! As we have noted, banks seldom keep excess reserves because they don't earn interest. Thus we have a multiple expansion of deposits.

The process works the same way if the government bond houses are not the ultimate sellers of the securities. Usually those sellers are individuals, corporations, or banks. If an individual sells a $10,000 bond to the government bond house, which, in turn, sells it to the Fed, the government bond house is only the middleman. When the Fed pays the government bond house, this money will be turned over to the person who sold the bond. When she deposits her check at her local bank, say the National State Bank of New Jersey, the check will still be sent to the New York Federal Reserve District Bank. Ten thousand dollars will be added to the reserves of the National State Bank, which is now free to lend it out.

When banks lend out money, the money supply increases. When the Fed buys $100 million of securities, it is making $100 million of reserves available to the banking system. Most of this money will be lent out, and through the deposit expansion multiplier, it will create a multiplied deposit amount. For example, if the reserve ratio were 10 percent, the multiplier would be 10 (Multiplier = 1/Reserve ratio = $\frac{1}{10}$ = 10). However, allowing for currency leakages and bank holdings of some excess reserves, we'll say that the multiplier is actually only 6. A $100 million open-market purchase will lead to about a $600 million expansion of deposits (and, therefore, a $600 million expansion of the money supply).

To fight inflation, the FOMC sells securities.

During periods of inflation, when the FOMC decides to sell securities, we have exactly the opposite set of events. If the FOMC were to give the government bond houses $100 million of securities with orders to sell them at whatever the market will bring, we can easily trace the steps.

Customers will be found, and they will pay by check. For example, a corporation with an account at Fulton National Bank in Atlanta might buy $50,000 of securities. When its check reaches the Atlanta Federal Reserve District Bank, $50,000 is deducted from the reserves of Fulton National Bank. Similar reserve deductions occur around the country. Soon reserves for the entire banking system are reduced by $100 million.

That's just the first step. The banks will probably be short of reserves as they carry little, if any, excess. Where do they get the money? They can borrow from their Federal Reserve District Bank's discount windows, but this will only tide them over temporarily, and they're reluctant to do this anyway. They can go into the federal funds market, which is an overnight market in which banks borrow from each other on a day-to-day basis if they are short of reserves. But because most banks are short because of FOMC sales, this source of funds has constricted.

Ultimately, the banks will have to curb their loans, which is what the FOMC wanted all along. Initially, then, we would expect that $100 million less reserves will mean $100 million less in loans. But *had* those loans been made, with a multiplier of six, there would have been some $600 million worth of loans, and the money supply would have been $600 million higher.

We're saying that if reserves are reduced by $100 million, this will, with a multiplier of six, ultimately reduce the money supply by $600 million. Or, put slightly differently, when reserves are reduced, the money supply will end up being lower than it would otherwise have been.

Are you ready to apply your knowledge of the monetary multiplier to determine the potential effect of the sale of some securities on the open market? Suppose the Fed buys $200 million of securities and the reserve ratio is 12 percent. By how much could our money supply increase?

Solution:

$$\underset{\text{reserves}}{\text{Excess}} \times \underset{\text{multiplier}}{\text{Monetary}} = \underset{\text{the money supply}}{\text{Potential expansion of}}$$

$$\$200 \text{ million} \times \tfrac{1}{12} \qquad =$$

$$\$200 \text{ million} \times \tfrac{100}{12} \qquad =$$

$$\$200 \text{ million} \times 8.3 \qquad = \$1,660,000,000^6$$

Discount Rate Changes

The discount rate is the interest rate paid by member banks when they borrow at the Federal Reserve District Bank. The main reason today's banks borrow is that they are having trouble maintaining their required reserves. In general, however, by resorting to the discount window, member banks are calling attention to their difficulties, perhaps inviting closer audits when their Federal Reserve inspectors visit. Also, there is always the chance of being turned down for these loans.

The original intent of the Federal Reserve Act of 1913 was to have the District Banks lend money to member banks to take care of seasonal business needs. In the busy period before Christmas, firms would borrow money from their banks, which would, in turn, borrow from the Federal Reserve District Banks. Borrowing, then, was really note discounting. You technically borrowed $1,000, but if the interest rate was 8 percent, the interest—$80 for a one-year loan—was deducted in advance. All you got was $920; you paid back $1,000.

How discounting works

This was called discounting. When the commercial banks took these IOUs or commercial paper to the Federal Reserve District Bank, they would borrow money to cover these loans. This was called rediscounting.

Today banks no longer rediscount their commercial paper. Instead, they borrow directly from the Federal Reserve and call the interest they pay the discount rate. Although each of the 12 District Banks sets its own discount rate, they agree virtually all the time—perhaps with an occasional prod from the Board of Governors—to charge the same rate.

Rather than borrow from the Fed, banks usually borrow excess reserves from each other, usually for no more than a few days at a time. The interest rate they pay is called the federal funds rate. Concerned about inflationary pressures, the Federal Reserve Open-Market Committee sold enough securities from February 1994 to February 1995 to double the federal funds rate. Since all other short term interest rates also move up sharply during this period, the economy began to slow in the first half of 1995.

Open-market operations are the Fed's day-to-day and most important policy weapon. After selling securities in the open market and still not getting the banks to cut back enough on their loans, the Fed will raise the discount rate. Because, however, member banks don't borrow heavily from the District Banks, raising the discount rate is more of a symbolic gesture. Although discount rate changes do occasionally have some impact on the financial markets,[7] more often than not these changes merely reflect the Fed's desire to keep the discount rate in line with other interest rates.

Changing Reserve Requirements

The Fed's ultimate weapon

A changing of reserve requirements is really the ultimate weapon of the Federal Reserve System. Like nuclear weapons, which are rarely—if ever—used, it can be nice to know that the mechanism is there.

---

[6]Because we rounded after one decimal, we got 8.3. If you rounded after four decimals, you would have gotten 8.3333, giving you a deposit expansion of $1,666,660,000.

[7]An unexpected rise in the discount rate sometimes causes about a 50-point drop in the Dow Jones Index of stock prices and a similar decline in the prices of bonds. Unexpected declines in the discount rate sometimes cause these markets to rally.

The Federal Reserve Board has the power to change reserve requirements within legal limits, but in practice it does this only once every few years. The limits for checkable deposits are between 8 and 14 percent.[8] Before the Board takes this drastic step, it usually issues numerous warnings.

The discount rate will be raised by the District Banks, often in unison, as engineered by the Board of Governors. The FOMC will be actively selling securities; credit will be getting tighter; the chairman will be publicly warning the banks that they are advancing too many loans. This is called moral suasion, and like other appeals to morality, it rarely achieves the desired results (unless the Fed has been following President Teddy Roosevelt's advice: "Speak softly and carry a big stick"). If it doesn't do the job—if the banks are still advancing too many loans and if the money supply is still growing too rapidly—the Fed reaches for its biggest stick and raises reserve requirements. The last time this happened, in October 1980, the resulting credit crunch sent the prime rate of interest soaring above 20 percent as the economy plunged into the worst recession since the Great Depression.

The basic reserve rate was set at 12 percent in 1980 for most checking deposits, but in April 1992 it was lowered to 10 percent. The Board of Governors took this strong measure to help the economy recover from the lingering effects of the 1990–91 recession. In banking circles this 10 percent rate is often referred to as the *reserve ratio,* ignoring the 3 percent ratio that must be held on the first $54 million of checking deposits.

This weapon is so rarely used because it is simply too powerful. For example, if the Federal Reserve Board raised the reserve requirement on demand deposits by just one half of 1 percent, the nation's banks and thrift institutions would have to come up with nearly $4 billion in reserves.

Why does the Fed rarely change reserve requirements?

Reserve requirements, then, are raised reluctantly by the Board of Governors, and only after all else fails. However, when the economy is gripped by recession, the Fed becomes less reluctant to turn to its ultimate weapon; but even then, reserve requirement changes are a last resort.

The Fed has three ways of increasing our money supply: lowering reserve requirements, lowering the discount rate, and buying government securities on the open market. What about printing currency? Does *this* raise our money supply? If you think the answer is yes, then you definitely should read the box about printing more money.

Summary: The Tools of Monetary Policy

What three things can the Fed do to fight a recession? List them right here:

1.

2.

3.

The answers are (1) lower the discount rate, (2) buy securities on the open market, and, ultimately, if these two don't do the job, (3) lower reserve requirements.

What three things can the Fed do to fight inflation? List them here:

1.

2.

3.

---

[8]If five members of the Board deem it desirable, the maximum can be raised to 18 percent, and if conditions are extraordinary, any rate whatsoever may be set.

Does Printing More Money Increase Our Money Supply?

When the Federal Reserve Banks issue currency, doesn't this increase our money supply? Surprisingly, the answer is no. Now I'm going to prove it.

What is the money supply? It's currency, demand deposits, and other checkable deposits held by the public. So the question is, When the Fed prints currency, how does it get into the hands of the public?

Suppose the Federal Reserve Bank of San Francisco issues 10 one-hundred-dollar bills and gives them to Security Pacific Corp., which pays by having its reserves lowered by $1,000. (Actually, its reserves stay the same, because this money goes into its vault.) Next, a local businesswoman writes a check for $1,000 on her account at Security Pacific and walks out of the bank with the 10 one-hundred-dollar bills.

Did that transaction increase the money supply? What do you think? On the one hand, when the teller gave the woman the cash, that increased the amount of money in the hands of the public by $1,000. But what the bank gave with that one hand, it took away with the other by decreasing her checking account by $1,000.

To recap: When the Federal Reserve Bank of San Francisco issued $1,000 in currency, did that lead to an increase in the money supply? No, it did not. When the Fed prints money, it does so to accommodate the needs of the public. If the public wishes to hold more of its money in the form of currency—and, parenthetically, less in the form of checking deposits—the Fed will accommodate these wishes.

While we're on the subject, I'd like you to take a look at the money you have in your wallet. You'll find the signature of the Secretary of the Treasury in the lower right of the face of each bill. Chances are Robert E. Rubin signed most of your money. You might even have a bill signed by James Baker or Donald Regan, both of whom served under President Reagan. What happened to all the currency issued before 1980? Nearly all of it was withdrawn from circulation as it wore out; it was replaced by crisp new bills. Does *this* increase our money supply? Obviously not. So the next time someone walks up to you on the street and asks you whether the Fed increases the money supply by issuing currency, tell him no.

The answers are (1) raise the discount rate, (2) sell securities on the open market, and, ultimately, if these two don't do the job, (3) raise reserve requirements. (For further results of monetary policy, see box "The Effectiveness of Monetary Policy in an Open Economy.")

The Fed's Effectiveness in Fighting Inflation and Recession

The Fed is more effective in fighting inflation than recession.

Federal Reserve policy in fighting inflation and recession has been likened to pulling and then pushing on a string. Like pulling on a string, when the Fed fights inflation, it gets results—provided, of course, it pulls hard enough.

Fighting a recession is another matter. Like pushing on a string, no matter how hard the Fed works, it might not get anywhere.

First we'll consider fighting inflation. Assume all three basic policy tools have been used: securities have been sold on the open market, the discount rate has been raised, and, ultimately, reserve requirements have been raised. The results are that bond prices have plunged, interest rates have soared, and money supply growth has been stopped dead in its tracks. Banks find it impossible to increase their loan portfolios. There's a credit crunch and there's credit rationing. Old customers can still borrow, but their credit lines are slashed. (My own line of credit, for example, was cut by Citibank during the 1980 credit crunch from $3,500 to $500.) Nearly all new customers are turned away.

The government fighting inflation is like the Mafia fighting crime.
Laurence J. Peter

During times like these, the rate of inflation has got to decline. It's hard to raise prices when no one is buying anything. No one can buy because no one has any money.

The Effectiveness of Monetary Policy in an Open Economy

Suppose the Fed tightens money and interest rates rise. Investors all over the world will be attracted to the higher interest rates they can earn by purchasing U.S. bonds, corporate bonds, and other assets. But in order to invest, they will need to exchange their money for U.S. dollars.

This will drive up the dollar relative to foreign currencies. In other words, you will now be able to get more marks, yen, and pounds for your dollars. Foreign goods will become cheaper to Americans and our imports will soar. Meanwhile, foreigners will be getting fewer dollars for their marks, yen, and pounds, so they will find American goods more expensive. And they will cut back on their purchases of those goods.

Let's recap: Tight money drives up interest rates, making American investments more attractive to foreigners. They will bid up the dollar, thus lowering our exports and raising our imports. So tight money works to lower our net exports (exports minus imports).

Did you get all that? We've really gotten a bit ahead of ourselves, because the effects of exchange rate changes on foreign trade are not analyzed until the next-to-last chapter of this book. But while we're at it, how would an expansionary monetary policy affect our net exports?

It would have just the opposite effect of a contractionary policy. Monetary expansion would lower our interest rates. Lower interest rates are not attractive to foreign investors, whose demand for U.S. dollars will drop. If the dollar falls relative to foreign currencies, that makes our exports cheaper and our imports more expensive. Thus, an expansionary monetary policy will raise our net exports and further stimulate our economy.

Of course, the Fed is somewhat reluctant to tighten up too much or too long because such a policy generally brings on recessions.

The Fed has a far harder time dealing with a recession. Again, assume the standard tools have been used: securities have been purchased on the open market, the discount rate has been lowered, and reserve requirements have been lowered. All this creates excess reserves for the banks. But now the $64 question: What do they *do* with these reserves?

Do they lend them out? Fine. To whom should they lend them? To a businessowner who needs a loan to keep going? To a firm that can't meet its next payroll without a loan? To an individual who has just lost her job and can't meet her car payments?

Never lend money to anyone who needs it.

All these examples bring to mind the first law of banking: Never lend money to anyone who needs it. If you ever want a bank loan, you've got to convince the loan officer that you don't really need the money. I don't mean to make the banks sound bad, but from their point of view, they simply can't afford to take the risks inherent in these loans. A banker's first concern must be "Will the bank be paid back?"

A bank is a place where they lend you an umbrella in fair weather and ask for it back again when it begins to rain.

—Robert Frost

During recessions, businesses that might have been good credit risks during prosperity have become poor risks. Individuals, too, lose creditworthiness during recessions, particularly if they've just been laid off. And so the very segment of the economic community most in need of help during recessions is least likely to be accommodated.

Meanwhile, many of the top credit-rated corporations are not coming in to borrow large sums of money. During recessions the companies to whom the banks will lend money are not borrowing. Why? Because business isn't so great for them either. Would you borrow to buy more equipment—even at low interest rates—if your equipment was one-third idle? Would you expand your factory if sales were down 20 percent—even if the interest rate fell to 4 percent?

In fact, in October 1982 the economy's capacity utilization rate had fallen to just 68.4 percent—an all-time low since this statistic was first compiled in 1948.[9] The Fed had by then loosened credit, but not until sales finally picked up in early 1983 did investments begin to rise appreciably.

---

[9]The capacity utilization rate is the percentage of the nation's plant and equipment that is being used. The full-employment and full-production section of Chapter 2 indicated that a capacity utilization rate of 85 to 90 percent would employ virtually all our usable plant and equipment.

All of this said, may we conclude that easy money has little or no effect in ending a recession? Not at all! It's like the adage "You can lead a horse to water, but you can't make him drink." But if that horse happens to be thirsty, just try to *stop* him from drinking.

The Fed was able to help end the recessions of 1980 and 1981–82 by relaxing credit and driving down interest rates. On the other hand, the excruciatingly slow and halting recovery of 1991–92 was not very responsive to the lowest interest rates in 15 years. Furthermore, even though the banks had plenty of money that they could have loaned out to individuals and business firms, many banks preferred to purchase short-term U.S. government securities.[10]

The Depository Institutions Deregulation and Monetary Control Act of 1980

I have waited until now to deal with the Depository Institutions Deregulation and Monetary Control Act of 1980. It is clearly the most important piece of banking legislation passed since the 1930s.

Economic historians will mark the 1970s and 1980s as decades of swift and significant change in American banking. During this period, the distinction between commercial banks and thrift institutions (savings banks, savings and loan associations, and credit unions) became blurred to the point where it's hard to tell what is a bank and what isn't.

What is a bank and what isn't?

Until 1980 there was a clear line of demarcation between commercial and thrift institutions. Banks (meaning commercial banks) could issue checking deposits; savings banks, savings and loan associations, and credit unions could not. The only problem was that more and more of the thrifts were doing just that. The way they got around the law was to call those checking deposits something else—namely, negotiable order of withdrawal accounts (or NOW accounts). Thus, technically, people who had deposits at these thrift institutions were not writing checks; they were writing negotiable orders of withdrawal (see box "Bankers Obey the Law").

While Federal Reserve regulation prohibited commercial banks from paying any interest on checking deposits, the thrifts were paying their depositors about 5 percent interest on their NOW accounts. Because these were technically savings accounts rather than checking accounts, it was OK to pay interest. Therefore, the thrifts had it both ways: They were able to give their depositors checking accounts and pay interest on them—which gave them a considerable competitive advantage over commercial banks.

The three key provisions of the Banking Act of 1980

The commercial banks complained to the Fed and to anyone else who would listen, but to little avail. Finally Congress took matters into its own hands and passed the Depository Institutions Deregulation and Monetary Control Act of 1980. It had three key provisions:

1. All depository institutions are now subject to the Fed's legal reserve requirements. Before this act, only those commercial banks that were members of the Federal Reserve—about one-third of all commercial banks were members—were subject to these requirements. The other commercial banks and thrift institutions were subject to state reserve requirements, which were substantially lower.

2. All depository institutions are now legally authorized to issue checking deposits. Furthermore, they may be interest bearing. Previously, commercial banks were forbidden to pay interest on checking accounts, while the thrift institutions claimed to be paying interest on savings accounts.

---

[10]Do you recall the crowding-out effect discussed in the appendix of Chapter 11? It shows how private borrowers are crowded out of financial markets by the U.S. Treasury, thus offsetting some of the effects of an expansionary fiscal policy.

"Bankers Obey the Law"*

Do bankers obey the law? In the last chapter we saw just how many savings and loan officials obeyed the law. And here we have thousands of S&Ls, savings banks, and credit unions openly flaunting the law by issuing NOW accounts. These accounts may not have been *called* checking accounts, but they looked like checking accounts, sounded like checking accounts, smelled like checking accounts, and were even represented to prospective customers as checking accounts. Now, if something *walks* like a duck and *talks* like a duck, it's reasonable to *call* it a duck.

How does it look to have thousands of bankers illegally issuing checking accounts and then denying they're doing anything illegal? After all, we're supposed to be a nation governed by law. The government obviously had to do something. But what? Haul these bankers into court like common criminals, throw the book at them, and lock them up in jail? What do *you* think?

If the law is being broken, what can you do? You can change the law. Which is exactly how this country got the Depository Institutions Deregulation and Monetary Control Act of 1980.

*These are the words of William Eiseman, director of personnel, Morgan Guaranty Trust and Security Company, in an interview with the author in 1975.

3. All depository institutions now enjoy all the advantages that only Federal Reserve member banks formerly enjoyed—including check clearing[11] and borrowing from the Fed (discounting).[12]

Remember that the main job of the Federal Reserve is to control the money supply. By bringing all depository institutions—especially the nonmember commercial banks and the savings banks that had NOW accounts—under the Fed's control, the Monetary Control Act made this job a lot easier.

The number of financial institutions is shrinking quickly.

Another important consequence of this law is that by the end of the 1990s, intense competition will reduce the 40,000-plus financial institutions that existed at the beginning of the 1980s to a little more than half that number. The lifting of the prohibition against interstate banking, combined with further advances in electronic banking, will create greater consolidation, with perhaps just 60 or 80 giant financial institutions doing most of the business. "Virtually all observers agree that the ability of the new financial system to generate credit and meet credit demands will be enhanced, because the system will consist of big, nationwide, all-purpose institutions."[13]

Fiscal and Monetary Policies Should Mesh

It should be apparent that there is little coordination in the making of fiscal and monetary policies. Indeed, there is little fiscal policy as such, but rather a series of compromises within Congress and between Congress and the president. Further, given the independence of the Federal Reserve Board, different groups of people are responsible for monetary and fiscal policy.

Because of the need for these policies to mesh rather than work at cross-purposes (as they sometimes have), we should consider ways to unify monetary and fiscal policy. One step in this direction would be to allow each newly elected president to appoint a new chairman of the Board.

---

[11]Check clearing is the mysterious process by which all the checks you wrote during the month are mailed to you by your bank at the end of the month. If you're not clear on how this gets done, you'd better check back to the box titled "Check Clearing" earlier in this chapter. The Federal Reserve System processes, or clears, billions of checks each year.

[12]"Reserves of nonmember depository institutions may be held at a correspondent depository institution holding required reserves at a Federal Reserve Bank, a Federal Home Loan Bank, or the National Credit Union Administration Central Liquidity Facility, if such reserves are passed through to a Federal Reserve Bank. The Board may, by regulation or order that is applicable to all depository institutions, permit them to maintain all or a portion of their required reserves in the form of vault cash." See *The Federal Reserve Bulletin,* June 1980, p. 446.

[13]*BusinessWeek,* November 17, 1980, p. 139.

Furthermore, it is quite frustrating for Americans trying to fix the responsibility and the blame for policy failures. In times of high rates of unemployment, inflation, and interest, it seems as though Congress, the president, and the Federal Reserve Board all invoke the immortal words of the late Freddie Prinz: "Is not my job."[14]

Questions for Further Thought and Discussion

1. Should the Federal Reserve Board of Governors remain independent? Argue this question from both sides.
2. Is the Federal Reserve more effective in fighting recessions or inflations? Explain your answer.
3. What is the most important function of the Federal Reserve? What other functions does it perform?
4. What are open-market operations? How are they conducted to fight inflation and recession?

---

[14]Freddie Prinz was the star of a TV show, "Chico and the Man," about 15 years ago. If we could elect a former actor as president, it seems appropriate that those responsible for fiscal and monetary policy all seem to be reading from other actors' scripts.

WORKBOOK FOR CHAPTER 13

Name _____   Date _____

Multiple-Choice Questions

Circle the letter that corresponds to the best answer.

1. Fiscal and monetary policy have
   a. the same means and ends   b. different means and
   ends   c. the same means and different ends
   d. different means and the same ends

2. Which statement is true?
   a. The United States has always had a central bank.
   b. The United States has never had a central bank.
   c. The United States had a central bank until 1913.
   d. The United States has had a central bank since 1913.

3. The most important Federal Reserve policy weapon is
   a. changing reserve requirements   b. changing the
   discount rate   c. moral suasion   d. open-market
   operations

4. To restrict monetary growth, the Federal Reserve will
   a. raise the discount rate and sell securities   b. raise
   the discount rate and buy securities   c. lower the
   discount rate and sell securities   d. lower the discount
   rate and buy securities

5. Monetary policy is conducted by
   a. the president only   b. Congress only   c. the
   president and Congress   d. the Federal Reserve

6. Which statement about the Federal Reserve Board of
   Governors is true?
   a. They serve seven-year terms.   b. There are 14
   members.   c. Every president appoints his own board.
   d. The members serve at the pleasure of the president,
   who can force their resignations at any time.   e. None
   of these statements is true.

7. Control of the Federal Reserve System is vested in
   a. the president   b. Congress   c. the Board of
   Governors   d. the District Banks

8. Basically the Board of Governors is
   a. independent   b. dependent on the president and
   Congress   c. powerless   d. on a par with the
   District Banks

9. Legal reserve requirements are changed
   a. very often   b. on rare occasions
   c. never   d. none of these

10. Which of these is a secondary reserve?
    a. Treasury bills   b. gold   c. vault cash
    d. deposits at the Federal Reserve District Bank

11. The larger the reserve requirement, the
    a. smaller the deposit expansion multiplier
    b. larger the deposit expansion multiplier   c. less
    the impact of an increase in reserves

12. Each of the following is a leakage from the deposit
    expansion multiplier except
    a. cash   b. the foreign trade imbalance
    c. excess reserves   d. all of these are leakages

13. Check clearing is done by
    a. the bank where a check is deposited   b. the bank
    on which a check is written   c. the Federal Reserve
    System   d. the comptroller of the currency

14. Open-market operations are
    a. the buying and selling of U.S. government securities
    by the Fed   b. borrowing by banks from the Fed
    c. the selling of U.S. government securities by the U.S.
    Treasury   d. raising or lowering reserve requirements
    by the Fed

15. When the Fed wants to increase the money supply, it
    a. raises the discount rate   b. raises reserve
    requirements   c. sells securities   d. buys
    securities

16. To buy securities, the Fed offers

    a. a low price and drives up interest rates   b. a low price and drives down interest rates   c. a high price and drives up interest rates   d. a high price and drives down interest rates

17. All open-market operations are carried out for the Fed by

    a. private government bond dealers   b. the U.S. Treasury   c. large Wall Street brokerage houses   d. none of the above

18. The original intent of the Federal Reserve Act was to have the District Banks lend money to

    a. individual borrowers, particularly business firms

    b. member banks to take care of seasonal needs

    c. the U.S. Treasury   d. none of the above

19. Which statement is true?

    a. The Fed is more effective at fighting inflation than fighting recession.   b. The Fed is more effective at fighting recession than fighting inflation.   c. The Fed is effective at fighting both recession and inflation.

    d. The Fed is effective at fighting neither inflation nor recession.

20. The Depository Institutions Deregulation and Monetary Control Act of 1980 had three key provisions, one of which was

    a. uniform reserve requirements for all financial institutions   b. zero reserve requirements for all time deposits   c. that no interest may be paid on checking deposits   d. that vault cash would no longer count toward reserves

21. The main job of the Fed is to

    a. control the rate of growth of the money supply   b. to manage the national debt   c. provide low-interest loans to all financial institutions   d. none of the above

22. One of the main results of the Depository Institutions Deregulation and Monetary Control Act of 1980 may be to

    a. lessen the number of financial institutions in the United States   b. increase the number of financial institutions in the United States   c. discourage the formation of big, nationwide, all-purpose financial institutions   d. make it easier for the member banks to borrow money from the Federal Reserve District Banks

23. Reserve requirements are changed

    a. once a week   b. three or four times a year   c. once every two or three years   d. once every eight or ten years   e. only if Congress passes a new law

24. Suppose that the deposit expansion multiplier were 7. After taking into account its three modifications, we might estimate the true deposit multiplier to be

    a. 14   b. 9   c. 7   d. 4   e. 1

25. Statement 1: Currency leakages take place especially during times of recession and low interest rates. Statement 2: The process of check clearing is being partially replaced by the electronic transferring of money.

    a. Statement 1 is true and statement 2 is false.

    b. Statement 2 is true and statement 1 is false.

    c. Both statements are true.   d. Both statements are false.

26. Which is the most accurate statement? The Federal Reserve

    a. markets new treasury bills, notes, certificates, and bonds   b. runs a check clearing operation for U.S. government checks, but does not handle checks written by private individuals or business firms   c. Open-Market Committee is part of the U.S. Treasury   d. buys and sells chunks of the national debt

27. The limits set by law for reserves on checking accounts are between

    a. 0% and 9%   b. 3% and 12%   c. 8% and 14%

    d. 12% and 18%

Fill-In Questions

1. The Federal Reserve System was established in the year

    _____.

2. There are _____ Federal Reserve districts.

3. The members of the Board of Governors are appointed by

_____, subject to

confirmation by the_____.

4. Control of the Federal Reserve is held by

_____.

5. Currently, nearly all checking deposits are subject to a

legal reserve requirement of _____ percent.

6. Time deposits are subject to no reserve requirement

because_____

_____.

7. All reserves pay an interest rate of _____

percent.

8. Primary reserves are held in the form of _____

_____ and _____

_____; secondary reserves are held in

the form of _____.

9. The process by which a check you write is deposited in

another bank, goes through the Federal Reserve System,

and is sent back to your own bank is known as

_____

_____.

10. The three goals of monetary policy are (1) _____

_____; (2) _____;

and (3)_____.

11. Open-market operations are the _____

_____.

12. If the Fed wants to increase the money supply, it will

follow these two steps: (1) _____

_____; (2) _____

_____; and if these do not prove

sufficient, it may _____.

13. If the Fed wanted to decrease the money supply, it would

go into the open market and _____

_____; this would also

_____ interest rates.

14. Open-market policy is conducted by the _____

_____, which is part of the Fed.

15. The main reason that banks borrow from the Fed is

because they _____.

16. The discount rate is defined as the _____

_____.

17. There are _____ members of the Federal Open

Market Committee; they are the _____

_____.

18. The Federal Reserve Board of Governors will _____

_____

only as a last resort.

19. It has been much easier for the Fed to fight

_____ than _____.

20. Until 1980 there was a clear line of demarcation between

commercial banks and the thrifts: commercial banks

could _____

while the thrifts could not.

21. A NOW account stands for _____

_____.

22. Under the Depository Institutions Deregulation and Monetary Control Act of 1980, all depository institutions are now subject to the Fed's _____; at the same time, all depository institutions are now legally authorized to issue _____.

23. The degree of coordination between fiscal and monetary policy today is _____.

24. Our paper currency is issued by _____ _____.

25. Our currency is backed by _____.

26. The part of our money supply issued by the Treasury is _____.

Problems

1. If you ran a bank with demand deposits of $20 million, you would need to hold reserves of how much?

2. If you ran a bank with demand deposits of $400 million, you would need to hold reserves of a little less than how much (assuming you don't remember the cutoff point)?

3. If there were a 15 percent reserve requirement, how much would the deposit multiplier be?

4. Using your answer from the previous problem, if the Federal Reserve increased bank reserves by $100 million, by how much would the money supply rise?

5. How much is the interest rate on a bond that has a face value of $1,000 and a selling price of $1,200 and that pays $120 interest?

6. If a bank has reserves of $21 million and demand deposits of $200 million, how much are the bank's: a. required reserves? b. excess reserves?

7. Approximately how much in reserves does a bank with $5 billion in demand deposits have to hold?

8. If a bank has reserves of $100 million and demand deposits of $700 million, how much are the bank's: a. required reserves? b. excess reserves?

9. How much reserves would a bank have to hold on: a. $1 billion of time deposits that will mature in less than 18 months? b. $1 billion of time deposits that will mature in more than 18 months?

10. Use the information in Table 1 to find this bank's required reserves.

Table 1

Demand deposits: $1 billion
Time deposits: $300 million

11. Use the information in Table 2 to find this bank's required reserves.

Table 2

Demand deposits: $1.4 billion
Time deposits: $1 billion

14 Twentieth-Century Economic Theory

Economists are not easy to follow when they talk about familiar, day-to-day events like unemployment rate changes and the rising consumer price index. When they talk theory, however, even their fellow economists have difficulty understanding, let alone agreeing with, what they are saying to each other. I'll repeat the words of George Bernard Shaw: "If all economists were laid end to end, they would not reach a conclusion."

John Maynard Keynes put all of this into perspective much more elegantly:

> The ideas of economists and political philosophers, both when they are right and when they are wrong, are more powerful than is commonly understood. Indeed, the world is ruled by little else. Practical men, who believe themselves to be quite exempt from any intellectual influences, are usually slaves of some defunct economist.

What conclusion will you reach at the end of this chapter? If you're like my fellow economists, you will choose one school of economic thought to defend while attacking each of the others. I hope you'll take each economic theory with a grain of salt, ferreting out what you can't accept while appreciating the cogency of the arguments that have been advanced. No attempt is being made to do more than outline some of the underlying ideas of each of the five main schools of this century. The appendix to this chapter presents "The Great Money Debate: The Keynesians versus the Monetarists."

Chapter Objectives

After you've read this chapter, you will have a better understanding of the basics of:

- The equation of exchange.
- The quantity theory of money.
- Classical economics.
- Keynesian economics.
- The monetarist school.
- Supply-side economics.
- The rational expectations theory.

The Equation of Exchange

Don't get the equation of exchange mixed up with the quantity theory of money.

Much of the Keynesian-Monetarist debate revolves around the quantity theory of money, which itself is based on the equation of exchange. So in the first two sections let's look at these two concepts before we deal specifically with the Classical School, the Keynesian School, or any of the other schools of twentieth-century economic theory. The equation of exchange and the quantity theory of money are easily confused, perhaps because the equation of exchange is used to explain the quantity theory. I warn my students every term about how easily the unwary test taker writes down the equation of exchange when asked for the quantity theory, or vice versa. Many of my students take these warnings to heart, remaining faithful to the tradition of confusing the two concepts on the next exam.

MV = PQ

The equation of exchange is

$$MV = PQ$$

What do these letters stand for? M represents the number of dollars in the nation's money supply—the currency, demand deposits, and checklike deposits.

The velocity of circulation, or the number of times per year that each dollar in our money supply is spent, is represented by V. If we were to multiple M times V, or MV, that would be our money supply multiplied by the number of times per year each dollar is spent—in other words, total spending. Total spending by a nation during a given year is GDP. Therefore,

$$MV = GDP$$

Now for the other side of the equation. P represents the price level, or the average price of all the goods and services sold during the year. Finally, there's Q, which stands for the quantity of goods and services sold during the year. Multiplying P times Q, we get the total amount of money received by the sellers of all the final goods and services produced by the nation that year. This is also GDP. Things equal to the same thing are equal to each other (MV = GDP; PQ = GDP); therefore MV = PQ.

We'll get a better idea of how this equation works by replacing the letters with numbers. For M we can substitute $900 billion, and we'll give V a value of 9,

$$MV = PQ$$

$$900 \times 9 = PQ$$

$$8,100 = PQ$$

This gives us a GDP of 8,100, or $8.1 trillion. As a form of shorthand, economists write billions of dollars without the dollar sign. The money supply of $900 billion becomes 900, and the GDP of $8,100 billion becomes 8,100.

So far we have MV = 8,100; therefore, PQ also = 8,100. How much are P and Q? We don't know. All we do know is that P × Q = 8,100.

What we'll do, so we can fool around with this equation, is arbitrarily assign values to P and Q. That might not be very nice or proper, but let me assure you that people do this sort of thing every day. Let's take P. Who can guess what the average price of all the final goods and services sold actually is? In other words, could you guess the average price of all those cars, houses, hot dogs, pairs of shoes, toothbrushes, cans of beer, cavity fillings, and so on? As there's no way of even guessing, we'll make the number $81. Why $81? Because it will be easy to work with. But perhaps $61.17 or $123.98 is what P actually denotes. We'll never know.

Now we'll consider Q. How many final goods and services were sold during the year? 23 billion? 345 billion? Again, we can't possibly know, so we'll assign a number. If we've already picked $81 for P, and PQ = 8,100, then Q must equal 100 (meaning, in economists' shorthand, 100 billion). Therefore:

$$MV = PQ$$

$$900 \times 9 = 81 \times 100$$

$$8,100 = 8,100$$

That's the equation of exchange. It must always balance, as must all equations. If one side rises by a certain percentage, the other side must rise by the same percentage. For example, if MV rose to 9,000, PQ would also rise to 9,000.

The Quantity Theory of Money

The crude version of the quantity theory

The quantity theory of money has both a crude version and a more sophisticated version. The crude quantity theory of money holds that when the money supply changes by a certain percentage, the price level changes by that same percentage. For example, if the money supply were to rise by 10 percent, the price level would rise by 10 percent. Similarly, if M were to double, then P would double. Using the same figures we assigned to the equation of exchange, let's see what happens if M and P double.

$$MV = PQ$$

$$900 \times 9 = 81 \times 100$$

$$1,800 \times 9 = 162 \times 100$$

$$16,200 = 16,200$$

If we double M, then MV doubles, and if we double P, PQ doubles. Because both sides of the equation must be equal, it appears that the crude quantity theory of money works out.

There are only two problems here. We are assuming V and Q remain constant. Do they? If they do, the crude quantity theory is correct. But what if they don't? For example, what if M, P, and Q all double? For the equation to balance, V would have to double. Similarly, what if M doubles and V declines by 50 percent? In that case, the rise in M would be canceled by the decline in V. If M doubles and MV stays the same, can we expect an automatic doubling of P?

Let's take a closer look at V and then at Q. Since 1950 V has risen fairly steadily from about three to nearly seven. In other words, individuals and businesses are spending their dollars much more quickly. Alternatively, they are making more efficient use of their money balances.

There are several explanations for the rise of V. First, there's inflation. Why hold large money balances when they lose their value over time? Second, why hold idle cash balances when they could be earning interest? Finally, the use of credit cards and automatic teller machines, especially during the last decade, has allowed people to carry less cash. As a result, V has more than doubled since the mid-1950s.

Now let's see about Q, the quantity of final goods and services produced. During recessions, production, and therefore Q will fall. For example, during the 1981–82 recession Q fell at an annual rate of about 4 percent during the fourth quarter of 1981 and the first quarter of 1982. During recoveries, production picks up, so we go from a declining Q to a rising Q.

Obviously, then, we cannot consider V or Q to be constants. Therefore, the crude version of the quantity theory is invalid.

The real problem with the early quantity theorists is that they overstated their case. Clearly, rapid monetary growth will invariably lead to inflation. But does a given rate of increase in the money supply lead to precisely the same rate of growth in the price level? Not in *my* book, which happens to be the one you are reading.

Today's modern monetarists, those who believe the key economic variable is changes in M, have come up with a more sophisticated quantity theory. They assume any short-term changes in V are either very small or predictable. The situation with Q, however, is another story.

Let's say M rises by 10 percent and V stays the same: MV will rise by 10 percent and PQ will rise by 10 percent. So far, so good. In fact, so far the crude and sophisticated quantity theories are identical. But what happens next is entirely up to the level of production, Q.

If there's considerable unemployment and we increase M, most, if not all, of this increase will be reflected in an increase in production, Q. Money flowing into the economy will lead to increased spending, output, and employment. Will it lead to higher prices as well? Probably not. Although our recent experience during recessions makes us a little more wary of large surges in the money supply, it is reasonable to expect most of the rise in M to be reflected in a rise in Q.

As we approach full employment, however, further increases in M will begin to lead, more and more, to increases in P, the price level (see Figure 1).[1] And it is there that the

During a period of very tight money in the late 1970s and early 1980s, V rose to nearly seven.

The sophisticated version of the quantity theory

The value of money . . . varies inversely as its quantity; every increase of quantity lowering the value, and every diminution raising it, in a ratio exactly equivalent.

—John Stuart Mill, *Principles of Political Economy*

---

[1]Do you recognize our old friend, the aggregate supply curve, which appeared in Figures 6 and 9 of Chapter 10?

Figure 1   Hypothetical Aggregate Supply Curve

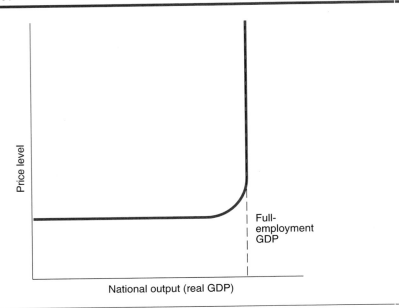

Sophisticated quantity theory
in brief

sophisticated quantity theory becomes operative. We therefore can make two statements summarizing the sophisticated quantity theory:

1. If we are well below full employment, an increase in M will lead mainly to an increase in Q.

2. If we are close to full employment, an increase in M will lead mainly to an increase in P.

That's the sophisticated quantity theory of money. Please don't confuse it with the crude quantity theory, and don't confuse either quantity theory with the equation of exchange.

What is the sophisticated quantity theory supposed to do? Like most theories, it makes a prediction. It its least rigorous version, it says that changes in M's rate of growth lead to similar changes in PQ's rate of growth. If M is increasing slowly, PQ will increase slowly; rapid growth in M leads to rapid growth in PQ. Although no precise mathematical relationship is claimed (as under the crude quantity theory), the monetarists say changes in M lead to predictable changes in PQ.

We've deftly sidestepped the whole question of whether V is stable in the short run. The monetarists tell us it is, and the validity of the modern or sophisticated quantity theory depends on the short-run stability of V. We'll deal with the question of the short-run stability of V in the appendix to this chapter.

Classical Economics

The United States suffered very bad recessions, even depressions, in the 1830s, 1870s, and 1890s, but always did eventually recover. If the government tried to get the country out of a recession, said the classicals, it only made things worse.

Recessions cure themselves.

The classical school of economics was mainstream economics from roughly 1775 to 1930. Adam Smith's *The Wealth of Nations,* a plea for laissez-faire (no government interference), was virtually the economics bible through most of this period. The classicals believed our economy was self-regulating. Recessions would cure themselves, and a built-in mechanism was always pushing the economy toward full employment.

As we saw at the beginning of Chapter 10, the centerpiece of the classical system was Say's law: Supply creates its own demand. Everything produced gets sold. Why? Because people work so that they can spend.

Say's law

Figure 2   The Interest Rate Mechanism

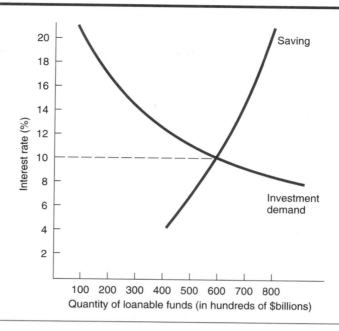

Savings will be invested.

What if people save some of their incomes? No problem, said the classicals, because that savings will be invested. With that, they pointed to Figure 2, which shows a graph of saving and investment. The two are equal at an interest rate of 10 percent.

What if the amount of money people wanted to save at 10 percent interest were greater than the amount businesspeople wanted to invest? Still no problem, said the classicals. The interest rate would fall automatically. People would be inclined to save less at lower interest rates, and businesspeople would be inclined to invest more. Eventually, the interest rate would fall far enough so that savings and investment would be equal.

Interest rate mechanism

Flexible wages and prices

The classicals also assumed downwardly flexible wage rates and prices. If there happened to be a temporary recession and business firms could not sell their entire inventories, they would simply lower their prices until their inventories were depleted. Similarly, if some workers were unemployed, they would offer to work for lower wages and would find new jobs.

Quantity theory of money

Another basic classical tenet was the quantity theory of money, which we discussed earlier in this chapter. Stated in its crudest version, when the money supply changes by a certain percentage, the price level changes by that same percentage. Thus, when the money supply is increased by 5 percent, the price level rises by 5 percent.

Resorting once again to the equation of exchange (whose components are defined in the first section of this chapter):

$$MV = PQ$$

V and Q are constant.

If M rises by 5 percent and P rises by 5 percent, that means V and Q remain constant. We shall hold a full-scale debate between the Keynesians and the monetarists about the stability of V in the appendix to this chapter and shall conclude that V is stable during nonrecession and peacetime years. And Q? Well, Q, the output of goods and services, rises during nonrecession years and falls during recession years.

Where does all this leave us as regards the quantity theory? In its crude version, which the classicals espoused, we could hardly expect V *and* Q to stay constant from year to year. So much, then, for the crude quantity theory.

Q: How many conservative economists does it take to screw in a lightbulb?
A: None. If the government would just leave it alone, it would screw in itself.

Finally, let's take a closer look at the classical contention that recessions are temporary phenomena, which, with the help of Say's law, the interest rate mechanism, and downwardly flexible wages and prices, cure themselves. This leads to the basic classical macroeconomic policy when there is a recession: Do nothing!

Government can't cure
recessions.

If the government attempted to cure a recession by spending more money or cutting taxes, these measures would not get the economy out of the recession. Why not? Because the recession would cure itself. Government intervention could not help, and it might even hurt.

What about monetary policy? If there were a recession, the standard monetary policy would be to increase the rate of growth of the money supply. What would this accomplish? Ask the classicals. Because the recession would be curing itself, output, Q, would go up automatically. Because V would be stable, a rise in M would simply be translated into a rise in P, so the attempt to cure the recession by means of monetary policy would only cause inflation.

The classical school dominated economic thought until the time of the Great Depression. If recessions cure themselves automatically, asked John Maynard Keynes in the 1930s, why is the entire world economy dragging along from year to year in unending depression? And if the economy isn't curing itself, said Keynes, government intervention is in order.

Keynesian Economics

Economics is the painful elaboration of the obvious.
—Anonymous

John Maynard Keynes wrote his landmark work *The General Theory of Employment, Interest, and Money* during the depths of the Great Depression. While President Herbert Hoover (perhaps the last political leader to uphold the theories of classical economics) was telling everyone who would listen that recovery was just around the corner, things were going from bad to worse. As the unemployment rate mounted, production plummeted, and soup kitchens proliferated, more and more Americans demanded that the federal government do something. When Franklin Roosevelt defeated Hoover by a landslide in 1932, he had a mandate for the government to do whatever was necessary to bring about recovery.

Keynes: The problem with recessions is inadequate aggregate demand.

Keynes provided a blueprint. The problem, he said, was inadequate aggregate demand. People were just not buying enough goods and services to employ the entire labor force. In fact, aggregate demand was so low that only the government could spend enough money to provide a sufficient boost.

Keynes defined aggregate demand as consumer spending, investment spending, and government spending (plus net exports, which at that time were negligible). Consumption is a function of disposable income. When disposable income is low, said Keynes, consumption is low. This was the problem Americans were having during the Great Depression.

The cure for recession is government spending.

Investment, which is largely a function of the marginal efficiency of investment, or the expected profit rate, was also very low during the Depression. So we could not hope that an upturn in investment would lead the way out of the Depression. The only hope was for the government to spend enough money to raise aggregate demand sufficiently to get people back to work.

What type of spending was necessary? Any kind, said Keynes. Quantity is much more relevant than quality. Even if the government employed some people to dig holes, said Keynes, and others to fill up those holes, it would still be able to spend the country out of these economic woes.

Where would the government get the money? There were two choices: print it or borrow it. If the government printed it, wouldn't that cause inflation? Keynes thought this unlikely; during the Depression, the country had been experiencing *de*flation, or falling prices. Who would even think of raising prices when he was having trouble finding customers?

In a campaign speech in Brooklyn in the fall of 1932, Roosevelt castigated Hoover for not balancing his budget.

What about budget deficits? Nothing improper about these, said Keynes. Although the common wisdom of the times was that the government must balance its budget, there was absolutely nothing wrong with deficits during recessions and depressions. It was necessary to prime the pump by sucking up the idle savings that businesses were not borrowing and using those funds to get the economy moving again.

Once government spending was under way, people would have some money in their pockets. And what would they do with that money? You guessed it—they'd spend it. This money would then end up in other people's pockets, and they, in turn, would spend it once again.

That money would continue to be spent again and again, putting more and more people back to work. In the process, the deficit would melt away. The government could cut back on its spending programs while tax receipts swelled, so we could view the budget deficits as a temporary expedient to get the economy off dead center.

But what of the classical automatic mechanism that ensured that the economy always moved toward full employment? In the long run, Keynes conceded, maybe it really did work. But in the long run, noted Keynes, "we are all dead."

Why invest in new plant and equipment when most of your capacity is idle?

Why didn't the classical mechanism work in the short run? Keynes observed that interest rates fell to about 2 percent during the Great Depression, but business firms still were not borrowing all that much to build new plant and equipment. After all, who in his right mind would invest in new plant and equipment when his factory was operating at only 30 or 40 percent of capacity? Besides, said Keynes, at an interest rate of 2 percent, many people would not be willing to lend out their savings. Why tie them up at such a low interest rate? Why not just sit on this money until interest rates rose again?

So much for the interest rate mechanism. With respect to downwardly flexible wages and prices, there were institutional barriers. Labor unions would oppose lowered wage rates, while highly concentrated industries would tend to prefer output decreases to price cuts during recessions.

If M rises, what if people don't spend additional money, but just hold it?

Keynes also raised some objections to the quantity theory of money. Most significant, he asked what would happen to the money that would be printed if the government did increase the money supply. The classicals had assumed it would be spent, thus pushing up the price level. This could happen, conceded Keynes, but during a bad recession perhaps people would just hold their money, waiting for interest rates to rise before they lent it out.

Wouldn't they spend it, as the classicals suggested? Poor people would. But if they were poor, what would they be doing with money in the first place? If the money supply were increased during a bad recession, said Keynes, that money would simply be held as idle cash balances by relatively well-to-do people. Nothing would happen to the money until the economy was well on its way toward recovery, interest rates rose, and more investment opportunities became available.

By the mid-1930s the classical school of economics had lost most of its adherents. Not everyone became a Keynesian. Conservative economists in particular could never fully reconcile themselves to the vastly increased economic role that the Keynesians awarded to the federal government. In fact, the remaining economic schools to be considered here—the monetarists, the supply-siders, and the rational expectationists—would all rail against the evils of big government.

Is Keynesian economics valid just during recessions?

But big government was here to stay. Although the massive spending programs of Franklin Roosevelt's New Deal did not get the country out of the Depression, the much bigger defense spending during World War II certainly did. There was no question that Keynes had been right, but since the war Americans had been plagued not just by periodic recessions but by almost unending inflation. There was growing feeling among the populace as well as professional economists that perhaps Keynesian economics was just recession and depression economics, that it could not satisfactorily deal with curbing inflation.

Keynesian economics may have reached its high point in 1964, when personal income tax rates were cut by about 20 percent. This tax cut, combined with accelerating military spending during the country's escalating involvement in the Vietnam War, brought about a rapid rate of economic growth in the mid- to late 1960s; but this growth was accompanied by increasing inflation, which reached double-digit proportions in the early 1970s. By the time President Richard Nixon proclaimed, "We are all Keynesians now," this school of economics had already been receiving a lot of bad press. In the 1970s being a Keynesian was out; to be in, you had to be a monetarist.

The Monetarist School

The Importance of the Rate of Monetary Growth

Monetarism begins and ends with one obsession: the rate of growth of the money supply. According to monetarists, most of our major economic problems, especially inflation and recession, are due to the Federal Reserve's mismanagement of our rate of monetary growth.

Milton Friedman, an economist who did exhaustive studies of the relationship between the rate of growth of the money supply and the rate of increase in prices, reached a couple of not surprising conclusions. First, the United States has never had a serious inflation that was not accompanied by rapid monetary growth. Second, when the money supply has grown slowly, the country has had no inflation.

In a study of the monetary history of the United States during the period of nearly a century after the Civil War, Friedman and his longtime collaborator Anna Jacobson Schwartz reached this conclusion: "Changes in the behavior of the money stock have been closely associated with changes in economic activity, money income, and prices."[2] Once again, the answer to all important economic questions is the rate of growth of the money supply.

Building on the quantity theory of money, the monetarists agreed with the classicals that when the money supply grows, the price level rises, albeit not at exactly the same rate. But they refuted Keynes's argument that if the money supply were raised during a recession, people might just hold on to these added funds. Like the classicals, the monetarists assumed that to get it is to spend it—not necessarily on consumer goods, but on stocks, bonds, real estate, and other noncash assets.

If people *did* spend this additional money, the prices of what they bought would be bid up. In other words, the monetarists were saying that the quantity theory basically holds true.

So far, so good. Now for recessions. What causes them? When the Federal Reserve increases the money supply at less than the rate needed by business—say, anything less than 3 percent a year—the economy is headed for trouble. Sometimes, in fact, the Fed does not let it grow at all and may even cause it to shrink slightly.

By and large the facts have borne out the monetarists' analysis. Without a steady increase in the money supply of at least 3 percent a year, there is a high likelihood of a recession.

The Basic Propositions of Monetarism

(1) The Key to Stable Economic Growth Is a Constant Rate of Increase in the Money Supply

Has our economic history been one of stable growth? No inflation? No recessions? Since World War II alone, we've had at least four waves of inflation and 10 recessions.

The monetarists place almost the entire blame on the Federal Reserve Board of Governors. If only they had been increasing the money supply by a steady 3 percent a year, we could have avoided most of this instability.

Let's trace the monetarist reasoning by analyzing the Fed's actions over the course of a business cycle. As a recession sets in, the Fed increases the rate of growth of the money supply. This stimulates output in the short run, helping to pull the economy out of the recession. In the long run, however, this expanded money supply causes inflation. So what does the Fed do? It slams on the monetary brakes, slowing the rate of growth in the money supply. This brings on a recession. And what does the Fed do in response? It increases the rate of monetary growth.

---

[2]Milton Friedman and Anna Jacobson Schwartz, *A Monetary History of the United States, 1867–1960* (Princeton, NJ: Princeton University Press, 1971), p. 676.

Stop-go monetary policy

"Is this stop-go, stop-go monetary policy any way to run an economy?" ask the monetarists. This type of policy inspires about as much confidence as the student driver approaching a red light. First he hits the brakes about 100 yards from the corner. Then, overcompensating for his error, he hits the accelerator much too hard. When the car shoots forward, he hits the brakes again, bringing the car to a dead stop about 50 yards from the corner. Then he repeats the whole process.

In the first half of the 1940s, the Fed helped finance the huge increase in the national debt (incurred by World War II) by pumping up the money supply by tens of billions of dollars. The 1950s, however, were a time of tight money, marked, incidentally, by three recessions.

In the late 1960s, an accelerating rate of monetary growth was accompanied by a rising rate of inflation, which, in the early 1970s, reached double-digit proportions. In 1973 the Federal Reserve Board put on the brakes, and we went into the worst recession we had suffered since World War II. In 1975 the Fed eased up and we recovered. Then, in late 1979, the brakes were applied. The prime rate of interest soared to more than 20 percent, and in January 1980 we went into a sharp six-month recession. What happened next? You guessed it. The Fed eased up again. Interest rates came down, and economic recovery set in. But in 1981 the Fed, alarmed at the rising inflation rate, stepped on the monetary brakes, and we entered still another recession in August 1981. The prime once again soared to more than 20 percent. This recession proved even deeper than that of 1973–75. In summer 1982 the Fed saw no course but to ease up on the brakes; sure enough, by November of that year the recession had ended.

(2) Expansionary Monetary Policy Will Only Temporarily Depress Interest Rates

In the short run, when the Fed increases the rate of monetary growth, interest rates decline. If the interest rate is the price of money, it follows that if the money supply is increased and there is no change in the demand for money, then its price (the interest rate) will decline.

In the long run, a rise in M pushes up inflation and interest rates.

The monetarists tell us that in the long run an increase in monetary growth will not lower interest rates; the increased money supply causes inflation. Lenders will demand higher interest rates to compensate them for being repaid in inflated dollars.

Let's say, for example, there's no inflation and the interest rate is 5 percent. This is the real rate of interest. The rate of inflation then rises to 8 percent; that means if it cost you $10,000 to live last year, your cost of living is now $10,800. If lenders can anticipate the rate of inflation, they will insist that they be paid not just for the real interest rate of 5 percent but also for the anticipated inflation of 8 percent. This raises the interest rate from 5 percent to a nominal rate of 13 percent.

When the Federal Reserve allows the money supply to grow quickly, interest rates are kept down for a while until lenders realize the rate of inflation (caused by faster monetary growth) is rising. They will then demand higher interest rates. Thus, a higher rate of monetary growth in the short run will keep interest rates low, but in the long run it will lead to higher interest rates.

(3) Expansionary Monetary Policy Will Only Temporarily Reduce the Unemployment Rate

The first two basic propositions partially explain the third. First, when monetary growth speeds up, output is expanded, but in the long run only prices will rise. Because rising output would lower the unemployment rate, in the short run unemployment is reduced. But in the long run, an increase in the rate of monetary growth will raise prices, not output, so the unemployment rate will go back up. We'll come back to why this happens.

The second basic proposition states that expansionary monetary policy only temporarily depresses interest rates. In the short run, more money means lower interest rates. These lower interest rates encourage more investment and, consequently, less unemployment.

But in the long run the added money in circulation causes inflation, which, in turn, raises interest rates. As interest rates rise, investment declines and the unemployment rate goes back up.

The monetarists have explained the temporary reduction in the unemployment rate more directly. As labor union members begin to anticipate inflation, they will demand higher wage rates. New labor contract settlements will reflect the higher cost of living, but these higher wage settlements will price some workers out of the market, thus raising the unemployment rate.

(4) Expansionary Fiscal Policy Will Only Temporarily Raise Output and Employment   Here we have another conflict—this time a basic one—between the monetarists and the Keynesians. The Keynesians believe fiscal policy, particularly heavy government spending, will pull us out of a recession. But how is this spending going to be financed? By borrowing. The Treasury goes into the market for loanable funds and borrows hundreds of billions of dollars to finance the deficit.

Crowding-out effect

The monetarists point out that such huge government borrowing comes directly into conflict with that of business firms and consumers. Not only will it be harder for these groups to borrow, but interest rates will be driven up. This crowding-out effect represents, according to the monetarists, a substitution of public for private spending. All we're really doing is spending more on government goods and services and less on consumer and investment goods and services. Aggregate demand is not increased.

How well would a budget surplus restrain inflation? Not very, say the monetarists. The Treasury would not be borrowing now, but rather repaying part of the national debt, which would tend to push down interest rates and make borrowing easier. Private borrowing would replace public borrowing. The hoped-for restraint would not materialize because private borrowers would now be spending these borrowed funds on goods and services. In effect, then, we would still have the same level of spending.

The Monetary Rule

Increase the money supply at a constant rate.

The policy prescription of the monetarists is simply to increase the money supply at a constant rate. When there is a recession, this steady infusion of money will pick up the economy. When there is inflation, a steady rate of monetary growth will slow it down.

You might ask why the money supply should be increased at all during inflation. There are two answers. First, the monetarists would tell you that if we didn't increase the money supply at all, we would be going back to the old, failed discretionary monetary policies of the past—the start-and-stop, start-and-stop policies that only made the business cycle worse. Second, over the long run the economy does need a steady infusion of money to enable economic growth.

The monetarists' steady monetary growth prescription is analogous to the feeding policy of the American Army. Every day, in every part of the world, at every meal, the soldiers walk along the chow line and receive, in addition to the main course and dessert, two pieces of white bread, two pats of butter, and one pint of whole milk. The main course is also dished out in equal portions. The food servers do not dole out portions whose sizes vary with that of the eater. They look from the serving pan to the eater's tray, slopping out serving spoonfuls of whatever it is that the Army decided to cook that day.

So, we have a 6-foot 6-inch 300-pound person getting the same size portion as does a 5-foot 6-inch 130-pound person. My theory is that the Army wants everyone to be the same size—a theory that seems to be borne out by the single uniform size that is issued. If everyone eats the same portion, presumably they will all end up this same size.

Perhaps the monetarists got the idea of increasing the money supply by a constant percentage by observing Army chow lines. They believe our economic health will be relatively good—if not always excellent—if we have a steady diet of money. No starts and stops, no extreme ups and downs, and, to complete the analogy, no very fat years and no very lean years.

The Decline of Monetarism

It's interesting that when the Fed really began to pay attention to what the monetarists were saying, this may have led to the ultimate decline of the monetarists. In October 1979

Federal Reserve chairman Paul Volcker announced a major policy shift. No longer would the Fed focus only on keeping interest rates on an even keel. From now on the Fed would set monetary growth targets and stick to them.

This new policy was followed for most of the next three years. The double-digit inflation that prevailed in 1979 and 1980 was finally brought under control by late 1982—but not until we had gone through a period of sky-high interest rates, very high unemployment, and two recessions.

Even though the Fed had finally followed the advice of the monetarists—at least to a large degree—and even though the nagging inflation of the last 15 years had finally been wrung out of the economy, people began to look elsewhere for their economic gurus. They looked to the White House, which had become a stronghold of the latest school of economics, the supply-side school.

Supply-Side Economics

Cut tax rates, government spending, and government regulation.

Supply-side economics came into vogue in the early 1980s when Ronald Reagan assumed the presidency. Supply-siders felt that the economic role of the federal government had grown much too large and that high tax rates and onerous government rules and regulations were hurting the incentives of individuals and business firms to produce goods and services. President Reagan suggested a simple solution: get the government off the backs of the American people. How? By cutting taxes and reducing government spending and regulation.

Raise aggregate supply.

The objective of supply-side economics, then, is to raise aggregate supply, the total amount of goods and services the country produces. The problem, said the supply-siders, is that high tax rates are hurting the incentive to work and to invest. All the government needs to do is cut tax rates, and voilà: up goes production.

Many of the undesirable side effects of high marginal tax rates are explained by the work effect, the savings and investment effect, and the elimination of productive market exchanges, which we shall take up in turn.

The Work Effect

Work–leisure decisions

People are often confronted with work–leisure decisions. Should I put in that extra couple of hours of overtime? Should I take on a second job? Should I keep my store open longer hours? If you answer yes to any of these, you'll have to give the government a pretty big slice of that extra income. At some point you may well conclude, "I'd have to be nuts to take on any extra work; I'd only be working for the government."

At what point do you start working for the government? When it takes 20 cents out of each dollar of extra income (a marginal tax rate of 20 percent)? When it takes 30 cents? Or 40 cents? Each of us makes his or her own decision about the cutoff point. If you are a wage-earner, you will have to pay Social Security tax, federal income tax, and, possibly, some state income tax. Back in 1980, before the passage of the Kemp-Roth tax cut and the tax cuts that came under the Tax Reform Act of 1986, people earning more than $50,000 a year often had marginal tax rates of more than 50 percent.[3] If you paid more than half of your overtime earnings in taxes, would *you* consider yourself to be working for the government?

Why work if the government gets most of your money?

Facing high marginal tax rates, many people refuse to work more than a certain number of hours of overtime or take on second jobs and other forms of extra work. Instead, they opt for more leisure time. In sum, high marginal tax rates rob people not only of some potential income but of the incentive to work longer hours. People working shorter hours obviously produce less, so total output is lower than it might have been with lower

---

[3]Under Kemp-Roth, personal income taxes were slashed 23 percent between 1981 and 1984. The top marginal tax rate was cut from 70 percent to 50 percent. Personal income tax rates were cut further under the Tax Reform Act of 1986 to marginal rates of 28 and 15 percent.

marginal tax rates. This and the saving-investment argument (considered next) are the two key points made by supply-siders for lower marginal tax rates.

The Saving and Investment Effect

High marginal tax rates discourage working, saving, and investing.

The supply-side economists really make two arguments against high marginal tax rates. The first is the work effect. Next is the saving and investment effect. When people save money, they earn interest on their savings. But a high marginal tax rate on interest income will provide a disincentive to save, or at least to make savings available for investment purposes.

Similarly, people who borrow money for investment purposes—new plant and equipment and inventory—hope that this will lead to greater profits. But if those profits are subject to a high marginal tax rate, once again there is a disincentive to invest.[4]

If people are discouraged from working, total output will be reduced. And if they are discouraged from saving and investing, the economy will be stagnant. Supply-side economists point to the economic stagnation of the late 1970s and early 1980s as proof of the basic propositions of their theory. On the other hand, the economic record during the Reagan years, particularly with respect to saving, investment, and economic growth, was nothing to write home about either.

The Elimination of Productive Market Exchanges

Most people have jobs at which they are good; an accountant, a carpenter, an automobile mechanic, and a gourmet chef are all relatively good at their professions. That's probably why they chose those lines of work to begin with—and all that on-the-job training didn't hurt either.

When you need your taxes prepared—especially if you stand to save several thousand dollars—you go to an accountant. When you need your transmission fixed, unless you're a skilled mechanic, you'll certainly be better off going to someone who is. In fact, one of the main reasons our standard of living is so high in the United States is because a large proportion of our labor force is composed of individuals with specialized skills.

What happens when your roof must be reshingled? Do you hire a roofer, or do you do it yourself? Do you do it yourself because it's cheaper?

Well, maybe it's cheaper and maybe it isn't. Suppose you can reshingle your roof in 100 hours and a roofer can do the job in 60 hours. If the roofer charges you $12 an hour (in addition to materials), it will cost you $720. How many hours would you have to work to earn $720? Suppose your clerical job pays $9 an hour and you are in the 40 percent marginal tax bracket. You take home only $5.40 an hour (that is, 60 percent of $9).

Do you hire the roofer or do it yourself? If you do it yourself, it will take you 100 hours. If you hire the roofer, you must pay him $720. How many hours would you have to work to bring home $720? Figure it out: $720/$5.40 = 133⅓ hours. I think even *I* would rather spend 100 hours on my roof than 133⅓ hours in front of a class. And I'm afraid of heights!

High tax rates discourage productive market exchanges.

There is a serious misallocation of labor when the productive market exchange— your clerical work for your roofer's labor—is eliminated; but because of the high marginal tax rate, it pays for you to work less at your regular job (at which you are presumably good) and more at household tasks (at which you are not so good). When you add up all the productive market exchanges short-circuited by high marginal tax rates, you may well be talking about hundreds of billions of dollars in misallocated resources.

The Laffer Curve

Policy prescription: Cut taxes!

Supply-side economists have one basic policy prescription: Cut tax rates! This will raise output. However, there *is* one slight problem. Won't federal tax revenue fall

---

[4]Under the Tax Reform Act of 1986, the basic corporate income tax rate was reduced from 46 percent to 34 percent.

The Laffer curve

Arthur Laffer, American economist
(Collections of the Library of Congress)

precipitously? Some supply-side economists feel this would not be an altogether bad idea. After all, the more the federal government takes in, the more it spends. All the Democrats did, they argue, was "tax, tax, tax, spend, spend, spend." But Arthur Laffer, an orthodox supply-side economics professor, said it isn't necessarily true that a tax rate cut will lead to a fall in tax revenue. *Au contraire.* (That's French for "just the opposite.")

Imagine that we're at point A on the Laffer curve drawn in Figure 3. We cut the marginal tax rate from 50 percent to 40 percent, and lo and behold, tax revenue rises from $1,200 billion to nearly $1,400 billion. Is this sophistry? (That's Greek for "pulling a fast one.")

Let's see how this works by looking at the case of a specific individual. Suppose this person pays $50,000 on an income of $100,000. If this person's tax rate were lowered to 40 percent, she would pay $40,000. Right? Wrong, say the supply-siders. She would now have an incentive to work harder. How much harder? Hard enough, say, to earn $130,000 by working every available hour of overtime or taking on a second job.

How much is 40 percent of $130,000? It comes out to exactly $52,000. How much did the government collect from her before the tax cut? Only $50,000. So by cutting tax rates, say the supply-siders, the government will end up collecting more revenue.

Is this true? If we look at the Laffer curve, it appears to be—at least at very high tax rates. But when the government cut tax rates in 1981 and 1982, tax revenue actually declined. Of course, there was a recession going on.

What if we were at, say, point C on the Laffer curve and we cut tax rates? What would happen to federal tax revenue? Obviously, it would decline.

The problem, then, is to figure out where we are on the Laffer curve, or what the parameters of the curve itself are, before we start cutting taxes. There really *is* a Laffer curve out there. The trouble is we don't know exactly where, so when we try to use it as a policy tool, it's kind of like playing an economic version of pin the tail on the donkey. When you play a game blindfolded, you run the risk of looking a lot like the six-year-old kids who miss the donkey completely. And this game is for somewhat higher stakes.

During the last two years of the Reagan administration, it had become apparent that supply-side economics was an idea whose time had gone. Although inflation had been brought under control and interest rates had declined as well (largely because of the efforts of the Federal Reserve), the supply-side policies had not yielded the rapid rate of

Figure 3   The Laffer Curve

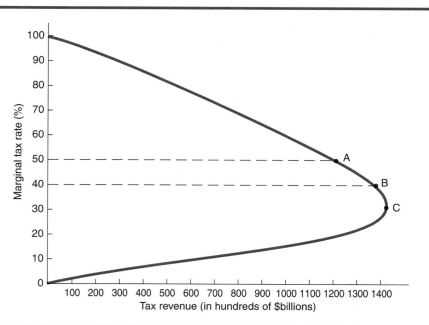

economic growth that the public had been led to expect. Perhaps the greatest legacies of supply-side economics were huge budget deficits and a monumental national debt.

Before we bury supply-side economics, we might note that in 1995 the new Republican congressional majority, in its quest to cut taxes and the federal budget deficit simultaneously, embraced a new term, "dynamic scoring." And what, exactly, is dynamic scoring? Apparently, it is a new term for the Laffer curve. If it yields the same results in the late 1990s as it did through the 1980s, then we can look forward to a rising tide of budgetary red ink.

In any case, after the Reagan years, conservative economists, many of whom had never been entirely comfortable with supply-side economics, had yet another banner to rally round. This one was called rational expectations.

Rational Expectations Theory

Most economists agree on two sets of policies.

Whatever else you have learned about economic policy, you have certainly learned that economists don't all agree on what policies we should follow. Nevertheless, with certain notable exceptions, most economists today would more or less agree on two sets of policies. To fight inflation, you want to lower the rate of growth of the money supply and reduce federal government budget deficits. And to fight recessions, you want to do the opposite: increase the rate of growth of the money supply and increase the size of the deficits. Although some economists would only partially acquiesce to these policies, there has been a greater consensus for these stated policies than for any others.

You probably never saw *Monty Python and the Holy Grail,* but in that movie there was a group of knights who distinguished themselves solely by saying "Neee." No matter what questions they were asked, they would always answer "Neee." Assuming "Neee" was Middle English for nay or no, those knights were the rational expectations theorists, or the new classical economists of their day.

Like the "old" classical economists, today's rational expectationists say no to any form of government economic intervention. Such intervention, no matter how well intentioned, would do a lot more harm than good. In fact, they maintain that anti-inflationary and antirecessionary policies, at best, would have no effect whatsoever. More likely, say the new classical economists, these policies would end up making things worse.

The view of Robert Lucas

Robert Lucas of the University of Chicago, a 1995 Nobel Prize–winner, is clearly top gun among the new classical economists. Lucas believes that people can anticipate government policies to fight inflation and recession, given their knowledge of policy, past experience, and expectations about the future. Consequently, they act on this anticipation, effectively nullifying the intended effects of those policies. What, then, should the government do? It should follow strict guidelines rather than try to use discretionary policy to tinker with the economy.

The three assumptions of rational expectations theory

Rational expectations theory is based on three assumptions: (1) that individuals and business firms learn through experience to anticipate the consequences of changes in monetary and fiscal policy; (2) that they act instantaneously to protect their economic interests; and (3) that all resource and product markets are purely competitive.

Now we'll translate. Imagine the Federal Reserve decides to increase the money supply's rate of growth sharply. Why would the Fed do this? To stimulate output and raise employment.

The scenario, according to the Fed, would be as follows: (1) the money supply rises; (2) business firms order more plant and equipment and more inventory; (3) more jobs are created and output rises; (4) wages do not rise right away, but prices do; (5) because prices rise and wages stay the same, profits rise; (6) eventually wages catch up to prices, profits go back down, and the expansion comes to an end.

This may have happened in the old days, say the rational expectations theorists, but surely people have learned something from all this experience. Everybody knows that when the Fed sharply increases the monetary growth rate, inflation will result. Business firms, of course, will raise prices. But what about labor? Anticipating the expected inflation, wage-earners will demand wage increases *now*. No more playing catch-up after the cost of living has already risen.

If wage rates are increased along with prices, do profits increase? No! If profits are not rising, there goes the main reason for increasing output and hiring more people—which, of course, was why the rate of monetary growth was raised in the first place.

Let's return to the rational expectations theorists' three assumptions. The first one is plausible enough—that through experience, we learn to anticipate the consequences of changes in monetary and fiscal policy. So, if a sharp increase in the rate of growth of the money supply always leads to inflation, eventually we will all learn to recognize this pattern. (See the box "Rational Expectations versus Adaptive Expectations.")

It would follow from the next two assumptions that the intended results of macroeconomic policy shifts will be completely frustrated. Why? If you knew that prices would be increasing, would you be willing to sit back and passively accept a decline in your standard of living? Wouldn't you demand a higher wage rate to keep pace with rising prices? The rational expectations theorists say people can always be expected to promote their personal economic interests, and furthermore, in a purely competitive market, they are free to do so.

In a purely competitive labor market, workers are free to leave one employer for another who offers higher wages. In a purely competitive products market, all firms are subject to the law of supply and demand, and will automatically pass along any wage increases in the form of higher prices.

Most macroeconomic policy changes are predictable.

Most macroeconomic policy changes, say the rational expectations theorists, are readily predictable. When there's inflation, there are extended debates in Congress, demands for cuts in government spending and tax increases, and a slowdown in the rate of monetary growth. Both Congress and the Federal Reserve generally telegraph policy moves, often months in advance. The point is that when these moves are made, no one is surprised. And because the public anticipates these policy changes, their intended effects

ADVANCED WORK

Rational Expectations versus Adaptive Expectations

How do we predict the future? The simplest way is to assume that past trends will continue. The *adaptive expectations hypothesis* is based on the assumption that the best indicator of the future is what happened in the past.

Suppose the price level has been rising at an annual rate of 6 percent for the last three years. Under adaptive expectations, people will expect prices to rise about 6 percent in year 4. Now let's add a wrinkle. Suppose that in year 4 the rate of inflation rises to 9 percent. So what rate of inflation do people now predict for year 5? They predict 9 percent. Well, suppose that in year 5 it rises to 14 percent. What will everyone predict for year 6? Fourteen percent? Fine. Except that in year 6 it goes down to 10 percent. So for year 7 everyone predicts 10 percent. But in year 7 the inflation rate falls to just 5 percent.

Under adaptive expectations, forecasts of the future rate of inflation may be right on the money, but they may also exhibit systematic error. When inflation is accelerating, forecasts will tend to be too low. And when inflation is decelerating (i.e., disinflation is taking place), then forecasts will tend to be too high.

The *rational expectations hypothesis* makes the assumption that people do not keep making the same mistakes over and over again when predicting future events. After getting burned once or twice, they do not systematically keep assuming that past trends will necessarily continue into the future.

The rational expectations hypothesis assumes that future expectations are based not just on past trends but on an understanding of how the economy works. For example, to form their expectation of the inflation rate, decision makers will use all available information, including past inflation rates, the impact of expected policy actions, and their knowledge of macroeconomic relationships within our economy.

So which hypothesis is right—rational expectations or adaptive expectations? To the degree that people have a sense of how our economy operates—and to the degree that they don't just blindly assume that past trends will continue into the future—the rational expectations hypothesis appears to have greater validity. But it falls far short of its adherents' claim that it is so powerful that it nullifies discretionary monetary and fiscal policy.

are canceled out by the actions taken by individuals and business firms to protect their economic interests. In the case of policies aimed at raising output and employment, all the government gets for its efforts is more inflation.

What should the government do?

What should the government do? It should do, say the rational expectations theorists, as little as possible. Like the classical economists, they believe the more the government tries to be an economic stabilizing force, the more it will destabilize the economy.

Basically, then, the federal government should figure out the right policies to follow and stick to them. What *are* the right policies? Funny you should ask. As you might expect, they've taken up the conservative economists' agenda: (1) steady monetary growth of 3 to 4 percent a year (the monetarists' monetary rule) and (2) a balanced budget (favored by the classical economists, among others).

Criticism of the rational expectations school

Like every other school of economics, the rational expectations school has certainly received its share of criticism. In fact, only a small minority of economists today would consider themselves new classical economists, mainly because this group just goes too far in ascribing rationality to both the general population and themselves.

Is it reasonable to expect individuals and business firms to predict the consequences of macroeconomic policy changes correctly when economists themselves come up with widely varying predictions, most of which are wrong? Economists place little faith in each other's rationality; is it rational for them to ascribe a greater prescience to the general population than they give themselves?

In a world of constant change, is it possible for people to accurately predict the economic consequences of policy changes? Indeed, when a continually changing cast of policy makers, each with his or her own economic agenda, seems to be calling for entirely new economic approaches every few years, it's awfully hard to tell the players without a scorecard—it's even harder to predict the final score.

A second criticism of the rational expectations school is that our economic markets are not purely competitive; some are not competitive at all. Labor unions are not an economist's idea of purely competitive labor market institutions. Nor would industries such as those that produce automobiles, petroleum, cigarettes, and breakfast cereals, each of which has just a handful of firms doing most of the producing, be considered very competitive.

Finally, critics raise the question of the rigidities imposed by contracts. The labor union with the two- or three-year contract cannot reopen bargaining with employers when greater inflation is anticipated because of a suddenly expansionary monetary policy. Nor can business firms that have long-term contracts with customers decide to charge higher prices because they perceive more inflation in the future.

An economist is someone who cannot see something working in practice without asking whether it would work in theory.
—Anonymous

Should we summarily dismiss the rational expectations school because it is so vulnerable to criticism? Most economists would probably concede that this school is correct in calling their attention to how expectations may affect the outcome of macroeconomic policy changes. In recent years, then, economists have become more aware that to the degree policy changes are predictable, people will certainly act to protect their economic interests. Because they will succeed to some degree, they will partially counteract the effect of the government's macroeconomic policy.

In other words, rational expectations theory has a certain validity, as do each of the other theories we discussed. The question we're left with is: How valid is each theory relative to each of the others? Perhaps this question is answered by the first and second laws of economics:

The First Law of Economics: For every economist, there exists an equal and opposite economist.

The Second Law of Economics: They're both wrong.

Conclusion

What policies should we follow?

What policies *should* we follow? Classical economists subscribed to Thomas Jefferson's dictum "The government that governs best, governs least." Because recessions will cure themselves, said the classicals, the government should adhere to a laissez-faire policy, allowing the private economic system to function without interference.

The Keynesians stress fiscal policy. During recessions, run federal budget deficits; during inflations, run surpluses. Monetary policy? The latter-day Keynesians conceded that an expansionary monetary policy would be helpful, but Keynesian economics has always stressed the primacy of fiscal policy.

The supply-side school, sometimes considered the flip side of the Keynesian school, stresses the importance of tax rate cuts to give people greater work incentives. Although supply-siders basically believe in balanced budgets, temporary deficits are justified as unfortunate by-products of the tax rate cuts.

The monetarists want rules—a 3 to 4 percent rate of monetary growth and balanced budgets. Why? Because we simply don't know enough about the workings of our economy to successfully practice discretionary macroeconomic policy.

Finally, we have the new classical economists, who believe macroeconomic stabilization policy is self-defeating because people not only anticipate government actions, they also protect their own economic interests so that the intended effects of the government policy are immediately and fully canceled out.

Murray Weidenbaum, who served as chairman of President Reagan's Council of Economic Advisors, puts a lot of what we've been talking about in this chapter into perspective:

> Each of the major schools of economic thought can be useful on occasion. The insights of Keynesian economics proved appropriate for Western societies attempting to get out of deep depression in the 1930s. The tools of monetarism were powerfully effective in squeezing out the inflationary force of the 1970s. Supply-side economics played an important role in getting the public to understand the high costs of taxation and thus to support tax reform in the 1980s. But sensible public policy cannot long focus on any one objective or be limited to one policy approach.[5]

Where does all of this leave us? It leaves us just about where we were at the beginning of this chapter: about the only thing economists can agree on is that they disagree.

Don't despair. After the great debate between the monetarists and the Keynesians in the appendix to this chapter, I'll try to tie things together in the next chapter on macroeconomic policy. I'll attempt to draw on the collective wisdom of the five schools of economics to attain the oft-stated goals of stable prices, high employment, and a satisfactory rate of economic growth.

Despite the fact that he [Labor Secretary John Dunlop] is an economist, basically I have great confidence in him.

—George Meany

Economics is the only field in which two people can share a Nobel Prize for saying opposing things.

—Roberto Alazar

Questions for Further Thought and Discussion

1. According to the classical economists, how did Say's law, the interest rate mechanism, and downwardly flexible wages and prices ensure that recessions would cure themselves?

2. According to John Maynard Keynes, what was the basic problem during recessions, and what was its solution?

3. What is the monetary rule and why is it favored by the monetarists?

4. What is the Laffer curve? How do supply-siders use it with respect to tax rates?

5. What are the three basic assumptions of the rational expectations theorists? Are they valid?

---

[5]Murray Weidenbaum, *Rendezvous with Reality* (New York: Basic Books, 1988), p. 23.

WORKBOOK FOR CHAPTER 14

Name _____ Date _____

Multiple-Choice Questions

Circle the letter that corresponds to the best answer.

1. Say's law states that
   a. supply creates its own demand   b. demand creates its own supply   c. demand will always exceed supply   d. supply will always exceed demand

2. The bible of classical economics was written by
   a. John Maynard Keynes   b. Milton Friedman
   c. Karl Marx   d. Adam Smith

3. According to the classical economists, if the quantity of money that people wanted to save was greater than the amount that people wanted to invest,
   a. there would be a recession   b. there would be inflation   c. the interest rate would fall   d. the interest rate would rise

4. The classical economists believed
   a. both wages and prices were downwardly flexible
   b. neither wages nor prices were downwardly flexible
   c. wages, but not prices, were downwardly flexible
   d. prices, but not wages, were downwardly flexible

5. The classicals believed recessions were
   a. impossible   b. potential depressions
   c. temporary   d. hard to end without government intervention

6. The problem during recessions, said John Maynard Keynes, was
   a. inadequate aggregate supply   b. inadequate aggregate demand   c. too much inflation   d. too much government intervention

7. According to Keynes, _____ was necessary to get us out of a depression.
   a. investment spending   b. consumer spending
   c. foreign spending   d. any kind of spending

8. Keynes believed budget deficits were
   a. to be avoided at all costs   b. bad during recessions   c. good during recessions   d. good all the time

9. The key to investment spending, said Keynes, was
   a. the interest rate   b. the expected profit rate
   c. foreign spending   d. government spending

10. Classical economics lost most of its popularity in
    a. the 1920s   b. the 1930s   c. the 1960s
    d. the 1980s

11. Big government was ushered in during the
    a. 1920s   b. 1930s   c. 1960s   d. 1980s

12. To the monetarists, the most important thing was
    a. the rate of growth of the money supply
    b. balancing the federal budget   c. raising the federal government's tax base   d. giving the Federal Reserve free reign

13. During a recession, if the money supply were increased,
    a. the Keynesians and the monetarists agree that people would probably just hold on to these funds
    b. the Keynesians and the monetarists agree that people would spend this money on assets of one kind or another
    c. the Keynesians believe people would probably just hold on to these funds, while the monetarists believe people would spend this money on assets of one kind or another

14. Which of the following is a basic proposition of monetarism?
    a. The key to stable economic growth is a constant rate of increase in the money supply.   b. Expansionary monetary policy will permanently depress the interest rates.   c. Expansionary monetary policy will permanently reduce the unemployment rate.

d. Expansionary fiscal policy will permanently raise output and employment.

15. The monetary rule states that

   a. the federal budget must be balanced every year
   b. the money supply must increase at the same rate as the price level   **c.** the money supply must remain a constant from year to year   **d.** the money supply must be increased at a constant rate

16. The monetarists criticized

   a. the stop-and-go policies of the Federal Reserve
   b. the ineffectiveness of monetary policy at fighting inflation   **c.** the importance given to money by the Keynesians   **d.** the Fed for keeping a heavy foot on the monetary brake and allowing the money supply to rise by only 3 percent a year

17. Supply-siders felt

   a. the federal government played too large an economic role   **b.** the federal government played too small an economic role   **c.** tax rates were too low   **d.** the federal government was not spending enough to meet the needs of the poor

18. According to the supply-siders, each of the following resulted from high marginal tax rates except

   a. the work effect   **b.** the savings-investment effect
   c. the elimination of productive market exchanges
   d. lagging demand for imported goods and services

19. Each of the following is associated with supply-side economics except

   a. Ronald Reagan   **b.** Arthur Laffer   **c.** Milton Friedman   **d.** Kemp-Roth

20. According to the Laffer curve, when very high marginal tax rates are lowered, tax revenue will

   a. decline considerably   **b.** decline slightly
   c. stay the same   **d.** increase

21. The rational expectations theorists said anti-inflationary policy will

   a. generally work   **b.** definitely do more harm than good   **c.** either do no good or do harm

22. According to the rational expectations theorists, everyone learns that when the Fed sharply increases monetary growth,

   a. inflation will result and people must move to protect themselves   **b.** a recession will result and people must move to protect themselves   **c.** people will continue to make the same mistakes over and over again

23. The effects of most macroeconomic policy changes, say the rational expectations theorists, are

   a. very hard to predict   **b.** very easy to predict
   c. slow—that is, they take place over a period of many years   **d.** irrational

24. The advice the rational expectations theorists give the federal government is to

   a. change macropolicy often   **b.** figure out the right policies to follow and stick to them   **c.** figure out what the public is expecting and then do the opposite

25. Which school would advocate government spending to end a recession?

   a. classical   **b.** Keynesian   **c.** monetarist
   d. supply-side   **e.** rational expectations

26. Which school would consider cutting tax rates as the cure for all our economic ills?

   a. classical   **b.** Keynesian   **c.** monetarist
   d. supply-side   **e.** rational expectations

27. MV = PQ

   a. all the time   **b.** most of the time   **c.** some of the time   **d.** never

28. The output of our economy is represented by the letter ___ in the equation of exchange.

   a. M   **b.** V   **c.** P   **d.** Q

29. If MV rises, PQ

   a. must rise   **b.** may rise   **c.** must stay the same   **d.** must fall

30. The crude quantity theory of money states that if MV rises by 20 percent, PQ will

   a. fall by 20 percent   **b.** fall   **c.** stay the same
   d. rise   **e.** rise by 20 percent

31. The modern monetarists believe

    a. V is very unstable   **b.** V never changes

    c. any changes in V are either very small or predictable

    d. if M rises, V will fall by the same percentage

32. As we approach full employment, what will probably happen?

    a. V will fall   **b.** Q will fall   **c.** Q will rise

    d. P will rise   **e.** P will fall

Fill-In Questions

1. Say's law states that _____ _____.

2. According to the classical economists, if there is a recession, the government should _____ _____.

3. The classicals, applying Say's law, believed all our income would be _____; all our production would be _____ and all our savings would be _____.

4. The classicals said if the amount of money people wanted to save was greater than the amount businesspeople wanted to invest, _____ _____.

5. The classical school dominated economic thought until _____.

6. John Maynard Keynes defined aggregate demand as _____ plus _____ plus _____.

7. According to Keynes, the most important determinant of the level of investment was the _____.

8. According to Keynes, the main institutional barriers to downward wage and price flexibility were (1) _____ _____ and (2) _____.

9. The main success of Keynesian economics in the 1960s was _____.

10. John Maynard Keynes said that during recessions and depressions, the main problem was _____ _____.

11. To solve that problem, Keynes suggested _____ _____.

12. Monetarism begins and ends with one obsession: _____ _____.

13. Milton Friedman concluded that we have never had a serious inflation that was not accompanied by _____ _____.

14. The monetarists believed that if the money supply were raised during a recession, people would _____ _____.

15. According to the monetarists, recessions are caused by _____.

16. The key to stable economic growth, according to the monetarists, is _____ _____.

17. The record of the Fed, say the monetarists, is analogous to _____ _____.

18. The monetary rule states that _____ _____.

19. The monetarists say expansionary monetary policy will _____ depress interest rates and the unemployment rate. They further say expansionary monetary policy will _____ raise output and employment.

20. Supply-side economics came into vogue in _____ _____.

21. The objective of supply-side economics is to _____ _____. The problem, said the supply-siders, was that _____ were hurting the incentive to work and invest.

22. The way to get people to work more, say the supply-siders, is to _____.

23. According to the Laffer curve, reducing very high marginal tax rates will result in _____ federal tax revenue.

24. The three assumptions on which rational expectations theory is based are: (1) _____;

(2) _____;

and (3) _____.

25. Most macroeconomic policy changes, say the rational expectations theorists, are _____ _____.

26. The rational expectations theorists have taken up two key items on the conservative economists' agenda:

(1) _____ and

(2) _____.

27. The main criticism leveled at the rational expectations theorists is that _____ _____.

Problems

1. If M were 600 and V were 10, how much would PQ be?

2. According to the crude quantity theory of money, if M were to increase by 10 percent, what would happen to V, P, and Q?

3. If M were 800, P were 20, and Q were 400, how much would V be?

4. Initially $M = 600$, $V = 8$, $P = 16$, and $Q = 300$. According to the crude quantity theory of money, if M rose to 720, how much would P be?

5. If P were 7 and Q were 800, how much would MV be?

The Great Money Debate: The Keynesians versus the Monetarists

The Keynesian and monetarist schools of economic thought have been spoiling for a fight since way back in Chapter 10. After keeping them apart all this time, I've decided to let them fight it out once and for all. After a preliminary bout following the objectives, you'll see the main event, a scheduled four-rounder for the economic title of the world. (Actually, the title is split several ways, but why get into that now?)

Appendix Objectives

These four topics will be debated:

- The stability of V.
- The transmission mechanism.
- Monetary policy.
- A question of timing.

Preliminary Debate

As I've frequently noted, the only thing on which economists seem to agree is that they disagree on just about everything. The two groups of economists who disagree with each other the most are the monetarists and the Keynesians. We're going to take up three major areas of disagreement, each of which happens to be related to money.

First, there's the question of how stable V, the velocity of money, happens to be. Then, there's the transmission mechanism, which is the mechanism by which changes in the demand for and the supply of money affect aggregate demand. Finally, we'll look at the effectiveness of monetary and fiscal policy.

The time has finally arrived to let the Keynesians and the monetarists duke it out. This appendix has been given over to them for that purpose. I'll step back and let them go at it, only occasionally intervening to separate them in the clinches and ring the bell at the end of each round. You'll decide who won the bout.

Round 1: How Stable Is V?

Velocity and Changes in the Money Supply

The Keynesians believe changes in the level of the money supply affect the level of aggregate demand through the interest rate. An increase in the money supply lowers the interest rate, raising investment and, consequently, aggregate demand. Similarly, a decrease in the money supply raises the interest rate, thus lowering investment and aggregate demand.

The monetarists see a more direct link between the money supply and the level of GDP than the Keynesians see. When the money supply is increased, it creates excess money balances held by individuals. This money burns a hole—so to speak—in their pockets, so they spend it. Poof! Up goes aggregate demand, or GDP.

Monetarists: Money burns holes in people's pockets.

A decrease in the money supply, say the monetarists, has the opposite effect. Consumers and business firms find themselves short of funds. They would like to carry certain money balances but find themselves carrying less. What do they do? They cut back on spending, and down goes aggregate demand.

In this reasoning, there is an implicit assumption about V (velocity), which, you may or may not recall, is part of the equation of exchange we discussed at the beginning of the chapter: MV = PQ (M is the money supply; V is the velocity of circulation, or the number of times each dollar in our money supply is spent during the year; P is the price level, or the average price of all final goods and services sold during the year; and Q is the quantity of transactions, or the number of things sold during the year, or simply output).

Monetarists: V must be constant.

If a rise in M raises PQ (or GDP), V must be constant. This, the monetarists maintain, is true in the short run, which might be for a year or two.

If velocity were a perfect constant—that is, a number that stayed exactly the same—changes in M would lead to precisely predictable changes in PQ or GDP. The application of monetary policy would become an exact science, something even the most ardent supporters of the Federal Reserve Board would not dare to hope for. Imagine the power of monetary policy if we knew that a 3 percent rise in the money supply, M, would lead to exactly a 3 percent rise in GDP (PQ). Unfortunately, V will not hold still for us. But the monetarists say V is relatively stable in the short run. And that's the next best thing.

How Stable Is Velocity in the Short Run?

Keynes: V is not stable.

The Keynesians and the monetarists clash sharply with respect to the short-run stability of V. In a word, the monetarists say V is stable, and the Keynesians say it isn't. Perhaps more significant, the monetarists claim V is predictable in the short run, while the Keynesians say it isn't.

The Keynesians maintain that V is sensitive to interest rate changes. When interest rates rise, people will be more likely to hold more interest-bearing assets and less money. Conversely, when interest rates decline, people tend to increase their money holdings. This responsiveness of money balances to interest rate changes is Keynes's speculative demand for money.

Now, if interest rates rise and people hold less money, they will have to make more efficient use of their money balances to meet their day-to-day transactions needs—V will rise. And if interest rates fall, people will tend to hold more money, some of which will lie idly, thus pushing down V.

Keynesians: A change in M may lead to a change in V in the opposite direction.

The Keynesian view of how changes in M affect V is diametrically opposed to the monetarist position. The latter, of course, holds that in the short run V will be constant, but the Keynesians say a change in M may lead to a change in V in the opposite direction.

The Keynesians maintain that a decline in the money supply pushes up interest rates. Consequently, people buy more bonds (whose prices have fallen). This churns the money supply, increasing velocity.

Similarly, if the money supply rises, interest rates fall, bond prices rise, and people sell some of the bonds they are holding.[1] They end up holding more cash, thereby decreasing velocity.

The Keynesians therefore conclude that velocity varies inversely with changes in the money supply. Consequently, an expansionary monetary policy may be partially or fully negated by a decline in velocity. And contractionary monetary policy may be similarly canceled by a rising velocity. Although changes in the money supply and velocity are inversely related, the Keynesians have no way to measure the magnitude of the changes in velocity caused by changes in the money supply.

It follows that there is no way, according to the Keynesians, of predicting how changes in the money supply will affect the price level.

The monetarists have identified three determinants of V in the short run.

The monetarists, however, dispute the Keynesians' claim that velocity is unstable in the short run. What determines velocity in the short run? The monetarists have identified

---

[1]The section How Open-Market Operations Work in Chapter 13 showed that bond prices and interest are inversely related.

three determinants: (1) the frequency with which people are paid; (2) people's inflationary expectations; and (3) the level of real interest rates.

The first determinant changes only very gradually. Employers, as a group, do not suddenly change from paying their employees once a week to once a month, or vice versa.

Expectations of inflation also do not suddenly arise, nor do they suddenly subside. It takes years for an inflation to gather momentum and for the public's perception of that inflation to take hold. Similarly, when inflation begins to subside, it will take a few years for inflationary expectations to subside as well.

Finally, we have real interest rates. These are the rates of return that bondholders receive after inflation. Suppose you receive 12 percent interest on a bond when there is currently a 5 percent inflation rate. We would say that the 12 percent interest rate is only the nominal rate, and that after the 5 percent rate of inflation is deducted, you are left with a real rate of interest of only 7 percent. Again, the monetarists believe that while nominal interest rates will rise and fall with the inflation rate, real interest rates remain relatively stable, at least in the short run.

Thus, the monetarists contend, because each of the three determinants of velocity is stable in the short run, then velocity must be stable in the short run as well.

Whether or not the monetarists have made a convincing case about the short-run stability of V, they have left themselves an escape hatch: V does not have to be stable in the short run for the sophisticated quantity theory to hold up. It just has to be predictable in the short run. Is it?

Again, the Keynesians just say no! They point to the experience of the 1930s and 1940s when V fluctuated widely, plunging from 4 in 1929 to 3 in 1932 and, after fluctuating widely through the rest of the decade, dropping to 2 during World War II. The monetarists prefer to look at the postwar period, particularly the 1960s and 1970s (see Figure A-1). "Aha!" reply the Keynesians, "Then why not look at the 1980s as well?" During this decade V certainly had its ups and downs.

The stability of V is in the eye of the beholder.

The stability of V is certainly in the eye of the beholder. But we can make a few generalizations. During wars and recessions, V is prone to decline as people tend to hold on to their money. We may account for V's decline in the mid-1980s by the change in how the Fed counted our money supply. Until then, only currency and demand deposits at commercial banks were counted. But suddenly the Fed was also including checklike deposits at thrift institutions. We can show the effect of this change algebraically: GDP is total spending. So is MV (the money supply multiplied by the number of times per year each dollar is spent). Therefore, MV = GDP.

MV = GDP

Now divide both sides of this equation by M.

$$MV/M = GDP/M$$

$$V = GDP/M$$

$V = \dfrac{GDP}{M}$

What happens to the value or size of V if M gets larger? It goes down.

Figure A-1   The Velocity of Money Circulation, 1964–97

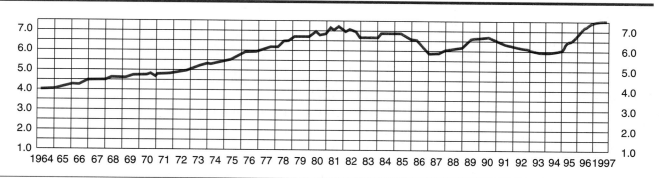

Source: *Economic Report of the President,* 1994, 1995, and 1998.

Quite possibly, then, the reason V declined in 1985 and 1986 was because of the change in the definition of M. We could conclude that except for times of war and recession, V has changed very little from one year to the next.

There has been a historical upward trend in V, which the monetarists readily acknowledge. This has been due to the expanded use of credit and credit cards, both of which, the monetarists would remind us, are fully predictable. Because people rely more on credit, they make better or more efficient use of their money balances, thereby pushing up V. In addition, there was a slow but steady decline in the money supply since 1994.

Is V predictable? The monetarists make an excellent case for the "normal years" of the last three and a half decades. But during the "abnormal years" of the Depression and World War II, V has been neither stable nor predictable. So we may conclude that as long as our economy behaves normally, V is predictable (if not completely stable) in the short run and that the sophisticated quantity theory does hold up.

Is V stable?

Round 2: The Transmission Mechanism

Introduction

Before championship bouts begin, we are usually treated to exhaustive analyses of the strategies and tactics of the two opponents. This section will do just that. The next three sections will bring you the Keynesian view, the monetarist view, and, finally, a comparison of the Keynesian and monetarist transmission mechanisms. The Keynesian position: an increase in the money supply depresses the interest rate. Given a certain MEI (marginal efficiency of investment) schedule, investment becomes more attractive and, therefore, increases. This, in turn, pushes up aggregate demand, and as we approach full employment, prices will rise as well. The monetarist position: a large increase in the money supply creates an imbalance in the money balances held by the public. People are holding more money than they wish to. What do they do? They spend this surplus on stocks and bonds, real estate, money market funds, and consumer durables. This, in turn, pushes up the prices of these assets. Finally, interest rates rise as lenders demand an inflation premium to compensate them for being repaid in inflated dollars.

Effects of a money supply increase: Keynesian and monetarist views

We can now sum up the effects of a money supply increase as seen by the Keynesians and the monetarists, respectively:

$$\text{Keynesians: M} \uparrow \rightarrow \text{Interest rates} \downarrow \rightarrow \text{Prices} \uparrow$$

$$\text{Monetarists: M} \uparrow \rightarrow \text{Prices} \uparrow \rightarrow \text{Interest rates} \uparrow$$

The monetarists and the Keynesians both believe large increases in the money supply will lead to rising prices. But they differ with respect to how interest rates and the level of investment are affected. The monetarists expect that rising prices will push up interest rates[2] and that, consequently, investment will fall. The Keynesians, on the other hand, look for a different sequence of events. A large increase in the money supply will push down interest rates and raise the level of investment.

When the Federal Reserve increases the money supply, what effect does this have on the level of interest rates, investment, and GDP? That depends on who answers this question.

The Keynesian View

Keynesians: A rise in M will lead to a decline in the interest rate.

A rise in the money supply will lead to a decline in the interest rate. At this lower interest rate, people will want to hold more money. Why? Number one: the opportunity cost of holding money (the interest rate) has gone down. Number two: at a lower interest rate,

---

[2]This is in the long run. They concede that in the short run interest rates may fall when the money supply goes up.

the price of bonds has gone up. Why buy bonds now? Why not wait until bond prices come back down?

We'll go over the entire process—what an increase in the money supply does to interest rates, the level of investment, and the level of GDP—step-by-step, using the graphs in Figure A-2. *Step 1* is shown in Figure A-2a. The demand for money, D1, is relatively flat. An increase of $100 billion in the money supply (from M1 to M2) leads to a decline of only 1 percent in the interest rate (from 10 percent to 9 percent).

Step 2. In Figure A-2b, what effect does this 1 percent decline in the interest rate have on the level of investment in the Keynesian system? It will raise investment, but not by much. Why? Because business firms are much more responsive to change in the expected profit rate (or the marginal efficiency of investment) than they are to interest rate changes.

Figure A-2b shows a relatively steep investment demand curve, I$_1$, which means investment will not rise much in response to a decline in the interest rate. Here, a 1 percent interest rate decline leads to a rise in investment of just $50 billion.

Step 3. Before we began this whole process, equilibrium GDP stood at 2,200. Now we have a $50 billion increase in investment. By how much will this raise GDP? That depends entirely on the size of the multiplier. Here we'll assume a multiplier of 2, so a $50 billion increase in investment leads to a $100 billion increase in GDP. This last move is shown in Figure A-2c.

Let's review the three steps of the Keynesian transmission mechanism. In this particular case, when the Fed raises the money supply by $100 billion, the interest rate falls by just 1 percent. This, in turn, leads to an increase in the level of investment of just $50 billion. Finally, with a multiplier of 2, the $50 billion rise in investment leads to a $100 billion rise in GDP. Perhaps $100 billion seems like a big increase, but it is relatively small when compared to the increase that takes place under the monetarist transmission mechanism.

The Monetarist View

Monetarists: A rise in M leads to a rise in spending.

Changes in the money supply, according to the monetarists, cause people to change their spending behavior. When the money supply rises sharply, people find themselves holding more money than they wish to. So what do they do? They spend it.

Figure A-2   The Keynesian Transmission Mechanism

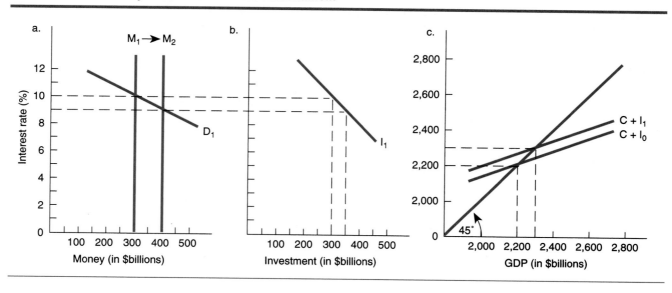

I don't mean they rush out to the shopping mall and buy up everything in sight. Rather, they add to their portfolios of assets. They might put the money into stocks and bonds, money market funds, real estate, or perhaps gold, a new car, or a video system.

People are constantly shifting their holdings among the various assets in their portfolios. If real estate becomes relatively attractive, they will shift into that from stocks and bonds and money market funds. If bond prices should fall (i.e., interest rates rise), people will put more money into bonds.

When the money supply is rising quickly, people will be pouring their excess cash balances into these various portfolio holdings, which, in turn, will drive up the prices of these holdings. This explains the heading for this section—the transmission mechanism. As the money supply grows, individual wealth holders transmit this increase into price increases. Put more succinctly by the monetarists, because money burns holes in people's pockets, they will spend it, thereby driving up prices.

Let's turn to Figure A-3.

Step 1. In Figure A-3a, when the Fed increases the money supply by $100 billion, from M1 to M2, this leads to a substantial decline in the interest rate—from 10 percent to 8 percent. Why? Because when people get their hands on this money, they buy things with it. Bonds are among the things they buy. When the demand for anything goes up, given a fixed supply, its price is driven up. Because bond prices and the interest rate are inversely related, as bond prices go up, interest rates fall.

Why does the interest rate come down so much? Because the demand for money, D_2, is relatively steep, according to the monetarists. Why? Because people have one basic reason to hold money: for transactions purposes. They will hold just enough money to handle their day-to-day personal and business needs, regardless of the interest rate. Thus, people would not alter their money balances much in response to even substantial interest rate changes.

Step 2. In Figure A-3b, a 2 percent decline in the interest rate (from 10 percent to 8 percent) leads to a big increase in investment, from $300 billion to $500 billion. Why so big? Because the investment demand curve, I_2, is relatively flat. In other words, according to the monetarists, investment is very responsive to interest rate changes.

Step 3. In Figure A-3c, this $200 billion investment increase gives rise to a $400 billion increase in GDP, assuming, once again, a multiplier of 2.

Let's review the steps. An increase of $100 billion in the money supply leads to a 2 percent decline in the interest rate, which, in turn, leads to a $200 billion increase in the level of investment. Assuming a multiplier of 2, GDP will then rise by $400 billion.

Figure A-3   The Monetarist Transmission Mechanism

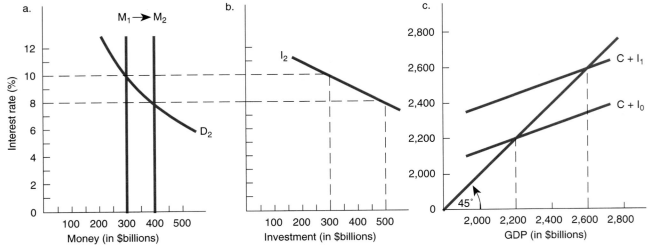

Comparison of Keynesian and Monetarist Transmission Mechanisms

The monetarists believe an increase in M will lead to a much greater increase in GDP than the Keynesians do.

When the money supply rises by $100 billion, why does the monetarist analysis lead to a GDP increase four times larger than that of the Keynesian analysis ($400 billion compared to $100 billion)?

There are two reasons. First, look at the slopes of the money demand curves, D_1 (in Figure A-2a) and D_2 (in Figure A-3a). Notice that D_2 is much steeper than D_1. In other words, the demand for money is much less responsive to the interest rate under monetarist analysis. The Keynesians believe people will want to hold a lot more money as the interest rate declines.

The second basic difference has to do with how responsive the demand for investment funds is to interest rate changes. The monetarists believe investment demand is very responsive to interest rate changes, while the Keynesians feel it is not.

These two very basic differences lead to very different conclusions. The Keynesians feel an increase in the money supply will not lead to a substantial increase in investment; the monetarists think it will. As we shall see, the Keynesians do not believe monetary policy can have a substantial impact on our economy, while the monetarists believe changes in the rate of growth of the money supply have a powerful economic effect.

Who Is Right?

We may conclude that, as in most economic disputes, both sides make some reasonable points. In this section I will explain the assumptions and disagreements that cause the Keynesians and the monetarists to reach such different conclusions about the outcome of the transmission mechanism, but I leave it to you to decide which school is right. Good luck!

Three basic disputes

We shall take up three basic disputes in turn: (1) the effect of an increase in the money supply on GDP; (2) the stability of velocity; and (3) the stability of the private sector.

Conflict number 1: the effects of an increase in the money supply on GDP. The Keynesians and monetarists are at loggerheads about the long-run consequences of a large-scale increase in the money supply when the economy is operating at less than full employment. The Keynesians maintain that interest rates will be reduced and investment encouraged to some degree. Consequently, there will be a moderate rise in output and employment. The monetarists, on the other hand, predict that in the long run, a large increase in the money supply will raise inflationary expectations. These will drive up prices, which will, in turn, push up interest rates, discourage investment, and drive down output and employment.

Thus the Keynesians think a large increase in the money supply will have a stimulating effect on output and employment, while the monetarists believe it will have the opposite effect.

Conflict number 2: how stable is velocity? In Round 1 of this chapter we reached this conclusion: In normal years (nondepression and nonwar years) V is at least predictable, if not stable, in the short run. Basically, then, we have upheld the monetarist position.

Conflict number 3: the stability of the private sector. The third bone of contention between the monetarists and the Keynesians has to do with the stability of the nongovernmental sector of the economy. The Keynesians think the private sector is inherently unstable because the expected profit rate, the marginal efficiency of investment, is subject to huge shifts. When these occur, investment will rise or fall substantially, dragging along aggregate demand.

The opposite view is held by the monetarists, who maintain that the business sector is inherently stable at full employment. Any economic instability is caused by the stop-and-go monetary policy of the Fed. If the Fed would merely follow their monetary rule—a steady annual monetary growth rate of 3 percent—the inherent stability of the private economy would correct any deviation from the full-employment norm.

Round 3: Monetary Policy

The common wisdom with respect to the proper monetary policy for the Fed to pursue has long been simple and explicit. During recessions, stimulate the economy by speeding up the rate of growth of the money supply; during inflations, cool down the economy by slowing that rate of growth. In this section, we'll examine the policy prescription of the Keynesians, who subscribe to the common wisdom, and that of the monetarists, who do not.

Fighting Recessions

Raise the rate of growth of M.

The Keynesians   During recessions, the Keynesians would advise the Fed to raise the rate of growth of the money supply. Will this bring the country out of the recession? No. Will it be of any help whatsoever? Maybe yes and maybe no. Like chicken soup, the Keynesians tell us, raising the rate of growth of the money supply will certainly not *hurt* us. Much better would be to cut taxes, and to raise government spending would be better still, but we're talking here only about monetary policy (not fiscal policy).

Increasing the rate of monetary growth would push down interest rates unless, of course, they are already around 2 percent. In that case, we would be in the liquidity trap. Raising the money supply any further would be of no help whatsoever.

But assuming the recession was not all that bad and interest rates were well above the 2 percent level, an increase in monetary growth would lower interest rates, thereby encouraging both business firms and individuals to borrow. But, as the Keynesians never tire of pointing out, the marginal efficiency of investment is much more important than the interest rate in determining the level of investment. Again, assuming the economy isn't in a deep recession, when the marginal efficiency of investment might be negative for most businesses, a decline in the interest rate relative to the marginal efficiency of investment would push up investment to some degree.

Don't change the rate of growth of M.

The Monetarists   Suppose the country is in the midst of a severe recession. What should the Fed do? Should it increase the rate of growth of the money supply, drive down interest rates, and make more money available for business investment, as the Keynesians suggest? The monetarists agree that such monetary stimulus could quickly get us out of the recession.

But why bother? they ask. The economy will get out of the recession all by itself, albeit at a somewhat slower pace. Suppose you're sick and your family doctor makes one of those rare home visits; you ask your doctor for some medication to make you better. "You don't need any medication," replies the doctor. "You're going to get better all by yourself." You may start to wonder what doctors are *for,* if not to write prescriptions.

The monetarists tell us the Fed doesn't really have to do anything because our economy will get better by itself. They go on to warn us that if the Fed were to increase the money supply too quickly or let it grow at too rapid a pace for too long, the result would be inflation. That's why, as with nature, it's always better to let things take their course.

Fighting Inflations

Slow the rate of growth of M.

The Keynesians   The Keynesians place much greater faith in the Fed's ability to slow down an inflation than in its ability to bring the country out of a recession. In short, by slamming on the monetary brakes, the Fed can send interest rates through the roof, making investment unprofitable even at high marginal efficiencies of investment.

The Fed can easily bring the economy to a grinding halt, something it has done most recently in 1980 and 1981. The back-to-back recessions Americans experienced in those years helped wring most of the inflation out of our economy.

This point is generalized by Lester Thurow:

> No one doubts that monetarism will stop inflation if it is practiced long enough and hard enough. At some point high interest rates stop all economic activity as well as inflation. But the

price is very high, not equitably distributed across the population, and not endurable in a democracy.[3]

A tight money policy is known in economists' circles as "pulling on a string" and is generally considered effective, if not always desirable—certainly not if it is overdone and causes a recession. Easy money is known as "pushing on a string," a policy that most Keynesians believe is much less effective in ending recessions than tight money is in ending inflations.

Follow the monetary rule.

The Monetarists   The monetarists actually agree with the Keynesians that tight money is a surefire way to halt inflation. But what then? they ask. If the Fed releases the brake too soon, we have another round of inflation. If it doesn't, we have a severe recession. Thus, once more we're faced with their only policy prescription: the monetary rule.

Round 4: A Question of Timing

The Lags

Timing, in economic policy as in most other areas, is of utmost importance. The effectiveness of both monetary and fiscal policy depends greatly on timing. Unfortunately, both of these policies are subject to three lags: the recognition, decision, and impact lags.

Suppose our economy enters a recession and the government provides a counteracting stimulus. What if this stimulus does not have full impact until recovery has set in? The end result of this well-intentioned government policy will be to destabilize the economy by making the recovery and subsequent prosperity far too exuberant. Similarly, if the government were to try to damp down an inflation, but the effects of its policy were not felt until the economy had already entered a recession, the policy would end up making the recession that much worse.

Recognition, decision, and impact lags

The recognition lag is the time it takes for policy makers to realize that a business cycle's turning point has been passed, or that either inflation or unemployment has become a particular problem. The decision lag is the time it takes for policy makers to decide what to do and to take action. And finally, the impact lag is the time it takes for the policy action to have a substantial effect. The whole process may take anywhere from about nine months to more than three years.

Fiscal Policy Lags

First, the president and Congress must recognize that there is a problem.

The lengths of the three lags under fiscal policy are not well defined. First, the recognition lag is the time it takes the president and a majority of both houses of Congress to recognize that something is broken and needs fixing—either an inflation or a recession. You would be amazed at how long this can take. In August 1981 we entered a recession, but in the spring of the following year President Reagan still could not bring himself to admit that we were actually in a recession (which, incidentally, proved to be the worst downturn since the Great Depression).

Congress, which at the time was divided between a Republican Senate and a Democratic House, also took some time to recognize the problem. This state of affairs was similar to that of 1967; inflation was beginning to get out of hand, but the president and Congress were reluctant to recognize the obvious.

Next, they must decide what to do about it.

Once the president *and* Congress recognize that something needs to be done about the economy, they must decide what action to take. After investigating the problem with his advisers, the president may make a fiscal policy recommendation to Congress. This recommendation, among others, is studied by appropriate subcommittees and committees, hearings are held, expert witnesses called, votes taken. Eventually bills may be passed by both houses, reconciled by a joint House-Senate committee, repassed by both

---

[3]Lester Thurow, *The Economist*, January 23, 1982.

houses, and sent to the president for his signature. This process usually takes several months. Finally, if the president likes the bill, he signs it. (If he doesn't, Congress may override his veto, but it usually doesn't.)

Finally, if will take time for their action to have an impact.

All this delay is part of the decision lag. We still have the impact lag. Once a spending bill, say a highway reconstruction measure, has been passed for the purpose of stimulating an economy that is mired in recession, a year may pass before the bulk of the appropriated funds is actually spent and has made a substantial economic impact. By then, of course, the country may already have begun to recover from the recession.

Monetary Policy Lags

Recognition lag is usually shorter for monetary than for fiscal policy.

One would expect monetary policy time lags to be somewhat shorter than fiscal policy time lags. The Board of Governors, which always has at least three or four professional economists among its membership, continually monitors the economy. Further, because the Board has only seven members, with the chair playing the dominant role, a consensus with respect to policy changes is reached far more easily than it is under our political method of conducting fiscal policy. While the legislative wrangling among the members of each house of Congress, between the two houses, and between the president and Congress may take several months, consensus among the seven members of the Fed is reached relatively quickly. The decision lag is thus fairly short.

How long is the impact lag—the time until monetary policy changes have a substantial effect? Economists estimate this time as anywhere from nine months to about three years. Further, there is some agreement that a tight money policy will slow down an inflation more quickly than an easy money policy will hasten a recovery. Still, there is no general agreement on whether monetary policy or fiscal policy is faster—or more effective.

While the goals of monetary policy and fiscal policy are identical—low unemployment and stable prices—the effects of each are felt in different economic sectors. Fiscal policy is generally directed toward the consumer sector (tax cuts) or the government sector (spending programs). Monetary policy, however, has its strongest impact on the investment sector. In brief, tight money discourages investment, and a rapidly growing money supply has the opposite effect. The only question, then, is how long it takes before the investment sector feels the impact of monetary policy changes.

Corporate investment does not fall off precipitously when the interest rate rises, nor does it shoot up when the interest rate falls. Although investment in plant and equipment becomes more attractive when the interest rate declines, as a rule large corporations take months, and sometimes years, to formulate investment plans. Therefore, transitory changes in the availability of investment funds or the rate of interest do not have a substantial impact on the level of investment in the short run. However, over a two- or three-year period, it's another story.

Thus, when we talk about the impact lag for monetary policy, we have to discuss that lag in terms of years rather than months. This is not to say that monetary policy changes have no impact for years, but rather that the substantial impact of these changes may not be felt for two or three years.

During a period of inflation, the proper monetary policy for the Fed to pursue is to slow down or even halt the growth of the money supply. But what if, by the time this is done and has had any impact, the economy has already entered a recession? Clearly it will make that recession even worse.

During a period of recession, what is the proper monetary policy? To speed up the rate of growth of the money supply. But suppose that by the time this policy has had any impact, recovery has begun? Oh no! Now this monetary expansion will fuel the next round of inflation.

To sum up, because of the recognition lag, the decision lag, and especially the impact lag, monetary policy is too slow to have its intended effect. By the time the monetary brakes are working to halt an inflation, the economy may have already entered a recession; and when an expansionary monetary policy is pursued to bring the economy out of a recession, recovery has already set in. Thus, because of the time lags, monetary policy may actually destabilize the economy. The Fed surely did not intend to have that effect, but the road to economic instability is often paved with good intentions.

The time lag in monetary policy invites a good-news/bad-news scenario. The good news is that there's a time lag. That's the *good* news? What's the *bad* news? It's a variable time lag. How variable? Monetarists believe it may be as short as six months or as long as two years.

Therefore, even if the Fed could take the time lag into account when it decides to slow the monetary growth rate to fight an inflation, how long a lag should it allow for? Six months? A year? A year and a half? Two years?

Fiscal versus Monetary Policy: A Summing Up

Keynesians: Fiscal policy is more powerful than monetary policy.

The Keynesians argue that fiscal policy is a much more powerful and reliable macropolicy tool than monetary policy. Why? Because fiscal policy, particularly increasing government spending during a recession, has a direct and substantial effect on GDP, whereas monetary policy is relatively weak and uncertain in effect.

When the government spends more money, G rises and has a multiplied effect on GDP. It happens one, two, three: (1) G rises; (2) it has a multiplied effect on GDP; and (3) GDP rises. That's fiscal policy—short and sweet.

But monetary policy, say the Keynesians, involves a longer and more variable sequence. Let's look at the effects of an expansion in the money supply. The Fed buys securities on the open market, creating more bank reserves. Will the banks lend out all these reserves? Only if they want to and are able to. Will there be a sufficient number of creditworthy borrowers who will want to borrow money during a recession to build new plant and equipment and expand their inventories?

If this money *is* lent out, the money supply will expand, but keep in mind the Keynesian assumptions of a relatively flat monetary demand curve and a relatively steep investment demand curve. A substantial increase in the money supply will lead to a relatively small decline in the interest rate. This, in turn, will lead to a small increase in investment and, eventually, a small increase in GDP.

Monetarists: Monetary policy is more powerful than fiscal policy.

Unlike the Keynesians, the monetarists believe a change in monetary policy has a short, direct, and powerful effect on GDP. An increase in M, assuming a stable or predictable V, will have a direct and predictable effect on PQ (which is GDP). The monetarists, like the classical economists before them, believe the private economy tends to operate near, or at, full employment. Therefore, any large increase in M will be translated into increases in P.[4]

Where does all this leave us? Who won the fight? I think you would agree that both the monetarists and the Keynesians got in some good licks. But who won? That's a good question. I don't know. Who do *you* think won?

Questions for Further Thought and Discussion

1. How does the Keynesian view of the transmission mechanism differ from the monetarist view?
2. How do the Keynesians' and the monetarists' policy prescriptions differ with respect to fighting (*a*) inflations and (*b*) recessions?
3. Is velocity stable in the short run? Where does the evidence point?

---

[4]If the economy is near or at full employment, Q can't increase much; the only give would be in P. Because PQ must rise in proportion to the increase in M, the rise in PQ will be all, or nearly all, in P.

WORKBOOK FOR APPENDIX TO CHAPTER 14

Name _____ Date _____

Multiple-Choice Questions

Circle the letter that corresponds to the best answer.

1. The two groups of economists who disagree with each other more than any others are the

    a. supply-siders and Keynesians   b. supply-siders and monetarists   c. monetarists and Keynesians

2. The Keynesians believe a change in the level of the money supply affects _____ through the interest rate.

    a. velocity   b. the level of aggregate supply
    c. the level of aggregate demand   d. the price level

3. One of the basic disagreements between the Keynesians and the monetarists is with regard to the

    a. stability of V   b. rate of growth of M
    c. level of prices   d. importance of real GDP versus nominal GDP

4. Which statement is true?

    a. Both the Keynesians and the monetarists believe V is sensitive to interest rate changes.   b. Neither the Keynesians nor the monetarists believe V is sensitive to interest rate changes.   c. The Keynesians believe V is sensitive to interest rate changes while the monetarists do not.   d. The monetarists believe V is sensitive to interest rate changes while the Keynesians do not.

5. The Keynesians say a change in M will lead to

    a. no changes in V   b. proportionate changes in V
    c. changes in V in the same direction   d. changes in V in the opposite direction

6. The Keynesians say a decline in the money supply

    a. pushes down interest rates and causes people to buy more bonds   b. pushes down interest rates and causes people to buy fewer bonds   c. pushes up interest rates and causes people to buy more bonds   d. pushes up interest rates and causes people to buy fewer bonds

7. Each of the following has been identified by the monetarists as a determinant of velocity in the short run except

    a. people's inflationary expectations   b. the frequency with which people are paid   c. changes in the level of output   d. the level of real interest rates

8. Is V predictable in the short run?

    a. The monetarists say yes and the Keynesians say no.
    b. The Keynesians say yes and the monetarists say no.
    c. The Keynesians and the monetarists both say yes.
    d. The Keynesians and the monetarists both say no.

9. Which statement is true about the Keynesian and monetarist transmission mechanisms when the money supply is increased?

    a. Under both, aggregate demand will rise.
    b. Under both, aggregate demand will decline.
    c. Under the Keynesian mechanism, aggregate demand will rise; but under the monetarist mechanism, it will fall.
    d. Under the monetarist mechanism, aggregate demand will rise; but under the Keynesian mechanism, it will fall.

10. According to the monetarists, when the money supply rises,

    a. interest rates rise   b. inflation declines
    c. people spend less on assets   d. people spend more on assets

11. An increase in M of $100 billion will lead to

    a. the same increase in GDP under the Keynesians as under the monetarists   b. a larger increase in GDP under the Keynesians than under the monetarists   c. a larger increase in GDP under the monetarists than under the Keynesians   d. none of the above

12. The Keynesians and the monetarists have three basic disputes connected with the transmission mechanism. They include each of the following except
    a. the effect of an increase in the money supply on GDP   b. the stability of interest rates   c. the stability of V   d. the stability of the private sector

13. The Keynesians believe monetary policy is
    a. more effective in fighting inflations than recessions
    b. more effective in fighting recessions than inflations
    c. effective in fighting both inflations and recessions
    d. effective in fighting neither inflations nor recessions

14. The monetarists say that if we are in a recession, the Fed should
    a. increase the rate of growth of M   b. decrease the rate of growth of M   c. do nothing

15. Which statement is true?
    a. The monetarists agree with the Keynesians that easy money is a good way to fight inflation.   b. The monetarists disagree with the Keynesians' contention that easy money is a good way to fight inflation.   c. The monetarists agree with the Keynesians' contention that tight money is a good way to fight inflation.   d. The monetarists disagree with the Keynesians' contention that tight money is a good way to fight inflation.

16. Each of the following is a policy lag except the _____ lag.
    a. psychological   b. impact   c. recognition
    d. decision

17. The lags under fiscal policy are _____ the lags under monetary policy.
    a. more clearly defined than   b. as well defined as
    c. less defined than

18. Monetary policy lags may last
    a. up to six months   b. up to one year   c. from six months to two years   d. from nine months to three years

19. Which statement is true?
    a. The Keynesians and the monetarists agree that fiscal policy is more effective than monetary policy.

b. The Keynesians and the monetarists agree that monetary policy is more effective than fiscal policy.
    c. The Keynesians believe more in fiscal policy and the monetarists in monetary policy.   d. The Keynesians believe more in monetary policy and the monetarists in fiscal policy.

20. The Keynesians assume a _____ monetary demand curve and a _____ investment demand curve.
    a. relatively flat, relatively flat   b. relatively steep, relatively steep   c. relatively steep, relatively flat
    d. relatively flat, relatively steep

21. The monetarists believe monetary policy has a _____ effect on GDP.
    a. direct and powerful   b. direct but not powerful
    c. indirect and powerful   d. indirect and weak

Fill-In Questions

1. The monetarists see a _____ between the money supply and the level of GDP.

2. If V were a perfect constant, a change in M would lead to a _____.

3. The Keynesians believe changes in the level of the money supply affect the level of aggregate demand through the _____.

4. The best course of action for the Fed, say the monetarists, would be to have the money supply grow at _____.

5. The monetarists say V is _____ and the Keynesians say V is _____.

6. If interest rates rise, according to the Keynesians, people hold less money and will have to _____.

7. Compared to the monetarist position, the Keynesian view of how changes in M affect V is _____.

8. The Keynesians maintain that an increase in M

   _____ interest rates.

9. The Keynesians say that V varies _____

   with M.

10. The monetarists have identified three determinants of V

    in the short run: (1) _____;

    (2) _____; and

    (3) _____.

11. You can most easily predict V in _____

    _____ years; it is harder to predict

    in _____ years.

12. According to the monetarists, a large increase in the

    money supply creates an _____

    _____. In response, people

    _____.

13. Both the Keynesians and the monetarists believe a large

    increase in M will lead to _____

    _____.

14. The monetarists expect rising prices to push up _____

    _____.

15. The effect of a large increase in the money supply on the

    level of investment, say the Keynesians, will be _____

    _____.

16. The long-run consequences of a large-scale increase in

    the money supply when the economy is operating at less

    than full employment will lead to _____

    _____ according to the Keynesians;

it will lead to _____

according to the monetarists.

17. The three basic disputes between the Keynesians and the

    monetarists with respect to the transmission mechanism

    are (1) _____;

    (2) _____;

    and (3) _____.

18. The Keynesians say that if we are in a recession, the Fed

    should _____,

    while the monetarists say the Fed should _____

    _____.

19. The Keynesians place much greater faith in the Fed's

    ability to fight _____ than to fight

    _____.

20. The three policy lags are (1) the _____

    _____ lag; (2) the _____

    _____ lag; and (3) the _____

    _____ lag.

21. The monetarists believe the monetary policy lags last

    between _____ and

    _____.

22. The Keynesians argue that _____

    policy is a much more powerful and reliable macropolicy

    tool than _____ policy.

23. Unlike the Keynesians, the monetarists believe changes in

    the monetary policy have a _____,

    _____, _____,

    and _____ effect on GDP.

15

A Guide to Macropolicy

The three main goals of macropolicy are stable prices, high employment, and a satisfactory rate of economic growth. All economists agree to these goals; they disagree about the means of achieving them.

This will necessarily be a very short chapter because virtually nothing I can say about macropolicy will not offend at least one school of economists. What I will propose here, while not particularly daring or innovative, will give the reader some sense of overall macropolicy, its potential, and its limitations.

Chapter Objectives

In this chapter we shall consider:

- Conventional monetary and fiscal policies to fight recessions and inflations.
- Incomes policies.
- How to attain a satisfactory rate of economic growth.

Fighting Recessions

We're going to talk about the conventional fiscal and monetary policies that are advocated by most economists. But as we saw in the last chapter, a significant minority opinion—especially among the monetarists and rational expectationists—runs counter to the majority opinion on macropolicy. So if you happen to disagree with conventional fiscal and monetary policy, just grit your teeth, work your way through the next few pages, and be thankful that this is a short chapter.

Conventional Fiscal Policy

Run deficits to fight recessions.

We'll begin with the simplest of fiscal policy measures drawn from Chapter 11; then we'll get a bit more fancy. The most conventional fiscal policy for fighting a recession is to run a budget deficit. Indeed, given the automatic stabilizers as well as our tax laws, deficits are virtually inevitable during recessions.

The question, then, is how big the deficits should be. Assuming the deficit rises about $30 billion for each point the unemployment rate rises and a 5 percent unemployment rate represents full employment, at a 6 percent unemployment rate, we should run a deficit of about $30 billion. How much should the deficit be when the unemployment rate is 7 percent? You got it—$60 billion. This is our famous full-employment balanced budget.

Conventional Monetary Policy

Speed up M growth to fight recessions.

Were we to enter a recession, the conventional monetary policy would be to speed up the rate of growth of the money supply. Here we need to be careful: if we were to speed it up too much, we would have to worry about an inflation and possibly rising interest rates, which, in time, would kill off any recovery. Surely there would be no justification for as much as a 10 percent rate of monetary growth over any extended period of time.

Two Policy Dilemmas

Suppose we are running a budget deficit of $90 billion and the annual rate of monetary growth is 8 percent. What could go wrong?

Huge budget deficits are financed by massive borrowings by the Treasury. As the economy begins to recover, business and consumer borrowing picks up as well. What does all this loan demand do to interest rates? It drives them up. And when interest rates, which were high even during the recession, rise still higher in the early stages of recovery, what happens next? The recovery collapses.

Thus, a budget deficit, designed to stimulate the economy, necessitates massive Treasury borrowing, driving up interest rates and ultimately choking off recovery.

Is there any way to resolve this dilemma? How about gradually reducing the deficit as the recovery progresses?

Let's consider rapid monetary growth. It stimulates recovery, making funds available to business firms and consumers. Interest rates may decline. So far, so good. But when we increase the money supply this rapidly, we also court inflation, and with inflation, people will demand more interest for their savings. With inflation and higher interest rates, it won't be long before the recovery sputters to a stop.

Can you think of a way out of this dilemma? We could try to reduce the rate of monetary growth as recovery begins to set in.

Fighting Inflation

Conventional Fiscal Policy

To fight inflation, reduce the deficit.

To fight inflation, we would immediately want to try to reduce the size of the federal budget deficit—if we happen to be running one. It would be too much of a shock to reduce it by more than $60 billion or $80 billion in one year, but in the face of persistent inflation, we would need to reduce the deficit year by year and ultimately run budget surpluses.

Conventional Monetary Policy

To fight inflation, slow the rate of M growth.

The obvious policy move here would be to slow down the rate of growth of the money supply. Indeed, if inflation were beginning to rage out of control, not only would the Fed have to stop the money supply from growing, but it would have to cause it to contract slightly.

Fighting Inflationary Recessions: Two More Policy Dilemmas

Some people think of inflations and recessions as separate problems. They once were. However, beginning with the recession in 1957–58, the price level has risen during every recession. To add insult to injury, during three of the four most recent recessions, 1973–75, 1980, and 1981–82, inflation was of double-digit proportions.

Let's review conventional fiscal policy to fight recession and inflation. To fight recession, we run budget deficits; to fight inflation, we run surpluses. Very well, then, what do we do to fight an inflationary recession? That's one dilemma.

We'll go on to the second dilemma. What is the conventional monetary policy to fight a recession? It's to speed up the rate of monetary growth. And to fight an inflation? Slow it down.

Here's the $64,000 question: How do we fight an inflation and a recession simultaneously using conventional fiscal and monetary policy? The answer: We can't.

Don't give up; there *is* hope.

One approach would be to try a combination of tight money to fight the inflation and a large budget deficit to provide the economic stimulus needed to fight the recession. The country kind of stumbled onto this combination during the recession of 1981–82, but not until the Fed eased up on the tight money part did the economy finally begin to recover. By then, much of the inflation had been wrung from the economy.

This suggests a second approach. First deal with the inflation, then cure the recession. In the early 1950s the United States suffered from a surge of inflation brought on by the Korean War. Three recessions occurred over the course of just eight years. By the end of the third recession, the consumer price index was virtually stable. Then, through almost the entire decade of the 1960s, the economy went through a recession-free expansion.

Conventional policies are not ideal for fighting inflationary recessions.

Conventional monetary and fiscal policy tools are sufficient to deal with simple recessions or inflations, but inflationary recessions pose additional problems. Conventional macropolicy cannot cure them without a great deal of suffering, especially by those who lose their jobs.

Incomes Policies: An Alternate Approach

Anti-inflationary monetary and fiscal policies damp down aggregate demand. Incomes policies seek to curb inflation without affecting aggregate demand. Why are they called *incomes* policies? Because they affect the nominal incomes that people receive. They also affect the prices that people pay for goods and services, thereby affecting their *real* incomes.

We shall consider two incomes policies designed to fight inflation: wage and price controls and tax-based incomes policies. Neither is especially popular with the economics profession.

Wage and Price Controls

During World War II, during the Korean War in the early 1950s, and again in 1971, the federal government imposed wage and price controls. These controls put a freeze on wages and prices, making it illegal to raise them.

The main argument for controls is that they break the back of inflationary expectations. This is in accordance with the adaptive expectations hypothesis we discussed in the last chapter, which is based on the assumption that the best indicator of the future is what happened in the past. If we freeze wages and prices after a period of inflation, then our past will soon be price and wage stability, or zero inflation. Once people see that inflation has ended, they will expect price stability to continue and will no longer demand inflationary wage increases or purchase a lot of goods and services today in the expectation that their prices will be going up tomorrow.

Two main arguments against controls

There are two main arguments against such controls. First, they interfere with the price mechanism (i.e., the law of supply and demand). Without question, this is the case. Because we are substituting a bureaucratic control system for an extremely complex and well-functioning private decision-making system, we would have to be desperate indeed to impose such a system. The controls cause shortages and impede production, so they will be either lifted or circumvented eventually.

A second objection to wage and price controls is that once they are removed, wages and prices will surge to make up for lost time. Indeed, this is exactly what happened both after World War II and in the mid-1970s, after the controls were removed.

Virtually all economists agree that wage and price controls cannot be used over an extended period of time because of their impact on efficiency. They may be effective in the short run—say, up to a year or so. But if people are aware that these controls will soon be phased out, they will expect a renewed bout of inflation. And so, with inflationary expectations high, there will indeed be another bout of inflation once the controls are lifted.

Tax-Based Incomes Policies

These policies involve the carrot-and-stick approach: the carrot is a tax cut, and the stick is a tax increase. If a corporation raises prices or grants wage increases beyond a certain predetermined percentage, say 4 percent, its corporate income tax rate is raised by a certain percentage. Similarly, if it holds wage and price increases below a certain percentage, its taxes are lowered.

Would this work? Some skeptics point to the large bureaucracy that would be needed to keep watch over such a system. Of course, if the government handed out only rewards for good behavior, the corporations could be counted on to give the good news to the IRS at the end of the tax year.

Attaining a Satisfactory Rate of Economic Growth

The U.S. growth rate has historically been 3.5 percent.

Historically, our economy has grown at a rate of nearly 3.5 percent a year. Most people would call that a satisfactory growth rate because it enabled the United States to become the world's leading economic power. Surely a rate of, say, 4 percent year after year would satisfy nearly everyone.

In the early 1970s, however, the growth rate began to lag. Two factors holding down the growth rate have been a low rate of investment (which, in turn, is largely due to a low savings rate) and a low rate of productivity increase.

In recent years Americans have been saving less than 5 percent of their incomes, compared to a rate of about 35 to 40 percent in China, a much poorer country. Furthermore, the federal government has been running huge budget deficits, which more than absorb all the personal savings we have been able to generate. In addition, we as a nation have been on an international buying spree, racking up huge trade deficits. Fortunately, foreigners have been recycling most of those dollars by buying up not only huge chunks of our national debt but also tens of billions of dollars in corporate bonds and stocks each year. Thus, essentially, foreign saving has enabled our businesses to continue investing in new plant and equipment.

Productivity is defined as output per unit of input. Labor productivity is measured by output per hour worked. Productivity is what makes our economy go. From 1963 to 1973 our productivity rose by nearly one-third. Between 1977 and 1994 it rose by only about 20 percent.

Lagging productivity and lagging investment are intertwined problems.

The problems of lagging productivity and lagging investment are intertwined. The less plant and equipment backing each worker, the lower our productivity will be. The lower our rate of productivity increase, the less plant and equipment will be produced (along with less consumer goods).

One way of channeling more income into saving is to make interest income tax free. Such a proposal would be objected to on the grounds that it was a giveaway to the rich, who derive a major portion of their incomes from interest. We'll overlook the fact that much of rich people's interest income is derived from tax-free state and municipal bonds, and address ourselves to the general objection that tax-free interest income would merely be a boon to the rich. Fine, let's limit tax-free interest to the first $5,000 of interest income.

Another possibility is a national sales tax, such as the value-added tax used in several European countries. At each stage of the production process, a uniform tax of, say, 2 percent is charged. Not only would such a tax discourage consumption and encourage saving, but it would drastically reduce the federal budget deficit.

One criticism of such a tax is that it would be regressive. While that is certainly true, its regressiveness could be greatly reduced by exempting food, most rents, and other goods and services purchased by the poor.

There is actually a whole medley of policy prescriptions for faster economic growth; we shall review these prescriptions in the next chapter. Right now we limit ourselves to the observation that because our growth has been lagging, we must be doing *some*thing wrong.

The Limits of Macropolicy

There is no question that the federal government can easily alter the course of our economy; but during the last decade, substantial changes took place that sharply limited its power. The internationalization of our economy has completely altered the rules of the macroeconomic policy game.

Marc Levinson noted these changes several years ago:

> International capital flows . . . have made it much more difficult for the central bank to plot the nation's monetary course.
>
> Suppose, for example, that the Fed wants to boost the economy's growth rate. When international capital flows were small, the central bank could stimulate borrowing by pumping up the money supply or cutting the discount rate. But now, lower real interest rates will spur investors to move their capital out of dollar-denominated investments. Economists can't even begin to estimate the likely extent of those capital flows.[1]

Levinson's analysis is supported by that of Kenichi Ohmae, who reasons that if the Fed tightens the money supply and pushes up interest rates, money will flow in from abroad, attracted by our relatively high interest rates. This will frustrate the tight-money and high-interest-rate objectives of the Fed, and, in effect, render the traditional instruments of monetary policy obsolete.[2]

As our economy becomes even more closely integrated into the world economy—a topic we'll pursue in the last two chapters in this book—it is clear that macropolicy will become less important. And so, as we begin counting down the years until the turn of the century, macropolicy may no longer be the only economic game in town. But it is still, by far, the biggest game.

Conclusion

Where does this leave us? Clearly, the economics profession does not have all the answers. But we do occasionally come up with some interesting questions, and we're very good at providing cogent explanations about why our predictions almost always seem to go awry.

As we approach the millennium, the problem of our lagging rate of economic growth has become quite apparent. How low *has* our growth been? *Why* has it been so low? *What* can we do to speed it up? I'm glad you asked. You'll find the answers in the next chapter.

Questions for Further Thought and Discussion

1. Outline the conventional monetary and fiscal policies for fighting an inflation. Then outline the conventional monetary and fiscal policies for fighting a recession. Why would an inflationary recession pose a dilemma for those who would attempt to apply conventional monetary and fiscal policies?

2. What are the two main incomes policies, and how are they used?

3. What are two main problems preventing us from attaining a satisfactory rate of economic growth? How could we try to solve these problems?

---

[1]Mark Levinson, "Economic Policy: The Old Tools Won't Work," *Dun's Business Month,* January 1987, pp. 30–33.

[2]Kenichi Ohmae, *The Borderless World* (New York: HarperCollins, 1990), p. xi.

WORKBOOK FOR CHAPTER 15

Name _____   Date _____

Multiple-Choice Questions

Circle the letter that corresponds to the best answer.

1. The conventional fiscal policy to fight a recession would be to
   a. increase the rate of monetary growth   b. decrease the rate of monetary growth   c. run budget deficits
   d. run budget surpluses

2. The conventional monetary policy to fight inflations would be to
   a. increase the rate of monetary growth   b. decrease the rate of monetary growth   c. run budget deficits
   d. run budget surpluses

3. One problem or dilemma we might face in fighting a recession is that
   a. we might end up with budget surpluses
   b. output might rise too quickly   c. interest rates might fall   d. interest rates might rise

4. During recessions, we want
   a. budget deficits and faster monetary growth
   b. budget deficits and slower monetary growth
   c. budget surpluses and faster monetary growth
   d. budget surpluses and slower monetary growth

5. During inflations, we want
   a. budget deficits and faster monetary growth
   b. budget deficits and slower monetary growth
   c. budget surpluses and faster monetary growth
   d. budget surpluses and slower monetary growth

6. Which statement is true?
   a. In recent years inflation and recession have become separate problems.   b. In recent years inflation and recession have become related problems.   c. Inflation and recession have never been related problems.
   d. Inflation and recession have always been related problems.

7. Each of the following could be used to fight inflation except
   a. tax-based incomes policies   b. wage and price controls   c. budget surpluses   d. budget deficits

8. Historically, we have had an annual growth rate of about
   a. 2 percent, which we have exceeded over most of the last 15 years   b. 2 percent, which exceeds the rate we have had over most of the last 15 years   c. 3½ percent, which we have exceeded over most of the last 15 years   d. 3½ percent, which exceeds the rate we have had over most of the last 15 years

9. In the 1970s and 1980s
   a. our saving rate and our productivity growth were both lagging   b. neither our saving rate nor our rate of productivity growth was lagging   c. our saving rate was lagging, but our rate of productivity growth was not   d. our productivity rate of growth was lagging, but our saving rate was not

10. In recent years macropolicy has
    a. become more powerful   b. become less powerful
    c. remained about as powerful as it was 15 years ago

Fill-In Questions

1. The three main goals of macropolicy are

   (1) _____; (2) _____

   _____; and (3) _____.

2. The conventional fiscal policy to fight a recession is to

   _____ while the conventional

   monetary policy is to _____

   _____.

3. The conventional fiscal policy to fight an inflation is to

   _____, while

the conventional monetary policy is to _____

_____.

4. One problem with both expansionary monetary and fiscal policies used to fight recessions is that they could lead to

_____.

5. The dilemma of fighting an inflationary recession with conventional fiscal policy would be _____

_____.

6. The dilemma of fighting an inflationary recession with conventional monetary policy would be _____

_____

_____.

7. Two incomes policies used to fight inflation are

(1) _____

and (2) _____.

8. Two factors that have held down the rate of growth are

_____

and _____.

9. Two possible ways of increasing our savings rate would

be _____

and _____.

16 Economic Growth and Productivity

All the way back in Chapter 1, I outlined the history of the American economy. Now I shall return to our country's recent economic history, this time examining the factors most responsible for slowing our economic growth these last 20 years. What are the causes of this slowdown, and what must we do to reverse this trend? To answer these questions, we need to put economic growth in a historical and international context.

Our problems pale in comparison to those of the less developed countries of Asia, Africa, and Latin America. They are just beginning the journey to development that we undertook more than two centuries ago. But, unlike us, they are beginning from a base of such abject poverty that many of them may never get far.

Chapter Objectives

The main topics of this chapter are:

- Economic growth in the United States: The record.
- The role of productivity.
- Why our productivity is increasing so slowly.
- The roles of savings, capital, and technology.
- The declining quality of our labor force.
- The law of diminishing returns.
- Economic growth in the less developed countries.
- The Malthusian theory of population.

The Industrial Revolution and American Economic Development

Prior to the Industrial Revolution about two centuries ago, one generation lived about as well as the next—or as badly. In fact, except for a few rich families, almost everyone was poor. Throughout the world, you were lucky if you had the basics—three square meals a day, some homespun clothes on your back, and a thatched roof over your head.

If you were *really* lucky, you might live to see your old age, which began around your 40th birthday. You lived and died within a few miles of where you were born, you spent most of your time farming, and you were illiterate. About the only good thing in life before the Industrial Revolution was that you never had to worry about finding a parking space.

The Industrial Revolution made possible sustained economic growth and rising living standards for the first time in history. The steam engine, the factory system, mass production, the mechanized cotton spindle, the blast furnace (for smelting iron), railroads, and scores of other innovations ushered in a massive increase in productivity and output.

Although living standards in the industrializing nations of Western Europe and in the United States rose steadily, not until the 1920s did the age of mass consumption truly arrive. Homes were electrified; electric appliances, telephones, and cars became commonplace; and most working people were even beginning to enjoy increasing amounts of

The Industrial Revolution made possible sustained economic growth and rising living standards for the first time in history.

leisure time. After the Great Depression and World War II, the industrialized nations were able to pick up where they had left off in 1930, and by 1990 living standards in most of these countries had tripled. Chapter 1 of this book traced American economic development over the last two centuries.

Starting in 1780, England needed 58 years to double its per capita GDP. The American industrial revolution following the Civil War was a bit faster, with per capita output doubling in 47 years. Beginning in 1885, Japan doubled its per capita GDP in 34 years.

But borrowing heavily on earlier technology and making use of a great influx of Japanese capital, South Korea doubled its per capita output in just 11 years, starting in 1966. And now, China is roaring along with its own industrial revolution, doubling its per capita output every 10 years.

The Industrial Revolution, which began in England around the middle of the 18th century, entered its second phase in America in the early years of this century. It was based on the mass production of cars, electrical machinery, steel, oil, and chemicals. But in the last two decades, the third phase of the Industrial Revolution has taken hold in Japan, Western Europe, and newly industrialized countries of Southeast Asia, as well as in the United States. This phase is based largely on consumer electronics, computer systems, communications systems, computer software, and advances in manufacturing processes.

The good news: we're still number one.

The American economy is the largest in the world and will continue to be in the foreseeable future. We have one of the world's highest standards of living and a larger stock of capital than any other country. Japan, our nearest competitor, has a GDP slightly more than half the size of ours. Well, that's the *good* news.

The bad news: we're losing our lead.

The *bad* news is that our standard of living, which was number one in the world 20 years ago, has barely increased over the last two decades. Our rate of capital formation is lower than Japan's, a country with only half our population and half our productive capacity. Our rate of productivity growth, or output per hour, has been growing at less than one-third the rate at which it grew in the 1950s and early 1960s. In short, we may still be the world's preeminent economic power, but we're steadily losing our lead.

Since the early 1970s our economy has been plagued by all sorts of problems—inflation, recession, high interest rates, a low savings rate, a trade imbalance, huge federal budget deficits, lagging productivity, and a ballooning national debt. In this chapter we will be particularly concerned with our low rates of savings and productivity. Our savings rate is among the lowest of all the industrial nations, as is the rate at which our productivity is increasing. These two factors are extremely important, because they presage relatively slow economic growth for the rest of the decade.

The Economic Growth of the United States

How have we been doing? Table 1 provides a summary of our economic performance since 1929. Since the 1960s, there has been a marked slowdown.

Table 1 **Percentage Change in Per Capita Real GDP, Selected Years**

Period	Percentage Change
1929–39	−6.1%
1939–49	35.8
1949–59	23.2
1959–69	30.1
1969–79	18.6
1979–89	17.4
1989–97	11.0

Sources: *Economic Report of the President,* 1998.

**Table 2   Median Family* Income,
Selected Years (in 1996 dollars)**

Year	Income
1980	40,079
1990	42,440
1996	42,300

*The term *family* refers to a group of two or more persons related by blood, marriage, or adoption, and residing together, as such persons are considered members of the same family.

Source: Bureau of the Census, *Current Population Reports,* 1997, P–60.

Median family income has increased only slightly since 1970.

Ready for some more bad news? It's right there in Table 2. Median family income, in 1996 dollars, has increased only slightly since 1970. If you're not clear on exactly what *median* family income is, I'll tell you. If we took every family in the country and lined them up in order of income, the median income would be that of the family right in the middle of the line. In 1996 the median American family had about $2,200 more income than it did back in 1980, and slightly less than it had in 1990.

Why Is Our Productivity Increasing So Slowly?

Slow productivity growth means slow economic growth.

First let's look at the record of productivity growth since 1950. Figure 1 shows that our output per hour rose by 87.9 percent between 1950 and 1973. But over the next 23 years it rose by only 36.2 percent. Before 1973 our output per hour rose an average of 3 percent each year, but since then it's risen at an annual average rate of just 1 percent.

Economic growth has declined since 1973 because our rate of productivity growth fell by two-thirds. Why did it fall? That's a simple question with a very complex answer.

Figure 1   Percentage Increase in Output per Hour, Business Sector, 1950–73 and 1974–97

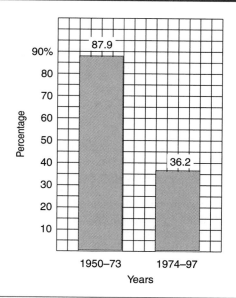

Sources: *Economic Report of the President,* 1983, 1998; *Economic Indicators,* February 1998.

Our Low Savings Rate

Low savings rate means low productivity growth.

There is no one clear reason why our rate of productivity increase slowed in the 1970s and 1980s, but a reason singled out by many economists is our low savings rate. Americans have been poor savers for generations, but through most years of the 1950s, 1960s, and 1970s, we still managed to put away around 7 to 8 percent of disposable income. This changed in the 1980s, however, when savings averaged just 5.4 percent of disposable income. Figure 2 shows a sharp decline from 1981 through 1989, and our savings rate remains below 5 percent, which makes it virtually the lowest in the industrial world.

The generations that came of age in the 1980s and 1990s have not done as well as their parents' generations.

Why do Americans save so little? Perhaps the explanation lies in the phenomenon called the "me generation" (see box). Perhaps Americans just want to have fun, and fun costs money. Whatever the reason—whether an inability to accept deferred gratification or the built-in savings disincentives of our tax laws—our savings rate is extremely low.

Personal savings is just one part of the total amount saved by Americans, which we call *gross saving*. Businesses save as well, and the government (I'm lumping together the

Figure 2   The Savings Rate: Saving as a Percentage of Personal Disposable Income, 1980–97

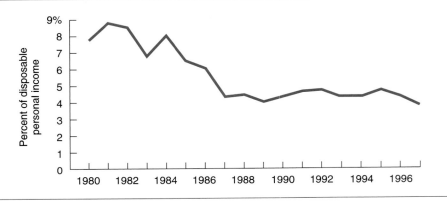

Source: *Economic Report of the President*, 1998.

The Me Generation and Generation X

"I want it *all* and I want it *now!*" That was the rallying cry of the "me generation," which came of age in the 1980s. These investment bankers, corporate lawyers, doctors, and computer whizzes gave new meaning to Thorstein Veblen's *conspicuous consumption.*

While most members of the so-called me generation may well have shared the material aspirations of their yuppie brethren, they just didn't have the dollars to make them happen. In fact, the generation of the 1980s has not done as well economically as their parents did when *they* were in their 20s.

In the 1960s most couples in their 20s could afford to buy a home; today less than one-third can. In terms of dollars of constant purchasing power, wages are virtually the same as they were 20 years ago. Family incomes have risen only because so many homemakers have gone back to work. Two may be able to live as cheaply as one, but only if they live on two salaries rather than one.

Harvard economist Benjamin Friedman wrote about an implicit compact between generations:

The thesis of this book is that the radical course upon which the U.S. economic policy was launched in the 1980s violated the basic moral principle that had bound each generation of Americans to the next since the founding of the republic; that men and women should work and eat, earn and spend, both privately and collectively, so that their children and their children's children would inherit a better world. Since 1980 we have broken with that tradition by pursuing a policy that amounts to living not just in, but for, the present. We are living well by running up our debt and selling off our assets. America has thrown itself a party and billed the tab to the future. The costs, which are only beginning to come due, will include a lower standard of living for individual Americans and reduced American influence and importance in world affairs.*

The so-called Generation X, which is coming of age in the 1990s, has clearly maintained the prolific spending habits of its generational precursors. Its members have also been "born to shop" and believe that you must "shop till you drop."

*Benjamin M. Friedman, *Day of Reckoning* (New York: Random House, 1988), p. 4.

federal, state, and local governments) engages in what economists term *dissaving,* or negative saving. Businesses save money through retained earnings (i.e., profits plowed back into the business), but most of their savings is in the form of depreciation (or capital consumption) allowances. These funds are used to replace the plant and equipment that has worn out or become obsolete, and they are also used to purchase additional plant and equipment.

The federal government ran budget deficits from 1970 through 1997, while the state and local governments have generally run surpluses. Beginning in the late 1970s, the federal deficits far outweighed the state and local surpluses, so the government contribution to the gross savings rate became a big minus.

What does our gross savings rate look like? In Figure 3 you can see an unmistakable downward trend from the late 1940s to the early 1990s, and then an apparent reversal beginning in 1993.

How does our gross savings rate compare with those of other leading industrial nations? Very badly. We're the low one over to the right in Figure 4. Our gross savings rate was about half that of Japan from 1975 through 1997.

Figure 3   U.S. Gross Savings Rate: Gross Saving as a Percentage of GDP, 1947–97

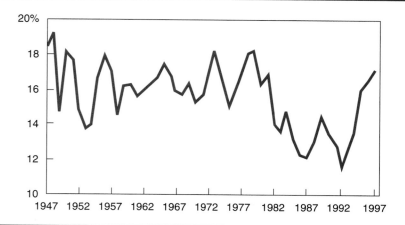

Source: *Economic Report of the President*, 1998.

Figure 4   Gross National Saving as a Percentage of GDP, Annual Average, 1981–90

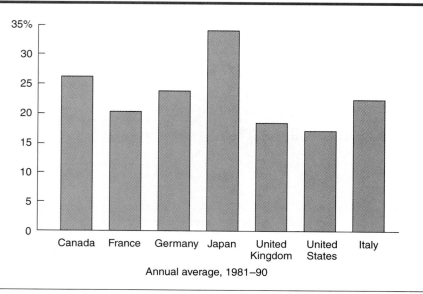

Source: Organization for Economic Cooperation and Development.

Because we save so little, we generate a very low flow of funds for investment. Over the last decade we've been running huge trade deficits, and foreigners have been recycling the dollars we sent them by making investments in the United States. Our investment is consequently much higher than it would otherwise have been due to this influx of dollars from abroad.

Foreign investors have been attracted by our high interest rates.

For foreigners, the key attraction of investing in the United States is the relatively high interest rates that we pay. Real interest rates (after subtracting the rate of inflation from nominal rates) were about three times as high in the United States as in Japan through most of the 1980s. This meant Japanese firms were borrowing at about one-third the interest rate that their American competitors were paying. This factor—which can be traced back to our low savings rate—has put American firms at a great disadvantage and is a major reason why we have been losing our product markets to Japanese competitors.

Our Low Rate of Investment

To increase our output at a satisfactory rate, we need to keep replacing worn-out and obsolete capital with the most up-to-date and technologically advanced plant and equipment. And we need not only to replace the capital that we've cast off, but also to keep increasing our capital stock.

Do you recall the production possibilities curves from Chapter 2? Figure 5 reproduces a few of them. The production possibilities curve provides a snapshot of our economy at full employment producing just two types of goods. Here they're capital goods and consumer goods. A country that devotes a higher proportion of its resources to capital goods than to consumer goods will grow faster than another country that initially has the same production possibilities curve but emphasizes consumer goods.

As you can see, the country shown in Figure 5B has a much higher rate of growth than the one in Figure 5A. And the reason why it has enjoyed this relatively high growth should be obvious. Perhaps the two countries in question are the United States and Japan (leaving aside the fact that Japan's economy is only a little more than half the size of

Figure 5   Capital Spending and Economic Growth

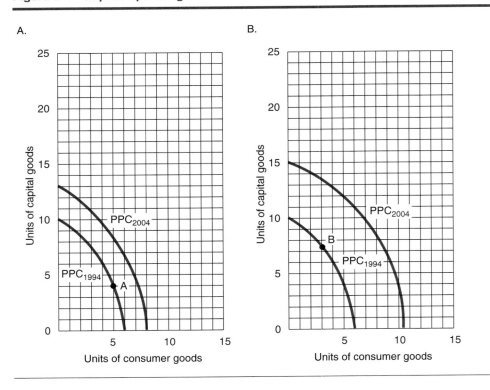

ours). The lesson our nation must learn is that until we begin to devote more resources to capital goods production and less to consumer goods production, our growth rate will continue to lag.

Over time the capital stock of every industrial nation grows. We call this *capital widening*. But rapid economic growth requires a rising amount of capital per worker. We call an increase in the ratio of capital to workers *capital deepening*.

There has been a marked slowdown in our country's capital-deepening process since the mid-1960s, as we can see from Table 3. From 1955 to 1965 capital grew five times faster than hours worked. By the 1990s that ratio had fallen to 1.2.

The Declining Quality and Quantity of Labor

In 1870, Americans, Germans, French, Japanese, and British workers averaged nearly 3,000 hours a year on the job. Now it is less than 2,000 hours, with much of the decline having come since World War II. How does our labor force stack up against those of the rest of the industrial world? Are we growing flabby and complacent? Some things are easier to measure than others, so we'll start with the easiest: the declining average workweek.

(1) The Declining Average Workweek The average workweek has declined from 60 hours in 1900 to less than 35 hours by the mid-1970s. Today most people put in the standard nine-to-five (or eight-to-four) with an hour for lunch. Flextime and four-day or three-day weeks (at 9 or 10 hours a day) are still the exception, not the rule. Until the 1920s most Americans were putting in a six-day week. From there we went to a standard Monday-to-Friday plus half a day on Saturday, and finally, by the late 1940s, we got it down to the five-day week.

In the 1950s, if George Washington's birthday fell on a Saturday, you had to celebrate it on your own time. But today his birthday (as well as several other holidays) is celebrated on Monday, ensuring that everyone not only has the day off but also gets to enjoy a three-day weekend. In fact, most full-time workers are guaranteed 10 paid holidays. When you figure in vacation time, paid sick leave, and personal leave, it's a wonder anyone ever has to show up to work at all. And if you run out of sick leave, you can always call in dead.

But as much as the average workweek has fallen and vacation days have increased, Americans work slightly more hours than do their counterparts in Japan and considerably more than those in Germany. And, unlike Western European workers who get about five weeks vacation, most Americans get relatively short vacations—usually just 2 or 3 weeks.

The Labor Department measures the average workweek per job, not per worker. What about all those people who hold two jobs, not to mention those who hold three? If you work 35 hours on one job and 25 hours on a second job, the Labor Department would say that you have an average work week of 30 hours. But, of course, you're actually working 60 hours.

According to an Economic Policy Institute study by Juliet Schor and Laura Leete-Guy, the average American worker now actually puts in about 140 more hours on the job

Table 3 Capital Deepening: Ratio of Growth of Capital to Hours Worked, 1955–96

Period	Ratio
1955–65	5.0
1965–73	2.4
1973–80	1.8
1981–89	1.5
1990–96	1.2

Sources: *Survey of Current Business,* August issues, 1967–97.

in a year than he did two decades ago. This has happened, they concluded, mainly because of the decline in real wages since 1973.

(2) Our Declining Educational System   Business firms are having trouble finding secretaries who can spell and put together grammatically correct sentences. Law firms spend millions of dollars teaching their attorneys how to write. And the impromptu remarks of our politicians—from ex-presidents George Bush and Ronald Reagan and ex-vice president Dan Quayle on down—are shot through with garbled syntax and grammatical errors (not to mention Quayle's tacking an *e* to the end of *potato* during an elementary school spelling bee).

More people are going to college, but our labor force is less educated.

It is truly paradoxical that at a time when more people than ever are attending college and millions of them are graduating every year, our labor force is less well-educated than those of previous generations. So I'll resolve the paradox. Our educational leaders figured out that they could get more students through the educational system by lowering standards every 10 or 15 years—kind of like a reverse game of limbo. They kept lowering the limbo stick and letting people step *over* it instead of having to squeeze *under* it. Peer pressure ("Don't appear too smart, or we won't accept you"), television (watching sitcoms rather than reading books), and less parental supervision (one-parent families or two parents holding down jobs) have also taken a toll.

Given the product of our educational system, it is no great surprise that the quality of our labor force has been derided, especially in comparison with those of other leading industrial nations. In an age when literacy, numerical skills, and problem-solving ability are crucial in the workplace, our schools are failing us (see the box "Our Failing Educational System"). A well-educated labor force is essential if we are going to be able to compete in the world economy.[1]

---

[1]The failings of our educational system are further enumerated near the end of Chapter 34 in *Economics* (or Chapter 18 in *Macroeconomics*).

Our Failing Educational System

By every measure, our educational system has been failing. Over the last 30 years verbal and math SAT scores have fallen sharply. Our literacy rate is among the lowest of those in industrial nations. American technological innovation, which was long on the cutting edge, has slacked off in recent years.

There is something very wrong with the way our children learn. By the time they reach high school, most of them still cannot do simple arithmetic without a calculator, and when they enter college, one out of three freshmen must enroll in at least one remedial course. If this is called higher education, one shudders to think of what is happening on the lower levels.

To be sure, education is basically a function of local government, with the state and federal governments providing some of the financing. On a state-by-state basis, however, some states spend three times as much per pupil as others do. And the variation among all the school districts in the nation is much wider, with the richest spending perhaps 8 or 10 times as much on each pupil as the poorest districts.

When Ronald Reagan took office in 1981, he called for a huge military buildup to counter what he perceived to be major weaknesses in our nation's defenses. Within six years defense spending more than doubled. He also appointed a commission to study our educational deficiencies. But when the commission reported that American education was swamped in a "sea of mediocrity," there was no perceptible presidential response.

Half the nation's math and science teachers are unqualified to teach those subjects. In Florida 61 percent of the new teachers of 6th through 12th-grade math flunked their math certification test, despite a required passing score of 61 percent.* We have an educational system that turns out 1 million functional illiterates a year. These young adults, who cannot read, write, or do simple numerical computations, are unqualified for any of the jobs opening up in our increasingly high-tech economy.

More spending will not, by itself, solve all our educational problems, but like chicken soup, it wouldn't hurt. More money for teachers' salaries will attract better and brighter teachers. More money spent on science labs, programs for gifted children, foreign language education, and computer facilities will reap substantial returns. We need to turn our educational system around, and we're not going to be able to do it on the cheap.

*Kurt Greenbaum, "Teachers Flunk Own Subjects," *Fort Lauderdale News*, June 15, 1991, p. 1B.

We have a permanent underclass comprising 10 percent of our population.

(3) The Permanent Underclass: Poverty, Drugs, and Crime   One of the major factors holding the United States back is a permanent underclass of nearly 10 percent of our population. These people are supported by our tax dollars, and many are members of third- and fourth-generation welfare families. No other industrialized nation in the world has such a large dependent population.[2]

Closely associated with poverty are drugs and crime. Although poor people are much more likely than any other population group to be afflicted by both drugs and crime, these problems have affected the lives of virtually every American. No community today is free of either drugs or crime, and they have taken an enormous toll, both economically and socially. Although we cannot quantify how the related problems of poverty, drugs, and crime have affected our rate of economic growth, they have clearly played a major role in lowering productivity and output, as well as our quality of life.

Poverty amid plenty

Poverty amid plenty is an apt description of America in the 1990s. Although we try to avoid making value judgments in economics, it amazes me that so many Americans do not feel an urgent need to alleviate the poverty that is all around us.

Just to begin to wipe out poverty and eradicate the epidemics of drugs and crime would take a massive effort. Somehow these 25 million Americans must be rewoven into our social fabric and become fully integrated, self-supporting members of our labor force. We *did* make a partial effort in the mid-1960s (President Lyndon Johnson's abortive War on Poverty), with mixed results, but since then we've done absolutely nothing. In terms of dollars, the bill would come to tens of billions a year, well into the next century. It comes down to two alternative questions: (1) Can we afford to *do* this? or (2) Can we afford *not* to?

This country was built by immigrants.

(4) Restrictions on Immigration   To say this country was literally built by immigrants would be no exaggeration. Immigration has been a tremendous source of strength to our nation. Even though immigrant families were always willing to start out on the bottom rung of the economic ladder and work their way up, the rise of "native American" groups eventually led to severe restrictions on the number of people allowed into this country (see the box titled "The Role of Immigration"). We have no way of measuring how much more dynamic and productive our economy would be if we still allowed unrestricted immigration as we did until the 1920s.

The Role of Technological Change   Way back in Chapter 2, I said that there are two basic ways to attain economic growth: (1) more inputs of capital and labor and (2) technological change. So far we've been talking about capital and labor. Now we'll turn to technological change.

Technological change enables us to produce more output from the same package of resources or, alternatively, to produce the same output with fewer resources. Technological change could be the creation of new or better goods and services. It also includes greater efficiency in market processes, improvements in the qualities of resources, improved knowledge about how to combine resources, and the introduction of new production processes.

Economic growth rate is largely determined by the rate of technological change.

The rate of technological change may well be the single most important determinant of a nation's rate of economic growth. Although the United States has long been at the cutting edge of technological change, the Japanese have applied that change to the production of high-quality manufactured goods—whether consumer electronics, cars, semiconductors, or steel. We keep coming up with great ideas, but the Japanese have been more adept at taking those ideas and running with them. For example, the industrial robot may have been invented in America, but Japanese companies employ almost three-quarters of the world's robots. Toyota, which uses robots extensively, produces half as many vehicles as General Motors with only 5 percent of GM's number of workers.

---

[2]Poverty will be discussed in the second part of Chapter 33 of *Economics* and Chapter 17 of *Macroeconomics*.

The Role of Immigration

The Daughters of the American Revolution, many of whom trace their ancestry back to the Mayflower, used to invite the president of the United States to address them every year. In 1933 Franklin Roosevelt, whose forebears arrived in New York while it was still a Dutch colony, was invited to speak. His first words were, "Fellow immigrants." Needless to say, the Daughters never asked him back.

Roosevelt's point, of course, was that we are indeed a nation of immigrants—regardless of when our families arrived. And each new wave of immigrants—whether from Europe, Africa, Latin America, or Asia—worked hard so that their children would have a better life. Hard work and deferred gratification were the hallmarks of each immigrant group.

Prior to the early 1920s, when a series of increasingly restrictive immigration laws were passed, virtually anyone who wanted to come here was welcome.* In the early years of this century, close to a million people came here each year, mostly from eastern and southern Europe. The prime motivation in restricting their numbers was to prevent further dilution of our vaunted northern European stock.

Immigrants are usually in their 20s or 30s, and they tend to be more adventurous, ambitious, and upwardly mobile than those who stay behind. As an added bonus, their educations have already been completed, so we reap the benefits while their native countries bear the costs. This phenomenon has been termed the *brain drain.*

Immigrants are often willing to work 14 or 16 hours a day, seven days a week. Within a couple of years, an immigrant has typically saved enough to open a small business. They may never get rich, but their children will go to college.

Until the 1920s immigrants were a tremendous source of economic strength. Not only did they help build the railroads, settle the West, staff the factories, and set up businesses, but they provided the energy, the ambition, and the drive that were often lacking in native-born Americans.

Today, with immigration restricted to slightly over 300,000 people a year, we are deprived of much of what made our economy go. There is no way to quantify how much this has cost us in terms of economic growth, but a remark overheard in the giant Hunts Point produce market in the Bronx sums it up well. An older man pointed at a hardworking Korean vegetable store owner and said to his friend, *"He works like our grandfathers used to work."*

This energy, ambition, and drive, is also vividly illustrated each year when the 40 finalists of the Westinghouse Science Talent Search competition are announced. In recent years nearly half the winners were foreign born or the children of immigrants. These young people are our future. Imagine if our educational system turned out millions just like them.

A study by the National Academy of Sciences released in May 1997 concluded that immigration added perhaps $10 billion a year to our GDP. But it did slightly reduce the wages and job opportunities of low-skilled American workers and temporarily placed a fiscal burden on state and local governments. On the average, the panel said, immigrant households have more school-age children and lower incomes, pay lower state and local taxes, and receive more state-financed social services than households of native-born Americans. But within 15 or 20 years the children of these families produce fiscal benefits as they finish school, start working, and begin to pay income and payroll taxes.

In 1996 Congress sharply cut back the federal benefits available to legal immigrants, while many Americans, perhaps forgetting their own origins, would like to restrict immigration even more. In addition, there is the question of illegal immigrants, who clearly outnumber those who settle here legally. However, we all need to remember that this nation was built by immigrants.

*Everyone, that is, except people from China and Japan. Fewer than 100 a year were allowed in under law and by the so-called Gentlemen's Agreement. From 1924 until after World War II, no one from Japan or China was allowed to enter the United States.

A nation's educational system plays a basic role in promoting a high rate of technological change. How well trained are its scientists and engineers, and how many graduate each year? How well trained are its workforce, its industrial managers, and its marketing people? Perhaps the answers to these questions are all too obvious with respect to the United States, given the performance of the American economy over the last two decades.

On the other hand (economists always seem to argue with both hands), over the last decade, computer literacy has increased exponentially. Today over 40 percent of all American homes have at least one personal computer and most ten-year-olds can use computers for a multitude of activities. And so, as basic reading, writing, and math skills have declined, computer skills have increased dramatically.

Three other factors retarding our growth rate are:
(1) Higher energy costs.
(2) Environmental protection requirements.
(3) Health and safety regulations.

Additional Factors Affecting Our Rate of Growth

In the 1970s six other factors retarding our rate of economic growth came into play: (1) higher energy costs, (2) environmental protection requirements, (3) health and safety regulations, (4) rising health care costs, (5) crumbling infrastructure, and (6) high military spending. When the OPEC nations quadrupled the price of oil in 1973, this not only set off a severe inflationary recession, but it permanently raised the cost of doing business and somewhat retarded our rate of growth. Similarly, environmental protection legislation requiring the expenditure of tens of billions of dollars to reduce air and water pollution also slowed economic growth. And then, too, new health and safety regulations—some of which were relaxed in the 1980s—ate up billions of dollars that would have otherwise been invested in plant and equipment or research and development.

None of this is to say that environmental protection and health and safety measures were not needed. Indeed, they probably reduced medical expenses and sick time significantly and substantially improved the quality of our lives. But they did divert resources from investment, consequently slowing our rate of growth by perhaps as much as 1 percent a year.

The effect of health care

Still another factor that has slowed growth has been our rising health care costs, which now claim more than 14 percent of our GDP. These impose a tremendous burden on taxpayers, who foot the bill for Medicare and Medicaid, and on private employers who must shell out tens of billions of dollars in medical insurance premiums.

The United States spends more on health care per capita than any other industrial nation, but the quality of that care has come under heavy criticism, and at least 37 million Americans have no medical insurance. One out of every seven dollars of our GDP goes toward health care, but we are clearly getting less per dollar than the citizens of any other industrial country. Again, while there is no way of quantifying how much the inefficiencies of our health care system have slowed our economic growth, they have clearly played a major role.

The effect of a deteriorating infrastructure

Also retarding economic growth is our virtually complete neglect of our nation's crumbling infrastructure. In the 1960s public investment in highways, bridges, ports, airports, water mains, sewers, and waterways was 2.3 percent of GDP. In the 1980s it was just 0.3 percent, about one-tenth the level of spending of several of our industrial rivals. Because we have deferred maintenance for so long, we're going to have to shell out a lot more to get things working again.

When you drive along our once glorious interstate highway network, you will often be slowed by long stretches of construction work, much of which could have been carried out years ago at considerably less cost. About 60 percent of our highways need work, ranging from repaving to major structural repairs, and perhaps "40 percent of all highway bridges—some 238,000 of them—are either structurally deficient or functionally obsolete."[3]

We have also allowed our railways to fall into disuse, or disappear altogether, while Japan and our trade rivals in Western Europe have been upgrading their own rail systems. Because of our relatively large geographic area, it is extremely important for us to upgrade our crumbling infrastructure to enhance economic growth and enable us to better compete in the international economic arena.

The effect of military spending

How has military spending affected our economic growth? To what degree has it drawn away resources that might otherwise have been used to build up our productive capacity? Between World War II and 1990, while we devoted about 6 percent of our GDP to defense, the Japanese held military spending to less than 1 percent. Until 1990 more than half of all the R&D spending by our government was on defense, and 40 percent of all our scientists and engineers worked on military projects. Today about 4 percent of our GDP is spent on defense.

Will we go the way of Spain in the early 17th century and England in the early years of this century? The United States now runs the risk of indulging in what historian Paul Kennedy terms *imperial overstretch:*

> Decision makers in Washington must face the awkward and enduring fact that the sum total of the United States' global interests and obligations is nowadays far larger than the country's power to defend them all simultaneously.[4]

---

[3]John Sedgwick, "Strong but Sensitive," *Atlantic Monthly,* April 1991, p. 72.
[4]Paul Kennedy, *The Rise and Fall of the Great Powers* (New York: Random House, 1987), p. 515.

How do we avoid this eventuality? "Without a rough balance between these competing demands of defense, consumption, and investment, a Great Power is unlikely to preserve its status for long."[5]

Most developed nations have experienced an eventual slowing of their growth rate. Mancur Olson, in his study titled *The Rise and Decline of Nations,* concludes that special interest groups—particularly labor unions, farmers' cooperatives, and employers' associations—become stronger as the economy grows.[6] These groups then make it more difficult to introduce new technologies that could continue to increase growth. For example, the International Longshoremen's Union prevented the containerization of freight for years until the shippers offered them an extremely lucrative retirement plan. And the farmers continue persuading Congress to provide them with billions of dollars a year in price supports and subsidies. An egregious practitioner of these politics is North Carolina Senator Jesse Helms, who, as the second-ranking Republican on the Senate Agriculture Committee (and its former chair), has seen to it that the tobacco growers of his state continued to receive their subsidies.[7]

How do we counteract the influence of these special interest groups? Olson suggests that we bring down the barriers to international trade. Look at what foreign competition has done for the automobile industry. The United Auto Workers Union has been forced to grant concessions to the big three automakers, resulting in lower costs and increased efficiency. And now Americans have a wider range of better-quality cars to choose from at lower prices. Olson also attributes the high growth rate of the Common Market nations to the effects of free trade on diluting the power of special interest groups.

In an extensive study of American economic growth over the 1929–82 period, Edward Denison attributed about half our growth to added inputs of labor and capital and the rest to increased productivity.[8] The main source of productivity growth was advances in knowledge obtained through research and development. A second major source was improvements in the quality of labor, primarily the consequence of improvements in education and training.

Why, then, has our rate of productivity growth been falling? To extend Denison's logic, we must look to lagging R&D spending and to a declining educational system.

The Productivity of Labor: An International Comparison

Are you ready for a big surprise? All right, then, here it comes. Which country in the world has the highest productivity per worker? Japan? Germany? Sweden? The answer is none of the above. That's right! The number one country in the world, the country with the highest productivity per worker, is—are you ready?—the United States.

How can that *be?* Our productivity growth has been slowing these last two decades, while that of our industrial rivals has grown much more rapidly. How could we possibly still be in the lead? The answer, of course, is that our lead was so big that even though a few other countries have been gaining, they haven't quite caught us yet. Indeed, since the early 1990s, as the economies of Western Europe and Japan slowed and unemployment mounted, we have probably increased our lead.

A series of studies by McKinsey, the giant consulting firm, has confirmed that American workers are the most productive in the world.[9] In 1990 the average full-time American worker produced $49,000 worth of goods and services, as opposed to $47,000 by the French worker, $44,200 by the German worker, and just $38,200 by the Japanese worker.

---

[5]Ibid., p. 446.

[6]Mancur Olson, *The Rise and Decline of Nations* (New Haven, CT: Yale University Press, 1982).

[7]In effect, then, the U.S. Department of Agriculture has subsidized the tobacco farmers, while the surgeon general was discouraging cigarette sales by forcing the companies to print a warning such as "Cigarette Smoke Contains Carbon Monoxide" on every pack of cigarettes and in every ad.

[8]Edward S. Denison, *Accounting for Slower Economic Growth* (Washington, DC: Brookings Institution, 1979).

[9]Studies were conducted in 1992, 1993, 1996, and 1997. The company has published an executive summary of the 1996 and 1997 studies.

Although international comparisons of productivity must be taken with at least a couple of grains of salt,[10] the McKinsey study is considered "the most authoritative to date," according to *New York Times* economics writer Sylvia Naser.[11] While we have been surpassed by the Japanese in several manufacturing industries, the U.S. economy shines in the service sector. For example, we are more than twice as efficient as the Japanese in general merchandise retailing "largely because Japan's zoning laws save mom-and-pop stores from annihilation by the Japanese equivalents of Wal-Mart."[12] Similarly, our deregulated telecommunications industry is at least twice as efficient as Germany's government monopoly.

In a nine-industry follow-up study, McKinsey determined that the average output per hour of German workers was 83 percent of the average output of American workers. And, according to the study, the average Japanese worker was just 79 percent as productive as the average American worker. Although Japanese workers are more productive than their American counterparts in making cars and steel, they lag far behind in making beer and in food packaging.[13]

The problem in Germany is "overengineering." Too much plant and equipment is allocated to each worker, leading to low levels of capacity utilization. In France, where the minimum wage is almost double that in the United States, and fringe benefits are also much higher, millions of lower-skilled workers are priced out of the labor market because employers simply cannot afford to hire them.[14]

Conclusion

Can we reattain a long-term annual growth rate of at least 3 percent? Our labor force grows by about 1 percent each year, so we'll need to sustain a productivity growth rate of at least 2 percent. We've certainly done that for most of our history, but if we are to do so again, we'll have to deal with all the factors that have been slowing productivity growth.

The Law of Diminishing Returns

Before we consider the problem of growth in less developed countries, let's look at the law of diminishing returns, which bears down on economic growth in every economy. We'll consider how this law applies to agricultural production and to office work.

Resources may be used in various proportions. For example, a farmer may either plant crops on 400 acres or cultivate 200 more intensively. Similarly, a bank may either install hundreds of ATMs or hire hundreds of real tellers. Using resources in different proportions will yield varying amounts of output. Let's look at one particular set of variations.

Next to the law of supply and demand, the law of diminishing returns is probably most often invoked. Unfortunately, this simple law is not clearly understood by those who so blithely drop its name. It should really be called the law of diminishing marginal output.

Using the data in Table 4, we see that one person working alone turns out two log cabins a week, while two people working together can turn out five per week. If you've ever attempted to move a 400-pound log, you know it's easier to have someone at the other end of the log. Perhaps three people can work together even more efficiently.

Increasing returns

The first three workers give us increasing returns (or increasing marginal returns). Working together, they can get a lot more done than if each worked alone. But notice

---

[10]Two reasons why international comparisons of worker output are difficult are (1) no two national accounting systems are identical, and (2) there are daily fluctuations in the exchange rates among the world's currencies.

[11]Sylvia Naser, "U.S. Output per Worker Called Best," *New York Times,* October 1, 1992, p. D1.

[12]Ibid.

[13]Sylvia Naser, "More Signs of a Productive U.S.," *New York Times,* October 22, 1993, p. D1.

[14]The minimum wage is discussed at the end of the chapter entitled "Labor Markets and Wage Rates" in *Economics* and *Microeconomics.*

Table 4   The Law of Diminishing Returns: An Example

Number of Workers	Total Output	Marginal* Output	
0	0	0	
1	2	2	Increasing returns
2	5	3	Increasing returns
3	9	4	Increasing returns
4	12	3	Diminishing returns
5	14	2	Diminishing returns
6	15	1	Diminishing returns
7	15	0	Diminishing returns
8	14	−1	Diminishing and negative returns
9	11	−3	Diminishing and negative returns

*Marginal output is the additional output produced by the last worker hired. Thus the first worker adds 2 units to output, so his marginal output is 2. The second worker hired adds 3 units of output (output has risen from 2 to 5), so his marginal output is 3. When a third worker is hired, total output jumps to 9. Marginal output has therefore risen by 4.

Diminishing marginal output

what happens when we hire a fourth worker. This person raises output, but only by 3. With the fourth worker we have the onset of diminishing returns (or diminishing marginal output).

Why is this so? Because three people may be an ideal number to move and lift 400-pound logs. The fourth worker is certainly a help, but proportionately, she doesn't add as much as the third worker.

A fifth worker adds still less to output (2 units) and a sixth worker even less (1 unit). In other words, five people can manage building log cabins almost as well as six. As we add the seventh worker, we find that he is superfluous. We would say, then, that from the fourth to the seventh worker, we have *diminishing returns.*

Negative returns

The eighth worker is actually in the way, having a marginal output of minus one. Returns become negative when this eighth worker is added. A ninth worker gets in the way even more. The eighth and ninth workers have negative returns.

What would be the maximum number of workers you would hire? The answer is six. If the wage rate were very low, you would hire up to six. The seventh worker, however, adds nothing to output, and the eighth and ninth get in the way, thereby reducing output.

The law of diminishing returns: If units of a resource are added to a fixed portion of other resources, eventually marginal output will decline.

The law of diminishing returns (or, technically, diminishing marginal output) is defined this way: *If units of a resource are added to a fixed proportion of other resources, eventually marginal output will decline.* If we were to keep adding labor to a fixed amount of land and capital, at some point the marginal output of labor would decline. In Table 4 this happens with the fourth worker, because her marginal output (3) is less than the marginal output of the third worker (4).

One of the major applications of the law of diminishing returns has been the Malthusian theory of population (see the box). The Reverend Thomas Robert Malthus predicted that diminishing returns would eventually lead to relatively low increases in food production. At the same time, the world's population would be doubling every generation. As the world's population outstripped the food supply, widespread famine would be inevitable. But the disaster that Malthus predicted never took place—at least it hasn't yet. We will be taking up the Malthusian theory at the end of this chapter.

The law of diminishing returns also helps explain the law of increasing costs, which was covered in the appendix to Chapter 2. Still another major application is the marginal revenue product schedule, the main topic of the chapter on demand in the factor market, which you'll find in *Economics* and *Microeconomics.*

Thomas Robert Malthus, English cleric and economist (The Granger Collection, New York)

Economic Growth in the Less Developed Countries

Well, enough about *our* problems. Now let's talk about other people's problems. Let's talk about people who *really* have problems—those who live in less developed countries.

The world can be divided into three groups of countries: the industrialized nations, the newly industrializing countries (NICs), and the less developed countries (LDCs). The big question, then, is how to get from LDC to NIC and, ultimately, to industrialized. And, parenthetically, at what cost?

The only way to industrialize

The only way to industrialize is to build up capital in the form of new plant and equipment. There are two main ways of doing this: working more and consuming less. As some of the poor nations of the world are barely at subsistence level, it's pretty hard for them to consume less. And because there is often a great deal of unemployment in preponderantly agricultural economies, those who want to work more have a hard time finding work.

Each of the LDCs shown in Table 5 has a per capita GDP of less than $200. The NICs, which have lifted themselves out of abject poverty during the last three or four decades, are well on their way to high standards of living. Among the industrial nations (shown in Table 6), it would appear that six have surpassed the United States. However, international comparisons should be made with a great deal of caution. Exchange rate fluctuations and varying systems of national income accounting make these comparisons somewhat problematical. Clearly the United States has one of the highest living standards in the world, but no one knows for sure who's number one—or who is number two, three, four, or five, for that matter.

Not all the LDCs have per capita incomes as low as $200, but two-thirds of the world's population live in countries with per capita incomes of less than $1,500. So what two out of every three people on this planet have in common is poverty.

Compounding the problems of the LDCs are rapidly growing populations. The Malthusian dilemma—a food supply growing at an arithmetic rate and a population growing at a geometric rate—is becoming a reality in some of the nations of sub-Saharan

Table 5   The 10 Poorest Countries in the World

	Country	GDP per capita ($)
1	Sudan	63
2	Somalia	74
3	Mozambique	80
4	Tanzania	85
5	Afghanistan	111
6	Ethiopia	130
7	Malawi	144
8	Burundi	146
9	Sierra Leone	152
10	Chad	186

Source: *Top 10 of Everything 1998* (New York: D. K. Publishing, 1997).

Table 6   The 10 Richest Countries in the World, 1996

	Country	GDP per capita ($)
1	Luxembourg	39,833
2	Switzerland	37,179
3	Japan	34,629
4	Bermuda	29,857
5	Denmark	28,104
6	Norway	26,477
7	United States	25,860
8	Germany	25,578
9	Austria	24,949
10	Iceland	24,605

Source: *Top 10 of Everything 1998* (New York: D. K. Publishing, 1997).

Africa, as well as in a few countries in Asia and in Latin America (see the box "The Malthusian Theory of Population"). Hundreds of millions face starvation, with virtually no chance to substantially raise their food output. The recurrent famines in Ethiopia and the Sudan may be mere dress rehearsals for a future crisis of much greater dimension.

Even more alarming in the long run, the birthrates of less developed nations show little indication of declining. And unless they decline, the emergency shipments of foodstuffs from the rest of the world are merely postponing the inevitable.

One way out of this dilemma may be the family planning programs that have been attempting to lower birthrates in the LDCs. Supported by government funding as well as grants from the Population Council, the International Planned Parenthood Federation, and the United Nations, the programs have had some success in lowering birthrates. With fewer mouths to feed, these countries now have more savings available for development (see the box "Family Planning and Economic Development").

Even *with* family planning programs, the populations of most LDCs continue to grow between 2 and 3 percent a year, and these countries must struggle to increase their

The Malthusian Theory of Population

Economics is called the "dismal science" largely because of the Malthusian theory. As it was originally formulated, the theory predicted that famine and warfare would, within perhaps a few generations, beset the world. This was inevitable because of a tendency for the world's population to double every 25 years.

The Reverend Thomas Robert Malthus wrote the first edition of the *Essay on the Principle of Population* in 1798. His two main points were that population tended to grow in a geometric progression—1, 2, 4, 8, 16, 32—and that the only ways to stop population from growing this rapidly were the "positive checks" of pestilence, famine, and war. Not a very pleasant outlook.

In his second edition, Malthus held out slightly more hope for holding down the rate of the population increase. It could be contained by the "preventive check" of "moral restraint," which meant not getting married until one could support a family (and, it went without saying, no fooling around before you got married).

Malthus also noted that the food supply could not increase as rapidly as population tended to because the planet was limited in size and there was only a fixed amount of arable land. He felt the food supply would ultimately tend to grow in an arithmetic progression—1, 2, 3, 4, 5, 6—and it would not take a mathematical genius to conclude that we would be in trouble within a few generations. The relevant figures are shown in the table below.*

The Malthusian theory is a variant of the law of diminishing returns. As increasing amounts of labor are applied to a fixed amount of land, eventually marginal output will decline.

Was Malthus right? Surely not in the industrialized countries, particularly the United States, Canada, and Australia, which are major exporters of wheat and other farm products. Two things happened in these countries to ward off Malthus's dire predictions. First, because of tremendous technological advances in agriculture—tractors, harvesters, better fertilizer, and high-yield seeds—farmers were able to feed many more people.† Second, as industrialization spread and more and more people left the countryside for the cities, the birthrate fell.

However, the less developed countries are caught in a double bind. The Malthusian positive check of a high death rate has been largely removed by public health measures, such as malaria control, smallpox vaccine, and more sanitary garbage disposal. But because these countries have not yet been able to industrialize and urbanize their populations, birthrates remain high. In most of Asia, Africa, and Latin America, populations are doubling every 30 to 35 years, putting hundreds of millions of people in peril of starvation. Famine is a reality in these countries, and it may well become even more widespread toward the end of this century.

*Malthus did not use actual years in his predictions; the years in the table are purely hypothetical to illustrate his theory. Also, Malthus did not predict that this would actually happen. Rather, he indicated that these were the tendencies, but that population increases could be checked by war, pestilence, famine, or moral restraint.

†Some observers have been encouraged by the so-called Green Revolution, which has enabled many large growers to double and triple yields by using better seeds and fertilizer. However, the prime beneficiaries have been the wealthy farmers and a few multinational agribusinesses, such as Dole, Del Monte, and Ralston Purina. They have profited by producing for export such crops as sugar, soybeans, bananas, and peanuts. But they have also forced millions of small farmers off the land and actually caused the production of indigenous food staples to decline, making these countries even more dependent on food imports.

Year	Food Production	Population
1800	1	1
1825	2	2
1850	3	4
1875	4	8
1900	5	16
1925	6	32

Family Planning and Economic Development

Remember the riddle of the chicken and the egg? There's a similar one in family planning and economic development: Which comes first, economic development or a falling birthrate? Historically, as a nation urbanized and industrialized, its birthrate eventually fell. According to a United Nations study, once a nation reaches a certain threshold, or stage of development, families will begin to choose to have fewer and fewer children.* The birthrate falls for three main reasons: (1) Children, who are economic assets on a farm, become just more mouths to feed in an urban setting. (2) Children used to be counted on for support in the parents' old age, but as development takes place, people are able to accumulate savings and will receive pensions when they retire. (3) As more children survive to adulthood, fathers don't need to have so many sons to ensure that at least one will survive to carry on the family name.

We know, then, that as development reaches a certain stage, the birthrate will fall. This enables a nation to save more, convert that savings into capital, and further increase its rate of economic growth. But why wait for birthrates to fall of their own accord? Why not induce them to fall by means of family planning programs *before* development has progressed very far?

Virtually every LDC has a policy of encouraging birth control to limit population growth. Some have had considerable success in lowering their birthrates, most notably China, Taiwan, Hong Kong, Singapore, South Korea, and several Caribbean nations.

*U.N. Department of Economic and Social Affairs, "With Special Reference to Conditions and Trends of Fertility in the World," *Population Bulletin* no. 7 (New York: 1965), chapter 9.

food supplies at that rate just to keep pace. To industrialize, they would need to attain a high enough economic growth rate to be able to produce capital goods as well as the basic consumer necessities. Thus many LDCs clearly will never be able to begin industrializing without outside help.

There *is* one additional source of capital: grants and loans from the industrialized nations. Over the last four decades hundreds of billions of dollars have been provided by the United States, the Soviet Union, Western Europe, and Japan. But now that many LDCs are deeply in debt (some have defaulted on their loans), it is unlikely that more credit will be extended. In fact, the interest that must be paid out each year by the LDCs has become a tremendous burden.

Grants and loans from industrialized nations

During the 1980s some nations *did* attain the status of NIC. The "four tigers" of Asia—South Korea, Taiwan, Hong Kong, and Singapore—as well as Malaysia, Brazil, Indonesia, and Thailand have done this, largely through foreign investment. Unwise

Chinese Economic Development

When the communists took over China in 1949, the country was one of the poorest nations in the world. After more than four decades of very rapid economic growth—punctuated by the chaotic setbacks of the Great Leap Forward in the 1960s and the Cultural Revolution of the 1970s—China is well along the path of economic development.

Although China's rulers have zigzagged from ideologically pure strong centralized control to the acceptance of a more freewheeling private sector, China's economic record is quite impressive. In 1949 the average Chinese person subsisted on less than $200 a year, but since then living standards have at least quintupled.

The industrial sector is three-tiered, with nearly two-thirds of the workers employed by the government and the rest working in cooperatives or for themselves. In the much larger agricultural sector, small groups of families work, on a cooperative basis, on plots averaging about 50 acres. Farm machinery is shared, and profits are divided at the end of the year.

Capitalism is most advanced in Guangdong Province, which lies adjacent to Hong Kong, where foreign corporations have set up factories that have become virtual export platforms, sending cheap manufactured goods to the United States and other industrial nations. Between 1978 and 1998 national output has more than quintupled. If this pace is maintained, within another three decades China may rival Japan for economic preeminence in Asia and perhaps in the rest of the world as well.

What is interesting about Chinese economic development is that the nation has gone from the ideological purity of the days of Mao Tse-tung to the rampant materialism that has been in evidence since his death in 1976. Most Chinese these days aspire to possess the "Big Eight Things": refrigerator, motorcycle, electric fan, color TV, tape recorder, camera, stereo, and washing machine.

Military spending and wars

investments in South Korea, Indonesia, and Thailand, many of which are in default, led to the Asian financial crisis that occurred in late 1997 and continued in early 1998.[15]

Still another problem is that virtually all LDCs spend a major part of their budgets on armaments, which diverts desperately needed funds from development. Warfare in Southeast Asia, Afghanistan, Ethiopia, Sudan, Peru, Somalia, and the Persian Gulf has further exacerbated the situation. The United States, the former Soviet Union, China, and several European nations have encouraged this unfortunate tendency by selling—or even giving—arms to developing nations.

China (see box "Chinese Economic Development") and India, the world's most populous nations, have made impressive strides toward development, although neither has yet attained NIC status (both, however, along with Pakistan, have managed to produce nuclear bombs). Today more than two-thirds of the people in the world live in LDCs, and nearly all of these people live at or near the subsistence level. Most live out their lives in abject poverty, with no hope that they or their children will have better lives.

Questions for Further Thought and Discussion

1. Why is our country's productivity increasing so slowly?
2. Explain the Malthusian theory of population. Is it relevant today anywhere in the world? Explain where and why.
3. How does the American savings rate compare to that of other leading industrial nations? What accounts for the difference?
4. What changes took place during the Industrial Revolution that made possible sustained economic growth?

---

[15]This crisis will be fully discussed in the last chapter.

WORKBOOK FOR CHAPTER 16

Name _____   Date _____

Multiple-Choice Questions

Circle the letter that corresponds to the best answer.

1. Our rate of productivity increase in the 1980s was
   _____ the rate of productivity increase in the 1960s.
   a. faster than   b. about   c. slower than

2. Compared to Japan, our rate of savings is _____ and
   our rate of capital formation is _____.
   a. higher, higher   b. lower, lower   c. higher,
   lower   d. lower, higher

3. Each of the following except _____
   slowed our rate of economic growth in the 1970s.
   a. research and development spending   b. pollution
   regulations and requiring pollution reduction
   c. health and safety regulations   d. rising energy
   costs

4. The key to productivity growth is
   a. an increasing labor force   b. technological
   change   c. expansion of land under cultivation
   d. the use of deteriorating and obsolete capital

5. Rising productivity could be each of these except
   a. more units of output from more units of input
   b. More output per unit of input   c. the same output
   from fewer units of input

6. Edward Denison attributes about _____ percent
   of our economic growth to increases in productivity.
   a. 10   b. 30   c. 50   d. 70   e. 90

7. Most of the people in the world live in
   a. LDCs   b. NICs   c. industrialized countries

8. During the last 10 years, Americans were saving about
   _____ percent of their disposable incomes.
   a. 3 to 6   b. 5 to 8   c. 7 to 10   d. 9 to 12

9. The prospects for LDCs to receive more foreign aid than
   they now receive are
   a. excellent   b. fair   c. poor

10 Sustained economic growth did not begin anywhere in the
   world until around
   a. 1450   b. 1600   c. 1750   d. 1900

11. Which statement is true with respect to the last 20 years?
    a. The American standard of living is rising very
    rapidly.   b. The American standard of living is rising
    very slowly.   c. The American standard of living is
    falling very slowly.   d. The American standard of
    living is falling very rapidly.

12. Compared to the 1950s, our rate of per capita real GDP
    growth is
    a. much faster   b. slightly faster   c. slightly
    slower   d. much slower

13. Which statement is true?
    a. The generation that came of age in the 1980s has a
    much higher standard of living than their parents'
    generation did when they came of age.   b. Most
    people in their 20s and 30s could be considered
    "yuppies."   c. The "me generation" gave new
    meaning to Thorstein Veblen's term *conspicuous
    consumption.*   d. None of these statements is true.

14. Compared to the gross savings rates of the other leading
    industrial nations, ours is
    a. among the lowest   b. about average
    c. higher than average   d. the highest

15. All other things remaining equal, which country in the figure
    below would you expect to have a higher growth rate?
    a. Country A   b. Country B   c. They would
    have the same growth rate.   d. There is no way of
    telling which would have the higher growth rate.

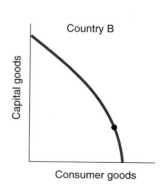

16. Our ratio of the growth of capital to hours worked has
_____ since the 1950s.
   a. declined sharply   b. declined slightly
   c. increased slightly   d. increased sharply

17. Which statement best reflects the role of our educational
system in preparing students for the workforce?
   a. More people than ever are attending college, so our
labor force is better educated than at any time in our
history.   b. Business firms are having trouble finding
secretaries who can spell and put together grammatically
correct sentences.   c. Most people in our labor force
are unable to perform their jobs because of their
educational shortcomings.   d. Increased spending on
teachers' salaries, science labs, and computer facilities
will completely solve any educational problems this
nation has.

18. Which statement is true?
   a. The permanent underclass is basically an economic
asset because it is a cheap source of labor.   b. The
permanent underclass has slowed our rate of economic
growth.   c. About 2 percent of all Americans are
members of the permanent underclass.   d. Because
the United States is a socially mobile society, there is no
such thing as a permanent underclass.

19. "Decision makers in Washington must face the awkward
and enduring fact that the sum total of the United States'
global interests and obligations is nowadays far larger
than the country's power to defend them all
simultaneously." This statement was made by
   a. Edward S. Denison   b. Paul Kennedy
   c. Benjamin M. Friedman   d. Mancur Olson

20. Which statement is false with respect to the period
1945–1990?
   a. More than half of all the research and development
spending by our government was on defense.
   b. Forty percent of all our scientists and engineers
worked on military projects.   c. We spent about
6 percent of our GDP on defense.   d. None of these
statements is false.

21. Mancur Olson suggests that the best remedy for
overcoming the economic influence of special interest
groups is
   a. bringing down the barriers to international trade
   b. having the federal government curb the influence of
special interest groups   c. raising tariffs on all
imports that are putting American workers out of work
   d. having the federal government nationalize all
industries dominated by special interest groups

22. The only ways to build up capital are to
   a. consume more and save more   b. consume less
and save less   c. consume more and save less
   d. consume less and save more

23. Most people in the world live on incomes of less than
_____ a year.
   a. $200   b. $1,500   c. $5,000   d. $10,000

24. Rapid population growth _____ the economic
development of LDCs.
   a. severely hampers   b. slightly hampers
   c. slightly helps   d. greatly helps

25. Malthus was correct in his predictions for
   a. at least some industrial countries and some LDCs
   b. at least some industrial countries but no LDCs
   c. at least some LDCs but no industrial countries
   d. neither the LDCs nor the industrial countries

26. Which statement is false?
   a. Children, who are economic assets on a farm, become
just more mouths to feed in an urban setting.
   b. Before economic development children are counted
on for support in their parents' old age, but as
development takes place, people become less dependent
on this form of old-age support.   c. As economic
development progresses, more children survive to
adulthood, and the birthrate begins to fall.   d. None
of these statements is false.

27. Since 1973 our productivity rose by more than 3 percent
in _____ year(s).
   a. 1   b. 4   c. 8   d. 11   e. 15

28. Which statement is true?

  a. We have been spending a larger percentage of our GDP on our infrastructure than Japan and most of the nations of Western Europe.   **b.** Our health care costs are now nearly 10 percent of our GDP.   **c.** American productivity is the highest in the world.   **d.** None of these statements is true.

29. Which statement is true?

  a. Americans work more hours and have a higher productivity than the workers of all other industrial nations.   **b.** The Japanese work more hours and have a higher productivity than the workers of any other industrial nation.   **c.** The Japanese work longer hours and Americans are more productive than the workers of any other industrial nation.   **d.** Americans work longer hours and the Japanese are more productive than the workers of any other industrial nation.

30. In general, as output rises you first attain

  a. increasing returns, then diminishing returns, then negative returns   **b.** diminishing returns, then negative returns, then increasing returns   **c.** negative returns, then increasing returns, then diminishing returns   **d.** increasing returns, then negative returns, then diminishing returns

31. The law of diminishing returns may also be called the law of

  a. diminishing marginal output   **b.** diminishing positive returns   **c.** negative returns   **d.** increasing returns

Fill-In Questions

1. An increase in the ratio of capital to workers is called

  _____.

2. Productivity is defined as _____

  _____.

3. Most Americans, French, Germans, Japanese, and British work a little under _____ hours a year.

4. In the early 1990s Americans were saving about

  _____ percent of their disposable incomes.

5. The Industrial Revolution began over _____

  centuries ago in _____.

6. Edward Denison attributes about _____

  percent of our economic growth to increases in labor and

  capital and about _____ percent to

  increases in productivity.

7. Instead of waiting for economic development to lower

  birthrates, many LDCs are counting on _____

  _____ to do this.

8. The country with the largest GDP in the world is

  _____.

9. Sustained economic growth was made possible by the

  _____.

10. Our real GDP in 1997 was more than _____

  times our real GDP in 1939.

Problems

1. Given the information in Table 1, fill in Malthus's predictions for the years 2025, 2050, and 2075.

Table 1

Year	Food Production	Population
2000	1	1
2025	_____	_____
2050	_____	_____
2075	_____	_____

2. a. Fill in the marginal output column of Table 2.

3. a. Fill in the marginal output column of Table 3.

Table 2

Number of Workers	Total Output	Marginal Output
0	0	
1	1	_____
2	3	_____
3	6	_____
4	9	_____
5	11	_____
6	13	_____
7	14	_____
8	14	_____
9	13	_____
10	11	_____
11	8	_____

b. Diminishing returns set in with the _____ worker.

c. Negative returns set in with the _____ worker.

Table 3

Number of Workers	Total Output	Marginal Output
0	0	
1	3	_____
2	7	_____
3	10	_____
4	12	_____
5	13	_____
6	13	_____
7	12	_____
8	10	_____

b. Given the information in Table 3, diminishing returns set in with the _____ worker.

c. Negative returns set in with the _____ worker.

17 Applications in Supply and Demand

Chapter 3 provided a bare-bones outline of supply and demand, but now you're going to get the real thing. We'll see how the forces of supply and demand interact to set prices and quantities bought and sold. This will set the stage for the next three chapters, which will delve still more deeply into the intricacies of supply and demand.

Chapter Objectives

Five questions are covered in this chapter:

- How much will a particular good or service cost?
- How much of it will be purchased?
- What is equilibrium?
- What are some applications of supply and demand?
- What are price floors and price ceilings?

In addition you will learn how to:

- Draw a graph of the demand curve.
- Draw a graph of the supply curve.
- Find equilibrium price and quantity.
- Determine the effects of changes in demand and supply.

Demand

The definition of demand is: the schedule of quantities of a good or service that people will buy at different prices.

Demand is defined as *the schedule of quantities of a good or service that people will buy at different prices.* At very high prices people don't buy many, and at lower prices they buy more.

An example of a demand schedule appears in Table 1. As price falls, the quantity demanded goes up. Why? Because as price declines, people are willing and able to buy more. From the buyer's standpoint, even if he wants a good or service, he won't buy it if he can't afford it. And if he can afford it but doesn't want it, he won't buy it.

In the definition of demand as a schedule of quantities that people are willing to buy at different prices, *willing* means having the ability to pay and desiring the product. Demand requires desire—and the ability to do something about it.

Stop! Read no further until you go out and buy yourself a package of graph paper. You're going to need nearly the whole package before you're finished with this chapter, and you'll go through at least another package before you finish this book. I'll wait right here until you get that graph paper.

Graphing step-by-step

This is a hands-on approach to economics. What we're going to do now is graph the demand schedule shown in Table 1. I'm going to talk you through this step-by-step. The first step is to set up the axes of the graph. The vertical axis measures price, and the horizontal axis measures quantity. This is a convention that we follow consistently in economics—price (or some other variable measured in money) goes on the vertical axis, and quantity (often output) is measured on the horizontal axis.

Setting up the vertical axis

Step 2 is to figure out our scales of measurement. On the vertical axis we measure price from $10 down to $6. There's a temptation to go all the way down to a price of zero, but if we give in to that temptation, our graph would end up looking something like the one in Figure 1.

And imagine if our prices ranged from $50 down to $46. If we were to come all the way down to zero, our demand curve would be squeezed into about an inch of space at the top of the graph paper. We want to draw the graph large enough so that we can read it easily. If we paint ourselves into a small corner of the graph paper by extending the vertical scale too low, we'll have trouble reading the graph. Ideally a graph should take up about two-thirds of a sheet of graph paper.

Setting up the horizontal axis   Step 3 is to set up the horizontal axis, or quantity scale. Most students prefer to have each line segment (or box) on the graph paper represent one unit of quantity, which is fine as long as you have enough segments to cover your whole range of quantities. If your quantity goes up to 80, you'll probably have to let each line on your graph paper represent two units or perhaps even four.

Ready for the fourth step? All right, then, here it comes. Put numbers on your quantity scale. Here you can start with 0 directly under the price scale and work your way across to the right. Go ahead and put in the numbers on your horizontal axis. I hope your numbers don't match mine in Figure 1.

What's wrong with my graph? The quantity scale is numbered consecutively by ones. It's too busy and much too hard to read. You'd be much better off numbering by fours—4, 8, 12, 16—or by fives—5, 10, 15, 20. It's easier to read a scale that has numbers that are an inch apart, rather than just ¼-inch apart.

Remember, you're the one who is going to have to read your graph and be able to reach accurate conclusions on the basis of your observations, so you want to get these

Table 1   Hypothetical Demand Schedule

Price	Quantity Demanded
$10	1
9	2
8	4
7	7
6	12

Figure 1

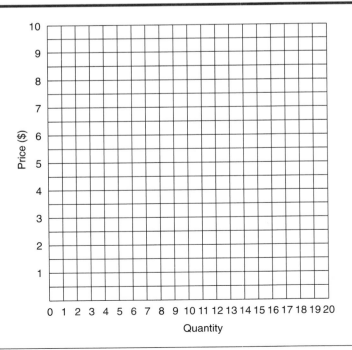

fundamentals down before you begin to lay out your graph. Enough said! It's time to draw the actual graph; set up your axes, and then you'll be ready for the next step.

Step 5: Place dots for each of the points (or coordinates) of your demand curve on the graph. I'll talk you through the first two points, and then you're on your own.

Refer to Table 1. Starting with a quantity of 1 and a price of $10, we go 1 space to the right of the origin (0) on the horizontal axis; then we move up 10 spaces. That gives us our first point.

To find the second point on the demand curve, we go 2 spaces to the right on the quantity axis and 9 spaces up. Similarly, to find our third, fourth, and fifth points, we move to the right on the horizontal axis and then straight up.

Now we're ready for our sixth and last step (which makes graphing twice as easy as the 12-step program that Alcoholics Anonymous, Overeaters Anonymous, and a lot of other groups will put you through): Connect the dots. Wait! I almost forgot to tell you something. Don't connect the dots with a ruler or any type of straightedge. Connect the dots freehand. Let your eyes guide you into drawing a smooth curve. Wait! I almost forgot to tell you something else. Use a pencil to draw your curve. Always draw your graphs in pencil. Can you guess why? You guessed it! If you mess up, you can erase your mistake and not have to start all over again. Before exams I warn my students about never drawing their graphs in ink. But about midway through the exam I hear paper being crumpled and students muttering under their breath. And they're the ones who tell me at the end of the test that I didn't give them enough time.

OK, I've said enough. Connect your dots and then see if your graph looks like the one I drew in Figure 2. If it does, great! If it doesn't, then check each of your dots with each of mine and see where you went astray. Throughout the next 11 chapters, I'll be asking you to do calculations and to draw graphs, and then to check your work. You'll be getting most things right, but remember that you can learn a lot from your mistakes.

Notice that the demand curve slopes downward and to the right as quantity rises. At high prices people buy little, but as price declines they buy more. We have an inverse relationship: As price comes down, quantity purchased goes up. This is the law of demand. More formally stated, the law of demand tells us that *the lower the price of a good or service, the greater the quantity that people will buy.* So the demand curve's downward slope reflects the law of demand.

So much for demand. Now we're ready for supply. We'll follow exactly the same procedure we followed for demand: we'll use data from a table to draw a graph of a supply curve. Then we'll put our two curves together in one graph to see one of the longest-playing acts in the entire history of economic thought: the law of demand and supply. Or is it the law of supply and demand? Actually, either one is fine.

Plotting the demand curve

The law of demand is: the lower the price of a good or service, the greater the quantity that people will buy.

Figure 2   Demand Curve

Supply

The definition of supply is: the schedule of quantities of a good or service that people will sell at different prices.

You can't repeal the laws of supply and demand.

—Anonymous

Plotting the supply curve

The law of supply is: the higher the price of a good or service, the greater the quantity that people will sell.

Supply is defined as *the schedule of quantities of a good or service that people will sell at different prices.* The figures in Table 2 show that as the price rises people are willing to sell more and more. There are two reasons for this. First, those already in business are willing to sell more in order to raise their profits. Second, new firms are attracted to the industry by the prospect of high profits.

This is the price mechanism in action. Suppose a bus line went out of business and the government appealed to people with cars to drive stranded commuters to work. Suppose you could even charge people. If the going rate were $1 per mile per passenger, you might well be tempted to start your own chauffeur service. The higher the price, the more firms will appear on the scene.

To draw a supply curve in Figure 3, we use the same type of graph we did in Figure 1. Starting with the point where quantity is 14 and price is $10, we go 14 spaces to the right from the origin (0), and then straight up 10 spaces. Using the same procedure, we plot the other four points and connect them to obtain our supply curve.

Go ahead and plot your graph. Remember to do it in pencil and to draw a smooth freehand curve. Then see whether it came out like mine in Figure 3.

You'll observe that the supply curve slopes upward and to the right as quantity rises. As price rises, then, quantity supplied rises as well. This is a direct relationship: Price and quantity supplied move in the same direction—which happens to be the law of supply. In more formal terms, *the higher the price of a good or service, the greater the quantity that people will sell.* So the upward slope of the supply curve reflects the law of supply.

Equilibrium

At equilibrium, quantity demanded and quantity supplied are equal. At a certain price, all buyers who are willing to buy will be able to. And all sellers who are willing to sell will also be able to. That price is the equilibrium price.

Table 2   Hypothetical Supply Schedule

Price	Quantity Supplied
$10	14
9	12
8	9
7	5
6	1

Figure 3   Supply Curve

The equilibrium point is where the demand and supply curves cross.

To find the equilibrium price and quantity, let's draw our demand and supply curves on the same graph. In Figure 4 we can find our equilibrium point by noting exactly where the curves cross. That tells us equilibrium price and quantity.

Where the demand and supply curves cross is a price of about $7.20, and the quantity is about 5. As a check, go back to the tables, which, if anything, are more accurate than the graph. This is because the graph is derived from the tables. Table 3 combines Table 1 and Table 2.

At a price of $8 in Table 3, the quantity demanded is 4 and the quantity supplied is 9. The difference between quantity demanded (4) and quantity supplied (9) is 5. At a price of $7, quantity demanded is 7 and quantity supplied is 5. At $7, quantity demanded (7) and quantity supplied (5) are only 2 apart. A price of $7 is much closer to equilibrium price than is $8. Remember that at equilibrium, quantity demanded equals quantity supplied. Because quantity demanded and quantity supplied are 2 apart at $7 and 5 apart at $8, $7 is much closer to equilibrium than $8.

If price is determined by supply and demand, we may ask whether one or the other is more important. More than a century ago the great classical economist Alfred Marshall wrote, "We might as reasonably dispute whether it is the upper or the under blade of a pair of scissors that cuts a piece of paper" as whether price is set by demand or supply.[1]

Price always tends toward its equilibrium level. If it should happen to be set higher, say $9, it will fall to $7.20. And if it's set lower than $7.20, it will rise.

It's easy to train economists. Just teach a parrot to say "supply and demand."

—Thomas Carlyle

Let's say the price is $9. A lot of unhappy sellers will say, "Here I go without a sale when I would have been willing to settle for a lower price." What do they do? They lower their price. And when they do—to, let's say, $8—most of the other sellers follow suit. Why? Because otherwise they'd sell nothing. Why would any buyer pay one seller $9 when the others are selling for $8?

---

[1]See Alfred Marshall, *The Principles of Economics,* 8th ed., 1920, p. 348. The first edition came out in 1890.

Figure 4   Demand, Supply, and Equilibrium

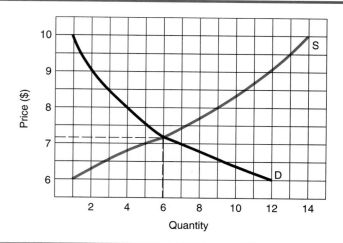

Table 3   Hypothetical Demand and Supply Schedules

Price	Quantity Demanded	Quantity Supplied
$10	1	14
9	2	12
8	4	9
7	7	5
6	12	1

As the price falls to $8, a few sellers—3, to be exact—will leave the market. In Table 3 we see that at $9 there are 12 sellers, but at $8 there are only 9. At the same time the number of buyers rises from 2 to 4.[2]

We're not yet at equilibrium, but we're getting closer. At $9 sellers outnumbered buyers 12 to 2. At $8 sellers outnumber buyers just 9 to 4. The price must be lowered to $7.20 for 6 buyers and 6 sellers to do business.

If price were below equilibrium, say at $6, the dissatisfied buyers would bid the price up. At $6 there would be 12 people willing to buy, but only 1 seller. Some of the buyers—7, in fact—would be willing to pay $7. So they'll say to the sellers, "Let's make a deal." These buyers will bid the price up to $7 and find 5 sellers willing to do business. We're still not quite at equilibrium. The price will be bid up slightly more to $7.20, bringing in one more seller and causing one more buyer to drop out of the market. At $7.20 there are 6 buyers and 6 sellers.

Above equilibrium price there are surpluses.

An alternative way to look at prices above and below equilibrium is in terms of surpluses and shortages. When the price is above $7.20, there is a surplus. Quantity supplied is greater than quantity demanded, and this difference is the surplus. For example, at a price of $9, the surplus is 10. How is the surplus eliminated? As we've just seen, by letting the price fall. The surplus, then, eliminates itself through the price mechanism.

Below equilibrium price there are shortages.

When the price is too low, there is a shortage. A shortage of 11 units occurs when the price is $6. But the shortage disappears when the price rises automatically to its equilibrium level of $7.20.[3]

Equilibrium price is the result of the forces of supply and demand. Together they determine equilibrium price. There will be no tendency for a price to change once it has reached its equilibrium. However, if either demand or supply (or both) changes, there will be a new equilibrium price.

A price is pushed toward equilibrium by the market forces of supply and demand. In other words, the price of any good or service is set by the law of supply and demand. That makes things easy for economists. Why are Rolls Royces so expensive? Supply and demand. Why is rice so cheap? Supply and demand. As long as the government does not interfere with the private market, the forces of supply and demand set the prices of everything. Or, as the popular saying goes, you can't repeal the law of supply and demand.

At equilibrium everyone is happy. Buyers can buy as much as they want. Sellers can sell as much as they want. Quantity demanded equals quantity supplied, and the market is said to *clear*.

Finding Equilibrium Price and Quantity

If we draw our graphs accurately, we can usually find equilibrium price and quantity in a couple of seconds, especially if we've used graph paper. But sometimes we need to do further analysis to find really accurate equilibrium prices and quantities. In this section we'll work out two such problems.

First, please draw a graph of the demand and supply curves for the information shown in Table 4.

Finding equilibrium price from the table

If you did a good job, your graph probably looks a lot like mine in Figure 5. Now comes the analysis. How much is equilibrium price? Go ahead and write down your best guess. What did you get? Maybe $12.50? I hate to tell you, but $12.50 is not the right answer. The way to find the right answer is to go back to Table 4 and do a little analysis. We want to find the price that is closest to equilibrium price. Is it $12 or $13? Take your time. Don't let me rush you. OK, time's up. Equilibrium price is a little closer to $13 than to $12.

How do I know this? Easy. At a price of $13, quantity demanded is 7 and quantity supplied is 12. So they're 5 units apart. Now check out the quantity demanded and the

---

[2]I have oversimplified here by assuming that each seller has one unit to sell and that each buyer buys just one unit. In real life buyers may purchase many units and sellers may supply many units.

[3]Shortages and surpluses are discussed much more extensively later in the chapter.

Table 4   Hypothetical Demand and Supply Schedules

Price	Quantity Demanded	Quantity Supplied
$15	2	19
14	4	17
13	7	12
12	12	6
11	20	3

Figure 5   Demand and Supply

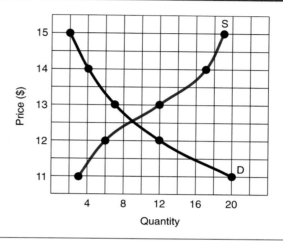

quantity supplied at a price of $12. Quantity demanded is 12 and quantity supplied is 6; they're 6 units apart. In other words, we are a little closer to equilibrium at a price of $13 than at a price of $12.

So what *is* the equilibrium price? Would $12.60 be correct? Sure. How about $12.58? Yes! $12.56? $12.61? $12.62? Any one of these is a fine answer, because each is a little closer to $13 than to $12. Anything between $12.55 and $12.65 is fine. We're not talking about economics being an exact science here, but more of an art.

Finding equilibrium quantity from the table

Now comes the more complex part of our analysis: finding equilibrium quantity. To find this, we'll break down our question into two parts: finding quantity demanded and then finding quantity supplied. We know that our equilibrium price is a little closer to $13 than $12, so our quantity demanded is a little closer to 7 than to 12. Because the midpoint between 7 and 12 is 9.5, we'll say, tentatively, that our quantity demanded is a bit less than 9.5—say, 9.4, 9.3, 9.2, or perhaps 9.1.

Now we'll do the same analysis with quantity supplied. Again, if equilibrium price is a little closer to $13 than to $12, quantity supplied is a little closer to 12 than to 6. Because the midpoint between 12 and 6 is 9, we're looking for a number a little higher than 9, say, 9.1, 9.2, 9.3, or 9.4. So what's our answer? I would say that equilibrium quantity is 9.2, or if I happened to get up on the other side of the bed that day, I'd say 9.3. In fact, I think anything within the range of 9.1 to 9.4 is acceptable. Why not 9.0 or 9.5? Well, 9.0 is the midpoint between our quantities supplied, 12 and 6. And 9.5 is the midpoint between our quantities demanded, 7 and 12.

Hey, that was so much fun, let's do another one. First draw a graph from the data in Table 5. Then, seeing where your demand and supply curves cross, estimate the equilibrium price and quantity. If your graph is drawn accurately, not only will it look a lot like Figure 6, but your equilibrium price and quantity will be pretty close to the mark. But we really need to check our table to make sure that our numbers are plausible.

What is the equilibrium price? At a price of $8, quantity demanded is 9 and quantity supplied is 16, so we're 7 units apart. At a price of $7, quantity demanded is 15 and

Table 5   Hypothetical Demand and Supply Schedules

Price	Quantity Demanded	Quantity Supplied
$10	2	22
9	5	20
8	9	16
7	15	9
6	24	1

Figure 6   Demand and Supply

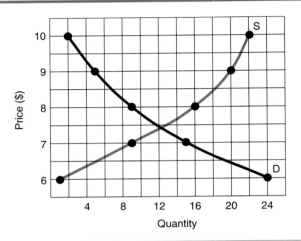

quantity supplied is 9, so we're 6 units apart. What do you think? I think equilibrium price is $7.42. And I'll take anything between $7.35 and $7.45.

Now how about equilibrium quantity? I'd really like you to do that whole dog and pony show I just did with quantity demanded and quantity supplied in the previous table. Work it out, and then come up with an equilibrium quantity.

Here's my own analysis. Quantity demanded is a little closer to 15 than to 9 (because equilibrium price is a little closer to $7 than to $8). Because the midpoint between 15 and 9 is 12, we're looking for a quantity demanded of 12.1, 12.2, 12.3, or 12.4. Quantity supplied is a little closer to 9 than to 16. Because the midpoint between these numbers is 12.5, we're looking at 12.4, 12.3, 12.2, or 12.1.

I'll call the equilibrium quantity 12.2. And I'll take anything between 12.1 and 12.4.

If you'd like to work through another problem, see the Extra Help box.

Is it necessary to do this analysis? Is it necessary to go back to the table to figure out equilibrium price and quantity? It isn't when you've got an equilibrium price that is clearly much closer to one dollar figure than to another. You'll be able to spot this when you draw your graph. But when the demand and supply curves cross about halfway between two prices, then you'll need to go back to the original data in your table to figure out more precisely where your equilibrium point lies.

Price Ceilings and Price Floors

You can't repeal the law of supply and demand.

One of the most popular sayings of all time is "You can't repeal the law of supply and demand." Maybe not, but our government sure has a lot of fun trying. Price floors and price ceilings, which Washington has imposed from time to time, have played havoc with our price system. And taxes on selected goods and services have also altered supply and demand.

What's the difference between a floor and a ceiling? If you're standing in a room, where's the floor and where's the ceiling? As you might expect, economists turn this

Finding Equilibrium Price and Quantity

You don't have to draw a graph to find the equilibrium price and quantity. There's enough information in Table A to find them. See what you can do.

A.

Price	Quantity Demanded	Quantity Supplied
$15	5	10
14	10	4

At a price of $15 quantity demanded is 5 and quantity supplied is 10, so they are 5 apart. At a price of $14 quantity demanded is 10 and quantity supplied is 4, so they are 6 apart. We are a little closer to equilibrium at a price of $15 than a price of $14. Let's call our equilibrium price $14.60 (or anything between $14.55 and 14.65).

Now let's zero in on quantity demanded and quantity supplied. Find the midpoint of quantity demanded (i.e.,

the midpoint between 5 and 10), and the midpoint of quantity supplied (i.e., between 10 and 4). They are shown in Table B.:

B.

	Quantity Demanded	Quantity Supplied
	5	10
Midpoint	7.5	7
	10	4

Now what kind of a number do we want for equilibrium quantity with respect to these midpoints? We want a number a little lower than the midpoint of 7.5 and a little higher than the midpoint of 7. Why not just split the difference and call it 7.25? If it makes you happier, call it 7.2. Or 7.3.

logic upside down. To find floors, we need to look up. How high? Somewhere above equilibrium price. And where are ceilings? Just where you'd expect economists to place them. We need to look down, somewhere below equilibrium price.

Figure 7 illustrates a price floor. Equilibrium price would normally be $10, but a price floor of $15 has been established. At $15 businesses are not normally able to sell everything they offer for sale. Quantity supplied is much larger than quantity demanded. Why? At the equilibrium price of $10, sellers are willing to sell less while buyers are willing to buy more.

Floors and surpluses

At a price of $15, there is a surplus of about 34 units. The government has created this price floor and surplus to keep the price at a predetermined level. This has been the case for certain agricultural commodities, most notably wheat and corn. It was hoped that these relatively high prices would encourage family farms to stay in business. That the

Figure 7   Price Floor and Surplus

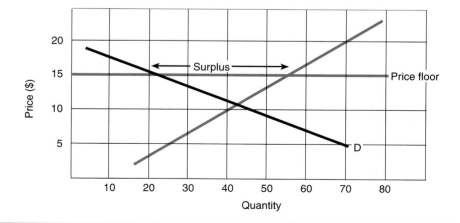

bulk of farm price support payments has gone to huge corporate farms has not discouraged Congress from allocating billions of dollars a year toward this end.

The way the government keeps price floors in effect is by buying up the surpluses. In the case of Figure 7, the Department of Agriculture would have to buy 35 units.

Another important price floor is the minimum wage. Today the vast majority of Americans are guaranteed a minimum of $5.15 an hour. Thus the wage rate, which is the price of an hour's labor, is, in effect, at least $5.15. We will be discussing this important price floor in great detail in a later chapter.

Price ceilings are the mirror image of price floors. An example appears in Figure 8.

Price ceilings are set by the government as a form of price control. "No matter what," the government tells business firms, "don't charge more than this amount."

Ceilings and shortages

A ceiling prevents prices from rising. The last time we had widespread price ceilings was during World War II. Because ceilings cause shortages, a rations system was worked out to enable everyone to obtain their "fair share" of such commodities as butter, meat, and sugar.

I remember World War II. I remember the ration books and the coupons you'd tear out when you went to the store. But chances are, even your parents don't remember the war, with its attendant shortages and rationing.

Ceilings and gas lines

You may remember the gas lines we had in 1979, and if you're a real old-timer, you may even recall the ones we had back in 1973. If not, imagine waiting a couple of hours in a line of cars six blocks long just to fill up your tank. What was the problem? In 1973 it was the Arab oil embargo, while the crisis in 1979 was set off by the Iranian Revolution.

How shortages are eliminated

In both cases, there was ostensibly an oil shortage. But according to the law of supply and demand, there can't really *be* any shortages. Why not? Because prices will rise. For example, in Figure 8, at a price of $25, there's a shortage. But we know the price will rise to $30 and eliminate that shortage. Why? Who drives it up? The dissatisfied buyers drive it up because they are willing to pay more than $25. Notice that as the price rises, the quantity demanded declines, while the quantity supplied rises. When we reach equilibrium price, quantity demanded equals quantity supplied, and the shortage is eliminated.

Now, I left you back in that gas line, and I know you don't want to wait two hours until it's your turn at the pump. Wouldn't you be willing to pay a few cents more if that meant you didn't have to wait? Let's suppose the gas station owner posted a higher price. What would happen? Some people would get out of line. What if he posted a still higher price? Still more people would leave the line. And as gas prices rose, more stations would miraculously open, and the others would stay open longer hours. What would happen to the gas lines? They'd disappear.

Figure 8   Price Ceiling and Shortage

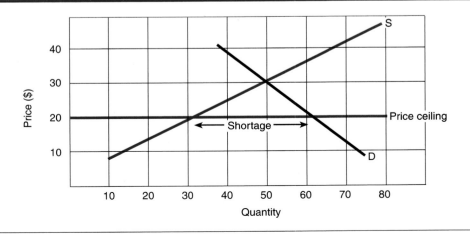

Who actually caused the shortage?

So now, let's ask the obvious question: What *really* caused the gasoline shortage? Who was the *real* villain of the piece? You guessed it! It was the federal government, which had set a ceiling on gasoline prices.

Let's return once more to Figure 8, the scene of the crime. What crime? How could you forget? Our government was caught red-handed, trying to violate the law of supply and demand.

In Figure 8, when a ceiling of $20 is established, there is a shortage of about 30 units. Had price been allowed to stay at the equilibrium level of $30, there would have been no shortage. However, at this lower price, business firms will sell 20 units fewer than they'll sell at equilibrium, and consumers will demand 10 units more. This explains the shortage.

One way the market deals with a shortage is to create what is known as a black market. Products subject to the price ceiling are sold illegally to those willing to pay considerably more. During World War II there was an extensive black market.

Usury laws put a ceiling on interest rates.

Two important price ceilings are rent control laws (see box "Rent Control: The Institution People Love to Hate") and usury laws, which put a ceiling on interest rates. Usury laws go back to biblical times when the prophets debated what, if anything, was a "fair" rate of interest. This same debate was carried on more than two millennia later by Christian scholars. And to this day we ask whether it is "moral" to charge high interest rates.

One dictionary definition of usury is "an unconscionable or exorbitant rate or amount of interest."[4] Many states have usury laws that prohibit banks, savings and loan

---

[4]*Webster's Collegiate Dictionary,* 10th ed., p. 1302.

Rent Control: The Institution People Love to Hate

Rent control is an institution that landlords, economists, libertarians, and nearly all good conservatives just love to hate. In fact, about the only folks who still seem to support rent control are the tenants whose rents are below what the market would have set and the politicians who voted for these laws in the first place.

Rent controls establish ceilings for how much rent may be charged for particular apartments and how much, if at all, these rents may be raised each year. The case for rent control is that it keeps down housing costs for the poor and the elderly. Actually, it keeps down housing costs for a lot of middle-class and rich people as well. Because the rent ceiling is established for each apartment regardless of who is living there, an awfully large number of people are paying a lot less than they could afford.

One of the perverse effects of rent control is to reduce vacancy rates. First, those paying low rents are reluctant to move. Second, real estate developers are reluctant to build apartment houses if their rents will be subject to controls. Still another perverse effect has been the large-scale abandonment of apartment buildings, especially in the inner cities, when landlords find that it makes more sense to walk away from their buildings than to continue losing money. These landlords had been squeezed for years by rising maintenance costs and stagnant rent rolls.

Richard Arnott has noted that "Economists have been virtually unanimous in their opposition to rent control." Why? Arnott provides a full list of reasons:

There has been widespread agreement that rent controls discourage new construction, cause abandonment, retard maintenance, reduce mobility, generate mismatch between housing units and tenants, exacerbate discrimination in rental housing, create black markets, encourage the conversion of rental to owner-occupied housing, and generally short-circuit the market mechanism for housing.*

After rent control was imposed in New York City in 1943, many landlords stopped taking care of their buildings and eventually walked away from 500,000 apartments.

Today nearly 200 cities, mostly in New York, New Jersey, and California, have some form of rent control. It is clear that this price ceiling has kept rents well below their equilibrium levels and consequently has resulted in housing shortages.

From a policy standpoint, do we want to eliminate rent controls? Would skyrocketing rents drive even more families into the ranks of the homeless? Perhaps a gradual easing of rent controls and their eventual elimination in, say, 10 or 15 years would send the right message to builders. But because these are local laws, only local governments can repeal them. And because the name of the political game is getting reelected, it is unlikely that many local politicians will find it expedient to repeal these popular laws.

* Richard Arnott, "Time for Revisionism on Rent Control?" *Journal of Economic Perspectives,* Winter 1995, p. 99.

Simultaneous Changes in Supply and Demand

Did you think we were finished? Hey, the fun has just begun. What happens to equilibrium price and quantity when supply rises (from S_0 to S_1) and demand falls (from D_0 to D_1) in Figure A?

A.

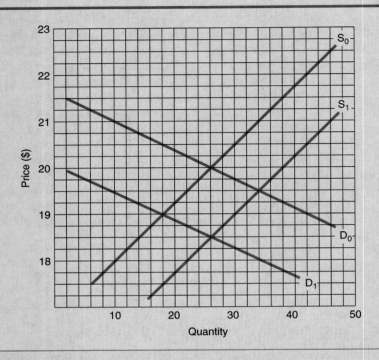

Equilibrium price falls from $20 to $18.50, while equilibrium quantity remains the same. Are you ready to generalize about what happens to equilibrium price and quantity when supply rises and demand declines? You're not?

Good. You want to see another couple of cases? Very good. If nothing else, you've learned not to trust me. Next case: Take a look at Figure B and tell me what happens to equilibrium price and quantity.

B.

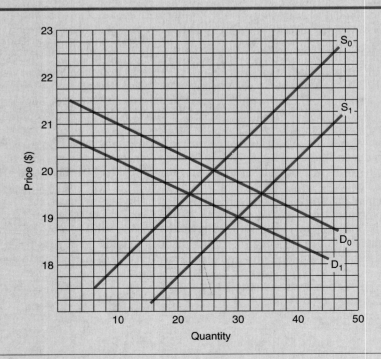

Price falls from $20 to $19, and quantity rises from 26 to 30. OK, we see that quantity rises again and that this time price falls. Just one more case and we're outta here.

What I'd like you to do now is find the new equilibrium point in Figure C.

C.

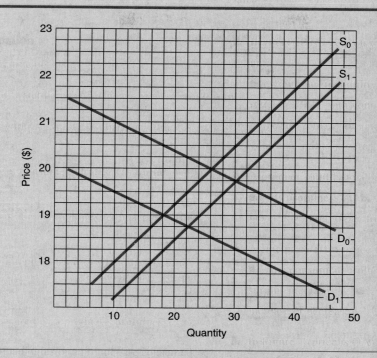

Equilibrium price falls from $20 to $18.75 while equilibrium quantity falls from 26 to 22. *Now* we're ready to generalize. All right, then, go ahead and generalize. I'll start you out. When supply rises and demand declines, equilibrium price . . . equilibrium price declines. And equilibrium quantity? It might rise, it might fall, and it might remain the same.

Figure D sums up our entire analysis. In the first of D's three graphs, an increase in demand and supply leads to an increase in both equilibrium price and equilibrium quantity. How about in the second graph? Here we have a decrease in equilibrium price and an increase in equilibrium quantity. And in the third? In this graph we have no change in equilibrium price and an increase in equilibrium quantity.

Are you ready for a sweeping generalization? All right, then, here it comes. An increase in both demand and supply will lead to an increase in equilibrium quantity, but equilibrium price may rise, fall, or remain the same.

D.

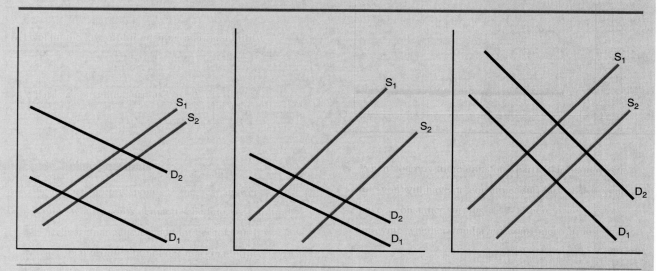

associations, and certain other financial institutions from charging above specified rates of interest. What effect, if any, do these laws have?

Until the late 1970s interest rates were well below their legal ceilings. But then came double-digit inflation rates; sharply rising interest rates; and, as these interest rates reached their legal ceilings, a full-fledged credit crunch. In other words, these interest rate ceilings created a shortage of loanable funds—which is exactly what one would expect to happen when a price ceiling is set below the market's equilibrium price. In this case we're talking about the market for loanable funds and their price, the interest rate.

The confusion over the location of price floors and ceilings on the graph may be overcome by considering what the government is doing by establishing them. Normally, price would fall to the equilibrium level, but a price floor keeps price artificially high. Think of a floor holding price above equilibrium; therefore, a price floor would be located above equilibrium price.

By the same logic, a price ceiling is intended to keep price *below* equilibrium. If not for that ceiling, price would rise. Therefore, a price ceiling must be located below equilibrium to keep price from rising to that level.

Keep in mind, then, that the normal tendency of prices is to move toward their equilibrium levels. A price ceiling will prevent prices from rising to equilibrium, while a price floor will prevent prices from falling to equilibrium.

Changes in Demand and Supply

Changes in Demand

Demand is defined as the schedule of quantities that people will purchase at different prices. A change or shift in demand occurs when there is any change in that schedule. If, at any price, people would buy more or less than they had been buying, there has been a change in demand. If, for example, at a price of $8 people now purchase a quantity of 5 instead of 4, demand has changed.

One of the reasons why demand changes is that there is a change in people's tastes. Concern about lung cancer reduces the demand for cigarettes, while concern about calories raises the demand for Tab, Diet Pepsi, Diet Coke, and other low-calorie soft drinks.[5]

Figure 9 illustrates an increase in demand. When demand rises from D_1 to D_2, we have a new equilibrium point. Price is now $8 and quantity is 9. Note that an increase in demand leads to a rise in equilibrium price and equilibrium quantity.

[5]Changes in demand and their causes will be discussed in the next chapter.

Figure 9   Increase in Demand

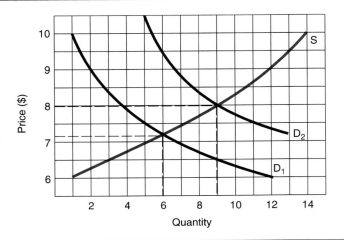

Changes in Supply

In Figure 10 we have a decrease in supply. Even though S_2 lies above S_1, we call this a decrease because sellers are willing to sell less at every price than they were when supply was S_1. A decrease in supply leads to a rise in price (to $8) and a decrease in the quantity sold (to 4).

A change in supply is generally prompted by a change in the cost of production. The price of pocket calculators, color TVs, and VCRs came down quickly during the late 1970s and early 1980s for this reason. These items' cost of production dropped, so more could be produced, increasing supply. Sometimes, however, supply may be reduced by monopoly action, thereby raising price. In 1973 the OPEC nations were able to quadruple world oil prices in just a few months.[6]

What happens when there are simultaneous changes in demand and supply? See the Advanced Work box "Simultaneous Changes in Supply and Demand" on previous spread.

Applications of Supply and Demand

Throughout this book we encounter many applications of supply and demand—so many, in fact, that I'm going to give you a quiz. But it will be an extremely easy quiz. There's just one answer to all these questions. Are you ready?

1. Interest rates are set by _____.
   Did you answer "supply and demand"? Good.
2. Wage rates are set by _____.
3. Rents are determined by _____.
4. The prices of nearly all goods are determined by _____.
5. The prices of nearly all services are determined by _____.

Occasionally, however, the government interferes with the price mechanism and imposes price floors (or minimums) or price ceilings (or maximums). This gets economists very upset because it not only prevents the most efficient allocation of resources but also makes it much harder to read our supply and demand graphs.

Let's take a closer look at the determination of the interest rate. I want to state right up front that there is no "interest rate" but rather scores of interest rates, such as mortgage rates, commercial loan rates, and short-term and long-term federal borrowing rates, as well as the interest rates paid by banks, credit unions, and other financial intermediaries.

---

[6]OPEC stands for Organization of Petroleum Exporting Countries.

Figure 10   Decrease in Supply

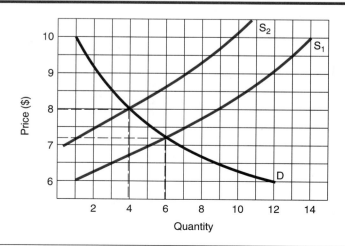

Figure 11 shows a hypothetical demand schedule for loanable funds and a corresponding hypothetical supply schedule.

We can see that $600 billion is lent (or borrowed) at an interest rate of 6 percent. In other words, the market sets the price of borrowed money at an interest rate of 6 percent. What would happen to the interest rate and to the amount of money borrowed if the supply of loanable funds increased?

Did you figure it out? If you did, then you can confirm your answers by glancing at Figure 12. A rise in the supply of loanable funds leads to a decrease in the interest rate to 4 percent and an increase in the amount of money borrowed to $800 billion.

Figure 11   Hypothetical Demand for and Supply of Loanable Funds

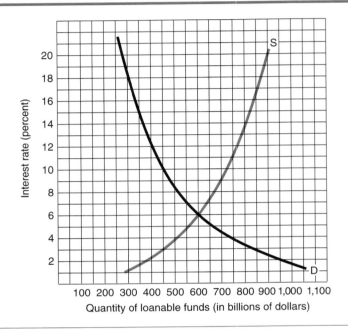

Figure 12   Hypothetical Demand for and Supply of Loanable Funds

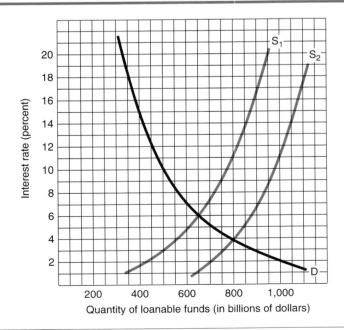

One more question: What happens to the interest rate and to the amount of money borrowed if the demand for loanable funds rises?

Did you say that the interest rate would rise and the amount of money borrowed would also rise? Good. Then what you must have done was to sketch a graph like the one shown in Figure 13. The interest rate rose to 9 percent, and the amount of money borrowed rose to $700 billion.

The Global Economy: Let Them Eat Bread

When told that the people had no bread, Marie Antoinette helped set off the French Revolution by replying, "Let them eat cake." Back in the 1980s, just before the breakup of the Soviet Union, the Soviets had the opposite problem. There was so much bread that even the cows were eating it.

The government had decided to keep the price of bread very low so that everyone could afford it, even cows. That's right! Soviet farmers found that it was cheaper to feed their cows bread than hay.

Here's how the system worked. Farmers shipped their wheat to mills to be ground into flour. From there it went to huge government bakeries where workers baked the flour into bread. A lot of that bread was then sent back to the farms, where it was fed to the cows. But after the breakup of the Soviet Union, the price of bread skyrocketed and the cows had to make do with hay and other less elegant fare.[7] The point is that the Soviet government attempted to dictate the prices of basic goods and services, but this prevented the price system from performing its most important function: rationing.

The Rationing Function of the Price System

If gasoline went up to $3 a gallon, would you cut back on your driving? Maybe you would try to do all of your shopping in one trip instead of in two or three. And if gasoline went still higher, maybe you would even agree to join a car pool.

---

[7]See Peter Passell, "Where Communist Economics Fell Short," *New York Times,* December 17, 1989, p. E–3.

Figure 13 **Hypothetical Demand for and Supply of Loanable Funds**

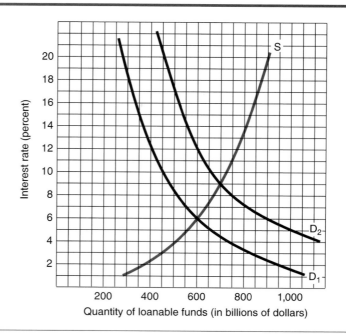

The price system is constantly sending buyers and sellers thousands of signals. The price of *this* service has gone through the roof. *That* product is on sale. *This* good is over-priced and *that* one is a bargain. When something becomes very expensive, we generally cut back. We do this not because the government ordered us to do so or because it issued ration coupons entitling everyone to only three gallons a week, but because the price system itself performed this rationing function.

At the beginning of Chapter 2, I defined economics as *the efficient allocation of the scarce means of production toward the satisfaction of human wants.* In a free-market, private-enterprise economy such as ours, we depend on the price mechanism, or the forces of supply and demand, to perform that job.

Questions for Further Thought and Discussion

1. Suppose market price is above equilibrium price. Is there a shortage or a surplus? Explain how it is eliminated.

2. Explain how the price system performs a rationing function.

3. Where is a price ceiling with respect to equilibrium price? What will be the relative size of quantity demanded and quantity supplied?

4. How is equilibrium price affected by changes in *(a)* demand and *(b)* supply?

Name _____   Date _____

Multiple-Choice Questions

Circle the letter that corresponds to the best answer.

1. An increase in supply while demand remains unchanged will lead to

   a. an increase in equilibrium price and a decrease in equilibrium quantity   **b.** a decrease in equilibrium price and a decrease in equilibrium quantity   **c.** an increase in equilibrium price and an increase in equilibrium quantity   **d.** a decrease in equilibrium price and an increase in equilibrium quantity

2. A decrease in demand while supply remains unchanged will lead to

   a. an increase in equilibrium price and quantity

   b. a decrease in equilibrium price and quantity

   c. an increase in equilibrium price and a decrease in equilibrium quantity   **d.** a decrease in equilibrium price and an increase in equilibrium quantity

3. As price rises

   a. quantity demanded and quantity supplied both rise

   b. quantity demanded and quantity supplied both fall

   c. quantity demanded rises and quantity supplied falls

   d. quantity demanded falls and quantity supplied rises

Use Table 1 to answer questions 4 and 5.

Table 1

Price	Quantity Demanded	Quantity Supplied
$12	10	15
11	14	10
10	20	5

4. The equilibrium price is about

   a. $11.25   **b.** $11.40   **c.** $11.50   **d.** $11.60

   e. $11.75

5. Equilibrium quantity is about

   a. 12   **b.** 12.3   **c.** 12.5   **d.** 12.8   **e.** 13

6. Demand for a good or service may be depicted in

   a. a table, but not a graph   **b.** a graph, but not a table   **c.** both a graph and a table   **d.** neither a graph nor a table

7. When quantity demanded is greater than quantity supplied, there

   a. is a shortage   **b.** is a surplus   **c.** may be either a shortage or a surplus   **d.** may be neither a shortage nor a surplus

8. When quantity supplied is greater than quantity demanded

   a. price will fall to its equilibrium level   **b.** price will rise to its equilibrium level   **c.** price may rise, fall, or stay the same, depending on a variety of factors

Use Figure 1 to answer questions 9 and 10.

Figure 1

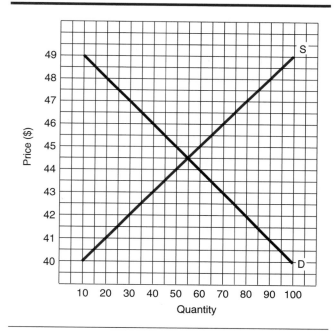

9. At a market price of $47, there is

   a. a shortage   **b.** a surplus   **c.** both a shortage and a surplus   **d.** neither a shortage nor a surplus

10. At a market price of $42, there is

    a. a shortage   **b.** a surplus   **c.** both a shortage and a surplus   **d.** neither a shortage nor a surplus

11. In Figure 2, an increase in demand and supply leads to

    a. an increase in equilibrium price and quantity

    b. a decrease in equilibrium price and quantity

    c. an increase in equilibrium price and a decrease in

equilibrium quantity   d.   a decrease in equilibrium price and an increase in equilibrium quantity

Figure 2

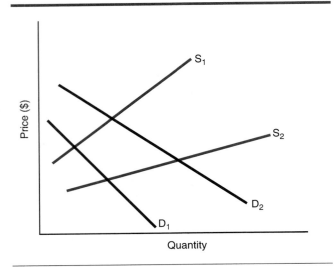

12. In general, an increase in demand and supply will lead to
    a.   a definite increase in equilibrium quantity   b.   a definite increase in equilibrium price   c.   a definite increase in equilibrium price and quantity   d.   a definite increase in neither equilibrium price nor equilibrium quantity

13. Our price system is distorted by
    a.   both price ceilings and price floors   b.   neither price ceilings nor price floors   c.   only price ceilings   d.   only price floors

14. Gas lines were caused by
    a.   price floors   b.   price ceilings   c.   both price floors and price ceilings   d.   neither price floors nor price ceilings

15. Statement 1: A change in supply is generally prompted by a change in the cost of production.
    Statement 2: Interest rates are set by supply and demand, but wage rates are not.
    a.   Statement 1 is true and statement 2 is false.
    b.   Statement 2 is true and statement 1 is false
    c.   Both statements are true.   d.   Both statements are false.

16. If the equilibrium price of corn is 30 cents an ear and the government imposes a floor of 40 cents an ear, the price of corn will
    a.   increase to 40 cents   b.   remain at 30 cents
    c.   rise to about 35 cents   d.   be impossible to determine

17. Usury laws tend to
    a.   create a shortage of loanable funds   b.   create a surplus of loanable funds   c.   make it easier to obtain credit   d.   have no effect on the amount of loanable funds available

18. If the price system is allowed to function without interference and a shortage occurs, quantity demanded will _____ and quantity supplied will _____ until the price rises to its equilibrium level.
    a.   rise, rise   b.   fall, fall   c.   rise, fall
    d.   fall, rise

19. Which statement is true?
    a.   A price floor is above equilibrium price and causes surpluses.   b.   A price floor is above equilibrium price and causes shortages.   c.   A price floor is below equilibrium price and causes surpluses.   d.   A price floor is below equilibrium price and causes shortages.

Fill-In Questions

1. As price falls, the quantity demanded_____.

2. The demand curve curves or slopes _____ _____.

3. As price falls, the quantity supplied _____.

4. At _____, quantity demanded and quantity supplied are equal.

5. At the equilibrium point of a graph, the demand and supply curves _____.

6. When quantity demanded is greater than quantity supplied, the price will _____.

7. If supply falls and demand remains the same, equilibrium

   price will _____ and equilibrium

   quantity will _____.

8. A change in supply is generally prompted by a change in

   the _____.

9. Interest rates are set by_____

   _____and _____.

10. What happens to interest rates when the demand for

    money rises?_____

11. When the supply of money falls, interest rates _____

    _____.

Use Figure 3 to answer questions 12 through 15.

Figure 3

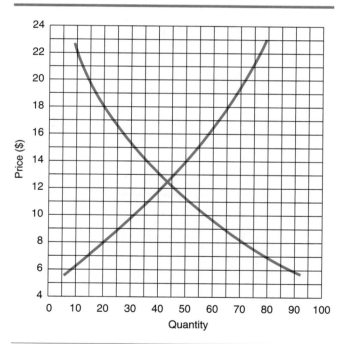

12. Equilibrium price is $ _____.

13. Equilibrium quantity is _____.

14. If price were $20, there would be a (shortage or surplus)

    _____ of _____.

15. If price were $8, there would be a (shortage or surplus)

    _____ of _____.

16. Price floors keep prices _____

    equilibrium price; price ceilings keep prices _____

    _____ equilibrium price.

17. Shortages are associated with price _____;

    surpluses are associated with price _____.

Problems

1. Given the information in Table 2, draw a graph of the demand and supply curves on a piece of graph paper.

Table 2

Price	Quantity Demanded	Quantity Supplied
$20	1	25
19	3	24
18	6	22
17	10	18
16	16	10
15	24	2

2. Equilibrium price is $ _____; equilib-

   rium quantity is _____.

3. Given the information in Table 3, draw a graph of the demand and supply curves on a piece of graph paper.

Table 3

Price	Quantity Demanded	Quantity Supplied
$15	1	27
14	4	25
13	9	21
12	16	12
11	22	6
10	26	2

4. Equilibrium price is $ _____;
   equilibrium quantity is _____.

5. In Figure 4, draw a new supply curve indicating a decrease in supply. State the new equilibrium price and
   quantity.

Figure 4

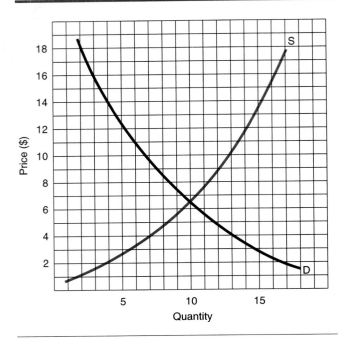

Table 4

Price	Quantity Demanded	Quantity Supplied
$6	12	19
5	18	13

8. Given the information in Figure 6: **a.** Is $12 a price ceiling or a price floor? **b.** Is there a shortage or a surplus? **c.** How much is it?

Figure 6

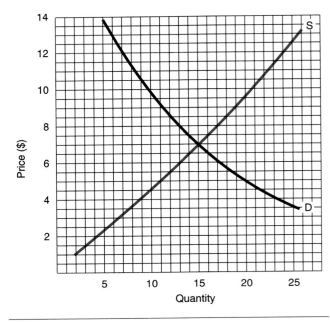

6. In Figure 5, draw a new demand curve indicating an increase in demand. State the new equilibrium price and quantity.

Figure 5

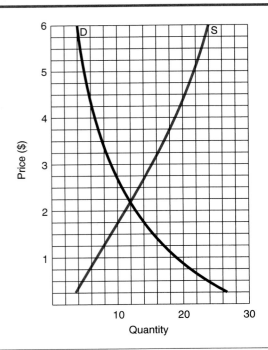

9. Given the information in Figure 7: **a.** Is $16 a price ceiling or a price floor? **b.** Is there a shortage or a surplus? **c.** How much is it?

Figure 7

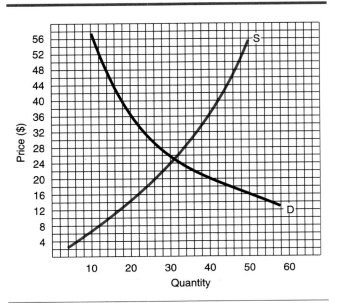

7. Given the information in Table 4, make your best estimate of equilibrium price and quantity. You don't need to draw a graph.

18 Demand

We need to use the definition of demand to find the answers to many of the questions in this chapter. In the last chapter demand was defined as *the schedule of quantities of a good or service that people will purchase at different prices.* That will be our starting point.

Chapter Objectives

In this chapter you will find out everything you always wanted to know about:

- Individual and market demand.
- Changes in demand.
- The elasticity of demand.
- Marginal revenue.
- Elasticity and total revenue.

Demand Defined

Definition of Demand

Demand is *the schedule of quantities of a good or service that people will purchase at different prices.* Let's look at the demand for sirloin steak. At $1 a pound, it would create traffic jams as people rushed to the supermarket; but at $3 a pound, sirloin steak would be somewhat less of a bargain. At $4 a pound, it would lose many of its previous buyers to chicken, chuck steak, and other substitutes.

As the price of an item goes up, the quantity demanded falls, and as the price comes down, the quantity demanded rises. This inverse relationship may be stated as the law of demand: *When the price of a good is lowered, more of it is demanded; when it is raised, less is demanded.*

The law of demand: When the price of a good is lowered, more of it is demanded; when it is raised, less is demanded.

Individual Demand and Market Demand

The law of demand holds for both individuals and markets. Individual demand is the schedule of quantities that a person would purchase at different prices. Market demand is the schedule of quantities that everyone in the market would buy at different prices.

Table 1 shows four examples of individual demand and then adds them up to total market demand. We add straight across. For example, at a price of $30, the quantity

Table 1   Hypothetical Individual Demand and Market Demand Schedules

| Price | Quantity Demanded by | | | | |
	Ross	George	Bill	Ron	Total
$30	0	1	2	1	4
25	2	1	3	3	9
20	3	2	5	4	14
15	3	3	6	6	18
10	4	5	7	7	23
5	5	6	7	8	26

The Work of Alfred Marshall

Much of the analysis in this chapter is based on the work of Alfred Marshall, the great English economist, whose work dates back about a century. When you read some

Stock Montage

of his observations, you'll probably think that all he's saying is just common sense and that you might have come up with the same observations yourself. And that may well be true. The only thing is that Alfred Marshall came up with them first.

Here, for example, is Marshall's one general law of demand: "The greater the amount to be sold, the smaller must be the price at which it is offered in order that it may find purchasers; or, in other words, the amount demanded increases with a fall in price, and diminishes with a rise in price."* I know—the man took the words right out of your mouth.

*Alfred Marshall, *Principles of Economics*, 8th ed., 1920, p. 99.

demanded on an individual basis is 0, 1, 2, and 1. Adding them together, we get total or market demand of 4. In the same way, by adding the individual quantities demanded at a price of $25, we get 9 (2 plus 1 plus 3 plus 3). And so forth.

What is the market?

There is one interesting question about market demand: What is the market? The market is where people buy and sell. Generally there is a prevailing price in a particular market. Take gasoline. In New York City the price of regular unleaded gas at most gas stations varied between $1.10 and $1.50 in March 1995. But just across the bay in New Jersey most stations charged between $1.00 and $1.25.

New York City and New Jersey are two separate markets for gasoline. People in New York would not go to New Jersey to save 10 or 15 cents a gallon because the trip would not only be inconvenient, it would cost them a $4 toll.

The market for gasoline is very local because the money you'd save by driving to the next market would be more than offset by the money it would cost you to go there. Another local market is for groceries. Again, you wouldn't drive to the other side of your city or perhaps three towns down the highway just to save a dollar or two.

The market for automobiles is regional. If you live in Boston and can save a couple of hundred dollars by going to a dealer in Providence, you probably will, but if you live in Chicago you won't go to San Francisco to save $200 on a car.

On a very local basis, then, prices for most goods will not vary much, but as the area covered grows larger, so do price variations. If people are willing to travel to get a bargain, the market will be much larger.

The market for some goods and services may be national or even international. A company shopping for a sophisticated computer system will look all over the world for the right system at the right price. And a man who needs brain surgery or a heart transplant will not go to his local doctor and ask her to operate in her office.

Changes in Demand

The definition of demand is our point of departure, so to speak, when we take up changes in demand. Once again, demand is the schedule of *quantities* that people purchase at different prices. A change in demand is a change in, or a departure from, this schedule.

Increases in Demand

Using the market demand schedule in Table 1, let's say the product in question becomes much more desirable, perhaps because it is suddenly discovered to be worth votes in presidential elections. The people listed in Table 1 just might be interested in this discovery and might well decide they are willing to pay even more for each unit.

An increase in demand is an increase in the quantity people are willing to purchase at all prices.

This takes us from Table 1 to Table 2, and it involves an increase in market demand. At each price, buyers are willing to buy more. Thus, by definition, there is an increase in demand. It is important to emphasize that an increase in demand is an *increase in the quantity people are willing to purchase at all prices.*

It will be helpful to illustrate this increase by means of a graph. This is done in Figure 1. Notice that the second demand curve, D_2, representing the increase in demand, is to the right of D_1. You should also note that at each price, the quantity demanded in D_2 is greater than the quantity demanded in D_1.

Decreases in Demand

A decrease in demand means people are willing to buy less at each price.

Now we're ready for a decrease in demand, also illustrated in Figure 1. You should be able to guess what the decrease would be. After all, there are only two curves on the graph, and if going from D_1 to D_2 is an increase—that's right!—going from D_2 to D_1 is a decrease.

A decrease in demand means *people are willing to buy less at each price.* In Figure 1, D_1 lies entirely to the left of D_2. If the curves were to cross, we would have neither an increase nor a decrease in demand; rather, we would have a change in demand.

Problems

Figure 2 illustrates a change in demand, whether we go from D_1 to D_2 or from D_2 to D_1. My students often dispute this point. In Figure 2, they argue, when price is more than

Table 2   Hypothetical Market Demand Schedule Illustrating an Increase in Demand

Price	(1) Quantity Demanded	(2) Quantity Demanded
$30	4	5
25	9	11
20	14	18
15	18	28
10	23	38
5	26	50

Figure 1   Increase in Demand

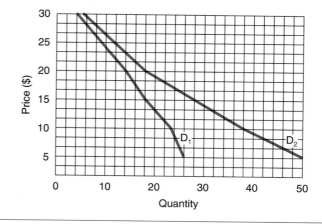

Figure 2

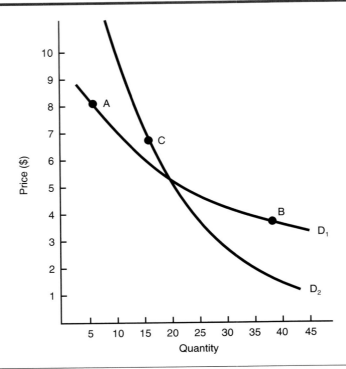

$5.25, going from D_1 to D_2 represents an increase in demand because people are willing to purchase more. And, they add, when we go from D_1 to D_2 at prices below $5.25, there is a decrease in demand.

Let's give it another try. If we go back to Table 2, we see that for every price the quantity demanded in the second column is greater than in the first. At $30, the quantity demanded in the second column is 5, compared with 4 in the first column. At $25, the second column has a quantity of 11, compared with 9 for the first column.

In Figure 1 we see that D_2 is entirely to the right of D_1. At each price ($30, $25, $20, $15, $10, and $5), the quantity demanded is greater for D_2 than for D_1. If D_1 and D_2 crossed, we could not say that for every price the quantity demanded was greater for D_2 than for D_1.

We must consider demand curves in their entireties, not just by fragments. Fifth Avenue and Broadway cross at 23rd Street. Above 23rd Street, Broadway is west of Fifth Avenue, and below 23rd Street it is east. Just as we cannot make the statement that Broadway is west of Fifth, we cannot say that one demand curve is greater than another if they cross.

Look again at Figure 2. Does going from point A to point B represent a change in demand? Going back once more to our definition of demand—the schedule of quantities that people will purchase at different prices—when we go from A to B, has there been any change in the demand schedule? If both A and B are on that schedule, there has been no change in demand.

On the graph we can easily see that both A and B are on the same demand curve. For a change in demand to have taken place, you would have to move off the demand curve. If you moved from point A on D_1 to point C on D_2, that would be a change in demand.

If the move from A to B is not a change in demand, what is it? It's simply a change in quantity demanded in response to a price change. Price fell, and quantity demanded rose. Incidentally, a favorite exam question is: If price falls and in response quantity demanded rises, does this represent a change in demand? *Please* answer no.

Here are some problems to see whether you're following what I'm talking about. Each is based on Figure 3. There are four possible answers: *(a)* a change in quantity

Figure 3

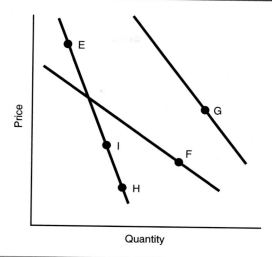

demanded, *(b)* a change in demand, *(c)* an increase in demand, and *(d)* a decrease in demand.

1. When we move from E to F, it is _____ .
2. A move from F to G is _____ .
3. A move from G to H is _____ .
4. A move from H to I is _____ .

Now we'll go over each of the answers. Moving from E to F is a change in demand because these points are on different demand curves that cross; neither is a higher demand curve because they cross. A higher demand would mean people would buy more at every price. When two curves cross, they don't fulfill this condition.

From F to G is an increase in demand because the demand curve on which G is situated is to the right of F's demand curve. Note that there is an increase in demand because people are willing to buy more at all prices on G's demand curve.

From G to H is a decrease in demand for the same reason. On H's demand curve, people are willing to buy *less* for every price than on G's curve.

From H to I is a change in the quantity demanded. As long as we remain on the curve, there's no change in demand.

We need to talk about an ordering or ranking of changes. You had four choices in these problems. The least significant change is a change in quantity demanded because we stay on the same curve. It's simply no big deal.

When we move off the curve, now *that's* something! If we move off the curve, where do we go? Presumably to some other curve. Which one? A higher one? A lower one? If we move to another demand curve that crosses the original curve, all we can say is that there's been a change in demand.

But if we move to a curve that is entirely to the right of the first curve, we clearly have an increase in demand. Saying we have an increase in demand is a much stronger statement than merely saying there's been a change in demand. Similarly, a decrease in demand is an equally strong statement.

The strongest thing we can say is that there has been an increase or a decrease in demand. The next strongest statement is that there has been a change in demand. The least powerful thing we can say is that there has been a change in quantity demanded. As we move from point to point, we try to make the strongest possible statement.

Go back to the second problem. When we go from F to G, there has been not merely a change in demand but an *increase* in demand. And in the third problem, when we go from G to H, why should we settle for a change in demand when we have a *decrease* in demand?

Now we'll try another set of problems using the same four possible answers. These are based on Figure 4.

5.   A move from J to K is _____ .
6.   A move from K to L is _____ .
7.   A move from L to M is _____ .
8.   A move from M to N is _____ .

Going from J to K is clearly a change in the quantity demanded because we stay on the same demand curve. From K to L is an increase in demand because L's demand curve is entirely to the right of K's curve. Similarly, from L to M is a decrease in demand because M's curve is entirely to the left of L's. If this isn't clear, see the Extra Help box.

Some students have questioned whether the curves would cross if they were extended. Obviously they would, but there are a couple of reasons why we can't extend the

Figure 4

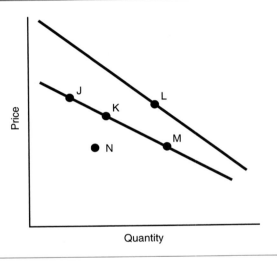

Differentiating between Changes in Demand and Changes in the Quantity Demanded

I have taught microeconomics well over 100 times. Go ahead and ask me which two concepts students mix up more than any others. Are you ready? Students are always confusing changes in demand with changes in quantity demanded. And when they're not doing that, they are confusing changes in quantity demanded with changes in demand.

I always like to come back to the definition of demand, which is *the schedule of quantities of a good or service that people purchase at different prices.* So a change in demand would be a departure from that schedule. Look again at the lower demand schedule in Figure 4. When

we go from point J to point K, there's been a change in quantity demanded (in response to a price change). In other words, price went down, so quantity demanded went up. But there was no change in demand. We see that graphically, because we stayed on the same demand curve, or schedule.

Now if we should go off that line, whether to point N or to any other point, then there's been a change in demand. We would *not* say that there has merely been a change in quantity demanded because we've left our demand curve, or schedule, and gone to some other one.

lines. First, how do we know that they would continue as straight lines? If we had additional demand data, perhaps we'd find that they don't cross after all. Second, we have plotted these curves over some relevant price range. They're not plotted at extremely low or extremely high prices because no seller would be interested in charging such prices. We must confine ourselves to the relevant price ranges within which the demand curves are drawn.

The move from M to N is a difficult one. We leave M's demand curve, so it's not a change in quantity demanded. Because N lies to the left of M's curve, it couldn't possibly lie on a demand curve to the right of M's curve. But—and once again we have the $64,000 question—is N on a curve to the left of the demand curve on which M is situated?

Think about possible demand curves. If N is on a demand curve that is parallel to M's curve, clearly there would be a decrease in demand. But what if N were on a demand curve that intersected M's curve? What would we have then? A *change* in demand!

These possibilities are illustrated in Figure 5. First we have D_2, which is roughly parallel to D_1 (on which M lies). D_3 and D_4 both cross D_1. Because we don't know on which of an infinite number of possible demand curves N is situated, we cannot assume there is a decrease in demand when we go from M to N. The most we can say is that there is a change in demand.

What Causes Changes in Demand?

Changes in Income

The demand for normal goods varies directly with income.

The demand for inferior goods varies inversely with income.

When your income goes up, you can afford to buy more goods and services. Suppose the incomes of most Americans rise. That means a greater demand for cars, new homes, furniture, steaks, and motel rooms. Similarly, if incomes decline, as they do during recessions, there will be a smaller demand for most goods and services.

Most goods are *normal goods*. The demand for these goods varies directly with income: when income goes up, the demand for these goods goes up (see the shift from D_1 to D_2 in Figure 1). When incomes decline, the demand for these goods declines as well (we go from D_2 to D_1).

However, certain goods are *inferior goods* because the demand for them varies inversely with income. For example, as income declines, the demand for potatoes, spaghetti, rice, and intercity bus rides increases. Why? Because these are the types of goods and services purchased by poorer people, and if income declines, people are poorer. As incomes rise, the demand for these inferior goods declines because people can now afford more meat, cheese, and other relatively expensive foods, and they'll take planes rather than ride in buses.

Figure 5

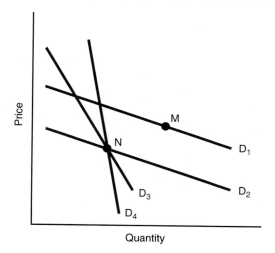

Changes in the Prices of Related Goods and Services   Suppose tunas suddenly discovered a way to evade tuna fishermen, the supply of tuna fish drastically declined, and the price of tuna fish shot up to $3 a can. What do you think would soon happen to the price of salmon, chicken, and other close substitute goods? Obviously, they would be driven up.

Let's see why this happens. First, the supply of tuna fish goes down and its price goes up. Most shoppers would say to themselves, "Three dollars a can! I've had tuna fish sandwiches for lunch every day of my life, but I'm not going to pay three dollars!" And so the former tuna fish buyers end up buying salmon and chicken. What has happened to the demand for salmon and chicken? It has gone up. And when the demand for something goes up, what happens to its price? It too goes up.

The prices of substitute goods are directly related.

Now we can generalize. The prices of substitute goods are directly related. If the price of one good goes up, people will increase their purchases of close substitutes, driving their prices up. If the price of one good comes down, people will decrease their purchases of close substitutes, driving *their* prices down.

The prices of another set of goods and services, those with complementary relationships, are inversely related. That is, when the price of one goes down, the price of the other goes up, or vice versa.

The prices of complementary goods are inversely related.

Suppose the price of videotape rentals falls from $2 a day to 50 cents a day. Many people will rush out to buy VCRs, driving up their prices. On the other hand, what will happen if gasoline goes up to $5 a gallon. People will drive a lot less. This will lower the demand for tires, pushing down their prices.

Changes in Tastes and Preferences   Suppose the American Cancer Society and the surgeon general mounted a heavy TV campaign with rock stars, professional athletes, movie actors and actresses, and other celebrities. The message: Stop smoking. Imagine what a successful campaign would do to cigarette sales.

Sometimes tastes and preferences change by themselves over time. Over the last two decades Americans have opted for smaller cars and less-fattening foods, and growing numbers of people have become more fashion conscious, buying only designer clothing and accessories. No member of my generation would have guessed that children would one day demand "fashionable" sneakers at more than $100 a pair.

Changes in Price Expectations   If people expect the price of a product to rise, they rush out to stock up before the price goes up. On the other hand, if the price is expected to fall, they will tend to hold off on their purchases.

When it appears that a war will break out, people will stock up on canned food, appliances, and anything else they think may be hard to buy in the coming months. On the other hand, when prices seem inordinately high, as the Manhattan co-op and condominium market did in early 1985, potential buyers will hold out for lower prices. Incidentally, the prices of co-ops and condominiums did come down considerably in 1985 and 1986, partly because buyers expected a decline and waited for it to happen.

Changes in Population   As the nation's population increases, the demand for a particular good or service tends to increase. Our population has been growing by more than 3 million each year, adding to the demand for food, housing, automobiles, medical care, and tens of thousands of other goods and services.

The changing age distribution of our population also affects demand. During the baby boom, 1946 to 1964, there was a tremendous rise in the demand for housing, and later, as these babies became teenagers, there was more demand for rock concert tickets, stereo systems, and designer jeans. In the first three decades of the 21st century, there will be a higher demand for retirement homes, nursing homes, wheelchairs, and bifocal glasses.

The Elasticity of Demand

Elasticity of demand measures the change in quantity demanded in response to a change in price. When price goes up, we know that quantity demanded declines. But by how much? Elasticity provides us with a way of measuring this response. And we measure the responsiveness of quantity demanded to a change in price by calculating the coefficient of price elasticity of demand (E_p) as follows:

Measuring Elasticity

$$E_p = \frac{\text{Percentage change in quantity demanded}}{\text{Percentage change in price}}$$

We'll start with this problem. A business firm has been selling 100 kitchen chairs a week. It runs a sale, charging $8 instead of the usual $10. People recognize this great bargain, and sales go up to 140 chairs. If P_1 is the initial price charged and P_2 is the sale price, Q_1 the initial quantity sold and Q_2 the quantity sold during the sale, we can calculate the coefficient of price elasticity of demand as follows:

Elasticity formula

$$E_p = \frac{\text{Percentage change in quantity demanded}}{\text{Percentage change in price}} = \frac{Q_2 - Q_1}{Q_2 + Q_1} \cdot \frac{P_2 + P_1}{P_2 - P_1}$$

This formula looks a lot more complicated than it is (see the box titled "Why We Don't Use a Simpler Elasticity Formula"). It simply calls for finding the percentage change in quantity and the percentage change in price, and then dividing the former by the latter. Go ahead and substitute into the formula in the space below and then solve.

Solution: $P_1 = 10$; $P_2 = 8$; $Q_1 = 100$; and $Q_2 = 140$.

$$\frac{140-100}{140+100} \cdot \frac{8+10}{8-10} = \frac{40}{240} \cdot \frac{18}{-2} = \frac{4}{24} \cdot \frac{9}{1} = \frac{1}{6} \cdot \frac{9}{1} = \frac{9}{6} = \frac{3}{2} = 1.5^1$$

Elasticity comes to –1.5, but by convention we ignore the sign (which, by the way, will always be negative for price elasticity of demand). In this case our answer is 1.5. A coefficient of 1.5 for price elasticity of demand means that for every 1 percent change in price, there will be a corresponding 1.5 percent change in quantity demanded.

Most students initially have some difficulty calculating elasticity, so we'll work out a few more problems. When you become confident that you can do this type of problem, you may skip the remaining problems and begin the next section.

Problem: Price is raised from $40 to $41, and quantity sold declines from 15 to 12. Solve in the space below.

---

[1]Where did 1.5 come from? To obtain the decimal value of a fraction, divide the bottom number into the top number.

ADVANCED WORK.......... Why We Don't Use a Simpler Elasticity Formula

Considering that elasticity is the percentage that quantity sold changes in response to a 1 percent change in price, wouldn't it be a lot easier to use the formula *percentage change in quantity divided by percentage change in price?* Some economists do use this formula. Let's try it for this problem. Price drops from $10 to $9, and quantity demanded rises from 100 to 120.

Using the formula:

$$\frac{\text{Percentage change in quantity}}{\text{Percentage change in price}}$$

we get:

$$\frac{20\%}{10\%} = 2$$

So far, so good. Now let's look at the same price range but reverse the direction so that price rises from $9 to $10 and quantity demanded falls from 120 to 100. Here our percentage change in quantity divided by percentage change in price would be:

$$\frac{16\frac{2}{3}\%}{11\frac{1}{9}\%} = 1.5$$

That's quite a discrepancy for the range of the demand schedule between $9 and $10. When price is lowered from $10 to $9, elasticity is 2, but when it is raised from $9 to $10, elasticity is only 1.5. Therefore, the same formula measuring elasticity over the same range of the demand curve yields two very different answers.

Let's try the more complex formula on the same data. Go ahead and do it in the space provided in the upper right part of this box, first trying the price decrease and then the price increase.

Solution: $P_1 = \$10$; $P_2 = \$9$; $Q_1 = 100$; and $Q_2 = 120$.

$$\frac{120 - 100}{120 + 100} \cdot \frac{9 + 10}{9 - 10} = \frac{\overset{1}{\cancel{20}}}{\underset{11}{\cancel{220}}} \cdot \frac{19}{1} = \frac{19}{11} = 1.72727 \,{}^*$$

(when price rises from $9 to $10)

$P_1 = \$9$; $P_2 = \$10$; $Q_1 = 120$; and $Q_2 = 100$.

$$\frac{100 - 120}{100 + 120} \cdot \frac{10 + 9}{10 - 9} = \frac{20}{220} \cdot \frac{19}{1} = 1.72727 \,{}^*$$

*You may round off at one decimal place for elasticity problems (1.72727 = 1.7) or at two places (1.73).

Solution: $P_1 = \$40$; $P_2 = \$41$; $Q_1 = 15$; and $Q_2 = 12$.

$$\frac{12 - 15}{12 + 15} \cdot \frac{41 + 40}{41 - 40} = \frac{3}{\underset{1}{\cancel{27}}} \cdot \frac{\overset{3}{\cancel{81}}}{1} = \frac{9}{1} = 9$$

Problem: Price is lowered from $5 to $4, and quantity demanded rises from 80 to 82.

Solution: $P_1 = \$5$; $P_2 = \$4$; $Q_1 = 80$; and $Q_2 = 82$.

$$\frac{82-80}{82+80} \cdot \frac{4+5}{4-5} = \frac{2}{\cancel{162}_{18}} \cdot \frac{\cancel{9}^1}{1} = \frac{2}{18} = \frac{1}{9} = .11$$

Problem: Price is raised from \$30 to \$33, and quantity demanded falls from 100 to 90.

Solution: $P_1 = \$30$; $P_2 = \$33$; $Q_1 = 100$; and $Q_2 = 90$.

$$\frac{90-100}{90+100} \cdot \frac{33+30}{33-30} = \frac{10}{190} \cdot \frac{63}{3} = \frac{1}{19} \cdot \frac{21}{1} = 1.11$$

The Meaning of Elasticity

What does all this mean? First, we say that when elasticity is greater than 1, demand is elastic. Remember, elasticity is the percentage change in quantity demanded brought about by a price change. In essence, it is percentage change in quantity divided by percentage change in price. Thus, for elasticity to be greater than 1, percentage change in quantity must be greater than percentage change in price. A price change of a certain percentage causes quantity to change by a larger percentage. When this happens, we say demand is elastic. For example, if the coefficient of price elasticity of demand is 10, that means for every 1 percent change in price, there will be a corresponding 10 percent change in quantity demanded. In this example, we would say demand is very elastic. We mean that the quantity demanded is responsive to price changes.

When demand is elastic, the quantity demanded is responsive to price changes.

When demand is elastic, it stretches as price changes. And when demand is not very elastic, it does not stretch much.

Elasticity is a simple number—2, 3.5, or 0.5, for example. It's a number that represents the percentage change in quantity demanded of a good resulting from each 1 percent change in that good's price. So an elasticity of 2 means that a 1 percent price change leads to a 2 percent change in quantity. What about elasticities of 3.5 and 0.5?

Inelastic demand is defined as an elasticity of less than 1; anything from 0 to .99 is inelastic. We can also make somewhat finer distinctions. An elasticity of .1 or .2 would be very inelastic, while one of .8 or .9 would be slightly inelastic. Similarly, an elasticity of 1.5 or 2 would be slightly elastic. And one of 8 or 10 would be very elastic.

The border between elastic and inelastic is 1. We call this *unit elastic*. Thus, if elasticity is less than 1, it is inelastic. If it is exactly 1, it is unit elastic. If elasticity is more than 1, it is elastic.

Now we'll deal with perfect elasticity and perfect inelasticity. Figure 6 shows a perfectly elastic demand curve. It is horizontal. Go ahead and calculate its elasticity from a quantity of 10 to a quantity of 20. Note that price remains fixed at \$8.

Solution: $P_1 = \$8$; $P_2 = \$8$; $Q_1 = 10$; and $Q_2 = 20$.

$$\frac{20-10}{20+10} \cdot \frac{8+8}{8-8} = \frac{10}{30} \cdot \frac{16}{0} = \frac{1}{3} \cdot \frac{16}{0} = \frac{16}{0} = \infty$$

How big is infinity? Big. Very, very big. How elastic is the demand curve in Figure 6? Very, very elastic. Infinitely elastic, or as we say here, perfectly elastic.

Now we'll move on to perfect inelasticity. If perfect elasticity is ∞, how large is perfect inelasticity? $-\infty$? Nope. Go back to what I said about the range of inelasticity—anything from 0 to .99. The lowest it can go is 0. That's perfect inelasticity.

Using the data in Figure 7, calculate the elasticity of the vertical demand curve. Quantity stays put at 15, but price varies. Let's say the price has fallen from 20 to 10. Calculate the elasticity. Again, use the formula, substitute, and solve.

Solution: $P_1 = 20$; $P_2 = 10$; $Q_1 = 15$; $Q_2 = 15$.

$$\frac{15-15}{15+15} \cdot \frac{10+20}{10-20} = \frac{0}{30} \cdot \frac{30}{10} = \frac{0}{30} \cdot \frac{3}{1} = \frac{0}{30} = 0$$

How many times does 30 go into 0? None. You can't divide *any* number into 0. Therefore, elasticity is 0. The elasticity of a perfectly inelastic line is 0. Did you follow this? Believe it or not, there are some people who didn't. If you happen to be one of them, try reading the box "Approaching Perfect Elasticity and Perfect Inelasticity Arithmetically."

Next we'll consider relative elasticity. If a vertical line is perfectly inelastic and a horizontal line is perfectly elastic, what about lines that are somewhere in between? Figure 8 has two such lines. The question here is, which of the two is more elastic, D_1 or D_2?

Figure 6   Perfectly Elastic Demand Curve

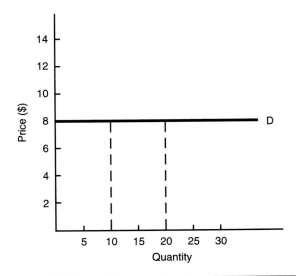

Figure 7   Perfectly Inelastic Demand Curve

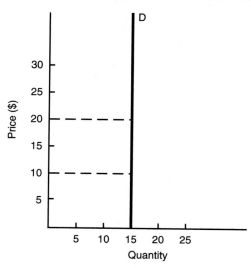

Figure 8   Relative Elasticity of Demand Curves

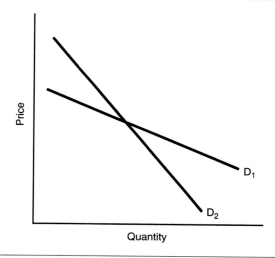

Approaching Perfect Elasticity and Perfect Inelasticity Arithmetically

Here is a set of questions for perfect elasticity.

How many times does 100 go into 100? _____

How many times does 10 go into 100? _____

How many times does 1 go into 100? _____

How many times does .1 go into 100? _____

How many times does .01 go into 100? _____

How many times does 0 go into 100? _____

   The right answers are 1; 10; 100; 1,000; 10,000; and finally, infinity, or ∞.

Now we'll do a corresponding set of questions for perfect inelasticity. Again we'll use 100.

How many times does 100 go into 100? _____

How many times does 100 go into 10? _____

How many times does 100 go into 1? _____

How many times does 100 go into .1? _____

How many times does 100 go into .01? _____

How many times does 100 go into 0? _____

   The right answers are 1; .1; .01; .001; .0001; and finally, 0.

D$_1$ is more elastic because it is closer to being horizontal. Remember, the more horizontal the demand curve is, the more elastic it is; and the more vertical the curve, the more inelastic it is.

Finally, we'll calculate the elasticity of a straight line. Surprisingly, it is not constant. Using Figure 9, let's calculate the elasticity at three points. First, do the calculations when price falls from $10 to $9 and quantity rises from 1 to 2.

Solution: P$_1$ = $10; P$_2$ = $9; Q$_1$ = 1; and Q$_2$ = 2.

$$\frac{2-1}{2+1} \cdot \frac{9+10}{9-10} = \frac{1}{3} \cdot \frac{19}{1} = \frac{19}{3} = 6.33$$

An elasticity of 6.33 is fairly high.

Moving right along, let's calculate the elasticity when price falls from $6 to $5 and the quantity demanded rises from 5 to 6.

Solution: P$_1$ = $6; P$_2$ = $5; Q$_1$ = 5; and Q$_2$ = 6.

$$\frac{6-5}{6+5} \cdot \frac{5+6}{5-6} = \frac{1}{11} \cdot \frac{11}{1} = 1$$

Figure 9   Straight-Line Demand Curve

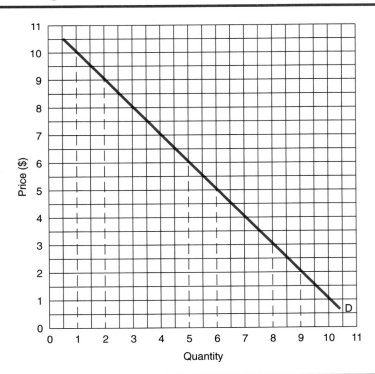

What we have here is unit elasticity, when a price change causes quantity demanded to change by the same percentage. Notice that in Figure 9 this occurs at the middle of the demand curve.

Now let's calculate the elasticity when price falls from $3 to $2 and quantity demanded rises from 8 to 9.

Solution: $P_1 = \$3$; $P_2 = \$2$; $Q_1 = 8$; and $Q_2 = 9$.

$$\frac{9-8}{9+8} \cdot \frac{2+3}{2-3} = \frac{1}{17} \cdot \frac{5}{1} = \frac{5}{17} = 0.29$$

The answer, .29, is rather inelastic. When we compare the three elasticities we calculated, this time moving to Figure 10, we reach this conclusion: A straight-line demand curve that moves downward to the right is very elastic at the top and progressively less elastic as we move down the curve. As we approach the bottom, demand becomes more and more inelastic.

Do you smoke? Well, whether you do or you don't, do you think the demand for cigarettes is elastic or inelastic? Are cigarettes a necessity? I'll let the smokers answer that one. Are there any close substitutes? Lollipops? Chewing gum? Hey, if these were such wonderful substitutes, you wouldn't have nearly so many people who still smoke.

In general, it would be safe to say that the demand for cigarettes is inelastic. How inelastic? If you're really curious, then check out the box "How Elastic *Is* the Demand for Cigarettes?"

Figure 10   Elasticity of Straight-Line Demand Curve

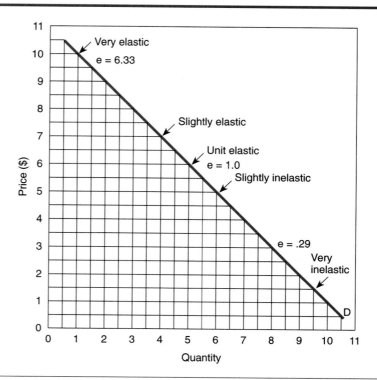

How Elastic *Is* the Demand for Cigarettes?

Let's face it: smokers have less fun. Everywhere they go there are No Smoking signs. To add insult to injury, the price of a pack of cigarettes has doubled in just a few years. And Bill and Hillary Clinton want to tax cigarettes even more.

Now you would think that an awful lot of people must have given up smoking. A study by Michael Grossman, Gary Becker, and Kevin Murphy found that a 10 percent increase in cigarette prices reduced current consumption among adults by 4 percent, and over a five-year period cigarette consumption fell by 7.5 percent.

Another study by the U.S. General Accounting Office revealed that the elasticity of demand for cigarettes among teenagers was somewhat higher—between .76 and 1.2.*

So is the demand for cigarettes elastic or inelastic? That depends on whose demand elasticity you are measuring. In general, however, we can say that the demand for cigarettes is slightly inelastic.

This raises an interesting public policy issue. The surgeon general keeps reminding us on every pack of cigarettes as well as in newspaper and magazine cigarette ads about all the terrible things smoking will do to us. But even more effective would be a hefty tax of two or three dollars on every pack, as there is in Canada, Great Britain, Ireland, Denmark, Norway, and a few other countries. Canada's tax of $3 per pack has helped cut per capita consumption by more than 50 percent since 1980.

*See The Margin, Fall 1991, p. 63.

Determinants of the Degree of Elasticity of Demand

The demand for certain goods and services is relatively elastic, while that for others is relatively inelastic. Consider heart medicine, for example. Suppose this medicine keeps you alive, and suppose its price doubles. Would you cut back on your purchases? Your demand curve would probably look like the one in Figure 11 or perhaps even like the one in Figure 7.

Do you agree that a person who needs heart medicine would cut back on the quantity she buys because its price doubles? A few people might do this. Why? Because they might not be able to afford it. Maybe one or two poor souls would say it's just not worth what they're being charged.

Figure 11   Relatively Inelastic Demand Curve

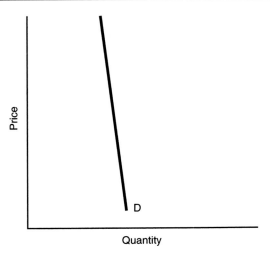

When AZT was first sold to people with AIDS, plenty of people simply couldn't afford to pay $800 to $1,000 a month. As its price came down, the quantity purchased rose somewhat. And so, Figure 11 might well represent the demand for a life-extending drug.[2]

What about relatively elastic demand? Take steak, for example. When its price goes too high, we substitute chicken, fish, and other meats for our steak dinners. The demand curve for steak might look something like the one in Figure 12.

What makes demand elastic or inelastic? By far the most important influence is the availability of substitutes. Steak has a number of reasonably close substitutes. If its price gets too high, people will buy other cuts of beef or fish and fowl instead. A relatively small percentage increase in price leads to a large percentage decline in quantity demanded.

In the case of heart medicine, demand is quite inelastic; there are no close substitutes. If price rises, quantity sold will not fall much.

There are other influences on the degree of elasticity in addition to the availability of substitutes. If the product is a necessity rather than a luxury, its demand will tend to be more inelastic. When the price of a movie ticket goes up by a dollar, you might stay home and watch television; but if the price of gasoline goes up by, say, 50 percent, you'll still buy it because you need to drive places.

Another factor affecting elasticity is the product's cost relative to the buyer's income. Once, after I had just purchased a spool of thread, my friend told me that I could have gotten it for 2 cents less in another store several miles away. Thread is not exactly a big-ticket item. But if you're earning $20,000 a year and you're interested in a $7,000 car, a price change of just 3 or 4 percent will determine whether you buy that car.

Over time the demand for a particular good often becomes more elastic. Take gasoline. If its price doubles, will people stop driving to work? To school? To the store? For the first year or two, there may be little you can do except cut back on your less essential driving. But when it comes time to buy a new car, you're likely to look for one that gives really good gas mileage. You may look for a job that's closer to home. Also, over time, the high price of gas may lead to the development of substitute fuels.

Finally, the number of uses a product has affects the elasticity of its demand. The more uses, the higher the elasticity. Salt, for example, has two main uses: to season food and to make your sidewalk less slippery when it snows. At $30 a pound, salt will still be purchased by most people to season food, but only when the price gets down to around 20 cents a pound will salt be used on the sidewalks.

---

[2]Why isn't the demand perfectly inelastic? Because at extremely high prices many people simply can't afford the drug.

Figure 12   Relatively Elastic Demand Curve

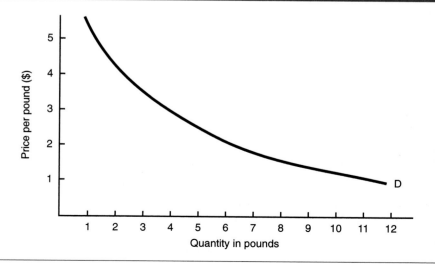

Advertising

What is the purpose of advertising? Everyone knows it's supposed to get the consumer to buy more of a product. Some industries (such as tobacco, toothpaste, breakfast cereals, and liquor) spend very heavily on advertising. In terms of what we've already discussed, we'll talk about how advertising affects demand.

In a nutshell, advertisers try to make demand for their products greater but, at the same time, less elastic. They want to push their firm's demand curve over to the right; but they also want to make it steeper or more vertical.

First, advertising seeks an increase in demand. In Figure 13, because of massive advertising, people are willing to buy more of the product at *all* prices. If D_1 is demand before advertising, D_2 would be demand after a successful advertising campaign.

Advertising is legalized lying.
—H. G. Wells

A second way in which advertising can influence a product's demand curve is by making it more inelastic. This is often done by means of brand identification. (See box "Which Motor Oil Is Number One?")

Two very similar products, Bayer aspirin and St. Joseph's aspirin for children, have been extremely well advertised. The fact that both are familiar product names alone attests to their popularity. If you go into the drugstore and see Squibb, Johnson & Johnson, and Bayer aspirin, which do you buy? Do you buy Bayer even if it's more expensive?

Aspirin is aspirin. What's in the Squibb and Johnson & Johnson bottles is identical to what Bayer puts in its bottles. But Bayer has convinced large numbers of people that somehow its aspirin is better, so people are willing to pay more for it. Right on the bottle it says "Genuine Bayer Aspirin," which may raise doubts about the aspirin sold by the competition. Bayer's advertising has been able to make its demand curve more inelastic.

Figure 13   Increase in Demand

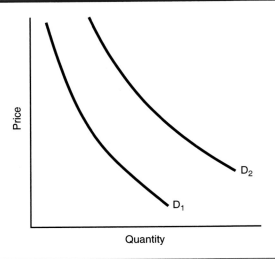

Which Motor Oil Is Number One?

May I ask you a personal question? You don't have to answer if you don't want to. All right, then, here goes. What's your favorite motor oil? I mean, deep down in your soul, do you believe that all motor oils are created equal, or do you believe that there's really one motor oil that provides better protection against engine wear during cold start-ups? A profound question.

If you were to believe the ads, almost every motor oil is superior to each of its rivals, a proposition that, of course, defies logic. Well, you no longer have to worry about these conflicting claims. According to a March 1992 ruling by Federal Judge Charles S. Haight in New York, virtually all motor oils are identical, despite conflicting claims by rival companies.*

*See Ronald Sullivan, "Quaker State Seeks Ruling against Castrol on Its Ads," *New York Times,* April 6, 1992, p. D7.

This company could raise its price yet not lose many sales. That is the essence of inelastic demand.

Advertising attempts to change the way we *think* about a product. It tries to make us think a product is more useful, more desirable, or more of a necessity. Ideally, an ad will make us feel we *must* have that product. To the degree that advertising is successful, the demand curve is made steeper and is pushed farther to the right, as from D_1 to D_2 in Figure 14.

An advertising campaign may attempt to convince consumers that a certain good or service is not only unique but actually a necessity. If you were running the advertising campaign for a medical group doing hair transplants, you would try to convince millions of middle-aged men that a transplant would not only change their lives, but that only your doctors could do it right. If your ads were completely successful, the demand curve for hair transplants from your firm would be perfectly inelastic.

Price elasticity of demand is closely related to the total revenue earned by a firm. We'll examine that relationship in the next section.

Total Revenue and Marginal Revenue

Total revenue is price times output sold.

If your firm sold four workstations at $3,200 each, how much would its total revenue be? The answer is $12,800. *Total revenue is price times output sold.*

Marginal revenue is the increase in total revenue when output sold goes up by one unit.

Now let's do marginal revenue. Suppose you sold five workstations instead of four. How much would your total revenue be? It would be $16,000 (5 × $3,200). Your marginal revenue from selling that fifth workstation would be $3,200. *Marginal revenue is the increase in total revenue when output sold goes up by one unit.* We can also say that marginal revenue is *the additional revenue derived from selling one more unit of output.*

We'll be assuming for the next four chapters that a seller can sell as much output as he or she wants at the market price. Thus, if the market price is $5, we can easily calculate the total revenue and marginal revenue. I'd like you to do that by filling in Table 3. Then you can check your work by looking at Table 4.

Graphing Demand and Marginal Revenue

Now we're ready to draw the graph of the demand and marginal revenue curves. The demand curve for this firm is the output, which runs from 1 to 6, at a price of $5. And the marginal revenue curve is the output, from 1 to 6, at whatever the price happens to be. Go ahead and draw a graph of the firm's demand and MR curves on graph paper.

Figure 14   An Increased and Less Elastic Demand

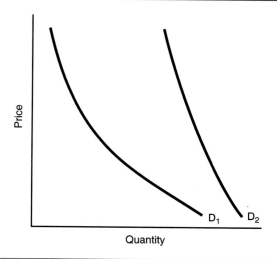

Table 3   Hypothetical Revenue Schedule

Output	Price	Total Revenue	Marginal Revenue
1	$5	_____	_____
2	5	_____	_____
3	5	_____	_____
4	5	_____	_____
5	5	_____	_____
6	5	_____	_____

Table 4   Hypothetical Revenue Schedule

Output	Price	Total Revenue	Marginal Revenue
1	$5	$ 5	$5
2	5	10	5
3	5	15	5
4	5	20	5
5	5	25	5
6	5	30	5

Now check your work against Figure 15. You should have drawn just one line, perfectly elastic, which serves as the firm's demand and MR curves. When price is constant, so is MR, and MR and demand are identical.

Elasticity and Total Revenue

Another aspect of elasticity has to do with a firm's total revenue. We want to see what effect elasticity has on total revenue when we raise or lower price.

First we'll go over total revenue or total sales. A firm will charge a particular price for some good or service, and it will be able to sell a certain quantity at that price. If the price were $7 and the quantity sold were 4, total revenue would be $28 ($7 × 4). That's all there is to it. If price were $12 and quantity sold 6, total revenue would be $72.

Figure 15   Demand and Marginal Revenue Curves

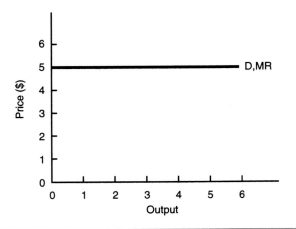

Suppose price were raised from $10 to $12 and quantity demanded fell from 20 to 12. Let's try a three-part question: (1) calculate elasticity; (2) state whether demand is elastic, unit elastic, or inelastic; and (3) calculate total revenue where price is $10 and $12. (See Table 5.)

Solution: $P_1 = \$10$; $P_2 = \$12$; $Q_1 = 20$; and $Q_2 = 12$.

$$\frac{12-20}{12+20} \cdot \frac{12+10}{12-10} = \frac{\cancel{8}^1}{\cancel{32}_4} \cdot \frac{\cancel{22}^{11}}{\cancel{2}_1} = \frac{11}{4} = 2.75$$

Table 5   Hypothetical Revenue Schedule

Price	Quantity Demanded	Total Revenue
$10	20	$200
12	12	144

If demand is elastic, a price increase will lead to a fall in total revenue.

We see, then, that *when demand is elastic, if we were to raise price, total revenue would fall.* This would make another good exam question: "If price rises and demand is elastic, total revenue will *(a)* rise, *(b)* fall, or *(c)* remain the same."

What do most students do when their instructor goes over this problem and tells them it might make a good exam question? They write down what appears in italic type in the previous paragraph. Then, on the exam, if they happen to remember that rule—there will be about 20 such rules to memorize—they'll get it right. After the test, the rule is forgotten along with 99 percent of the other material that was memorized.

In this course you can figure out a lot of the answers to exam questions right on the spot. Take the exam question I quoted: "If price rises and demand is elastic, total revenue will *(a)* rise, *(b)* fall, or *(c)* remain the same." To figure this out, make up a problem like the one we just did. The key here is that you want demand to be elastic. That means percentage change in quantity is greater than percentage change in price.

To derive our next rule, we'll use the same problem we've just solved (when elasticity was found to be 2.75). Try this question: "If price declines and demand is elastic, total revenue will *(a)* rise, *(b)* fall, or *(c)* remain the same." In that problem, when price dropped from $12 to $10, what happened to total revenue?

Seeing that total revenue rose from $144 to $200, we can state our second rule. *When demand is elastic, if we were to lower price, total revenue would rise.*

Now we're ready for the third and fourth rules. What happens to total revenue when demand is inelastic and price is raised? You can make up your own problem, or if you like, use the data from our straight-line graph in Figure 9. When price was raised from $2 to $3, quantity demanded declined from 9 to 8. How much, then, is total revenue at a price of $2 and at a price of $3?

If demand is inelastic, a price increase will lead to an increase in total revenue.

At a price of $2, it is $18 ($2 × 9); at a price of $3, it is $24 ($3 × 8). We now have our third rule. *When demand is inelastic, if we were to raise price, total revenue would rise.*

Can you guess the fourth rule? Using the same data but reversing the process (i.e., lowering price), we would find: *When demand is inelastic and price is lowered, total revenue will fall.* (Price goes from $3 to $2, and total revenue falls from $24 to $18.)

As a businessperson facing an inelastic demand curve, you would never lower your price because your total revenue would decline. You would be selling *more* units and getting *less* revenue. If someone offered to buy 8 units from you for $24, would you agree to sell 9 units for $18? Think about it. What would happen to your total revenue? What would happen to your total cost? Obviously, your total revenue would decline from $24 to $18. And your total cost? Surely it would cost you more to produce 9 units than 8 units. If your total revenue goes down and your total cost goes up when you lower your price, it would hardly make sense to do so.

Try another one. If price is $8 and output ranges from 1 to 6, compile a table of output, price, total revenue, and marginal revenue in the space below. Then draw a graph of the demand and marginal revenue curves on graph paper.

How did you do? Better this time? Do your table and graph check out with mine? (See Table 6 and Figure 16.) See, there's really nothing to it. In this and the next chapter, the demand and marginal revenue curves will be the same perfectly straight horizontal line.

Table 6   Hypothetical Revenue Schedule

Output	Price	Total Revenue	Marginal Revenue
1	$8	$ 8	$8
2	8	16	8
3	8	24	8
4	8	32	8
5	8	40	8
6	8	48	8

Figure 16   Demand and Marginal Revenue Curves

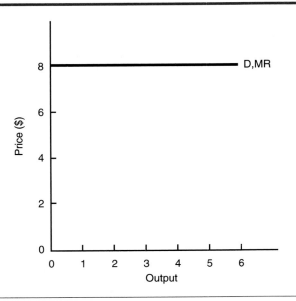

Last Word

Virtually all of the concepts developed in this chapter will be applied in the next dozen chapters, so it is extremely important for you to be comfortable working with them. After you have completed the workbook questions, please take the time to go back over anything that you don't fully understand. Repetition may not be much fun, but it can sure pull up your grade in this course.

Questions for Further Thought and Discussion

1. As you move down a straight-line demand curve, what happens to its elasticity? Can you prove this?
2. If demand is elastic and price is raised, what happens to total revenue? Can you prove this?
3. Explain how the price of a good is affected by changes in the prices of *(a)* substitute goods; *(b)* complementary goods.
4. Explain the difference between a change in demand and a change in the quantity demanded.

WORKBOOK FOR CHAPTER 18

Name _____ Date _____

Self-Review Examination

Questions 1–6: Answer true or false.

_____ 1. An increase in demand is illustrated graphically by a shift upward and to the right by the demand curve.

_____ 2. If price falls and, in response, quantity demanded rises, this represents an increase in demand.

_____ 3. A perfectly elastic demand curve has an elasticity of zero.

_____ 4. When demand is elastic and price is raised, total revenue will fall.

_____ 5. When demand is inelastic and price is lowered, total revenue will rise.

_____ 6. Elasticity of demand is found by dividing the percentage change in price by the percentage change in quantity.

7. Suppose demand is very, very elastic. What would happen to total revenue if you: a. raised your price? b. lowered your price?

8. What is unit elasticity?

Multiple-Choice Questions

Circle the letter that corresponds to the best answer.

1. If demand is inelastic and price is raised, total revenue will
   a. rise   b. fall   c. stay the same
   d. possibly rise or possibly fall

2. If demand is elastic and price is lowered, total revenue will
   a. rise   b. fall   c. stay the same
   d. possibly rise or possibly fall

3. Goods for which demand is directly (positively) related to income are called
   a. substitute goods   b. complementary goods
   c. inferior goods   d. normal goods

4. Demand is elastic when
   a. percentage change in price is greater than percentage change in quantity   b. percentage change in quantity is greater than percentage change in price   c. the demand curve is vertical   d. price increases raise total revenue

5. An increase in the demand for steak could be caused quickly by a(n)
   a. fall in the price of steak   b. increase in the supply of steak   c. expectation of a future cutback in the supply of steak   d. a decline in the price of chicken

6. The demand for an inferior good is
   a. positively related to its own price   b. negatively related to income   c. unaffected by consumer tastes and preferences   d. insensitive to changes in prices of its complements

7. Each of the following may lead to a change in the demand for product A except
   a. a change in the price of product A   b. a change in people's taste for product A   c. a change in people's incomes   d. a change in the price of product B (a substitute for product A)

8. The retail market for gasoline is
   a. local   b. regional   c. national
   d. international

9. Suppose the price of a service falls and people buy more of that service. What has happened?
   a. Quantity demanded changed   b. Demand changed.
   c. Demand increased.   d. Demand decreased.

10. The most important determinant of the degree of elasticity of demand is
   a. whether the item is a big-ticket item   b. whether the item is a luxury   c. how many uses the product has   d. the availability of substitutes

447

11. The advertiser wants to push her product's demand curve
   a. to the right and make it more elastic   b. to the
   right and make it less elastic   c. to the left and make
   it more elastic   d. to the left and make it less elastic

12. Change in which of the following would not quickly
    cause a shift in demand?
    a. number of buyers   b. tastes   c. buyers'
    perception of quality of product   d. income
    e. price

13. A decrease in demand means that the quantity demanded
    a. does not fall at any price   b. falls only at the
    equilibrium price   c. falls at a few prices   d. falls
    at most prices   e. falls at all prices

14. Which statement is true about the graph in Figure 1?
    a. Demand is perfectly elastic.   b. Demand is
    perfectly inelastic   c. Demand is more elastic at point
    X than at point Y.   d. Demand is more elastic at point
    Y than at point X.

Figure 1

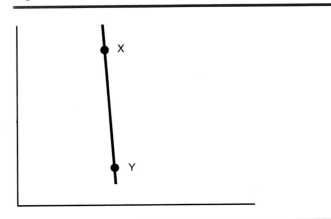

15. As income rises, the demand for inferior goods
    a. rises   b. falls   c. stays about the
    same   d. cannot be determined

For questions 16 through 21, use choices **a** through **d** (the same choice may be used more than once) and refer to Figures 2 and 3.
   a. change in quantity demanded   b. change in
   demand   c. increase in demand   d. decrease in
   demand

___ 16. A move from I to J

___ 17. A move from J to K

___ 18. A move from K to L

___ 19. A move from M to N

___ 20. A move from N to O

___ 21. A move from O to P

Figure 2

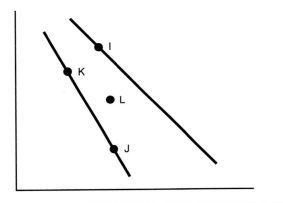

Figure 3

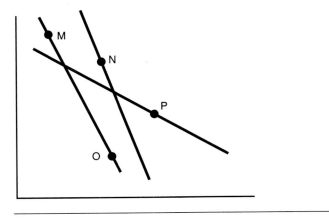

22. A 5 percent increase in the price of sugar causes the quantity demanded to fall by 15 percent. The demand for sugar is

   a. perfectly elastic   **b.** elastic   **c.** unit elastic

   d. inelastic   **e.** perfectly inelastic

23. If the price of cameras falls, there will be a(n)

   a. decrease in the demand for film   **b.** decrease in the quantity of cameras demanded   **c.** decrease in the supply of cameras   **d.** increase in the demand for cameras   **e.** increase in the quantity of cameras demanded

24. The market demand for a good will decrease

   a. as income decreases if the good is an inferior good

   b. if the market price of a substitute good increases

   c. as income decreases if the good is a normal good

   d. if the market price of a complementary good decreases   **e.** as the number of consumers in the market increases

25. Demand is elastic if

   a. percentage change in quantity is greater than percentage change in price   **b.** percentage change in price is greater than percentage change in quantity

   c. percentage change in quantity demand is zero

   d. percentage change in price is zero   **e.** percentage change in quantity is equal to percentage change in price

Problems

1. Use the data in Table 1 to draw a graph of this company's demand and marginal revenue curves in Figure 4.

Table 1

Output	Price
1	$8
2	8
3	8
4	8
5	8

Figure 4

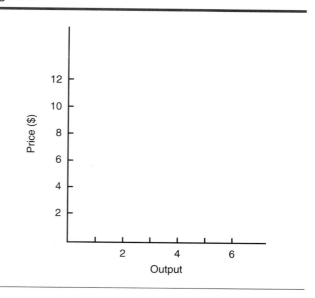

2. If price were increased from $40 to $42 and quantity demanded fell from 50 to 45, calculate elasticity; state whether demand is elastic, unit elastic, or inelastic; and find how much total revenue was when price was $40 and $42.

3. If price were lowered from $50 to $43 and quantity demanded rose from 15 to 16, calculate elasticity; state whether demand is elastic, unit elastic, or inelastic; and find how much total revenue was when price was $50 and $43.

4. Draw a demand curve, D_1. Then draw a second demand curve, D_2, that is less elastic.

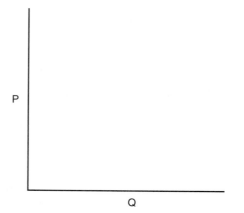

5. Draw a demand curve, D_1. Then draw a second demand curve, D_2, that illustrates a decrease in demand.

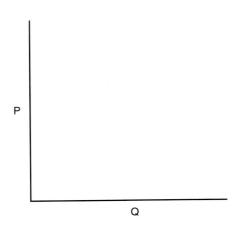

6. Draw a perfectly elastic demand curve and state its elasticity.

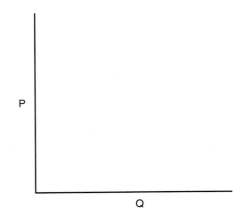

7. On the demand curve shown in the accompanying graph, label the curve where it is very elastic, unit elastic, and very inelastic.

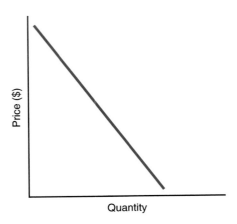

8. If elasticity of demand is 2 and price is raised from $10 to $11, by what percentage will quantity demanded fall?

9. If elasticity of demand is .5 and price is lowered from $20 to $19, by what percentage will quantity demanded rise?

CHAPTER

19 Theory of Consumer Behavior

Why do people buy goods and services? Because they derive some utility or usefulness from them. We measure that utility by how much consumers are willing to pay.

Chapter Objectives

When you have completed this chapter you will know everything you'll ever need to know about:

- Marginal utility.
- The law of diminishing marginal utility.
- Total utility.
- Maximizing utility.
- The water–diamond paradox.
- Consumer surplus.

Utility

What Is Utility?

Utility is measured by how much you are willing to pay for something.

People often confuse utility and usefulness. "Why did he buy that thing? It has no utility." In economics that would be a self-contradicting statement. Utility means only that you think enough of something to buy it.

Suppose you were ravenously hungry and came upon a hamburger stand. If the attendant told you that he had just one hamburger left—you're hungry enough to put away four—and that you'd have to pay $3 for it, would you buy it?

If you did, that hamburger would have given you at least $3 worth of utility. What if you had refused to pay $3, but when he lowered the price to $2.75 you bought it? Then that hamburger's utility would have been $2.75.

You were still hungry and soon came upon a second hamburger stand. You said to yourself as you approached, "I'd be willing to spend $2 on a second hamburger." Why not $2.75? Because you're not as hungry as you were before you wolfed down that $2.75 hamburger.

Suppose you spent $2 on a second hamburger and would be willing to pay just $1 for a third. Notice how the utility derived from consuming that third hamburger is much less than what the second one was worth.

If you managed to find someone who would let you have that third hamburger for no more than a dollar, what then? You'd try to get a fourth hamburger for a quarter. Why only a quarter? Because you're feeling a little piggy, and besides, I need you to be a little hungry still so I can illustrate a couple of things.

Table 1 sums things up. That's your demand schedule for hamburgers when you're ravenously hungry.

Table 1   Hypothetical Demand Schedule for Hamburgers

Price	Quantity Demanded
$2.75	1
2.00	2
1.00	3
.25	4

Table 2   Hypothetical Marginal Utility Schedule

Units Purchased	Marginal Utility
1	$2.75
2	2.00
3	1.00
4	.25

Marginal Utility

You've seen that the first hamburger you consumed had a utility of $2.75, the second had a utility of $2, the third, $1, and the fourth, 25 cents. Thus you just derived your marginal utility schedule. It appears in Table 2.

Marginal utility is *the additional utility derived from consuming one more unit of some good or service.* What happens to your marginal utility as you consume more and more hamburgers? It declines from $2.75 to $2 to $1 to 25 cents.

We've come to the *law of diminishing marginal utility.* As we consume more and more of a good or service, we like it less and less. That might be OK for an exam answer, but I have to be a bit more elegant here, so let's restate the law as follows. *As we consume increasing amounts of a good or service, we derive diminishing utility, or satisfaction, from each additional unit consumed.*

Think about it. How many movies would you want to go to in a day? In a week? How many plane trips to Europe would you want to take in a week? How many times do you want to take this economics course?

Total Utility

Are you ready to put all of this together? Let's hope everything *will* come together when we look at total utility. Total utility is *the utility you derive from consuming a certain number of units of a good or service.* To get total utility, just add up the marginal utilities of all the units purchased. Table 3 does this for your hamburgers.

Let's go over Table 3 column-by-column. The first two columns come from Table 1, which is your hypothetical demand schedule for hamburgers. The third column, "Marginal Utility," shows how much utility you derive from the first, second, third, and fourth hamburgers.

Can you figure out how we got the fourth column, "Total Utility"? Start with a total utility of $2.75. That's the marginal utility of the first hamburger. How much is the

Table 3   Hypothetical Utility Schedules

Price	Units Purchased	Marginal Utility	Total Utility
$2.75	1	$2.75	$2.75
2.00	2	2.00	4.75
1.00	3	1.00	5.75
.25	4	.25	6.00

Marginal utility

The law of diminishing marginal utility

Total utility

second hamburger worth to you? It's worth $2; so what's the total utility of two hamburgers? It's $4.75—$2.75 for the first hamburger plus $2 for the second.

How much is the total utility of three hamburgers? It's $5.75—$2.75 for the first plus $2 for the second plus $1 for the third. And finally, how much is the total utility of four hamburgers? It comes to $6 ($2.75 + $2 + $1 + $.25).

There are two ways to find total utility. First, we can add up the marginal utilities of the items purchased, in this case hamburgers. A shortcut would be to add the marginal utility of the last hamburger purchased to the total utility of the previous hamburgers purchased. For example, the total utility of three hamburgers is $5.75. The marginal utility of the fourth hamburger is $.25; just add that to the $5.75 to get a total utility of $6 for four hamburgers.

Are you comfortable calculating marginal utility and total utility? If you are, please go directly to the next section, on maximizing utility. But if you need more practice, then you'll find help in the box "Calculating Marginal Utility and Total Utility."

Maximizing Utility

How much we buy of any good or service depends on its price and on our marginal utility schedule. Go back to the hamburger example. We can see in Table 3 how many hamburgers we'd buy at each price. Unlike that example, however, in real life there's usually only one price. No one will offer us that first hamburger at $2.75, the second at $2, the

Calculating Marginal Utility and Total Utility

We'll start with a demand schedule for University of Memphis sweatshirts, shown in the first table (A). We can use this demand schedule to derive a marginal utility schedule and a total utility schedule for Karen Jones. How much utility does she derive from that first sweatshirt? Obviously, she gets $15 worth. So now you have her marginal utility and total utility from one sweatshirt. Put those numbers in Table A below and then complete the table.

The second table shows Karen Jones's marginal utility and total utility schedules. Make sure that your figures in Table A match mine in Table B.

Did you get everything right? If you did, you may skip the rest of this box. But stay with it if you need more help.

Look at the marginal utility column. Now look at the price column (to the far left on Table B). You'll notice that

they're identical. Check back to Table 3. You see that the price column and the marginal utility column are also identical. So when you're filling in the marginal utility column, just copy the price column.

Now let's tackle total utility. Marginal utility and total utility are identical at a quantity of one. At a quantity of two, total utility is found by adding the marginal utility at quantity one plus the marginal utility at quantity two. So total utility ($27) = $15 + $12. How do we find total utility at a quantity of three? We add the first three marginal utilities: $15 + $12 + $10 = $37.

At a quantity of four, total utility ($44) = $15 + $12 + $10 + $7. At a quantity of five, total utility ($49) = $15 + $12 + $10 + $7 + $5. And at a quantity of six, total utility ($53) = $15 + $12 + $10 + $7 + $5 + $4.

A.

Price	Quantity Demanded	Marginal Utility	Total Utility
$15	1	_____	_____
12	2	_____	_____
10	3	_____	_____
7	4	_____	_____
5	5	_____	_____
4	6	_____	_____

B.

Price	Quantity Demanded	Marginal Utility	Total Utility
$15	1	$15	$15
12	2	12	27
10	3	10	37
7	4	7	44
5	5	5	49
4	6	4	53

third at \$1, and the fourth at a quarter. For every good or service at any given time, there's just one price.

What we do, then, with our limited incomes is try to spend our money on what will give us the most satisfaction or utility. Keep in mind that as we consume more and more of any good or service, according to the law of diminishing marginal utility, its marginal utility declines. How much do we buy? We keep buying more and more until our marginal utility declines to the level of the price.

Because we buy a good or service up to the point at which its marginal utility is equal to its price, we could form this simple equation:

$$\frac{\text{Marginal utility}}{\text{Price}} = 1$$

Marginal utility = 1
Price

For example, if the price of hamburgers were 25 cents, we'd buy four hamburgers. The marginal utility of the fourth hamburger would be 25 cents. So

$$\frac{\text{Marginal utility}}{\text{Price}} = \frac{25¢}{25¢} = 1$$

A person distributes his income in such a way as to equalize the utility of the final increments of all commodities consumed.
— W. Stanley Jevons,
Theory of Political Economy

If we buy hamburgers up to the point where $\frac{\text{MU of hamburgers}}{\text{P of hamburgers}} = 1$, we will do the same with everything else we buy. How many CDs or cassettes do we buy? We keep buying them until their MU falls to the level of their price. If there are 93 different CDs we like equally, do we buy them all, even if we have the money? Maybe we buy two or three. The first one we buy is worth more to us than the price if we go ahead and buy a second one; and that second one is worth more than the price if we buy a third CD. If we stop at three, the third CD is worth the price, but a fourth would not be.

We keep buying CDs until their MU declines to the price level. In fact, the same thing can be said about everything we buy. To generalize,

General utility formula

$$\frac{\text{MU}_1}{\text{P}_1} = \frac{\text{MU}_2}{\text{P}_2} = \frac{\text{MU}_3}{\text{P}_3} = \frac{\text{MU}_n}{\text{P}_n}$$

The next time you're in Burger King, or any other eating establishment for that matter, I'd like you to use this general utility formula. Perhaps you'll come up with results that are similar to those shown in the box "Getting Your Priorities Straight at Burger King."

We have been making an implicit assumption throughout our discussion of utility: we are getting bargains on each unit we purchase until the last one. The MU of that last one is just equal to price, but the MU of the earlier units purchased is greater than price. This is the assumption on which consumer surplus is based.

Suppose that a good or service were free. How many units would you consume? You would keep consuming units until the item's marginal utility fell to zero.

If movies were free, you might go to three or four a week. I once knew a guy who went to four a day. Not only did he love movies, but he didn't work, go to school, or engage in any other productive activity.

We have seen that as we consume more units, not only does marginal utility decline, but total utility keeps rising. But what happens when marginal utility falls to zero? At that point we don't consume any more of that good or service. And our total utility is at a maximum.

If, for some reason, we consumed still another unit, our marginal utility would become negative. That unit would be worth less than zero. An extra hamburger that would make us sick or a movie that we didn't have time to see or didn't really *want* to see would decrease total utility. And so, in conclusion, we maximize our total utility when our marginal utility falls to zero.

You are ravenously hungry, so you decide to do lunch at Burger King. You're going to try something a little different this time—hamburgers, french fries, and a Coke or two. If Table A represents your demand for hamburgers, fill in your marginal utility schedule:

A.

Price	Quantity Demanded	Marginal Utility
$3	1	_____
2	2	_____
1	3	_____

Your marginal utility schedule is identical to the prices you are willing to pay for the first, second, and third burgers—$3, $2, and $1, respectively.

Table B shows your demand for french fries. Please fill in the marginal utility column.

B.

Price	Quantity Demanded	Marginal Utility
$1.50	1	_____
1.00	2	_____
.50	3	_____

What did you get? I hope it was $1.50 for the first order of fries, $1 for the second, and $.50 for the third.

All of this has made you thirsty. How about some Coke? Fill in your marginal utility schedule in Table C.

C.

Price	Quantity Demanded	Marginal Utility
$1.50	1	_____
.50	2	_____

The first Coke gives you a marginal utility of $1.50, while the second yields only $.50 worth.

It's finally time to get to the point. Suppose hamburgers were $3. How many would you buy? Did you say one? Good! And how many orders of fries would you buy if they went for $.50 an order? Did I hear you say you'd buy three? All *right!* And if Cokes were $.50? You'd buy two.

Now let's put all these numbers into our formula:

$$\frac{MU_1}{P_1} = \frac{MU_2}{P_2} = \frac{MU_3}{P_3}$$

I'd like you to substitute the marginal utilities and prices of (1) hamburgers, (2) french fries, and (3) Cokes. I'll start you off:

$$\frac{\$3}{\$3} = \underline{\qquad} = \underline{\qquad}$$

Have you filled in your fries and Cokes? I'll bet you got this:

$$\frac{\$3}{\$3} = \frac{\$.50}{\$.50} = \frac{\$.50}{\$.50}$$

Let's see how many burgers, fries, and Cokes you'd chow down if burgers were $1, fries were $1, and Cokes were $1.50. Write down your answers.

You would have purchased three burgers, two fries, and one Coke. Now set up your MU/Price equation, substituting your fingers for burgers, fries, and Cokes.

$$\frac{MU_1}{P_1} = \frac{MU_2}{P_2} = \frac{MU_3}{P_3}$$

$$\underline{\qquad} = \underline{\qquad} = \underline{\qquad}$$

By now you should be able to do all of this in your sleep—provided it hasn't already put you to sleep. Here are the results:

$$\frac{\$1}{\$1} = \frac{\$1}{\$1} = \frac{\$1.50}{\$1.50}$$

Why did you shift from one burger to three? Because their price came down. And why did you buy fewer fries and Cokes? Because their prices rose. Now we come to that elusive point I've been trying to make. We're always maximizing our utility. We'll buy more and more of a particular good or service until its MU declines to its price (remember our law of diminishing marginal utility).

You maximized your utility by purchasing one hamburger when its price was $3, three fries at $.50 each, and two Cokes at $.50 each. But when the price of hamburgers fell to $1, you bought three. And you bought just two orders of fries when their price rose to $1 and just one Coke at $1.50. The next time you're dining at Burger King, Wendy's, White Castle, or any other gourmet eatery, ask the manager to charge the two sets of prices I've suggested to see how her customers will respond. Perhaps she'll tell you that you haven't read far enough in this text. After you've read about maximizing profits in the chapter on cost and profit, you'll never suggest such an outlandish idea. Oh well, it can't hurt to ask.

The Water–Diamond Paradox

How come water, which is essential to life, is so cheap, while diamonds, which are not at all essential, are so expensive? We now have enough utility theory under our belts to resolve this apparent paradox.

First, the law of diminishing marginal utility tells us that as we consume increasing amounts of a good or service, we derive decreasing utility (or satisfaction) from each additional unit consumed. Second, we know from the general utility formula that we'll keep buying more of a good or service until its marginal utility falls to the level of its price. Therefore:

$$\frac{\text{MU of water}}{\text{P of water}} = \frac{\text{MU of diamonds}}{\text{P of diamonds}}$$

The price of water in most parts of the world is low because it is abundant. But the price of diamonds is high because they are not abundant.

We consume a great deal of water, so the marginal utility of the last gallon consumed is as low as its price. But we buy very few diamonds, so the marginal utility of the last carat purchased is very high.

Imagine what would happen if diamonds were to become plentiful and water were to become scarce. The marginal utility of water would go way up, along with its price. And the marginal utility and price of diamonds would fall. Not only that, but there would no longer be a water–diamond paradox.

Consumer Surplus

You may remember the great English economist Alfred Marshall from the last chapter. About a century ago he wrote these words:

> The price which a person pays for a thing can never exceed, and seldom comes up to, that which he would be willing to pay rather than go without it, so that the satisfaction which he gets from its purchase generally exceeds that which he gives up in paying away its price; and he thus derives from the purchase a surplus of satisfaction.
>
>   It may be called consumer's surplus.

Definition of consumer surplus

Today we define consumer's surplus, or consumer surplus, a little more succinctly: Consumer surplus is *the difference between what you pay for some good or service and what you would have been willing to pay.*

I used to live in a very classy neighborhood. In fact, this neighborhood was so classy that none of the supermarkets bothered to stay open on Sunday. One tiny grocery store was open all the time, and I made a point of never shopping there because the place was an unbelievable rip-off.

As fate would have it, a friend who was visiting on a Sunday wanted meatballs and spaghetti. I warned her that the only place to buy it was at that store. She went there and came back with an eight-ounce can. "How much?" I asked.

"Don't ask," she replied.

Later I saw the price on the can. It was $4.99.

Why did I tell that whole story, and what does it have to do with consumer surplus? First of all, was my friend ripped off? The answer, surprisingly, is no. Forget about the store being open on Sunday, the convenience, and all the rest. The bottom line is, my friend bought that can of meatballs and spaghetti. If it wasn't worth at least $4.99 to her, she wouldn't have bought it.

When you're really thirsty, wouldn't you be willing to pay $3 for a bottle of soda? Luckily, you don't have to—unless, of course, you live in my old neighborhood, you have no soda in the house, and it's a Sunday. Usually, when you buy something, you actually would have been willing to pay even more.

In the previous section, we said a person keeps buying more and more of a good or service until that person's marginal utility for that item falls to the price level. Therefore,

Figure 1   Consumer Surplus

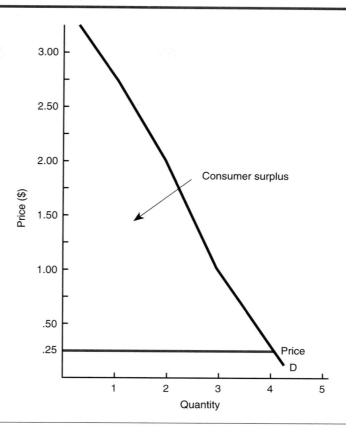

each unit purchased except the last one was a bargain because MU was greater than price. This can be seen in Figure 1, where we once again use the hamburger example from the beginning of the chapter.

If the price of hamburgers were a quarter, you would purchase four and the consumer surplus would be the triangular area above the price line in Figure 1. The total consumer surplus would be based on the difference between what you paid for each hamburger (25 cents) and what you would have been willing to pay. You would have been willing to pay $2.75 for the first one, so your consumer surplus on the first hamburger is $2.50. You would have been willing to pay $2 for the second, so on that one your consumer surplus is $1.75. Similarly, on the third hamburger your consumer surplus is $1.00 − .25 = $.75. On the fourth hamburger, MU = Price (25 cents = 25 cents), so there is no consumer surplus. Your total consumer surplus would be $2.50 + $1.75 + $.75 = $5. Looked at another way, your total utility derived from the four hamburgers is $6, and if you pay 25 cents for each of four hamburgers, $6 minus $1 equals a consumer surplus of $5.

The next time you go shopping, don't complain about being ripped off. No one ever paid more than he or she was willing to pay; no one ever bought anything whose price exceeded its utility; and anyone who ever bought several units of the same product at a fixed price enjoyed a consumer surplus.

Let's calculate another consumer surplus. I'm getting a little tired of hamburgers, so let's do exercise sessions with a personal trainer. Enough sessions and you'll be on the next U.S. Olympic team. Use just the information in Table 4 to find the consumer surplus you'll enjoy by purchasing four sessions.

The key thing to remember in solving this problem is the definition of consumer surplus: the difference between what you pay for something and what you would have been willing to pay. How much did you pay for four sessions? If you bought four, then the price must have been $25; so you paid $100 (4 × $25). Now, how much would you have

**Table 4   Hypothetical Demand Schedule for Sessions
with a Personal Trainer**

Price	Quantity Demanded	Marginal Utility	Total Utility
$50	1	_____	_____
40	2	_____	_____
30	3	_____	_____
25	4	_____	_____
20	5	_____	_____
15	6	_____	_____

**Table 5   Hypothetical Utility Schedule for Sessions
with a Personal Trainer**

Price	Quantity Demanded	Marginal Utility	Total Utility
$50	1	$50	$ 50
40	2	40	90
30	3	30	120
25	4	25	145
20	5	20	165
15	6	15	180

been *willing* to pay for these four sessions? In other words, how much total utility do you derive from four personal training sessions? To find that out, we need to fill in Table 5.

We see from Table 5 that four sessions have a total utility of $145. If you have to pay only $100 for these sessions, then your consumer surplus is $45 ($145 − $100).

Next question: How much would your consumer surplus be if you purchased six sessions? Work it out right here:

You would have been willing to pay $180 for the six sessions, as that's the total utility you would derive from these sessions. But you would buy six sessions only if the price were $15 per session. So you would have to pay $90 (6 × $15) for these sessions. Your consumer surplus would be $180 − $90 = $90.

If you're not understanding this, then you need a little more practice, which you'll get in the box "Finding the Consumer Surplus." But if you're on top of this concept, go directly to the workbook section.

Questions for Further Thought and Discussion

1. Explain the law of diminishing marginal utility, and give an example to illustrate it.
2. If you were to consume five hamburgers at Wendy's, would you enjoy a consumer surplus? Explain your answer.
3. How do we measure utility? Are interpersonal comparisons valid? Why or why not?

Finding the Consumer Surplus

Use the demand schedule in Table A to find the consumer surplus if a quantity of six is purchased.

A.

Price	Quantity Demanded	Marginal Utility	Total Utility
$100	1	_____	_____
80	2	_____	_____
65	3	_____	_____
55	4	_____	_____
50	5	_____	_____
45	6	_____	_____

How much do we have to pay for six units? The answer is $270 (6 × 45). Next, how much would we be willing to pay for these six units? Your filled-in table should look like B, which indicates that the total utility of six units is $395.

B.

Price	Quantity Demanded	Marginal Utility	Total Utility
$100	1	$100	$100
80	2	80	180
65	3	65	245
55	4	55	300
50	5	50	350
45	6	45	395

Now all we have to do is simple subtraction. We start with what we are willing to pay for six units, a total utility of $395, and subtract what we have to pay, $270. The calculation is $395 − $270 = $125. Thus $125 is our consumer surplus.

Can you find how much the consumer surplus would be if we purchased five units? Figure it out in this space.

Total utility of five units is $350. We would have to pay $250 (5 × $50). Consumer surplus is $350 − 250 = $100.

How much would the consumer surplus be if we bought three units?

Total utility of three units is $245. We would have to pay $195 (3 × $65). Consumer surplus is $245 − $195 = $50.

Name _____   Date _____

Self-Review Examination

Questions 1–8: Answer true or false.

_____ 1. The diamond–water paradox has never been resolved.

_____ 2. Total utility will rise as long as marginal utility is rising.

_____ 3. The concept of consumer surplus was formulated by Alfred Marshall.

_____ 4. Total utility is at a maximum when marginal utility is zero.

_____ 5. We are maximizing our utility when the marginal utility of each good or service we purchase is equal to its price.

_____ 6. Utility is measured by a product's usefulness.

_____ 7. As increasing amounts of a product are consumed, marginal utility will decline.

_____ 8. If you were to purchase five drinks at $1 each, you would enjoy a consumer surplus

9. State the general utility formula.

10. Define marginal utility.

11. Explain the law of diminishing marginal utility.

12. What is a consumer surplus?

Multiple-Choice Questions

Circle the letter that corresponds to the best answer.

1. If we know a person's demand schedule, we can find
   a. her marginal activity, but not her total utility
   b. her total utility, but not her marginal utility
   c. both her total utility and her marginal utility
   d. neither her total utility nor her marginal utility

2. If a service is free, you will consume more and more of it until
   a. your marginal utility is zero   b. your total utility is zero   c. both your marginal utility and your total utility are zero   d. neither your marginal utility nor your total utility is zero

3. A product's utility to a buyer is measured by
   a. its usefulness   b. its price   c. how much the buyer is willing to pay for it   d. none of the above

4. As the price of a service rises
   a. the consumer surplus decreases   b. the consumer surplus increases   c. the consumer surplus may increase or decrease

5. In Figure 1 (price is OA) consumer surplus is bounded by
   a. OBD   b. OACD   c. ABC   d. none of these

Figure 1

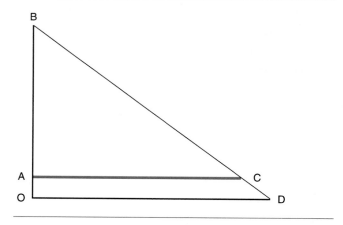

6. When you buy three units of a particular good or service
   a. you will have no consumer surplus   b. you will have a consumer surplus   c. there is no way of knowing whether you have a consumer surplus

7. A person would be maximizing her total utility when
a. she had a consumer surplus   b. her marginal utility was zero   c. her marginal utility was equal to her total utility   d. she had no consumer surplus

8. Which statement is true?
a. Most people have the same utility schedules.
b. Most people enjoy a consumer surplus for at least some of the things they buy.   c. We will consume additional units of a product until our consumer surplus is zero.   d. The utility of a product is measured by its usefulness.

9. Which statement is false?
a. The water–diamond paradox can be resolved with the help of the law of diminishing marginal utility.   b. We will consume a service when its marginal utility is equal to its price.   c. The law of diminishing marginal utility has little validity today.   d. None is false.

10. As you purchase more and more of any good or service, your
a. total utility and marginal utility both decline
b. total utility and marginal utility both rise
c. total utility rises and marginal utility declines
d. total utility declines and marginal utility rises

11. A person will buy more and more of a good or service until
a. marginal utility is greater than price   b. price is greater than marginal utility   c. price is equal to marginal utility

12. In Figure 2 (price is JK) consumer surplus is bounded by
a. JKMN   b. JLN   c. KLM   d. none of these

Figure 2

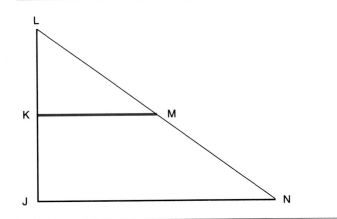

13. If the marginal utility you derived from the last video game you played was $1.75 and the game cost 50 cents to play
a. you have been playing the game too long   b. you haven't been playing the game long enough   c. there is no way to determine whether you have played the game long enough

Problems

1. Suppose Table 1 shows your demand schedule for cans of soda. a. What is your total utility from three cans of soda? b. What is your marginal utility from the third can of soda? c. If price were $1.50, how much would your consumer surplus be?

Table 1

Price	Quantity Demanded
$3.00	1
2.00	2
1.50	3

2. Suppose Table 2 shows your demand schedule for CDs. a. What is your total utility from four CDs? b. What is your marginal utility from the fourth CD? c. If the price is $2, how much will your consumer surplus be?

Table 2

Price	Quantity Demanded
$10	1
8	2
6	3
4	4
2	5

3. Suppose that at three units purchased, marginal utility is $8 and total utility is $30. If the marginal utility of the fourth unit purchased is $6, how much is the total utility of four units?

20 Supply

In the preceding chapters we've covered applications in supply and demand; demand; and utility and consumer surplus. Now we're ready to tackle supply. You'll find that much of this chapter parallels what was covered in the chapter on demand, so we don't need to cover this material in as much depth. In a sense, then, we won't be breaking new ground until the last part of the chapter, when we discuss tax incidence.

Chapter Objectives

The main topics that will be covered are:

- Definition of supply.
- Individual and market supply.
- Changes in supply.
- Elasticity of supply.
- Tax incidence.

Supply Defined

Definition of supply

Supply is *a schedule of quantities of a good or service that people are willing to sell at various prices.* As prices rise, they are willing to sell more. Thus we have a positive or direct relationship between price and quantity: as price rises, quantity supplied rises; as price falls, quantity supplied falls.

You may ask *why* quantity supplied rises as price rises. Let me answer by asking *you* a question. Can you type? I mean, can you type at all? Even using the two-finger method with four mistakes on each line? Most people can type at least that well.

What happens when your professor wants a term paper typed? "I don't own a PC." "My typewriter is broken." "My PC is down." "I don't know how to type." "I have a broken hand—tomorrow I'll bring in the cast."

But if the professor insists on a typed term paper, somehow everyone eventually comes up with one. Some students pay people to type the papers. Some students even pay people to *write* them. If the going rate were $2 a page and you were a terrible typist, you might well go out and hire a typist.

What if suddenly millions of term papers were assigned and because of the unprecedented demand for typists, the price was bid up to $20 a page. Would *you* pay someone $20 a page to do what you could do yourself? Why stop there? Twenty dollars a page! Why not set yourself up in business as a typist?

Let's analyze what has happened. At very low prices, many students are willing to hire typists; but at very high prices, they'd not only do their own typing, but they'd hire themselves out as typists. This helps explain why, at very high prices, the quantity supplied will be high.

Try this one on for size. Over the last 20 or 30 years doctors have become very reluctant to make house calls. "You broke your leg, have a 108-degree fever, and you're hallucinating? You must be if you think I make house calls. Why don't you hop right over to the office and we'll have a look at you?" How do you get this joker to make a house call?

Do what you do when you want a ringside table at a club; grease the guy's palm. Tell your doctor there's an extra $100 in it for him if he can make it over to your place before your mortician. Now there's one fella who *does* make house calls. Or maybe the "extra" would have to be slightly higher, but you get the point.

Individual Supply and Market Supply

Individual supply is *the supply schedule of a single firm.* As we've seen, the higher the price, the greater the quantity of output supplied by an individual firm.

Market supply is *the sum of the supply schedules of all the individual firms in the industry.* Table 1 presents a simplified supply schedule for the American automobile industry (excluding imports).

There are two main simplifications in this supply schedule. Obviously, Lincoln Continentals, Ford Mustangs, Oldsmobile Cutlass Supremes, and Honda Accords, as well as the whole range of Chryslers, Chevys, and Buicks, vary greatly in price, so we'll assume each of these nine American car manufacturers produces an identical car. A second simplification is that these companies would actually be willing to sell *any* car at relatively low prices.

The right-hand column of Table 1 gives us the market supply. It is, of course, the sum of the individual supplies of the nine companies; and as we see in Figure 1, the market supply curve, like each individual supply curve, moves upward to the right. At higher and higher prices the market will supply an increasing number of cars.

There are two reasons for this. As we have illustrated, as price rises each of the existing firms will produce and sell more cars; but at high enough prices, other firms—both domestic and foreign—will be attracted to the industry. Why does the quantity supplied rise as price goes up? Because existing firms will raise their outputs, and new firms will be attracted to the industry.

We will carry this analysis further in the next chapter. We will soon see that the ease with which firms may enter the industry is a key characteristic of perfect competition.

Table 1   Hypothetical Supply of American Cars, 1998 (in thousands)

Price	GM	Ford	Chrysler	Japanese Transplants*	Total
$14,000	5,311	2,356	1,245	535	9,447
12,000	4,617	1,984	991	384	7,976
10,000	4,002	1,584	762	270	6,618
8,000	3,623	1,216	601	208	5,648
6,000	3,190	996	491	181	4,858

*In 1994 Honda, Nissan, Nummi, Diamond-Star, Autoalliance, and Subaru-Isuzu produced cars in the United States.

Changes in Supply

In Chapter 18 of *Economics* and Chapter 6 of *Microeconomics,* we solved a series of problems dealing with changes in demand. This section presents a similar group of problems, this time dealing with changes in supply. The first set is based on Figure 2. You have four choices: (a) a change in quantity supplied, (b) a change in supply, (c) an increase in supply, and (d) a decrease in supply.

1. A move from E to F is _____ .
2. A move from F to G is _____ .
3. A move from G to H is _____ .
4. A move from H to I is _____ .

Figure 1   Hypothetical Supply of American Cars, 1998

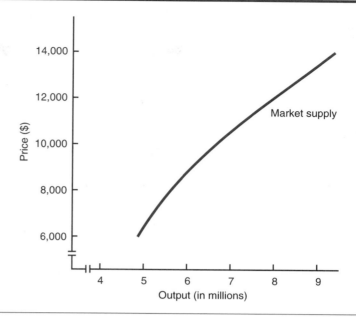

Note: We don't go down to 0 on the price scale; we don't go down to 0 on the output scale. We don't need those figures, so why put them in the graph?

Figure 2

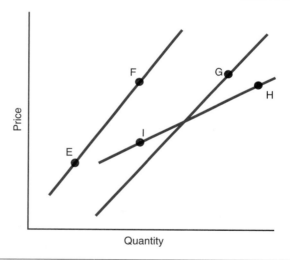

When we go from E to F, there is merely a change in the quantity supplied because we never leave the supply curve.

The move from F to G is an increase in supply. Why an increase? Because we are going to a higher supply curve; G is situated on a supply curve that provides greater quantities at *all* prices than the one on which F is located.

The move from G to H is a change in supply. Although we leave G's supply curve—that's the change—we cannot say whether the change is an increase or a decrease because H is located on a supply curve that crosses G's.

Finally we have the move from H to I, which is similar to the move from E to F. It is also a change in the quantity supplied.

Now we'll do another set of problems, using Figure 3.

5. A move from J to K is _____ .
6. A move from K to L is _____ .
7. A move from L to M is _____ .
8. A move from M to N is _____ .

The move from J to K is an increase in supply because we have moved to a higher supply curve (at *every* price, more is offered for sale).

When we go from K to L we stay on the same supply curve, so it is just a change in the quantity supplied.

The move from L to M is the opposite of that from J to K, so it is a decrease in supply.

Finally, the move from M to N is a change in supply. Because we don't know the shape of the supply curve on which N is situated, we don't know whether it crosses the one on which M is located. Thus the most definitive thing we can say is that there has been a change in supply. If this section wasn't clear, see the box "Differentiating between Changes in Supply and Changes in Quantity Supplied" for extra help.

Figure 3

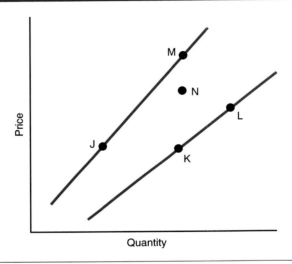

Differentiating between Changes in Supply and Changes in Quantity Supplied

Let's go back to the definition of supply, which is *the schedule of quantities of a good or service that people will sell at various prices.* So a change in supply is a departure from that schedule. A move from K to L on the higher supply curve in Figure 3 is *not* a change in supply. Why not? Because we stay on that supply curve. So a move from K to L is a change in quantity supplied. When we leave that supply curve, as we do when we go from point L to point N, a change in supply has taken place.

The supply curve is the graphic representation of the supply schedule. Any departure from that schedule is a change in supply. But if we just slide along the supply curve, in response to a change in price, then what we have is a change in the quantity supplied.

Let's move on to Figure 4. When we go from S_2 to S_1, we say that there has been an *increase* in supply. But doesn't S_2 look higher than S_1? It may *look* higher, but what's important here is that S_1 lies entirely *to the right* of S_2. And so, at every price, sellers on S_1 are willing to sell larger quantities than sellers on S_2 will sell.

Changes in Cost of Production

The main reason for changes in supply is changes in the cost of production. If the cost of raw materials, labor, capital, insurance, or anything else goes up, then supply goes down. For example, consider what happened when oil prices quadrupled back in 1973. Within months electric bills rose sharply. Why? Was there a heat wave and people kept their air conditioners on all day? In the *winter? That's* when electric bills went up.

Let's analyze this electricity price increase with a simple supply and demand graph. Figure 4 shows that the sudden sharp increase in the cost of oil (which is used to generate much of our electricity) had the effect of reducing our supply of electricity from S_1 to S_2, which, in turn, pushed up the price of electricity from P_1 to P_2.

The same analysis applies to changes in other costs of doing business—for example, interest, rent, and wages. An increase in these costs tends to reduce supply, while a decrease in costs pushes up the supply of that good or service.

Better management and technology

What else can lead to changes in supply? An advance in technological know-how can push up supply, as can better management or even higher working morale. If supply *does* go up, what happens to price?

Before answering this question, you might want to glance again at Figure 4. Go from S_2 to S_1. You can see that price falls from P_2 to P_1. So an increase in supply leads to a decrease in price.

Changes in taxes

Still another factor that affects supply is taxes. Their basic effect is to reduce supply. For example, a move from S_1 to S_2 in Figure 4 might reflect a tax increase. The effect of taxes on supply will be taken up later in this chapter.

Expectation of price increases

We'll consider one more influence on supply: the expectation of future price changes. If prices are expected to rise sharply, suppliers will try to hold current production off the market in anticipation of these higher prices. Suppose you make hula hoops and you have inside information that their price will triple in a few weeks. What do you do? You hold your hoops off the market, thereby reducing supply and driving up price. On the other hand, if you expect a steep drop in prices, what will you do? You'll try to offer your entire inventory at lower prices, which amounts to increasing supply.

Figure 4   Hypothetical Demand and Supply for Electricity

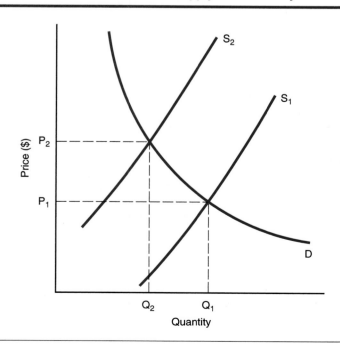

Elasticity of Supply

Our analysis of the elasticity of supply parallels our analysis of the elasticity of demand, which, as you may recall, went on for page after page in the chapter on demand. This time around we'll take some shortcuts. Let's begin with the formula for the price elasticity of supply. Because it is identical to the formula for the elasticity of demand, I won't even repeat it.

Next, let's discuss the meaning of the elasticity of supply. Not surprisingly, it has pretty much the same meaning as the elasticity of demand. It measures the responsiveness of the quantity supplied to changes in price. A high elasticity of, say, 10 means a 1 percent change in price brings about a 10 percent change in quantity supplied. And, similarly, an elasticity of 0.2 means a 10 percent change in price gives rise to just a 2 percent change in quantity supplied.

Now we'll look at a few graphs illustrating elasticity of supply. We'll start with perfect elasticity, then look at perfect inelasticity, and close with relative elasticity.

Figure 5 shows a perfectly elastic supply curve, which is exactly the same as a perfectly elastic demand curve. Figure 6 shows a perfectly inelastic supply curve, which would be identical to a perfectly inelastic demand curve.

Figure 5   Perfectly Elastic Supply Curve

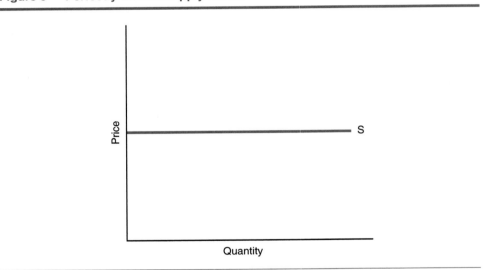

Figure 6   Perfectly Inelastic Supply Curve

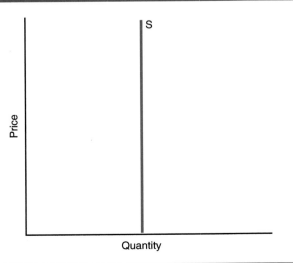

Supply tends to be inelastic during very short periods of time. In the United States right after World War II, it was nearly impossible to get a car at *any* price. It took time to convert from tank, jeep, and plane production back to turning out those shiny new Hudsons, Studebakers, Kaiser-Fraisers, Nashes, and Packards. Even if you were willing to part with a big one—that's right, a thousand bucks—you still had to put your name on a yearlong waiting list. Supply became more elastic after a few years, as more firms entered the industry and existing firms increased their output.

Finally, take a look at relative elasticities of supply in Figure 7. Which curve is more elastic? You should recognize S_2 as the more elastic because it is closer to horizontal and quantity supplied would be fairly responsive to price changes.

Figure 7   Relative Elasticities of Supply

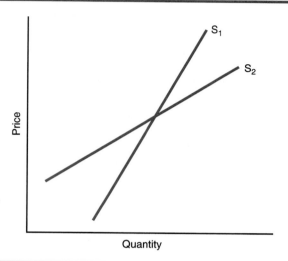

In the next section we'll be using supply and demand analysis to see how taxes affect equilibrium price and quantity. And we'll see how the elasticities of supply and demand determine the relative tax burden imposed on buyers and sellers.

Tax Incidence

Tax incidence tells us who really pays a tax, or who bears the burden. In cases like the personal income tax and the payroll tax, which are both direct taxes, the burden clearly falls on the taxpayer. But when we're dealing with indirect taxes such as excise and sales taxes, the incidence is less clear.

A tax lowers supply and raises price.

A tax on a good or service will raise its price. In terms of supply, such a tax, in effect, lowers supply. This is so because at every price sellers will be offering less for sale. Supply is defined as the quantities people sell at different prices, so this tax will shift the supply curve to the left.

As a result of the tax, people are willing to sell less at every price. That is a decrease in supply.

Who bears the burden of a tax? Most people would say the consumer does. After all, doesn't the seller merely act as the agent for the government and collect the tax? Or, put slightly differently, doesn't the seller just pass the tax on to the consumer?

There's only one way to find out, and that's to do a few measurements. We'll begin with price and output. Assume supply is S_1 in Figure 8; how much are price and output? Price is $8, and output is 8.

Ready for a curveball? Here it comes. How much do you think the tax is if it lowers supply from S_1 to S_2? Hint: Measure it vertically. Did you get $3 (the vertical distance from S_1 to S_2 at an output of 8)? Good! We're about halfway to figuring out who bears the burden of this tax.

Figure 8   Decrease in Supply

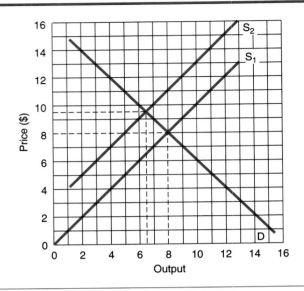

Figure 9   Decreases in Supply Due to Tax

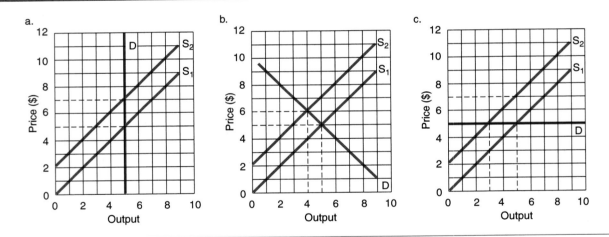

A tax increase leads to a decrease in supply.

We've represented a tax increase as a decrease in supply, from S_1 to S_2. So we need to find the new price and quantity. What are they? Price climbs to $9.50, while quantity falls to 6.5. OK, who bears the burden of this tax? Ask yourself, Was the consumer any worse off after the tax increase? She *was?* Why? Because she had to pay a higher price. How *much* higher? One dollar and 50 cents higher. She had to absorb half of the $3 tax.

What factor determines the tax burden?

In this case, then, the tax burden is shared by the buyer and the seller. Can you guess what factor determines where the burden falls? It's the relative elasticities of supply and demand. This is illustrated in the three panels of Figure 9. In Figure 9a (the left panel) we have a perfectly inelastic demand curve. When a $2 tax is imposed, who pays it? Obviously, the buyer does. In Figure 9b (the middle panel), where the elasticities of demand and supply are equal, the tax burden is shared equally. And when demand is perfectly elastic, as in Figure 9c (the right panel), the burden falls entirely on the seller, because price stays at $5 and the seller must absorb the entire $2 tax.

When demand is perfectly inelastic, the burden falls entirely on the buyer.

Let's step back a bit and generalize. When demand is perfectly inelastic (Figure 9a), the buyer bears the entire tax burden. And when demand is perfectly elastic (Figure 9c), the tax burden falls entirely on the seller. In other words, as elasticity of demand rises, the tax burden is shifted from the buyer to the seller.

Figure 10   Decreases in Supply Due to Tax

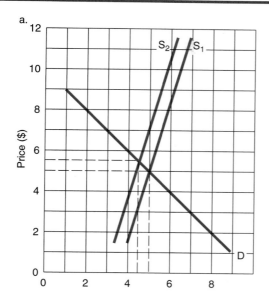

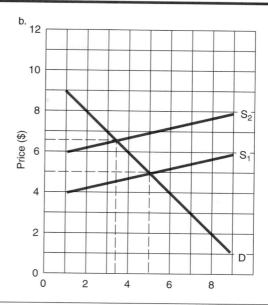

When supply is perfectly inelastic, the burden falls entirely on the seller.

We may do a parallel analysis on the elasticity of supply. But we're not going to. We'll just summarize the results. When supply is perfectly inelastic, the seller bears the entire tax burden. And when supply is perfectly elastic? You guessed it: the buyer bears the entire burden. To conclude, as the elasticity of supply rises, the tax burden shifts from the seller to the buyer.

We are left with two conclusions: (1) As elasticity of demand rises, the tax burden is shifted from the buyer to the seller. (2) As the elasticity of supply rises, the tax burden is shifted from the seller to the buyer.

Who bears the burden of a tax? It all comes down to the elasticities of demand and supply. We need to make one more set of comparisons. We need to compare the relative elasticities of demand and supply. This is shown in Figure 10, where a tax of $2 has been imposed. In Figure 10a (the left panel), where supply is relatively inelastic (to demand), the tax is borne largely by the seller (because price rises just 50 cents, from $5 to $5.50). But when supply is relatively elastic (in Figure 10b, the right panel), price rises from $5 to $6.50. This means the buyer must pay $1.50 of the $2 tax.

Once you're really good with tax burdens, all you'll need to do is glance at a graph and you'll know the relative tax burdens of the buyer and the seller. Then, if you find yourself in a juice bar and the guy next to you starts complaining about taxes, you can whip out some graph paper and show him all about the relative elasticities of supply and demand. And, who knows, he might even buy you a glass of carrot juice.

Questions for Further Thought and Discussion

1. How do the relative elasticities of demand and supply affect the relative tax burdens of the buyer and the seller?

2. Explain the difference between a change in supply and a change in the quantity supplied. Make up an example to illustrate this.

3. What are the factors that cause changes in supply? Try to use examples from actual firms or industries.

WORKBOOK FOR CHAPTER 20

Name _____   Date _____

Multiple-Choice Questions

Circle the letter that corresponds to the best answer.

1. As price rises

   a. supply rises   b. supply falls   c. quantity supplied rises   d. quantity supplied falls

2. A perfectly elastic supply curve is

   a. a horizontal line   b. a vertical line   c. neither a horizontal nor a vertical line

3. Over time the supply of a particular good or service tends to

   a. become more elastic   b. become less elastic

   c. stay about the same

4. A shift in the supply curve for gasoline in the United States would result if

   a. people decided to travel more by automobile

   b. the OPEC nations decided to stop sales of crude oil to the United States   c. the price of gasoline increased

   d. the price of gasoline decreased   e. the price of mass transit increased

5. If the price of a product rises and as a result businesses increase their production, then

   a. supply has increased   b. supply has decreased

   c. quantity supplied has increased   d. quantity supplied has decreased   e. both supply and quantity supplied have increased

6. Changes in supply may be caused by changes in

   a. the cost of factors of production   b. the level of technology   c. the number of suppliers   d. all of the above   e. none of the above

   For questions 7 through 12, use choices **a** through **d** and Figures 1 and 2. Each choice may be used more than once.

   a. change in quantity supplied   b. change in supply

   c. increase in supply   d. decrease in supply

Figure 1

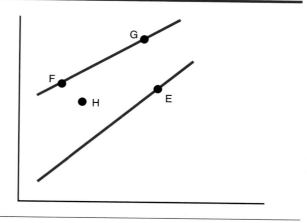

Figure 2

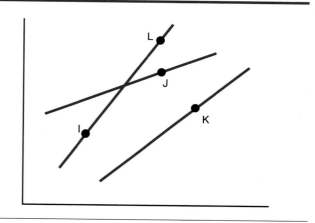

_____ 7. A move from E to F

_____ 8. A move from F to G

_____ 9. A move from G to H

_____ 10. A move from I to J

_____ 11. A move from J to K

_____ 12. A move from K to L

13. When demand is perfectly elastic, a tax increase is borne
    a. only by the buyer   b. only by the seller
    c. mostly by the buyer   d. mostly by the seller

14. If supply is perfectly inelastic, a tax increase is borne
    a. only by the buyer   b. only by the seller
    c. mostly by the buyer   d. mostly by the seller

15. A tax will
    a. lower price and raise supply   b. lower price and lower supply   c. raise price and lower supply
    d. raise price and raise supply

16. When demand is relatively inelastic and supply is relatively elastic, the burden of a tax will be borne
    a. mainly by sellers   b. mainly by buyers
    c. equally between sellers and buyers   d. it is impossible to determine the relative burdens of the tax

Use Figure 3 to answer questions 17 through 20.

Figure 3

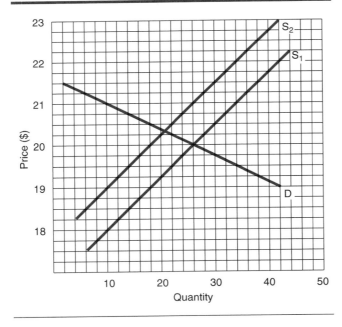

17. How much is the tax?
    a. $.35   b. $.50   c. $.65   d. $1.00
    e. $1.50

18. About how much of the tax is paid by consumers in the form of higher prices?
    a. 10 cents   b. 20 cents   c. 35 cents
    d. 50 cents   e. 65 cents

19. About how much of the tax is paid by the sellers?
    a. 80 cents   b. 65 cents   c. 50 cents   d. 35 cents   e. 10 cents

20. As a result of the tax, the consumption of this good falls by about
    a. 4   b. 5   c. 6   d. 7   e. 8

21. The imposition of a tax
    a. raises both supply and demand   b. lowers neither supply nor demand   c. lowers only supply
    d. lowers only demand

22. An increase in the wage rate paid to construction workers will tend to
    a. decrease the demand for homes   b. cause a movement along the supply curve for new homes
    c. decrease the supply of new homes   d. increase the supply of new homes

23. If the price of laser surgery to correct near-sightedness falls by 50 percent, in the long run
    a. industry supply will rise   b. industry supply will fall   c. industry demand will rise   d. industry demand will fall

Fill-In Questions

1. Supply is defined as _____

   _____.

2. Over time the elasticity of supply for a particular good or service tends to become _____

   _____.

3. A tax on a service that has a relatively elastic demand and a relatively inelastic supply will be borne mainly by the

   _____

   _____.

4. An increase in supply is shown graphically by a shift of

   the supply curve to the _____ .

5. The main reason for changes in supply is changes in the

   _____ .

6. A perfectly elastic supply curve can be shown graphically

   as _____ .

7. A tax cut _____ supply.

Problems

1. Draw a perfectly elastic supply curve.

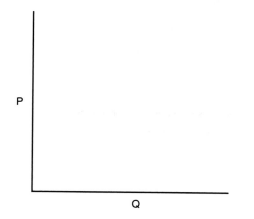

2. Draw a perfectly inelastic supply curve.

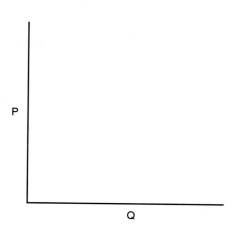

3. Draw a supply curve, S_1. Then draw a more elastic supply curve, S_2.

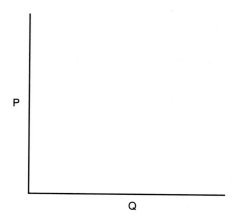

4. Draw a supply curve, S_1, and a second supply curve, S_2, that represents an increase in supply.

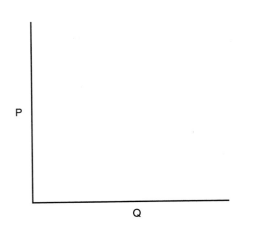

5. In Figure 4: **a.** How much is the tax? **b.** How much of this tax is borne by the buyer and how much is borne by the seller?

Figure 4

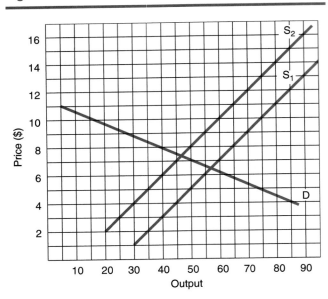

21 Cost and Profit

The most important equation of any business firm is: Total revenue – Total cost = Profit. In Chapter 18 we looked at total revenue, and now we'll look at total cost and profit.

Chapter Objectives

This chapter introduces each of these concepts:

- Fixed costs, variable costs, and total cost.
- Marginal cost.
- Short run and long run.
- Shut-down and go-out-of-business decisions.
- Average cost.
- Graphing the AFC, AVC, ATC, and MC curves.
- Profit maximization and loss minimization.

Costs

In a business firm costs are half the picture. The other half is sales or total revenue. The equation that every businessperson knows better than anything else in the world is:

$$\text{Sales} - \text{Costs} = \text{Profit}$$

It can also be stated this way:

$$\text{Total Revenue} - \text{Total Cost} = \text{Profit}$$

If you write it vertically—

$$\begin{array}{r} \text{Total Revenue} \\ -\ \underline{\text{Total Cost}} \\ \text{Profit} \end{array}$$

—you can quickly grasp what is meant by looking at "the bottom line."

We are going to analyze costs in two ways. First we'll divide them into fixed and variable costs. A little later we'll divide them into costs in the short and long runs.

Fixed Costs

Fixed costs stay the same no matter how much output changes.

Examples of fixed costs are rent, insurance premiums, salaries of employees under guaranteed contracts, property taxes, interest payments, and most of the depreciation allowances on plant and equipment. Even when a firm's output is zero, it incurs the same fixed costs.

Fixed costs are sometimes called *sunk costs* because once you've obligated yourself to pay them, that money has been sunk into your firm. Fixed costs are your firm's overhead. The trick, as we'll see in the next chapter, is to spread your overhead over a large output.

Variable Costs

Variable costs vary with output.

When output rises, variable costs rise; when output falls, variable costs fall. What are examples of variable costs? The most important is wages, particularly the wages of production workers. If you cut back on output, you lay off some of these people. If you reduce output to zero, none of them will be paid.

Another variable cost is fuel. When you raise or lower output, you vary your fuel bill. The same is true with raw materials (for example, steel, glass, and rubber in automobile production). Electricity, telephone use, advertising, and shipping are other variable costs.

Sometimes, however, a cost may be fixed *or* variable. Take electricity. An office that is open from nine to five may have a fixed electric bill. But a factory powered by electricity may have a variable electric bill. Similarly, if a firm's phone bill is always about the same, then telephone use is a fixed cost. But if the bill rises considerably during selling seasons or other busy times, then it's a variable cost.

Total Cost

Total cost is the sum of fixed cost and variable cost.

The data in Table 1 illustrate the relationship of total cost, fixed cost, and variable cost. Notice that as output rises, fixed cost stays the same and variable cost rises. Notice also how the increase in total cost is due to the increase in variable cost. These relationships may also be observed in Figure 1, which is based on Table 1.

Table 1   Hypothetical Cost Schedule for a Business Firm

Output	Fixed Cost	Variable Cost	Total Cost
0	$1,000	$ 0	$1,000
1	1,000	500	1,500
2	1,000	900	1,900
3	1,000	1,300	2,300
4	1,000	1,800	2,800
5	1,000	2,400	3,400
6	1,000	3,200	4,200

Figure 1   Fixed, Variable, and Total Cost

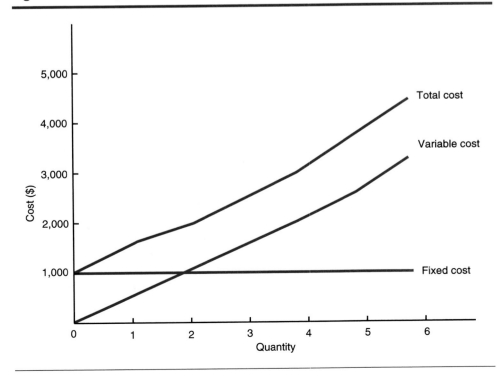

Marginal Cost

If we look again at Table 1, we can calculate the marginal cost of producing one unit of output: $500. That is because the total cost of producing one unit of output is $1,500 and the total cost of producing zero units of output is $1,000 (we still have fixed costs of $1,000 even at zero output). The additional cost of producing that first unit is $500.

Now figure out the marginal cost of the second, third, fourth, fifth, and sixth units of output. Write them down and then check your answers against these. The marginal cost of the second unit is $400 ($1,900 − $1,500); the third unit is also $400 ($2,300 − $1,900); the fourth unit is $500 ($2,800 − $2,300); the fifth is $600 ($3,400 − $2,800); and the sixth is $800 ($4,200 − $3,400).

Here's another problem to work out. Fill in the columns for total cost and marginal cost in Table 2. Try to do this in ink so you won't be able to sell back this book. If everyone does this, we'll double sales. After you've done this problem, you can check your answers against those in Table 3.

Table 2   Hypothetical Cost Schedule for a Firm

Output	Fixed Cost	Variable Cost	Total Cost	Marginal Cost
0	$500	$ 0	_____	_____
1		200	_____	_____
2		300	_____	_____
3		450	_____	_____
4		650	_____	_____
5		950	_____	_____
6		1,500	_____	_____

Table 3   Hypothetical Cost Schedule for a Firm

Output	Fixed Cost	Variable Cost	Total Cost	Marginal Cost
0	$500	$ 0	$ 500	—
1		200	700	$200
2		300	800	100
3		450	950	150
4		650	1,150	200
5		950	1,450	300
6		1,500	2,000	550

Before we get into the short run and the long run, I'd like to go back over fixed cost, variable cost, and total cost when the output is 0. Suppose that at an output of 0 fixed cost is $200. How much is variable cost and total cost?

At an output of 0, variable cost is always 0. Therefore the total cost (fixed cost + variable cost) is $200. At an output of 0, total cost is equal to fixed cost. Let's do one more. At an output of 0, if fixed cost is $1,000, how much is variable cost and total cost?

Variable cost is 0 and total cost is $1,000.

The Short Run and the Long Run

The present time is always in the short run. The short run extends for some time into the future—sometimes a few weeks, possibly a few years. During the short run a firm has two options: it can continue operating, or it can shut down and produce no output. In the long run it also has two options: to stay in business or to go out of business.

The Short Run

As long as there are any fixed costs, we are in the short run. How long is the short run? In some businesses, only a couple of minutes.

When I was growing up in New York during the years immediately following the Civil War, there was a guy who would make an announcement on the subway train as it went over the Manhattan Bridge. Then he'd open his raincoat; he had hundreds of ball-point pens hanging in rows from the lining of the coat. He was selling pens. He would tell us that he had a short-term lease, which was true. It took the train about five minutes to go over the bridge, and then his lease was up. That was the length of his short run.

Most firms have considerably longer short runs. A steel firm might need a couple of years to pay off such fixed costs as interest and rent. Even a grocery store would need several months to find someone to sublet the store and to discharge its other obligations.

The Long Run

The long run is the time at which all costs become variable costs.

Although it's defined in the left-hand margin, the long run never exists except in theory. Why not? Because you'll never have a situation in which all your costs are variable. It would mean no rent, no interest, no insurance, no depreciation, and no guaranteed salaries. That would indeed be a hard way to do business.

Toward the end of the short run, as the times for paying off various fixed costs approach, you have to decide whether you're going to stay in business. If you are, when your lease is up, you sign a new one. When a machine wears out, you replace it. And so forth.

You never really reach the long run. Like Moses, you can see the mountains of Canaan from afar, but you never get to set foot in the promised land. On any given day you can gaze out beyond your short run to your long run, but as you proceed through the short run, you have to make decisions that will push your long run farther and farther into the future.

The Decision to Shut Down

A firm has two options in the short run.

A firm has two options in the short run: it can either operate or shut down. If it operates, it will produce the output that will yield the highest possible profits; if it is losing money, it will operate at that output at which losses are minimized.

If the firm shuts down, its output is zero. Shutting down does not mean zero total costs. The firm must still meet its fixed costs. Look at Table 1 again. At an output of zero, fixed costs—and therefore total costs—are $1,000.

Why can't the firm go out of business in the short run? Because it still has fixed costs (see box "What's the Difference between Shutting Down and Going Out of Business?").

extra HELP

What's the Difference between Shutting Down and Going Out of Business?

One big difference between shutting down and going out of business is that after you've shut down you're still paying bills, but when you've gone out of business you're "free at last!"* That's right! Once you've legally left the industry, you have no more bills to pay because you have no more costs—fixed *or* variable.

When you've shut down operations, you may still owe money on your lease, insurance premiums may be due, and you may still be paying off a loan. There may be employees under contract who have been guaranteed salaries even if there is no work for them. In addition, if you have a shut-down plant, you might need to hire people to maintain the equipment, keep the pipes from freezing, and keep out intruders. And if there are hazardous waste materials on the premises, these may have to be disposed of before you can legally go out of business.

*This expression was the stirring conclusion of Martin Luther King, Jr.'s 1963 "I have a dream" speech. He was not, of course, discussing the difference between shutting down and going out of business.

These obligations must be discharged. Any plant, equipment, inventory, and raw materials must also be sold off. All of this takes time. How long? In some types of business, such as retail food, garment manufacturing, TV production, and most service industries, it would be a matter of two or three months. But in heavy industry, such as iron and steel, nonferrous metals, automobiles, oil refining, and other types of manufacturing, it might take a couple of years.

We'll work out some problems involving the shutdown decision. If a firm has fixed costs of $5 million, variable costs of $6 million, and prospective sales of $7 million, what does it do in the short run? It has a choice: (1) operate or (2) shut down.

If you owned this firm, what would you do? No matter what you do, you'll lose money. If you operate, your total cost will be $11 million ($5 million fixed cost plus $6 million variable cost). Sales − Costs = Profit, so $7 million − $11 million = −$4 million. That's not too good.

How much will you lose if you shut down? You will still have to pay out $5 million in fixed costs. Your variable cost will be zero. How much will your sales be? Zero. If you shut down, you produce nothing. If you shut down, your fixed and total costs are the same—$5 million. As sales are zero, you lose $5 million by shutting down.

What do you do? Shut down and lose $5 million, or operate and lose $4 million? Remember, in the short run, these are your only options. What you do is operate. It's a lot better to lose $4 million than to lose $5 million. How can you go on month after month—and possibly year after year—losing so much money? You can't. In the long run you have the added option of going out of business.

Here's another problem. What does this firm do in the short run if its fixed costs are $10 million, its variable costs are $9 million, and its prospective sales are $8 million? Will the firm operate or shut down? Back up your answer with numbers after you've figured out the right choice.

If the firm shuts down, it will lose its $10 million in fixed costs. If it operates, it will have sales of $8 million and total costs of $19 million ($10 million fixed plus $9 million variable). If the firm operates, it will lose $11 million (sales of $8 million minus costs of $19 million). And so the firm will shut down because it's obviously better to lose $10 million than $11 million.

This whole discussion of losing money may seem depressing and perhaps beside the point. Why go into business in the first place if you're going to lose money? Remember, however, that most businesses eventually fail. Many others, at one time or another, lose money. Although we will continually stress the fact that businesspeople are always striving to maximize their profits, when faced with losses they strive just as hard to minimize those losses. Perhaps they try even harder because their economic survival is at stake. During the recession years of 1980 and 1981 Chrysler and Ford were struggling to hold their losses to $1 billion. In the early years of this decade IBM and General Motors laid off tens of thousands of employees in an effort to cut multibillion-dollar losses.

We'll try one more problem. What does a firm do in the short run with prospective sales of $10 million, variable costs of $12 million, and fixed costs of $8 million?

If the firm shuts down, it will lose its $8 million in fixed costs. If it operates, it will lose $10 million (sales of $10 million minus total costs of $20 million). Clearly, it shuts down.

A firm will operate in the short run when prospective sales exceed variable costs.

We are now ready for another rule. When does a firm operate in the short run? *A firm will operate in the short run when prospective sales exceed variable costs.* Go back to the first problem. Prospective sales were $7 million, and variable costs were $6 million. By operating, it added $7 million in sales and had to pay out only an additional $6 million in costs. By operating, it cut its losses by $1 million.

A firm will shut down in the short run when variable costs exceed prospective sales.

A firm will shut down when variable costs exceed prospective sales. Check back on the second and third problems. In the second problem, when variable costs are $9 million and prospective sales are $8 million, the firm saves $1 million by shutting down. In the third problem, variable costs are $12 million and prospective sales $10 million, so $2 million is saved by shutting down.

Stop! We need to pause, catch our breath—and summarize the last three problems. Table 4 provides that summary.

Table 4   Summary Table of Last Three Problems
(All dollar figures in millions)

	Problem 1	Problem 2	Problem 3
Fixed costs	5	10	8
Variable costs	6	9	12
Prospective sales	7	8	10
Decision	Operate	Shut down	Shut down

In the short run a firm has two options: (1) operate, (2) shut down. It operates when prospective sales exceed variable costs. And when variable costs are greater than prospective sales, it shuts down. What if variable costs equal prospective sales? Flip a coin.

The Decision to Go Out of Business

In the short run the businessowner must decide whether to operate or shut down. In the long run the owner is faced with two different options. The long-run choices are easier: (1) stay in business or (2) go out of business. If a firm has prospective sales of $4 million, fixed costs of $3 million, and variable costs of $2 million, what does it do in the long run?

This firm will go out of business because in the long run it will be losing money. Prospective sales of $4 million − Total costs of $5 million ($3 million fixed + $2 million variable) = −$1 million profit.

What would you do in the long run if your firm's prospective sales were $8 million, fixed costs were $4 million, and variable costs were $3 million?

You would stay in business because you would make a profit of $1 million (sales of $8 million minus costs of $7 million).

In summary, then, we have two long-run options: (1) stay in business, (2) go out of business. If a firm's prospective sales are greater than its total costs (variable cost plus fixed cost), it will stay in business. But if total costs exceed prospective sales, the firm will go out of business.

We'll need to qualify this. If a firm lost one dollar, that loss would obviously be unlikely to drive it out of business. Some very large firms—the airline Pan Am comes to mind because I once owned some of its stock—have lost hundreds of millions of dollars for several years running and *still* have not gone out of business.[1] Fine. They are the exceptions that prove the rule (see box "Does Everybody Who's Losing Money Go Out of Business?"). The rule is that if your total costs exceed your prospective sales, you'll go out of business in the long run.

---

[1]Pan Am finally did go out of business in 1991.

Does Everybody Who's Losing Money Go Out of Business?

Mom and Pop run a little grocery in a tiny town somewhere in northwestern Nebraska. You can go there anytime between 6:00 A.M. and midnight to buy some of the stuff you forgot to pick up at the supermarket. And if you forget your wallet, no problem. Your credit is good there.

If Mom and Pop ever sat down and figured out how much money was coming in each week and how much they were paying out, they'd probably close up their store and go to work for someone else. Or maybe not. There's a lot to be said for being your own boss and making your own hours, even if they do happen to be from 6:00 A.M. to midnight.

Now according to our analysis, if sales are lower than variable costs, the firm will shut down. And if sales do not cover total costs in the long run, the firm will go out of business. But maybe Mom and Pop's store is the exception that proves the rule. The rule says you go out of business if you're not at least breaking even. But if you look hard enough, you'll almost always be able to find some people who don't follow this rule.

Average Cost

In this section we'll find average fixed cost, average variable cost, and average total cost. To get each, we do simple division, dividing by output.

Average Fixed Cost

Average fixed cost (AFC) is fixed cost divided by output.

$AFC = \dfrac{Fixed\ cost}{Output}$

Average fixed cost gets progressively smaller as output rises because we are dividing a larger and larger number into one that stays the same. If fixed cost is $1,000 how much will average fixed cost be at one unit of output?

$$\text{Average fixed cost (AFC)} = \frac{\text{Fixed cost}}{\text{Output}} = \frac{1,000}{1} = 1,000$$

Now figure out AFC at two units of output. Just plug the numbers into the formula.

$$\text{AFC} = \frac{\text{Fixed cost}}{\text{Output}} = \frac{1,000}{2} = 500$$

Calculate AFC for three, four, five, and six units of output to the nearest dollar in the space below. Use your figures to fill the AFC column of Table 5.

Table 5   Hypothetical Cost Schedule

Output	Variable Cost	Total Cost	Average Fixed Cost	Average Variable Cost	Average Total Cost
1	$ 500	$1,500	_____	$500	$1,500
2	800	1,800	_____	400	900
3	1,000	2,000	_____	_____	_____
4	1,300	2,300	_____	_____	_____
5	1,700	2,700	_____	_____	_____
6	2,400	3,400	_____	_____	_____

Solutions:

$$\text{AFC} = \frac{\text{Fixed cost}}{\text{Output}}$$

$$\frac{1,000}{3} = 333; \quad \frac{1,000}{4} = 250; \quad \frac{1,000}{5} = 200; \quad \frac{1,000}{6} = 167$$

Average Variable Cost

Average variable cost (AVC) is variable cost divided by output.

Unlike fixed cost, variable cost rises with output. What about AVC? Usually it declines for a while as output increases. Eventually, however, AVC will level off and begin to rise.

Table 5 shows a variable cost schedule. I've worked out the AVC for 1 and 2 units of output. I'd like you to work out the rest and fill in that column of the table.

$$\text{Average variable cost (AVC)} = \frac{\text{Variable cost}}{\text{Output}} = \frac{500}{1} = 500$$

$$\frac{800}{2} = 400$$

$$AVC = \frac{Variable\ cost}{Output}$$

Average Total Cost

Average total cost (ATC) is total cost divided by output.

Like AVC, ATC declines with output for a while but eventually levels off and then begins to rise. We'll see that ATC lags slightly behind AVC, leveling off when AVC begins to rise and not rising until after AVC is well on the way up.

We'll use Table 5 to get in some practice. I'll work out ATC for the first two outputs, and you work out the rest.

$$\text{Average total cost (ATC)} = \frac{\text{Total cost}}{\text{Output}} = \frac{1,500}{1} = 1,500$$

$$\frac{1,800}{2} = 900$$

$$ATC = \frac{Total\ cost}{Output}$$

You'll find everything worked out in Table 6. I'd like you to note that AFC and AVC add up to the ATC at each output. You can use this as a check on your work. If they don't add up, you've made a mistake.[2]

We'll work out one more table and then move on to a graph. Table 7 has all the numbers you'll need to calculate AFC, AVC, and ATC. Please fill in Table 7, including the marginal cost (MC). Assume fixed cost is $500. Check your work using Table 8.

---

[2]You may have noticed that AFC and AVC don't add up to ATC when the output is 3. This slight discrepancy is actually due to rounding: 333⅓ + 333⅓ = 666⅔. I rounded 333⅓ down to 333 and 666⅔ up to 667, so if the sum of AFC and AVC doesn't exactly equal ATC, it is probably due to rounding.

Table 6   Hypothetical Cost Schedule

Output	Variable Cost	Total Cost	Average Fixed Cost	Average Variable Cost	Average Total Cost
1	$ 500	$1,500	$1,000	$500	$1,500
2	800	1,800	500	400	900
3	1,000	2,000	333	333	667
4	1,300	2,300	250	325	575
5	1,700	2,700	200	340	540
6	2,400	3,400	167	400	567

Table 7   Hypothetical Cost Schedule

Output	Variable Cost	Total Cost	AFC	AVC	ATC	Marginal Cost
1	$ 200	___	___	___	___	___
2	300	___	___	___	___	___
3	420	___	___	___	___	___
4	580	___	___	___	___	___
5	800	___	___	___	___	___
6	1,200	___	___	___	___	___
7	1,900	___	___	___	___	___

Table 8   Hypothetical Cost Schedule

Output	Variable Cost	Total Cost	AFC	AVC	ATC	Marginal Cost
1	$ 200	$ 700	$500	$200	$700	$200
2	300	800	250	150	400	100
3	420	920	166.67	140	306.67	120
4	580	1,080	125	145	270	160
5	800	1,300	100	160	260	240
6	1,200	1,700	83.33	200	283.67	400
7	1,900	2,400	71.43	271.43	342.86	700

Graphing the AFC, AVC, ATC, and MC Curves

Much of microeconomic procedure involves three steps: filling in a table, drawing a graph based on that table, and doing an analysis of the graph. We're ready for the second step.

Plan your graph before you draw it.

When you draw a graph, you should plan it first. Label both axes. Figure out how high you'll need to go. Then figure out your scale. Will each box on your graph paper represent $5, $10, or $20? To draw a proper graph, you need graph paper.

Your output will be from 1 to 7. What will be the highest point on your graph? Both ATC and MC have highs of $700. So the vertical axis should go up to $700. When students begin to draw graphs, they connect all the points with straight lines, often using rulers. For starters, don't use a ruler to connect the points. You're drawing curves, not a series of straight lines that meet each other at odd little angles.

The AFC curve, which is not used very often in microeconomic analysis, is plotted in the accompanying box "Distinguishing between Fixed Cost and Average Fixed Cost." I'd like you to draw a graph of the AVC, ATC, and MC curves. If you've drawn them correctly, they'll come out like those in Figure 2.

Distinguishing between Fixed Cost and Average Fixed Cost

Using a piece of graph paper, see whether you can draw the average fixed cost curve, using the data in Table 8. Then on the same graph, draw the fixed cost curve. If your graph looks like the one in this box, then you don't need any extra help.

If your AFC curve looks different, make sure you plotted each point correctly. If you're having trouble plotting points, you definitely need to reread the early sections of Chapter 17 (Chapter 5, *Macroeconomics*), where I went over how to plot graphs.

The AFC curve sweeps downward to the right, getting closer and closer to the output axis. When drawn correctly, it should be a very smooth curve.

The fixed cost curve is always a perfectly horizontal line. In this case, fixed cost is $500, so the fixed cost curve runs straight across the graph at a cost of $500. It stays fixed at $500 no matter what the output.

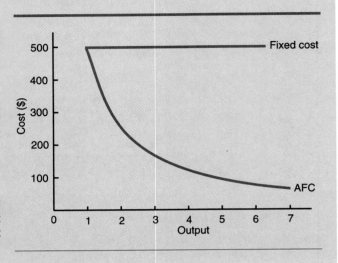

Figure 2   Average Total Cost, Average Variable Cost, and Marginal Cost

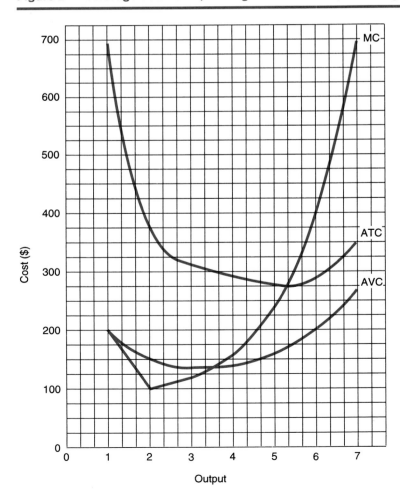

Computing Your Exam Average

We'll digress for a moment by discussing grades on exams. Suppose you took three exams and scored 80, 70, and 60. Your average would be 70. What if, on the next exam, you got a 66? What would your average be? It would be 276/4 = 69.

Suppose on the next exam you got a 67? Now what would your average be? It would be 343/5 = 68.6.

If you got a 68 on the next exam, what would happen to your average? 411/6 = 68.5.

If your next exam mark was exactly 68.5? 479.5/7 = 68.5. No change.

If you scored a 69 on the next exam, what would your average be? 548.5/8 = 68.56.

All of this is meant to show you how the marginal score affects the average score. Notice that as long as the marginal score is below the average score, the latter is declining, but when the marginal score is 68.5, it is equal to the average score. And the average score is neither rising nor falling; it is at its minimum point.

Similarly, when MC intersects AVC and ATC, it does so at *their* minimum points. As long as MC is below AVC, AVC must be falling. Once MC cuts through the AVC curve, the latter begins to rise. The same is true of the relationship between MC and ATC.

Why does the MC curve pass through the AVC and ATC curves at their minimum points?

The most important thing is the shape of the AVC and ATC curves. Both are U shaped, and both are intersected by the MC curve at their minimum points.

Why does the MC curve pass through the AVC and ATC curves at their minimum points? The basic reason is that each marginal value changes the average value. If you *really* want to know why, see the box entitled "Computing Your Exam Average."

Incidentally, when you draw the curves, if you start with the MC curve, it will be much easier to draw in the AVC and ATC curves.

We'll try another problem. First fill in Table 9. A completed version appears in Table 10. Assume here that fixed cost is $400.

Table 9   Hypothetical Cost Schedule

Output	Variable Cost	Total Cost	AFC	AVC	ATC	Marginal Cost
1	$100	_____	_____	_____	_____	_____
2	150	_____	_____	_____	_____	_____
3	210	_____	_____	_____	_____	_____
4	300	_____	_____	_____	_____	_____
5	430	_____	_____	_____	_____	_____
6	600	_____	_____	_____	_____	_____
7	819	_____	_____	_____	_____	_____

Table 10   Hypothetical Cost Schedule

Output	Variable Cost	Total Cost	AFC	AVC	ATC	Marginal Cost
1	$100	$500	$400	$100	$500	$100
2	150	550	200	75	275	50
3	210	610	133	70	203	60
4	300	700	100	75	175	90
5	430	830	80	86	166	130
6	600	1,000	67	100	167	170
7	819	1,219	57	117	174	205

I hope your table matches Table 10. Now we're ready for the graph. We'll use only three of the curves in the analysis that comes a little later in the chapter—the AVC, ATC, and MC. The AFC curve doesn't serve any analytic purpose, so from here on we won't draw it.

Now I'd like you to draw a graph of the AVC, ATC, and MC curves on a piece of graph paper. Remember, start with the MC curve because you need that curve to help you plot the minimum points of the AVC and ATC curves. Still not convinced? Then just trust me.

Compare your graph with the one in Figure 3. How did your minimum points come out on the AVC and ATC curves? If you drew your curves in the order I suggested—MC first, then AVC and ATC—your MC should have intersected both the AVC and ATC curves at their minimum points (see box "The Shapes of the AVC and ATC Curves").

Before we move on to the even more spectacular analysis toward the end of the chapter, we'll do a bit of preliminary analysis. Read off the minimum points of the AVC and ATC curves. At what outputs do they occur? Write down these two points: the output at which the minimum point of the AVC occurs and how much AVC is at that point. Then do the same for the minimum point on the ATC curve.

Your answers should be within these ranges: For AVC, your output should be somewhere between 3.3 and 3.4. AVC is a bit less than $70. How *much* less? Probably around $69, or $69 and change. Where do we get these numbers? If you were careful when you drew your graph—if you weren't, use mine—AVC is $70 at an output of 3. MC is still a bit below AVC at $60. As output goes beyond 3, MC continues to rise while AVC declines slightly.

For ATC, your output should be around 5.7 or 5.8. ATC is between $165 and $165.90. Notice that the MC curve intersects the ATC curve between outputs of 5 and 6, but closer to 6. Notice that at an output of 5 ATC is $166, and at an output of 6, it is $167, but because the MC curve cuts the ATC curve at its minimum point, ATC must be *less* than $166.

Figure 3   Average Variable, Average Total, and Marginal Cost

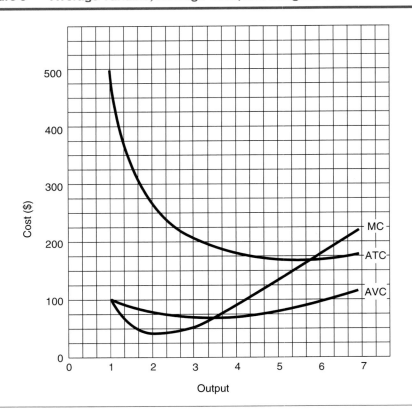

The Shapes of the AVC and ATC Curves

I've made a big deal about the MC curve intersecting the AVC and ATC curves at their minimum points. And you may have noticed that as output increases, the AVC reaches a minimum and begins to rise before the ATC reaches a minimum and begins to rise. For example, in Figure 2 the AVC reaches a minimum at an output of 3.5 and the ATC reaches a minimum at 5.1. And in Figure 3 the minimum point of the AVC is 3.3 and the minimum point of the ATC is 5.7.

First, let's talk about why the AVC and ATC curves are U shaped. As output rises, initially both average variable cost and average total cost decline. Why? Because of economies of scale. I mentioned these in the appendix to Chapter 2 and will deal with them more extensively in the next chapter. As a business firm grows larger, it can usually cut its costs by taking advantage of quantity discounts, using expensive but highly productive equipment, and developing a highly specialized and highly skilled workforce. But as output continues to expand, these economies of scale are outweighed by diseconomies of scale, such as the managing of a bloated bureaucracy and the rising costs of resources. Again, diseconomies of scale will be fully discussed in the next chapter.*

Why does the AVC curve reach a minimum before the ATC curve? Average total cost is the sum of average fixed cost and average variable cost. We know that as long as output is expanding, AFC is declining. But as you can see from Figures 2 and 3, AFC declines at a declining rate (i.e., more and more slowly) as output rises. Average variable cost, on the other hand, reaches a minimum and then begins to rise at an increasing rate (i.e., faster and faster). Eventually the increase in AVC is greater than the decrease in AFC. At that point ATC begins to rise.

*The rise of the ATC is also explained by the law of diminishing returns, which was discussed toward the end of Chapter 16.

It might seem to you that we are reading Figure 3 with great precision, perhaps a little too *much* precision. For example, to the naked eye, is it really clear that the minimum point of the ATC curve is between $165 and $165.90? Hardly. But we use Table 10 to guide us. We want a number that is slightly less than $166. Why not $164.25? All right, all right—you're twisting my arm. I personally think $164.25 is a bit low. On an exam I'd mark it right, but I can't vouch for *your* professor.

If you *really* want to get a closeup view of these turning points, you'll find them in the accompanying Extra Help box. One way or another, you need to understand that the minimum point on the AVC curve is a shade below $70, while the minimum point on the ATC curve is just below $166.

Profit Maximization and Loss Minimization

We're finally ready to do some marginal analysis, which is the basis of much of microeconomic decision making. The big decision we'll be making here is choosing the output at which the business firm should produce. If we choose correctly, profits will be maximized (or losses minimized).

We'll decide on output two ways. First we'll use the data in Table 11. Just subtract total cost from total revenue. Do this for each unit of output. Put your answers in the total profits column.

It would appear from Table 11 (I've done a separate profits table, Table 12) that profits are maximized at an output of 6, with 7 a close second. But we're missing something if we're trying to pinpoint exactly where we maximize our profits. The maximum profit point may well be between two numbers. In fact, we'll soon see that it is between outputs of 6 and 7, and somewhat closer to 7. How? By doing marginal analysis.

Profit maximization point: MC = MR

In a nutshell, *profits are maximized when marginal cost is equal to marginal revenue.* We're going to draw a graph. Then we'll see how much output is when profits are maximized, after which we'll see how much profits are at that output. I guarantee they'll be more than the $200 they are at an output of 6.

The graph we'll draw will need just three curves: MC, MR, and ATC. Remember that the demand curve and the marginal revenue curve are identical, but be sure to label that curve properly.

A Closer Look at the Minimum Points of the AVC and ATC Curves

The basic point we've been making, just in case you somehow missed it, is that the MC curve hits the minimum points of the AVC and ATC curves. As output rises, AVC declines less and less steeply, reaches a minimum when the MC curve crosses, and then begins to rise. Ditto for the ATC curve.

Using the same data from Table 10 that was used to draw Figure 3, I've redrawn the AVC and ATC curves at their critical turning points in Figures A and B. As you can see, *my* minimum AVC is $69.50 and *my* minimum ATC is $165.50.

A.

B.

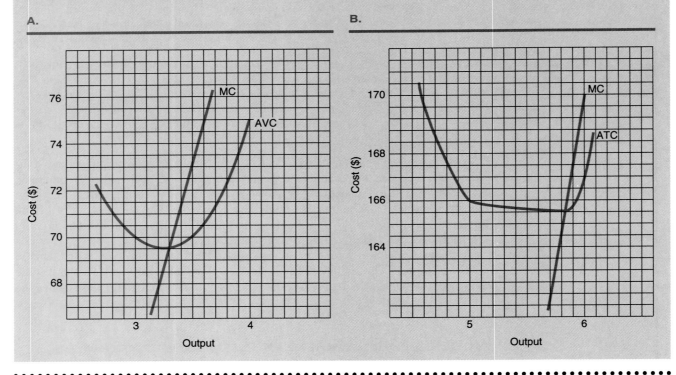

Table 11   Hypothetical Revenue, Cost, and Profit Schedule

Output	Price	Total Revenue	Marginal Revenue	Total Cost	ATC	Marginal Cost	Total Profits
1	$200	$ 200	$200	$ 500	$500	$100	_____
2	200	400	200	550	275	50	_____
3	200	600	200	610	203	60	_____
4	200	800	200	700	175	90	_____
5	200	1,000	200	830	166	130	_____
6	200	1,200	200	1,000	167	170	_____
7	200	1,400	200	1,205	176	205	_____

Table 12   Hypothetical Profits Schedule

Output	Total Profits
1	−$300
2	−150
3	−10
4	100
5	170
6	200
7	195

Your graph should have come out looking something like Figure 4. Marginal cost and marginal revenue are equal at an output of about 6.7. If your output is something like 6.68 or 6.75, that's close enough—in fact, maybe you're closer to the truth than I am (see box "Making Sure We're Maximizing Total Profit"). Occasionally that happens.

Calculating total profit can be as easy as four minus two equals two (or total revenue minus total cost equals total profit). That's easy as long as we happen to know how much total revenue and total cost are. Which we do, of course, for each of the outputs in Table 11.

But how do we go about calculating total profit when output is not a whole number? Well, for starters, we can't just read off total revenue and total cost from a table and do simple subtraction. How do we find total profit, for example, at an output of 6.7, where we happen to be maximizing our profits?

The easiest way of finding total profit at 6.7 units of output is to find profit per unit of output and multiply that figure by output. How do we find profit per unit of output (or profit margin)? We subtract ATC from price: Profit per unit = Price − ATC.

So we need to find three things: (1) output, (2) price, and (3) ATC. Then we plug them into this equation: Total profit = (Price − ATC) × Output.

Figure 4   Finding the Most Profitable Output

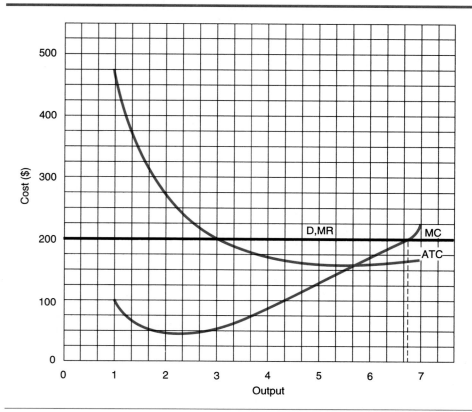

Making Sure We're Maximizing Total Profit

We know we always maximize total profit where the MC and MR curves cross. In Figure 4 they cross at an output of 6.7. Total profit comes to $201, which is a bit more than the profit of $200 at 6 units of output shown in Table 12. What if, according to *your* graph and *your* observation, ATC were somewhat higher than $170, or your output were a bit lower than 6.7, and your total profit came out to *less* than $200?

Then you would know something is wrong. Because you *do* maximize your total profit when MC equals MR. So,

what can you do? Three variables are used to calculate total profit: output, price, and ATC. Price is given (it's $200 in this problem), so it can't be changed. Can you change output to increase your total profit? Why *not*? You may raise it a bit—but not beyond, say, 6.75. What about ATC? Lower it. If $170 is OK, what about $169? That's OK, too. What about $167? Definitely not! Because $167 is the ATC at an output of 6, and your output is about 6.7. Thus you have a little room to maneuver, by lowering ATC and/or raising output, until your total profit rises above $200.

In this problem, we already know output (6.7) and price ($200); we just need to find ATC. We want to find ATC at an output of 6.7. See if you can find it on the graph in Figure 4.

What's your answer? Did you get something around $172? Maybe $171? Maybe $173?

There's no *one* correct value for ATC at an output of 6.7. We're making an observation on a graph. Everyone draws a graph a bit differently, and everyone *reads* a graph somewhat differently as well. So, on *my* graph, the ATC looks like $170 to *me,* but on *your* graph, ATC may look like $171 to *you.* Or $173, for that matter. Whose ATC is more accurate? If you're good at drafting, then *your* graph (and observation) is better. Hey, I *failed* mechanical drawing at Brooklyn Tech when I was 14 years old, and my drawing hasn't improved all that much over the course of the intervening century.

Back to our problem. We now have our three variables: output, price, and ATC. So plug them into the equation and find total profit.

$$\text{Total profit} = (\text{Price} - \text{ATC}) \times \text{Output}$$

Solution:

$$\text{Total profit} = (\text{Price} - \text{ATC}) \times \text{Output}$$
$$= (\$200 - \$170) \times 6.7$$
$$= \$30 \times 6.7$$
$$= \$201$$

Remember that we are maximizing our total profit at an output of 6.7, so total profit will be greater than it would be at any other output. We know from Table 12 that total profit is $200 at an output of 6, so we must show a higher profit at an output of 6.7. Because $201 is higher than $200, we're OK. But if *you're* still not OK, then you need to look again at the box "Making Sure We're Maximizing Total Profit."

Let's try another problem. First we can approximate total profits in Table 13. Write in the total profits figures (total revenue minus total cost). Then we'll use marginal analysis.

As you will have calculated (and as I have in Table 14), total profits appear to be maximized at an output of 5. That is, total losses are minimized here. You may have

Table 13   Hypothetical Revenue, Cost, and Profit Schedule

Output	Price	Total Revenue	Marginal Revenue	Total Cost	ATC	Marginal Cost	Total Profits
1	$450	$ 450	$450	$1,500	$1,500	$500	_____
2	450	900	450	1,800	900	300	_____
3	450	1,350	450	2,000	667	200	_____
4	450	1,800	450	2,300	575	300	_____
5	450	2,250	450	2,700	540	400	_____
6	450	2,700	450	3,400	566.67	700	_____

Table 14   Hypothetical Profits Schedule

Output	Total Profits
1	−$1,050
2	−900
3	−650
4	−500
5	−450
6	−700

noticed that MC is still below MR. We have not maximized our profits—or minimized our losses—until MC rises to meet MR.

Let's plot the graph and see where we minimize our losses. We'll need three curves: the demand/marginal revenue curve, the MC curve, and the ATC curve.

According to Table 14, we minimize our losses at an output of 5, when total losses equal $450. Do we do any better with marginal analysis? First, we find our best output, which comes to about 5.2 in Figure 5 (anything between 5.15 and 5.25 is acceptable). MC crosses ATC at 533. Now we calculate total losses at output 5.2.

$$\text{Total profit} = (\text{Price} - \text{ATC}) \times \text{Output}$$

$$= (\$450 - 533) \times 5.2$$

$$= (-\$83) \times 5.2$$

$$= -\$431.60$$

It looks as though we can cut our losses to $431.60 by producing at an output of 5.2 instead of at 5. Please remember that we can use the total profit formula to find total losses, which are negative total profits.

Producing exactly where MC equals MR enables us to maximize total profit (or minimize total losses). Let's see why. MR is the additional revenue from selling one more unit of output. MC is the additional cost from producing one more unit of output. Thus, by producing and selling more, we're adding to our costs and to our revenues.

How far should we go? As long as we're adding more to our revenue than to our costs, our total profit is rising. For example, if MC is 10 and MR is 18, by producing and selling that unit our total profit has gone up by 8. Suppose the MC of the next unit is 13 and the MR is 18. By producing *that* unit, our total profit goes up by 5. Now if, on producing yet another unit, MC goes to 17 while MR is 18, it still pays to expand because we're adding one more dollar to our profits. If MC of the next unit is 24 and MR is 18, we won't produce that unit; but theoretically, if we could produce a small part of it, we would because *then* we would be maximizing our profits.

Figure 5   Finding the Most Profitable Output

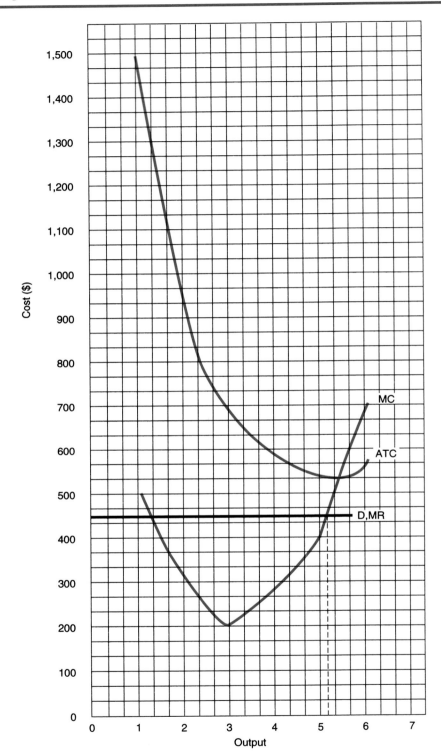

Questions for Further Thought and Discussion

1. How would you distinguish between the short run and the long run?
2. At the output at which a firm maximizes its profits, what two variables are equal? At the output at which a firm minimizes its losses, what two variables are equal?
3. On what basis does a firm decide whether or not to shut down? On what basis does it decide whether or not to go out of business?

WORKBOOK FOR CHAPTER 21

Multiple-Choice Questions

Circle the letter that corresponds to the best answer.

1. Richard and Spiro's used car lot has prospective sales of $5 million, fixed costs of $8 million, and variable costs of $4 million. In the short run the firm will _____, and in the long run it will _____.

   a. shut down, go out of business   b. shut down, stay in business   c. operate, stay in business

   d. operate, go out of business

2. The decision to shut down is made in

   a. both the short run and the long run   b. neither the short run nor the long run   c. the long run

   d. the short run

3. When MC is rising but still below ATC, then

   a. ATC is declining   b. ATC is constant

   c. ATC is rising   d. there is no way of determining what ATC is doing

4. In general a firm's

   a. total cost rises as output rises up to a certain point and then begins to decline   b. marginal cost rises as output rises up to a certain point and then begins to decline   c. average total cost declines as output rises up to a certain point and then begins to rise

5. If AVC is declining, then

   a. marginal cost must be less than AVC

   b. marginal cost must be greater than ATC

   c. AVC must be greater than AFC

6. Which of the following is most likely to be a variable cost?

   a. real estate taxes   b. rental payments of IBM equipment   c. interest on bonded indebtedness

   d. fuel and power payments

7. If a firm is producing a level of output at which that output's marginal cost is less than the price of the good

   a. it is producing too much to maximize its profits

   b. it is probably maximizing its profits   c. higher profits could be obtained with increased production

   d. none of the above

8. Which of these statements is false?

   a. When the firm shuts down, output is zero.

   b. When variable cost is zero, output is zero.

   c. When output is zero, total cost is zero.

   d. None of these is false.

9. Total cost is the sum of

   a. marginal cost and fixed cost   b. marginal cost and variable cost   c. variable cost and fixed cost

10. In the short run

    a. all costs are fixed costs   b. all costs are variable costs   c. some costs are fixed costs   d. all costs are marginal costs

11. Which statement is true?

    a. A firm will operate in the short run when prospective sales exceed fixed costs.   b. A firm will operate in the short run when prospective sales exceed variable costs.   c. A firm will shut down when total cost exceeds prospective sales.   d. None of these statements is true.

12. A firm has a fixed cost of $100,000, and variable cost is $90,000 at an output of one. How much is marginal cost at an output of one?

    a. $10,000   b. $90,000   c. $100,000

    d. $190,000   e. There is insufficient information to answer the question.

13. A profit-maximizing firm will increase production when
    a. price is less than marginal cost   **b.** price equals marginal cost   **c.** price exceeds marginal revenue   **d.** price exceeds marginal cost

14. In the short run, a firm has two options:
    a. stay in business or go out of business   **b.** stay in business or shut down   **c.** operate or go out of business   **d.** operate or shut down

15. As output expands to larger and larger numbers, _____ continues to decline.
    a. AFC   **b.** AVC   **c.** ATC   **d.** MC

16. A firm will operate at that output where MC equals MR
    a. only when it is maximizing its profits   **b.** only when it is minimizing its losses   **c.** both when it is maximizing its profits and when it is minimizing its losses   **d.** neither when it is maximizing its profits nor minimizing its losses

17. The salaries paid to people who are in the middle of three-year guaranteed contracts are
    a. a fixed cost   **b.** a variable cost   **c.** a fixed cost or a variable cost   **d.** neither a fixed cost nor a variable cost

18. The marginal cost curve intersects _____ at its/their minimum point(s).
    a. the ATC, but not the AVC   **b.** the AVC, but not the ATC   **c.** both the ATC and the AVC   **d.** neither the ATC nor the AVC

19. Average variable cost is found by dividing
    a. variable cost by output   **b.** output by variable cost   **c.** marginal cost by output   **d.** output by marginal cost

20. Statement 1: AVC can never be higher than ATC. Statement 2: AVC and marginal cost are equal at an output of one.
    a. Statement 1 is true and statement 2 is false.
    b. Statement 2 is true and statement 1 is false.
    c. Both statements are true.   **d.** Both statements are false.

21. Which statement is false?
    a. AFC plus AVC equals ATC.   **b.** Marginal cost equals AVC at an output of one.   **c.** AVC equals ATC at an output of one.   **d.** None is false.

22. Statement 1: Price is equal to total revenue divided by output. Statement 2: AFC rises as output rises.
    a. Statement 1 is true and statement 2 is false.   **b.** Statement 2 is true and statement 1 is false.   **c.** Both statements are true.   **d.** Both statements are false.

Fill-In Questions

1. Fixed cost plus _____ equals total cost.

2. In the long run a business has two options: to _____ _____ or to _____.

3. Variable costs change with _____.

4. Total cost is the sum of _____ and _____.

5. Marginal cost is the _____.

6. At zero units of output, total cost is equal to _____ _____.

7. The short run is the length of time it takes all fixed costs to become _____.

8. In the short run a firm has two options: (1) _____ or (2) _____ .

9. A firm will operate in the short run as long as _____ _____ are greater than _____ _____; a firm will operate in the long run as long as _____ are greater than _____.

10. Total revenue divided by output equals _____.

Problems

1. Fill in Table 1.

Table 1

Output	Fixed Cost	Variable Cost	Total Cost	Marginal Cost
0	$800	—	____	____
1		$100	____	____
2		150	____	____
3		200	____	____
4		270	____	____
5		360	____	____

2. If a firm's prospective sales are $5 billion, its fixed costs are $3 billion, and its variable costs are $1.5 billion, what does it do: **a.** in the short run? **b.** in the long run?

3. If a firm's prospective sales are $20 million, its fixed costs are $12 million, and its variable costs are $22 million, what does it do: **a.** in the short run? **b.** in the long run?

Answer questions 4 through 9 using Table 2.

Table 2

Output	Variable Cost	Total Cost	AVC	ATC	Marginal Cost
1	$ 400	____	____	____	____
2	700	____	____	____	____
3	900	____	____	____	____
4	1,350	____	____	____	____
5	2,000	____	____	____	____
6	3,000	____	____	____	____

4. Given: Fixed cost = $500; price = $475. Fill in Table 2.

5. On a piece of graph paper, draw a graph of the demand, marginal revenue, ATC, AVC, and MC curves.

6. How much is output?

7. Find total profit.

8. State the minimum point of the ATC curve in dollars and cents.

9. State the minimum point of the AVC curve in dollars and cents.

22 Supply in the Short Run and the Long Run

In this chapter we shall derive a firm's short-run and long-run supply curves, as well as its shut-down and break-even points. We shall also examine economies and diseconomies of scale, and the long-run planning envelope curve.

Chapter Objectives

After reading this chapter you will be familiar with:

- The short-run supply curve.
- The long-run supply curve.
- The shut-down and break-even points.
- Economic efficiency.
- The long-run planning envelope curve.

The Short-Run and Long-Run Supply Curves

Derivation of the Firm's Short-Run and Long-Run Supply Curves

This section is basically a proof of why an individual firm has a certain supply curve. We'll draw on several concepts developed in this and the previous chapter. When we finish we'll have four more rules that the firm always follows. I'll show you how these rules are derived. You now have the analytic equipment to follow the proof.

A firm will always produce where MC equals MR.

We'll start by citing the profit maximization rule. *A business firm will always choose that output where MC equals MR.* Because maximizing profits is the main—some economists say the only—objective of the business firm, we'll accept this without proof.

Remember that marginal cost is the additional cost of producing one more unit of output. And marginal revenue is the additional revenue from selling one more unit of output. Because marginal revenue is identical to price, we could say that a firm will maximize its profit at the output at which marginal cost equals price.

A firm will operate in the short run if sales are greater than variable costs.

Let's get back to those problems from the last chapter dealing with prospective sales, fixed cost, and variable cost. We derived a rule with respect to prospective sales and variable costs. *A firm will operate if sales are greater than variable costs; a firm will shut down if variable costs are greater than sales.*

We're going to derive two simple corollaries that we'll use in place of these axioms. But first, let's change the word *sales* to *total revenue*. What two things do we multiply to get total revenue? Can you remember? We multiply price times output. So we can then say this: A firm will shut down if variable cost is greater than total revenue (or price × output). Suppose we divide variable cost by output and total revenue by output:

$$\frac{\text{Variable cost}}{\text{Output}} > \frac{\text{Price} \times \text{Output}}{\text{Output}} = ?$$

What is variable cost divided by output? It's average variable cost, or AVC. And what's Price × Output divided by Output? It's price.

We can now substitute these terms into our statement: A firm will shut down if AVC is greater than price. Alternately, a firm will operate if price is greater than AVC.

Can we derive a similar corollary for the following statement? *A firm will go out of business if total cost is greater than total revenue.* I know *I* can, but can *you* do it? I'll wait right here while you work it out in this space:

How did you do? Did you get *this?*

$$\frac{\text{Total cost}}{\text{Output}} > \frac{\text{Price} \times \text{Output}}{\text{Output}}$$

And this?

$$\text{ATC} > \text{Price}$$

Once you have these two variables, you get this: If average total cost (ATC) is greater than price, the firm will go out of business. Alternately, a firm will stay in business if price is greater than ATC.

At any given time, a business firm will have a certain set of cost curves: AVC, ATC, and MC. These curves are determined mainly by the firm's capital stock—its plant and equipment. Over time the curves can change; but at any given time they're fixed. What concerns us here is the MC curve. We can assume it doesn't change.

What about MR? That changes with price. There is an infinite number of possible prices. Because the firm will always operate where MC equals MR, there is an infinite number of possible prices and therefore an infinite number of MRs, but only one MC curve. It follows, then, that we could slide along the MC curve so that no matter what the MR, MC would equal MR.

Let's go over these points. MC must equal MR. MC stays the same. MR can change—to any value. Whenever price changes we have a new MR line, but the MC curve remains the same. The MC will equal MR, but at some other point on the MC curve.

This can be illustrated. In Figure 1 we'll start with MC = MR at an output of 9. MR = $43. At an output of 8, MC = MR = $28. At an output of 7, MC = MR = $19. And so forth down the MC curve.

When we get below an output of about 6.1, we run into a problem. We're losing money. In the long run no firm will stay in business if it's losing money, so for every output above 6.1 we can just move along the MC curve and, in effect, we will be moving along the firm's long-run supply curve.

Now hold it right there! What did I just say? I said, "We can just move along the MC curve and, in effect, we will be moving along the firm's long-run supply curve." So now I'm calling the firm's MC curve (above a certain output) that firm's long-run supply curve. Where did *that* come from? It came from our definition of supply, which was given at the beginning of Chapter 20 (Chapter 8 in *Microeconomics*): *Supply is a schedule of quantities of a good or service that people are willing to sell at various prices.* This is exactly what we've derived by examining the firm's MC curve at various prices.

At outputs below 6.1, the firm is losing money because ATC is above price. Remember that price and MR are the same. Below an output of 6.1, MC is less than ATC; and because the firm will produce where MC equals MR, it should be obvious that below an output of 6.1, MR is less than ATC. In other words, the firm would be receiving less for each unit sold than the cost of producing that unit.

This is consistent with what we concluded toward the end of the last chapter—that in the long run a firm will go out of business if total cost is greater than sales. It is exactly

Figure 1   Derivation of Firm's Short-Run and Long-Run Supply Curves

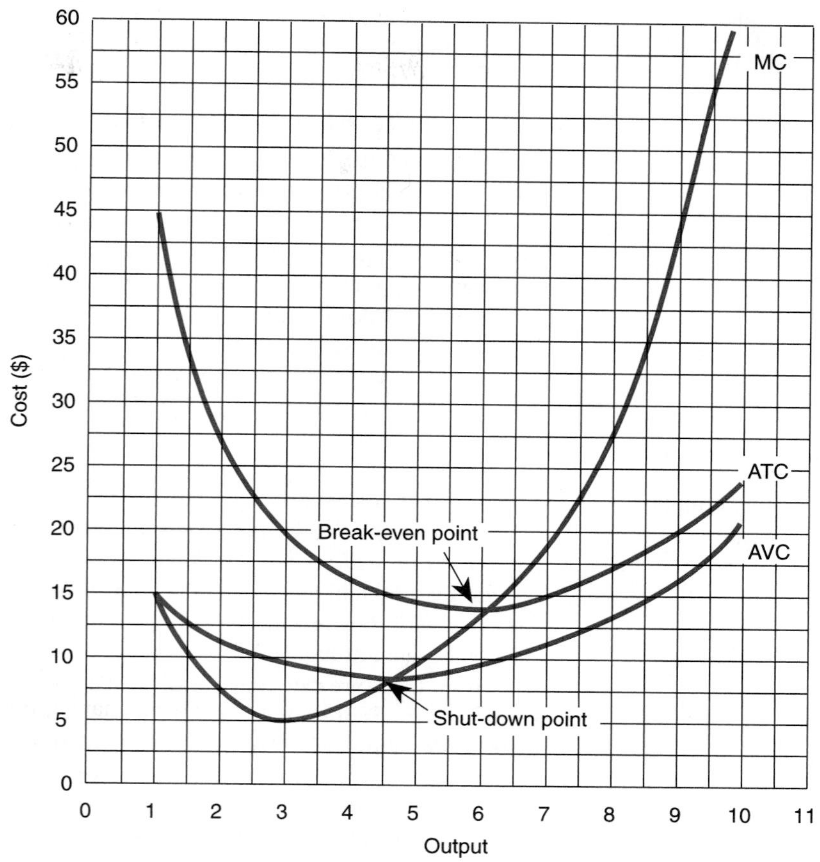

the same thing to say that a firm will go out of business if ATC is greater than price (or MR). Why? Because if we divide total cost by output, we get ATC. If we divide total revenue by output, we get price.[1] In other words, if we would go out of business if total cost were greater than sales, we'd also go out of business if ATC were greater than price.

Let's go on to the firm's short-run supply curve. If we continue our way down the firm's MC curve below an output of 6.1, we find that at an output of 5, MC = MR = $10. At an output of 4, MC = MR = $7. But we see in Figure 1 that at an output of about 4.5, the MC curve passes through the AVC curve, signifying the minimum point of the AVC. This means any price (and MR) below that point (about $8.40) will be below AVC.

We know from the previous chapter that if variable cost exceeds sales, the firm will not operate in the short run. Now we have AVC exceeding price, and this amounts to the same thing as variable cost exceeding sales.

If we were to divide variable cost by output, we'd get AVC. If we were to divide sales by output, we'd get price. Again, we see that when AVC is greater than price, it is the same as saying that variable cost is greater than sales. And the firm does not operate; it shuts down.

Thus the firm's short-run supply curve does not go below the point at which MC is lower than AVC. In this case, the short-run supply curve does not go below an output of 4.5. We call this the shut-down point. *The firm's short-run supply curve begins at the shut-down point and moves up the firm's MC curve as far as it goes.* It does *not* stop at the point at which the MC curve intersects the ATC curve. The short-run supply curve runs all the way up the firm's MC curve.

---

[1]Total revenue = Price × Output. Total revenue/Output = Price.

Long-run supply curve

The firm's long-run supply curve also runs up the MC curve, beginning at the point at which the MC curve intersects the ATC curve. That is called the break-even point. In this case, it is at an output of 6.1. *A firm's long-run supply curve begins at the break-even point and runs all the way up the MC curve.*

Finding the Firm's Shut-Down and Break-Even Points

Now let's identify the firm's shut-down and break-even points. In other words, how much is AVC at the shut-down point and how much is ATC at the break-even point?

To help answer these questions as accurately as possible, we'll use Table 1, on which Figure 1 is based. The shut-down point is at an output of 4.5. At this output, AVC is at a minimum. From the table we see that at an output of 4, AVC is $8.50, and at an output of 5, it is $8.80. Do *not* assume $8.50 is a minimum point. That minimum occurs at an output of 4.5 and is, say, $8.40. The same is true at the break-even point. It lies at an output of 6.1, not 6, as some casual observers might have it. At an output of 6, MC is below ATC. In Table 1, MC = $14 and ATC is $14.67. ATC hits its minimum at an output of 6.1 and is perhaps $14.65.

Shut-down and break-even points

These points—the break-even and shut-down points—become important when we determine the lowest prices acceptable to the firm in the long run and in the short run. *In the short run, if price is below the shut-down point, the firm will cease operations, and in the long run it will go out of business if price is below the break-even point.*

In this problem the shut-down point is at $8.40, so if the price is less than $8.40, the firm will shut down in the short run. In the long run, if the price is less than $14.65, the firm will go out of business.

Here, then, are our four rules. In the short run: (1) if price is below the shut-down point, the firm will shut down; (2) if price is above the shut-down point, the firm will operate. In the long run: (3) if price is below the break-even point, the firm will go out of business; (4) if price is above the break-even point, the firm will stay in business.

Before reading any further, please ask yourself, Self, did I really understand these last two sections? If you didn't, you have plenty of company. I'll bet if you reread the last few pages, your comprehension will be better the second time around.

Table 1   Hypothetical Schedule of Costs*

Output	Variable Cost	Total Cost	AVC	ATC	Marginal Cost
1	$ 15	$ 45	$15	$45	$15
2	22	52	11	26	7
3	27	57	9	19	5
4	34	64	8.50	16	7
5	44	74	8.80	14.80	10
6	58	88	9.67	14.67	14
7	77	107	11	15.29	19
8	105	135	13.33	16.88	28
9	148	178	16.23	19.78	43
10	210	240	21	24	62

*Fixed cost = $30.

A Summing Up

We're going to do a little more graphical analysis. I'll supply the graph (Figure 2), and you supply the analysis. Figure 2 is based on Table 2.

First, calculate total profit. Follow our usual three-step method: (1) write down the formula, (2) plug in the numbers, and (3) solve.

Figure 2   The Shut-Down and Break-Even Points

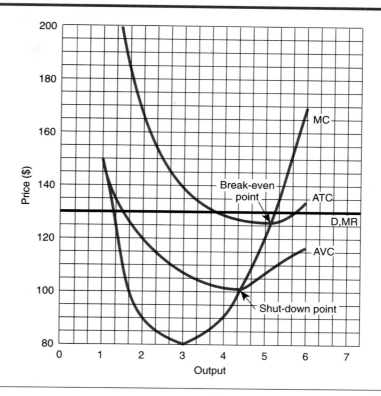

Table 2

Output	Variable Cost	Total Cost	Average Variable Cost	Average Total Cost	Marginal Cost	Total Profit
1	$150	$250	$150	$250	$150	–$120
2	240	340	120	170	90	–80
3	320	420	106.67	140	80	–30
4	410	510	102.50	127.50	90	+10
5	530	630	106	126	120	+20
6	700	800	116.67	133.33	170	–20

Solution:

$$\text{Total profit} = (\text{Price} - \text{ATC}) \times \text{Output}$$

$$= (\$130 - \$126) \times 5.25$$

$$= \$4 \times 5.25$$

$$= \$21$$

You'll want to watch out for a couple of things here. First, when you're picking an ATC, remember it will be the ATC at the output at which you are maximizing your total profit. That output looks like 5.25 or so. At *that* output, ATC is *more* than it is at the break-even point (i.e., the minimum point of the ATC curve). I see it as $126. *You* may see it as $126.15.

A second thing to watch out for is that your total profit *must* come out to more than any total profit shown in Table 2. Why? We are maximizing our total profit at an output of 5.25, so the profit we calculate must be larger than the profit at any other output.

Because the largest profit shown in the table is $20 (at an output of 5), *your* total profit *must* be larger than $20. Even if it comes out to $20.01, that's big enough.

Ready for some more analysis? What is the lowest price the firm will accept in the short run? If price is less than that figure, what will the firm do?

The firm will not accept a price lower than $101 in the short run (you may see this as $100.50 or $101.25, which is fine). If the price is less, the firm will shut down.

What is the lowest price the firm will accept in the long run? If price is less than that figure, what will the firm do?

The firm will not accept a price of less than $125.50 in the long run. Why can't we use $126? Because the *minimum* point on the firm's ATC curve—the break-even point—occurs at an output of slightly more than 5, and we know from Table 2 that ATC is $126 at an output of 5. Therefore, if price is less than $125.50 (I'll take anything from $125.90 down to $125), the firm will go out of business in the long run.

Here is one last set of questions. How much will the firm's output be in the short run and the long run if the price is $170? In both the short run and the long run, the output will be 6. At an output of 6, MC is $170, so MC equals MR, and the firm is maximizing its profit.

If the price is $115, find output in the short run and the long run. In the short run output will be about 4.85 (MC equals MR). How much will output be in the long run? This is a trick question. The answer is zero. Why? Because $115 is below the firm's break-even point, so it is less than the lowest price the firm would accept in the long run (i.e., the lowest price that could induce the firm to stay in business).

And finally, if the price is $90, what will the firm's output be in the short run and the long run? The answer to both questions is zero. In the short run, because the price is lower than the shut-down point, the firm will shut down and produce nothing. And in the long run the firm will go out of business.

If all of this is not perfectly clear, then work out the problems in the box "Finding the Firm's Short-Run and Long-Run Supply Curves, and Shut-Down and Break-Even Points."

Efficiency

So far, we've concentrated on a firm's most profitable output. But we are concerned with more than just profits in economics. We are also concerned with efficiency.

Efficiency is such an important economic concept that it is part of the definition of economics: *Economics is the efficient allocation of the scarce means of production toward the satisfaction of human wants.* It's time to explain just what the word *efficient* means.

We say that a firm is operating at peak efficiency if its average total cost is held to a minimum. How much would that output be in Figure 3? The answer is 10. You'll notice that the peak efficiency output is also where the break-even point is located.

How much is the most profitable output in Figure 3? It is 11. OK, if you owned this firm, would you produce at an output of 10 or 11? I hope you said 11. Given the choice of operating at peak efficiency or most profitably, we assume that every businessowner would choose the latter.

This is not to say that a businessowner may ignore efficiency. Indeed, we shall see in the next chapter that the perfect competitor is driven to produce at peak efficiency in the long run.

Figure 3   The Most Efficient Output

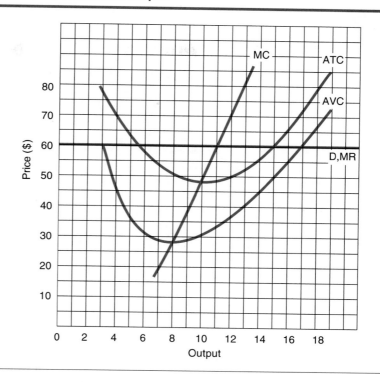

Figure 4

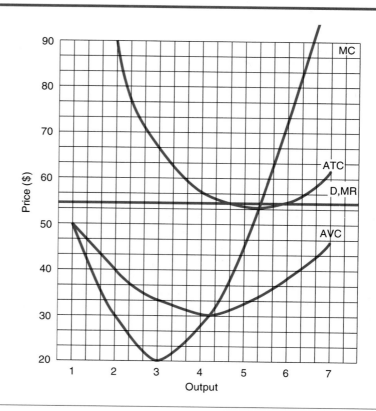

Source: Table 3 on following spread.

Finding the Firm's Short-Run and Long-Run Supply Curves, and Shut-Down and Break-Even Points

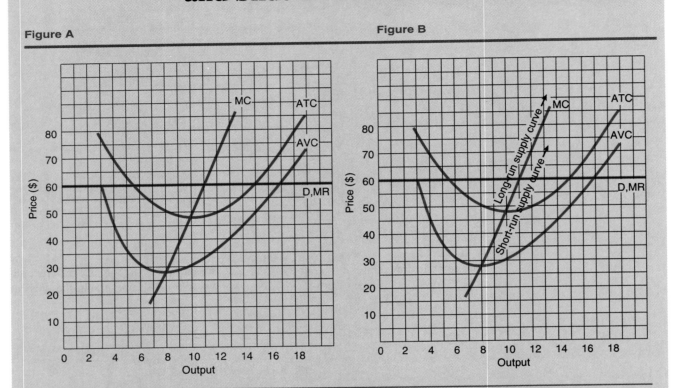

Figure A

Figure B

First I'd like you to label the firm's short-run and long-run supply curves in Figure A. Then label the shut-down and break-even points.

Once you've done that, check your work against mine in Figure B. Next I'd like you to write down the lowest price this firm would accept in the short run and the lowest price it would accept in the long run.

The lowest price the firm would accept in the short run is $28; the lowest price it would accept in the long run is $48.

Last set of questions: (1) If the price is $50, what will the firm's output be in the short run and in the long run? (2) If the price is $40, what will the firm's output be in the short run and in the long run? (Answers appear below Figure B.)

Answers: (1) If the price is $50, the firm will have an output of 10.1 in both the short run and the long run. (2) If the price is $40, the firm will have an output of 9.1 in the short run. In the long run it will go out of business; so its output will be 0.

Review: Efficiency and Profit Maximization

We're going to work out one last problem which ties together several of the things we've been doing so far. First, use the data in Table 3 to draw a graph of this firm's demand, marginal revenue, average total cost, average variable cost, and marginal cost curves. Then see if your graph looks like Figure 4.

Table 3

Output	Variable Cost	Total Cost	Average Fixed Cost	Average Variable Cost	Average Total Cost	Marginal Cost
1	$ 50	$150	$100	$50	$150	$50
2	80	180	50	40	90	30
3	100	200	33.33	33.33	66.67	20
4	128	228	25	32	57	28
5	168	268	20	33.60	53.60	40
6	228	328	16.67	38	54.67	60
7	322	422	14.29	46	61.71	94

Note: Fixed cost = $100; price = $54.

Use your graph to find: *(a)* the firm's output; *(b)* the lowest price the firm would accept in the short run; *(c)* the lowest price the firm would accept in the long run; *(d)* the firm's most efficient output; and *(e)* total profit.

Have you done all that? Then I want you to compare your results with mine. Since your graph is drawn a little differently from mine, we came up with slightly different answers. Indeed, even if we were making observations from the same graph, the chances are that our answers would not all be exactly the same.

(a) 5.7

(b) $31.75

(c) $53.00

(d) 5.67

(e) Total profit = (Price – ATC) × Output
$$= (\$54 – \$53.20) \times 5.7$$
$$= \$.80 \times 5.7$$
$$= \$4.56$$

Let's talk about each of these answers. *(a)* The firm's output is where the MC and MR curves cross, which appears to be at an output of 5.7. Observing your own graph, you may well have come up with a slightly different answer. *(b)* The lowest price the firm would accept in the short run is at the shut-down point. Your answer needs to be slightly less than $32, which is AVC at an output of 4. (See Table 3.) *(c)* Similarly, the lowest price the firm would accept in the long run is a little less than $53.60, the ATC at an output of 5. I saw this break-even point as $53.00, but again, our observations may well differ slightly.

Now we come to the interesting stuff. First, *(d)* the firm's most efficient output. I saw the break-even point occurring at an output of 5.67. You may have seen it as slightly more or less than this number. The important thing here is to observe that the most efficient output is slightly less than the most profitable output. I saw them as 5.67 and 5.7, respectively. You may have seen them as 5.65 and 5.68. Or even as 5.6 and 5.7.

You may ask, can you really *see* all this in Figure 4? Well, it's one thing to *see* it, and another to know it's there. How do you know just what's there? By going back to Table 3. At an output of 5, ATC is $53.60. It falls a little more until the break-even point, where, at an output of 5.67, the ATC is $53.00. Then it begins to rise again.

In the meanwhile the MC, which intersected the ATC at $53, goes on to intersect the MR curve at $54, which would be at an output just a tiny bit higher. So the most profitable output *must* be a drop higher than the most efficient output.

And finally, *(e)* the calculation of total profit. We know the price is $54 and we've estimated output to be 5.7. What about ATC? Well, the ATC we need to use is the ATC at an output of 5.7. Since we've estimated the ATC at the most efficient output to be $53.00, we need to make the ATC at this slightly higher output be just a little bit higher than $53.00, so we'll make it $53.20. Certainly $53.10, $53.25, or $53.30 would also be fine.

There's just one more thing we need to check. Do we show a high enough profit? To know for sure we need to go back to Table 3 and find the total profit at an output of 5. How much is it?

It comes to $2 (total revenue of 5 × $54 = $270) – total cost ($268). So any total profit of somewhat more than $2 would be fine. We found it to be $4.56. If you used an ATC of, say, $53.50, and our output of 5.7, you would have found total profit to be $2.85 or (price of $54 – ATC of $53.50) × output of 5.7.

Let's take a closer look at two of the critical points of the graph—the most efficient output and the most profitable output. You'll find this in the accompanying Extra Help box.

Economies and Diseconomies of Scale

Large-scale enterprise is expected to be more efficient than small business. And in general, we expect large firms to be able to undersell small firms. One reason for this belief is that large firms can often get quantity discounts when they buy raw materials or inventory (Safeway even uses a system of central buying and warehousing). A manufacturer will be able to give you a better price if he has to deliver 10,000 cartons of tuna fish to one warehouse rather than 100 cartons to five different stores. Also, it costs less to sell your final product in quantity than to sell it piece by piece. For this reason, a wholesaler has much lower prices than a retailer. Buying and selling in large quantities, then, is one reason for economies of scale.

As a firm grows, it takes advantage of being established. Its salespeople are known, it has established outlets and delivery routes, and its brand name becomes familiar. These advantages will mount as the firm continues to grow.

Believe it or not, all of this is actually leading somewhere. It is leading to an analysis of the four types of competition, beginning with perfect competition. Now that you have all the analytical tools, you'll get a chance to use them.

In 1776 in *The Wealth of Nations,* Adam Smith noted three other advantages. When a firm is large enough to provide specialized jobs for its workers, economies of scale will follow. He used a pin factory as an example.

One worker, said Smith, "could scarce, perhaps, with his utmost industry, make one pin in a day, and certainly could not make twenty." He then described how pin making has become specialized: "One man draws out the wire, another straights it, a third cuts it, a fourth points it, a fifth grinds it at the top for receiving the head."[2]

There are three distinct advantages to producing pins in this manner. First, the workers become good at their jobs—better than they would be if they went from one function to another. Second, they don't waste time going from one task to another. Third, the factory can employ specialized and expensive equipment because it will be fully used. For example, a special die to draw the wire can be purchased because it will be used continually; and a machine to cut the wire can be purchased for the same reason.

---

[2]Adam Smith, *The Wealth of Nations* (London: Methuen, 1950), Book 1, Chapter 1, pp. 8–9.

A Closer Look at the Most Efficient and Most Profitable Outputs

Figure C highlights two relationships. First, we can see that the output at which the firm operates at peak efficiency, 5.67, is clearly less than the output at which it maximizes its profit (5.7). And second, the ATC at output 5.67 ($53.00) is just a drop lower than it is at an output of 5.7 ($53.20).

Figure C

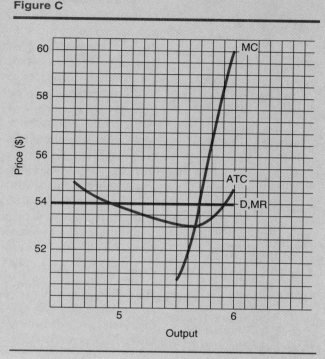

Smith estimated that 10 people working together in a factory could produce 48,000 pins a day, which is a prime example of economies of scale.

Economies of scale enable a business firm to reduce its costs per unit of output as output expands. Often these cost reductions can be passed on to the consumer in the form of lower prices. One outgrowth of expansion is increasing specialization. People's jobs become more and more specialized, as they did in Adam Smith's pin factory. And with the growth of specialization are sown the seeds of inefficiency, rising costs, and diseconomies of scale.

As a firm grows larger, it will create a bureaucracy. Early in the firm's history, the founder hired all her employees personally. As the firm grew, she had her foreman do the hiring. Today, if you try to get a job at a large company, you have to go through the personnel department, then meet your prospective supervisor, then meet your prospective supervisor's supervisor, and perhaps meet several other members of "the team"—or work your way through some other variation of this process.

Expansion means complexity, and complexity means decay.

A huge hierarchy of corporate authority is established—a hierarchy that might have once made sense, but that now may either have little relevant function or actually work at cross-purposes. The American automobile industry is a good case in point. Fewer than half the employees of GM, Ford, and Chrysler actually make cars. The rest do sales, advertising, market research, litigation, accounting, personnel work, budgeting, or public relations and the like for their companies—anything but make cars.

During the blackouts and energy shortages of the mid- to late 1970s, when Consolidated Edison (Con Ed) was having trouble generating enough electricity to keep New York City going, the company ran a series of ads telling its customers to keep their lights on (don't turn your lights off when you go out of your house or a burglar will know no one is home). This was a typical case of one hand of the corporate bureaucracy apparently not knowing what the other hand was doing.

Parkinson's Law

You may have heard of C. Northcote Parkinson, who formulated Parkinson's Law: "Work expands so as to fill the time available for its completion." Just picture all those seemingly busy bureaucrats scurrying around, firing off memos, talking on the phone, and rushing to meetings. But no discernible output results. Parkinson added a corollary: "Work expands to occupy the people available for its completion." If Parkinson is right, then large organizations are filled with important-looking people who appear very busy but are doing virtually no real work.

Even the quantity discounts enjoyed by large firms will eventually disappear as the firms use up so many resources that they bid up their prices. If a company rents office space, it can save money by renting several floors in a building. But if the firm needs a large percentage of the total downtown office space in a city, it will end up paying more per square foot. Similarly, suppliers who gladly give quantity discounts for large orders will have to raise their prices to a customer who purchases their entire output. Furthermore, other customers will bid up prices rather than see their own supplies cut off.

Depicting the stages of growth of several large corporations, we start with the initial spurt, during which economies of scale are operative and unit costs are declining. As the companies continue to mature and output continues to rise, their unit costs stay about the same. This stage is sometimes called *proportional returns to scale*.

In the final stage, which several large corporations have reached—the most conspicuous being International Harvester, Continental Illinois Bank, and Bank of America—diseconomies of scale set in. The corporate dinosaurs, beset with rising unit costs, are now so huge that they may no longer be able to compete. The only question is whether their status as an endangered species will permit them to continue functioning, or whether they will be permitted to die natural deaths.[3]

The Long-Run Planning Envelope Curve

We have been making an implicit assumption about the business firm. We've assumed it has been operating with a plant of given size. What's wrong with assuming that? Nothing, unless the firm alters the size of its plant.

What is a plant?

What is a plant? It's a factory, office, store, or any combination of factories, offices, or stores. The plant used by Procter & Gamble consists of hundreds of factories and offices. The plant of Kmart consists of hundreds of stores, factories, and offices, and the plant of Kone's ice-cream parlor on Kings Highway in Brooklyn consists of that one store (and, some would say, of the Kone "boys," who must now be in their 80s).

What happens to the supply of a firm when its plant size is altered? If the plant becomes larger, the firm's ATC and MC curves shift to the right. The firm's MC curve, which is its supply curve—above the shut-down point in the short run and above the break-even point in the long run—shifts to the right. This means supply increases.

If a firm were to build a larger factory, it might be able to lower its costs. For example, looking at Figure 5, ATC_2 reflects lower costs than does ATC_1 for outputs greater than 150. And ATC_3 reflects lower costs than does ATC_2 for outputs of more than 250.

---

[3]The government has grudgingly resorted to a third alternative: a bailout. Penn Central, Lockheed, and Chrysler have all received government loans to keep them afloat. In addition, the Federal Reserve and the Federal Deposit Insurance Corporation have pumped billions of dollars into failing banks to keep them going, while the savings and loan bailout will ultimately cost U.S. taxpayers several hundred billion dollars.

Figure 5   Varying Factory Capacities

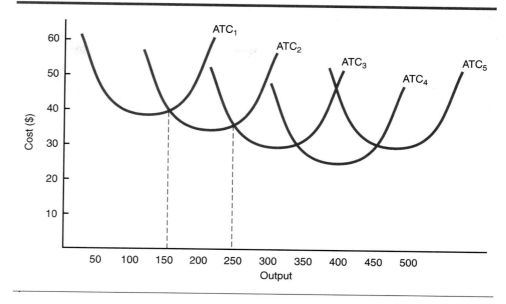

How much would it cost to produce at ATC$_1$'s break-even point? How much would it cost to produce at the break-even points of ATC$_2$ and ATC$_3$?

Notice we have declining costs: $39 at the break-even point of ATC$_1$, $34 at that of ATC$_2$, $30 at that of ATC$_3$, and $26 at that of ATC$_4$. Why are costs declining? For a variety of reasons, which could be lumped under the heading of economies of scale. These economies include quantity discounts by making massive purchases from trade suppliers and the three economies noted in Adam Smith's discussion of mass production in a pin factory. These economies are specialization at a particular job, the use of specialized machinery, and the time saved by not having workers go from job to job.

Just as a firm may realize economies of scale as output rises, a certain point is reached when ATCs begin to rise. Here the diseconomies of scale set in. Basically, the firm grows so large that management becomes inefficient. One hand does not know what the other is doing. Divisions of a corporation begin to work at cross-purposes.

When a firm grows, it increases its plant.

Thus, as the firm grows in size and output, it increases its plant. ATC will fall through a certain range of output, but eventually it will begin to rise. This is seen in Figure 4. Costs decline from ATC$_1$ to ATC$_2$ to ATC$_3$ to ATC$_4$. After ATC$_4$, they begin to rise.

In the short run, a firm is stuck with a certain size plant. If output were 175 and the firm were operating with ATC$_1$, the firm can do nothing about it in the short run. But in the long run, it would expand so it could operate a plant that would be better suited to producing at 175. That plant would be signified by ATC$_2$. If it were producing in plant ATC$_5$ with an output of 500, if output should decline to 275 and that decline were perceived as a permanent decline, the firm would contract its plant size to ATC$_3$.

These changes in the size of plant are long-run changes; they take time. New factories, offices, and stores would have to be constructed. Old ones would have to be sold or sublet. In the long run, a firm could be virtually any size, provided, of course, it had the requisite financing to expand.

We can say that there are an infinite number of plant sizes. Theoretically, then, Figure 4 could consist of an infinite number of ATC curves, one for each size plant.

Now we come to the firm's long-run planning envelope curve. If the firm were to stay with one size plant over the long run, its long-run supply curve would simply run along the MC curve above the break-even point, as it does in Figures 3 and 4. If the firm were to consider many different plant sizes, we would need to take this fact into account.

Figure 6   The Long-Run Planning Envelope Curve

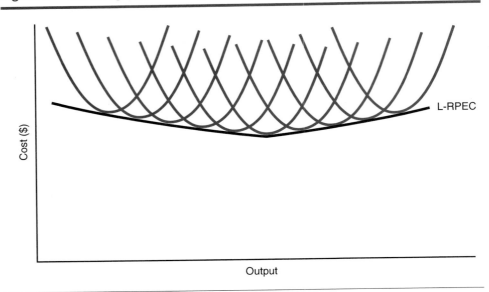

We do this by means of the long-run planning envelope curve (L-RPEC), shown in Figure 6. Here we have combined the break-even points of several different-sized plants, represented by their ATCs. The long-run planning envelope curve, which is tangent to these curves, is also U shaped. It reaches a low point at the break-even point of the lowest ATC curve. This point represents the lowest possible cost at which the product can be produced. A firm will produce at that output and with a plant of that size only if that is the output at which it would maximize its profits.

Questions for Further Thought and Discussion

1. How do you find the most efficient output, and how do you find the most profitable output?

2. What are economies of scale? Please give an example. What are diseconomies of scale? Please give an example.

3. What is the long-run planning envelope curve?

Name _____ Date _____

Multiple-Choice Questions

Circle the letter that corresponds to the best answer.

1. We find price by dividing

   a. total revenue by output   b. output by total revenue   c. total cost by output   d. output by total cost

2. In Figure 1, at which output is the firm operating most efficiently?

   a. 30   b. 39   c. 46   d. 50

Figure 1

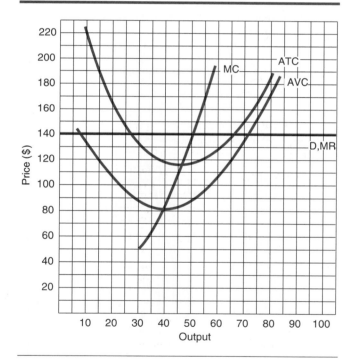

3. The marginal cost curve intersects the ATC curve at its

   a. minimum point, which is the break-even point

   b. maximum point, which is the break-even point

   c. minimum point, which is the shut-down point

   d. minimum point, which is the shut-down point

4. Parkinson's Law is an example of

   a. the long-run planning envelope curve

   b. diseconomies of scale   c. Adam Smith's pin factory   d. the firm's search for its most profitable output

5. The lowest point on a firm's short-run supply curve is at the

   a. break-even point   b. shut-down point

   c. most profitable output point   d. lowest point on the marginal cost curve

6. As output increases, eventually

   a. economies of scale become larger than diseconomies of scale   b. diseconomies of scale become larger than economies of scale   c. economies of scale and diseconomies of scale both increase   d. economies of scale and diseconomies of scale both decrease

7. When marginal cost is rising but is less than average total cost, we are definitely below the

   a. shut-down point   b. break-even point

   c. maximum profit point

8. The marginal cost curve intersects the average variable cost curve at the

   a. shut-down point   b. break-even point

   c. maximum profit point

9. In Figure 2, if you want to produce an output of 100, in the long run you will choose a plant whose size is represented by

   a. ATC_1 b. ATC_2 c. ATC_3 d. ATC_4

   e. ATC_5

Figure 2

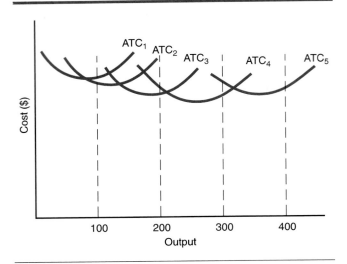

10. In Figure 2, if you want to produce an output of 200, in the long run you will choose a plant whose size is represented by
    a. ATC$_1$ b. ATC$_2$ c. ATC$_3$ d. ATC$_4$
    e. ATC$_5$

11. The firm's long-run supply curve runs along its _____ curve.
    a. ATC   b. AVC   c. MC   d. MR

12. The firm's long-run planning envelope curve
    a. is based on the assumption that a plant's size cannot be altered in the long run   b. exists only in theory, but never in reality   c. consists of many different plant sizes   d. is identical to the firm's short-run position

13. Adam Smith noted each of the following economies of scale except
    a. specialization   b. employment of expensive equipment   c. saving of time that would otherwise be spent going from one task to another   d. diminishing returns

14. Statement 1: The firm's short-run supply curve runs up the marginal cost curve from the shut-down point to the break-even point.
    Statement 2: The firm will not accept a price below the break-even point in the short run.
    a. Statement 1 is true and statement 2 is false.

b. Statement 2 is true and statement 1 is false   c. Both statements are true.   d. Both statements are false.

Fill-In Questions

1. The minimum point of the firm's AVC curve is called the _____; the minimum point of the firm's ATC curve is called the _____.

2. If we connect the break-even points of several different-sized plants, we can draw the firm's _____ curve.

3. We say that a firm is producing at peak efficiency if it operates at _____.

4. Total revenue divided by output equals _____.

Problems

Use Figure 3 to answer questions 1 through 4.

Figure 3

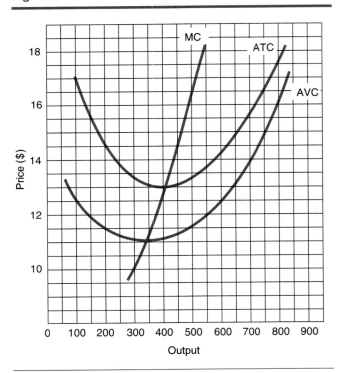

1. If the price is below $11, what will the firm do: **a.** in the short run? **b.** in the long run?

2. If the price is between $11 and $13, what will the firm do: **a.** in the short run? **b.** in the long run?

3. If the price is above $13, what will the firm do: **a.** in the short run? **b.** in the long run?

4. How much will output be in the short run if the price is **a.** $16? **b.** $13? **c.** $11? **d.** $10?

5. Please label the firm's break-even point, shut-down point, short-run supply curve, and long-run supply curve in Figure 3.

6. In Figure 3, how much is the firm's **a.** most efficient output? **b.** most profitable output if price is $14.50?

Use the information in Figure 4 to answer questions 7 through 11.

Table 1

If Price Were:	What Would the Firm Do in the:		How Much Would Output Be in the Short Run?
	Short Run?	Long Run?	
$125	_____	_____	_____
100	_____	_____	_____
80	_____	_____	_____
70	_____	_____	_____

12. You should do this problem in four steps. First: Fill in Table 2. Assume fixed cost is $100 and price is $64.

Figure 4

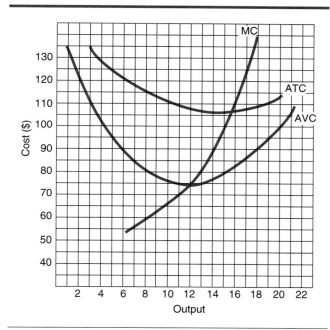

Table 2

Output	Variable Cost	Total Cost	Average Variable Cost	Average Total Cost	Marginal Cost
1	$ 30	_____	_____	_____	_____
2	50	_____	_____	_____	_____
3	80	_____	_____	_____	_____
4	125	_____	_____	_____	_____
5	190	_____	_____	_____	_____
6	280	_____	_____	_____	_____

Second: Fill in Table 3.

Table 3

If Price Were:	What Would the Firm Do in the:		How Much Would Output Be in the Short Run?
	Short Run?	Long Run?	
$90	_____	_____	_____
40	_____	_____	_____
20	_____	_____	_____

7. What is the lowest price the firm would accept in the short run?

8. What is the lowest price the firm would accept in the long run?

9. On Figure 4, label the shut-down and break-even points.

10. On Figure 4, label the short-run and long-run supply curves.

11. Fill in Table 1.

Third: Draw a graph of the firm's demand, marginal revenue, average variable cost, average total cost, and marginal cost curves on a piece of graph paper. Be sure to label the graph correctly. On the graph, indicate the break-even and shut-down points and the firm's short-run and long-run supply curves.

Fourth: Calculate total profit in the space below, then answer questions **a** through **d**.

a. The minimum price the firm will accept in the short run is $ _____. **b.** The minimum price the firm will accept in the long run is $ _____. **c.** The output at which the firm will maximize profits is _____. **d.** The output at which the firm will operate most efficiently is _____.

23 Perfect Competition

Economics, like other pursuits that attempt to explain life on this planet, seeks to organize its observations into recognizable categories, or, less charitably, into convenient pigeonholes. And so we have placed the nearly 20 million business enterprises found in this country into four precisely defined categories, which we shall be discussing in this chapter and in the three that follow. Although these categories do not always provide a good fit, they do help us understand how businesses operate, and how their prices, outputs, and profits are determined.

Perfect competition, as economists wistfully point out, is an ideal state of affairs, which, unfortunately, does not exist in any industry. Why bother, then, with a nonexistent form of competition? The reason is kind of similar to the Judeo-Christian tradition. We're all sinners, but we still need to know right from wrong.

Perfect competition attains the ideal of always being right. It is held up as what we should strive to approach, even if we can never hope to attain its state of grace. But who knows—maybe we'll get lucky.

For our purposes, perfect competition will be considered an unattainable standard by which the other forms of competition—monopoly, monopolistic competition, and oligopoly—will be judged. Thus, even though it doesn't exist, perfect competition has its uses.

Chapter Objectives

In this chapter you will be introduced to these terms and concepts:

■ The characteristics of perfect competition.
■ The perfect competitor's demand curve.
■ The short run and the long run.
■ Economic and accounting profits.
■ Decreasing, constant, and increasing cost industries.

Definition of Perfect Competition

Under perfect competition, there are so many firms that no one firm is large enough to have any influence over price. What is influence? If any action taken by the firm has any effect on price, that's influence. If a firm, by withholding half of its output from the market, were able to push up price, that would be influence. If a firm doubled its output and forced down price, that too would be influence. Even if a firm made prices go up by leaving the industry, *that* would be influence on price.

The industry operating under perfect competition includes many firms. How many? So many that no single firm has any influence on price. How many would *that* be? There's no exact answer, but we can agree on some numbers. Would a million firms be many? Obviously, yes. Would 80,000? Definitely. Ten thousand? Yes. Would three be many? No! Ten? No! Seventeen? No.

There's no clear dividing line. Students don't seem very happy with "more than 17 but fewer than 10,000." If you want my guess—and it's only an arbitrary number—I'd

---

Identical Products Are in the Minds of the Buyers

Are all hamburgers identical? Is the Whopper identical to the Big Mac? Are Wendy's hamburgers identical to those of White Castle? Maybe *you* can differentiate among these choices, but what if every buyer in the market considered them identical? They *would* be identical.

This identity takes place in the minds of the buyers. If

they think all cars—Toyotas, Fords, Volkswagens, Plymouths, and Cadillacs—are the same, they're the same. If all buyers are indifferent about whether they're offered station wagons, stretch limos, or subcompacts, all cars are identical. A car is a car. Remember: the customer is always right.

---

say perhaps 200 firms would constitute many. But that's just *my* guess, and in microeconomics there's no one correct answer to this question of how many is many.

The perfect competitor is a price taker rather than a price maker. Price is set by industrywide supply and demand; the perfect competitor can take it or leave it.

Another part of the definition of perfect competition has to do with the product. *For perfect competition to take place, all the firms in the industry must sell an identical, or standardized, product.* That is, those who buy the product cannot distinguish what one seller offers from what another seller offers. So, in the buyer's mind, the products are identical. The buyer has no reason to prefer one seller to another (see box "Identical Products Are in the Minds of the Buyers").

A perfectly competitive industry has many firms selling an identical product.

Now we can define perfect competition. A perfectly competitive industry *has many firms selling an identical product.* How many is many? So many that no one firm can influence price. What is identical? A product is identical in the minds of buyers if they have no reason to prefer one seller to another.

Two additional characteristics are perfect mobility and perfect knowledge.

We've already discussed the two most important characteristics—actually, requirements—of perfect competition: many firms and an identical product. Two additional characteristics are perfect mobility and perfect knowledge.

Firms must be free to move wherever there's an opportunity for profits. Land, labor, and capital will move where they can secure the highest possible return. An entrepreneur will give up his or her business and work for someone else if the wage offered is higher than the firm's profit.

Perfect mobility

Usually certain barriers to entry in various markets inhibit mobility. Licenses, long-term contracts, government franchises, patents, and control over vital resources are some of these barriers. Under perfect competition, there would be perfect mobility, and none of these barriers could exist. As in an open game of poker, anyone with a sufficient stake is welcome to play. In fact, hundreds of firms are entering or leaving each year. There are no significant barriers to entry, with the possible exception of money.[1]

Perfect knowledge

Perfect knowledge or information is another characteristic. Everyone knows about every possible economic opportunity. One example would be the market for audiologists in New York; everyone knows every job that exists and every opening when it occurs. In fact, if one person leaves one job for another, several other people become involved in a game of musical chairs as each fills the next vacated position. The audiologist from New York Eye and Ear who fills the position at Brooklyn Jewish Hospital leaves a position vacant at New York Eye and Ear. His or her position is taken by someone from Long Island College Hospital, which now leaves that person's position open. And so forth.

Agriculture, particularly wheat growing, has been held up as an example of perfect or near-perfect competition. The rise of the giant corporate farm has made this example somewhat obsolete, but economists haven't been able to come up with any other examples of perfect competition.

---

[1]To go into any business these days, you not only need to lay out several thousand dollars for rent, inventory, equipment, advertising, and possibly salaries, but you also need money on which to live for at least six months.

Figure 1 Perfect Competition: How Price Is Set

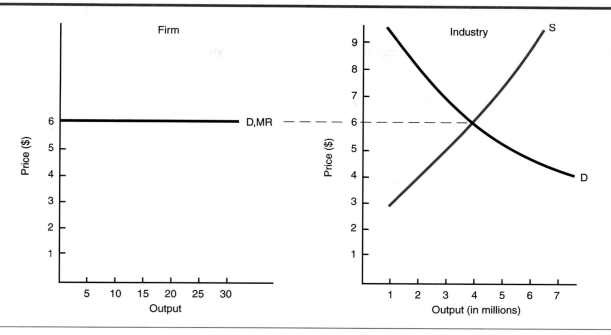

The Perfect Competitor's Demand Curve

Horizontal demand curve

The perfect competitor faces a horizontal, or perfectly elastic, demand curve (see Figure 1). As we noted in the last chapter, a firm with a perfectly elastic demand curve has an identical MR curve. This is significant because the firm can sell as much as it wants to sell at the market price. It's not necessary to lower price to sell more.

What determines the market price? Supply and demand. Figure 1 has a supply curve and a demand curve. Where they cross is the point of market price.

In our graph, the market price is $6. The firm can sell all it wants to sell at that price. What would happen if it should raise its price one penny to $6.01? It would lose all its sales to its many competitors who would still be charging $6, so the firm would never raise its price above market price.

Would a firm ever lower its price below market price, say to $5.99? Why would it do that? To get sales away from its competitors? There is no need to do this because the perfect competitor can sell as much as he or she desires at the market price. There is no point in charging less.

Why is the demand curve flat instead of curving downward to the right?

If the firm's demand curve is derived from the intersection of the industry demand and supply curves, why is it flat? Why isn't it sloping downward to the right like the industry demand curve? Actually, it is. I know it doesn't look that way, but it really is.

Look at the scale of industry output in Figure 1; it's in the millions. The output scale of the individual firm goes up to 30. When the industry demand curve slopes downward to the right, it does so over millions of units of output. For example, as the price falls from $6 to $5, output goes from 4 million to 5.5 million. In fact, it takes a price change of just $1 to bring about a change in the quantity demanded of 1.5 million units.

The graph on the left side of Figure 1 deals with output changes between 0 and 30 units. It would take a far greater change in output to change price, even by one cent. That's why the demand curve of the individual firm is seen as flat; and that's why the firm is too small to have any effect on price.

Theoretically, the firm's demand curve slopes ever so slightly downward to the right. But we can't see that slope, so we draw a perfectly horizontal curve and consider it perfectly elastic.

The Short Run

In the short run the perfect competitor may make a profit or lose money. In the long run, as we'll see, the perfect competitor just breaks even.

Figure 2 shows one example of a perfect competitor in the short run. Is the firm making a profit or is it losing money? How do you know?

You can always tell by looking at the demand curve and the ATC curve. If the demand curve is above the ATC curve at any point, the firm will make a profit. If the demand curve is always below the ATC curve, the firm will lose money.

In this case, the firm is losing money. How much? You should be able to figure that out for yourself. Go ahead. You'll find the solution in Figure 3.

Did you get a loss of $20? If you didn't, check your price and output. Clearly, the price is $6 and the output is 8. What about ATC? I saw it as $8.50. But suppose you saw it as $8.45. Then your total loss would have come to $19.60. Would this be wrong? It would be no more wrong than $20. When I drew this graph, I wanted ATC to be exactly $8.50, but if it looked to you like $8.45, then that's what it is.

Here's another problem. In this case, is the firm losing money or is it making a profit? Check out the demand and ATC curves. How much is the profit or loss? Figure it out; you have the tools. The problem is Figure 4; the solution is Figure 5.

Figure 2   The Perfect Competitor in the Short Run

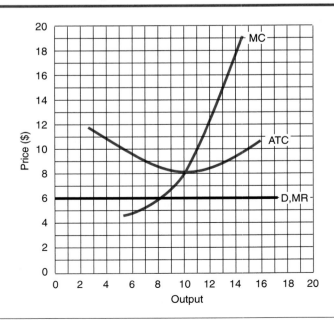

Figure 3   The Perfect Competitor in the Short Run: Solution

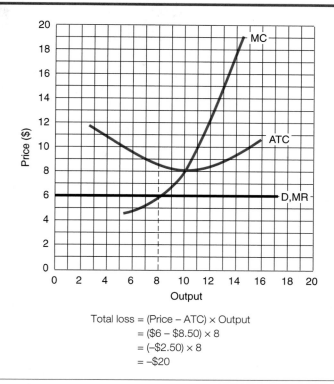

Total loss = (Price − ATC) × Output
= ($6 − $8.50) × 8
= (−$2.50) × 8
= −$20

Figure 4   The Perfect Competitor in the Short Run

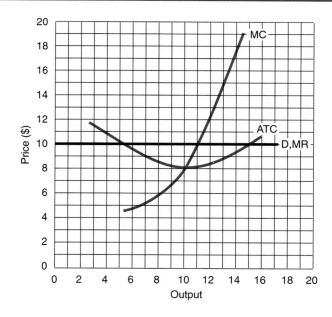

Is this graph beginning to look familiar? It should be. In Figures 2 and 3 the firm is losing money—$20 to be exact—but this same firm looks a lot better in Figures 4 and 5, where it is turning a profit of $20.90.

How can this same firm doing the same thing be making a profit in one set of graphs and taking a loss in another set? The answer lies in the forces beyond its control. What *kind* of forces? The forces of supply and demand. Let's look at them.

Figure 5   The Perfect Competitor in the Short Run: Solution

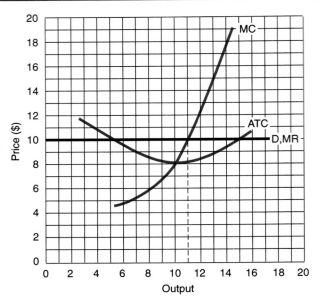

Total profit = (Price − ATC) x Output
              = ($10 − $8.10) x 11
              = ($1.90 x 11)
              = $20.90

If you read ATC as anywhere between $8.10 and $8.25 (and calculated a total profit of anything between $19.25 and $20.90), then you're right on the mark. But for analytic purposes, we'll need to show a profit of more than $20 (see box "Maximizing Total Profit and Maximizing Profit per Unit").

Figure 6   Taking a Loss in the Short Run: The Firm and the Industry

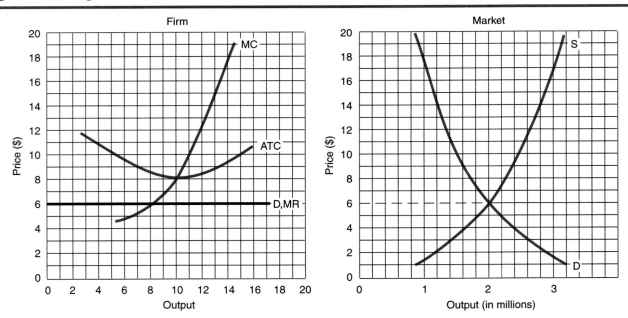

A double graph appears in Figure 6. The left side reproduces Figure 2 (or 3), which shows the firm losing money. The right side shows industry supply and demand.

Price is the same for the firm and the industry.

The important thing to notice is that price is the same for the firm and the industry. The price is set by industry supply and demand. It then becomes the demand/MR curve for the firm, which can sell as much as it wants at that price. Also notice that the amount the firm does choose to sell is determined by the intersection of the firm's MC curve with its demand/MR curve. (For a further discussion of graphs, see box "Maximizing Total Profit and Maximizing Profit per Unit.")

The same thing is happening in Figure 7, the left side of which is taken from Figure 4 (or 5), where the firm is making a profit. Again, notice the price set in the industry market is identical to the price taken by the firm.

In the short run a firm will either make a profit or take a loss. There is a remote possibility that it will break even, but that possibility is about the same as the possibility of a tossed coin landing on its edge instead of on its head or tail. It's not something you can count on happening with much regularity.

ADVANCED WORK

Maximizing Total Profit and Maximizing Profit per Unit

To find total profit we use the following formula: (Price – ATC) × Output. For instance, we calculated the total profit in Figure 5 to be $20.90 by using that formula. The formula for profit per unit of output is simple: Price – ATC.

To summarize, our total profit is the profit we make by selling our entire output. In other words, it's our profit per unit multiplied by our output. And our profit per unit is the profit we make on each unit of output sold.

When do we maximize our profit per unit? Obviously when the difference between price and ATC is at a maximum. This can be found by visually inspecting Figure 5. Price, which is read from the demand curve, is $10. At what output is ATC at a minimum? At the break-even point, where the MC curve crosses the ATC curve. The break-even point is at an output of 10.

How much is ATC at an output of 10? It's $8. How much is profit per unit at an output of 10? It's $2. Well, you may ask, why not produce at an output of 10 and maximize our profit per unit? That's a good question you're asking. Can you tell me why we are better off producing 11 units of output, even though we have a profit margin (or profit per unit) of only $1.90?

Think about it. All right, then, did you figure out that at 11 units of output we make a larger total profit ($1.90 × 11 = $20.90) than at 10 units of output ($2 × 10 = $20)? Remember, we assume that every businessowner has one main objective: to maximize profits. So if you have to choose between maximizing your total profit or maximizing your profit per unit, you'll go for total profit every time.

Figure 7   Making a Profit in the Short Run: The Firm and the Industry

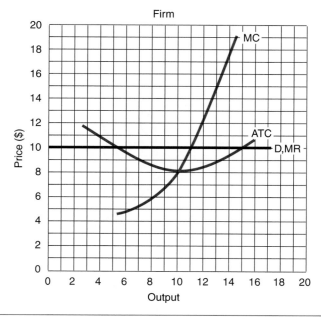

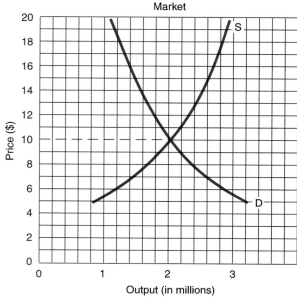

The Long Run

In the long run, firms may enter or leave the industry.

In the long run there is time for firms to enter or leave the industry. This factor ensures that the firm will make zero profits in the long run. What was an unlikely outcome for the firm in the short run—zero profits—becomes an absolute certainty in the long run.

Remember that in the long run, no firm will accept losses. It will simply close up shop and go out of business. Given the situation in Figure 2 (and 3 and 6), where the individual firm is losing money, it will leave the industry. But as I said at the beginning of the chapter, one firm cannot influence price, so if one firm leaves the industry, market price will not be affected.

If one firm is losing money, presumably others are, too; given the extent of the short-run losses this individual firm is suffering, chances are other firms are also ready to go out of business. When enough firms go out of business, industry supply declines from S_1 to S_2, which pushes price up from $6 to $8. This price rise is reflected in a new demand curve for the firm on the left side of Figure 8. In short, a decline in industry supply from S_1 to S_2 pushes up the firm's demand curve from D_1 to D_2.

There is a secondary effect on the firms that remain in the industry. Each will expand output slightly to the right. On the left side of Figure 8, we see that the firm's output rises from 8 to 10.

Figure 9 is based on Figure 7. It shows the long-run effect of a short-run profit. If one firm is making a profit, we can assume others are, too. New firms will spring up, and entrepreneurs will enter the industry to get their share of the profits. As more and more firms enter the industry, market supply increases, pushing the supply curve to the right (see the right side of Figure 9). As market supply rises, market price comes down until it reaches $8.

Here, once again, industry price and the price taken by the individual firm are equal. The output for the individual firm has been reduced slightly; but, more significantly, the new firms that entered the industry have increased market supply. This, in turn, reduced the price to $8, and profits for the individual firm are now zero. Along with this, as we can see on the left side of Figure 9, output has fallen from 11 to 10.

The left side of Figure 8 and the left side of Figure 9 look identical. Notice that the ATC and the demand/MR curves are tangent (just touching). At the point of tangency, MC equals MR, so that is where the firm produces. ATC equals price at that point, so profit is zero.

Figure 8   Going from Taking a Loss in the Short Run to Breaking Even in the Long Run

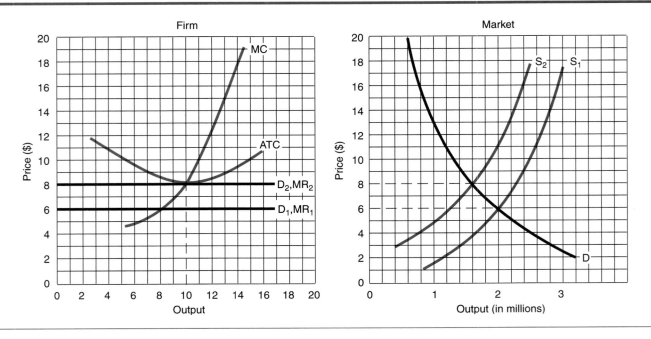

Still another way to find total profit and total loss is to draw a couple of dashed lines on a graph to form a box. By multiplying the height and length of this box, or rectangle, you can find a firm's total profit or total loss. This method is illustrated in the box "Showing Total Profits and Losses Graphically."

Let's slow down for a minute to catch our breath. We've talked about the firm making a profit or taking a loss in the short run and just breaking even in the long run. But to make sure that you're clear on what the firm's long-run situation looks like, I'm going to draw yet another graph. Figure 10 shows the firm's demand and MR curve tangent to the ATC curve. So, what are the firm's long-run price and output? Have you figured them out? The price is $18.50, and the output is 11.

Figure 9   Going from Making a Profit in the Short Run to Breaking Even in the Long Run

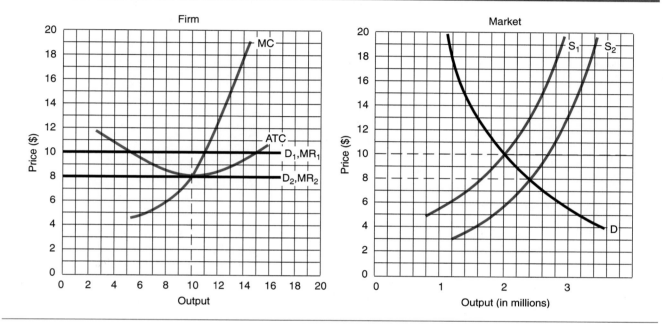

Figure 10   The Perfect Competitor in the Long Run

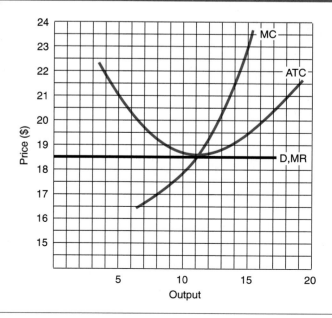

ADVANCED WORK ••••••• Showing Total Profits and Losses Graphically

Face it. Economists sometimes like to show off a little, and one way we really get to shine is when we draw some truly elegant graphs. So buckle your seat belt because we are about to take off.

What I'm going to show in this graph is how, by drawing just a couple of dotted lines and then multiplying two numbers, you can quickly calculate a firm's total profit. In Figure A here, I've done this. First, I drew a vertical dotted line down from the intersection of the MR and MC curves at 50 units of output. Then I drew a horizontal dotted line from the ATC curve at 50 units of output straight across to the price scale.

Figure A

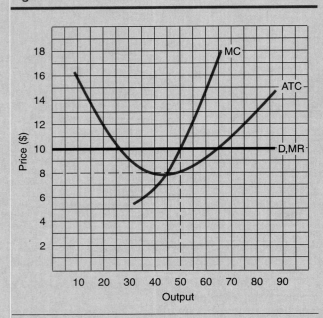

Now it's easy to find total profit. It is the area of the box that is bounded by the two dotted lines, the demand curve, and the price scale. To find that area, simply multiply the distance of the vertical line ($2) and the horizontal line (50 units of output). How much is $2 × 50? It's $100.

Of course, we could have used the tried-and-true method:

Price	$10
- ATC	− 8
	$ 2 × output (50) = $100

We can also find total loss graphically by drawing just two dotted lines and multiplying. I've worked out a problem in Figure B.

Figure B

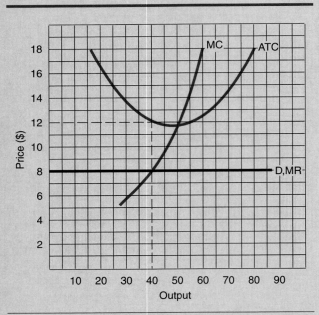

Our loss box is $4 × 40, or a loss of $160. Just like our box for total profit, it is bounded by the two dotted lines, the demand curve, and the price scale. Again, we can find our loss this way:

Price	$ 8
- ATC	−12
	$ 4 × output (40) = $160

Efficiency

Efficiency defined

In economics we have some rather peculiar definitions. We define *efficient* as cheap. When a firm is an efficient producer, it produces its product at a relatively low cost. A firm operates at peak efficiency when it produces its product at the lowest possible cost. That would be at the minimum point of its ATC curve—the break-even point.

For the perfect competitor in the long run, the most profitable output is at the minimum point of its ATC curve. Check it out in Figure 10. At any other output, the firm would lose money; just to stay in business, it must operate at peak efficiency.

This is the hallmark of perfect competition. The firm, not through any virtues of its owners but because of the degree of competition in the marketplace, is forced to operate at peak efficiency. As we'll see in the next three chapters, the other forms of competition do not force peak efficiency.

Perfect competition is very good for the consumer. She or he can buy at cost. That's right, price is equal to ATC. Remember, there's no economic profit. And consumers have the firm's competitors to thank for such a low price. Competition will keep business-owners honest—that is, if there's enough competition.

Economic and Accounting Profits

We keep saying that profits are zero. Who would stay in business with no profits? Actually, there *are* profits. A firm's accountant might tell the businessowner that the firm made $85,000 (in the long run), but an economist would say the firm made no profit whatsoever.

Accounting profits

Accounting profits are what's left over from sales after the firm has paid all its explicit, or dollar, costs—rent, wages, cost of goods sold, fuel, taxes. What the business-owner keeps are the accounting profits. But the economist makes some additional deductions, called "implicit costs."

Implicit costs are a business firm's *opportunity costs.* What is an *opportunity cost?* Near the beginning of Chapter 2, I said: *The opportunity cost of any choice is the forgone value of the next best alternative.* If you choose to work for yourself, the opportunity cost of that choice is the income you forgo by not doing the same work for someone else. And what is the opportunity cost of investing $1 million of your own money in your business? It's the interest you could have earned on your money by investing it in an equally risky business owned by someone else.

Economic profits

What, then, are the implicit (or opportunity) costs of a family business? These costs include a return on your investment, wages that you and your family members could have earned doing the same work for another firm, rent on the space used in your house, and wear and tear on your car to the degree that it is used for your business. Your accountant will probably include these last two costs but will not deal with the first two.

Suppose you've invested $100,000 of your own money in your business. You could have earned $15,000 in interest had you lent these funds to another business of comparable risk. If you and your spouse, instead of working 12 hours a day for your business, had worked for another firm, the two of you would have earned $70,000. The economist will subtract these $85,000 in economic costs from your $85,000 in accounting profits. And poof—your economic profits are zero.

Why, you ask, should economic costs be subtracted from accounting profits? Because they represent alternatives that you have forgone to have your own business. You *could* have earned $15,000 interest on your $100,000 by investing it elsewhere, and you and your spouse *could* have earned $70,000 by working for someone else. The cost of not availing yourselves of these opportunities—your opportunity cost—is $85,000. Being in business for yourselves cost you $85,000.

Being in your own business is working 80 hours a week so that you can avoid working 40 hours a week for someone else.
—Ramona E. F. Arnett

Why stay in business if your economic profit is zero? Because you *are* still making accounting benefits. And you wouldn't do any better if you invested your money elsewhere and worked for someone else; you'd be in exactly the same economic situation. And, of course, by having your own business, you're your own boss.

When economic profits become negative—particularly if these losses are substantial and appear permanent—many people will close their businesses and go to work for other companies. Going back to our example, they will then be able to earn $85,000 a year ($15,000 in interest and $70,000 in wages).

On the other hand, when there are economic profits in the short run, more people are attracted to the industry. Market supply goes up as more firms are formed by people who perceive that they could do better working for themselves than for other people. Eventually, in the long run, economic profits in the industry fall to zero. At that point, no one else enters the industry.

Decreasing, Constant, and Increasing Cost Industries

The long-run planning envelope curve, pictured in Figure 6 in the last chapter, really makes two statements. For virtually every industry, a firm will be able to lower its ATC if it can expand up to a certain point. If it expands beyond that point, ATC will rise.

This gives us two concepts: decreasing costs and increasing costs. In a decreasing cost industry, firms can expand and lower their costs, while in an increasing cost industry, any expansion will lead to rising costs. There's also a third possibility: a constant cost industry, where ATC does not change as output rises.

Decreasing cost industries   In a decreasing cost industry, firms can realize lower ATCs by increasing their output. They can take advantage of economies of scale—discounts from buying or selling large quantities, declining average fixed cost as output expands, and lower costs resulting from specialization. Decreasing cost industries are characterized by firms operating on the declining segments of their ATC curves, illustrated in Figure 11. (See box "Technological Advance and Decreasing Costs") for another aspect of decreasing costs.)

Increasing cost industries   In an increasing cost industry, diseconomies of scale overwhelm economies of scale. These diseconomies drive costs up, pushing firms into the rising segment of their ATC

Figure 11   Decreasing, Constant, and Increasing Cost

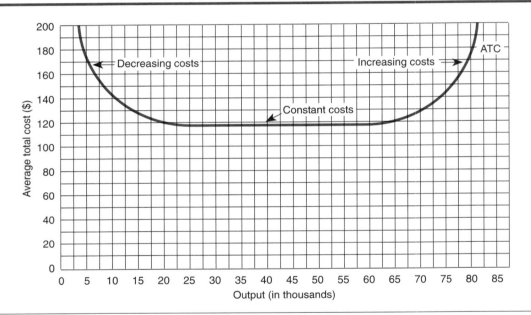

When we talk about constant cost and rising cost industries, we are implicitly assuming no technological progress. To avoid rising costs, a firm must innovate and jump down to a lower ATC curve. Although America has long been on the cutting edge of technological development, Japanese manufacturers have been much more adept at streamlining their production processes and, in effect, jumping down to progressively lower ATCs.

Think of how much the prices of VCRs, CD players, personal computers, and laser printers have come down in recent years. And think of the great progress, though much less measurable, that has been made with respect to product quality. The Japanese challenge to America and to the rest of the world is to find ways to constantly improve product quality while cutting production costs.

This analysis goes well beyond the scope of this book, but it is central to the problems U.S. manufacturers have had competing with Japanese manufacturers. If you would like to imagine an alternate analysis, then try to picture a series of ATC curves getting progressively lower, as technological advances keep lowering the cost of production.

curves. What are these diseconomies? One prime example would be managerial inefficiencies—the cost of maintaining a huge bureaucracy, the difficulties of communication among the bureaucracy's myriad branches, and the attendant duplication and waste. Another factor is diminishing returns, which set in while the ATC curve is in its early stages of decline and become increasingly important as output continues to rise. (For a full discussion of diminishing returns, see the next-to-last section of Chapter 16 of *Economics* and *Macroeconomics*.)

Constant cost industries

We've looked at decreasing cost industries and increasing cost industries. What about constant cost industries, where ATC does not change as output rises? For example, look at ATC for outputs between 25 and 58 in Figure 11. What can we say about economies of scale and diseconomies of scale? We can say that they are in balance, with economies of scale and diseconomies of scale just canceling each other out between outputs of 25 and 58.

Factor costs—wages, rent, and interest—are by far the most important determinants of whether costs are falling, constant, or increasing. Usually factor costs will eventually rise, which ultimately makes every industry an increasing cost industry. As more and more land, particularly in a given locality, is used by the expanding industry, rent will be bid up. And as more labor and capital are used by the industry, wages and interest rates will be bid up as well.

All industries, then, are really increasing cost industries, but the range of output within which they happen to operate is often one of decreasing or constant costs.

Decreasing Costs and the Breakdown of Perfect Competition

If a firm continually expands to take advantage of decreasing costs, its output will keep increasing. At some point it will become so large that it will have a discernible influence over price in the industry. At that point, by definition, the industry will cease to be perfectly competitive.

If we were to take our original firm—the one presented in Figure 1—with an original output of 20 or 30 units, how much would it have to expand to end perfect competition? If industry output were 4 million, as shown in Figure 1, and any firm in that industry began producing, say, 80,000 units (2 percent of output), perhaps that would be enough. If not 80,000, then 100,000 or 150,000 would be enough. At some point every economist would agree (though some observers say all economists *never* agree) that the firm is too big for perfect competition to exist.

Where Do We Go from Here?

One down, three to go. Perfect competition was the first of our four competitive models. It is a theoretical model that may not exist in the real world. But it serves as a standard by which we measure the next three competitive models.

Monopoly, which is on the opposite end of the competitive spectrum, provides a model of an industry in which there is a solitary firm. That comes next in our discussion, to be followed in succeeding chapters by monopolistic competition and oligopoly.

Questions for Further Thought and Discussion

1. Does the perfect competitor always break even in the long run? Explain why or why not.
2. If the perfect competitor is losing money in the short run, what happens in the market to drive up price?
3. Two characteristics of perfect competition are perfect mobility and perfect knowledge. Make up an example of each.

Name _____   Date _____

Multiple-Choice Questions

Circle the letter that corresponds to the best answer.

1. Perfect competition is
   a. the prevalent form of competition in the United States   b. the only form of competition in the United States   c. found occasionally   d. probably impossible to find

2. Under perfect competition
   a. many firms have some influence over price   b. a few firms have influence over price   c. no firm has any influence over price

3. Under perfect competition, there are
   a. many firms producing an identical product   b. a few firms producing an identical product   c. many firms producing a differentiated product   d. a few firms producing a differentiated product

4. The perfect competitor is
   a. a price maker rather than a price taker   b. a price taker rather than a price maker   c. a price taker and a price maker   d. neither a price maker nor a price taker

5. The determination of whether two products are identical
   a. is done by market research   b. takes place in the minds of the buyers   c. is done by the government
   d. is done by the sellers

6. The perfect competitor's demand curve is
   a. always horizontal   b. always vertical
   c. sometimes horizontal   d. sometimes vertical

7. Which statement about the perfect competitor is true?
   a. She may charge a little below market price to get more customers.   b. She may charge a little above market price to imply that her product is superior.
   c. She will always charge the market price.
   d. None of these statements is true.

8. Each of the following is a characteristic of perfect competition except
   a. many firms   b. identical products   c. perfect mobility   d. varying prices charged by different firms

9. In the short run the perfect competitor will probably
   a. make a profit or break even   b. take a loss or break even   c. make a profit or take a loss

10. In the long run the perfect competitor will
    a. make a profit   b. break even   c. take a loss

11. Under perfect competition _____ profits are always zero in the long run.
    a. accounting   b. economic   c. both economic and accounting   d. neither accounting nor economic

Use the choices below to answer questions 12 and 13.
   a. in the long run making a profit   b. in the long run breaking even   c. in the long run taking a loss
   d. in the short run making a profit   e. in the short run breaking even   f. in the short run taking a loss

12. Figure 1 shows the perfect competitor _____ .

Figure 1

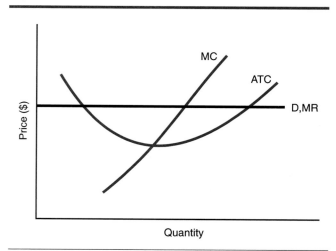

13. Figure 2 shows the perfect competitor _____ .

Figure 2

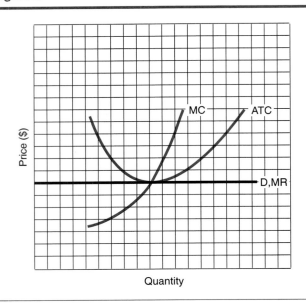

Quantity

14. The perfect competitor's demand and marginal revenue curves are
    a. identical only in the long run   b. identical only in the short run   c. never identical   d. always identical

15. Decreasing, constant, and increasing costs refer to
    a. accounting costs   b. economic costs
    c. marginal costs   d. average total costs

16. Which statement is true?
    a. Accounting profits are greater than economic profits.
    b. Economic profits are greater than accounting profits.
    c. Accounting profits are equal to economic profits.

17. The most efficient output
    a. is always equal to the most profitable output for the perfect competitor   b. is never equal to the most profitable output for the perfect competitor   c. is equal to the most profitable output for the perfect competitor only in the long run   d. is equal to the most profitable output for the perfect competitor only in the short run

Use Figure 3 to answer questions 18 through 21.

18. Total profit
    a. is the rectangle bounded by EFJI   b. is the rectangle bounded by EFGH   c. is the rectangle bounded by HGJI   d. cannot be found on this graph

19. Output
    a. is OK   b. is OL   c. is OM   d. cannot be found on this graph

20. Profit per unit is
    a. MF   b. MG   c. MJ   d. FJ   e. GJ

21. The firm's most efficient output
    a. is OK   b. is OL   c. is OM   d. cannot be determined on this graph

Figure 3

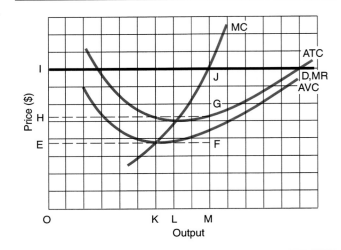

Output

Fill-In Questions

1. Under perfect competition there are so many firms that no one firm has any influence over _____ .

2. Under perfect competition all sellers sell a(n) _____ product.

3. The determination that a product is identical takes place in _____ .

4. The perfect competitor's demand curve is a

   _____; the marginal revenue curve is a

   _____.

5. A perfect competitor would never charge more than

   market price because _____

   _____; the perfect competitor would

   never charge less than market price because _____

   _____.

6. In a perfectly competitive industry, price is set by

   _____

   and _____.

7. The four main characteristics of perfect competition are

   (1) _____;

   (2) _____;

   (3) _____;

   and (4) _____.

8. In the short run the perfect competitor may make a

   _____ or take a _____;

   in the long run the perfect competitor will_____

   _____.

9. In a perfectly competitive industry, if firms are making

   profits, _____,

   which will result in zero profits in the long run; if there

   are losses in the short run, _____

   _____, resulting in zero profits (and

   losses) in the long run.

10. In the long run, economic profits are_____

    _____.

11. The perfect competitor operates at the _____

    _____ point of her average total cost

    curve in the long run.

12. In a decreasing cost industry, a firm that is a perfect

    competitor cannot keep growing because ultimately it will

    _____.

13. If the firms in a competitive industry are earning profits,

    in the long run new firms will_____.

    But if most firms are losing money, then in the long run

    some of the firms will _____.

14. If the firms in a competitive industry are losing money, in

    the long run the market price will _____.

    But if most firms are making a profit, then in the long run

    the market price will _____.

Problems

1. **a.** Find the total profit or total loss of the firm shown in
   Figure 4. **b.** Is the firm in the short run or the long run?
   c. How much is the firm's most efficient output? **d.** What
   is the lowest price the firm would accept in the long run?

Figure 4

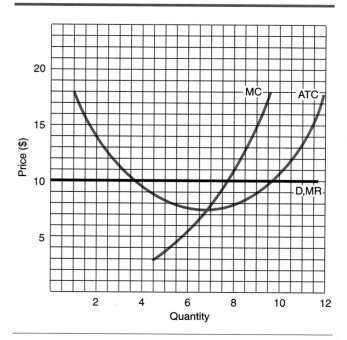

2. **a.** Find the total profit or total loss of the firm shown in Figure 5. **b.** Is the firm in the short run or the long run? **c.** How much is the firm's most efficient output? **d.** What is the lowest price the firm would accept in the long run?

Figure 5

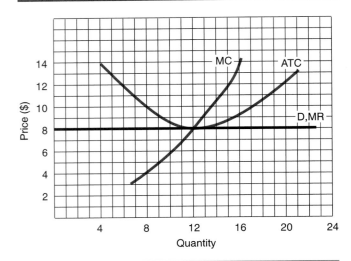

3 **a.** Find the total profit or total loss of the firm shown in Figure 6. **b.** Is the firm in the short run or the long run? **c.** How much is the firm's most efficient output? **d.** What is the lowest price the firm would accept in the long run?

Figure 6

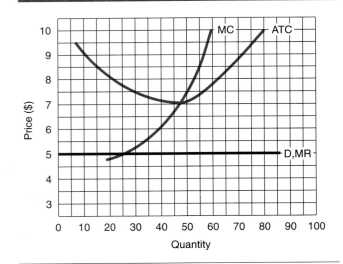

4. Given sales: $400,000; total costs: $250,000; return you could have earned by investing your money elsewhere: $15,000; wages you and your family members could have earned doing the same work for another firm: $40,000. How much are your family business's **a.** accounting profits? **b.** economic profits?

5. Given the industry supply and demand shown on the right side of Figure 7, use the left side of the figure to draw the perfect competitor's demand, marginal revenue, average total cost, and marginal cost curves for its long-run situation.

Figure 7

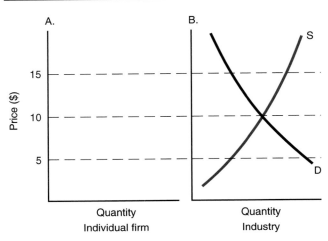

6. Given sales: $5 million; explicit costs: $3 million; return you could have earned by investing your money elsewhere: $50,000; wages you and your family members could have earned doing the same work for another firm: $120,000. How much are your family business's **a.** accounting profits? **b.** economic profits?

7. If economic profits are $250,000 and implicit (or opportunity) costs are $100,000, how much are accounting profits?

24 Monopoly

We've talked enough about perfect competition, an ideal state that probably does not exist. Welcome to the real world of imperfect competition. We'll begin here with monopoly and then go on to monopolistic competition and oligopoly in the next two chapters. When we've completed our analysis of these competitive states, you will probably conclude what I concluded a long time ago: that nobody's perfect.

When you were a kid, did you ever play the game of Monopoly? The whole idea was to control strips of properties, such as Boardwalk and Park Place. Some people get to play Monopoly even after they've grown up—and they get to keep all the money. In this and the next three chapters, we'll see how this game is played by the big kids.

Chapter Objectives

We'll look at these topics:

- The graph of the monopolist.
- How the monopolist's profits are calculated.
- The monopolist in the short run and the long run.
- Barriers to entry.
- Limits to monopoly power.
- Economies of scale and natural monopoly.
- What makes bigness bad?

Monopoly Defined

A monopoly is a firm that produces all the output in an industry.

A monopoly is the only firm in an industry. There's nobody else selling anything like what the monopolist is producing. In other words, there are no close substitutes.

Examples of monopoly include DeBeers diamonds, the local gas and electric companies, and, until recently, AT&T. During the years after World War II, IBM, Xerox, and Alcoa (Aluminum Company of America) also had monopolies.

What are close substitutes?

One might ask how close substitutes would need to be to disqualify firms from being monopolies. Surely a Cadillac Seville is a reasonably close substitute for a Lincoln Continental. Further, there are many close substitutes for a Xerox photocopying machine, but there are no close substitutes for diamonds, gas, electricity, and telephone calls.

We need to ask *why* there are no close substitutes for the monopolist's good or service. Has the monopolist erected barriers to keep out potential competitors, or is there some other explanation as to why the monopolist is the sole producer? We'll talk about barriers to entry later in the chapter.

We should also distinguish between local and national monopolies. Someone may be the only doctor in the vicinity and have a local monopoly, but there are more than 500,000 doctors in the United States. A hardware store, grocery, drugstore, or dry cleaners may have a monopoly in its neighborhood, but each may have several competitors within a few miles.

The Graph of the Monopolist

Monopoly is the first of three types of imperfect competition. Monopolistic competition and oligopoly follow in the next two chapters. The distinguishing characteristic of imperfect competition is that the firm's demand curve is no longer a perfectly elastic horizontal line; now it curves downward to the right. This means the imperfect competitor will have to lower price to sell more.

Using the data in Table 1, we'll draw our four standard curves: demand, marginal revenue, marginal cost, and average total cost. First, fill in Table 1 and check your figures against those in Table 2. Please observe that the demand and marginal revenue schedules no longer coincide. After you've completed Table 1, use these figures to draw a graph of the aforementioned curves on a piece of graph paper.

A common mistake students make when filling out Table 1 is to use some number (in this case, 20) for MC at one unit of output. We'll review exactly what MC is; then we'll see why there's no way of finding MC at one unit of output.

Do you recall the definition of marginal cost? MC is *the additional cost of producing one more unit of output.* Remember that as output rises, fixed cost stays the same and variable cost rises. So far, so good. The only problem is we don't know how much fixed cost is at one unit of output; nor do we know how much variable cost is at one unit of output. The MC of the first unit of output would be total cost at output one minus total cost at output zero. How much is total cost at output zero? It's fixed cost. But we don't know fixed cost, so we can't figure out MC at output one. For the remaining outputs, we *can* figure out MC because we know how much total cost rises.

Look at the graph you drew and see whether it matches the one in Figure 1. The ATC and MC curves are the same as they were for the perfect competitor. I hope your MC intersects your ATC at its minimum point. Also note that the demand and marginal revenue curves slope downward to the right. At one unit of output, the demand and

Table 1   Hypothetical Demand and Cost Schedule for a Monopoly

Output	Price	Total Revenue	Marginal Revenue	Total Cost	ATC	MC
1	$16	_____	_____	$20	_____	_____
2	15	_____	_____	30	_____	_____
3	14	_____	_____	36	_____	_____
4	13	_____	_____	42	_____	_____
5	12	_____	_____	50	_____	_____
6	11	_____	_____	63	_____	_____
7	10	_____	_____	84	_____	_____

Table 2   Hypothetical Demand and Cost Schedule for a Monopoly

Output	Price	Total Revenue	Marginal Revenue	Total Cost	ATC	MC
1	$16	$16	$16	$20	$20	—
2	15	30	14	30	15	$10
3	14	42	12	36	12	6
4	13	52	10	42	10.50	6
5	12	60	8	50	10	8
6	11	66	6	63	10.50	13
7	10	70	4	84	12	21

Figure 1   The Monopolist Making a Profit

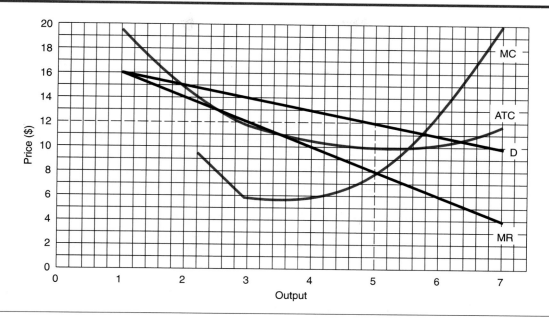

marginal revenue curves share the same point—$16—but the MR curve then slopes down much faster. In fact, when the demand curve is a straight line, the marginal revenue curve is also a straight line that falls twice as quickly. If you want to know why, take a look at the box "Why the MR Curve Declines Faster than the Demand Curve."

When the demand curve falls $1 to $15 at two units of output, the MR curve falls $2 to $14. At three units of output, when the demand curve falls $1 to $14, the MR curve falls $2 to $12.

Calculating the Monopolist's Profit

At what output does the monopolist produce?

Now we'll get down to business. At what output does the monopolist produce? Go ahead and perform the marginal analysis to determine the most profitable output. I'll tell you the first step. Look at Figure 1 and find the point at which your marginal cost curve crosses your marginal revenue curve. That's your output. Do your calculations right here:

Why the MR Curve Declines Faster than the Demand Curve

In Table 2, when the output is one, price is $16; but to sell two units of output, the seller must lower price to $15. Two units at $15 equals $30 (total revenue). Notice that the seller can't charge $16 for the first unit and $15 for the second. That's because the seller has to post one price. (If the seller manages to charge more than one price, we have price discrimination, which we'll talk about in the next chapter.)

When price is lowered to $15, total revenue is $30. Marginal revenue is $14 (total revenue of $30 at two units of output minus total revenue of $16 at one unit of output). At two units of output, because we charge a price of $15, the point on the demand curve is $15. So, at two units of output, we have $15 on the demand curve and $14 on the MR curve.

To sell three units, the seller must lower price to $14. That yields a total revenue of $42 and a MR of $12 ($42 − $30). So, at three units of output, we're at $14 on the demand curve and $12 on the MR curve.

Let's summarize. If the seller lowers price to sell more output, the price is lowered on all units of output, not just on the last one. This drives down MR faster than price (which is read off the demand curve). Notice also that the MR curve descends twice as quickly as the D Curve.

According to Figure 1, MC equals MR at 5 units of output. Using the formula for total profit, we find:

$$\text{Total profit} = (\text{Price} - \text{ATC}) \times \text{Output}$$
$$= (\$12 - \$10) \times 5$$
$$= \$2 \times 5$$
$$= \$10$$

We have a conflict here that didn't exist under perfect competition. The perfect competitor produced at the most profitable output, which in the long run always happened to be the most efficient output. But we see that the monopolist does not produce where output is at its most efficient level (the minimum point of the ATC curve). Remember, *every firm will produce at its most profitable output, where MC equals MR*. If that does not happen to be the most efficient output and if, for example, that firm is a bakery—get ready for a terrible pun—then that's the way the cookie crumbles. Finding the monopolist's price and output is a little harder than finding the price and output for the perfect competition. If you need more practice, see the box "How to Find the Monopolist's Price and Output."

Looking at Figure 1, let's compare the price of the monopolist with that of the perfect competitor. In the very long run the perfect competitor would charge $9.90, the minimum point of its ATC curve, while the monopolist's price is $12. Next, let's compare output. The perfect competitor would produce at an output of 5.5, which is where ATC is at its minimum, but the monopolist's output is 5.

To summarize, the monopolist makes a profit, whereas in the long run the perfect competitor makes no profit. The monopolist operates at less than peak efficiency, while

Every firm produces where MC = MR.

In the long run, the monopolist makes a profit, but the perfect competitor does not.

How to Find the Monopolist's Price and Output

Let's go over how the monopolist sets price step-by-step, using Figure 1. Step 1: The monopolist chooses her output by finding where the MC and MR curves cross. Step 2: By moving down along the dashed line, we find that the output she chose is 5.

Step 3: We move up the dotted line from MC = MR to the demand curve. Step 4: We move horizontally along the dotted line to a price of $12.

Here's another one for you to work out. How much is the output and price of the monopolist represented by Figure A?

If we move down from where the MC and MR curves cross, we find that the output is 20. To find price we go up from where the MC and MR curves cross to the demand curve, and then horizontally to the price axis. This gives us a price of $9.

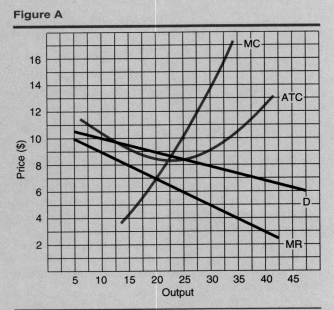

Figure A

the perfect competitor operates at peak efficiency (the lowest point on the ATC curve). Finally, the perfect competitor charges a lower price and produces a larger output than the monopolist.[1]

This last point bears some explanation. The monopolist operates on a much larger scale than does the individual perfect competitor. But the sum of output under perfect competition would be larger than it would be under monopoly.

I haven't bothered to distinguish between the short run and the long run mainly because the monopolist has no rivals. With perfect competition, the fact that the firms entered the industry (attracted by profits) or left the industry (driven out of business by losses) made the short run differ from the long run. Under monopoly, even larger profits wouldn't attract rival firms; otherwise, there would no longer be a monopoly. If a monopoly were losing money, in the long run it, too, would go out of business.

How could a monopolist lose money?

You might ask, How could a monopoly lose money? What if, given both the demand for its product and its ATC schedule, no matter what the output, the firm lost money?

I once started a mail-order business. I had invented a fantastic liquid diet. Interested? OK, here it is. Just drink these liquids—skim milk, Alba '70 shakes, clear soup, plain nonfat yogurt (liquid or frozen), grapefruit, watermelon, fruit pops, fruit juice, and vegetable juice (and take a daily vitamin pill)—and you'll lose about a pound a day. It also helps to run 25 to 30 miles a week.

I had what I thought was a great slogan: "What have you got to lose?" But I needed to advertise, rent a post office box, and print up my diet. I charged $2. What happened? What do you *think* happened? I spent about $350 and got 20 or 30 orders. If you happen to want to go into the diet business, I'll sell you *my* business—cheap. And then *you'll* have a monopoly (even though this diet has imitators, none comes close).

So I was a monopolist, but I lost money. You can be a monopolist, too. Start an autograph club. For just $1, people can send for your signature; no one else can start up this business. The only problem is that nobody else would want to. But you'll be a monopolist. That is, you'll be one until you get sick and tired of losing money.

Review of the Monopolist's Economic Analysis

I'm throwing a lot of new stuff at you, so let's step back for a few minutes and review the monopolist's table and graph. (For extra help, see the box "How to Read a Graph.") Microeconomics is based largely on the three-step problems you've come to know and love: (1) filling in the table, (2) drawing the graph, and (3) doing the analysis.

You may begin by filling in Table 3 and then seeing whether your numbers correspond to the data in Table 4.

Next comes the graph. Draw the demand, marginal revenue, marginal cost, and average total cost curves on a piece of graph paper. Then check your work with that in Figure 2.

Are you ready to do some analysis? Ready or not, we need to find the monopolist's total profit. Do that right here. Then check your work with the calculations that follow.

---

[1]In theory, the perfect competitor produces 5.5 units and the monopolist 5. But because the perfect competitor is a tiny firm, we can't really compare its output with that of the monopolist, who produces the industry's entire output. Thus, when we say the perfect competitor would produce an output of 5.5, we must realize that the firm would no longer be a perfect competitor. Do you follow this? If you don't, don't worry. This is only a footnote.

How to Read a Graph

Let's go over some of the points we've already covered. Refer to the graph in Figure B below. How much is the output of this monopolist? Write down your answer. Next question. How much is price? Again, write down your answer. Finally, how much is total profits? Work it out in the space here.

We'll go over each of these questions in turn. First, *our output is always determined by the intersection of the MC and MR curves.* That occurs at an output of about 4.25.

How much is price? First, *price is read off the demand curve.* Remember that. Where on the demand curve—at what output? At the maximum profit output we just found—4.25. How much is price at that output? It appears to be about $9. And how much is ATC? Go straight up from where MC crosses MR to the ATC curve. It looks like about $7.50.

Next we calculate total profits.

$$\text{Total profits} = (\text{Price} - \text{ATC}) \times \text{Output}$$

$$= (\$9 - \$7.50) \times 4.25$$

$$= \$1.50 \times 4.25$$

$$= \$6.38$$

You may have noticed that once we find output (where MC = MR), everything else lines up. Price is located on the demand curve above the output of 4.25. ATC is on the ATC curve, also above an output of 4.25. When we find total profits, we plug price, ATC, and output into our formula.

Figure B

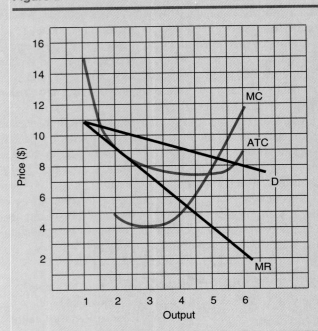

Table 3

Output	Price	Total Revenue	Marginal Revenue	Total Cost	ATC	MC
1	$21	____	____	$30	____	____
2	20	____	____	40	____	____
3	19	____	____	48	____	____
4	18	____	____	57	____	____
5	17	____	____	70	____	____
6	16	____	____	93	____	____

Table 4

Output	Price	Total Revenue	Marginal Revenue	Total Cost	ATC	MC
1	$21	21	21	$30	30	—
2	20	40	19	40	20	10
3	19	57	17	48	16	8
4	18	72	15	57	14.25	9
5	17	85	13	70	14	13
6	16	96	11	93	15.50	23

Figure 2   The Monopolist Making a Profit

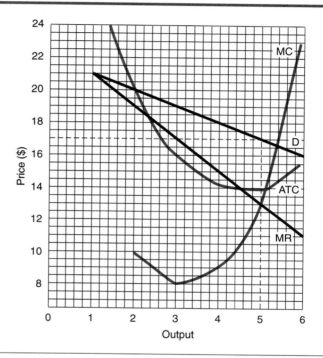

$$\text{Total profit} = (\text{Price} - \text{ATC}) \times \text{Output}$$
$$= (\$17 - \$14) \times 5$$
$$= \$3 \times 5$$
$$= \$15$$

I'm not going to let you off the hook just yet. Try these three questions.

1. At what output would the firm produce most efficiently?
2. At what output would the perfect competitor produce in the long run?
3. What price would the perfect competitor charge in the long run?

Here are the answers.

1. The output at which the firm would produce most efficiently would be about 5.1, which is the minimum point of the ATC curve.
2. The perfect competitor would produce at an output of 5.1 in the long run.
3. In the long run the perfect competitor would charge a price of about $13.97 (the minimum, or break-even, point of the ATC curve).

The Monopolist in the Short Run and the Long Run

No distinction is made for the monopolist between the short and long runs. Why not? Because no other firms will enter or leave the industry; by definition, the monopolist is the only firm.

If the firm is losing money, is it in the short run or the long run? What do *you* think?

It must be in the short run because no firm will stay in business if it's losing money. Not even the Chicago Cubs. For years the Wrigley family (as in Wrigley's chewing gum) lost money on the Cubs. It was an expensive hobby. Eventually it became too expensive even for the Wrigleys, who evidently decided that they could double their pleasure *and* their fun by selling the team.

If the monopolist is making a profit, is it in the long run or the short run? Can you tell? Think about it.

If the firm were in the short run, would this monopolist stay in business? Yes! And so it would continue to make a profit. In the long run, then, it would be making a profit. Therefore, there is no way to distinguish between the long run and the short run if the firm is making a profit.

Let's sum things up. If the firm is making a profit, for analytic purposes, it doesn't matter whether it's in the short run or the long run. If the firm is losing money, it must be in the short run; in the long run it will go out of business.

Demand and Supply under Monopoly

Because the monopolist is the only seller in the industry, she not only faces the entire market demand curve, but her supply curve *is* the market supply curve. Look again at Figure 2. The market demand curve is labeled D. And the market supply curve? Can you find it? It's labeled MC. That's *right*—the monopolist's supply curve is her MC curve. Her supply curve begins at the break-even point (i.e., the minimum point of the ATC curve) and runs up the MC curve. (Because we're not distinguishing between the monopolist's short run and long run, we won't bother with a short-run supply curve.)

Are All Monopolies Big Companies?

The answer is no. Many monopolies are tiny firms operating in very tiny markets. What matters is size relative to the market—the proverbial big fish in the small pond.

The chances are there's only one bookstore on your college campus. That store would have a monopoly even though it's not nearly as big as some of the Barnes and Nobles superstores. The only video rental store in a small town would have a monopoly. There are tens of thousands of gas stations, convenience stores, restaurants, cleaners, and repair shops that have monopolies in their communities.

Barriers to Entry

We'll consider each of four barriers to entry in turn: (1) control over an essential resource, (2) economies of scale, (3) legal barriers, and (4) economies of being established.

Control over an Essential Resource   We tend to think of resources as natural resources—oil, coal, iron ore, arable land—but in economics, the basic resources are land, labor, and capital. The Metropolitan Opera has a near monopoly because it has most of the world's opera stars (labor) under contract.

Until the early 1960s the National Football League (NFL) had a monopoly, but this was challenged by the American Football League. The NFL had virtually all the established star football players under contract, so the AFL went after college stars. In 1965 the New York Jets signed University of Alabama star quarterback Joe Namath for the then unheard-of sum of $427,000; that action broke the back of the NFL's monopoly.

DeBeers Diamond Company in South Africa owns four-fifths of the world's diamond mines, and the International Nickel Company of Canada controls about 90 percent of the world's nickel reserves. The Standard Oil Company controlled the oil industry in the 1880s until the early 1900s because it owned more than 90 percent of the nation's oil fields and refineries. At that same time the American Tobacco Company controlled 90 percent of U.S. tobacco production.[2]

Economies of Scale   Typically, heavy industry—iron and steel, copper, aluminum, and automobiles—has high setup costs. But once your plant and equipment are set up, you can take advantage of economies of scale by increasing your output.

In the 1980s General Motors, Ford, and Chrysler were able to realize these economies much more than could American Motors and Volkswagen of America, both of which were relatively small.[3] Thus we are really talking about two necessary conditions for realizing economies of scale: having the wherewithal to set up and having sufficient demand for your product.

Imagine how difficult it would be to set up a rival phone network or even a rival electric company in a large city. What protects monopolies from potential rivals is that they're selling enough units to have a relatively low ATC (see Figure 3). If you were to enter the industry, how could you hope to have the capital to set yourself up to compete effectively?

Figure 3 illustrates the problem of economies of scale faced by the small producer of cars. At relatively low levels of production, say 100,000 to 200,000 cars, the firm will not be able to take advantage of the economies of mass production that are available to rival firms. According to this illustration, ATC continues to decline appreciably through an output of at least 700,000.

Legal barriers include licensing, franchises, and patents.

Licensing

Legal Barriers   These include licensing, franchises, and patents. The whole idea is for the government to allow only one firm or a group of individuals to do business.

Licensing prevents just anybody from driving a taxi, cutting hair, peddling on the street, practicing medicine, or burying bodies. Often the licensing procedure is designed

---

[2]In 1911 the Supreme Court broke up these monopolies. (See the chapter titled "Corporate Mergers and Antitrust.")

[3]American Motors was absorbed by Chrysler, and Volkswagen stopped producing cars in the United States.

Figure 3   Hypothetical Production Costs for Cars

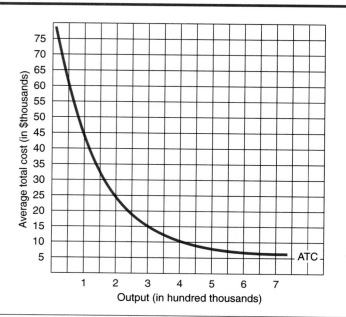

Patents

to hold down the number of people going into a certain field and thereby keep prices in that field high.

Patents are granted to investors so that they have a chance to get rich before someone else uses their ideas. They have 17 years to get their act together. In some cases, perhaps most notably U.S. Shoe Machinery Company, a firm buys up patents and uses them to prevent competition. A common practice is to obtain a patent on a new product or process and then, before the 17 years are up, obtain a new patent on some improvement or innovation. Japanese firms have been able to dominate the consumer electronics industry by successfully obtaining patents on each innovation to the original product.

Government franchises

The most important legal barrier is the government franchise. When it gives out a good number of franchises—to local radio stations, for example—the government does not introduce a significant barrier. However, cable TV in many localities is another story. There have been scandals in various towns and cities across the nation—most notably in Wisconsin, Pennsylvania, and New York. Anxious cable companies have quite blatantly offered bribes to local officials, usually in the form of large blocks of company stock, to secure cable franchises.[4]

The most important form of local franchise is the public utility—your gas and electric companies. There's only one to a locality. The local government grants the franchise, and, like it or not, the company's got you. Monopolies don't have to worry about giving poor service at outrageous prices. Where else can you go? (See box "At Rutgers Coke Is the Only Choice.")

Economies of Being Established   Companies that have been operating for many years have recognizable brand names, and their sales representatives have established territories. Most important, the seller and buyer have a long-standing relationship. A retailer can count on her supplier for fast, reliable service.

A new company, with newly hired sales reps just learning their routes, will have a hard time prying customers from a well-established competitor. How can you convince a retailer to buy your product or service when she never saw you before and is unfamiliar with what you're selling? For these reasons, the economies of being established make it difficult to take market share from a company that may have been doing business before you were born.

Another advantage of being established is setting the industry standard, as does Microsoft in computer software and Matsushita in VCR format. Why does *your* VCR have a VHS format rather than a (Sony) Betamax format? Mainly because nearly all available tapes are VHS. Back in the late 1970s when Sony and Matsushita went head-to-head, Sony's one-hour tapes were too short for movies. Since Matsushita produced two-hour tapes, their VHS format very quickly became the industry standard.

And talking about the advantages of being established, it's hard not to notice that virtually everyone drives a car powered by gasoline. Would you believe that the Stanley

---

[4]The most celebrated case involved John Zaccaro, husband of Geraldine Ferraro, the Democratic Party's 1984 vice presidential nominee. Zaccaro was accused of demanding a $1 million bribe to secure a cable contract for a company that aspired to wire the borough of Queens in New York City. He was acquitted.

At Rutgers Coke Is the Only Choice

Outbidding Pepsi by about $2.5 million, the Coca-Cola Company paid Rutgers, the State University of New Jersey, some $10 million in 1994 for exclusive rights to sell its products to some 48,000 students on three campuses over the next decade. On-campus food and beverage vendors may sell only Coca-Cola Company beverages, which include Nestea iced tea, Sprite, Minute Maid drinks, and, of course, every variety of diet and regular Coke. The football coach will even be doused with Powerade, rather than Gatorade.

Rutgers, of course, is not the first school to sell an exclusive franchise to a private vendor. The next time you're in your school cafeteria or snack bar, see whether it sells both Coke and Pepsi. If it doesn't, you'll know who's got the franchise.

Steamer set a world speed record of 122 miles an hour way back in 1909? That's right—a steam-powered car. If the manufacturer had not priced it as a luxury vehicle and instead had striven for economies of scale as Henry Ford was doing, we might all be driving Stanley Steamers. And perhaps sometime soon, more and more of us will be driving electric cars. Which brings us to the limits of monopoly power.

Limits to Monopoly Power

Limits to the four barriers to entry

First, we'll consider limits to the four barriers to entry. We saw how the National Football League lost its monopoly when it lost control over an essential resource—star football players. Similarly, Alcoa, which at one time controlled nearly all the world's known bauxite (aluminum ore) reserves, lost its monopoly when other reserves were discovered.[5]

Economies of scale and high capital requirements are a significant barrier to entry, but by 1990 Nissan, Honda, Toyota, Mazda, and Mitsubishi joined the parade of American automobile producers. Of course, each of these producers was set up by its friendly giant company back home.

Finally, even legal barriers have been overcome. Rival phone companies have gone to court to win the right to plug into the AT&T network while providing a competing and generally lower-priced long-distance service. In general, however, government franchises are there for a reason: in some industries it makes economic sense to have only one firm in a given locality; so the franchise may well be a barrier we don't want to overcome.

The ultimate limit to monopoly power may come from the government or from the market itself. If a firm gets too big or too bad, the federal government may decide to trim that firm's sails. We'll take this issue up in the chapter "Corporate Mergers and Antitrust."

The market limits monopoly power through the development of substitutes.

Let's consider how the market limits monopoly power, basically through the development of substitutes. Take Kleenex, for example. To this day, some people call tissues "Kleenexes." In the late 1940s Kleenex was the only paper tissue on the market, so *tissues* and *Kleenexes* could properly be considered synonymous. But over the years scores of competitors have sprung up, and today the market share of Kleenex is very small indeed.

Another interesting case is that of Xerox. Having invented the first "dry" photocopy machine, Xerox had the market all to itself during the late 1950s and early 1960s. Shortly thereafter, IBM, Savin, Canon, Sharp, Pitney-Bowes, Multilith-Addressograph, and a multitude of other firms began marketing their own photocopiers. Nonetheless, to this day when someone needs a photocopy, chances are he or she will ask you to "xerox" it—which is a lot easier than asking you to "multilith-addressograph" it.

Economies of Scale and Natural Monopoly

Two justifications for monopoly

There are really only two justifications for monopoly: economies of scale and natural monopoly. Economies of scale justify bigness because only a firm with a large output can produce near the minimum point of its long-run ATC curve. When the firm's output is so large that it is almost equal to the output of the entire industry, this state of monopoly is justified by calling it efficient. Of course, we have just seen that the firm is not operating at the minimum point of its ATC curve (see Figure 2), but that's another story.

Natural monopoly is closely related to economies of scale. Some think a natural monopoly occurs when someone gains complete control of the wheat germ supply or of the entire crop of Florida oranges. Close, but no cigar. Cigar? No, even Cuban cigars are not a natural monopoly.

---

[5]The Alcoa case is discussed in the chapter "Corporate Mergers and Antitrust."

Examples of natural
monopolies

Examples of natural monopolies are the local gas and electric companies, the local phone companies, and local cable TV companies. Why are these natural monopolies? Because they can provide cheaper service as monopolies than could several competing firms. Let's see why.

In Figure 4, one electric company serves an entire suburban town. Pictured here is one street in that town, its houses lined up properly just as they might be anywhere in suburbia. Every house on the block uses the same company. After all, what choice do they have?

Figure 5 shows four competing electric companies on an identical street of an identical town somewhere else in suburbia. Notice the four power lines running along the street. In this town there's freedom of choice; you can hook up with any of these four companies.

Figure 4   One Electric Company Serving One Block

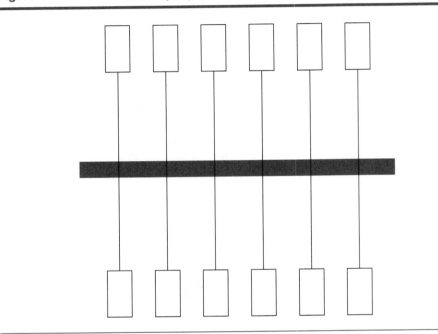

Figure 5   Four Electric Companies Serving One Block

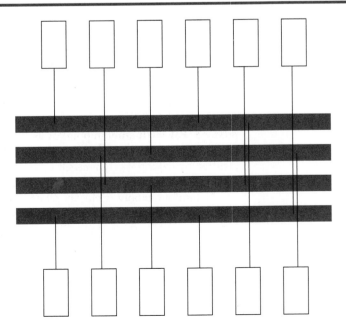

Are We Paying Too Much for Electricity?

Local electric companies, although closely regulated by state power commissions, charge widely varying rates across the country. Indeed, people living in New York pay 13.6 cents per kilowatt hour, while those in Washington state pay only 5.0 cents. In 1994 California, a high-cost state, authorized commercial and industrial energy-users to buy power from out-of-state utilities beginning in 1996, and residential energy-users six years later. Under this plan, California's three major utilities will have to transmit over their lines power that customers buy from other utilities. If other states follow California's lead, we may all find our electric bills going down instead of up.

Will the Local Companies Lose Their Monopolies?

Even the monopolies held by local phone companies are slowly being chipped away by rival firms that provide high-volume users with low-priced service. To date, these companies have captured less than 2 percent of this hundred-billion-dollar market, but their share may expand rapidly over the next few years.

According to a *New York Times* article by Edmund L. Andrews, officials in Illinois, New York, and several other states are "beginning to adopt rules that make it easier for aspiring rivals to connect their optic lines and switches to public networks, giving them access to the entire phone system—the coverage they need to carry calls the last mile or the last blocks to low-volume users that otherwise would be uneconomical for them to serve."* Before the millenium AT&T, MCI, Sprint, and other long distance carriers may also be providing local service.

*Edmund L. Andrews, "The Local Call Goes Up for Grabs," *New York Times,* December 29, 1991, section 3, p. 1.

There's only one problem with this arrangement. It's much more expensive. You see, each company, assuming customers are evenly distributed, does only one-quarter of the business that would be done by a company that had a monopoly. While it must construct the same system of power lines, it realizes only one-quarter of the output. Its costs are much higher than those of the monopoly.[6]

From society's viewpoint, these higher costs reflect a great waste of resources. Why construct four parallel power lines when one will do as nicely? And, one might add parenthetically, why dig up the street four times rather than once to lay and repair the cables?

This is the case for natural monopoly. It's cheaper, it's more efficient, and it's more convenient. The bottom line is that our bills are much lower (see box "Are We Paying Too Much for Electricity?").

Imagine if we had six or eight competing local phone companies.

Another case for natural monopoly can be made with respect to local telephone service. Imagine if we had four, six, or eight competing phone companies. Placing a call would be like playing Russian roulette. Imagine your surprise if you actually got through! (See the box titled "Will the Local Companies Lose their Monopolies?")

It would not be easy to conduct business. "Let's see now, I call this client on the orange phone, my lawyer on the gray phone, and my accountant on the yellow phone." And what if the president needs to reach his opposite number in the Kremlin in a hurry and can't remember: "Was it the red phone for the Kremlin and the green phone for McDonalds—or was it the other way around?" You can imagine the puzzlement in Moscow at getting an order for two Big Macs and a large order of fries.

When Is Bigness Bad?

From what we've seen so far, monopoly isn't *all* bad. At times only a monopolist can fully take advantage of economies of scale; and in certain instances, particularly with respect to local public utilities, there are natural monopolies. In the case of Xerox, Kleenex,

---

[6]Technically, these are average fixed costs. They're four times as high as that of the electric company that has a monopoly. For example, if it cost $4 million to lay cable through a town, and if 40,000 families lived in the town, the monopoly would have an AFC of $100 ($4,000,000/40,000). Each of the four competing companies would have an AFC of $400 per family ($4,000,000/10,000).

and IBM, these innovative companies once had monopolies simply because each was the first to enter its field.

Why, then, do so many people dislike monopolies? For one thing, monopolies tend to be inefficient. As illustrated in Figure 6 later in the chapter, a monopoly does not produce at the minimum point of its ATC curve. Furthermore, by always restricting output to some point to the left of that minimum, the monopoly is preventing resources from being allocated in the most efficient manner. Land, labor, and capital that would have otherwise flowed into the monopolized industry are kept out and will eventually find their way into other industries where they will not be as efficiently used.

Politically, big business has always been extremely powerful, especially when several large firms have joined together in common cause. The power of the oil-auto-construction lobby has been awesome in the post–World War II period. This group managed to get an oil depletion allowance through Congress that reduced the income taxes of oil firms by 27 percent. (No other industry got this tax break.) To stimulate housing, there were Federal Housing Administration and Veterans' Administration mortgages plus, of course, the interest deduction on the personal federal income tax. To get people to these houses and from city to city, Congress appropriated the funds to build a national highway network (through the Highway Trust Fund). One of the legacies of these policies has been our utter dependence on gasoline and the consequent energy crises of 1973 and 1979.

Economic power is easily converted into political power.

We've seen, then, that economic power is easily transformed into political power and that political power is used to enhance economic power. A large corporation rarely hesitates to use its vast power to get what it wants. The law firms of many legislators do business with large corporations. Legislators' lawyers also sit on the boards of banks, insurance companies, and other firms that do business with the nation's largest corporations. Although corporate campaign contributions are illegal, corporate (voluntary) political action committees (PACs) have contributed hundreds of millions of dollars to congressional and presidential campaign coffers, not to mention the tens of millions in personal contributions by corporate officials and major stockholders.

Old soldiers never die; they just fade away.
—General Douglas MacArthur

Large firms, most notably defense contractors, often do sizable business with the government. The standard career path for higher-ranking military officers is to step into the top job slots with defense contracting firms upon their retirement from the military. To modify the legendary words of General Douglas MacArthur, old soldiers never die, they just get jobs with Lockheed, General Dynamics, Pratt and Whitney, Boeing, General Electric, McDonnell Douglas, and the rest of the defense establishment. In the words of another old general, Dwight D. Eisenhower, "Beware of the military-industrial complex."

Beware of the military-industrial complex.
—General Dwight D. Eisenhower

One may argue that our country's lightning victory over Iraq in what Saddam Hussein had forecast would be "the mother of all battles" showed that our sophisticated weaponry really did work and that the trillions of dollars we had spent were not wasted after all. But the question we need to address is not whether we are getting the most bang for our bucks, but instead whether so many of our resources should continue to be expended on armaments considering that the disintegration of the Soviet Union has left us as the world's only superpower.

Bigness can also mean inefficiency.

Bigness can also mean inefficiency. Near the end of the chapter "Supply in the Short Run and the Long Run," we talked about corporate bureaucracies and diseconomies of scale. This problem has become acute among the giant firms that are often referred to as "corporate dinosaurs." The box titled "The Corporate Hierarchy" takes a critical look at this growing problem.

Another problem is that the monopolist may engage in price discrimination, which involves dividing buyers into two or more markets and setting different prices in different markets. This practice, which we'll discuss thoroughly in the next chapter, is not confined to big firms; any imperfect competitors, whether big or small, may engage in price discrimination.

Bigness may be bad for the economy, but our society is prepared to take only limited action against it and only when a large company breaks the rules. Our main set of rules is our antitrust laws, which we'll get to in a few chapters.

The Corporate Hierarchy

Americans are fond of creating pecking orders, and the bureaucratic managerial structures set up to run America's large corporations are prime examples. In Japan, where the corporate hierarchy is substantially flatter, chief executive officers earn 16 or 18 times what their average employees earn. But in the United States the average CEO pulls down 100 to 120 times the earnings of the average worker.

There's a place for everything, and everything in its place. Follow this aphorism and your home will be neat as a pin. Unfortunately, when it's applied to the American corporation, the results are not nearly as copacetic.

In some companies—banks and insurance companies may be the best examples—there are three or four company cafeterias and dining rooms. You know exactly who eats in which. And if you forget, you'll quickly be reminded. To modify our aphorism, there's a place for everyone, and everyone in her or his place.

Hierarchies are necessary if we're going to have any kind of control. And they're necessary if we're going to build empires. That's right—control and empire-building are what American corporations are all about.

Empire-building within the corporation is not an entirely American phenomenon, but it has been raised to an art form in this country. The more people you supervise and the more tasks your group performs—however little they contribute to actual production of goods and services—the more money you'll earn and the higher the trajectory of your career path will be.

The economies of the Soviet Union and its Eastern European satellites were based on a command structure. Marching orders were issued from the top and made their way down through the ranks. Here's what we're going to produce, said the planners, and here's how we're going to do it, comrades. And after it's produced, we'll tell you where to send it and how much to charge.

This structure is not efficient. It allows no feedback from consumers, no competition, and very few work incentives. But it's just the structure our own huge corporations have. The tip of the hierarchy passes orders down to the troops. The rank-and-file worker is rarely consulted and does not identify with the company or with the product it produces. Furthermore, the people who are making the decisions at the top have virtually no contact with their customers. The end result is often a high-cost, low-quality product.

Our leading corporations have become so complex, so overmanaged, so distant from their customers, and so alienating to their rank-and-file employees that it is a wonder they have been able to function as well as they have. Perhaps the dilemma is best summed up by management consultant Ichak Adizes: "Good organizations should be structured by geniuses so that idiots can run them. Unfortunately, most American organizations are structured by idiots so that it takes a genius to run them."*

*Quoted in Steven Schlosssstein, *The End of the American Century* (New York: Congdon & Weed, 1989), p. 108.

When Is Bigness Good?

To be big is not necessarily to behave badly. Natural monopolies, for example, taking advantage of economies of scale, deliver services much more cheaply than could a multitude of competing firms. And in general, large firms can take advantage of economies of scale.

Sometimes a firm, such as Xerox, IBM, or Microsoft, is the first to enter an industry. Should we ask such a firm to wait until each of its competitors can catch up? Or do we allow them to grow very large? Perhaps the question we should ask is whether a firm is big because it is very bad or because it is very good.

The Economic Case against Bigness

The best of all monopoly profits is a quiet life.
—John Hicks

I'll start with the obvious. Does the monopolist operate at the minimum point of his ATC curve? No! Just glance back at Figures 1 and 2.

Because the monopolist is not pressed by competition, there is no great incentive to control costs or to use resources efficiently. Indeed, there is no need to spend much money on research and development, to improve manufacturing processes, to develop new products, or to be responsive to customer needs.

A monopolist can charge his customers higher prices and provide poorer service than he would if he had competitors. I mean, where else can you go? Have you ever lost your temper dealing with your local bank (assuming it's the only one in town), the phone company, or the gas or electric company? You've heard the phrase "The customer is always right"? Not when you're dealing with a monopoly.

One of the most important effects of the growing amount of foreign competition, especially from the Japanese, is the new emphasis on product quality. American cars, specialty steel, machine tools, and a whole host of consumer products have all enjoyed tremendous quality improvement over the last 10 years. It is a virtual certainty that without the spur of foreign competition, the quality standards of American products would not have improved so greatly.

Two Policy Alternatives

Two ways to prevent public utilities from charging outrageous prices are: (1) government regulation and (2) government ownership.

We have accepted certain instances of monopoly—mainly, local public utility companies. These companies are natural monopolies and provide the public with better and more cheaply priced service than it would get from most competing firms. How can we prevent these public utilities from taking advantage of their power and charging outrageous prices? There are two ways: (1) government regulation and (2) government ownership.

Government Regulation   Suppose Figure 6 represents the market situation of the Rochester Electric Company, which is now regulated by the New York State Public Service Commission.

The commission would have two objectives: a lower price for electricity consumers and a higher output of electricity than we see in Figure 6. To accomplish both ends, the commission would set the price of electricity at about $10.75, which is lower than the current market price of $11.10. How much would output now be? How about total profits?

Using the formula for total profits, we get:

$$\text{Total profits} = (\text{Price} - \text{ATC}) \times \text{Output}$$
$$= (\$10.75 - \$9.30) \times 5.25$$
$$= \$1.45 \times 5.25$$
$$= \$7.61$$

This is illustrated in Figure 6. Consumers now pay a lower price and receive more electricity than they would have under an unregulated monopoly. But this is not a perfect solution because even the regulated natural monopoly does not necessarily produce at the minimum point of its ATC curve.

Government Ownership   The second option for a natural monopoly is government ownership. The post office, the Tennessee Valley Authority, the New York State

Figure 6

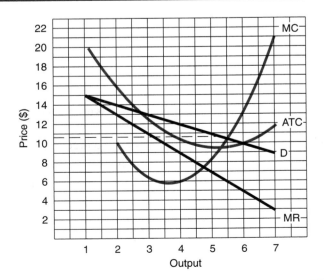

Are government-owned enterprises inefficient?

Power Authority, the New Jersey Transit System, and the Metropolitan Transit Authority of Boston are all examples.

Are these inefficient government boondoggles whose jobs could be better done by private enterprise? Consider the origins of the New Jersey public transportation system. When the private bus lines were unable to operate even with massive public subsidies, the state of New Jersey reluctantly took them over.

The case of the Tennessee Valley Authority (TVA) is even stranger. TVA uses itself as a yardstick with which to measure the costs of power provided by privately owned utilities. The latter complain about "unfair" government competition, and they do have a point because TVA sometimes provides electricity at half the cost of that incurred by privately owned companies.

This is rather interesting when one considers the origins of TVA. Much of rural Tennessee, Arkansas, and Alabama, as well as parts of other states near the Tennessee Valley, were not provided with electricity by private power companies as late as the early 1930s because they were not deemed worthy customers. They were too poor, they lived too far apart, and it was simply not economically feasible to run transmission cables into this part of the country. So TVA, without competing with private companies, went into this area and provided it with electricity at half the going rate.

Let private enterprise do the job— if it can.

The general thrust of public policy in the area of natural monopoly is to let private enterprise do the job but to regulate prices closely. Only as a last resort, when private enterprise is unwilling or unable to do the job, does the government take on the job itself.

Conclusion

Is monopoly good, bad, or indifferent? One fair conclusion is that natural monopoly would be good, if only its power were not abused. But monopolies based on other factors—I refrain from calling them "unnatural monopolies"—must be looked on with suspicion. They may be up to no good, and they also may be illegal.

In a sense, virtually all firms are monopolies. The last gas station before the turnpike entrance, the only bar on your block, and the only grocery in your neighborhood that stays open until midnight are all monopolies. The test they must pass is whether or not there are close substitutes.

Who decides this? The buyers do. If the buyers in your local area think that your store is the only game in town—that no one else even comes close—then you have a monopoly. But let's not get carried away. No one is going to drive 50 miles just to buy your gas, drink your beer, or buy a quart of milk at your store. What you've got is a very local monopoly. You may even be earning an economic profit, but you're not exactly Exxon.

From this discussion we shall make a very neat segue into monopolistic competition, which is the subject of the next chapter. By blending some elements of monopoly and some elements of perfect competition, we will obtain a mixture of firms that we encounter every day in the real world.

Questions for Further Thought and Discussion

1. Are very large firms economically justifiable? What are the pros and cons of bigness?

2. A monopolist can control her price or the quantity she sells, but she can't control both. Explain this statement.

3. Make the case for natural monopolies.

4. Are all monopolies large firms? Make up an example of a monopoly that is a small firm.

5. Is bigness good or bad? Argue both sides of the argument.

WORKBOOK FOR CHAPTER 24

Name _____ Date _____

Multiple-Choice Questions

Circle the letter that corresponds to the best answer.

1. Which statement is true?

   a. All monopolists' products have close substitutes.

   b. Most firms in the United States are monopolies.

   c. There are no monopolies in the United States.

   d. A monopoly is a firm that produces all the output in an industry. e. None of these statements is true.

2. The monopolist is

   a. an imperfect competitor and has a horizontal demand curve b. an imperfect competitor and has a downward sloping demand curve c. a perfect competitor and has a horizontal demand curve

   d. a perfect competitor and has a downward sloping demand curve

3. A downward sloping demand curve means

   a. you have to lower your price to sell more

   b. demand falls as output rises c. demand rises as output rises d. total revenue declines as price is lowered

4. The monopolist's demand and marginal revenue curves

   a. are exactly the same b. are completely different

   c. coincide only at one unit of output d. cross

5. The monopolist produces

   a. where MC equals MR b. at the minimum point of ATC c. at maximum output d. when price is highest

6. If a monopolist has a straight-line demand curve, its marginal revenue curve

   a. will be the same as the demand curve b. will fall twice as quickly as the demand curve c. will lie below the demand curve at all points d. will cross the demand curve

7. Which statement is true?

   a. The monopolist and the perfect competitor both produce where MC equals MR. b. Neither the monopolist nor the perfect competitor produce where MC equals MR. c. The monopolist, but not the perfect competitor, produces where MC equals MR. d. The perfect competitor, but not the monopolist, produces where MC equals MR.

8. Which statement is true about economic profit in the long run?

   a. Both the monopolist and the perfect competitor make one. b. Neither the monopolist nor the perfect competitor makes one. c. Only the perfect competitor makes one. d. Only the monopolist makes one.

9. Which statement is true?

   a. The monopolist cannot lose money. b. The monopolist always operates a large firm. c. The monopolist will not lose money in the short run.

   d. The monopolist will not lose money in the long run.

10. Price is always read off the _____ curve.

   a. MC b. MR c. ATC d. demand

11. The most efficient output is found

   a. where MC and MR cross b. at the bottom of the ATC curve c. when the demand and MR curves are equal d. where the ATC and demand curves cross

12. When the monopolist is losing money

   a. we are in the short run b. we are in the long run c. it is impossible to tell if we are in the short run or the long run d. we have to go back and check our work because monopolists don't lose money

13. The basis for monopoly in the automobile industry would most likely be

    a.   control over an essential resource   b.   economies of scale   c.   legal barriers

14. Which statement is true?

    a.   It is impossible for monopolies to exist in the United States.   b.   Once a monopoly is set up, it is impossible to dislodge it.   c.   Monopolies can be overcome only by market forces.   d.   Monopolies can be overcome only by the government.   e.   None of these statements is true.

15. Which of the following is a natural monopoly?

    a.   the National Football League   b.   a local phone company   c.   DeBeers Diamond Company

    d.   IBM

16. Which statement is true?

    a.   Big business has a great deal of economic power but very little political power.   b.   Big business has a great deal of political power but very little economic power.   c.   Big business has a great deal of economic and political power.   d.   Big business does not have much political or economic power.

17. An example of government ownership of a monopoly is

    a.   the Tennessee Valley Authority   b.   the New York State Public Service Commission

    c.   AT&T   d.   General Motors

18. Who said, "Good organizations should be structured by geniuses so that idiots can run them. Unfortunately, most American organizations are structured by idiots so that it takes a genius to run them"?

    a.   Ichak Adizes   b.   Robert Frost   c.   John Hicks   d.   General Douglas MacArthur

    e.   President Dwight D. Eisenhower

19. The average American CEO pulls down _____ times the earnings of the average worker.

    a.   10 to 15   b.   25 to 40   c.   100 to 120

    d.   400 to 500   e.   1,000 to 1,200

20. Which statement is true?

    a.   The monopolist is just as driven as the competitive firm to control costs and use resources efficiently.

    b.   The monopolist often charges his customers higher prices and provides poorer service than he would if he had competitors.   c.   Growing foreign competition has had no effect on the quality of American products.   d.   None of these statements is true.

Fill-In Questions

1. A monopoly is a firm that produces _____ _____.

2. A monopoly is a firm that has _____ _____ substitutes.

3. The demand curve of an imperfect competitor slopes _____.

4. The monopolist always produces at that output at which _____ is equal to _____.

5. If a firm's demand curve is a straight line sloping downward to the right, its marginal revenue curve will be

    a _____ _____.

6. In the long run the perfect competitor makes _____ profit; in the long run the monopolist makes _____ profit.

7. The four barriers to entering a monopolized industry are

    (1) _____;

    (2) _____;

    (3) _____;

    and (4) _____.

8. There are really only two justifications for monopoly:

   (1) _____

   and (2) _____ .

9. Local gas and electric companies, the phone company, and local cable TV companies are all examples of _____ _____ monopolies.

10. The main economic criticism of monopolies and big business in general is that they are _____ .

11. Economic power is easily translated into _____ _____ .

12. One group of firms that does a lot of business with the government is _____ .

13. President Eisenhower warned us, "Beware of the _____ _____."

14. There are two ways to prevent public utilities from taking advantage of their power: (1)_____ and (2) _____ _____ .

Problems

1. **a.** Fill in Table 1. **b.** Using your own piece of graph paper, draw a graph of the firm's demand, marginal revenue, marginal cost, and average total cost curves. **c.** Calculate the firm's total profit. **d.** If the firm operates at optimum efficiency, how much will its output be? **e.** If the firm were a perfect competitor, how much would its price be in the long run?

Table 1

Output	Price	Total Revenue	Marginal Revenue	Total Cost	ATC	MC
1	$19	____	____	$25	____	____
2	18	____	____	40	____	____
3	17	____	____	50	____	____
4	16	____	____	58	____	____
5	15	____	____	65	____	____
6	14	____	____	74	____	____
7	13	____	____	87	____	____

2. **a.** Fill in Table 2. **b.** Using your own piece of graph paper, draw a graph of the firm's demand, marginal revenue, marginal cost, and average total cost curves. **c.** Calculate the firm's total profit. **d.** If the firm operates at optimum efficiency, how much will its output be? **e.** If the firm were a perfect competitor, how much would its price be in the long run?

Table 2

Output	Price	Total Revenue	Marginal Revenue	Total Cost	ATC	MC
1	$22	____	____	$30	____	____
2	21	____	____	42	____	____
3	20	____	____	51	____	____
4	19	____	____	60	____	____
5	18	____	____	70	____	____
6	17	____	____	82	____	____
7	16	____	____	98	____	____

3. a. Using the data from Figure 1, calculate the firm's total profit. **b.** If the firm operates at optimum efficiency, how much will its output be? **c.** If the firm were a perfect competitor, how much would its price be in the long run?

4. a. Using the data from Figure 2, calculate the firm's total profit. **b.** If the firm operates at optimum efficiency, how much will its output be? **c.** If the firm were a perfect competitor, how much would its price be in the long run?

Figure 1

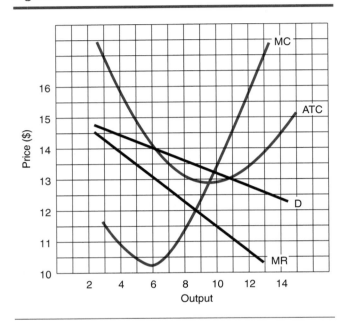

Figure 2

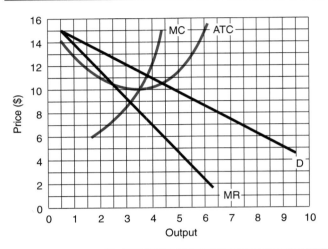

25 Monopolistic Competition

More than 99 percent of the nearly 20 million business firms in the United States are monopolistic competitors. So the least we can do is give them a chapter all to themselves.

Chapter Objectives

When you have completed this chapter you will be familiar with:

- The monopolistic competitor in the short and long runs.
- Product differentiation.
- Price discrimination
- The characteristics of monopolistic competition.

Monopolistic Competition Defined

Definition of monopolistic competition

Monopolistically competitive industry has many firms selling a differentiated product. How many is many? So many that no one firm has any significant influence over price. Although this is our working definition, monopolistic competitors do have some influence over price because their products are differentiated. But it's a *small* influence.

We now encounter a differentiated product for the first time. Notice that the definition of monopolistic competition differs from that of perfect competition only in the element of a differentiated product. You'll remember that under perfect competition, all the sellers sold an identical product.

Why did we say the product was identical? Because none of the buyers differentiated among the products for sale. Each was considered the same: number 2 wheat is number 2 wheat; a large grade A egg is a large grade A egg.

The difference between identical and differentiated

If the buyer doesn't differentiate among the versions of the product sold, the products are identical. If he or she does differentiate, the product is then differentiated. Who determines whether the product is differentiated or identical? The buyer—that's who.

The Monopolistic Competitor in the Short Run

The monopolistic competitor can make a profit or take a loss in short run.

Like the perfect competitor, the monopolistic competitor can make a profit or take a loss in the short run; but in the long run the firm will break even. The reason the monopolistic competitor makes zero economic profits in the long run is the same as that under perfect competition.

In the long run, if firms are losing money, many will leave the industry, lowering industry supply and raising market price. And if, in the long run, firms are realizing substantial profits, new firms will be attracted to the industry, thus raising supply and lowering market price. But we're getting ahead of ourselves.

Figure 1 shows a monopolistic competitor in the short run. Notice how its demand and MR curves slope downward, like those of the monopolist. Theoretically, we may opt for a somewhat more elastic demand curve for the monopolistic competitor than for the monopolist because the latter faces the demand curve for the entire industry. The

Figure 1 Monopolistic Competitor Making a Profit in the Short Run

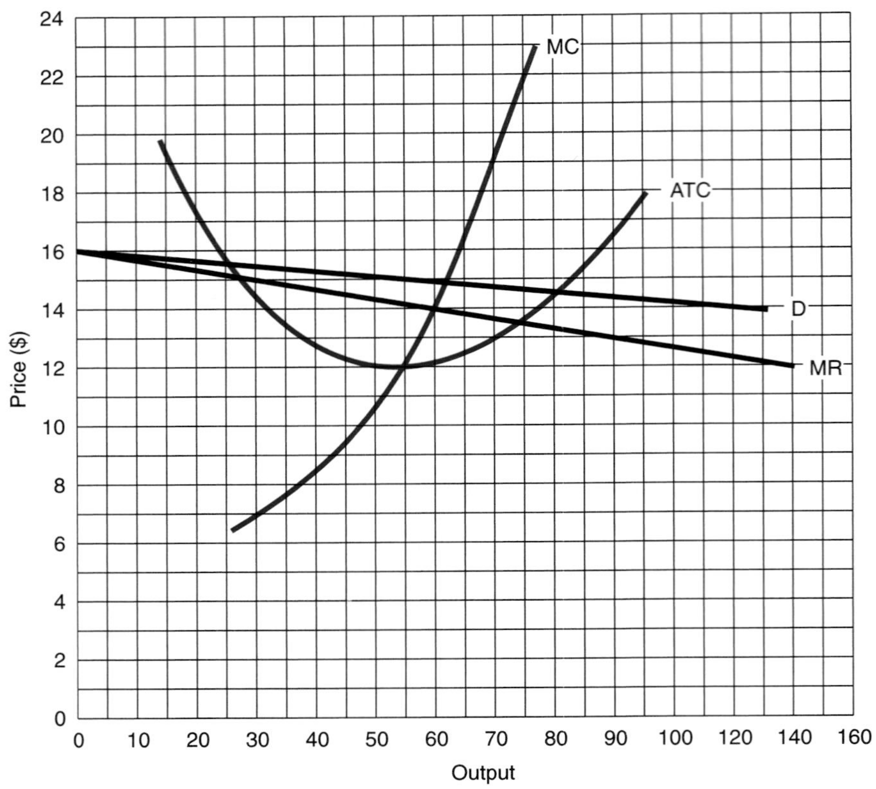

Very elastic demand curve

monopolistic competitor, as only one firm in a crowded industry, must have a very elastic demand curve because there are many close substitutes for the firm's product. In fact, no one can get too far out of line with respect to price because buyers are always ready to purchase substitutes from a rival firm.

Getting back to Figure 1, how much is the firm's output? How much is its price? How much profit does it make? Work it out right here:

First the output. When MC equals MR, output is 60. We find that at an output of 60, the price, which we read off the demand curve, is \$15, and the ATC is \$12.10 or so. Now we can write down our standard equation, substitute, and solve:

$$\begin{aligned}\text{Total profit} &= (\text{Price} - \text{ATC}) \times \text{Output}\\ &= (\$15 - \$12.10) \times 60\\ &= \$2.90 \times 60\\ &= \$174\end{aligned}$$

Now we're ready for Figure 2, which also shows the monopolistic competitor in the short run. How much is output? Is the firm making a profit or taking a loss? How much is it?

Figure 2   Monopolistic Competitor Taking a Loss in the Short Run

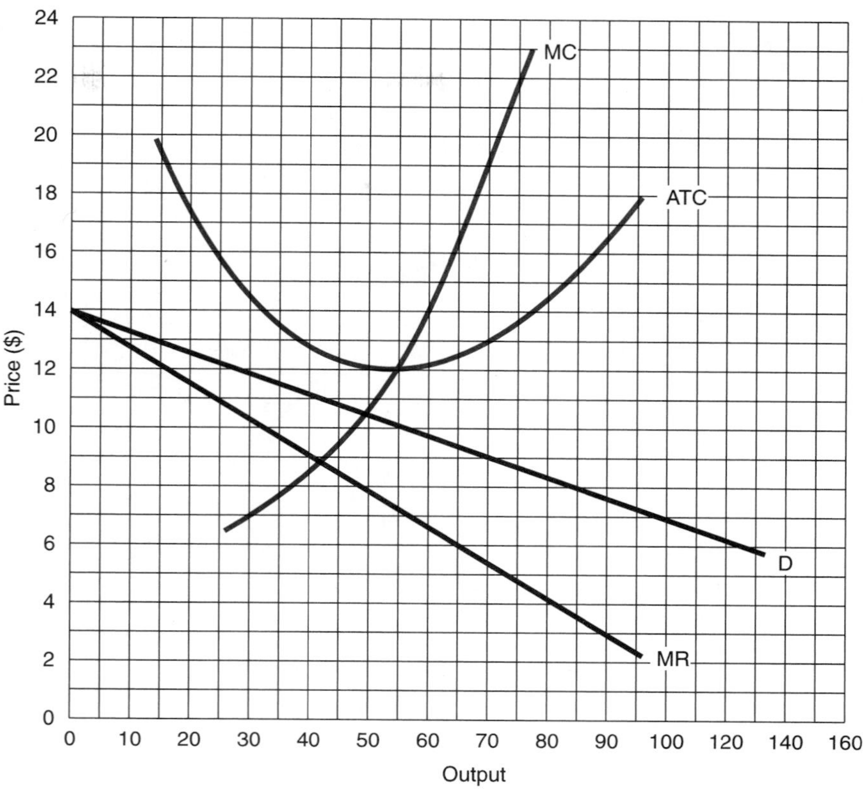

$$\text{Total profit} = (\text{Price} - \text{ATC}) \times \text{Output}$$

$$= (\$11 - \$12.80) \times 42$$

$$= -\$1.80 \times 42$$

$$= -\$75.60$$

I'm not above admitting that even *I* cannot read my *own* graphs with any greater precision than the average reader. So, if your price, output, ATC, and, consequently, loss are a little different from mine—no problem. I'll accept any loss that's within the range of, say, $70 to $80.

The Monopolistic Competitor in the Long Run

The monopolistic competitor makes zero economic profits in the long run.

As I said earlier, in the long run the monopolistic competitor makes zero economic profits. If there are short-run profits, more firms will enter the industry, driving down market price and profits. If there are losses, some firms will leave the industry, pushing up market price and reducing losses.

Figure 3 is a model of the monopolistic competitor in the long run. Notice how the point at which the MC and MR curves cross is directly below the price. Output is 40, and price is $12.25. Notice also that price is equal to ATC at that output.

Were the firm to produce at any other output, what would happen to its profits? I'm sure you figured out that they would be losses. At any other output, the demand curve lies below the ATC curve, so price is less than ATC.

Notice that the price in Figure 3 is higher than the minimum point of the ATC curve. This means that in the long run price is higher under monopolistic competition than it is under perfect competition.

Figure 3   Monopolistic Competitor Breaking Even in the Long Run

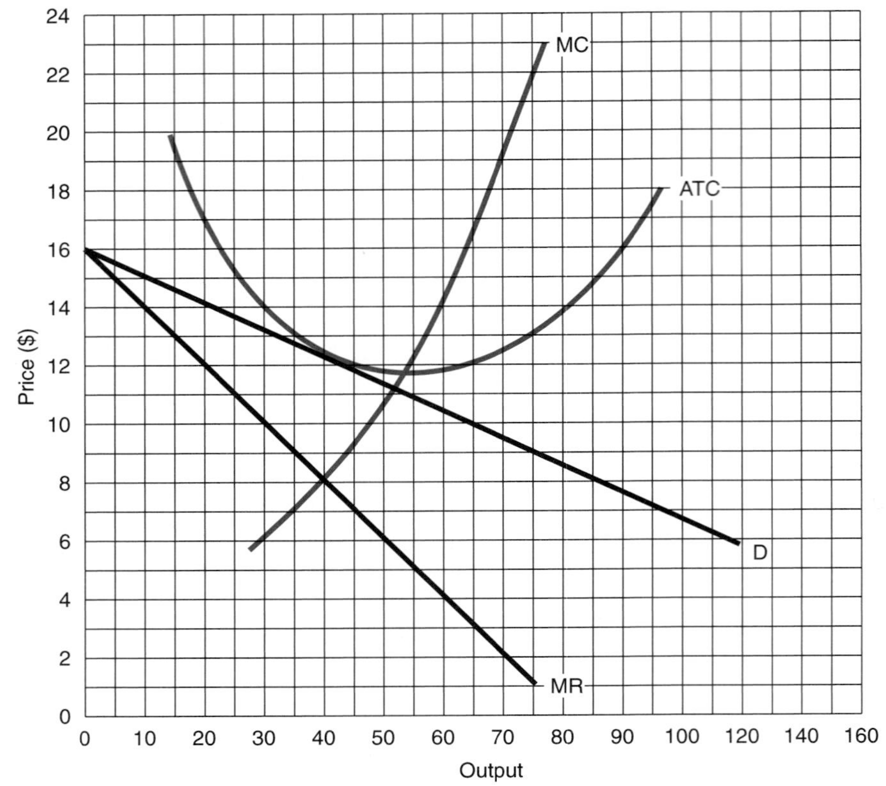

Who is more efficient: the perfect competitor or the monopolistic competitor?

What about output? Again, because the monopolistic competitor produces to the left of the minimum point of its ATC curve, output is lower than it is under perfect competition.

Finally, we have efficiency. Who is more efficient: the monopolistic competitor or the perfect competitor? There is one test for efficiency: What is your ATC? Because the perfect competitor produces at the minimum point of its ATC curve and the monopolistic competitor does not, clearly the perfect competitor is more efficient.

To sum up, both the monopolistic competitor and the perfect competitor make zero economic profits in the long run. The monopolistic competitor charges a higher price and has a lower output than the perfect competitor. And the perfect competitor is a more efficient producer than is the monopolistic competitor.

I'm going to make a confession now that may shake you up a little. The graphs drawn in Figures 1, 2, and 3 have demand curves that really should not be as inelastic as they appear. Nearly all economics textbook writers are guilty of this sin, so I didn't want to be left out. You'll probably be able to get through the rest of your life without being asked why these demand curves should be flatter, or more elastic. In the box "Who's Got the Flatter Demand Curve?" I plead guilty of drawing demand curves of insufficient elasticity, but I *do* have an explanation.

Product Differentiation

The crucial factor is product differentiation.

Product differentiation is crucial to monopolistic competition. In fact, the product differentiation is really what stands between perfect competition and the real world. People differentiate among many similar products.

What makes one good or service differ from another? We need only for the buyer to believe there's a difference, because product differentiation takes place in the buyer's mind. What's the difference between a Buick Electra and a Chrysler Imperial—besides

ADVANCED WORK

Who's Got the Flatter Demand Curve?

Whose demand curve is flatter, the monopolistic competitor's or the monopolist's? Because the monopolist faces the industry's entire demand curve, its demand curve is less flat, or more inelastic, than that of the monopolistic competitor, which is one of many competing firms. Under monopolistic competition, even small price increases will drive many customers to rival firms.

In terms of elasticity, it is fair to say that the monopolistic competitor faces a more elastic, or flatter, demand curve than does the monopolist. But this difference in elasticity would not be apparent if you were to compare the graphs in this chapter with those in the previous chapter. For analytic purposes, I made the demand curves for the monopolistic competitor steeper, or more inelastic, than I should have. I wanted to be sure that these graphs looked notably different from those of the perfect competitor. But in the real world, in which nearly all firms happen to be monopolistic competitors, each firm's demand curve would be nearly horizontal. Such a demand curve is shown in the figure here.

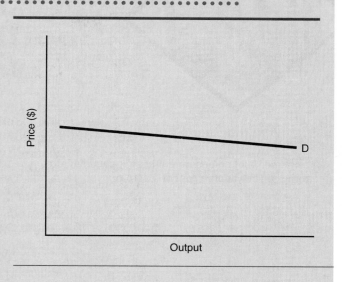

$8,000? There is absolutely no difference between these two cars *if* the buyer sees no difference. Suppose someone is given the choice and says, "I don't care. They're both the same to me." To this buyer, the cars are identical. One is longer, maybe; one has nicer upholstery.

In the real world, however, buyers generally do differentiate. "I like the refreshing taste of Kools." "I'm a man, so I smoke Chesterfields, even though they're killing my throat." "I'm a modern woman [in contradistinction to an ancient woman], so I smoke Virginia Slims." "I'm a modern man, so I smoke Virginia Slims." Huh?

Americans are provided with a wide array of shampoos, breakfast cereals, candy bars, facial and bath soaps, soft drinks, ballpoint pens, and thousands of other consumer goods. Similarly, we can choose from among huge numbers of lawyers, accountants, physical therapists, chiropractors, advertising agencies, public relations firms, service stations, and restaurants. People living in other countries rarely get to make all the consumer choices that Americans are called upon to make and consequently do not engage in nearly as much product differentiation as American consumers do.

We're always differentiating.

We're always differentiating, and our basis doesn't have to be taste, smell, size, or even any physical differences among the products. Two CD shops might carry the same poor excuse that passes for music these days—it can only be played loud, so those young people suffering from hearing loss can still pick up some of the sounds. Both shops charge exactly the same prices. Both shops are conveniently located. But one is always crowded and the other is always empty.

Why? Ambience. Perhaps one place lets you play a CD before you buy it. Perhaps one place will take special orders for you. Perhaps the salesclerks and owners are nice, helpful people, while in the other store they're all grouches.

Now we're dealing with a differentiated product. The CDs are the same. The prices are the same. But one store's got ambience up to here, and the other has to send out for it. The buyer prefers Mr. Nice Guy's store over the grouch's store, so we have a differentiated product.

When sellers try to get buyers to differentiate between their products and those of competitors, the sellers do so based on more than physical differences between their product and other versions of it. Also used are convenience, ambience, reputations of the sellers, and appeals to your vanity, unconscious fears, and desires, as well as snob appeal.

The Typical Monopolistic Competitor

Nearly all business firms in the United States are monopolistic competitors. They are monopolistic rather than perfect competitors. They are monopolistic rather than perfect competitors because, in the mind of the buyer, their products are differentiated from one another. The monopolistic element is the uniqueness of each seller.

You walk into your neighborhood tavern. By the time you have bellied up to the bar, your drink is waiting for you. OK, so it's only a Diet Coke with a twist of lemon. It's the thought that counts. The bartender, by silently placing your usual in front of your spot at the bar has announced, "This woman is one of my regulars. She doesn't even have to say anything. I know what she drinks, and I know where she likes to sit."

The bartender has accorded you a certain status, a sense of belonging. It's something the perfect competitor can't provide, unless, of course, *all* bars happen to do this. Walk into a strange bar and see whether the bartender puts a drink down in front of you before you've ordered. If this happens—*and* if it's what you always order—then that drink's on me.

The monopolistic competitor tries to set his or her product apart from the competition.

Each monopolistic competitor attempts to set his or her firm apart from the competition. The main way of doing this is through advertising. As we saw in the "Demand" chapter, when this is done successfully, the demand curve faced by the monopolistic competitor becomes more vertical or inelastic. Buyers are willing to pay more for this product because they believe it's wonderful. Or they'll undergo acts of great physical endurance: "I'd walk a mile for a Camel."

Typical monopolistic competitors are beauty parlors and barbershops, grocery stores, drugstores, restaurants and fast-food emporiums, gas stations, dry cleaners and laundries, (small) accounting and law firms, doctors, dentists, electricians, plumbers, and all the other small businesses you'd see along any Main Street, USA. Each has many competitors, and each produces a differentiated product.

Think of all the 7-Elevens, diners, coffee shops, greasy spoons, beauty parlors and barbershops, mom-and-pop groceries and general stores, bars, hamburger joints, and millions of other tiny retail stores where people spend time eating, drinking, getting groomed, or picking up a couple of everyday household items. Most of them dispense one thing, and you won't find it on the menu. It's local gossip. People stop by in the morning with last night's news, and later that afternoon they come to pick up that day's latest scoop. If you lived in a small town, where would *you* rather do business?

You eat in one luncheonette rather than any of the others because the counterman talks to you while you're having lunch or the waitress keeps your coffee cup filled. You prefer one grocery because they'll take your order over the phone. You'd rather shop in a particular drugstore because it has a much more cheerful atmosphere than all the other drugstores in town.

Why do business at one store rather than at its competitors?

Ambience, cleanliness, personal attention, convenience of location, easy credit, free delivery service, and good service in general are all reasons why buyers might shop at one store rather than at its competitors. Thus product differentiation does not necessarily mean there are any physical differences among the products. They might all be the same, but how they're sold may make all the difference.

On the other hand, there are, of course, some very real physical product differences. Different brands of orange juice, beer, cigars, ice cream, and hamburgers *do* taste different and *are* different in physical composition. Buyers often differentiate based on real physical differences among products. But differentiation takes place only in the buyer's mind, and it may or may not be based on real physical differences.

Price Discrimination

Price discrimination sounds like a terrible thing, something that violates our basic constitutional rights. Sometimes it's bad, and other times it's not bad at all. In fact, price discrimination is often a disguised subsidy to the poor.

Price discrimination occurs when a seller charges two or more prices for the same good or service. Doctors often charge rich patients 10 times what they charge poor patients for the same service. Airlines sometimes allow riders under 16 years of age to fly for half the regular fair ("youthfare").

The most notorious example of price discrimination was probably that of A&P markets during the 1940s. A&P had three grades of canned goods: A, B, and C. Grade A was presumably of the highest quality, B was fairly good, and C was—well, C was edible. My mother told me that she always bought grade A, even though it was the most expensive. Nothing but the best for our family.

Our family was friendly with another family in the neighborhood. The husband, a man in his early 50s, found out he had stomach cancer. "Aha!" exclaimed my mother, "Mrs. S. always bought grade C!"

A few years later the Federal Trade Commission (FTC) prohibited A&P from selling grades A, B, and C. The FTC didn't do this because of Mr. S.'s stomach cancer, but because there was absolutely no difference among the grades.

Why had A&P concocted this elaborate subterfuge? Because it was worth tens of millions of dollars in profits! Consider a can of green peas that had the demand schedule in Table 1.

To keep things simple, suppose A&P had a constant ATC of 20 cents a can. How much should it charge? To figure this out, add a total cost column to Table 1 and then a total profit column. Now figure out the total profits at prices of 50 cents, 40 cents, and 30 cents, respectively.

In Table 2 these calculations are worked out. If A&P could charge only one price, it would be 50 cents; total profit would be $30. Now let's see how much profit would be if A&P were able to charge three different prices.

At 50 cents, A&P would be able to sell 100 cans. These are sold to the people who won't buy anything if it isn't grade A. Then there are those who would like to buy grade A but just can't afford it. These people buy 40 cans of grade B. Finally, we have the poor, who can afford only grade C; they buy 30 cans.

All this is worked out in Table 3. Total revenue now is $75 for the 170 cans sold, and total cost of 170 cans remains $34. This gives A&P a total profit of $41.

Why is total profit so much greater under price discrimination ($41) than it is under a single price ($30)?[1] Because the seller is able to capture some or all of the consumer surplus. (Consumer surplus was covered in the "Demand" chapter.) People are willing to buy 100 cans at 50 cents, 40 more at 40 cents, and another 30 at 30 cents. But the people who buy only grade A will buy *all* their cans of green peas at that price, while those buying

---

[1]Total profit would be $30 at 50 cents; it would be $28 at 40 cents; it would be $17 at 30 cents.

Table 1   Hypothetical Demand Schedule for Canned Peas

Price	Quantity Demanded	Total Revenue
$.50	100	$50
.40	140	56
.30	170	51

Table 2   Hypothetical Demand Schedule for Canned Peas

Price	Total Revenue	Total Cost	Total Profit
$.50	$50	$20	$30
.40	56	28	28
.30	51	34	17

Table 3   Hypothetical Demand Schedule for Canned Peas, by Grades

Grade	Price	Quantity Demanded	Total Revenue	Total Cost	Total Profit
A	$.50	100	$50	$20	$30
B	.40	40	16	8	8
C	.30	30	9	6	3
			$75	$34	$41

grade B will buy all their peas at 40 cents and grade C buyers will buy all their peas at 30 cents. By keeping its markets separate rather than charging a single price, A&P was able to make much larger profits.

The firm that practices price discrimination needs to be able to distinguish between two or more separate groups of buyers. The doctor clearly does this when he or she sizes up the patient's ability to pay, so when you go to the doctor, wear your most raggedy clothes, ask whether food stamps are accepted, and be sure to say you're a college student.

To practice price discrimination, you need to be able to (1) distinguish between at least two sets of buyers and (2) prevent one set of buyers from reselling the product to another set.

In addition to distinguishing among separate groups of buyers, the price discriminator must be able to prevent buyers from reselling the product (i.e., stop those who buy at a low price from selling to those who would otherwise buy at a higher price).[2] If the 15-and-a-half-year-old buys an airline ticket at half fare and resells it to someone who is 35 years old, the airline loses money. Most 15-and-a-half-year-olds don't have lots of money, so the special fare is a way of filling an otherwise empty seat; but when the 35-year-old flies half-fare and would have been willing to pay full fare, the airline loses money. In the case of A&P, there was no problem preventing the grade C customers from reselling their food to the grade A customers because shoppers voluntarily separated themselves into these markets.

Price discrimination is woven into our economic fabric, and in most cases it is basically a mechanism for rationing scarce goods and services. For example, because nearly everyone seems to want to go to the movies at eight on Saturday night, the theaters encourage moviegoers to see films at other times by charging considerably less. But the main motivation for price discrimination is, of course, to raise profits. If price discrimination were carried to its logical conclusion, we would have perfect price discrimination (see box).

Is the Monopolistic Competitor Inefficient?

It appears from our analysis of the long-run position of the monopolistic competitor in Figure 3 that the firm does not produce at the minimum point of its ATC curve. Economists criticize monopolistic competition as wasteful on two counts: too many firms in the industry and overdifferentiation.

Are there too many firms in monopolistically competitive industries?

Are there too many beauty parlors? Not if you want to get your hair done on Friday or Saturday afternoon. Too many gas stations? Not when there are gas lines. Too many Chinese restaurants? Not on Sundays. Are there too many grocery stores and too many real estate offices? Only when they're not busy. But most business firms, which apparently carry excess capacity during certain times of the day or the week, are set up to handle peak loads, so there aren't necessarily too many monopolistic competitors.

With respect to the second criticism, is there really overdifferentiation? Perhaps there don't seem to be substantial differences among grocery stores, drugstores, luncheonettes, dry cleaners, and ice-cream parlors, but consider the alternative. Consider the drab monotony of the stores in much of Eastern Europe, including the old Soviet Union. Maybe

---

[2]Remember when you passed your 12th birthday and could no longer get into the movies at the children's price? Did you ever get a younger-looking kid to buy your ticket for you and try to pass yourself off as under 12 to the ticket taker? What? You *still* do it?

ADVANCED WORK

Perfect Price Discrimination

If price discrimination were carried to its logical conclusion, we would have perfect price discrimination. Every buyer in the market would lose his or her entire consumer surplus in the process.

Let's review the definition of consumer surplus, which was discussed in the "Demand" chapter: *Consumer surplus is the difference between what you pay for some good or service and what you would have been willing to pay.* We'll start with a very simple situation. Amanda is willing to pay $30 for a pair of jeans, and Kristin is willing to pay $25. If the seller were to charge $20, then Amanda would enjoy a consumer surplus of $10 and Kristin would enjoy one of $5. But if the seller *knew* how much each woman was willing to pay for a pair of jeans, and if the seller were able to tell Amanda that the price was $30 and tell Kristin separately that the price was $25, he would completely eliminate their consumer surpluses.

Now we'll add another wrinkle. Suppose Amanda is willing to pay $30 for the first pair of jeans and $20 for the second. And suppose Kristin is willing to pay $25 for the first pair and $15 for the second. If the seller knew this and was able to take advantage of this information, he would charge Amanda $30 for the first pair and $20 for the second. And Kristin would be charged $25 for the first pair and $15 for the second.

Now we'll wind things up. Imagine there are 20 buyers in the market for jeans. The seller has somehow found out exactly how much each pair of jeans is worth to each of the buyers. By charging them *exactly* those prices, he will have managed to carry out perfect price discrimination. Of course, it would be virtually impossible to carry out price discrimination on such a large scale. But when you think about all those ridiculous sets of rules the airlines set up—tickets must be purchased 7 or 14 or 21 days in advance, no refunds, no changes, and you've got to stay over for at least one Saturday night—what they're really trying to do is squeeze out as much of their customers' consumer surpluses as they can.

this lack of differentiation, this standardization, enables the sellers to cut costs somewhat. But is it worth it?

What are you really buying when you go to a fancy restaurant? Surely not just a meal. Undoubtedly you'll order something on a somewhat higher culinary plane than a Big Mac, large fries, and a Coke, but is that meal worth $80? It is when it is served by a waiter with a phony French accent, there are flowers on your table, nice linen tablecloths, candlelight, soft music, and a solicitous maitre d', plus the restaurant is a restored 18th-century carriage house. (See the box titled "Selling Status.")

Is monopolistic competition wasteful and inefficient?

Monopolistic competition, with its attendant product differentiation, may be viewed as wasteful and inefficient, and a case can easily be made that it is. Think of all the money spent on advertising, packaging, marketing, and sales promotion, as well as interiors, facades, and window displays. These expenses add perhaps 10 or 20 percent to the prices of most things we buy; so we may well ask, Is it worth it? You decide.

I'll bet you're saying to yourself, "There he goes again, copping out and passing the buck." And you're right. You see, the buck stops with you because it's *your* buck and it's *your* decision about how to spend it.

Do you want to spend it on advertising, ambience, service, and convenience, or are you basically a no-frills person? Do you usually buy no-frills brands in the supermarket, fly coach rather than first-class, drive an economy car, and consider dinner in a fast-food emporium "eating out"? If you have answered yes to each of these questions, you are indeed a no-frills person who knows the value of a dollar.

Can you imagine a no-frills world?

On the other hand, if you answered no to all of the above, you are clearly a person of refined taste and high style—a very au courant person (that's French for "up-to-date"). Whether we like it or not, product differentiation is the way monopolistic competitors compete. And whether we're aware of it or not, our entire environment is flavored by product differentiation. Imagine that next December every commercial Christmas display is done in black and white. Imagine what our supermarkets would look like with all black-and-white boxes, jars, and cans. And imagine what people would look like if they all wore the same styles and colors. In a word, product differentiation adds flavor, texture, and variety to our lives. Whether we want to pay the price is a matter of individual taste.

Finally, let's consider the nature of competition. Monopolistic competitors *do* compete with respect to price, but they compete still more vigorously with respect to

Selling Status

Have you ever thought about opening a restaurant? Restaurants are getting to be pretty complicated places considering that local laws usually dictate that you segregate your diners by smoking preference (pro or con). Why not segregate *your* diners by status?

That's *right!* We've got a table for two in our low-status section. What's that? Oh, there's a 15-minute wait for a high-status table. What's the difference? Well, if you need to ask, then you probably *belong* in the low-status section.

Do the high-status diners get better food? No, the food's the same. And the service? The same. Then what *is* the difference? Price. That's right—we charge twice as much for the same food and service in the high-status section as in the low-status section.

How can we get away with that? It's easy. Everyone knows who's in which section. We know the cheapos and the big spenders, the tightwads and the sports.

Why are people willing to pay twice as much for the same food and the same service? They're paying for status. And by selling status, you can really boost your profits. So go ahead and open your restaurant. And save a nice table for me. In which section? I'll give you three guesses.

ambience, service, and the rest of the intangibles that attract customers. In this arena American business does engage in lively, innovative competition. The next time you're walking along a shopping street, take note of how the storekeepers try to entice you with their window displays. To the degree that they're successful, they have induced you to differentiate their products from all the others. That is what monopolistic competition is all about.

Questions for Further Thought and Discussion

1. In what respects does a monopolistic competitor differ from a perfect competitor?
2. Explain why the monopolistic competitor breaks even in the long run.
3. Is the monopolistic competitor inefficient? Try to argue the question from both sides.
4. What are the two necessary conditions under which price discrimination can take place? Give an example of price discrimination.

WORKBOOK FOR CHAPTER 25

Name _____   Date _____

Multiple-Choice Questions

Circle the letter that corresponds to the best answer.

1. Monopolistic competition differs from perfect
    competition only with respect to
    a. the number of firms in the industry   b. product
    differentiation   c. barriers to entry   d. economies
    of scale

Figure 1

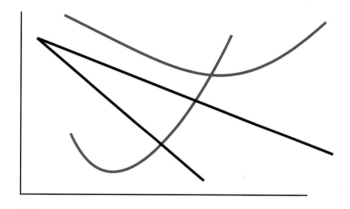

2. In the long run the monopolistic competitor in Figure 1 is
    a. more efficient than the perfect competitor
    b. less efficient than the perfect competitor
    c. as efficient as the perfect competitor

3. In the short run the monopolistic competitor will be
    a. definitely making a profit   b. definitely taking a
    loss   c. definitely breaking even   d. either taking
    a loss or making a profit

4. In the long run the monopolistic competitor will be
    a. making a profit   b. taking a loss   c. breaking
    even

5. The demand curve of a monopolistic competitor is
    a. flatter than that of the perfect competitor and steeper
    than that of the monopolist   b. flatter than that of the
    monopolist and steeper than that of the perfect competitor
    c. identical to the perfect competitor's demand curve
    d. identical to the monopolistic competitor's marginal
    revenue curve

6. Product differentiation can take place
    a. only if there are physical differences among the
    products   b. only if there are no physical differences
    among the products   c. whether or not there are
    physical differences among the products

7. Which statement is true?
    a. When you decide which doctor to go to, your only
    concern is the quality of the medical service you will
    receive.   b. People differentiate among goods and
    services based not only on physical differences but also
    on ambience, convenience, and service.
    c. Monopolistic competitors are usually large firms.
    d. None of these statements is true.

8. Which of the following would not be a monopolistic
    competitor?
    a. Joe's barbershop   b. a mom-and-pop grocery
    store   c. a storefront lawyer   d. a restaurant
    e. all are monopolistic competitors

9. Which statement about price discrimination is true?
    a. It generally hurts the poor.   b. It is inherently
    evil.   c. It involves charging at least two separate
    prices for the same good or service.   d. It generally
    involves deceiving the consumer.

10. Each of the following is an example of price
    discrimination except
    a. Airline "youthfares"   b. higher-priced movie
    tickets after 5:00 P.M. and on weekends   c. doctors
    charging more to patients who need lab tests
    d. A&P's old grades A, B, and C

11. In the long run in monopolistic competition
    a. most firms make a profit   b. the absence of entry
    barriers ensures that there are no profits
    c. economies of scale ensure that there are no profits
    d. most firms lose money

12. Which statement is true?
    a. Most firms in the United States are monopolistic
    competitors.   b. Most firms in the United States are

perfect competitors.   **c.**   Most consumers would prefer lower prices and less product differentiation.

d.   None of these statements is true.

13. Perfect price discrimination eliminates _____ of the customer's consumer surplus.

    a.   all   **b.**   most   **c.**   some   **d.**   none

14. Which statement is true about perfect price discrimination?

    a.   It is very common.   **b.**   It is illegal   **c.**   The larger the market, the more likely one is to find it.

    d.   None of these statements is true.

15. Price discrimination

    a.   often works to the advantage of the poor

    b.   generally helps rich customers.   **c.**   is very hard to find in the United States   **d.**   is illegal in the United States

16. Under perfect price discrimination

    a.   consumer surplus is zero   **b.**   consumer surplus is maximized   **c.**   consumer surplus is a constant no matter what price is charged   **d.**   consumer surplus rises as price is lowered

17. Statement 1: Monopolistic competitors are usually very large companies.

    Statement 2: Nearly half of all business firms in the United States are monopolistic competitors.

    a.   Statement 1 is true and statement 2 is false.

    b.   Statement 2 is true and statement 1 is false.

    c.   Both statements are true.   **d.**   Both statements are false.

Fill-In Questions

1. A monopolistically competitive industry has

   _____ firms producing a _____

   _____ product.

2. The most crucial feature of monopolistic competition is

   _____.

3. The monopolistic competitor gets people to buy his or her product by providing better

   (1) _____;

   (2) _____;

   and (3) _____.

4. A monopolistic competitor makes a profit only in the

   _____.

5. The monopolistic competitor's demand curve slopes

   _____.

6. Price discrimination occurs when a seller charges _____

   _____ for the same good or service.

7. The reason A&P sold grades A, B, and C of the same product was to _____.

8. The firm that practices price discrimination needs to be able to distinguish _____

   _____; the seller also must be able to

   prevent _____.

9. The monopolistic competitor _____

   produces at the minimum point of his or her ATC curve.

Problems

1. Given the information in Figure 2, how much profit does this monopolistic competitor make?

2. Is the firm in Figure 2 operating in the short run or the long run? How do you know?

3. Draw a graph of a monopolistic competitor in the long run on a piece of graph paper.

Figure 2

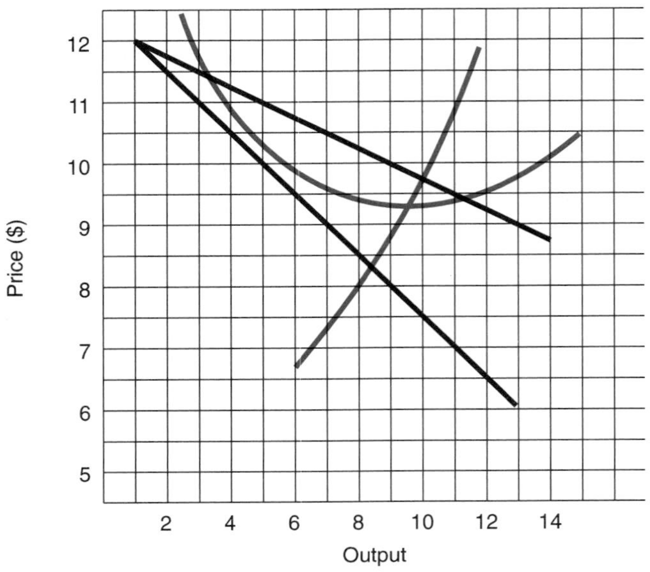

26 Oligopoly

The prefix *oli,* contrary to popular opinion, does not stand for Colonel Oliver North. It means "few." An oligarchy is a government controlled by only a few rulers. An oligopoly is an industry controlled by only a few firms.

Chapter Objectives

In this chapter we'll cover these topics:

- Concentration ratios.
- The Herfindahl–Hirschman index.
- The competitive spectrum.

Oligopoly Defined

An oligopoly is an industry with just a few sellers.

An oligopoly is *an industry with just a few sellers.* How few? So few that at least one firm is large enough to influence price.

Oligopoly is the prevalent type of industrial competition in the United States as well as in most of the noncommunist industrial West. Table 1 lists some of the more important American industries that are oligopolies. In terms of production, the vast majority of our GDP is accounted for by firms in oligopolistic industries.

Is product identical or differentiated?

Is the product identical or differentiated? It doesn't matter. In the case of the steel, copper, and aluminum industries, the product happens to be identical; but in most other cases, the product is differentiated.

The crucial factor under oligopoly is the small number of firms in the industry. Because there are so few firms, every competitor must think continually about the actions of its rivals. What each does could make or break the others. Thus there is a kind of interdependence among oligopolists.

In 1953 Charles Wilson, then secretary of defense in President Eisenhower's cabinet and former president of General Motors, made this statement to a congressional committee: "For years I thought what was good for our country was good for General Motors, and vice versa." Although this seemingly innocuous statement offended many people, Wilson was merely pointing out the economic importance of his former employer.

Big business is oligopoly.

General Motors has been our country's largest or second-largest industrial company for more than five decades, producing over half of all American-made cars. The company typifies American business. When we talk about big business in the United States, we're talking about oligopolies such as GM, Ford, Exxon, Mobil, IBM, Xerox, Boeing, and all the other industrial giants that have become household names.

Because the graph of the oligopolist is similar to that of the monopolist, we will analyze it in exactly the same manner with respect to price, output, profit, and efficiency. Price is higher than the minimum point of the ATC curve, and output is somewhat to the left of this point. And so, just like the monopolist, the oligopolist has a higher price and a lower output than does the perfect competitor.

The oligopolist, like the monopolist and unlike the perfect competitor, makes a profit. With respect to efficiency, because the oligopolist does not produce at the minimum point of its ATC curve, it is not as efficient as the perfect competitor.

We're going to consider a whole range of oligopolistic models, from close collusion to cutthroat competition. Each type, theoretically, has its own graph, but we'll only do the graphs of the two extreme cases (Figure 2, a few pages ahead, and Figure A-7 in the appendix to the chapter). First, however, we'll look at concentration ratios and the Herfindahl–Hirschman index, two measures of the degree of oligopoly in various industries.

Two Measures of the Degree of Oligopolization

Looking at the percentage share of sales of the leading firms is one way of measuring how concentrated an industry is. This is called the industry's concentration ratio. A second way to measure this is to calculate the Herfindahl-Hirschman index, which, it turns out, is a lot easier to do than to say.

Concentration Ratios

The total percentage share of industry sales of the four leading firms is the industry concentration ratio.

Economists use concentration ratios as a quantitative measure of oligopoly. *The total percentage share of industry sales of the four leading firms is the industry concentration ratio.* Industries with high ratios are very oligopolistic.

How much is the concentration ratio for an industry whose four largest firms produce, respectively, 10, 8, 7, and 5 percent of the industry's output? Work it out right here:

Just add them together to get 30.

The concentration ratios in Table 1 range from 85 in office typewriters, canned soup, and tires and tubes to 99 in disposable diapers and 100 in tennis balls and instant breakfasts. In the last two industries the entire output is produced by no more than four firms. Remember that the concentration ratio is the total percentage share of industry sales of the four leading firms. As you'll observe in Table 1, the four leading firms in tennis balls are PepsiCo, General Corp., Spalding, and Dunlop. But only three firms in instant breakfasts—Carnation, Pillsbury, and Dean Foods—produce the entire industry output.

Two key shortcomings

Two key shortcomings of concentration ratios should be noted. First, they don't include imports. For example, in the auto industry (not shown in Table 1, with a concentra-

Table 1   Concentration Ratios in Selected Industries

Product	Largest Firms	Concentration Ratio
Instant breakfast	Carnation, Pillsbury, Dean Foods	100
Tennis balls	PepsiCo, General Corp., Spalding, Dunlop	100
Disposable diapers	Procter & Gamble, Kimberly-Clark, Curity, Romar Tissue Mills	99
Telephone service	AT&T, General Telephone and Electronics, United Telecommunications, Continental Telephone	98
Razor blades	Gillette, Warner-Lambert, Procter & Gamble, Philip Morris	98
Cameras and film	Eastman Kodak, Polaroid, Bell & Howell, Berkey Photo	98
Chewing gum	Wm. Wrigley, Warner-Lambert, Squibb, Philip Morris	97
Electric razors	Norelco, Remington, Warner-Lambert, Sunbeam	96
Telephones	Western Electric, General Telephone, United Telecommunications, Continental Telephone	95
Car rentals	Hertz, Avis, National, Budget	94
Cigarettes	Philip Morris, RJR Nabisco, Brown & Williamson, Lorillard	93
Photocopiers	Xerox, Minnesota Mining & Manufacturing (3M), SCM, Addresso-Multigraph	90
Breakfast cereals	Kellogg, General Mills, General Foods, Quaker Oats	87

tion ratio of 76), foreign cars account for about one-third of the American market. Although Honda is listed among the top four American automakers, the concentration ratio does not take into account the 2 million Japanese imports, not to mention the hundreds of thousands of Volkswagens, Saabs, BMWs, Audis, Jaguars, Porsches, and Rolls Royces the United States also imports.

Concentration ratios have become less meaningful as foreign imports have increased. For instance, we get 80 percent of our consumer electronics and 53 percent of our oil from abroad, so concentration ratios in these industries are meaningless. Perhaps in a world with unrestricted international trade, which would make our world a veritable global village, we could replace national concentration ratios with international concentration ratios. In the meantime we'll go with what we have in Table 1.

The second shortcoming is that the concentration ratios tell us nothing about the competitive structure of the rest of the industry. Are the remaining firms all relatively large, as in the cigarette industry, which has a total of just 13 firms, or are they small, as in the aircraft and engine parts industry, which totals about 190 firms? This distinction is important because when the remaining firms are large, they are not as easily dominated by the top four as are dozens of relatively small firms.

The American automobile industry, which was long a classic example of oligopoly, has been changing drastically in recent years (see box "Oligopoly in the Automobile Industry"). Not only have imports made a substantial impact, but now six Japanese carmakers have set up operations in *this* country. The imports have made the automobile industry's concentration ratio much less relevant, while the transplants have been reducing that ratio. But these developments have been an unmitigated boon to the car buyer, who is reaping the benefits of lower prices and much higher quality.

The Herfindahl–Hirschman Index (HHI)

The Herfindahl–Hirschman index is the sum of the squares of the market shares of each firm in the industry.

The Herfindahl–Hirschman index (HHI) is *the sum of the squares of the market shares of each firm in the industry.* We'll start with a monopoly. One firm has all the sales, or 100 percent of the market share. So its HHI would be 100^2, or $100 \times 100 = 10,000$.

Oligopoly in the Automobile Industry

The automobile industry has long been considered the archetypal American oligopoly. Until the arrival of Volkswagen in Pennsylvania (which closed up shop in 1988), followed by the six Japanese "transplants," the entire industry consisted of just four firms. More than 95 percent of our cars were made by the Big Three—General Motors, Ford, and Chrysler—and the rest by American Motors, which has since merged with Chrysler. So until very recently the American automobile industry had a concentration ratio of 100.

But there were two major changes during the last two decades. The first was set off by the gasoline shortages we had in 1973 (the Arab oil embargo) and 1979 (the Iranian Revolution). The higher gas prices that followed made fuel-efficient cars—particularly Japanese cars—much more attractive to the American buyer. Imports, which had been limited to just 10 percent of the market, shot up to about 30 percent by the mid-1980s.

Of equal long-run significance to the industry has been the advent of the Japanese transplants, which began setting up assembly lines during the 1980s. Today these firms assemble three out of every ten American cars, and before long, when we talk about the Big Three, their names will be GM, Ford, and Honda.

The table below shows cars and trucks made in the United States during January 1998.

Company	Number of U.S.-Made Cars and Trucks
General Motors	288,398
Ford	257,999
Chrysler	148,202
Honda	57,551
Toyota	40,066
Nissan	31,988
Nummi	29,651
Subaru-Isuzu	16,616
Mitsubishi	12,253
Autoalliance	9,050
BMW	4,556
Navistar	4,484
Mercedes	4,166
Miscellaneous	4,769
Total number of cars and trucks made in the U.S.	909,749

Source: *Automotive News*, February 9, 1998.

Now that's some big Herfindahl–Hirschman index! In fact, they just don't come any bigger than that. What is the HHI of *every* monopoly? That's right—it's 10,000.

Now *you'll* get a chance to compute a few HHIs. Find the HHI of an industry with just two firms, both of which have 50 percent market shares. Work it out right here:

Solution: $50^2 + 50^2 = 2,500 + 2,500 = 5,000$

Now let's add another wrinkle. Find the HHI of an industry that has four firms, each with a 25 percent market share:

$$
\begin{aligned}
\text{Solution: } & 25^2 + 25^2 + 25^2 + 25^2 \\
& = 625 + 625 + 625 + 625 \\
& = 2,500
\end{aligned}
$$

Can you see where all this is going? The less concentrated an industry, the lower its HHI. And here's one last question. Imagine an industry with 100 firms, each with an equal market share. Without going through all the work, see if you can figure out the HHI.

It would come to 100: $1^2 + 1^2 + 1^2 \ldots + 1^2 = 100$.

The Justice Department uses the HHI to decide whether an industry is highly concentrated. This measure is preferred to four-firm concentration ratios because the index is based on the shares of *all* firms in an industry.

The Competitive Spectrum

We shall now consider the possible degrees of competition, from cartels and open collusion down through cutthroat competition. These possibilities are shown in Figure 3, toward the end of this section.

Cartels

A cartel is an extreme case of oligopoly.

With so few firms in our basic industries, there is a strong temptation for the leading firms to band together to restrict output and, consequently, increase prices and profits. An extreme case is a cartel, where the firms behave as a monopoly in a manner similar to that of the Organization of Petroleum Exporting Countries (OPEC) in the world oil market.

Given a certain market demand for a good or service over which an oligopoly exercises little control, firms that openly collude can control industry supply and, to a large degree, market price. For example, by withholding part or most of supply, the colluding firms can bid the market price way up. This was done by OPEC in 1973 when the price of oil quadrupled (see Figure 1).

If the cartel is able to operate successfully, securing the full support of all its members (who don't try to undercut the cartel price to sell some extra output under the table), its situation will approximate that of a monopoly. Just like a monopoly, which faces the entire market demand curve, the cartel will control the entire industry supply. OPEC, which controlled most of the world's oil exports, was able to take advantage of a relatively inelastic demand for oil by withholding supply in late 1973 and early 1974, thereby quadrupling world oil prices.

Figure 1   Withholding Supply to Raise Price

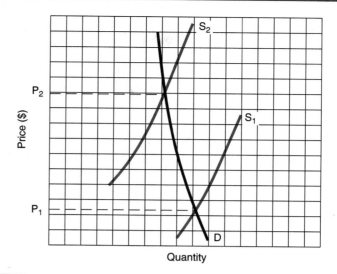

In the chapter "Corporate Mergers and Antitrust," we'll talk about the formation of trusts or cartels in the late 19th century in many basic American industries, most notably oil, which led to the Sherman and Clayton acts, outlawing such behavior. Today the only cartels we need to worry about are those existing outside our borders.[1]

Open Collusion

Open collusion operates like the Mafia.

Slightly less extreme than a cartel would be a territorial division of the market among the firms in the industry. This would be a division similar to that of the Mafia, if indeed there really is such an organization. An oligopolistic division of the market might go something like this. All prostitution, dope, loan-sharking, and gambling in New England is run by Steve (The Fence); New York is run by Frankie (Big Frank); Philly and Atlantic City are run by Max (Tiny); the Midwest is run by Mike (The Banker); Florida by Joey (Three Fingers); the Gulf Coast by Paddy (The Professor); the mountain states by Benny (Dog Ears); and the West Coast by Anthony (Fat Tony).

Nobody messes with anyone else's territory. The arrangement will continue until there is a new power alignment within the family or a new firm tries to enter the industry.

This cozy arrangement would give each operation a regional monopoly. On a national basis, each operation's market situation is depicted by Figure 2.

You may have noticed that this graph is identical to that of a monopoly. Although the firm may have only 15 or 20 percent of the market, its pricing behavior is that of the monopolist, and the results are similar. Compared to the perfect competitor, the colluding oligopolist charges a higher price (not one equal to the minimum point of the ATC curve); has a higher ATC (and is therefore less efficient); restricts output (i.e., operates to the left of the minimum point of the ATC); and finally, unlike the perfect competitor, makes a profit.

These are extreme cases, but they would be illegal, even during the last few years of less-than-stringent enforcement of the antitrust laws. Now, as we move to somewhat less extreme cases of collusion, we begin to enter the realm of reality. This brings us to the celebrated electric machinery conspiracy case.

---

[1]Locally, however, there are mob-run cartels, involving legal and illegal activities. After a 10-year investigation of the Mafia's longtime control of the garbage-hauling industry in the suburbs north of New York City, in 1997 five people and 13 garbage-hauling companies pleaded guilty to setting up a property rights system in which they claimed the permanent right to the locations where they picked up garbage, shared profits from their contracts, and disguised their profit sharing through sham transactions and false tax returns.

Figure 2   The Colluding Oligopolist

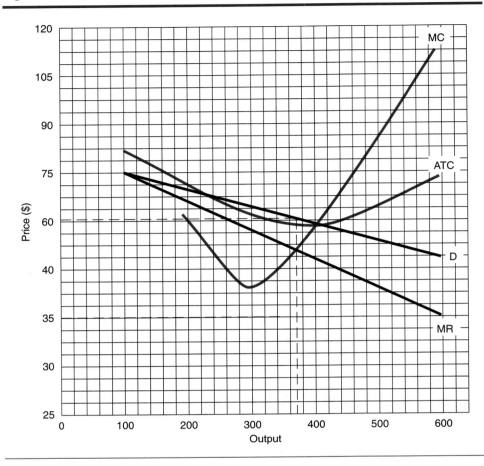

Covert Collusion: The Electric Machinery Conspiracy Case

In the late 1950s officials of General Electric, Westinghouse, Allis-Chalmers, and other leading electrical firms met periodically at various hotels and motels around the country. These secret meetings were set up to fix the prices of electric transformers, turbines, and other electrical equipment. Although government contracts were awarded based on the lowest sealed bid, the conspirators rigged the bidding so that even the lowest bid would be extremely profitable. In fact, the firms took turns making low bids. The public, too, was bilked of hundreds of millions of dollars in higher prices.

Finally, in 1961, the U.S. Supreme Court found seven high-ranking company officials guilty of illegal price-fixing and market-sharing agreements. They were given fines, which their companies took care of, and short jail sentences, during which time their salaries were paid. On release from jail each was given back his old job. Talk about tying yellow ribbons round the old oak tree!

As a footnote to this story, some 11 years later two of the companies involved in the 1961 case, General Electric and Westinghouse, were charged with fixing prices on turbine generators. Oh well, nobody's perfect.

Was this case the tip of the iceberg or an unfortunate aberration, a group of unethical executives who gave big business a black eye? There have been other cases. Some of the executives of Marcor Paper Company (now a division of Mobil Oil), which made containers, and a few other container manufacturers also received short jail sentences for illegal price-setting. The Archer Daniels Midland Company admitted fixing the prices of lysine and citric acid, and paid $100 million in fines, by far the largest judgment ever obtained by the Justice Department. But there is not any overwhelming evidence that big business is any more corrupt than any other sector of American life, although that is a somewhat underwhelming testimonial.

Price Leadership

Playing follow-the-leader

Short of meeting in hotel rooms to set prices secretly, do oligopolists conspire in less overt fashion? Until the 1930s U.S. Steel exercised open price leadership in the steel industry. On one day U.S. Steel would post a price for a particular type of steel, and the next day Bethlehem, Republic, Armco, Inland, and the rest of the industry would post an identical price, down to the last hundredth of a cent.

At the turn of the century the leaders of the major steel firms actually collectively agreed on prices at dinners held periodically by Judge Gary, president of U.S. Steel. Since those days not only has it become much more difficult to get away with collusion, but the companies could no longer take the full cost of these dinners as tax write-offs because only 80 percent of business "entertainment" expenses are deductible.

The cigarette industry provided another instance of price leadership.

> Between 1923 and 1941, virtual price identity prevailed continuously among the "standard" brands. During this period there were eight list price changes. Reynolds led six of them, five upward and one downward, and was followed each time, in most cases, within 24 hours of its announcement. The other two changes were downward revisions during 1933 led by American and followed promptly by the other standard brand venders.[2]

The prime rate set by big banks is a form of price leadership.

Another form of price leadership that has sprung up in recent years is the setting of the prime rate of interest by the nation's leading banks. That rate might stay the same for several months until suddenly 2 of the top 10 banks raise their prime by a quarter of a percent, and within 24 hours, the rest of the nation's 9,000-odd banks raise theirs a quarter of a percent. What is interesting here is that rarely do the same banks change the rate two times in a row, but in virtually every instance the other 9,000-some banks play follow-the-leader. Bankers and other oligopolists engaging in price leadership would have us believe that they are "locked in competition" and that the forces of supply and demand dictate the same price to everyone. But this explanation strains credulity because no two firms—and certainly not 9,000—face exactly the same demand schedules or have the same cost schedules.

Collusion is most likely to succeed when there are few firms and high barriers to entry.

When is collusion most likely to succeed? Mainly when there are few firms in the industry and when there are high barriers to entry. Basically, it's much easier to keep secrets—when you're violating the antitrust laws, you have to keep secrets—when there aren't too many people to deal with. In a far-fetched example, in the 1950s the American Communist Party was considered a group of people conspiring to advocate the violent overthrow of the American government. It turned out that several thousand of their somewhat fewer than 20,000 card-carrying members were actually FBI agents or paid informers. Some conspiracy!

Conspiracies need to be kept very small. When entry barriers, particularly capital requirements, are high enough, conspirators don't have to worry about new firms entering the industry and, presumably, being taken into the conspiracy.

Conclusion

A community of interest

Perhaps there is no collusion at all, or at least not much. But there is surely a certain community of interest, a community that may go well beyond the confines of specific industries. This idea is explored in the box entitled "The Old Boy Network at Six Big Banks." It could also apply to the Texas oil interests, the Michigan automobile industry, the Silicon Valley computer establishment in California, and the high-tech complex along Route 128 in the Boston suburbs.

Let's take a look at the chart in Figure 3. At one end we have the cartel, which no longer operates within the American economy although it may be found in world markets

---

[2]F. M. Scherer, *Industrial Pricing: Theory and Evidence* (Skokie, IL: Rand McNally, 1970), p. 38.

The Old Boy Network at Six Big Banks

Directors of supposedly competing banks are meeting with each other continually—on the boards of other companies.

People of the same trade seldom meet together, even for merriment and diversion, but the conversation ends in a conspiracy against the public, or in some contrivance to raise prices.

—Adam Smith,
The Wealth of Nations

Under the Clayton Antitrust Act, it is illegal for a person to sit on the boards of two competing firms, as this would tend to lessen competition. But there is a way around this prohibition; it is called the "indirect interlock," by which members of the boards of competing firms serve together on the boards of companies in nonrelated industries.

Although it could be argued that boards of directors have little power and that interlocking directorships are irrelevant, this situation is at least evidence of the trend toward economic concentration. As recent statistics show, the share of business done by the biggest industrial, retail, and financial corporations has been increasing steadily. On the indirectly interlocked directorates of these firms sit many men who know each other, share certain economic and political views, and yet are often connected with supposedly competing businesses. Are these men really competing, or is competition merely a facade behind which they pursue their common business interests?

The collapse of Penn Central in 1970 provides a good example of possible abuses of power through bank interlocks. Thomas Perkins served on the boards of both Morgan and Penn Central; Stuart Saunders, board chairman of Penn Central, served on Chase's board. It so happened that, shortly before it became publicly known that Penn Central was nearly bankrupt, Morgan and Chase sold off much of their holdings in Penn Central.

Of course, membership on boards is not the only meeting ground for industrial competitors. Country clubs, dining clubs, trade associations, professional societies, and other social institutions provide ample opportunity for collusion. Nevertheless, there seems to be a growing community of interest among the Big Six New York banks. When each extends a line of credit to Exxon, where directors of four of the banks serve on the board, there is a common bond among the banks. This bond is cemented by similar shared loans to other companies on whose boards sit representatives from these same banks.

There has got to be a great temptation to cooperate, to refrain from rocking the boat. Although it violates no antitrust statute, this arrangement could undermine competition. Unfortunately, there are probably no legal remedies because the indirect interlock is more a symptom of economic concentration than a conspiracy to create it.

One might also wonder how a director divides his loyalties between AT&T and Chase or Citibank. Are these roles of simultaneous creditor and debtor so inconsistent as to be, perhaps, schizophrenic? Or is this apparent dichotomy overcome by a stronger loyalty—to the small group of men who hold most of the country's economic power?

Source: Reprinted from Stephen L. Slavin, "The Old Boy Network at Six Big Banks," *Business and Society Review* (Fall 1977), p. 62.

Figure 3   The Competitive Spectrum

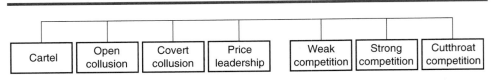

(most notably in the oil market). At the opposite end of the spectrum we have the cutthroat competitor, the firm that will stop at nothing to beat out its rivals. Industrial espionage and sabotage, underselling, disparaging of rival products, and other unfair competitive practices are the trademarks of such firms. We'll be considering the case of the cutthroat oligopolist in the appendix to this chapter.

Near the middle are the mildly competing oligopolists and the occasionally cooperating oligopolists. Sometimes their leaders are called corporate statesmen.

Where on this spectrum is American industry?

Where on this spectrum is American industry? Where do we place the industries listed in Table 1? Near the middle? Toward the cutthroat end of the spectrum? Or toward the cartel end?

The answer is that there *is* no answer. You won't pin me down on this one. There are two reasons why there is no answer to this question.

First, there is no one place where American industry is located because different industries have different competitive situations. In short, some oligopolistic industries are more competitive than others, so to say that *all* industries are located at a certain point on the spectrum—regardless of where—has got to be wrong.

Second, there is widespread disagreement about the degree of competition in any given industry. Take banking, for example. If one were to judge the degree of competitiveness among banks by all the newspaper advertising they do to attract depositors and to get people to take out car loans and mortgages, it would appear that this is a very competitive industry. But one would reach quite a different conclusion by observing that when one or two major banks change their prime rate of interest, within a day or so all the other major banks, not to mention the rest of the banks around the country, play follow-the-leader.[3]

Whatever the degree of collusion, it would be hard for firms in oligopolistic industries to ignore each other's actions and anticipated reactions with respect to price and output. In the appendix to this chapter we'll investigate the situation of oligopoly with no collusion. This is at the other end of the spectrum from cartels (see Figure 3), with which we began our discussion.

Questions for Further Thought and Discussion

1. The American automobile industry is an archetypal oligopoly. Show why this statement is true.

2. Where is American industry on the competitive spectrum? Instead of answering this question, you may criticize it.

3. What are the two measures of the degree of oligopolization. Work out a numerical problem using each of them.

---

[3]Bankers would tell us that they're not oligopolists to begin with, and that in any event, their concentration ratio is no more than about 15. On the other hand, there is no question that the 20 largest banks in the country do more than one-third of all the banking business.

WORKBOOK FOR CHAPTER 26

Name _____   Date _____

Multiple-Choice Questions

Circle the letter that corresponds to the best answer.

1. Which statement is true?

    a. All oligopolies have only a few firms.   **b.** Most oligopolies have only a few firms.   **c.** Some oligopolies have only a few firms.

2. The auto industry has a concentration ratio of more than _____ percent.

    a. 10   **b.** 30   **c.** 50   **d.** 70   **e.** 90

3. Which statement is closest to the truth?

    a. The six big New York banks engage in cutthroat competition.   **b.** The six big New York banks are perfect competitors.   **c.** There is some evidence of possible conflict of interest when people sit on the boards of banks and large industrial corporations and have financial ties to the banks.   **d.** Those who sit on the boards of large New York banks simultaneously sit together on the boards of other large corporations but have little in common.

4. Price is

    a. always read off the demand curve   **b.** sometimes read off the demand curve   **c.** always read off the marginal revenue curve   **d.** sometimes read off the marginal revenue curve

5. In the U.S. today collusion is

    a. illegal and does not exist   **b.** illegal and does exist   **c.** legal and does not exist   **d.** legal and does exist

6. Which statement is true?

    a. All firms in oligopolistic industries are large.   **b.** Most firms in the United States are oligopolies.   **c.** The crucial factor in oligopolistic industries is product differentiation.   **d.** Most of our GDP is produced by oligopolies.

7. Which of the following is not an oligopolist?

    a. Exxon   **b.** General Motors   **c.** your local phone company   **d.** Xerox

8. Which statement about oligopolies is false?

    a. They operate at the minimum points of their ATC curves.   **b.** They charge higher prices than perfect competitors.   **c.** They make profits in the long run.   **d.** They cannot legally form cartels in the United States.

9. Which statement is false?

    a. The cigarette and auto industries have high concentration ratios.   **b.** OPEC is a cartel.   **c.** Most oligopolies engage in outright collusion.   **d.** None of these statements is false.

10. The electric machinery case involved

    a. a cartel   **b.** covert collusion   **c.** cutthroat competition   **d.** none of the above

11. The least competitive industry is one that has

    a. price leadership   **b.** covert collusion   **c.** overt collusion   **d.** a cartel

12. Which statement is true?

    a. A person who sits on the board of Chase may also sit on the board of Citibank.   **b.** The people who run our large banks share a community of economic interest.   **c.** People on boards of major banks rarely run into each other.   **d.** Most members of bank boards are involved in conflicts of interest.

13. Which statement is true?

    a. Most of American industry is engaged in cutthroat competition.   **b.** Most of American industry does not compete.   **c.** Some oligopolistic industries are more competitive than others.   **d.** None of these statements is true.

14. An industry that is highly concentrated might have a Herfindahl–Hirschman index of

    a. 20,000   b. 2,000   c. 800   d. 100   e. 1

15. An industry that has 100 firms, each with a 1 percent market share, would have a Herfindahl–Hirschman index of

    a. 1   b. 10   c. 100   d. 1,000   e. 10,000

Use Table 1 to answer questions 16 through 19.

Table 1

Industry X		Industry Y		Industry Z	
Firm	Market Share (%)	Firm	Market Share (%)	Firm	Market Share (%)
1	25	1	35	1	30
2	25	2	20	2	30
3	15	3	15	3	20
4	10	4	15	4	10
5	10	5	10	5	5
6	10	6	5	6	5
7	5				

16. The highest concentration ratio

    a. is in Industry X   b. is in Industry Y   c. is in Industry Z   d. cannot be determined

17. The highest Herfindahl–Hirschman index

    a. is in Industry X   b. is in Industry Y   c. is in Industry Z   d. cannot be determined

18. Which statement is true?

    a. Industry X is more concentrated than Industry Y.

    b. Industry Y is more concentrated than Industry Z.

    c. Industry Z is more concentrated than Industry X.

    d. Industries X, Y, and Z have the same concentration ratio.

19. Which statement is true?

    a. Industry X has a higher Herfindahl–Hirschman index than Industry Y.   b. Industry Y has a higher Herfindahl–Hirschman index than Industry Z.

    c. Industry Z has a higher Herfindahl–Hirschman index than Industry X.   d. Industries X, Y, and Z have the same Herfindahl–Hirschman index.

20. Which statement is true?

    a. Most cars sold in the United States are either imported or made by Japanese firms in this country.

    b. Three out of every 10 new cars in the United States was assembled by a Japanese company.   c. There are now 12 Japanese companies building cars in the United States.   d. None of these statements is true.

21. Imports have made the automobile industry's concentration ratio much _____ relevant, while the Japanese transplants have been _____ that ratio.

    a. more, reducing   b. more, increasing   c. less, reducing   d. less, increasing

22. A monopoly would have a concentration ratio of _____ and a Herfindahl–Hirschman index of _____.

    a. 100, 100   b. 10,000, 10,000   c. 10,000, 100   d. 100, 10,000

23. Which statement is true?

    a. The higher the Herfindahl–Hirschman index, the higher the degree of concentration.   b. The lower the Herfindahl–Hirschman index, the higher the degree of concentration.   c. The Herfindahl–Hirschman index remains constant as the degree of concentration rises.

    d. There is no relationship between the Herfindahl–Hirschman index and the degree of concentration.

Fill-In Questions

1. An oligopoly is an industry with _____ _____.

2. One measure of the degree of competitiveness (or of oligopoly) is called a _____.

3. The oligopolist_____ at the minimum point of her ATC curve.

4. The total _____ of industry sales by the four leading firms is the industry concentration ratio.

5. The most important cartel in the world today is

_____.

6. An important Supreme Court case involving covert

collusion was the _____ case.

7. U.S. Steel and a few cigarette companies were all

engaged in _____

to attain their economic ends.

8. Most of the dominant banks in the United States are

located in_____.

Problems

1. Given the information in Table 2, calculate the concentration ratio of this industry. *Show your work.*

Table 2

Firm	Percent of Sales
A	14%
B	4
C	23
D	5
E	2
F	8
G	17
H	10
I	2
J	15
Total	100%

2. a. How much is the concentration ratio in the industry
shown in Table 3?
   b. Calculate the Herfindahl–Hirschman index in this
industry.

Table 3

Firm	Market Share
1	30%
2	20
3	20
4	10
5	10
6	5
7	5

3. a. How much is the concentration ratio in the industry
shown in Table 4?
   b. Calculate the Herfindahl–Hirschman index in this
industry.

Table 4

Firm	Market Share
1	40%
2	15
3	10
4	10
5	10
6	5
7	5
8	5

Oligopoly without Collusion

Welcome to the world of cutthroat competition, the world in which oligopolistic firms take no prisoners. Although we won't be getting into industrial espionage, you can be sure that industrial spies are lurking everywhere. Each firm wants to know exactly what its competitors are doing and how they will react to any changes in price that it might initiate. The dynamics of oligopoly under cutthroat competition are very different from those of oligopoly with collusion.

Appendix Objectives

After you've read this appendix, you'll know all about:

- Cutthroat competition.
- The kinked demand curve.
- Administered prices.

The Kinked Demand Curve

Cutthroat competition: an extreme case

Before changing price, a firm will try to gauge its competitors' reactions.

Now we deal with the extreme case of oligopolists who are cutthroat competitors, firms that do not exchange so much as a knowing wink. Each is out to maximize its profits. These oligopolists are ready to cut the throats of their competitors, figuratively speaking, of course.

The uniqueness of this situation leads us to the phenomenon of the kinked demand curve, pictured in Figure A1. For the first time in this textbook, we have a firm's demand curve that is not a straight line.

Figure A1   The Kinked Demand Curve

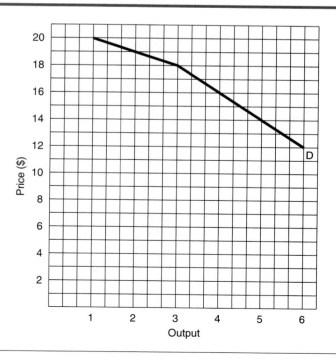

If I raise my price, they won't raise theirs.

If I lower my price, they lower theirs.

Two characteristics of straight-line demand and MR curves always hold true.

Why does the demand curve of the fiercely competing oligopolist have a kink? The answer is that it is based on the oligopolist's assumption about his rivals' behavior in response to his own actions. The oligopolist can do three possible things: raise price, lower price, or not change price.

Suppose the price has been the same for a fairly long period of time. The oligopolist thinks about raising price. If I raise my price, what will my competitors do? Who knows? What would *I* do if one of my rivals raised her price? If I did nothing, I would get some of my rival's customers, so I wouldn't change my price.

Even though I hate to admit it, my competitors are as smart as I am, so if *my* response to a rival's price increase is to keep my price the same and get some of my rival's customers, surely my rivals would respond in the same way to my price increase. Therefore, I don't raise my price.

What about lowering my price and stealing some of my competitors' customers? Now I ask myself, how would *I* react? I'd immediately lower my price in response to a move by one of my competitors. And my competitors would lower their prices in response to my lowering mine. So I won't lower my price.

If I don't lower my price (because my competitors would follow) and if I don't raise my price (because my competitors won't follow), what *do* I do? Nothing. I leave my price where it is.

What makes sense for me also makes sense for my competitors. None of them will raise or lower price. We all keep price where it is, and that happens to be at the kink in the demand curve.

This explains why price does not change often under extremely competitive oligopoly. A firm is afraid to make a move for fear of what its rivals might or might not do. Underlying that fear is the memory of price wars touched off by one firm lowering its price. Hence it's better to leave well enough alone.

Let's examine the kinked demand curve more closely. It's really two demand curves in one, the left segment being relatively elastic (or horizontal) and the right less elastic (more vertical).

In Figure A2 both segments of the demand curve have been extended. This was done to set up the next step, the MR curves of Figure A3. Before we can figure out the oligopolist's actual MR curve, we'll have to see how each of the MR curves in Figure A3 is drawn.

First, look at MR_1, which corresponds to D_1. Notice that it is equal to D_1 at one unit of output and that it slopes downward to the right, falling twice as quickly as D_1. These two characteristics of straight-line demand and MR curves always hold true. *If a demand curve is a straight line, its MR curve will also be a straight line that will coincide with it at one unit of output and decline twice as quickly.* (By convention, we refer to demand and MR curves as curves, even if they happen to be straight lines.)

Let's take a look at MR_2, which corresponds to D_2. Notice how D_2 and MR_2 are equal at one unit of output and how MR_2 slopes downward to the right, falling twice as quickly as D_2. Using this information, we're ready to draw a graph for an oligopolist. I'll do one and then you'll do a couple.

First, we'll go over the demand curve in Figure A4, which is the now-familiar kinked curve. The price and output are always at the kink, so in this instance, price is $18 and output is three.

Now for the MR curve. We have each of the points. We can connect the points between one and three units of output and also between four and six units of output. The problem is what we do about drawing the MR curve between the third and fourth units.

Let's go back for a minute to Figure A3, where we drew two MR curves, MR_1 and MR_2. Each curve met its corresponding demand curve at one unit of output, so we need to do the same thing in Figure A4.

Notice how the MR curve is already extended to one unit of output. Let's extend the lower segment of the MR curve running from outputs four to six all the way up to one unit of output. Notice how it is equal to the extended demand curve in Figure A4.

Now we're all set. The actual MR curve is the heavy line from outputs one through three. Then it drops straight down and continues along the heavy line from output three through output six. The key is to extend the MR curve from the third to the fourth unit.

**Figure A2   The Kinked Demand Curve as a Combination
of Two Demand Curves**

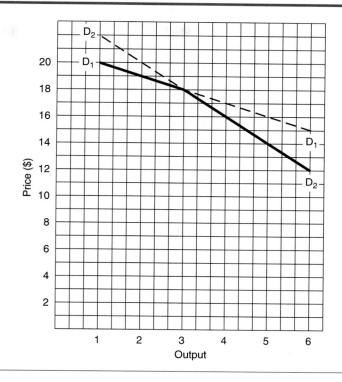

**Figure A3   The Kinked Demand Curve and Two Corresponding
Marginal Reserve Curves**

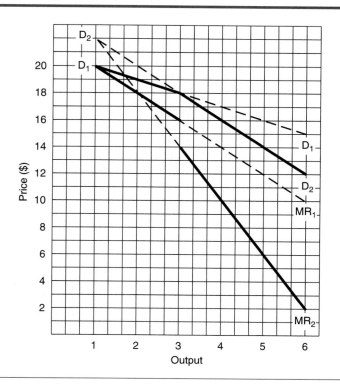

**Figure A4   The Kinked Demand Curve and the Discontinued
Marginal Reserve Curve**

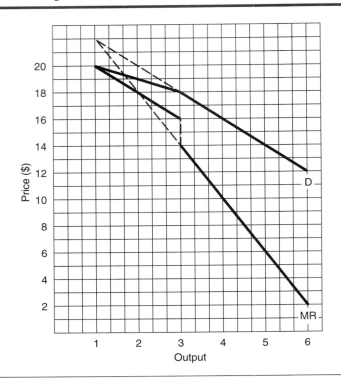

A common mistake is to connect the one-to-three segment with the four-to-six segment, as I've done in Figure A5. You have to drop straight down at three units of output
and then extend the MR curve from three to four at the same slope or angle at which it
has been running from four to six. Let's see what you can do.

Filling in and using the data from Table A1, draw the firm's demand and MR curves.
A tricky part comes when we do the MR curve at its discontinuity (when it drops straight
down). This part always lies directly below the kink in the demand curve.

First, check your figures for Table A1 with mine in Table A2. Then check your
graph with that in Figure A6. How much is output? How much is price?

The output is at the kink in the demand curve, which occurs at four units of output.
At that output, price is $47. The key in the graph, of course, is the discontinuity of the
MR curve, which is directly below the kink. By extending the lower segment of the MR
curve (which runs from seven to five units of output) up to four units of output, all you
need to do is draw the vertical dotted line connecting the two MR segments.

At this point we're ready to add the ATC and MC curves, draw a graph, and do some
analysis. I'd like you to (1) fill in Table A3; (2) on a sheet of graph paper, draw a graph
of the firm's demand, MR, MC, and ATC curves; and (3) find the firm's output, price,
and total profit.

First, check your figures with those of Table A4. Next, check your graph with the
one shown in Figure A7. Finally, how much are output, price, and total profit?

Output, which is directly under the kink, is four. Price, which is at the kink, is $27.
Remember that price is *always* read off the demand curve. And now, total profit:

$$\text{Total profit} = (\text{Price} - \text{ATC}) \times \text{Output}$$

$$= (\$27 - \$24) \times 4$$

$$= \$3 \times 4$$

$$= \$12$$

Figure A5   A Common Error in Drawing the Marginal Reserve Curve

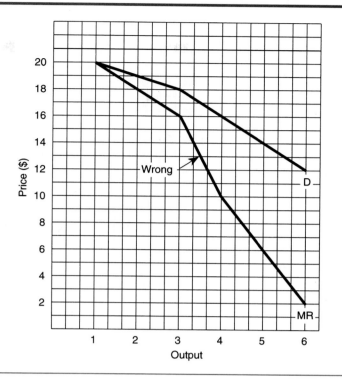

Table A1   Hypothetical Demand Schedule for Competing Oligopolist

Output	Price	Total Revenue	Marginal Revenue
1	$50	____	____
2	49	____	____
3	48	____	____
4	47	____	____
5	44	____	____
6	41	____	____
7	38	____	____

Table A2   Solution to Table A1

Output	Price	Total Revenue	Marginal Revenue
1	$50	$ 50	$50
2	49	98	48
3	48	144	46
4	47	188	44
5	44	220	32
6	41	246	26
7	38	266	20

Figure A6   The Cutthroat Oligopolists' Demand and Marginal Reserve Curves

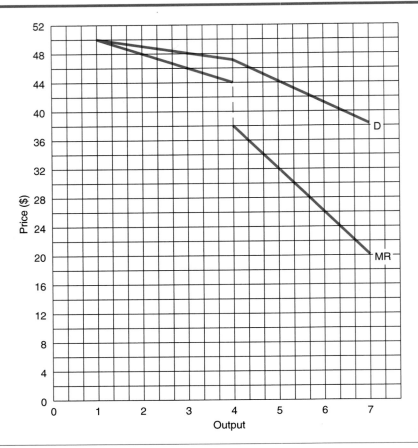

**Table A3   Hypothetical Demand and Cost Schedule
for a Competitive Oligopolist**

Output	Price	Total Revenue	Marginal Revenue	Total Cost	ATC	Marginal Cost
1	$30	_____	_____	$ 40	_____	_____
2	29	_____	_____	60	_____	_____
3	28	_____	_____	75	_____	_____
4	27	_____	_____	96	_____	_____
5	24	_____	_____	125	_____	_____
6	21	_____	_____	162	_____	_____
7	18	_____	_____	210	_____	_____

Table A4   Solution to Table A3

Output	Price	Total Revenue	Marginal Revenue	Total Cost	ATC	Marginal Cost
1	$30	$ 30	$30	$ 40	$40	—
2	29	58	28	60	30	$20
3	28	84	26	75	25	15
4	27	108	24	96	24	21
5	24	120	12	125	25	29
6	21	126	6	162	27	37
7	18	126	0	210	30	48

Figure A7   The Cutthroat Oligopolist

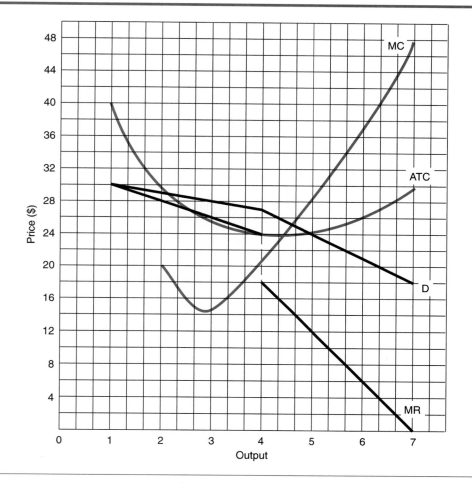

Can you come up with an easier way of finding the firm's total profit? Look at Table A4 again. Did you figure it out yet? Just subtract total cost from total revenue at an output of four ($108 – $96 = $12). Once you know the output, all you need to do is subtract TC from TR.

In passing, let us note that the oligopolistic firm does not produce at the minimum point of its ATC curve, so we do not have peak efficiency even though there is considerable competition. Price tends to stay at $27. This is the main reason why, under competition, oligopolists' prices tend to be "sticky." We call such sticky prices *administered prices,* which is the topic of the last section of this appendix.

Administered Prices

Administered prices are set by large corporations for relatively long periods of time, without responding to the normal market forces, mainly, changes in demand. For example, although demand fell substantially during the Great Depression, many firms, most notably the railroads, did not lower their prices.

We already saw how, under the constraints of fierce competition, the oligopolist is reluctant to raise or lower price. Prices are said to be sticky.

If we take the firm's MC curve as its supply curve, we will see that the oligopolist operates within a fairly wide range of possible MRs before it is necessary to change price. Look back at Figure A6. Because of the discontinuity of the MR curve (the vertical broken line), the firm will charge the same price at the same output no matter how much MC varies within the range of $38 to $44. In Figure A7, MC can vary from $18 to $24 and still equal MR.

Administered prices are peculiar to oligopoly. Perfect competitors and monopolistic competitors are too small to dictate price. Monopolists will change their output and price in response to changes in demand in order to maximize their profits. But under competitive oligopoly, the firms will rarely shift output or price because they will continue to maximize profit as long as MC is within the range of MR.

Thus administered prices can occur only under oligopoly and are most likely under very competitive oligopoly. While oligopoly is the dominant type of competition in American industry, many would question just *how* competitive our oligopolies are.

Questions for Further Thought and Discussion

1. Explain the cutthroat competitor's reasons for not raising or lowering his price, thereby accounting for the kink in his demand curve.

2. What are administered prices, and how are they set?

Name _____ Date _____

Multiple-Choice Questions

Circle the letter that corresponds to the best answer.

1. Compared to the perfect competitor in the long run, the cutthroat oligopolist has a

   a. lower price and lower profits   b. higher price and higher profits   c. higher price and lower profits

   d. lower price and higher profits

2. According to the theory of the kinked demand curve, if a firm were to raise its price, its competitors would

   a. lower theirs   b. raise theirs   c. keep theirs the same

3. According to the theory of the kinked demand curve, if a firm were to lower its price, its competitors would

   a. lower theirs   b. raise theirs   c. keep theirs the same.

4. The kinked demand curve depicts

   a. cutthroat competition   b. cartels   c. collusive oligopoly   d. price leadership

5. The kinked demand curve is associated with

   a. sticky prices   b. OPEC   c. covert collusion

   d. none of the above

6. The discontinuity in the oligopolist's marginal revenue curve occurs

   a. to the right of the kink   b. to the left of the kink

   c. directly below the kink   d. at different places at different times

7. Administered prices are most likely to occur under

   a. perfect competition   b. monopolistic competition

   c. monopoly   d. oligopoly

Fill-In Questions

1. The sign of cutthroat competition on a graph would be the

   _____ .

2. One of the outcomes of the kinked demand curve is

   _____ prices.

3. Administered prices are set by _____

   for_____ without responding to

   _____ .

4. Administered prices are peculiar to _____

   _____ .

Problems

1. **a.** Fill in Table 1. **b.** Use Figure 1 to draw a graph of the demand, marginal revenue, average total cost, and marginal cost curves for this firm. **c.** Calculate total profit. Show your work in the space provided.

Table 1

Output	Price	Total Revenue	Marginal Revenue	Total Cost	ATC	Marginal Cost
1	$50	____	____	$ 60	____	____
2	48	____	____	100	____	____
3	46	____	____	132	____	____
4	44	____	____	168	____	____
5	40	____	____	212	____	____
6	36	____	____	270	____	____
7	32	____	____	343	____	____

Figure 1

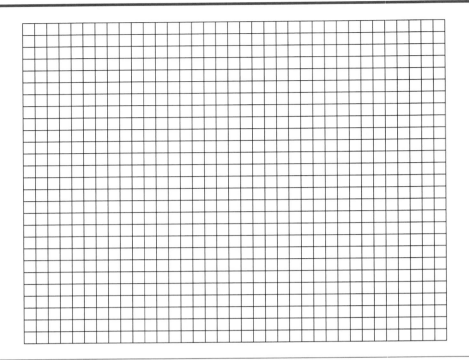

2. Given the information in Figure 2, calculate the firm's profit.

Figure 2

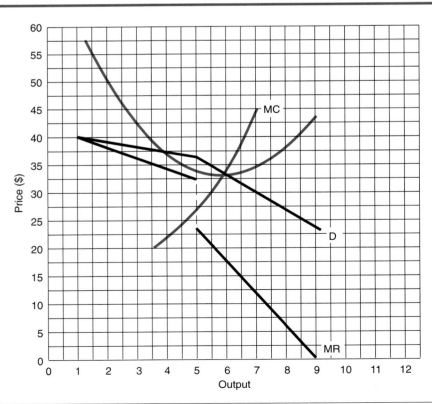

27 The Four Types of Competition: A Review

This chapter will summarize some of the high points of the preceding four chapters, especially the graphs. No new material will be introduced. In fact, virtually all the graphs are taken from the earlier chapters.

Chapter Objectives

This chapter provides a review of:

- Perfect competition.
- Monopoly.
- Monopolistic competition.
- Oligopoly.

Perfect Competition

Definition of perfect competition

A perfectly competitive industry has many firms selling an identical product. How many is many? So many that no one firm can influence price. What is identical? A product is identical in the minds of buyers when they have no reason to prefer one seller to another.

The short run

Figure 1 shows the perfect competitor taking a loss in the short run. Figure 2 shows the perfect competitor making a profit in the short run. Neither of these possibilities exists in the long run, when the perfect competitor makes zero economic profit.

The long run

In the long run, if the firm has been losing money, it may well leave the industry. Enough firms will leave to reduce market supply and raise price enough to eliminate the

Figure 1   Perfect Competitor Taking a Loss in the Short Run

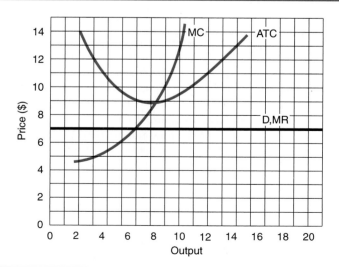

Figure 2   Perfect Competitor Making a Profit in the Short Run

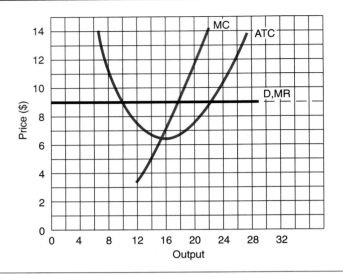

Figure 3   Perfect Competitor Breaking Even in the Long Run

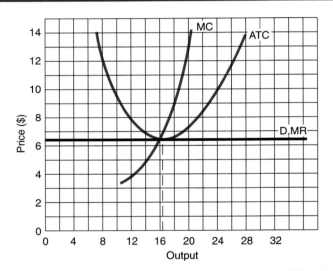

economic losses of the firms that remain in the industry. Thus, in the long run, the perfect competitor will make zero economic profit.

In the long run, if the firm has been making a profit, additional firms will have been attracted to the industry, raising industry supply and reducing market price. Thus, in the long run, profit is reduced to zero. The long-run situation of the perfect competitor is shown in Figure 3.

In the long run the perfect competitor's price is equal to the low point on the firm's ATC curve. Because the firm produces at that output, it operates at peak efficiency. That is, it operates at the minimum point of its ATC curve, which means it produces at the lowest possible cost.

Monopoly

Definition of monopoly

A monopoly is a firm that produces all the output in an industry. There's nobody else selling anything like what the monopolist is producing. In other words, there are no close substitutes.

There is no distinction between the short run and the long run.

There is no distinction between the short run and the long run under monopoly because the monopolist is the only firm in the industry. No firms enter or leave, as they do with perfect competition. The market demand curve *is* the monopolist's demand curve.

Figure 4 shows the monopolist's market situation. The firm has a higher price than does the perfect competitor because a monopolist's price is higher than the minimum point of its ATC curve. Similarly, output is restricted because the monopolist produces at some point to the left of that minimum ATC point. Finally, the monopolist makes an economic profit in the long run because price (read from the demand curve) is higher than ATC.

Figure 4   The Monopolist

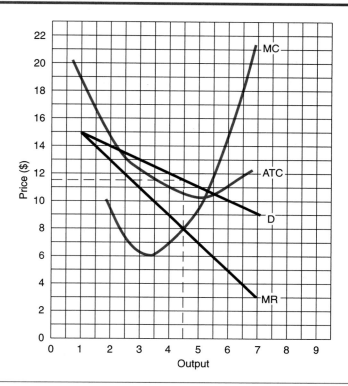

Monopolistic Competition

A monopolistically competitive industry has many firms selling a differentiated product. How many is many? So many that no one firm has any significant influence over price.

If the buyer doesn't differentiate among the various products sold, the product is identical. If the buyer does differentiate, the product is differentiated. Who determines whether the product is differentiated or identical? The buyer does.

Like the perfect competitor, the monopolistic competitor can make a profit or take a loss in the short run but in the long run, the firm will break even. The reason the monopolistic competitor makes zero economic profits in the long run is the same as that under perfect competition.

In the long run, if firms are losing money, then many will leave the industry, thus lowering industry supply and raising market price. If firms are realizing substantial profits in the long run, then new firms will be attracted to the industry, thus raising supply and lowering market price.

The monopolistic competitor is shown making a short-run profit in Figure 5 and taking a short-run loss in Figure 6. Finally, Figure 7 shows the long-run situation of the monopolistic competitor when economic profit is zero.

Definition of monopolistic competition

The short run

The long run

Under monopolistic competition, the firm's price is higher than the minimum point of its ATC curve, and output is restricted to a point to the left of the minimum ATC. The firm does not produce at peak efficiency because ATC is not at its minimum, and again, there are zero economic profits.

Figure 5   The Monopolistic Competitor Making a Profit in the Short Run

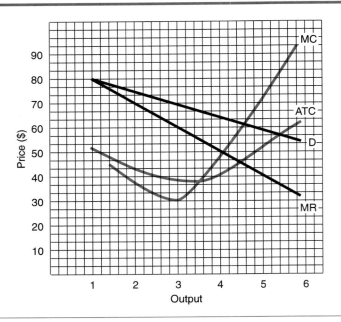

Figure 6   The Monopolistic Competitor Taking a Loss in the Short Run

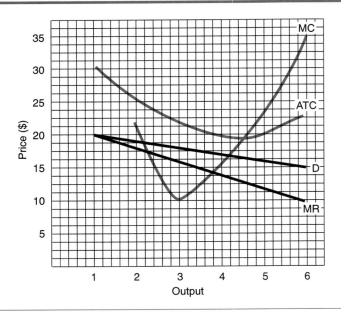

Figure 7   The Monopolistic Competitor Breaking Even in the Long Run

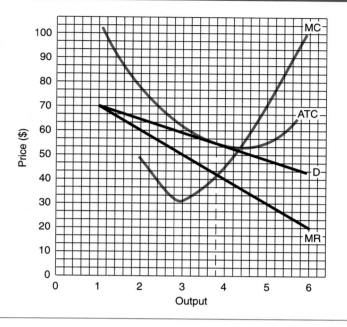

Oligopoly

An oligopoly is an industry with just a few sellers. How few? So few that at least one firm is large enough to influence price.

In Figure 8 we have the noncompeting oligopolist, and in Figure 9 the competing oligopolist. Both charge prices higher than the minimum point of their ATC curves, both restrict output to a point to the left of the minimum ATC, neither operates at peak efficiency, and both make an economic profit.

Figure 8   The Colluding Oligopolist

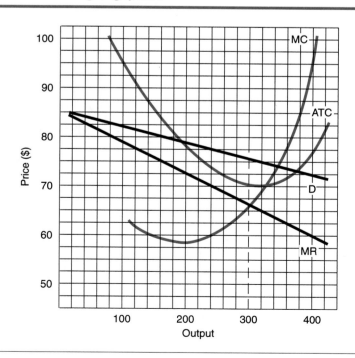

Figure 9   The Competing Oligopolist

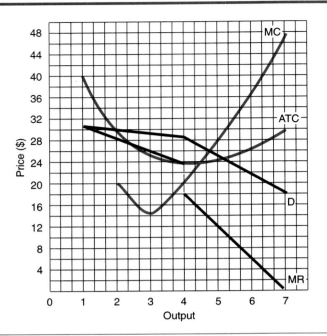

Perfect Competition versus Imperfect Competition

The perfectly competitive model is an ideal, rarely if ever attained in a world of imperfect competition. Indeed, more than 99 percent of the business firms in the United States are monopolistic competitors. Virtually all of the rest are oligopolies and monopolies. Now let's look at some tables listing the characteristics of perfect competition and imperfect competition, which includes monopoly, oligopoly, and monopolistic competition.

Summary Tables

Tables 1, 2, and 3 summarize what we've covered here with respect to number of sellers, type of product, price, output, profit, and efficiency.

Table 1   The Four Types of Competition: Number of Sellers and Type of Product

Type of Competition	Number of Sellers	Type of Product
Perfect competition	Many	Identical
Monopoly	One	—
Monopolistic competition	Many	Differentiated
Oligopoly	Few	Either identical or differentiated

Table 2   The Four Types of Competition: Price and Output

Type of Competition	Price	Output
Perfect competition	At minimum ATC	At minimum point of ATC
Monopoly	Higher than minimum ATC	Restricted (to left of minimum ATC)
Monopolistic competition	Higher than minimum ATC	Restricted (to left of minimum ATC)
Oligopoly	Higher than minimum ATC	Restricted (to left of minimum ATC)

Table 3   The Four Types of Competition: Profit and Efficiency

Type of Competition	Profit	Efficiency
Perfect competition	Zero economic profit	Peak efficiency
Monopoly	Makes an economic profit	Less than peak efficiency
Monopolistic competition	Zero economic profit	Less than peak efficiency
Oligopoly	Makes an economic profit	Less than peak efficiency

Questions for Further Thought and Discussion

1. How does perfect competition compare to monopolistic competition with respect to price, profit in the long run, average total cost, and output?

2. How does perfect competition compare to monopoly with respect to price, profit in the long run, average total cost, and output?

3. How does perfect competition compare to oligopoly with respect to price, profit in the long run, average total cost, and output?

Name _____ Date _____

Multiple-Choice Questions

Write in the letter that corresponds to the best answer for questions 1 through 8, using choice **a**, **b**, **c**, or **d**.

    a. perfect competitor/competition

    b. monopolist/monopoly   **c.** monopolistic competitor/competition   **d.** oligopolist/oligopoly

1. A firm in an industry with many sellers selling a differentiated product would be a(n) _____.

2. A firm that faces the entire demand curve of an industry would be a(n) _____.

3. In the long run only a(n) _____ operates at the minimum point of its ATC curve.

4. The crucial factor in _____ is the low number of sellers.

5. The crucial factor in _____ is product differentiation.

6. Under _____ and _____, there are no profits in the long run.

7. A firm with many sellers and an identical product is a(n) _____.

8. The kinked demand curve takes place under competitive _____.

Fill-In Questions

1. How many firms is many? So many that _____
   _____.

2. A product is identical in the _____
   _____.

3. Under any type of competition, if firms are losing money in the long run, _____.
   _____. If firms are making a profit in the long run, _____
   _____.

4. In the long run the perfect competitor's price is equal to the _____ on the firm's ATC curve. Therefore, the firm is operating at _____ _____ efficiency.

5. A monopolist's product has no _____
   _____.

6. The monopolist's price is _____ than the perfect competitor's; in the long run the monopolist's profit is _____ than the perfect competitor's.

7. A monopolistically competitive industry has _____ _____ firms selling a _____ product.

8. Product differentiation takes place in the _____ _____.

9. In the long run the monopolistic competitor's price is _____ the minimum point on its ATC curve.

10. An oligopoly is an industry with _____
    _____.

11. Only the _____ in the _____ produces at the minimum point of its ATC.

Problems

Use graph paper to do these problems.

1. Draw the graph of the demand, marginal revenue, marginal cost, and average total cost curves of the perfect competitor in the **a.** short run, making a profit; **b.** short run, taking a loss; **c.** long run.

2. Draw the graph of the monopolist.
3. Draw the graph of the monopolistic competitor in the **a.** short run, making a profit; **b.** short run, taking a loss; **c.** long run.
4. Draw the graph of the competitive oligopolist.

28 Corporate Mergers and Antitrust

Have you been thinking about going to law school? I'm sure you know that many graduates of our country's top law schools are getting starting salaries of $85,000. It isn't bad work—if you can get it.

But would this work make you happy? In this chapter you'll actually get a chance to find out because I'm going to let you practice corporate law without a license. Unfortunately, I'm not going to be paying you, but I'm sure that when you've gotten through this chapter you'll agree that the experience has been priceless.

The whole trick of being a lawyer is figuring out how to bill clients for as many hours as possible at a rate of at least $300 an hour. In fact, one prominent attorney, who happened to die of overwork, went straight up to heaven where he was greeted by Methuselah, who until that point held the title as the world's oldest man. Methuselah shook the attorney's hand and told him he was honored to meet the world's oldest man. The attorney was confused. "But you're Methuselah and I'm just another overworked attorney who died from a massive heart attack at the age of 40."

"I *was* expecting an older-looking man," Methuselah conceded, "but you've *got* to be older than I am—at least according to your time sheets."

There are, of course, literally hundreds of lawyer jokes that have made the rounds, but this one has always been my favorite. Now we'll turn to more serious matters and talk about growing corporate concentration and antitrust enforcement.

There has been an unmistakable trend toward bigness in business since the mid-1980s. Corporate mergers and takeovers have become so common that anything less than a billion-dollar deal is not even considered financial news. Let's see how this trend developed and how the government has attempted to regulate it.

Chapter Objectives

When you complete this chapter you will be familiar with each of the following:

- The explanation of antitrust.
- Major antitrust laws.
- Modern antitrust.
- Types of mergers.
- The effectiveness of antitrust.
- The trend toward bigness.

A Historical Perspective on Corporate Concentration

The history of the American economy since the Civil War has been one of growing corporate concentration. Like the tides, this concentration has had its ebbs and flows.

A high-water mark was reached in the early years of this century when J. P. Morgan put together a couple of huge deals with his fellow captains of industry, Andrew Carnegie, Edward Harriman, and John D. Rockefeller. Then, in the years before World War I, came the first trustbusters, Presidents Teddy Roosevelt and William Howard Taft. A new wave of corporate mergers took place in the 1920s, only to be succeeded by the antitrust enforcement policies of Presidents Franklin Roosevelt and Harry Truman in the 1930s and 1940s. After that, a new wave of mergers continued for the next five decades.

During the last century and a quarter, a few hundred huge companies came to dominate our economy. There have been a few reverses—the 1911 breakup of the Standard Oil and American Tobacco trusts, and the antitrust enforcement of the 30s and 40s, and the more recent breakup of AT&T—but the trend has been unmistakable.

Antitrust

The Political Background

The common view is that during the 19th century the federal government rarely intervened in the economy, allowing businesses to go their own ways. There were, however, two major forms of intervention, both of which were key issues in the events leading up to the Civil War.

First, at various times the government passed a high protective tariff that generally made certain imports more expensive and greatly aided northern manufacturers. Second, the transcontinental railroad, which completely bypassed the South, was built with a tremendous amount of federal aid. This aid took the form of 10-mile strips of land on alternating sides of the track, so that for every mile of track built, the railroad received 10 square miles of land.

Both policies were benevolent with respect to big business, so few protests were raised about government intervention in that arena. Furthermore, with the election of Abraham Lincoln in 1860, the Republican Party would dominate the federal government for the next 70 years. In fact, only two Democrats were elected president during those years: Woodrow Wilson, who squeaked in after a three-way race with two Republicans, and Grover Cleveland, whose politics were as conservative as those of most Republicans.

This was the political backdrop against which the first antitrust legislation was passed in 1890. The Sherman Antitrust Act was passed by a Republican Congress and signed by a Republican president. For "the party of big business" to have passed a law such as this, the economic situation had to have been pretty desperate.

The late 19th century was the era of the "trust." Trusts were cartels that set prices and allocated sales among their member firms. In some cases, most blatantly oil, a single company was formed that controlled most or all production in the industry. The Standard Oil trust, which was carved out of 39 independent oil companies by John D. Rockefeller, controlled 90 percent of all U.S. oil production, refining, and marketing. In 1892 40 independent sugar companies formed the American Sugar Refining Company. Still other trusts were formed in meat packing, leather, whiskey, tobacco, electrical goods, coal, steel, and the railroads.

In his landmark work on those times, Matthew Josephson pictured

> an America in which the citizen was born to drink the milk furnished by the milk Trust, eat the beef of the beef Trust, illuminate his home by grace of the oil Trust, and die and be carried off by the coffin Trust.[1]

Even more grating were the insults hurled at the public by those who ran these huge industrial empires. Probably the most famous was the remark by railroad tycoon Billy Vanderbilt: "The public be damned. I am working for my stockholders."[2]

The Sherman Antitrust Act

In 1890 Congress passed the Sherman Antitrust Act to curb the trust movement. Senator John Sherman, brother of General William Tecumseh Sherman (of Civil War fame and to

What is a trust?

John D. Rockefeller, American oil magnate (The Granger Collection, New York)

---

[1]Matthew Josephson, *The Robber Barons* (New York: Harcourt Brace Jovanovich, 1962), p. 358.
[2]Ibid., p. 187.

this day voted the least popular person by the citizens of Atlanta), was one of the most powerful politicians of his day. Senator Sherman was so popular that the leaders of his party kept urging him to run for president. He did seek the Republican nomination in 1880, 1884, and 1888, but was never nominated. Interestingly, his older brother, the general, discouraged his own presidential nomination by declaring, "I will not accept if nominated and will not serve if elected."

Senator Sherman had mixed feelings about the growing concentration of corporate power and its abuses. After all, he was a leader of the Republicans, the party of big business. He hoped his law would slow the powerful trend toward monopolization of American industry, but the language of the law was left rather vague.

The key passage

The key passage stated that "every contract, combination in the form of trust or otherwise, in restraint of commerce among the several states, or with foreign nations, is hereby declared illegal." It went on to state, "Every person who shall monopolize, or conspire with any other person or persons to monopolize any part of the trade or commerce of the several states, or with foreign nations, shall be guilty of a misdemeanor."

It was left to the courts—most specifically, the Supreme Court—to interpret this language. Who were these justices? They had been appointed by the Republican presidents who had served since the time of Lincoln, so the justices were conservative. And they were old. Generally, as people get older, their politics grow more conservative—and these men were conservative to start with.

Addyston Pipe case

The only case of significance to come before the Court during the first 20 years the law was on the books was *Addyston Pipe and Steel* in 1899. Six cast-iron pipe producers in Ohio and Pennsylvania had set up a bidding ring. These six firms would take turns making the low bid. This blatant price-fixing was found to be a clear violation of the Sherman Act. In a revealing footnote to the case, the six firms found a legal solution to their problem: they merged.

Standard Oil and *American Tobacco* cases

Finally, after years of preparation by the Roosevelt and Taft administrations, suits were brought against two of the biggest trusts of the day, the Standard Oil and American Tobacco trusts. Standard Oil was split into 34 separately owned companies, the five largest of which are known today as Exxon, Mobil, Sohio (Standard Oil of Ohio), Amoco, and Chevron (see box "The Breakup of Standard Oil"). The American Tobacco Company was broken up into three companies: the American Tobacco Company, Liggett & Myers, and P. Lorillard.

Were these trusts broken up because they were big? No! Bigness per se did not offend the Court. The trusts were broken up because they had behaved badly.

What had the Standard Oil trust done that was bad? It had forced the railroads, which were then the basic means of shipping oil, to give it rebates or discounts not just on the oil it shipped but even on the oil shipped by its competitors. You can justify asking for a rebate on your *own* freight charges, but imagine forcing the railroads to pay you a rebate on your competitors' freight charges. Basically, it was using its tremendous market power to force its rivals out of business.[3]

The problem with the Supreme Court's interpretation of Sherman was that it did not prohibit monopoly per se, but prohibited only certain illegal tactics that had been practiced by Standard Oil and American Tobacco. Clearly the Court was even more conservative than other Republican branches of government. Nevertheless, the breakup of these companies was a radical measure that indicated how serious the problem of monopolization had become to the rest of the business establishment. In a sense, then, their breakup was deemed necessary to preserve the status quo.

The rule of reason

From this decision the Supreme Court formulated its "rule of reason," which set the tone for antitrust enforcement for the next two decades. Bigness itself was no offense as long as that bigness was not used against rival firms.

Mere size is no offense.

The rule of reason was applied in the *U.S. Steel* case of 1920 when the Wilson administration sought the same legal remedy against the steel trust that had been applied nine years earlier against the oil and tobacco trusts. The Court concluded that the U.S.

---

[3]The Interstate Commerce Act of 1887 prohibited granting rebates to large shippers.

The Breakup of Standard Oil

In 1911 the Supreme Court ordered the breakup of the Standard Oil Company for violating the Sherman Act. The five largest pieces were Standard Oil of New York, New Jersey, Ohio, Indiana, and California.

Standard Oil of New York evolved into Standard Oil Company of New York, into SOCONY-Mobil-Vacuum, and finally, into Mobil Oil, the nation's second-largest oil company today.

Standard Oil of New Jersey became ESSO, and nearly 20 years ago it became Exxon, which is the largest oil company in the world.

Standard Oil of Ohio (Sohio), Standard Oil of Indiana (Amoco), and Standard Oil of California (Chevron or SoCal) are still known by their original names.

Additional derivative firms include Continental Oil (now part of Du Pont), Marathon Oil (which merged with U.S. Steel), and Atlantic Richfield.

The Rockefeller family and Chase Manhattan Bank, while holding large blocks of stock in each of these companies, own too little to exercise control.

Steel Corporation, which produced more than half of the nation's steel, did not violate the Sherman Act just because it was big. The Court pronounced: "The corporation is undoubtedly of impressive size. . . . But we must adhere to the law, and the law does not make mere size an offense, or the existence of unexerted power an offense." And the very existence of competitors disproved the contention that U.S. Steel had misused its power.

So not *all* trusts were illegal, but only *unreasonable* restraints of trade. Remember the fairy tale of the three little pigs accosted by the big bad wolf, who told them, "I'll huff and I'll puff and I'll blow your house down"? Well the Supreme Court's rule of reason said that the wolf not only had to be big and bad, but he actually had to blow that house down. Bigness and bad intentions alone were not illegal per se. So even though the folks running U.S. Steel had intended to drive out their competitors, the fact that they had not succeeded was proof enough that they had done nothing illegal.

The Clayton Antitrust Act

For the first time since before the Civil War, the Democrats finally sat in the driver's seat, with Woodrow Wilson occupying the White House and a Democratic majority in both houses of Congress. In 1914 they passed two laws aimed at bolstering the Sherman Act by specifically outlawing all the bad business practices that continued to go unpunished.

The Clayton Act prohibited practices that lessened competition or tended to create a monopoly.

The Clayton Antitrust Act prohibited five business practices when their effect was to "substantially lessen competition or tend to create a monopoly."

1. *Price discrimination.* I took this up in the chapter on "Monopolistic Competition," using the examples of airlines charging half fare to teenagers, doctors charging widely varying rates based on patients' incomes, and the grades A, B, and C set up by A&P. Generally, the courts have not held price discrimination to be illegal.

2. *Interlocking stockholding.* This occurs when one firm buys the stock of another. Although it goes on every day, on occasion the courts will find it illegal. In the 1950s, Du Pont, together with Christiana Securities, both controlled by the Du Pont family, were forced to sell the huge block of General Motors stock they had accumulated.[4] The question is whether a stock acquisition is deemed to lessen competition.

3. *Interlocking directorates.* It is expressly forbidden for a person who is a director of one corporation to sit on the board of another corporation that is in the same industry. This obvious conflict of interest could easily be detected as corporate boards are widely published. (To some degree indirect interlocks sidestep this prohibition. See the box in the "Oligopoly" chapter titled "The Old Boy Network at Six Big Banks.")

---

[4]Du Pont bought about 25 percent of General Motors's stock in 1919. Over the next four decades GM bought most of its seat-cover fabrics, paints, and glues from Du Pont. In 1957 the Supreme Court found that other firms had been unfairly excluded from selling paint, glues, and fabrics to GM and forced Du Pont to sell its GM stock.

4. *Tying contracts.* It is illegal to sell one product on the condition that another product or products be purchased from the same seller. For example, the law prohibits General Electric from telling a buyer it can purchase GE toasters only if it also purchases GE lightbulbs.

5. *Exclusive dealings.* It is illegal to tell a retailer that he or she must not carry some rival firm's product line. For example, RCA cannot tell an appliance dealer that if he wants to carry RCA televisions and VCRs, he can't also carry Sony and Sharp competing products.

The Clayton Act also expressly exempted labor unions from prosecution under the Sherman Act. This was significant because, until the 1911 oil and tobacco cases, the prime target of the Sherman Act had been the Hatters Union in Danbury, Connecticut, back in 1908. The Court construed the union to be a monopoly in restraint of trade; it was fined the huge sum of $210,000 (the equivalent of more than $3 million in today's dollars).

The Federal Trade Commission Act (1914)

FTC as a watchdog

The Federal Trade Commission (FTC) was set up as a watchdog against the anticompetitive practices outlawed by the Sherman and Clayton acts. Although empowered to investigate anticompetitive business practices and issue cease-and-desist orders, the courts stripped most of its powers by the 1920s. In 1938 the Wheeler-Lea Amendment gave the Federal Trade Commission what has become its most important job: preventing false and deceptive advertising.

Pizzeria Uno, one of the nation's leading restaurant chains, had been advertising its low-fat pizzas. In 1996 the Federal Trade Commission forced the company to concede that its ads were false and misleading, and to cease making these claims. By no stretch of the imagination did these pizzas meet the FTC's definition of low fat—three grams per portion. Pizzeria Uno's slices contained 14 to 36 grams of fat. They may make great pizza, but it only goes to show that you can't eat your pie and be skinny too.

In recent years the FTC has been playing a much more active role in approving or disapproving mergers. In 1995 it blocked the proposed merger of the Rite Aid and Revco drugstore chains, contending that the combination would leave millions of consumers with no low-cost outlet for prescription drugs. That same year, it did allow the merger of two pharmaceutical giants, Ciba-Geigy and Sandoz, but only after forcing them to divest themselves of $1 billion in assets to prevent the combined company from dominating several market segments.

When Staples and Office Depot proposed merging in 1997, they agreed to sell hundreds of their stores. Nevertheless the FTC did not approve the deal, arguing that the office supply superstores were a market in themselves, distinct from the much larger market for office goods sold through catalogues, discount chains, and stationery stores.

In the same year the FTC approved the merger of Boeing, which builds 60 percent of the world's commercial aircraft, and MacDonnell Douglas, whose market share had shrunk to just under 10 percent (the remaining 30 percent is built by Airbus Industrie, the European consortium). One reservation the FTC had concerning the merger was Boeing's 20-year contracts to be sole supplier of new jets to American, Delta, and Continental airlines. The European Commission, which is the executive arm of the 15-nation European Union, considered these supply arrangements a threat to the survival of Airbus, and was set to reject the merger.

How, you may ask, can these European guys reject a merger between two American firms? Although the Commission could not technically block the deal, it could make it difficult for Boeing-MacDonnell to do business in Europe by imposing fines of up to 10 percent of the company's worldwide revenues. One day before the Commission was to vote, Boeing-MacDonnell blinked. It agreed to alter its use of the exclusive aircraft supply contracts.

In early 1998 the European Commission, along with antitrust regulators in Australia and Canada, apparently forced the cancellation of an announced merger between two Big

Six accounting firms, Ernst & Young and KPMG Peat Marwick. One of the concerns was that the merger would lead to the layoff of thousands of employees, this at a time of high unemployment in Europe.

Modern Antitrust

Partial Breakdown of the Rule of Reason

Alcoa case

Keep in mind that the Supreme Court continued to be dominated, right into the 1940s, by a conservative majority who had been appointed by the almost unbroken string of Republican presidents who served from the Civil War to the Great Depression. To ensure that the Sherman Act was not applied too vigorously, the justices developed the "rule of reason" doctrine. First applied in the 1911 *Standard Oil* case and then refined in the 1920 *U.S. Steel* case, the rule prevailed until the Alcoa case of 1945. Until then, you had to be big *and* bad before the Court would find you guilty under Sherman.

The membership of the Supreme Court changed radically during the Roosevelt and Truman administrations, which extended for 20 years. In a landmark 1945 decision, the Court found that the Aluminum Company of America (Alcoa), which held 90 percent of the aluminum market, was an illegal monopoly.

The two arguments that Alcoa presented in its defense were rejected. The first, based directly on the rule of reason, was that although it did have a nominal monopoly on aluminum production, it had not intended to exclude competitors and had not, in fact, behaved badly. This argument was rejected by the Court, which noted that the absence of competitors was itself proof of monopolizing.

The second argument advanced by Alcoa was to define the relevant market more broadly than just aluminum. Steel, copper, and even recycled aluminum should be included as well, which would reduce Alcoa's market share from 90 percent to about one-third. This argument, too, was rejected by the Court.

Judged Learned Hand said, "Congress did not condone 'good trusts' and condemn 'bad' ones; it forbade all." A 90 percent share of the market "is enough to constitute a monopoly; it is doubtful whether 60 or 64 percent would be enough, and certainly 33 percent is not."

The Alcoa *decision eclipsed the rule of reason.*

The *Alcoa* decision appeared to sweep away the last vestiges of the rule of reason, making monopoly itself, and not merely monopolization, illegal. This change was underscored by the fact that Alcoa had been big but hadn't been bad.

The *Alcoa* case represented the high-water mark of antitrust enforcement. Eight years later, in the *Du Pont* case, the defendant was able to use the relevant market argument that Alcoa had unsuccessfully raised. Du Pont and a licensee had 100 percent of the nation's cellophane market (and 75 percent of the market for transparent wrapping material). But the Court accepted the argument that the relevant market included all "flexible packaging materials," such as aluminum foil and waxed paper. Du Pont had only 18 percent of the flexible packaging materials market, which would hardly constitute a monopoly. (See the box for a description of four landmark cases.)

The 60 Percent Rule

A firm must be big and bad.

What has apparently evolved from these antitrust decisions is what might be called "the 60 percent rule." Should a firm have a share of at least 60 percent of the relevant market *and* should that firm have behaved badly toward its competitors, it would then be subject to prosecution. However, whether it would be prosecuted would depend on the political and economic outlook of the current administration, and whether it would be found guilty would depend on the outlook of the nine Supreme Court justices.

The Celler-Kefauver Antimerger Act

After a 15-year slowdown caused by the Great Depression and World War II, the pace of the merger movement picked up again. In fact, during the decade following the war,

Four Landmark Cases

The government has brought suit against three virtual monopolies: Xerox, AT&T, and IBM. The government won a clear-cut victory in the Xerox suit in 1975, attained a compromise in the AT&T suit in 1982, and unceremoniously aborted the IBM suit in the same year. The jury is still out, so to speak, on the Microsoft case, which has been dragging on since 1995.

Xerox

This case hinged on whether the relevant market was (as Xerox maintained) *all* paper copiers, which would have given the company less than 50 percent of the market in 1973, or just plain paper copiers (as the government maintained), which would have given Xerox close to 100 percent of the market. What's the difference between a plain paper copier and other copiers? Believe me, you would know by the results. "Other" copiers (which are now obsolete) used coated paper that gave off a chemical smell and was rather disgusting to touch.

Xerox, which held the patents on its paper copiers, agreed to license these patents to its competitors. By this time Japanese competitors were also entering the American market, so Xerox's market share of the plain paper market fell below 50 percent.

AT&T

AT&T was accused of having a monopoly on local phone service (which it could hardly contest) and of making it hard for its long-distance competitors (such as MCI and Sprint) to use its local phone network. In exchange for giving up its 22 local phone companies, AT&T was not only allowed to keep its long-distance service, Bell Labs, and Western Electric, but it was allowed to enter the telecommunications-computer field.

IBM

Originally initiated in 1969, this suit continued for 13 years until the Reagan Justice Department decided to drop it. In 1969 IBM had about 70 percent of the mainframe computer market, which it still held in 1982. But the word processor and minicomputer markets had become important segments of the overall computer market during this period. Thus, the Justice Department reasoned that the changing computer market had made IBM's continued dominance in mainframes much less relevant.

Microsoft

Windows, the Microsoft operating system, runs on more than 90 percent of the 100 million PCs sold in the world each year. The Justice Department was concerned that the company would use this virtual monopoly to force computer makers to use software products it might create in the future, further extending that monopoly.

In 1995 Microsoft signed a consent decree with the government which prohibits the company from tying the purchase of one product to another, but does allow it to develop "integrated" products. In October 1997 the Justice Department brought suit, contending that Microsoft was violating its consent decree by forcing PC makers to take its Internet Explorer browser as a condition of licensing Windows. The company contends that Explorer and Windows are not separate products, but a single integrated product.

In December 1997 Judge Thomas Pennfield Jackson of the U.S. District Court in Washington ruled that Microsoft must separate its Internet browser software from its industry-dominating Windows 95 operating system. He wrote, "The probability that Microsoft will not only continue to reinforce its operating system monopoly by its licensing practices, but might also acquire yet another monopoly in the Internet browser market, is simply too great to tolerate indefinitely until the issue is finally resolved."

Initially Microsoft claimed that it was simply not possible to separate the browser from the current operating system without paralyzing a PC. Judge Jackson, however, countered that he had removed the browser in about 90 seconds from his own PC.

In January 1998 Microsoft agreed to Judge Jackson's order by allowing PC makers to remove the Explorer icon. However, a ruling in the overall consent-decree case was not expected until at least June 1998, and in all probability, the case may drag out well beyond then.

For two decades Microsoft has made computers more powerful and easier to use for millions of consumers by adding more to its program, from point-and-click icons to facsimile software. But its growing market power has enabled the company to crush competitors, thus eliminating competition and innovation and probably harming consumers. What were once separate products, such as the browser, were pulled in to become features of Microsoft's Windows operating program. It may be years before the courts finally resolve these antitrust issues.

Source: John Markoff, "Judge's Rule Is a Setback for Microsoft," *New York Times*, December 12, 1997, p. D1.

Bethlehem Steel–Youngstown Sheet and Tube case

some 2,000 mergers involving large corporations took place. The Celler-Kefauver Act in 1950 was an attempt to slow that pace.

The act forbade companies from merging with or acquiring other companies where the effect "may be substantially to lessen competition, or tend to create a monopoly." Its first test came in the 1958 *Bethlehem Steel–Youngstown Sheet and Tube* case. The Court agreed with the Justice Department that a merger between the number two and the number six steel producers would violate the Celler-Kefauver Act. Even mergers that threatened to reduce *potential* competition were prohibited by the courts in subsequent cases. But all the act really seemed to do was slow down the flood tide of mergers that continued right through the 1960s.

The problem that succeeding Justice Departments had to deal with was the *type* of merger that was now taking place: the conglomerate merger. The laws on the books—the Sherman, Clayton, and Celler-Kefauver acts—were certainly adequate to deal with mergers that lessened actual or potential competition. But none addressed mergers that do not directly threaten competition in any given industry because they occur between firms in different industries.

In the next section, we will take up three types of mergers— horizontal, vertical, and conglomerate—and a fourth type that has become very important in recent years, a sort of diversifying merger.

Baseball's Antitrust Exemption

If you happen to be a serious student of the game of baseball, you're probably aware that in 1922 Congress exempted professional baseball from the provisions of antitrust legislation. Although major-league baseball is clearly a monopoly, the reasoning was that baseball is a sport, not a business. Whether it's a sport, a business, or both, the prolonged 1994–95 baseball strike prompted many members of Congress to consider rescinding baseball's antitrust exemption. I'll have more to say about the baseball strike in the chapter titled "Labor Unions."

Types of Mergers

Horizontal Mergers

Conventional mergers

A horizontal merger is the conventional merger. Two firms in the same industry form one larger company. Usually a larger firm swallows a smaller one. When John D. Rockefeller was running Standard Oil, he swallowed 39 competing firms.

Horizontal integration has become particularly prevalent among the airlines. In recent years Eastern Airlines, Mohawk, Pan Am, National, PeoplesExpress, USAIR, Continental, and Texas Air were all involved in mergers. In addition, there are indications that the pharmaceutical, health care, and telecommunications industries may have begun a period of horizontal mergers.

The legal problem with horizontal mergers is that they appear to violate the Sherman Act. Two competing firms that merge may well lessen competition. The question is, Where do the Justice Department and the courts draw the line? Several years ago Chrysler, the number three firm in the automobile industry, was permitted to merge with American Motors, which was number four. So where do we draw the line? If the number two firm merges with the number three firm, does this lessen competition? The answer depends on the makeup of the administration at the time, which may vary from the relatively restrictive Roosevelt and Truman administrations to the relatively permissive Reagan administration, as well as on the makeup of the courts, which see personnel shifts as justices retire and presidents appoint new ones.

Vertical Mergers

Vertical mergers

When firms that have been engaged in different parts of an industrial process or in manufacturing and selling join together, we have a vertical merger. A maker of TVs and stereos that bought out a retail chain and marketed its TVs and stereos through this new outlet would be an example. If an auto company merged with a steel mill, a tire company, or a glass manufacturer, we would have a vertically integrated company.

Janet Lowe described this process in the entertainment field:

The purchase of the entertainment giant MCA by Matsushita and Columbia Pictures by Sony represented an effort to complete a vertical structure by these two companies. They already produce much of the high-technology equipment used in the entertainment industry; the companies wanted to add to that the technology of programming that was transmitted by their own equipment.[5]

Conglomerate Mergers

Two companies in unrelated fields

A conglomerate merger occurs between two companies in unrelated industries—telephones and hotels, real estate and auto parts, oil and steel. A conglomerate, the product of such mergers, is a group of unrelated companies under one corporate umbrella. The term comes from the Latin *conglomerare,* meaning "to roll together."

The huge wave of conglomerate mergers in the 1960s was the cutting edge of the long-term trend toward corporate concentration. About 80 percent of the mergers during that decade were of the conglomerate variety. In recent years, that figure has fallen to about 50 percent. Firms that were minuscule in the 1950s became corporate giants over the course of 10 or 15 years. In fact, by the late 1950s conglomeration was not only a shortcut to rapid corporate growth, but it was virtually the only available opportunity left for such growth.

The spectacular growth of the larger conglomerates was summarized by Anthony Sampson.

> James Ling of Ling-Temco-Vought built up an obscure defense contractor in 1960 into the 14th biggest American industrial company in 1969, including a meat-packing business, an airline, a car rental firm, and a big manufacturer of jet planes. Charles Bluhdorn . . . set up Gulf & Western in 1956, when it was making car bumpers in Grand Rapids, and then bought up 92 companies, making anything from zinc and sugar to cigars and Paramount films. Thornton bought up a small electronics firm, Litton Industries, for a million dollars and added 103 companies in nine years, with products from ships and calculating machines to textbooks and seismic equipment.[6]

How did they do it? Gulf & Western happened to have a friend at Chase Manhattan, which financed many of its acquisitions. Chase then got the accounts of the acquired firms, and often the cash of these firms was used to make still further acquisitions.

In 1972 ITT agreed to sell off some of its component firms.

ITT is really a case unto itself. We tend to think of this firm as just a telephone company, but some of the firms that have been associated with it at one time or another are very familiar names—Avis, Sheraton Hotels, Hartford Insurance, Levitt Houses (builders of Levittowns in Pennsylvania and on Long Island), and Wonder Bread. As the biggest conglomerate in the United States, it is an almost self-sufficient company. Its executives at one time could have attended conventions in Sheraton hotels in many different cities, all of which might have been insured by Hartford. They could have used Avis cars and eaten sandwiches dispensed by Canteen machines and made with Wonder bread. Of course, all of this was before June 13, 1995, when ITT announced its plans to break up into three separate companies—an industrial products manufacturing business; an insurance company; and a casino, hotel, and sports company. If other conglomerates follow suit, perhaps the latter half of the 1990s will be called the age of deconglomeration.

Conglomerating has several advantages. In addition to providing ready-made markets for the goods and services produced by various divisions, the very diversity of the company is insurance against economic adversity. A downturn in one industry will not hurt too much because the firm is diversified into many industries. A strike in one component firm or division will shut down only a small part of the entire conglomerate because virtually all unions are organized along industry or craft lines. For example, if the Screen Actors Guild (Ronald Reagan was its first president) went on strike, Viacom, which owns Paramount, would hardly notice.

There are tax advantages to conglomeration.

There are also tax advantages to conglomerating. If you purchase a firm that then loses money, those losses may be subtracted from your profits before you pay taxes. For example, if a conglomerate makes $200 million, it will have to pay about $70 million in

---

[5]Janet Lowe, *The Secret Empire: How 25 Multinationals Rule the World* (Burr Ridge, IL: Business One Irwin, 1992), p. 65.

[6]Anthony Sampson, *The Sovereign State of ITT* (New York: Fawcett Crest, 1974), p. 152.

taxes. But if it picks up a firm that lost, say, $100 million, its income is now $100 million and it will have to pay only about $35 million in corporate income tax.

Also important is the power derived from forming a big company. Roy Ash of Litton Industries became President Richard Nixon's director of management and budget. G. William Miller went from the presidency of Textron to Federal Reserve chairman and then secretary of the Treasury under President Jimmy Carter. Within the corporate world itself, it's much more fun and it's much more ego gratifying to see your company grow from a nothing into a major force in just a few years. ITT, Tenneco, Gulf & Western, TRW, and Viacom all started out as minnows and have grown into corporate whales.

The king of conglomerates today is General Electric, a mix of manufacturing, finance, and broadcasting, including NBC. Walt Disney now owns not just hotels and theme parks, but ABC as well. And what ever became of ITT? It split into three separate companies, and one of its progeny has split in three again.

Deregulation

Ronald Reagan spoke to the frustrations of millions of people who ran businesses of all sizes when he said back in 1980 that he would "get the government off the backs of the American people." Reagan estimated that American businesses spent upwards of $100 billion a year just to follow all the federal rules and regulations and to employ people to fill out all the required forms. Did he succeed in cutting the red tape? Not really, inasmuch as the pile of paperwork imposed by the federal government is higher now than ever. But he did continue deregulating American industry, something that had been started a couple of years earlier under President Jimmy Carter. The box "The Deregulation Scorecard" discusses the effects of the deregulation of three major industries—the airlines, long-distance trucking, and long-distance phone calling.[7]

At this juncture the results of deregulation have been quite good. Clearly prices have been held down by competition among the long-haul trucking firms, the long-distance phone companies, and the airlines. Since 1979 the number of trucking companies has tripled to 45,000. AT&T now goes head-to-head with MCI, Sprint, and dozens of smaller companies. But fierce competition has driven several major airline carriers out of business, most notably Eastern and Pan Am.

The effects of the Reagan revolution on the environment, as well as on worker health and safety; the cutting down of the redwoods (Reagan once remarked, "If you've seen one redwood, you've seen 'em all"); and the actions of James Watt, the ecological disaster Reagan appointed as secretary of the interior, are all extremely important issues, but I just can't include them in a book this size (notice how I *did* manage to editorialize about them anyway).

How Effective Is Antitrust?

What do we want antitrust to do?

What do we want antitrust to do? If we want to create something approximating perfect competition, antitrust has failed miserably. If we would like to prevent further oligopolization of American industry, it has been a qualified success. *How* qualified?

As Al Smith, the governor of New York more than 60 years ago, used to say, "Let's look at the record." Since the Sherman Act (1890) and the Clayton Act (1914), we have seen industrial concentration become still greater. When firms in the Fortune 100 merge—Du Pont and Continental Oil, U.S. Steel and Marathon Oil, Occidental and Cities Service, General Electric and RCA, and Texaco and Getty Oil—the degree of concentration increases. Were mergers to continue at this pace, by the early part of the next century just a handful of companies would be doing most of the nation's business.

---

[7]The railroads (1976–80) and the natural gas industry (1978) were also deregulated. In Chapter 12 (of *Economics* and *Macroeconomics*) we talked about the disastrous effects of deregulation on the savings and loan industry.

The Deregulation Scorecard

Under the administrations of Jimmy Carter and Ronald Reagan, a great deal of deregulation took place in banking, the airlines, long-distance trucking, and long-distance phone calling. In banking, the country ended up with the savings and loan debacle (discussed in Chapter 12 of *Economics* and *Macroeconomics*), which will ultimately cost American taxpayers about $300 billion. But the effects of deregulation in the other industries have been much more salutary.

The airline industry is still in flux after a series of bankruptcies and mergers, but labor productivity rose 20 percent during the first five years of deregulation, costs have been cut, and in general airfares have been held below where they would have been without deregulation.

Before deregulation, the Interstate Commerce Commission sometimes forced truckers to take roundabout routes and to return with empty trucks from long hauls. In the first 10 years after deregulation, many new firms were attracted to the industry, and shipping rates have decreased substantially.

The key to long-distance phone calling is the breakup of AT&T, with the parent company still in the long-distance business but the regional Baby Bells spun off into independent companies that handle local and intrastate (within a state) calls. AT&T, MCI, Sprint, and a host of new competitors are falling all over themselves to provide customers with low-priced, quality service. The words of Alfred Kahn, who was chairman of the Civil Aeronautics Board when deregulation was coming into vogue, were an excellent forecast of things to come: "I have more faith in greed than in regulation."*

In a study of the effects of deregulation, Robert Crandall and Jerry Ellig concluded that

> Within 10 years, prices were at least 25 percent lower, and sometimes close to 50 percent lower. . . . Consumers gained substantially—not just because of rate reductions, but also because of improvements in the quality of service.†

New York Times, October 7, 1980.
†Robert Crandall and Jerry Ellig, *Economic Deregulation and Consumer Choice: Lesson for the Electric Industry* (Fairfax, VA: Center for Market Processes of George Mason University, 1996), p. 3.

Things could have been a lot worse without antitrust.

On the other hand, things could have been a lot worse. Without antitrust, there would have been no legal means for the government to curb even those mergers that most blatantly stifled competition. Furthermore, many firms hesitate to merge because they are fairly certain the Justice Department *would* take legal action.

Few of the recent mergers have involved leading firms in any industry. Presumably, even the rather permissive Reagan Justice Department would have stepped in to block the merger of, say, General Motors (number one) and Ford (number two). But it didn't stop Chrysler (number three) and American Motors (number four).

In the spring of 1995 Microsoft, the world's largest software company, announced its intention to acquire Intuit in what would have been the largest deal ever in the software industry. But the Antitrust Division of the Justice Department soon filed suit to block the deal, saying it would lead to higher prices for consumers and less innovation in the market for personal finance software. Within a month Microsoft abandoned its planned acquisition because of the suit and the possibility of protracted litigation.

Just a few weeks later, IBM, the world's largest computer maker, and Lotus, a large software rival of Microsoft, managed to work out a $3.5 billion deal, to which the Federal Trade Commission and the Justice Department quickly gave their blessing. Now why did the government approve this deal but veto the Microsoft–Intuit merger? Did you figure out the answer? Microsoft and Intuit both make software. When the largest software company tried to merge with a rival, the government said no. But IBM makes computers and Lotus makes software, so the government said yes.

If we judge the antitrust record not just on the basis of what *has* happened but also on what *has not* happened, it doesn't look all that bad. Should it have been better? Some critics point out that antitrust really freezes the status quo. Small firms are sometimes prevented from merging, while larger firms are left alone. To allow more competition, the critics say, the number 9 and 10 firms should be able to merge, and the number 1 and 2 firms should not.

This criticism is not completely valid, at least in regard to the activities of recent years, because small firms *do* merge. And so do not-so-small firms.

Is antitrust a misguided numbers game?

Antitrust enforcement may hinder American competition with foreigners, especially the Japanese. For example, 7 of the 10 largest banks in the world are Japanese; Chase Manhattan, our largest, is number 16.

Other critics argue that antitrust policy is a misguided numbers game. By worrying only about the number of competitors in an industry or the degree of concentration, the Justice Department ignores the role of dynamic competition. The innovator may attain a temporary monopoly—such as those held by Kleenex, Xerox, and IBM—but other entrepreneurs will quickly imitate the new product or process if it is successful.

Again, this view has a certain validity; no one would want the government to stifle industrial creativity. However, the whole focus of antitrust policy has been on mergers and not on firms that generate their own growth. The point that antitrust cannot play it solely by the numbers is nonetheless well taken.

The Trend toward Bigness

One of the refreshing things about economics is that we can all look at exactly the same data and come to widely varying conclusions. One view—to which I don't happen to subscribe—is that economic competition has grown in recent years for three reasons. First, there's much more foreign competition. However, as huge foreign firms buy up American firms (we'll talk about this in the final chapter, "International Finance") or squeeze them out of business, we may end up with *less* competition than we had before the foreign firms began competing. The second reason is the declining importance of manufacturing (which is dominated by relatively large firms) relative to the service industries (where smaller firms prevail); this makes for a lot more competition. And third, the rise of new industries, such as production of microcomputers and computer software, has created many small, highly competitive firms.

All that said, my own opinion, if it has somehow eluded you, is that by and large American business is steadily becoming more and more concentrated. Even in the computer software industry, tiny firms like Microsoft grow into giants overnight. Let's take a closer look at manufacturing.

In 1929, after a decade of considerable consolidation (General Motors alone gobbled up more than 100 independent carmakers), the 200 largest firms produced less than 40 percent of our manufactured goods. Today they produce over 60 percent.[8]

If you care to glance back at Table 1 of the "Oligopoly" chapter, you'll see still more evidence of corporate concentration. But I've saved my best shot for last: Table 1 of this chapter.

By the mid-1980s the corporate takeover frenzy really set in. White knights, corporate raiders, junk bonds, and leveraged buyouts may not have done much to spur investment in plant, equipment, or research and development, nor did they stimulate economic growth, but they definitely expanded our vocabulary.

By early 1993 several of the leading players were no longer in the game. Ivan Boesky, who had paid a $100 million fine for engaging in insider trading, had served a short jail term and then disappeared from public view. Michael Milken, the man who invented the junk bond (which was used to finance many of the takeovers) had paid $1.1 billion in fines and settlements for securities fraud and had finished serving a 22-month prison term. And his employer, Drexel Burnham Lambert, which had led the charge into the junk bond business, had gone bankrupt.

As you can see in Table 1, 16 of the largest mergers in U.S. history took place in 1996 and 1997. And of the top 15 mergers of all time, eight were in communications. One may wonder, after the break-up of AT&T back in 1982 (see box, "Four Landmark Cases"), if we may not be heading for another communications monopoly.

---

[8] For a study that reaches the opposite conclusions, see William G. Shepherd, "The Causes of Increased Competition in the U.S. Economy, 1939–1980," *Review of Economics and Statistics* (November 1982).

Table 1   The Largest U.S. Corporate Mergers and Acquisitions

Target Name	Acquirer Name	Year	Value of Transaction in $ Billion*
Citicorp	Travelers Group	1998	70.0
NationsBank	Bank America	1998	60.00
MCI Communications Corp.	WorldCom Inc.	1997	41.9
RJR Nabisco Inc.	Kohlberg Kravis Roberts & Co.	1988	30.6
Banc One	First Chicago NBD	1998	30.0
NYNEX Corp.	Bell Atlantic Corp.	1996	21.3
MCI Communications Corp.	British Telecommunications	1996	18.9
Capital Cities/ABC Inc.	Walt Disney Co.	1995	18.9
Corestates Financial	First Union	1997	17.1
Pacific Telesis Group	SBC Communications Inc.	1996	16.4
McCaw Cellular Commun Inc.	American Telephone & Telegraph Co.	1993	15.7
Warner Communications Inc.	Time Inc.	1989	14.1
Barnett Banks, Jacksonville, FL	NationsBank Corp., Charlotte, NC	1997	13.8
MFS Communications Co. Inc.	WorldCom Inc.	1996	13.6
Kraft Inc.	Philip Morris	1988	13.4
Gulf Oil Corp.	Standard Oil Co. of California	1984	13.4
McDonnell Douglas Corp.	Boeing Co.	1996	13.4
ITT Corp.	Hilton Hotels Corp.	1997	12.4
Squibb Corp.	Bristol-Myers Co.	1989	12.1
Northrop Grumman Corp.	Lockheed Martin Corp.	1997	11.8
Continental Cablevision Inc.	US West Media Group	1996	11.4
HFS Inc.	CUC International Inc.	1997	11.3
First Interstate Bancorp, CA	Wells Fargo & Co.	1995	10.9
Morgan Stanley Group Inc.	Dean Witter Discover & Co.	1997	10.6
Conrail Inc.	Investor Group	1996	10.4
Getty Oil Co.	Texaco Inc.	1984	10.1
Chase Manhattan Corp.	Chemical Banking Corp.	1995	9.9
Boatmen's Bancshares, St. Louis	NationsBank Corp., Charlotte, NC	1996	9.7
Paramount Communications	Viacom Inc.	1993	9.6
American Cyanamid Co.	American Home Products Corp.	1994	9.6
Hughes Aircraft Co.	Raytheon Co.	1997	9.5

*Securities Data includes assumption of debt in its calculation of the value.

Source: Securities Data Co.

Corporate Raiders, White Knights, Stock Repurchases, and Leveraged Buyouts

Any way you slice it, corporate takeovers and the financial defenses erected against them have diverted tens of billions of dollars a year from investment in new plant and equipment. Furthermore, the wave of leveraged buyouts and hostile takeovers has forced corporate officers to focus on short-term profitability rather than on long-term growth. Then, too, costly takeovers financed by mountains of debt have placed corporations in precarious financial straits.

In the 1980s hundreds of billions of dollars changed hands in scores of big-name mergers. Yet no new refineries were built because Chevron spent more than $13 billion to buy Gulf. Nor did the $30.6 billion R. J. Reynolds–Nabisco merger result in the erection of new production facilities to turn out still more cigarettes or breakfast cereals. And when the overextended Campeau Corporation purchased Allied Stores and Federated Department Stores for a total of more than $6 billion in the late 1980s, the whole structure came crashing down into bankruptcy before the decade was out.

Corporate officers knew that their restive stockholders watched the quarterly profit figures as avidly as they watched the stock market ticker. If those profits dipped for even one quarter, the corporation could easily become the target of an unfriendly takeover. So anything that might even temporarily depress profits—spending on research and development, a new factory, or a better computer system—was often vetoed, although it probably would have enhanced growth and profits three, four, or five years down the road.

Corporations are in hock up to their eyeballs, largely because of the takeover frenzy of the 1980s. Right now corporate debt is more than $3.5 trillion, a sum that is only slightly smaller than the national debt. Irving Kristol has noted that "the debt to equity ratio of American corporations is on the rise as corporation after corporation frantically tries to escape dismemberment."*

Can we blame the corporate takeover fever of the last decade for our lagging investment in plant and equipment? While there were plenty of other problems that we discussed in the last few chapters, it's obvious that the takeovers and their accompanying mountain of debt made a bad situation a lot worse.

*The Wall Street Journal, May 13, 1988, p. 16.

The trend toward consolidation in banking accelerated in 1997 and early 1998. NationsBank, through mergers in 1996, 1997, and 1998, became the largest bank (see Table 1).

What effect have corporate takeovers had on our economy? Have they been a drain on investment funds? Does the threat of a takeover keep management on its toes, or does it force management to take costly defensive measures and reinforce an outlook that can see no further than the quarterly profit figure? (See box "Corporate Raiders, White Knights, Stock Repurchases, and Leveraged Buyouts" on the previous page.)

Sorry, I don't have the answers to these questions, but my asking them should give you a pretty good clue. You might try to imagine how much our country's economic performance could be improved if we could harness all the energy and financial resources that go into financial manipulations and use them for truly productive purposes.

Will the government do anything? Even if it were to begin to move against future mergers, it would be years before these cases were actually settled. It is probably safe to say, then, that the latest wave of mergers, which began in the 1950s and accelerated during the last decade, will continue unabated until at least the beginning of the 21st century.

In April 1998, Travelers Group, an insurance brokerage firm, and Citicorp, the nation's second largest bank, announced their plans to carry out the largest merger in corporate history. If it goes through, it will create the world's largest financial-services concern. However, in the spring of 1998, it was uncertain whether the government would approve either this merger or the second largest merger—that between Worldcom and MCI.

Questions for Further Thought and Discussion

1. How effective is antitrust?
2. Trace the strength of the corporate merger movement since the early 1980s.
3. What was the historical and political background against which the Sherman Antitrust Act was passed?
4. Trace the use of the rule of reason since it was first applied in the *U.S. Steel* case.

Multiple-Choice Questions

Circle the letter that corresponds to the best answer.

1. Which statement is true?

   a. Since the Civil War the United States has seen a steady expansion of corporate concentration.

   b. Since the Civil War, corporate concentration has become much less pronounced.   c. Corporate concentration has remained about the same since the Civil War.   d. None of these statements is true.

2. The first trustbusters were Presidents

   a. Teddy Roosevelt and William Howard Taft

   b. Franklin Roosevelt and Harry Truman

   c. Dwight D. Eisenhower and John Kennedy

   d. Jimmy Carter and Ronald Reagan

3. A key passage of the _____ Act stated that "every contract, combination in the form of trust or otherwise, in restraint of commerce among the several states, or with foreign nations, is hereby declared illegal."

   a. Clayton   b. FTC   c. Celler-Kefauver   d. Sherman

4. The trusts won only the _____ case.

   a. *Addyston Pipe*   b. *U.S. Steel*   c. *American Tobacco*   d. *Standard Oil*

5. In 1911 the Supreme Court decided to

   a. allow the trusts to keep functioning as they had in the past   b. break up the trusts   c. let the trusts off with small fines   d. put the leaders of the trusts in jail

6. Until the *Alcoa* case, the Supreme Court generally held that

   a. bigness was all right as long as the company wasn't bad   b. bigness was all right under any circumstances   c. a company could do as it pleased as long as it wasn't big

7. The Supreme Court's rule of reason was applied

   a. from the time of the Civil War   b. from 1911 to 1945   c. after 1945   d. after 1970

8. The high-water mark of antitrust enforcement was marked by the _____ case.

   a. *Alcoa*   b. *U.S. Steel*   c. *Addyston Pipe*   d. *IBM*

9. The Clayton Antitrust Act prohibited each of the following except

   a. price discrimination   b. interlocking stockholding   c. interlocking directorates   d. trusts

10. The most important job of the Federal Trade Commission today is to

    a. prevent false and deceptive advertising   b. break up unlawful trusts   c. issue cease-and-desist orders when anticompetitive business practices occur   d. promote commerce with foreign nations

11. The rule of reason today is

    a. outlawed   b. partially in force   c. completely irrelevant

12. Antitrust today could best be summed up by the

    a. 90 percent rule   b. 60 percent rule   c. rule of reason   d. one-year rule

13. Labor unions became exempt from antitrust enforcement under the _____ Act.

    a. Sherman   b. Clayton   c. FTC   d. Celler-Kefauver

14. The Celler-Kefauver Act was aimed at mergers that

    a. may substantially lessen competition or tend to create a monopoly   b. result in the formation of conglomerates   c. result in diversifying the products and services produced by a corporation   d. may help competition but reduce the number of firms in the industry

617

15. In the 1950s and 1960s the predominant form of merger was the _____ merger.

    a. horizontal **b.** vertical **c.** conglomerate

    d. diversifying

16. In recent years, the government decided to drop the _____ _____ case.

    a. *U.S. Steel* **b.** *AT&T* **c.** *Xerox* **d.** *IBM*

17. When two firms in the same industry form one larger company, this is a _____ merger.

    a. horizontal **b.** vertical **c.** conglomerate

    d. diversifying

18. ITT, Ling-Temco-Vought, Textron, and Gulf & Western are all the products of _____ mergers.

    a. horizontal **b.** vertical **c.** conglomerate

    d. diversifying

19. Since 1929 the percent of American manufactured output produced by the 200 largest industrial firms has

    a. decreased **b.** stayed about the same

    c. increased substantially **d.** doubled

20. Since the early 1980s the size of companies acquired in mergers has been

    a. getting smaller **b.** staying about the same

    c. getting larger

21. In general, the deregulation of the airlines and interstate trucking led to

    a. lower costs and lower prices **b.** higher costs and higher prices **c.** higher costs and lower prices

    d. lower costs and higher prices

Fill-In Questions

1. The first trustbuster presidents were _____ _____ and _____ .

2. In 1911 the Supreme Court broke up the _____ _____ and the _____ .

3. In the late 19th century trusts were formed. They were _____ ; the largest trust was the _____ _____ trust.

4. "Every person who shall monopolize, or conspire with any other person or persons to monopolize, any part of the trade or commerce of the several states, or with foreign nations, shall be guilty of a misdemeanor" was a key passage of the _____ Act.

5. The first case to be tried under the Sherman Act was the _____ case; the companies were found _____ of _____ .

6. In 1911 the Supreme Court broke up the _____ _____ trust into three component parts:

    (1) _____ ;

    (2) _____ ;

    and (3) _____ .

7. The Supreme Court broke up the trusts in 1911 because they _____ .

8. "Bigness was no offense" was the underpinning of the _____ .

9. A _____ makes the sale of one product conditional on the purchase of another product or products from the same seller; _____ stipulate that a retailer must not carry some rival firm's product line.

10. Expressly forbidding a person who is a director of one corporation to sit on the board of another corporation in the same industry is a provision of the_____ _____ Act.

11. _____ used the relevant market argument successfully in its case, just eight years after the *Alcoa* case.

12. The Celler-Kefauver Act forbids a company's merger with, or acquisition of, other companies where the effect may be _____ _____.

13. By the 1950s and 1960s, the most prevalent type of merger was the _____ merger.

14. The government's reason for dropping the *IBM* case was that _____.

15. A vertical merger takes place when two firms that _____ _____ join together, while a horizontal merger takes place when two firms that _____ _____ join together.

16. Had there been no antitrust, there probably would have been _____ _____.

17. The largest mergers have taken place in the _____ _____ industry.

18. In 1929 the largest 200 firms produced about _____ _____ percent of U.S. manufactured goods; today they produce _____ percent.

29 Demand in the Factor Market

Every few chapters you probably hear gears grinding as we shift and head off in another direction. So buckle up because here we go again. This time we're moving away from how businesses compete to how they manage their resources. In the preceding six chapters we analyzed the behavior of firms as sellers in the market for final goods and services; now we'll analyze how they behave in the market for factors of production.

Chapter 2 talked about the factors of production, or resources. This chapter looks into how their prices are determined.

Right now we'll look at demand in the factor market. We'll develop the concept of marginal revenue product, on which demand is based. This will set up the next three chapters, where we'll deal specifically with labor unions and the determination of wages, rent, interest, and profits.

Our main endeavor in this chapter is to use the concept of marginal revenue product to determine how many units of a factor will be hired by perfect and imperfect competitors. As we shall see, the law of demand and supply plays a central role.

Chapter Objectives

The chief concepts we'll cover are:

- Derived demand.
- Productivity.
- Marginal revenue product.
- Changes in resource demand.
- The substitution and output effects.
- Optimum resource mix for the firm.

Derived Demand

Previous chapters dealt with the demand for goods and services. Demand for these goods and services is sometimes called *final demand.* Examples of final demand are the demand for cars, TVs, haircuts, medical services, or gasoline.

What is derived demand derived from?

Now we'll look at *derived demand,* which is the demand for resources. There are four resources: land, labor, capital, and entrepreneurial ability. The demand for these resources is derived from the demand for the final products. For example, the demand for land on which to grow corn is derived from the demand for corn, and the demand for labor with which to produce cars is derived from the demand for cars.

A change in final demand brings about a change in derived demand. The Arab oil embargo and the quadrupling of oil prices in 1973 led to a decline in the demand for large cars. This caused massive layoffs in Detroit. Thus a decline in the demand for the final product, cars, led to a decline in the derived demand for the resource of autoworkers. Simultaneous with the falling demand for American cars, the Russian wheat crop failed and the Soviet Union made massive purchases of American wheat. This, in turn, drove up the demand for farm labor and farmland in the United States.

Productivity

In addition to the demand for the final product, two other factors influence the demand for the productive resources (land, labor, capital, and entrepreneurial ability). First we'll consider the productivity of the resource and then the relative prices of substitutable resources.

Productivity is *output per unit of input.* What exactly is meant by *productivity* and *unit of input?* Productivity itself is really measured by what is produced. "I had a productive night," my friend confided over a plate of lo mein in an all-night Chinese restaurant after a party. "Productive?" I asked. "Sure," he said, "I got 16 phone numbers." That's productive! Especially since he's 84 years old.

What about units of input? Inputs measure the four resources—land, labor, capital, and entrepreneurial ability. Thus, a unit of input might be an hour of labor, an acre of land, or an automobile assembly line.

Let's put these concepts together. Productivity is output per unit of input. If John produces 8 microchips per hour and Sally produces 16, Sally is twice as productive as John. If 30 bushels of wheat are harvested from acre one and 10 bushels from acre two, acre one is three times as productive as acre two.

The more productive a resource is, the more it will be in demand. Obviously, acre one is in much greater demand than is acre two. This would be reflected in both their prices and their rents. Similarly, Sally can obtain much higher wages than John because she is so much more productive.

Prices of Substitute Resources

A given good or service can usually be produced in many different ways. The producer can use various combinations of resources. The Chinese, for example, didn't have many capital goods available a few decades ago, so when they built a factory they used a very labor-intensive method of construction. Thousands of workers dug the hole for the foundation, carting off the dirt in wicker baskets. In the United States, where we have a great deal of capital equipment, we use a capital-intensive method of production. Bulldozers and other earth-moving equipment get the job done with much less labor.

In each country the cheapest production method available is used. China happens to be a labor-intensive country because capital is relatively expensive. In the United States we use a capital-intensive method because labor is relatively expensive.

Photocopy machines are so expensive in China that you won't find them in many neighborhood stores, and they certainly aren't standard equipment in home offices. Suppose you need to send out 50 copies of your résumé. Will you type out each copy or type one and photocopy the rest? Figure it out. Do you type individual résumés when you're looking for a job, or do you get a hundred photocopied or offset for 5 cents apiece? If the wage rate were just 10 or 15 cents an hour—as it still is in some of the poorer countries of the world—you'd be typing your résumés.

When wages rise, many companies seek to substitute machinery for relatively expensive labor. By automating, they will be able to lower their costs of production. If land became more expensive, farmers would work each acre much more intensively, substituting labor and capital for relatively more expensive land.

The demand for a resource is its marginal revenue product schedule. After we see how this schedule is derived, we'll return to our discussion of the determinants of the demand for a resource and how changes in those determinants change that demand.

Marginal Revenue Product (MRP)

The demand for resources is derived mainly from the demand for the final product. Resource productivity and the relative prices of substitutable resources also help determine price. Now we're ready to see how a firm decides how much of a resource to purchase.

How much of a resource a firm will purchase depends on three things: (1) the price of that resource, (2) the productivity of that resource, and (3) the selling price of the final product that the resource helps to produce. We'll go through a few numerical examples to find out how much land, labor, and capital will be purchased by a firm. Along the way, I'll introduce three new terms: *marginal physical product, marginal revenue product,* and *marginal revenue product schedule.* The last is the firm's demand schedule for a given resource. (See the box "The Concept of Margin in Economic Analysis.")

Table 1 has an output schedule for a firm that is using up to 10 units of labor. I'd like you to fill in the column for marginal physical product, remembering to do it in ink so we can sell a lot of new books. Just treat marginal physical product as you've treated marginal cost and marginal revenue. Marginal physical product is simply the additional output produced by one more unit of input (in this case, one more unit of labor).[1]

Table 1   Hypothetical Output of Labor Hired by a Firm

Units of Labor	Output	Marginal Physical Product
1	15	_____
2	29	_____
3	41	_____
4	51	_____
5	58	_____
6	62	_____
7	63	_____
8	63	_____
9	62	_____
10	60	_____

---

[1]You'll notice that the second worker adds less to output than the first worker, and that the third adds less to output than the second. Why? Diminishing returns is why. If you're really interested in the whys and wherefores of diminishing returns, this topic was discussed toward the end of Chapter 16 of *Economics* and *Macroeconomics.*

ADVANCED WORK .... **The Concept of Margin in Economic Analysis** ....

We discussed diminishing returns in Chapter 16 of *Economics* and *Macroeconomics.* If you were to glance back at that section, you'd see that the marginal physical product we're computing here is identical to the marginal output we computed there.

Indeed, all of our marginal concepts—marginal physical product, marginal output, marginal cost, marginal revenue, and the soon-to-be-introduced marginal revenue product—are cut from the same cloth, so to speak. Let's define each.

- Marginal output, or marginal physical product, is the additional output produced by one more unit of a resource.

- Marginal cost is the cost of producing one additional unit of output.

- Marginal revenue is the additional revenue for selling one more unit of output.

- Marginal revenue product is the additional revenue obtained by selling the output produced by one more unit of a resource.

The concept of margin is central to economic analysis. These marginal concepts enable us to figure out exactly what mix of resources we should use, what output we should produce, and what price we should charge in order to maximize our profits—which remains, of course, our bottom line.

I hope your marginal physical product schedule checks out with mine in Table 2. Notice that the marginal physical product is zero with the 8th worker and negative with the 9th and 10th workers. The 8th worker adds nothing to output, while the 9th and 10th workers are in the way. No business firm would hire more than seven workers under these circumstances, even if the wage rate were a penny an hour. (For extra help, see the box "Productivity and Marginal Physical Product.")

Table 3 has a column for price. Why is it always the same no matter how large output is? Because in this case we're dealing with a perfect competitor. Later in the chapter we'll have an imperfect competitor. If a monopolist, monopolistic competitor, or oligopolist wants to sell more, she must lower price.

Go ahead and fill in the third column of Table 3. That should be a cinch for you by this time. Now for the fifth column, total revenue product. Try your luck on this one.

Let's check your methodology. Did you multiply output (column 2) by price (column 4)? If you did, you definitely got total revenue product (column 5) right because it's pretty hard to multiply a number by 10 and get the wrong answer.

MRP is the additional revenue obtained by selling the output produced by one more unit of a resource.

Oh yes, I almost forgot! How do we find marginal revenue product? First, we'll define it. MRP is *the additional revenue obtained by selling the output produced by one more unit of a resource.* To find MRP, just take the difference in total revenue product between units of land. We'll start with the first unit of land; it produces a total revenue product of $200. Because zero units of land produce no revenue, the MRP of the first unit of land is $200. How about the second unit of land? Just take the total revenue produced by two units of land and subtract the total revenue produced by one unit of land. And so forth. After you've done that for all nine units, check your results with those in Table 4.

Table 2   Hypothetical Output of Labor Hired by a Firm

Units of Labor	Output	Marginal Physical Product
1	15	15
2	29	14
3	41	12
4	51	10
5	58	7
6	62	4
7	63	1
8	63	0
9	62	−1
10	60	−2

Productivity and Marginal Physical Product

The relationship between productivity and marginal physical product, or marginal output, could stand some clarification. Suppose a machine operator produces 100 units per hour. That's her productivity. A second machine operator is hired. If their combined output is 198, then their average productivity is 99 (198/2 = 99).

We can also say that the marginal output, or marginal physical product, of the second worker is 98. However, we're not saying that the second worker is not as productive as the first worker, but just that if a second worker were added, output would rise by 98.

Table 3   Hypothetical Marginal Revenue Product Schedule

(1) Units of Land	(2) Output	(3) Marginal Physical Product	(4) Price	(5) Total Revenue Product	(6) Marginal Revenue Product
1	20	____	$10	____	____
2	38	____	10	____	____
3	53	____	10	____	____
4	65	____	10	____	____
5	73	____	10	____	____
6	78	____	10	____	____
7	80	____	10	____	____
8	80	____	10	____	____
9	79	____	10	____	____

Table 4   Hypothetical Marginal Revenue Product Schedule

(1) Units of Land	(2) Output	(3) Marginal Physical Product	(4) Price	(5) Total Revenue Product	(6) Marginal Revenue Product*
1	20	20	$10	$200	$200
2	38	18	10	380	180
3	53	15	10	530	150
4	65	12	10	650	120
5	73	8	10	730	80
6	78	5	10	780	50
7	80	2	10	800	20
8	80	0	10	800	0
9	79	−1	10	790	−10

*There's a much easier way of finding the marginal revenue product. Just multiply the marginal physical product by the price. This works for the perfect competitor; unfortunately, it doesn't work for the imperfect competitor. To avoid confusion, as well as to ensure that we get the right answers when we find the MRP for the imperfect competitor, let's stick with our method of using total revenue product to find the MRP.

You may have noticed that you can also find MRP by multiplying marginal physical product by price. In Table 4, one unit of land has a MRP of 20 and a price of $10 (20 × $10 = MRP of $200). The second unit of land has a MRP of 18 and a price of $10 (18 × $10 = $180). Can you use this shortcut to find MRP? You can when you're finding the MRP of the perfect competitor. But in another couple of pages we'll be finding the MRP of the imperfect competitor. To do that you'll have to use our original method—taking differences in total revenue product produced by additional units of a resource.

Let's do some marginal analysis.

Now we're ready to do some marginal analysis using Table 4. How many units of land would you hire if you needed to pay $200 rent per unit? Think about it. How much is that land worth to you? The answer lies in the MRP schedule, which is the firm's demand schedule for land.

OK, time's up. You'd hire just one unit of land because only that first unit is worth $200. Sorry if you missed that one, but don't despair. I'll give you another chance. How many units of land would you hire if the rent were $150? Go back to the MRP schedule.

What do you say? Three units? Did you say three units? If you did, then you may proceed to the next plateau.

Careful now. How many units of land would you hire if its price were $90? Assume the land is indivisible. That means you can't subdivide it. OK, what's your answer? Four units? Five units? Sorry, only one guess to a customer. The answer is: four units. Why not five? Because the fifth unit of land is worth only $80 according to your own MRP schedule. Would you shell out $90 for something worth only $80 to you? I hope you wouldn't.

Let's work out one more MRP schedule. Fill in Table 5, and then check your work with the figures in Table 6.

One last question: Is the firm whose MRP schedule is shown in Table 6 a perfect competitor or an imperfect competitor? The envelope, please. The answer is: The firm is a perfect competitor. How do we know? We know because the firm can sell its entire output at the same price—$12.

Graphing the MRP

In Figure 1 I've drawn a graph of the MRP schedule shown in Table 4. This curve represents the firm's demand curve for land. As you would expect, it slopes downward to the right. Now I'd like you to draw a graph of the MRP schedule shown in Table 5. Draw it on your own piece of graph paper. Then see whether it matches my graph in Figure 2.

Table 5   Hypothetical MRP Schedule

(1) Units of Land	(2) Output	(3) Marginal Physical Product	(4) Price	(5) Total Revenue Product	(6) Marginal Revenue Product
1	18	———	$12	———	———
2	34	———	12	———	———
3	48	———	12	———	———
4	59	———	12	———	———
5	68	———	12	———	———
6	74	———	12	———	———
7	77	———	12	———	———
8	78	———	12	———	———

Table 6   Hypothetical MRP Schedule of the Perfect Competitor

(1) Units of Land	(2) Output	(3) Marginal Physical Product	(4) Price	(5) Total Revenue Product	(6) Marginal Revenue Product
1	18	18	$12	$216	$216
2	34	16	12	408	192
3	48	14	12	576	168
4	59	11	12	708	132
5	68	9	12	816	108
6	74	6	12	888	72
7	77	3	12	924	36
8	78	1	12	936	12

Figure 1   The Marginal Revenue Product Curve

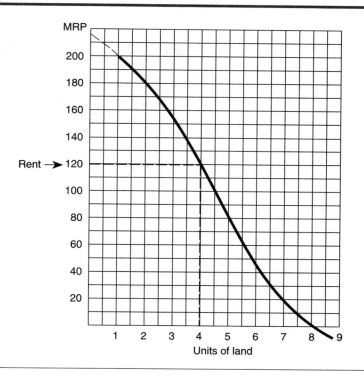

Figure 2   The Marginal Revenue Product Curve of the Perfect Competitor

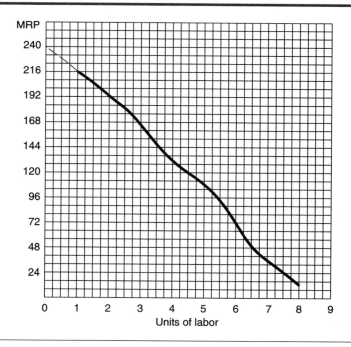

Let's do some graphical analysis.   Are you ready for a little graphical analysis? In Figure 1 I've assumed a rent of $120. How many units of land are hired? Four. How much rent is collected? Total rent is $480 (4 × $120).

The triangular area at the top of Figure 1 is what we call the producer's surplus. This is the difference between how much this land is worth to the firm and how much it actually had to pay in rent. How much it actually paid in rent is shown in the rectangle below the triangle. Producer's surplus parallels consumer's surplus (how much consumers would be willing to pay for a final product minus how much they had to pay), which we covered in the chapter on utility.

Now we'll use Figure 2 to answer two more questions. How many workers would be hired if the wage rate were $72? How much would the firm's wage bill be? If you draw in your wage rate line, both answers will be staring you in the face.

The firm would hire six workers and would have a wage bill of $432.

While we're hot, we'll do another set. How many workers would be hired if the wage rate were $144 (assuming workers are indivisible), and how much would the firm's wage bill come to?

Three workers would be hired, and the firm would pay a total of $432 in wages.

The MRP of the Imperfect Competitor

How do we distinguish between the perfect competitor and the imperfect competitor?

How do we distinguish between the perfect competitor and the imperfect competitor? Suppose we compare the demand curve of the perfect competitor with those of the monopolist, the monopolistic competitor, and the oligopolist. While the perfect competitor has a horizontal demand curve, the demand curves of the others slope downward to the right. A horizontal demand curve reflects the fact that the firm can sell its entire output at a constant price. A downwardly sloping demand curve means the firm must continually lower its price to sell more and more output.

We're concerned here with how a downwardly sloping demand curve for the final product affects the demand for resources. In Table 7 we have the same outputs and marginal physical products as in Table 6, but instead of a constant price, it lowers as output increases. This reflects the downwardly sloping demand curve of the imperfect competitor.

Fill in the columns for total revenue product and MRP in Table 7, and then check your work with the data in Table 8. After that, draw an MRP curve in Figure 3 and see whether it matches the curve shown in Figure 4.

Does your Table 7 match my Table 8? If it does, go on to the next paragraph. If it doesn't, then please read the box "Finding the Imperfect Competitor's MRP."

How many workers would the firm hire if the wage rate were $150? How much would the wage bill come to? At a wage rate of $150, two workers would be hired, so the firm's wage bill would be $300.

Table 7   Hypothetical MRP Schedule

(1) Units of Land	(2) Output	(3) Marginal Physical Product	(4) Price	(5) Total Revenue Product	(6) Marginal Revenue Product
1	18	18	$12	_____	_____
2	34	16	11	_____	_____
3	48	14	10	_____	_____
4	59	11	9	_____	_____
5	68	9	8	_____	_____
6	74	6	7	_____	_____
7	77	3	6	_____	_____
8	78	1	5	_____	_____

Table 8   Hypothetical MRP Schedule of the Imperfect Competitor

(1) Units of Land	(2) Output	(3) Marginal Physical Product	(4) Price	(5) Total Revenue Product	(6) Marginal Revenue Product
1	18	18	$12	$216	$216
2	34	16	11	374	158
3	48	14	10	480	106
4	59	11	9	531	51
5	68	9	8	544	13
6	74	6	7	518	−26
7	77	3	6	462	−56
8	78	1	5	390	−72

Figure 3

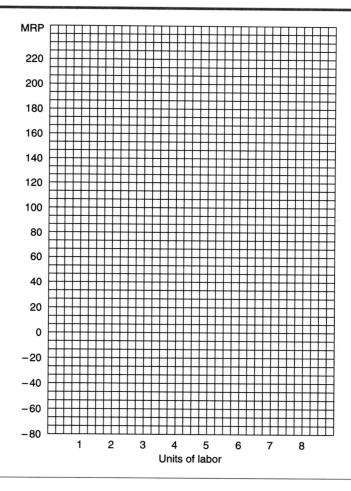

If the wage rate were $51, how many workers would be hired? How much would the firm's wage bill be? At a $51 wage rate, four workers would be hired, and the firm would pay $204 in wages.

You may have noticed that the MRP curve of the perfect competitor (shown in Figure 2) is much flatter (or more elastic) than the MRP curve of the imperfect competitor (shown in Figure 4). Why? Because the imperfect competitor must lower price to sell additional output.

If we take a numerical example from Tables 6 and 8, this will become clear. Using Table 6 of the perfect competitor, one unit of labor produces 18 units of output, which is

The MRP curve of the perfect competitor is flatter than that of the imperfect competitor.

Figure 4   The Marginal Revenue Product Curve of the Imperfect Competitor

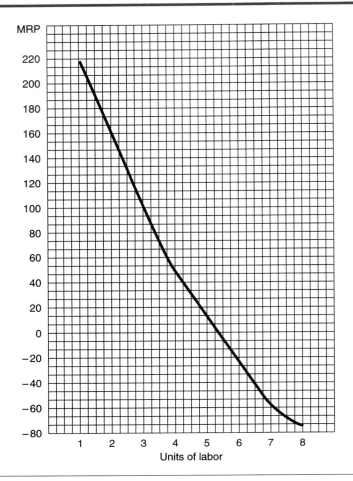

Finding the Imperfect Competitor's MRP

How much was your MRP for two units of labor in Table 7? Was it $176? And for the third unit of labor, was your MRP $140? What you did, then, was try to find MRP by multiplying marginal physical product by price, and that simply does not work for the imperfect competitor.

What *does* work in finding the MRP of the second unit of labor is subtracting the total revenue product of the first unit of labor from the total revenue product of the second unit of labor. Go back to Table 7 and do that. Did you get $158? Good. Now find the MRP of the third unit of labor. Subtract the total revenue product of the second unit of labor from the total revenue product of the third unit of labor. I'll bet you got $106.

For practice, fill in the following table:

Units of Labor	Output	Marginal Physical Product	Price	Total Revenue Product	Marginal Revenue Product
1	10		8		
2	19		7		
3	27		6		

How did you do? I hope your table is identical to this:

Units of Labor	Output	Marginal Physical Product	Price	Total Revenue Product	Marginal Revenue Product
1	10	10	8	80	80
2	19	9	7	133	53
3	27	8	6	162	29

sold at $12, yielding total revenue product of $216. Two workers produce 34 units of output sold at $12 each for a total revenue product of $408.

The imperfect competitor (Table 8) has somewhat different data. The first worker produces 18 units sold at $12 each for a total revenue product of $216; but two workers producing 34 units sold at just $11 produce a total revenue product of only $374.

Why do two workers under perfect competition produce a product sold for $408 while the same two workers under imperfect competition produce a product sold for only $374? The answer is that the perfect competitor can sell as much as she wants to sell at a constant price, while the imperfect competitor must lower her price to sell additional units of output.

The MRP schedule is derived from the total revenue product schedule. It follows that because the total revenue product of the imperfect competitor rises more slowly than that of the perfect competitor, the imperfect competitor's MRP schedule will decline more rapidly.

To facilitate a comparison of the MRP curves of the perfect competitor and the imperfect competitor, I've put the two curves together in Figure 5. Why should the MRP curve of the imperfect competitor decline so much more rapidly than that of the perfect competitor? For the same reason the MRP schedule in Table 8 declines much more rapidly than that shown in Table 6. The reason is that the imperfect competitor must lower price to sell additional units of output, while the perfect competitor can sell all of her output at the same price.

Figure 5   **The Marginal Revenue Product Curves of the Perfect and Imperfect Competitors**

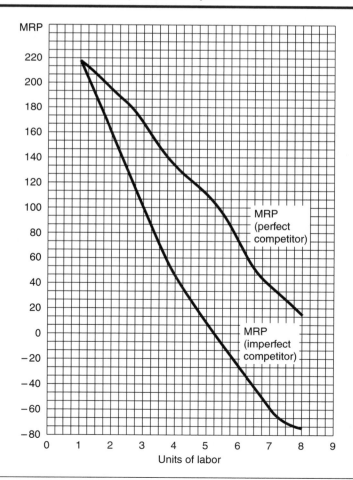

Changes in Resource Demand

Changes in Resource Demand versus Changes in Quantity of Resource Demanded

The firm's MRP curve is its demand curve for a resource.

A firm's demand for a factor of production or resource is depicted by the firm's MRP curve. So far we've been looking at movements along that curve. For instance, when rent declines, the firm will lease more units of land. This shift would be a downward movement along the MRP curve for land. Similarly, a rise in the wage rate would result in a decline in the number of workers hired. We would slide up the firm's MRP curve for labor.

At the beginning of the "Demand" chapter, I put on a dog and pony show to help you distinguish between changes in demand and changes in the quantity demanded. When the demand schedule is plotted on a graph, a change in demand means that we move to a different demand curve. A change in the quantity demanded means that we go from one point on a demand curve to another.

So our analysis of MRP parallels our earlier analysis of demand for a final product. Now, however, we're talking about a firm's demand for a resource. In other words, *the MRP schedule is a firm's demand schedule for a resource.* As the price of that resource declines, the firm demands larger quantities.

Shifts in the MRP curve

Now we're ready—or at least *I* am—to discuss shifts in the MRP curve (rather than shifts along the curves). A shift from MRP_1 to MRP_2 in Figure 6 represents an increase in the demand for capital. How would a decrease in the demand for capital be represented? By a shift from MRP_2 to MRP_1.

The Four Reasons for Changes in Resource Demand

Four things cause shifts in the MRP curve: (1) changes in the demand for the final product, (2) productivity changes, (3) changes in the prices of other resources, and (4) changes in the quantities of other resources.

Figure 6   A Shift in the Marginal Revenue Product Curve

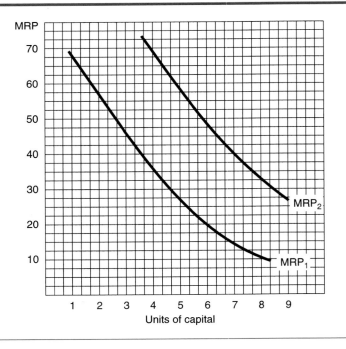

The most important influence on resource demand is a change in the demand for the final product.

Changes in the Demand for the Final Product   This is by far the most important influence on the demand for a factor of production. A firm that had no sales would have no demand for land, labor, capital, or entrepreneurial ability. Looking at things more optimistically, let's suppose the demand for the final product shown in Table 4 were to rise so much that its price was driven from $10 to $20. What would happen to the firm's MRP curve?

Would the MRP schedule in Table 4 be raised or lowered (i.e., will the firm's demand for land be raised or lowered)? There's only one way to find out. Turn back to Table 4, change price from $10 to $20, and recalculate the MRP schedule. Once you've done the necessary calculations, check your work with that in Table 9. Obviously, MRP doubled.

Next, I'd like you to superimpose the new MRP curve on Figure 1. Label it MRP$_2$. How does it look? If you did it correctly, it should look like MRP$_2$ in Figure 7, which would lead you to the inescapable conclusion that a rise in the demand for the final product leads to a rise in the demand for the factors of production. You can therefore derive that a fall in the demand for the final product will lead to a fall in the demand for the factors of production.

Productivity Changes   Productivity is output per unit of input. If output per unit of input is doubled, what will happen to productivity? Check it out. This time use the data in Table 6. Double the marginal physical product and multiply each figure by price.

What happened to your MRP? It doubled at each price, right?

What raises productivity?

Now we'll ask what raises productivity. Nearly all of any increase comes from two sources: better capital and better trained and educated labor. The computerization of the American industrial and service sectors has been the main factor responsible for the productivity increases of the last 25 years. Not only have we introduced more and better computer systems, but many members of our labor force, particularly workers in office jobs, have acquired the necessary skills to use them.

Changes in the Prices of Other Resources   There are four factors of production. Sometimes one factor may be used as a substitute for another. When land is scarce, as it is in Bangladesh, labor is substituted for land. Each acre of land is cultivated much more intensively than it would be in the United States. When a new machine replaces several workers, we are substituting capital for labor.

Substitute Factors If the price of a factor of production, say labor, goes up, business firms tend to substitute capital or land for some of their now more expensive workers. This is the substitution effect. Similarly, a decline in the wage rate will lead to a substitution of labor for capital or land. We're assuming, of course, that the price of capital or land hasn't changed (or if it has, it hasn't fallen as much as the wage rate).

The substitution effect

The output effect

There's also an output effect, which works in the opposite direction. When the price of any resource rises, this raises the cost of production, which in turn lowers the supply of

Table 9   Hypothetical MRP Schedule

(1) Units of Labor	(2) Output	(3) Marginal Physical Product	(4) Price	(5) Total Revenue Product	(6) Marginal Revenue Product
1	20	20	$20	$400	$400
2	38	18	20	760	360
3	53	15	20	1,060	300
4	65	12	20	1,300	240
5	73	8	20	1,460	160
6	78	5	20	1,560	100
7	80	2	20	1,600	40
8	80	0	20	1,600	0
9	79	−1	20	1,580	−20

Figure 7   A Shift in the Marginal Revenue Product Curve

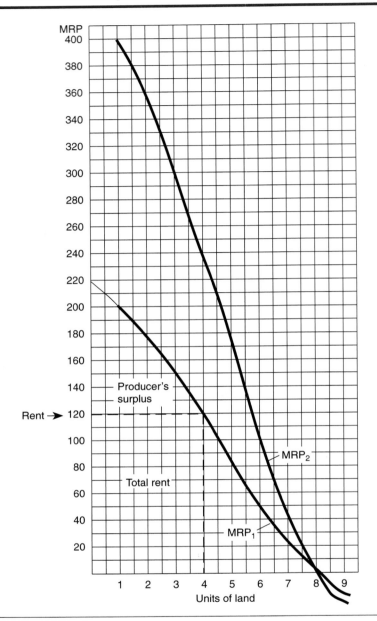

the final product. When supply falls, price rises, consequently reducing output. In other words, according to the output effect, if the cost of a factor of production rises, output will decline, thereby reducing the employment of all factors of production. Conversely, a decline in the cost of a factor will raise output, thereby raising the use of all factors of production.

In sum:

1. The substitution effect: If the price of a resource is raised, other resources will be substituted for it. If the price of a resource is lowered, it will be substituted for other resources.

2. The output effect: If the price of a resource rises, output of the final product will decline, thereby lowering the employment of all resources. If the price of a resource falls, output of the final product will rise, thereby increasing the employment of all resources.

The two effects are contradictory.

What we have, then, are contradictory effects. When the price of a resource rises, for example, the substitution effect dictates that more of the other resources will be used, thus increasing their employment. But the output effect pushes their employment down.

Which effect is stronger?

Which effect is stronger? Take the case of the introduction of computers in offices. The substitution effect pushed down the employment of labor, but the output effect pushed it way up. White-collar employment has risen sharply since the introduction of computers, so the output effect has clearly outweighed the substitution effect.

Now you *know* I'm going to present a case where the substitution effect outweighs the output effect. Output rose with the mechanization of agriculture in the South during the late 1940s, but more than three-quarters of the agricultural labor force in the deep South was forced off the land. Here the substitution effect (of capital for labor) swamped the output effect.

Sometimes, then, the substitution effect is stronger than the output effect, while at other times the opposite holds true. Thus, if you are asked whether automation raises or lowers the employment of labor, you will sound well informed when you explain that it will raise employment if the output effect is stronger and lower it if the substitution effect dominates.

Complementary Factors   Although resources are usually substitutable at least to some degree, they also usually work well together. In fact, you need at least some labor to produce virtually every good or service, and labor productivity may be greatly enhanced by land, capital, and entrepreneurial ability.

Complementary factors of production

We say that two factors are complements in production if an increase in the use of one requires an increase in the use of the other. If a bicycle messenger service purchased 100 new bicycles, it would need to hire 100 messengers to ride them; or if 100 new messengers were hired, the firm would need to purchase 100 bicycles.

To carry our example further, suppose the price of bicycles rose considerably. What would happen to the firm's demand for bicycles (or capital)?

You said it would go down, right? What would happen to the firm's demand for riders (labor)? It, too, would go down.

What if, instead, the wage rate for bicycle riders rose sharply? What would happen to the firm's demand for bicycle riders and for bicycles? It would fall.

Now we can generalize. When the price of a resource rises, the demand for a complementary resource will fall; when the price of a resource falls, the demand for a complementary resource rises.

Changes in the Quantities of Other Resources   If we go back to one of the eternal questions of economics—Why are workers in one country more productive than those in another country?—the answer is that they have more land, capital, and entrepreneurial ability with which to work.

Why are workers in one country more productive than those in another country?

As already noted, the farmer in Bangladesh has a lot less land with which to work than the American farmer has, and the Chinese construction worker has a lot less capital backing him than his American counterpart does. It would follow that an increase in land would greatly raise the productivity of the farmer in Bangladesh, while the Chinese construction worker's productivity would soar if he were given heavy construction equipment.

We can conclude, then, that an addition of complementary resources would raise the MRP of any given resource, while a decrease in complementary resources would have the opposite effect.

Optimum Resource Mix for the Firm

So far, we have been deciding how much of a resource should be hired by a firm. We hire more and more labor until the MRP of the last worker hired is equal to the going wage rate. Similarly, we hire land until the MRP of the last unit of land hired is equal to the going rent. Finally, more and more capital is hired until the last unit of capital hired is equal to the interest rate.

We can generalize by saying that the firm will use increasing amounts of a resource until the MRP of that resource is equal to its price. We'd hire workers until the MRP of labor equals the price of labor (or the wage rate). Suppose we divide both sides of the equation by the price of labor.

$$(1)\ \text{MRP of labor} = \text{Price of labor}$$

$$(2)\ \frac{\text{MRP of labor}}{\text{Price of labor}} = \frac{\text{Price of labor}}{\text{Price of labor}}$$

This may be simplified to:

$$(3)\ \frac{\text{MRP of labor}}{\text{Price of labor}} = 1$$

$\frac{\text{MRP of labor}}{\text{Price of labor}} = 1$

Remember, anything divided by itself equals one.

Now let's do the same thing with land.

$$(1)\ \text{MRP of land} = \text{Price of land}$$

$$(2)\ \frac{\text{MRP of land}}{\text{Price of land}} = \frac{\text{Price of land}}{\text{Price of land}}$$

$\frac{\text{MRP of land}}{\text{Price of land}} = 1$

$$(3)\ \frac{\text{MRP of land}}{\text{Price of land}} = 1$$

And with capital:

$$(1)\ \text{MRP of capital} = \text{Price of capital}$$

$$(2)\ \frac{\text{MRP of capital}}{\text{Price of capital}} = \frac{\text{Price of capital}}{\text{Price of capital}}$$

$\frac{\text{MRP of capital}}{\text{Price of capital}} = 1$

$$(3)\ \frac{\text{MRP of capital}}{\text{Price of capital}} = 1$$

Next, we may combine the three equations into one.

$\frac{\text{MRP of labor}}{\text{Price of labor}} =$
$\frac{\text{MRP of land}}{\text{Price of land}} =$
$\frac{\text{MRP of capital}}{\text{Price of capital}} = 1$

$$\frac{\text{MRP of labor}}{\text{Price of labor}} = \frac{\text{MRP of land}}{\text{Price of land}} = \frac{\text{MRP of capital}}{\text{Price of capital}} = 1$$

A firm will keep hiring more and more of a resource up to the point at which the MRP is equal to its price.

After all, things equal to the same thing (in this case, 1) are equal to each other.

The reason I dragged you through all of this (in addition to showing off my algebra) is to reinforce the conclusion we reached a few minutes ago: *A firm will keep hiring more and more of a resource up to the point at which its MRP is equal to its price.* This great truth enables us to do another set of problems. You can have slept through everything up to this point and still get this right.

Given the data in Table 10, how many units of land, capital, and labor would you hire? It's easy. Reread the italicized statement in the previous paragraph.

The answers? Do we have the envelope? Ah yes. We would hire three units of land, five units of capital, and four units of labor.

Table 10   Hypothetical MRP Schedules for a Firm

Units of Land	MRP of Land	Units of Capital	MRP of Capital	Units of Labor	MRP of Labor
1	$12	1	$15	1	$30
2	10	2	13	2	26
3	8	3	10	3	21
4	6	4	7	4	15
5	4	5	3	5	8
6	2	6	0	6	1
Rent = $8		Interest = $3		Wage rate = $15	

Next we're going to take up each of the four resources in turn, beginning with labor in the next two chapters. The questions we will answer are why the wage rates are what they are, and why rent, interest, and profit are what *they* are.

Questions for Further Thought and Discussion

1. If automatic dishwashers and human dishwashers can be substituted for one another, and if the wage rate for dishwashers rises, what happens to the demand for automatic dishwashers according to *(a)* the substitution effect and *(b)* the output effect?

2. As output rises, which MRP curve declines more quickly—the MRP of the perfect competitor or the MRP of the imperfect competitor? Explain your answer.

3. How is the demand for a resource affected by *(a)* changes in the demand for the final product and *(b)* productivity changes?

WORKBOOK FOR CHAPTER 29

Name _____   Date _____

Multiple-Choice Questions

Circle the letter that corresponds to the best answer.

1. Derived demand is the demand for

   a. final goods and services   b. resources

   c. final goods as well as services and resources

   d. neither final goods and services nor resources

2. When the demand for wheat rises, the demand for farm labor

   a. rises   b. falls   c. may rise or fall

3. The demand for resources is based on

   a. only the demand for the final product   b. only the productivity of the resource   c. both the demand for the final product and the productivity of the resource

   d. neither the demand for the final product nor the productivity of the resource

4. Which statement is true?

   a. Resources and final products are both measured by units of input.   b. Resources and final products are both measured by units of output.   c. Resources are measured by units of input, and final demand is measured by units of output.   d. Resources are measured by units of output, and final products are measured by units of input.

5. Which statement is true?

   a. Productivity is output per unit of input.

   b. Productivity is input per unit of output.

   c. Productivity is neither of the above.

6. Relative to the Chinese economy, the U.S. economy is

   a. more capital intensive   b. more labor intensive

   c. more labor intensive and more capital intensive

   d. less labor intensive and less capital intensive

7. The added output for which one additional input of labor is responsible is its

   a. marginal revenue product   b. marginal physical product   c. average revenue product   d. average physical product

8. A rise in the wage rate would lead to a movement

   a. down the MRP curve and a rise in the number of workers hired   b. down the MRP curve and a decline in the number of workers hired   c. up the MRP curve and a decline in the number of workers hired   d. up the MRP curve and a rise in the number of workers hired

9. The firm's demand schedule for a resource is its _____ schedule.

   a. MPP   b. MRP   c. total revenue

   d. output

10. The MRP curve for the perfect competitor is _____ the MRP curve for the imperfect competitor.

    a. identical to   b. steeper than   c. flatter than

11. The triangular area above the rent line and below the MRP line in Figure 1 is called the _____.

    a. total rent   b. consumer's surplus

    c. producer's surplus   d. none of the above

12. In Figure 1 total rent would be

    a. $300   b. $500   c. $800   d. unknown

Figure 1

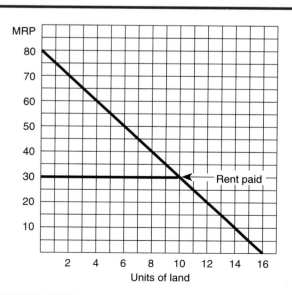

13. An increase in the demand for capital would be reflected in a movement to the

    a. left of the firm's MPP curve   b. left of the firm's MRP curve   c. right of the firm's MPP curve

    d. right of the firm's MRP curve

14. The firm will hire workers until the wage rate and the _____ of the last worker hired are equal.

    a. marginal physical product   b. MRP

    c. output

15. A firm will operate at that point where _____ is equal to one.

    a. the marginal physical product of capital/price of capital   b. the MRP of capital/price of capital

    c. the price of capital/marginal physical product of capital   d. the price of capital/MRP of capital

16. A firm will keep hiring more and more of a resource up to the point at which its MRP is equal to

    a. one   b. its marginal physical product   c. its price   d. its output

17. If the MRP of the last worker hired is lower than the wage rate, the firm has

    a. hired too many workers   b. hired too few workers   c. hired the right number of workers

18. If the wage rate is higher than the MRP of the last worker hired,

    a. the firm might be able to profitably hire at least one more worker   b. the firm has already hired too many workers   c. there is no way of knowing whether the firm has too few or too many workers

19. The most important influence on a firm's demand for a factor of production is

    a. the quantities of other resources   b. the prices of other resources   c. its productivity   d. the demand for the final product

20. If the price that a perfect competitor receives for her final product doubles, the firm's MRP schedule will

    a. rise   b. fall   c. double at each price

    d. stay about the same

21. The most effective way to increase the productivity of labor would be to

    a. increase capital   b. increase labor   c. lower capital   d. shift workers from white-collar work to blue-collar work

22. Capital and labor are _____ factors of production.

    a. substitute   b. complementary   c. both complementary and substitute   d. neither complementary nor substitute

23. Automation will raise the level of employment if the

    a. output effect is equal to the substitution effect

    b. output effect is greater than the substitution effect

    c. substitution effect is greater than the output effect

24. A firm will try to be in each of these situations except

    a. MRP of capital = Price of capital   b. MRP of land/Price of land = 1   c. 1 − Price of labor = MRP of labor   d. MRP of land/Price of land = MRP of labor/Price of labor

Fill-In Questions

1. Derived demand is the demand for _____.

2. A firm will use increasing amounts of a resource until the _____ of that resource is equal to its _____.

3. Productivity is defined as _____ per unit of _____.

4. If Melissa produces twice as much per hour as Adam, we would say that she is _____ as productive as he is.

5. Our economy is relatively _____ intensive, while the Chinese economy is relatively _____ intensive.

6. If farmland became five times as expensive, farmers would use much more _____ and _____ per acre.

7. When the productivity of a resource rises, its

_____ and its

_____ also rise.

8. When the price of a substitute resource declines, the price

of a resource will_____.

9. The MRP of the fourth unit of output = the

_____ less

the _____.

10. The MRP is the additional _____

obtained by _____.

11. The producer's surplus of rented land is the difference

between how much this land is _____

_____ and how much_____

_____.

12. The optimum resource mix for a firm is denoted by this

equation:

_____ / _____ =

_____ / _____ =

_____ / _____ = 1.

13. A firm will keep hiring more and more of a resource up to

the point at which its _____

_____ is equal to _____.

14. The MRP curve of the perfect competitor declines

_____ than that of the imperfect

competitor.

15. A firm will keep leasing additional units of land until the

MRP of that land is equal to the _____.

16. An increase in the productivity of labor will

_____ the MRP of labor.

17. The four reasons for changes in resource demand are:

(1) _____;

(2) _____;

(3) _____;

and (4) _____.

18. If the price of labor goes up and a firm replaces some

workers with machines, this is the _____

effect; when the price of a resource declines and the level

of production consequently rises, this is the _____

_____ effect.

19. If labor and capital are complementary resources and the

price of labor goes up, then the employment of capital

_____.

Problems

1. **a.** Fill in Table 1. **b.** Using the data in Table 1, draw a graph of the firm's MRP curve on a piece of graph paper. **c.** Is the firm a perfect or an imperfect competitor? **d.** If the wage rate were $60, how many workers would be hired? How much would the total wage bill come to? **e.** If the wage rate were $35, how many workers would be hired? How much would the total wage bill come to?

Table 1

(1) Units of Labor	(2) Output	(3) Marginal Physical Product	(4) Price	(5) Total Revenue Product	(6) Marginal Revenue Product
1	15	____	$6	____	____
2	28	____	6	____	____
3	40	____	6	____	____
4	50	____	6	____	____
5	57	____	6	____	____
6	62	____	6	____	____
7	64	____	6	____	____
8	65	____	6	____	____

2. a. Fill in Table 2. **b.** Using the data in Table 2, draw a graph of the firm's MRP curve on a piece of graph paper. **c.** Is the firm a perfect or an imperfect competitor? **d.** If the wage rate were $250, how many workers would be hired? How much would the total wage bill come to? **e.** If the wage rate were $99, how many workers would be hired? How much would the total wage bill come to?

Table 2

(1) Units of Labor	(2) Output	(3) Marginal Physical Product	(4) Price	(5) Total Revenue Product	(6) Marginal Revenue Product
1	22	_____	$20	_____	_____
2	43	_____	19	_____	_____
3	63	_____	18	_____	_____
4	81	_____	17	_____	_____
5	96	_____	16	_____	_____
6	109	_____	15	_____	_____
7	119	_____	14	_____	_____
8	127	_____	13	_____	_____

3. Given the data in Table 3, how many units of land, labor, and capital would you hire?

Table 3

Units of Land	MRP of Land	Units of Capital	MRP of Capital	Units of Labor	MRP of Labor
1	$20	1	$35	1	$31
2	17	2	33	2	24
3	13	3	27	3	16
4	8	4	20	4	9
5	2	5	12	5	5
6	1	6	4	6	2
Rent = $8		Interest = $27		Wage rate = $24	

30 Labor Unions

In previous chapters we saw that the price of every final product—cars, gasoline, sugar, steak, shoes—is determined by two things: supply and demand. This held true whether the firm was a perfect competitor, a monopolistic competitor, a monopolist, or an oligopolist.

We have talked quite a bit about the demand for labor and the other factors of production. Now we'll deal specifically with how wage rates are set. In this chapter we'll look at how labor unions affect the supply of labor. Then, in the next chapter, we'll examine the overall supply of labor and the demand for labor, and we'll reach a conclusion that will startle no one: Every wage rate is determined by supply and demand.

America needs a raise.
—John Sweeney,
President, AFL–CIO

Chapter Objectives

These are the high points of this chapter:

- A short history of the labor movement.
- Labor legislation.
- The economic power of unions and employers.
- The economic power of monopsonies.
- Collective bargaining.
- The strike.

A Short History of the American Labor Movement

The Early Years

Labor unions were considered subversive until the 1940s.

Labor unions are a traditional American institution, with their own national holiday, replete with parades, speeches, and picnics. This, of course, was not always so. Until the 1940s most Americans had unfavorable opinions of unions. In the popular mind, they were subversive organizations set up to obtain exorbitant wage increases and possibly overthrow the American economic system. And union leaders were regarded as racketeers, communists, or political bosses.

Some of these views were not wide of the mark, and to this day labor unions and their leaders do not always put the national good before their more immediate goals. But most Americans have come to accept unions as part of the national scene, little different from other U.S. institutions.

The AF of L rang in the modern era of unions in 1886.

Although the trade union movement in the United States is some two centuries old, most labor historians consider the modern era to have begun with the founding of the original American Federation of Labor in 1886 or with its predecessor, the Knights of Labor, which rose to prominence in the mid-1880s. Within the ranks of these organizations there was an almost continual struggle between those who sought specific gains—better wages, hours, and working conditions—and those who advocated more far-reaching reforms—a universal eight-hour day, elimination of the wage system, and the establishment of producers' cooperatives to replace private enterprise.

Terence Powderly, who in 1879 attained the office of Grand Master Workman of the Knights of Labor, held the view that wage increases of a few cents an hour were entirely inadequate because workers were entitled to the full price of their labor. But the strike, which Powderly termed a "relic of barbarism," was not the proper means of securing gains. The Knights, whose membership was open to all except doctors, lawyers, bankers, and saloonkeepers, would use reason, persuasion, and, if necessary, arbitration. You can guess how far this got them.

Fortunately or unfortunately, depending on your viewpoint, many of the member unions of the Knights went out on strike in the early 1880s. Often they won. Their biggest victory was in 1885, when Jay Gould's Wabash Railroad gave in. Ironically, the ranks of the Knights of Labor, whose leadership opposed the strike, rose from only 100,000 members in 1880 to some 700,000 in 1886.

Haymarket affair

But what goes up must come down, at least sometimes. What became known as the Haymarket affair took place in 1886. At a rally sponsored by various labor organizers in Chicago's Haymarket Square, a terrible tragedy occurred. It had been raining and the leaders were preparing to end the rally when a bomb was thrown into a group of policemen, eight of whom were killed. The organizers of the rally were blamed and quickly tried and eight were found guilty of murder. One committed suicide, four were hanged, and the other three received long prison terms. Later, considerable evidence was brought forth to show that all eight were innocent and that no union members had been involved in the killings. But public opinion had already turned against the Knights.

By the late 1880s the American Federation of Labor, or the AF of L (AFL) as it became known, had become the predominant labor organization. Samuel Gompers, who served as its president until his death in 1924, stressed the importance of "bread-and-*Bread-and-butter unionism*
butter unionism." Why the AF of L succeeded where the Knights had failed is explained largely by their opposing philosophies as well as by the changing conditions of the American economy.

The wage relationship was here to stay.

The emergence of the large corporation, which replaced the small workshop, meant the wage relationship was here to stay. Forget about small producers' cooperatives and start worrying about securing enough bargaining strength to obtain better wages, hours, and working conditions. An individual worker has little bargaining power against a huge corporation, but thousands of workers, banded together in craft unions—the ironworkers, cigar makers, carpenters—did have a certain amount of leverage. They could, if they didn't get what they wanted, withhold their labor. In other words, they could go out on strike.

This might not sound all that radical, but during the first three decades of the 20th century most Americans saw unions as subversive, foreign, and, in some cases, downright evil. Employers fought them tooth and nail. Union members were blacklisted, those suspected of having union sympathies were fired, court orders were obtained to prohibit strikes as well as milder forms of union activity, and sometimes private detectives, labor goons, and sympathetic local police were used to put down strikes violently.

Key Labor Legislation

Wagner Act

National Labor Relations Act (Wagner Act, 1935)   The Wagner Act and the Taft-Hartley Act are by far the two most important pieces of labor legislation. The Wagner Act, named for New York senator Robert Wagner, committed the federal government not only to promoting collective bargaining but also to actually supporting union organizing. Twelve years later the Taft-Hartley Act was put forth as a measure to redress this imbalance by protecting "employers' rights."

Prohibition of unfair labor practices

The Wagner Act prohibited employers from engaging in such "unfair labor practices" as (1) coercion or interference with employees who are organizing or bargaining; (2) refusal to bargain in good faith with a union legally representing employees; and (3) in general, penalizing employees for union activity.

The act set up a three-member (now a five-member) board to protect workers in organizing unions and to administer representation elections (i.e., to determine which union will represent the workers of a company). If 30 percent of the employees in an entire company, or just one unit of that company, decide to be represented by a union, these people petition the National Labor Relations Board to conduct an election. If the union gets a majority of votes, it then represents *all* the employees of that company or unit, even those who are not members of the union.

The Wagner Act put the force of the government behind collective bargaining.

This law put the force of the federal government behind collective bargaining, at the same time lending unions a certain legitimacy. It established unions as an American institution. In addition, the Wagner Act provided the necessary machinery to ensure that large corporations would allow unions to organize and would bargain in good faith.

During World War II strikes were considered unpatriotic; but 1946 set a record for strikes—a record that still stands. The late 1940s were a time of inflation and prosperity, and labor used the strike weapon to get what it considered its fair share of the economic pie. Partially in response to these disturbances, the Republicans captured control of Congress in 1946 for the first time in 14 years. They felt they had a mandate not only to redress the imbalance between the power of labor and the power of management, but as many observers noted, "to put labor in its place."

Taft-Hartley Act

Taft-Hartley Act (1947)   The Taft-Hartley Act has three main provisions: (1) it allows the president to call an 80-day "cooling-off" period; (2) it allows the states to ban the union shop; and (3) it severely limits the closed shop.

Strikes that "imperil the national health or safety" may be halted by court order at the request of the president, who determines which strikes imperil Americans' health and safety. If a settlement is not reached during the 80 days allowed, the union may resume the strike.

Section 14b: right-to-work laws

The most controversial part of the law is Section 14b. This section allows the states to enact "right-to-work" laws, which prohibit union shop contracts. (About 20 states—mainly in the South—have laws prohibiting contracts that require union membership as a condition of employment.)

Closed shop

The act severely limits the extent of the closed shop (closed to nonunion members). However, unions have sometimes gotten around this prohibition by calling a closed shop a union shop (see the box).

Jurisdictional disputes and secondary boycotts are prohibited.

Taft-Hartley also prohibits jurisdictional disputes and secondary boycotts. A jurisdictional dispute occurs when two unions, each vying to organize a company, picket that company, which has no dispute with either union. A secondary boycott is directed against a company that isn't party to a strike, such as a trade supplier or a customer or a retail outlet.

Eighty-day cooling-off period

The 80-day cooling-off period puts the union at a strategic disadvantage. For 80 days the company can stockpile inventory, making it easier for it to weather a strike and perhaps less likely to make concessions. On the other hand, by committing itself to ensuring

---

The Closed Shop, Union Shop, Open Shop, and "Right-to-Work" Laws

(1) Closed shop An employer may hire only union members. The Taft-Hartley Act outlawed this arrangement, but sometimes union hiring halls operate as de facto closed shops. If an employer, generally a construction firm, hires only those sent by the union, we have a closed shop, even though it is nominally a union shop.

(2) Union shop Under a union shop contract, all employees must join the union, usually within 30 days after they are hired. This arrangement effectively increases union membership because many workers would not have joined unless they were forced to. A variation of the union shop is the agency shop, in which you don't have to join the union, but you must pay dues.

(3) Open shop No one is forced to join the union, although it does represent all the workers in contract negotiations. Union members often resent nonmembers who are "getting a free ride," because they don't have to pay dues.

(4) Right-to-work laws Section 14b of the Taft-Hartley Act permitted the states to pass laws prohibiting the union shop. Some 20 states have done this, which means in those states you can work in a shop that is organized without having to join the union. Organized labor has struggled in vain since 1947 to get this controversial section repealed because these right-to-work laws have been responsible for lower union membership in the states that passed them.

labor peace, not to mention to protecting the nation's health and safety, the administration is more likely to put pressure on both parties to settle their dispute.

At every Democratic presidential convention until 1988, delegates representing labor unions got the convention to adopt a platform plank demanding the repeal of Section 14b of the Taft-Hartley Act. Even when the Democratic party swept to victory, capturing the presidency and Congress, as it did in 1948, 1960, 1964, and 1976, somehow leaders never got around to Section 14b.

In the late 1950s widespread publicity about labor racketeering and corruption, highlighted by televised congressional committee hearings, created a demand for remedial legislation. The jailing of Teamster president Dave Beck, complaints from union members that their unions were undemocratic and curbed dissent, and widespread instances of conflict of interest (where union officials had financial interests in the companies with whom they conducted labor negotiations) led to the Landrum-Griffin Act.

Landrum-Griffin Act

Why was this law necessary?

Landrum-Griffin Act (1959)   This act had four main provisions: (1) a "bill of rights" for union members; (2) provision of election procedures; (3) limits on takeovers of locals by national unions; and (4) a listing of the financial responsibilities of union officials.

Why was this law necessary? Consider this provision from its bill of rights: "No member of any organization may be fined, suspended, expelled, or otherwise disciplined except for nonpayment of dues . . . unless such member has been (a) served with written specific charges; (b) given a reasonable time to prepare his defense; and (c) afforded a full and fair hearing."

Why outline election procedures? Because in many unions the leadership was able to perpetuate itself in office. Why limit takeovers of locals? Because this device was often used to silence opposition. Finally, the main reason to deal with union finances was to cut down on embezzlement of union funds (see the box "The Special Case of the Teamsters").

The Labor Movement since the New Deal

The atmosphere surrounding labor organizing in the 1930s was poles apart from that of the earlier decades of the century. Where there had been prosperity, there was depression. The government, which had been an enemy, was now an ally. And the national mood had changed. Those who ran corporate America had made a mess of things. Perhaps the unions, which stressed higher pay, better working conditions, and job security, were really on the right track.

The Special Case of the Teamsters

Talking about union corruption without mentioning the Teamsters would be like talking about communism without mentioning Karl Marx. The Teamsters were so crooked that the federal government had to step in to run their 1991 election. Ronald Carey, who won a hard-fought race, is the first president in memory not to serve under a cloud of suspicion. Peter Kilborn placed the union's leadership in clear perspective:

Three of the six previous general presidents since 1952—David Beck, James R. Hoffa, and Roy L. Williams—have been sent to prison for crimes like tax evasion, jury tampering, and fraud. A fourth, Frank E. Fitzsimmons, let the mob drain the workers' pension funds while looking the other way, but was never charged. Jackie Presser, president from 1983 to 1988, died while under indictment for embezzlement. The last president before Carey, William

McCarthy, rigged the bidding on the contract to print the teamsters' magazine so his son-in-law could get it.*

When Ronald Carey was reelected in 1996 over James P. Hoffa, son of the late Teamsters president, Hoffa protested that Carey won only because Carey used hundreds of thousands of dollars of the union's money (which would have been illegal). Federal investigators agreed with this allegation and Carey was forced to resign. A new election was called for some time in 1998 and not only was Carey barred from running again, but early in the year Hoffa's own election activities were under investigation, with the possibility that he too may be barred from running.

*Peter T. Kilborn, "Carey Takes the Wheel," *New York Times*, June 21, 1992, Section 6, p. 27.

Figure 1 **Union Membership, 1900–**

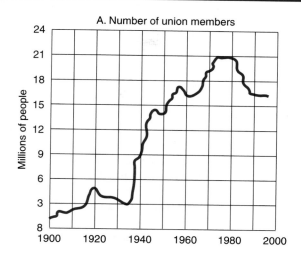

A. Number of union members

B. Union membership as a percentage of the civilian labor force

Union membership rose spectacularly in the mid-1930s.

As you can see from Figure 1, union membership rose spectacularly from the mid-1930s to the mid-1940s. The major impetus was the Wagner Act, which more than anything else legitimized unions and facilitated their organizing workers in the nation's basic industries of auto, steel, and rubber. During this time a split developed within the AFL, leading to the formation of the Congress of Industrial Organizations (CIO) in 1935. The split was caused by a dispute over whether to organize along craft lines, as the AFL had been doing for 50 years, or along industry lines, as advocated by the leaders of the CIO.

Craft unions

Craft unions are organized along the lines of particular occupations, such as air traffic controllers, plumbers, operating engineers, airline pilots, or teachers. In general these are relatively well-paid jobs requiring years of training.

Industrial unions

Industrial unions, such as the United Steel Workers, the United Auto Workers, and the United Mine Workers, are organized along industry lines, without regard to craft. Lumped together in one union are skilled and unskilled workers doing varied types of work. What bonds them is that they all work in the same industry.

In some industries, particularly those with unskilled or semiskilled mass-production workers, it makes more sense to organize along industrial rather than craft lines. Unlike plumbers or airline pilots, the people who put together cars can be trained in a couple of hours—and replaced just as quickly. They simply don't have a craft that sets them apart from their co-workers.

The conflict within the AFL over whether to organize along craft or industrial lines led to the great schism of the organization in 1935. Most of the AFL leadership, who headed the craft and building trades unions, believed that machinists, for example, whether employed in autos, steel, or any other industry, should be organized into a machinists' union. But the leaders of the breakaway Congress of Industrial Organizations believed all the workers in an industry should be organized into an industrywide union regardless of craft.

AFL–CIO merger

In the mid- to late 1930s there was a tremendous spurt of labor organizing by the CIO in steel, autos, rubber, oil, and other areas of heavy industry. The AFL also began organizing along industrial lines during this period. As we can see in Figure 1, these were the golden days of union organizing.

The Taft-Hartley Act unintentionally sparked efforts to reunite the AFL and the CIO. The main obstacle to the merger was no longer the philosophical one of whether organization should be carried out along craft or industrial lines. That issue had been settled by the late 1930s when the AFL began to organize its own industrial unions.

The problem that still had to be resolved was jurisdictional. Unions belonging to the AFL and to the CIO had been organizing workers in the same fields, often competing with each other. The member unions involved entered into "no-raiding" agreements and even appointed umpires to resolve any cases the unions could not settle between themselves. The way was then cleared for the merger, which took place in 1955.

Union membership reached an all-time peak of 33 percent in the mid-1950s (see Figure 1B). But in actual numbers, it peaked at 21 million in the early 1970s (see Figure 1A). Today only one out of seven workers is a union member. The country has shifted from a manufacturing economy to a service economy, and it's much harder to organize computer programmers, word processors, financial analysts, and insurance adjusters than it is to organize factory workers.

One of the factors, then, affecting union membership is the decline of manufacturing employment, particularly in the nation's industrial heartland. In a sense, the auto and steel industries are in a long-term decline that began during the 1973–75 recession and intensified during the recession of 1981–82. This decline has been largely offset by the rapid unionization of public employees during the 1960s, particularly on the state and local levels. However, the rapid rise in the public employment rolls of the 1960s and 1970s has not continued in later decades.

In the 1990s, while Boeing, McDonnell Douglas, IBM, Sears, General Motors, and other huge corporations were laying off hundreds of thousands of workers, smaller firms in services and high-tech industries were hiring. But small firms are costly to organize, and unions have traditionally been weak in service and high-tech industries. Still another factor in the erosion of union membership has been the growth of foreign competition, especially in heavy manufacturing such as steel, autos, and mining. Even when foreign firms set up operations in the United States—most notably in the auto industry—they have been extremely successful in preventing unions from organizing their plants.

Still another factor is the current optimistic economic mood. Decades ago, many Americans grew up in pro-union households and saw themselves as members of the working class. But now many see themselves as part of an upwardly mobile middle class that views unions as irrelevant.

The South continues to be the least unionized section of the country. Long the target of AFL–CIO organizers, this region has remained a tough nut to crack. Right-to-work laws, strong local conservatism, and antiunion feeling, as well as the economic power of the local firms, have kept labor organizing at a low ebb.

Which is the biggest labor union today? As you can see in Table 1, it's the National Education Association, with 2.3 million members. Until just a few years ago the Teamsters Union headed the list, but the deregulation of the trucking industry, which I talked about two chapters back, led to the formation of tens of thousands of tiny independent, nonunion trucking firms.

The two largest labor union mergers in history were announced recently. The United Auto Workers, the United Steel Workers, and the International Association of Machinists, each of whom has been losing members, are expected to finalize the formation of a single union with nearly 2 million members by 1999. In 1997 the National Education Association, with 2.3 million members, and the American Federation of Teachers, with over 900,000 members, announced a merger that would create the largest union in the nation's history, with 3.2 million members. It is scheduled to take place in 2002.

Union membership as a percentage of the labor force has been falling since the mid-1950s (see Figure 1B), but the decline in big craft and industrial unions has been even

Table 1   Membership of Top 10 Labor Unions, 1995

Union	Membership
National Education Association	2,300,000
International Brotherhood of Teamsters, Chauffeurs, Warehousemen and Helpers of America	1,400,000
American Federation of State, County, and Municipal Employees	1,200,000
United Food and Commercial Workers, International Union	1,000,000
Service Employees International Union	1,000,000
American Federation of Teachers	900,000
International Union, United Automobile, Aerospace and Agricultural Implement Workers of America	800,000
International Brotherhood of Electrical Workers	700,000
Communications Workers of America	500,000
International Association of Machinists and Aerospace Workers	500,000

Source: *The Wall Street Journal Almanac,* 1998.

faster. Their decline was offset by the rapid unionization of government employees during the 1970s and 1980s. Can you pick out those unions in Table 1? They are the National Education Association (number 1); the American Federation of State, County, and Municipal Employees (number 3); the Service Employees International Union (number 5) (a substantial minority of members are government employees); and the American Federation of Teachers (number 6).

The future of unionism may indeed lie with public sector workers. Nearly 40 percent of all government workers, but only 10 percent of all private sector workers, were union members in 1996. Rutgers University economist Leo Troy predicts that the AFL will become a predominantly public sector institution early in the 21st century.[1] Nevertheless, AFL president John Sweeney has initiated a huge organizing drive aimed at *all* workers.

The Economic Power of Labor Unions

Are labor unions too powerful?

Are labor unions too powerful? When a powerful union like the United Steel Workers not only shuts down the steel industry but depresses several related industries, as it did for 116 days in 1959, is this something the country can afford to tolerate? Or when the Teamsters, the International Longshoremen, or any other union's members walk off their jobs because they disapprove of certain business decisions, must the rest of us suffer? Don't unions have too much political power, having at their disposal millions of dollars as well as hundreds of thousands of campaign workers? Finally, aren't unions really forcing up prices and causing inflation?

Many people accuse unions of being monopolies. Indeed, they were prosecuted under the Sherman Antitrust Act during the first two decades of this century. In a sense, of course, unions *are* monopolies. For example, the painters', plumbers', carpenters', longshoremen's, and teamsters' trades are nearly 100 percent unionized. Aren't these monopolies?

We define a monopoly as the seller of a good or service for which there are no close substitutes. Of course, labor is not really a good or service but rather a factor that helps produce a good or service. But if we brush aside that technicality, then for all intents and purposes unions are sometimes monopolies.

Unions have two ways of asserting power: inclusion and exclusion.

Unions have two basic ways of exerting power. One way is to take in as members virtually everyone who works in a particular craft or industry. This is the *method of inclusion,* and it could give the union a monopoly. Examples are the United Steel Workers, the United Auto Workers, and the Teamsters.

A second way of exerting power, which is quite common in the building trades, is the *principle of exclusion.* You don't take in just anyone. There are tests, you might need

---

[1]*Fortune,* June 10, 1996, p. 26.

experience, and believe it or not, it probably wouldn't hurt to know someone—preferably a close relative like a father or an uncle—who happens to be an influential member of the union. By keeping people out, you keep down the supply of carpenters, plumbers, bricklayers, and electricians, and amazingly, wages go all the way up.

The principle of exclusion works like a charm. Wages were extremely high in the building trades for most of the 1960s and the nonrecession years of the 1970s. In recent years things have not been so great, perhaps because of a nationwide construction slump caused by high interest rates, and possibly because the high union scale wage rates have priced new building construction out of the market.

Let's see what the principles of inclusion and exclusion look like graphically. In Figure 2A we have the inclusive union, generally a large industrial union such as the United Steel Workers. The union tries to obtain a high standard wage from U.S. Steel (now part of USX), Bethlehem, Republic, and the other companies. But at a high wage rate, the companies will hire fewer workers than they would have hired at lower wages.

We get the same results from the exclusive union (see Figure 2B). This time, however, the union has restricted the supply of workers by allowing only certain people into its ranks. It's clear, then, that both exclusion and inclusion will lead to higher wages.

Are unions too powerful? Public opinion is divided on this issue, but before we even attempt to answer this question, we should look at the other side of the coin. Are large corporations too powerful?

The Economic Power of Large Employers

We've seen that workers, who were once powerless to bargain individually with huge corporate employers, have formed unions that have become quite powerful. One is apt to forget that these corporations have remained very powerful, and some—myself included—would say that this power has become increasingly concentrated because of the rapid pace of corporate mergers.

The case of monopsony

Let's consider an extreme case of corporate power, that of monopsony. The seller of a product for which there are no close substitutes is a monopolist. Monopsony is the market situation in which there is only a single buyer for a product. The most common kind of monopsony is a labor market where there is only a single employer. The Hershey Company in Hershey, Pennsylvania, was once an example. At one time or another General Electric in Schenectady, New York; J. P. Stevens in several towns in the South; and

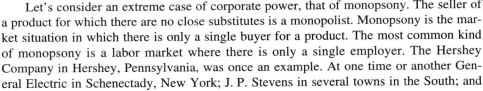
Figure 2   Inclusive and Exclusive Unions

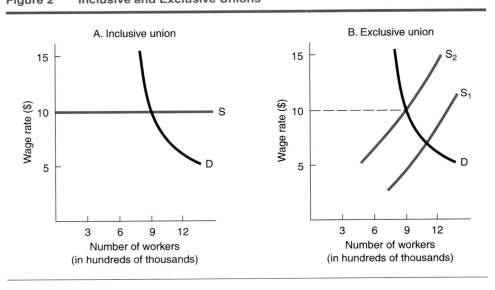

the military bases in various towns around the country have completely dominated the local job markets. Sometimes 60 to 80 percent of the jobs in these areas have been provided by a single employer. Technically, a monopsonist is a single buyer, but these towns came pretty close. The late Senator Henry "Scoop" Jackson of Washington was long known as the senator from Boeing because of the huge defense contracts he was able to secure for the Seattle firm. Incidentally, in the mid-1970s when defense spending was cut, Seattle went into a depression.

In this chapter we are concerned with the monopsonist as the dominant employer in a locality, but a monopsonist, in more general terms, faces the entire supply curve of anything being sold—labor, other resources, or any good or service. Perhaps the prime example today exists in Japan's Toyota City, with its rings of auto supplier firms radiating outward from the Toyota Motor Company headquarters. This city of 325,000 is a prime example of a company town, where nearly everyone is employed, directly or indirectly, by the same company.

The monopsonist faces the entire supply curve of labor.

The monopsonist faces the entire supply curve of labor. Because that curve sweeps upward to the right (that is, to induce more people to work more, you have to pay them a higher wage rate), the monopsonist who wants to hire more workers will have to offer a higher wage rate. The best-known monopsonists these days are professional baseball, football, and basketball leagues (see box "Professional Sports as Monopsonies").

The question is really one of relative power. Historically, workers have increased their power relative to large corporations by forming unions, but there is wide variation in the division of power between corporations and unions in different industries. The International Ladies Garment Workers Union (ILGWU) was relatively weak until the 1930s but became the dominant force in an industry characterized by thousands of tiny manufacturers. This situation changed somewhat during the last two decades, as mergers among these firms left the manufacturers' side dominated by 10 or 12 large corporations.

The Oil and Chemical Workers Union is pitted against Big Oil, which is not just a national power but an international one as well. Another apparently weak union was the Amalgamated Clothing and Textile Workers Union, which merged over 20 years ago. But that is only half true. It is weak relative to the textile giants, Burlington Industries and J. P. Stevens, but its situation in the men's clothing industry is analogous to that of the ILGWU in women's clothing. In 1995 the ILGWU merged with the Amalgamated Clothing and Textile Workers Union to form UNITE.

Professional Sports as Monopsonies

If you happen to be a professional athlete, you probably don't have many prospective employers to whom you can sell your services. Take baseball. If you're a really good prospect, the chances are you'll be drafted by one of the major-league teams, and if you're *really* good, you'll work your way up to the big leagues. But then you'll have to play for the team that drafted you for another five years before you may become a free agent and sell your services to other teams willing to bid on them.

Professional football had virtually no free agency until 1993. Until then if you were one of the better players in the National Football League, you were virtually tied to your team for your entire career, unless you were traded to another team. Every 8 or 10 years a rival league would spring up and a bidding war would ensue, driving up salaries. In the 1960s there was the American Football League, which later merged with the National Football League. In the 1970s we had the World Football League, and in the 1980s the United States Football League. These two leagues folded, but not before they pushed up salary levels in the National Football League.

The National Basketball Association, which has dominated professional basketball since the 1940s, eventually merged with the American Basketball Association, but not until a costly bidding war had raised salaries into the millions.

Today the professional baseball, football, and basketball leagues have pure monopsony power. So, too, does professional hockey, which endured labor stoppages before the play-offs in 1992 and during the 1994–95 season. Although professional athletes are handsomely paid, and although they do enjoy some degree of free-agent power, their salaries would be even higher if there were more bidders for their services.

Collective Bargaining

The Collective Bargaining Process

Collective bargaining is the main arena of the power struggle between labor and management. In general, labor tries to secure substantial increases in wages, fringe benefits, and perhaps better working conditions. Management, of course, offers considerably less than labor wants. And so they bargain. But backing up their bargaining power are their two ultimate weapons: for labor, it is the strike; for management, it is the ability to take a strike.

Some observers say the lockout is management's ultimate weapon. That's like saying that if labor's ultimate weapon is to punch management in the nose, management can beat labor to the punch, so to speak, by punching itself in the nose. If a strike hurts the company by cutting off production, so does a lockout. Surely it doesn't make a whole lot of sense to lock out workers who were about to leave anyway (see box "The Baseball Lockout").

No, the ultimate weapon of management is the ability to take a strike. To carry my analogy further, a good fighter must be able to take a punch. Perhaps in other fields the term *glass jaw* or *canvas back* might be laudatory, but not in boxing—and not in collective bargaining. If the union knows management cannot withstand a strike, it will certainly push much harder for a favorable settlement.

The ability to take a strike, of course, varies from firm to firm and from industry to industry. Generally, manufacturing fares better than services because the manufacturer can build up inventories in anticipation of a strike. On the rare occasions when the Taft-Hartley Act is invoked by the president, such a company can add even more to its stockpiles during the 80-day halt of the strike. As a strike wears on, orders can be filled from this large inventory. Also, delivery times can be stretched out from, say, the normal two months to three or four months. When the strike is over, workers can be put on overtime and extra workers temporarily hired to help build up the depleted inventories and fill any backlog of orders.

In 1989 Seattle-based Boeing Aircraft Company was able to withstand a strike easily because it had built up a large inventory of planes. This gave the company much greater power to hold out than the workers had. When a settlement was reached after a few months, Boeing got nearly all it had originally asked for.

Firms in service industries are less able to take a strike than those in manufacturing because they do not have an inventory to help them cushion the effects of lost production. An airline, an insurance company, a bank, a computer firm, or a real estate company cannot make up lost sales because their competitors will have picked up the slack.

A diversified firm, particularly a large conglomerate, can ride out a strike more easily than can the firm that produces a single good or service. A strike will affect only one or two divisions; the others will keep operating. Similarly, a large firm has a better

---

The Baseball Lockout

In 1990 the major-league baseball owners locked the players out of spring training. *Why?* Because their collective bargaining agreement with the players' union had expired and negotiations had bogged down. But why call a lockout? After all, didn't a lockout hurt the owners as well as the players? Yes, it did. And didn't the lockout have the same basic effect as a strike? Yes, it did.

So why did the owners lock out the players from spring training? Because they surmised that a collective bargaining agreement could not be reached and that the players would strike at a time of their own choosing, presumably sometime during the season, just as they had

back in 1981. The owners figured a work stoppage was nearly inevitable and a lockout at the beginning of spring training would hurt them less (and the players more) than would a strike sometime during the season. *Why?* Because the owners would lose out on a lot of TV and ballpark admissions revenue if the season were interrupted. Furthermore, the players, most of whom had had little or no income during the previous winter, were less able to withstand a lockout in February than they would be the loss of income during a strike. Remember: a key factor in deciding when to begin a strike is the day after payday.

chance of surviving a strike than a small firm does because it has greater financial resources. Finally, a multinational corporation might simply shift operations to another country in the event of a strike.

All this brilliant analysis notwithstanding, one can occasionally draw exactly the opposite conclusion about negotiating strength varying with the ability to take a strike. It's like the rhetorical question "Would you hit a person wearing glasses?" Then, of course, you put on a pair of glasses.

What does this have to do with the ability to take a strike? I'm glad you asked. If you worked for a company that might go under, would you call for a strike? You'd probably win the strike and be out of a job. That's why the United Auto Workers did not dare call a strike in the 1970s and early 1980s, although they could have easily defeated Chrysler. To carry this a bit further, if a company like Chrysler is financially weak, you won't ask for much of a wage increase. In fact, during the 1981–82 recession, some unions actually negotiated not only no wage increases but even wage reductions. Saving jobs, especially during the economic doldrums of the early 1990s, has often led to wage reductions.

Both union and management bargaining teams operate under certain constraints.

Both the union and management bargaining teams operate under certain constraints. This union team cannot go back to its membership without some minimally acceptable package. Often they talk of trying to "sell" a particular agreement to the union's members. Regardless of whether a vote is taken on the proposal (sometimes the union negotiating team has carte blanche to reach a binding settlement), if that settlement is unacceptable to the rank and file, the negotiating team will soon be out of a job.

Industrial relations are like sexual relations. It's better between two consenting parties.
—Vic Feather,
British trade-union leader

Among the management team's constraints, the first is money. How much can the company afford? Of course, how much it *says* it can afford and how much it *actually* can afford may be widely divergent figures. But the team cannot go beyond what top management is willing to pay, or it, too, will be out of a job.

Furthermore, there is the issue of management prerogatives, which are jealously guarded. If the management team were to agree to allow the union to share in the company's decision making, this would not be received too favorably by the folks upstairs.

Besides power, what about negotiating skills? Although good negotiators come away with better settlements than bad negotiators do, the real test of a good negotiator is getting the best possible package—or from the management standpoint, giving away the smallest possible package—*without* precipitating a strike.

Anybody can avoid a strike by reaching a disadvantageous agreement, just as anyone can allow a strike to develop by being intransigent. The trick is to get the best possible deal without a strike. And that takes a good negotiator.

The pressure to reach a settlement without a strike is considerable.

The pressure on both sides to reach a settlement without a strike is considerable. The cost of a strike to management can be extremely high. For example, General Motors lost $90 million a day in sales during the 67-day strike in 1970, and the striking members of the United Auto Workers did not fare much better, losing an estimated $50 million to $60 million a day in pay.

I don't mean to give the impression that collective bargaining is solely a test of power. Real issues are presented and discussed. The rising cost of living, health insurance, worker productivity, as well as previous settlements are generally bandied about. For example, during a period of inflation the union team will be sure to point out that its members have lost ground in terms of actual purchasing power over the life of the expiring contract. One might add, parenthetically, that they would be hard put to go back with any wage settlement that did not at least keep pace with the cost of living. Today about one-quarter of union contracts have escalator, or COLA (cost-of-living allowance), clauses, which provide protection against inflation during the life of the contract.

COLAs

Productivity increases

Productivity increases are a key issue because they provide the basis for pay increases. If workers produce more, they have a good argument for increased pay; and if more is produced, the company can afford to pay more. Unfortunately, productivity—output per labor hour—is not often measured with accuracy. A union might argue that productivity is rising 4 percent a year, and management might just as reasonably counter that the figure is only 2 percent. It's practically impossible for one side to convince the other that it has a monopoly on the truth.

Finally, there's the issue of pattern-setting wage increases. For example, after the uniform services (police, fire, and sanitation) negotiations are completed in New York, the city then begins negotiations with the other municipal unions. The bargaining teams for those unions do not want to go back to their members with less than the other guys got. It's as simple as that. During periods of rapid inflation, with the added pressure of keeping up with the rising cost of living, the unions sometimes view the pattern-setting settlements as minimums that must be exceeded. This tends to create still newer pattern setters, which themselves become goals to be surpassed.

The Collective Bargaining Agreement

Collective bargaining negotiations will end with either an agreement or a strike. (The lockout option, as I pointed out, is really no option at all and has rarely been used since the 1930s.) Less than 5 percent of these negotiations end in strikes, but as we know, no news is good news, or to put it another way, the media always plays up the bad news.

The collective bargaining agreement is a contract running from a page or two up to several hundred pages. The first key provision is wages and hours. The second is job security and seniority. Other areas often covered include grievance procedures, working conditions, and the role of the union in the day-to-day running of the firm. Also spelled out in the contract are health benefits, the number of paid holidays, paid sick leave and personal leave days, and vacation days.

The focal point of the negotiations is generally the amount by which wage rates will be increased. In fact, progress reports on the negotiations generally refer to the latest wage offer. Everything else gets lumped together as "other issues."

Job security and seniority are also important contract provisions. Generally, the last people hired are the first to be laid off. Seniority is often the most important criterion for promotion as well. This has tended to pit older, more experienced workers against younger workers, but a union negotiating team will almost always regard seniority as sacrosanct, especially because older workers tend to dominate most unions.

Company officials typically dislike union wage scales and seniority provisions because they require everyone to be paid at the same rate regardless of individual productivity differences. Furthermore, officials are legally bound to lay off the least senior workers during bad economic times—times when it would make more sense to lay off the least efficient workers. Union officials counter that it would be arbitrary and unfair to use any criterion other than seniority as the basis for wage rates, promotion, and order of layoffs.

Another important provision in many contracts is the grievance procedure, which is spelled out step-by-step. For example, an assembly line worker whose supervisor yelled at her might first have to go to her shop steward, who then talks to the supervisor. If the grievance is not settled at that level, it might go to the chief steward and the head of the department. Beyond that, the contract may specify two or three still higher levels. However, most grievances are settled at the steward–supervisor level.

Other grievances may involve interpretations of the contract—when is a worker entitled to overtime, who is more qualified for promotion, whether an employee is eligible for full benefits during pregnancy leave.

The Strike

The public eye is captured by the most spectacular strikes—the 1981 air traffic controllers' and baseball players' strikes, followed the next year by the National Football League Players Association's strike.[2] Yet none of these strikes directly affected more than a few thousand workers, and there was very little effect on our economy.

In fact, very few strikes have disrupted the U.S. economy. Since the passage of the Taft-Hartley Act in 1947, only two have caused major economic disruption: the 1959

---

[2]The 1987 football strike had even less economic impact, mainly because the NFL was able to field teams of strikebreakers (called "scabs"), who jumped at the chance to play professional football.

steel strike and the United Auto Workers' strike against General Motors in 1970. The worst year, 1946, was an aberration because the unions had been restricted from striking during the war while inflation was pushing up the cost of living. With the exception of 1946, in no year did strikes result in as much as a 1 percent loss in total labor-hours worked.

The major-league baseball strike that wiped out the 1994 play-offs and World Series probably comes to mind first when we think of strikes these days (see box "The Baseball Strike"). But the United States doesn't have nearly as many big strikes as it did back in the 1950s, 1960s, and 1970s, when the Labor Department recorded more than 300 strikes a year involving large groups of workers. That number now averages only 35 a year.

One might ask why unions go on strike when what they are fighting over—the 10 or 15 cents an hour—cannot possibly compensate for the wages lost during the strike. For example, suppose labor and management are 1 percent apart when the strike is called. In one week the workers will have lost 1/50, or 2 percent, of their annual pay. A strike lasting one month means forgoing 8 percent of their annual pay.

Why go on strike then? I'll give you four good explanations. First, most union members don't make these calculations. Second, sometimes the opposing sides are not 1 percent apart, but 3 or 4 percent apart. Third, you're hoping the strike will be settled quickly. I've walked a few picket lines in my day, and the prime topic of conversation is whether or not "they" are meeting.

The fourth reason is a combination of machismo and credibility. In New York many people remember Mike Quill, who was president and chief negotiator for the Transit Workers Union (TWU) in the 1950s and 1960s. It seems that every New Year's Eve there were two shows on television: Mike Quill and Guy Lombardo.

Every other New Year's Eve the city's contract with the Transit Workers Union would expire, and negotiations always went down to the wire. Most people in New York got around by public transportation in those days, and we never knew if we'd make it home from the parties. Usually the negotiators would "stop the clock" (which meant that although the contract had expired at midnight, as long as negotiations were proceeding no strike would be called).

Finally, at about 4:00 A.M., the mayor would announce that the city had "found" the money to give the TWU most of what it wanted, and a strike would be averted in the nick of time. But many people began to doubt whether Quill would actually have the guts to call a strike. As Quill got older, his Irish brogue got thicker, and by Christmas 1965 the word was out that Quill was ready for a strike. Of course, no one knew for sure because it had become pretty hard to understand what he was saying due to the brogue. John

Four good explanations for why people strike

The Baseball Strike

Although there have been several work stoppages in baseball, as well as in other professional sports, the strike that began on August 12, 1994, and lasted until a federal judge issued an injunction against the owners on March 31, 1995, was the longest work stoppage in professional sports. The players' union and the baseball club owners had been negotiating for more than a year, but by August 1994 it was apparent to both sides that there was no chance of reaching an agreement. The players realized that without a collective bargaining agreement a strike or a lockout was inevitable, so they decided to strike at a time when a labor stoppage would hurt the owners much more than themselves.

The strike not only wiped out the last six weeks of the regular season, the play-offs, and the World Series, but it continued right through spring training in 1995. The base-ball clubs hired replacement players, hoping to induce some striking players to cross the picket lines and go back to work on the owners' terms; more importantly, owners needed to stage baseball games to collect TV revenue, which provides the owners with most of their income.

The turning point came when the National Labor Relations Board concluded that the owners had not bargained in good faith with the players' union, and sought an injunction in federal court. As soon as the injunction was granted, the players agreed to return to work. Almost immediately after they did, the club owners voted to accept the players' offer to return to work and replacement players were dismissed. But as of late summer 1995, no collective bargaining agreement had been reached, so there remained the prospect of yet another work stoppage.

Lindsay, the patrician mayor-elect, would be taking office at 12:01 A.M. on January 1. Robert Wagner, the outgoing mayor, had failed to reach a settlement with Quill, so he flew to Mexico during the last hours of his term, throwing the whole mess into Lindsay's lap.

Quill and Lindsay sat across the table from each other, and it quickly became apparent that Quill was not overly fond of the young mayor. When the city put forth an offer, Quill turned it down with scorn. "Do you take me for a schmuck?"[3] asked Quill, somewhat managing to make himself understood. "You're offering *bubkes*."[4]

Lindsay whispered to an aide, "*Schmuck* I know, but what is *bubkes?*" It didn't really matter because Quill was bound and determined to call a strike. Why? Some people thought he hated Lindsay, but there was a better reason. Quill had to put up or shut up. He was like the boy who cried wolf; if he cried wolf this one last time, no one would believe the transit workers would ever strike.

You have to strike sometime to maintain credibility.

You have to strike *sometime* to maintain credibility. If management gets the idea you are afraid to strike, they won't make a decent offer. Why should they? But as I've emphasized, strikes are the exception, not the rule. Therefore what it really comes down to in collective bargaining—the incentive to settle—is the threat of a strike. That threat rather than its occasional occurrence provides the motivation necessary to make collective bargaining work.

The 15-day walkout by 185,000 Teamsters against United Parcel Service in August 1997 was the biggest strike in a quarter of a century. The two key issues were the conversion of part-time to full-time jobs, and a proposed change in the pension plan.

Over the past four years UPS had added 8,000 full-timers, who averaged $19.95 an hour, and 38,000 part-timers, who earned about $9.50 an hour. The strikers demanded that 10,000 part-time positions be converted into full-time jobs over the next four years. UPS offered to convert 1,000 part-time to full-time jobs over five years.

The dispute over the pension plan was less clearcut. Under the existing plan, UPS paid into a multiemployer plan. Because UPS was, by far, the largest contributor, it basically guaranteed the pensions not just of UPS retirees, but of Teamsters who had retired from many other companies, some of which had defaulted on their pension contributions. The Teamsters wanted to keep things as they were, but UPS wanted to switch to a company-controlled plan, which, it said, would raise pensions by as much as 50 percent.

The company repeatedly requested that President Bill Clinton invoke the Taft-Hartley Act, but the president refused on the grounds that the national health and safety were not imperiled. Perhaps not, but not only was UPS losing $50 million a day and union members trying to get by without their wages, but hundreds of thousands of small businesses were especially hard hit by the strike. After 15 days, UPS finally blinked. Under the terms of the settlement, the pension plan was left intact, and the company agreed to convert 10,000 part-time jobs into full-time jobs over the next five years. In addition, over the next five years, full-time workers would receive a pay increase of $3 an hour, and part-timers would receive a $4-an-hour pay increase.

In recent years most strikes have not ended as successfully for labor unions as the Teamsters strike against UPS. The hiring of permanent replacement workers (see accompanying box) during strikes has enabled employers to force workers back to their jobs at Caterpillar, Bridgestone-Firestone, and at newspapers in New York and Detroit. There was even a failed attempt in Congress to pass a law banning the hiring of permanent replacement workers during strikes back in 1994. As long as the Republicans maintain control of Congress, there is virtually no chance that such legislation will be passed.

Averting Strikes: Mediation and Arbitration

Collective bargaining is the basic way of averting strikes. The two sides sit down together and, after some tough bargaining, hammer out an agreement that each can live with.

---

[3]Fool, idiot (slang, from Yiddish).

[4]Peanuts, an insultingly small amount (in Yiddish).

Hiring Permanent Replacement Workers at Caterpillar

Have you ever heard the question "Will it play in Peoria?" Peoria, an old industrial town in central Illinois, is the location of the headquarters of Caterpillar, the world's largest manufacturer of construction equipment.

Unlike nearly every other large American manufacturing firm, Caterpillar makes about 75 percent of its products in the United States and ships nearly 60 percent of them abroad. In April 1992 the company's 12,600 blue-collar workers returned to their jobs after ending a five-month strike. Although the United Auto Workers' local leaders were very unhappy with management's last offer, they recognized that the strikers' resolve had started weakening when Caterpillar began arranging to hire permanent replacement workers.

Greyhound bus services and Eastern Airlines had also hired permanent replacement workers during strikes, but both companies ended up in bankruptcy. However, Caterpillar was in an excellent position to make good on its threat, because more than 8,000 people had already applied for replacement jobs. This tactic may tip the collective bargaining scales in favor of management in future negotiations in other manufacturing industries.

In the summer of 1994, 15,000 members of the United Autoworkers Union struck again at Caterpillar in a dispute over the firing of union members. By the spring of 1995, close to half had given up and gone back to their jobs when it became clear that the company could withstand the strike by using a factory work force of UAW returnees and office workers, along with temporary and permanent new employees.

The 1994–95 baseball strike, during which replacement players were hired, ended with the players returning to work, but with no collective bargaining agreement. During yet another strike at Bridgestone-Firestone that began in July 1994, the tire company hired 2,300 permanent replacement workers in four factories in the Midwest. That strike continued until May 1995 when union members voted to return to their jobs without winning a single concession from management. In many other labor disputes in recent years, the mere threat of permanent replacements has blunted the spirit to fight.

After a union-organized two-year nationwide boycott of Bridgestone-Firestone tires, in November 1996, the company promised to take back those strikers who were still displaced by replacement workers, and to give workers their first across-the-board raise since 1982.

But what if they can't reach an agreement? Or what if they can't even agree to sit down together in the same room? In those cases, a mediator or an arbitrator may be called in, either by the parties themselves or by the federal government.

A mediator is literally a go-between. President Jimmy Carter forged the Camp David accords by running back and forth with proposals and counterproposals by Israel's Menachem Begin and Egypt's Anwar Sadat. A labor mediator tries to speed up the process of negotiations, getting each side to give a little more and take a little less. Often he or she sits down with each side separately and then, when an agreement seems possible, gets both sides together for what is, the mediator hopes, the final bargaining session.

The mediator does not have the power to impose a settlement but can play a valuable role as an expediter. The job of an arbitrator is to impose settlements. This takes the decision out of the hands of labor and management, making arbitration a situation both sides usually want to avoid. Under compulsory arbitration, a labor contract or law actually stipulates that if the two parties cannot reach an agreement, an arbitrator will make the decision.

Have Unions Raised Wages?

Unions have raised wages—but by how much?

Have unions raised wages? The answer is yes. The only question is, By how much? Various studies done in the 1960s and 1970s indicate that unions—among them the Teamsters and the unions of electricians, airline pilots, and plumbers—have raised the wages of their members by 10 to 45 percent. According to the U.S. Department of Labor, in 1997 the hourly wages of union workers were 20 percent greater than those of nonunion workers, and their fringe benefits were typically worth two to four times as much.

Unions have tended to spring up in relatively productive occupations, often in very profitable industries. There is evidence that even without unions the pay would be better than in the other nonunionized sectors. Perhaps we will see some decline in the pay differentials between unionized and nonunionized work with the decline of the nation's industrial sector.

One field that demonstrates the power of labor organization is medicine. That's right! And the American Medical Association (AMA), although it would consider a union label beneath contempt, has been amazingly successful in raising the median wage rate of doctors—which is well in excess of $200,000 a year—by restricting their numbers. The process works the same with sheet metal workers, bricklayers, and electricians, but the AMA does it better.

Unions *do* raise wages, and they provide a badly needed measure of job security. Until unions were organized, workers were powerless to bargain with huge corporate employers. Now many fear the power has shifted too far the other way.

Questions for Further Thought and Discussion

1. Which key provisions of the Taft-Hartley Act persuaded union leaders that the law was antilabor?
2. What are the basic provisions of a collective bargaining agreement?
3. Explain the differences between mediation and arbitration.
4. Explain how a monopsonist operates in the labor market, and illustrate your explanation with an example.

WORKBOOK FOR CHAPTER 30

Name _____ Date _____

Multiple-Choice Questions

Circle the letter that corresponds to the best answer.

1. Unions have

    a. increased wages   b. decreased wages   c. had
    no effect on wages

2. Which statement is true about labor unions in the United
   States?

    a. They have always been very popular.   b. They
    did not gain widespread acceptance until the 1940s.

    c. They have never gained widespread acceptance.

    d. None of these statements is true.

3. The Knights of Labor

    a. were philosophically opposed to strikes but
    occasionally engaged in strikes   b. were
    philosophically in favor of strikes but almost never struck

    c. were philosophically opposed to strikes and never
    struck   d. were philosophically in favor of strikes but
    never engaged in strikes

4. The American Federation of Labor became the nation's
   predominant labor organization in

    a. the early 19th century   b. the 1880s   c. the
    early 20th century   d. the 1940s

5. The AFL has always been basically interested in

    a. better wages, hours, and working conditions

    b. the formation of small producers' cooperatives

    c. the creation of true socialism   d. none of the
    above

6. The act that supported union organizing was the

    a. National Labor Relations Act   b. Taft-Hartley
    Act   c. Landrum-Griffin Act   d. Sherman
    Antitrust Act

7. Employers' rights were protected in the

    a. National Labor Relations Act   b. Taft-Hartley
    Act   c. Landrum-Griffin Act   d. Sherman
    Antitrust Act

8. Jurisdictional disputes and secondary boycotts are
   prohibited under the _____ Act.

    a. National Labor Relations   b. Taft-Hartley

    c. Landrum-Griffin   d. Sherman Antitrust

9. Limits on takeovers of locals by national unions and a
   listing of the financial responsibilities of union officials
   were provisions of the _____ Act.

    a. National Labor Relations   b. Taft-Hartley

    c. Landrum-Griffin   d. Sherman Antitrust

10. Under a(n) _____ shop, an employer
    may hire only union members.

    a. closed   b. union   c. open

11. Right-to-work laws promote the formation of

    a. closed shops   b. union shops   c. open shops

12. In 1935 the

    a. AFL was organizing along industry lines and the CIO
    was organizing along craft lines   b. AFL was
    organizing along craft lines and the CIO was organizing
    along industry lines   c. AFL and the CIO were both
    organizing along craft lines   d. AFL and the CIO
    were both organizing along industry lines

13. The AFL and CIO split up in _____ and
    got back together in _____.

    a. 1915, 1935   b. 1935, 1955   c. 1955, 1975

    d. 1975, 1985

14. The only pro-labor name among the following is

    _____.

    a. Landrum   b. Griffin   c. Taft   d. Hartley

    e. Wagner

15. Which statement is true?

    a. No union is a monopoly.   b. Some unions are
    monopolies.   c. All unions are monopolies.

16. Which statement is true with respect to the two basic ways unions have of exerting power?

    a. Only inclusion leads to higher wages. **b.** Only exclusion leads to higher wages. **c.** Both inclusion and exclusion lead to higher wages. **d.** Neither inclusion nor exclusion leads to higher wages.

17. A monopsony is

    a. the only seller of a product for which there are no close substitutes **b.** the only buyer of a product for which there are no close substitutes **c.** both the seller and the buyer of a product for which there are no close substitutes **d.** neither the seller nor the buyer of a product for which there are no close substitutes

18. Each of the following companies except _____ was once a monopsony.

    a. General Electric **b.** J. P. Stevens **c.** the Hershey Company **d.** AT&T

19. The ultimate weapon that management can use against unions is

    a. collective bargaining **b.** the strike **c.** the ability to take (or withstand) a strike **d.** the lockout

20. The firm with the least ability to withstand a strike would be a

    a. manufacturing firm **b.** service firm **c.** diversified firm

21. A collective bargaining negotiation is

    a. solely a test of power **b.** solely a presentation and discussion of real issues **c.** both a test of power and a presentation and discussion of real issues **d.** neither a test of power nor a presentation and discussion of real issues

22. Pattern-setting wage increases tend to be viewed as

    a. minimums by unions engaged in subsequent bargaining **b.** maximums by unions engaged in subsequent bargaining **c.** irrelevant by unions engaged in subsequent bargaining

23. Collective bargaining negotiations _____ end with a strike.

    a. always **b.** usually **c.** occasionally **d.** never

24. The two key areas covered by provisions of collective bargaining agreements are

    a. wages and hours, and job security and seniority **b.** wages and hours, and working conditions **c.** job security and seniority, and working conditions

25. The job of a(n) _____ is to impose a settlement.

    a. arbitrator **b.** mediator **c.** collective bargaining team leader

26. Most strikes

    a. cause widespread economic disruption **b.** cause little economic disruption **c.** cause no economic disruption

Fill-In Questions

1. Until the decade of the _____, most Americans had an unfavorable opinion of labor unions.

2. The Knights of Labor sought to use _____, _____ and, if necessary, _____, to win their demands.

3. The two most important pieces of labor legislation were the_____ Act and the _____ Act.

4. The Wagner Act prohibited employers from engaging in such "unfair labor practices" as

    (1) _____;

    (2) _____;

    or (3) _____.

5. The apparatus for conducting union representation elections was set up under the _____ _____ Act.

6. The _____ Act put the force of the federal government behind collective bargaining.

7. Jurisdictional disputes and secondary boycotts are prohibited under the _____ Act.

8. Under the _____ shop, an employer may hire only union members.

9. Under the _____ shop, no one is forced to join the union.

10. Industrial unions are organized along _____ _____ lines, while craft unions are organized along _____ lines.

11. The biggest spurt in union membership occurred during the decade of the _____.

12. The conflict within the AFL over whether to organize on a craft basis or an industrial basis led to _____ _____.

13. The _____ continues to be the least unionized section of the country, mainly because of

(1) _____;

(2) _____;

(3) _____;

and (4) _____.

14. Unions have two basic ways of exerting power. They are to (1) _____ and

(2) _____.

15. A monopsony is _____ _____.

16. _____ is the main arena of the power struggle between labor and management.

17. The ultimate weapon for labor is _____, while the ultimate weapon for management is _____ _____.

18. At collective bargaining sessions, management operates under two main constraints:

(1) _____

and (2) _____.

19. Collective bargaining negotiations will end with either _____ or _____.

31 | Labor Markets and Wage Rates

In the last chapter we talked about how labor unions affect the supply of labor. That influence has declined sharply over the last 40 years. Today only one out of seven Americans holding a job is a union member, so when we talk about the supply of labor, we're talking mainly about people who are not union members.

Chapter Objectives

In this chapter you'll learn about:

- The supply of labor.
- The demand for labor.
- High wage rates and economic rent.
- Real wages and productivity.
- The minimum wage dispute.

Income Disparity

In the United States, as well as in most other countries, there is a wide disparity in income. People like Roger Clemens, John Elway, Michael Jordan, Albert Belle, Michael Jackson, David Letterman, Jay Leno, Oprah Winfrey, and the presidents of major corporations, as well as heart surgeons and even the writers of best-selling economics textbooks, make millions of dollars a year. And, of course, the rest of us barely scrape by on $100,000 a year—or even less.

Nineteen ninety-seven was a very good year for movie-maker Steven Spielberg, who pulled down $283 million. Michael Jordan was paid $30 million to play basketball, and a lot more for doing commercials, and perhaps two dozen baseball and basketball players earn over $10 million. But the typical American wage earner earned between $20,000 and $30,000.

I'm going to try to answer the question of why people earn such widely varying incomes. There are several reasons for this disparity, but the bottom line remains the same. You guessed it: supply and demand.

The Supply of Labor

Noncompeting Groups

Skilled, semiskilled, and unskilled labor

There are various classes, or strata, of labor. There is skilled labor, which includes carpenters, plumbers, machinists, computer programmers, printers, schoolteachers, and airline pilots. There is semiskilled labor, such as assembly-line workers, file clerks, receptionists, and supermarket checkers. Finally, there is unskilled labor, which includes freight handlers, dishwashers, porters, janitors, and gas station attendants.

There are also professional (who are the amateurs?), managerial, sales, and service occupations. *The Dictionary of Occupational Titles* lists tens of thousands of job classifications, each of which has its own special code. If you happen to collect unemployment insurance benefits, when you go to the state employment office the employment officer will put a sticker in your booklet listing your code so that your skill is readily identifiable.

Although strike activity has diminished in recent years, a few long and bitter strikes have taken place. One strike-breaking tactic, which President Ronald Reagan seemed to popularize in 1981 when he sought to end the air traffic controllers' strike, is to hire permanent replacement workers. This tactic was employed more recently by Eastern Airlines, Greyhound bus services, and Caterpillar (see box titled "Hiring Permanent Replacement Workers at Caterpillar" at the end of the previous chapter).

In a sense, there are thousands of noncompeting groups. But that doesn't mean there's no overlap or that people with one skill do not compete for jobs with those who have other skills. In fact, an employer is often faced with the decision to hire either a skilled worker for high pay or a lower-paid trainee. One might say that in the long run we are all potential competitors for the same jobs.

Suppose hundreds of thousands of jobs as major-league ballplayers became available. Perhaps the major leagues expanded to Mars, Venus, and Jupiter. I know I haven't revealed this to many people, but I still harbor ambitions to have a major-league career.[1] And so do a lot of other economics professors. We could start our own teams—the Keynesians, the Monetarists, the Rational Expectationists.

Let's return to the point I was making. If the opportunities arise in certain fields—professional sports, engineering, accounting, computer programming, medicine—people will go through the necessary training and compete for jobs. If there are large numbers of relatively high-paying jobs, people currently in those fields will eventually be joined by huge numbers of competitors.

We are all competitors in the same employment pool.

In still another sense, we are all competitors in the same employment pool. Certain skills are partially substitutable for other skills. One 100-word-per-minute typist is a perfect substitute for another 100-word-per-minute typist; but an electrician who can type 20 words per minute is only a partial substitute. Similarly, a plumber's assistant is a partial substitute for a plumber, and a file clerk is an even more partial substitute for a plumber's assistant.

In the long run most of us can learn to do many different jobs. In some cases it takes just a few hours, but it takes many years to learn other skills. In the short run, however, we are all partial substitutes for one another. The question is, how partial?

There *are* noncompeting groups, but these distinctions tend to blur in the long run. To the degree that there is a good deal of labor mobility—the ability to change occupations and/or geographic locations—there is less demarcation among the nation's various occupational groups.

The Theory of the Dual Labor Market

Primary and secondary labor markets

Obviously, we are not all in the same labor market, primarily because we are separated by skill, ability, and training. A more radical theory than that of noncompeting groups places the entire labor force into two broad categories: the primary and secondary labor markets.

The primary market has most of the good jobs, which not only pay well but offer good opportunities for advancement. Examples of such jobs include the skilled crafts, management, the professions, and virtually all the other jobs requiring college degrees. (See box "Are You in the Primary Market or in the Secondary Market?")

The secondary market consists of all the jobs that are left over. The pay is low, and there is little chance for advancement. Often these jobs are temporary, and the people who hold them are called "disposable workers." These jobs include work in laundries,

[1]For those who are skeptical about this, I quote a sentence about me on page 187 of *The Einstein Syndrome: Corporate Anti-Semitism in America Today* by Stephen L. Slavin (Lanham, MD: University Press of America, 1982): "He plans to enter the free agent draft this fall and pursue a major league baseball career."

Are You in the Primary Market or in the Secondary Market?

Thirty years ago, you could graduate from high school, get married, have kids, and have a decent life in a blue-collar town.

—Gary Bauer, president of the Family Research Council
(quoted in *BusinessWeek*, March 13, 1995, p. 74)

Former Secretary of Labor Robert Reich noted that "The fundamental fault line through the labor force divides workers by education and skills." In 1979 a male college graduate earned 49 percent more than a man with just a high school diploma; by 1992 the gap had widened to 83 percent.* Heightened international competition, along with rapid technological change, largely accounts for the 23 percent plunge in real hourly wages for high school dropouts from 1973 to 1993.

Does this mean that a college degree will almost double your earnings? Increasingly, the answer is no.

Historically a college degree has been the passport that allowed millions of Americans to move from the secondary labor market to the primary labor market. In the first decades of this century many individuals from poor and working-class families worked their way through college. But in the years immediately following World War II millions of returning veterans were able to go to college under the G.I. Bill of Rights, which paid their tuition and most or all of their living expenses as well.

Those who graduated returned to the labor market, getting jobs as accountants, engineers, attorneys, corporate managers, and other professionals. The American economy continued to expand quite rapidly through the early 1970s, creating millions of positions for college graduates to fill.

In the late 1960s and early 1970s, when the baby boomers began reaching college age, the philosophy of open admissions gained widespread acceptance, giving rise to another major expansion of the college population, especially at two-year community colleges. But since 1973 our economic growth has slackened, and fewer jobs that require a college degree have been created each year.

Today nearly one out of five adults has a college degree, and educational standards have fallen substantially. A diploma remains a *necessary* condition for a person to move from the secondary to the primary labor market. But that diploma is no longer a *sufficient* condition. You not only need a college degree, but you also need to be educated (the two are not necessarily synonymous)—and maybe a little lucky or well-connected. On the other hand, if you *don't* have a college degree, your chances of ever getting a job in the primary market are nil—unless, of course, your parents own the company.

*Robert Reich, "The Fracturing of the Middle Class," *New York Times,* August 31, 1994, p. A19.

hospitals, fast-food chains, and clothing factories. These positions are often filled by minority group members and women.

The rich stay rich, and the poor stay poor.

The dual labor market theory is a class theory of employment. The rich stay rich, and the poor stay poor. The college degree seems to be a dividing line, a line that is seldom passed by those from poorer economic backgrounds.

One problem with this theory is that it doesn't account for the huge middle level of occupations—nursing, teaching, social work, and noncollege-graduate positions in insurance, banking, and retailing. But the theory *does* support the contention that there are noncompeting groups in the labor market. The only question is, how many?

The Backward-Bending Labor Supply Curve

When we talk about the supply of labor, I ask my students whether they would be willing to do clerical work for $5.15 an hour. Nobody would. How about $10 an hour? A lot of hands go up. And at $100 an hour, everyone volunteers.

The substitution effect

This demonstrates the *substitution effect.* As the wage rate rises, people are willing to substitute more work for leisure time because leisure time is becoming more expensive. Imagine if an hour of leisure time cost you $100! Suppose the wage rate were increased to $1,000 an hour. Now an hour of leisure time would cost you $1,000! That's a lot of money to give up for just one hour of watching TV, playing bingo, or hanging around the shopping mall.

Something else is happening as your wage rate keeps getting higher. You're making all this money. You're rich! You're making $1,000 an hour. But if you keep working more and more hours, when are you going to be able to spend your money? When are you going to have time to see your family and friends? And when are you going to have time to sleep?

The income effect

How many hours would you work picking up money?

At some point, as your wage rate continues to rise, you will say to yourself, "I want more leisure time for myself, if only so that I'll be able to spend some of my money." Now you're willing to give up some income in exchange for more leisure time. We call this the *income effect.*

Let's see how the substitution and income effects work for *you.* How would you like a job picking pennies up off the floor? You get to keep all the pennies you pick up. What's the catch? There *is* no catch. Just tell me how many hours per week you'd be willing to work.

Of course some people would not stoop so low as to take a job picking up pennies. How about nickels? Dimes? Quarters? Half-Dollars? How about dollar bills? All right, I'll even let you pick up five-dollar bills. What I want to know is how many hours per week you would be willing to work picking up each of these denominations of coins and bills.

Write down your answers. Then compare them to mine in Table 1. Of course, there *is* no "right" answer. Everyone has his or her own schedule of hours of willingness to work.

Table 1   Hypothetical Work Schedule Picking Up Money

Type of Money	Hours per Week
Pennies	35
Nickels	50
Dimes	58
Quarters	61
Half-dollars	63
Dollar bills	65
Five-dollar bills	62

Most people would work more hours to pick up nickels than they would to pick up pennies. And more hours to pick up dimes than to pick up nickels. That's the substitution effect at work: they're substituting more work for leisure time. But at some point their hours reach a maximum. In this example, people would work 65 hours to pick up dollar bills. Beyond that point, the income effect will outweigh the substitution effect, as they give up some income in exchange for more leisure time.

Turning to Figure 1, we see that as the wage rate rises from very low levels to higher and higher levels, people substitute extra work for leisure time. That's the substitution effect. And it happens up to point J. Beyond point J the curve begins to move upward to the left as the wage rate continues to rise. That's the income effect.

To summarize: The substitution effect means that you trade away leisure time for more money, and the income effect means that you trade away some money for more leisure time. At wage rates below point J on the curve, the substitution effect outweighs the income effect. At point J the two effects just offset each other. Above J the income effect outweighs the substitution effect.

We call curve S in Figure 1 the individual labor supply curve. Perhaps the typical individual will work a maximum of 60 or 70 hours a week. I had a friend called Shrieking Jack. (Never mind how he got the name. Believe me, it fit.) He used to work 108 hours a week.

"Why, Jack, why do you do it?" Jack pointed at his brand-new Chevy Impala—remember the cars that had what looked like bow ties on their rear ends? "With time and a half and double time on both jobs, I paid for that car in three weeks! Of course, I had to work 324 hours." Then he shrieked.

We can now generalize our findings in Figure 2. Here we have the general supply curve of labor. Why is it general? Because nearly everyone will increase hours of work up to a point as the wage rate rises and then cut back. Of course, people will cut back at different points, some at 30 hours, some at 40, some at 60 or 80, and Shrieking Jack at 108.

Figure 1   **Hypothetical Individual Labor Supply Curve**

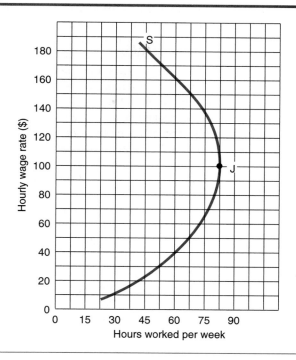

Figure 2   **Hypothetical General Supply Curve for Labor**

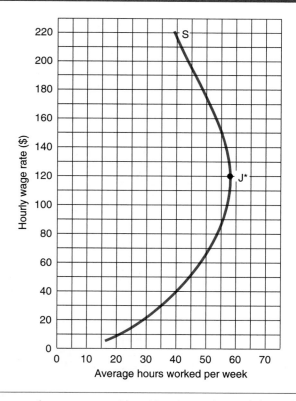

*At about $120 an hour, on the average, people would work a maximum of about 58 hours. This is designated by point J.

At relatively low wage rates, the substitution effect outweighs the income effect, but at some point, as the wage rate rises, the two are in balance (point J). Finally, as the wage rate is increased still further, the income effect overcomes the substitution effect.

Do you recall that the chapter "Demand in the Factor Market" introduced a different substitution effect? The idea was that if the price of, say, labor went up, business firms would tend to substitute capital or land for some of their now more expensive workers. So *that* substitution effect described substituting one resource for another. In *this* chapter we just finished talking about another substitution effect that describes how, as wage rates rise, people are willing to substitute more work for leisure time. Economists are usually good at giving the same concept two or three different names. In the case of the substitution effect, however, we've given the same name to two different concepts.

But the argument can be made that these two concepts are basically the same. In both cases, when the price of A (labor, leisure) gets high enough, we begin to substitute B (capital, work).

Although we talk about a general supply curve for labor, because there are different types of work (and noncompeting groups to perform each of these jobs), there are many different labor supply curves in the short run. For example, the general supply curve for heart surgeons might look like the one in Figure 3A, while that of clerical workers looks like the one in Figure 3B. If the wage rate for heart surgeons is $1,475 an hour, we find that we are above point J, and the supply curve has already begun to bend backward. The wage rate for clerical workers is $7 or $8 an hour, so we are well below point J in Figure 3B.

The popular name among economists for the general supply curve is the backward-bending supply curve. This shows that economists are capable, every so often, of fooling around. What's so funny about a backward-bending supply curve? I'm not too sure myself, but it's about the funniest thing we've been able to come up with.

Figure 3   Hypothetical General Supply Curve for Labor—Examples

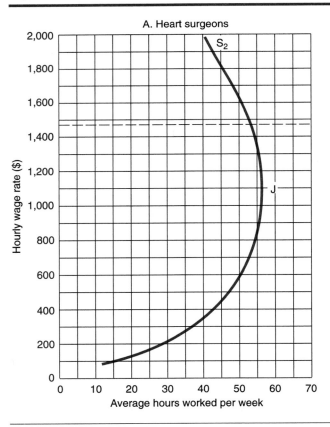

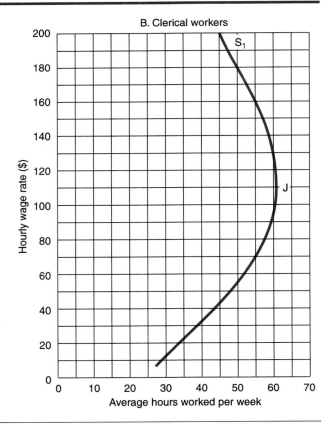

The Demand for Labor

The Marginal Revenue Product Schedule

You may have noticed that I have been trying to impress on you the idea that the wage rate is determined by two factors, supply and demand. We just covered supply. Demand is the firm's MRP schedule for labor. In the more general sense, the demand for a particular type of labor is the sum of all the firms' MRP schedules.

Demand for labor is represented by the MRP schedule.

Like nearly all demand curves we've encountered, the general demand curve for labor, shown in Figure 4, slopes downward to the right. It conforms to the law of demand, a concept first introduced in Chapter 3: *When the price of a good is lowered, more of it is demanded; when it is raised, less is demanded.* Because every firm's MRP curve slopes downward to the right (as the wage rate, or price of labor, declines), it follows that the general demand curve for labor, which is the sum of these curves, also slopes downward to the right.

We may ask what determines the demand for labor or, more specifically, the MRP schedule of each firm. Remember that the demand for each factor of production—land, labor, capital—is a derived demand. It is derived from the demand for the final product.

Firms hire labor because that labor produces a final product, which is then sold. Not all labor is identical. Some people are more productive because they are better trained, more skilled, or have more natural ability.

Obviously, workers who are more productive will generally be more in demand and better paid than less productive workers. The more highly skilled machinist and the better basketball player will usually earn more than their less productive colleagues.

Some people become more productive because of education and training, some because of work experience, and, of course, some are just born with greater natural ability. High school graduates earn considerably more than those who never got past the eighth grade, and there is also a wide differential between the earnings of high school graduates and college graduates. But perhaps too much is made of these differences, which may be

Figure 4   Hypothetical General Demand Curve for Labor

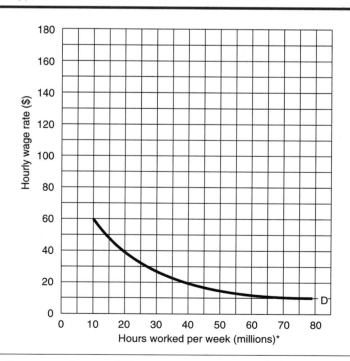

*We have gone from average hours worked per week to millions of hours worked per week to reflect the total labor market with millions of people selling their labor.

explained on the basis of general ability and connections as well as education. For example, the average college graduate has a considerably higher IQ than a high school graduate has, but you won't raise your IQ by going to college. Furthermore, the college graduate comes from a family with better business connections than the high school graduate's family has.

Productivity: the role of education

What I'm getting at is that relatively high productivity cannot be completely explained by education when we compare high school and college graduates. Furthermore, we have many cases where people of widely varying productivity earn the same wages regardless of education or ability. These things don't matter in an office or factory where there is a standard wage rate for any worker who has put in a certain number of years on the job; everyone gets the same pay no matter how productive he or she is. Labor unions, civil service rules, and institutional custom often enforce these standards. In sum, productivity partially explains wage differentials, but it is not the entire story.

Specialized skills

Closely related to worker productivity are specialized skills possessed by some workers, which also influence the demand for labor. Generally, the highly skilled worker or the highly trained specialist will earn higher wages than the person with less developed skills. Specialists in medicine and dentistry, in law, and in engineering are usually among the best paid practitioners of their professions. This is especially true when their skills are in relatively high demand in relation to their supply.

Finally, some workers are in demand because of the natural abilities they possess. Obvious examples abound in show business and professional athletics. A little later we'll consider the special cases of David Letterman and Willie Mays.

Nonhomogeneous Jobs

Still another factor accounting for different wage rates is worker preference with respect to working hours and conditions. Those willing to work longer hours, night shifts, and weekends will usually earn higher wages than will those who work the standard Monday-to-Friday, nine-to-five workweek; those who work under unsafe conditions earn higher wages as well. Pay differentials are institutionalized, for example, for window washers who work above the 20th floor.

Pay differentials adjust for harder, more unpleasant, less convenient work.

Harder, more unpleasant, or less convenient work is usually somewhat better paid than the more conventional occupations. Night workers and those who work overtime get pay differentials. The out-of-town salesman is better paid than his home territory counterpart, while the sandhog who builds tunnels is given much shorter hours and higher pay than most other construction workers.

More than a century ago John Stuart Mill took a diametrically opposite view of how well people were paid to do undesirable work:

> The really exhausting and the really repulsive labours, instead of being better paid than others, are almost invariably paid the worst of all . . . The hardships and the earnings, instead of being directly proportional, as in any just arrangements of society they would be, are generally in an inverse ratio to one another.[2]

How do we get people to pick up our garbage?

Do you happen to know the year in which Martin Luther King, Jr., was assassinated? It was 1968. And in which city? Memphis. What was King doing in Memphis? He was leading a strike of sanitation workers. The Memphis sanitation workers were predominantly black, and they were paid little more than minimum wage. Because there was so much employment discrimination against blacks, especially in the South, many black men were forced into doing this undesirable work at very low wages.

But the situation was different in New York City. Not only were sanitation workers relatively well paid, but few were black or Hispanic. In fact, for years public school teachers complained that garbage men were paid more than *they* were. So New York got its garbage picked up by paying white men very well to do it; Memphis got *its* garbage picked up by not allowing black or Hispanic men to do more desirable types of work.

---

[2]John Stuart Mill, *Principles of Political Economy,* ed. Ashley, p. 388.

How does our society get its dirty work done? By paying people enough to make it worth their while? Or by calling on oppressed minorities to work as migrant farm laborers, bedpan orderlies, janitors, dishwashers, and launderers? This disturbing question may be argued persuasively from either side.

Graph of the Demand for Labor

In the chapter "Demand in the Factor Market," we saw that the demand curve for labor—the MRP schedule—slopes downward to the right. Similarly, the general demand curve for labor, which encompasses the sum of the demand curves of every firm, also slopes downward to the right. This curve is shown in Figure 4.

The Wage Rate: Supply and Demand

Here's what we've all been waiting for. Oh, I know, it's a bit anticlimactic, but who needs surprises? It's all there in Figure 5. You may ask, where did Figure 5 *come* from? Can you guess? Glance back at Figures 2 and 4. That's right—I just copied the general labor supply curve from Figure 2 and the general labor demand curve from Figure 4.

Much of this course is based on a simple law: the law of supply and demand. When quantity demanded is equal to quantity supplied, we've got our price. In this case the price of labor, or the wage rate, is about $16 an hour. But remember, this is only a *hypothetical* wage rate. How much is the *actual* wage rate? A lot lower? In many cases, yes. It all depends on the type of work you do and on the demand and supply schedules in each of hundreds, or even thousands, of job markets.

High Wage Rates and Economic Rent

In the early 1950s, when the Giants still played baseball at New York's Polo Grounds, Willie Mays joined the team as a young rookie and quickly established himself as the

Figure 5   Hypothetical General Demand and Supply Curves for Labor

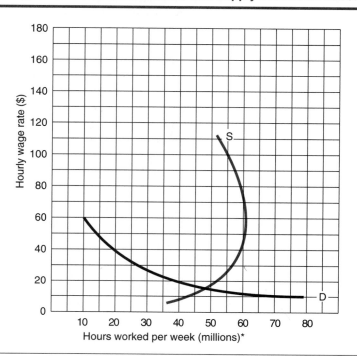

*We have gone from average hours worked per week to millions of hours worked per week to reflect the total labor market with millions of people selling their labor.

most exciting player in the game. Like most ballplayers of his generation, Mays came from an economically deprived background and was eventually earning unheard-of sums of money.

There was something mysterious about Mays that aroused the curiosity of his teammates. He would often disappear on summer afternoons when no games were scheduled, but he never said where he was going. Some of his friends worried about a 20-year-old country kid and what could happen to him in the big bad city.

It turns out that on those summer afternoons Willie Mays, center fielder for the New York Giants, was playing stickball in the streets of Harlem with the neighborhood kids. Why was he doing this? Because he loved playing ball.

Professional baseball, football, basketball, tennis, and other sports give a few thousand people a chance to make a living playing kids' games. Although they negotiate for huge salaries, many, like Willie Mays, would have been willing to play for a lot less. Maybe it's a chance to prolong one's childhood for a few more years. Perhaps that's what gave Roger Kahn the idea for the title of his story of the 1953 Brooklyn Dodgers, *The Boys of Summer*.

Whenever a person gets paid more than the minimum she would be willing to accept, we call the excess over the minimum *economic rent*. For example, I might be willing to accept just $20,000 to be an economics professor. As I am now collecting a salary of $950,000, my economic rent is $930,000.

In January 1998 the ABC, CBS, and Fox networks agreed to collectively pay $17.6 billion for the rights to broadcast National Football League games for the next eight years. Question: What effect did this deal have on the players' salaries and on their economic rent? Obviously it raised both salaries and economic rent.

How much does David Letterman make? Although Mr. Letterman asked me not to disclose his exact earnings, it was estimated at about $30 million a year. I will try to put aside my personal misgivings about a mere show business personality earning even more than I do.

Have you ever gone to a club, maybe to hear a particular singer or a certain group, and been subjected to a comedian as the preshow act? While you're waiting, this comic comes out and announces, "On my way over to the club tonight . . ." Each joke is worse than the last. You look at your friends and ask why you have to pay good money to listen to this clown. Finally, the comic is finished and the crowd claps wildly as he makes his exit. He knows and everybody else knows his act bombed, but the audience is clapping in sarcasm, out of relief that he's leaving, in anticipation of the featured act, or maybe some combination of the three.

Why do comedians make so much money

If you wonder why David Letterman, Jay Leno, Eddie Murphy—or any of the other half dozen or so top stand-up comedians—make so much money, just take a look at the competition. It's like the guy who ends up in a prison where everyone knows the jokes by number. Finally, he gets up the courage to yell out "66!" No one laughs. "Why?" he asks his cellmate. "It's all in the way you *tell* it." And people like David Letterman know how to tell it. The split-second timing, the deadpan expression, the scornful look (at Paul Shaffer)—these are the successful comedian's stock-in-trade. But only a handful are as gifted as Letterman, Leno, and Murphy.

It all comes back to supply and demand.

We come back again to supply and demand. There may be thousands of would-be comics occasionally getting a gig here and there, but there are perhaps half a dozen really good ones. Thus, we have a graph like that in Figure 6, in which the wage rate comes to $30 million.

Now David Letterman probably could scrape by on $10 million a year if he really had to. If that were his secret bottom line—if he was really willing to work for that paltry sum—his economic rent would be some $20 million.

Is David Letterman overpaid? The question boils down to supply and demand. Good stand-up comedians, great athletes, cosmetic surgeons, and authors capable of writing best-sellers are all in relatively short supply. If supply is relatively low in relation to demand, the resulting wage rate will be high.

These explanations as to why a tiny fraction of our population makes so much more than the rest of us, cloaked in such terms as *marginal revenue product* and *economic rent*,

Figure 6   Determination of Economic Rent by Supply and Demand

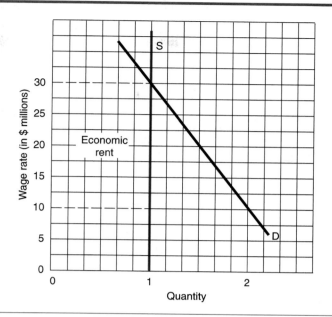

may still leave us wondering if these folks are *really* worth such huge incomes. For another view, see the box "Winner-Take-All Markets."

Real Wages and Productivity

When I was a boy growing up in Brooklyn during the Spanish-American War, I got a part-time job selling subscriptions to a local newspaper called the *Kingsway Courier*. The subscription manager, who doubled as the sports editor, told us he was a $12,000-a-year man. Understand that he was trying to impress us—when I was a kid, earning $12,000 meant selling 60,000 subscriptions.

If you were offered a job today at a salary of, say, $100,000, you probably would be inclined to take it. But what if you were locked into that salary for life? Isn't it conceivable that by the time you reach middle age, $100,000 won't buy all that much? With the cost of living quadrupling since 1970, who knows what will happen to prices over the next 20 or 30 years?

Winner-Take-All Markets

Why do the chief executive officers of large American corporations earn on average 150 times the salary of the average production worker? Japanese CEOs earn only 16 times the average Japanese worker's salary, and German CEOs, only 21 times the average German worker's salary. Are American CEOs so much more valuable than their German and Japanese counterparts?

Robert Frank and Philip Cook note that top corporate executives in the United States, unlike their foreign counterparts, are relatively free to move from firm to firm, going to the highest bidder, in what the authors call "winner-take-all markets." These are markets in which a handful of top performers walk away with the lion's share of total rewards. This payoff structure has always been common in entertainment and professional sports, but in recent years it has permeated many other fields—law, journalism, consulting, investment banking, corporate management, design, fashion, even the hallowed halls of academe.* The star system is distorting American society by diverting talented young people into competition that most will lose.

*Robert Frank, "Talent and the Winner-Take-All Society," *The American Prospect,* Spring 1994, p. 95. See also, Robert Frank and Philip Cook, *The Winner-Take-All Society* (New York: Free Press, 1995).

What are real wages?

By real wages, economists mean what you can actually buy with your wages. If the rate of inflation were 10 percent a year, you'd need a 10 percent pay raise each year just to maintain your standard of living. And a person who earned $10,000 in 1970 would need about $40,000 today to continue living the same lifestyle.

Most of us are not content just to maintain the same standard of living from year to year. We like to see it go up, if not steadily from one year to the next, at least in sizable jumps every four or five years. Why can't we do this by giving everyone pay increases—increases that more than keep pace with inflation?

What can you buy with your earnings?

The key question is, What can you buy with this money? You can't buy more unless we produce more. In short, the national standard of living cannot rise unless national production rises.

When we talk about the relationship between real wages and production, the important factor is output per labor-hour. In other words, how much do people produce in an hour? For real wages to grow, output per labor-hour must grow. In fact, this is an almost exactly parallel relationship.

Between 1947 and 1978 output per labor-hour rose 104 percent. During this period real wages rose 105 percent. But since 1978 things haven't gone so well. Output per labor-hour has risen only about 1 percent a year since 1978. And real wages have not increased at all.

Real wages and output per labor-hour have a parallel relationship.

The historical relationship between real wages and output per labor-hour is a fact—and you can't argue with a fact. Any efforts to raise real wages must center on raising output per labor-hour. It is not enough to raise money wages without raising output; to do that would only cause inflation. Then we'd all be making $100,000 a year, but our living standard would be the same as when we were earning considerably less.

American wages versus wages in other industrial countries

How do American wages stack up against those of other industrial countries? Not all that impressively. As you can see from a glance at Figure 7, the United States ranks third out of the nine leading industrial nations, with our average hourly manufacturing wage rate (including fringe benefits) of $17.10. Until the late 1970s or early 1980s this country paid higher wages than any other nation. Looking ahead, when we take into account our lagging productivity growth, it would be a good bet that our country will fall further

Figure 7   Hourly Wage and Fringe Benefits in Manufacturing, 1994

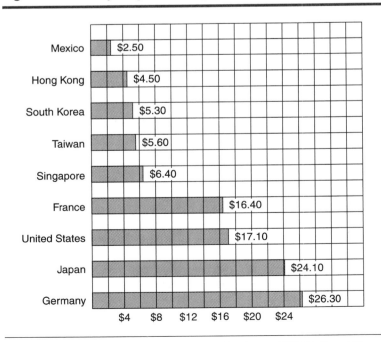

Sources: National Science Foundation, Morgan Stanley, and DRI/McGraw-Hill.

behind the leaders. But before you get too depressed, keep in mind that international comparisons of wages and living standards have long been suspect and need to be taken with at least a couple of grains of salt.

Real Wages versus Nominal Wages

In an earlier chapter of *Economics* and *Macroeconomics* I spent several pages, replete with bells and whistles, explaining how to convert nominal (or money) GDP into real GDP, which measures the economy's output of actual goods and services. Along the way we reviewed how to calculate percentage changes. Now we'll apply the same methodology to converting money (or nominal) wages into real wages.

Here's our first problem: Your wage rate rises from $5 an hour in 1993 to $8.40 an hour in 1999. Meanwhile, the consumer price index (CPI) rises from 100 in 1993 (the base year) to 120 in 1999 (the current year). How much is your real hourly wage in 1999, and by what percentage has it increased since 1993?

Solution:

$$\text{Real wages (current year)} = \text{Money wages (current year)} \times \frac{\text{CPI (base year)}}{\text{CPI (current year)}}$$

$$= \frac{\$8.40}{1} \times \frac{100}{120}$$

$$= \frac{\$8.40}{1} \times \frac{10}{12}$$

$$= \frac{\overset{.70}{\cancel{\$8.40}}}{1} \times \frac{10}{\underset{1}{\cancel{12}}}$$

$$= \$7.00$$

We found, then, that your real wage rate is $7 an hour in 1999. You'll notice that when I substituted numbers into the formula, I placed $8.40 over 1. I did this because I wanted to cross multiply. When you set up future problems, always put your money wages over 1.

For the second part of the problem we want to find the percentage increase in real wages from 1993 to 1999. We just found real wages of $7 for 1999. How much were real wages in 1993? There's only one choice—$5, which was given. Because 1993 was the base year, we're comparing what an hour's wages bought you in 1993 to what an hour's wages buy you in 1999.

So what is the percentage change when we go from $5 to $7?
Solution:

$$\text{Percentage change} = \frac{\text{Change}}{\text{Original number}}$$

$$= \frac{\$2}{\$5}$$

$$= .4$$

$$= 40\%$$

When we convert a decimal to a percentage, we move the decimal point two places to the right and add a percentage sign: .4 = .40 = .40.% = 40%.

If calculating percentage changes is not your strong suit, then please read the box titled "Calculating Percentage Changes," which you'll find about halfway through Chapter 8 in *Economics* and *Macroeconomics*.

Here's the next problem. Mr. Zitnik, who was earning $20,000 in 1994, received several promotions and is earning $32,500 in 1997. Over this same period the CPI rose to 125. Assume that 1994 was the base year. How much are Mr. Zitnik's real wages in 1997, and by what percentage did they change since 1994? Work out your solution to both parts of the problem right here, and then check your work.

Solution:

$$\text{Real wages (1997)} = \text{Money wages (1997)} \times \frac{\text{CPI (1994)}}{\text{CPI (1997)}}$$

$$= \frac{\$32,500}{1} \times \frac{100}{125}$$

$$= \frac{\overset{260}{\cancel{\$32,500}}}{1} \times \frac{100}{\underset{1}{\cancel{125}}}$$

$$= \$26,000$$

$$\text{Percentage change} = \frac{\text{Change}}{\text{Original number}}$$

$$= \frac{\$6,000}{\$20,000}$$

$$= .30$$

$$= 30\%$$

Are you getting the hang of this? We'll try one more, but I'll warn you in advance, it's a little tricky. All set? All right, then, here it comes: Ms. Klopman has been working at the same job since 1989, the base year. She was making $400 a week at that time, and now, in 1999, she is earning $540 a week. If the CPI rose to 180 in 1999, how much are Ms. Klopman's real wages in 1999, and by what percentage did they change? (Be careful how you answer this.)

Solution:

$$\text{Real wages (1999)} = \text{Money wages (1999)} \times \frac{\text{CPI (1989)}}{\text{CPI (1999)}}$$

$$= \frac{\$540}{1} \times \frac{100}{180}$$

$$= \frac{\overset{3}{\cancel{\$540}}}{1} \times \frac{100}{\underset{1}{\cancel{180}}}$$

$$= \$300$$

$$\text{Percentage change} = \frac{\text{Change}}{\text{Original number}}$$

$$= \frac{-\$100}{\$400}$$

$$= \frac{-1}{4}$$

$$= -.25$$

$$= -25\%$$

Between 1989 and 1999 Ms. Klopman's money wages rose from $400 to $540, but they rose more slowly than the CPI rose. Her *real* wages fell from $400 to just $300, a decline of 25 percent.

What has happened to real wages in the United States since the 1970s? Have they gone up or down? Most people's real wages went down. You'll see that immediately when you look at Figure 8.

Real wages peaked in the late 1970s, reached a low during the 1981–82 recession, rose again until 1986, and declined once more in the late 1980s. During the first half of the 1990s, real wages have been flat, remaining just below the 1989 level.

Figure 8 **Index of Real Wages, 1975–98 (base: second quarter of 1989 = 100)**

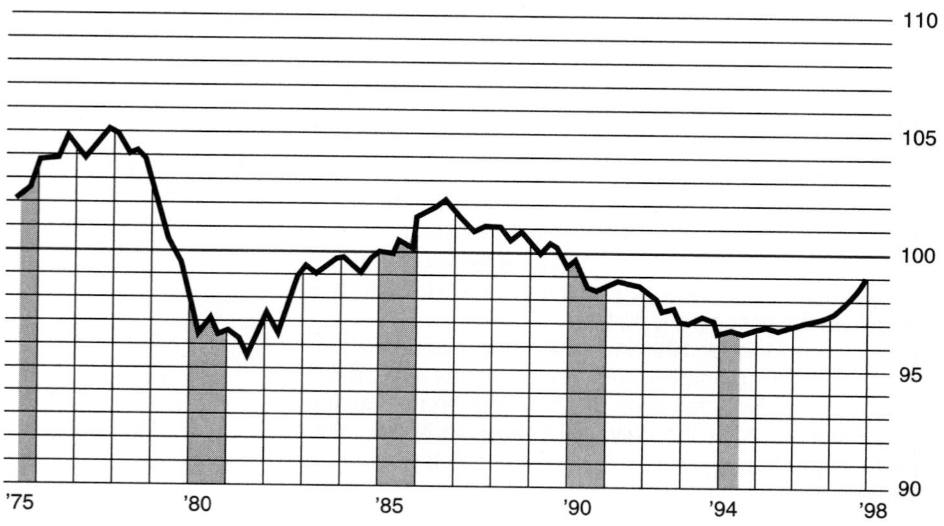

Source: Bureau of Labor Statistics, employment cost index.

The Minimum Hourly Wage Rate

The Fair Labor Standards Act

In 1938 Congress passed the Fair Labor Standards Act calling for a 25-cent-an-hour minimum wage (raised to 30 cents in 1939, a standard workweek of 44 hours (reduced to 40 hours in 1940), and the payment of time and half for overtime. You know, of course, that 25 cents bought a lot more in 1938 than it does today.

Since then the minimum wage has been raised periodically, but these raises have not kept pace with inflation. In 1990 it was raised from $3.35 to $4.25, and in 1996 it was raised again to $4.75, and to $5.15 in mid-1997. Most Americans earn a lot more than the minimum wage, but about 10 million workers who were earning under $5.15 received increases. In addition, as a ripple effect, several million others who were earning $5.15 or slightly more also got pay raises.

Does raising the minimum wage cause some unemployment? In the box "The Minimum Wage and the Unemployment Rate," we'll try to gauge the effect of the 1996–97 minimum wage increase, and then, using Figures 9, 11, and 12, we'll use demand and supply analysis to see how raising the minimum wage might cause some unemployment.

Should There Be a Minimum Wage Rate?

Conservatives: The minimum wage law hurts the very people it is supposed to help.

According to many conservative economists, the minimum wage law hurts the very people it is supposed to help—young workers, the unskilled, and those whose productivity is low. These economists use marginal revenue product analysis (which we covered a couple of chapters back) to support their claim that the basic effect of the minimum wage is to cause millions of marginal workers to be unemployed. And they point to the rising teenage unemployment rate as their proof.

Figure 9 shows a hypothetical MRP curve for unskilled labor (i.e., the demand for unskilled labor) and a hypothetical labor supply curve. It is obvious that at $5.15 an hour, the current minimum wage, there is a surplus of unskilled labor. By allowing the wage rate to fall to the equilibrium level, substantially more people would find work.

To fix the minimum of wages is to exclude from labour many workmen who would otherwise have been employed; it is to aggravate the distress you wish to relieve.

—Jeremy Bentham,
A Manual of Political Economy

Many younger workers are familiar with the catch–22 of job interviews: "Come back when you have some experience." Where are you supposed to get that experience when you can't get that first job? The conservative economists would help younger workers get that experience by suspending the minimum wage. Once they acquired the requisite experience, they would be able to get jobs that pay at least the minimum wage.

Between 1973 and 1997 real hourly wages fell for most Americans. The graph in Figure 10A shows real hourly wages by level of education for men; the graph in Figure 10B shows the same thing for women. As you can see, the only workers who made gains during this period were women with at least some college education.

The Minimum Wage and the Unemployment Rate

Opponents of the minimum wage rate claim that it causes substantial unemployment. In October 1996 the minimum wage was raised from $4.25 to $4.75; in July 1997 it was raised to $5.15. What happened to the unemployment rate? Let's go to the instant replay, which is shown in the accompanying table.

After the October 1996 increase, there was a slight increase in the unemployment rate over the next three months, but then it fell even lower during the next spring and summer. After the July 1997 increase in the minimum wage (from $4.75 to $5.15) the unemployment rate inched down a bit more during the rest of the year.

Monthly Unemployment Rate, 1996, 1997, and 1998

	1996	1997	1998
January	5.7	5.3	4.7
February	5.5	5.3	4.6
March	5.7	5.2	4.7
April	5.5	5.0	
May	5.5	4.8	
June	5.3	5.0	
July	5.4	4.9	
August	5.2	4.9	
September	5.2	4.9	
October	5.2	4.8	
November	5.3	4.6	
December	5.3	4.7	

Figure 9   Hypothetical Demand and Supply Schedules for Unskilled Labor

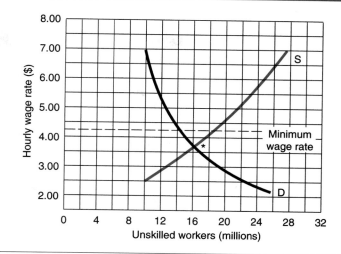

*According to hypothetical schedules, equilibrium wage rate is $3.75. At minimum wage rate of $4.25, there is a surplus of about 4 million workers. These are people who would be willing to work at $3.75 but can't find jobs. If the minimum wage were lowered or suspended for teenagers, more of them would be able to find employment. The question is, How many?

Figure 10A   Real Hourly Wages for Men by Level of Education, 1973 and 1996

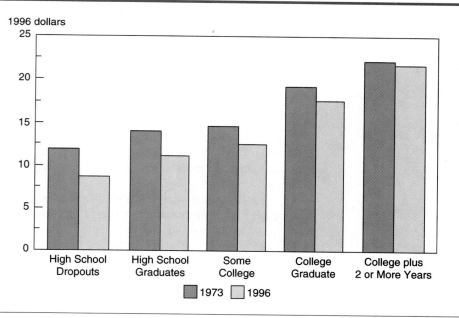

Source: Economic Policy Institute.

For those who remember Richard Nixon and the many "irregularities" of his presidency, one of the less publicized capers involved Ray Kroc, the guiding spirit of McDonald's. It seems that McDonald's, along with scores of other corporations, illegally contributed to Nixon's campaign war chest. In return the president tried to exempt teenage employment from the minimum wage law. Undoubtedly, he was concerned with the high teenage unemployment rate and was anxious to help young people acquire meaningful work experience.

This raises another issue. My students—many of whom staff the fast-food emporiums of America—claim they do the same work as older workers. Were the minimum

Figure 10B   Real Hourly Wages for Women by Level of Education, 1973 and 1996

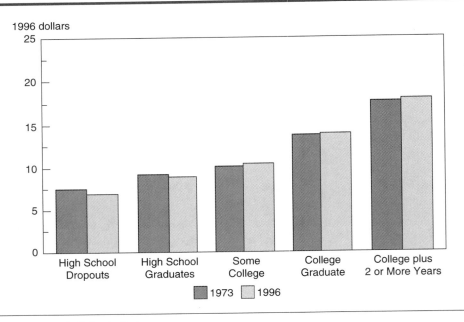

Source: Economic Policy Institute.

wage lowered for teenagers, this would just be an excuse to pay them even less. In fact, the whole attack on the minimum wage is suspect on the same grounds.

Who in America can live on $5.15 an hour? And who is worth *less* than $5.15 an hour? Wasn't the idea of minimum wage legislation to help abolish sweatshop wage levels? Would those who would abolish the minimum wage have us return to those conditions?

President Ronald Reagan did not propose abolishing the minimum wage, but just lowering it during the summer months for teenagers, from $3.35 an hour to $2.50 an hour.[3] This way, Mr. Reagan reasoned, millions of teenagers would gain valuable work experience. Year after year he sent this proposal to Congress, and year after year Congress ignored it.

In France the minimum wage is just over $10 an hour. In early 1994, with one in four people under the age of 25 unable to find work, the government decreed that employers would be allowed to pay young men and women between 30 and 80 percent of the monthly minimum wage, depending on their qualifications. Enraged at the prospect of having to work for as little as $300 a month, hundreds of thousands of students and other young people marched through the streets of Paris and more than a dozen other French cities, forcing the government to withdraw the decree.

Those who would lower or eliminate the minimum wage make two implicit assumptions, which become apparent when we look at Figures 11 and 12. They assume a very elastic (or flat) MRP (or demand) curve for inexperienced or low-skilled labor and a very elastic supply of that labor.

This occurs only in Figure 11A. As we can see, the elimination of the minimum wage (set hypothetically at $4.25 an hour) allows the wage rate to fall to an equilibrium level of $3.45 an hour. The big news here is the huge jump in employment, from 7 million to almost 18 million. This shows us graphically (no pun intended) what *could* happen if we abolished the minimum wage. But *will* it happen? It will if both the MRP (or demand) for unskilled labor and the supply of unskilled labor are very elastic.

To "help" teenagers, President Reagan proposed lowering their minimum wage to $2.50 an hour.

-----
[3]The minimum wage was $3.35 per hour from 1982 until 1990.

Figure 11   Elastic Labor Demand and Supply

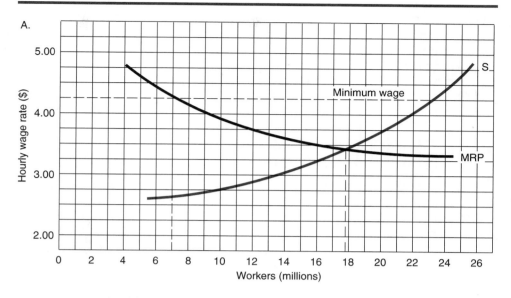

Elastic Demand and Inelastic Supply of Labor

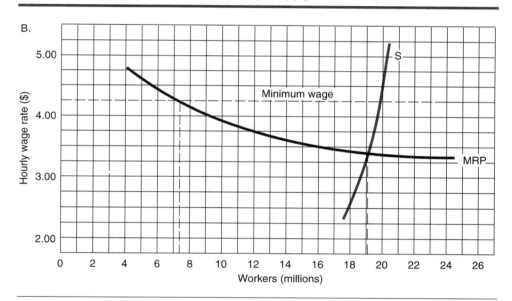

Figure 11B shows an elastic demand with an inelastic supply of unskilled labor. When the minimum wage is eliminated, there is a large jump in employment. In Figure 12A (inelastic demand, elastic supply) and Figure 12B (inelastic demand, inelastic supply), we see only tiny rises in employment in response to the abolition of the minimum wage.

Let's sum up the prospects of an employment rise if we get rid of the minimum wage. Question number one: Will employment of unskilled and inexperienced workers rise if we eliminate the minimum wage? Answer: Yes! Check it out. When we drop the minimum wage in Figures 11 and 12, employment *does* rise. Question number two: How much does it rise? Answer: It rises very little unless the demand for labor is very elastic. Is it very elastic? It well *could* be, but I wouldn't bet on it.

One must also question the validity of the MRP argument. There is no question that teenagers, particularly nonwhite teenagers, are the last hired and the most poorly paid. Is this because they are relatively unskilled and inexperienced? Or is it because they are discriminated against? And are older workers more productive?

**Figure 12   Inelastic Demand
and Elastic Supply of Labor**

**Inelastic Labor
Demand and Supply**

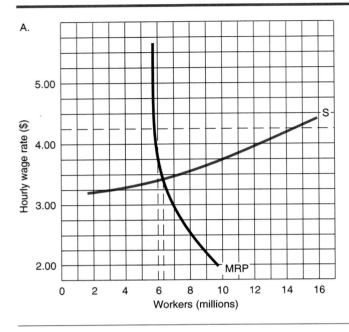

A.

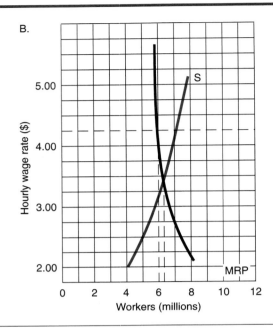

B.

Let's take a parallel case. In the average college today a young assistant professor, fresh out of graduate school, is paid less than half the salary of an older full professor, who, incidentally, generally has a lighter teaching load. Can we possibly base this huge pay differential on productivity?

Wages are set institutionally.

Wages are set institutionally, with little regard to marginal analysis. Labor unions, corporate bureaucracies, and government agencies all play roles. Suppose you go to the personnel officer of some large corporation and say you are willing to work for that company at less than the entry-level wage. You'll be laughed right out of the office.

Who earns the minimum wage? In 1998 nearly 10 million Americans did. They included hamburger flippers, gas station attendants, garment workers, salesclerks, and janitors. About two-thirds were adults, while most of the rest were teenage members of low-income families for whom the wages were an important source of income.

Where does all this leave us? Because wages are set institutionally rather than by marginal analysis, it makes little sense to abolish the minimum wage law. On the other hand, there is some truth to the contention of conservative economists that *some* teenagers are priced out of the labor market by the minimum wage. The question is, How many?

One might also raise the question of the teenage labor supply. How many unemployed teenagers would, if given the opportunity, work for less than the minimum wage? We don't know. Again, the question is, How many?

The wage rate is set by the law of supply and demand.

If my analysis of how wage rates are set leaves you less than fully satisfied, you still have the economist's one eternal truth: the price of labor, like the price of just about everything else, is set by the law of supply and demand. Now we shall see how well that eternal truth holds up with respect to rent, interest, and profits.

Questions for Further Thought and Discussion

1. Are you in the primary labor market or the secondary labor market? Use your answer to show how these markets differ.

2. Explain why the backward-bending labor supply curve has this shape.

3. Should there be a minimum wage rate for teenagers? Present both sides of the issue.

4. What is economic rent? Make up an example that illustrates this concept.

WORKBOOK FOR CHAPTER 31

Name _____

Multiple-Choice Questions

Circle the letter that corresponds to the best answer.

1. According to the backward-bending supply curve, as the hourly wage rate increases from 0 to $10,000 the number of hours per week worked by the average person will

    a. be constant   b. decrease, then increase

    c. increase, then decrease   d. increase steadily

    e. decrease steadily

2. The demand for labor in a particular market is

    a. the sum of all the individual labor supply curves

    b. the sum of all the firms' MRP curves   c. the sum of all the individual labor supply curves and all the firms' MRP curves   d. none of these

3. Which statement is true?

    a. Differences in wage rates are explained entirely by differences in productivity.   b. Differences in wage rates are explained entirely by differences in education and training.   c. Differences in wage rates are explained entirely by whom you know (rather than what you know).   d. None of these statements is true.

4. The possibility of earning economic rent is great if

    a. the supply of a factor is very high relative to demand

    b. the demand for a factor is very high relative to supply   c. both demand for a factor and supply of a factor are high   d. both demand for a factor and supply of a factor are low

5. If you are earning $20,000 a year today and you were to earn $40,000 a year 10 years from today, your

    a. real wages and money wages will both have increased   b. real wages and money wages will both have decreased   c. real wages will have increased

    d. money wages will have increased

6. In general, when output per labor-hour increases, real wages

    a. rise by about the same percentage   b. rise by a larger percentage   c. rise by a smaller percentage

    d. stay about the same   e. fall

7. Conservative economists believe the minimum wage law

    a. helps all workers equally   b. hurts all workers equally   c. hurts teenagers more than other workers

    d. helps teenagers more than other workers

8. President Reagan advocated

    a. lowering the minimum wage for teenagers

    b. raising the minimum wage for teenagers

    c. exempting teenagers from the minimum wage entirely

9. If the minimum wage were eliminated, the employment of marginal workers would

    a. rise a lot   b. rise a little   c. stay exactly the same   d. fall a little   e. fall a lot   f. fall by an indeterminate amount   g. rise by an indeterminate amount

10. There would be a very large increase in employment of low-wage workers if the minimum wage law were abolished and the MRP of workers were

    a. very elastic and the supply of workers were very elastic   b. very elastic and the supply of workers were very inelastic   c. very inelastic and the supply of workers were very elastic   d. very inelastic and the supply of workers were very inelastic

11. When the minimum wage is abolished, the wage rate for marginal workers will

    a. fall and employment will fall   b. fall and employment will rise   c. rise and employment will rise   d. rise and employment will fall

12. Which statement is true?

    a.   Over time the distinctions among noncompeting groups tend to blur.   b.   Over time the distinctions among noncompeting groups tend to become sharper.

    c.   Over time there is no tendency for the distinctions among noncompeting groups to change.

13. Which statement is true?

    a.   The primary job market has most of the good jobs.

    b.   The secondary job market has most of the good jobs.

    c.   Neither the primary nor the secondary job market has the best jobs.   d.   None of these statements is true.

14. According to the theory of the backward-bending labor supply curve,

    a.   first the substitution effect sets in, then the income effect   b.   first the income effect sets in, then the substitution effect   c.   the substitution effect and the income effect set in at the same time   d.   there is neither a substitution effect nor an income effect

15. Which statement is true about incomes in the United States?

    a.   Almost everyone earns about the same income.

    b.   Almost everyone is either very rich or very poor.

    c.   There is a wide disparity in income.   d.   None of these statements is true.

16. Which statement(s) is/are true?

    Statement 1. A college diploma is still a necessary condition for a person moving from the secondary to the primary labor market, but that diploma is no longer a sufficient condition.

    Statement 2. The earnings differential between high school graduates and college graduates narrowed from 1979 to 1992.

    a.   Statement 1 is true and statement 2 is false.

    b.   Statement 2 is true and statement 1 is false.

    c.   Both statements are true.   d.   Both statements are false.

17. In the United States the CEOs of large corporations earn about _____ times the salary of the average production worker.

    a.   25   b.   75   c.   150   d.   500   e.   1,500

18. Hourly wages and fringe benefits in U.S. manufacturing are _____ than those in Japan and _____ than those in Germany.

    a.   higher, higher   b.   lower, lower   c.   higher, lower   d.   lower, higher

19. Which statement is true?

    a.   The average hourly wage in the United States is $5.15 an hour.   b.   If the minimum wage rate for teenagers were lowered, more teenagers would find jobs.   c.   The hourly wage rate in the United States is higher than that in any other country.   d.   The minimum wage rate in France is much lower than that in the United States.

Fill-In Questions

1. The dual labor market consists of a _____

    market and a _____

    market.

2. The substitution effect (on the backward-bending labor

    supply curve) takes place when _____

    _____.

    The income effect takes place when _____

    _____.

3. At very low wage rates the _____

    effect outweighs the _____ effect;

    at very high wage rates the _____

    _____ effect outweighs the

    _____ effect.

4. The wage rate is always determined by two factors:

    _____ and _____.

5. Economic rent is _____

    _____.

6. By real wages, economists mean what you can _____

    _____.

7. If we abolished the minimum wage law, employment of

   low-wage workers would _____

   _____.

8. President Reagan wanted to lower the minimum wage

   rate for _____; he thought

   this would result in _____.

9. If the minimum wage were eliminated, wages would

   definitely _____ for some

   marginal workers, and the employment of marginal

   workers would definitely _____.

10. If the minimum wage were abolished, there would be a

    substantial increase in the employment of marginal

    workers only if the MRP for marginal labor were very

    _____ and the supply of marginal

    labor were very _____.

Problems

1. Ms. Spielvogel was paid $400 a week in 1987, the base
   year. By 1995 she was earning $900. If the consumer
   price index was at 180 in 1995, how much were Ms.
   Spielvogel's real wages that year, and by what percentage
   had they changed?

2. Mr. Yeltsin made $24,000 in 1991, the base year. By
   1998 he is earning $36,000. If the CPI has risen to 120 by
   1998, how much are Mr. Yeltsin's real wages that year,
   and by what percentage have they changed since 1991?

Refer to Figure 1 to answer Problems 3 and 4.

3. An increase in the minimum wage to $6 would cause

   _____ million people to lose their jobs.

4. An increase in the minimum wage to $7 would cause

   _____ million people to lose their jobs.

Figure 1

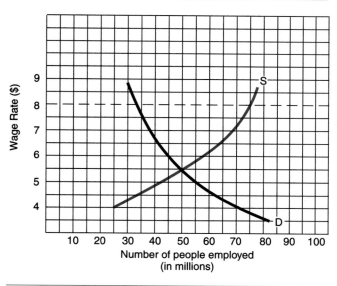

32 Rent, Interest, and Profit

We're ready to tackle the payments to the remaining three factors of production—land, capital, and entrepreneurial ability. As you might have expected, rent and interest are determined by supply and demand. Profits, however, are determined somewhat differently.

Chapter Objectives

We'll take up each of these topics in turn:

- What is land?
- Economic rent.
- Are prices high because rents are high, or are rents high because prices are high?
- What is capital?
- How is the interest rate determined?
- The net productivity of capital.
- The capitalization of assets.
- The present value of future income.
- How are profits determined?
- Theories of profit.

Rent

What Is Land?

Land is a resource or a factor of production. The owner of land is paid rent for allowing its use in the production process. The amount of rent paid for a piece of land is based on the supply of that land and the demand for that land.

This raises four questions: (1) Exactly what *is* land? (2) How does one piece of land differ from another? (3) How is the supply of land derived? (4) How is the demand for land derived?

Exactly What Is Land?   Land is land. An acre of land in Lake Forest, Illinois, an affluent Chicago suburb, is a suitable site for building a home. A half acre in downtown Los Angeles could be used for an office building, and 160 acres in Kansas might do well for growing wheat. How land is used depends on its location, its fertility, and whether it possesses any valuable minerals.

Sometimes we confuse land with what is built on it.

Sometimes we confuse land with what is built on it. A plot of land with apartment houses, stores, or office buildings will bring a lot more rent than a plot that lies vacant. But, strictly speaking (in economic terms), we pay rent on the land itself. We'll call the payments on buildings and other capital goods a form of interest, which we'll cover in the next part of this chapter.

How Does One Piece of Land Differ from Another?   As I just noted, a plot of land may have a few alternative uses. If it is used at all, it will be used by the highest bidder—the one willing to pay the most for it. For example, real estate developers bought up hundreds of dairy farms in central New Jersey over the last two decades. The developers made these farmers offers they could not refuse. In effect, then, the land was worth more as housing sites than as farms.

The basic way in which one piece of land differs from another is location. Only four plots of land can be located at the four corners of one of the most expensive pieces of real estate in the world, Fifth Avenue and 57th Street in Manhattan. Land that is just off this intersection is nearly as expensive. Land near airports, near highway interchanges, in shopping malls, or in the downtown sections of cities is more expensive than less desirably located land.

How Is the Supply of Land Derived?   The supply of land is virtually fixed. Aside from the efforts of the Dutch to reclaim small parcels of land from the North Sea, and relatively minor dredging and draining projects around the world, about one-quarter of the earth's surface is land. Until we're ready for interplanetary travel, everything we've got to work with is on the earth's surface. To go one step further, at any given location there's a fixed amount of land.

Of course, we can make more efficient use of that land. In cities, for example, we build straight up so that thousands of people can work on just one acre. Unfortunately, we've been unable to duplicate this feat in the suburbs because of the extensive acreage we've found it necessary to devote to parking lots.

There is a finite amount of land.

Any way we slice it, we have a finite amount of land. In economics we say the supply of land is fixed. We represent the supply of land as a vertical line, such as the one in Figure 1. We're lumping all land together in that graph, but technically there are tens of thousands of different supplies of land because each location differs from every other location.

The demand for land is derived from a firm's MRP curve.

How Is the Demand for Land Derived?   The demand for land, like the demand for labor and capital, is derived from a firm's MRP curve. The land will go to the highest bidder; the demand curve in Figure 1 represents the MRP schedule of the firm willing to pay the most for the land.

Why does the demand curve for land slope downward to the right? You may remember that a firm's MRP curve declines with output because its marginal physical product declines with output (due to diminishing returns). In addition, if the firm is an imperfect

Figure 1   Determination of Rent

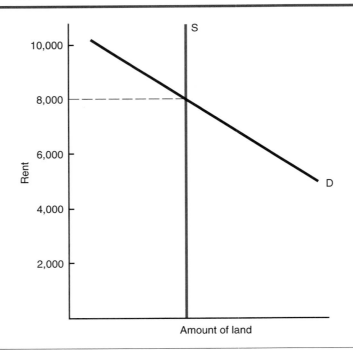

competitor, it must lower its price to increase sales, thereby further depressing MRP as output expands.

How Is Rent Determined?

From what I've been saying in the last 10 chapters and from the big buildup I gave you in the last section, you do not have to be a great economist to answer the question of how rent is determined. It is determined by the law of supply and demand. In Figure 1, we find that rent is $8,000.

Just to make sure you've got this straight, if the demand for land were D_1 in Figure 2, how much would the rent be?

Did you say $120,000? Good. If demand for land were D_2, how much would rent be?

Was your answer $160,000? All right, then. Did you notice that when the demand for land rises, the rent goes up as well? This is exactly what you'd expect under the law of supply and demand.

There is one peculiarity, though. You've noticed that the supply of land is fixed, or perfectly inelastic. Because supply doesn't change, changes in price are brought about by changes in demand.

We can use this information to analyze rents charged on three different plots of land. Suppose plot 1 is 100 miles from the nearest city and is not in demand for any use. How much rent does it bring?

It brings nothing because no one wants to use it. It's what we call marginal land. Suppose someone sets up a store on this land with the permission of the landlord but pays no rent. Very few people shop in this store because it's in the middle of nowhere. If the store owner's capital costs are $10,000, the cost of his labor is $20,000, and his sales are $30,000, he will make zero economic profits.

Now we'll move on to plot 2, just 30 miles from the center of town. This store also has capital costs of $10,000 and labor costs of $20,000, but its sales are $45,000. Guess how much rent this store owner will pay?

She will pay $15,000. You see, business is so good at this location that if the rent were anything less than $15,000, the guy who built his store on the marginal (or free) land in the boondocks would have bid $15,000. The location of the land closer to town, where so many more potential customers pass by, makes plot 2 worth $15,000 to at least one firm.

Figure 2   Increase in Demand for Land

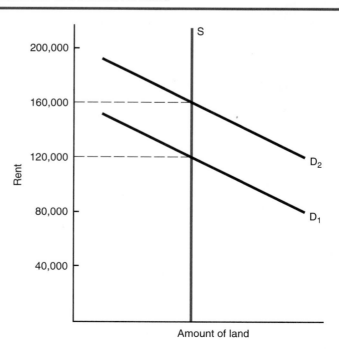

Finally, we have plot 3, right in the center of town where people pass by in droves. How much rent will someone pay for this plot? It will bring much more than $15,000. If the costs of capital are $10,000, the costs of labor $20,000, and sales $100,000, how much will this land rent for?

It will rent for $70,000. If it were renting for less, someone would come along and offer the landlord $70,000. The owner of the store on plot 1 certainly would; and so would the owner of the store on plot 2.

Now I'd like you to try this one on for size. Suppose costs remain the same, but sales on plot 1 rise to $40,000. Will the owner of plot 1 pay any rent? How much? He will pay $10,000 in rent.

If sales on plot 2 rise to $55,000, how much rent will it bring? It will bring $25,000.

If sales on plot 3 rise to $110,000, how much rent will it bring? It will bring $80,000.

To summarize, location is the basic differentiating factor in the rents of various plots of land, and the demand for each piece of land determines how much rent is paid.

Economic Rent

Payment in excess of what people would be willing to accept is economic rent.

In the last chapter, I introduced the concept of economic rent, the amount of money certain people are paid beyond what they would be willing to work for. For example, baseball players who love the sport, like the legendary Willie Mays, are willing to play for a lot less than they're paid, and perhaps David Letterman would actually accept a measly $10 million a year instead of whatever it is that he earns. The surplus is called economic rent.

Economic rent, then, is the payment above the minimum necessary to attract this resource to the market. Rent paid to landlords (exclusive of any payment for buildings and property improvements) is, by definition, economic rent.

Should landlords be paid anything at all?

We may ask whether landlords should indeed be paid any rent at all for their land. After all, the land was always there; it certainly wasn't created by the landlords. (See the box "Who Created the Land?") Whether they expropriated it, inherited it, or even purchased it, the land really belongs to society. About a century ago a man named Henry George even started a single-tax movement whose objective was to finance government solely by taxing land rent. George reasoned that the land did not really belong to the landlords and the payment of rent did not increase production (because the land is there for the taking), so why not tax away this unearned surplus?

What Henry George overlooked

Henry George, American economist

Although this tax proposal has been criticized on several counts,[1] it does have considerable merit. A tax on land would raise revenue, and such a tax would fall largely on unproductive resource owners.

But Henry George overlooked an important attribute of rent: as the price for the use of land, it serves as a guidance mechanism, directing the most productive (i.e., highest-paying) enterprises to the most desirable (i.e., expensive) land. Because the most desirable locations bring the highest rents, they are inevitably occupied by the highest bidders. If we taxed away these rents, we might conceivably have some effect on the allocation of land. For instance, if I owned a plot of land in midtown San Francisco and all my rent were taxed away, I might just as soon rent it to a candy store as to a fancy boutique.

Are Prices High because Rents Are High, or Are Rents High because Prices Are High?

Do certain stores charge high prices because they have to pay high rents?

How many times have you gone into a store in a high-rent district and been overwhelmed by the prices? Didn't you say to yourself, "Their prices are high because the owner has to pay such a high rent"? Fair enough. A store situated in an expensive area has to charge high prices to make enough money to pay its greedy landlord.

We're going to digress for a couple of minutes and a couple of centuries because this same question came up in early 19th-century England. David Ricardo, the great

---

[1] It would raise only a small fraction of needed government revenue; landlords sometimes improve the land; and rent on land is not the only kind of income that is unearned.

ADVANCED **W**ORK Who Created the Land?

Do you remember the very first words of the Bible? "In the beginning God created the heaven and the earth" (Genesis 1:1). This raises an interesting question. Why do landlords get to charge rent on this land? If you have ever posed this question, let's look at Leviticus (25:23): "The land shall not be sold for ever: for the land is mine; for ye are strangers and sojourners with me."

Pierre-Joseph Proudhon carried this reasoning to its logical conclusion: "Who is entitled to the rent of land? The producer of the land without doubt. Who made the land? God. Then, proprietor, retire!" Just to sum things up, Proudhon asked himself this question: What *is* property? His answer? "Property is theft!"

A very strong current in economic thought denies the landlord's claim to rent. However, the problem we have had since being banished from the Garden of Eden is that we need to deal with scarcity, and rent is an excellent means of efficiently allocating the use of scarce land.

Pierre-Joseph Proudhon, French journalist (Brown Brothers)

David Ricardo, English economist (The Granger Collection, New York)

High rents don't cause high prices.

economist, set the record straight: "Corn is not high because a rent is paid, but a rent is paid because corn is high."[2]

The price of corn (and wheat) was high because there was a great demand for it caused by the Napoleonic Wars. Because the supply of farmland in England was entirely under cultivation (and therefore fixed), a rise in the demand for corn raised the demand (or the MRP) for farmland, thereby driving up rents.

Now, back to the present. You've seen that stores in expensive neighborhoods charge high prices and pay high rents. But why do they pay high rents? Because they outbid all the other prospective tenants. Why did they bid so high? Because they wanted the desirable location. Stores located in busy shopping areas pay much higher rents than do stores in less busy areas. Why? Because their locations are so desirable that their rents are bid up.

Now we'll look at the same question from the other side. Suppose a store happens to pay a low rent—say a mom-and-pop grocery not far from where you live. How do its prices compare with supermarket prices? They're higher, right? But you'd expect them to be lower, if low rents lead to low prices.

Here's the final word. High rents don't cause high prices. Desirable locations attract many prospective renters, who bid up rents because they believe they will get a lot of business. In other words, following Ricardo's analysis, rents are high because the demand for the final product—and consequently the derived demand—is high.

Interest

What Is Capital?

Capital consists of office buildings, factories, stores, machinery and equipment, computer systems, and other synthetic goods used in the production process. When we invest, we are spending money on new capital. When we build an office park, a shopping mall, or an assembly line, or when we purchase new office equipment, we are engaged in investment.

---

[2]David Ricardo, *The Principles of Political Economy and Taxation,* ed. L. Reynolds and W. Fellner (Burr Ridge, IL: Richard D. Irwin, 1963), p. 34.

Economists feel good when they can think in terms of stocks and flows. The stock of capital increases by means of a flow of investment. Suppose you have half a glass of water; that's your capital stock. You can fill up that glass by letting tap water flow into it; that's your investment flow. When you've filled your glass, you have doubled your capital stock.

To use a machine example, say you have a capital stock of four machines. You buy two more. That's your investment for the year. Now you have a capital stock of six machines.

How Is the Interest Rate Determined?

The law of supply and demand

You guessed it! The interest rate is determined by the law of supply and demand. Figure 3 shows this.

The demand for capital is the firm's MRP schedule for capital. As we've seen, MRP curves always slope downward to the right.

The supply of loanable funds, however, unlike the supply of land (which is perfectly inelastic), slopes upward to the right. You may remember that the backward-bending labor supply curve of the previous chapter slopes upward to the right, until, at extremely high wage rates, it bends backward.

Why does the supply of loanable funds or savings slope upward to the right? Because the amount of money people save is somewhat responsive to interest rates. The higher the interest paid, the more people will save.

Interest Rates and Consumer Loans

Do banks charge too much interest on credit card loans?

Usury laws place limits on how much interest may be charged.

Do high interest rates deter borrowing for consumer loans? Obviously they do. And do the banks charge too much on credit card loans? They *do?* Then maybe a legal ceiling should be placed on the interest that may be charged on these and other loans.

Although there is no federal law on the books, many states have what are called usury laws, which place legal ceilings on the interest rates that may be charged on certain types of loans. (See the box "Usury in Ancient Times.") Usury is defined as charging "an unconscionable or exorbitant rate of interest." Usury laws are intended to curb this greedy practice. But, as the old saying goes, the road to hell is paved with good intentions.

Usury laws, however popular with the public, drive many economists wild. Why? There are two reasons. First, these laws may hurt the very people they are intended to

Figure 3   Determination of the Interest Rate

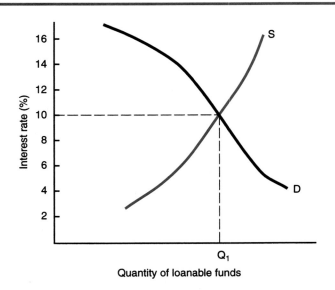

ADVANCED WORK

Usury in Ancient Times

Mosaic laws in the book of Deuteronomy strictly forbid not only usury (lending money at exorbitant interest rates), but even the taking of any interest. In those days loans were made mainly for charitable purposes, so the prohibition made a great deal of sense.

Aristotle considered the charging of interest to be the most unnatural method of accumulating wealth:

> The most hated sort, and with the greatest reason, is usury, which makes a gain out of money itself, and not from the natural objects of it. For money was intended to be used in exchange, but not to increase at interest . . . Of all modes of getting wealth this is the most unnatural.*

These same views continued to be reflected in the rules of the Church, which prevailed until the end of the Middle Ages. With the rise of commerce, however, the basic purpose of most loans changed, and the prohibitions against taking interest were dropped. But what constitutes a "fair" rate of interest on consumer loans continues to be debated to this day.

*Aristotle, *Politics,* ii, p. 1258.

Aristotle, Greek philosopher (The Granger Collection, New York)

help by creating a shortage of loanable funds. This is illustrated in Figure 4, at which we'll look more closely in a minute.

A second reason why economists love to hate usury laws is that these laws blatantly interfere with the price mechanism, more familiarly known as the law of supply and demand. Prices signal the buyers and sellers in the market. When prices are low buyers try to buy more, and when they're high sellers offer more of their goods or services for sale. Because the interest rate is the price of money, a high price signals sellers to provide more loanable funds, while discouraging borrowers from borrowing. A high enough interest rate would completely eliminate the shortage of loanable funds.

Let's look at Figure 4 to see how the price mechanism would work. First, if there *were* a legal ceiling on interest rates of 16 percent, there would be a shortage of how much? It looks to me like $350 billion ($550 billion demanded – $200 billion supplied). And how much is the equilibrium interest rate? That's right—it's 24 percent. So if we eliminated the interest ceiling, the interest rate would quickly rise to 24 percent, and the shortage would be eliminated.

Usury laws are price ceilings.

You may recall our discussion of price ceilings and price floors in the chapter titled "Applications in Supply and Demand." Usury laws are price ceilings because they prevent the interest rates from rising to their equilibrium levels. In other words, usury laws place an upper limit on interest rates. Consequently, there are a lot more borrowers in the market than sellers, which creates a shortage of loanable funds.

So how exactly do usury laws hurt borrowers? They hurt the borrowers with relatively poor credit ratings. For example, if the interest rate were fixed at 16 percent, lenders would be willing to lend out only about $220 billion, all of which would go to people they considered the most creditworthy borrowers. The rest of us would be completely left out. Some of us would go to consumer finance companies (e.g., Household Finance, Seaboard Finance, and Beneficial Finance); these might not be covered by usury laws and could therefore charge higher interest rates. Or we might go to loan sharks who often charge a straight 10 percent interest—that's 10 percent a week! So the next time you think you're paying an arm and a leg in interest on a bank credit card, consider the alternative.

Figure 4   Interest Rate Ceiling

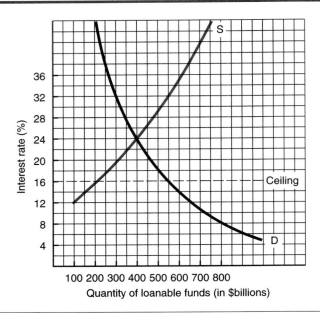

While I'm still up on my soapbox, I'd like to make the connection between usury laws and other legal obstacles to the price mechanism. Farm price supports, or price floors, are one such obstacle. In the last chapter we discussed the minimum wage law, another price ceiling. Wage and price controls were mentioned a few times in the earlier chapters of *Economics* and *Macroeconomics*. Still another legal interference with the law of supply and demand is rent control, which puts a ceiling on how much rent landlords may charge for apartments.

Economists dislike the laws that set up these obstacles because they interfere with the price mechanism and often end up harming the very people they were intended to help. That said, a case can be made for each one of these laws. And while in general most economists would prefer not to tamper with the forces of supply and demand, many of us are prepared to make certain exceptions. My own predilection is for minimum wage laws, which I believe do a lot more good than harm. The issue comes down to making judgment calls. And those judgment calls are yours—not mine.

Determination of the Level of Investment

How much investment an individual business firm does depends on its MRP and the current interest rate. We'll suppose the interest rate is 10 percent, as shown in Figure 5. At that rate the firm will undertake $40 million of investment projects. At lower interest rates the firm would invest more than $40 million, and at higher rates it would invest less. If the interest rate were 18 percent, how much would be invested? While you're at it, how much would be invested at an interest rate of 4 percent?

At an interest rate of 18 percent, about $13 million would be invested; at 4 percent, investment would be $60 million.

Many firms have a drawerful of investment projects just waiting to be carried out. If they were arranged in order of their profitability, they would be, in effect, the firm's MRP curve. A firm will undertake its most profitable projects first, then its somewhat less profitable ones, and finally, its least profitable ones. But it will be limited by interest rates. The lower the rate of interest, the more investment projects will be undertaken. To see how this works from the viewpoint of the individual firm, we'll work out a numerical problem in the next section.

Figure 5   Net Productivity of Capital

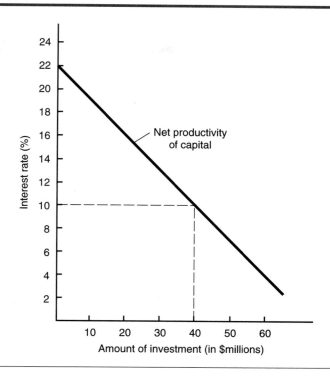

The interest rate is especially important for long-term investment projects.

The interest rate is especially important for long-term investment projects. Let's look at a long-term project that might be carried out in the United States—a country with relatively high interest rates—or in Taiwan, where interest rates have been substantially lower. Let's use this rather extreme example: If the interest rate were 10 percent in the United States but only 3 percent in Taiwan, a 20-year investment of $1,000 would need to yield more than $6,730 in the United States but anything over $1,810 in Taiwan. Don't worry about the arithmetic—just look at the bottom line.

The Net Productivity of Capital

To help us figure out whether a certain capital project should be undertaken, economists have developed the concept of net productivity of capital, which translates into the expected profit rate.

The expected profit rate

To get this figure, which we'll express as a percentage, we need to follow two easy steps:

1. Subtract all costs (including an allowance for a normal profit) from sales. This gives us the dollar value of net productivity.

2. Assuming this value is positive, we divide it by capital cost to give us the net productivity of capital, which we express as a percentage.

Net productivity of capital =
$$\frac{\text{Dollar value of net productivity}}{\text{Capital cost}}$$

To summarize: (1) Sales – Costs (including a normal profit) = Dollar value of net productivity. (2) Net productivity of capital = Dollar value of net productivity / Capital cost.

I just tried to slip a new term by you. Until now I've never said a word about *normal profits.* We can consider them compensation for a businessowner's implicit costs—a term that was defined in an earlier chapter. But if you're *really* curious about normal profits, check out the box on them.

I'll illustrate this with a problem. Find the net productivity of capital if Sales = $150,000; Labor costs = $30,000; Raw materials = $10,000; Fuel and maintenance = $5,000; Normal profit = $5,000; and Capital cost = $80,000.

Figure out the net productivity of capital by following the two steps we've just outlined. Then check with the solution below. Wait! I forgot to tell you something. When you're subtracting all those costs, don't forget to include the $80,000, which is your capital cost.

Solution: Sales ($150,000) – Costs (including a normal profit) ($30,000 + $10,000 + $5,000, + $5,000 + $80,000 = $130,000) = Dollar value of net productivity ($20,000).

$$\frac{\text{Dollar value of net productivity (\$20,000)}}{\text{Capital cost (\$80,000)}} = \text{Net productivity of capital (25 percent)}$$

A 25 percent net productivity of capital looks pretty good. Would you go ahead and invest in this capital good? Yes, you would. Unless . . . Unless what? What if you needed to borrow the money to invest? Would you *still* go ahead? You would unless the interest rate you had to pay exceeded 25 percent. Of course, that isn't very likely, but it *could* happen. In 1980 and 1981 the prime rate of interest—the rate charged by banks to major corporations—went above 20 percent. That meant smaller businesses were charged 22, 23, or 24 percent. And some less creditworthy borrowers found themselves paying more than 25 percent.

What if you didn't need to borrow? Would you go ahead and invest in a capital good that would yield a 25 percent return? Not if interest rates were above 25 percent. Why not? Because you would get more than a 25 percent return by simply lending out your funds. Why invest in your own business for a 25 percent return when you could do better elsewhere?

Of course, it is unusual for interest rates to be anywhere *near* 25 percent. What if your net productivity of capital were 25 percent and the interest rate were 10 percent? Would you invest? Definitely! If the interest rate were 20 percent, would you invest? Yes, you would. We'll say you'd invest right up to the point (or just short of the point) at which the interest rate equals your net productivity of capital.

The Capitalization of Assets

Economists seem unable to leave well enough alone. No sooner do they give us a rule to follow—keep investing until your net productivity of capital declines to the level of the interest rate—than they come up with an alternate way of dealing with capital investment. In this case, we have the concept of capitalization of assets.

ADVANCED WORK .... Normal Profits ....

Let's begin by reviewing *accounting profits, implicit costs,* and *economic profits*—all terms that were introduced previously. Suppose a firm had sales of $800,000 and paid out $500,000 in wages, rent, cost of materials, and advertising, which left it accounting profits of $300,000. Now suppose that had this businessowner and her husband worked the same hours for someone else, they could have earned $80,000. In addition, they had $200,000 of their own money tied up in their business and could have received 10 percent interest if they had lent it to another firm.

How much, then, are their implicit costs and their eco-

nomic profits? Their implicit costs are $100,000 ($80,000 + $200,000 × .10 = $80,000 + $20,000). The economic profits are found by subtracting implicit costs from accounting profits: Accounting profits ($300,000) – Implicit costs ($100,000) = Economic profits ($200,000).

Now we're ready to talk about normal profits. They are basically compensation for the firm's implicit costs. Or more formally, *normal profits are the return to businessowners for the opportunity cost of their implicit inputs.* All that said, what we're left with is a new equation: Accounting profits – Normal profits = Economic profits.

If an asset yields X dollars per year in profits, how much is that asset worth?

This concept enables a business firm to make a decision about whether to purchase a particular piece of machinery, some equipment, a building, or another capital asset. If a particular asset yields X number of dollars per year in profits, how much is that asset worth? To find out we need to know one more thing: the current interest rate.

Let's set up an illustration. Suppose the going interest rate is 10 percent. If you bought a corporate bond, you'd get a 10 percent return. Why not invest the money in your own business by purchasing a machine? The question is, How much is that machine worth to you?

If the machine yields an annual return of $80, which goes on forever, should you buy it? That depends on two things: (1) its price and (2) the going rate of interest. We already know that the going rate of interest is 10 percent.

What if the machine would cost you $100? Would you buy it? Think about it. What would your annual rate of return be (as a percentage)?

It would be 80 percent ($80/$100). Would you buy that machine? You'd be crazy not to. An 80 percent return! How much would your rate of return be if you put your money into corporate stocks or bonds? A paltry 10 percent!

What if the machine cost $400? Would you buy it? You would? All right! That would still be a 20 percent return ($80/$400).

OK, are you ready? What is the maximum you would be willing to pay for this machine? Figure it out.

Time's up! Your answer, please. Was your answer $800? Then you're right. Why $800? Because $800 would yield a return of 10 percent ($80/$800). You would be willing to pay $800 for the machine, but not a penny more. Why no more? Because if you paid more than $800, your rate of return would fall below the 10 percent return you could earn elsewhere.

I know you'd hate to have to go through all these steps every time you contemplated buying a machine or any other capital good, so I'll tell you what I'm gonna do. I'm gonna give you an easy formula. All you'll have to do is plug in a couple of numbers and you'll have the answer staring you in the face. Are you ready? Then here it comes.

Value of asset =
Annual income
from asset
Interest rate

$$\text{Value of asset} = \frac{\text{Annual income from asset}}{\text{Interest rate}}$$

OK, try this one. How much is the value of a building that provides an annual income of $200 when the going interest rate is 8 percent?

Solution: $$\frac{\text{Annual income from asset}}{\text{Interest rate}} = \frac{\$200}{.08} = \$2,500$$

What would happen to the value of an asset if interest rates fell? Figure *that* out.

It would rise. For instance, if the interest rate fell to 4 percent, what would the value of this asset rise to?

Solution: $$\frac{\$200}{.04} = \$5,000$$

If interest rates rise, what happens to the value of an asset? It falls. This is so because once you have your money tied up in a particular asset, you no longer have alternative investment opportunities. If those opportunities improve (i.e., the interest rate rises), then you're stuck with a relatively low-yielding asset; it isn't worth as much as it was formerly. If you tried to sell it, you would get less than you paid for it. You may recall our discussion in Chapter 13 in *Economics* and *Macroeconomics* (in the open-market operations section) in which we concluded that interest rates and bond prices were inversely related.

On the upside, if interest rates fall, the value of your asset rises. The yield you're getting is better than that of alternative assets. So, if you can predict interest rate changes accurately, you stand to make a lot of money. Unfortunately, no one has come up with a formula for that. About the best I can do is to tell you to buy when interest rates are high and sell when they're low.

The Present Value of Future Income

Economists are fond of saying that a dollar today is worth more than a dollar you will have in the future. Why? Inflation?

While it's true that most of us have never known anything *but* inflation in our lifetimes, a dollar today would be worth more than a future dollar even if there were no inflation. If no inflation were expected in the future, lenders would charge borrowers what we call the real rate of interest.[3]

Waiting necessarily commands a price.
—Gustav Cassel,
The Nature and Necessity of Interest

Let's say you have a dollar today and no inflation is expected over the next year. If you can get 5 percent interest by loaning out your dollar, that means one year from now you will have $1.05. On the other side of the coin, so to speak, the person who borrows the dollar from you today is willing to pay you $1.05 in one year. Why, then, is a dollar today worth more than a future dollar? Because it can be lent out to earn interest.

Next question. If a dollar today is worth more than a future dollar, how *much* more is it worth? If the interest rate were 8 percent, how much would $100 today be worth in terms of dollars you will have one year from now?

The correct answer is $108. Naturally, we have a formula to figure these problems out.

The present value of a dollar received one year from now is $1/(1 + r)$, when r is the interest rate. Substitute .08 for r (remember 8 percent is equivalent to the decimal .08) in the formula, and see what you get.

Did you get 92.59 cents? (The actual answer is 92.592592592, with the three numbers repeating themselves ad infinitum.) So a dollar one year from now would be worth only 92.59 cents today.

What if the interest rate were 5 percent? How much would a dollar received one year from now be worth today?

Solution:
$$\frac{1}{1 + r} = \frac{1}{1.05} = 95.24 \text{ cents}$$

We'll do one more—when the interest rate is 12 percent.

---

[3]During times of inflation, the expected inflation rate is factored into the interest rates charged to borrowers. You may recall this from the section headed Anticipated and Unanticipated Inflation in Chapter 9 of *Economics* and *Macroeconomics*.

Solution:

$$\frac{1}{1+r} = \frac{1}{r} = \frac{1}{1.12} = 89.29 \text{ cents}$$

We can say, then, that when the interest rate rises, the present value of future dollars will decline; when the interest rate falls, the present value of dollars held in the future will rise.

We can use a general formula for the present value of dollars held any number of years into the future:

$$\text{Present value of a dollar received } n \text{ years from now} = \frac{1}{(1+r)^n}$$

Remember that time is money.
—Benjamin Franklin

If you're uncomfortable with algebra, don't worry. Once you plug in the numbers for r and n, it's no longer algebra, but just arithmetic.

The letter n is an exponent. It tells us to multiply what's inside the parentheses by itself n times. If the numbers inside the parentheses are $(1 + .12)$ and n is 3, what should we do? We should multiply $1.12 \times 1.12 \times 1.12$.

Now we'll work out a couple of problems using the formula. If the interest rate is 6 percent and you will be paid a dollar in two years, what is the present value of that dollar? Work it out to the nearest cent right here:

Solution:

$$\frac{1}{(1+r)^n} = \frac{1}{(1.06)^2} = \frac{1}{(1.06) \times (1.06)} = \frac{1}{1.1236} = 89 \text{ cents}$$

Let's recap, and then we'll work out one more problem. The higher the interest rate, the lower the present value. And the longer you must wait for your money, the less it is worth to you today. Another way of looking at these relationships is to see what a rising interest rate and a rising waiting period do to the denominator of the formula. Clearly they raise it, which lowers the present value of the asset.

What is the present value of $1,000 that will be paid to you in three years if the interest rate is 5 percent? Work it out to the nearest cent.

Solution:

$$\text{Present value} = \$1,000 \times \frac{1}{(1+r)^n}$$

$$= \$1,000 \times \frac{1}{(1.05)^3}$$

$$= \$1,000 \times \frac{1}{(1.05)(1.05)(1.05)}$$

$$= \$1,000 \times \frac{1}{1.157625}$$

$$= \$1,000 \times .863838$$

$$= \$863.84$$

Now that I've put you through all those moves computing present value, I'm going to show you a shortcut. You may be able to find a table like the one in the box "How Much Is $100 Received in the Future Worth to You Today?" Or if you have a really good pocket calculator, you should be able to find present value a lot faster. But if *n* is only 1 or 2, then I'm sure you can work out most problems with this handy formula in just a minute or two.

Profits

Profits, the last topic of this chapter, does not lend itself to any mathematical formulas or computations. Indeed, except for some problems at the end of this chapter, you have seen the last of the mathematical computations you will be asked to perform in this book. The entire study of profits, unlike that of rent and interest, is hotly debated by economists, politicians, and social critics. Let's begin by looking at how profits are determined and how large they are, and then I'll outline a few theories of profits.

How Are Profits Determined?

Profits are considered a residual left after payment of rent, interest, and wages.

Until now I've been saying that the law of supply and demand determines the price of just about everything. Now I'm going to have to change my tune. Economists treat profits as a residual left to the entrepreneur after rent, interest, and wages have been paid. One could argue that because these three resource payments are determined by supply and demand, then what's left over, profits, are indirectly determined by supply and demand.

What do *you* think? Does that sound plausible? Should we just leave it at that? Profits are indirectly determined by supply and demand?

ADVANCED WORK

How Much Is $100 Received in the Future Worth to You Today?

This may not be a question people commonly ask you, but it is an interesting one, at least to economists. First, you may give a general answer: less than $100. But how *much* less than $100? That depends on two factors—when you will receive that $100 and what the interest rate is. The table here gives us a lot of answers.

So, what is the present value of $100 received four years from now if the interest rate is 12 percent? It's $63.55. And how much is the present value of $100 re-

ceived in 15 years if the interest rate is 6 percent? It's $41.73.

Are you ready for a couple of generalizations? All right, then, here they come. First, as the interest rate rises, the present value declines. Second, as your years of waiting for your money increase, the present value declines. To generalize, the present value of a future dollar payment is inversely related to both the interest rate and how long you have to wait for your money.

Years in the Future	2 Percent	4 Percent	6 Percent	8 Percent	12 Percent
1	98.04	96.15	94.34	92.59	89.29
2	96.12	92.46	89.00	85.73	79.72
3	94.23	88.90	83.96	79.38	71.18
4	92.39	85.48	79.21	73.50	63.55
5	90.57	82.19	74.73	68.06	56.74
6	88.80	79.03	70.50	63.02	50.66
7	87.06	75.99	66.51	58.35	45.23
8	85.35	73.07	62.74	54.03	40.39
9	83.68	70.26	59.19	50.02	36.06
10	82.03	67.56	55.84	46.32	32.20
15	74.30	55.53	41.73	31.52	18.27
20	67.30	45.64	31.18	21.45	10.37

Considering that this section goes on for another few pages, apparently *I'm* not too thrilled with leaving it at that. After all, if profits are the catalytic agent, the prime motivating factor, the ultimate reward for the entrepreneur, surely we can do better than to treat them as a mere residual. True, the business firm must pay rent, interest, and wages, and it may keep any remaining profits, but surely profits are a little more exciting than that, if I may be so bold.

How Large Are Profits?

What do we know about profits so far? At the beginning of Chapter 4, we talked about their role as an economic incentive under capitalism. The lure of profits is what gets business firms to produce the huge array of goods and services that provide the industrial countries of the world with such high standards of living.

We also know that economists derive profits somewhat differently from the way accountants derive them. Both subtract explicit costs (out-of-pocket or dollar costs, such as wages and salaries, cost of materials, fuel, electricity, rent, insurance, and advertising) from sales. But economists also subtract implicit costs (opportunity costs of additional resources used, such as the wages the owner of the firm and family members could have earned working elsewhere, and interest on money tied up in the firm that could have been earned by investing it elsewhere). Subtracting both explicit and implicit costs from sales means that economic profits are somewhat lower than accounting profits.

In 1997 corporate profits before taxes were $743 billion, and proprietors' income was $545 billion. Profits, then, were a total of $1,288 billion of a national income of $6,657 billion paid to all the factors of production, or almost 20 percent.

Keep in mind that these were all accounting profits. Well over half the profits of proprietorships and a somewhat smaller share of corporate profits were implicit costs, so economic profits were probably over $500 billion, or about 8 percent of national income.

While we're on the subject, I should mention that wages and salaries (including fringe benefits) came to $4,703 billion in 1997, and that figure does not include implicit wages of at least another $350 billion. The rest of national income is made up of rent and interest; so, any way you slice it, wages and salaries come to almost 80 percent of national income, profits are about 8 percent, and rent and interest payments account for the rest.

Large corporations have no implicit costs, but the majority of the nation's 4 million corporations are very small businesses with substantial implicit costs.

Theories of Profit

Economic profit is the payment for entrepreneurial ability—whatever *that* is. The entrepreneur is rewarded for recognizing a profit opportunity and taking advantage of it. There are four somewhat overlapping theories of how the entrepreneur earns a profit: (1) as a risk taker; (2) as an innovator; (3) as a monopolist; and (4) as an exploiter of labor. We'll take up each in turn.

Capitalism without bankruptcy is like Christianity without hell.
—Frank Borman

The Entrepreneur as a Risk Taker   Have you ever played the lottery? Did you ever hit the number? The $5 or $10 that most lottery players spend each week is a very risky "investment." Why do it? Because the payoff is so high. And if you don't play, then you can't even *dream* of winning.

To win you have to risk loss.
—Jean-Claude Killy

The only way to get people to make risky investments is to offer high rates of return. In general, the riskier the investment, the higher the average rate of return. I mean, would *you* play the lottery if your chance of winning were one in a million and the payoff were 10 percent? Or 100 percent? Or even 1,000 percent?

To get people to make risky investments, offer them high rates of return.

Not too many folks are drilling for oil these days, but at one time you could hardly move without running into an oil well in wide stretches of Texas, Oklahoma, and a few other Southwestern states. Wildcatters may do all kinds of geological surveys and probability studies, or they may just trust dumb luck. Either way, you're taking one big risk when you start drilling down 5,000 feet or more. You're spending tens of thousands of dollars and you're either going to hit a gusher or you're going to come up dry. But as they say, nothing ventured, nothing gained.

Frank Knight, American economist
(The University of Chicago)

Distinction between invention
and innovation

Schumpeter's theory of
innovation

Joseph Schumpeter, American
economist (Courtesy of the Harvard
University Archives)

Distinction between capitalist
and entrepreneur

Natural scarcities versus
contrived scarcities

According to Frank Knight's classic *Risk, Uncertainty, and Profit,* all economic profit is linked with uncertainty. Think of the telephone, the television, the automobile, and the airplane. Who knew for certain that they would work technologically and catch on commercially? Think of the wildcat oil-well drillers. These people took risks and made huge fortunes, but a lot of other people took risks and failed. As many rich Texans have long been fond of saying, money is just a way of keeping score.

Frank Knight saw profit as the reward for risk bearing. And those profits, while relatively uncertain and unstable, are also much higher than the normal profits earned by the owners of mainstream business enterprises.

The Entrepreneur as an Innovator   We need to distinguish between invention and innovation. An invention is a new idea, a new product, or a new way of producing things. An innovation is the act of putting the invention to practical use. Sometimes the inventor comes up with something commercially feasible, but for one reason or another—usually a shortage of capital—she does not market it. The Wright brothers, for example, never made a penny from commercial air flight, although Alexander Graham Bell, of all people, tried to steal their ideas.

Joseph Schumpeter, one of the foremost business cycle theorists, stressed the preeminence of innovation as the basis for economic advance.

Whenever a new production function has been set up successfully and the trade beholds the new thing done and its major problems solved, it becomes much easier for other people to do the same thing and even to improve upon it. In fact, they are driven to copying it if they can, and some people will do so forthwith. It should be observed that it becomes easier to do the same thing, but also to do similar things in similar lines—either subsidiary or competitive ones—while certain innovations, such as the steam engine, directly affect a wide variety of industries. . . . Innovations do not remain isolated events, and are not evenly distributed in time, but . . . on the contrary they tend to cluster, to come about in bunches, simply because some, and then most, firms follow in the wake of successful innovation.[4]

Schumpeter went on to say that "risk bearing is no part of the entrepreneurial function."[5] That's done by the capitalist who puts up the money. If the entrepreneur himself puts up the money, then he bears the risk of losing it as a capitalist, not as an entrepreneur. Finally, Schumpeter notes that in a purely competitive economy, profit "is the premium put upon successful innovation in capitalist society and is temporary by nature: it will vanish in the subsequent process of competition and adaption."[6]

If we distinguish, then, between the capitalist and the entrepreneur, the reward for entrepreneurship would be profits due to innovation. The capitalist's return would be interest, not profits. The capitalist's interest rate would depend on the risk.

So far we've depicted the entrepreneur as a risk taker and an innovator. No more Mr. Nice Guy. From here on, we'll see the entrepreneur cast in the role of economic villain.

The Entrepreneur as a Monopolist   Do the monopolist and the oligopolist, for that matter, make a profit? They sure do! In the previous chapters devoted to these kinds of firms, we concluded that they were able to make profits because of a shortage of competition. If this shortage of competitors is due to hard work, foresight, and innovation, one could hardly complain about the evils of big business.

Still, we need to make a distinction between "natural scarcities" and "contrived scarcities." A firm that develops a technology before anyone else (as IBM and Xerox both did) or one that possesses a unique location (as does the owner of land at a busy intersection) is the beneficiary of a natural scarcity and consequently earns monopoly profits.

Then there are the other guys, who have created or are able to take advantage of a contrived scarcity. The controllers of patents and those who own or have cornered the market on a vital resource (DeBeers Diamonds, the National Football League) will almost always restrict output so they can earn monopoly profits. These are the economic

[4]Joseph A. Schumpeter, *Business Cycles* (New York: McGraw-Hill, 1964), p. 75.
[5]Ibid., p. 79.
[6]Ibid., pp. 79–80.

Which Theory of Profits Do We Apply?

Can you imagine what would happen if a pharmaceutical company came up with a drug that really *did* promote substantial hair growth? Its marketers would probably use the advertising slogan "Gone today, hair tomorrow." Or what if the company discovered a drug that cured sexual impotence? I'll leave it up to you to coin a slogan. Or how about a company that produced a drug that made wrinkles disappear?

Now try to imagine what would happen to the profits of a company that discovered a miracle drug that could grow hair again *and* cure impotence *and* remove wrinkles. No, I'm not going to give you a hot stock tip. I'm just leading up to a question.

Which theory of profits do we apply to this example? Innovation? Certainly this company is an innovator. Monopoly? Until its patent runs out, the firm has a monopoly. Is the firm being rewarded for being a risk taker? I think we can argue that it took the risk of spending millions on research that might pay off big—but might not pay off at all.

So we can't neatly pigeonhole this entrepreneurial profit in any of these three categories. But if you *had* to pick one, which one would you pick? Which one would I pick? I'd have to go with profit as a reward for innovation. But it's not an easy call.

---

bad guys because they are holding output below the levels at which the public wishes to purchase. (See the box "Which Theory of Profits Do We Apply?")

Marxist exploitation theory

The Entrepreneur as an Exploiter of Labor   Karl Marx based his theory of profits on the supposition that the capitalist exploits the worker. To illustrate this relationship, we'll take a simple numerical example. Suppose a worker needs to work 12 hours a day to have enough money to buy food. But suppose he could produce this food in just six hours working for the capitalist. The reason he can produce so much food is because he uses the capitalist's machinery.

The worker produces enough food for two people in 12 hours. The capitalist gives him just enough wages to buy one day's food and keeps the other day's food for himself. Thus, a capitalist's role is to exploit his employees. Not bad work if you can get it.

Surplus value

Marx calls the expropriation of the proceeds of six hours of labor time "surplus value." The capitalist uses this to buy more capital. Then he will be able to exploit even more workers.

Capital, then, comes from the surplus value that has been stolen from the worker, and that surplus value represents the capitalist's profit.

Conclusion

What does all of this add up to? Which theory of profits is correct? Well, you know my style by now. I ask you what you think, I let you sweat for a while, and then, finally, I reveal the truth to you. I'll give you some time to go back over each of the four theories of profit. Imagine we're playing a couple of minutes of music while the clock is ticking away. OK—time's up! What's your answer?

Whichever answer you chose is right because there is a lot of truth in each of the four theories—even the Marxist theory. After all, more than 1 billion Chinese can't all be completely wrong! Furthermore, it's undeniable that monopolists *do* make profits. And surely there are plenty of profits earned by innovators and risk takers.

What we may conclude, then, is that everybody's right. And we may conclude that nobody has a monopoly on the truth.

Questions for Further Thought and Discussion

1. Are prices high because rents are high, or are rents high because prices are high? Use an example to illustrate your answer.

2. What are usury laws? Why do economists hate them?

3. Explain why a dollar today is worth more than a dollar you will have in the future.

4. How are profits determined?

Name _____ Date _____

Multiple-Choice Questions

Circle the letter that corresponds to the best answer.

1. Which statement is true?

    a. All land has the same economic value.   **b.** The most important factor affecting rent is location.

    c. The economic value of a plot of land is determined exclusively by the raw materials it contains   **d.** None of these statements is true.

2. The supply of land

    a. is fixed   **b.** varies from time to time   **c.** rises with demand   **d.** is higher in urban areas than in rural areas

3. Land is most efficiently used in

    a. cities   **b.** suburban areas   **c.** rural areas

4. The rent on a particular piece of land is based on

    a. the supply of land   **b.** the buildings located on that land   **c.** the MRP schedule of the highest bidder   **d.** the MRP schedule of the lowest bidder

5. When the demand for a plot of land rises,

    a. its supply will fall   **b.** its supply will rise

    c. its price will fall   **d.** its price will rise

6. The supply of land is

    a. perfectly elastic   **b.** perfectly inelastic

    c. relatively elastic   **d.** variable in elasticity

7. Rent on marginal land is

    a. very high   **b.** above zero   **c.** zero

    d. negative

8. Each of the following is a valid criticism of Henry George's ideas except that

    a. a tax on land would raise only a small fraction of needed government revenue   **b.** landlords sometimes improve the land   **c.** like rent, other kinds of income are unearned   **d.** a tax on land would result in a decrease in the supply of land

9. Which statement is true?

    a. Prices are high because rents are high.   **b.** Rents are high because prices are high.   **c.** David Ricardo believed high rents would drive English farmers out of business.   **d.** None of these statements is true.

10. As interest rates rise

    a. more investment will be undertaken   **b.** less investment will be undertaken   **c.** there is no change in the level of investment

11. The net productivity of capital is found by

    a. adding capital cost to dollar value of net productivity   **b.** subtracting capital cost from dollar value of net productivity   **c.** multiplying capital cost by dollar value of net productivity   **d.** dividing dollar value of net productivity by capital cost   **e.** dividing capital cost by dollar value of net productivity

12. A firm will not carry out an investment project if the net productivity of capital is

    a. greater than the interest rate   **b.** equal to the interest rate   **c.** smaller than the interest rate

13. In general, when your net productivity of capital is 25 percent, you

    a. will not invest   **b.** will invest   **c.** will be indifferent about whether you invest because you will break even exactly

14. Whether you purchase a new machine or a new building depends on

    a. only its price   **b.** only the going rate of interest

    c. both its price and the going rate of interest

    d. neither its price nor the going rate of interest

15. The value of an asset is equal to

    a. the annual income from the asset plus the interest rate   **b.** the annual income from the asset times the interest rate   **c.** the annual income from the asset divided by the interest rate   **d.**   the interest rate divided by the annual income from the asset

16. If there were no inflation, a dollar today would be worth
    a.   exactly the same as a dollar received in the future
    b.   more than a dollar received in the future   **c.**   less than a dollar received in the future

17. Which statement is true?
    a.   Profits are determined by supply and demand.
    b.   Profits are solely a reward for risk taking and innovation.   **c.**   Profits are derived solely from the exploitation of workers.   **d.**   None of these statements is true.

18. Which statement is true?
    a.   Profits are about one-quarter of GDP.   **b.**   Profits are about 1 percent of GDP.   **c.**   Accounting profits are larger than economic profits.   **d.**   None of these statements is true.

19. Which economist believes all profits are linked with uncertainty and risk?
    a.   Frank Knight   **b.**   Joseph Schumpeter   **c.**   Karl Marx   **d.**   John Maynard Keynes

20. "Innovations do not remain isolated events, and are not evenly distributed in time, but . . . on the contrary they tend to cluster, to come about in bunches, simply because some, and then most, firms follow in the wake of successful innovation." Who made this statement?
    a.   Frank Knight   **b.**   Joseph Schumpeter   **c.**   Karl Marx   **d.**   John Maynard Keynes

Use Figure 1 to answer questions 21 through 23.

21. The horizontal dotted line is
    a.   a price ceiling   **b.**   a price floor   **c.**   either a price ceiling or a price floor   **d.**   neither a price ceiling nor a price floor

22. If there were no usury law, the interest rate would be _____ percent.
    a.   18   **b.**   20   **c.**   23   **d.**   26   **e.**   28

Figure 1

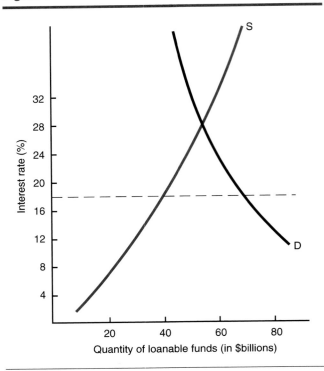

23. With this usury law in effect there is a _____ of _____ billion.
    a.   shortage, $28   **b.**   surplus, $28   **c.**   shortage, $55   **d.**   surplus, $55

24. The present value of a dollar declines as
    a.   the interest rate declines and the number of years you wait for your money declines   **b.**   the interest rate rises and the number of years you wait for your money rises   **c.**   the interest rate declines and the number of years you wait for your money rises   **d.**   the interest rate rises and the number of years you wait for your money declines

Fill-In Questions

1. The amount of rent paid for a piece of land is based on the

   _____ and the _____ .

2. In economic terms, we pay rent only on _____

   _____ .

3. Plots of land are differentiated mainly with respect to

   _____ .

4. The amount of land in the world is virtually _____ _____.

5. In a demand and supply graph for land, supply is represented by a(n) _____ line.

6. The main thing Henry George advocated was a _____ _____.

7. An important attribute of rent overlooked by Henry George was its role as a _____, _____ directing the most productive enterprises to the _____ _____.

8. Rent is high because _____ _____.

9. We can add to our stock of _____ by means of a flow of _____.

10. The interest rate is determined by the law of _____ _____ and _____.

11. The demand for capital is the firm's _____ _____ schedule for capital.

12. The supply of loanable funds slopes upward to _____ _____.

13. The amount of investment undertaken by an individual business firm depends on its MRP and the _____ _____.

14. To derive the net productivity of capital, we subtract _____ _____ from _____ to get the dollar value of net productivity and then divide that figure by _____.

15. A firm will keep carrying out additional investment projects as long as its _____ _____ is higher than the _____.

16. The value of an asset is found by dividing the _____ _____ by the _____.

17. If interest rates rise, the value of an asset will _____ _____.

18. If the interest rate were 7 percent, $100 today would be worth _____ in dollars you will have one year from now.

19. If interest rates fall, the present value of future dollars will _____.

20. Economists treat profits as a _____ left to the entrepreneur after _____, _____, and _____ have been paid.

21. Economic profits are somewhat lower than accounting profits because we are subtracting both _____ and _____ costs from sales.

22. In 1997, total profits (corporate pretax profits and proprietors' income) were $_____ billion.

23. Profits are about _____ percent of national income.

24. The four somewhat overlapping theories of how the entrepreneur is able to earn a profit are: (1)_____; (2) _____; (3) _____; and (4) _____ _____.

Problems

1. Given the information in Figure 2, how much will the firm invest if the interest rate is a. 15 percent? b. 10 percent? c. 5 percent?

Figure 2

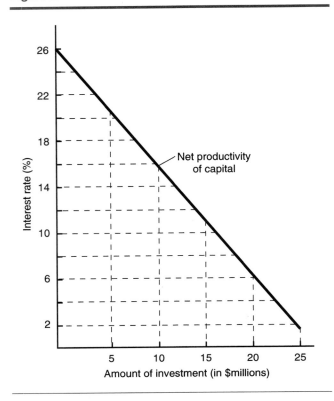

Net productivity of capital

Interest rate (%)

Amount of investment (in $millions)

2. Find the net productivity of capital if Sales = $200,000; Labor costs = $50,000; Raw materials = $20,000; Advertising = $5,000; Fuel and maintenance = $5,000; Normal profit = $25,000; and Capital cost = $75,000.

3. How much is the value of a machine that provides an annual income of $500 when the going rate of interest is 7 percent?

4. How much is the value of a shopping mall that provides an annual income of $20 million when the going interest rate is 9 percent?

5. If the interest rate is 10 percent and a dollar will be paid to you in three years, what is the present value of that dollar (to the nearest 10th of a cent)?

6. What is the present value of $10,000 that will be paid to you in four years if the interest rate is 8 percent? Work it out to the nearest cent.

7. Find the net productivity of capital if Sales = $800 million; Labor costs = $400 million; Raw materials = $75 million; Insurance = $5 million; Advertising = $30 million; Fuel and maintenance = $20 million; and Capital cost = $200 million.

8. How much is the value of a building that provides an annual income of $200,000 when the going rate of interest is 10 percent?

9. If the interest rate is 12 percent and a dollar will be paid to you in four years, what is the present value of that dollar (to the nearest cent)?

33 Income Distribution and Poverty

The economic history of the United States has been one of tremendous growth, a rising standard of living, and a home in the suburbs for most American families. But income has not been distributed evenly, and tens of millions of Americans have been left far behind. Indeed, poverty amid plenty has been one of the basic failures of our society.

This chapter is divided into two parts: income distribution and poverty. If income were distributed evenly, every American would have an income of more than $25,000 a year—that's every man, woman, and child—and there would be no poverty. In fact, if income were distributed evenly, there would be virtually nothing to write about income distribution and poverty.

Chapter Objectives

When you have finished this chapter, you will know the answers to these questions:

- How unequal is income distribution in the United States?
- What determines how income is distributed?
- How does the distribution of income differ from the distribution of wealth?
- How is poverty defined?
- Who are the poor?
- What are the main government transfer payments to help the poor?
- What are the causes of poverty?
- What are the solutions?

Income Distribution in the United States

The Poor, the Middle Class, and the Rich

How unequal is income distribution in the United States? To answer this question, we must first answer three subsidiary questions: How unequal are the incomes of (1) the poor and the rich? (2) blacks and whites? and (3) males and females? There are no big surprises here. The rich make more money than the poor; whites make more than blacks; and men make more money than women. The question is, How much more?

Do you know what a quintile is? I'll bet no one ever asked you *that* before. A quinquennial is an event that occurs every five years; a quintuplet is one of five babies born at the same time. A *quintile* is one-fifth, just like a quarter is one-fourth. We'll use this term to measure income distribution.

The poor are in the lowest quintile, the middle class in the next three quintiles, and the rich in the upper quintile. Is it accurate to say that 20 percent of our population is poor, 60 percent is middle class, and 20 percent is rich? Maybe not. But because social scientists can't agree about where to draw the dividing lines between the poor and the middle class and between the middle class and the rich, this arbitrary arrangement is as good as any other. And besides, we get to deal with nice round numbers—20, 60, and 20.

Who is rich, who is middle class, and who is poor?

The Lorenz curve

Now we're going to analyze a Lorenz curve, named for M. O. Lorenz, who drew the first one in 1905. Let's begin by looking at the axes of Figure 1. On the horizontal axis

Figure 1   Hypothetical Lorenz Curve

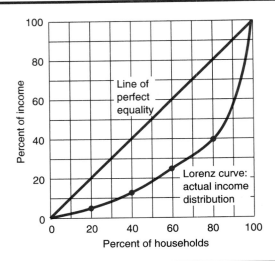

we have the percentage of households, beginning with the poor (0 percent to 20 percent), running through the middle class (20 percent to 80 percent), and ending with the rich (80 percent to 100 percent). The vertical axis shows the cumulative share of income earned by these households.

Figure 1 has just two lines. The straight line that runs diagonally from the lower left to the upper right is the line of perfect equality. You'll notice that the poorest 20 percent of the households receive exactly 20 percent of the income, and that 40 percent of the households receive exactly 40 percent of the income. In other words, every household in the country makes exactly the same amount of money.

The curve to the right of the straight diagonal line is the Lorenz curve, which tells us how income is actually distributed. What percent of income does the poorest 20 percent of all households receive? And how much does the next poorest 20 percent receive? Put your answers here:

Lowest fifth:

Second fifth:

Third fifth:

Fourth fifth:

Highest fifth:

The lowest fifth receives just 5 percent of all income; the second fifth receives 7.5 percent; the third fifth receives 12.5 percent; the fourth fifth receives 15 percent; and the highest fifth receives 60 percent. (If you don't know how I got these numbers, please read the box "Finding the Percentage of Income Share of the Quintiles in Figure 1.")

What do you think of *that* income distribution? Not very equal, is it? You'll notice the Lorenz curve is pretty far to the right of the diagonal line. That diagonal is the line of perfect equality, so the farther the Lorenz curve is from it, the less equal the distribution of income becomes.

Definition of the Lorenz curve

Do you know what I forgot to do? I forgot to define the Lorenz curve. Do *you* want to take a stab at a definition? Here's mine: *A Lorenz curve shows the cumulative share of income earned by each quintile of households.*

Finding the Percentage of Income Share of the Quintiles in Figure 1

The lowest quintile receives 5 percent of all income. Right? How much does the second quintile get? It gets 7.5 percent. Where did we get that number? What is the percentage share of income earned by the lowest 40 percent of households? It looks like 12.5 percent—right? Now if the bottom quintile earns 5 percent, and the lowest two quintiles earns a total of 12.5 percent, how much do households in the second-lowest quintile earn? They earn 7.5 percent (12.5 percent – 5 percent).

Next question: How much is the cumulative percentage share of income of the lower 60 percent of households? It comes to 25 percent. So how much is the third quintile's income share? It's 12.5 percent (25 percent – 12.5 percent). In other words, we take the lower 60 percent of households' share (25 percent) and subtract from it the combined share of the lower two quintiles (12.5 percent).

The lower 80 percent receives 40 percent of income. From that, we subtract the income share of the lower 60 percent (25 percent), which leaves the fourth quintile with a 15 percent income share. One more quintile to go—the highest quintile. If 100 percent of all households receive 100 percent of all income and the lowest 80 percent of all households receive a total of 40 percent, what's left for the top quintile? You got it—60 percent.

Figure 2   Lorenz Curve of Income Distribution in the United States, 1996

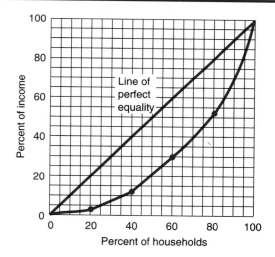

Source: U.S. Bureau of the Census, *Current Population Reports, Series P–60.*

How does our own income distribution look? It's plotted for you in Figure 2. Once again, figure out the distribution of income, and write your answers here:

Lowest fifth:

Second fifth:

Third fifth:

Fourth fifth:

Highest fifth:

Table 1   Percentages of Total Income before Taxes Received by Each Fifth of American Families, 1960 and 1996

Income Rank	1960	1996
Lowest fifth	4.8%	3.7%
Second fifth	12.2	9.0
Third fifth	17.8	15.1
Fourth fifth	24.0	23.3
Highest fifth	41.3	49.0

Source: U.S. Bureau of the Census, *Current Population Reports, Series P–60.*

Check your answers against those in the right-hand column of Table 1. Your figures don't have to match mine exactly because we're both making our own observations from the graph.

Has income become more equally distributed since 1960?

Now, let's compare the distribution of income in 1996 with that in 1960. Has income become *more* evenly distributed or *less* evenly distributed? A society in which the poorest fifth of the population gets less than 4 percent of the income and the richest fifth gets nearly half has a very uneven distribution of income. Since 1960, the top fifth's share of income rose from 41.3% to 49.0%, whereas the share of each of the lower four-fifths declined. In short, then, the rich are getting richer and the poor are getting poorer. You can see this even more vividly in the box "Winners and Losers, 1977–92."

Distribution of Wealth in the United States

The rich are different from you and me

—F. Scott Fitzgerald

Yes, they are different. They have more money.

—Ernest Hemingway

What did we learn from all those income figures in the last section? That rich people have higher incomes than poor people? But we already knew that. That rich people can enjoy a higher standard of living? We knew that, too. But we can surmise something else from these income distribution figures. The same guys who were pulling down $300,000 last year were doing it the year before and the year before that. So, over time, they were able to buy nice first homes, second homes, fancy cars, and expensive clothes; to go skiing on weekends; and maybe even to put a little bit aside for a rainy day.

And what about the working class and the poor? What have they got to show for all their years of work? Maybe a modest little home with a second mortgage, a beat-up car, and a lot of bills. Which brings us to an important conclusion: if we're going to compare living standards, we need to look not just at income distribution but at accumulated wealth. We do this in the box titled "Millionaires and Billionaires."

Has the distribution of wealth become less equal since 1980? Is it fair to call the decade of the 1980s the age of greed? Researchers at the Federal Reserve and Internal Revenue Service reported that in 1976 the richest 1 percent of our population held about 20 percent of the nation's wealth. By 1989 their share had climbed to 37 percent. They held a collective net worth (what they owned minus what they owed) of $5.7 trillion—more than was held by the bottom 90 percent of Americans (84 million households with about $4.8 trillion in net worth).[1]

Although more than 100 million Americans directly or indirectly (mainly through pension plans) own some corporate stock, the top 5 percent of all households own 77 percent of equity holdings. The bottom 80 percent own only 1.8 percent.[2]

Wealth includes housing and other real estate, checking and savings accounts, certificates of deposit, stocks and bonds, and other valuable assets. One reason for the greater concentration of wealth in the hands of the rich is the slashing of federal income tax rates paid by the very rich. In 1981 the top tax bracket was 70 percent; by 1991 it was just

---

[1]See Sylvia Nasar, "Fed Gives New Evidence of 80s Gains by Richest," *New York Times,* April 21, 1992, p. A1; Gar Alperovitz, "Distributing our Technological Inheritance," *Technology Review,* October 1994, p. 32. A Twentieth Century Fund study found that between 1980 and 1990, the share of wealth held by the top 1 percent rose from 20 percent to 35.7 percent. See *Newsweek,* May 1, 1995, p. 62D.

[2]James M. Poterba and Andrew A. Samwick, *Brookings Papers on Economic Activity,* vol. 2, 1995.

◤**A**DVANCED **W**ORK ··········· Winners and Losers, 1977–92 ···········

The 15-year period from 1977 to 1992 was great for the rich, but not so great for the rest of us. The table here shows the percentage change in average after-tax family income for six income groups from 1977 to 1992. The top 1 percent did the best, with a 99 percent increase in average family income from 1977 to 1992. The top fifth also enjoyed a big gain—25.1 percent. But everyone else lost ground. The average family income of the fourth fifth fell by 12.1 percent, and that of the lowest fifth fell by 11.1 percent.

Income Group	Percent Change
Top 1 percent	+99.0%
Highest fifth	+25.1
Second fifth	−0.3
Third fifth	−7.5
Fourth fifth	−12.1
Lowest fifth	−11.1

Source: *Fortune*, June 29, 1992.

The top 1 percent of American families did very well indeed over the 15-year period from 1977 to 1992. Their average income doubled, while the average incomes for the lower four-fifths of American families actually declined. Keep in mind that these are averages, so not every family

in the top 1 percent actually experienced an income gain, and not every family in the lower four-fifths suffered an income loss. In the second fifth, for instance, there was virtually *no* change in average family income. Furthermore, there was a substantial amount of shifting of families among these different income groups. For example, a family may have risen from the second fifth to the highest fifth, or fallen from the third fifth to the lowest fifth.

It does not take a rocket scientist to figure out that income distribution was a lot less equal in the early 1990s than it was in the late 1970s. We know that changes in our tax laws have been a major factor. Income tax rates were cut, especially for the rich, while Social Security tax rates were raised, taking a large bite out of the incomes of the working poor, the working class, and the lower-middle class. Indeed, two-thirds of all Americans pay more today in Social Security tax than they do in personal income tax.

The rich also reaped huge capital gains in the 1980s, largely from increases in stock prices, real estate, and investments in their own businesses. During this same period the average hourly wage rate fell by more than 10 percent. Meanwhile the relatively high-paying manufacturing sector has been shedding hundreds of thousands of jobs every year, while employment in the relatively low-paying service sector has been rising rapidly.

31 percent.[3] But the main reason why the distribution of wealth in America is becoming less equal is because the distribution of income is becoming less equal. In summary, the rich are getting richer and the poor are getting poorer.

Distribution of Income: Equity and Efficiency

Philosophers and economists have wrestled with these questions for centuries, but they still have not reached a conclusion. First we'll consider what a fair and just distribution of income would be, and then we'll talk about how income distribution affects the efficient operation of our economy.

The utilitarian view

We'll begin with the utilitarian view based on the law of diminishing marginal utility, which was discussed with great eloquence in the chapter on the theory of consumer behavior in *Economics* and *Microeconomics*. On the off chance that you don't fully recall this important law, I'll restate it: *As we consume increasing amounts of a good or service, we derive diminishing utility or satisfaction from each additional unit consumed.*

Poverty is an anomaly to rich people; it is very difficult to make out why people who want dinner do not ring the bell.

—Walter Bagehot

Let's seat a rich person and a poor person side by side in a booth at McDonald's and place a Big Mac in front of each of them. The rich person and the poor person wolf down the burgers with equal delight. So we place a second Big Mac in front of each of them and, if their appetites are big enough, a third and a fourth. When will they stop chowing down? When they've had enough. Who will stop first—the poor person or the rich person? We don't know. Would it be reasonable to guess that they would stop at about the same time? I think so.

What does all of this prove? It proves that Big Macs are enjoyed by people from all income groups. It also indicates that poor people and rich people get about the same

_____

[3]In 1993 it was raised to 39.6 percent.

Millionaires and Billionaires

Whenever there is excessive wealth, there is also in the train of it excessive poverty; as where the sun is brightest the shade is deepest.

—Walter Savage Landor, "Aristoteles and Callisthenes," *Imaginary Conversations*

Remember our discussion of millions, billions, and trillions way back in Chapter 5 of *Economics* and *Macroeconomics*? One million is written in digits with a one followed by two sets of three zeros: 1,000,000. And one billion? A one is followed by three sets of three zeros: 1,000,000,000.

So, what's a millionaire? Someone who earns a million dollars a year? No! No? That's right! To be a millionaire, all you need is a net worth of 1 million dollars. Take a minute to figure out your own net worth. Add up all your assets—your stocks and bonds, your bank deposits, and all your property. Don't forget your car, your summer cottage, or even your clothes, jewelry, and valuable stamp collection. After you've added up all your assets, do the same thing with your liabilities—that's everything you owe. Be sure to include your mortgage debt, bank loans, credit card balances, car loan, and any outstanding student loans.

Once you've added up all your assets and all your liabilities, subtract your liabilities from your assets:

Assets – Liabilities = Net worth

How much is your net worth? More than 1 million dollars? Then you're a millionaire. What happens if your liabilities are greater than your assets? Then you have a negative net worth. And what if your liabilities are 1 million dollars more than your assets? Then congratulations are in order because you are a negative millionaire.

Being a millionaire is not such a big deal in this country because there are 6 million of them. Think about it. If you owned a house that was situated in Palm Beach, Provincetown, Grosse Point, Westport, Palm Springs, Newport, or Manhattan's Park Avenue or Sutton Place, you'd be a millionaire simply because of where you lived. So, if you want to become an instant millionaire, all you need to do is move to a more affluent neighborhood.

The really rich are our billionaires—the folks with net worth in 10 figures. Yet even these people are becoming rather common. A total of 143 individuals or families have a net worth of at least $1 billion. In 1994 there were just 69.

The Forbes 1997 Top Ten List of American Billionaires

Name and Rank	Main Source of Income	Net Worth (in $ billions)
1. William Henry Gates III	Microsoft (cofounder)	40.0
2. Warren Edward Buffett	Stock market	21.0
3. Paul Gardner Allen	Microsoft (cofounder)	17.0
4. Lawrence J. Ellison	Oracle (founder)	9.2
5. Gordon Earle Moore	Intel (cofounder)	8.8
6. Steven Anthony Ballmer	Microsoft (employee)	8.3
7. John Werner Kluge	Metromedia (founder)	7.8
8. Ronald Owen Perelman	Stock market	6.5
9. Walton family: Helen, Jim, John, Alice, and S. Robson	Wal-Mart Stores (widow and children of founder Sam Walton)	6.4 each
10. Jay Arthur Pritzker	Finance, hotels	6.0
Robert Alan Pritzker	Manufacturing, service	6.0

Source: *Forbes*, October 13, 1997.

satisfaction from Big Macs, Whoppers, Bruce Springsteen concerts, and all the other available goods and services.

The only problem is that the poor person can't afford to buy nearly as much as the rich person can. The rich person can buy all the Big Macs he wants, but the poor person can afford just one—without enough money remaining for a side of fries. What if the rich person gave one dollar to the poor person? The rich person would have more than enough money left. He can afford to buy all the Big Macs *and* french fries he'll ever want and *still* have plenty of money left over.

OK, so would it be such a bad thing for the rich guy to fork over a buck or two to the poor guy? After all, that money would mean a whole lot more to the poor guy. But now we'll carry this redistribution scheme to its logical conclusion. Let's have everyone who's earning more than the average income give his surplus to everyone who is earning less. When we've finished, we'll all have exactly the same income. I have just stated the utilitarian case for equality.

Short of genius, a rich man cannot imagine poverty.

—Charles Péguy

What do *you* think? Is this fair? What about the people who worked hard for their money, putting in hours of overtime, holding down two jobs, and never seeing their families or friends? And what about the lazy bums who don't even bother looking for a job because they know they'll have exactly the same income as the working stiffs?

So much for a fair and just distribution of income. How does income distribution affect our economic efficiency? Well, for starters, what would an equal distribution of income do to work incentives? Would *you* work hard if you'd end up with exactly the same income as a lot of people who just sat at home and waited for their checks? Two of the things that make our economy go are the carrot and the stick. The carrot is all the money you can make by working hard. And the stick is that if you don't work, you don't eat.

How does income distribution affect our economic efficiency?

Another incentive that would suffer is the incentive to save. Considering that the interest you'd get from your savings would be divided among everyone, why bother to save at all? Why invest, for that matter? Why bother to engage in any productive activities whatsoever, when we'll all end up with the same income no matter what we do?

Of course, if we were to pursue this reasoning to its logical conclusion, we would end up with very little output (because only a few workaholics would still be producing) and therefore very little real income.

So what should we do? Neither extreme seems desirable. Complete income equality would rob us of our productive incentives. And great income inequality would mean a great deal of human suffering, because many of the poor would not be able to afford even the basic necessities of life.

Whatever the means of income redistribution, the ends are always the same—to take from the rich and give to the poor. Robin Hood may not have won favor with the Sheriff of Nottingham or with the rich people he robbed, but most folks agree that the rich—*and* the middle class—should give some of their money to the poor. The only question is, How much?

What Determines Income Distribution?

What *does* determine income distribution? Remember the adage "It's not *what* you know; it's *who* you know"? (Actually, it's *whom* you know.) So is *that* all there is? Connections?

Did David Rockefeller rise quickly through the ranks to attain the presidency of Chase Manhattan Bank back in the 1960s solely because he had a Ph.D. in economics, while I couldn't even get an interview? (I really couldn't.) Not that his family's huge holding of Chase Manhattan stock had anything to do with it. In general, it is fair to say that connections don't hurt, but once you have your foot in the door you've got to have *something*. I might be able to get you a tryout with the Atlanta Braves, but if you can't pitch—or hit—don't hold out for *too* big a signing bonus.

Some people make a lot more money than most others do. Why? Is it training, education, intelligence, inborn skills, physical attributes, or just plain luck? Yes. Yes? Yes, it's all of the above. And don't forget about job discrimination. Few WASP males have encountered it, but just ask most women, blacks, Hispanics, and members of other racial, religious, and ethnic minorities about it.

Close to two-thirds of all personal income is earned in wages and salaries, so we'll concentrate on the factors causing these incomes to vary so widely. And then we'll take a look at property income, which accounts for a little less than one-quarter of all personal income. Finally, we'll look at government transfer payments, which account for the rest.

Why do some people earn more than others?

Differences in Wages and Salaries Why do doctors make more than word processors? Why do professional athletes make more than cashiers? The questions may change from chapter to chapter, but the answer remains the same: supply and demand. Basically, the people in certain occupations are in relatively short supply. Relative to what? Relative to the demand for their services.

A doctor must go through not just four years of college and four years of medical school but also a year's internship and at least three years of residency. Consider all those years of little or no income, all that money going toward tuition and living expenses, all those student loans to pay back. And, incidentally, consider all that malpractice insurance that still has to be paid out in the years to come.

Doctors are in short supply relative to the demand for medical services. And they're kept in short supply by the American Medical Association, as noted in the chapter on labor unions in *Economics* and *Macroeconomics*. But I've overlooked the intelligence and ability of the person who becomes a doctor. These factors also greatly influence how much doctors earn. One might ask why, then, Ph.D.s in history, philosophy, or even economics don't earn what doctors do. Once again, we're back to supply and demand. I'm still waiting for that long-predicted Ph.D. shortage to materialize so college teaching salaries will finally start going up.

How important is education?

How important is education? We *do* know college graduates earn a lot more than high school graduates; M.B.A.s, particularly those who have taken the trouble to attend Harvard, Columbia, Wharton, or the University of Chicago, are getting starting salaries of $80,000 or $90,000; and graduates of our more illustrious law schools are pulling down similar salaries. (See Table 2.)

How many times have you heard that in today's high-tech economy, you not only need to know reading, writing, and arithmetic, but you must be computer literate as well? As the blue-collar workforce shrinks, more and more people are getting office jobs, and there's a computer terminal on almost every desk. Are training and education important? You tell *me*.

Everyone tells us that the longer we stay in school, the more money we'll make for the rest of our lives. Is this true? Yes, it is. The average college graduate will earn almost three times the income earned by someone who has not completed the eighth grade. Why? Because of everything the college graduate learned in school? Not necessarily. Because of the college diploma, which is the minimum entrance requirement for many jobs? Possibly.

Why does a college graduate earn more than a grade school dropout?

The main reasons the college graduate earns so much more than the grade school dropout are that the college graduate is probably smarter, richer, and more motivated; has better connections; and comes from a home with a more supportive learning environment. In other words, the personal characteristics of the two people, rather than their respective educations, determine their earning power. This is not to say that education does not affect earning power at all or that many poor people, given the opportunity, could not do well in school and go on to brilliant careers selling junk bonds or even writing economics textbooks.

But before we get too excited about the importance of education and training as determinants of income, we might want to take a look at the role credentials play in the hiring process. According to Kenneth Arrow and Michael Spence, employers use years of schooling as a screening device.[4] *Does* more schooling make you more productive? My

---

[4]See Kenneth Arrow, "Higher Education as a Filter," *Journal of Public Economics* 2 (July 1973), pp. 193–216; Michael Spence, "Job Market Signaling," *Quarterly Journal of Economics* 87 (August 1973), pp. 355–74.

Table 2   The 10 Best-Paid CEOs in 1997

Rank	Name	Company	Total Compensation (in $ millions)
1	Sanford I. Weill	Travelers Group	$152.6
2	Ray R. Irani	Occidental Petroleum	108.2
3	Louis V. Gerstner Jr.	I.B.M.	91.5
4	George M.C. Fisher	Eastman Kodak	63.8
5	L. Dennis Kozlowski	Tyco International	62.3
6	Jill E. Barad	Mattel	56.2
7	Eugene M. Isenberg	Nabors Industries	52.0
8	Reuben Mark	Colgate-Palmolive	35.5
9	William J. Schoen	Health Mgmt. Associates	31.3
10	Eckhard Pfeiffer	Compaq Computer	30.2

Source: *The New York Times,* April 15, 1998, Section 3, p. 1.

nephew Jonah tells me that what he learned in law school has virtually nothing to do with what he's been doing these last 15 years in mergers, acquisitions, and trusts and estates. The title of Robert Fulghum's best-seller sums it up: *All I Really Need to Know I Learned in Kindergarten.*

How important is talent?

How important is talent? Sometimes it's very important. Michael Jackson has brought home about $60 million a year since 1989. In the mid-1990s Oprah Winfrey (her mother loved Harpo Marx and named her after him by spelling his name backward) earned an average of $150 million a year. Another field where talent usually rises to the top is sales. Those with the best communication skills and the most extroverted personalities generally do the best, whether they're selling real estate, used cars, insurance, or aluminum siding.

And yet talent is usually not a decisive factor in determining how much people earn. In most organizations, both public and private, new employees are hired at the same starting salaries, and they advance in lockstep from one pay level to the next. More than talent and ability, and education or training, the most important factor in determining pay level seems to be seniority.

The 1960s and 1970s were decades of great social upheaval. The women's liberation movement and the civil rights movement sought to place women, blacks, and other minorities squarely in the socioeconomic mainstream. Although these movements and the public- and private-sector hiring programs they engendered have had a major impact in promoting equal economic opportunity, employment discrimination persists.

Through the 1960s women working full time were stuck earning around 60 percent of what men earned. In 1973 the median wage for women was just 63 percent of that for men. By 1996 it had risen to 74 percent. The average college-educated woman, however, still earns less than the average high school–educated man.

Blacks have traditionally earned 60 percent of what whites earned.

Employment discrimination can be measured in two basic ways: by relative income and by occupation. Traditionally, blacks have earned about 60 percent of what whites have earned, while women working full time have also earned about 60 percent of what was earned by their male counterparts. Moreover, women have traditionally entered very specific occupations, most notably the three Ss (schoolteacher, secretary, and social worker) as well as nurse, cashier, waitress, maid, telephone operator, and dressmaker. In fact, these occupations were long considered "women's work." Blacks and Hispanics also were confined largely to low-paid factory work, janitorial duties, and, until the late 1940s, farm labor.

Women have traditionally earned 60 percent of what men have earned.

Unemployment is an important determinant of income level.

Unemployment—or, more broadly, the lack of employment—is an important determinant of the income level of millions of Americans. We'll start with the fact that over the last four decades the unemployment rate for blacks has been consistently double that of whites. As noted previously, when it's a recession for whites, it's a depression for blacks.[5]

During the last two major recessions—in 1975 and in 1982—the unemployment rate for blacks topped 20 percent while the unemployment rate of black teenagers rose above 50 percent. Hispanics have suffered nearly as much as blacks from a lack of employment opportunities during the years since World War II.

But the official unemployment rate gives only a partial picture because millions of jobless people who aren't actively looking for employment (called "discouraged workers" by the Bureau of Labor Statistics, which compiles the official unemployment rate)[6] are not included in the official rate.

Property Income   Wages and salaries accounted for 62 percent of personal income in 1997, property income accounted for 26 percent, and government transfer

---

[5]See the box with this title in the chapter on economic fluctuations, unemployment, and inflation in *Economics* and *Macroeconomics.*

[6]For a detailed discussion of this topic, see the section headed How the Unemployment Rate is Computed in the chapter on economic fluctuations, unemployment, and inflation in *Economics* and *Macroeconomics.*

payments for 12 percent. As you might have suspected, most property income goes to the rich. These payments are in the form of rent, interest, dividends, and profits (which include capital gains).

Property income has two basic sources: savings and inheritance. Under current tax laws Americans may inherit nearly $700,000 from each estate without paying federal taxes, but very few people inherit anything approaching this figure. The Rockefellers, Mellons, Gettys, Fords, Du Ponts, and Kennedys are the exceptions that prove the rule—most of the rich are self-made millionaires (or billionaires, for that matter).

The two largest sources of wealth, exclusive of inheritance, have been the fortunes made in the stock market and the starting up of new companies. In the computer field alone, great fortunes were made by Lawrence Ellison (Oracle), Gordon Earle Moore (Intel), Steve Jobs (Apple), Kenneth Olsen (Digital), William Gates, Paul Gardner Allen, and Steven Anthony Ballmer (Microsoft), An Wang (Wang Laboratories), and David Packard (Hewlett-Packard), and, of course, Ross Perot (Electronic Data Systems) and Sam Walton (Wal-Mart). Stock market investors who hit it big include Warren Buffet, Edward Crosby Johnson III, and Ronald Owen Perelman.

Property income may also be derived from ownership of stocks, bonds, bank deposits, and other assets. Because the poor and the working class hold little property, little (if any) of their income comes from this source. Those in the middle class derive somewhat more of their income from property, but rarely more than 10 percent. And the rich? Well, the superrich, those whose annual incomes easily surpass $1 million, get most or all of their income from rent, interest, and profits. The people who live exclusively on their property income are sometimes called rentiers, which simply means they don't have to work for a living.

Income from Government Transfer Payments   In addition to wages, salaries, and property income, some people receive government transfer payments. For retirees, Social Security benefits may be their main means of support. For most people collecting unemployment benefits, these checks are their sole means of support. And public assistance recipients all depend on these benefits plus food stamps for their entire income.

Social Security benefits, which constitute more than two-thirds of all federal government transfer payments, are not aimed specifically at the poor, but they do help millions of older people rise above the poverty line. Similarly, Medicare helps the elderly regardless of income level. Unemployment benefits, which go to less than half of the unemployed, happen to go disproportionately to those in lower income groups.

The public assistance and food stamp programs are targeted solely at poor people. The basic philosophy is to provide subsistence to those who are down on their luck and in dire need of help. However, as we shall see in the second part of this chapter, in recent decades a permanent underclass has become completely dependent on government aid.

Virtually all of us agree that a certain amount of income redistribution is needed, but where we part company is in specifying just how much should be redistributed. We all want to see a more equitable and yet more efficient society, but we are far from reaching a consensus as to how that can be attained.

This brings us to the question of poverty in America. We're painfully aware that it's out there, but we're not sure what should be done about it. Like other subjects in economics, poverty and income distribution raise a lot of interesting questions. Unfortunately, there don't seem to be many answers.

Poverty in America

In this part of the chapter we'll examine the dimensions of the poverty problem in the United States, some of its causes, how we're dealing with it, and some possible remedies. But first we need to define poverty.

Some people's money is merited. And other people's money is inherited.

—Ogden Nash

The largest sources of wealth

Social Security benefits constitute more than two-thirds of all federal government transfer payments.

Poverty Defined

The relative concept of
poverty

There are two basic ways to define poverty: as a relative concept and as an absolute concept. So far, by defining the poor as the lowest income quintile (i.e., the lowest 20 percent) in the nation, we set up poverty as a relative concept. In other words, this group of people is poor relative to the rest of the population.

But there are a couple of problems with this definition. First, suppose everyone's standard of living quadrupled from one year to the next. We'd *still* be calling those in the lowest quintile poor, even though most of the "poor" would be living better this year than the entire middle class lived last year. Although Jesus *did* say, "Ye have the poor always with you" (Matthew 26:11), *these* poor people would be driving late-model cars, living in nice houses, and eating in fancy restaurants three or four nights a week.

A second difficulty with the concept of relative poverty is that the lowest income quintile is infinitely better off than the average citizens of the world's poorest nations. In Bangladesh, Ethiopia, and Somalia, most people struggle to survive on maybe $200 or $300 a year. Even our homeless population fares considerably better than that. So when we use the relative concept of poverty, we need to keep asking, "Relative to what?"— which gets to be pretty boring after a while.

The absolute concept of
poverty

What about the absolute concept of poverty? Well, there's one basic problem here, too. Who gets to determine the dividing line between poor and not poor, and how is that determination reached? The best approach is to set up a minimum basic standard of living and figure out how much it costs to maintain that standard from year to year. So far, so good. OK, so who gets to set up this basic living standard, and what goods and services should go into it?

The most widely used poverty standard is the official poverty line calculated each year by the U.S. Department of Agriculture. The department bases its estimate on the assumption that poor families spend about one-third of their incomes on food. Each year it calculates the minimum food budget for a family of four for one week, multiplies that figure by 52 for the family's annual food budget, and then triples that figure to get the official poverty line. In 1996 that line was set at $16,036 for a family of four.

The official poverty line

Can a family of four live on $16,036? It all depends on what you mean by living. Is it enough to put food on the table, clothes on your back, and a roof over your head? In some parts of the country, the answer is yes. In the more expensive cities such as New York, Boston, and San Francisco, as well as in many suburban communities, especially in the Northeast, $16,036 won't provide even the bare necessities, largely because of relatively high rents. Of course, all we're talking about here is a definition. When we get to the topic of public assistance in a few pages, we'll see that virtually none of the nation's thousands of locally administered welfare programs brings any of the poor up to the poverty line. Indeed, few even come close.

Once the poverty line has been established, we can find the poverty rate by dividing the number of poor people by the total population of the country. In other words, the poverty rate is the percentage of Americans who are poor.

The Census Bureau has been tracking the poverty rate since 1960. As you can observe in Figure 3, there was a sharp decline throughout the 1960s and early 1970s. In 1973 the rate bottomed out at 11.1 percent, about half the 1960 rate. The main causes of the decline were the prosperity of the 1960s and the War on Poverty conducted by the administration of President Lyndon Johnson. The federal government spent tens of billions of dollars on education, job training, and the creation of government jobs for millions of poor people.

But recessions in 1973–75, 1980, and 1981–82 pushed the poverty rate back up to 15.2 percent in 1983. Furthermore, President Ronald Reagan, who believed antipoverty programs were just "throwing money at problems," persuaded Congress to dismantle some of these programs. Reagan argued that his economic program—basically, massive tax cuts—would create enough jobs in the private sector to put millions of poor people to work in productive (rather than make-work) jobs. Indeed, from 1983 to 1989 1 million poor people or so were added to the employment rolls. Although the majority of these

Figure 3   U.S. Poverty Rate: Percentage of Individuals below the Poverty Line, 1960–96*

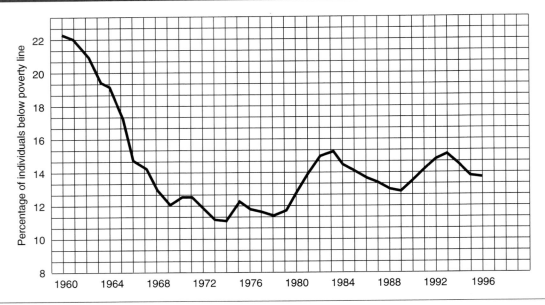

*In 1993 the Census Bureau adopted a different system of statistical weighting from the one used in previous years.
Source: U.S. Bureau of the Census.

jobs were relatively low-paying positions in the service sector, the poverty rate *did* decline from 15.2 percent in 1983 to 12.8 percent in 1989. It rose again during the recession of 1990–91, peaking in 1993. The poverty rate has fallen steadily since then to 13.7 percent in 1996, a period of rapid economic growth and falling unemployment. But in 1996 there were still 36.5 million Americans living below the poverty line.

Some conservative critics point out that the poverty rate would be substantially lower if we counted the value of noncash, or in-kind, benefits given to the poor by the government. These include Medicaid, housing subsidies, low-rent public housing, food stamps, and school lunches (we'll discuss the main government transfer programs in detail in an upcoming section). If these in-kind benefits were counted, the poverty rate would have been 10.8 percent in 1996 rather than the reported 13.7 percent.

The poverty rate would be substantially lower if we counted the value of in-kind benefits.

Who Are the Poor?

Who *are* the poor? Old people? Traditionally, people older than 65 have had a much higher poverty rate than the general population, but the advent of Medicare, higher Social Security benefits, and supplementary Social Security benefits over the last two decades has reduced the poverty rate for older Americans to well below the overall rate. In 1996 it was 10.8 percent.

Most poor people are white.

Are most poor people black? No, most poor people are white. It *is* true that almost three out of ten blacks are poor, but only 12.6 percent of our population is black; therefore 26.5 percent of all poor people are black. Figure 4 shows the relative poverty rates for white, black, and Hispanic Americans. Although one out of every three blacks lives below the poverty line, the poorest population group is Native American. The National Indian Policy Center says that 47.3 percent of the people living on Indian reservations and trust lands are poor.

OK, so our first two stereotypes of the poor as elderly and black or Hispanic were wrong. Ready for another shocker? Where do the majority of the poor live? In the cities? Wrong again! Most poor people actually live outside the cities. They live in the suburbs, in small towns, and in rural areas. While it *is* true that the majority of the poor are white residents of the suburbs, small towns, or the countryside, a disproportionate number of

Figure 4   Poverty Rates by Race, 1996

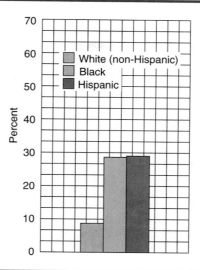

Source: U.S. Bureau of the Census.

the poor are urban blacks and Hispanics. So if you want to be poor, you can increase your chances substantially by being black or Hispanic and living in a large city.

Speaking of improving your chances of being poor, if you happen to be a member of a female-headed household with children, your chances improve to about one out of two. And if that household happens to be black or Hispanic, then you stand an even better chance. To a large degree, then, your chances of being rich or poor in the United States have a lot to do with how skillfully you have chosen your ancestors.

God must love the poor—he made so many of them.
—Abraham Lincoln

So who *are* the poor? About three-quarters are single mothers and their children. People living in the rural South and in the Appalachian region have relatively high poverty rates. In fact, the poverty rate in Mississippi is three times that of Connecticut. Migrant farm workers, native Americans, and recent immigrants are also more likely than the general population to be poor.

And then there are the people who once held jobs in declining industries like steel, automobiles, rubber, oil, textiles, and apparel, as well as in mining and farming. Many have been forced to take minimum-wage jobs in service industries, and others have found no jobs at all.

Americans work at or close to the minimum wage in fast-food restaurants, laundries, and hospitals, on farms, and even in illegal sweatshops around the country. A person earning $5.15 an hour for 35 hours a week earns an annual income of just $9,373 (before taxes), which would clearly leave a family of four—or three, for that matter—well below the poverty line.

The working poor

All the people employed at or just above the minimum wage could be considered the working poor. Most of them receive little or no government benefits yet somehow manage to make ends meet from paycheck to paycheck. But even if they don't get one cent from the government, they are still part of our poverty problem. (And what about the homeless? See box.)

The long-term unemployed

Finally, there are the chronically (long-term) unemployed and the discouraged workers. Although the U.S. unemployment rate has been relatively low during the last few years, this measure does not take into account the millions of Americans who have been out of work for years. The official unemployment statistics count only those who have actively sought employment; people who have given up looking for jobs are not included. The Bureau of Labor Statistics calls the latter group "discouraged workers." If the long-term unemployed—both officially unemployed and officially discouraged—were fully accounted for, we would be talking about another 8 or 10 million people.

The Homeless

The law, in its majestic equality, forbids the rich as well as the poor to sleep under bridges, to beg in the streets, and to steal bread.

—Anatole France

There have always been homeless people in America—the hobo jungles of the Depression era, the skid rows (or skid roads, as they are known in the West), and, of course, the isolated shopping-bag ladies and other folks who lived out on the street, in doorways, or in train stations. But now there are literally millions of them. In a nation of some 270 million people, between 2 and 3 million are homeless.* During the winter of 1996–97 New York City provided temporary shelter to more than 20,000 homeless people every night. And advocates of the homeless have estimated that another 60,000 to 90,000 sleep in privately run shelters, in bus and railroad terminals, or out on the street.

A convergence of four trends has multiplied the number of homeless people who congregate in all our large cities. Since World War II the number of entry-level factory jobs has steadily declined in every large city. Meanwhile, the availability of cheap housing (basically furnished rooms) has also declined as the cities' more dilapidated neighborhoods were demolished to make way for urban renewal projects.

A third trend has been gentrification, which has pushed rents through the roof, so to speak, in New York, San Francisco, Boston, Chicago, and most other major cities. Finally, the deinstitutionalization of the mentally ill over the last two decades (without the promised halfway houses to treat and shelter them) has further added to the homeless population.

The U.S. Department of Health and Human Services estimates that one-third of the homeless are mentally ill. That agency also estimates that half of the homeless are alcoholics or drug addicts, and few are receiving treatment. Interestingly, about one-quarter of the homeless work full time, according to the U.S. Conference of Mayors. The problem for them is being trapped between jobs that pay too little and housing that costs too much.

*There are widely varying estimates of the number of homeless people in the United States. Christopher Jencks (*The Homeless,* Cambridge, MA: Harvard University Press, 1994, chapter 1) makes an estimate of 400,000 to 500,000 for 1987 and presumably would make a much higher estimate today. While a reliable census of the homeless isn't possible, if we include individuals and families who are temporarily staying with relatives and friends, an estimate of 2 to 3 million is reasonable.

Child Poverty

Perhaps the most striking thing about poverty in America is how it affects children. Senator Daniel Patrick Moynihan, a longtime advocate of welfare reform, has put it starkly: "At any given moment, about one child in four is born poor. Over time, upward of one in three will be on welfare at some point. One in two will live in a single-parent, female-headed household."[7]

Particularly hard hit by poverty are black children and Hispanic children (see Figure 5). "Children are our future" may be a cliché, but they are nevertheless a future that we neglect at our peril.

The overall poverty rate for children in the United States was 20.6 percent in 1996, the highest of any developed country. Only Australia, Canada, Ireland, and Israel have child poverty rates of over 10 percent. While the stereotype of the indigent elderly persists, our children are much more likely to be living in poverty.

Large-scale, high-rise, low-income public housing projects have been especially good breeding grounds for this culture of poverty. In these neighborhoods at least three-quarters of the families are on welfare, most of the girls get pregnant before they are 18, and there is a great degree of drug dependency and an extremely high rate of violent crime (see box "Poverty and Crime"). The gangs are the real authority in the ghetto, according to Nicholas Lemann. The gang "forces kids, through physical terror, to give up school and work and become professional criminals."[8] To some degree this phenomenon has evolved in poor Hispanic and non-Hispanic white neighborhoods as well.

The civil rights revolution led by the Reverend Martin Luther King, Jr., in the early 1960s and the federal civil rights legislation passed in its wake gave rise to a tremendous black exodus from the ghettos as central city housing barriers came tumbling down.

---

[7]Daniel Patrick Moynihan, "Half the Nation's Children: Born without a Fair Chance," *New York Times,* September 25, 1988. p. E25.

[8]Nicholas Lemann, "The Origins of the Underclass," *Atlantic Monthly,* June 1986, p. 39.

Poverty and Crime

What is bringing home the issue of poverty to most Americans is the accompanying issue of crime. Although ghetto residents remain the prime victims of street crime, adjacent working-class neighborhoods, outlying areas of the cities, and even the suburbs have been subjected to this rising wave of crime.

Drugs, particularly crack, have been the catalyst, and few Americans feel truly safe anymore. The existence of a permanent underclass not only means continued high costs of public assistance, but it helps sustain the crime and drug epidemic eating away at the heart of America.

Drugs and crime, which are embedded in the ghetto culture, threaten to engulf the rest of the nation unless a major effort is made to alleviate poverty. Nancy Reagan's best intentions notwithstanding, we will need to do a lot more than ask youngsters to "just say no."

Figure 5   Poverty Rates of Selected Population Groups, by Race, 1996

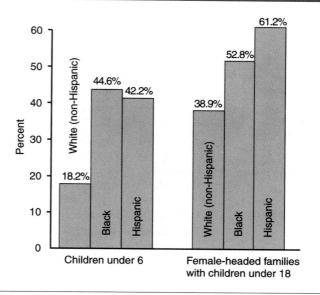

Source: U.S. Bureau of the Census.

Everyone who could get out got out. These middle-class and working-class families fled the squalor, crime, and inferior schools of the ghettos for the apartments and private homes formerly owned by the white middle- and working-class families who had already made their own exodus—to the suburbs.

Later in the chapter we'll be discussing William Julius Wilson's view of how these events brought about the formation of a permanent black underclass in the ghettos of the nation's large cities. Right now let's see how the federal government has dealt with this great upsurge in urban poverty.

A decent provision for the poor is a true test of civilization.
—Samuel Johnson

The Main Government Transfer Programs

The Social Security Act of 1935

The Social Security Act of 1935 set up three major programs: Social Security, unemployment insurance, and public assistance. Taxes paid by workers and their employers financed the first two programs. Public assistance, which was intended to help families experiencing temporary economic distress, was the only means-tested program. To obtain public assistance (or relief, as it was then called), you needed to demonstrate that your income or means of support was insufficient to cover your basic needs.

Medicare and Medicaid

Two major programs, Medicare and Medicaid, were added in the mid-1960s under President Johnson's Great Society program. Medicare, which was really a supplement to Social Security, provided retirees and their families with free or very low-cost medical care. Free medical care was provided to the poor under Medicaid.

There are about 40 million Americans who have no health insurance. Nearly all are among the working poor—too young to receive Medicare and too well-off to receive Medicaid. Their low-paying jobs do not provide health insurance, so they often must go without any medical care whatsoever.

Today more than one out of every ten Americans receives food stamps. The food stamp program, which also began in the 1960s, enabled the very poor as well as the working poor to buy enough food. Like Medicare and Medicaid, it has expanded tremendously since the late 1960s.

Have these programs worked? Yes, they have. Each has accomplished what it was set up to do. But there are three major problems: (1) their costs have gone through the roof; (2) they have fostered a permanent dependency on government support among millions of poor families; and (3) they have not ended poverty.

Public assistance has been the greatest disappointment. About half the money spent goes to female-headed families that stay on the program for eight years or more. Intended to provide "temporary relief," public assistance has instead engendered a permanent dependence in millions of families.

The number of people receiving public assistance remained remarkably steady—at about 11 million—from 1975 through 1989. Although we were hit with back-to-back recessions from 1980 to 1982, which ordinarily would have produced an increase in the rolls, the Reagan administration managed to institute sharp eligibility cutbacks, which prevented such an increase. But the welfare rolls shot up from 11 million in mid-1993 to a peak of 14.4 million in March 1994. The main reason for this increase was the recession of 1990–91. By early 1994, the benefits of the subsequent economic expansion finally began to reach people at the bottom of the economic ladder. Another important factor has been that many states have restricted eligibility for welfare.

One misconception about welfare mothers is that they keep having more and more children so that they can collect bigger checks. Indeed, many states no longer increase the size of a welfare grant if more children are born into a family. But 72 percent of all welfare families have only one or two children.

A welfare culture has evolved over the last four decades, giving rise to second-, third-, and fourth-generation welfare families. Typically, teenage girls become pregnant, keep their babies, go on welfare, do not marry, and have no hope of becoming self-supporting. In a sense, the young mothers are provided with surrogate husbands in the form of public assistance checks. Eventually their children grow up, become teenage parents themselves, and continue the welfare pattern through another generation. The challenge we face is how to break this pattern and help these families become self-supporting.

What we keep coming back to is the overwhelmingly high poverty rate of children. Some 22 percent of Americans now aged 18 to 20 spent at least one year on welfare before they were 18; for 18- to 20-year-old blacks, that figure is 72 percent.

The words of one welfare mother are especially poignant: "I'm sorry I got myself into this and my children into this. And I don't know how to get them out of it. If I don't get them away from here, they're going to end up dead, in jail, or like me."[9]

Theories of the Causes of Poverty

Any theory of poverty must take into account our entire socioeconomic system, how it is set up, how it is run, and who gets what. Poor people live on the margin or even beyond the system. They are basically superfluous and rarely have much impact on the system. They are an unfortunate presence, by-products that have been discarded but are grudgingly tolerated by society's "productive" members.

At least a dozen theories of poverty have attracted support, and each has at least *some* apparent validity. But because there are so many different poverty groups, no single theory can have universal applicability. We'll begin by briefly outlining a few theories,

---

[9]See Celia W. Dugger, "On the Edge of Survival: Single Mothers on Welfare," *New York Times*, July 6, 1992, p. B6.

and then we'll look at the two with the largest number of adherents: the conservative and liberal theories.

The Poor Are Lazy   This theory was popular through most of the 19th century and right up to the time of the Great Depression. God's chosen people, who were destined to go to heaven, worked hard all their lives and were rewarded by attaining great earthly riches. And the poor? Well, you can figure out for yourself where they were headed. This theory went down the tubes when the Great Depression hit and millions of relatively affluent Americans were thrown out of work, lost their life savings, and had to ask the government for handouts.

The Heritage of Slavery   Because blacks were brought here in chains and held back for three centuries by slavery and a feudal sharecropping system in the South, the current poverty of many blacks can be explained by centuries of oppression. Not only were blacks systematically excluded from all but the most menial jobs, but they were denied the educational opportunities open to almost all other Americans. Mortgage loans, restaurant meals, hotel and motel lodging, union membership, and apartment rentals were routinely denied. In effect, then, blacks were systematically excluded from the nation's economic mainstream until the 1960s. Is it any wonder, ask adherents of this theory, that after so many years of oppression both during and after slavery, many blacks still find themselves mired in poverty?

Full-time working women have earned 60 percent of what full-time working men earned.

Employment Discrimination   All the way back in Chapter 2 we talked about how employment discrimination causes our economy to operate at less than its full potential. Employment discrimination has been especially strong in holding down the incomes of women, blacks, Hispanics, and other minorities. The fact that women working full-time have generally earned about four-fifths of what their male counterparts have earned clearly points toward discrimination. Similar figures for blacks and Hispanics arouse the same suspicion.

But other factors have also contributed to these wage differentials—education, training, and experience, and, in the case of many women, the years taken off work to raise children. Social scientists generally believe that about half of these wage differentials result from employment discrimination and the other half from other factors. As more employment opportunities become available to women and to minorities, we may see a narrowing of wage differentials. Meanwhile, employment discrimination has obviously been playing a major role in the poverty of women, blacks, Hispanics, and other minorities.

Black Male Joblessness   Back in 1970, about 33 percent of all black families were headed by women. By 1997, the number had jumped to over 60 percent. The growing perception of a permanent welfare population of single black mothers and their children has raised the question of where the young black males are who got them pregnant. In college? Playing major-league ball? Hardly.

Only half of all black males aged 16 to 64 are employed.

While more than four-fifths of all white males aged 20 to 44 are employed, only about half of their black counterparts have jobs. What are the rest of them doing? Some are officially unemployed, and some are "discouraged workers" who have stopped looking for work. And where are the rest of these guys? Some may be working in the underground economy—in either the legal or illegal sector. And others have just slipped through the cracks. (See the box "The Darity–Myers Thesis.")

The decline in manufacturing has been especially brutal to young black men. According to William Julius Wilson, "48 percent of all employed black males, ages 20 to 24, were in well-paid, blue-collar, semiskilled crafts positions in 1974. By 1986, that figure had declined to 25 percent."[10]

---

[10]See Bob Herbert, "Who Will Help the Black Man?" *New York Times Magazine,* December 4, 1994, p. 74.

The Darity–Myers Thesis: The Economic Marginality of Young Black Men

William A. Darity, Jr., and Samuel L. Myers, Jr., argue that "black men have become less useful in the emerging economic order; they are socially unwanted, superfluous, and marginal."* Consequently there is a shrinking pool of marriageable black men. This growing marginality has led to drug abuse, violent crime, incarceration, and a high death rate, further depleting the ranks of marriageable young black men. Cutting welfare benefits, Darity and Myers observe, will do nothing to lower the number of black female-headed households, because the underlying problem is finding meaningful employment for millions of black men.

Their conclusion is bleak:

The decline in the supply of marriageable mates has dire consequences for the future of black families. If the effects of violent crime, homicide, incarceration, and other aspects of the marginalization of black men rob the next generation of fathers and husbands and the next generation's mothers form families at earlier and earlier ages, then our best estimates suggest that the vast majority of all black families will be female headed by year 2000. These families will be poor and increasingly isolated from the mainstream of American society. Curbing welfare will have no effect in halting this trend. And, unfortunately, not much hope seems to exist for slowing the withdrawal of young black men from productive spheres of the economy.

*William A. Darity, Jr., and Samuel L. Myers, Jr., "Family Structure and the Marginalization of Black Men: Policy Implications," presented at the American Economic Association Meetings, Washington, D.C., January 1995.

The absence of eligible males does explain why there are so many single young black women, but it doesn't explain why these women are having so many children. Some conservatives, most notably Charles Murray,[11] believe that they allow themselves to get pregnant because they want to get on welfare. However, substantial research indicates that although public assistance is the main source of support once these girls give birth, peer pressure, the wish to go through the rite of passage into womanhood, and the desire for something to love are the real motivating factors.[12]

Let's pause here for a minute to catch our breath. We've been talking for a while about the causes of what is mainly black poverty. Keep in mind that most poor people are white. But when we distinguish between short-term poverty and a permanent underclass, we are talking mainly about a problem that has affected blacks, who constitute about 60 percent of the long-term poor.

Poverty Breeds Poverty   Poverty itself generally breeds poverty. Before birth an infant may suffer from poor prenatal care or even acquire an addiction to drugs, particularly crack. During childhood inadequate nutrition and a lack of medical and dental care also take their tolls. An unsafe—or even violent—environment, emotional deprivation, and a broken home also militate against a normal childhood. This situation makes it extremely difficult to do well in school, so the easiest course is to give up.

Inadequate Human Capital   Human capital is defined as the acquired skills of an individual—education, training, and work habits. People who grew up poor usually had poor home learning environments, attended poor schools, dropped out before graduation, acquired little useful work experience, did not develop good work habits, and have poorly developed communication skills. In sum, they are virtually unemployable in today's economy.

The Conservative View versus the Liberal View

Now we're ready for the Super Bowl of poverty theory debate—the conservatives versus the liberals. Representing the conservative view will be Charles Murray, whose book

---

[11]Charles Murray, *Losing Ground: American Social Policy, 1950–1980* (New York: Basic Books, 1984).

[12]P. Cutright, "Illegitimacy and Income Supplements," *Studies in Public Welfare,* paper no. 12, prepared for the use of the Subcommittee on Fiscal Policy of the Joint Economic Committee, Congress of the United States (Washington, DC: Government Printing Office, 1973); C. R. Winegarden, "The Fertility of AFDC Women: An Economic Analysis," *Journal of Economics and Business* 26 (1974), pp. 159–66; William Julius Wilson, *When Work Disappears* (New York: Knopf, 1996), pp. 107–9.

Losing Ground depicts overly generous public assistance programs as perpetuating a dependent underclass. William Julius Wilson is perhaps the most prominent of Murray's liberal critics, so he'll represent their view.[13]

The conservatives and liberals agree on ends but disagree on means.

The conservatives and the liberals agree completely on ends—getting the long-term poor off welfare and into self-supporting employment—but they disagree completely on the appropriate means. Basically, the liberals favor the carrot approach, while the conservatives advocate the stick.

Did the Great Society program help alleviate poverty?

During the Great Depression, President Franklin Roosevelt's New Deal program attempted to lift one-third of all Americans out of poverty. Poverty wasn't rediscovered until the 1960s,[14] and the response was President Lyndon Johnson's Great Society program. Did this program and its extension through the 1970s actually help alleviate poverty? Here's Murray's response:

> In 1968, as Lyndon Johnson left office, 13 percent of Americans were poor, using the official definition. Over the next 12 years, our expenditures on social welfare quadrupled. And, in 1980, the percentage of poor Americans was—13 percent.[15]

Charles Murray, American economist (© 1993 Susan Muniak)

Murray draws this conclusion: By showering so much money on the poor, the government robbed them of their incentive to work. Using the archetypal couple, Harold and Phyllis, he shows how in 1960 Harold would have gone out and gotten a minimum-wage job to support Phyllis and their newborn baby. But 10 years later the couple would be better off receiving public assistance and food stamps, living together without getting married, and having Harold work periodically. Why work steadily at an unpleasant, dead-end job, asks Murray, when you can fall back on welfare, food stamps, unemployment insurance, and other government benefit programs?

All of this sounds perfectly logical. But Murray's logic has been shot full of holes by his critics. We'll start with welfare spending. Although payments did increase from 1968 to 1980, when we adjust them for inflation these payments actually decreased between 1972 and 1980. Wilson really lowers the boom:

> The evidence does not sustain Murray's contentions. First, countries with far more generous social welfare programs than the United States—Germany, Denmark, France, Sweden, and Great Britain—all have sharply lower rates of teenage births and teenage crime.
>
> Second, if welfare benefits figured in the decision to have a baby, more babies would be born in states with relatively high levels of welfare payments. But careful state-by-state comparisons show no evidence that [public assistance] influences childbearing decisions; sex and childbearing among teenagers do not seem to be a product of careful economic analysis.[16]

Another problem with Murray's analysis is that the unemployment rate doubled between 1968 and 1980 yet the poverty rate remained constant. Why? Because of all the social programs that were in place—unemployment insurance, public assistance, food stamps, and Medicaid, among others. Although there was substantial economic growth throughout most of the 1970s, this growth was insufficient to absorb all of the housewives and baby boomers who had entered the labor market. And so the odd man out was the black male.

Murray's use of statistics and the conclusions he derives from them raise even more questions. If, instead of comparing the poverty levels in 1968 (when the Great Society program had pretty much run its course) and 1980 (when the poverty level had been rising due to long-term economic stagnation), he had looked at the period of 1965 to 1974 (when social spending was rising), he would have concluded that the percentage of Americans below the poverty line had been cut by more than 40 percent.

Still more to the point, social scientists warn of the difficulty of measuring the effects of a nonevent. The nonevent in question is the absence of antipoverty programs in the

---

[13]Wilson would probably reject any label, but his views are supported by nearly all liberals.

[14]Interest was sparked by Michael Harrington's book *The Other America* (New York: MacMillan, 1962).

[15]Murray, *Losing Ground,* p. 8.

[16]William Julius Wilson, Introduction to Lisbeth B. Schorr and Daniel Schorr, *Within Our Reach* (New York: Doubleday, 1989), p. xxv.

1960s and 1970s. Had there been no such programs, would more people have been poor—as the liberals (and numerous other observers) maintain—or would there have been even less poverty, as Murray insists?

Murray believes that not only did the social programs of the 1960s and 1970s not work but they actually caused more poverty by destroying the incentive to work. Murray's view is seconded by Mickey Kaus:

> Although welfare might not *cause* the underclass, it *sustains* it. With [welfare] in place, young girls look around them and recognize, perhaps unconsciously, that girls in their neighborhood who have had babies on their own are surviving, however uncomfortably (but who lives comfortably in the ghetto?). Welfare, as the umbilical cord through which the mainstream society sustains the isolated ghetto society, permits the expansion of this single-parent culture.[17]

One conservative approach to welfare dependence is noted in the box "Dealing with Teenage Pregnancies."

Murray blamed the antipoverty programs for increasing poverty, but he really had it backward: These programs prevented a bad situation from getting worse. During a time of rising unemployment, particularly among black males, it was actually a triumph of social policy to keep the poverty rate from rising.

All of this said, Murray's thesis should not be dismissed out of hand. There *are* plenty of people out there who choose welfare as the easy way out. Even more to the point, a culture of poverty *has* developed during the last four decades. Had he said that the largesse of the federal government had induced a sizable minority of the poor to succumb to the joys of living on the dole, he would have had a valid point. Murray simply overstated his case.

In his landmark work *The Truly Disadvantaged,* Wilson begins by describing the black ghettos as they were more than 40 years ago. Sure there was crime, but it was still safe to walk the streets at night. And sure there was joblessness, but nothing like what there has been these last 20 years. Then he goes on to describe other social problems:

> There were single-parent families, but they were a small minority of all black families and tended to be incorporated within extended family networks and to be headed not by unwed

The offer of alms increases the supply of beggars.
—Simon Newcomb

William Julius Wilson, American sociologist (The University of Chicago)

Forty years ago the ghettos were a lot kinder and gentler places to live.

---

[17]Mickey Kaus, "The Work Ethic State," *New Republic,* July 7, 1986, p. 24.

Dealing with Teenage Pregnancies

The birthrate among teenage girls in the United States is higher than that of any other industrial country—twice as high as the British and Canadian rates, more than three times the French rate, and more than four times the rates of the Swedes and Dutch. Among girls under 15, the contrasts are even sharper. For white teenagers alone, our birthrates are higher than those of teenagers in any other Western country.*

Think of a girl growing up in a slum who has had two or three children before she is out of her teens. By the time she's in her 40s she will have 8 or 10 grandchildren, virtually all of whom will be on welfare. Think of what a burden she and her offspring will be to our society.

Poverty is not only perpetuated but also expanded by the more than 200,000 babies born each year to poor, unwed teenage mothers. If the number of these births could be substantially reduced, we would go a long way toward reducing poverty. So the big question is, How do we get these girls to stop having babies?

Every proposal—unrestricted and free abortions, free contraceptives, sex education, and tubal ligations and vasectomies (i.e., sterilization)—is highly controversial. Nevertheless, hundreds of thousands of children are having children every year, and our society has been unable to take any meaningful steps to deal with this growing problem.

In 1992 New Jersey became the first state to deny extra welfare benefits to women who had additional children. Formerly, these families would have received $64 per month upon the birth of each child. Many other states have imposed identical restrictions. It remains to be seen whether these measures will have any appreciable effect. It should be noted that almost three-fourths of the families receiving public assistance have only one or two children.

*Frances Fox Piven, a liberal, notes that these other rich countries provide far more generous assistance to single mothers. See "From Workhouse to Workfare," *New York Times,* August 1, 1996, p. A27.

teenagers and young adult women but by middle-aged women who usually were widowed, separated, or divorced. There were welfare recipients, but only a very small percentage of the families could be said to be welfare-dependent. In short, unlike the present period, inner-city communities prior to 1960 exhibited the features of social organization—including a sense of community, positive neighborhood identification, and explicit norms and sanctions against aberrant behavior.[18]

So what happened? What happened was the civil rights revolution led by Martin Luther King, Jr., in the early 1960s and the subsequent legislation that lowered racial housing and employment barriers. Until then the big-city ghettos had been socioeconomically integrated. But this quickly changed by the late 60s as millions of blacks, who had been penned up in the ghettos, were finally able to move out. They moved into the houses and apartments that had been vacated by the whites who had fled to the suburbs.

How did this outward migration affect those who were left behind?

The outward migration of middle- and working-class blacks had a significant impact on those left behind.

The exodus of middle- and working-class families from many ghetto neighborhoods removes an important "social buffer" that could deflect the full impact of the kind of prolonged and increasing joblessness that plagued inner-city neighborhoods in the 1970s and early 1980s. . . . Even if the truly disadvantaged segments of an inner-city area experience a significant increase in long-term joblessness, the basic institutions in that area (churches, schools, stores, recreational facilities, etc.) would remain viable if much of the base of their support comes from the more economically stable and secure families. Moreover, the very presence of these families during such periods provides mainstream role models that help keep alive the perception that education is meaningful, that steady employment is a viable alternative to welfare, and that family stability is the norm, not the exception.[19]

What's left behind is a neighborhood of impoverished people. Wilson notes that in 1980 only 7 percent of all poor whites lived in areas of extreme poverty, but 32 percent of all poor Hispanics and 39 percent of all poor blacks lived in such areas.[20] These areas became increasingly unsafe and were eventually shunned by those who didn't live in them, further isolating those who remained.

This isolation makes it harder to find a job; few ghetto dwellers are tied into the job network. And because few relatives or neighbors have steady work, tardiness and absenteeism are not considered aberrant behavior. Consequently, those who do find jobs seldom hold them very long.

So the key is jobs—or rather the lack of them:

Lack of jobs is the key.

The black delay in marriage and the lower rate of remarriage, each associated with high percentages of out-of-wedlock births in female-headed households, can be directly tied to the employment status of black males. Indeed, black women, especially young black women, are confronting a shrinking pool of "marriageable" (that is, economically stable) men.[21]

Wilson also notes that the cities have lost far more than 2 million jobs in manufacturing and the wholesale and retail trades since the end of World War II. The loss of these jobs, as well as technological changes creating the need for a more highly trained and educated labor force, has made the job prospects of inner-city blacks and Hispanics bleak indeed.

Still another consequence of widespread joblessness is that most poor children fail to perceive any connection between schooling and future employment. When it comes to school, they think, Why bother? "In such neighborhoods, therefore, teachers become frustrated and do not teach and children do not learn."[22]

The migration of black middle- and working-class families from the ghettos removed the key social constraint against crime. And the erection of huge, highrise, low-income

---

[18]William Julius Wilson, *The Truly Disadvantaged* (Chicago: University of Chicago Press, 1987), p. 3.

[19]Ibid., p. 56.

[20]Ibid., p. 58.

[21]Ibid., p. 145.

[22]Ibid., p. 57.

public housing projects further destroyed the remaining sense of community. Place together a large number of female-headed families with a large number of teenage children (who commit more crime than any other population group) and you've got the recipe for not only high crime rates but almost complete social breakdown.

Wilson's thesis is a direct repudiation of Murray's, which blames public assistance and other social programs for the emergence of the permanent black underclass. Wilson finds no evidence to support that contention. Instead, he blames a whole range of social and economic forces, including past employment discrimination.

Has the government done too much for the poor?

The arguments that Wilson has advanced would not persuade many Americans, who would remain convinced that Murray and his conservative allies are right—that the government has done entirely too much for the poor, especially poor blacks and Hispanics. As Wilson himself has acknowledged, no government program that is perceived as helping only the poor is likely to gain the support of a majority of Americans. At a time when more and more people—white as well as black (see box titled "The Permanent White Underclass")—are faced with bleak economic prospects, the government will have to come up with programs that are geared toward helping tens of millions of working-class Americans, not just the poor.

Solutions

All poor people have one thing in common: They don't have nearly enough money. Or, in the words of the great wit Finley Peter Dunne, "One of the strangest things about life is that the poor, who need the money the most, are the very ones that never have it." So why not simply *give* it to them? In the box titled "The Negative Income Tax," a program that would do just that is described.

The basic liberal solution—in addition to combating employment discrimination—is to provide the poor with better education and training, and with millions of government jobs. The conservatives have placed their faith in providing the poor with jobs mainly in the private sector. But the basic strain running through conservative thought about welfare recipients may be summed up in just three little words: Cut 'em off. A solution with widespread support, workfare, combines the liberal carrot of training and jobs with the conservative stick of cutting off the benefits of those who refuse to seek training or work.

The Conservative Solutions   To end the poor's dependency on government largesse, Charles Murray would simply pull the plug on the life-support system:

> [Scrap] the entire welfare and income-support structure for working-aged persons, including [public assistance], medicaid, food stamps, unemployment insurance, workers' compensation, subsidized housing, disability insurance, and the rest. It would leave the working-aged person with no recourse whatsoever except the job market, family members, friends, and public or private locally funded services.[23]

---

[23]Murray, *Losing Ground,* pp. 227–28.

The Permanent White Underclass

There *is* no permanent white underclass. No? Tell that to the folks unkindly referred to as white trash. Tell that to the unemployed 50-year-old ex-autoworker whose wife works at the 7-Eleven and who makes ends meet with food stamps. Tell it to the high school dropout who hangs around drinking beer with his buddies all day. Or maybe talk to the crack-addicted unwed teenage mother whose alcoholic father used to beat her.

The permanent poverty problem among whites is not nearly as bad as it is among blacks and Hispanics, but it's growing quickly. You may have noticed that most of the street beggars and the homeless all across the United States are white. And there are millions of them. Look at them. They may be our future.

ADVANCED WORK
The Negative Income Tax

The negative income tax is the logical extension of the federal personal income tax. People earning relatively high incomes pay nearly 40 percent of their incomes to the IRS. Those earning somewhat less are taxed at 28 percent, while those earning more moderate amounts are taxed at a 15 percent rate. And millions of low-income families pay nothing, so we can say their tax rate is 0 percent. Now, what about *really* poor families—those below the poverty line? Most of them are on welfare and Medicaid and receive food stamps. The negative income tax would largely or entirely replace these programs by simply sending the poor enough money to live on.

Isn't this just calling welfare by another name? Yes and no. Yes, it's still giving money to the needy, but it has five clear advantages over public assistance, food stamps, and Medicaid.

First, if money is mailed out by the IRS rather than by the hodgepodge of local departments of welfare, perhaps two or three billion dollars a year could be saved in administrative costs. More than 100,000 people are employed by county and municipal welfare departments, not to mention tens of thousands more employed by various state and federal bureaus and agencies whose sole purpose is to oversee the work done by the local departments. If all these people suddenly vanished, no one would miss them, least of all the poor.

A second advantage of the negative income tax over the current public assistance programs is that the poor would be freer to choose how to spend their money. Economists have long recognized that consumers spend their money most efficiently when they are free to buy what they want. Food stamps and Medicaid both place rigid restrictions on the types of food and medical services consumed by the poor. Add to that the administrative cost of these programs, and we may be talking about another two or three billion dollars of waste.

Of course, one may ask how many of the negative income tax dollars sent to the poor would be spent on crack or liquor or gambling—or whether even more children would turn up at school each morning without having had breakfast. On the other hand, how did you spend your last income tax refund? Oops—sorry—I should never have asked.

Third, this system would provide everyone in the United States with a guaranteed annual income. Instead of thousands of widely varying welfare programs, with payments in some states four or five times those in others, every poor person would get the same amount of money.

Finally, the negative income tax would afford the poor a certain measure of dignity, because the assistance would take the form of an income tax refund. This would be no small thing to people who endure the stigma of being on the dole, living in public housing projects, going to public health clinics, and having to pay for their grocery purchases with food stamps. Although some welfare critics have painted pictures of welfare queens and welfare

chiselers living in great opulence, most people dependent on public assistance lead miserable lives, have very low self-esteem, and are barely able to keep the wolf from the door. Anything that provides a modicum of self-respect to welfare recipients would greatly improve the "welfare mess" that has become a permanent part of American life.

To illustrate how the negative income tax would work, the table below illustrates the negative income tax for a family of four. In the first column we have earned income. This could be from wages and salaries, unemployment benefits, child support payments, or any other cash income. The subsidy, or negative income tax, is shown in the second column. When earned income is zero, the family receives $5,000 from the government. In other words, every family would have a guaranteed annual income of $5,000.

Earned Income	+	Subsidy	=	Total Income
–0–		$ 5,000		$ 5,000
$ 2,000		4,000		6,000
4,000		3,000		7,000
6,000		2,000		8,000
8,000		1,000		9,000
10,000		–0–		10,000

As earned income rises, the subsidy declines. For every $2 earned income rises, by how much does the subsidy decline? That's right—it goes down by $1. In effect, every $2 of additional earnings is taxed by $1, which gives us a marginal tax rate of 50 percent.*

If we add the first two columns across, we get total income. A family with an earned income of $6,000 would receive a subsidy of $2,000, giving it a total income of $8,000. As earned income rose, the subsidy would decline until, at an earned income of $10,000, the subsidy would be zero.

Thus, at income levels of less than $10,000, the family receives the negative income tax. At an income of exactly $10,000, there is no negative income tax. And at incomes above $10,000, the family will be paying income tax, albeit not at a 50 percent marginal tax rate.

The negative income tax has several drawbacks. First, despite administrative cost savings, it will cost the Treasury a good deal more than all the federal, state, and local aid to the poor combined. Second, it will still leave most of the nonworking poor well below the poverty line. Alternatively, if a guaranteed minimum income level of, say, $15,000 were set, the program would become prohibitively expensive.

A third problem has to do with work incentives. A 50 percent marginal tax rate may be too great a disincentive to work. But a much lower rate would mean raising the total income ceiling well above $10,000. In that case, families considerably above the poverty line would not be

(continued)

paying personal income taxes and yet they would be receiving negative income tax.

A few halfhearted attempts to enact a negative income tax were made in the 1970s, but Congress never passed the necessary legislation. Today the concept of the negative income tax lives only in economics texts.

Nevertheless, the earned income tax credit, which is written into our Internal Revenue Code, does provide a kind of backdoor negative income tax to low-wage workers. In 1997 a family with two children could receive as much as $3,656 a year from the credit. Families earning more than $29,290 are ineligible.

*The marginal tax rate is found by dividing additional taxes paid by additional taxable income.

A somewhat more humane approach is advocated by Mickey Kaus: Replace all government aid with

> an offer of employment for every American citizen over 18 who wants it, in a useful public job at a wage slightly below the minimum wage. . . . If you showed up, and worked, you would be paid for your work. If you don't show up, you don't get paid. Simple.[24]

Urban enterprise zones

Jack Kemp, who served as housing secretary under President George Bush, has long advocated urban enterprise zones, which provide businesses with substantial tax incentives to set up operations in specially designated poor neighborhoods. Although Kemp had been pushing this proposal for more than 15 years, by the end of the 1990s only a handful of states had set up enterprise zones. After the massive riot in South-Central Los Angeles and smaller riots in Atlanta and other major cities that occurred in response to the Rodney King verdict in 1992,[25] the federal government began to set up additional enterprise zones. However, the Clinton administration did not extend this initiative.

The Liberal Solutions   While the conservatives claim the government has done too much for the poor, the liberals believe much too little has been done. Barbara Ehrenreich and Frances Fox Piven, for example, point out that an increasing number of jobs do not pay enough to subsist on.[26] The solution? Government jobs.

Jobs, jobs, jobs

Government jobs doing what? Jobs rebuilding the nation's crumbling highways and bridges, and staffing hospitals, schools, libraries, and day care centers. Jobs rebuilding dilapidated inner-city housing and cleaning up toxic waste dumps. In the 1930s, the Works Progress Administration (WPA) of the New Deal employed millions of Americans building highways, airports, bridges, parks, and school buildings. Much of this infrastructure is badly in need of repair. In addition we need millions of people to staff day care centers, libraries, and after-school programs. Why not create a labor-intensive, minimum-wage, public service jobs program of last resort for today's low-skilled and jobless workers?[27]

But some liberals acknowledge that even a massive jobs program won't get *all* of the poor off the dole. Remember that nearly all these people are women with young children.

More is needed than providing jobs.

Our country will need to go beyond providing jobs if we are to succeed in greatly reducing poverty. The lives of those in the permanent underclass are filled with hopelessness and despair. The lack of jobs put most of these families into this predicament, but it will take more than jobs, three or four generations later, to get them out of it.

Dr. David Rogers, president of the Robert Wood Johnson Foundation, remarked that "human misery is generally the result of, or accompanied by, a great untidy basketful of intertwined and interconnected circumstances and happenings"[28] that all need attention if

---

[24]Kaus, "The Work Ethic State," p. 30.

[25]You probably recall that the rioting was set off when a jury inexplicably acquitted four Los Angeles police officers after their videotaped beating of Rodney King, a man who was offering no resistance.

[26]Barbara Ehrenreich and Frances Fox Piven, "The Alarm Clock Syndrome," *New Republic,* October 6, 1986, p. 18.

[27]See William Julius Wilson, *When Work Disappears* (New York: Knopf, 1996), pp. 225–38; and Sheldon Danziger and Peter Gottschalk, *America Unequal* (Cambridge, MA: Harvard University Press, 1995), p. 174.

[28]Robert Wood Johnson Foundation, *Annual Report,* 1984.

a problem is to be solved. This point was amplified by Lisbeth and Daniel Schorr in their landmark work *Within Our Reach:*

> The mother who cannot respond appropriately to a child's evolving needs while simultaneously coping with unemployment, an abusive husband or boyfriend, an apartment without hot water, insufficient money for food, and her own memories of past neglect—even a mother who is stressed to the breaking point can be helped by a neighborhood agency that provides day care, counseling, and the support that convinces her that she is not helpless and alone.[29]

America's War on Poverty, launched by President Lyndon Johnson during the mid-1960s and extended under the administration of Richard Nixon through the mid-1970s, did not wipe out poverty, but it did cost the taxpayers tens of billions of dollars. Conservative critics said it was merely throwing money at problems. The liberal solution to poverty at the end of the 20th century continues to call for massive government spending programs, which leaves this approach still vulnerable to the charge that it is just throwing money at problems.

Workfare   Most Americans would never tolerate simply cutting off all government aid, nor would many of us be willing to subsidize a negative income tax. But workfare—a conjunction of work and welfare—is now the law of the land. As a compromise between liberals and conservatives, this concept has widespread support.

Workfare is now the law of the land.

After a 20-year struggle Senator Daniel Patrick Moynihan shepherded the Family Assistance Act of 1988 through Congress. Although it was not nearly as far-reaching as he had hoped to make it, the law does mark a substantial departure from established policy.

These are the law's key provisions:

- The mother or father in a two-parent family is required to provide at least 16 hours a week of community service (i.e., partially work off the family's check).
- Every state is required to enroll at least 20 percent of its welfare recipients in education and training programs.
- Child care is provided to enable women to join the labor force.
- Between 1990 and 1994 the federal government provided the states with $3.3 billion to implement this program.
- States must ensure that all child-support orders provide for immediate wage withholding.
- States must obtain both parents' Social Security numbers before issuing birth certificates and must establish automated systems for tracking down absent parents.

Does workfare work?

Well before the passage of the Family Assistance Act of 1988, workfare had already been a limited success, most notably in Massachusetts, Oklahoma, and California. Each state managed to place some longtime welfare recipients in jobs paying more than the minimum wage. The problem, some critics say, is that workfare merely skims off the cream—those most highly skilled and motivated—while ignoring the hard-core, long-term recipients.

Welfare Reform: The Personal Responsibility and Work Opportunity Act of 1996   This was the most significant piece of welfare legislation since the Social Security Act of 1935. Despite its impressive title, one thing it had in common with the Family Assistance Act of 1988 was that it did not create one new job. These are its main provisions:

- The federal guarantee of cash assistance for poor children is ended.
- The head of every welfare family would have to work within two years or the family would lose benefits.

---

[29]Lisbeth B. Schorr and Daniel Schorr, *Within Our Reach* (New York: Doubleday, 1989), p. 151.

- After receiving welfare for two months adults must find jobs or perform community service.
- Lifetime welfare benefits would be limited to five years. (Hardship exemptions would be available to 20 percent of families.)
- Each state receives a lump sum to run its own welfare and work programs.
- Future legal immigrants barred from welfare assistance.
- $24 billion cut from food stamp program.
- Up to 20 percent of those on public assistance—the ones who are least employable—will be allowed to remain on the rolls beyond the time limit.

For the first time since 1935 the federal government no longer guaranteed support to all of America's children. Critics have pointed out that the law requires some four million mothers, nearly all with little education and poor job skills, to somehow go out and find jobs that will support their families. And most significantly, the law creates no new jobs, pays for no training programs, and makes no provision for additional free or low-cost day care facilities. Within a few years, some critics have said, we will see millions of children out on the streets starving to death.

The real question is whether these families can survive. Those women who do find jobs will probably lose their Medicaid eligibility. And for every $100 they earn, they will lose $24 in food stamps, and if they have a federal housing subsidy, they will face a $30 rent increase. On the other hand, a study by Kathryn Edin and Laura Lein found that virtually all poor single mothers—whether working or receiving public assistance—had to supplement their income with money from relatives, boyfriends, or the absent father of their children.[30] In addition many worked off the books. Are these sources of supplemental income already stretched to their limits, or can they be stretched further?

Although it is still too soon to evaluate this law, almost two million people left the welfare rolls between August 1996, when it was signed by President Clinton, and the spring of 1998. Because of economic expansion, over two million people had already left the rolls between March 1994 and August 1996. So it is reasonable to assume that many people would have left welfare for the workforce even if no welfare reform law had been passed. One might argue, however, that many people left the welfare rolls in anticipation of being forced off. But there's no denying that some four and a half million people have gone off public assistance between March 1994 and December 1997, when the welfare rolls dropped below 10 million for the first time in more than 25 years.

For at least a couple of years prior to the passage of the 1996 welfare reform law, nearly all the states had been trying a variety of carrot and stick measures to move adults from welfare to work. In addition, the unemployment rate fell below 6 percent in September 1994, and has been below 5 percent since July 1997.

The clock is ticking for all but the 20 percent of all welfare recipients who will be permitted to remain on the rolls even after their two-year time limit runs out.[31] Presumably by late 1998 millions of single mothers and their children will be thrown off the rolls, although they will still receive food stamps, Medicaid, and possibly housing assistance. If and when this happens, we will find out if the dire predictions of millions of people starving in the streets will come true.

Conclusion[32]

For more than three decades presidents have railed against welfare dependency and promised to get these people back to work (see box "Presidential Statements on Ending Welfare Dependency"). By early 1995 President Bill Clinton and a majority of Democrats and Republicans in Congress agreed that anyone on welfare should either get a job or

---

[30]Kathyrn Edin and Laura Lein, *Making Ends Meet* (Ithaca, MY: Cornell University Press, 1997).

[31]In many states the limit is less than two years.

[32]Or concluding editorial, depending upon whether or not you agree.

Presidential Statements on Ending Welfare Dependency

Lyndon B. Johnson (1964) This Administration today, here and now, declares unconditional war on poverty.

Jimmy Carter (1977) The welfare system is a disgrace. It is antiwork, antifamily, inequitable in its treatment of the poor, and wasteful. We must make a complete and clean break with the past.

George Bush (1992) We need to say, "Get a job or get off the dole."

Bill Clinton (1991) In a Clinton Administration, we're going to put an end to welfare as we know it.

be cut off within two years. Experts estimate that at least 2 million families have become long-term, repeat users of public assistance.

A 1994 study by the Urban Institute found that 64 percent of the women who join the welfare rolls leave within two years, usually because they find work. But three-quarters return to welfare. Why? Low wages, lack of health insurance, and fights with supervisors are the main reasons given. But these women also cited jealous interference, and even physical assaults, from boyfriends threatened by the prospect of their financial independence.

The average welfare grant for a mother with two children is $4,400, but it would cost about $12,000 to enroll her in a work program, mainly because of the costs of her supervision and day care for her children. A program enrolling 2 million women would cost an extra $15 billion a year.

House Speaker Newt Gingrich has suggested that some children might be better off in orphanages than living on welfare. But welfare is indisputably cheaper. The average family on welfare—a mother with two children—receives benefits of about $15,000 a year in cash, food stamps, Medicaid, housing, and other services. One year in an orphanage costs at least $38,000 per child, and at some orphanages the cost is twice that.

There is virtually complete agreement all across the political spectrum that the only way to break the cycle of poverty and welfare dependency is to put every able-bodied person to work. The federal government needs to do for the poor what it did for the working and middle classes during the Great Depression. We need a full-scale jobs project patterned after the WPA (Works Progress Administration), which provided productive jobs for millions of Americans. We can put people to work rebuilding our crumbling infrastructure of highways, bridges, schools, hospitals, and public transportation networks.

Whether we create more jobs through direct government employment, government contracts with private industry, or tax incentives to firms willing to set up shop in poor neighborhoods, the bottom line is that we need to put at least 8 million Americans back to work. If we can do this, the rest of the pieces will eventually fall into place.

Questions for Further Thought and Discussion

1. What's the difference between the distribution of income and the distribution of wealth? Describe the distribution of income and the distribution of wealth in the United States.

2. Discuss the basic determinants of income distribution.

3. Who are the poor in the United States? A few population groups have very high incidences of poverty. Explain why people in each of these groups tend to be poor.

4. There are several theories of the causes of poverty. Why can't a single theory explain all the poverty in the United States?

5. Compare and contrast the conservative and liberal views of poverty.

WORKBOOK FOR CHAPTER 33

Name _____ Date _____

Multiple-Choice Questions

Circle the letter that corresponds to the best answer.

1. Most social scientists define the poor as being the lowest
   _____ percent of our income recipients.
   a. 10   **b.** 20   **c.** 3.   **d.** 40   **e.** 50

2. When we compare the people who were poor five years
   ago with those who are poor today, we find that they are
   a. an entirely different group of people   **b.** a
   slightly different group of people   **c.** exactly the same
   group of people

3. Which statement is false?
   a. A rich person and a poor person get the same
   satisfaction from eating a Big Mac.   **b.** The utilitarian
   case for equality is to redistribute income from the rich to
   the poor.   **c.** Most Americans would agree to having
   a completely equal distribution of income.   **d.** None
   of these statements is false.

4. An equal distribution of income would
   a. hurt both the work incentive and the incentive to
   save   **b.** hurt neither the work incentive nor the
   incentive to save   **c.** hurt the work incentive but not
   the incentive to save   **d.** hurt the incentive to save but
   not the work incentive

5. Doctors earn more than people in other professions
   basically because
   a. they need to be compensated for all those years they
   spent in school   **b.** they are in short supply relative to
   the demand for their services   **c.** it costs a lot more to
   be a doctor—office expenses, support staff, and
   malpractice insurance—than it does to be in almost any
   other profession   **d.** doctors put in longer hours than
   most other people

6. In most large public and private organizations the most
   important factor in determining pay level seems to be

   a. talent and ability   **b.** education and training
   c. seniority   **d.** connections

7. Employment discrimination
   a. has ceased to exist   **b.** is as strong as ever
   c. continues to persist but is less widespread than it was
   20 years ago

8. Women working full-time earn about _____
   percent of what is earned by their male counterparts.
   a. 25   **b.** 50   **c.** 75   **d.** 100

9. Each of the following is a major source of great wealth
   except
   a. earning large salaries   **b.** starting up new
   companies   **c.** real estate   **d.** inheritance

10. Which is not aimed solely at the poor?
    a. food stamps   **b.** public assistance   **c.** Social
    Security

11. The unemployment rate for blacks is generally _____
    the rate experienced by whites.
    a. about half of   **b.** slightly lower than
    c. about the same as   **d.** slightly higher than
    e. about double

12. Which statement is false?
    a. About three-fourths of the poor are single mothers
    and their children.   **b.** About half of the poor are
    elderly.   **c.** People living in the South are more likely
    to be poor than those living in the rest of the
    country.   **d.** None of these statements is false.

13. About _____ million Americans are homeless.
    a. 2 to 3   **b.** 6 to 8   **c.** 12 to 15   **d.** 20 to 25
    e. 40 to 50

14. Which statement is true?
    a. Most poor people are black.   **b.** Most black
    people are poor.   **c.** People over age 65 have a higher

poverty rate than the overall rate for Americans.

    d.   None of these statements is true.

15. Darity and Myers predict that

    a.   welfare reform will lead to a sharp decline in the number of black families living below the poverty line.

    b.   Cutting welfare benefits will increase the ranks of marriageable young black men.   c.   the underlying cause of poverty is too much government intervention.

    d.   there will be an increasing number of black families headed by females.

16. "The exodus of middle- and working-class families from many ghetto neighborhoods removes an important 'social buffer' " was said by

    a.   Nicholas Lemann   b.   Charles Murray

    c.   Mickey Kaus   d.   William Julius Wilson

17. Which statement is true?

    a.   Virtually none of the homeless have jobs.

    b.   Many of the homeless are mentally ill.   c.   The homeless are concentrated in a few large cities.

    d.   None of these statements is true.

18. About one out of every _____ children is born into poverty.

    a.   two   b.   four   c.   seven   d.   nine

19. Social scientists believe _____ the differential between what women and men earn can be explained by employment discrimination.

    a.   almost all of   b.   about half of   c.   only a small part of

20. Which statement is false?

    a.   Poverty breeds poverty.   b.   Poor people have low human capital.   c.   The liberals and conservatives disagree on how to get people off the welfare rolls and into self-supporting jobs.   d.   None of these statements is false.

21. It would not be reasonable to say that poor people

    a.   are grudgingly tolerated by society's "productive" members   b.   are largely superfluous to our socioeconomic system   c.   are basically self-supporting   d.   are poor for a variety of reasons

22. Workfare was basically

    a.   a program set up to remove at least half the people from the welfare rolls by 2002   b.   a very expensive program that will increase welfare dependency

    c.   a compromise between liberals and conservatives

    d.   a federal jobs program

23. Under a negative income tax program, as the earned incomes of poor people rose, the money they would receive from the government would

    a.   fall   b.   stay the same   c.   rise

24. The superrich get most of their income from

    a.   rent, interest, and profits   b.   wages   c.   illegal transactions   d.   none of the above

25. The richest fifth of all American families receives _____ percent of our total income.

    a.   almost 35   b.   almost 50   c.   more than 60

    d.   more than 75

26. The most important piece of welfare legislation since 1935 was passed in the year

    a.   1974   b.   1980   c.   1988   d.   1993

    e.   1996

27. Under current law no person may receive welfare benefits for

    a.   more than four consecutive years   b.   more than five years over a lifetime   c.   more than five consecutive years   d.   more than ten years over a lifetime

Fill-In Questions

1. There are basically two ways to measure employment discrimination: by _____ and by _____.

2. Traditionally, blacks have earned about _____ percent of what whites have earned.

3. Property income has two original basic sources:

(1) _____

and (2) _____ .

4. The two biggest benefit programs aimed solely at the poor

are _____ and

_____ .

5. About one out of every _____ black

Americans is poor.

6. About _____ percent of all poor

people are black.

7. The basic problem with the absolute concept of poverty is

finding the _____

_____ .

8. The negative income tax has five clear advantages over

welfare, Medicaid, food stamps, and other programs to

aid the poor. List at least three:

(1) _____ ;

(2) _____ ;

and (3) _____ .

9. The superrich get most of their incomes from _____

_____ .

10. The poverty line is set by the _____ .

11. Setting up a _____ program was

the basic provision of the Family Assistance Act of 1988.

12. _____ has long

advocated setting up urban enterprise zones.

Problems

Use Figure 1 to answer questions 1 through 4.

Figure 1

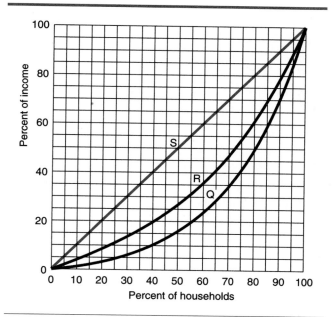

1. How much is the percentage of income received by the lowest quintile on line R?
2. How much is the percentage of income earned by the highest quintile on Lorenz curve Q?
3. How much is the percentage of income received by the highest quintile on line R?
4. How much is the percentage of income received by the middle three quintiles on line S?

Use this information on a hypothetical negative income tax program to answer questions 5 through 7. Every family has a guaranteed annual income of $8,000. For every $2 earned income rises, the subsidy goes down by $1.

5. If the family earned $2,000: a. How much of a subsidy would it receive? b. Calculate the family's total income.

6. If the family earned $5,000: **a.** How much of a subsidy would it receive? **b.** Calculate the family's total income.

7. At what level of earned income would the subsidy be zero?

34 International Trade

Trillions of dollars' worth of business in international trade is conducted every year. Certain trading nations—Japan, the United Kingdom, Hong Kong, Korea, and Taiwan among them—draw their economic lifeblood from foreign trade, while others, such as the United States, France, Germany, Russia, and China, are relatively self-sufficient. Yet even the United States has become increasingly dependent on imported TVs, VCRs, compact cars, oil, and other consumer goods.

How this trade is conducted is the subject of this chapter; how it is financed is the subject of the next. The thread that runs through international trade and finance is specialization and exchange. If all the nations of the world were self-sufficient, there would be no international trade and little need for international finance. But if that were to happen, the world would have a much lower standard of living.

Chapter Objectives

These are the topics we'll cover:

- Specialization and trade.
- Domestic exchange equations.
- Absolute advantage and comparative advantage.
- Tariffs or quotas?
- The arguments for protection.
- The causes of our trade imbalance.
- What we can do to restore our balance of trade.
- Our trade deficits with Japan and China.
- GATT and NAFTA.

More Imports than Exports

America is being flooded with imports, and millions of workers are being thrown out of work. Americans are buying not just foreign-made cameras and VCRs, but also foreign-made steel, textiles, apparel, personal computers, typewriters, and toys. But why worry? After all, the world is now a global village, and we all buy from and sell to each other. Why should we buy something from an American firm when we can get a better deal from a foreign firm?

International trade is really good for everyone. As consumers, we are able to purchase a whole array of goods and services that would not have otherwise been available—at least, not at such low prices. Hence, we can thank international trade for much of our high standard of living. As producers, we are able to sell a great deal of our output abroad, thereby increasing our employment and profits. So far, so good. The only trouble is that during the last two decades we were buying a lot more from foreigners than they were buying from us.

So what do we *do?* Do we throw up protective tariff barriers to keep out lower-priced foreign imports? Or, like the old Avis rent-a-car commercials, do we just try harder? In Part I we'll consider the theory of international trade, why such trade is so wonderful, and why we should not do anything to impede its flow. In Part II we'll take a closer look at the practice of international trade and try to zero in on the causes of our trade imbalance and what we can do to redress it. And then, in Part III, we'll look at why we've been running huge trade deficits with Japan.

Part I: The Theory of International Trade

The trend in our balance of trade is alarming.

Recent years have seen a growing consensus in the United States that we need more protection against the import of foreign goods. As Japanese cars, Korean VCRs, Brazilian steel, Canadian lumber, and Hong Kong textiles have flooded American markets, we have seen an alarming trend in our balance of trade. Indeed, we went from a positive balance of $9 billion in 1975 to a negative balance of $160 billion in 1987.

What caused this dramatic turnaround? What can we do to reverse this trend? Should we restrict this profusion of imports, or should we listen to the reasoning of the economics profession, which is nearly unanimous in arguing for free trade?

Specialization and Trade

Specialization is the basis for international trade.

The basis for international trade is specialization. Different nations specialize in the production of those goods and services for which their resources are best suited. Such an allocation of the world's resources lends itself to the efficient production of goods and services. If you check back with our definition of economics in Chapter 2—the efficient allocation of the scarce means of production toward the satisfaction of human wants—you'll see that international specialization and trade conform to that definition.

If we go from individual specialization and trade to national and international specialization and trade, we'll see that each induces an efficient allocation of resources.

An individual who attempts to be entirely self-sufficient would have to make his or her own nails, grow his or her own food, spin his or her own cloth, sew his or her own clothes, make his or her own tools, ad infinitum. It is much easier and a lot cheaper to work at one particular job or specialty and use one's earnings to buy those nails, food, clothes, and so on.

It pays for nations to specialize, just as it pays for individuals.

What makes sense individually also makes sense internationally. Thus, just as it pays for individuals to specialize and trade, it pays for nations to do so. And that's exactly what we do: On a national basis we specialize and trade. But it would be impossible to do this unless there were a big enough market in which to buy and sell the goods and services we produce. Of course, the United States has long been the world's largest national market.

Adam Smith recognized the advantages of foreign trade more than two centuries ago when he wrote:

> If a foreign country can supply us with a commodity cheaper than we ourselves can make it, better buy it of them with some part of the produce of our own industry, employed in a way in which we have some advantage. The general industry of the country . . . will not thereby be diminished . . . but only left to find out the way in which it can be employed with the greatest advantage.[1]

Suppose there are just two products in the world: photocopy machines and VCRs. The United States as well as every other industrialized country has the necessary resources and technology to produce both. The production possibilities curve in Figure 1A shows a hypothetical range of various combinations of outputs of photocopiers and VCRs.

You may recall from the discussion of the production possibilities curve in Chapter 2 that a couple of assumptions are made: (1) a nation is using all its resources to produce just two products, and (2) it is using the best available technology. You may further recall

---

[1] Adam Smith, *The Wealth of Nations,* vol. 1, ed. Edwin Cannan (London: University Paperbacks by Methuen, 1961), pp. 478–79.

Figure 1   Production Possibilities Curves

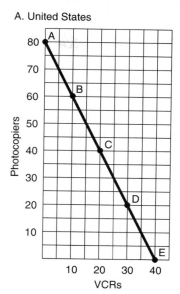

A. United States

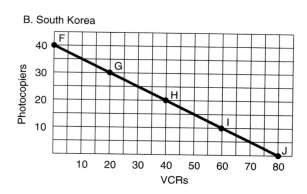

B. South Korea

that if a nation is operating on its production possibilities curve, it is operating at full capacity and full employment.[2]

You may also have noticed that the production possibilities curves in Figure 1 are straight lines rather than the rounded (concave to the origin) curves of Chapter 2. This reflects constant opportunity costs; in Chapter 2 we showed increasing opportunity costs.[3]

Just by glancing at Figure 1 you will see that the United States is better at making photocopiers and South Korea is better at making VCRs. Before we conclude that the United States should specialize in photocopy machines and South Korea in VCRs, let's consider what would happen if each nation produced both products and they didn't trade.

Domestic Exchange Equations

If we examine a few points along the U.S. production possibilities curve (Figure 1A), we will find various combinations of photocopiers and VCRs that we could produce. At point A, with all of the country's resources devoted to photocopier production, the U.S. output is 80 copiers. At point B we make 60 copiers and 10 VCRs. At C it's 40 copiers and 20 VCRs; at D it's 20 copiers and 30 VCRs; and at E we make 40 VCRs.

From this information we can derive this equation:

Domestic exchange equation for the United States

$$2 \text{ photocopiers} = 1 \text{ VCR}$$

In other words, the opportunity cost of producing one more VCR is two photocopiers. Alternatively, the cost of producing two more copiers would be one VCR.

Let's turn now to Figure 1B, which depicts the production possibility curve of South Korea. At point F this country would make 40 photocopy machines. At G production would total 30 photocopiers and 20 VCRs. Thus the opportunity cost of 20 additional VCRs would be 10 copiers. Obviously, then, the South Korean domestic exchange equation is:

Domestic exchange equation for South Korea

$$1 \text{ photocopier} = 2 \text{ VCRs}$$

---

[2]What I am hinting at in a not very subtle way is that if you don't recall these things, it would be a very good idea to reread the production possibility curve section of Chapter 2.

[3]In the real world every industry eventually faces increasing opportunity costs. But here we use constant opportunity costs because straight lines lend themselves much better to our analysis than do curved lines.

A comparison of the American and South Korean domestic exchange equations tells us that the South Koreans are twice as efficient at VCR production as they are at making photocopy machines; Americans have precisely the opposite situation. Again, instinct tells us that it would make economic sense for South Korea to devote all its resources to VCR production and to trade its VCRs for American photocopiers, in whose production we would specialize.

The Terms of Trade

We're finally ready to set up trading between South Korea and the United States. We know that South Korea will trade its VCRs for our photocopiers. What we don't know are the terms of trade. Specifically, how many VCRs will South Korea be willing to trade for each copier? Alternatively, how many copiers will the United States be willing to trade for each VCR?

South Korea will trade its VCRs for our photocopiers, and we will trade our copiers for their VCRs.

To help answer these questions, we will make a couple of simple observations. Let's look at the American domestic exchange equation again:

$$2 \text{ photocopiers} = 1 \text{ VCR}$$

Surely the United States would be unwilling to trade more than two photocopiers for one VCR. But what if South Korea offered *more* than one VCR for two copiers? This would be a better deal for the United States than trying to produce VCRs by itself. Let's see why.

By devoting a fixed amount of resources, the United States could produce either two copiers or one VCR. If it devoted those resources to producing two copiers and trading them for more than one VCR, the United States would be better off than it would have been using those resources to produce just one VCR.

The same logic applies to South Korea, whose domestic exchange equation is

$$2 \text{ VCRs} = 1 \text{ photocopier}$$

Obviously, South Korea would be unwilling to trade two VCRs for anything less than one photocopier. If South Korea could trade two VCRs and get more than one photocopier in exchange, it would be better off concentrating on VCR production and trading some of them for copiers.

Two general observations

We can now make two general observations:

1. No nation will engage in trade with another nation unless it will gain by that trade.
2. The terms of trade will fall somewhere between the domestic exchange equations of the two trading nations.

The first observation is virtually a truism, but the second may require further elaboration. We'll state the two domestic exchange equations sequentially and then derive the terms of trade.

United States:	2 photocopiers = 1 VCR
South Korea:	1 photocopier = 2 VCRs

Looking at these two equations, we ask ourselves whether the United States and South Korea can do business. The United States is willing to trade two photocopiers for more than one VCR; the South Koreans are willing to trade two VCRs for more than one copier. Can a trade be worked out to the satisfaction of both parties? Go ahead and try to work out such an exchange. How many copiers for how many VCRs?

Use trial and error. Would the United States accept 1½ VCRs for 2 copiers? Yes! Would South Korea give up 1½ VCRs for 2 copiers? Yes! That's one possibility for what we call their terms of trade.

Here's another. Would the United States accept 2½ VCRs for 2 copiers? Obviously. Would the South Koreans give up 2½ VCRs for 2 copiers? Yes. There's another possibility. In fact, we could easily demonstrate a large number of possible terms of trade.

What are the terms of trade between the United States and South Korea?

At this point you may well ask, What *are* the terms of trade? The best we can do is say they will definitely be between the two domestic exchange equations. But where?

That depends on the forces of supply and demand in the world market. Let's suppose VCRs are selling for $200 and copiers are also selling for $200. What do you think the terms of trade for these two products will be?

I hope you said one copier for one VCR. Would these terms of trade satisfy both the United States and South Korea? The answer is definitely yes.

Over the last two centuries economists have insisted that when two countries trade, both gain from the trade. Now we'll prove it. Figure 2 includes the production possibilities curves of the United States and South Korea from Figure 1 and shows their trade possibilities curves. The last tell us that these countries are trading copiers for VCRs on a one-for-one basis.

Both countries end up with more copiers and more VCRs.

In effect, through international trade both countries end up with more copiers *and* more VCRs. Suppose the United States had been operating at point C of its production possibilities curve (before discovering the benefits of international trade). At C we produced 40 copiers and 20 VCRs. But if we concentrate our resources on copier production (i.e., produce 80 copiers) and trade some copiers for VCRs, we go to point K of our trade possibilities curve. At K we have 50 copiers and 30 VCRs. What we've done, then, is produce 80 copiers and trade 30 of them for 30 VCRs.

You can easily demonstrate that South Korea experiences similar gains from trade. Start at point H on its production possibilities curve and figure out how much better off South Korea is at point L of its trade possibilities curve. Do your calculations in this space.

South Korea produces 80 VCRs and sells 30 of them to the United States in exchange for 30 copiers. It now has 50 VCRs and 30 copiers. At point H it had only 40 VCRs and 20 copiers. Its gain is 10 VCRs and 10 copiers.

Figure 2   Trade Possibilities Curves: The United States and South Korea

A. United States

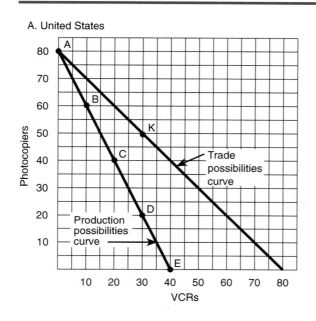

B. South Korea

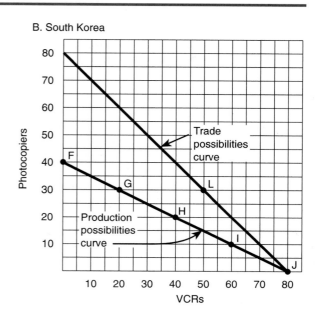

Absolute Advantage and Comparative Advantage

In the trade example we just used, you may have inferred that South Korea makes VCRs more efficiently (that is, at a lower cost per unit) than the United States does and that the United States is more efficient than South Korea in photocopier production.

This may well be the case, but we don't have cost figures. If it *does* cost the United States the same amount to make a copier as it costs South Korea to make a VCR, clearly we're better at making copiers and they're better at making VCRs.

Absolute Advantage   *Absolute advantage is the ability of a country to produce a good or service at a lower cost than its trading partners.* For example, Saudi Arabia, which can produce crude oil at a much lower cost than can either the United States or Japan, exports hundreds of billions of barrels a year to each of these nations.

Let's assume that the United States *does* make copiers for exactly the same production costs as does South Korea for its VCRs. Expressed somewhat differently, it takes the United States an expenditure of the same resources to produce a copier as it does Korea to make a VCR. Suppose it costs South Korea $200 to make a VCR; it follows that it costs the United States $200 to make a copier.

Try this one on for size. If the United States attempts to produce its own VCRs, how much will it cost to make them? If you're not sure, look at Figure 2A. With the same amount of resources, we produce 80 copiers (point A) or 40 VCRs (point E), so it costs us twice as much to make a VCR as a copier (i.e., it costs $400 per VCR).

South Koreans have an absolute advantage at making VCRs.

The bottom line is that Americans can buy South Korean VCRs at half the price that American manufacturers would charge. Thus the South Koreans have an *absolute advantage* in making VCRs. They're better than we are at making VCRs, so we would do well to take advantage of their low prices while we concentrate on making things we're good at making.

In this problem we are particularly good at making copiers. In fact, we are so good that we enjoy an absolute advantage over South Korea. And so, just as we find it advantageous to buy their VCRs, they buy American copiers rather than produce their own.

Americans have an absolute advantage at making copiers.

With absolute advantage it should be obvious that each country sells what it produces most efficiently and buys what it produces least efficiently. What about countries that do not enjoy an absolute advantage in producing anything? If your country can't make anything for less than other countries, what can it sell? In the next section, we'll find out.

Comparative Advantage   In the previous problem South Korea was better at making VCRs than it was at making copiers. How much better? A glance back at Figure 2 shows us that South Korea could turn out twice as many VCRs as copiers, using the same resources.

How about the United States? Using the same resources, the United States could turn out twice as many copiers as VCRs.

We found that there was a basis for trade because both countries stood to gain. Now let's go a step further and ask whether there would be any basis for trade if South Korea were more efficient than the United States at making both VCRs *and* copiers. What do you think? No? Guess again.

Imagine there are only two countries in the world (the United States and South Korea) and they produce only two goods (VCRs and copiers). To keep things simple, we'll assume the only resource used to make these goods is labor. We know it takes South Korea twice as much labor to produce a copier as a VCR.

Suppose it takes 10 hours to make a VCR in South Korea and 20 hours to make a copier. Using the same analysis for the United States, suppose it takes 30 hours to make a copier and 60 to make a VCR. This information is summarized in Table 1.

Table 2 shows how many VCRs and copiers the United States and South Korea can make in 600 hours of labor. Because the United States can make one copier in 30 hours, in 600 hours it can make 20 copiers. Similarly, the United States can make 10 VCRs in 600 hours because it takes 60 hours to make one.

Table 1   **Hours of Labor Required to Produce Copiers and VCRs in the United States and South Korea**

Country	Copiers	VCRs
United States	30 hours	60 hours
South Korea	20	10

Table 2   **Copiers and VCRs Produced by the United States and South Korea Using 600 Hours of Labor**

United States	20 copiers or 10 VCRs
South Korea	30 copiers or 60 VCRs

What if the United States used 300 hours of labor to build copiers and 300 to build VCRs? In that case, we would have 10 copiers and 5 VCRs. Similarly, South Korea would produce 15 copiers and 30 VCRs. Therefore the United States and Korea could turn out a total of 25 copiers and 35 VCRs without trading. This is shown in Table 3.

Are you wondering what all this is leading up to? It's all leading up to Table 4, which will demonstrate how a shift in VCR and copier production will lead to an increased output of both VCRs and copiers. That's right! You're going to try to figure out which country should raise VCR production and which should increase its production of copiers. Use Table 3 as your starting point.

You may have reasoned that because South Korea is relatively efficient at making VCRs, it will raise its VCR output while reducing its output of copiers. The United States will do the opposite. If that's what you figured, you figured right.

In Table 4 the United States shifts all 600 hours of labor into copier production and consequently produces 20 copiers. South Korea, on the other hand, shifts 120 hours of its labor from copiers to VCRs. Thus in 420 hours it turns out 42 VCRs; in 180 hours it makes 9 copiers.

When we add up the total output of copiers and VCRs in Table 4, we find that we have exceeded the outputs in Table 3. There is a gain of 4 copiers (from 25 to 29) and 7 VCRs (from 35 to 42).

Table 3   **Copiers and VCRs Produced by the United States and South Korea Using 600 Hours of Labor***

United States	10 copiers and 5 VCRs
South Korea	15 copiers and 30 VCRs
Total	25 copiers and 35 VCRs

* Each country devotes 300 hours to VCR and 300 hours to copier production.

Table 4   **Copiers and VCRs Produced by the United States and South Korea Using 600 Hours of Labor***

United States	20 copiers and 0 VCRs
South Korea	9 copiers and 42 VCRs
Total	29 copiers and 42 VCRs

*The United States devotes 600 hours to copier production; South Korea devotes 180 hours to copier production and 420 to VCR production.

If South Korea and the United States are the only two countries in the world and copiers and VCRs are their only products, then we are ready to trade. The trade will be American copiers for South Korean VCRs. As we did in the previous problem, let's have a one-for-one exchange.

A one-for-one trade leaves both countries better off than they were before they specialized. Let's say South Korea trades 8 VCRs for 8 copiers. South Korea now has 34 VCRs and 17 copiers, while the United States ends up with 8 VCRs and 12 copiers (see Table 5).

How does this compare with what each country had before specialization? For this comparison, look back at Table 3. South Korea has a net gain of 2 copiers and 4 VCRs, while the United States has 3 more VCRs and 2 more copiers. These gains are summarized in Table 6.

This is what is meant by a trade that helps both parties. We see that even though one nation is better at producing both products, it still pays for each nation to specialize in the production of the product it is relatively good at making and to trade for the product the other is relatively good at making.

Let's go back once again to the concept of opportunity cost. What is the opportunity cost of producing one VCR for the United States? In other words, to raise VCR output by one unit, what do you give up? You give up two copiers. What is the opportunity cost of producing one VCR in South Korea? You guessed it: one-half of one copier.

Now we'll consider the opportunity cost of producing copiers. In the United States it's one-half of one VCR; in South Korea it's two VCRs. In other words, the opportunity cost of producing VCRs is lower in South Korea. How about the opportunity cost of producing copiers? It's lower in the United States.

The law of comparative advantage: Total output is greatest when each product is made by the country that has the lowest opportunity cost.

We're finally ready for the law of comparative advantage, which is what this section is all about. Are you ready? OK, here it comes. *The law of comparative advantage states that total output is greatest when each product is made by the country that has the lowest opportunity cost.* In our example, copiers should be made in the United States and VCRs in South Korea. This is so because the United States has a comparative advantage in copiers while South Korea has one in VCRs. This is true even though South Korea can make both copiers and VCRs at a lower cost than the United States can. (See the box "Absolute Advantage versus Comparative Advantage.")

Just for a change of pace, let's look at a couple of graphs instead of at tables. In Figure 3 we show the production possibilities curves of Canada and Belgium. See if you can answer these four questions: (1) Which country has a comparative advantage in producing telescopes? (2) Which country has a comparative advantage in producing microscopes? (3) Which country has an absolute advantage in producing telescopes? (4) Which country has an absolute advantage in producing microscopes?

Canada has a comparative and an absolute advantage in producing telescopes, while Belgium has a comparative and absolute advantage in producing microscopes.

Obviously Canada should be trading some of its telescopes for some of Belgium's microscopes. Canada would be willing to trade two telescopes for more than one

Table 5   **Copiers and VCRs Owned by the United States and South Korea after United States Trades 8 Copiers for 8 VCRs**

United States	12 (20 − 8) copiers and 8 (0 + 8) VCRs
South Korea	17 (9 + 8) copiers and 34 (42 − 8) VCRs

Table 6   **U.S. and South Korean Gains from Trade**

United States	2 (12 − 10) copiers and 3 (8 − 5) VCRs
South Korea	2 (17 − 15) copiers and 4 (34 − 30) VCRs

Absolute Advantage versus Comparative Advantage

One of the things economists are fond of saying is that you can't compare apples and oranges. Here's a corollary: you can't compare absolute advantage and comparative advantage. The words may not exactly trip off your tongue, but still they ring true. Let's see why.

First, what *is* absolute advantage? It means that one country is better than another at producing some good or service (i.e., it can produce it more cheaply). For example, the United States enjoys an absolute advantage over Japan in building commercial aircraft. But the Japanese enjoy an absolute advantage over the United States in making cameras. They can turn out cameras at a lower cost than we can, while we can build planes at a lower cost than the Japanese can.

So absolute advantage is a comparison of the cost of production in two different countries. What about comparative advantage? Let me quote myself: "The law of comparative advantage states that total output is greatest when each product is made by the country that has the lowest opportunity cost."

So we can say that as long as the relative opportunity costs of producing goods differ among nations, there are potential gains from trade even if one country has an absolute advantage in producing everything. Therefore *absolute* advantage is not necessary for trade to take place, but *comparative* advantage is.

Figure 3   Production Possibilities Curves

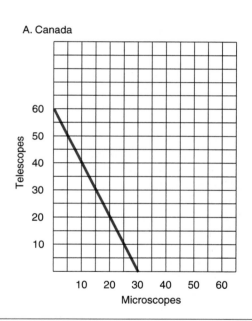

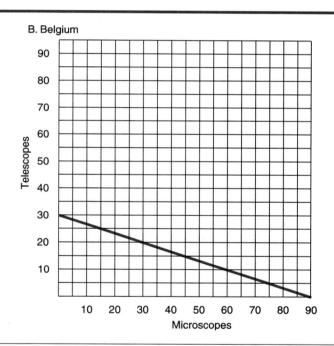

microscope. And Belgium would be willing to trade three microscopes for more than one telescope. So clearly, they will be able to do business. The big question is: What are their terms of trade?

If Belgium and Canada were the only countries in the world, then their terms of trade would be determined by their relative bargaining power. But in today's world of international trade, their terms of trade are determined by the relative prices of microscopes and telescopes in the international market. So let's make it very easy. If telescopes sold for $1,000 and microscopes also sold for $1,000, then what are our terms of trade?

Our terms of trade would be 1:1, or one telescope for one microscope. We're ready, now, to add trade possibilities curves to our production possibilities curves. We've done that in Figure 4.

Now we can prove graphically how much better off a nation is when it trades. The production possibilities curve shows various combinations of two goods that a nation can produce. If it doesn't trade, then it will produce and consume one of these combinations.

Figure 4   Production Possibilities Curves and Trade Possibilities Curves

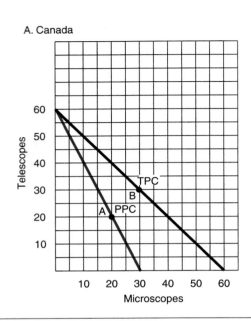

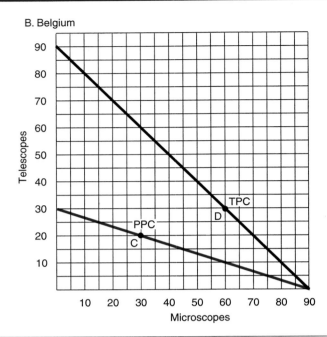

Suppose that Canada does this at point A—20 microscopes and 20 telescopes. But if Canada specialized in making just telescopes, it could make 60 telescopes (and no microscope) and trade away 30 of them to Belgium in exchange for 30 microscopes. This would place Canada at point B of its trade possibilities curve.

Talk about having your cake and eating it too! Specialization and trade enables Canada to go from point A (20 telescopes and 20 microscopes) to point B (30 telescopes and 30 microscopes). So by trading Canada gains 10 telescopes *and* 10 microscopes.

Now let's see how Belgium does by trading 30 of its microscopes for 30 of Canada's telescopes. We'll start at point C on Belgium's production possibilities curve. At that point Belgium is producing and consuming 20 telescopes and 30 microscopes. By specializing in making microscopes, Belgium produces 90, sends 30 of them to Canada in exchange for 30 microscopes, and ends up at point D of its trade possibilities curve. At that point it has 30 telescopes *and* 60 microscopes. Compared to point C, Belgium has 30 more microscopes and 10 more telescopes.

You may still have your doubts about these transactions. How can *both* countries gain by trading? Their gain really comes from specialization. Canada is especially good at making telescopes, while Belgium is better at making microscopes. It's as simple as that.

The Arguments for Protection

As America continues to hemorrhage manufacturing jobs, there is a growing outcry for protection against the flood of foreign imports. But American consumers are virtually addicted to Japanese cars; South Korean VCRs, TVs, and other consumer electronics; and hundreds of other manufactured goods from all over the world. How do we justify taxing or excluding so many things that so many Americans want to buy?

Four main arguments for protection

Four main arguments have been made for protection. Each seems plausible and strikes a responsive chord in the minds of the American public. But under closer examination, all four are essentially pleas by special interest groups for protection against more efficient competitors.

We'll first consider the argument that certain industries, while not as efficient as their foreign competitors, are essential to the defense of the country. The next three arguments, especially the last two, are related. Each uses the premise that industries based in foreign countries are not competing fairly with their American counterparts.

The infant industry argument is addressed to American consumers who would be seduced into buying foreign goods by their temporarily lower prices. The low-wage and the employment arguments are addressed to the workers who would be hurt by foreign competition. Interestingly, the owners of American companies who would stand to gain the most from protection are conspicuously silent about the benefits they would receive from protection.

(1) The National Security Argument   Originally this argument may have been advanced by American watchmakers, who warned the country not to become dependent on Swiss watchmakers because in the event of war Americans would not be able to make the timing devices for explosives without Swiss expertise. Yet during one long, drawn-out war, World War II, the United States was able to develop synthetics, notably rubber, to replace the supplies of raw materials that were cut off. And the Germans were able to convert coal into oil. It would appear, then, that the Swiss watch argument may have been somewhat overstated.

If our country were involved in a limited war, it is conceivable that our oil supplies from the Mideast might be cut off (although no American president would stand by passively while this happened), but we could probably replace these imports by producing more oil ourselves. When Iraqi forces invaded Kuwait in 1990 President George Bush was able to put together an international coalition that quickly defeated Iraq. And if there were a third world war we would certainly not have to worry about a cutoff of needed war material because the war would last only a few minutes.

If the national security argument is applied only to limited or local wars rather than to worldwide wars, it is possible that we do need to maintain certain defense-related industries. A justification that the United States should make its own aircraft, ordnance (bombs and artillery shells), and nuclear submarines might well be valid on a national security basis. But these industries have done extremely well in international markets and are hardly in need of protection.

Does our dependence on foreign suppliers make us vulnerable in time of war?

Nevertheless, as our dependence upon Japanese technology grows, particularly in the area of semiconductor components, the national security argument has gained some validity. The time may come when major defense contractors become dependent on Japanese suppliers for critical components of entire weapons systems. Although that day might not arrive until after the turn of the century, we had better start worrying right now.

Of course, with the disintegration of the Soviet bloc and the end of the 45-year-old cold war, the world seems considerably safer. On the other hand, the continued spread of nuclear arms technology may soon make the national security argument much more relevant.

(2) The Infant Industry Argument   In the late 18th century American manufacturers clamored for protection against "unfair" British competition. British manufacturers were "dumping" their products on our shores. By pricing their goods below cost, the British would drive infant American manufacturers out of business. Once their American competition was out of the way, the British companies would jack up their prices.

Are American industries still infant industries?

Whatever validity this reasoning once had has long since vanished. American manufactured products are no longer produced by infant industries being swamped by foreign giants. About the best that can be said is that some of our infant industries never matured, while others went well beyond the point of maturity and actually attained senility. Perhaps a senile industry argument might be more applicable to such stalwarts as steel, textiles, clothing, and automobiles.

An argument *can* be made that in a world of rapid technological change, a perfectly grown-up industry may become a helpless infant at any time. And hence some temporary protection is needed to allow American producers to catch up with the competition. The auto and steel industries provide excellent cases in point. After receiving some protection from foreign competition during the 1980s, both have made impressive comebacks through the first half of the 1990s.

How can the United States compete against countries that pay "coolie wages"?

(3) The Low-Wage Argument   The reasoning here is best summed up by this question: How can American workers compete with foreigners who are paid "coolie wages"?

Certain goods and services are very labor intensive (i.e., labor constitutes most or nearly all of the resource costs). Clothing manufacturing, domestic work, rice cultivation, most kinds of assembly-line work, and repetitive clerical work are examples. There is no reason for American firms to compete with foreign firms to provide these goods and services. If we look at our national experience over the last 150 years, Americans have always left the least desirable, most labor-intensive, low-paying work to immigrants. The Irish did the domestic work, built the railroads and canals, and did much of the rest of the backbreaking work of the mid-19th century. Then, in sequence, the Germans, Chinese, Italians, Poles, other Eastern Europeans, Jews, Mexicans, and, more recently, Vietnamese and Koreans have been accorded the lowest place on the economic totem pole. And, of course, a special place near the bottom has long been reserved for blacks and Hispanics—not because they were recent immigrants, but simply because they were systematically excluded from the economic mainstream by discrimination.

Those were the rules of the game, and by and large they served us well. Gradually they started to change in the early 1970s as a growing number of relatively cheap foreign imports began to dominate the American market.

What happened? What brought about these changes? First, Japan and West Germany, which had been rebuilding their industrial plants from scratch since World War II, had finally attained parity with the American industrial plant. At the same time their workers were being paid, on the average, less than half the wages of American workers. But in the 1970s the wages of both German and Japanese workers rose very sharply relative to those of American workers (the average German worker earned more than the average American worker by 1980). Throughout the 1970s, however, our trade balances with both these countries continued to deteriorate.

Why are some countries high-wage countries, while others are low-wage countries?

Why *are* certain workers paid higher wage rates than others? Why *are* some countries high-wage countries, while others are low-wage countries? In general, high-wage workers produce more than low-wage workers. The main reason workers in high-wage countries produce more is that they have more capital with which to work than do workers in low-wage countries.

And so labor was paid more in the United States than anywhere else in the world during the three decades following World War II because we had more capital (plant and equipment) per worker than any other country. But as other countries succeeded in rebuilding and adding to their capital, our advantage began to disappear.

A new group of industrializing nations, among them South Korea, Taiwan, Thailand, Indonesia, Singapore, and Brazil, is challenging the older industrial powers. By combining capital with low wage rates, they are able to undersell even Japan (see box "Having the Best of Both Worlds"). Although the wage rates in these emerging industrial nations will rise over time to reflect the growing productivity of their workers, they *do* have a clear competitive edge over higher-wage nations.

The question, then, is how to deal with low-wage competition. The answer is to deal with it the way we always have. We have always imported labor-intensive goods—sugar, handmade rugs, wood carvings, even Chinese back scratchers—because they were cheap. And we always let immigrants do the most backbreaking, low-paying, thankless labor. By specializing in the production of goods and services in which we excel, we can use the proceeds to buy the goods and services produced by people who are forced to work for low wages.

(4) The Employment Argument   Hasn't the flood of imports thrown millions of Americans out of work? The answer is, yes—but.

First we'll deal with the yes. There is no denying that hundreds of thousands of workers in each of the industries with stiff foreign competition—autos, steel, textiles, clothing, consumer electronics, and petroleum—have lost their jobs due to this competition. If we

Having the Best of Both Worlds

The low-wage countries of Asia, Africa, and Latin America have a competitive advantage. So do the high-capital countries of Japan, the United States, Canada, and the European union. Why not combine the best of both worlds—low wages and high capital?

That's just what American multinational corporations have done around the world. Just across the Rio Grande in northern Mexico, thousands of factories churn out everything from cars and refrigerators to water beds and garage-door openers; they then ship most of these goods back into the United States. The factories are called *maquiladoras,* from the Mexican word for handwork. The workers are seldom paid much more than $1 an hour, or maybe a quarter of the U.S. minimum wage of $5.15.* There is great concern that the free trade agreement that President George Bush negotiated with Mexico in 1992 will eventually lead to a flood of low-priced Mexican goods, but that flood began *years* ago.

Japanese multinational corporations have invested heavily in Mexico, Brazil, and the nations of the Pacific Rim. They are farming out the less profitable tasks, such as assembly work, while keeping the most advanced high-value work, such as product design and engineering, in Japan. In Thailand, for instance, Japan has established more than 50 electronics companies since 1985. While Japan's consumer electronics exports to America have been falling, exports of microwave ovens, VCRs, and TVs from Japanese companies in Thailand have soared.

*General Motors pays its American assembly-line workers about $18 an hour plus about another $18 an hour in fringe benefits; it pays its Mexican assembly-line workers $1.50 an hour and almost no fringe benefits.

had restricted our imports of these goods by means of tariffs or quotas, most of these workers would not have lost their jobs.

If we restrict our imports, our exports will decline.

Unfortunately, the governments of our foreign competitors would reciprocate by restricting our exports. Furthermore, a nation pays for its imports by selling its exports.[4] By curbing our imports, we will be depriving other nations of the earnings they need to buy our exports. In sum, if we restrict our imports, our exports will go down as well.

Even such unabashed free traders as President Reagan's Council of Economic Advisors conceded that 25,000 to 30,000 jobs may be lost for each additional billion dollars of imports. They go on to say, "Protection may save jobs in import-competing industries, but this is likely to be matched by the less visible loss of jobs elsewhere in the economy."[5]

The jobs we save in steel, autos, textiles, clothing, consumer electronics, and petroleum will be lost in our traditional export industries—machinery, office equipment, aircraft, chemicals, and agricultural products. From an economic standpoint, this would involve a considerable loss because we would be shifting production from our relatively efficient export industries to our relatively inefficient import industries. Is that any way to run an economy?

What about the workers who lose their jobs because of imports?

Nevertheless, you may ask about the human cost. What happens to the workers who are thrown out of work by foreign competition? Should their employers help them or should the government? And what can be done to help them?

Ideally, these displaced workers should be retrained and possibly relocated to work in our relatively efficient industries. Those who cannot be retrained or cannot move should be given some form of work, if only to keep them off the welfare rolls.

Who should help these displaced workers adjust? In a sense, their employers are responsible because these people were loyal and productive employees for perhaps 20 or 30 years. Unfortunately, the companies that should bear most of the responsibility for helping their employees are hardly in a position to do so. After all, they wouldn't be laying off workers if business were good to begin with.

That leaves the party of last resort: the federal government. What does the federal government do for workers who are displaced by foreign competition? Not very much.

---

[4]The United States, Argentina, Brazil, Mexico, Poland, and several other countries have discovered another way of paying for imports. Together they have borrowed hundreds of billions of dollars a year to finance their spending binge. In the next chapter we'll take a closer look at this borrowing.

[5]*Economic Report of the President,* February 1986, pp. 107–8.

These workers receive extended unemployment benefits, are eligible for job retraining, and may receive some moving expenses. But the bottom line is that a middle-aged worker who loses her $15-an-hour job will probably not find another one that pays close to that, and government programs will not begin to compensate for this loss.

Does this mean we should keep out foreign goods that displace so many workers? No, not at all. We need better government retraining programs to get these people into well-paid, productive jobs.

Tariffs or Quotas

Politically, it is very hard to resist the pleas of millions of Americans who have been losing their jobs because of imports. Furthermore, some powerful industries have been hurt by imports, most notably the auto industry. Surely General Motors, Ford, and Chrysler are not without influence in the halls of Congress.

Although economists are loathe to be in such a situation, suppose it came down to choosing between the two main forms of protection: tariffs and import quotas. Which would be better? Or, more accurately, which is the lesser of two evils? Perhaps an apt analogy for this choice is picking the good guy of the 20th century with Hitler and Stalin as the only nominees.

A tariff is a tax on imports. Throughout most of U.S. history until World War I, the tariff was our main source of federal revenue. The United States, which has lower tariffs than most other countries, charges less than 10 percent of the value of most imports.

A quota is a limit on the import of certain goods. Sometimes this is a legal limit (as in the case of textiles and sugar), and sometimes it is a "voluntary" limit (as was the case with cars from Japan). In the early and mid-1980s the Japanese limited their export of cars to the United States to fewer than 2.5 million a year, but only because of the threat of more stringent legal limits in the form of higher tariffs.

A third interference with free trade is export subsidies. Although several countries, most notably Japan and South Korea, do subsidize their export industries, this is a relatively minor expedient in the United States. The effect of export subsidies, of course, is to make the products cheaper, an effect that many Americans complain gives foreign competitors an "unfair advantage."

Both tariffs and quotas raise the price that consumers in the importing country must pay. However, there are three important differences in the effects of tariffs and quotas.

First, the federal government receives the proceeds of a tariff. Under import quotas there *are* no tax revenues.

Second, a tariff affects all foreign sellers equally, but import quotas are directed against particular sellers on an arbitrary basis. For example, in 1986 various Japanese car manufacturers had widely varying quotas, but the import of South Korean Hyundais was unrestricted.

A third difference involves relative efficiency. Efficient foreign producers will be able to pay a uniform tariff that less efficient producers will not be able to meet. But arbitrary import quotas may allow relatively inefficient foreign producers to send us their goods while keeping out those of their more efficient competitors. This comes down to somewhat higher prices for the American consumer because less efficient producers will charge higher prices than more efficient producers.

Figure 5 illustrates the effects of a tariff. A $50 tariff on cameras raises the price of a camera from $200 to about $245. And it causes the quantity purchased to fall from 2.25 million to 2.1 million.

Incidentally, a tariff, like any other excise tax, causes a decrease in supply—that is, a smaller quantity is supplied at every possible price. The effect of taxes on supply was discussed at length in the chapter on supply in *Economics* and *Microeconomics*.

To summarize, tariffs are better than quotas, but free trade is best. In the long run, the American consumer must pay for trade restrictions in the form of higher prices. (See the box "What Does It Cost to Save Jobs?")

A tariff is a tax on imports.

A quota is a limit on the import of certain goods.

Tariffs are better than quotas, but free trade is best.

Figure 5   A Tariff Lowers Supply

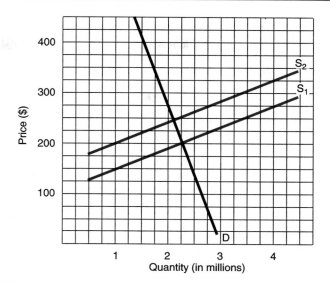

What Does It Cost to Save Jobs?

Almost everything costs something. How much does it cost to save an American job from foreign competition? Sometimes it costs hundreds of thousands of dollars a year.

Various estimates have been made for jobs in different industries. In specialty steel it costs consumers about $1 million a year in the form of higher prices to save one American job. To save a job making television sets in the United States costs more than $400,000 a year. Saving other jobs in steel production, shipping, and chemicals also costs the American consumer hundreds of thousands of dollars.

We need to ask ourselves: Is it worth all this money to save certain jobs? Would American consumers support high tariffs or import quotas if they knew how much it cost to save each job?

Former Secretary of Labor Robert Reich has noted that much of what we produce is purchased by other industries:

For one thing, every time one industry gained protection, another industry, dependent on the first for material or components, found itself squeezed. Once the steel industry successfully warded off cheaper foreign steel, the Big Three American automakers discovered that they had to pay 40 percent more for it than did their global competitors, thus putting the American automakers at a greater competitive disadvantage and, paradoxically, making them all the more needful of protection. The same proved true for American apparel manufacturers when textiles were first protected, and American computer manufacturers when foreign semiconductors were blocked from the American market.*

*Robert Reich, *The Work of Nations* (New York: Knopf, 1991), p. 78.

Conclusion

No nation was ever ruined by trade.
    —Benjamin Franklin

The case for free trade is one of the cornerstones of economics. (See box "Petition of the Candlemakers to Shut out the Sun.") Economics is all about the efficient allocation of scarce resources, so there is no reason why this efficient allocation should not be applied beyond national boundaries. A baseball team that has more pitchers than it knows what to do with but needs a good-hitting shortstop will trade that extra pitcher or two for the shortstop. It will trade with a team that has an extra shortstop but needs more pitching. This trade will help both teams.

International trade helps every country; we all have higher living standards because of it. To the degree that we can remove the tariffs, import quotas, and other impediments to free trade, we will all be better off.

It has been estimated that lower-priced imports kept the rate of inflation one or two points below what it would otherwise have been since the mid-1980s. This is still another important reason for not restricting imports.

Petition of the Candlemakers to Shut out the Sun

The case of protection against "unfair" competition was extended to its absurd conclusion by Frédéric Bastiat, a mid-19th-century French economist who wrote an imagined petition to the Chamber of Deputies. Parts of that petition follow.

> We are suffering from the intolerable competition of a foreign rival, placed, it would seem, in a condition so far superior to ours for the production of light, that he absolutely inundates our national market with it at a price fabulously reduced. The moment he shows himself, our trade leaves us—all consumers apply to him, and a branch of native industry, having countless ramifications, is all at once rendered completely stagnant. This rival . . . is no other than the Sun. What we pray for is, that it may please you to pass a law ordering the shutting up of all windows, skylights, dormerwindows, outside and inside shutters, curtains, blinds, bull's eyes; in a word, of all openings, holes, chinks, clefts, and fissures, by or through which the light of the sun has been in use to enter houses . . .*

*Frédéric Bastiat, *Economic Sophisms* (Edinburgh: Oliver and Boyd, Tweeddale Court, 1873), pp. 49–53.

Frédéric Bastiat, 19th-century French economist. *Courtesy Roger-Viollet.*

Imports pressure American companies to become more efficient. It is obvious, for example, that Toyota, Nissan, Honda, and the other Japanese automakers drove Detroit to make far better cars with far fewer workers than it used to. Indeed, our annual productivity gains of 10 percent would have been inconceivable without the spur of Japanese competition. Our chemical, steel, pharmaceutical, computer, textile, apparel, commercial aircraft, machine tool, paper copier, and semiconductor industries have all been spurred to much higher levels of efficiency by their foreign competitors.

None of this is to deny that there are problems. The millions of workers who are losing their jobs due to foreign competition cannot be expected to cheerfully make personal sacrifices in the interest of the greater national economic well-being. Nor will the American people stand by patiently awaiting the readjustment or deindustrialization of our economy to conform to the new world economic order. In the long run we may all be better off if there is worldwide free trade, but, as John Maynard Keynes once noted, "In the long run we are all dead."

The economics profession nearly unanimously backs free trade.

While the economics profession is nearly unanimous in advocating free trade, there is nearly complete disagreement over what to do about our huge trade deficit. If we do nothing, as fervent free traders advocate, can we count on our trade imbalance to eventually correct itself? Or will foreigners—especially the Japanese—continue to outsell us? These are just two of the questions I'll try to answer in the second part of this chapter.

Part II: The Practice of International Trade

Our balance of trade versus our balance of payments

Let's distinguish between our balance of payments and our balance of trade. Our balance of trade, which we'll be discussing in this section, *compares the dollar value of merchandise and services we buy from foreigners with the dollar value of the merchandise and services they buy from us.* Our balance of trade is the main component of our overall balance of payments, which is *our country's record of all transactions between its residents and the residents of all foreign nations.* We'll get to our balance of payments in the next chapter.

Figure 6 shows how dependent we have become on the global economy. During the 1990s, our merchandise imports and exports have sharply increased as a percentage of goods produced by our economy. Until the mid-1970s, our imports and exports were each less than 10 percent of our domestic goods output.

What do we import and what do we export? We import and export both goods and services. The goods we import include cars, VCRs, TVs, computer chips, cameras, wine, oil, toys, clothing, and steel. Among the goods we export are cotton, wood, wheat, cars, tractors, and airplanes.

We import and export services such as hotel stays, restaurant meals, and car rentals for tourists, movies, TV programming, compact disks, computer software, banking, insurance, legal, and accounting services. In recent years we have been running a large and growing balance of trade in services. In 1997 we exported $102 billion more in services to foreigners than we imported from them.

When foreign tourists fly to the United States on American airlines and spend billions of dollars on hotels, meals, and local transportation, they are contributing to our positive balance of trade in services. So the next time you see Japanese tourists snapping pictures of one of our national monuments, walk up to them and thank them. They might even ask you to pose with them.

Our balance of trade in goods is a completely different story. From the outbreak of World War I until 1970 we maintained a positive trade balance in merchandise. By the late 1970s we were beginning to run substantial deficits. In 1984 the trade deficit broke the $100 billion mark, and rose to $202 billion by 1997.

Figure 7 shows us three things: our trade balance in goods (or merchandise); (2) our trade balance in services; and (3) our overall trade balance, the sum of the balance in goods and services. Since the mid-1970s, we've been running trade deficits in merchandise and trade surpluses in services. But as you can see, the deficits in goods have far outweighed the surpluses in services, leaving us with large and growing overall trade deficits.

We can expect an even larger trade deficit in 1998 as Indonesia, South Korea, and Thailand struggle to set their economies right, overcome their financial crises, and export

Figure 6   Merchandise Imports and Exports as Percentage of Goods Produced in the United States, 1990–97

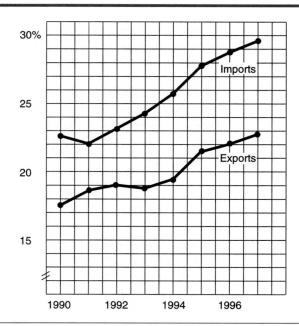

Source: *Economic Report of the President,* 1998; *Survey of Current Business,* February 1998.

Figure 7   U.S. Balance of Trade in Goods and Services, and Overall Balance, 1970–97 (in billions of dollars)

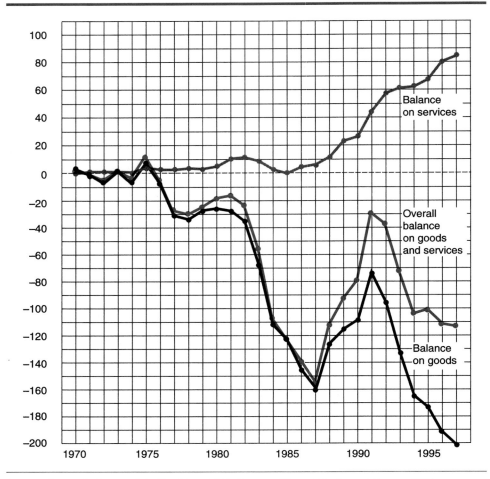

Source: *Economic Report of the President*, 1985; *Survey of Current Business*, February 1998.

their goods at bargain basement prices in an attempt to jump-start their economies. We'll talk about the East Asian financial crisis more extensively in the next chapter.

We cannot keep running trade deficits indefinitely because at some point—perhaps 10 or 15 years from now—the rest of the world will no longer want to keep sending us more goods than we are sending them. Right now, foreigners are quite happy to accept our dollars in payment for the goods we buy. Most of those dollars are sent back to the United States to purchase real estate, corporate stock, and U.S. government securities. In the next chapter we'll consider the question of what will happen if and when foreigners are no longer willing to accept our dollars in payment for their exports. Right now we'll look at the causes of our merchandise trade imbalance and then at what we can do to correct it.

What Are the Causes of Our Merchandise Trade Imbalance?

We have been losing market share both at home and abroad.

Not only have we been losing our national markets to foreign imports, but we have been losing our share of *foreign* markets as well. In 1969 we made 90 percent of our nation's machine tools, 88 percent of our cars, and 82 percent of our TVs. And today? We make half our machine tools; we make just over 60 percent of our cars (not counting the output of the Japanese transplants); and our only remaining TV maker, Zenith, moved its only remaining production facilities to Mexico in 1992.

In the 1970s, 8 of the top 10 makers of semiconductors were American. By the end of the 1980s, 8 of the top 10 were Japanese, 1 was Korean, and 1 American. In the 1970s the world's top 10 banks were all American; today none is. And now there are signs that we may even be losing our lead in commercial aircraft manufacturing and in computer software engineering.

Why have we been losing our markets to foreign competitors, and why have we been running such large trade deficits? Before we turn to the underlying reasons, I want to mention three of the most obvious culprits: our huge bill for imported oil and our very large trade deficits with Japan and China. Together, these three account for nine-tenths of our overall deficit. I've summarized the U.S. problem with oil imports in the box titled "Our Oil Import Bill," but our trade problems with Japan and China will be dealt with separately in Part III of this chapter.[6]

The three biggest culprits are our oil bill and our deficits with Japan and China.

Why did the United States, which has run positive trade balances practically every year since the turn of the century, begin running small negative trade balances in the 1970s and huge ones in the 1980s? There is no single answer to this question, but each of several theories provides part of the answer.

A rising dollar makes our exports more expensive and our imports cheaper.

(1) The Rise of the Dollar   Between 1980 and 1985 the dollar rose by 74 percent against the world's major currencies. How much of this increase was due to our huge budget deficits is still being debated, but the effect of this spectacular increase in the dollar's value on our balance of trade is clear. A rising dollar depresses our exports because it makes our goods more expensive relative to foreign goods. Similarly, it makes imported goods cheaper relative to American products, thus encouraging the consumer to switch.

In 1980 our balance of trade stood at –26 (that is, –$26 billion). By 1985 it stood at –122. There is no way to determine how much of this decline was caused by the rising dollar, but it seems likely that the rising dollar played a large role. The dollar rose substantially in 1995, 1996, and early 1997, especially against the yen. This rise was accompanied by a rise in our merchandise trade deficit from $166 billion in 1994 to $202 billion in 1997. Let's look at several other factors that have also contributed to our huge merchandise trade imbalance.

(2) Our Low Saving Rate   Americans have become notoriously poor savers, averaging less than 5 percent of their disposable personal income since the mid-1980s. The

---

[6]Our deficits with Japan averaged over $50 billion from 1986 through 1997. Sony now makes TVs in Westmoreland County, PA.

Our Oil Import Bill

In 1990, for the first time in our history, we imported half of the oil we consumed. To lend some perspective, in 1973, when the Arab oil embargo produced our first oil-price shock, we imported just 39 percent of our oil. And in 1979, when Iran cut production after the fall of the Shah, we imported 45 percent. Yet both times the price of oil went through the roof and we had gas lines six blocks long.

So are we vulnerable to future shocks? Yes, we are. And over time we'll become even more vulnerable. American domestic production has been declining, as the output from fields in Alaska's North Slope declines and many other fields mature. In 1997 our bill for oil imports was $72 billion, and it probably will be rising during the rest of the decade.

Most Americans believe gasoline taxes are too high and only grudgingly went along with the 12-cent-a-gallon increase that was part of the deficit reduction package passed by Congress in October 1990. But American gasoline taxes (federal plus state and local), at 41 cents a gallon, on average, are the lowest in any major industrial country. The French and the Italians pay over $3 a gallon in tax, the Germans, $2.75.

Would Americans be willing to pay an extra two or three bucks a gallon? Never! Even if it meant we'd be able to cut our foreign energy dependence in half and maybe even cut our trade deficit in half as well? Still no! Hey, there are priorities around here, buddy. And nobody messes with American priorities. Americans like to drive, and they like their gasoline to be cheap—no matter who has to pay for it in the long run.

Japanese have been putting away more than 20 percent a year. The Germans, the South Koreans, the Taiwanese, and other people experiencing a rapid rate of economic growth—and, not coincidentally, a positive balance of trade—have all had very high savings rates.

A penny saved is a penny earned.
—Benjamin Franklin

If you don't save, you can't invest, and if you don't invest, you don't grow. It's as simple as that. Compounding our difficulties is that our federal budget deficits have been sopping up more than half our savings, which leaves the private sector with just one option: borrow from foreigners. This strategy has worked up to a point. While tens of billions of dollars in investment funds have been flowing in from abroad each year, they have come here only because of our relatively high interest rates.

We are consuming more than we are producing, borrowing more than we are saving, and spending more than we are earning.
—Murray Weidenbaum

(3) The High Cost of Capital   Because the Japanese, with a population half the size of ours, generate the largest pool of savings in the world, Japan's cost of capital measured by real interest rates (i.e., nominal interest rates less the rate of inflation) has been just one-third that in the United States over the last two decades. One of the few things on which all economists agree is the central role of interest rates in determining the level of investment.

Mainly because of our low saving rate and partially because of our huge budget deficits, high real interest rates have discouraged investment in plant and equipment as well as in technological innovation. Indeed, these high real interest rates have attracted investment funds from the Japanese and other foreign sources. This inflow has only partially offset the lack of investment funds generated by American savers. Consequently investment and, ultimately, American productivity have been lagging well below the rates of the three decades following World War II.

(4) Defense Spending   The defense expenditures of the United States have dwarfed those of every other industrial power, except, incidentally, those of the former Soviet Union. One-third of our research-and-development (R&D) spending goes toward defense, and until 1990 about half of our engineers and scientists were involved in military projects.

Can we afford to devote such a large proportion of our resources to defense, especially when the countries we are presumably defending spend so little? While 4 percent of our GDP goes toward defense, the Japanese spend barely 1 percent of theirs. Nearly all of their R&D dollars and engineering and scientific talent go into the production of goods and services, which have been displacing those made in America. One can only ask whether we have our priorities straight, and whether, in a time of diminishing military tension, we should be diverting our dollars to defense from areas where they could be used more productively.

Our schools are turning out students who cannot read or write.

(5) Education   The American educational system, once second to none, is now second to practically everyone's. The illiterate high school graduate is no longer the rare exception, and about one-third of all college freshmen need remedial work in the three Rs—reading, writing, and arithmetic. Nearly every college—even in the Ivy League schools—has special classes for students unprepared to do college work. In test after test, Americans rank at or near the bottom of the industrial countries.

And that's the good news. The worst is yet to come. "Twenty million to 30 million adults cannot read, write, or calculate well enough to function effectively at work," according to a series on education in the *New York Times*.[7] And recent research suggests "American schools are graduating students who lack even the skills needed to fill existing assembly-line jobs, let alone the sophisticated new jobs that increasingly dominate the economy."[8]

---

[7]Joseph Berger, "Companies Step In Where the Schools Fail," *New York Times,* September 26, 1989, p. A1.

[8]Edward B. Fiske, "Impending U.S. Jobs 'Disaster': Work Force Unqualified to Work," *New York Times,* September 25, 1989, p. A1.

Half of our high school math and science teachers are unqualified to teach those subjects. Richard Lamm, former governor of Colorado, put together some interesting numbers pinpointing what we're up against:

> An average eighth grader in Japan knows more mathematics than a graduate of an M.B.A. program in the United States. An average 17-year-old American knows half as much math as an average Swedish 17-year-old. Homework in Japan is about two hours a day, compared to approximately half an hour in the United States. Japanese students go to school 240 days a year, while U.S. students go 180 days a year. By the time a Japanese student graduates from high school, he or she has had as much classroom time as an American college graduate.[9]

More capital, higher productivity, and higher wages.

(6) The Role of Multinationals

Before the 1960s the vast low-wage workforces of the world's poorer nations were no threat to the workers in the high-wage economies like the United States. Our workers were many times more productive than those in the poorer nations because they had so much more capital to work with.

All of this began to change in the 1960s as multinational corporations began to move their manufacturing operations offshore to take advantage of this low-wage labor pool. By providing these workers with sufficient plant and equipment, the multinationals were able to increase their productivity to the level of American assembly-line workers.

Much of the manufacturing of apparel, shoes, toys, and consumer electronics, which had been done largely by the "four tigers," has been shifting to China, India, Indonesia, the Philippines, Thailand, and other low-wage countries. Capital has long been much more mobile than labor, and that capital has been flowing very rapidly to the low-wage nations.

The hollow corporation

The term *hollow corporation* has gained currency in the last decade as more and more companies put their names on imported goods. These companies' sole function is to sell such goods as the Dodge Colt or the Panasonic typewriter, both of which are made in Japan. Yet our import business is not dominated by firms that market goods for the Japanese and other foreign producers, but rather by our own multinational corporations that have shifted most of their production overseas. Joel Kurtzman describes their operations:

> These multinationals have transformed themselves from producers of goods to importers and marketers of goods made overseas by their foreign divisions and affiliates. Because so many of our imports come to us in the form of trade between the different divisions of American multinationals, the balance-of-payments deficit has become structurally integrated into our economy.[10]

Keep in mind, then, that these are American firms that are marketing foreign-made products in this country without incurring the wrath that has become known as Japan bashing and, more recently, Korea bashing and China bashing. Over the last three and a half decades, while the share of the world's manufacturing held by the United States has declined by more than 40 percent, the share held by multinationals has remained a steady 18 percent.[11]

Americans are in for the short run; the Japanese are in for the long run.

(7) A Longer Time Horizon

U.S. corporations clearly have a much shorter time horizon than do their Japanese competitors. American management's fanatical concern with the bottom line, with the quarterly profit figure, has been exacerbated in the last decade by fears of stockholder unrest and hostile takeovers. Most stockholders are in for the short run—maybe a few months, possibly a year or two—but long-term investments in R&D, in new plant and equipment, and in product development do not pay off for at least a few years.

---

[9]Richard D. Lamm, "Crisis: The Uncompetitive Society," in *Global Competitiveness: Getting the U.S. Back on Track*, ed. Martin K. Starr (New York: W. W. Norton, 1988), p. 25. Our failing educational system was discussed at greater length in Chapter 16 of *Economics* and *Macroeconomics*.

[10]Joel Kurtzman, *The Decline and Crash of the American Economy* (New York: W. W. Norton, 1988), p. 131.

[11]Ibid., pp. 133–34.

Michael Dertouzos, Richard Lester, and Robert Solow contrast this approach with that of the Japanese competition:

> Japanese firms have been willing to take on high levels of debt in order to invest in new production capacity and marketing infrastructure ahead of the growth in demand; in effect, they have been investing to grow demand. Thereafter they have priced their products aggressively and often far below costs in the early phases of a developing market. . . . Costs decline more rapidly as the manufacturer learns how to build the product more efficiently and as the growing production volume offers a larger base of units over which to spread fixed costs.[12]

Obviously, no one theory explains the success of the Japanese or our own relative decline. It follows that there is no single remedy for our huge trade imbalance. We do know something is seriously wrong with the way we're running our economy, and unless we can figure out what it is and fix it, our nation will fall to the second or third rank of economic powers.

What Can We Do?

Devalue the dollar.

One thing that should have helped reduce our negative merchandise trade balance was a fall in the value of the dollar relative to other currencies. Indeed, the dollar did fall back to its 1980 level by 1989 and continued to sink. Our negative trade balance, which had peaked at -160 in 1987, fell below -100 in the early 1990s.

Why didn't it fall all the way back to its 1980 level of -26? One explanation is that Japan, the "four tigers" (Taiwan, Korea, Singapore, and Hong Kong), and some of our other trading partners whose sales to us expanded between 1980 and 1985 refused to give up those gains. As the dollar declined, so did their prices. What they did, then, was defend their markets by cutting their profit margins, even taking occasional losses.

The J-curve effect

Another explanation is provided by the J-curve effect (sorry, no pictures). When the dollar is devalued, the trade deficit actually continues to rise for another year or year and a half—which is exactly what happened from 1985 through 1987, when our deficit went from -122 to -145 to -160.

At the onset of devaluation, why do things get worse before they begin to get better? The first thing to happen is that our exports become cheaper to foreigners (i.e., our exports' prices decline), while imports to the United States become more expensive (their prices rise). Hence foreigners are getting higher prices for the goods they send us, but we're getting lower prices for our exports. Do you follow so far?

But if the prices of our exports decline, won't foreigners buy more? Yes—only not right away. It takes time for advertisements to wean them away from domestic products. And don't forget that our foreign competitors are reluctant to give up market share, especially on their home turf.

The same goes for imports. It takes a year or two to get Americans to switch from foreign imports to American goods, and again, our foreign rivals will cut prices to hold their market share.

Clearly the 1980–85 dollar rise does not fully explain the huge jump in our trade deficit; if it did, then the 1985–94 devaluation should have returned the deficit to its 1980 level. All the other causes outlined in the previous section have also played roles. So, as we cast about for remedies, let's see what else we can fix.

We need to put a lid on consumption.

The core of our trade problem is that the so-called "me generation" of the 1980s went on a spending spree that has continued through the 1990s and that it still hasn't paid for. We need to put a lid on consumption; then, we hope, all the other pieces will fall into place.

Various measures could be taken to curb consumption and, concurrently, raise saving. A national sales tax or, alternatively, a value-added tax (like those in several

---

[12]Michael L. Dertouzos, Richard K. Lester, and Robert M. Solow, *Made in America: Regaining the Productive Edge* (Cambridge, MA: MIT Press, 1989), pp. 55–56.

European countries) would not only hold down consumption but would also raise tens of billions of dollars in federal revenue. A value-added tax, unlike a sales tax, is collected at each stage of the production process.

We need to save more.

Economists have always believed in providing incentives to get people to "do the right thing" (which was even made into a film by Spike Lee). One thing we want people to do is save more, and the way to get them to do that is to make at least some of their savings tax free.

Bring back the tax-free IRA.

Individual retirement accounts (IRAs) were tax free from 1982 to 1986, when the personal savings rate averaged 7.2 percent. But from 1987, when the tax exemption was removed, through 1994, the savings rate averaged just 4.5 percent. It would appear that by bringing back the tax-free IRA and lowering taxes on, say, the first $1,000 of interest earned on bank accounts and other forms of savings, we could push up our savings rate well above 5 percent. One might note that the Japanese have built powerful savings incentives into their tax code.

Defense spending should fall.

One of the few bright spots in recent years has been our declining defense spending. What we must guard against, however, are the blandishments of the defense establishment to "not let down our guard" (i.e., keep spending money on new weaponry). But if the former Soviet Union continues cutting defense spending, the pressure to cut our own spending may prove irresistible.

Educating our future labor force is the key.

Turning around our failing education system may be the key to turning around our economy. One part of the problem, which may be a little too sensitive to discuss (but I'll discuss it anyway), is that our best and our brightest do not become teachers. In fact, those majoring in education have consistently scored among the lowest of all students taking the Scholastic Aptitude Test (SAT). Who scored the lowest? Those with the lowest scores were physical education majors. (But then, how do you *teach* gym?)

My own plan is to pay teachers enough to attract bright and highly motivated people, allow the schools to expel "students" who are consistently disruptive, and abolish all college departments of education. The latter not only offer courses of almost no intellectual substance, but they perpetuate standards that rarely soar to even a level of mediocrity. I would also get rid of any teacher who could not read at an eighth-grade level. I might extend the school day and the school year, make two hours of homework a night mandatory, and abolish automatic promotion. If this program were followed—and I have no illusions that it ever will be—our schools would no longer graduate illiterates and semiliterates, who are completely unqualified for today's workforce.

We need to take a longer view.

Getting American corporations to take the longer view, well beyond the quarterly profit figure, would require major changes in the way we do business. Prohibiting hostile takeovers and enacting changes in the capital gains law (perhaps offering tax write-offs on profits from investments held at least five years) would be good for starters. But such measures are just not in the cards, so corporate America will keep thinking short term.

Protectionist legislation is a real possibility.

Protectionist legislation is a real possibility if our foreign competitors are indeed dumping goods below cost on our shores. Although the economics profession and many people in government remain firmly opposed to any interference with free trade, the pressure for such measures will continue to grow if our trade deficit does not shrink to an acceptable level.

Part III: Our Trade Deficit with Japan and China

For most of the 1980s and 1990s, Japan was not only our fiercest trade competitor, but was running huge trade surpluses with us. In the long run, however, our largest trade deficits may be with China, whose surplus in 1997 was virtually equal to that of Japan. (See Figure 8.)

But don't believe everything you see in Figure 8. Our deficits with Japan are substantially underestimated because Japanese multinational corporations have shifted much of their production offshore to Thailand, Indonesia, Malaysia, Singapore, China, Korea, and Mexico. For instance, that Sony TV that you just bought may well be one of the 14

Figure 8   U.S. Merchandise Trade Deficit with Japan and China,* 1990–97

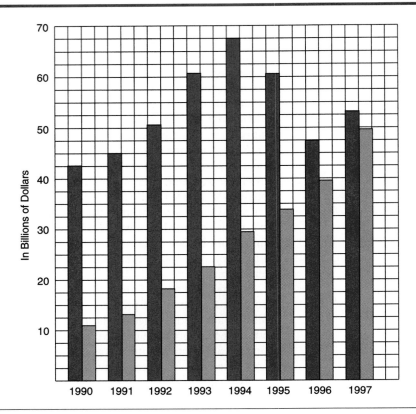

Source: *Economic Report of the President,* 1998; *Survey of Current Business,* July 1997; February, 1998.
*Japan is represented by the darker bars and China by the lighter bars.

million sets turned out just across the Rio Grande in Tijuana. (See again box "Having the Best of Both Worlds" earlier in this chapter.)

There are two factors that compromise our official trade deficits with China. Until July 1, 1997, when China repossessed Hong Kong, a substantial part of the goods shipped here were made in China. If these goods were counted as imports from China—and not from Hong Kong—our trade deficits with China would have been a great deal higher.

On the other hand, our exports to China are also underestimated. Chinese officials themselves admit that high tariffs have led to rampant smuggling of cigarettes and other consumer goods. In 1997 out of about 100 billion American and other foreign-brand cigarettes that were sold in China, not a single one was legally imported.

Many goods once made elsewhere in Asia—in Japan, Taiwan, Singapore, South Korea—are now produced in foreign-owned factories that have been moved to China. Our growing deficit with China is largely offset by declining deficits with other Asian nations.

The Ongoing Trade Negotiations with Japan

We negotiate concessions from Japan, but our deficit does not fall.

Year after year we are running trade deficits with Japan averaging more than $50 billion. And year after year we negotiate with them to open up their markets to our exports. You may even remember President George Bush's ill-fated trip to Japan a few years ago, the main purpose of which was to convince the Japanese to increase their imports of American autos and auto parts by $10 billion a year. And then, in 1993, President Bill Clinton went to Tokyo to secure additional assurances that Japan's markets would become more open to foreign imports. Well, the negotiations were billed as great successes, but we're still waiting for the results.

In May 1995, after months of unsuccessful negotiations with the Japanese, President Clinton slapped a 100 percent tariff on the 13 top models of Japanese cars. The tariff would be rescinded if an accord were reached by the end of June to open the Japanese market for American cars and car parts.

Just hours before the deadline, Japanese and American negotiators struck a deal. In exchange for President Clinton's rescinding the tariff, the Japanese agreed to purchase more foreign auto parts, encourage dealers to sell more foreign cars, open the Japanese market for repair parts, and Toyota, Honda, and Mitsubishi agreed to build more cars in the United States. The bad news was that the Japanese did not agree to specific numerical goals. The good news was that the United States and Japan averted a possible trade war.

To lend some perspective to our trade negotiations with the Japanese, we have pried concession after concession from them for years, but our deficit rose for the first four years of the 1990s, reaching a record $67 billion in 1994 (see Figure 8). Even more to the point, they continued to pick off our high-tech industries one by one and, with them, millions of high-paying jobs. Although we saw some improvement in 1995 and 1996, in 1997 our deficit was still over $50 billion.

Japanese Trading Practices

Are the Japanese dumping?

Are the Japanese dumping, or selling their products below cost, to drive American producers out of business? Because they are selling many of their products below cost, it is reasonable to ask whether they are unfairly—and, according to our laws, illegally—competing by dumping their products on our shores. Clearly, the *effect* of selling below cost is to drive out American competitors. But what is their *motivation?* Perhaps Japanese firms' motivation in charging so little is to minimize their losses in the short run by producing and selling a large volume of output, and spreading their fixed costs to take advantages of economies of scale. This, of course, is exactly what every economist would tell a firm to do.

But when we look at the other side of the coin, at how Japanese society pulls together to keep foreign manufacturers out of the Japanese market, at how the Japanese consumer is willing to pay double what the American consumer pays for the same Japanese products, it is fair to say that driving American competitors out of business provides a great deal of the motivation for Japanese manufacturers to sell us their goods below cost—at least in the short run. (The question of whether Japanese markets are closed to imports is discussed in the accompanying box.)

The fundamental difference between ourselves and the Japanese is product quality.

Other theories attempting to explain the success of Japanese manufacturers attribute much of it to the just-in-time manufacturing system, to the lifetime employment practices of large corporations, to a strong work ethic, to weak labor unions, and to worker involvement in decision making. All of these certainly describe important differences between the Japanese workplace and ours, and they also likely account for much of the Japanese success. However, A. Blanton Godfrey and Peter Kolesar believe the fundamental difference between ourselves and the Japanese is product quality: "The failure of American competitiveness is largely a failure to manage for quality, while the key to the Japanese success is an almost compulsive and fanatical attention to managing for quality."[13]

The same conclusion was reached by the MIT Commission on Industrial Productivity: "Mass production was the driving force behind American postwar prosperity, but it is often no longer an appropriate model for managers and workers in the changed circumstances of today."[14] The commission uses the Japanese automobile industry as an example of how product quality can be raised:

> The Japanese have succeeded by providing different products for each segment of the market. To do so efficiently and profitably, they have developed technologies, product development

[13]A. Blanton Godfrey and Peter J. Kolesar, "Role of Quality in Achieving World-Class Competitiveness," in *Global Competitiveness: Getting the U.S. Back on Track,* ed. Martin K. Starr (New York: W. W. Norton, 1988), p. 216.

[14]Dertouzos et al., *Made in America,* p. 46.

Are Japanese Markets Closed to Imports?

The Japanese have always considered themselves different, and the rest of us are forced to agree with them. An insular society shut off from the rest of the world until the mid-19th century, the Japanese are an ethnically and culturally homogeneous nation. They have no immigrant population to speak of, and more than almost any other people, the Japanese are just plain clannish. Is it any wonder, then, that they prefer doing business among themselves rather than with outsiders?

American exporters have long complained that Japanese markets were largely closed to them. The record shows that our exports to Japan have been inordinately low, even in fields where we are selling a superior product at prices well below those charged by Japanese producers. And yet Japan's tariff barriers are by and large no higher than our own.

One trade barrier is the *keiretsu* (economic group), which is described by Clyde Prestowitz as an alliance "linked by cross-shareholdings, common banking affiliations, and the use of the same trading company to procure raw materials and to distribute products."* This makes for quite a tidy arrangement. Although group members don't always deal with each other, they usually do. After all, what is a *keiretsu* for?

Less formal but very powerful obstacles are placed in the way of imports. These are described by Murray Sayle, an Australian journalist who lived in Japan for several years:

> The Japanese exporter to the United States needs only to offer a better or cheaper product, and he's honorably in. But the would-be exporter to Japan finds the marketplace already seized up solid with a dense network of "friendships," of layer upon layer of middlemen who have been doing business together for years, and who are, of course, all Japanese.†

The relationship between the large manufacturer and the supplier is an especially close one. In fact, the vaunted just-in-time inventory control system is based on it. As Prestowitz notes, "When the whole production system depends on precisely timed delivery of zero-defect products, it is absolutely critical to have a high degree of confidence in the supplier. Such confidence requires working closely with him and even assisting him in parts design and the manufacturing process."‡ The bond between these firms is not easily severed by outsiders, especially foreign outsiders.

*Clyde V. Prestowitz, Jr., *Trading Places* (New York: Basic Books, 1988), p. 157.
†Murray Sayle, "The Japanese Exporter: Japan Victorious," *New York Review of Books,* March 28, 1985.
‡Prestowitz, *Trading Places,* p. 165.

---

methods, and patterns of workplace organization that allow them to reduce the volume of production and increase the speed with which new products are brought to market.[15]

The Japanese compete on the basis of price and quality.

What it all comes down to is that the Japanese compete not just on the basis of price but on the basis of product quality. They have taken our system of mass production one step further, turning out a wide range of customized variations, while we continue to concentrate on single standardized products.

The Japanese have also been extremely adept at borrowing and adapting more advanced technology that was developed abroad. Between 1950 and 1980 Japan spent nearly $10 billion in licensing fees to American and European companies, in return receiving technology that had cost between $500 billion and $1 trillion to develop.[16]

Table 7 tells almost as much about our trade relationship with Japan as does Figure 8. What do we sell the Japanese? Agricultural products. And what do we buy from them? Manufactured products. When a nation supplies another nation with raw materials and gets back, in return, manufactured goods, it is a colonial relationship. You don't have to be a rocket scientist to figure out which nation is the colony.

Do the Japanese want to play the game of international trade on a level playing field? Are they fair and honorable competitors? Wrong questions! That's right! We should have been asking two entirely different questions: What's your game? And, Can anybody play? (If these questions sound familiar, I stole them from the lyrics of an old popular song, "Carrie Anne.")

Japan picks winners, and then makes sure they win.

Their game is to pick industries that look like long-run winners for Japan—cars, consumer electronics, computer chips, cameras—and to give them backing not just from the

---

[15]Ibid., p. 48.

[16]See Robert Reich, "The Quiet Path to Technological Preeminence," *Scientific American,* October 1989, p. 43.

**Table 7   Our Six Leading Exports to
and Six Leading Imports from Japan, 1996**

What We Sell the Japanese

1.	Corn seed
2.	Soybeans
3.	Coal
4.	Wood
5.	Cotton
6.	Wheat

What the Japanese Sell Us

1.	Automobiles
2.	Tape recorders
3.	Trucks
4.	Office machines
5.	Parts for office machines
6.	Computer chips

Source: *1998 Information Please Business Almanac and Sourcebook.*

government but from fellow industrialists, from employees, consumers, and basically from the entire society. The government provides R&D funding, helps keep out imports, and holds down the interest rate, so the new industry has virtually unlimited low-interest funding. Competitors cooperate rather than compete. The Japanese consumer automatically prefers indigenous products—no matter how costly or qualitatively inferior—to foreign imports. And as a whole the Japanese people prefer doing business among themselves rather than with foreigners. In the box titled "How the Japanese Drove American TV Manufacturers Out of Business," I discuss in more detail the Japanese game of international trade and how it is played.

The Japanese five-step program to attain market dominance.

The Japanese method of attaining market dominance in industries targeted by the Ministry of International Trade and Industry (MITI) is a carefully formulated five-step operation:

1. Keep foreign producers out of the Japanese market.
2. License technology from American producers who find they cannot sell in Japan no matter how low their prices are.
3. Obtain investment capital and maintain an orderly market for targeted domestic producers.
4. Sell in the American and other foreign markets below cost (and sometimes at half the price charged in Japan).
5. Drive American and other foreign competitors out of business and attain a dominant market share.

That's their game. And can anybody play? Well, obviously, no one else can play in Japan. But couldn't we play this game ourselves? Again, the answer is no.

To play this game, you need a very cohesive society, even a homogeneous one. And like Ivory Soap, the Japanese are almost 99 and 44/100ths percent ethnically pure. Furthermore, the government traditionally—in contradistinction to our own—plays a nurturing role with its industrial firms. And Japanese firms, while they *do* compete, will generally close ranks to keep out foreigners.

Can we play the Japanese game?

To return—finally!—to the original question: Can anybody play Japan's game? Can we? Only truly cohesive societies can pull off the economic miracle that Japan pulled off after 1945. Only a country whose industrialists can all pull together, and whose people virtually refuse to do business with or buy from anyone who is not a native, can accomplish what Japan accomplished. South Korea, a nation sometimes described as a Japanese clone, has managed a similar economic miracle since the mid-1950s.

How the Japanese Drove American TV Manufacturers Out of Business*

You'd have to be at least in your mid-50s to remember those old Dumonts, RCAs, GEs, and Sylvanias, with their nine-inch screens, back in the late 1940s. Howdy Doody, Gene Autrey, Hopalong Cassidy, and Farmer Gray cartoons were all the rage. Well, TV programming has come a long way, but it's still by and large produced by American companies. However, TV manufacturing, like so much else in consumer electronics, has come to be dominated by the Japanese. Today there are no American companies still making television sets in this country.

It all started back in 1956 when a cartel of Japanese television makers was formed. The Home Electric Appliance Market Stabilization Council had two objectives: first, to gain complete control of the Japanese TV market, and then, to gain control of the far larger American market.

At the time GE, Westinghouse, and RCA produced the state-of-the-art TVs. Because the cartel effectively excluded the sale of American TV sets in Japan, these companies "each licensed and then transferred its monochrome technology to members of the cartel. In 1962, RCA went one step further and licensed its color technology to the Japanese."†

Next came the plan's second phase. The American market would be inundated with television sets that would be sold well below cost. To subsidize this venture, the Japanese consumer was charged double what Americans paid. Indeed, while Americans were paying an average of just $350 a set, Japanese consumers were forking out $700 for identical TVs.

The cartel's members also paid illegal rebates of $40 a set to some 80 American importers, including Alexander's and Sears.

These illegal rebates were paid in several ways. Some Japanese manufacturers deposited money for their American co-conspirators in secret bank accounts in Switzerland, Hong Kong, or Japan. Others sent telegraphic transfers of money marked as "credits" for spare parts. Still others gave American importers extended payment terms for their purchases—and forgave the interest. Japanese firms also provided offsetting discounts on other merchandise sold to TV importers, as well as payments disguised as "market research."

The objective was to destroy the American industry by selling goods extraordinarily cheaply, often at prices far below production costs. To avoid detection by the U.S. government and lawsuits by American manufacturers, the participants in this scheme filed falsified documents with the Customs Service.‡

Within a few years the American TV manufacturers got wind of what was happening and filed a complaint with the U.S. Treasury Department that Japan was dumping TV sets on the U.S. market at prices well below production costs. It took three years for the Treasury Department to conclude that they were right—that the Japanese were indeed dumping. Still, virtually nothing was done. Meanwhile, American TV makers were being forced out of business one after another, until none was left.

*Much of this information may be found in chapter 6 of Pat Choate's book *Agents of Influence* (New York: Touchstone, 1990). Choate ran for vice president in 1996 on the Reform Party ticket with Ross Perot.
†Ibid., p. 80.
‡Ibid., p. 81.

Well, you might ask, why can't we just put up high tariffs to keep out imports? Good question! Aside from the fact that our competitors would reciprocate with tariffs of their own to keep out American goods, there's an even more important reason. Americans would simply not stand for it. It would mean no VCRs, no TVs, and no cameras. Most of all, it would mean a sharp decline in our standard of living, which most Americans would find intolerable. High tariffs might well have been feasible 20 or 30 years ago, but not today when the American consumer has become so dependent on foreign imports.[17]

The Japanese consumer has long accepted a lower standard of living because it was necessary for the greater economic good. But how many Americans would be willing to make that sacrifice? Certainly not those whose lifestyle is best described as "born to shop" and "shop till you drop." The concept of subordinating our personal interests to those of our society is as foreign to us as our concept of the ascendancy of the individual is to the Japanese.

So to return one last time to the question, Can anybody play the Japanese economic game? No, not anybody. And surely not us.

---

[17]American manufacturers—indeed, manufacturers around the world—have become extremely dependent on imported components and raw materials. We depend heavily on foreigners for such manufacturing inputs as oil, machine tools, computer chips, and steel.

The Word War

In the last few years Americans have engaged in an ongoing debate with the Japanese over whom to blame for the huge trade imbalance between our two countries. Stephen Cohen has compared this economic relationship "to a stormy marriage to which the two partners bring complementary neuroses, along with irreplaceable benefits." But underlying the relationship are some fundamental societal differences that help explain why we have run such large trade deficits with Japan. Cohen describes these differences:

> The United States as a whole maximizes consumption and recreation, pursues instant gratification, extols the spirit of the individual, and adheres to a belief in the glory of the free market. Japan as a whole opts to work, to save, to sublimate the self to the interests of a larger group, to plan and to sacrifice for the long run, and to adhere to an economic system based primarily on enhancing the size and power of entrenched domestic interests.[18]

Most of our trade problem is due to our own shortcomings. How do we explain why Japanese automobile firms can produce better cars on American soil than our own Big Three can? How do we explain why about 20 percent of our workforce (albeit not 30 percent, as Yosio Sakurauchi, speaker of the lower house of Japan's parliament, would have it) is functionally illiterate? And how do we explain our lagging productivity, our low rate of capital formation, our dearth of engineering graduates, our humongous corporate executive salaries, and the relatively low quality of so many of our products? Moreover, how do we explain our huge federal budget deficits? Well, all right—nobody's perfect. But much of our trade problem that isn't explained by these failures may be blamed on the Japanese, who take advantage of our relatively open markets while denying us access to their own.

The size of the Japanese market is second only to our own, so if our goods continue to be denied access, we cannot attain the same economies of scale that Japanese producers enjoy. These markets must be opened; alternatively, ours must be closed. Without access to the Japanese market (as well as a large share of our own), we cannot compete in broad sectors of the high-tech market.

We need to be asking the Japanese some hard questions: Why do we manage to export our manufactured goods to other industrial countries without much ado, while it's such a struggle to export them to Japan? Why do so many other countries also complain about how Japan's markets are closed? And why have the Japanese been running huge bilateral trade surpluses in manufactured goods with nearly *all* their trading partners—even the newly industrialized economies of Southeast Asia?

Our Trade Deficit with China

When we began trading with China in the mid-1970s, after President Richard Nixon's historic trip to open relations with that nation, American exporters had great hopes that the world's most populous nation would eventually become the world's largest consumer market. Two decades later, toys, athletic shoes, clothing, and other relatively low-price manufactured goods are flooding into the United States, along with an increasing stream of higher-priced goods such as tools, auto parts, electronic gear, microwave ovens, and personal computers. Although U.S. exports to China are growing rapidly, our exports are only about one-quarter of our imports.

Why are we importing so much from China? Mainly because U.S. retailers are seeking the cheapest goods available and finding them in China. Wal-Mart Stores imported nearly $2 billion worth of goods in 1997, and Kmart and Toys 'R' Us also found that the price was right in China.

One of the big trade issues between China and the United States is that thousands of Chinese factories, many controlled by top officers of the Chinese army, have been making unauthorized, or knock-off, copies of American movies, CDs, and most important, computer software. According to a *New York Times* article, an American official

---

[18]Stephen Cohen, *Cowboys and Samurai* (New York: HarperBusiness, 1991), p. 3.

said that Chinese officials disputed the United States estimates that 95 percent of computer software used in China was pirated and asserted that it was closer to 25 to 30 percent—and that they would take steps to lower that amount.[19]

Trading with China and Japan: More Differences than Similarities

In all major respects our trade imbalance with China is very different from that with Japan. Our deficit with China is rising rapidly, while our deficit with Japan peaked in 1994, and is in long-term decline.

Our trading position with Japan is very much like a colony and a colonial power. As you saw in Table 7, we send agricultural products to Japan in exchange for manufactured goods. In the years before the American Revolution, the British strongly encouraged their American colonies to send them raw materials in exchange for manufactured goods. Which, incidentally, was one of the grievances over which we rebelled.

Our trading relationship with the Chinese is very different. We send airplanes, computers, movies, compact disks, cars, cigarettes, power-generating equipment, and computer software in exchanges for toys, clothing, shoes, and low-end consumer electronics.

Still another difference between China and Japan is that the latter was never open to foreign direct investment. Japanese factories are Japanese-owned. But China, since the mid-1980s, has been open to foreign direct investment, which has been attracted mainly by extremely low wages, about $50 a month, except in the southern provinces surrounding Hong Kong. American, Japanese, British, Korean, and Taiwanese corporations have invested some $200 billion to set up assembly lines that use semiskilled labor to turn out cheap manufactured goods. Foreign-owned companies are then required to export a certain percentage of what they produce.

The percentage of its exports made by enterprises with foreign investment grew from 1 percent in 1985 to nearly 50 percent in 1998. So we have American multinational corporations using cheap Chinese labor to produce toys, clothing, watches, shoes, and other low-end consumer products for the American market. Much of what they're sending to us used to come from Japan back in the 1950s. "Made in Japan" has been replaced by "Made in China."

Japanese gains in the production of semiconductors, machine tools, steel, autos, TVs, and VCRs have led directly to the loss of millions of well-paying American jobs. Although Chinese products may compete on a broader scale with American goods in the future, Chinese exports so far have generally not translated into job losses in the United States. China's leading exports are products that have not been produced in large quantity by American factories for more than a decade.

The Chinese, like the Japanese before them, have insisted on licensing agreements and large-scale transfer of technology as the price for agreeing to imports. These agreements, of course, lead to the eventual elimination of imports from the United States. However, the Chinese have taken this process one step further. Sometimes, instead of entering into licensing agreements, Chinese factories simply manufacture pirated versions, or knock-offs, of American videos, CDs, computer software, and designer apparel.

In another 30 or 40 years the chinese economy may well surpass those of the United States and Japan. But right now China's GDP is about one-eighth the size of ours, and it is still primarily an agricultural nation. Unlike Japan, China supplies us with low-end manufactured products, and is a growing market for our main exports.

You probably don't remember the 1988 vice presidential debate, but you might remember this quote. After Vice President Dan Quayle had compared himself to President John Kennedy, Senator Lloyd Bentsen told him, "John Kennedy was a friend of mine. You're no John Kennedy." Now that our trade deficit with China is nearly as large as our deficit with Japan, you might wonder if history is repeating itself. It isn't. Japan is an ad-

---

[19]Seth Faison, "U.S. and China Sign Accord to End Piracy of Software, Music Recordings and Film," *New York Times,* February 27, 1995, p. D6.

vanced industrial power in direct competition with the United States. China is a newly industrializing country that will not become a direct competitor for another two or three decades. China is not yet another Japan.

Part IV: Trade Issues at the End of the Century

Our continuing trade deficits with Japan and our overall imbalance of trade are issues we have been dealing with for quite some time. But three new areas of controversy arose in the mid-1990s—the NAFTA and GATT agreements and our rapidly growing trade deficit with China. As our deficit with Japan continues to shrink, these three trade issues will take center stage.

NAFTA

The North American Free Trade Agreement, which was ratified by Congress in 1993, created a free-trade area including Canada, the United States, and Mexico, a market fast approaching 400 million consumers. Here is how the agreement is described in the 1994 *Economic Report of the President:*

> In addition to dismantling trade barriers in industrial goods, NAFTA includes agreements on services, investment, intellectual property rights, agriculture, and strengthening of trade rules. There are also side agreements on labor adjustment provisions, protection of the environment, and import surges.[20]

How well has the agreement worked so far? Has a flood of cheap Mexican goods resulted in "the sound of jobs being sucked out of the United States"? Hardly. Despite the precipitous fall of the peso against the dollar and other currencies in late 1994, our trade with Mexico was up about 20 percent and we continued to run a very small trade surplus.

In early 1995, however, the full effects of the peso's fall turned our small trade surplus with Mexico into an annual deficit of over $15 billion. The effect of NAFTA on jobs is more difficult to discern. Clearly the threat of moving operations to Mexico, where hourly wages and fringe benefits average about $1.35 an hour, has had a depressing effect on American factory wages. But there is little evidence that the agreement has cost more than 200,000 jobs, which is less than 2 one-thousandths of our total employment.

NAFTA was an extension of an earlier trade agreement with Canada, our most important trading partner, with whom we have been running a $10 billion to $15 billion trade deficit in recent years. Under the agreement, duties on most goods will be phased out soon after the turn of the century.

GATT

The General Agreement on Trade and Tariffs was drafted in 1947 and has since been signed by more than 100 nations. GATT is a uniform system of rules for the conduct of international trade. Its latest version, which was ratified by Congress in 1994, was the culmination of years of negotiations. It will reduce tariffs worldwide by an average of 40 percent, lower other barriers to trade such as quotas on certain products, and provide patent protection for American software, pharmaceuticals, and other industries.

Will GATT hurt our trade balance, unleash a flood of cheap foreign imports, and result in the loss of millions of American jobs? Although some industries will be affected adversely, the positive appears to outweigh the negative. First of all, on the average, foreign countries have more trade restrictions and tariffs on U.S. goods than we have on theirs, so GATT should help us much more than it hurts us. For the first time intellectual property rights like patents, trademarks, and copyrights will be protected. GATT will also open markets for service industries such as accounting, advertising, computer services, and engineering—fields in which Americans excel.

---

[20]See page 225 of the *Report.*

Finally, GATT brings agriculture under international trade rules for the first time. Many countries heavily subsidize their farmers (in 1997 the United States spent $7 billion in crop subsidies), but European subsidies dwarf those paid to American farmers. Clinton's Council of Economic Advisors noted that, "Since the United States has a strong underlying comparative advantage in agriculture, the mutual reduction in trade barriers and subsidization will be to the distinct advantage of U.S. producers."[21] Proportionately, the Europeans will have to reduce their subsidies a lot more than we'll have to, making American crop exports even more competitive.

Will the last round of GATT live up to its advanced billing? If the world's trading nations adhere to the agreement, world trade should expand substantially, so that every nation gains, and there will be no losers.

Final Word

In order to reduce our overall trade deficit further we need to make a combination of four things happen. First, we need to raise our rate of productivity growth and keep improving the quality of American goods and services. Second, we need to lower our dependence on oil imports, perhaps by raising the tax on gasoline. Third, we must reduce our trade deficit with Japan—a problem we share with many other nations. And finally, we need to do something about our rapidly rising deficit with China.

We simply cannot allow ourselves to continue running huge trade deficits. In addition to sinking future generations into debt, we have been losing hundreds of thousands of high-paying manufacturing jobs every year.

Although economists remain opposed to tariffs and other trade barriers, pressure is building to do something to curb the flood of imports, especially those from Japan. Although there has been strong protectionist political pressure in recent years, this pressure may abate as our trade deficit declines.

Questions for Further Thought and Discussion

1. Explain what comparative advantage is. Make up an example to illustrate this concept.
2. What is wrong with having tariffs and quotas? Which is the lesser of two evils, and why?
3. To what degree are we at fault for our huge trade deficit with Japan? To what degree are the Japanese at fault?
4. What would you suggest we do to reduce our trade deficit?
5. We run huge trade imbalances with two countries. Explain the cause of the imbalances.

---

[21]*Economic Report of the President,* 1995, p. 208.

WORKBOOK FOR CHAPTER 34

Name _____   Date _____

Multiple-Choice Questions

Circle the letter that corresponds to the best answer.

1. Our balance of trade
   a. has always been positive   b. turned negative in
   the mid-1970s   c. turned negative in the mid-1980s
   d. has always been negative

2. Which makes the most sense economically?
   a. individual self-sufficiency   b. national self-
   sufficiency   c. national specialization   d. none of
   these

3. If the United States were to devote all its resources to
   producing washing machines, it could turn out 50 billion
   a year; if it devoted all its resources to producing cars, it
   could turn out 10 billion a year. Our domestic exchange
   equation is
   a. 5 cars = 1 washing machine   b. 5 washing
   machines = 1 car   c. ⅕ of a washing machine = 1 car
   d. ½ of a car = 1 washing machine

4. If the United States were to trade its cars for another
   country's washing machines, it would not trade one car
   unless it received at least _____
   washing machines. (Use data in question 3.)
   a. at least one   b. more than one   c. at least
   five   d. more than five

5. Which statement is false?
   a. No nation will engage in trade with another nation
   unless it will gain by that trade.   b. The terms of
   trade will fall somewhere between the domestic exchange
   equations of the two trading nations   c. Most
   economists advocate free trade.   d. None of these
   statements is false.

6. If Hong Kong can make TVs more efficiently than France
   can, it enjoys
   a. a comparative advantage   b. an absolute
   advantage   c. no advantage

7. Under the law of comparative advantage, total output is
   greatest when each product is made by the country that
   a. enjoys an absolute advantage   b. has the lowest
   opportunity cost   c. has the lowest wage
   rates   d. has the lowest degree of specialization

8. The least applicable argument for protecting American
   industry from foreign competition would be the _____
   _____ argument.
   a. national security   b. infant industry   c. low-
   wage   d. employment

9. Imports would be lowered by
   a. tariffs only   b. import quotas only   c. both
   tariffs and import quotas   d. neither tariffs nor import
   quotas

10. Of these three choices—tariffs, quotas, and free trade—
    economists like _____ the most and
    _____ the least.
    a. tariffs, quotas   b. tariffs, free trade   c. free
    trade, tariffs   d. free trade, quotas   e. quotas, free
    trade   f. quotas, tariffs

11. Our biggest trade deficit was a little over _____
    billion.
    a. $125   b. $165   c. $205   d. $245
    e. $285

12. In the 1980s Japanese real interest rates were about
    a. triple ours   b. one-and-a-half times ours
    c. about the same as ours   d. somewhat lower than
    ours   e. one-third ours

13. Each of the following has contributed to our trade deficit
    except
    a. high military spending   b. the high cost of
    capital   c. the cost of our educational
    system   d. our short time horizon

14. Since the 1950s the percentage share of the world's manufacturing of

a. multinationals and of U.S. firms has declined

b. multinationals and U.S. firms has risen

c. multinationals has declined and of U.S. firms has risen   d. multinationals has risen and of U.S. firms has declined

15. Which statement is false?

a. The J-curve theory explains why devaluation does not lead to an immediate reduction in the trade deficit.

b. The 1980–85 rise in the dollar does not fully explain the rise in the trade deficit.   c. A declining dollar will eventually reduce the trade deficit.   d. None of these statements is false.

16. Each of the following would reduce our trade deficit except

a. getting American corporations to take the shorter view and focus on the quarterly profit figure

b. cutting defense spending   c. increasing investment   d. improving our educational system

17. The best example of unfair Japanese trade practices may be found in the _____ industry.

a. computer software   b. photocopier

c. camera   d. textile   e. TV manufacturing

18. Statement 1: If we eliminated our trade deficit with Japan and our oil import bill, we would be running trade surpluses.

Statement 2: Americans pay lower taxes on gasoline than do the citizens of most of the nations in Western Europe.

a. Statement 1 is true and statement 2 is false.

b. Statement 2 is true and statement 1 is false.

c. Both statements are true.   d. Both statements are false.

19. Statement 1: Japanese industrialists pay much lower interest rates than do American industrialists.

Statement 2: Between 1950 and 1980 Japan paid about $10 billion to acquire technology that had cost between $500 billion and $1 trillion to develop.

a. Statement 1 is true and statement 2 is false.

b. Statement 2 is true and statement 1 is false.

c. Both statements are true.   d. Both statements are false.

20. Statement 1: It costs more to save an American job making specialty steel from foreign competition than it does to save a job making television sets.

Statement 2: Although saving American jobs from foreign competition may raise prices, the cost is well worth it.

a. Statement 1 is true and statement 2 is false.

b. Statement 2 is true and statement 1 is false.

c. Both statements are true.   d. Both statements are false.

21. To save a job making television sets in the United States from foreign competition would cost consumers about _____ a year in the form of higher prices.

a. $400   b. $4,000   c. $40,000   d. $400,000

e. $4 million

Questions 22–24 refer to Table 1.

Table 1

	One Nigerian Worker	One Romanian Worker
Basketballs	5	12
Barbi Dolls	10	18

22. Nigeria has an absolute advantage in the production of

a. basketballs   b. Barbi Dolls   c. both basketballs and Barbi Dolls   d. neither basketballs nor Barbi Dolls   e. none of the above

23. The opportunity cost of producing one basketball in Romania is

a. ⅔s of a Barbi Doll   b. 1 Barbi Doll   c. 1½ Barbi Dolls   d. 4 Barbi Dolls   e. 6 Barbi Dolls

24. Romania has a comparative advantage in the production of

a. basketballs   b. Barbi Dolls   c. both basketballs and Barbi Dolls   d. neither basketballs nor Barbi Dolls   e. none of the above

Fill-In Questions

1. The basis for international trade is _____ _____.

    Use Figure 1 to answer questions 2 through 6.

Figure 1

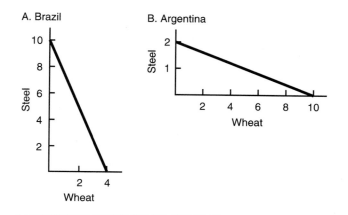

A. Brazil   B. Argentina

2. Brazil is better at producing _____

    than at producing_____.

    Argentina is better at producing _____

    than at producing_____.

3. The domestic equation of exchange for Brazil is

    _____. The domestic equation

    of exchange for Argentina is _____.

4. If Argentina and Brazil traded, Argentina would trade

    _____ for _____,

    while Brazil would trade _____

    for _____.

5. Brazil would be willing to trade one ton of steel for more

    than _____ ton(s) of

    wheat. Argentina would be willing to trade five tons of

    wheat for more than _____

    ton(s) of steel.

6. State the terms of trade in steel and wheat.

    a. One ton of steel will be exchanged for more than

        _____ and less than

        _____ tons of wheat.   b. One

        ton of wheat will be exchanged for more than _____

        _____ and less than _____

        tons of steel.

7. If one country is better at growing wheat than another

    country, it enjoys a(n) _____

    advantage in wheat production.

8. The law of comparative advantage states that total output

    is greatest when each product is made by the country that

    has the _____

    _____.

9. Four main arguments have been made for trade

    protection: (1) the _____ argument,

    (2) the _____argument; (3) the

    _____ argument; and (4) the

    _____ argument.

10. Although economists dislike both, they would prefer

    tariffs to _____.

11. A tariff is a tax on _____;

    a quota is a limit on_____.

12. If it costs three times as much to make a car in Nigeria as

    it does in Mexico and it costs twice as much to grow

    wheat in Mexico as it does in Nigeria, we say Mexico

    enjoys an absolute advantage in the production of

    _____, and Nigeria

enjoys an absolute advantage in the production of

_____.

13. A company that puts its name on imported goods is called

a _____

corporation.

14. One thing we could do to reduce our trade imbalance is to

_____

_____ the dollar.

15. Our trade deficit hit a peak in the year _____,

when it was $_____ billion.

16. _____ was the last year in which we

ran a trade surplus.

Problems

Assume Bolivia and Chile use the same amount of resources to produce tin and copper. Figure 2 represents their production possibilities curves. Use it to answer questions 1 through 8.

1. What is the domestic exchange equation of Bolivia?

2. What is the domestic exchange equation of Chile?

3. Bolivia would be willing to trade 5 tons of tin for how much copper?

4. Chile would be willing to trade 15 tons of copper for how much tin?

5. Bolivia has a comparative advantage in the production of which metal?

6. Chile has a comparative advantage in the production of which metal?

7. Bolivia has an absolute advantage in the production of which metal?

8. Chile has an absolute advantage in the production of which metal

Figure 2

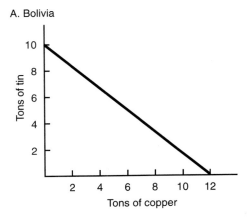

A. Bolivia

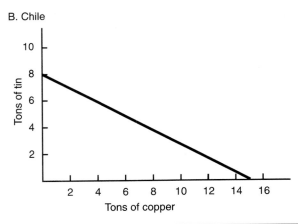

B. Chile

35 International Finance

International trade is just one part of international finance, which encompasses foreign investment, exchange rates, and other international transactions as well as the finance of international trade. After we've examined the entire picture of international trade and finance, you'll see that the United States is in an increasingly weak position and that some day in the not-too-distant future not only will American economic influence around the world have greatly diminished, but foreigners will be calling the shots in our own economy.

Chapter Objectives

These are the topics we'll cover:

- Financing international trade.
- The balance of payments.
- Exchange rate systems.
- The decline and fall of the American economy.

The Mechanics of International Finance

Think of international trade and finance as an extension of our nation's economic activities beyond our borders. Instead of buying microchips from a firm in California, we buy them from a firm in Japan. Instead of selling Cadillacs in Miami, we sell them in Rio de Janeiro. And rather than building a factory in Chicago, we build one in Hong Kong.

We discussed the whys and wherefores of international trade in the last chapter; now we'll see how that trade is financed. Ideally, our exports should pay for our imports; but since the mid-1970s the United States has had a very large negative balance of trade. That is, our imports have grown much faster than our exports.

The balance of trade is part of the balance of payments.

The balance of trade is only part of the big picture of international finance. That picture includes imports and exports of services as well as goods. Also included are investment income, transfers of funds abroad, and capital inflows and outflows. The whole shooting match is called the balance of payments, which we'll take up after we look at the mechanics of financing trade. Toward the end of this part of the chapter we'll talk about international exchange rate systems, including the gold standard.

Financing International Trade

When an American importer buys $2 million of wine from a French merchant, how does she pay? In dollars? In francs? In gold? Gold is used only by governments, and then only on very rare occasions, to settle international transactions. Dollars, although sometimes acceptable as an international currency, are not as useful as francs to the French wine merchant. After all, the merchant will have to pay his employees and suppliers in francs.

There's no problem exchanging dollars for francs in either the United States or France. Many banks in New York have plenty of francs on hand, and virtually every bank in the country can get francs (as well as yen, marks, pounds, and other foreign currencies) within a day or two. In Paris and every other French city dollars are readily available from banks. On any given day—actually, at any given minute—there is a market exchange rate of francs for dollars; all you need to do is find the right teller and you can exchange your dollars for francs or francs for dollars within minutes.

Financing international trade is part of the economic flow of money and credit that crosses international boundaries every day. For the rest of this chapter we'll see where these funds are going and, in particular, how the United States is involved. We'll begin with the U.S. balance of payments, which provides an accounting of our country's international financial transactions.

The Balance of Payments

Often people confuse our balance of payments with our balance of trade. Actually, the balance of trade is a major part of the balance of payments. *The entire flow of U.S. dollars and foreign currencies into and out of the country constitutes the balance of payments,* while the trade balance is just the difference between our imports and our exports.

Until the mid-1970s we generally had a positive balance of trade; that is, the value of our exports was greater than that of our imports. All this changed drastically due to the quadrupling of oil prices in late 1973, as well as several other factors I'll be enumerating toward the end of this chapter. But an unmistakable trend, which had been going on for decades, foreshadowed the negative trade balances we have been experiencing every year since 1976.

The balance of payments has two parts: the current account and the capital account.

The balance of payments consists of two parts. First is the current account, which summarizes all the goods and services produced during the current year that we buy from or sell to foreigners. The second part is the capital account, which records the long-term transactions that we conduct with foreigners. The total of the current and capital accounts will always be zero; that is, our balance of payments never has a deficit or a surplus. When we look at these accounts in more detail, the picture should become clearer.

Table 1 shows the U.S. balance of payments in 1997. The great villain of the piece is our huge merchandise trade deficit of $202 billion. The next item, services, comprises mainly income from insurance, tourist spending, and legal financial services. Now we have income from investments. From the turn of the century to the early 1980s the United States had a substantial net investment income because Americans invested much more abroad than foreigners invested in the United States. Because of our huge trade deficits in recent years, however, foreigners have been left holding hundreds of billions of dollars, most of which they have invested in the United States. The return on this investment has been growing rapidly. In fact, in 1997, for the first time since the early years of this cen-

Table 1   U.S. Balance of Payments, 1997* (in $ billions)

1. **Current account**	
2. Merchandise	
3. Exports	+678
4. Imports	−880
5. Balance of trade	−202
6. Services	
7. Exports	+253
8. Imports	−168
9. Balance of services	+ 85
10. Income from investments	
11. Income receipts	+236
12. Income payments	−250
13. Net investment income	− 14
14. Net unilateral transfers abroad	− 39
15. **Balance on current account**	−168
16. **Capital account**	
17. Capital inflows	+690
18. Capital outflows	−427
19. **Balance on capital account**	+263
20. Statistical Discrepancy	− 95
21. **Totals**	0

Source: *Survey of Current Business,* April 1998.

*Figures may not add up due to rounding.

tury, the flow of income from investments—interest, profits, dividends, and rent—turned negative. Why? Because foreigners have invested a lot more in the United States than Americans have invested abroad.

Finally, we have net transfers, which include foreign aid, military spending abroad, remittances to relatives living abroad, and pensions paid to Americans living abroad. Because the United States does not receive foreign aid, no foreign troops are stationed here, and few personal remittances or pensions are paid to U.S. residents from abroad, net transfers will continue to be a negative figure into the foreseeable future.

Our balance on the current account is a clear indicator of how we're doing. To arrive at that balance in Table 1, just add items 5 (balance of trade), 9 (balance of services), 13 (net investment income), and 14 (net unilateral transfers abroad). Adding −202, +85, −14, and −39, we get −168 (figures don't add up exactly due to rounding). A negative balance on the current account of $168 billion means that we went $168 billion deeper into debt with foreigners.

Our current account deficit is balanced by our capital account surplus.

When we add up the numbers that go into our current account, it is easy to see why this figure is negative and why our current account deficit has been growing in recent years. (See Figure 1.) But what international finance takes away with one hand, it pays back with the other. Thus, by definition, our current account deficit is balanced by our capital account surplus.

What have foreigners done with the dollars they have earned from trading with us as well as from their other current account dealings with us? Nearly all of this money has been reinvested in the United States in the form of corporate stocks and bonds; U.S. Treasury bills, notes, and bonds; and real estate and direct investment in plant and equipment.

Prior to the early 1980s Americans were investing much more in foreign countries than foreigners were investing in the United States. But as our balance of trade worsened it was inevitable that the flow of capital would be reversed. Some relatively minor items

Figure 1   Current Account Surpluses and Deficits, 1965–97

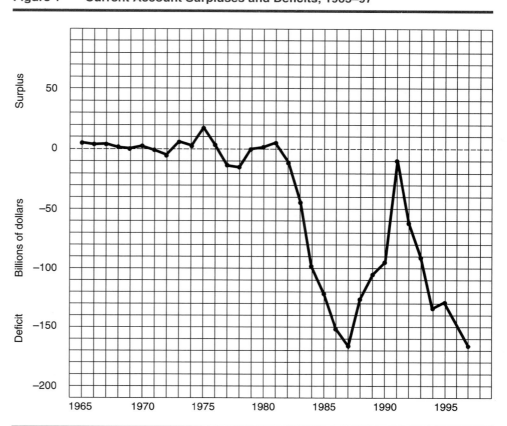

Source: *Survey of Current Business*, April 1998.

Technically, the balance of payments has no deficits or surpluses.

are included in the capital account, most notably the statistical discrepancy. Now, $33 billion is a pretty big discrepancy. This money flowed into the United States but was never recorded.[1]

Technically there are no balance-of-payment deficits or surpluses because the current account deficit, by definition, will be balanced by a capital account surplus. In 1997 we ran a $168 billion current deficit, which was matched by a $263 billion capital account surplus plus the $95 billion statistical discrepancy.

Was this a coincidence? Not at all! As you can see in Figure 1, we've been running substantial current account deficits since 1982, but they have been matched dollar-for-dollar by capital account surpluses plus or minus statistical discrepancies.

The way it works is that we buy much more from foreigners than they buy from us. In effect, they lend or give us the money to make up the difference between our imports and our exports. It would not be an exaggeration to say that we borrow so much from foreigners to finance our current account deficits that we sell them pieces of the American rock, so to speak. Those pieces consist mainly of corporate stock and real estate, but they also lend us tens of billions of dollars each year in the form of purchases of corporate and government bonds and other debt instruments.

Now that foreigners own more investment assets in the United States than Americans own abroad, they are receiving more interest, rent, dividends, and profits than we are. In the early 1980s, when we held more assets abroad than foreigners held in the United States, Americans earned a net investment income of over $30 billion a year. This net inflow fell sharply over the next decade as foreigners bought up more and more American stocks, bonds, and real estate, and purchased American corporations or built their own factories, office buildings, and retail outlets. In 1997 there was a net outflow of $14 billion in investment income.

In future years, we can expect this net outflow of investment income to continue to grow. Unless we can reduce our deficit in the trade of goods and services, our current account deficit will keep growing, and foreigners will have little choice but to keep sending most of those dollars back here to buy up more and more of our assets.

We go deeper and deeper into debt each year.

While technically we don't run balance-of-payments deficits, we *do* go deeper and deeper into hock each year. Should this last another three or four decades, foreign investors will own most of the country, so it is hard to refrain from calling the huge shortfalls in our balance-of-payments account "deficits."

Exchange Rate Systems

The basis for international finance is the exchange of well over 100 national currencies. Until the 1930s the world's currencies were based on gold. Since then a relatively free-floating exchange rate system has evolved. Under this system exchange rates are determined largely by the forces of supply and demand. In other words, how many yen, marks, francs, or pounds you can get for your dollars is determined largely by the impersonal forces of the market.

Three distinct periods

We'll consider three fairly distinct periods in the recent history of exchange rates. First, we'll examine the period before 1934, when most of the world was on the gold standard. Second, we'll look at the period from 1934 to 1973, when international finance was based on fixed exchange rates. Finally, we shall review the period from 1973 to the present, when we have had relatively freely floating exchange rates.

---

[1]Statistical discrepancy is another way of saying, "Something's just not adding up." This very issue came up once in a course taught by the late Oskar Morgenstern, the mathematical economist.

Sometime during the 1930s Austria exported 10,000 horses to Czechoslovakia, but the Czechs had no record of having imported 10,000 horses. "Did the horses disappear into thin air when they crossed the border?" asked Morgenstern. No, he concluded. The 10,000 horses were swallowed by a statistical discrepancy.

The Gold Standard

Exactly what is the gold standard?

There has been a lot of talk in recent years about a return to the gold standard, but it's not going to happen. Exactly what *is* the gold standard, what are its advantages, and what are its disadvantages? Funny you should ask.

A nation is on the gold standard when it defines its currency in terms of gold. Until 1933 the U.S. dollar was worth 1/23 of an ounce of gold. In other words, you could buy an ounce of gold from the Treasury for $23 or sell this department an ounce for $23. Paper money was fully convertible into gold. If you gave the Treasury $23, you would get one ounce of gold—no ifs, ands, or buts. In 1933, just before we went off the gold standard (along with the rest of the world), we raised the price of gold to $35 an ounce, which meant a dollar was worth 1/35 of an ounce of gold.

To be on the gold standard, a nation must maintain a fixed ratio between its gold stock and its money supply. That way, when the gold stock rises, so does the money supply. Should gold leave the country, the money supply declines.

That brings us to the third and last requirement of the gold standard: there must be no barriers to the free flow of gold into and out of the country.

When we put all these things together, we have the gold standard. The nation's money supply, which is based on gold, is tied to the money supply of every other nation on the gold standard. It is the closest the world has ever come to an international currency. This system worked quite well until World War I, when most of the belligerents temporarily went off the gold standard because many of their citizens were hoarding gold and trying to ship it off to neutral nations.

How the gold standard works

Ideally, here is how the gold standard works. When Country A exports as much as it imports from Country B, no gold is transferred. But when Country A imports more than it exports, it has to ship the difference, in gold, to the trading partners with whom it has trade deficits.

Suppose the United States had to ship 1 million ounces of gold to other countries. This would lower our gold stock and, consequently, our money supply. When our money supply declined, so would our price level. This would make our goods cheaper relative to foreign goods. Our imports would decline and our exports would rise because foreigners would find American imports cheaper than their own goods.

A self-correcting mechanism

What we had, then, was a self-correcting mechanism. A negative balance of trade caused an outflow of gold, a lower money supply, lower prices, and ultimately, fewer imports and more exports. Thus, under the gold standard, negative trade balances eliminated themselves.

After World War I the nations that had left the gold standard returned to the fold, but some nations' currencies were overvalued (relative to their price in gold) while others' currencies were undervalued. Adjustments were difficult because the nations whose currency was overvalued would have faced a gold drain and, consequently, lower prices and lower wages. But wages and prices are rarely downwardly flexible.

An alternative was to devaluate—that is, lower the price of money in relation to gold. For example, a 10 percent devaluation would mean that instead of getting 10 pounds for an ounce of gold, you now get 11. As the Great Depression spread, one nation after another devaluated, and within a few years virtually everyone was off the gold standard.

Evaluation of the gold standard

Let's step back for a moment and evaluate the gold standard. It *did* work for a long time, automatically eliminating trade surpluses and deficits. And it *did* stimulate international trade by removing the uncertainty of fluctuating exchange rates.

But the gold standard has a downside. First, it will work only when the gold supply increases as quickly as the world's need for money. By the early 20th century this was no longer the case. Second, it will work only if participating nations are willing to accept the periodic inflation and unemployment that accompany the elimination of trade imbalances. In today's world political leaders must pay far more attention to their domestic constituencies than to their trading partners. Finally, strict adherence to the gold standard would render monetary policy utterly ineffective. If gold were flowing into the United States, the

Federal Reserve would be powerless to slow the rate of monetary growth and the ensuing inflation. And if there were an outflow of gold, the Federal Reserve would be unable to slow the decline in the money supply and thereby prevent the advent of a recession.

With the breakdown of the gold standard in the 1930s, protectionism returned as one nation after another raised tariff barriers higher and higher. Devaluation followed devaluation until the entire structure of international trade and finance was near complete collapse. Then came World War II—and with it, a great revival of economic activity. While the war was still raging, the Bretton Woods conference was called to set up a system of international finance that would lend some stability to how exchange rates were set.

The Gold Exchange Standard, 1934–73

Fixed exchange rates

The Bretton Woods (New Hampshire) conference set up the International Monetary Fund (IMF) to supervise a system of fixed exchange rates, all of which were based on the U.S. dollar, which was based on gold. The dollar was defined, as it had been for the last 10 years, as being worth 1/35 of an ounce of gold, so gold was $35 an ounce, and dollars were convertible into gold at that price.

Other currencies were convertible into dollars at fixed prices, so these currencies were indirectly convertible into gold. But this was short of a gold standard because the money supplies of these nations were not tied to gold and no longer would trade deficits or surpluses automatically eliminate themselves. If a nation ran consistent trade deficits, it could devalue its currency relative to the dollar. A devaluation of 10 percent or less could be done without the IMF's permission (larger cuts required permission).

The new system functioned well for 25 years after World War II. The United States ran almost continual balance-of-payment deficits during the 1950s and 1960s, which eventually led to an international financial crisis in 1971. But until that year these deficits contributed to international liquidity. This is because U.S. dollars as well as gold were held as reserves for international payments by virtually every country in the world but the United States.

During this period millions of American tourists went abroad (while fewer foreign tourists could afford to come here) and spent billions of dollars a year. More than 1 million American troops were stationed in Western Europe, Korea, Japan, and scores of other countries, and they spent most of their pay locally. Meanwhile, it took billions of dollars a year to supply these troops with food and other daily necessities, most of which were purchased locally. Finally, we dispensed billions of dollars a year in foreign economic and military aid.

So you may think of the United States during the 1950s and 1960s as a kind of financial Johnny Appleseed, walking the earth throwing U.S. dollars to the wind. Had any other nation spread its currency around the way we did, that currency would have quickly found its way back to its treasury to be redeemed in gold. But not the almighty U.S. dollar, which for years was literally as good as gold.

Why were U.S. dollars so acceptable?

Why were U.S. dollars acceptable to other nations? First, the United States held the largest stock of gold in the world and stood ready to sell that gold at $35 an ounce to the central banks of every nation. Second, the American economy was by far the largest and strongest in the world.

By the late 1960s, as our gold stock dwindled and as foreign governments found themselves with increasing stocks of dollars, these nations began to ask some embarrassing questions. If the United States continued to run balance-of-payments deficits, would we be able to redeem the dollars they were holding for gold at $35 an ounce? Would the United States be forced to devalue the dollar, thus making other countries' dollar holdings less valuable?

Sure enough, in 1971 President Richard Nixon announced that the United States would no longer redeem dollars for gold. In one fell swoop the Bretton Woods agreement to maintain fixed exchange rates went out the window. The dollar would now float, and with it, every other currency. Now the forces of demand and supply would determine exchange rates.

Why did the U.S. balance of payments deteriorate in the 50s and 60s?

Let's step back for a minute and ask why the U.S. balance of payments deteriorated so badly during the 50s and 60s. There were several reasons, but one that is easily overlooked is really the most important. You see, our positive balance of payments and, in particular, our huge trade surpluses in the late 1940s were only a temporary situation brought about by World War II. Of all the major belligerents, only the United States escaped unscathed from the vast war damage. The industrial machines of Germany and Japan, not to mention those of England, France, Italy, and the rest of Europe, were reduced to rubble.

Renewed foreign competition

Thus our industrial goods had virtually no competition in the world's markets until well into the 1950s, when the postwar recovery finally took hold. At that time the best our competitors could do was narrow our leads in some areas and provide products we didn't bother to manufacture, most notably small cars. But by the early 1950s our huge trade surpluses began to narrow.

Military and foreign aid spending

A second reason for our growing payments deficits was our huge military and foreign aid spending. American soldiers stationed abroad required the expenditure of billions of dollars a year, as did the military and economic aid we provided to our foreign friends and allies. The cost of the Vietnam War must be added to the bill too.

Increasing private investment abroad

A third factor was rapidly increasing U.S. private investment abroad, which went from an annual rate of just $2 billion in the early 1950s to $8 billion in the late 1960s.

Inflation

Then there was inflation, particularly in the late 1960s and through the 1970s and early 1980s. Because our inflation rate was higher than those of most of our trading partners, some American goods were priced out of both foreign and domestic markets.

Oil price shocks

Just two more to go. First is the oil price shock of 1973, when oil prices quadrupled, and the subsequent shock of 1979, when oil prices again rose sharply (not to mention the oil shock of 1990). This put our balance of trade into the negative column and has helped keep it there.

The productivity factor

Finally, we have the productivity factor. Believe it or not, the United States still produces more goods and services than any other country in the world (Japan, number two, produces a little more than half as much), and American workers are still the world's most productive. The problem is that we have been losing our productivity lead. That, combined with Americans' prodigious appetite for consumer goods—both American and foreign—and their refusal to save, has added considerably to our mounting trade deficits.

The Freely Floating Exchange Rate System, 1973 to the Present

To return to 1971, when our payments deficits finally forced us to abandon the gold exchange standard—and forced the rest of the world off as well—the IMF needed to set up a new system fast, and that system was, in computer terminology, a default system.

We were back to the law of supply and demand.

We were back to the old system that economists fondly refer to as the law of supply and demand. How does it apply to foreign exchange? The same way it applies to everything else.

Figure 2 shows hypothetical supply and demand curves for German marks. Inferring from these curves, you can get 1.5 marks for a dollar, or one mark for 67 cents—and vice versa.

Who sets this exchange rate? Basically, the forces of supply and demand do. The question then is, Where does the supply and demand for marks come from?

The demand curve for marks represents the desire of Americans to exchange their dollars for marks. Why do they want marks? To buy German goods and services, stocks, bonds, real estate, and other assets.

Likewise, the supply curve of marks represents the desire of German citizens to purchase American goods, services, and financial assets.

Now we get to the beauty of the law of supply and demand. The point at which the two curves cross tells us the exchange rate of marks and dollars. In Figure 2 we have a rate of five marks for one dollar.

Figure 2   Hypothetical Demand for and Supply of German Marks

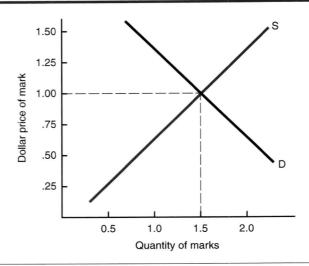

With freely floating exchange rates, currencies will sometimes *depreciate* in value relative to other currencies. If the pound, for instance, depreciates with respect to the lira, it may fall from one pound equals 300 lira to one pound equals 280 lira. Similarly, a currency can *appreciate* in value relative to another currency. Before appreciation 20 francs equaled one mark, but after the franc appreciated 19 francs equaled one mark.

We don't have completely free-floating exchange rates.

If we had completely free-floating exchange rates (i.e., no government interference), the market forces of supply and demand would set the exchange rates. To a large degree, this is what happens; but governments do intervene, although usually for a limited time. In other words, government intervention may temporarily influence exchange rates, but exchange rates are set by the forces of supply and demand in the long run.

Three factors influence the exchange rates between countries. (Let's continue to use the United States and Germany as an example.) The most important factor is the relative price levels of the two countries. If American goods are relatively cheap compared to German goods, there will be a relatively low demand for marks and a relatively high supply of marks. In other words, everyone—Germans and Americans—wants dollars to buy American goods.

A second factor is the relative growth rates of the American and German economies. Whichever is growing faster generates a greater demand for imports. If the American economy is growing faster, it will raise the demand for marks (to be used to buy imported goods from Germany) while decreasing the supply of marks (the Germans will hold more marks and fewer dollars because they are not buying many American goods).

The third and final factor is the relative level of interest rates in the two countries. If the interest rates are higher in Germany than they are in the United States, American investors will want to take advantage of the higher rates by buying German securities. They will sell their dollars for marks, driving up the price of marks. In effect, then, the demand for marks will rise and their supply will decline.

In 1980 and 1981 U.S. interest rates went through the roof. Banks, the U.S. Treasury, and major corporations were paying more than 15 percent—and sometimes more than 20 percent—to borrow money. These high rates, which were double or triple what could be earned abroad, made the American dollar exceedingly attractive to foreigners, because they generally needed to convert their currencies into dollars to invest here. So it was our relatively high interest rates that provided most of the impetus for the rising dollar during the first half of the 1980s (see Figure 3).

Figure 3   International Exchange Rates, 1967–97

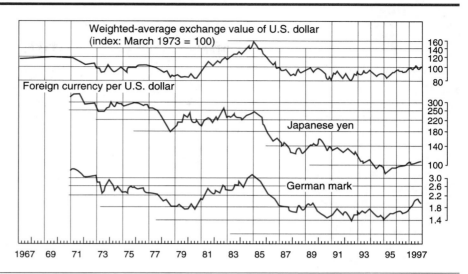

Source: *Business Cycle Indicators*, March 1998.

Remember that the exchange rate reflects the demand of foreigners for U.S. dollars and the demand of Americans for foreign currencies. By the late 1980s American interest rates had fallen to the levels of foreign interest rates. This cut sharply into the foreign demand for U.S. dollars, pushing the dollar all the way back down (see Figure 3). The cheaper dollar, incidentally, helped reduce our huge imbalance of trade by the early 1990s. If Figure 3 confuses you, then help is on the way. You'll find it in the box "Interpreting the Top Line in Figure 3."

Two of our major trading partners are Germany and Japan. Figure 3 shows how the dollar has fluctuated against the mark and the yen since 1971.

When we had fixed exchange rates in the 1950s and 1960s, there were no fluctuations in the exchange rate between dollars and yen or between dollars and marks. Since then, of course, there has been nothing *but* fluctuation. In addition, the dollar has been on a long-term downward trend against both the mark and the yen. In the 1950s you could get 350 yen for your dollar, but in early 1998 you could get only about 130 yen. Similarly, in the 1950s you could get more than four marks for one dollar, but in early 1998 you could get about 1.8 marks for a dollar.

How Well Do Freely Floating (Flexible) Exchange Rates Work?

So far, so good.

Until 1973 most countries had fixed exchange rates because they feared flexible rates would fluctuate wildly. Has that happened since 1973? While there certainly have been some ups and downs, most notably with the dollar, we can still say so far, so good.

The dollar declined by well over 20 percent relative to other major currencies during the late 1970s, but this trend was completely reversed in the early 1980s. Between 1980 and early 1985 its value rose by 74 percent. But then another major decline set in (see Figure 3). International trade and finance have adjusted extremely well to these ups and downs, while government intervention has not been a major factor. Barring a major international financial crisis—such as a chain of loan defaults by Third World countries or the refusal of foreign investors to extend further credit to the U.S. government and to American corporations—we will continue to have freely floating exchange rates. While far from perfect, it may be the best system we have known.

Interpreting the Top Line in Figure 3

The graph line at the top of Figure 3 shows how the U.S. dollar has fluctuated against other major currencies since 1967. When the line rises, that means the dollar has risen in value against a weighted average of 10 major foreign currencies. What does this mean in plain English?

First, a weighted average of currencies is similar to your grade point average. If you're really curious about how weighted averages are constructed, look at the box "Construction of the Consumer Price Index" in the chapter on economic fluctuations in *Economics* and *Macroeconomics*.

Figure 3 charts an index of the dollar's relationship to other major currencies, with a base of March 1973. Let's say that in March 1973 a dollar traded for 50 francs. We set that base year at 100. Suppose the index rises to 200 a few years later. Then you might be able to get 100 francs for your dollar.*

The index did rise from the low 80s in 1980 to just over 145 in 1985; so the dollar rose by about 75 percent. What did this mean to American consumers? It meant that on the average they could get about 75 percent more foreign currency for their dollars than they could have just five years before.

Suppose a Honda Accord cost 1,000,000 yen in 1985. If 250 yen exchanged for one dollar, the car cost an American $4,000 (1,000,000/250). By 1988 you could get only 125 yen for your dollar. If that new Accord still cost 1,000,000 yen, how many dollars did you need to buy it? Don't wait for me to tell you. I'd like you to work out the answer here:

Here's the solution: 1,000,000/125 = $8,000.

When the dollar rises in value, foreign goods become cheaper; at the same time American goods become more expensive to foreigners. What do you think this does to our trade balance? That's right—it makes it worse. Since the late 1980s the index has generally fluctuated within a range of 80 to 100. Most economists believe that the dollar has fallen low enough to reduce our trade deficit.

*This is, of course, an oversimplification, because the dollar will not have risen by 100 percent against every currency during this period. It will have risen by more than 100 percent against some and by less than 100 percent against others.

The Euro

As of January 1, 1999, most of Western Europe will have a single currency, the euro. The European Monetary Union will have eleven members—Austria, Belgium, Finland, France, Germany, Ireland, Italy, Luxembourg, Netherlands, Portugal, and Spain. To qualify, each nation needed to meet three criteria—an annual budget deficit of less than 3 percent, an inflation rate of less than 3 percent, and a public debt of less than 60 percent of GDP. Having a common currency will not only facilitate trade among the members, but it may also spur economic growth.

The Peso Crisis and the Decline of the Dollar

In late 1994 the Mexican peso went into a steep decline, followed almost immediately by a steady decline in the dollar. By the spring of 1995 the declines in both currencies had been arrested, but not until after the international currency markets had been thoroughly roiled.

The Mexican Peso Crisis of 1994–95   During its last few years in power—1992, 1993, and 1994—the government of President Carlos Salinas de Gortari kept the peso artificially high by keeping key statistics out of the public domain—how much Mexico's foreign reserves had been depleted to prop up the peso and how dependent it had become on short-term money from abroad. Rather than tie up these funds in factories and other assets that cannot be swept out of the country with a few strokes of the keyboard, the Salinas government encouraged foreign investors to buy short-term notes called *tesobonos*.

The artificially high peso encouraged Mexicans to import goods while it discouraged foreigners from buying Mexico's exports. To cover its increasing trade and current account deficits, Mexico borrowed increasing amounts from foreign investors, mainly in the form of *tesobonos*. On December 22, 1994, after the peso came under intense pressure in foreign exchange markets, the Mexican government decided to abandon the fixed exchange rate between the dollar and the peso, allowing the peso to float. Rather than float, however, the peso sank like a stone, from 3.5 pesos to 7 to the dollar by early March, prompting a $53 billion U.S.-led bailout.

President Clinton, perhaps motivated by a fear that a collapse of the Mexican economy would lead to a flood of illegal immigrants, cobbled together a huge loan package. By executive order, he used $20 billion in U.S. Treasury funds, persuaded the Federal Reserve to lend an additional $4.5 to $6 billion, got the International Monetary Fund to come up with $10 billion, and secured the rest from other leading industrial nations. The lenders required Mexico to adhere to strict targets for money supply, domestic credit, government spending, and foreign borrowing.

On March 9, 1995, the Mexican government announced a far-reaching austerity plan that raised taxes and pushed up interest rates, resulting in a higher rate of inflation and interest rates, and consequently, the layoffs of hundreds of thousands of workers. But the plan had the desired effect on currency speculation, because the peso regained more than a quarter of its value over the next seven weeks and stock prices rose more than 65 percent over this period. Still the Mexican economy was in a deep recession through much of 1995. By 1996 the Mexican economy had not only recovered, but that nation's financial house was back in order, and it had begun repaying its foreign loans.

The 1995 Decline of the Dollar   Because the value of the dollar vis-à-vis other currencies is set by the market forces of supply and demand, and because over $1 trillion a day passes through the hands of currency traders, if these people think that the dollar is overvalued relative to other currencies, they will sell dollars. In 1994, when we ran a trade deficit of $166 billion and a current account deficit of $134 billion, the currency traders began selling dollars, mainly for Japanese yen and German marks.

The dollar, which had been holding its own against most other major currencies in the early 1990s (see Figure 3), fell substantially throughout 1994 and then more sharply in early 1995. Why? There were three main reasons. First, our huge current account deficit in 1994 sent another $156 billion abroad, adding to the hoard of more than a trillion dollars that foreigners already held. The second reason for the fall of the dollar was that its demand as a reserve currency was falling. According to figures from the International Monetary Fund, the dollar accounted for 70 percent of all central bank reserves in 1984; by the beginning of 1994 the number had sunk to 61 percent. Finally, our $25 billion contribution to the bailout of the Mexican peso associated the dollar with a sharply declining currency. Interestingly, as the peso recovered about a quarter of its value in March and April of 1995, the dollar, which had been falling sharply against the mark and the yen, finally stopped falling against these two currencies (see Figure 3).

To summarize, what happened to the supply of dollars outside the United States in 1994 and early 1995? And what happened to the demand for U.S. dollars? Clearly the supply went up and the demand went down. Now if the supply of anything goes up while the demand for it goes down, what happens to its price?

Its price must go down. This is illustrated in Figure 4, which shows a change in the supply of dollars and the demand for dollars relative to yen. Although this graph is hypothetical, it does show how the dollar's value is determined by the forces of supply and demand.

The East Asian Financial Crisis

In late 1997 a financial crisis hit South Korea, Indonesia, and Thailand, and threatened to spread through the rest of Asia and even beyond. Indeed, it was so reminiscent of the

Figure 4   Hypothetical Supply of and Demand for Dollars Relative to Yen

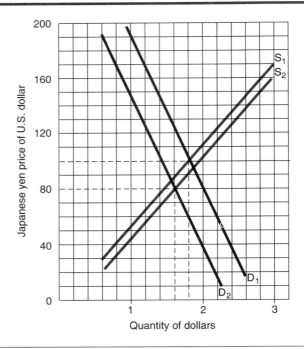

Mexican peso crisis that it appeared to be, in the words of baseball philosopher Yogi Berra, "déjà vu all over again."

Here's what happened. Japanese, Western European, and American banks lent nearly $400 billion to South Korean, Thai, and other East Asian banks. Nearly all these loans were very short term, having maturities of less than one year, and had to be repaid in yen, pounds, francs, marks, or dollars.

A Korean bank, for example, relent this money to local businesses, many of whom, it turned out, were poor credit risks. When they defaulted, the bank could not repay its creditors. To make matters worse, the Korean currency, the won, fell precipitously against the yen, pound, franc, mark, and dollar. This placed Korean (as well as Thai and Indonesian) banks in danger of default. The problem was compounded because so many of these short-term loans were falling due. Normally, of course, the Japanese, Western European, and American banks would have automatically renewed the loans, but now they refused to do so without credible guarantees that they would eventually be repaid. The International Monetary Fund, with strong backing from the governments of the world's leading industrial powers, agreed to provide over $100 billion—twice the cost of the Mexican bailout—to South Korea, Indonesia, and Thailand.

The bailout worked. The financial crisis had apparently receded by February 1998. But one may ask whether by making the lenders whole, this did not encourage more careless lending and future crises. If lenders were confident that they would be bailed out whenever they got into trouble, they would continue to make loans that should not have been made.

The Decline and Fall of the American Economy

What follows could be criticized as overly subjective (as opposed to having just the right degree of subjectivity), polemical, and not neutral enough for a principles of economics text. I would be forced to plead guilty as charged. What has happened to the international economic standing of this country in recent years would be hard to describe in neutral terms, so I leave it to my fellow textbook authors to provide blander, less subjective descriptions.

From Largest Creditor to Largest Debtor

During the second half of the 19th century the United States borrowed heavily from Great Britain and other European nations to finance the building of railroads and the construction of much plant and equipment. Our country was a classic debtor nation, importing manufactured goods, exporting agricultural products, and borrowing capital in order to industrialize.

During World War I the United States became the world's leading creditor nation.

On the eve of World War I with the process of industrialization largely completed, we finally became a creditor nation. In 1914 foreigners owed us more than we owed them. Our creditor status rose substantially during the war as we loaned the Allies billions of dollars. We became the world's leading creditor nation, a position we held until 1982.

What happened to make us lose this position and even fall into debt? The most obvious cause of this enormous turnabout was the shift in our balance of trade, which we talked about in the last chapter. But three other important forces have also been at play. First, our role as the world's leading economic and military power after World War II became a huge drain on our resources and ultimately contributed to our downfall. Second, our federal budget deficits, which began to get out of hand in the 1970s, became overwhelming in the early 1980s. Finally, as our status shifted from creditor to debtor, the inflow of interest, rent, dividends, and profits eventually reversed itself and became a growing outflow of funds.

Military spending

The Vietnam War shattered not only the myth of our military omnipotence but the myth of our economic omnipotence as well. We simply could not afford to station hundreds of thousands of troops all over the world, extend billions of dollars in military and economic aid each year, and at the same time, balance our current account.

The role of budget deficits

We had overestimated ourselves as the leader of the free world. Moreover, we were trying to lead the world by running budget deficits. Throughout the 1960s we ran small deficits, although President Lyndon Johnson's bookkeeping magic allowed us to show a small surplus in 1969. It was our last to date.

In the 1970s our deficits rose to double-digit figures—$23 billion in 1971, $53 billion in 1975, and $74 billion in 1976. But, in the words of Ronald Reagan, "You ain't seen nothin' yet!" Throughout the 1980s and the first half of the 1990s we ran triple-digit deficits. However, by fiscal year 1998 the deficit had virtually disappeared.

Low savings

Americans were saving so little, there was simply not enough money available to finance the deficit *and* provide business firms with investment funds. So what did we do? We borrowed from foreigners, who not only covered half the deficits but provided tens of billions more for private investment. They did not do this out of the goodness of their hearts but because the interest rates we were paying—the interest rates we were *forced* to pay—were considerably higher than they could have earned at home.

We have to pay more rent, interest, dividends, and profits to foreigners.

As our foreign debt continues to mount, the interest, rent, dividends, and profits we have to pay to foreigners will continue to grow. Although our net debt is now approaching $1 trillion (i.e., foreign assets in the United States less American assets abroad), American investments abroad are somewhat more risky and thus yield higher returns than more conservative foreign investments in the United States. Nevertheless, the net inflow of factor payments (i.e., what we receive less what foreigners receive) has dropped from $22 billion in 1987 to just $15 billion in 1994. By the late 1990s foreigners will be earning a net investment return of approximately $40 billion to $50 billion a year. Add that to our trade deficit, and we're obviously in big trouble.

You can really see it coming by looking at Figure 5. In 1985 we became a debtor nation, and since that year, foreign investment in the United States has far outstripped our investment abroad. These trends will continue into the foreseeable future as foreigners continue accumulating dollars and using them to buy up our assets (see box "From Number One Creditor to Number One Debtor").

What can we do?

Is there anything we can do to stanch this outflow of dollars and bring down our current account deficit? It follows from what we've been discussing that we need to do three things: (1) lower the trade deficit; (2) lower military spending abroad; and (3) reduce the net outflow of factor payments.

Figure 5   U.S. Assets Abroad and Foreign Assets in the United States, 1983–97

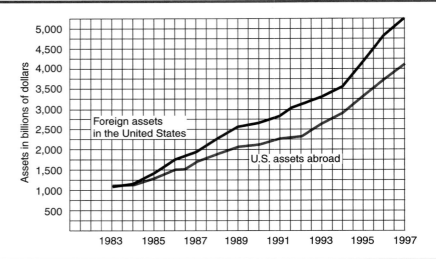

Source: *Economic Report of the President,* 1992 and 1995; *Survey of Current Business,* April 1998.

From Number One Creditor to Number One Debtor

In just three years the United States went from being the world's leading creditor to the world's leading debtor (see Figure 5). Well, look at the bright side: we're still number one. In fact, we've surged past Brazil, Argentina, and Mexico, each of which had long been vying for the title of world's premier debtor.

This debt doesn't even count the more than $1 trillion that foreigners are holding.* And unless drastic mea-sures are soon taken, we will fall far deeper into debt. At this writing, the prospects for such measures are not good.

*See the box titled "How Much Money Is Out There Anyway?" in the chapter on money and banking in *Economics* and *Macroeconomics.*

Some economists believe the trade deficit will eventually disappear when the dollar has fallen far enough. If and when it does, our standard of living will be lower because imports will be more expensive (coincidentally raising the inflation rate by one or two points). In addition, the lower dollar will make American stocks, bonds, and real estate purchases even greater bargains for foreign investors.

And now for some good news. The breakup of the Soviet empire and the disintegration of the Soviet Union itself have made it feasible to begin major withdrawals of American troops stationed abroad. A secondary effect has been the reduction of defense spending. On the other hand—there is almost always an other hand in economics—our involvement in the Persian Gulf, Bosnia, and elsewhere has sharply limited what once was termed our "peace dividend."

Finally, there is the net outflow of factor payments. This figure is a residual that will rise and fall depending on our success in dealing with the trade deficit, military spending abroad, and the budget deficit. As long as our indebtedness to foreigners continues to grow—and the only question is how *fast* it will grow—the net outflow will continue to rise.

Yet many of our dollars remain abroad where they circulate as a medium of exchange. The Federal Reserve estimates that 60 percent of all the U.S. currency being printed is eventually used as unofficial legal tender in China, Russia, Mexico, Romania, Tajikistan, Vietnam, and dozens of other countries. Lithuania, Argentina, and Brazil have formally pegged their currencies to the dollar, while many others have done so informally. In effect, then, much of the world is unofficially on the dollar standard.

As long as we can maintain a low inflation rate and currency stability, the world may continue to accept our dollars in exchange for a multitude of goods and services. We're certainly getting a great deal. We get to buy tens of billions of dollars' worth of stuff each year and pay for it just by printing money. So it would not be unreasonable to say that dollars are our largest export.

In any case, we must wonder about the implications of our nation's huge debt. Joel Kurtzman pretty much sums up our dilemma:

> It is extremely unlikely we will ever again be able to act as freely as we once did economically. We may never again have a free enough hand to stimulate the kind of investment we need to become competitive once more. The reason our investments will be slim in the future is that we must keep our interest rates high enough to convince foreigners to loan us money. High rates may be able to pull in enough money to fund our nation's annual budget deficit, but they powerfully discourage longer-term productive investment.[2]

The U.S. Treasury depends on the foreign saver to finance the deficit.

The foreign saver, who finances about half of our budget deficit, has a strong voice in setting the interest rates—not just for U.S. government securities but indirectly for other interest rates as well. As our dependence on funds from abroad grows, we are abdicating not just our role as the world's leading economic power but our economic sovereignty. It is humiliating each time the U.S. Treasury must go, tin cup in hand, to solicit Japanese investors to purchase U.S. government securities. As time goes by, decisions affecting the American economy will be made not in New York and Washington but in Tokyo, London, Frankfurt, and other financial capitals outside the United States.

We are living for today and not worrying about tomorrow.

As a nation we are living for today and not worrying about what will happen tomorrow. "America has thrown itself a party and billed the tab to the future," says Harvard economist Benjamin Friedman.[3] But all parties must end sometime, and someone is going to be left with a mess to clean up. (See the box "The Role of Drug Money" for a discussion of another aspect of our living for today.)

This cleaning up will be left to the next generation. Lawrence Malkin puts it in these stark terms:

> Since the United States has been borrowing for today's consumption and not for productive investments . . . it is the young who will have to earn the interest in the future to pay for the present spending spree by their elders. The transfer will be less obvious than the way in which they already pay part of their salary through the Social Security system to finance their elders' consumption. But the result will be the same. The children will have to pay it back.[4]

---

[2]Joel Kurtzman, *The Decline and Crash of the American Economy* (New York: W. W. Norton, 1988), p. 145.

[3]Benjamin M. Friedman, *Day of Reckoning* (New York: Random House, 1988), p. 4.

[4]Lawrence Malkin, *The National Debt* (New York: New American Library, 1987), p. 120.

The Role of Drug Money

There are no hard figures or even reliable estimates on the amount of money sent abroad to pay for cocaine and heroin imports. But considering that the United States is clearly the world's leading drug importer, it is reasonable to say that more than $20 billion is sent abroad to drug growers and traffickers. The transfer of funds is done by cash or electronically through the worldwide banking network and is not easy to trace.

How does this affect our balance-of-payments deficit? It doesn't, except that we often run "statistical discrepancies" of some $25 billion to $35 billion. Now where could

all that money be coming from? And where could it be going?

Some of it is coming back into the United States to purchase legitimate businesses, some to buy luxury condominiums along South Florida's "Gold Coast," and some may even be going to help finance our federal budget deficits. The point is, however reprehensible the drug dealers are, the economic effect of their transactions is similar to the effects of any other imports. The bottom line is that Americans are buying today's pleasures with tomorrow's income.

Warning: Do Not Read beyond This Point if You Think This Book Has a Happy Ending

These last two sections were not written for the faint of heart, the superpatriotic, or the easily depressed. What I have to say may startle you or make you angry, but if you dare to read on, you will learn what I *really* think will happen to our country over the next 20 years. How much of this is mere conjecture and how much is straight fact will be left for you to decide. But whatever the truth may be, one thing has become increasingly clear: Our country is going down the tubes.

Living beyond Our Means

The root cause of our problems has been that we as a nation have been consuming more than we have been producing, spending more than we have been earning, or, in short, living for today without providing for tomorrow. In the 19th century, when this country also ran up a large international debt, we were financing capital expansion. This investment in the future enabled us to vastly expand our production and quickly pay off our debt.

Today we are following a radically different course. We are not borrowing from abroad to finance capital expansion but rather to pay for a massive spending spree. What are we buying? We're buying consumer electronics, cars, designer clothes, and oil.

We are a nation of consumption junkies.

America has become a nation of consumption junkies. This is not, in itself, such a terrible thing if we support our habit. But we can't. So we ask foreigners to indulge us. And so far they have—at a price. We've been giving them IOUs in the form of U.S. dollars, and more and more, foreigners have been cashing them in for pieces of America. It seems as though everyone—the British, the Japanese, the Dutch, the Canadians, the Germans—owns a piece of the rock. We can only wonder how many more pieces we have left to sell.

We are selling off the rock—piece by piece.

Since the early 1980s we've seen a massive recycling of dollars. As our trade deficits mounted, the dollars we sent abroad were lent back to us as foreigners took advantage of our relatively high interest rates to purchase Treasury securities and corporate bonds. But they have increasingly been using their dollar stash to buy up pieces of America in the form of real estate and corporate stock. One might say foreigners are now not just America's creditors but its owners as well.

On the Other Hand . . .

Now that I've presented the downside of our economic prospects, let's look at the upside. American workers remain the most productive in the world, especially in the production of services. In the spring of 1998 we had very low unemployment and inflation and our federal budget deficit was disappearing. And while our trade deficit remains much too high, if the dollar does not rise, we can expect the trade deficit to fall as we enter the new millennium.

Closing Word: Will Foreigners Soon Own America?

Over the last three decades foreigners have accumulated well over 1 trillion U.S. dollars (a sum exceeding our current money supply). Most of this money is being held abroad. But in recent years as our trade deficit soared, and especially following the depreciation of the dollar, foreigners have been using their holdings of U.S. dollars to buy up large chunks of America.

Will foreigners soon own most of this country?

Is it true that foreigners will soon own most of our country? Is it true that their most conspicuous purchases—CBS Records and Columbia Pictures by Sony, a controlling interest in Rockefeller Center by Mitsubishi, the ill-fated Federated and Allied stores deals by Campeau (the Canadian investor), and the acquisition of Firestone Tire by Bridgestone—are just a harbinger of things to come? Well, there's some good news and some bad news. The good news is that of the roughly $22 trillion of real assets in this country, foreigners own no more than 10 or 12 percent. And the bad news? At the rate they're going, within another 20 years they'll own more than one-third.

In industry after industry, foreigners have been buying great hunks of our productive facilities. At last report they owned half of the cement industry, one-third of the chemical industry (including 4 of the top 10 firms), and even such American institutions as *TV Guide,* Burger King, Bloomingdale's, Jordan Marsh, A&P, *Woman's Day,* Twentieth Century Fox, Colt 45, Lone Star Beer, Carvel's, 7-Eleven, Smith and Wesson (handguns), Ball Park (hot dogs), Tiffany's, and RCA Records.

The American automobile industry is an interesting case. The Japanese transplants have reached over 20 percent of the U.S. capacity, but they have been built from the groundup rather than simply acquired. Honda, now America's number four automaker, may soon overtake Chrysler. In fact, the transplants are actually exporting cars, some of them to Japan.

The Japanese have three good reasons for building plants in the United States. They save a couple of hundred dollars right off the top in shipping costs for every car built here. Second, they have billions of dollars that they need to invest, so why not build plants in a politically stable country with a fairly well-educated labor force? And perhaps most important in the long run, by substituting cars put together here for cars made in Japan, they are placing themselves within any tariff wall that may be erected in coming years.

Martin Feldstein, who once served as the chair of President Reagan's Council of Economic Advisors, cited these and other factors:

> The United States is, of course, fundamentally attractive to foreign investors because of its massive $5 trillion marketplace, its political stability, its continuing flow of technological and product innovations, and its relatively flexible labor and product markets. The recent tax changes increase the appeal of location in the United States to businesses that produce substantial taxable profits or high professional incomes. The sharp decline in the dollar also makes American assets more attractive to foreign buyers and lowers the relative cost of production in the United States.[5]

The Japanese own L.A.'s Arco Plaza; New York's Empire State Building and Exxon Building; Washington, D.C.'s U.S. News & World Report Building; Atlanta's IBM Tower; Las Vegas's Dunes Hotel; and most of the major hotels on Waikiki Beach. The British have $1 billion invested in Washington, D.C., real estate, including part ownership of the famed Watergate complex. And Canada's Olympia & York, the world's largest real estate company, owns several office buildings in midtown Manhattan. In fact, foreign interests hold close to half the office space in downtown Los Angeles, about 40 percent in Houston, one-third in Minneapolis, and a good 20 percent in New York City.

Another sector with a strong foreign presence is banking. Foreign banks hold about 20 percent of all the banking assets in the United States and provide perhaps 30 percent of all business loans. The heaviest concentration of foreign banking interests is in California, where the Japanese alone hold more than one-third of that state's banking assets and control 5 of the 10 largest banks. The main reason for this imposing presence is the number of other Japanese firms that these banks service.

Investment banking also has attracted Japanese and European money. Shearson Lehman Brothers, Goldman Sachs, Wertheim & Co. (now Wertheim Schroder & Co.), and First Boston (now C. S. First Boston) are all owned in part by foreigners, while Aubrey G. Lanston was purchased outright by the Industrial Bank of Japan.

Before we get too upset with the Japanese, we need to consider two factors. First, which foreign country owns a larger chunk of America than any other? Disregard your first guess—it's not Japan. Great Britain owns more of us than any other foreign country.

America has been selling off the family jewels to pay for a night on the town.
—Representative John Bryant, D-Texas

Japanese automobile transplants

Why do the Japanese want to make cars here?

Foreign real estate holdings

Foreign bank ownership

---

[5]"The United States in the World Economy: Introduction," in *The United States in the World Economy,* ed. Martin Feldstein (Chicago: University of Chicago Press, 1988), p. 7.

And one more word about the Japanese. Largely because of financial problems at home—their recent stock market crash and their plunging real estate prices—they have greatly scaled back on their American investments.

The top 10 foreign-based publishers now account for over 40 percent of American book sales. Some of the familiar publishing companies now owned by foreigners include Addison-Wesley, Penguin/Putnam, HarperCollins, Little Brown, Henry Holt, Farrar Straus & Giroux, Harlequin, Bantam/Dell/Doubleday, Macmillan, and Random House.

Meanwhile advertising, which Americans presumably invented, has been taken over by the British, who now own three of the top five U.S. agencies. We can only wonder what will come next. There's still a lot out there for foreign investors to buy. The question I leave you with is this: What's going to happen when there's nothing left to sell?

Questions for Further Thought and Discussion

1. What is meant by our balance of payments? Explain what current account and capital account are.
2. What is the gold standard? How does it work?
3. Why does the dollar fluctuate with other currencies?
4. How did the United States go from being the world's largest creditor nation to the world's largest debtor?
5. Will foreigners soon own America?

WORKBOOK FOR CHAPTER 35

Name _____ Date _____

Multiple-Choice Questions

Circle the letter that corresponds to the best answer.

1. Which statement is true?

   a. The dollar rose from 1980 to 1985 and then declined.

   b. The dollar declined from 1980 to 1985 and then rose.

   c. The dollar has been rising since 1980.   d. The dollar has been falling since 1980.

2. We became a debtor nation in

   a. 1975   b. 1980   c. 1986   d. 1990

3. In 1994 our net foreign debt was over _____ billion.

   a. $150   b. $250   c. $350   d. $500

4. Which statement is true?

   a. In the 1980s we did not receive many dollars in investment funds from foreigners.   b. In the 1980s foreign investment funds were attracted by our high interest rates.   c. Our military spending has helped reduce our current account deficit.   d. None of these statements is true.

5. During the 1980s

   a. both American investment abroad and foreign investment in the United States increased   b. both American investment abroad and foreign investment in the United States decreased   c. American investment abroad increased and foreign investment in the United States decreased   d. American investment abroad decreased and foreign investment in the United States increased

6. The world's leading debtor nation is

   a. Argentina   b. Brazil   c. Mexico   d. the United States

7. Which statement is true?

   a. Foreigners own most of the assets in the United States.   b. We own more assets in foreign countries than foreigners own in the United States.

   c. Foreigners own half of our cement industry and one-third of our chemical industry.   d. None of these statements is true.

8. Which statement is false?

   a. The Japanese produce more than half of all cars built in the United States.   b. The number four automobile producer in the United States is Honda.   c. The Japanese will soon own about 20 percent of the capacity for producing cars in the United States.   d. None of these statements is false.

9. An American importer of Italian shoes would pay in

   a. dollars   b. gold   c. lira

10. The total of our current and capital accounts

    a. will always be zero   b. will always be negative   c. will always be positive   d. may be positive or negative

11. In recent years we bought _____ from foreigners than they bought from us, and we invested _____ in foreign countries than foreigners invested in the United States.

    a. more, more   b. less, less   c. less, more   d. more, less

12. Today international finance is based on

    a. the gold standard   b. a relatively free-floating exchange rate system   c. fixed rates of exchange

13. The international gold standard worked well until

    a. World War I   b. 1940   c. 1968   d. 1975

14. If we were on an international gold standard,

    a. inflations would be eliminated   b. recessions would be eliminated   c. trade deficits and surpluses would be eliminated   d. no nation would ever have to devalue its currency

795

15. Which of the following is false?

    a. The gold standard will work only when the gold supply increases as quickly as the world's need for money.   b. The gold standard will work only if all nations agree to devalue their currencies simultaneously.   c. The gold standard will work only if participating nations are willing to accept periodic inflation.   d. The gold standard will work only if participating nations are willing to accept periodic unemployment.

16. The gold exchange standard was in effect from

    a. 1900 to 1934   b. 1934 to 1973   c. 1955 to 1980   d. 1973 to the present

17. The United States first began running balance-of-payments deficits in the

    a. 1940s   b. 1950s   c. 1960s   d. 1970s   e. 1980s

18. Today currency exchange rates are set by

    a. the International Monetary Fund   b. the U.S. Treasury   c. bilateral agreements between trading nations   d. supply and demand

19. The most important influence on the exchange rate between two countries is

    a. the relative price levels of the two countries

    b. the relative growth rates of the two countries

    c. the relative level of interest rates in both countries

    d. the relative wage rates of both countries

20. Devaluation would tend to

    a. make the devaluating country's goods cheaper

    b. make the devaluating country's goods more expensive   c. have no effect on the value of the devaluating country's goods

Fill-In Questions

1. The entire flow of U.S. dollars and foreign currencies into and out of the country constitutes our _____ _____.

2. Nearly all the dollars that foreigners have earned from trading with the United States have been _____ _____ in the form of _____ _____.

3. The two parts of the balance of payments are the _____ _____ account and the _____ account.

4. The basis for international finance is the exchange of _____.

5. A nation is on the gold standard when it _____ _____.

6. To be on the gold standard, a nation must maintain a fixed ratio between its gold stock and _____ _____.

7. Under the gold standard, if country J imports more than it exports, it has to ship _____ _____ to the trading partners with whom it has trade deficits. This will depress country J's _____, and its price level will _____.

8. Under the gold standard, if country K's price level declines, its imports will _____ and its exports will_____.

9. For the 25 years following World War II, dollars functioned well as reserves for two reasons:

    (1) _____

    and (2) _____.

10. The three reasons for the deterioration of our balance of payments in the 1950s and 1960s were:

    (1) _____ ;

    (2) _____ ;

    and (3) _____ .

11. Today exchange rates are set by _____

    and _____ .

12. The three factors that influence the exchange rates between countries are (1) _____

    _____ ;

    (2) _____ ;

    and (3) _____

    _____ .

GLOSSARY

Ability-to-Pay Principle   The amount of taxes that people pay should be based on their ability to pay (i.e., their incomes).

Absolute Advantage   The ability of a country to produce a good at a lower cost than its trading partners.

Accelerator Principle   If sales or consumption is rising at a constant rate, gross investment will stay the same; if sales rise at a decreasing rate, both gross investment and GDP will fall.

Accounting Profit   Sales minus explicit cost. Implicit costs are not considered.

Aggregate Demand   The sum of all expenditures for goods and services.

Aggregate Supply   The nation's total output of goods and services.

Antitrust Laws   These laws, including the Sherman and Clayton acts, attempted to enforce competition and to control the corporate merger movement.

Arbitration   An arbitrator imposes a settlement on labor and management if they cannot reach a collective bargaining agreement.

Automatic Stabilizers   Programs such as unemployment insurance benefits and taxes that are already on the books to help alleviate recessions and hold down the rate of inflation.

Autonomous Consumption   The minimum amount that people will spend on the necessities of life.

Average Fixed Cost   Fixed cost divided by output.

Average Propensity to Consume   The percentage of disposable income that is spent; consumption divided by disposable income.

Average Propensity to Save   The percentage of disposable income that is saved; saving divided by disposable income.

Average Tax Rate   The percentage of taxable income that is paid in taxes; taxes paid divided by taxable income.

Average Total Cost   Total cost divided by output; represented by ATC.

Average Variable Cost   Variable cost divided by output; represented by AVC.

Backward-Bending Labor Supply Curve   As the wage rate rises, more and more people are willing to work longer and longer hours up to a point. They will then substitute more leisure time for higher earnings.

Balance of Payments   The entire flow of U.S. dollars and foreign currencies into and out of the country.

Balance of Trade   The difference between the value of our imports and our exports.

Balanced Budget   When federal tax receipts equal federal government spending.

Bank   A commercial bank or thrift institution that offers checkable deposits.

Benefits-Received Principle   The amount of taxes people pay should be based on the benefits they receive from the government.

Bonds   (See government bonds or corporate bonds.)

Break-Even Point   The low point on the firm's average total cost curve. If the price is below this point, the firm will go out of business in the long run.

Budget Deficit   When federal tax receipts are less than federal government spending.

Budget Surplus   When federal tax receipts are greater than federal government spending.

Business Cycle   Increases and decreases in the level of business activity that occur at irregular intervals and last for varying lengths of time.

CPI   (See consumer price index.)

Capital   All means of production (mainly plant and equipment) created by people.

Capitalism   An economic system in which most economic decisions are made by private owners and most of the means of production are privately owned.

Cartel   A group of firms behaving like a monopoly.

Circular Flow Model   Goods and services flow from business firms to households in exchange for consumer expenditures, while resources flow from households to business firms in exchange for resource payments.

Classical Economics   Laissez-faire economics. Our economy, if left free from government interference, tends toward full employment. The prevalent school of economics from about 1800 to 1930.

Closed Shop   An employer may hire only union members; outlawed under the Taft-Hartley Act.

Collective Bargaining   Negotiations between union and management to obtain agreements on wages, working conditions, and other issues.

Communism   An economic system characterized by collective ownership of most resources and central planning.

Comparative Advantage   Total output is greatest when each product is made by the country that has the lowest opportunity cost.

Competition   Rivalry among business firms for resources and customers.

Concentration Ratio   The percentage share of industry sales by the four leading firms.

Conglomerate Merger   Merger between two companies in unrelated industries.

Consumer Price Index   The most important measure of inflation. This tells us the percentage rise in the price level since the base year, which is set at 100; represented by CPI.

Consumer Surplus   The difference between what you pay for some good or service and what you would have been willing to pay.

Consumption   The expenditure by individuals on durable goods, nondurable goods, and services; represented by C.

Consumption Function   As income rises, consumption rises, but not as quickly.

Corporate Bonds   This is a debt of the corporation. Bondholders have loaned money to the company and are its creditors.

Corporate Stock   Share in a corporation. The stockholders own the corporation.

Corporation   A business firm that is a legal person. Its chief advantage is that each owner's liability is limited to the amount of money he or she invested in the company.

Cost-Push Inflation   Rising costs of doing business push up prices.

Creeping Inflation   A relatively low rate of inflation, such as the rate of less than 4 percent in the United States in recent years.

Crowding-Out Effect   Large federal budget deficits are financed by Treasury borrowing, which then crowds private borrowers out of financial markets and drives up interest rates.

Cyclical Unemployment   When people are out of work because the economy is operating below the full-employment level. It rises sharply during recessions.

Deflation   A general decline in the price level.

Deflationary Gap   Occurs when equilibrium GDP is less than full-employment GDP.

Demand   A schedule of quantities of a good or service that people will buy at different prices; represented by D.

Demand, Law of   When the price of a good is lowered, more of it is demanded; when the price is raised, less is demanded.

Depository Institutions Deregulation and Monetary Control Act of 1980   This made all depository institutions subject to the Federal Reserve's legal reserve requirements and allowed all depository institutions to issue checking deposits.

Depression   A deep and prolonged business downturn; the last one occurred in the 1930s.

Derived Demand   Demand for resources derived from demand for the final product.

Diminishing Returns, Law of   If units of a resource are added to a fixed proportion of other resources, marginal output will eventually decline.

Direct Tax   Tax on a particular person. Most important are federal personal income tax and payroll (Social Security) tax.

Discount Rate   The interest rate charged by the Federal Reserve to depository institutions.

Diseconomies of Scale   An increase in average total cost as output rises.

Disequilibrium   When aggregate demand does not equal aggregate supply.

Disposable Income   Aftertax income. Term applies to individuals and to the nation.

Economic Growth   An outward shift of the production possibilities frontier brought about by an increase in available resources and/or a technological improvement.

Economic Problem   When we have limited resources available to fulfill society's relatively limitless wants.

Economic Profit   Sales minus explicit costs and implicit costs.

Economic Rent   The excess payment to a resource above what it is necessary to pay to secure its use.

Economies of Scale   Reductions in average total cost as output rises.

Elasticity of Demand   Measures the change in quantity demanded in response to a change in price.

Entrepreneurial Ability   Ability to recognize a business opportunity and successfully set up a business firm to take advantage of it.

Equation of Exchange   Shows the relationship among four variables: M (the money supply), V (velocity of circulation), P (the price level), and Q (the quantity of goods and services produced). MV = PQ.

Equilibrium   When aggregate demand equals aggregate supply.

Equilibrium Point   Point at which quantity demanded equals quantity supplied; where demand and supply curves cross.

Exchange Rates   The price of foreign currency; for example, how many dollars we must give up in exchange for marks, yen, and pounds.

Excise Tax   A sales tax levied on a particular good or service; for example, gasoline and cigarette taxes.

Expected Rate of Profit   Expected profits divided by money invested.

FDIC   (See Federal Deposit Insurance Corporation.)

Federal Deposit Insurance Corporation   Insures bank deposits up to $100,000.

Federal Reserve System   Central bank of the United States, whose main job is to control our rate of monetary growth.

Fiscal Policy   Manipulation of the federal budget to attain price stability, relatively full employment, and a satisfactory rate of economic growth.

Fiscal Year   Budget year. U.S. federal budget fiscal year begins on October 1.

Fixed Costs   These stay the same no matter how much output changes.

Frictional Unemployment   Refers to people who are between jobs or just entering or reentering the labor market.

Full Employment   When a society's resources are all being used with maximum efficiency.

Full-Employment GDP   That level of spending (or aggregate demand) that will result in full employment.

GDP   (See gross domestic product.)

Government Bonds   Long-term debt of the federal government.

Gross Domestic Product   The nation's expenditure on all the goods and services produced in this country during the year at market prices; represented by GDP.

Gross Investment   A company's total investment in plant, equipment, and inventory. Also, a nation's plant, equipment, inventory, and residential housing investment.

Herfindahl–Hirschman Index   A measure of concentration calculated as the sum of the squares of the market share of each firm in an industry.

Horizontal Merger   Conventional merger between two firms in the same industry.

Hyperinflation   Runaway inflation; in the United States, double-digit inflation.

Income Effect   A person's willingness to give up some income in exchange for more leisure time.

Incomes Policy   Wage controls, price controls, and tax incentives used to try to control inflation.

Increasing Costs, Law of   As the output of a good expands, the opportunity cost of producing additional units of this good increases.

Indirect Tax   Tax on a thing rather than on a particular person; for example, sales tax.

Induced Consumption   Spending induced by changes in the level of income.

Inflation   A general rise in the price level.

Inflationary Gap   Occurs when equilibrium GDP is greater than full-employment GDP.

Interest Rate   Interest paid divided by amount borrowed.

Interlocking Directorates   When one person serves on the boards of at least two competing firms.

Investment   The purchase or construction of any new plant, equipment, or residential housing, or the accumulation of inventory; represented by I.

Keynesian Economics   As formulated by John Maynard Keynes, this school believed the private economy was inherently unstable and that government intervention was necessary to prevent recessions from becoming depressions.

Labor   The work and time for which employees are paid.

Labor Force   The total number of employed and unemployed people.

Laffer Curve   Shows that at very high tax rates, very few people will work and pay taxes; therefore government revenue will rise as tax rates are lowered.

Laissez-Faire   The philosophy that the private economy should function without any government interference.

Liquidity Trap   At very low interest rates, said John Maynard Keynes, people will neither lend out their money nor put it in the bank, but will simply hold it.

Long Run   When all costs become variable costs and firms can enter or leave the industry.

Lorenz Curve   Data plotted to show the percentage of income enjoyed by each percentage of households, ranked according to their income.

M   The money supply—currency, checking deposits, and checklike deposits (identical to M1).

M1   Currency, checking deposits, and checklike deposits.

M2   M1 plus savings deposits, small-denomination time deposits, and money market mutual funds.

M3   M2 plus large-denomination time deposits.

Malthusian Theory of Population   Population tends to grow in a geometric progression (1, 2, 4, 8, 16), while food production tends to grow in an arithmetic progression (1, 2, 3, 4, 5).

Marginal Cost   The cost of producing one additional unit of output; represented by MC.

Marginal Propensity to Consume   Change in consumption divided by change in income; represented by MPC.

Marginal Propensity to Save   Change in saving divided by change in income; represented by MPS.

Marginal Revenue   The revenue derived from selling one additional unit of output; represented by MR.

Marginal Revenue Product   The demand for a resource, based on that resource's marginal output and the price at which it is sold; represented by MRP.

Marginal Tax Rate   Additional taxes paid divided by taxable income.

Marginal Utility   The additional utility derived from consuming one more unit of some good or service.

Maximum Profit Point   A firm will always produce at this point; marginal cost equals marginal revenue.

Measure of Economic Welfare   A measure developed by James Tobin and William Nordhaus that modifies GDP by excluding "economic bads" and "regrettable necessities" and adding household, unreported, and illegal production.

Mediation   A third party acts as a go-between for labor and management during collective bargaining.

Minimum Wage   The legal minimum that may be paid for one hour of labor. For most of the 1980s that minimum was $3.35; it is now $5.15.

Monetarism   A school of economics that places paramount importance on money as the key determinant of the level of prices, income, and employment.

Monetary Policy   Control of the rate of monetary growth by the Board of Governors of the Federal Reserve.

Money   Main job is to be a medium of exchange; also serves as a standard of value and a store of value.

Money Supply   Currency, checking deposits, and checklike deposits (M or M1).

Monopolistic Competition   An industry that has many firms producing a differentiated product.

Monopoly   An industry in which one firm produces all the output. The good or service produced has no close substitutes.

Monopsony   A market in which a single buyer has no rivals.

Multiplier   Any change in spending (C, I, or G) will set off a chain reaction leading to a multiplied change in GDP. Equation is $1/(1 - MPC)$.

NNP   (See net national product.)

National Debt   (See public debt.)

National Income   Net domestic product minus indirect business taxes.

Natural Monopoly   An industry in which a single firm can provide cheaper service than could several competing firms.

Net Investment   Gross investment minus depreciation.

Net National Product   Gross domestic product minus depreciation.

Net Productivity of Capital   The expected annual profit rate.

Nominal Interest Rate   The real interest rate plus the inflation rate.

Noncompeting Groups   Various strata of labor that do not compete for jobs; for example, doctors and secretaries, skilled and unskilled workers.

Oligopoly   An industry with just a few firms.

Open Economy   An economy linked to the rest of the world through international trade.

Open-Market Operations   The purchase or sale of Treasury securities by the Federal Reserve; main monetary policy weapon.

Open Shop   When no one is forced to join a union even though the union represents all the workers in contract negotiations.

Opportunity Cost   The forgone value of what you give up when you make a choice.

Output Effect   When the price of any resource rises, the cost of production rises, which, in turn, lowers the supply of the final product. When supply falls, price rises, consequently reducing output.

P   The price level, or the average price of all goods and services produced during the current year.

Paradox of Thrift   If everyone tries to save more, they will all end up saving less.

Partnership   A business firm owned by two or more people.

Payroll Tax   (See Social Security tax.)

Per Capita Real GDP   Real GDP divided by population.

Perfect Competition   An industry with so many firms that no one firm has any influence over price, and firms produce an identical product.

Permanent Income Hypothesis   Formulated by Milton Friedman, it states that the strongest influence on consumption is one's estimated lifetime income.

Personal Income   Income received by household, including both earned income and transfer payments.

Price Ceiling   Government-imposed maximum legal price.

Price Discrimination   Occurs when a seller charges two or more prices for the same good or service.

Price Floor   Government-imposed minimum price (used almost exclusively to keep agricultural commodity prices up).

Price Leadership   One firm, often the dominant firm in an oligopolistic industry, raises or lowers price, and the other firms quickly match the new price.

Price System   Mechanism that allocates resources, goods, and services based on supply and demand.

Prime Rate   Rate of interest that banks charge their most creditworthy customers.

Production   Any good or service for which people are willing to pay.

Production Possibilities Frontier   A curve representing a hypothetical model of a two-product economy operating at full employment.

Productivity   Output per unit of input; efficiency with which resources are used.

Progressive Tax   Places greater burden on those with best ability to pay and little or no burden on the poor (e.g., federal personal income tax).

Proprietorship   A business firm owned by just one person.

Public Debt   The amount of federal securities outstanding, which represents what the federal government owes (the accumulation of federal deficits minus surpluses over the last two centuries).

Public Goods   Goods that are consumed equally by everyone whether they pay or not.

Q   Output, or number of goods and services produced during the current year.

Quantity Theory of Money   Crude version: Changes in the money supply cause proportional changes in the price level. Sophisticated version: If we are well below full employment, an increase in M will lead to an increase in output. If we are close to full employment, an increase in M will lead mainly to an increase in P.

Rational Expectations Theory   This is based on three assumptions: (1) that individuals and business firms learn through experience to anticipate the consequences of changes in monetary and fiscal policy; (2) that they act immediately to protect their economic interests; and (3) that all resource and product markets are purely competitive.

Real GDP   GDP corrected for inflation; actual production.

Real Interest Rate   Nominal interest rate minus inflation rate.

Real Wages   Nominal wages corrected for inflation.

Recession   A decline in real GDP for two consecutive quarters.

Regressive Tax   Falls more heavily on the poor than on the rich; for example, Social Security tax.

Required Reserve Ratio   Percentage of deposits that must be held as vault cash and reserve deposits by all depository institutions.

Required Reserves   Minimum vault cash or reserves; held at the Federal Reserve District Bank.

Right-to-Work Laws   Under the Taft-Hartley Act, states are permitted to pass these laws, which prohibit the union shop. (Union membership cannot be made a condition of securing employment.)

Rule of Reason   Mere size is no offense. Market conduct rather than market share should determine whether antitrust laws have been violated.

Saving Function   As income rises, saving rises, but not as quickly.

Say's Law   Supply creates its own demand.

Short Run   The length of time it takes all fixed costs to become variable costs.

Shut-Down Point   The low point on the firm's average variable cost curve. If price is below the shut-down point, the firm will shut down in the short run.

Social Security Tax   A tax paid equally by employee and employer, based on employee's wages. Most proceeds are used to pay Social Security retirement and Medicare benefits.

Specialization   Division of productive activities so that no one is self sufficient.

Stagflation   A period of either recession or stagnation accompanied by inflation.

Stock   (See corporate stock.)

Strike   When a collective bargaining agreement cannot be reached, a union calls for a work stoppage to last until an agreement is reached.

Structural Unemployment   When people are out of work for a couple of years or longer.

Substitution Effect   If the price of a resource, say labor, goes up, business firms tend to substitute capital or land for some of their now-expensive workers. Also, the substitution of more hours of work for leisure time as the wage rate rises.

Supply   A schedule of quantities that people will sell at different prices; represented by S.

Supply, Law of   When the price of a good is lowered, less of it is supplied; when the price is raised, more is supplied.

Supply-Side Economics   Main tenets: economic role of federal government is too large; high tax rates and government regulations hurt the incentives of individuals and business firms to produce goods and services.

Tariff   A tax on imported goods.

Terms of Trade   The ratio of exchange between an imported good and an exported good.

Total Cost   The sum of fixed and variable costs.

Transfer Payment   Payment by one branch of government to another or to an individual. Largest transfer payment is Social Security.

Transmission Mechanism   The series of changes brought about by a change in monetary policy that ultimately changes the level of GDP.

Unemployment Rate   Number of unemployed divided by the labor force.

Union Shop   All employees must join the union, usually within 30 days after they are hired.

Utility   The satisfaction you derive from a good or service that you purchase. How much utility you derive is measured by how much you would be willing to pay.

Variable Costs   These vary with output. When output rises, variable costs rise; when output declines, variable costs fall.

Velocity   The number of times per year each dollar in the money supply is spent; represented by V.

Vertical Merger   The joining together of two firms engaged in different parts of an industrial process, or the joining of a manufacturer and a retailer.

Wage and Price Controls   Rules established by the government that either place a ceiling on wages and prices or limit their rate of increase.

Workfare   A plan that requires welfare recipients to accept jobs or to enter training programs.

INDEX

REAL GROSS DOMESTIC PRODUCT IN CHAIN–WEIGHTED DOLLARS, 1929–97 (1992 = 100)*

Year	GDP	Personal Consumption Expenditures Total	Gross Private Domestic Investment Total	Net Exports			Government Purchases					Percent Change from Prior Year GDP
								Federal				
				Net	Exports	Imports	Total	Total	National Defense	Non-Defense	State and Local	
1929	942.6	636.0	174.9	2.2	41.3	39.1	129.2	25.1	—	—	104.0	—
1930	858.9	596.4	122.9	−.3	34.2	34.5	139.9	28.0	—	—	111.9	−8.9
1931	792.9	574.6	100.0	−2.6	28.3	31.0	143.9	28.6	—	—	115.5	−7.7
1932	687.8	537.7	28.7	−2.8	22.5	25.2	138.2	27.4	—	—	108.5	−13.3
1933	673.4	513.2	30.5	−3.4	22.8	26.3	135.5	35.4	—	—	101.2	−2.1
1934	725.6	551.8	47.1	−1.1	25.6	26.8	150.7	45.9	—	—	94.5	7.7
1935	781.4	559.5	78.2	−8.3	27.3	35.7	156.8	46.1	—	—	113.1	7.7
1936	892.2	612.9	103.0	−5.8	29.0	34.9	182.1	72.8	—	—	109.1	14.2
1937	930.7	636.1	120.9	−2.2	36.6	38.8	174.6	67.4	—	—	112.9	4.3
1938	893.4	621.9	78.9	4.8	35.2	30.4	186.4	71.5	—	—	114.9	−4.0
1939	964.3	675.2	95.7	5.3	37.5	32.2	200.0	97.6	17.4	56.0	124.9	7.9
1940	1,039.2	687.7	139.7	9.4	43.1	33.5	207.3	87.4	45.0	54.5	119.9	7.8
1941	1,227.8	721.8	171.4	3.2	44.8	41.6	331.6	215.6	169.0	40.5	114.9	18.2
1942	1,473.6	721.1	93.4	−12.7	30.2	42.9	678.1	564.9	484.2	28.2	107.2	20.0
1943	1,766.9	742.4	61.5	−37.2	25.6	57.8	995.2	895.9	781.8	17.9	99.4	19.9
1944	1,915.5	769.9	67.9	−33.3	28.4	72.9	1,113.2	1,014.3	882.0	21.3	96.0	8.4
1945	1,838.4	819.5	94.7	−27.4	37.6	65.0	951.3	852.1	748.1	12.7	99.2	−4.0
1946	1,459.1	893.6	212.8	30.4	76.5	46.1	310.8	201.2	166.1	29.4	109.7	−20.8
1947	1,436.9	898.4	228.0	48.1	90.7	42.6	251.0	127.0	97.7	33.6	124.0	−1.5
1948	1,491.1	932.5	263.6	19.0	69.6	50.6	276.0	144.9	94.6	50.2	131.1	3.8
1949	1,497.4	953.6	214.9	19.8	68.7	48.7	308.9	160.3	105.6	54.7	147.4	.4
1950	1,627.0	1,002.8	296.4	3.7	60.8	57.0	326.3	167.0	125.1	41.9	159.3	8.7
1951	1,787.5	1,014.7	296.6	12.7	73.8	61.0	455.4	294.0	257.5	36.5	161.4	8.8
1952	1,863.8	1,059.1	323.2	2.6	71.5	68.7	536.3	372.3	326.5	45.8	164.0	4.3
1953	1,933.2	1,012.2	275.6	−8.1	79.7	76.4	561.8	389.6	329.6	60.0	172.2	3.7
1954	1,919.8	1,132.4	268.5	−2.6	71.3	73.9	521.5	335.7	288.7	47.0	174.3	−.7
1955	2,028.2	1,200.9	326.6	−6.0	77.7	83.6	506.6	307.9	267.8	40.4	198.4	5.6
1956	2,068.7	1,231.5	323.7	−1.4	89.5	89.7	509.3	303.7	266.3	37.4	205.5	2.0
1957	2,108.4	1,268.7	306.1	−2.1	97.5	95.7	533.7	316.7	279.6	37.0	217.0	1.8
1958	2,097.9	1,287.1	283.0	−19.3	84.5	78.6	546.0	312.0	265.2	46.8	234.0	−.5
1959	2,212.3	1,394.6	274.2	−34.8	71.9	106.6	618.5	360.5	307.6	58.8	256.8	5.5
1960	2,261.7	1,432.6	270.5	−21.3	86.8	108.1	617.2	349.4	301.3	54.1	267.2	2.2
1961	2,309.8	1,461.5	265.2	−19.1	88.3	107.3	647.2	363.0	313.8	55.5	283.8	2.1
1962	2,449.1	1,533.8	298.5	−26.5	93.0	119.5	686.0	393.2	332.4	66.8	292.1	6.0
1963	2,554.0	1,596.6	318.1	−22.7	100.0	122.7	701.9	391.8	324.0	72.9	309.7	4.3
1964	2,702.9	1,692.3	344.6	−15.9	113.3	129.2	715.9	385.2	309.9	79.2	330.9	5.8
1965	2,874.8	1,799.1	392.5	−27.4	115.6	143.0	737.6	385.2	303.8	84.6	353.2	6.4
1966	3,060.2	1,902.0	423.5	−40.9	123.4	164.2	804.6	429.1	348.2	85.7	375.9	6.4
1967	3,140.2	1,958.6	406.9	−50.1	126.1	176.2	865.6	471.7	393.5	84.7	394.2	2.6
1968	3,288.6	2,070.2	429.8	−67.2	135.3	202.5	892.4	476.3	400.9	82.5	416.5	4.7
1969	3,388.0	2,147.5	454.4	−71.3	142.7	214.0	887.5	459.9	381.6	84.3	428.0	3.0
1970	3,388.2	2,197.8	419.5	−65.0	158.1	223.1	866.8	427.2	349.0	83.0	440.0	.0
1971	3,500.1	2,279.5	467.4	−75.8	159.2	235.0	851.0	397.0	313.7	86.3	454.4	3.3
1972	3,690.3	2,415.9	522.1	−88.9	172.0	261.0	854.1	390.2	300.3	91.9	464.5	5.4
1973	3,902.3	2,532.6	583.5	−63.0	209.6	272.6	848.4	371.1	281.2	91.5	478.5	5.7
1974	3,888.2	2,514.7	544.4	−35.6	229.8	265.3	862.9	368.8	273.5	96.4	495.6	−.4
1975	3,865.1	2,570.0	440.5	−7.2	228.2	235.4	876.3	367.9	269.7	99.1	510.0	−.6
1976	4,081.1	2,714.3	536.6	−39.9	241.6	281.5	876.8	364.3	264.7	100.4	514.3	5.6
1977	4,279.3	2,829.8	627.1	−64.2	247.4	311.6	884.7	370.1	266.4	104.3	516.4	4.9
1978	4,493.7	2,951.6	686.0	−65.6	273.1	338.6	910.6	377.7	266.7	111.4	534.7	5.0
1979	4,624.0	3,020.2	704.5	−45.3	299.0	344.3	924.9	383.3	271.0	112.7	543.5	2.9
1980	4,611.9	3,009.7	626.2	10.1	331.4	321.3	941.4	399.3	280.7	119.0	543.6	−.3
1981	4,724.9	3,046.4	689.7	5.6	335.3	329.7	947.7	415.9	296.0	120.4	532.8	2.5
1982	4,623.6	3,081.5	590.4	−14.1	311.4	325.5	960.1	429.4	316.5	113.3	531.4	−2.1
1983	4,810.0	3,240.6	647.8	−63.3	303.3	366.6	987.3	452.7	334.6	118.5	534.9	4.0
1984	5,138.2	3,407.6	831.6	−127.3	328.4	455.7	1,018.4	463.7	348.1	115.9	555.0	6.8
1985	5,329.5	3,566.5	829.2	−147.9	337.3	485.2	1,080.1	495.6	374.1	121.8	584.7	3.7
1986	5,489.9	3,708.7	813.8	−163.9	362.2	526.1	1,135.0	518.4	393.4	125.2	616.9	3.0
1987	5,648.4	3,822.3	820.5	−156.2	402.0	558.2	1,165.9	534.4	409.2	125.3	631.8	2.9
1988	5,862.9	3,972.7	826.0	−114.4	465.8	580.2	1,180.9	524.6	405.5	119.1	656.6	3.8
1989	6,060.4	4,064.6	861.9	−82.7	520.2	603.0	1,213.9	531.5	401.6	130.1	682.6	3.4
1990	6,138.7	4,132.2	817.3	−61.9	564.4	626.3	1,250.4	541.9	401.5	140.5	708.6	1.3
1991	6,079.0	4,105.8	737.7	−22.3	599.9	622.2	1,258.0	539.4	397.5	142.0	718.7	−1.0
1992	6,244.4	4,219.8	790.4	−29.5	639.4	669.0	1,263.8	528.0	375.8	152.2	735.8	2.7
1993	6,389.6	4,343.6	863.6	−70.2	658.2	728.4	1,252.1	505.7	354.4	151.2	746.4	2.3
1994	6,610.7	4,486.0	975.7	−104.6	712.4	817.0	1,252.3	486.6	336.9	149.5	765.7	3.5
1995	6,742.1	4,595.3	991.5	−98.8	791.2	890.1	1,251.9	470.3	322.6	147.5	781.6	2.0
1996	6,928.4	4,714.1	1,069.1	−114.4	857.0	971.5	1,257.9	464.2	317.8	146.1	793.7	2.8
1997	7,191.4	4,869.7	1,192.2	−142.1	964.4	1,106.5	1,270.6	457.8	305.0	148.3	812.9	3.8

* Years 1929–58 approximated with constant 1992 prices.

CONSUMER PRICE INDEX, 1925–97
(1982–84 = 100)

Year	Index (all items)	Percent Change
1925	17.5	3.5
1926	17.7	−1.1
1927	17.4	−2.3
1928	17.1	−1.2
1929	17.1	0.6
1930	16.7	−6.4
1931	15.2	−9.3
1932	13.7	−10.3
1933	13.0	0.8
1934	13.4	1.5
1935	13.7	3.0
1936	13.9	1.4
1937	14.4	2.9
1938	14.1	−2.8
1939	13.9	0.0
1940	14.0	0.7
1941	14.7	9.9
1942	16.3	9.0
1943	17.3	3.0
1944	17.6	2.3
1945	18.0	2.2
1946	19.5	18.1
1947	22.3	8.8
1948	24.1	3.0
1949	23.8	−2.1
1950	24.1	5.9
1951	26.0	6.0
1952	26.5	0.8
1953	26.7	0.7
1954	26.9	−0.7
1955	26.8	0.4
1956	27.2	3.0
1957	28.1	2.9
1958	28.9	1.8
1959	29.1	1.7
1960	29.6	1.4
1961	29.9	0.7
1962	30.2	1.3
1963	30.6	1.6
1964	31.0	1.0
1965	31.5	1.9
1966	32.4	3.5
1967	33.4	3.0
1968	34.8	4.7
1969	36.7	6.2
1970	38.8	5.6
1971	40.5	3.3
1972	41.8	3.4
1973	44.4	8.7
1974	49.3	12.3
1975	53.8	6.9
1976	56.9	4.9
1977	60.6	6.7
1978	65.2	9.0
1979	72.6	13.3
1980	82.4	12.5
1981	90.9	8.9
1982	96.5	3.8
1983	99.6	3.8
1984	103.9	3.9

Data beginning 1978 are for all urban ~~consu~~mers: earlier data are for urban wage ~~earner~~s and clerical workers. Annual "per-~~cent ch~~ange" measured December to ~~Decemb~~er.

~~Source: U~~.S. Department of Labor. ~~Bureau of Labor~~ Statistics.

CONSUMER PRICE INDEX, 1925–97
(continued)

Year	Index (all items)	Percent Change
1985	107.6	3.8
1986	109.6	1.1
1987	113.6	4.4
1988	118.3	4.6
1989	124.0	4.6
1990	130.7	6.1
1991	136.2	3.1
1992	140.3	2.9
1993	144.5	2.7
1994	148.2	2.7
1995	152.4	2.5
1996	156.9	3.3
1997	160.5	1.7

CHAIN–WEIGHTED PRICE DEFLATORS FOR GROSS DOMESTIC PRODUCT, 1959–97
(1992 = 100)

Year	Index (all items)	Percent Change
1959	23.0	—
1960	23.3	1.4
1961	23.6	1.2
1962	23.9	1.3
1963	24.2	1.2
1964	24.6	1.5
1965	25.0	1.9
1966	25.7	2.8
1967	26.6	3.2
1968	27.7	4.4
1969	29.0	4.7
1970	30.6	5.3
1971	32.1	5.2
1972	33.5	4.2
1973	35.4	5.6
1974	38.5	8.9
1975	42.2	9.4
1976	44.6	5.8
1977	47.5	6.4
1978	50.9	7.3
1979	55.3	8.5
1980	60.4	9.3
1981	66.1	9.4
1982	70.2	6.3
1983	73.2	4.2
1984	75.9	3.8
1985	78.6	3.4
1986	80.6	2.6
1987	83.1	3.1
1988	86.1	3.7
1989	89.7	4.2
1990	93.6	4.4
1991	97.3	3.9
1992	100.0	2.8
1993	102.3	2.6
1994	105.9	2.4
1995	108.0	2.5
1996	111.0	2.3
1997	115.2	2.0

Source: U.S. Department of Commerce, Bureau of Economic Analysis.

INTEREST RATES, 1929–97
(percent per annum)

Year	Prime Rate Charged by Banks	Discount Rate, Federal Reserve Bank of New York
1929	5.50–6.00	5.16
1933	1.50–4.00	2.56
1939	1.50	1.00
1940	1.50	1.00
1941	1.50	1.00
1942	1.50	1.00
1943	1.50	1.00
1944	1.50	1.00
1945	1.50	1.00
1946	1.50	1.00
1947	1.50–1.75	1.00
1948	1.75–2.00	1.34
1949	2.00	1.50
1950	2.07	1.59
1951	2.56	1.75
1952	3.00	1.75
1953	3.17	1.99
1954	3.05	1.60
1955	3.16	1.89
1956	3.77	2.77
1957	4.20	3.12
1958	3.83	2.15
1959	4.48	3.36
1960	4.82	3.53
1961	4.50	3.00
1962	4.50	3.00
1963	4.50	3.23
1964	4.50	3.55
1965	4.54	4.04
1966	5.63	4.50
1967	5.61	4.19
1968	6.30	5.16
1969	7.96	5.87
1970	7.91	5.95
1971	5.72	4.88
1972	5.25	4.50
1973	8.03	6.44
1974	10.81	7.83
1975	7.86	6.25
1976	6.84	5.50
1977	6.83	5.46
1978	9.06	7.46
1979	12.67	10.28
1980	15.27	11.77
1981	18.87	13.42
1982	14.86	11.02
1983	10.79	8.50
1984	12.04	8.80
1985	9.93	7.69
1986	8.83	6.33
1987	8.21	5.66
1988	9.32	6.20
1989	10.87	6.93
1990	10.01	6.98
1991	8.46	5.45
1992	6.25	3.25
1993	6.00	3.00
1994	7.15	3.60
1995	8.83	5.21
1996	8.27	5.02
1997	8.44	5.00

Source: Board of Governors of the Federal Reserve System.